1 MONTH OF
FREE
READING

at
www.ForgottenBooks.com

By purchasing this book you are
eligible for one month membership to
ForgottenBooks.com, giving you
unlimited access to our entire
collection of over 1,000,000 titles via
our web site and mobile apps.

To claim your free month visit:
www.forgottenbooks.com/free904824

ISBN 978-0-266-88750-8
PIBN 10904824

For support please visit www.forgottenbooks.com

COMMONWEALTH OF AUSTRALIA.

HISTORICAL RECORDS

OF

AUSTRALIA.

SERIES I.

GOVERNORS' DESPATCHES TO AND FROM ENGLAND.

VOLUME VI.

August, 1806—December, 1808.

Published by:

THE LIBRARY COMMITTEE OF THE COMMONWEALTH PARLIAMENT.

1916.

SYDNEY:
WILLIAM APPLEGATE GULLICK, GOVERNMENT PRINTER.
———
1916.

Governor Bligh.

Around the story of the life of William Bligh and of his administration of the government of New South Wales, more romance and misrepresentation have gathered than around the story of any other governor of the colony. The distortion of facts has been due in part to bitter party animosities, already prevalent in the colony, and in part to new antagonisms created by the determined, somewhat tactless action of a rugged, irascible nature. Throughout his life, Bligh possessed in a remarkable degree the faculty of making bitter and vindictive enemies. In the words of George Caley, he was " a man whom nature has intended to be the subject of abuse."

Prior to accepting the government of New South Wales, Bligh had spent his life in the navy. He was accustomed to the stern realities of service on the quarter-deck of a ship of the line. He was used to the rough manners of the navy and to the forceful and virile speech of the period. At that time, the press gang and its methods had full swing; stern measures were necessary to repress the opposition of men impressed; floggings were frequent; the seamen had long been restless, and this feeling had culminated in the mutiny at the Nore; human life was thought little of; men were punished severely for small offences; commissions were readily obtainable by purchase. Life generally was stern and hard. Men served their country in naval, military, and civil capacities with a keen intensity; but at the same time they sought with eagerness the emoluments and perquisites of office.

The birth and parentage of William Bligh are obscure. His own statement is not definite. He said* that he was born about 1753, probably at Tinten or Tynten in the parish of St. Tudy, Cornwall, and was the son of Charles and Margaret Bligh. Other

* See R. Polwhele's " Biographical Sketches in Cornwall," ii, 19.

accounts* affirm that his birth took place at Plymouth on the 9th of September, 1754, and that he was the son of John Bligh, of Tretawne in the parish of St. Kew, Cornwall.

On the 1st of July, 1762, he entered the navy as captain's servant to John Storr on the *Monmouth,* a ship of 60 guns, and in that capacity served seven months and three weeks. After his discharge his career is not known, until he shipped as A.B. on the *Hunter* on the 27th of July, 1770. He was made midshipman on the same ship on the 5th of February following, and was transferred as midshipman to the *Crescent* on the 22nd of September, 1771, and to the *Ranger* on the 2nd of September, 1774. From the *Ranger* he was discharged on the 17th of March, 1776, and on the 1st of July in the same year was appointed master of the sloop *Resolution,* under Captain James Cook, for his third and last voyage of discovery. Bligh, in his previous career, must have distinguished himself, for Cook selected him for this expedition, and thought that he " could be usefully employed in constructing charts." After the death of Cook and the return of the *Resolution* to England, the crew were paid off on the 24th of October, 1780. Under Admiral Parker, Bligh was present at the battle off the Doggerbank on the 5th of August, 1781. On the 5th of October following, he received his commission as fifth lieutenant on the *Berwick,* and was transferred to a similar rank in the *Princess Amelia* on the 30th of December. On the 20th of March, 1782, he was commissioned as sixth lieutenant on the *Cambridge,* and fought under Lord Howe at Gibraltar.

On the 14th of January, 1783, Bligh was placed on the half-pay list and obtained permission to seek employment in merchant vessels. During the next four years he sailed several voyages to different parts of the world. In a ship called the *Britannia,* he sailed for Jamaica under employment to a Mr. Campbell, a West Indian merchant. Fletcher Christian, afterwards leader of the *Bounty* mutineers, was a member of the *Britannia's* crew. Bligh rated him as a gunner, but gave instructions that he should be regarded as an officer. In the words of Edward Lamb, second in command of the *Britannia,* Christian was very indifferent in his duties, but Bligh treated him as a brother, was " blind to his faults, and had him to dine and sup every other day in the cabin."

* *cf.* Maclean's " Deanery of Trigg Minor."

Bligh returned from the West Indies on the 6th of August, 1787. During his absence, an expedition was organised with the object of transplanting bread-fruit and other trees and plants from the island of Otaheite to the West Indies. Sir Joseph Banks, who, for reasons unknown, had become a great patron of Bligh, had secured for him the command of this expedition. Accordingly, Bligh was appointed lieutenant and commander of the *Bounty,* an armed storeship of 215 tons, with a complement of forty-five men. Bligh's final instructions were issued on the 20th of November, and he sailed from Spithead on the 23rd of December, 1787. On the 26th of October, 1788, the *Bounty* anchored in Matavai bay, Otaheite. She remained there until the 25th of December, when she was removed to the neighbouring harbour of Toahroah. After securing the desired bread-fruit trees, Bligh sailed on the return voyage on the 4th of April, 1789. Twenty-four days later, when near Tofoa in the Friendly Islands, twenty-five of the crew, under the leadership of Fletcher Christian, the master's mate, mutinied and seized the ship.

Bligh and eighteen companions, provided with scanty provisions, were cast adrift by the mutineers in the ship's launch. In this open boat he successfully accomplished a daring voyage of about 3,600 miles to Koepang in Timor, without charts and through little known seas. At Timor, he purchased a small schooner and sailed for Batavia. From Java, he travelled *viâ* the Cape of Good Hope to England, and arrived at Portsmouth on the 14th of March, 1790. In November of the same year, he was tried and honourably acquitted by a court martial on the loss of the *Bounty.*

The story of Bligh's wonderful voyage in an open boat, the subsequent discovery of the survivor and descendants of the mutineers on Pitcairn Island under romantic and idyllic conditions, and the false use of the circumstances of the mutiny made by Bligh's enemies to damage his reputation have all tended to give an undue prominence to this minor episode in the history of the navy. It has been frequently asserted that the mutiny was due to the severity and harsh measures adopted by Bligh in his command, but probably no more unjust charge could have been made. Sworn testimonies* are extant which are directly contradictory to this

* These are contained in the "Answer," published in 1792 by Bligh in reply to Edward Christian's criticism.

assertion. It is recorded that though, when things went wrong, Bligh frequently damned his men, " *he was never angry with a man the next minute* "; that he was not fond of flogging, and that " some deserved hanging who had only a dozen "; and that he was a father to every person on the ship. Christian received many special favours from Bligh. He was given the use of Bligh's cabin and liquor; he was taught navigation and drawing; he was asked to dine every third day with Bligh.

The actual causes of the mutiny were undoubtedly the attractions to the toil-hardened sailors of a life of indolence and sensuality at Otaheite. In his reports, Bligh mentioned these as the cause of the mutiny. The amours of the staff and crew of the *Endeavour,* when captain Cook visited the same island in 1769, are well known, and a mutiny was narrowly averted on that ship, the men having the same motives as Christian and his colleagues. Christian was twenty-four years of age, and, according to Lamb's testimony, during the voyage of the *Britannia* he had shown that he " was then one of the most foolish young men I ever knew in regard to the sex." In a spurious account* of Christian's travels, published in 1796, the cause of the mutiny is indicated. It is stated that Bligh, on his arrival at Otaheite, ordered the crew to be examined for venereal disease, as " the ladies in this happy island are known not to be the most reserved in granting their favours. . . . . . The women at Otaheite are not only constitutionally votaries of Venus, but join to the charms of person such a happy cheerfulness of temper and such engaging manners that their allurements are perfectly irresistible." In the same book, testimony in Bligh's favour is given: " At the same time, it is but justice that I [Christian] should acquit Captain Bligh in the most unequivocal manner of having contributed in the smallest degree to the promotion of our conspiracy by any harsh or ungentlemanlike conduct on his part. So far from it that few officers in the service, I am persuaded, can in this respect be found superior to him, or produce stronger claims upon the gratitude and attachment of the men whom they are appointed to command."

After his return to England, the crew of the *Bounty* was paid off on the 22nd of October, 1790, and Bligh was put on the half-

* " The Voyages and Travels of Fletcher Christian," etc., London, H. D. Symonds, 1796.

pay list with the rank of commander. Three weeks later he was given the command of the *Falcon,* and on the 15th of December he was promoted to the rank of captain. On the 7th of January, 1791, he was again placed on the half-pay list. In the meantime, a second expedition to obtain the bread-fruit trees from Otaheite was organised. The ship *Providence,* of 24 guns, and the brig *Assistant,* as a tender, were selected, and Bligh was appointed to the command on the 16th of April, 1791. The fact that Bligh was selected a second time for such a command indicates that the Admiralty did not consider that his conduct had contributed towards the mutiny. Bligh sailed from England on the 2nd of August, 1791. He was successful in securing the bread-fruit trees, and after landing some at Jamaica and some at St. Vincent's, he returned to England on the 4th of August, and the *Providence* was paid off on the 6th of September, 1793. For his services in successfully transplanting the bread-fruit trees, Bligh was awarded the gold medal of the Society of Arts.

During Bligh's absence eleven of the *Bounty* mutineers had been brought to England and tried by court martial on the 12th to 18th of September, 1792. At this time strong efforts were made by the friends of the mutineers to vilify Bligh's character. Edward Christian, brother of the mutineer, wrote many letters to the press alleging cruelty and harshness against Bligh in his command, but at the court martial no evidence in proof of this was tendered. Christian wrote a commentary on the court martial, and this provoked a rejoinder from Bligh in a pamphlet* which he published.

Similar allegations were made against Bligh in his second voyage. Matthew Flinders, who sailed as midshipman on the *Providence,* stated that Bligh's harshness caused discontent. The facts were that during the voyage from Otaheite a shortage of water occurred; as the bread-fruit trees were the primary object of the expedition, Bligh put the men on a short allowance in order that the plants might be watered. Someone secretly watered the plants with salt water, and Bligh threatened to flog the ship's company. This incident is certainly insufficient to justify the

* " An Answer to certain assertions," etc., by Captain Wm. Bligh, London, 1792.

statement that Bligh's harshness caused any permanent discontent. In a letter to the *Times,* dated 16th July, 1794, Edward Harwood, the surgeon during the voyage, wrote: " Captain Bligh's general conduct during the late expedition, which was crowned with the most ample success, his affability to his officers and humane attention to his men gained him their high esteem and admiration, and must eventually dissipate any unfavourable opinion hastily adopted in his absence." This opinion is confirmed by a notice in the *Kentish Register,* dated 6th September, 1793, which reported the paying off of the crew of the *Providence*: " The high estimation in which Captain Bligh was deservedly held by the whole crew was conspicuous to all present. He was cheered on quitting the ship to attend the Commissioner, and at the dock gates the men drew up and repeated the parting acclamation."

The adverse criticism to which Bligh was subjected appears to have had some influence on Lord Chatham, for he showed some diffidence in receiving Bligh at the Admiralty. This feeling must have been of short duration, for in 1794 Bligh was in service* off Ushant in command of the *Warrior,* of 74 guns. On the 30th of April, 1795, he was commissioned as captain of the *Calcutta,* and was employed in the North Sea with Admiral Duncan's squadron. On the 7th of January, 1796, he was given the command of the *Director,* of 64 guns. In this ship he was present first at the mutiny of the Nore in 1797, where he distinguished himself by his intrepidity and resourcefulness, and later in the year at the battle of Camperdown. In that engagement, the *Director* was in the larboard division of Vice-Admiral Onslow's squadron, and first silenced and then boarded the *Vryheid,* flagship of Admiral de Winter.

On the 3rd of July, 1800, the *Director* was paid off, and Bligh placed on the half-pay list. In the following September he was occupied in surveying the Irish coasts. On the 13th of March, 1801, he was given the command of the *Glatton,* on the 12th of April of the *Monarch,* and on the 8th of May of the *Irresistible.*

* This service is not recorded at the Admiralty. Between the 6th of September, 1793, and the 30th of April, 1795, Bligh's name is on the half-pay list. It has been generally accepted on Bligh's own statement.

In the *Glatton*, he was present in the action off Copenhagen, and for his services on that occasion was personally thanked by Lord Nelson.

On the 21st of May, 1801, Bligh was elected a fellow of the Royal Society. In the following year, Bligh was again put on the half-pay list when the *Irresistible* was paid off on the 28th of May. On the 2nd of May, 1804, he was appointed to the command of the *Warrior*, and was detailed for service in the channel. Whilst in command of this ship, Bligh was tried by court martial on charges preferred by his lieutenant. The latter had been ordered on deck when suffering from an injury to the foot. Bligh was acquitted by the court, but was cautioned to be more careful in the use of his words.

Whilst in command of the *Warrior*, Bligh was offered and accepted the government of New South Wales. The offer was conveyed to him by Sir Joseph Banks in a letter, dated 15th March, 1805. The fact that the salary attached to the governorship was increased from £1,000 to £2,000 *per annum* proves that it was the desire of the government to induce officers of a higher rank to accept the office. In his letter to Bligh, Sir Joseph Banks stated: " In conversation, I was this day asked if I knew a man proper to be sent out in his [Governor King's] stead—one who has integrity unimpeached, a mind capable of providing its own resources in difficulties without leaning on others for advice, firm in discipline, civil in deportment, and not subject to whimper and whine when severity of discipline is wanted to meet emergencies. I immediately answered: As this man must be chosen from among the post captains, I know of no one but Captain Bligh who will suit." Banks was not blind to the faults of his friends, for example the irascibility of Governor King. But he sincerely held the highest opinion of Bligh. What Bligh's enemies called unnecessary harshness was regarded by Banks as necessary " severity of discipline."

Bligh had been inured to the stern realities of exploring in unknown seas during his voyage under Captain James Cook and in the two expeditions under his own leadership. His long experience on the quarter-decks amidst the hardships of naval warfare had hardened him. In consequence, Bligh was a strict disciplinarian, and unfortunately had acquired an exaggerated coarseness of speech, which rebuffed an importunate petitioner, made him a man of few friends, and gave his enemies an opportunity to cavil. He was a fellow of the Royal Society, and a man of varied and considerable attainments, if it is possible to judge from the books he requisitioned for use at the government house in Sydney. Apart from the standard legal, geographical, and historical works, these included such varied books as Malthus on Population, Fontana on Venoms and Poisons, Dickson's System of Agriculture, Cooper's complete Distiller, Emmerson's Mechanics, Kiel's Astronomy, and a work on experimental researches in permanent dyes. The appointment of Bligh to the government of New South Wales placed a martinet in command of a colony whose inhabitants, during the thirteen years since the departure of Governor Phillip, had developed habits of unbridled license. Governor Hunter had attempted to stem the torrent, and had failed. Governor King had announced drastic reforms which he had proved unable to carry out. Governor Bligh was sent out with instructions to curb the will of a people who had become emboldened by their previous success, and his failure was perhaps almost inevitable. It was impossible for the efforts of any governor to be crowned with success until the disturbing elements, the New South Wales Corps and its partisans, were removed.

Bligh sailed from England on board the transport *Sinclair* in February, 1806, under the convoy of H.M.S. *Porpoise,* commanded by Joseph Short. During the voyage many disputes arose between Short and Bligh, and Bligh's participation in them was criticised adversely by the secretary of state.* On an examination of the evidence given at the inquiries† held in Sydney in connection with Short's conduct, it is clear that his command was irregular and that he was a difficult man to work with. It is probable that in the disputes with Bligh, his superior officer, Short was in the wrong, notwithstanding the criticism of the secretary of state.

Governor Bligh arrived off Port Jackson on the 6th of August, 1806, and made his official landing at 11 a.m. on the 8th. He

* *See* page 80.   † *See* page 44 *et seq.* and page 65 *et seq.*

assumed the government on the 13th, and his commission as captain-general and governor-in-chief was read with full ceremony in front of government house at noon on that day.

Bligh resided in Sydney as governor-elect for four days, and during that time he took the extraordinary action* of accepting land grants from the retiring governor, Philip Gidley King. On the 10th of August, 1806, three grants were given by King to Bligh. The first, " for a private residence near Sydney," consisted of 240 acres to be known by the name of Camperdown. This land adjoined the Grose Farm on the south side of the Parramatta-road, and now forms the suburb of Camperdown. The second " for a private residence near Parramatta " comprised 105 acres, to be known by the name of Mount Betham. It lay on the north side of the river at the town of Parramatta. The third, " for a private residence between Sydney and Hawkesbury," comprised 1,000 acres, to be known as Copenhagen, and lay on the south-western side of the Hawkesbury road in the neighbourhood of Rouse hill. The subsequent history of the grant at Parramatta illustrates the opinion held on these transactions. After Bligh's death, these lands were inherited by his six daughters as co-heiresses. In 1840, the validity of the grants was questioned, and a suit for impeachment was threatened. Action was avoided by the surrender to the crown of the grant at Parramatta on condition that legal proceedings with a view to the impeachment of all three grants should be abandoned. This surrender was completed on the 24th of February, 1841, by Sir Maurice O'Connell, who had married Mrs. Mary Putland, one of Bligh's daughters. The acceptance of a compromise by the crown, instead of full impeachment of all three grants, indicates that there was an element of doubt as to the validity of the grants. At the same time it seems strange that there should have been a delay of so many years before any definite action was taken.

The grant of 790 acres to be known as " Thanks " to Mrs. Anna Josepha King, the wife of Governor King, by Governor Bligh on the 1st of January, 1807, has been discussed in a previous volume.*

Soon after his assumption of the government, Bligh had experience of the party feeling current in the colony. On the 14th

* *See* page xv, volume IV.

of August, 1806, an address* of welcome was presented to him, signed by George Johnston for the military, Richard Atkins for the civil, and John Macarthur for the free inhabitants. Bligh accepted this address in good faith, but in the following month addresses† were presented to him from the free inhabitants at Sydney and the Hawkesbury. In these addresses the validity of Macarthur's signature was repudiated, the Sydney settlers stating " had we deputed anyone, John McArthur would not have been chosen by us, we considering him an unfit person to step forward upon such an occasion, as we may chiefly attribute the rise in the price of mutton to his withholding the large flock of wethers he now has to make such price as he may choose to demand."

Philip Gidley King sailed from Port Jackson in H.M.S. *Buffalo* on the 10th of February, 1807. During these first six months of his administration Bligh attempted no reforms, but devoted himself to the task of acquiring a full acquaintance with the general condition of the colony. He called for reports on the public buildings, on the administration of the commissariat, and on the state of agriculture and the colony generally. Through no fault of his own, however, Bligh encountered opposition from the commencement of his administration. Within a fortnight of his arrival Bligh was presented with private letters written by under secretary Cooke, stating the intentions of Lord Camden to authorise grants of 600 acres to Joseph Short, commander of H.M.S. *Porpoise*, and of 1,000 acres to John Townson, a retired captain of the N.S.W. Corps. As neither Governor King nor himself had received " any authority according to the tenor of Mr. Cooke's letter," Bligh refused to make the grants, and on the 26th of August, 1806, wrote to the secretary of state for instructions. At the same time he authorised the applicants " to look out for the respective tracts they would approve of," which would be granted to them when he " received directions to locate the same." The neglect of the department to give orders to Bligh was unfortunate for Joseph Short, as he had brought out a considerable investment to be utilised on his anticipated grant.

During these first six months Bligh experienced considerable difficulty in the naval administration owing to the conduct of

---

*See page 566.   † *See* pages 568 and 570.

Short, which necessitated the holding of two courts of inquiry.* These resulted in Short being sent to England under arrest for trial by court martial on charges preferred by his lieutenant. At the time of the court martial Bligh's refusal to give Short a land grant, a refusal which was perfectly justified, although it entailed considerable loss to Short, was utilised by Bligh's enemies to vilify his administration.

Although Bligh's administration and character were represented falsely on many occasions, the exchange of land grants with Governor King and the development of Bligh's farm at the Hawkesbury admit fairly of adverse criticism. On the 1st of January, 1807, Bligh purchased some land at the Hawkesbury.† Andrew Thompson acted as Bligh's overseer. If the evidence of Thompson in a sworn deposition‡ can be relied upon, Bligh erected buildings on his farm of the value of £1,000 at the cost of the crown; he employed twenty to thirty convicts victualled by the crown; he drew on the public stores at the Hawkesbury for articles for his private use; he stocked his farm by drawing animals heavy with young from the public herds, and after the young were born the mothers were returned without their progeny. Bligh and Thompson§ assert that the undertaking was of the nature of an experimental farm designed to demonstrate the value of industry and good management under conditions prevalent in the colony. If this was so, the experiment was valueless, for Bligh gave himself concessions far in excess of those proposed for settlers,|| and Thompson admitted this in the statement¶ " that a common Farmer, who has to pay for everything, would by no means have such profits." Thompson asserted that the live stock and articles drawn from the public herds and stores were to be paid for in the produce of the farm. At that time very extended credits were given to settlers by government. As Bligh purchased his farm in January, 1807, and he was deposed in January, 1808, it is clear that the average duration of his credit did not exceed six months, and this was not excessive. Because Bligh had paid nothing into the public stores in return for goods and stock

---

* *See* page 44 *et seq.* and page 65 *et seq.*
† *See* note 106.   ‡ *See* page 359.   § *See* page 366.
|| *See* page 168.   ¶ *See* page 367.

delivered before January, 1808, it is unfair to assume that he did not intend to pay anything. It is not possible, therefore, to accept the charge put forward by the insurrectionaries that Bligh was guilty of conversion of public property to private uses. At the same time it was a grave error of judgment and utterly indefensible for a governor to engage in farming, which secured a pecuniary profit to himself in his private capacity, when the success of the enterprise was dependent largely on concessions granted by himself in his official capacity.

On the 14th of February, 1807, Governor Bligh initiated his first big reform by the publication of a general order which prohibited absolutely " the exchange of spirits or other liquors as payment for grain, animal food, labour, wearing apparel or any other commodity whatever." Severe penalties were ordered for offences against this regulation; for a prisoner, the punishment was 100 lashes and hard labour for twelve months; for a settler, free by servitude, pardon, or emancipation, deprivation of all indulgences from the crown, imprisonment for three months, and a fine of £20; for all other persons, deprivation of all indulgences from the crown and a fine of £50. This regulation was the first indirect cause which led to the deposition of Bligh. Although a wise and salutary measure, it operated adversely against the pecuniary interests of all classes of the community. John Macarthur and William Minchin admitted in their evidence at the court martial on George Johnston that everyone in the colony, officials, military, and all others, trafficked in spirits by necessity for want of a proper currency. Spirits were imported at a few shillings per gallon, and were bartered at 100 to 200 *per cent.* profit. Imported spirits were distributed according to the rank and influence of the individual, and it is clear that the senior officials and most favoured individuals reaped the greater profit. The colonists in general lacked the public spirit that should have won support for this well-advised reform, while pecuniary loss provoked opposition that was active though secret. Lieutenant-colonel Foveaux stated* that the result of the restrictions was to make " the gentleman and the Man of character, who would blush at being detected in an

* *See* page 642.

illicit transaction, the tributaries of the daring and unprincipled Smuggler and distiller." This testimony from Foveaux, who was an open antagonist of Bligh, indicates the peculiar attitude of many colonists who were opposed to Bligh. Although unwilling to commit a breach of the regulations openly, they connived at and participated in the profits of an illicit traffic. As in the case of the abolition of slavery by the British Parliament, and in the case of the prohibition of Kanaka labour on the Queensland sugar plantations, the pecuniary interest of the individual had been injured in the endeavour to procure the welfare of the community at large.

On the 9th of March, 1807, the ship *Dart,* belonging to John Macarthur and Messrs. Hulletts, of London, arrived in Port Jackson. In her two stills were imported; one had been sent out to the order of captain Abbott, and the second had been consigned to John Macarthur by his agent, who acted also for Abbott. The second still had been sent out without Macarthur's foreknowledge. Bligh ordered these stills into the public stores to be returned to England. This action produced no opposition, although it had important consequences at a later date.

The first open and active opposition to Bligh was shown by John Macarthur. It arose out of a verdict given by Bligh sitting in the court of appeal. It had been the practice in giving promissory notes to express payment in some form of barter, owing to the lack of specie. Wheat notes were given as follows: the sterling value of the note was divided by the current selling price of a bushel of wheat, and the note made out for the corresponding number of bushels. The value of wheat naturally fluctuated. At the Hawkesbury, it had been fixed at 9s. 3d. per bushel by general order in January, 1806. Owing to the severe losses by floods in March, 1806, the government price offered in the December following was 13s. 9d. In June, 1807, private sales were transacted at 28s. Macarthur held a wheat note given by Andrew Thompson at prices current before the flood. On this note, Macarthur sued in the civil court for the specific performance of the contract on the basis of the bushels of wheat expressed. The court gave the decision that the note was an expression of value and not of quantity of produce. Against this verdict Macarthur appealed in

July, 1807, and Bligh dismissed the appeal without hearing the appellant. By this decision, Macarthur was compelled to accept a reduction in the number of bushels expressed in the note *pro rata* with the increased price of wheat between the dates on which the bill was drawn and on which it was liquidated. Thereafter, Macarthur ceased to visit at government house. The governor showed no resentment of this action, and subsequently called on Macarthur when he was reported to be ill.

In July, 1807, D'Arcy Wentworth, an assistant surgeon, was tried by a court martial for contempt and disobedience of orders on the complaint of captain Abbott. The court, under the presidency of major Johnston, found him guilty and sentenced him to be publicly reprimanded. On the 23rd of July, Wentworth was ordered to return to his duties, but two days later was suspended from office by orders of the governor. Wentworth immediately made application to Bligh for the reasons of his suspension; and when these were refused he sought permission to visit England, but this request was also refused. Bligh had caused a private inquiry* into the conduct of Wentworth, and he transmitted the charges to England without giving Wentworth the opportunity of making any reply. This action of Bligh was manifestly unjust. The court martial had been instigated by one of the military party, and it is probable that Bligh's inquiries arose out of the trial. However, the military party, after the arrest of Bligh, took up Wentworth's cause, when he was tried and honourably acquitted by court martial.† Wentworth's suspension provoked his bitter hostility to Bligh.

In the meantime, Bligh had been making inquiries into the land tenures in the town of Sydney. He submitted a lengthy report on the subject in his despatch, dated 31st October, 1807. Bligh noted irregularities in many of the leases,‡ and on the 23rd of July issued a general order directing six named persons to quit and remove their houses from lands adjoining government house on or before the 1st of November following. These persons had received permissive occupancies from Governor King. Amongst other leases adversely commented on in his despatch there was a

* *See* page 188.   † *See* page 446 *et seq.*   ‡ *See* note 38.

lease to John Macarthur, near St. Phillip's church. This lease was dated 1st January, 1806, but Bligh asserted* that it was given after the 12th of July, 1806, which statement is probably correct.† It is very likely that this and other leases were given by King as a *placebo* to some of his active opponents. Bligh prevented Macarthur taking possession of the lease, as it encroached on the church lands.

In October, 1807, Bligh was again in open conflict with Macarthur. Bligh gave orders that the complete stills, which had been imported in the *Dart*, should be shipped on the *Duke of Portland* for their return to England. After their arrival the coppers had been removed to Macarthur's house to unpack the sundries which they contained, and had not been returned to the public store. When he heard of Bligh's orders, Macarthur endeavoured to obtain permission to sell the complete stills to some ship going to India or China, or, if this was objected to, to retain the copper only for domestic use. These requests were ignored. After some petty objections raised by Macarthur, the coppers were removed from the house of Garnham Blaxcell, Macarthur's partner, under the superintendence of Robert Campbell, junior, acting by the orders of the naval officer, but without the consent of Macarthur. Macarthur at once brought an action‡ against Campbell, junior, for wrongful seizure of his property, and secured a majority verdict in his favour on the ground that Campbell, junior, held no official status. The vindictive words used by Macarthur in his address to the court indicate that it was a malicious prosecution directed at Bligh. The deportation of the stills was justified fully, and the only error was committed by the naval officer when he directed his nephew, R. Campbell, junior, to remove the coppers, instead of personally superintending.

In the more important of his official acts, Bligh had been in the right. But in smaller matters he had acted unwisely, and his conduct had caused offence. By this time, there had developed, especially amongst the military, a feeling of rancour and bitterness. This was due to small causes, to his coarseness of speech, to the directness of his remarks, and to his disregard for the feelings

* *See* page 424.   † *See* note 128.   ‡ *See* page 174.

of others. Major Johnston, in October, 1807, wrote to the military
secretary of the Duke of York, and asked him to intervene between
the governor and the commanding officer of the military. Johnston
complained of Bligh's " interfering in the interior management of
the Corps by selecting and ordering both officers and men on
various duties without my knowledge; his abusing and confining
the soldiers without the smallest provocation and without ever consulting me as their commanding officer; and again, his casting
the most unreserved and opprobrious censure on the Corps at
different times in company at Government House." Johnston
was of a pacific nature, but it is clear that he was antagonised by
the manners which Bligh had learnt on the quarter-deck.

Prior to the arrival of the schooner *Parramatta,* at the end of
November, Bligh had acquired an unenviable position. John
Macarthur and D'Arcy Wentworth were his open enemies ; George
Johnston, John Harris, William Minchin, and the military generally
were in covert antagonism to him ; many of the merchants were
opposed to him owing to restriction of their trade. On the other
hand, the middle and lower orders of settlers were warmly attached
to him on account of his actions for their relief after the Hawkesbury floods. In the meantime Bligh's enemies in England had not
been idle. The opposition commenced by the friends of the mutineers of the *Bounty* had been continued. In Bligh's absence, many
calumnies had been circulated, just as had happened under the
administration of governors Hunter and King. Short had obtained
a hearing, and his reports had gained credence to Bligh's prejudice. Bligh was accused of selling provisions at high prices for
his own emolument during the scarcity in the colony. An agitation for Bligh's recall was commenced, and Francis Grose, who
had become a general, was suggested openly as his successor.
As the appointment of Grose would have thrown the colony
entirely into the hands of the military, it is highly probable that
the agitation was originated by the friends of the military party
in New South Wales. The opinion held in the office of the secretary of state is unknown, but the extent of the agitation may be
gathered by the fact that the *Morning Herald* on the 1st of
February, 1808, actually announced the recall of Bligh. This
was incorrect.

In June, 1807, the schooner *Parramatta*, which belonged to John Macarthur and Messrs. Hulletts, of London, had cleared for Otaheite. John Hoare, a convict for life, secreted himself on board her, and at Otaheite escaped in the *General Wellesley* to India. By the port regulations, the master of every vessel at Port Jackson had to give security, himself in £800 and two inhabitants in £50 each, not to carry off any person without the governor's sanction. Macarthur and his partner, Garnham Blaxcell, were the bondsmen for the *Parramatta*. When the schooner returned in November, 1807, the naval officer sued for the amount of the bond in the civil court, and it was decided that the bond was forfeited. An appeal against this verdict was entered. In the meantime the naval officer refused to allow the vessel to be entered, retained the ship's papers, and placed two police officers on board in charge. Macarthur deeply resented this, and on the 7th of December notified* the master and crew of the schooner that he had abandoned her, and that they were no longer to expect pay or provisions. Seven days later the master and crew came on shore, and made affidavits† at the judge-advocate's office that they had left the ship on account of Macarthur's action. These affidavits were necessary, as it was contrary to the port regulations for seamen to remain on shore in Sydney. Up to this moment Macarthur was wholly in the wrong, and deliberately set the law at defiance. The decision of the civil court for the forfeiture of the bonds was given on a question of fact. The naval officer was justified in holding the schooner until the penalties were liquidated. The lodging of an appeal could have had only the object of delay. No fact justified Macarthur in abandoning the schooner and forcing the crew to commit a breach of the port regulations.

Acting under instructions from Bligh, judge-advocate Atkins wrote‡ on the same day (14th December) to summon Macarthur to appear on the following day and answer for his conduct. Macarthur somewhat contemptuously declined to appear.§ This was an error of judgment on the part of Macarthur, though strictly within his legal rights. The letter was virtually a command from

* *See* page 295.
† *See* page 307.   ‡ *See* page 307.   § *See* page 296.

the representative of the King, and certainly should not have been resented by him. On the 15th of December Atkins issued a warrant* for the arrest of Macarthur, and according to Atkins' evidence, Bligh approved of his action. In issuing this warrant, Atkins was wrong. The letter to Macarthur was not a summons, and, until a legal summons had been served and ignored, no warrant for Macarthur's arrest should have been issued. Bligh had the misfortune of having a man as his legal adviser who was untrained in the law and addicted to alcoholic excess.† The warrant was served by a constable. Macarthur spurned the constable, told him that he would never submit until he was forced, and added that Bligh and his friends would soon make a rope to hang themselves. This action was an open defiance of the civil power. On the following day a bench of magistrates,‡ which included major Johnston, decided that a second warrant should be issued for his arrest. This was executed, and Macarthur was brought before Atkins and admitted to bail. On the 17th of December, he was again brought before a bench of magistrates,§ consisting of the judge-advocate, John Palmer, and two of the military party, George Johnston and Edward Abbott. By this bench he was committed to take his trial before the criminal court, and was admitted to bail.

The court of criminal jurisdiction did not meet until the 25th of January, 1808, but in the interval Macarthur was not idle. Four days after his committal he called upon Atkins for payment of a bill drawn in 1793. When payment was not made, he applied to Bligh for relief in a memorial,‖ dated 29th December, and in reply was informed " that a Court of Civil Jurisdiction is open to take cognizance of all Civil Actions." He repeated his applications to the governor without success on the 1st and 12th of January.

Macarthur then attempted to make use of his lease near St. Phillip's church, which had been submitted by Bligh to the consideration of the secretary of state. For this purpose he engaged some soldiers of the New South Wales Corps to erect a fence around the allotment, which included a public well. Bligh was compelled publicly to put a stop to this work.

On the 20th of January Macarthur made a strong effort¶ to obtain a copy of his indictment, but this request was refused.

* *See* page 310.   † *See* page 150.
‡ *See* page 312.   § *See* page 314.   ‖ *See* page 231.   ¶ *See* page 228.

Two days later, when the members of the criminal court had been nominated, he wrote a letter* to Bligh protesting against Atkins sitting as judge-advocate. In reply, he was told that the law must take its course. In this action, Macarthur was clearly in the wrong. At the trial of major Johnston in England in 1811, the judge-advocate general stated that " it was perfectly incompetent to any person brought before that Court to offer a challenge against the Judge-Advocate sitting upon it; he might as well offer a challenge against a Judge in this country sitting at the Assizes. The Governor has no more right to change the Judge-Advocate who sits upon that Court than he has to change a Judge in England or anywhere else."

There is no doubt that Macarthur, prior to his trial, had determined to force a crisis with Bligh. Whether the actual usurpation of the government had been determined will probably never be known. There are indications that some conspiracy was on foot. On the 11th of January the removal of captain Abbott from his command at Parramatta to headquarters was proposed. Abbott was a magistrate, and this change would have given the military party a preponderancy on the bench of magistrates at Sydney. This plan was checkmated by Bligh, who sanctioned the change to take place on the 27th of January, but dispensed with Abbott's services as a magistrate. Abbott, in a private letter to Philip Gidley King, dated 13th February, 1808, stated that he had advised major Johnston that, in the event of taking the step to arrest Bligh, to send for lieutenant-governor Paterson, then stationed at Port Dalrymple, immediately afterwards. As Abbott was at Parramatta on the 26th of January, it is clear that this advice must have been given previously, and that the decision to make the arrest was not the mere impulse of the moment. Abbott, however, did not confirm this statement in his evidence at the trial of Johnston. At that trial Bligh swore that the screws were taken out of the breeches of the two field pieces at government house on the night of the 25th of January. Private Gillard swore that he removed the elevating screws from the same guns a few days before the 26th of January, by order of lieutenant Minchin. On the 24th of January, Edward and Hannibal Macarthur,

* *See* page 229.

Nicholas Bayly, and Garnham Blaxcell (Macarthur's two bails-men), and the six officers who were nominated for the criminal court on the following day, all dined together at a mess dinner of the New South Wales Corps. John Macarthur was not present at the dinner, but spent the evening walking to and fro on the parade in front of the mess-room. It seems highly probable that the usurpation was the result of a well-considered plan, in which the prime mover was John Macarthur; that major Johnston was the passive figure-head of a more active and energetic party behind him; that many of the malcontents against Bligh were averse to extreme measures; and that the trial of Macarthur was made the cause of action by the prisoner and his immediate adherents to force Bligh's hands and to implicate the waverers and provoke them to take a decisive step.

The criminal court met for the trial of Macarthur* in the morning of the 25th of January. The members were the judge-advocate and six military officers. As was the custom, the oath was administered to the six officers by the judge-advocate, but, before Atkins had taken his oath, Macarthur entered a protest against him sitting as judge-advocate. The letters patent constituting the courts of justice enacted that the criminal court should consist of the judge-advocate for the time being and six officers of his Majesty's sea or land forces. These were one and indivisible. Until all the members of the court were sworn in, no legal court was constituted. The six officer members of the court therefore could only hear the protest in a private capacity, as they had no judicial standing until the court was legally complete. As has already been stated, no protest could stand, and the governor had no power to remove or supersede the judge-advocate. Before the meeting of the court, Macarthur was in possession of Bligh's opinion† on the merits of a protest against Atkins, and he knew that it would not be entertained. In the deliberations of a criminal court, the judge-advocate acted as an exponent of the law to his colleagues, but in the consideration of the verdict his vote was equal only to that of any other member of the court. As six of the seven members of the court were military officers, and probably in sympathy with him, Macarthur had little reason to fear the

*See page 221 et seq.　　†See page 229.

verdict. The only inference that can be drawn from these facts is that Macarthur, in making this irregular protest, deliberately attempted to upset the administration of the colony, to force an immediate issue with Bligh, and to implicate openly the members of the court in an illegal procedure. It is probable that this action was taken on Macarthur's initiative, with the connivance of the extremist members of the military party. For some months previously, it must be remembered, Macarthur was not on terms of intimacy with Johnston and several of the senior officers.

At this stage, Bligh sought the advice of major Johnston, and at 5.30 p.m. on the 25th of January wrote requesting to see him without delay. Johnston sent a verbal message in reply that he was too unwell to attend. He had been present at the mess dinner on the night before, and had met with an accident on his return to Annandale. It is recorded that his face was much bruised and his arm in a sling for several days, and it is probable that a temporary incapacity was serious enough to affect Johnston's judgment for the time.

Early in the morning of the 26th of January, Macarthur was arrested and lodged in gaol on a warrant, issued by Atkins, Arndell, Campbell, and Palmer, for his alleged escape from the custody of the provost-marshal. Probably the magistrates were wrong in issuing this warrant. Macarthur's bailsmen were responsible for his appearance before the criminal court. As no criminal court had yet been legally formed, it is probable that technically Macarthur had not surrendered to his bail, was not in the custody of the provost-marshal, and that his bailsmen were still responsible for his appearance.

At 10 o'clock the six members of the criminal court met, and forwarded to Bligh Macarthur's protest against Atkins and their own protest against the imprisonment of Macarthur. Bligh did not reply to these letters, and at 3 o'clock the members adjourned. Shortly afterwards Bligh forwarded a summons to each member to appear before him on the following day to answer certain charges. The crimes they were charged with were treason and usurpation of the government. It is probable that the issue of this summons or some similar action by Bligh was the aim and object of the provocative conduct of Macarthur and the extremists. Bligh immediately communicated to Johnston the charges against the officers, and suggested that during his (John-ston's) illness captain Abbott should take the military command. In reply to Bligh's letter, Johnston sent a verbal message " that he was so ill as to be unable to write, but that he would get a person to write an answer in the evening."

Johnston received Bligh's letter at Annandale shortly after 4 o'clock, and notwithstanding his refusal to wait on Bligh, he hastened to the barracks, then situated around the site of Wynyard-square. It is evident that Johnston made no effort to achieve a peaceable settlement, but on the contrary was determined to let matters take their course. Soon after his arrival at the barracks Johnston committed the first open act of rebellion and usurpation of the civil power, when he assumed the title of lieutenant-governor and signed the warrant for the release of Macarthur from gaol. Macarthur had been confined in gaol throughout the day. The promptitude with which Johnston ordered the release is additional evidence that the insurrection was a preconceived plan. Macarthur was released, and shortly after 7 o'clock government house was surrounded by the soldiers, Bligh was arrested, and the colony was in the hands of rebels.

It is needless to discuss the problem as to which individuals were actually privy to the final decision for the arrest of Bligh. The opinion of the English counsel who were consulted was " that the evidence to be collected from the correspondence prin-cipally affects John McArthur, Nicholas Bayly, Doctor Townson, John Blaxland, Garnham Blaxcell, and Thomas Jamieson, as having previously concerted together with Major Johnston the arrest and imprisonment of Governor Bligh, and having after-wards borne a part in the assumed Government."

A careful study of the papers will show that very few of the malcontents were desirous of extreme measures. The large majority of the insurrectionaries were men who sought unre-strained freedom of action, and a few weeks after the arrest of Bligh they were just as antagonistic to Johnston's administration as they had been to Bligh's. After the arrest misrepresentations were industriously circulated by the rebels to justify their action. It was stated even that Bligh had shown cowardice and was found under a servant's bed. A picture illustrating this episode was freely exhibited by sergeant-major Whittle, and is still extant. Bligh's friends circulated pipes discrediting the leading rebels. In consequence it is impossible to reach a definite conclusion on many of the issues which were raised.

Governor Bligh was the victim of circumstances when he failed to maintain the government of the colony. Since the departure of Governor Phillip, in 1792, officials had received many privileges and perquisites, which, though inconsistent with the public welfare, had been excused by the fact that, owing to the high cost of living, the man who held a situation under government could barely subsist on his pay. Bligh put an end to these privileges and perquisites. He refused land grants, restricted assigned labour, and prohibited the barter of spirits. He acted with the best intentions, and his reforms were urgently needed. But he paid too little regard to the necessity of conciliating, so far as might be, powerful interests and powerful individuals. The determination of his actions and the coarseness of his speech gave, perhaps, unnecessary offence, but by no means justified the opposition to and the usurpation of his government.

A fact of importance is that at the critical moment in the story, the second in command in the colony was major Johnston. It was generally acknowledged that Johnston was " a well disposed good natured man—a cheerful companion and an idol of the soldiers and the lower order of society." His well meaning good nature made him an easy tool in the hands of men determined to overcome any obstacles which might interfere with their personal interests. Probably at no other time would Macarthur have been successful in attaining his ends. If lieutenant-governor Paterson had been present at headquarters, Macarthur would have been unsuccessful, for Paterson had a strong distrust of him. Lieutenant-colonel Foveaux had similar feelings, and when he superseded Johnston Macarthur was retired into private life. It was otherwise with Johnston, and Macarthur was able to mould his views, with the result that during the insurrection and Johnston's subsequent administration, Macarthur held the actual command. This view is well borne out by the subsequent action of the English government. In 1809, Johnston and Macarthur sailed for England in the *Admiral Gambier*. The government were desirous of dropping all further inquiry into the rebellion, but Johnston forced an issue. He was tried by court martial in 1811, convicted of mutiny, and cashiered, a mild penalty for such a crime. He was allowed to return to the colony in 1812, and at the time of his death, in 1823, Lachlan Macquarie stated that the war office was favourably considering his reinstatement to his former rank in the army. Macarthur, on the other hand, was prevented from returning to the colony until the year 1817, except at the risk of standing his trial before the criminal court on his arrival in Sydney.

When Governor Macquarie arrived, in 1810, he made a general summary of the circumstances of the arrest. He stated:—

" It occurs to me that your Lordship may perhaps wish to know my opinion and Sentiments with regard to the extraordinary transactions and disturbances that took place here, as connected with the arrest of Governor Bligh, and the subversion of his Government, by Lieut.-Colonel Johnston, at the head of the New South Wales Corps, on the 26th of January, 1808.

" I have taken particular pains to discover the cause which gave rise to that most daring event, and to the mutinous conduct of Lt.-Colonel Johnston and the New South Wales Regiment, and find it extremely difficult to form a just Judgment on this delicate and mysterious subject, Party rancour having run so high as to preclude the possibility of arriving at the truth without a very minute and legal investigation of the whole business.

" But, in justice to Governor Bligh, I must say that I have not been able to discover any Act of his which could in any degree form an excuse for, or in any way warrant, the violent and Mutinous Proceedings pursued against him on that occasion, very few complaints having been made to me against him, and even those few are rather of a trifling nature.

" On the other hand, there cannot be a doubt but that Governor Bligh's administration was extremely unpopular, particularly among the higher orders of the People; And from my own short experience, I must acknowledge that he is a most unsatisfactory Man to transact business with, from his want of candor and decision, in so much that it is impossible to place the smallest reliance on the fulfilment of any engagement he enters into."

All the unbiassed contemporary opinions are in full accordance with Macquarie's summary.

After the insurrection Bligh was kept in confinement until February, 1809, when he was allowed to embark on H.M.S. *Porpoise* for the purpose of sailing direct for England. Bligh, however, sailed for Tasmania, and returned to Port Jackson after the arrival of Governor Macquarie. He took his final departure on the 12th of May, 1810. During the two years that elapsed between his arrest and departure, Bligh committed many breaches of faith in his negotiations with the insurrectionaries. These can be regarded only as distinct blemishes on an otherwise clean fighting career. On several occasions he pledged his word of honour, which he did not keep. His plea, that a promise to a rebel was not binding, can scarcely be accepted.

After his return to England, Bligh was promoted, in July, 1811, to the rank of rear-admiral of the blue squadron, and in June, 1814, to that of vice-admiral, but remained on the half-pay list. He died in Bond-street, London, on the 7th of December, 1817, and was buried in Lambeth churchyard.

The administration of Governor Bligh and its results form one of the most important milestones in the development of the civil life of Australia. Had this stormy epoch been eliminated from the history of this continent, progress might have been retarded indefinitely. In the interval between the departure of Governor Phillip in 1792, and the arrival of Governer Bligh, the administration of the colony had fallen into the hands of what was to all intents and purposes a small oligarchy, consisting of the military officers and a few wealthy partisans. Their one object was to acquire wealth. Everything was subordinated to this desire, with the result that the many outside the oligarchy were forced to lose the profits of their honest labour in the ruinous traffic which benefited chiefly the members of the ruling class. Bligh recognised the evil, and his deposition was brought about because it was perceived that this was the only means to prevent immediate and complete reform. But his arrest did not result in the failure of his efforts and a permanent reversion to the former conditions. It concentrated the attention of the English authorities on the conditions of the colony. It forced them to initiate immediate reforms. It directly caused the recall of the New South Wales Corps, which, by long residence, had become the most powerful and perhaps the most evil factor in the community. It indirectly led to the reform of the law courts, to the removal of the restrictions on trade and commerce, and to the general betterment of the conditions of life in the colony.

George Johnston.

George Johnston was born at Annandale, Dumfrieshire, Scotland, on the 19th of March, 1764. On the 6th of March, 1776, he obtained a commission as second lieutenant of the 45th company of marines. During the years 1777 and 1778, he was stationed at New York and Halifax. On the 27th of April, 1778, he was promoted to the rank of first lieutenant in the 91st company. In the years 1779 and 1780, he was employed recruiting in England. In 1781, he was despatched to the East Indies, and remained there until December, 1785. During this period he served on board H. M. ships *Sultan* and *Worcester*, and on four occasions was in action with the French fleet. In one engagement, he was severely wounded. He served under Earl Percy, who, after succeeding to the dukedom of Northumberland, became a patron of Johnston. In January, 1786, he obtained leave of absence for six months, and on resuming duty was attached to headquarters. Towards the end of the year, he was transferred as first lieutenant to the detachment of marines intended to form the garrison for the settlement at Botany Bay. In December, he embarked on board the *Lady Penrhyn*, a transport in the first fleet. When Governor Phillip examined Port Jackson in January, 1788, it is claimed that Johnston was the first man to land in that harbour. During the first twelve months of the settlement, Johnston acted as adjutant of orders to Governor Phillip. After the death of captain Shea, on the 2nd of February, 1789, he received the command of the vacant company as captain-lieutenant. In 1790, he was in command of the marines on detached duty at Norfolk Island. In 1791, the detachment of marines was relieved by the New South Wales Corps, and at the same time was given the option of being discharged or of remaining in the colony. Many availed themselves of the privilege, and were enlisted in an auxiliary or fifth company in the corps. Johnston, who had returned from Norfolk Island with the marines, took command of this company, and a commission as captain was issued to him on the 25th of September, 1792. He was one of the first land-owners from the class of officers, and was granted 100 acres at Annandale by lieutenant-governor Grose on the 12th of February, 1793. In January, 1796, he was nominated by Governor Hunter to relieve Philip Gidley King in the command at Norfolk Island, but owing to ill-health he was unable to fulfil this duty. In the following September he was appointed aide-de-camp to the governor. In 1800, Johnston received his brevet rank as major. In the same year he was placed under arrest by lieutenant-colonel Paterson on charges of " paying spirits to a serjeant as part of his pay at an improper price, contempt, and disobedience of orders." He protested against trial by court martial in the colony, and his objection was upheld by Governor Hunter, who, in consequence, ordered him to England under arrest. He sailed in October, 1800, on H.M.S. *Buffalo.* In England his trial was quashed.* He returned to the colony on the 14th of December, 1801, on board the transport *Minorca,* but it was not until the 17th of October, 1802, that he was released from arrest and his reconciliation with lieutenant-colonel Paterson was announced.†

In January, 1803, Johnston took the temporary command of the New South Wales Corps during the illness of lieutenant-colonel Paterson. At this time inquiries and courts martial were being held in connection with certain libellous pipes about Governor King which had been circulated. These involved the governor in serious disputes with the military. During a court martial on Anthony Fenn Kemp, of which Johnston was president, John Harris, the judge-advocate and prosecutor, was charged with " scandalous infamous behaviour " in disclosing the votes of members at previous courts martial. Thereupon the court martial on Kemp was adjourned, and the trial of Harris demanded by Johnston.‡ The results of this action seriously interfered with the administration of the colony, and a bitter correspondence§ ensued. Johnston demanded the appointment of a judge-advocate in place of Harris. This request was strongly resisted by King,

---

* *See* page 270, volume III. † *See* page 322, volume IV. .
‡ *See* page 177, volume IV. § *See* page 177 *et seq.*, volume IV.

but he ultimately gave way " to Secure the Peace of the Colony by the Criminal Courts not continuing suspended for want of Members to compose it and on no other consideration." This conflict between the military and King has a remarkable similarity to the final dispute between the military and Bligh. The action taken by Johnston was extremely doubtful. The papers that are available do not demonstrate how far his action was due to his personal initiative, how far to the instigation of a party behind him, as the papers in his actions against Bligh do.

In March, 1804, Johnston commanded the military sent in pursuit of the convicts who had risen in rebellion at Castle Hill. He acted with great courage and daring when he encountered the rebels at Vinegar Hill, and completely routed them. When lieutenant-colonel Paterson was detailed for the command of the settlement at Port Dalrymple, in 1804, the command of the New South Wales Corps devolved on Johnston, and he retained it until the arrival of lieutenant-colonel Foveaux, on the 28th of July, 1808. On the 1st of January, 1806, he received his commission as major.

In spite of a certain weakness of decision, Johnston's character was an admirable one. He was " a well disposed good natured man." He had few if any personal enemies, and was popular with all persons he came in contact with. In his routine military administration he was methodical and just, and was the idol of the rank and file. His very good nature made him the easy tool of conspirators, and this was his undoing. Prior to the rebellion, he resented the interference of Governor Bligh in military matters, but when making his report to the military secretary to the Duke of York on this subject, his diffidence and fairness were shown when he stated: " I will detail to you . . . . some of the most glaring acts of Governor Bligh's indecorous and, *I hope I might be pardoned if I said,* oppressive conduct."

Prior to the arrest of Bligh, the malcontents probably held frequent conferences with Johnston, for without him action was impossible. Captain Abbott stated that the arrest had been discussed, but it is probable that Johnston was averse to extreme action. When John Macarthur arrived at the barracks after his liberation on the 26th of January, 1808, Johnston is reported to have said: "God's curse! What am I to do, Macarthur? Here are these fellows advising me to arrest the Governor!" to which Macarthur replied: "Advising you; then, Sir, the only thing left for you to do is to do it. To advise on such matters is legally as criminal as to do them." If this conversation is correctly recorded it is proof that Johnston was the tool in the hands of the malcontents, and also that Macarthur at least recognised the guilt of the action.

Both at the time of the arrest and throughout his administration, Johnston failed to assert his personal authority, and it was generally recognised that the actual administration was in the hands of Macarthur. Johnston therefore was only the figure-head under whom the maladministration for the following six months was carried on.

His first official act was to assume the title of lieutenant-governor. This was quite unjustifiable. By the letters patent appointing each governor, the senior officer on the station was appointed administrator in the event of the death or absence of the governor or lieutenant-governor, and a lieutenant-governor was appointed only by a commission from the King. After this, acts of rebellion succeeded one another rapidly. On the 27th of January the judge-advocate, commissary, provost-marshal, naval officer, and, three days later, the chaplain, were suspended from their duties. If the rebellion had been only against the person of Governor Bligh, it is difficult to understand why these officers should have been promptly relieved of their duties before giving evidence of unwillingness to continue acting, unless the object of the rebels was to obtain a complete control of all branches of the government. During the first few days of power, an insurrectionary committee sat to examine Bligh's public and private papers, with the object of securing incriminating evidence against him. With the possible exception of the papers in connection with Bligh's farm, this search was a total failure, and is decidedly discreditable to the honour of the insurrectionaries.

The legal administration under Johnston was a parody of justice. On the 30th of January, a meeting of the criminal court was ordered for the trial of Macarthur. This trial was a pitiable farce. The indictment prepared by Atkins was read, but there was no prosecutor. Under these circumstances the prisoner, Macarthur, had unlimited license; there was no one to object to his questions; no one to cross-examine or refute the evidence he tendered; no one to question his conduct in producing extracts from Bligh's correspondence. Captain Abbott advised Johnston of the shameful character of the proceedings, but the trial was allowed to be completed without interruption.

The court martial on D'Arcy Wentworth* on the 17th of February was also a mockery, as there was no prosecutor. On the 10th of February, Thomas Jamison demanded a court martial† on himself, but when Bligh refused to prosecute, no trial was held. The holding of the one trial and the refusal of the other were decidedly inconsistent actions. William Gore was convicted of perjury without trial after taking action similar to that of Macarthur at his first trial, in entering a protest against the constitution of the court. The trial of John and Gregory Blaxland and Simeon Lord was allowed to develop into the persecution of the prosecutor. Two men, Oliver Russell and Robert Daniels, were convicted and sentenced for perjury without trial.‡ In the case of Russell and Daniels, Johnston recognised the flagrant injustice committed, and released the two prisoners.

By the end of March a very strong party had arisen in opposition to the Johnston-Macarthur administration. To checkmate this, Johnston ordered Charles Grimes and John Harris to carry his despatches to England. On the 26th of April, he wrote a letter§ to all officers stationed at Sydney challenging them to produce charges against Macarthur, but the officers tactfully refused. The settlers' antipathy to Macarthur is shown by their address|| to Johnston on the 11th of April. According to the testimony¶ of Thomas Arndell, Macarthur endeavoured to silence all expression of opposition by the refusal of the individual's right to petition the representative of the king.

By his arrest of Bligh, Johnston took over the administration of a colony in which existed many discontented and discordant factions. The removal of Bligh did nothing to remove these causes of trouble, and the ease with which the rebellion was

* See page 446 et seq.   † See page 442 et seq.   ‡ See page 484.
    § See page 518. || See page 572.   ¶ See page 573.

accomplished increased rather than allayed the restlessness. The general peace of the colony was in a worse condition after than before the arrest.

Johnston was superseded in the administration by the arrival of his senior officer, lieutenant-colonel Foveaux, on the 28th of July. After living for some months in retirement, he sailed for England in company with Macarthur in the *Admiral Gambier,* in March, 1809, and arrived there on the 9th of October following. In the meantime counsel had been consulted on behalf of the crown, and had given their opinion that major Johnston, Macarthur " and the persons concerned with them were guilty of a conspiracy and high misdemeanor in the arrest and imprisonment of Governor Bligh "; that the military concerned should be tried by a court martial in England, and all others by a criminal court in the colony. The authorities were unable to take action until the witnesses for the prosecution arrived, on the 25th of October, 1810, and it is doubtful whether any action would have been taken if Johnston and his party had not been so persistent in their agitation for an inquiry.

Johnston, who had been promoted lieutenant-colonel on the 25th of April, 1808, was tried by court martial, held at the Royal Hospital, Chelsea, on the 7th of May, 1811, and continued by adjournments until the 5th of June following. He was found guilty of mutiny, and sentenced to be cashiered.

Johnston returned to the colony in October, 1812, and lived in retirement on his estate called " Annandale," near Sydney. He died, universally respected, on the 3rd of January, 1823. At the time of his death his case was being considered by the war office, and it is probable that he would have been reinstated to his former rank in the army if he had lived a few months longer.

Joseph Foveaux.

JOSEPH FOVEAUX was born in the year 1765 of French parents resident in England. His career it not known until he obtained by purchase a commission as lieutenant in the New South Wales Corps on the 5th of June, 1789. He attained successive promotions to the rank of captain and major in the colony, the last being dated the 10th of June, 1796. Prior to his appointment as commandant at Norfolk Island, on the 26th of June, 1800, his official colonial career was undistinguished. During his residence in the colony he acquired considerable property, and in December, 1801, he sold his estate of 1,770 acres at Toongabbe, together with 1,350 sheep, to John Macarthur for the sum of £2,000.

On the 9th of June, 1801, his commission as lieutenant-governor of Norfolk Island was signed, and on the 29th of April, 1802, as lieutenant-colonel of the New South Wales Corps. He retained the command at Norfolk Island until the 9th of September, 1804, when he sailed for England in the whaler *Albion* on leave of absence for reasons of health. His administration of the island was memorable chiefly for the severity he adopted in the suppression of an attempted rising amongst the convicts. Whilst in England he drew up a report on the proposed evacuation of Norfolk Island, and his suggestions were adopted.

He returned to the colony on the 28th of July, 1808, and on the following day relieved Johnston in the administration of the government. The *camaraderie* and mutual support prevalent amongst the officers of the New South Wales Corps are well shown by his action on his arrival. On the 28th of July, Foveaux first learned of the arrest of Governor Bligh, and " determined on the same day to continue the arrest and to carry on the government in his own name. This resolution seems to have been taken almost sooner than it was possible to have received the necessary information "[*] to form his own opinion as to the advisability of Bligh's deposition.

The most important episodes of Foveaux's administration were a continuation of the efforts to induce Bligh to leave the colony, the granting of lands in the city of Sydney, the endeavour to secure the cancellation of the contract[†] between Messrs. Campbell and Hook and lieutenant-governor Collins, the erection of commissariat stores and barracks, and the drastic action[‡] he adopted with regard to the ship *Rose*.

* From a legal opinion given by T. G. Harris for the crown.
† *See* page 645.   ‡ *See* page 648 *et seq.*

Foveaux was relieved of the government by the arrival of lieutenant-governor Paterson on the 1st of January, 1809. He remained in the colony until the 17th of March, 1810, when he sailed for England in the brig *Experiment.* After the death of David Collins, Foveaux was an applicant for the post of lieutenant-governor at Hobart, but the secretary of state would not entertain his candidature. The counsel acting for the crown had reported that Foveaux was liable to be tried by court martial on a charge of mutiny in continuing the arrest and imprisonment of Governor Bligh. In consequence, he was under a cloud until the trial of Johnston was concluded, and it was decided to take no further proceedings in connection with Bligh's arrest. On the 4th of June, 1811, he was appointed inspecting field officer of the recruiting district for Cork and Waterford. A month later he was appointed lieutenant-colonel to the Greek regiment of light infantry. On the 4th of June, 1814, he was promoted to the rank of major-general, and on the 22nd of July, 1830, to that of lieutenant-general. He died on the 20th of March, 1846, at New-road, London.

FREDK. WATSON.

January, 1916.

DESPATCHES.

HISTORICAL RECORDS

OF

AUSTRALIA.

SERIES I.

GOVERNOR BLIGH'S COMMISSION.*

George the Third, by the Grace of God, &c., the United Kingdom of Great Britain and Ireland, King, Defender of the
Faith.

To Our Trusty and Well beloved William Bligh, Esquire, Greet-
ing: Whereas We did, by Our Letters Patent, under Our Great Recital of King's
Seal of Our United Kingdom of Great Britain and Ireland, commission.
bearing date, at Westminster, the twentieth day of February, in
the forty-second year of Our Reign, Constitute and Appoint Our
Trusty and Well-beloved Philip Gidley King, Esquire, to be Our
Captain-General and Governor-in-Chief in and over Our Territory called New South Wales, extending from the Northern Cape
or Extremity of the Coast called Cape York, in the latitude of
Ten Degrees thirty seven minutes south to the Southern extremity of the said Territory of New South Wales, or South
Cape, in the latitude of forty-three Degrees thirty-nine minutes
South, and of all the Country Inland to the Westward as far as
the One hundred and thirty fifth Degree of East Longitude,
reckoning from the Meridian of Greenwich, including all the
Islands adjacent in the Pacific Ocean within the Latitudes aforesaid of Ten Degrees thirty seven minutes South, and forty-three
Degrees thirty-nine Minutes South, and of all Towns, Garrisons,
Castle, Forts, and all other Fortifications or other Military Works
which might be erected upon the said Territory or any of the said
Islands for and during Our Will and Pleasure, as by the said
recited Letters Patent, relation being thereunto had may more
fully and at large appear: Now Know you that we have revoked Revocation of letters patent.
and determined, and by these presents Do revoke and determine,
the said Letters Patent, and every Clause, Article, and Thing
therein contained; And further Know You that We, reposing
Especial Trust and Confidence in the Prudence, Courage, and

Loyalty of You, the said William Bligh, of Our Especial Grace, certain knowledge, and Meer Motion, have thought fit to Con-

Bligh to be Governor-in-Chief.

stitute and Appoint You, the said William Bligh, to be Our Captain-General and Governor-in-Chief in and over Our Terri-tory called New South Wales, extending from the Northern Cape

Territorial jurisdiction.

or Extremity of the Coast, called Cape York, in the Latitude of Ten Degrees thirty-seven Minutes South, to the Southern Ex-tremity of the said Territory of New South Wales, or South Cape, in the Latitude of forty-three Degrees thirty-nine minutes South, and of all the Country Inland to the Westward, as far as the One hundred and thirty-fifth Degree of East Longitude, reckoning from the Meridian of Greenwich, including all the Islands adjacent in the Pacific Ocean within the Latitudes afore-said of Ten Degrees Thirty-seven Minutes South, and Forty-three Degrees Thirty-nine minutes South, and of all Towns, Garrisons, Castles, Forts, and all other Fortifications or other Military Works, which are or may be hereafter erected upon the

General instructions.

said Territory, or any of the said Islands; And We do hereby require and Command You to do and execute all things in due manner that shall belong to Your said Command, and the Trust We have Reposed in You, according to the several Powers and Directions granted or appointed You by this present Commission, and the Instructions and Authorities herewith given to you, or by such further Powers Instructions, and Authorities as shall at any time hereafter be granted or appointed You under Our Signet and Sign-Manual, or by Our Order in Our Privy Council, or by Us through one of Our Principal Secretaries of State. And

Oaths of office to be taken.

Our Will and Pleasure is that You, the said William Bligh, after the Publication of these Our Letters Patent, do in the first place take the Oaths appointed to be taken by an Act passed in the first year of the Reign of King George the First, Intituled "An Act for the further Security of His Majesty's Person and Govern-ment and the Succession of the Crown in the Heirs of the late Princess Sophia, being Protestants, and for extinguishing the Hopes of the pretended Prince of Wales and his Open and Secret Abettors," as altered and Explained by an Act passed in the sixth year of Our Reign, Intituled "An Act for altering the Oath of Abjuration and the Assurance, and for amending so much of an Act of the seventh Year of her late Majesty Queen Anne, In-tituled 'An Act for the Improvement of the Union of the Two Kingdoms,' as after the time therein limited requires the delivery of certain Lists and Copies therein mentioned to persons In-dicted of High Treason or Misprison of Treason"; As also that You make, use, and subscribe the Declaration mentioned in an Act of Parliament made in the twenty-fifth year of the Reign of

King Charles the Second, Intituled "An Act for preventing Dangers which may happen from Popish Recusants"; And likewise that You take the usual Oath for the due execution of the Office and Trust of our Captain-General and Governor-in-Chief in and over our said Territories and its dependencies for the due and impartial administration of Justice. And further, that you take the Oath required to be taken by Governors in the Plantations to do their utmost that the several Laws relating to Trade and Plantations be duly observed, which said Oaths and Declaration Our Judge-Advocate in our said Territory is hereby required to tender and administer unto You, and in Your Absence to Our Lieutenant-Governor, if there be any upon the place; All which being duly performed, you shall administer unto Our Lieutenant-Governor, if there be any upon the place, and to Our Judge-Advocate, the Oaths mentioned in the first mentioned Act of Parliament, altered as above, as also cause them to make and subscribe the aforementioned Declaration. And We do hereby authorize and empower you to keep and use the Public Seal, which will be herewith delivered to you or shall hereafter be sent to You, for sealing all things whatsoever that shall pass the Great Seal of Our said United Territory and its Dependencies. We do further Give and Grant unto You, the said William Bligh, full power and authority from time to time and at any time hereafter, by yourself or by any other to be authorized by you in that behalf, to administer and give the Oaths mentioned in the said first-recited Act of Parliament, altered as above, to all and every such Person or Persons as you shall think fit who shall at any time or times pass into Our said Territory or its Dependencies, or shall be resident or abiding therein. And We do hereby authorize and empower you to constitute and appoint Justices of the Peace, Coroners, Constables, and other necessary Officers and Ministers in Our said Territory and its Dependencies for the better administration of Justice and putting the Laws in execution, and to administer or cause to be administered unto them such Oath or Oaths as are actually given for the execution and performance of Offices and Places. And We do hereby Give and Grant unto You full power and authority where you shall see Cause or shall judge any Offender or Offenders in Criminal Matters, or for any Fines or Forfeitures due unto Us, fit Objects of Our Mercy, to Pardon all such Offenders, and to remit all such Offenders' Fines and Forfeitures (Treason and Wilful Murder only excepted), In which Cases You shall likewise have power, upon extraordinary occasions, to grant reprieves to the Offenders until and to the Intent Our Royal Pleasure may be known therein. And whereas it belongeth to Us, in right of Our Royal Pre-

Marginal notes:

Oaths to be taken by the lieutenant-governor and judge-advocate.

Custodian of the public seal.

Power to administer oaths of allegiance.

To appoint justices of the peace and officers of the law.

To pardon and reprieve.

rogative, to have the Custody of Idiots and their Estates, and to take the Profits thereof to Our Own use, finding them necessaries; And also to provide for the Custody of Lunatics and their Estates, without taking the Profits thereof to Our Own Use. And whereas such Idiots and Lunatics and their Estates remain under our immediate Care, great Trouble and Charges may arise to such as shall have occasion to resort unto Us for directions respecting such Idiots and Lunatics and their Estates, We have thought fit to entrust You with the Care and Commitment of the Custody of the said Idiots and Lunatics and their Estates. And

To pass grants for the custody of lunatics and their estates. We do by these presents Give and Grant unto You full Power and Authority, without expecting any further special Warrant from us from time to time, to Give Order and Warrant for the preparing of Grants of the Custodies of such Idiots and Lunatics and their Estates as are or shall be found by Inquisitions thereof to be taken by the Judges of Our Court of Civil Jurisdiction, and thereupon to make and pass Grants and Commitments, under Our Great Seal of Our said Territory, of the Custodies of all and every such Idiots and Lunatics, and their Estates, to such Person or Persons, Suitors in that behalf, as according to the Rules of Law, and the use and practice in those and the like Cases you shall judge meet for that Trust, the said Grants and Commitments to be made in such manner and form, as nearly as may be, as hath been heretofore used and accustomed in making the same under the Seal of Great Britain, and to contain such apt and Convenient Covenants, Provisions, and Agreements on the parts of the Committees and Grantees to be performed, and such security to be by them given, as shall be requisite and needful.

To levy armed forces. And We do hereby Give and Grant unto You, the said William Bligh, by Yourself or by your Captains or Commanders, by you to be authorized, full power and authority to levy, Arm, Muster, Command, and Employ all persons whatsoever residing within Our said Territory and its Dependencies under your Government, and as occasion shall serve, to march from one place to another, or to embark them for the resisting and withstanding of all Enemies, Pirates, and Rebels, both at Sea and Land; and such Enemies, Pirates, and Rebels, if there shall be occasion to pursue and prosecute in or out of the limits of Our said Territory and its Dependencies, and (if it shall so please God) them to vanquish, apprehend, and take, and being taken according to Law, to put to Death, or keep and preserve alive at your dis-

To proclaim martial law. cretion, and to execute Martial Law in time of Invasion, or other times, when by Law it may be executed; and to do and execute all and every other Thing and Things which to Our Captain-General and Governor-in-Chief Doth or ought of Right to belong.

And We do hereby give and grant unto you full Power and Authority to erect, raise, and build in Our said Territory and its Dependencies such and so many Forts, Platforms, Castles, Cities, Boroughs, Towns, and Fortifications, as You shall judge necessary, and the same or any of them to fortify and furnish with Ordnance and Ammunition and all sorts of Arms fit and necessary for the Security and Defence of the same, or any of them to demolish or dismantle as may be most convenient. And for as much as divers Mutinies and Disorders may happen by persons shipped and employed at Sea during the time of War, And to the end that such persons as shall be shipped and employed at Sea during the time of War may be better Governed and Ordered, We do hereby give and grant unto you, the said William Bligh, full power and Authority to constitute and appoint Captains, Lieutenants, Masters of Ships, and other Commanders and Officers, and to grant to such Captains, Lieutenants, Masters of Ships, and other Commanders and Officers, Commissions to execute the Law Martial during the time of War, according to the directions of an Act passed in the twenty-second year of the Reign of Our late Royal Grandfather, Intituled "An Act for amending, explaining, and reducing into One Act of Parliament the Laws relating to the Government of His Majesty's Ships, Vessels, and Forces by Sea." And the same is altered by An Act passed in the nineteenth year of Our Reign, Intituled "An Act to explain and amend an Act made in the twenty-second year of the Reign of his late Majesty, King George the Second, Intituled 'An Act for amending, explaining, and reducing into One Act of Parliament, the Laws relating to the Government of His Majesty's Ships, vessels, and Forces by Sea,'" and to use such Proceedings, Authorities, Punishments, Corrections, and Executions upon any Offender or Offenders who shall be mutinous, seditious, disorderly, or any way unruly, either at Sea, or during the time of their abode or residence in any of the Ports, Harbours, or Bays of Our said Territory, as the Case shall be found to require, according to Martial Law, and the said directions during the time of War, as aforesaid: Provided that nothing herein contained shall be construed to the enabling you, or any of You, Authority to hold Plea or have any jurisdiction of any Offence, Cause, Matter, or Thing committed or done upon the High Sea, or within any of the Havens, Rivers, or Creeks of Our said Territory and its dependencies under Your Government, by any Captain, Commander, Lieutenant, Master, Officer, Seaman, or other person whatsoever, who shall be in actual service and Pay, in or on Board of Our Ships of War, or other Vessels acting by immediate Commission, or Warrant from Our Commissioners

To erect fortifications.

To exercise sovereign naval powers.

With certain limitations.

for executing the Office of Our High Admiral of Our United
Kingdom of Great Britain and Ireland, or from Our High
Admiral of Our United Kingdom of Great Britain and Ireland
for the time being, under the Seal of Our Admiralty; But that
such Captain, Commander, Lieutenant, Master, Officer, Seaman,
Soldier, or other person so offending shall be left to be proceeded
against and tried as the merits of their Offences shall require,
either by Commission under Our Great Seal of this Kingdom as
the Statute of the twenty-eighth of King Henry the Eighth
directs, or by Commission from Our Commissioners for executing
the Office of Our High Admiral of Our United Kingdom of Great
Britain and Ireland or from Our High Admiral of Our United
Kingdom of Great Britain and Ireland for the time being, according to the aforesaid Act, intituled "An Act for amending, explaining, and reducing into one Act of Parliament the Laws
relating to the Government of His Majesty's Ships, Vessels, and
Forces by Sea," as the same is altered by an Act passed in the
nineteenth Year of Our Reign, Intituled "An Act to explain and
amend an Act made in the twenty-second year of the reign of
His late Majesty King George the second, Intituled 'An Act
for amending, explaining, and reducing into One Act of Parliament the Laws relating to the Government of His Majesty's

The trial of offences committed at sea. Ships, Vessels, and Forces by Sea'": Provided nevertheless that
all Disorders and Misdemeanors committed on Shore by any
Captain, Commander, Lieutenant, Master, Officer, Seaman, Sol-
dier, or any other person whatsoever, belonging to any of Our
Ships of War, or other Vessels acting by immediate Commission
or Warrant from Our Commissioners for executing the Office of
Our High Admiral of Our United Kingdom of Great Britain and
Ireland, or from Our High Admiral of our United Kingdom of
Great Britain and Ireland for the time being under the seal of
Our Admiralty, may be tried and punished according to the Laws
of the place where any such Disorders, Offences, and Misdemeanors shall be committed on shore, notwithstanding such
Offender be in Our actual service and borne in Our Pay on
Board any such Our Ships of War or other Vessels acting by
immediate Commission or Warrant from Our Commissioners for
executing the Office of Our High Admiral of our United Kingdom of Great Britain and Ireland, or from Our High Admiral
of Our United Kingdom of Great Britain and Ireland for the
time being as aforesaid, so as he shall not receive any protection
for the avoiding of Justice for such offences committed on shore
from any pretence of his being employed in Our Service at Sea.

Power to control finances. Our Will and Pleasure is that all Public Monies which shall be
raised be issued out by Warrants from you, and be disposed of by

you for the support of the Government, or for such other purpose
as shall be particularly directed, and not otherwise. And We do To grant land.
hereby Give and Grant unto You full Power and Authority to
agree for such Lands, Tenements, And Hereditaments as shall be
in Our Power to dispose of and them to Grant to any Person or
Persons upon such Terms and upon such moderate Quit Rents,
Services, and Acknowledgements to be thereupon reserved unto
Us according to such Instructions as shall be given to You under
Our Sign-Manual, which said Grants are to pass and be sealed by
Our Seal of Our said Territory and its Dependencies, and, being
entered upon Record by such Officer or Officers as you shall
appoint thereunto, shall be good and effectual in Law against Us,
Our Heirs and Successors. And We do hereby Give you, the To control
said William Bligh, full power to appoint Fairs, Marts, and commerce.
Markets, as also such and so many Ports, Harbours, Bays, Havens,
and other Places for the conveniency and security of Shipping,
and for the better loading and unloading of Goods and Mer-
chandizes, as by you shall be thought fit and necessary. And We
do hereby require and command all Officers and Ministers, Civil
and Military, and all other Inhabitants of Our said Territory and
its Dependencies, to be obedient, aiding and assisting unto You,
the said William Bligh, in the execution of this Our Commission,
and of the Powers and Authorities herein contained, And in Case
of your Death or Absence out of Our said Territory, to be
obedient, aiding, and assisting unto such Person as shall be
appointed by Us to be Our Lieutenant-Governor or Commander-
in-Chief of Our said Territory and its Dependencies, To whom
We do, therefore, by these presents, Give and Grant all and
singular the Powers and Authorities herein granted to be by him
executed and enjoyed during Our Pleasure, or until your Arrival
within Our said Territory and its Dependencies. And if, upon Provision
Your Death or Absence out of the said Territory and its Depen- for vacancy
in office.
dencies, there be no Person upon the place commissioned or
appointed by Us to be Our Lieutenant-Governor, or Commander-
in-Chief of Our said Territory and its Dependencies, Our Will
and Pleasure is that the Officer Highest in Rank, who shall be at
the time of Your Death or Absence upon Service within the same,
and who shall take the Oath and subscribe the Declaration
appointed to be taken and subscribed by you, or by the Commander-in-Chief of Our said Territory and its Dependencies,
shall take upon him the Administration of the Government, and
execute Our said Commission and Instructions, and the several
Powers and Authorities therein contained, in the same manner
and to all intents and purposes as other Our Lieutenant-Governor
or Commander-in-Chief should or ought to do in Case of your

Absence, until your return, or in all Cases until Our further
Pleasure be known therein. And We do hereby Declare, Ordain,
and Appoint that You, the said William Bligh, shall and may
hold and execute and enjoy the Office and Place of Our Captain-
General and Governor-in-Chief in and over Our said Territories
and its Dependencies, together with all and singular the Powers
and Authorities hereby granted unto You, for and during Our
Will and Pleasure. In Witness, &c., the twenty-fourth day of May.
By writ of Privy Seal. ·

INSTRUCTIONS TO GOVERNOR BLIGH.

George R.   25th May, 1805.

INSTRUCTIONS for our trusty and well-beloved William Bligh,
Esquire, &c., &c.

1st. With these our Instructions you will receive our Commission under our Great Seal, constituting and appointing you to be
our Captain-General and Governor-in-Chief of our Territory
called New South Wales, extending from the Northern Cape or
Extremity of the Coast called Cape York, in the Latitude of Ten
Degrees thirty-seven Minutes South, to the Southern Extremity
of the said Territory of New South Wales, or South Cape, in the
Latitude of Forty-three Degrees Thirty-Nine Minutes South, and
of all the Country Inland to the Westward, as far as the One
hundred and Thirty-fifth Degree of East Longitude, reckoning
from the Meridian of Greenwich, including all the Islands adjacent in the Pacific Ocean, within the Latitudes aforesaid of the
Ten Degrees Thirty-seven Minutes South and Forty-three Degrees thirty-nine Minutes South, and of all Towns, Garrisons,
Castles, Forts, and all other Fortifications or other Military
Works which now are or may be hereafter erected upon the said
Territory, or any of the said Islands, with directions to obey
such Orders and Instructions as shall from time to time be
given to you under our Signet and Sign Manual, or by our
Order in our Privy Council. You are therefore to take upon
you the execution of the Trust we have reposed in you, and as
soon as conveniently may be, with all due solemnity to cause our
said Commission under Our Great Seal of the United Kingdom
of Great Britain and Ireland, constituting you Our Governor
and Commander-in-Chief as aforesaid, to be read and published.

2nd. It is Our Royal Will and Pleasure that you do pursue
such measures as are necessary for the Peace and Security of the
same and for the safety and preservation of the Public Stores and
Stock of every description, and that you do proceed without
delay to the Cultivation of the Lands, the Curing of Fish and
other Provisions, distributing the Convicts for those and other

Marginal notes:
Term of office.

Instructions to Governor Bligh.

Territorial jurisdiction.

Commission to be read in public.

General instructions.

purposes in such manner and under such Inspectors or Overseers, and under such regulations as may appear to you to be necessary and best calculated for procuring Supplies of Grain and ground Provisions, and for Curing of Fish and other Provisions, and for rendering their Services most useful to the Community.

The assortment of Tools and Utensils which have been from time to time provided for the use of the Convicts and other Persons who compose the said Settlement, are to be distributed according to your discretion, and guided by such further Instructions as you may receive from us through one of our principal Secretaries of State, and according to the Employment assigned to the several Persons. In the distribution, however, you will use every proper degree of Economy and be careful that the Commissary do transmit an Account of the Issues from time to time to the Commissioners of our Treasury and to one of our principal Secretaries of State, to enable them to judge of the propriety or expediency of granting further Supplies. The Clothing of the Convicts and the Provisions issued to them and the Civil and Military Establishments must be accounted for in the same manner pursuant to such instructions in that behalf as you from time to time shall receive from the Commissioners of our Treasury or one of our principal Secretaries of State.

3rd. AND WHEREAS the Commissioners of our Admiralty have commissioned certain of our Ships to be employed at our said Settlement under your Orders, for the purpose of supplying the same with Live Stock and other necessaries from such Places as shall be found most convenient for that purpose, you are, in consequence thereof, to consider the providing such Supplies of Live Stock and necessaries as an object of the first Importance, and you are to follow without delay such Directions in the Execution thereof as you shall from time to time receive from us under our Sign Manual, or from one of our principal Secretaries of State in that behalf, and all such Live Stock as shall be brought into our said Settlement by means of our aforesaid Ships, or otherwise at the Public Expense, are to be considered as Public Stock and for the use of the Settlers and emancipated Convicts being Settlers, and under no pretext whatever to be sold, given away, made over or transferred by them or any of them to whom such Live Stock shall be granted by you without your special leave and license in writing first had and obtained for that purpose, on pain of forfeiting the same, which shall in such Case revert and be added to the Public Stock of our said Settlement.

4th. And as the Increase of the Stock of Animals must depend entirely upon the measures you may adopt for their preservation, you are hereby particularly charged and directed to be extremely

Instructions
to Governor
Bligh.
cautious in preventing all Cattle, Sheep, Hogs, etc., which are to be preserved as much as possible for propagating the Breed of such Animals, from being slaughtered or taken away from our said Settlement on any pretence whatever by any Vessels or Craft which shall come there, untill a competent Stock may be acquired to admit of your supplying the Settlement from it with Animal Food without having further recourse to the Places from whence such Stock may have originally been obtained.

The products
of convict
labour.
5th. It is our Will and Pleasure that the Productions of all descriptions acquired by the Labour of the Convicts shall be considered as a Public Stock, which we so far leave to your disposal that such parts thereof as may be requisite for the subsistence of the said Convicts and their Families, or the subsistence of the Civil and Military Establishments of the Settlements, may be applied by you to that Use. The remainder of such Productions you will reserve as a Provision for such further number of Convicts as you may expect will from time to time be sent from hence to be employed under your directions in the manner pointed out in these our Instructions to you; and you are always to take

The
assignment
of the services
of convicts.
care on the Arrival of such Convicts to obtain an Assignment to you or the Governor-in-Chief for the time being from the Masters of the Ships bringing the said Convicts, of the Servitude of such Convicts whose Services are assigned either for the remainder of the Terms which shall be specified in their several Sentences or Orders of Transportation, or for such less time as shall be specified in their respective Sentences in that behalf.

Voyages of
discovery to
be made.
6th. And whereas we are desirous that some further Information should be obtained of the several Ports or Harbours upon the Coasts and the Islands contiguous thereto within the limits of your Government, you are, whenever any of our said Ships can be conveniently spared for that purpose, to send one or more of

Intercourse
with the
natives.
them upon that Service. You are to endeavour by every possible means to extend your Intercourse with the Natives and conciliate their affections, enjoining all our Subjects to live in Amity and Kindness with them; and if any of our Subjects shall wantonly destroy them, or give them any unnecessary interruption of the exercise of their several occupations, It is our will and pleasure that you do cause such offenders to be brought to Punishment according to the degree of the Offence. You will endeavour to procure from time to time Accounts of the number of Natives inhabiting the Neighbourhood of our said Settlement, and report your opinion to one of our Secretaries of State in what manner the intercourse with these People may be turned to the advantage thereof.

7th. And it is further our Royal Will and Pleasure that you do, by all proper Methods, enforce a due observance of Religion and good order among the Inhabitants of the said Settlement, and that you do take particular care that all possible attention be paid to the due celebration of Public Worship.

8th. And whereas it hath been represented to us that great Evils have arisen from the unrestrained Importation of Spirits into our said Settlement from Vessels touching there, whereby both the Settlers and Convicts have been induced to barter and exchange their Live Stock and other necessary articles for the said Spirits, to their particular loss and detriment, as well as to that of our said Settlement at large, We do, therefore, strictly enjoin you, on pain of our utmost displeasure, to order and direct that no Spirits shall be landed from any Vessel coming to our said Settlement without your Consent, or that of our Governor-in-Chief for the time being previously obtained for that purpose, which orders and directions you are to signify to all Captains or Masters of Ships immediately on their arrival at our said Settlement, and you are, at the same time, to take the most effective Measures that the said orders and directions shall be strictly obey'd and complied with.

9th. And whereas we have, by our Commission, bearing date the twenty-fourth day of May, 1805, given and granted unto you full power and authority to emancipate and discharge from their Servitude any of the Convicts under your superintendance who shall, from their good Conduct and a disposition to Industry, be deserving of Favor, It is our Will and Pleasure that in every such case you do issue your Warrant to the Surveyor of Lands to make Surveys of and mark out in Lots such Lands upon the said Territory as may be necessary for their Use, and when that shall be done that you do pass Grants thereof with all convenient speed to any of the said Convicts so emancipated, in such conditions and acknowledgements as shall hereafter be specified, Viz.:—

To every Male shall be granted Thirty acres of Land, and in case he shall be married Twenty Acres more, and for every Child who may be then at the Settlement at the time of making the said Grant, a further Quantity of Ten Acres, free of all Fees, Taxes, Quit Rents, or other acknowledgements whatsoever, for the space of Ten Years; provided that the Person to whom the said Land shall have been granted shall reside within the space and proceed to the Cultivation and Improvement thereof, reserving only to us such Timber as may be growing or to grow hereafter upon the said Land, which may be fit for Naval Purposes, and an Annual

Instructions
to Governor
Bligh.
Quit Rent of Six Pence for every Thirty Acres after the expiration of the Term or Time before-mentioned. You will cause Copies of such Grants as may be passed to be preserved, and make a regular return of the said Grants to the Commissioners of our Treasury, and the Lords of the Committee of our Privy Council for Trade and Plantations.

Assistance to
be given to
emancipists.
10th. And whereas it is likely to happen that the Convicts who may, after their emancipation in consequence of this Instruction, be put into Possession of Lands, will not have the means of proceeding to their Cultivation without the Public Aid, It is our Will and Pleasure that you do cause every such Person you may so emancipate to be supplied with such a Quantity of Provisions as may be sufficient for the sustenance of himself and also of his Family until such time as their Joint Labour may reasonably be expected to enable them to provide for themselves, together with an Assortment of Tools and Utensils, and such a Proportion of Seed Grain, Cattle, Sheep, Hogs, &c., as may be proper and can be spared from the General Stock of the Settlement.

Prohibition
of foreign
intercourse.
11th. And whereas it is our Royal Intention that every sort of intercourse between our said Settlement, or other Places which may be hereafter established on the Coast of New South Wales and its Dependencies, and the Settlements of our East India Company, as well as the Coasts of China and the Islands situate in that part of the World to which any Intercourse has been established by any European Nation, should be prevented by every possible means, It is our Royal Will and Pleasure that you do not upon any Account allow Craft of any Sort to be built for the use of Private Individuals which might enable them to effect such Intercourse, and that you do prevent any Vessel which may at any time hereafter arrive at the said Settlement from any of the Ports beforementioned from having any Communication with any of the Inhabitants residing within your Government without first receiving especial Permission from you for that purpose.

Grants of land
to free
settlers.
12th. And whereas certain of our Subjects now resident within our said Settlement, and others from hence or from other Parts of our Dominions, may be desirous of becoming Settlers in our said Settlement, our Will and Pleasure is that in case such Persons shall apply to you for Grants of Lands you do afford them every encouragement that can be given in that undertaking without subjecting the Public to any Expense, and that Grants of Land to such Amount as you shall judge proper be made out for each Person applying, not exceeding One Hundred Acres over and above the Quantity hereinbefore directed to be granted to such Convicts as shall be emancipated or discharged from their Servitude, free of all Fees, Taxes, Quit Rents, and other acknowledge-

ments for the space of Ten Years, but after the expiration of that Instructions to Governor Bligh. time to be liable to an Annual Quit Rent of One Shilling for every fifty Acres.

13th. It is nevertheless our Royal Intention, in case of any peculiarly meritorious Settler or well-deserving emancipated Convict becoming a Settler as aforesaid, that you shall be at liberty to enlarge the said Grants so respectively to be made to such Settler or emancipated Convict as aforesaid, by the addition of such further number of Acres to be granted to them respectively, as you in your discretion shall judge proper, subject nevertheless to our approbation thereof upon your transmitting to one of our Principal Secretaries of State, which you are hereby directed to do by the first opportunity, your reasons for making the same. The granting of additional lands.

14th. And whereas such Persons as are or shall become Settlers upon our said Continent of New South Wales, or the said Islands dependent thereupon, may be desirous of availing themselves of the labour of part of the Convicts who are or may be sent there, It is our will and pleasure that, in case there should be a prospect of them employing any of the said Convicts to advantage, that you assign to each Grantee the Service of any number of them that you may judge sufficient to answer their purpose, on condition of their maintaining, feeding, and Clothing such Convicts in such manner as shall appear satisfactory to you and to our Governor of New South Wales for the time being. The assignment of convicts to settlers.

15th. You are to take Care that all Grants to be given of Lands in our said Continent or Islands be made out in due form, and that the Conditions required by these our Instructions be particularly and expressly mentioned in the respective Grants, that the same be properly registered, and that regular returns thereof be transmitted by the proper Officers to our Commissioners of our Treasury and to the Committee of our Privy Council appointed for all matters of Trade and Foreign Plantations, within the space of Twelve Months after the passing of such Grant. The method of granting lands.

16th. It is also our Will and Pleasure that in all Grants of Land to be made by you as aforesaid, regard be had to the profitable and unprofitable Acres, so that each Grantee may have a proportionable number of one sort and of the other, as likewise that the breadth of each Tract to be hereafter granted be one-third of the length of such Tract, and that the length of such Tract do not extend along the Banks of any Bay or River but into the Main Land, that thereby the said Grantees may have each a convenient share of what accommodation the said Harbour or Rivers may afford for Navigation or otherwise. General conditions for land grants.

17th. It is also our will and pleasure that between every thousand Acres of Land so to be allotted to Settlers or emanci- Crown reservations.

Instructions
to Governor
Bligh.
pated Convicts, being Settlers as aforesaid, you do reserve not
less than five hundred Acres adjacent thereto for the benefit of
us, our Heirs and Successors, which spaces so reserved you are
not to grant without our especial direction and license; but you
are at liberty to lease the same for any Term not exceeding
fourteen Years, and on such Terms and Conditions as you shall
judge advantageous to our Service, subject to such orders as
shall be given to you in that behalf under our Sign Manual or by
one of our Principal Secretaries of State.

The formation
of townships.
18th. And whereas it has been found by experience that the
settling Planters in Townships* has very much redounded to
their advantage, not only with respect to the assistance they have
been able to afford each other in their Civil Concerns, but likewise with regard to their Security, you are therefore to lay out
Townships of convenient size and extent in such Places as you
in your discretion shall judge most proper, having as far as may
be natural boundaries extending up into the Country and com-
prehending a necessary part of the Sea Coast when it can be
conveniently had.

The building
of towns.
19th. You are also to cause a proper place in the most convenient part of each Township to be marked out for the building
of a Town sufficient to contain such a number of Families as you
shall judge proper, to settle them with Town and Pasture Lots
convenient to each Tenement, taking Care that the said Town be
laid out upon or as near as conveniently may be to some
navigable River or the Sea Coast; and you are to reserve to us
proper Quantities of Land in each Township for the following
Purposes, Viz., For erecting Fortifications and Barracks, or for
other Military or Naval Services, and more particularly for the
building a Town Hall and such other Public Edifices as you shall
deem necessary, and also for the growth and production of Naval
Timber, if there are any Wood-lands fit for that purpose.

Reservation
of church
lands.
20th. And it is our further Will and Pleasure that a particular
Spot, in or as near each Town as possible, be set apart for the
Building of a Church, and Four hundred Acres adjacent thereto
allotted for the maintainance of a Minister, and Two hundred for
a Schoolmaster.

Fees on
land grants.
21st. And whereas it is necessary that a reasonable Compensation shall be made to the Surveyor-General of our Lands for
surveying and laying out the said Lands, for the use of such
Persons who may be disposed to become Settlers in the said
Continent or Islands dependent thereupon, We have thought fit
to establish the Table of Fees hereunto annexed, which you are
to allow him to demand from all Persons whatsoever, excepting
the Non-commissioned Officers and Men of the Detachment of

* Note 2.

our Marine Corps, or to the Convicts, emancipated or discharged, Instructions
to Governor
Bligh. who are not to be subjected to the Payment of such Fees.

22nd. You are to cause the above-mentioned Table of Fees to be hung up in one of the most Public Places, that all Persons concerned may be apprized of the Charges which may be demanded from them on their taking up Lands within the said Continent, or Islands dependant thereupon.

List of Fees upon Grants of Land.

Governor's Fees.

Schedule of fees on land grants.

	£	s.	d.
For the Great Seal to every Grant not exceeding 1,000 Acres	0	5	0
For all Grants exceeding 1,000 Acres, for every 1,000 each Grant contains	0	2	6
For a License of Occupation	0	5	0

Secretary's Fees.

	£	s.	d.
For every Grant passing the Seal of the Province, if under 1,000 Acres	0	5	0
Between 1,000 and 5,000 Acres	0	10	0
All above	0	15	0
In Grants of Land, when the number of Proprietors shall exceed 20, each Right	0	2	6
In Ditto, where the number of Proprietors shall not exceed 20, the same as for Grants, in proportion to the Quantity of Land.			
For every License of Occupation of Land	0	2	6
For every Grant of Land, from 1,000 to 20,000 Acres; take for the first 1,000 Acres 15s., and for every 1,000 Acres more	0	2	6

Fees to be taken by the Chief Surveyor of Land.

	£	s.	d.
For every Lot under 100 Acres	0	2	6
From 100 to 500 Acres	0	5	0
Above 500 Acres	0	7	6
Every Township, if above 20 Rights, each Right	0	2	6

Auditors' Fees.

	£	s.	d.
For auditing every Grant	0	3	4

Register's Fees.

	£	s.	d.
For recording a Grant of Land for or under 500 Acres ...	0	1	3
For recording a Grant of Land from 500 to 1,000 Acres ..	0	2	6
For every 1,000 Acres to the Amount of 20,000	0	0	6
For recording a Grant of a Township	1	0	0

Additional Instructions to Governor Bligh.*

Sir, Downing Street, 20th Novr., 1805.

You are already in possession of His Majesty's Instructions for the guidance of your conduct as Governor of His Settlements in New South Wales and its Dependencies and have

* Note 3.

Instructions
to Governor
Bligh.
had the opportunity of perusing the whole of the Correspondence between that Government and the Secretary of State to the latest period.

I have therefore at present only to draw your attention to those objects which appear to me to claim the most particular consideration, leaving such as are of less importance to the control of that discretionary power, which has been entrusted to you, in the confidence of your zeal and ability to employ it for the benefit of the Colony and in the furtherance of His Majesty's gracious and benevolent Intentions.

Supplies of
provisions.
And first the progress made by the Settlement within these few years towards furnishing the Provisions requisite for the support of the Inhabitants is happily such as to call for little or no further assistance from England in this particular, excepting in regard to a certain quantity of Salt meat for the consumption of those who are victualled from the Government Stores at Port Jackson and in the subordinate Settlements, which will be continued as long as the necessity of drawing them from England exists.

Proposed
future
shipments
of stores.
The Supplies of Live Stock must hereafter be left entirely to the enterprize of Individuals, and the demands upon this Country will I trust in future be confined to the Stores indispensably requisite for the Clothing and maintenance of the Convicts remaining at the Charge of-Government, and for enabling them to proceed with the Public Works on which they are usually employed; and to those Articles which it may be necessary to continue for some time longer, for the purpose of being exchanged in Barter with the Settlers.

Proposed
freedom of
trade and
commerce.
Nothing, I conceive, will more essentially contribute to bring forward the Supplies, which the Country is become able to furnish in most of the Articles of first necessity, such as Corn, Poultry, Vegetables, etc. than the abolition of all restrictions in the disposal of those Supplies and in like manner it seems desireable that you should take the earliest opportunity of revising the regulations at present existing for fixing prices on Goods imported into the Colony, which I apprehend must (excepting in a few particular instances) operate to the disadvantage of the Inhabitants.

You will therefore understand that it is not judged necessary for you to interfere in future in respect to the demands of Adventurers bringing Articles for Trade to the Colony, further than to prevent improper communications between the Ships and the Convicts, excepting with regard to the Article of Spirits.

The traffic
in spirits.
In this particular the exertions of Governor King have been productive of the most beneficial consequences, and I strongly

recommend you to persevere in the system he has so wisely laid Instructions to Governor Bligh. down of a rigorous prohibition of this pernicious beverage without a regular licence from you for the purpose.

I need scarcely observe that the Articles sent out for Barter are to be disposed of as usual, but I think it proper to call your attention to a charge which I perceive is made of 15 per Cent. to Commission charged by the commissary. the Commissary General for the superintendance of the Sales of these Goods. It seems to be a very high allowance and to require explanation.

It is my intention to propose to Parliament to provide for an Establishment for Port Dalrymple. establishment at Port Dalrymple upon the same footing as that which has been fixed for the Derwent; and it is His Majesty's pleasure that you do not permit any new settlements to be formed from Head Quarters. The detachment at Newcastle may be con- The settlement at Newcastle. tinued on its present footing, but should not be extended beyond what is necessary for the security of the Convicts employed in working the Coal Mines and cutting Cedar.

I cannot approve of so great an importation of Cattle into the Importation of cattle to Port Dalrymple. Settlement of Port Dalrymple, where I apprehend they can scarcely yet have the means of providing in a proper manner for their Security without neglecting the Cultivation of the ground or the erection of requisite Buildings. If a proper opportunity should offer, some proportion should be sent to the Derwent; but this I leave entirely to your discretion.

Lieutenant Colonel Foveaux will avail himself of the first The evacuation of Norfolk Island. opportunity to return to his Duty and will afford you the most material assistance in completing the measures to be taken for the evacuation of Norfolk Island, in conformity to the Instructions for that purpose, contained in Lord Buckinghamshire's* letter of the 24th June, 1803.

You will inform Lieutenant Governor Collins that all his Collins to report to Bligh. Reports and Requisitions are to be addressed to you as Governor in Chief, and that it will be unnecessary for him to correspond with me excepting when an opportunity may offer of forwarding Copies of his communications to you, which he is never to neglect.

You will of course take a proper opportunity, if you shall think Visits to dependent settlements. it desirable, to visit the dependent Settlements, and to examine the actual state of them, and will communicate to me the result of your proceedings for His Majesty's information.

All the Supplies demanded by Governor King have been for- Shipments of supplies. warded by the William Pitt and Tellicherry which sailed a short time since and by the Lady Magdelina Sinclair, and various Articles which have been judged desirable either in consequence of your suggestion or by the Accounts of Persons lately arrived

Instructions to Governor Bligh.

from New South Wales have been added.   A proportion of Clothing also beyond the quantity specified by Governor King has been sent out, as it had been provided for a particular service and not being applicable to use in England would have been damaged by remaining in Store.

I have only to add that such points of Governor King's late Dispatches as seemed to require the opinion of His Majesty's Law Officers have been referred for consideration, as soon as I receive their Reports they shall be communicated to you.

Regulation of intercourse with Americans.

I am not enabled to give you my Instructions as to the conduct to be observed to Americans frequenting the Shores of New Holland for the purpose of fishing and traffic, that question being still under the consideration of the Committee of His Majesty's Privy Council for Trade and Plantations. If they shall attempt to make any Settlement on any particular spot you will give them notice of His Majesty's Right of Sovereignty and in all cases warn them to depart; and it will be in your discretion to regulate their Importation of any Articles of Traffic into the Colony as you see occasion, and to establish such Duties and Prohibitions as may prevent their interfering with the Trade of His Majesty's Subjects.

Encouragement of education and religion.

I am to draw your particular attention towards forming some plan for the Education and particularly the religious Education of the Colony. The Duties levied for the support of the Orphan House when the Buildings are completed may be partly applicable to this important object. But I am to desire that immediately on your arrival you do state the necessity of making some Establishment for the Religious Education of the Inhabitants and that you do consult the principal Inhabitants and particularly Mr. Marsden on the best plan to be adopted and transmit to me their sentiments in conjunction with your own.

School teachers to be sent to the colony.

As considerable difficulty may occur in finding proper Persons within the Colony capable of instructing the Children of the Settlers I have directed enquiries to be made and shall hold out encouragement to a few correct and intelligent Persons to proceed to the Colony for this purpose.

Education of the children.

In a Settlement, where the irregular and immoral habits of the Parents are likely to leave their Children in a state peculiarly exposed to suffer from similar vices, you will feel the peculiar necessity that the Government should interfere in behalf of the rising generation and by the exertion of authority as well as of encouragement, endeavour to educate them in religious as well as industrious habits—it is reasonable that the more wealthy Inhabitants should bear the charge of educating their own Children; but it is His Majesty's gracious Direction that the Expence, indispensably required to give effect to this interesting object, Instructions to Governor should not be withheld from the Public Funds and you are Bligh. authorized to make such advances upon this account as you may Expense to be deem requisite to afford the means of education to the Children borne by the Crown. of the Colony.   I have, &c.,

CASTLEREAGH.

CAPTAIN KING TO THE RIGHT HON. WILLIAM WINDHAM.

(Despatch per ship Britannia.)

1806.
18 Aug.

Sir,   Sydney, New South Wales, 18th August, 1806.

I have the honor to enclose a Letter from Lieutenant Despatch from lieut.-governor Governor Paterson to my Lord Castlereagh, dated 12th August Collins. last—referring to one to Earl Camden, dated November 14th, 1805.

As those Letters with my former Communications on that Subject have been transmitted, I shall not trespass further on Your time than by referring to those documents, And such further Information as may be required of me on my return to England.   I have, &c.,

PHILIP GIDLEY KING.

[Enclosure.]

[A copy of this letter will be found in volume I, series III.]

GOVERNOR BLIGH TO THE RIGHT HON. WILLIAM WINDHAM.

(Despatch No. 1, per ship Britannia ; acknowledged by Viscount Castlereagh, 31st December, 1807.)

Government House, Sydney,

Sir,   New South Wales, 26th August, 1806.   26 Aug.

The opportunity by which I now have the honor to write to you will only allow me to state generally my arrival here, and entering into the Government of the Colony ; perhaps my enlarged details will arrive as soon as this by the Ships which are to follow, and I shall have more due time to make my dispatches of the consequence which circumstances at this time render them.

I arrived on the 6th Instant, in the Sinclair, Transport, with Arrival of His Majesty's Ship Porpoise, after a stormy passage of fifty-one Governor Bligh. days from the Cape of Good Hope, from whence I wrote the necessary information attending the Voyage that far.

The necessary arrangements would have been finally closed Illness of with Governor King, but I am concerned to say a severe illness captain King. of the Gout has delayed it, which, however, I hope will not be of

1806.
26 Aug.

King to sail
in H.M.S.
Buffalo.
long duration, and that he will be able to sail in the Buffalo, the Ship he Commands, in the course of a Month, it being his anxious desire to do so. He will be particularly able to describe the state of this Colony, which at present I lament in representing is in considerable want of Grain from the overflowing of the Hawkesbury. This Evil I shall endeavour to provide against in future, if I find it practicable to put my Plans into execution to prevent so heavy a calamity as loss of Property and Food.

Governor King informs me his dispatches will before this have acquainted you of the misfortune, which unhappily I cannot immediately relieve.

Scarcity of
grain for seed.
A great want of Grain for Seed also pervades the Settlement, to remedy which my only hope is a supply from Norfolk Island, whither I shall send a Colonial Vessel without delay.

Distress in
the colony.
In addition to this misfortune, the Vessels that have arrived here came short victualled under expectations of plentiful supplies; so that I take the Government labouring under distress and embarrassment, but which I trust and hope will in part be removed by the ensuing Crops. It will, nevertheless, be some Years before the Individuals can realize their property again with all the assistance I may be able to give them; while I feel confident in due time to be able to restore it, and place them in greater opulence and comfort.

Importation
of rice from
India.
The Sydney, an East India Ship, was sent from hence to Calcutta to procure a Supply of Rice, the 14th April last, but it is feared she will not return until January next.

Increase in
expenditure.
This circumstance will increase the expence of the Colony, and I am to observe also that it will be still increased by putting the Public Stores and Buildings into repair, without which they will become of no use.

Failure of
imported seed.
The Wheat and Barley which has been sent out in the Sinclair will not grow, so that the intentions of Government in giving a supply of Seed is of no effect.

I find also that the Grain sent out in the Pitt was in the same state; and I recommend, instead of packing it in Casks, it should be put in Bags, stowed in an airy part of the Ship, and frequently aired.

Had I known what had been ordered out in the Sinclair, the Grain should have been landed in good order.

Convicts ex
Fortune and
Alexander.
The Fortune and Alexander have landed their Convicts in good Health, and the former sailed for Bengal, the 19th Instant.

I beg leave to inclose the *Sydney Gazettes,* and I have the honor to be, with the highest respect, &c.,

WM. BLIGH.

GOVERNOR BLIGH TO THE RIGHT HON. WILLIAM WINDHAM.

(Despatch No. 2, per ship Britannia; acknowledged by Viscount Castlereagh, 31st December, 1807.)

Sir,   Sydney, New South Wales, 26th August, 1806.

On the 20th Instant Captain Short, Commander of His Majesty's Ship Porpoise, presented to me a Letter, dated 8th July, 1805, from Mr. Cooke, stating the intentions of My Lord Camden, giving me directions to locate to him Six hundred Acres of Land. *Directions for land grant to Short,*

Mr. Townson, late a Captain in the New South Wales Corps, a respectable Gentleman, and who has come out with means to do so, has presented me with a similar document for One Thousand Acres. As I am under uncertainty how to proceed, as Governor King nor myself have received any authority according to the tenor of Mr. Cooke's Letter, I beg leave to request instructions on the subject. *and to Townson.*   I have, &c.,

WM. BLIGH.

———

GOVERNOR BLIGH TO SECRETARY MARSDEN.

(Per ship Britannia.)

His Majesty's Ship Porpoise,

Sir,   Sydney Cove, New South Wales, 26th August, 1806.

I have the honor to acquaint you for the information of my Lords Commissioners of the Admiralty that I arrived here on the 6th Instant, and found His Majesty's Ship Buffalo fitting out to receive Governor King who will proceed to England in her in the course of a Month. The opportunity I now have is an uncertain one, which with my recent arrival to take the Command of the Colony makes it necessary to defer my regular dispatches until the Buffalo sails. From the Cape of Good Hope I sent accounts of my proceedings, from whence we sailed on the 17th of June, and performed this passage in fifty one Days. *Arrival of Governor Bligh.* *Passage from the Cape of Good Hope.*

The Stores sent out in the Porpoise for the Buffalo and Clothing for the New South Wales Corps have received great injury for want of being properly stowed and aired during the fine weather, and the loss is severely felt. Captain Short has informed me he had no Charge of them, but I nevertheless ordered a Survey thereon, the report of which I beg leave to inclose, and to refer their Lordships to my former dispatches respecting Captain Short's behaviour to me, and requesting he might be superceded from under my Command. *Shipment of stores and clothing in H.M.S. Porpoise.*

I have, &c.,

WM. BLIGH.

1806.
26 Aug.

Survey of
stores on
H.M.S.
Porpoise.

[Enclosure.]

SURVEY OF STORES ON H.M.S. PORPOISE.

By William Bligh, Esqr., etc., etc.

You are hereby required and directed to proceed on board His Majesty's Ship Porpoise, and there take a strict and careful Survey of Stores which have been sent out to His Majesty's Ship Buffalo and this Colony reporting to me such as are damaged, the state they are in, and the cause of such defects.

Given, etc., this 18th day of August, 1806, in Sydney Cove, Port Jackson.

WM. BLIGH.

Captain Houstoun
Mr. Jno. Oxley, Lieutenant
None Master   } of H. M. Ship Buffalo.
Mr. Willm. Jackson, Boatswain
Mr. Jackson, Master of the Ship Sinclair
Mr. Moore, Master Builder.
Attested: RD. ATKINS, J.-A.

PURSUANT to an Order from Captain William Bligh, Esqr., etc., etc.

We whose names are undersigned have taken a strict and careful Survey on the Stores brought out by that Ship for the use of His Majesty's Ship Buffalo and do find as follows Vizt. Cables of 14½ Inch, four in No. Rotten and decayed in many places but may be converted to make Rope etc. Hawser of Eight Inch, One in No., cut entirely through by an Iron bound Cask being stowed in the heart of the Tier, besides being decayed in various places—Rope 3 Inch One Coil partly damaged. Rope 2. Do. Do. Do. 1½ Inch One Coil entirely rotten and decayed ¾ Inch two Coils entirely rotten and decayed, One Coil of 1 Inch entirely rotten and decayed, One Case No. 11 containing one Bolt of No. 4 Canvass entirely destroyed, Twenty-three Yards of Red Fearnought, White Fearnought 60 Yards, some fit for use the other entirely rotten and decayed, Hammocks 12 in No. damaged but repairable, Foresails Two in No. decayed but repairable, Fore Topsails One in No. rotten and decayed and unfit for its proper Service.

Mainsail One in No. damaged but repairable
Fore Staysail One   Do.   Do.   Do.
Main Topmast-Staysail Do.   Do.   Do.

Marine Cloathing, Eleven Jackets, four pair of Breeches, One Waistcoat, Eight Pair of Stockings, Twenty four Shirts, 12 Haversacks, entirely rotten and destroyed, and we are of opinion that the above Stores have been damaged and destroyed, from the above damp of the Ship and from the Hatches being Caulked down and not being aired since they were originally stowed at Deptford—And we farther declare that we have taken this Survey with such Care and Equity that we are ready if required to make Oath to the impartiality of our proceedings.

Given under our hands on board His Majesty's Ship Porpoise in Sydney Cove, Port Jackson, this 19th day of August, 1806.

J. HOUSTOUN, 2nd Commander ⎫
J. OXLEY, Lieutenant ⎬ H. M. Ship Buffalo.
WM. JACKSON, Boatswain ⎭
J. H. JACKSON, Master of the Ship Sinclair.
THOS. MOORE, Master Builder.

Attested: RD. ATKINS, J.-A.

CAPTAIN KING TO THE RIGHT HON. WILLIAM WINDHAM.

(Per ship Richard and Mary.)

Sir,   Sydney, New South Wales, 6th September, 1806.

With this I have the honor to transmit Duplicates of my late Dispatches, dated as p. Margin,* and those which I had written previous to Governor Bligh's Arrival, when I had the honor to receive My Lord Castlereagh's Dispatches, dated as per Margin.† Immediately on their receipt, I directed the Harrington to be liberated, and the Bonds given by the Commander, &c., were given up. For the proceedings which took place prior to my receiving that dispatch, and on hearing that War had taken place between England and Spain, I respectfully request Your reference to the accompanying Duplicate, dated 26th July, 1806.

Should the great Multiplicity of perhaps more important public Affairs have prevented your being informed of my Conduct and the Motives by which I have been guided in administering the Government of this Colony, you will readily conceive the great Satisfaction I experienced on receiving my Lord Castlereagh's dispatch, dated 20th Nov'r last, which contained such an honourable and gratifying testimonial of the Royal Approbation of my Conduct in the Arduous task I have had to perform.

Agreeable to His Majesty's Commands, I am possessing Governor Bligh of every Document and Circumstance which may tend to the future Welfare of these remote parts of His Majesty's Dominions.

* 5th April, 1806 ; 30th June ; 26th July.   † 20th Novr. ; 21st Novr., 1805.

1806.
6 Sept.

Proposed
date of
departure.

Having given the Government up to Governor Bligh on the 13th ulto. with every Mark of respect and Ceremony due to his Situation, I propose sailing for England in His Majesty's Ship Buffalo between the 28th instant and 5th October and hope to arrive in England about the latter end of April.*

I have, &c.,
PHILIP GIDLEY KING.

CAPTAIN KING TO SECRETARY MARSDEN.

(Per ship Richard and Mary.)

Sir,   Sydney, New South Wales, 6th September, 1806.

Instructions
to King
to report
for orders.

Although it is possible I may arrive in England as soon, or a Short time, after this Letter may reach You, Yet I consider it my Duty to acknowledge the receipt of their Lordships' directions, dated 15th Nov'r, 1805, requiring me, as soon as I was relieved in the Government by Captain Bligh, to repair, without loss of Time, with His Majesty's Ship Buffalo, to Spithead, to await their Lordships' further Orders.

King's
proposed
movements.

Captain Bligh arrived here the 7th of August, and on the 13th of that Month I gave the Government up to him, with every mark of Respect and Ceremony due to his Situation. I intend to sail between the 28th instant and 5th October, And shall attempt the Western Passage, through Bass's Straits, in which case I propose touching at the Cape of Good Hope; But should the prevalence of the Westerly or South-West Winds oblige me to make the passage by Cape Horn, it is my intention to touch at St. Catherine's or Rio de Janeiro.

I have, &c.,
PHILIP GIDLEY KING.

THE RIGHT HON. WILLIAM WINDHAM TO GOVERNOR BLIGH.

(Despatch per ship Brothers; acknowledged by Governor Bligh, 31st October, 1807.)

18 Sept.

Permission
granted to
Mrs. Chapman
to become a
settler.

Sir,   Downing Street, 18 Septr., 1806.

Mrs. Chapman, a Widow Lady, having applied to me for Permission to proceed to New South Wales with a View of establishing herself there as a Governess and Teacher, I have given the necessary Directions for her being provided with a Passage to Port Jackson on board of one of the Ships taken up by the Transport Board for the Conveyance of Convicts and Stores.

As there can be no doubt but that Benefit may accrue to the Settlement from the Residence of a respectable Person of Mrs. Chapman's Description, it is highly proper that She should

* Note 5.

receive suitable Encouragement, and I am to desire that you will have a Grant of Land consisting of fifty Acres, situated as conveniently as circumstances will permit, to be made out in her Name with the usual Reservations, and that you will allow to Mrs. Chapman the Assistance of one Female Convict, who is to continue to be clothed and victualled from the Public Stores until such Time as Mrs. Chapman shall be in Circumstances to enable her to dispense with such Indulgence; you will in all other Respects afford her due Encouragement and Assistance in establishing herself in the Settlement.   I have, &c.,

W. WINDHAM.

1806.
18 Sept.

Land grant for
Mrs. Chapman.

SIR GEORGE SHEE TO GOVERNOR BLIGH.

(Per ship Brothers; acknowledged by Governor Bligh, 31st October, 1807.)

Sir,   Downing Street, 6th Octr., 1806.

Mr. Blaxland has undertaken at Mr. Windham's desire to give a Passage to two Otaheite Boys, whom it has been judged proper to send back to their Native Country, and Mr. Windham has directed me to desire that you will reimburse all reasonable expences incurred by Mr. Blaxland on their Account. Mr. Windham also directs me to recommend the Boys to your Care and Protection until you may have an Opportunity of forwarding them to Otaheite; and he requests you will send them there under the Care of some proper Person as soon as you conveniently can.

I have, &c.,

GEO. SHEE.

6 Oct.

Return of two
natives of
Otaheite from
England.

CAPTAIN KING TO THE COMMISSIONERS OF THE NAVY.

(Per ship Alexander.)

His Majesty's Ship Buffalo,

Gentlemen,   Port Jackson, 1st Novr., 1806.

I have received Your Letter of the 7th December, 1805, And can by no Means Account for Your not having then received the Vouchers for Naval Stores purchased for the use of H. M. Ship Buffalo on the 13th September, 1804, As it appears from my Entry that one was put up and two only remaining. I have considered it necessary to forward one of them, And have to request that You will please to give directions for the imprest standing against me on that Account to be taken off. I have also the honor to transmit you an Account Current for the different Sums drawn by me on Your Board between the 13th day of March 1803 and the present date with attested Vouchers for each transaction.

1 Nov.

Vouchers for
naval stores.

1806.
1 Nov.
The Boatswain and other people are made acquainted with the Stoppage against their Wages for the Overpay they received for extra Work on the 25th September 1804.

I have, &c.,
PHILIP GIDLEY KING.

[Enclosures.]
[Copies of the account and vouchers are not available.]

GOVERNOR BLIGH TO THE RIGHT HON. WILLIAM WINDHAM.
(Despatch marked " General No. 3," per ship Alexander; acknow-
ledged by Viscount Castlereagh, 31st December, 1807.)

5 Nov.

Sir,   Sydney, New South Wales, 5th November, 1806.

By Ships* which sailed on the 26th August and 7th September, I had the honor to inform you of my arrival and taking the Command of this Colony. Since that time I have been arduously
Visits of inspection to country districts. employed in visiting the different parts of it, and endeavouring to possess myself of a general knowledge both of its state and the immediate things to be done for its advantage, concerning which my constant attention for some time longer will be required to mature the plans which may be adopted.

Under such a necessary mode of beginning, I trust, Sir, you will see that my resting the information of the state of the Colony to Governor King's Despatches made up to the time of my arrival is proper, except any observations on my part which tend to shew what has been done since or changes taken place.

Distress caused by the floods in the Hawkesbury. The distresses occasioned by the Inundation of the Hawkesbury River has required great attention to relieve the wants of the unfortunate Settlers in that part of the Country, and the losses they sustained powerfully effecting the other parts of the Colony, very extensive aid in Provisions has been necessary to be given the poor generally.

Scarcity of grain for seed. In the midst of those difficulties, great exertions have been necessary to the preservation of the ensuing Harvest of Wheat and Barley, and planting Maize Corn to secure Seed, for which I have adopted every means, and have every hope that we shall do well, although the ensuing Crop will not be very abundant; but here I must express my confidence that the Calamity will make the grower of Corn more cautious, and set a juster value on the produce of his Land.

The Harvest will soon begin; some Barley will be cut in the course of a Week if the Weather turns fine, but at present it is
Cultivation of potatoes. unseasonable. The Gardens are now giving Supplies of Potatoes, and, as I demanded personally the exertions of every one to this culture, I have the satisfaction to know we have so succeeded that

* Note 6.

in the course of a Month I shall be able to reduce our expences of victualling from the Public Stores, and the Settlers in general convinced they must depend more on themselves than they have done hitherto.

Government Farm, at Castle Hill, has at present One Hundred and Fifty Acres of Wheat; but it has been so much worn out the returns will be but small; in Maize we shall be productive, and particularly in the later Crops, the Worm having done some injury in the beginning of the season. Public agriculture at Castle Hill.

When the Wheat comes in, we shall be prepared to receive it securely, to which end such Artificers as we have here have been employed repairing the Granaries and finishing a New Wind Mill.

The Public Stores and Government Houses require great repairs, and building the church here, and what will be required at Parramatta, will considerably add to the expences of the first Year or two of my Government; nevertheless, the aggregate will, I trust, be found moderate. Public buildings in want of repair.

In the customs and manners of the people here a great deal is to be corrected. The Settlers in general, and particularly those from Prisoners, are not honest, have no prudence, and little industry, besides being burthened with debts; great chicanery is used in all their dealings, and much litigation. All this will require a vast deal of attention on my part to remove, to which end the rising generation shall be watched over and educated, while the pernicious customs of the place shall be checked by every means in my power. Character and condition of the settlers.

To the general expences which the Colony bears will be observed as soon as I can have time to ascertain them the very great proportion of Old and Infirm Persons who do no work for Government; and I take the liberty to make this observation on account of the selections of Prisoners which appear to have been sent out from England. Cost of the aged and infirm to the Crown.

By my Letter A accompanying this Despatch you will observe, Sir, I have been under the necessity to direct the Commissary to draw two Sets of Bills on His Majesty's Treasury, the one for Two Hundred and Fifty Pounds was occasioned by Governor King's sending a Ship called the Sophia to Port Dalrymple which did not return in his time; and the other for a Supply of Spirits for His Majesty's Colonial Vessels. Bills drawn.

Demands also are made for Supplies of Stores and Provisions for the Year 1807, supposing those made in 1805 to be on their way, and to these are annexed the Remains of Stores up to the 12th August last; and that of Provisions on the 1st Instant. Requisitions for stores.

The Demand for Stationery is likewise absolutely necessary being in great want thereof.

1806.
5 Nov.

Projected
departure of
King.

Governor King, who has suffered much ill health and has but little intermission from the Gout, expects to sail the latter end of this Month, by whom I shall have the honor of again writing to you.

This conveyance will take the *Gazettes* from the 31st August last to the 2nd Instant; the others of prior date were sent with my former Despatches.   I have, &c.,
                                              WM. BLIGH.

[Enclosure No. 1.]

Requisition
for articles
for barter.

LIST of Articles to be sent for Barter with the Inhabitants of New South Wales for the year 1807.

Quality.	Quantity Wanted.	Quality.	Quantity Wanted.
Port Wine	20 Pipes	Iron Pots 1 to 4 Galls	300 No.
Yellow Soap	10,000 lbs	,, Saucepans	200 ,,
Hops............	10 packets	Weights from ¼ to 28 lbs......	20 Sets
White Paint	2,000 lbs	Frying Pans	200 No.
Black	200 ,,	Fish Hooks as pr Drawing....	100 Gross
Paint Oil....................	200 Gns.	Sheet Lead	2 Rolls
Paint Brushes in Sorts	1 Gross	Solder for do ....:......	200 lbs
Shoe Brushes..	1 ,,	Iron assorted	6 Tons
Window Glass	2000 feet	Scissars	200 Prs
do 10/12.........	1000 ,,	Combs, Ivory Small Tooth ..	1000 No.
do 10/6	1000 ,,	Pins	50 lbs
do 8/6	1000 ,,	Locks Drawer	50 No.
Copper Bell Wire	200 lbs.	,, Stock—sorted	100
Earthen Ware sorted	10 Crates	,, Pad	50
Nails 6d	100,000 No.	Raven Duck	2000 yds
,, 8	100,000 ,,	Superfine Blue Cloth	400 ,,
,, 10	100,000 ,,	Coat Buttons, gilt and plated	12 Gross
,, 12	100,000 ,,	Women's Shoes	500 pr.
,, 18	300,000 ,,	Fig Blue	100 lbs
,, 20	200,000 ,,	Irish Linen	2000 yds
,, 24	50,000 ,,	Pullicat Handk'fs	400 No.
,, 30	50,000 ,,	Linen Check	1000 yds
,, 40	50,000 ,,	Coloured Threads...........	200 lbs
Hair Sieves Sizes	24 No.	White Do	100 ,,
Wire Sieves Sets for Wheat ⎫		Black Barcelona Hkfs	200 No.
Flour packed in light Cases ⎭	40 Sets	Coloured do	200 ,,
Hats fine	500 No.	Flannel	200 yds
Cotton Wick	200 lbs	Printing Paper	20 Reams
West India Hoes broad	200 No.	Durant sorted	200 Pieces
Scythe Blades	24 ,,	Twist....................	10 lbs
Sickles	1000 ,,	Sewing Silk................	10 ,,,
Spades with Handles	500 ,,	Men's Shoes (good)	2000 pr
Saws, Pit	24 ,,	do Boots (assorted of a good	
,, Cross Cut	24 ,,	Quality)...........	200 ,,
,, Hand	24 ,,	Fool's cap plain..............	20 Reams
Files—Pit, Cross and Hand	1000	Plain Post thick	10 ,,
Saws		do thin	10 ,,
do sorted	500	Pot Paper	10 ,,
Tin double	6 Cases		

N.B.—It is necessary that the Articles supplied are of good quality or they will not be purchased.

Approved—WM. BLIGH.   JOHN PALMER, Commiss'y.

[Additional Enclosures.]

[Copies of these are not available.]

1806.
5 Nov.

GOVERNOR BLIGH TO THE RIGHT HON. WILLIAM WINDHAM.

(Despatch No. 4 and A, per ship Alexander; acknowledged by Viscount Castlereagh, 31st-December, 1807.)

Sir,   Sydney, New South Wales, 5th November, 1806.

Referring to Governor King's separate Letter A., dated 12th August, 1806, which goes with this Despatch, I have the honor to acquaint you that I have given the Commissary direc- **Freight of the** tions to pay the Owner of the Sophia the Sum of Two Hundred **ship Sophia.** and Fifty Pounds Sterling being the agreed Sum for that Vessel's Service in carrying People, Provisions and Stores from hence to Port Dalrymple as stated in the above mentioned Letter.

And as a proportion of Spirits here is requisite to issue as a **Purchase of** Ration to His Majesty's Colonial Vessels, I directed Five Hun- **spirits for** dred and Seventy Seven Gallons to be purchased for that pur- **vessels.** pose, for the payment of which I ordered the Commissary to draw Two Sets of Bills of Exchange on His Majesty's Treasury and have the honor to inclose Vouchers for those Services which I hope will be approved of.   I have, &c.,

WM. BLIGH.

[Enclosure No. 1.]

VOUCHER FOR THE FREIGHT OF THE SHIP SOPHIA.   **Voucher for**
                                                       freight of
Sydney, New South Wales.   **ship Sophia.**

RECEIVED this 13th day of Sept. 1806 of John Palmer Commissary of Stores and Provisions one Set of Bills of Exchange on the Right Honorable the Lords Commissioners of His Majesty's Treasury at Ninety Days sight in my favor for the Sum of Two Hundred and fifty Pounds Sterling being payment of Freight of the Ship Sophia to Port Dalrymple and from thence to this place.

For which I have Signed five Receipts of this tenor and Date.

ROB. CAMPBELL.

I do hereby Certify that the above sum was paid by my order.

WM. BLIGH.

[Enclosure No. 2.]

VOUCHER FOR THE PURCHASE OF SPIRITS.   **Voucher for**
                                               the purchase
Sydney, New South Wales, 13 Sept., 1806.   **of spirits.**

John Palmer Esqr. Commissary to His Majesty's
    Territory of New South Wales.

To Messrs. Campbell and Co.

To 577 Gallons Spirits @ 9/- pr. Gall. ...... £259 13 ⸗0

RECEIVED this Thirteenth Day of Septr. One thousand Eight Hundred and Six of John Palmer Esqr. Commissary One Set of Bills of Exchange On the Right Honorable the Lords Commissioners of His Majesty's Treasury at Ninety Days sight for

1806.
5 Nov.

Voucher for
the purchase
of spirits.

the Sum of Two Hundred and Fifty Nine Pounds thirteen Shillings Sterling being payment for the above Spirits.

For which I have signed five Receipts of this tenor and date.

CAMPBELL AND CO.

We the undersigned do hereby Certify that the above purchase has been made on the Most Moderate terms.

RD. ATKINS, J.-A.

THOS. JAMISON, J.P.

I do hereby Certify that the above was purchased by John Palmer Esqr. Commissary Agreeable to my Order.

WM. BLIGH.

GOVERNOR BLIGH TO THE RIGHT HON. WILLIAM WINDHAM.

(Despatch No. 5, per ship Alexander; acknowledged by Viscount Castlereagh, 31st December, 1807.)

Sir,   Sydney, New South Wales, 5th November, 1806.

Transmission of Sydney Gazettes.

I beg leave to inclose the *Gazettes* of this place from the 31st August 1806 to the 2nd November following those from the 10th August being sent by the Britannia.   I have, &c.,

WM. BLIGH.

GOVERNOR BLIGH TO THE RIGHT HON. WILLIAM WINDHAM.

(Despatch No. 6, per ship Alexander; acknowledged by Viscount Castlereagh, 31st December, 1807.)

Sir,   Sydney, New South Wales, 5th November, 1806.

In my former Despatches I had to mention that Captain Short of His Majesty's Ship Porpoise and Captain Townson late of the New South Wales Corps had presented to me Letters from Mr. Secretary Cooke that it was the intentions of my Lord Camden to give them Grants of Land, since which Mr. G. Bunker, Master of the Elizabeth South Whaler, has presented me a similar Letter on his part, and in consequence thereof although I consider myself not authorised to comply fully until I receive authority so to do, I have directed the respective Persons to look out for such quantities of Land for farther approval, but not otherwise to be retained in their possession.

I have, &c.,

WM. BLIGH.

Proposed land grant to G. Bunker.

GOVERNOR BLIGH TO THE RIGHT HON. WILLIAM WINDHAM.

(Despatch per ship Alexander; acknowledged by Viscount Castlereagh, 31st December, 1807.)

Sir,   5th November, 1806.

Returns of New South Wales Corps.

I have the honor to transmit the Monthly Returns of the New South Wales Corps from the 1st September, 1806, to the 1st November following.   I have, &c.,

WM. BLIGH.

[Enclosure.]

MONTHLY RETURN of His Majesty's New South Wales Corps, commanded by Colonel Francis Grose, Sydney, 1st November, 1806.

1806.
5 Nov.

Returns of New South Wales Corps.

Companies.	Colonel.	Lieut.-Colonel.	Major.	Captains.	Lieutenants.	Ensigns.	Adjutant.	Paymaster.	Qu'r-master.	Surgeon.	Ass't Surgeon.	Serjeants present.	Drummers present.	Present fit for duty.	Sick.	On command.	Furlough.	Recruiting.	Total.	Serjeants.	Drummers.	Rank and file.	Inlisted.	Dead.	Discharged and recommended.	Discharged and not recommended.	Deserted.
Colonel Grose's	:	:	:	:	:	:	1	1	1	1	1	7	1	49	3	8	:	:	60	:	:	:	:	1	:	1	:
Lieut.-Col. Paterson's	:	1	:	:	:	:	:	:	:	:	:	:	:	5	1	54	:	:	60	:	:	:	:	:	:	:	:
Major Foveaux's	:	:	:	:	:	1	:	:	:	:	:	1	:	16	1	43	1	:	60	:	:	:	:	:	:	:	:
Captain Johnston's	:	:	:	1	:	1	:	:	:	:	:	1	2	45	:	15	:	:	60	:	:	:	:	:	:	:	:
„ Abbott's	:	:	:	:	:	:	:	:	:	:	:	1	1	7	2	50	1	:	60	:	:	:	:	:	:	:	:
„ Wilson's	:	:	:	1	:	1	:	:	:	:	:	2	2	48	2	10	:	:	60	:	:	:	:	:	:	:	:
„ Savory's	:	:	:	:	:	:	:	:	:	:	:	3	2	37	2	20	1	:	60	:	:	:	:	:	:	:	:
„ Grosser's	:	:	:	:	:	:	:	:	:	:	:	2	2	46	2	11	1	:	60	:	:	:	:	:	:	:	:
Total	:	1	:	2	:	3	1	1	1	1	1	17	10	253	13	210	4	:	480	:	:	:	:	1	:	1	:

N.B.—Three Serjeants one Drummer and Forty Six Rank and File Supernum'y doing duty with the Reg. not included.

GENERAL RETURN of His Majesty's New South Wales Corps, 1st November, 1806.

Absent Officers' names and ranks.	From what time.	By whose leave.
Colonel Grose	15th Decem'r, 1794	His Majesty's.
Major Foveaux		
Captain Savory	Not joined	
" Grosser	do	
Lieutenant Bayly		Resignation given in; Commanding Officer's leave of Absence.
Ensign Cressy	25th April, 1805	Commanding Officer's leave of absence.
Lieutenant Anderson	25th May, 1805	Resignation given in; Commanding Officer's leave of Absence.

Names of Officers present.	Names and rank of officers on duty, and what duty.	Vacant officers, and by what means.
Lt Colonel Paterson.	Captain Kemp, Port Dalrymple.	Lieut't Davies, dead.
Captain Jan.	Lieut't Moore, do	
" Wilson (Resignation given in and on leave of ... till His Majesty's pleasure is known).	Lieut't Laycock, do	Assist't Surgeon Roberts, dead.
Ensign Lawson.	Ensign Piper, do	Ensigns Barrallier and Wilson, Promoted.
" Draffen.		
" Cox.		
Pay Master Cox (suspended).	Lieut't Piper, at Norfolk Island.	Serjeans on Command, 11.
Qr. Master Laycock, in Arrest under Sentence of a Court Martial.	Captain Abbott, at Parramatta.	Drummers do 6.
Surgeon Harris.	Lieut't Brabyn do	
Asst Surgeon Smith Appointed by the Commanding Officer to act as Asst Surgeon till His Majesty's pleasure is known.		

W. PATERSON, Lt.-Col., Commanding.

GOVERNOR BLIGH TO SECRETARY MARSDEN.

(Despatch per ship Alexander.)

1806.
5 Nov.

Sir,   Sydney, New South Wales, 5th November, 1806.

His Majesty's Ship the Supply having been found unser- *Condition of the hulk Supply.* viceable and cut down to a Hulk in the Harbour by Governor King's Order after a regular Survey, she continued so for the use of putting Casks and Lumber occasionally into her; but, becoming more rotten and leaky induced him to represent the same to me on my arrival, and that it would be necessary to break her up.

In consequence of this representation, and seeing the great *The hulk Supply to be broken up.* risk of her sinking, I ordered a Survey, by the Report of which I have directed her to be broke up, and the Iron and Copper which may be taken off her to be delivered into Government Stores for the use of the Public Service, and accounts of the Issues to be kept by the Commissary and carried to the Credit of the Commissioners of His Majesty's Navy.

I beg leave to inclose Copies of Governor King's Letter; and the Order and Report of Survey.   I have, &c.,
                                        WM. BLIGH.

[Enclosure No. 1.]

GOVERNOR KING TO CAPTAIN BLIGH.

Sir,   Sydney, 12th August, 1806.

His Majesty's late Armed Vessel Supply, which was con- *King's report on the hulk Supply.* demned by Survey in 1799, has been ever since at the King's Moorings in this Cove, and about three Years ago was cut down. From the very rotten State she is now in it is requisite to keep a Number of Men employed at least one day in the Week to keep her from sinking. As I had not a Sufficient Number of persons that I conceived properly qualified to Survey her so as to warrant my ordering her to be broke up, And the great inconvenience that will attend her sinking where she lays, I beg to suggest the propriety of her being surveyed, and if the Report meets Your Approbation I would recommend her being broke up, as the remaining Iron and Copper work about her will be very useful for the Government purposes in the Colony.

I have, &c.,
                                        PHILIP GIDLEY KING.

MR. THOMAS MOORE TO GOVERNOR BLIGH.

Sydney, 13th August, 1806.

I BEG leave to acquaint your Excellency that H. M. Ship Supply, *Moore's report on the hulk Supply.* which was condemned in Ninety Seven, and since that Period

1806.
5 Nov.
has been used as a hulk, is now in so Rotten and leaky a state
that she is in danger of sinking at her Moorings; which will be a
great Annoyance to the Harbour and a loss to Government.

I have, &c.,

THOS. MOORE.

[Enclosure No. 2.]

Survey of
the hulk
Supply.

ORDER FOR THE SURVEY OF THE HULK SUPPLY.

By William Bligh, Esquire, etc., etc.
WHEREAS the Supply Hulk lying at this place is represented to
be rotten, irreparable, and in danger of sinking at her Moorings.

You are hereby required and directed to proceed with the Persons hereinafter named on board the said Hulk and taking a
careful Survey of the same, report to me your opinion thereon.

Given, etc., this 4th Day of September, 1806.

WM. BLIGH.

To Joseph Short, Esq., 2nd Captain of His Majesty's Ship Por-
poise; John Houstoun, Esqr., 2nd Commander of His
Majesty's Ship Buffalo; Mr. Thomas Moore, Master Builder;
Mr. Roger Best, Carpenter of H. M. Ship Buffalo; Mr.
Benjn. Bannister, Carpenter of H. M. Ship Porpoise.

[Enclosure No. 3.]

[*A copy of the report on the survey is not available.*]

GOVERNOR BLIGH TO SECRETARY MARSDEN.

(Despatch per ship Alexander.)

Sir,   Sydney, New South Wales, 5th November, 1806.

Reports to the
Adm'ralty.
I beg leave to inform my Lords Commissioners of the
Admiralty that this conveyance, by a Ship called the Alexander
for London, takes all the necessary documents relative to my
situation in obedience to their Lordships' Commands, as likewise
the circumstances which have taken place.

Projected
departure of
King.
Governor King in His Majesty's Ship Buffalo will sail in the
course of this Month, the extensive concerns of this Colony
together with a want of Bread having detained him longer in
settling than was expected.

Loss of the
whaler
Britannia.
The only Nautical occurrence is in the discovery of a Shoal*
by the loss of the Britannia Whaler, Nathaniel Goodspeed Commander, a statement of which is inclosed.

The Colony has suffered materially in Grain by an Inundation
of the River Hawkesbury as also the Settlers by loss of property.
The present Harvest will however relieve their wants in that
particular, and it is hoped that due precautions will prevent
their again suffering a similar calamity.   I have, &c.,

WM. BLIGH.

* Note 7.

[Enclosure.]

1806.
5 Nov.

PROTEST OF LATE SHIP BRITANNIA, NATHANIEL GOODSPEED, MASTER.

Protest of the late ship Britannia.

BY this public Instrument of Protest be it known unto all Men who shall see these presents that on the third day of October in the Year of Our Lord, One thousand, Eight hundred and Six before me, Richard Atkins Esquire, His Majesty's Judge Advocate and Notary public for the Territory of New South Wales and its Dependencies, Personally appeared Mr. Nathaniel Goodspeed, late Master of the Ship Britannia of London, William Dyer, Second Mate of the said Ship, John Douglas, Boat Steerer, and John Curtis, Boat Steerer, who being duly sworn on the holy Evangelists of Almighty God did solemnly depose to be true the sundry Matters and things hereinafter mentioned in this Instrument of Protest viz.

That on August twenty-fourth, One Thousand Eight hundred and Six, at Noon, the Latitude by Observation was 30° 38' South, and the Longitude, by Lunar Observation at 3 P.M., was 156° 40' East, by Dead reckoning 157° 40' East; to the best of my recollection the course steered by Compass from Noon was west until 8 p.m., at the rate of four knots an hour. We then steered N.W., going nearly at the same rate until 2 A.M., when we discovered Breakers ahead, close to the Ship. We immediately put down the Helm, the Wind being nearly aft at the time; but, unfortunately, the Ship did not answer her helm quick enough to clear the said Breakers. Our Ship striking aft first, she fell round off, and was hove bodily on the said Breakers, which proved to be a Bed of Coral Rocks;* after Striking two or three times she broke her back, her Stern and bow dropping down and Midships hove up. The Sea was then breaking violently upon the Ship, so as rendered it impossible to have got her off, or even were it possible to have got her off, She would have immediately Sunk on account of the aforesaid Disaster. We were then under the Necessity of having recourse to our Boats to Save our lives; the first Boat we attempted to lower into the Water was unfortunately Stove by a Surge of the Sea, and the lives of the Crew was with difficulty Saved. We then had recourse to the others, And at two and half A.M. we were fortunate enough to get Safe from the Ship, clear of the Breakers, with two Boats, Nineteen Men being on board of them, myself included; there then remained on board the Wreck five Men, who could not get on board the Boats time enough before we were obliged to push from the Ship on Account of the Breakers; nor could we venture to approach the Ship again until daylight. The people on board lowered a rope from the Jib Boom end into the Water; we then

* Note 7.

1806.
5 Nov.
———
Protest of the
late ship
Britannia.

ventured under the Boom with one of our Boats, when the Second
Mate and one of the Seamen were hauled on board, and with their
Assistance the people on board were enabled to launch another
Boat into the Water and get safe thro' the Breakers with about
forty pounds of Biscuit and ten Gallons of Water. The timbers
of the Ship at that time were Sticking thro' her Sides.

At low Water Saw a quarter of a Mile of dry Sand, but at high
Water there was no part dry; the Shoal lay N.E. and S.W.
Seven or Eight Miles, and about five or Six in breadth.

We left the Ship with three Boats, but four days after one of
them, in a Gale of Wind, Separated from us, and has not been
Since heard of. We were then Steering for New South Wales.
On the 29th of August we made the Land, and on the 8th of
September made New Castle, where we were treated with kind-
ness, and on the thirteenth of September we happily arrived at
Port Jackson.

And that against the aforesaid Wind, Weather Coral Rocks and
subsequent loss of the said Ship they the aforesaid Deponents
do most solemnly protest.

Sworn before me this 3rd day of October, 1806.

Notice of protest regularly entered. A true Copy.

R. ATKINS, J.-A. and N.P.

———

GOVERNOR BLIGH TO SECRETARY MARSDEN.

(Per ship Alexander.)

Sir,   Sydney, New South Wales, 5th November, 1806.

Transfer of
the crew of
the Lady
Nelson from
the books of
the Buffalo
to those of
the Porpoise.

The Lady Nelson Brig having been employed as a Tender
to His Majesty's Ship Buffalo with a Lieutenant and fourteen
Men and borne on her Books for Wages and Victuals pursuant
to their Lordships' orders to Governor King of the 4th March
1802, I have in consequence of Governor King's representation
to me directed the said Officer and Men to be turned over to His
Majesty's Ship Porpoise under my Command.

I herewith beg leave to inclose a Copy of their Lordships'
Order, dated 4th March, 1802, to bear the Lady Nelson's Crew
as Supernumeraries; a Copy of Governor King's Letter, dated 3rd
of September, 1806, requesting my order to discharge the Lady
Nelson's Crew to the Porpoise; a Copy of my Order to Governor
King to discharge the said Crew, dated 4th September 1806; and
a Copy of my Order to Captain Short to receive them of the
same date.   I have, &c.,

WM. BLIGH.

[Enclosure No. 1.]

ADMIRALTY WARRANT FOR THE CREW OF THE LADY NELSON.

BY the Commissioners for executing the Office of Lord High Admiral of the United Kingdom of Great Britain and Ireland etc.

The crew of the tender Lady Nelson to be borne on the books of the Buffalo.

WHEREAS we think fit that Fifteen Men shall be borne on a Supernumerary List for Wages and Victuals in the Ship you Command for the purpose of being lent to the Lady Nelson Tender when employed upon the Business of Surveying. You are hereby required and directed to bear the said Men on a Supernumerary List for Wages and Victuals accordingly and when she is employed in the abovementioned Service to deliver into the Charge of the Lieutenant whom you may appoint to Command her, the Stores and Provisions necessary on that Occasion who is to consider himself accountable for the same.

Given under our Hands, the 4th March, 1802.

T. TROWBRIDGE.
JAS. ADAMS.
J. MARKHAM.

[Enclosure No. 2.]

CAPTAIN KING TO GOVERNOR BLIGH.

Government House, Sydney,
New South Wales, 3rd Sept., 1806.

Sir,

Having by Order of my Lords Commissioners of the Admiralty dated 4th March, 1802, borne fourteen Men and one Lieutenant on the Books of His Majesty's Ship Buffalo under my Command as Supernumeraries for Wages and Victuals, for the purpose of being lent to the Lady Nelson Tender, I have to request your Order for their discharge into the Porpoise, under your Command, the said Tender devolving on you on my proceeding to England in His Majesty's Ship Buffalo.

Discharge of the Lady Nelson's crew from the Buffalo to the Porpoise.

I have, &c.,
PHILIP GIDLEY KING.

[Enclosure No. 3.]

GOVERNOR BLIGH'S ORDERS RE CREW OF THE LADY NELSON.

By William Bligh, Esquire, etc., etc

YOU are hereby required and directed to discharge from His Majesty's Ship Buffalo, the Officer and Men which are borne by Admiralty Order, dated 4th March, 1802, on the Supernumerary List as the Lady Nelson's Crew into His Majesty's Ship Porpoise, taking care to comply with the Act of Parliament.

Given, etc., this 4th day of September, 1806.

WM. BLIGH.

To Philip Gidley King, Esquire.

1806.
5 Nov.

The Lady
Nelson to be
tender to the
Porpoise.

By William Bligh, Esquire, etc., etc.

You are hereby required and directed to receive from His Majesty's Ship Buffalo, The Lady Nelson as a Tender to His Majesty's Ship Porpoise, and to bear on your Books, as discharged from those of His Majesty's Ship Buffalo with proper Lists for Wages and Victuals, Lieutenant Symonds and fourteen Men as Supernumeraries belonging to the said Tender.

You will also direct the Warrant Officers to charge themselves with the Stores, and govern yourself always in Receipts and Expenditure for her use, according to the Rules of the Navy, observing the strictest Frugality.

Given, etc., this 4th day of September, 1806.

WM. BLIGH.

To Joseph Short, Esquire, 2nd Captain of His Majesty's Ship Porpoise, Sydney Cove.

CAPTAIN KING TO SECRETARY MARSDEN.
(Per ship Alexander.)

8 Nov.

Causes of
delay in King's
departure.

Sir,   H. M. Ship Buffalo, Port Jackson, 8th Novr., 1806.

As settling the Colonial Accounts and arranging many public Objects to facilitate my Successors gaining a complete public Knowledge of the Trust he has undertaken and the necessity of waiting until some Supplies of Bread can be got from the coming Harvest I shall not be able to leave this place before the latter end of the Month.

Services of
lieutenant
Houston.

Lieutenant Houstoun who has acted by my order as Second Commander of the Buffalo since Captain Kent was lent to the Investigator has been very active in the Command of the Ship on the different Voyages she has gone to Norfolk Island And the New Settlements And is a very Sober and assiduous good Officer.

Services of
John Oxley.

Mr. John Oxley has acted as Lieutenant of the Buffalo since March 1805 on Lieut. B. Kent being lent to the Investigator. He is a very Active Sober and attentive young Man. As no opportunity offered of his passing his Examination for a Lieutenant until the Arrival of Capt. Bligh I have requested that Officer to give Mr. Oxley another Actg. Order after the date of his passing.

Services of
William Kent.

Mr. William Kent also passed at the same time, and has acted as Lieutenant of the Buffalo by my Order since Augt. 1805 on Acting Lieut. Robbins being lent to go to Valparaiso as stated in a former Letter. That Officer not being returned it is my intention to keep him open on the Books until the probability of his joining the Buffalo in those Seas is over, when I shall give Mr. Kent another Acting Order consequent on his passing his Accounts as Lieutenant of the Buffalo.

1806.
8 Nov.

Mr. James Symons, having served as my Acting Lieutenant of the Lady Nelson and having conducted himself in the Command of that Vessel much to my Satisfaction. On his passing his Examination I have requested Captain Bligh to give him an Acting Order.

Services of James Symons.

In stating the above Circumstances respecting those Officers I trust their Lordships will approve of my Motives in noticing those Gentlemen who have been so much out of that line of Service that might have brought them forward to their Lordships' Notice much sooner.   I have, &c.,

PHILIP GIDLEY KING.

THE RIGHT HON. WILLIAM WINDHAM TO GOVERNOR BLIGH.
(Despatch per transport Duke of Portland; acknowledged by Governor Bligh, 31st October, 1807.)

Sir,   Downing Street, 6th Decr., 1806.

6 Dec.

Mr. Bell, having been recommended to me in the strongest Manner by Persons of great Respectability, has received my permission to proceed to New South Wales as a Settler, and I take this Opportunity to recommend him and his Family to your Protection. You will direct a Grant of Five hundred Acres of Land to be made out in his Favor, subject to the usual Reservations; and you will afford him such Assistance of Convicts and Stores as he is entitled to expect and as can be spared consistently with other Claims: Mr. Bell takes out with him Property to the Amount of more than Five hundred Pounds.
       I have, &c.,

Recommendation of and land grant for Bell.

W. WINDHAM.

SIR GEORGE SHEE TO GOVERNOR BLIGH.
(Per transport Duke of Portland.)

Sir,   Downing Street, 8th Decr., 1806.

8 Dec.

Since Mr. Secretary Windham's Letter to you of the 18th September last relative to Mrs. Chapman's Estab't in the Settlement under your Command was written, that Lady has married, and I have now to acquaint you that her Husband Mr. Marchant has received Mr. Windham's Permission to accompany her to Port Jackson.   I have, &c.,

Marchant granted permission to become a settler.

GEORGE SHEE.

GOVERNOR BLIGH TO SECRETARY MARSDEN.
(Despatch per H.M.S. Buffalo.)

Sir,   Sydney, New South Wales, 12th December, 1806.

12 Dec.

I beg leave to inclose to You, for the information of my Lords Commissioners of the Admiralty, the proceedings of a

1806.
12 Dec.

Inquiry into
the conduct
of Short,
Tetley, and
Lye.

Court of Enquiry on the conduct of Joseph Short, Esquire, Commander of His Majesty's Ship Porpoise, and Lieutenant Tetley and Mr. Daniel Lye, Master, which I was under the necessity of ordering on account of the respective Charges in the Letters of representation which accompany the Minutes and verbal information I had received of Captain Short's severity. Annexed to these documents is my Order for a Survey on Mr. Lye's state of confinement, the Report of the Surgeons thereon, my Order to liberate Mr. Lye in consequence thereof, and Captain Short's Letters to obviate my Order.   I have, &c.,

WM. BLIGH.

[Enclosure No. 1.]

LIEUTENANT TETLEY TO GOVERNOR BLIGH.

His Majesty's Ship Porpoise,
Sydney Cove, Port Jackson,
Sir,   New South Wales, 15th November, 1806.

Lieutenant
Tetley's charges
against captain
Short.

I am sorry to be under the Necessity of Writing You on so unpleasant an affair as that of making some Serious Complaints against Joseph Short, Esquire, Second Captain of His Majesty's Ship under Your Command, for having at different times appropriated the Ship's Stores to his own private use; that he has lent Men from the Ship to private persons on Shore, whereby the Service has materially suffered; The Articles of War were never but once read since the Ship was Commissioned, Nor any officer's Commissions ever read; The Boats' Crews have been kept up at different times most of the Night, either waiting for Captain Short or taking his Friends on Shore, And I have every reason to Suppose that, if an Opportunity offered, they would desert in Consequence; Since the Order of the 4th September respecting provisions he has had more than his Allowance; that he has at different times behaved to me in a cruel and oppressive Manner, and made use of the most unofficer-like language to me on the Quarter-Deck when in the Execution of my duty, and endeavoured to depreciate me in the Opinion of the Officers and Ship's Company; And I beg leave to say that, in Consequence of the ill-usage I have received from Captain Short, my peace of Mind is broke and my health much injured; That I have sufficient Witnesses (as per Margin*) to Substantiate the truth of my Assertions; And I hope you will, Sir, take Steps most conducive to the good of the Service.

I have, &c.,
J. S. TETLEY.

* Messrs. Lye, Baxter, Calver, Hobbs, Bannister, Hardinge, Jno. Seymour, Corp'l Stephens, Jas. Allen, Wm. Harvey.

[Enclosure No. 2.]

DANIEL LYE TO GOVERNOR BLIGH.

His Majesty's Ship Porpoise,

Sir,   Sydney Cove, 22nd November, 1806.

Having a few days since waited on You with a Complaint against Captain Short, which You requested I would let You know by Letter, Captain Short having behaved in an unofficer-like and improper Manner to me and other Officers in the Ship, which has caused me to be very unhappy and uncomfortable for some time past, I therefore conceive it my Duty to point out to You the Unofficer-like Conduct of Capt'n Short, for which I have sufficient Witnesses, named per Margin,* to Substantiate the Charges which I shall bring against him. On the Ship's Arrival in False Bay, being late in the Afternoon, it falling nearly calm, We were obliged to come to Anchor about three Miles from Simon's Bay; at 7 o'Clock in the Evening the Harbour-Master came on board; when Capt'n Short came on Deck to receive him he was so much intoxicated that it was with great difficulty he could Stand, The Ship all this time being at an unsafe place at Anchor had it come on to blow from the N.E., but the light Airs of Wind prevented us getting to any other Anchorage that Night, and on the 13th of June Capt'n Short came off to the Ship so much intoxicated that without Assistance he could not get up the Ship's Side. I think it my duty also to point out that Capt'n Short has made a wasteful Expence of His Majesty's Stores in converting them to his own private use, Having likewise wanted the Gunner at the Cape of Good Hope to expend two of the Ship's Musquets, which the Gunner refused to do. The Articles of War have never been read since the Ship left England, which I think has been the Means of so many Punishments being inflicted in the Ship, owing to the People being ignorant of the Articles they are liable to fall under. Since the Ship has been in Port Jackson the Boats' Crews have been kept up almost every Night from 11, 12, and sometimes till 2 o'Clock in the Morning, when the Ship's Company is always turned out to whip the Chair up; And I am confident, if the Ship was in any other Port than this, the greatest part of the Ship's Company would have deserted. I hope, Sir, You will take those Charges into Consideration, And take such Steps as You think necessary for the good of His Majesty's Service to bring Capt'n Short to Justice, as it is impossible for the Officers of the Ship to live where such flagrant Abuses exist.   I have, &c.,

Attested: WM. BLIGH.   DAN'L LYE.

* Mr. Tetley, 1st Lieut't; Fran's Calver, Gunner; Wm. Hobbs, Boats'n; Benj'm Bannister, Cr.

1806.
12 Dec.

[Enclosure No. 3.]

DANIEL LYE TO GOVERNOR BLIGH.

Sir,   H. M. Ship Porpoise, 9th December, 1806.

Lye's complaint
as to his
confinement.

I beg leave to acquaint You that I have been close confined under an Arrest since the 28th of November and not even allowed to come out of my Cabin to my Meat, for Charges I am not yet acquainted with. I wrote to Capt. Short the 1st day of December, requesting to know the Charges for which I was so closely confined, but he has thought proper not yet to acquaint me with them. I wrote to the Surgeon the 2nd of December, finding myself unwell from the closeness of my Confinement, stating also to him the Small Size of my Cabin, from the Heat of the Climate, and the unpleasant Smells which comes from the next Cabin owing to a Woman and a family of Children being there, which the Officers of the Gun-Room can Witness, requesting him if I was not released from such close Confinement to enclose my Letter to You, of which there has been no further Notice taken of Since, nor has he come near me since to enquire if I was well or not. I hope, Sir, You will take my unpleasant State of confinement into Consideration, And take such Steps as You think proper, refering to my Letter of the 22nd of November, to crush such oppressive treatment.   I have, &c.,

Attested: WM. BLIGH.   DAN'L LYE.

[Enclosure No. 4.]

THIS Letter is wrong dated; as Mr. Murphy delivered it with 2 Order Books into my hands from the Ship by Captn. Short's Orders this Morning, 10th Decr. 1806, And might have been sent to me if written on the 1st having received Letters dated Subsequent to it from Captn. Short.   W.B.

CAPTAIN SHORT TO GOVERNOR BLIGH.

Sir,   His Majesty's Ship Porpoise, 1st December, 1806.

Lye placed in
confinement.

I beg leave to acquaint You that on Friday, the 28th ultimo, I confined Mr. Lye, Acting-Master of this Ship for disobedience of my Orders. I have for a length of time had great reason of Complaint against him, both for disobedience of my Orders and treating me with Contempt. I have also to charge

Captain Short's
charges against
Tetley and Lye.

him, with Lieut. Tetley, of talking in presence of the Ship's Company in language tending to make them discontented and to create Mutiny. I beg to lodge a Complaint against Lieut. Tetley for the above, together with other practices highly detrimental to His Majesty's Service, and such as tended to create insubordination in His Majesty's ship he was first Lieutenant of. I therefore Submit it to your Judgment the Steps to be taken;

But assure you that it is highly requisite for the discipline of the Ship that an Enquiry should be made; the reason I have not confined Lieutenant Tetley is my having no other Officer on board.*

1806.
12 Dec.

Short's request
for an inquiry.

I have enclosed the Order Books, which I hope will prove to You my Attention to the discipline of this Ship, as well as to your several Orders. I am, &c.,

Attested: WM. BLIGH. JOSEPH SHORT.

[Enclosure No. 5.]

GOVERNOR BLIGH TO CAPTAIN SHORT.

Sir, Government House, Sydney, 10th December, 1806.

On my Return from my Journey throughout the Settlement I received this Morning by the hands of Mr. Murphy, Midshipman of the Porpoise, Your Letter dated the 1st instant. I apprehend the date is wrong, as he had just received it from You, and a Letter Subsequent to it dated the 5th instant, which has been delivered to me by a Messenger in the Country.

Letters acknowledged.

I have to inform You likewise that on my Setting out on my Journey, Lieutenant Tetley wrote me a Letter complaining of you, And that Mr. Lye about the same time came with a Complaint to the same Effect, which I directed him to State in writing, but would not have any Conversation with him on the Subject, and since that he has written a Second Letter.

Charges made against Short.

In Consequence, therefore, of these Circumstances and Your request, I have directed Captain King, Captain Houstoun, and Lieutenant Oxley to proceed on board the Porpoise and enquire into the Representations You have made, as likewise those of Lieutenant Tetley and Mr. Lye, with directions to report to me thereon. I am, &c.,

An inquiry ordered.

WM. BLIGH.

The Enquiry will take place at ten o'Clock to-Morrow Morning.
Attested: WM. BLIGH. WM. BLIGH.

[Enclosure No. 6.]

CAPTAIN SHORT TO GOVERNOR BLIGH.

His Majesty's Ship Porpoise,
Sir, Sydney Cove, 11th December, 1806.

In Answer to Yours of Yesterday's date I beg to acquaint You that there was no Mistake in the date of my Letter, As it was reported You was coming to Sydney daily I had it wrote to Send You on Your Arrival, as an Enquiry could not take place

Explanation of date of letter.

---

* *Marginal note.*—John Bowman, Adam Brown, Wm. Harvey, when working in between the Heads. Mr. Harding, Mr. Oldrey, Mr. Basden, Mr. Pineo to prove the Speeches. Also their disobedience of my Orders. Also Mr. Tetley being drunk in his Watch, and Mr. Lye damning me, wishing the Boat to sink alongside.

1806.
12 Dec.
until Your coming to this, I thought it sufficient time to acquaint
You of my Complaint. As to Mr. Tetley's and Mr. Lye's Complaints against me I hope I have never given them just Ground
for, Neither do I know what they are—But conscious of having
done my duty as an officer will enable me with pleasure to meet
the strictest Scrutiny into my Conduct.

I am, &c.,

Attested: Wm. Bligh.   JOSH. SHORT.

[Enclosure No. 7.]

Warrant for
holding an
inquiry on
H.M.S.
Porpoise.
WARRANT TO HOLD AN ENQUIRY ON H.M.S. PORPOISE.

By William Bligh, Esquire, etc., etc.

JOSEPH SHORT ESQUIRE, Commander of His Majesty's Ship Porpoise under my Command, requesting an Enquiry into the Conduct of Lieutenant Tetley and Mr. Lye, Master, belonging to the
said Ship, And these officers having in the first instance likewise
made heavy Complaints against him their Said Commander, I
therefore put You in Possession of their respective Letters requiring and directing You to proceed on board the said Ship
taking with You to Your Assistance Captain John Houstoun and
Lieutenant John Oxley of His Majesty's Ship Buffalo and
Enquire into the same, presenting to me a Statement, And Your
Opinion thereon.

Given, etc., this 10th day of December, 1806.

WM. BLIGH.

To Philip Gidley King, Esq.,
    Captain of His Majesty's Ship Buffalo.
    Attested: Wm. Bligh.

[Enclosure No. 8.]

ENQUIRY INTO THE COMPLAINTS OF CAPTAIN SHORT,
LIEUTENANT TETLEY AND DANIEL LYE.

Proceedings of
inquiry into
the conduct of
Short, Tetley,
and Lye.
PURSUANT to an Order from William Bligh, Esquire, principal
    Captain of H. M. Ship Porpoise, dated the 10th Decr., 1806,
    And to us directed.

In Compliance therewith we proceed to enquire into the respective
Complaints exhibited by the 2d. Captain, 1st. Lieutenant and Master
against each other.

MR. BASDEN, Purser of H.M. Ship Porpoise, called in to give testimony on the Charges alledged by Lieutenant Tetley against Captain
Short, Commander of the Porpoise.

Q. 1, by Court.—Does it come within Your personal knowledge
that Captain Short has at different times appropriated the Ship's
Stores to his own private use; If it does, relate the times and Circumstances ?—A. It does not come within my knowledge that
Captain Short has ever taken Stores out of the Ship for his own
private Use.

Q. 2.—Has Captain Short ever appropriated any Provisions or Stores under Your Charge to his own private Use?—*A.* No more than he is entitled to.

1806.
12 Dec.

Proceedings of inquiry into the conduct of Short, Tetley, and Lye.

Q. 3.—Does it come within Your knowledge that he has lent Men from the Ship to private persons on Shore whereby the Service has materially suffered?—*A.* I remember Captain Short directing Lieutenant Tetley to lend one of the Seamen to some person on Shore for a few hours, but I do not imagine the Service could suffer from it. I do not recollect the Seaman's Name, but believe the person he was lent to was Mr. Fitz. I do not know that the Man lent in consequence of that direction.

Q. 4.—How often has the Articles of War been read Since the Ship was commissioned, or since Your Appointment?—*A.* I have heard the Articles of War read by Captain Short to the Ship's Company, the hands being turned up for that purpose; reading the Articles of War took place when the Ship was in England, But cannot say whether it was more than once; does not remember their being read during the Voyage nor Since our Arrival in this Country, but that the Articles of War was read before punishment was inflicted relating to the Crime.

Q. 5.—Have You reason to believe that from the Boat's Crews being kept up at different times most of the Night, either waiting for Captain Short or taking his Friends on Shore, or any other oppressive Act of Captain Short, that the Boat's Crew or any other of the Ship's Company would in Consequence thereof desert if an Opportunity offered?—*A.* I have never known the Boat's Crews to be kept up past 12 o'Clock Except three or four times; Neither do I, to the best of my knowledge, believe that any would desert, or that Captain Short has ever treated the Ship's Company with Oppression.

Q. 6.—Has Captain Short received more than his Allowance of Provisions Since The Order, 4th September last?—*A.* Since that period Captain Short has not received more than his Allowance of provisions.

The Mess Book for October and November produced. It does not appear to us in the Article of Bread that he has exceeded his Allowance, And by the same Book he has drawn more than the Allowance of Beef; But Mr. Basden States that the Overplus of Beef is occasioned by more of that Article coming on board than will keep in this warm Climate; the Surplus has generally been divided between the Gun-room and the Cabin; the Mess Book for September being destroyed, No reference can be had to that Month; And he appears to have taken no Spirits whatever in the Months of October, November, and December. Mr. Basden also desires to state that upon balancing the Account, Captain Short will be found not to have exceeded his Allowance in any one Species.

Q. 7.—Relate every instance wherein Captain Short has behaved in a cruel and oppressive Manner to Lieutenant Tetley, using unofficer-like language to him on the Quarter Deck when in the Execution of his Duty, and endeavouring to depreciate him, Lieutenant Tetley, in the Opinion of the Officers and Ship's Company?— *A.* I never knew Captain Short behave to Lieutenant Tetley in an Oppressive or cruel Manner, And have never heard any unofficer-like language from Captain Short to him, And have never known Captain Short to depreciate Lieutenant Tetley in the Opinion of either Officers or Ship's Company, to the best of my knowledge.

1806.
12 Dec.

Proceedings of
inquiry into
the conduct of
Short, Tetley,
and Lye.

MR. LYE, Master of the Porpoise, called :—

Q. 1 being put.—*A.* I have heard of such things; but they do not come within my personal knowledge, Except the Circumstance of Some Green Baize which he has seen the Taylor using for different purposes in Captain Short's Cabin.

Q. 3 put.—*A.* At the Cape of Good Hope the Armourer was lent to a Mr. Rozelle for about a fortnight, And that the Arms suffered materially during his Absence for Want of being cleaned; And at this place, during the time the Ship was refitting, James Allen was lent from the Ship to Mr. Fitz and Mr. Luttrell to work in their Gardens; I think he was away for 16 days.

Q. 4 put.—*A.* I recollect their being read Once in England, not once on the Voyage, And once since the Ship's Arrival here, the 8th of the present Month, by Lieutenant Tetley, in Consequence of Captain Short's direction to him.

Q. 5 put.—*A.* I have known Boats' Crews to be kept up from 11 to 2 in the Morning, and have overheard the people to murmur at being kept up, And from that Circumstance think they would have deserted if they had been in a convenient Port; And does not know of any oppressive Act of Captain Short that would induce them to desert Except the above, if it may be so termed.

Q. 6 put.—*A.* I cannot positively say he has.

Q. 7 put.—*A.* I remember hearing Captain Short saying to Lieutenant Tetley that he knew he kept an Almanac against him, Lieutenant Tetley denying it. Captain Short said he despised him And his Mean Actions; but cannot recollect the date, but think it was about a Month or two ago; At the time, the Ship's Company was clearing the Long Boat.

DAN'L LYE, Acting Master.

MR. CALVER, Gunner, called :—

Q. 1 put.—*A.* Not any of my Stores, nor of any others to my knowledge.

Q. 2 answered by the above.

Q. 3 put.—*A.* I remember one Man being lent—the Armourer—at the Cape of Good Hope, And corroborates the Evidence of Mr. Lye as to that Circumstance, and further States that having occasion to clean the Navel Bolts, for want of the Armourer to drive them out, was obliged to employ a Soldier on that Service, who broke the Cheek of the Carriage, which in his Opinion has rendered the Carronade unserviceable; And that he had pointed out to Captain Short the Necessity of the Armourer being employed on that Service, who said that any other person would do as well. With respect to James Allen being lent, corroborates Mr. Lye, but cannot recollect the time or to whom he was lent.

Q. 4 put.—*A.* I cannot recollect any other time than last Sunday, the 8th Instant.

Q. 5 put.—*A.* I have heard some murmuring among the Ship's Company at being obliged to Set up so late at the time the Ship was fitting, but have no reason to think they would desert in Consequence of it, Altho' one of the Boats Crew has deserted Since our Arrival here, But I cannot State his reason.

Q. 6 put.—*A.* Evidence can give no Opinion.

Q. 7 put.—*A.* I have heard altercations between them, but cannot Speak as to the time or Circumstance, And corroborates the Evidence of Mr. Lye with respect to Captain Short having Said that Lieutenant Tetley kept an Almanac against him and the language made use of on that occasion.

1806.
12 Dec.
———
Proceedings of
inquiry into
the conduct of
Short, Tetley,
and Lye.

FR'S CALVER.

MR. HOBBS, boatswain, being called:—

Q. 1 put.—*A.* I recollect Captain Short appropriating about Six Yards of Baize and Canvas for Dish Stands; And on another occasion, the Bolt of Baize was sent for, and a quantity cut off to cover a Desk; That he, the Boatswain, was supplied with 20 Yards of Green Baize, which was used by Captain Short for different purposes in his Cabin, Except what covered a Sett of Side Ropes and Chair Slings, and Side Ropes for an Accommodation Ladder.

Q. 2 put, and answered by the 1st.

Q. 3 put.—*A.* At the Cape of Good Hope, the Man I had appropriated to me for a Yeoman was mostly ashore attending the washing, and corroborates the former Evidence respecting James Allen being lent, as also the testimony of Mr. Lye and Mr. Calver, respecting the Armourer being lent at the Cape of Good Hope.

Q. 4 put.—*A.* I do not recollect their having been read except last Sunday.

Q. What Officers' Commissions have You heard read?—*A.* I do not recollect any Commissions being read but Captain Bligh's, which was read at Sea. Captain Short's was also read at the same time.

Q. 5.—*A.* He corroborates Mr. Calver in that respect.

Q. 6 put.—*A.* But cannot recollect he has.

Q. 7 put.—*A.* Altercations so often happen between the Captain and Officers that he cannot charge his Memory with anything particular.　　　　　　　　　　　　　　　　　　　　　WM. HOBBS.

MR. BANNISTER, Carpenter, called:—

Q. 1 put.—*A.* I know of no other Circumstance than Captain Short's appropriating about 100 feet of wainscot for the purpose of making Shelves to contain Books in the Great Cabin.

Q. 2.—*A.* Answered by the first.

Q. 3 put.—*A.* Not within my own knowledge.

Q. 4 put.—*A.* I never heard them read but on Sunday last.

Q. 5 put.—*A.* Not to my knowledge.

Q. 6 put.—*A.* But Evidence cannot Speak to it.

Q. 7 put.—*A.* Corroborates the former Evidence of this Charge.

Q. What Officers' Commissions have you heard read?—*A.* The same as Mr. Hobbs.　　　　　　　　　　　　　BENJ'N BANNISTER.

MR. HARDING called:—

Q. 1 put.—*A.* from my own personal knowledge I cannot say I do, but recollect the Shelves in the Great Cabin being made out of the Ship's Stores.

Q. 2 put.—*A.* But cannot speak to it.

Q. 3 put.—*A.* He recollects a Man being lent at the Cape of Good Hope (the Armourer), but for what purpose he cannot say; Also another Man at this place, but cannot say to whom or for what reason.

Q. 4 put.—*A.* He cannot recollect how often except last Sunday.

Q. 5 put.—*A.* He has heard the Ship's Company murmur on that occasion, which he attributed to the Short Complement and Boats' Crew kept up, Consequently the hard work occasioned thereby, but does not think it would cause them to desert.

1806.
12 Dec.

Proceedings of
inquiry into
the conduct of
Short, Tetley,
and Lye.

Q. 6 put.—A. The Evidence cannot take upon himself to Answer.

Q. 7 put.—A. I have heard harsh language made use of by Captain Short to Lieutenant Tetley, but never particularly noticed the Expressions, as I always made a point of retiring when an Altercation took place between them.

Q.—What Officers' Commissions have You heard read since You belonged to the Ship?—A. I have heard Captain Bligh's Commission read as first Captain, and Capt'n Short's Commission, or Order, as Second Captain—no others.

Q.—When did You join the Porpoise?—A. On the 7th of May, 1805.

F. L. HARDINGE.

JOHN SEYMOUR, the Armourer, called:—

Q. 3 put.—A. I understood I was lent to the Fiscull* at the Cape of Good Hope, where I remained for three or four days.

JNO. SEYMOUR.

CORP'L STEPHENS called:—

Q. 1 put.—A. I cannot say he ever did.

Q. 3 put.—A. Not to my knowledge.

Q. 4 put.—A. Three times—twice by Capt'n Short and once by Lieut. Tetley.

Q. 5 put.—A. They have been often kept up, but I cannot Say they would desert.

Q. 7 put.—A. I do not know of any instance.

Q.—Have you ever heard any of the Officers' Commissions read?—A. I have heard Capt'n Bligh's and Capt'n Short's and no others.

WM. STEPHENS.

JAMES ALLEN called:—

Q. 1 put.—A. I do not recollect.

Q. 3 put.—A. I have worked for Mr. Fitz, by his Order, for three weeks.

Q. 4 put.—A. I never recollect their being read but twice.

Q. 5 put.—A. Cannot say.

Q. 7 put.—A. He being below Cannot speak to this Charge.

his
JAMES X ALLEN.
mark

WILLIAM HARVEY, Boatswain's Mate, called:—

Q. 1 put.—A. I do not know of any.

Q. 3 put.—A. Corroborates the Circumstances as to Allen being lent.

Q. 4 put.—A. Cannot recollect, Except last Sunday, when they were read by Lieutenant Tetley.

Q. 5 put.—A. I cannot say they would desert.

Q. 7 put.—A. It does not come within my knowledge.

WM. HARVEY.

End of Examination and Evidence of the Enquiry on Lieutenant Tetley's Letter, dated 15th November, 1806.

Mr. Daniel Lye, Master's Letter, of the 22nd November, 1806, being read to the Court,—

LIEUTENANT TETLEY called:—

The Court directed him to relate:—

Q. 1.—Whether he ever saw Captain Short being so much intoxicated that it was with great difficulty he could stand when on the Quarter-Deck, and the Duty of the Ship going forward?—A. The Night he entered the outer part of Simon's Bay, the Harbor-Master

* Note 8.

came on board. I acquainted Captain Short that he wished to know the particulars relative to the Ship's Arrival at that place. Captain Short appeared drunk, and ridiculed the Officer, which the Harbour-Master expressed himself hurt at; that the Ship, at the time, was at Single Anchor—an unsafe Situation—and further States that on or about the 13th of June last Captain Short went out of the Ship in a State of intoxication.

1806.
12 Dec.

Proceedings of Inquiry into the conduct of Short, Tetley, and Lye.

Q. 2.—Does it come within Your knowledge that Captain Short has made a wasteful Expense of His Majesty's Stores, and converted them to his own private use?—*A.* Yes. Shortly after our leaving Gravesend the Carpenter mentioned to me that there was no Wood on board to repair the Boats with, the Joiner, Corporal Stephens, having used the wood for furniture for Captain Short. At another time the Carpenter informed me that the Table I had lent from the Gun-room to the Midshipman's berth, had been cut up by the Captain's Order, to make a Writing desk for him. Two Cotts, and Canvas for two more Cotts designed for the passengers, was never appropriated to their use, altho' applied for by them, But the Canvas made into a Cott for Captain Short. At the time we arrived at the Cape, I desired the Boatswain to get a pair of Side-ropes covered. He told me there was no Green Baize in the Ship. He had sent between 30 and 40 Yards into the Cabin to Captain Short, and had never received any back; That the Tailor had informed him it was made into Dish Stands and other uses for the Cabin. On Our passage between the Cape of Good Hope and Port Jackson, the Boatswain informed me that there were no log-lines in the Ship. and that for some time past he had been using Fishing lines for that purpose, and that he accounted for there being no log-lines by saying that Captain Short had used them for every trifling occasion, both in the Cabin and upon Deck. On the 28th day of April, 1806, It will appear by the Ship's Log, that one of the Jolly-Boat's Davits were carried away. No such thing took place, as it was in my particular watch that the Circumstance was mentioned, And that an Anchor-Stock had been cut up previous to this to repair the Boats in room of the Wainscots that had been used in the Cabin, And that Mr. Lye, the Master, informed me the Anchor-Stock had been expended to replace the Davits that were never carried away. He also says he heard Captain Short desire the Gunner to expend two Musquets as lost out of a Boat at the Cape of Good Hope, which the Gunner objected to, as no Musquets were lost at the time.

Q.—How often have You heard the Articles of War read Since You joined the Ship?—*A.* Once at Spithead, and once last Sunday; But whenever a Man was punished the Article under which he lay was always read.

Q.—Have the Boats' Crews been kept up every Night from 11, 12, and sometimes 2 o'Clock in the Morning, when the Ship's Company have been turned out to whip the Chair up?—*A.* It has frequently in this port happen'd till within the last fortnight.

Q.—Are You of Opinion that if the Ship was in any other Port than this, that the greater part of the Ship's Company would desert thro' that Cause?—*A.* One Man has already deserted since our Arrival, and another attempted to do so; that much murmuring has existed among the people, which leads me to suppose that might be the Case.

J. S. Tetley.

1806.
12 Dec.

Proceedings of
inquiry into
the conduct of
Short, Tetley,
and Lye.

MR. CALVER, the Gunner, called:—

Q. 1 put.—*A.* I saw him once at night when the Ship was in Symon's Bay, but no duty was going on at the time.

Q. 2 put.—*A.* He does not know of any wasteful Expence of stores, but recollects that Cap't Short asked him, after leaving the Cape of Good Hope, to expend two Musquets in a Boat that was swamped there, which he declined, as the Musquets were not lost.

                                                    •   FR'S CALVER.

MR. HOBBS, the Boatswain, called :—

Q. 1 put.—*A.* I have seen him two or three times intoxicated, but not so much so that he could not Stand; the only particular time was at the Cape of Good Hope, when he (Capt'n Short) was going on Shore to a Ball.

Q.—Did You ever tell Mr. Tetley that You have sent about 30 or 40 Yards of Green Baize into the Cabin, and had received none back?—*A.* I told him I had sent all the Green Baize I had, and rec'd none back.

Q.—Was the Canvas that was drawn for the Passengers' Cotts appropriated for that purpose?—*A.* As the passengers nor none of the Officers applied for them, I did not issue them; the Canvas is now on board, and remains on my Charge as Cotts.

Q.—Has Captain Short had any part of that Canvas for a Cott for his own Use?—*A.* No; the Canvas drawn for the Cotts being No. 3, And that made into a Cott for the Captain lately, No. 5.

Q.—Do you know of any wasteful Expence of the log-lines?—*A.* There has been a Number used for the Cabin; Several carried away, but not allowed to be expended by Capt'n Short.

                                                    WM. HOBBS.

MR. BANNISTER, Carpenter, called:—

Q. 1 put.—*A.* I have seen him at different times when he has appeared to me to be intoxicated, but cannot recollect any particular time.

Q.—Did You cut an Anchor Stock up on the passage to repair the Boats?—*A.* Yes.

Q.—What became of the plank You was supplied with for that purpose?—*A.* Used for making Scupper-Shoots, by the Captain's orders.

Q.—How did you expend the Anchor Stock?—*A.* Replacing one of the Quarter Davits.

Q.—To your knowledge, was that Quarter Davit carried away, or did you work the Anchor Stop up to replace it?—*A.* It was not carried away, but I was ordered by the Captain to expend it, with which I complied, not being better acquainted with the Service.

                                                    BENJ'N BANNISTER.

MR. PINEO called :—

Q.—Did Mr. Lye, since his Confinement, report to You his being unwell from the Closeness of his Confinement, the small Size of his Cabin, the heat of the Climate, and the unpleasant Smell of the next Cabin owing to a Woman and family of Children being there, by Letter?—*A.* He did. I visited him immediately in Consequence of it; and seeing his Cabin Door shut And Window leading into the Gun-room being also shut, I could not think he could suffer from a close Confinement, and there appear'd no Symptoms of ill-health.

                                                    O. PINEO.

Mr. Pineo withdrawn.

1806.
12 Dec.

Proceedings of
Inquiry into
the conduct of
Short, Tetley,
and Lye.

The Sergeant of Marines, called and asked If any Orders were given to the Centinels to prevent Mr. Lye's Door and Window of his Cabin being opened, who says that no Such Orders were given, but that Captain Short the day after Mr. Lye being Confined, gave directions that the door might be kept open.

JAS. PETTY, St. R. Ms.

MR. PINEO again called :—

Q.—Did Mr. Lye request You to forward the Letter he wrote to You to Captain Bligh?—A. He did, which I communicated to Captain Short as my immediate Commanding Officer.

Q.—As Mr. Lye complained of being ill, Did You not conceive it Your Duty to visit him since his first Complaint?—A. I do; but from my Situation in the Gun-Room, and frequently hearing him converse, I had no Apprehension of his being indisposed.

Q.—How long do You suppose Mr. Lye can remain in that close State of Confinement without his Health being endangered?—A. That will depend upon the State of the weather and other Circumstances which I cannot foresee.

O. PINEO.

The Charge against Captain Short by Mr. Lye, the Master, being ended, Captain Short is called and requested to State the Witnesses he wishes to have brought forward in Support of the charges alleged by him against Mr. Lye, the Master of the Porpoise, and Lieutenant Tetley.

JOHN BOWMAN, Gunner's Mate, called :—

Q. 1.—Do You know of Mr. Lye disobeying Captain Short's Orders at any time?—A. I was on the Quarter Deck on the 28th November last assisting unfurling the Awning, and heard Captain Short order Mr. Lye to go forward and order the Stream Cable to be boused in, which Mr. Lye said he would do; But that as the people were all employed there was no one forward to do it. Captain Short again told him to go forward and see it done, to which Mr. Lye replied that he would, but that the Awning was not furled. Captain Short then ordered him to his Cabin.

Q. 2.—Do You know of no other instance of Mr. Lye's disobeying Captain Short's Orders?—A. None; Except the Night we were working between the Heads, when I heard Captain Short desire Mr. Lye to go forward and take his Great Coat off, And not to Set a bad example to the Ship's Company. Whether he complied I cannot say, As my Attention was taken up in Steering the Ship.

Q. 3.—Did You ever see Mr. Lye treat Captain Short with Contempt?—A. Never.

Q. 4.—Did You ever hear Mr. Lye or Lieutenant Tetley talk in the presence of the Ship's Company in language tending to make them discontented and to create Mutiny?—A. Never in my life; quite the contrary.

Q. 5.—Do You know of any practices used by Lieutenant Tetley tending to create insubordination in this Ship of which he is first Lieutenant?—A. No.

Q. 6.—Have You ever seen Lieutenant Tetley intoxicated or drunk in his Watch?—A. Never.

his
JOHN x BOWMAN.
mark

1806.
12 Dec.

Proceedings of
inquiry into
the conduct of
Short, Tetley,
and Lye.

ADAM BROWN, Seaman, called:—

Q. 1 put.—A. I was on the Quarter-Deck when Captain Short ordered Mr. Lye to see the Slack of the Stream Cable taken in. Mr. Lye said he would go when the Awning was out of the way, and corroborates Bowman's Evidence on that Question.

Q. 2 put.—A. I know of none.

Q.—Can you speak to any disobedience of Orders when the Ship was working between the heads?—A. None.

Q. 3 put.—A. Never.

Q. 4 put.—A. Never.

Q. 5 put.—A. Never.

Q. 6 put.—A. No.   ADAM BROWN.

WM. HARVEY, Boatswain's Mate, called:—

Q. 1 put.—A. Corroborates the former Evidences.

Q. 2 put.—A. He knows of none.

Q. 3 put.—A. Not to my knowledge.

Q. 4 put.—A. No.

Q. 5 put.—A. No.

Q. 6 put.—A. No.   WM. HARVEY.

MR. HARDING called:—

Q. 1 put.—A. I know of none, But that some altercation took place.

Q. 2 put.—A. When working between the Heads, respecting the Captain's ordering Mr. Lye to take his great Coat off.

Q. 3 put.—A. Never.

Q. 4 put.—A. Positively never.

Q. 5 put.—A. I know of none.

Q. 6 put.—A. I have seen Mr. Tetley after dining in the Cabin, or with a party, gay, but never incapable of doing his Duty.

                                                J. L. HARDINGE.

MR. OLDREY, called:—

Q. 1 put.—A. I do not, indeed, Except once when we were working between the heads I heard Captain Short desire Mr. Lye to take off his Great Coat. It was in the Evening, and Mr. Lye replied he thought he might wear what Cloaths he thought proper; and I did not see him take it off.

Q. 3 put.—A. No.

Q. 4 put.—A. Never.

Q. 5 put.—A. Never:

Q. 6 put.—A. Never.   W. OLDREY.

MR. BASDEN, Purser, called:—

Q. 1 put.—A. I remember one instance when the Ship was working between the Heads I heard Captain Short desire Mr. Lye to take off his Great Coat, which he did not do; And that he has gone on Shore since lying in this Harbour when left Commanding Officer, which was contrary to Capt'n Short's Order, which I believe is in the Order Book.

Q. 3 put.—A. I have heard Mr. Lye make use of replies to Capt'n Short which I have thought unbecoming an Officer to his superior, but cannot recollect the Circumstances.

Q. 4 put.—A. I have heard Lt. Tetley say before the Ship's Company it was a Shame the people should be kept up so late, and should not wonder if they were to desert.

Q. 5 put.—A. I know of none.

1806.
12 Dec.

Proceedings of
inquiry into
the conduct of
Short, Tetley,
and Lye.

Q. 6 put.—*A.* I have—once.
Q. 7.—Was he incapable of doing his duty?—*A.* He was asleep on the After Gun on the Quarter-Deck.
Q.—Was there any other person on deck that Saw him in that State besides Yourself?—*A.* There was a petty Officer and the Man at the Wheel. I do not recollect the petty officer's Name, but the Name of the Man was John Woodhouse.

W. B. BASDEN.

MR. PINEO called:—

Q. 1 put.—*A.* No, I never did.
Q. 2 put.—*A.* As the first.
Q. 3 put.—*A.* I have seen him turn his Back when Capt'n Short has given him Orders, and Answer him in a very rough Manner, but cannot recollect any particular Circumstance.
Q. 4 put.—*A.* I have heard language from both of them which I have considered as being very improper, such as reflecting on the Mode of carrying on duty in the Ship; the Boats' Crews being kept up was enough to make Men run away; And particularly Mr. Lye saying that he wished the Boat would sink alongside; the best of his recollection, this language took place in the Gun-room, when it was reported the Captain was coming alongside. I have also heard Mr. Lye say if he had Capt'n Short in some other place he would retaliate or resent Injuries he had received, But cannot say whether this was in the Gun-Room or before the Ship's Company; and I have heard him damn Capt'n Short in the Gun-room.
Q. 5 put.—*A.* I do not recollect any but what is stated in my Answer to the 4th question.
Q. 6 put.—*A.* I have seen him intoxicated and asleep in his watch.
Q.—Was any other person present?—*A.* Mr. Basden, the purser, was present.
Q.—At what period of the Voyage was this?—*A.* On the passage from England to the Cape.
Q.—Had You and Mr. Basden had any Conversation on that Subject at the time You say he was drunk in his Watch?—*A.* We had. We expressed our sorrow at Seeing an Officer in that Situation.
Q.—From Your own Observation, do You consider Mr. Tetley addicted to getting drunk when at Sea?—*A.* I should not call him a Sober Man. O. PINEO.

MR. BASDEN called in again:—

Q.—Was any of the Gentlemen of the Gun-Room on Deck at the time you observed Mr. Tetley to be drunk?—*A.* Not at the time I was, to the best of my knowledge; And I was not on deck myself more than ten Minutes.
Q.—Can You take it upon yourself to say that Mr. Pineo was not present with You, and that You did not converse together upon the Impropriety of an Officer being in that Situation?—*A.* I do not remember, not having taken an Account, and so long a time having elapsed. W. B. BASDEN, purser.

JOHN WOODHOUSE called:—

Q. 6 put.—*A.* I never have.
Q.—Do You recollect the Circumstance of Mr. Basden taking the Helm from You when you was at the Wheel?—*A.* He never took the Helm from me, but I remember his looking at the Compass one Night when I was at the Wheel. Lt. Tetley had the Watch at the

1806.
12 Dec.

Proceedings of
inquiry into
the conduct of
Short, Tetley,
and Lye.

time, but was not intoxicated. I never took a turn at the Wheel but twice during the Voyage, which enables me to Speak more particularly to this Circumstance.

Q.—Do You recollect who was Mate or Midshipman of the Watch at that time?—A. I do not recollect.

Q.—Was Mr. Pineo on deck at the time?—A. I cannot recollect.

JOHN WOODHOUSE.

MR. HARDING called:—

Q.—On Lieut't Tetley's Watch from England towards the Cape of Good Hope, was You Mate of his Watch?—A. I was.

Q.—Do You recollect Mr. Tetley being drunk and asleep Sitting on a Carronade in any first or other Watch during that Passage?—A. I do not.

Q.—If Lieut't Tetley was seen in that Situation by any other Person walking the Quarter-Deck, could it escape Your Observation?—A. No, as I always reported the Log to him every hour; And if he had been asleep I must have known it, as he is very difficult to wake when asleep.

Q.—From Your Own Observation, and as Mate of Lieut't. Tetley's Watch, do you consider him as a person addicted to getting drunk?—A. I do not.   J. HARDINGE.

FINDING.

In giving Our opinions on the above, it appears to us that Captain Short had appropriated to his use Some Yards of Green Baize and about 100 feet of Wainscot for conveniences about his Cabin, And that a false Entry has been made in the Ship's log-Book respecting a Davit being carried away, And that the Carpenter was directed to expend an Anchor Stock to replace the Davit, the Anchor Stock having been previously cut into boards to replace the Wainscot used in Captain Short's Cabin. It also appears that Captain Short desired the Gunner to expend two Musquets when none were deficient. Respecting Captain Short's lending Men from the Ship, It appears that the Armourer was lent for some days to a person at the Cape of Good Hope, by which the Service was injured by a Carronade being disabled, And the Arms in a bad Condition. It also appears that the Boatswain's Yeoman was lent as a Gardener to Mr. Fitz at the time the Ship was refitting. From the testimony adduced, It does not appear to us certain that the Articles of War have been read more than twice Since the Ship has been in Commission, And that no other Officers' Commissions have been read than those of Captains Bligh and Short. It appears that the Boats' Crew have been repeatedly kept up in this port after the hour of twelve at Night at a time the Ship was refitting, but no reason to Suppose they would desert beyond Conjecture. It also appears that much harsh language has been used by Captain Short to Mr. Tetley, as particularized by the Master Gunner's and Carpenter's Testimony. With respect to the Charge of Drunkenness alleged against Captain Short, We conceive that his being in that State at the Cape of Good Hope appears to be verified by the Evidence of the Boatswain, Gunner, and Carpenter—not laying any Stress on Lieut. Tetley's testimony on that behalf. On Captain Short's Charge against Mr. Lye for disobedience of Orders, We do not in our Conscience believe that any Censure, beyond a Reprimand, would be made by a Court-Martial, judging from the kind of testimony produced to us; Nor do we conceive that the testimony

produced to verify Lt. Tetley and Mr. Lye's treating Captain Short
with disrespect and exciting insubordination and Mutiny among the
Ship's Company is at all proved; Nor can we help pointing out to
Your Attention the Evidence of the Purser and Surgeon respecting
Lieutenant Tetley being drunk in his Watch, which we consider to
be entirely Shaken, from the variation there appears in their Evidence of Mr. Pineo being on Deck with Mr. Basden at the time he
says he Saw Lieutenant Tetley drunk and asleep on his Watch,
which Charge we consider as further invalidated by the testimony
of the Mate of the Watch, the Man at the Helm, and all the other
Evidences questioned on that behalf. Having given Our Opinion
on the Charges contained in the respective Letters, We must Submit
to Your Consideration how far the Charges against Mr. Lye contain
sufficient Grounds for his being kept in the State of Arrest he is now
in to be tried by a Court-Martial, which cannot be held in this
Country, Nor can the prisoner and his Evidences be sent from hence
for that purpose without a total hindrance of the Ship's Services,
for Want of Officers and Men; And also Submit to Your determination whether there appears to be grounds sufficient for a Court
Martial on Captain Short.*

Proceedings of inquiry into the conduct of Short, Tetley, and Lye.

Given under our hands, on board H. M. Ship Porpoise, in
Sydney Cove, Port Jackson, the 12th December, 1806.

PHILIP GIDLEY KING, Principal Commander.
JNO. HOUSTOUN, Acting Second-Commander.
J. OXLEY, Acting-Lieutenant of His Majesty's
Ship Buffalo.

Attested: WM. BLIGH.

[Additional Enclosures.]

[*Copies of the papers relating to the medical examination and
confinement of Daniel Lye are not available.*]

THE RIGHT HON. WILLIAM WINDHAM TO GOVERNOR BLIGH.

(Despatch No. 1, per transport Duke of Portland; acknowledged by
Governor Bligh, 31st October, 1807.)

Sir,· Downing Street, 18th Decr., 1806.

The Commanding Officer of the New South Wales Corps
will receive by the present Opportunity the Orders of His Royal
Highness the Commander in Chief to discharge G. L. M. Huon
de Kerillac† a French Emigrant of a distinguished Family who
has been for some time serving as a private Soldier in that Regiment. As soon as his Discharge is received I am to desire that
you will do everything in your Power to contribute to the comfortable Establishment of M. Huon de Kerillac and afford him
every assistance that he can reasonably expect, and that he is a
Relation of the late venerable Bishop of St. Pol de Peon and
strongly recommended to me by the Marquis of Buckingham I
am sure you will feel Pleasure in complying with my Wishes in
his favor. I have, &c.,
W. WINDHAM.

Discharge of Huon de Kerillac from the New South Wales Corps.

* Note 9. † Note 10.

1806.
18 Dec.

THE RIGHT HON. WILLIAM WINDHAM TO GOVERNOR BLIGH.

(Despatch No. 2, per transport Duke of Portland; acknowledged by
Governor Bligh, 31st October, 1807.)

Sir,   Downing Street, 18th Decr., 1806.

Grant of land
for Richard
Guise.

    An Application for a Grant of Land in New South Wales
having been made to me by Richard Guise, formerly a Serjeant
in the New South Wales Corps, who has been strongly recommended by Lieut: Col. Foveaux, and stated by him to be possessed
of at least £1,000: I am to desire that you will cause to be made
out to him in the usual Form and subject to the customary Reservations a grant of 300 Acres and that you will give him every
Encouragement to which he may appear entitled, together with
such Assistance of Convicts as you may be enabled to afford him
consistently with a due Attention to the Claims of other
Individuals.   I have, &c.,
                                          W. WINDHAM.

THE RIGHT HON. WILLIAM WINDHAM TO GOVERNOR BLIGH.

(Despatch No. 3, per transport Duke of Portland; acknowledged by
Governor Bligh, 31st October, 1807.)

Sir,   Downing Street, 18th Decr., 1806.

Recommenda-
tion of Thomas
Hansen.

    An Application for a Grant of Land in New South Wales
having been made by Thomas Hansen who has been recommended
by Mr. Mellish and Mr. Mather, and who states that he has purchased an Estate of about 250 Acres in New South Wales, I am
to desire that you will give him every Encouragement to which
he may appear entitled, together with such Assistance of Convicts, as you may be enabled to afford him consistently with a due
Attention to the Claims of other Individuals.
                                          I have, &c.,
                                          W. WINDHAM.

THE RIGHT HON. WILLIAM WINDHAM TO GOVERNOR BLIGH.

(Despatch No. 4, per transport Duke of Portland; acknowledged by
Governor Bligh, 31st October, 1807.)

Sir,   Downing Street, 18th Decr., 1806.

Grant of land
for captain
Kent.

    An Application for a Grant of Land in New South Wales
having been made to me by Captn. Kent of the Navy, who was
employed many years on Services connected with the Colony, and
who states that he is actually possessed of a considerable Quantity of Stock there, I am to desire that you will cause to be made
out to him, in the usual Form and subject to the Customary
Reservations, a Grant of 2,000 Acres, and that you will give him
every Encouragement to which he may appear entitled, together

with such Assistance of Convicts as you may be enabled to afford him consistently with a due Attention to the Claims of other Individuals.

I have, &c.,
W. WINDHAM.

THE RIGHT HON. WILLIAM WINDHAM TO GOVERNOR BLIGH.

(Despatch No. 5, per transport Duke of Portland; acknowledged by Governor Bligh, 31st October, 1807.)

Sir, Downing Street, 18th Decr., 1806.

An Application for a Grant of Land in New South Wales having been made to me by Sir Arthur Paget in favor of John Derry, William Emmett and Richard Wrather, these Persons having stated that they are possessed of Property to the Amount of £500 between them; I am to desire that you will cause to be made out in the usual Forms and subject to the Customary Reservations, a Grant of One Hundred Acres to each of them, and that you will give them every Encouragement to which they may appear entitled together with such Assistance of Convicts as is usual and as you may be enabled to afford them consistently with a due Attention to the Claims of other Individuals.

Grants of land for Derry, Emmett, and Wrather.

I have, &c.,
W. WINDHAM.

GOVERNOR BLIGH TO SECRETARY MARSDEN.

(Despatch per H.M.S. Buffalo.)

Government House, Sydney,
Sir, New South Wales, 21st December, 1806.

21 Dec.

Inclosed are three Letters which I have as a part of my Duty to request you to present to My Lords Commissioners of the Admiralty.

Captain Short's charges against captain King.

The first Letter is from Captain Short to Captain King, late Governor of this Colony, under evident signs of alarming him on the score of keeping a false Muster.

The second is Captain Short's Letter to me stating his surprise at Mr. Jamison being left behind when the Lady Nelson sailed, of his being only Twelve Years of Age although mustered as Ordinary Seaman on the Buffalo's Books as belonging to the Lady Nelson Tender, and to clear himself of a Charge of a false Muster that might be made against him he waited for my orders on the occasion; in answer to which I referred him to Instructions and Rules of the Service.

The third is a Letter from Governor King to me, on my communicating to him the one which I had received from Captain Short.

The Youth alluded is Thirteen but tall and stout and I should have guessed his Age about Fifteen or Sixteen, and thought him a very desirable person to act as a Midshipman in this Country, and I think could not any where have been objected to. Captain Short made no objection to him when turned over with the Crew of the Lady Nelson from the Buffalo to the Porpoise: on the contrary seemed to approve of him by giving him permission to attend School, where he was when the Lady Nelson sailed, and on finding her gone returned to the Porpoise, and Captain Short again gave him leave to remain ashore as he had done before.

The internal Duty and Regulation of the Porpoise in every degree has rested with Captain Short, he has had it at his own discretion to rate or disrate as he found best for the good of the Service and I am under the necessity of declaring as my opinion that Governor King has acted for the best and not through any motive to which Captain Short alludes.

Governor King will attend their Lordships to answer farther for himself if necessary but does not hesitate to complain of this illiberal attack from Captain Short.

                                        I have, &c.,
                                            WM. BLIGH.

[Enclosure No. 1.]

CAPTAIN SHORT TO CAPTAIN KING.

Sir,   His Majesty's Ship Porpoise, 17 Decr., 1806.

I think it requisite to acquaint you that meeting young Mr. Jamison on Saturday last I asked him his Age, when he told me 12 Years, I was much surprized on coming on board and referring to the List sent from the Buffalo with the Lady Nelson's Ships Company to find he had been borne as an Ord'y Seaman since the 20th August, 1803, at which time he could not 'have been more than 9 Years of Age, As I cannot commit myself by being bro't under the Charge of false Muster, I shall be obliged to write to Capt. Bligh on the Subject but before I took that step I thought it friendly to acquaint you of the Circumstance and shall wait your Answer.

                                        I am, &c.,
                                            JOSEPH SHORT.

A true Copy: PHILIP GIDLEY KING.

[Enclosure No. 2.]

CAPTAIN SHORT TO GOVERNOR BLIGH.

Sir,   H.M.S. Porpoise, Sydney, Decr. 18, 1806.

Mr. Jamison came to me last Saturday and said he was left behind from the Lady Nelson (which had sail'd that Morn'g) which I was much surprized at as I repeatedly gave Mr. Symonds

1806.
21 Dec.

Short's
complaint to
Bligh about
Jamison.

directions not to leave any of his Crew behind without your orders, I also find Mr. Jamison is only Twelve years of age altho' he has been Mustered as an Ord'y Seaman on the Buffalo's Books as belonging to the Lady Nelson since the 20th of Augt. 1803, on seeing him last Saturday I asked him his age when he informed me as above; to clear myself of a charge of false Muster that may hereafter be made should I continue to bear a boy rated as such, I think it my Duty in the first place to represent it to you—and shall wait your orders on the Occasion.

~ Understanding from Mr. Basden it is your order that the Ship's Company goes on half allowance of Spirits, I am to request your written order to pass the ship's amount for the same.

I am, &c.,
JOSEPH SHORT.

[Enclosure No. 3.]

CAPTAIN KING TO GOVERNOR BLIGH.

His Majesty's Ship Buffalo,

Sir,   Port Jackson, December 20th, 1806.

King's
repudiation
of Short's
charges.

If I was astonished when I shewed you Cap. Short's letter to me of the 17th Inst. alluding to what he insinuates as a False Muster respecting Mr. Jamison's Age and Rating on the Buffalo's Books; I certainly felt the intention of that letter more forcibly when you informed me of his Official Letter to you of the 18th Instant.

When the Lady Nelson and her Complement were discharged from the Buffalo to the Porpoise on the 4th last September; If Capt. Short had then enquired the Youth's Age and Rating (as he then saw him) and reported to you at that time what he has since found it convenient to do, It certainly would have been an act of Duty; But his reporting it now, Four Months after the Youth was received on board the Porpoise by Capt. Short, and was actually entered on the Porpoise's Books, and so recently after the late Enquiry (at which I presided) into the Unpleasant Events between him and his Officers, I cannot help thinking that his troubling you at this time arises more from a Malignant Motive than a bare discharge of Duty, which requires me to state the following facts.

Statement as to
the status of
Jamison.

In October 1802, I received an Admiralty order dated March 4th, 1802, To bear 15 Men in a Supernumerary List for Victuals and Wages on the Buffalo's Books to Man the Lady Nelson, considered as a Tender to the Buffalo; An Acting Lieut. was appointed by me to Command her, and some well behaved Convicts who had been Seamen were Emancipated to Serve in her.

1806.
21 Dec.

Statement as to
the status of
Jamison.

In August 1803, I sent Mr. Jamison (who was then, and is now, a Stout active Youth) on board to act as Midshipman, No Boys of Classes, or Servants, being received by the Admiralty Order for her Establishment, he was rated Ordinary, has been constantly Mustered, and except Twice has constantly gone to Sea in that Vessell.

Since receiving Capt. Short's Letter of the 17th Inst. I have examined the Lady Nelson's List on the Buffalo's Books, And find that Mr. Jamison's Age was perhaps erroneously stated to be Thirteen in August 1802, which I am convinced was suggested by his Appearance, and with no Intention to insert a wrong Age to his entry.

As a Choice of Persons to serve on board His Majesty's Ships and Vessells on this particular Service, cannot be had, and the Youth in question having Acted as a Midshipman and been constantly mustered, I cannot do myself the injustice to think for a moment that this Transaction can warrant Captain Short's harsh allusion to a False Muster, Than which, nothing could be more against my Ideas of the Service and my inclination.

Having stated these Facts, I hope you will see no impropriety in my Requesting you to enclose this Letter, with Capt. Short's Letter to me of the 17 Inst. and his to you on this Subject; to My Lords Commissioners of the Admiralty.

I have, &c.,
PHILIP GIDLEY KING.

GOVERNOR BLIGH TO SECRETARY MARSDEN.

(Despatch per H.M.S. Buffalo.)

23 Dec.

Tetley placed
in confinement
by Short.

Sir,   Sydney, New South Wales, 23rd December, 1806.

In addition to the transactions which caused me to order a Court of Enquiry on the 10th Instant on Captain Short and his Officers which is herewith sent, I regret to be under the necessity of transmitting for the information of my Lords Commissioners of the Admiralty another Letter from Lieutenant Tetley stating the severity of Captain Short's conduct to him, confining him a Prisoner to the Ship, and threatening him with high charges against his Life; requesting a Court Martial might be held on Captain Short.

Release of
Tetley by
Bligh.

I also beg leave to inclose the Order I gave in consequence to liberate Lieutenant Tetley as the Public Service and our remote situation would not allow of the confinement of Officers unless absolutely necessary.   I have, &c.,
WM. BLIGH.

[Enclosure No. 1.]

LIEUTENANT TETLEY TO GOVERNOR BLIGH.

H. M. Ship Porpoise,

Sir,   Sydney Cove, December 20th, 1806.

Disagreeable as it is to me to be under the Necessity of Tetley's
troubling You with such repeated Complaints of Captain Short's complaint
Conduct to me—Yet a Sense of the Duty I owe the Public and relating to
myself impels me to it. I was in hopes after the Court of En- Short's conduct.
quiry, that Captain Short's Conduct would soften towards me;
on the contrary it has been, if possible, more harsh and insulting,
he having actually made me a Prisoner to the Ship and told me
that he never would quit me until I had answered for the high
Charges he had against my life. I have therefore to request that
a Copy of this Letter as also of my Letter to You dated Novr.
15th, 1806, may be transmitted to the Admiralty for the purpose
of a Court Martial being held on Captain Short, as I feel myself so degraded by Captain Short's Conduct in the Eyes of the
Officers and Ships Company that my Situation is truly distressing.   I have, &c.,

Attested: WM. BLIGH.   J. S. TETLEY.

[Enclosure No. 2.]

ORDERS FOR THE RELEASE OF LIEUTENANT TETLEY FROM RESTRAINT. Orders for the
release of
By William Bligh, Esquire, etc., etc. Tetley from
restraint.
WHEREAS from the nature of the Service we are on and our
remoteness from England Courts Martial cannot be held or
Charges of Offences submitted to my Lords Commissioners of the
Admiralty but in a long course of time, and the confinement
of Officers and Men would be oppressive as likewise detrimental
to the public Service unless for heinous Crimes, the nature
of which I shall cause to be enquired into or form a judgement thereon; and Lieutenant Tetley having stated by Letter to
me of the 20th Instant your having made him a prisoner to the
Ship:—It is my Order that when any Officer belonging to His
Majesty's Ship Porpoise under my Command be put in arrest
or confined Prisoner to the Ship I am to be informed thereof
immediately, and in case of my absence from Head Quarters
through my Aid du Camp.

And you not having made any report to me of Lieutenant
Tetley being confined to the Ship, you will allow that Officer the
usual recreation of leave when he can be spared from his duty.

Given, etc., this 23rd of December, 1806.

WM. BLIGH.

Attested: WM. BLIGH.

1806.
27 Dec.

GOVERNOR BLIGH TO SECRETARY MARSDEN.

(Despatch per H.M.S. Buffalo.)

Sir,   Sydney, New South Wales, 27th December, 1806.

Inquiry into the complaint of Short against Tetley and Lye.

    I beg leave to enclose farther Complaints of Captain Short against Lieutenant Tetley and Mr. Daniel Lye, Master, and of his confining Lieutenant Tetley to the Ship and Mr. Lye a second time to his Cabin. Upon which a second Court of Enquiry was held; the proceedings are here inclosed and shew the Charges were not proved—suspicions of the Purser and Surgeon's Evidences, and declaring that there was no cause for the confinement of Mr. Lye to his Cabin or Lieutenant Tetley to the Ship; but that their opinion was, that His Majesty's Service, as far as related to the Porpoise being useful to the Public Duties of this Colony, were entirely suspended until some change took place.

    Annexed to these proceedings is my Order for the release of Lieutenant Tetley and Mr. Lye, and a Letter from Lieutenant Tetley again complaining of Captain Short's great severity ordering Pistols to be got ready and threatening that he would soon use them—that his Life was not safe, and that he was degraded as an Officer by Captain Short.

I have, &c.,
WM. BLIGH.

[Enclosure No. 1.]

CAPTAIN SHORT TO GOVERNOR BLIGH.

His Majesty's Ship Porpoise, Sydney Cove,
Sir,   25th December, 1806.

Short's complaint of the conduct of Lye and Tetley.

    I beg leave to acquaint you that, on my returning on board this Ship last Evening, about half-past 10 o'Clock, Mr. Basden acquainted me that Lieutenant Tetley and Mr. Lye had been making use of most provoking and unofficer-like Language in the Gun-Room, in a tone of voice to be heard by the Ship's Company between Decks—one remark of Mr. Tetley's that the Porpoise was a perfect Hell afloat, and he did not care who heard him say so; also, that there were some damned Rascals in her—one he could point out in a few Minutes, that was now taking down what was said (Mr. Basden was the only person writing in his Cabin with the door open), and that would not mind swearing a Man's life away, with many other expressions equally improper. Mr. Lye, joining in the Conversation, said he only wished to have his revenge on two Scoundrels in this Ship, which he would have, and that there was a gang of Villians on board not fit to black Shoes, and that he knew them all, with other expressions highly

improper. Mr. Basden soon after went on Deck, Mr. Lye follow- 1806.
27 Dec.
ing him, and twice intentionally run against him, which Mr.
Basden took no Notice of, but crossed the Deck for the purpose Short's
complaint of
of avoiding a repetition of the insult. Mr. Lye followed him and the conduct of
Lye and Tetley.
twice repeated it, with an intent to provoke him to quarrel; at
this time I came on board and heard the above, and hearing
Lieutenant Tetley had drank too much, I ordered Mr. Lye, who
was Officer of the Watch, to have the lights in the Gun-room put
out, fearing, if I sent for Lieutenant Tetley in such a situation,
he might make use of irritating expressions, and meaning to
inquire into it this Morning; but after going to my Cabin I
heard a noise in the Gun-room, and going on Deck I observed
the Lights was not out there, on which I directed Mr. Lye to
go down himself and see them out; this order I repeated four or
five times before I could get him to obey it. I then returned to
my Cabin, but shortly after I heard loud talking on Deck and
Mr. Lye ordering Mr. Basden to walk on the other side of the
Quarter-Deck; when I went up Mr. Basden informed me Mr.
Lye had again shoved against him when passing; on my asking
Mr. Lye his reasons for behaving in such a manner he gave me
very provoking impertinent answers, when, observing he was half
Drunk, I remarked it to him, and advised him to be very careful
of his Conduct—that he had already been guilty of Mutiny, and
if he did continue it I should be obliged to confine him in his
Cabin, where he should remain until he was tryed by a Court-
Martial; he directly turned his back in a most contemptious and
provoking manner, and said *"that does not rest with you"*; his
repeating this Language, I could bear it no longer, but ordered
him a Prisoner in his Cabin. I also beg to add that this Morning Mr. Pineo reported to me that himself and Mr. Tetley was
walking on different sides of the Quarter-Deck; Mr. Tetley came
over to him and said, " 'Do you know what my opinion of you
is?" Mr. P. asked him whether was speaking to him on duty or
privately; his Answer was "On duty," and that his opinion was,
"You are a damned Scoundrel and Villian for joining in opinion
with the Captain just now."

After stating the above, I beg to say that the Conduct of Lieutenant Tetley and Mr. Lye is such as to inflame the minds of the
Officers and Ship's Company; that I am confident if they are permitted to do duty will create a Mutiny. I have not confined Mr.
Tetley, but have stopt his leave from going on shore, and have
given orders to Mr. Pineo to take no private notice of a thing
mentioned on a public Quarter-Deck and on Duty.

I am, &c.,
Jos'h. Short.

[Enclosure No. 2.]

GOVERNOR BLIGH TO CAPTAIN SHORT.

An inquiry
to be held.

Sir,   Government House, Sydney, 25th December, 1806.
        I have received your Letter of to-day and will direct an
Enquiry to be made without delay into the Charges therein
contained against Lieutenant Tetley and Mr. Lye, Master of the
said Ship.   I am, &c.,
        Attested: WM. BLIGH.   WM. BLIGH.

[Enclosure No. 3.]

GOVERNOR BLIGH TO LIEUTENANT TETLEY AND MR. LYE.

                            Government House, Sydney,
        Gentlemen,   25th December, 1806.
Notification of   Captain Short by Letter of this Date having charged you
inquiry to
Tetley and Lye. (yesterday) with Drunkenness, Contempt, Unofficerlike conduct,
and behaviour such as to inflame the Minds of the Officers and
Ships Company and to create Mutiny.; this is therefore to inform
you that an Enquiry into the same will take place without delay.
                                               I am, &c.,
        Attested: WM. BLIGH.   WM. BLIGH.

[Enclosure No. 4.]

Warrant for
holding inquiry.

WARRANT FOR HOLDING INQUIRY.

                            By William Bligh, Esquire, etc., etc.
JOSEPH SHORT ESQUIRE Commander of His Majesty's Ship Por-
poise under my Command having by his Letter of yesterday's
date reported to me that on his returning on board that Ship at
half past Ten o'Clock in the Evening of the 24th Instant Mr.
Basden the Purser acquainted him that Lieutenant Tetley and
Mr. Lye had been making use of unofficerlike and provoking
Language in the Gun Room; that Mr. Lye had been following
Mr. Basden on Deck and intentionally run against him to pro-
voke him to quarrel; of Mr. Lye's using provoking and insulting
Language, and giving impertinent answers to Captain Short; of
Lieutenant Tetley's insulting Mr. Pineo the Surgeon; That
Lieutenant Tetley and Mr. Lye were at that time in a state of
intoxication; and that Lieutenant Tetley and Mr. Lye's conduct
is such as to inflame the Minds of the Officers and Ships Com-
pany and if they are permitted to do duty it will create a
Mutiny.
        I therefore with this put you in possession of the said Letter
of Captain Short's and do hereby require and direct you to proceed on board the said Ship, taking to your assistance Captain
John Houstoun and Lieutenant John Oxley of His Majesty's
Ship Buffalo, and enquire into the same reporting to me whether

1806.
27 Dec.
———
Warrant for
holding inquiry.

under these Charges and full meaning of Captain Short's Letter there is a necessity for the good of the Service that Mr. Lye should be confined a Prisoner to his Cabin and Lieutenant Tetley to the Ship; taking into consideration every circumstance to guide your opinions, particularly our remote situation from England and the state of the Colony.

Given, etc., this 25th of December, 1806.

WM. BLIGH.

To Philip Gidley King, Esqr.,
Captain of His Majesty's Ship Buffalo.
Attested: WM. BLIGH.

[Enclosure No. 5.]

PROCEEDINGS OF INQUIRY.

Proceedings of
inquiry into
the charges of
Short against
Tetley and Lye.

PURSUANT to an Order from William Bligh Esquire Captain General and Governor in Chief, etc., etc.

CAPTAIN SHORT's Letter dated Decr. 25th to Captain Bligh being read to Mr. Basden Purser, from the "Words "I beg leave" to "provoke him to quarrel," and from the Words "Mr. Basden informed me" to "when passing," and being asked if those were his complaints to Captn. Short: Mr. Basden answered, that he represented it to Captn. Short for the purpose of screening himself from such insults in future, not intending it to be brought before a Court Martial, or Court of Inquiry, but that he intends on the repetition of such insults to take proper measures for preventing it.

Question.—In the conversation you state to have taken place in the gunroom, did they make use of your name?

Answer.—No they did not—but their conversation was so pointed that I could not but take it to myself.

Question.—Did Mr. Tetley appear drunk that Evening.

Answer.—He had taken a chearful Glass, but did not appear incapable of doing his duty.

Question.—What further passed than is stated in Captn. Short's Letter respecting Mr. Tetley and Mr. Lye—in which yourself was not concern'd.

Answer.—I heard Mr. Lye, say upon Captn. Shorts telling him that there were more charges against him than he could answer for, and if he continued to follow that conduct and treat him with such disrespect and contempt, he w'd confine him to his cabin, where he should remain till he was tried by a Court Martial, Mr. Lye, turned round, and said that was more than he could answer to do. Mr. Basden says he does not know what passed between Captn. Short and Mr. Lye to produce that conversation.

Question.—Who was upon the deck at the time this conversation passed?

Answer.—To the best of my knowledge, Mr. Hobbs, Mr. Newson, Mr. Oldrey, and Mr. Harding.

Question.—From your knowledge do you know what passed Mr. Tetley and Mr. Pineo.

Answer.—No I do not.

W. B. BASDEN.

1806.
27 Dec.

Proceedings of
inquiry into
the charges of
Short against
Tetley and Lye.

MR. PINEO, Surgeon, Called :—

and that part of Captn. Short's Letter, beginning with the words: "Mr. Pineo reported to me" and ending "with the Captn. Just now" being read to Mr. Pineo, and asked whether he stated it as a complaint to Captn. Short, intending it to be brought before a Court Martial or Court of Inquiry, or that Captn. Short should redress it himself—and whether the words stated to have been made use of in the Letter occurred.

Answer.—I reported it to Captn. Short, for the purpose of getting advice, as the words were stated to have been spoken on duty,— and that the Statement in the Letter was correct.

Question.—Do you know of any conversation between Mr. Tetley and Mr. Lye, on the Evening of the 24th Decr. supposed to relate to Mr. Basden.

Answer.—No I do not, I was on Shore.

Question.—Of your knowledge, do you know of any dispute that took place, between Captn. Short and Mr. Lye on the Evening of the 24th Decr.

Answer.—I came on board with Captn. Short in the Evening of the 24th Mr. Basden complained to Captn. Short of some conversation that he stated to have taken place in the Gunroom between Mr. Tetley and Mr. Lye, that I followed Captn. Short to his Cabin, and that to the best of my knowledge Captn. Short desired Mr. Lye to see the Lights put out, which he cannot take upon himself to say Mr. Lye disobeyed. Captn. Short went upon deck, and he remained in the Cabin, I heard Captn. Short caution Mr. Lye not to treat him with insolence and disrespect repeatedly and to take care of himself Mr. Lye made answer that he would see to that, that he would take care of himself—I afterwards heard Captn. Short caution him again, and tell him he would confine him to his cabin, and try him by a Court Martial, Mr. Lye replied, in a very insolent manner, that does not rest with you, Sir, during which time I remained in the Captn's Cabin, and the conversation passed upon deck, but was within my hearing.

O. PINEO.

MR. CALVER, Gunner, called,

and asked what he knows of any circumstance that occurred between the Captn. and Officers on the Evening of Decr. 24th and where was he between 8 o'Clock and ½ past ten that Evening.

Answer 1st.—I was in the Gunroom sitting with the 1st Lieut. and Master—and when the Captn. came on board I went upon the deck. I returned to the Gunroom, and when the Lights were order'd out I went to my Cabin, and when the Serjt. of Marines came to put my Light out I went to the Captn. who gave me leave for my light. I heard Captn. Short Blame Mr. Lye for not putting the Lights out, Mr. Lye assured him that he had done it, hearing that conversation I went to Captn. Short and told him I had seen Mr. Lye blow the Light out himself. Captn. Short replied he was asking me no questions and desired me to go away, and that was all I heard until 12 when I received Orders that no Light should be kept in except Mr. Basden and Mr. Pineo's.

Question.—As you was in the Gunroom in Company with Mr. Tetley and Mr. Lye from 8 till ½ past ten, did you hear any improper or insulting Language from either or both those Officers respecting Mr. Basden or any other Officer of the Ship.

1806.
27 Dec.

Proceedings of
inquiry into
the charges of
Short against
Tetley and Lye.

Answer.—In the course of conversation, they lamented the present unhappy state of the Ship, and hoped that there would be better times, that no particular allusions were made to any Officer—and that it appeared to him to be a private conversation.

Question.—Do you suppose, that conversation could be heard by any person before the Gunroom Bulkhead.

Answer.—No.

Question.—Did Mr. Tetley or Mr. Lye appear Intoxicated.

Answer.—They had been taking a Chearful Glass, but were not the worse for liquor.

FRS. CALVER.

MR. NEWSON called and the 1st question put to Mr. Calver, being asked him.

Answer.—I was upon deck. I recollect Captn. Short ordering Mr. Lye to put the lights out which was done; there were high words passing between Captn. Short and Mr. Lye, but did not pay any attention, he being on the opposite side of the D'k—I heard nothing further between Captn. Short and Mr. Lye.

Question 2nd.—What conversation did you hear between Mr. Lye and Mr. Basden.

Answer.—I heard Mr. Lye desire Mr. Basden to walk upon the Opposite side of the deck—Mr. Lye being Officer of the Watch.

Question 3rd.—Did you see Mr. Lye use any personal violence to Mr. Basden, either by shoving or otherwise.

Answer.—No.

Question 4th.—Did you hear Mr. Lye make use of any disrespectful Language to Captn. Short.

Answer.—No.

JNO. NEWSON.

MR. OLDREY the 1st Question put.

Answer.—I was upon deck it being my watch, I heard Captn. Short order Mr. Lye to put the Lights out, Mr. Lye said, the Serg't of Marines had reported them out. Captn. Short ordered him to go and see them put out himself Mr. Lye went down with the Serg't of Marines and put them out, and then went to the Captn.; some words ensued Captn. Short went below and afterwards came upon deck; Captn. Short told Mr. Lye he was drunk—he made answer he was not. Captn. Short said you are, Sir, Mr. Lye assured him he was not drunk. Captn. Short said that he would prove that he was. Mr. Lye said that he could prove to the contrary—A few words past, the Captn. said he (Mr. Lye) was Guilty of Mutiny. These Mr. Lye requested I would notice. A short time afterwards the Captn. Ordered Mr. Lye to his Cabin.

Question 2nd put.

Answer.—I heard Mr. Basden say to Mr. Lye do you mean to insult me. Mr. Lye said he was Officer of the watch and that he should not walk the Midship part of the Qur. Deck, Mr. Basden passed close to Mr. Lye, Mr. Lye told him if he did not give him room he (Mr. Basden) should go on the other side of the Qr. deck. Mr. Basden made some answer, Mr. Lye told him if he was not quiet, he should order him to his cabin. Captn. Short came on deck, and asked him (Mr. Lye) who he was ordering to his cabin, and then that part of the conversation, between Captn. Short and Mr. Lye, respecting his being drunk took place, as already related.

1806.
27 Dec.

Proceedings of
inquiry into
the charges of
Short against
Tetley and Lye.

Question.—Did you hear Mr. Lye when he was ordered under arrest say to Captn. Short, it was more than he could answer for doing.

Answer.—No I did not.

Question.—Did it appear to you that in the course of the dispute between Captn. Short and Mr. Lye, that Mr. Lye made use of any mutinous or disrespectable Language towards Captn. Short.

Answer.—No it did not.

Question.—Did it appear to you that Mr. Lye was intoxicated?

Answer.—No Sir, he did not appear to me so.

WM. OLDREY.

WILLIAM LINGER Private of Marines called,

and the different Questions put, declares he knows nothing about the Business except hearing Captn. Short order Mr. Lye to his Cabin.

his
WILLIAM x LINGER.
mark

MR. HOBBS—Boatswain, being called,

and the different Questions put, he being named by Mr. Basden as an Evidence, says that he is entirely ignorant of any circumstance that occurred that Evening he being forward it being Christmas Eve, enjoying himself with his friends.

WM. HOBBS.

In considering the assertions contained in the preceding testimonies, We do not consider that any material point in Captain Short's Letter is proved in a satisfactory manner by a second Witness to any one Charge, And from the unhappy differences that have increased to such an alarming degree on board the Porpoise, between the 2nd Captain and Officers, and in which there appears the utmost personal rancour, we consider that the testimony of Mr. Basden, the Purser, and Mr. Pineo, the Surgeon, are by no means free from personal rancour, prejudice, and partiality, and in viewing the whole from the testimony adduced, we conceive that there is no existing cause for Mr. Lye being put under Arrest, or Mr. Tetley's being confined to the Ship. But we are decidedly of opinion that His Majesty's Service, as far as relates to the Porpoise being useful to the Public Duties of this Colony, are entirely suspended by the unfortunate differences that exist on board that Ship between the 2nd Commander, Surgeon, and Purser, and the 1st Lieutenant and Master, which may lead you to cause some change or separation to take place amongst those Officers, which Measure alone can tend to render that Ship fit for any Public Service.

Given under our Hands on Board His Majesty's Ship Porpoise, this 26th day of December, 1806, Sydney Cove.

PHILIP GIDLEY KING, Commander of H. M.
Armed Vessel Buffalo.
JNO. HOUSTOUN, Second Commander Do.
J. OXLEY, 1st Lieut. Do. Do.

[Enclosure No. 6.]

GOVERNOR BLIGH'S ORDERS TO CAPTAIN SHORT.

By William Bligh, Esquire, etc., etc.

Bligh's orders
for the
liberation of
Tetley and Lye.

IN conseqeunce of your Letter to me of the 25th Instant against
Lieutenant Tetley and Mr. Lye Master, of His Majesty's Ship
Porpoise under my Command, and that you had put them in
confinement, And a Court of Enquiry having been held thereon :—
This is therefore to require you to liberate the said Officers
according to the Opinion of the said Court until the circumstances can be enquired into by Order of My Lords Commissioners of the Admiralty.

Given, etc., this 27th day of December, 1806.

WM. BLIGH.

Attested : WM. BLIGH.

[Enclosure No. 7.]

LIEUTENANT TETLEY TO GOVERNOR BLIGH.

His Majesty's Ship Porpoise,
Sir,   Sydney Cove, Decr. 28th, 1806.

I have to acquaint you that on your Order for the release
of Mr. Lye from confinement, the hands being turned up for the
purpose of reading the Order to them—Captn. Short ordered me
to go forward with the Prisoner Mr. Lye, I told him I did not
consider myself a Prisoner (being in the actual execution of my
duty, he having ordered me to turn the hands and call the
Officers) he immediately ordered the Corporal of Marines to lay
hold of me, and take me to where Mr. Lye was placed amongst
the Ship's Company. Captn. Short then read the 19, 20 and 23
Articles of War, observing at the same time that we fell under
those Articles and would suffer under them, turning at the same
time to Mr. Pineo the Surgeon and Mr. Basden the Purser, and
• told them that he conceived they had done their duty as Officers
and Gentlemen—" and I have only to do my duty by reading
Captn. Bligh's order to me," which he read to liberate Mr. Lye.
Captn. Short then desired the Gunner and Armourer to be sent
for (the Ship's Company still being on Deck) and ordered Three
brace of Pistols to be cleaned and flinted and six Cartouch boxes
with ball ammunition ready, the hands were then ordered to their
duty, when the Gunner reported to Captn. Short that the Pistols
were ready and in the Colour Chest on Deck, and Captn. Short
said he would soon use them and hoped that there was good
flints in them and that when he wanted them that they would be
of Service.

From the above circumstances you will perceive the unofficer
and ungentlemanlike manner in which I have been treated;

Tetley's
complaint as
to Short's
conduct.

1806.
27 Dec.

Tetley's
complaint as
to Short's
conduct.

Captain Short has by degrading me in the face of the Ship's
Company rendered it impossible for me to maintain that respect
which is due to me as first Lieutenant of this Ship. I am also
from various circumstances induced to believe that my Life is not
safe under his Command, the above Charges I can substantiate
by the evidence of the undermention'd Persons.

I have, &c.,

J. S. TETLEY.

Messrs. Lye, Harding, Newsom, Phillips, Oldrey, Bannister,
Calver, Wm. Harvey, Jno. Seymour.

Attested: WM. BLIGH.

————

THE RIGHT HON. WILLIAM WINDHAM TO GOVERNOR BLIGH.

(Despatch No. 6, per transport Duke of Portland; acknowledged by
Governor Bligh, 31st October, 1807.)

30 Dec.

Sir,   Downing Street, 30th December, 1806.

Lord Castlereagh's letter of the 13th July, 1805, replied to
all the Dispatches from New South Wales, which had been
received prior to that date; and such further communications
as appeared necessary at the time of your departure from here
for your Government, I take for granted, were either made to
you by my Predecessor in office, or introduced into your instructions.*

The evacuation
of Norfolk
Island.

The subject most necessary at present to advert to is the withdrawing of the Establishment from Norfolk Island.

The ground on which this measure was determined on appears
to have been the very great expence at which the Settlement was
maintained, and the very great difficulty with which a communication between it and Port Jackson was preserved—a difficulty arising from the danger of approaching an Island without a
Port secure from Tempests, or even a Road in which Ships could
safely anchor.

On these and other grounds, it seems that an Order was con-
veyed by Lord Buckinghamshire,† when Secretary of State, dated
June, 1803, for removing a part of the Settlement of Norfolk
Island to Port Dalrymple, or to some other situation on Van
Dieman's Land.

Terms offered
to settlers at
Norfolk Island.

The mode of removal proposed was that the Settlers, together
with their Live and Dead Stock, should be conveyed to the place
of their destination at the public Expence, and that, on their
arrival there, Grants of Land should be made to them in the proportion of four Acres for every one the property of each Individual which he should leave in a state of cultivation; and two

* Note 11.   † Note 4.

Acres for every one of waste or uncultivated Land which he should have in his possession; that each Settler should receive Rations from the public Stores for twelve months, together with the labor of two convicts for the same period, and every other usual aid which should be found necessary to enable him to provide for himself and his family; also, that such proportion of the live Stock of each Settler as he should not have the means of removing should be taken by Government and paid for at a fair Valuation in money, or in such Articles of Necessity as the public Stores of New South Wales might furnish.

1806.
30 Dec.

Terms offered
to settlers at
Norfolk Island.

The expediency was at the same time suggested of leaving a small Establishment and a few Inhabitants on Norfolk Island for the purpose of raising Maize to fatten Swine, to be salted and cured for the use of the other Settlements, and of sending persons from Port Jackson at the close of each summer to assist in effecting this object.

Maintenance
of a small
establishment
on the island.

It appears by the correspondence that the substance of these instructions having been communicated to the Settlers by Lieutenant-Colonel Foveaux, many of them at first expressed perfect readiness to remove, but that they wished in general to postpone their departure until their Crops, then in the Ground, should be saved.

Opinions of
the settlers re
the proposed
evacuation.

It further appears that the Crops, when saved, proved inadequate even to the supplying of food for the Stock to be removed during the Voyage to the Van Dieman Land, and that the Settlers had hesitated afterwards in agreeing to the removal, a Reluctance produced chiefly, it would seem, by some Stipulations which were proposed to them by the Lieutenant-Governor in consequence of a Dispatch which he had received from Governor King.

The Settlers, it seems, at length represented to the Lieutenant-Governor (who was at that time about to return to England for the Recovery of his Health) that the terms proposed were inadequate to compensating the losses and privations which they should suffer by their removal to a New Settlement, and that many local considerations, such as the Nature of the tenures under which they held their lands and houses, the obligations between Debtors and Creditors, and other Circumstances, would prevent them from accepting the proposed terms.

In consequence of these representations, considered as they were by the Lieutenant-Governor as being entitled to attention, and in consequence of impediments arising from a deficiency of food for the Stock of the Settlers, and of the want of sufficient means of conveyance, no steps were at that time taken for carrying His

1806.
30 Dec.

Removal of
convicts and
four settlers
from the island.

Majesty's Instructions into effect. It appears, however, from a dispatch lately received from your predecessor, dated 20th July, 1805,* that a considerable Number of the Convicts had been moved to Port Dalrymple, but that only four Settlers had withdrawn from the Island; and by a subsequent dispatch from him, dated 8th September, 1805, it appears that Governor King had sent the Buffalo to carry from Norfolk Island to Port Dalrymple such Settlers as should choose to remove.

Expense of maintaining the settlement.
These Measures, however, can have had but little effect in promoting the object of freeing Government from the Expence of maintaining an Establishment in Norfolk Island, the necessity for Courts of Justice, for a Military Commandant, for a Detachment of Troops, a Chaplain, Storekeeper, and for other subordinate Officers, must still have continued, as well as the necessity of maintaining a constant communication with Port Jackson, and the consequent Expence would inevitably increase according as the population of the Island should advance, Experience having proved that the Crops become more subject to blight according as the Clearing the Land proceeds—inasmuch as that the Crops have latterly almost entirely failed; at least, it is evident that as the Crops would become less equal to the wants of the Settlement every year, a proportionate Increase of Supplies from $port$ Jackson would every year become more requisite.

Independently of these Considerations, too, there appears to be very little doubt but that the Settlement of Port Jackson and the adjoining territory will very shortly afford to its Inhabitants abundant means of subsistence, and that the subordinate Settlements of Hobart Town and Port Dalrymple possess every advantage which fertility of soil can confer.

It being evident upon the whole that very little, if any, advantages can be expected from a partial Evacuation of Norfolk Island, Commensurate with the Expence of maintaining that Settlement,

The complete evacuation to be effected.
I have it in Command to desire that you will take the Measures forthwith for withdrawing the Settlers and all the Inhabitants, together with their live and dead Stock, the Civil and Military Establishment, and the Stock belonging to Government, observing the following regulations, taken chiefly from a plan delivered in by Lieutenant-Governor Foveaux as the General Rule for your proceedings.† You are to understand, however, that you are at liberty to exercise your discretion in respect to partial deviations from these Regulations in instances in which you have reason to think that such Deviations may be necessary, Communicating the Grounds and Extent of such Deviation for His Majesty's information.

* Note 12.   † Note 13.

The Settlers and other Inhabitants are to be divided into two Classes—

The *first* to consist of discharged Seamen, Marines, and Old Servants of Government, who have proved themselves to be industrious and deserving of favour;

Classification of the settlers on Norfolk Island.

The Second to consist of persons who have formerly been Convicts, but who have conducted themselves with propriety, or who have large families, or from other Causes, may have claims to particular Attention;

And the Third to comprehend the remainder of the Inhabitants possessing Land or buildings, but who have no particular pretensions to the favour of Government.

To all persons in each of these Classes, Grants of Land are to be made (free of Expence), on their arrival either in the New Settlement of Port Dalrymple or of Hobart's Town (according to their option), in the proportion of two Acres for every one of cleared Ground, and of one Acre for every Acre of Waste Land of which they shall have been possessed in Norfolk Island. Convenient Buildings are to be erected on each Allotment for the residence of the Settlers at the Public Expence, in the Manner hereafter explained, of equal Value with the Houses which they shall have left Behind.

Concessions offered to settlers removed to Tasmania.

The *Settlers* of the first Class, with their respective Families, are to be victualled and Clothed for two years at the Public expence; they are to be allowed the labour of *four* Convicts for the first nine Months, and of two for fifteen Months longer, the Convicts also to be victualled and Clothed at the public Expence.

Assistance to be granted to settlers of the first class;

Those of the second Class are to be victualled and Clothed, as also the respective families of those composing it, for two years at the Public Expense, and to be allowed the labour of *two* Convicts for the same period.

of the second class;

And the Settlers of the *third Class* are to be victualled and Clothed from the public Stores for twelve Months, to be allowed the labour of two Convicts for the same period, and to be in other respects assisted as New Settlers.

of the third class.

All these Classes are to be supplied from the Public Stores with implements of Husbandry, as well as with such other Implements and Tools equivalent to such as they shall have been possessed of, and may not have it in their power to remove.

In regard to all persons not comprised within any of these Classes, a discretionary power must be vested in the Officer entrusted with the Execution of the Service of removing the Settlement either to afford pecuniary Compensation to the Individuals for the Property they may leave behind, or to certify the

Compensation for settlers unclassified.

1806,
30 Dec.
Claims of each to Dwellings at the public charge, as proposed for settlers of the first Class.

Limit fixed for pecuniary compensation.

The Officer in question is at the same time to be restricted from exceeding on any account the Sum of £1,000 in affording pecuniary Compensation.

Live stock to be purchased by government.

In the Event, however, of its being found absolutely necessary that any of the persons comprised within the above Classes should leave behind them any part of their live Stock, such Stock is to be taken by Government at a fair Valuation, and paid for in such Articles of clothing, or other necessaries, as the public Stores may furnish, and as may be best suited to the Situation and wants of the individuals.

Arrangements for the civil officers.

With regard to the Officers on the Civil Establishment of Norfolk Island whose Services shall be no longer necessary, it is His Majesty's Pleasure that such of them as you may judge duly qualified shall be appointed to fill corresponding Situations in the subordinate Settlements of Port Dalrymple and Hobart's Town as Vacancies may arise, and in the meantime that they shall continue upon half Pay.

Judge-advocate Hibbins to be discharged.

I am, however, under the necessity of excepting from this Indulgence the Deputy Judge-Advocate, Mr. Hibbins, whose conduct in the transaction in which Mr. Clarke was concerned was such that I am to desire you will signify to him that His Majesty has no further Occasion for his Services.

The means of removing the Settlers must be supplied by the Colonial Vessels.

Lieut.-colonel Foveaux to superintend if possible.

In carrying this measure into effect it would be highly desirable that Lieutenant-Colonel Foveaux should be employed; but as the health of that Gentleman does not admit of his proceeding to New South Wales by the Ships now under dispatch, it will be advisable that the removal of the Settlement should not, on this account, be delayed.

Should Lieutenant-Colonel Foveaux, however, arrive at Port Jackson before the final Arrangement for carrying these Instructions into effect shall have been completed, you will not fail to intrust him with the execution of the Service.

I have, &c.,
W. WINDHAM.

[Enclosure.]

Foveaux's observations on the proposed evacuation of Norfolk Island.

LIEUTENANT-GOVERNOR FOVEAUX'S OBSERVATIONS CONCERNING THE REMOVAL OF THE SETTLEMENT AT NORFOLK ISLAND.

26th March, 1805.

ON my communicating My Lord Hobart's instructions concerning the removal I found many of the Settlers disposed to accept the offered terms; in fact, the idea of doing so continued pretty

1806.
30 Dec.

Foveaux's
observations on
the proposed
evacuation of
Norfolk Island.

general for some time, and several gave in their Names for this purpose, which I transmitted to Governor King. The only objection stated to an immediate removal was the extreme want of the Settlers, owing to the great scarcity of Maize and Wheat, a quantity of which they were desirous of taking with them, as they did not like the Idea of depending wholly on the Ration that might be allowed from the Public Stores on their arrival at the new Settlement. From hence arose the desire of stopping until such time as their Crops were ready to take off the ground; but on the arrival of the Integrity, Colonial Cutter, on the 4th of August last from Port Jackson, and in consequence of a Letter from Gov'r King dated 20th July, 1804, which I communicated to two of the principal Settlers who had given in their Names to remove, as also to two free Men who came from Port Jackson to settle here, that inclination which was before so manifest almost totally disappeared and out of Forty-one who had given in their Names to remove, only ten remained willing to go; the others requested their names to be withdrawn from the List altogether.

Concerning the removal of a part of the Establishment from the Island, from the immediate consideration of its great expense, I do not exactly perceive how any material reduction of Expense could be made; for so long as there shall remain an Establishment, however small, it will be necessary to Keep up the Courts of Justice. The great inconvenience for want of them was long experienced by Governor King during his administration, and on his representation, I believe, the Patents for holding them were granted. This service will require that a sufficient number of Officers should be retained. As to the plan proposed by Governor King of sending Officers in a Vessel annually for settling such Civil or other matters as may occur during the Year, I have to observe that, independent of the inconvenience which would attend the delay of Public Justice, there will be found other difficulties and obstacles. Disputes too frequently happen among the better orders of Society, and much more so among that description which composes the chief number of the Inhabitants of this Island. From the consequent variety of Causes, the necessary delay of a Vessel off this Island, particularly if a hired one, would be attended with an Expense more than equal to the saving to be obtained by the plan.

As to any advantage to be derived from the circumstance of sending a Vessel in the Summer Season to take from off the Settlers' hands such Pork as they may be enabled to salt during the Winter, admitting the quantity to be such as to make it an object to Government, I am convinced under all circumstances, and particularly from that of there being no Harbour or safe

1806.
30 Dec.

Foveaux's
observations on
the proposed
evacuation of
Norfolk Island.
place of anchorage for a Vessel, that the difficulty and danger for
the Shipping would more than counterbalance any benefit to be
derived therefrom; besides, it is obvious that the supply to be
obtained from this Settlement must at all times be very precarious.

The last Salting Season, in order to encourage the Settlers, I
offered sixpence per lb., being an addition of one penny beyond
what is given for fresh Pork, besides allowing them at the rate of
twenty lb. of Salt to the hundred lb. of Pork for Salting. When
the Pork was received a great part was found so badly cured that
it was returned on the Settlers' hands, and consequently became a
total loss to them; in fact, it requires large convenient buildings
for this purpose, which the Settlers have neither the ability or
inclination to erect, it being so very uncertain whether the
quantity of Pork they may obtain may requite them for the
Expense, trouble, and risk they run in curing it.

As to any Saving which might be made by raising Pork here,
and salting it, I am clearly of opinion, from my Knowledge of
Port Jackson, that the Inhabitants of that place will be able, in a
short time, to supply Government with Animal Food at a much
cheaper rate than could be raised and taken from hence, after
including the necessary expense of Freight, &c.

That the rearing of Swine on this Island has become more
uncertain and doubtful, each year's experience serves to prove;
and, notwithstanding the Fertility of the Soil, the success of the
Crops are, from various causes, equally precarious. In the year
1801, from these causes, the Island was reduced to the most
unpleasant extremity, and such was the scarcity of Grain and
Animal Food, there was an absolute necessity for sending out the
Boats to get Fish, from which uncertain dependence the Island
was for some time, and in a great measure, supported. In 1802
the Crops succeeded better, but from that period to the present
they have either failed generally, or being so very indifferent as
scarcely to reward the Labor of the Settlers. They have, therefore, not been in a situation to supply the Public Stores for some
time past with a sufficient quantity of Pork to victual those necessarily dependent upon the Crown; indeed, had it not been for the
favourable produce of the Crops of Wheat raised for Government
in 1802, there would have been a necessity long ago to have had
recourse to Port Jackson for Supplies; but even as it is, and
although a small supply of Flour has been lately sent from Port
Jackson, there is a necessity for issuing a reduced Ration, which
took place in July last, and must have commenced sooner had
it not been for the favourable circumstance just mentioned.
Should the present Crops (which are in a very doubtful state)

fail, the consequence would be that such as are victualled from the
Public Stores, as well as many of the Settlers, who are already
reduced to great distress from the present scarcity, must be supported from Port Jackson; for, notwithstanding Swine of a
certain age will live upon the Herbage of the Island, Yet they
never attain a state of perfection without Corn, and from the
extreme scarcity now existing there has been a great fatality
among the younger Kind of Swine, by which the Settlers have
suffered very much indeed.

1806.
30 Dec.

Foveaux's
observations on
the proposed
evacuation of
Norfolk Island.

It might be imagined that the Settlers, under all these circumstances, would be desirous of removing to some of the new Settlements; but as many of them came in the first expedition, they
are acquainted with the difficulties and hardships they must
encounter at an infant Settlement before they could fix their
Families in any tolerable degree of comfort. They therefore feel
but little inclination to remove from habitations and other little
enjoyments which they actually possess, to an unknown Country,
where they will have to provide themselves, and begin the World
again.

However, should the idea once prevail that a gradual reduction
will, at all Events, decidedly take place, and that the Government
will positively give up the Settlement altogether, I have no doubt
but the Disposition for removal will again become general; even
now I am persuaded there are some who would, were it not for
their pecuniary embarrassments, being much involved in debt,
remove immediately. This obstacle could only be obviated by a
general removal, when, of course, the Creditor would have the
same means of obtaining justice at the new Settlement as now
on this Island.

How far it may be proper to hold out further encouragement,
or make a distinction in favor of those who have obtained a
greater degree of comfort and convenience by Labour and industry, or of those who came out free, or have been discharged in
the Country from the Marines, is a matter that requires some
consideration.

Should Government have it in Contemplation to abandon the
Settlement, I conceive the removal of the whole Establishment
within as short a Period as the necessary precautions for the
supply of Provisions, &c., will admit of, would be the least expensive, as from the great inconvenience attending the communication between this Island and Port Jackson, and the necessity
there would be for Keeping up an Establishment, even though a
reduction thereof should take place, it must occur that little
difference can be made in the expense, which object can only be
effected, in my Opinion, by a total removal; and although this

1806.
30 Dec.

Foveaux's
observations on
the proposed
evacuation of
Norfolk Island.

measure might be attended with a temporary inconvenience to the Inhabitants, yet I am persuaded, from a due consideration of all circumstances, they would ultimately benefit by the change.

As to any saving by reducing the Salaries of a few Civil Officers, or discharging others from their situations, as pointed out by Governor King's Letter, I should hope that when the great hardship that Individuals must experience from such a measure is considered, as well as the Minuteness of the Saving, that Government will not see a necessity for having recourse to such an expedient. Besides, should the Settlement be removed, it is to be hoped that those persons who have long been the Servants of Government may at least receive similar situations at some of the New Settlements; and as some of them have been at a great expense in erecting Houses for themselves, I should humbly rcommend that such expense be made good to them, or that Habitations of equal value may be erected for them in some of the new Settlements at the expense of Government. There are, besides, some other inhabitants, having families, in possession of habitations, although not of any great value, who would suffer much by the necessity of a removal, and may be, I conceive, fairly entitled to some consideration of the same Nature.

Foveaux's
suggestions
for the
compensation
of the settlers.

LIEUTENANT-GOVERNOR FOVEAUX'S OBSERVATIONS concerning the removal of the Settlers and other Inhabitants from Norfolk Island, with his Opinion respecting the Encouragement which might be held out to them as an Inducement for such removal; to which is annexed a List of the Names of the Settlers with the Number in their respective Families now residing on the Island, divided into three Classes. Also an Account of the Quantity of Land and Stock in their possession. A List of Officers and Superintendants holding Land &c. and an account of Buildings belonging to Inhabitants to which is added their supposed Value.

THOSE Settlers coming under the denomination of the first Class, being either discharged Seamen or Marines, or such as have been a long time in the employ of Government and conducted themselves faithfully, besides being Men of an industrious Turn, I conceive are entitled to a greater degree of Encouragement than the others, and would recommend that they should severally be victualled and clothed, with their respective Families, for two Years, and be allowed the Labour of four Men for nine Months on being put in possession of their Land at the new Settlement, which would enable them to plant and sow in the ensuing season; At the end of Nine Months to take away two of the four Men, and to victual and clothe the other two Men for Fifteen

Months longer, making up the period of Victualling and clothing as follows, viz.:—For the Settler and his Family and two Servants two Years, and the extra two Men nine Months.

To the second Class of Settlers, that they should be victualled and clothed with their respective Families and be allowed the Labour of two Men for two Years, to be victualled and clothed at Government's Expense from the time of their being put in Possession of their Land. And to the Third Class of Settlers I would recommend the exact Conditions pointed out in my Lord Hobart's Instructions, excepting only a reduction of the Quantity of Land. To the Superintendants and Soldiers who possess Land I conceive it may be proper to allow the Labour of two Men on the same Conditions as those of the Second Class of Settlers.

Respecting the Land, I would recommend the following proportion, *i.e.*, for every Acre brought under Cultivation, in the proportion of two Acres for one; and for every Acre of Waste Land, an equal Quantity; and as an Equivalent for this reduction, I would recommend that convenient Buildings should be erected on each Settler's Farm at the Public Expense, at least of equal Value with those they may leave behind them; for it is not altogether the Object of the Settler to obtain large possessions of Land; his principal Aim will be to make himself and Family as comfortable as possible, and to clear as much Land as will support them at the Expiration of the Period for which they are to be victualled at the Public Expense. As the Inhabitants who are in the possession of Buildings will be material Sufferers in the Event of a removal, I am of Opinion it would be proper to pay them the Value of their Buildings, of which I have annexed a Statement, or to erect Buildings for them of equal Value at the Public Expense, at Port Jackson or some of the near Settlements, leaving the place at their own Option. And as some of these People in particular would be put to great Inconvenience and Distress by loss of their Avocation on a removal, a further Indulgence might be added by victualling them and Families for a few months at the Public Expense, until they could obtain some Employment, or to allow them to become Settlers at Port Jackson, if there are not too many at that place already.

Although I am aware that these proposals may appear very liberal, and will be attended with considerable Expense, Yet I am of Opinion, when all Circumstances are duly considered, that Offers of less Encouragement could not well be made; and should it be the Wish of Government to abandon the Settlement, it will be the readiest way to facilitate that Object, for notwithstanding many of the Settlers labour under great Inconvenience from the precarious Success of their Crops, still they manage to support

1806.
30 Dec.

Foveaux's
suggestions
for the
compensation
of the settlers.
themselves and Families. Some of them, with respect to dwellings and other Conveniences, feel tolerably comfortable. Others,
having large Families and being advanced in Years, will feel little
Inclination to remove without some probable appearance that
they may benefit by the Change, and even with this Encouragement, was there a Certainty the Settlement would not be entirely
given up, there are some who would rather chuse to remain where
they are.   J. FOVEAUX.

THE RIGHT HON. WILLIAM WINDHAM TO GOVERNOR BLIGH.

(Despatch No. 7, per transport Duke of Portland; acknowledged by
Governor Bligh, 31st October, 1807.)

Sir,   Downing Street, 30th December, 1806.

Despatches
acknowledged.

Dispatches of the numbers and dates specified in the Margin* have been received from Governor King since the date of
your Instructions, and your Letters of the 15th of March, 1st
of April and 30th of May have also been received.

The dispute
between Bligh
and Short.

The unfortunate difference or misunderstanding between you
and Captain Short, which forms the subject of your letter,†
appears, I must observe, to have arisen from very trivial Causes,
and to have proceeded to a length to which it could not possibly
have advanced had you both been impressed with a just sense,
situated as you were, of the propriety, if not necessity, of preserving a good understanding with each other.

The Questions on which your Differences arose seem to be
proper for the Admiralty, and only for the Admiralty, to whom
you observe you have transmitted Copies of your Letter to
decide.

Subject-matter
of King's
despatches.

I shall postpone, at present, entering at any Length upon the
subject of the Communications which Governor King's Dispatches contain, since, as you are directed in your Instructions
to report generally upon the state of the Colony, and as you will
naturally convey to me all the Information which you may be
able to obtain upon the different points adverted to in the Dispatches, I shall hope to receive full and detailed Information
from you in your first Dispatches from New South Wales upon
these Points.

Shipments
of supplies.

The Supplies required by Captain King have been provided
and have been shipp'd on board the Duke of Portland and Young
William according to Invoices which you will receive from the
Transport Board.

Salt Provisions for One Year's Consumption for the Settlements under your Government are also shipped on board of the

* No. 1, 2, 3, 4, 5, July 20, 1805. Military, Septr. 8 (*see* note 14).   † Note 9.

abovementioned Vessels; But owing to the deficiency in the King's Stores of the Quantity necessary for the extraordinary demands this Year of salted Pork, the whole of the supply consists of Beef. As Pork, however, is more easily procured than Beef in New South Wales, I apprehend that no Inconvenience can possibly result from this Change.

The Objections made by Captain King to locating the land adjoining Mount Taurus to Mr. McArthur will be further considered when your Observations upon the point shall be received.

The Report of His Majesty's Law Officers* upon the Case of the Ship "Harrington" was transmitted to Captain King in Novr. last with Instructions for the Release of that Ship and her Crew.

Captain King's Conduct† in resisting the Attempt of the House of Messrs. Campbell and Co. to introduce into the Colony a quantity of Spirits contrary to the Orders of Government was highly proper, and I trust that the Principle on which the prohibition rests will always be rigidly attended to.

I herewith inclose the Report of His Majesty's Judge-Advocate on the proceedings transmitted in Governor King's letter of ——‡ respecting Mr. Savage, and I cannot help expressing my regret at observing in the Correspondence with New South Wales so many Instances of Courts-Martial upon points which might be disposed of without reference to this Country.

No Notice has been taken of Mr. Crossley's Appeal, because the necessary Security for the prosecution thereof has not been entered into by him or by any Person on his Part in England.

I have the satisfaction to acquaint you that Measures have been taken for augmenting the New South Wales Corps to 800 Men, and that when an Opportunity shall offer the Officers and Men who have been added to the Regiment are to proceed to their Destination. W. WINDHAM.

Marginal notes:
- 1806. 30 Dec.
- Land grants to Macarthur at the Cowpasture.
- The case of the brig Harrington.
- Approbation of King.
- The court martial on assistant-surgeon Savage.
- The appeal of Crossley to the privy council.
- Augmentation to the N.S.W. Corps.

THE RIGHT HON. WILLIAM WINDHAM TO GOVERNOR BLIGH.

(Despatch per transport Duke of Portland; acknowledged by Governor Bligh, 31st October, 1807.)

Sir, Downing Street, January, 1807.
Since closing my despatches to you of the 30th Ult'o, I have received three letters from Lieut.-Governor Collins, dated the 17th and 25th of June, and the 2nd of Aug't last, in which he states that the Settlement under his care has been so much neglected that he has been under the necessity of reducing the Ration of Provisions; also that the Provisions sent to him from Port Jackson and Norfolk Island had been of the worst possible

Marginal notes:
- 1807. — Jan.
- Condition of the commissariat at Hobart.

* Note 15.   † Note 16.   ‡ Blank in the original (*see* note 17).

1807.
— Jan.
Quality. He acknowledges that previously to the 17th of June
he had rec'd a quantity of Salted Pork from Port Jackson, and
a proportion of the Articles consigned to him from England by
the Ship William Pitt; but he adds that intimation had been
given him that he might expect a small Supply of Flour and
Barley Meal, but that no vessel had reached Hobart Town on the
2nd of August following with that Supply. On referring to the
The settlement formed by Collins. correspondence in this office respecting the Settlement at Hobart
Town, I find that Lieut.-Governor Collins left England in April,
1803, with Instructions to Settle the people who accompanied
him at Port Phillip, in Bass's Straits, but with discretionary
power to fix on any other part of the Coast of New South Wales
in preference, provided he should do so with the concurrence and
approbation of Gov'r King, to whom copies of the Instructions
were forwarded, and He (Gov'r King) was at the same time
apprized that the new Settlements were to be considered as
Dependencies upon his Gov't, also that the Lieut.-Government
was to be placed under his orders. It further appears that Lieut.-
Governor Collins found Port Phillip to be deficient in many of
the requisites for a Settlement, and therefore fixed his Establishment on the River Derwent, with the concurrence and approbation
of Governor King, who had before formed a small Settlement
there under the charge of Lieut. Bowen, of the Navy.

King's reports on the commissariat at Hobart. In January, 1805, Governor King it appears informed[*] the
Secretary of State that Lieut.-Governor Collins had at that time
45 weeks flour and 35 weeks salt meat, and that as soon as a
convenient opportunity offered, it was his (Gov'r King's) intention to compleat the salt Provisions to a due proportion with the
flour, of which there was sufficient to last until Oct'r, 1805, before
which period he expected Supplies from England. Gov'r King
at the same time enclosed the copy of a letter which he had
written to Lieut.-Governor Collins informing him that his Report
on the subject of a Survey of Flour and other Provisions, and
calculation of time they would last, had set his, the Governor's,
mind at ease, but that he should not, notwithstanding, neglect
any opportunity that might offer of adding to the Stores of
Provisions at Hobart Town, observing that he could not but
approve of his reasons for directing that the wheat carried on
speculation should be purchased, notwithstanding the Sophia,
which carried his letter, had three weeks provisions on Board for
26 female Convicts, the overplus of which was to be delivered to
the Dep'y Comm'y. In a dispatch from Gov'r King, dated the
30th of April, 1805, after stating that the quantity of Wheat
remaining in the Colony was equal to 57 weeks Consumption, and

* Note 18.

that no further supply of Grain or Flour could be required from England, observes that at Hobart Town there was Flour and Wheat to last till Jan'y, 1806, and at Port Dalrymple to last to the middle of August, and he adds that as further Supplies of Grain were on their way, shipped by Individuals at their own risk, to be delivered into Government Stores, *those Settlements would undergo no reduction in their full rations.*

In July, 1805, Governor King states that by a late opportunity he had sent a small Supply of Salt meat to Lieut.-Governor Collins, and that the Buffalo was then refitting in order to proceed to Norfolk Island to take a further proportion of Grain and such Pork as might be ready salted, to proceed with it to Port Dalrymple and to the Derwent; he adds that the remains of the Salt Pork did not exceed 64 weeks for the people victualled from the Stores, including the Supplies he should necessarily send to the Derwent, Port Dalrymple, &c., and, therefore, suggests the propriety of a Supply being sent out.

The last cited letter from Governor King was received on the 15th April, 1806. Two Ships had in the meantime sailed from Europe with Provisions and Stores, as stated in the margin,* and would probably have arrived in March or April; indeed, it appears from Lieut.-Governor Collins's letter that one (the William Pitt) had reached Port Jackson about this time.

I need not state to you that Stores and Provisions to a considerable amount were also sent out by the Lady Magdalena Sinclair and the Porpoise, and I entertain no doubt but that you will have availed yourself of the ample means at your disposal to relieve Lieut.-Governor Collins from the difficulties and embarrassment of which he complains, and which must, I take for granted, have been occasioned by some accidental cause which he does not state.

In L't-Gov'r Collins's Letter, dated 2nd August, he encloses a Demand for Hospital Supplies, many of the Articles specified in which appear very far indeed to exceed the probable occasion for them. He requires, for Instance, 400 Gals. of Wine, a Quantity exceeding 6 Hogsheads, and he at the same time states there is not a Man sick in the hospital.

It is not necessary to animadvert on this Demand; but it is necessary that a Caution should be given by you to L't-Gov'r Collins and the other L't-Gov'rs, by which they may be aware that they are answerable for every Demand which receives their Sanction, and that when Demands apparently so disproportionate as the one in question is to the Occasion, are made, extreme inattention of Officers on Duty in not preventing or observing upon

* The margin is blank (*see* note 19).

1807.
— Jan.
such Demands in the Dispatches must be attributed to them. The Demands for Medicines are not complied with, because a quantity sufficient for two Years' consumption was sent by the L'y M. Sinclair.   W. WINDHAM.

GOVERNOR BLIGH TO SECRETARY MARSDEN.

(Despatch per H.M.S. Buffalo.)

2 Jan.

Naval orders
given by Bligh.

Sir,   Sydney, New South Wales, 2nd January, 1807.
        I beg leave to inclose for the information of My Lords Commissioners of the Admiralty Copies of the Orders alluded to in my general Letter* up to the time of putting Captain Short under an Arrest.   I have, &c.,
                                                 WM. BLIGH.

[Enclosure.]

NAVAL ORDERS GIVEN BY GOVERNOR BLIGH.

Short ordered
to England
for trial by
court martial.

BY William Bligh Esquire Captain of His Majesty's Ship Porpoise and Senior Officer of His Majesty's Ships and Vessels employed on the Coast of New South Wales.

WHEREAS by the Reports of the Courts of Enquiry which have been held in consequence of your Letters of Complaints against Lieutenant Tetley and Mr. Daniel Lye, Master, of His Majesty's Ship Porpoise, and their Complaints against you have arisen to such a pitch that His Majesty's Service as far as relates to the Porpoise being useful to the Public Duties of the Colony are entirely suspended; and that these circumstances of complaint should be enquired into and which only can be done but by your going to England where Courts Martial may be held, or as my Lords Commissioners of the Admiralty may direct the Cases to be determined—this is therefore to require and direct you to give up the Command of His Majesty's Ship Porpoise for the time being, Lieutenant John Putland having my Order to hold it during your absence, and proceed to England in His Majesty's Ship Buffalo Captain King, late Governor of this Colony, having my Orders to receive you; And on your arrival in England you are to inform the Secretary of the Admiralty for your farther proceedings, and for which this shall be your Authority.

Given, etc., this 1st day of January, 1807.

To Joseph Short, Esq.,   WM. BLIGH.
        Commander of His Majesty's Ship Porpoise.

You will transmit in writing to me a List of such Witnesses as are necessary on the occasion.   WM. BLIGH.

Attested: WM. BLIGH.

* Note 20.

By William Bligh, Esquire, etc., etc.

YOU are hereby required and directed to receive on Board His Majesty's Ship Buffalo under your Command Joseph Short, Esquire, Commander of His Majesty's Ship Porpoise for a passage to England, bearing him on your Supernumerary List according to the Rules of the Service.

Short to travel on the Buffalo.

Given, etc., this 1st January, 1807.

WM. BLIGH.

Philip Gidley King, Esq.,
Captain of His Majesty's Ship Buffalo.
Attested: WM. BLIGH.

By William Bligh, Esquire, etc., etc

YOU are hereby required and directed to hold yourselves in readiness to repair to England in His Majesty's Ship Buffalo, on account of charges and Complaints between Joseph Short Esquire Commander and yourselves. And you are to transmit to me such Witnesses as you deem necessary taking care to confine them to few.

Tetley and Lye to return to England.

Given, etc., this 1st of January, 1807.

WM. BLIGH.

To Lieutenant Tetley and Mr. Daniel Lye, Master,
of His Majesty's Ship Porpoise.
Attested: WM. BLIGH.

By William Bligh, Esquire, etc., etc.

IN consequence of Joseph Short Esquire having violently opposed his being superceded from His Majesty's Ship Porpoise under my Command in order to his proceeding to England in His Majesty's Ship Buffalo to decide by Court Martial Charges which he has made against his Officers and they against him, and swearing by God he would not allow Lieutenant John Putland's Acting Commission to be read to act in his absence until the Pleasure of my Lords Commissioners of the Admiralty be known: You are hereby required and directed to proceed on board His Majesty's Ship Porpoise and calling all the Officers and Ships Company together you are to put the said Joseph Short Esquire under an Arrest and proceed to read the said Acting Commission accordingly to the Officers and Ships Company.

Short to be placed in arrest.

Given, etc., this 1st January, 1807.

WM. BLIGH.

To John Houstoun, Esq.,
Second Commander of His Majesty's Ship Buffalo.
Attested: WM. BLIGH.

1807.
2 Jan.

Short placed
in arrest on
H.M.S.
Buffalo.

By William Bligh, Esquire, etc., etc.
WHEREAS by my Order of the 1st instant You was directed to
receive Captain Short for a passage to England And he on that
day having been put under an Arrest for disobedience of my
Orders by refusing to give up the Command of the Porpoise,

You are hereby required and directed to receive him the said
Captain Short on board His Majesty's Ship under Your Command as a prisoner at large And on Your Arrival in England to
inform My Lords Commissioners of the Admiralty thereof.

Given, etc., this Second day of January, 1807.

WM. BLIGH.

To Philip Gidley King, Esquire,
Captain of H. M. Ship Buffalo.
Attested: WM. BLIGH.

GOVERNOR BLIGH TO SECRETARY MARSDEN.

(Despatch per H.M.S. Buffalo.)

Sir,   Sydney, New South Wales, 2nd January, 1807.

Lieutenant
Putland
appointed to
command
H.M.S.
Porpoise.

His Majesty's Service demanding the most prompt
measures to put a stop to the differences between Captain Short
and his Officers and place His Majesty's Ship Porpoise in a
proper and quiet state for the benefits which were due to the
Ship's Company, it became necessary for me to appoint Lieutenant John Putland* to Command her until the pleasure of My
Lords Commissioners of the Admiralty be known, which I hope
and trust will meet their Lordship's approbation and that I may
be allowed to recommend him, he having been Eight Years a
Lieutenant, and deserving of the honor and trust reposed in him,
besides being the only Commissioned Officer remaining under my
Command; and was the first Lieutenant made by Lord Nelson
at the Battle of the Nile.   I have, &c.,

WM. BLIGH.

[Enclosure.]

WARRANT OF APPOINTMENT TO LIEUTENANT PUTLAND.

Warrant to
Putland as
commander
H.M.S.
Porpoise.

BY William Bligh Esquire Captain of His Majesty's Ship Porpoise and Senior Officer of His Majesty's Ships and Vessels
employed on the Coast of New South Wales.

To Lieutenant John Putland, hereby appointed to Act
as Commander of His Majesty's Ship Porpoise until
the Pleasure of the Right Honorable the Lords Commissioners of the Admiralty be known.

WHEREAS His Majesty's Service requires that Joseph Short
Esquire Commander of His Majesty's Ship Porpoise should proceed to England in His Majesty's Ship Buffalo.

* Note 21.

By Virtue of the Power and Authority to me given I do hereby constitute and appoint You Acting Commander of His Majesty's Ship Porpoise willing and requiring you forthwith to repair on board and take upon you the Charge and Command of Acting Commander in her accordingly; strictly charging and commanding all the Officers and Company of the said Ship to behave themselves jointly and severally in their respective Employments with all due Respect and Obedience unto you their said Acting Commander. And you likewise to observe and execute the general Printed Instructions and such Orders and Directions as You shall from Time to Time receive from me or any other your superior Officer for His Majesty's Service; hereof, nor you, nor any of you may fail, as you will answer the contrary at your Peril, And for so doing this shall be your Warrant.

(Marginal notes:) 1807. 2 Jan. — Warrant to Putland as commander H.M.S. Porpoise.

Given, etc., the First day of January, 1807.

Attested: WM. BLIGH. WM. BLIGH.

GOVERNOR BLIGH TO SECRETARY MARSDEN.

(Despatch per H.M.S. Buffalo.)

Sir, Sydney, New South Wales, 3rd January, 1807. *(Marginal:)* 3 Jan.

I beg to lay before My Lords Commissioners of the Admiralty (in addition to my former Charges against Captain Short to my arrival at the Cape of Good Hope) that on the 1st Instant having given an Order to Captain Short of His Majesty's Ship Porpoise under my Command to give up the Command of the said Ship to proceed to England in His Majesty's Ship Buffalo, and also an Order to Lieutenant John Putland to command her in his absence, Captain Short refused to obey such Order. That on my being acquainted therewith, I sent Captain Houstoun of the Buffalo with Lieutenant Putland on board to put the said Order into execution, but Captain Short persisting in the refusal and swearing violently by God he would not allow the Commission to be read, they returned on Shore again, when I gave Captain Houstoun the Order to put Captain Short under an Arrest for such disobedience; I therefore have to request their Lordships will be pleased to take into their consideration, how far Captain Short may be tried for the same in my absence, such Persons being sent home (on his own account) named in the Margin* will prove the violence and disobedience I complain of; particularly Captain Houstoun of His Majesty's Buffalo.

(Marginal notes:) Short's refusal to obey Bligh's orders. — Short placed under an arrest.

* *Marginal note.*—Lieut. Tetley, Mr. Danl. Lye, Master; Mr. Pineo, Surg.; Mr. Basden, Purser; Mr. Calver, Gunner; Mr. Harding, Mr's Mate; Mr. Newsom, Mid. Of His Majesty's Ship Porpoise.

1807.
3 Jan.

I beg leave to inclose Captain Houstoun's and Lieutenant Putland's Letters stating Captain Short's conduct, on the 1st Instant.

I have, &c.,

WM. BLIGH.

[Enclosure No. 1.]

CAPTAIN HOUSTON TO GOVERNOR BLIGH.

His Majesty's Ship Buffalo,

Sir,   Port Jackson, Jany. 2nd, 1807.

Houston's
report on
Short's refusal
to give up his
command.

In case of any explanation being hereafter required from me in consequence of my proceeding on board .His Majesty's Ship Porpoise with your verbal Order to See that Lieut. Putland's Order to take upon himself the command of that Ship was read to the Officers and Ships Company, I think it necessary to inform you that on my Repairing on board for that Purpose I made Captain Short acquainted therewith, and was answered by him that he considered Lieutenant Putland whenever he came on board that Ship as Subservient to him, that he commanded the Ship, and in a Most *passionate and Violent Manner declared that his commission should not be read by God,* because he would require his attendance as one of his Principal Evidences and likewise required time to Settle his accounts, and have Surveys held on the Ships Stores as should Lieutenant Putland's commission be allowed to be read he would Step into his Shoes and be oblidged to humble himself to Captain Putland to be allowed to get his things over the Side, when immediately I returned on Shore to make Your Excellency acquainted with Captain Short's determination and Receive your written order of the 1st instant which I yesterday Saw put into full effect.

I have, &c.,

JNO. HOUSTON.

[Enclosure No. 2.]

LIEUTENANT PUTLAND TO GOVERNOR BLIGH.

His Majesty's Ship Porpoise, Sydney Cove,

Sir,   Port Jackson, 1st January, 1807.

Putland's
report on
Short's refusal
to give up his
command.

In obedience to your Directions of this day's date I repaired on board His Majesty's Ship Porpoise to read your Commission appointing me Acting Commander during Captain Short's absence, having previously delivered to him your Letter requiring him so to do. He decidedly refused to let it be read; and now on my going on board a second time accompanied by Captain Houstoun according to your directions, Captain Short behaved very violent and said by God it should not be read and that he would not give up the Command of the Ship, and when I came on board he considered me as second Lieutenant only.

On going on board the third time Captain Houstoun presented your Order and put Captain Short under an Arrest; Your Acting Order to Command was then read and I took the Command accordingly.   I have, &c.,

1807.
3 Jan.

JNO. PUTLAND.

Sworn before me this 12th day of Jany., 1807: RD. ATKINS, J.-A.

GOVERNOR BLIGH TO SECRETARY MARSDEN.

(Despatch per H.M.S. Buffalo.)

Sir,   Sydney, New South Wales, 7th January, 1807.

7 Jan.

I beg leave to transmit for the information of My Lords Commissioners of the Admiralty, the Letters of Captain Short, Lieutenant Tetley, and Mr. Daniel Lye Master, of His Majesty's Ship Porpoise, containing Lists of the Witnesses they require on the Charges exhibited by them against each other.

Lists of witnesses required for the court martial.

I have, &c.,
WM. BLIGH.

[Enclosure No. 1.]

MR. DANIEL LYE TO GOVERNOR BLIGH.

H. M. Ship Porpoise,
Sir,   Sydney Cove, January 6th, 1807.

Having received Orders from you to prepare to return to England in H. M. Ship Buffalo, for the purpose of defending myself of Charges brought against me by Captn. Short, and likewise for the purpose of substantiating Charges I have brought against Captn. Short, I have the Honour of transmitting to you the Names of those Witnesses whose testimony I conceive Necessary for effecting the Above purposes.

Witnesses required by Lye.

And have, &c.,
DAN'L LYE.

Names of witnesses:—Lieut. Tetley, Messrs. Calver, Hobbs, Bannister, Harding, Oldrey, Jno. Bowman, Adam Brown, Wm. Harvey, Jas. Allen, Jno. Seymour, Jas. Riley.

[Enclosure No. 2.]

LIEUTENANT TETLEY TO GOVERNOR BLIGH.

Sir,   H. M. Ship Porpoise, Sydney Cove, Jany. 6th, 1807.

Having received your orders to prepare to return to England in H. M. Ship Buffalo, for the purpose of defending the Charges brought against me by Capt. Short of this Ship: as also

Witnesses required by Tetley.

1807.
7 Jan.

Witnesses
required
by Tetley.

for the purpose of substantiating the Charges I have brought against Capt. Short, I have the honor of transmitting to you the names of those Witnesses, whom I conceive essentially necessary for effecting the above.   I have, &c.,

                                        J. S. TETLEY.

Names of witnesses:—Messrs. Lye, Basden, Calver, Hardinge, Newsome, Oldrey, Hobbs, Bannister, Phillips, Jno. Seymour, Jas. Allen, Wm. Harvey, Corpl. Stephens.

[Enclosure No. 3.]

CAPTAIN SHORT TO GOVERNOR BLIGH.

                        H. M. Ship Porpoise, Sydney Cove,
        Sir,   3rd January, 1807.

Witnesses
required by
Short.

        I beg leave to send you a List of Witnesses which I wish to take home, and am to request you will permit me to remain on board the Porpoise some days for the purpose of closing the Ships Accounts and getting my things removed.

                                I am, &c.,
                                        JOSH. SHORT.

List of witnesses:—Lieut. Jno. Putland, Messrs. Pineo, Basden, Hobbs, Calver, Bannister, Harding, Newson, Oldrey, Phillips, John Seymour, Arm'r, Adam Brown, John Bowman, Jas. Allen, Henry Ade, Wm. Hy. Carpenter, Wm. Stephens (Corporal Marines).

[Enclosure No. 4.]

CAPTAIN SHORT TO GOVERNOR BLIGH.

                        H. M. Ship Porpoise, Sydney Cove,
        Sir,   8th January, 1807.

Putland's and
Harding's
depositions
to be taken.

        I beg leave in Answer to yours of Yesterday to observe that I have not included any more Witnesses in my List than I deem absolutely requisite as the Offences were committed at different times, and before different Persons, but as it may be a great inconvenience for Mr. Putland to go home, under these circumstances I have no objection to have his Deposition taken before the Judge Advocate although I am fearfull the Court will not look at it; I also beg to observe the Mr. Harding having served so much of his time, and his having pointed out to me the great inconvenience it would be to him to return home, If it meets your Approbation I have no objection to dispence with his under the same Circumstances.

                                I am, &c.,
                                        JOSH. SHORT.

GOVERNOR BLIGH TO SECRETARY MARSDEN.

(Despatch per H.M.S. Buffalo.)

Sir,   Sydney, New South Wales, 7th January, 1807.

Inclosed are reports from the Boatswain and Carpenter of
His Majesty's Ship Porpoise under my Command, Stating their
deficiency of Stores, as found by survey to be owing to Captain
Short ordering them to be used but not allowing them to be
regularly expended, and praying that the same might be presented to free them from the Amount being charged against
their Wages.   I have, &c.,
                                WM. BLIGH.

Deficiency in the stores of the Porpoise.

[Enclosure.]

MESSRS. HOBBS AND BANNISTER TO GOVERNOR BLIGH.

H. M. Ship Porpoise, Port Jackson,
Sir,   7th January, 1807.

We beg leave to represent to Your Excellency that as a
very great deficiency of the Stores upon our Charge will appear
from the Survey taken on the 29th and 30th of last month and
what should actually remain on board by the working Abstract,
and as we are both young Officers we hope you will pardon us for
the intrusion we are now committing; being totally unacquainted
with the Service, we both thought it was our duty to comply with
any directions Captain Short thought proper to give us with
respect to our Stores, although it was not given in writing, and
accordingly entered in our rough Expences the particular purposes for which those Stores were made use of; Captain Short
having objected to sign to them has been the cause of the deficiency above Complained of. We therefore beg leave to inclose
to your Excellency a fair statement of the Stores so made use of
and hope you will have the goodness to forward it to the Navy
Board in order that we may not be made accountable for what
has been ordered by our Commander and which our total ignorance of the service made us assent to.

Boatswain's and carpenter's explanation of the deficiency of stores.

                    We have, &c.,
                    WM. HOBBS, Boatswain.
                    BENJ. BANNISTER, Carpenter.

GOVERNOR BLIGH TO SECRETARY MARSDEN.

(Despatch per H.M.S. Buffalo.)

Sir,   Sydney, New South Wales, 9th January, 1807.

The Public Service has obliged me to request of You to
lay before my Lords Commissioners of the Admiralty transactions

1807.
9 Jan.

The disputes
between Short,
Tetley, and Lye.

which have taken place in His Majesty's Ship Porpoise under
my Command between Captain Short, Lieutenant Tetley, and
Mr. Daniel Lye, Master.

I have endeavoured to arrange the circumstances clearly as
they have taken place, but nevertheless think this general Letter
and Statement necessary in order to show the connection of the
different Papers, as well as to express to their Lordships my
disapprobation of Captain Short's conduct; particularly his irritating manner and the want of due care in the management and
appropriation of the Ship's Stores, as well as those put on board
for the use of the Buffalo and the Colony as stated in my Letter
of the 26th August last; and likewise for his not taking in a
sufficient quantity of Provisions and Purser's Necessaries, which
by the Warrant Officers' Statement appear to be extremely unjustifiable besides distressing to those Men in passing their
Accounts; and preventing the harmony which ought to have been
in the Ship, and affecting the welfare of this Colony.

These circumstances having been enquired into, it became
absolutely necessary to send home Captain Short under the
Charges made against him by Lieut. Tetley and Mr. Lye the
Master, as likewise they to answer the complaints he afterwards
made against their proceedings.

Should what I have stated on my part, as Charges against
Captain Short, be cognisable by a Court Martial in my absence,
I imagine the same Witnesses which accompanied him will prove
his unofficerlike conduct and violence to me, stated to their
Lordships in my former Despatches;* as also my present Charge
for his disobedience of my orders.

That the Porpoise may remain effective, I have exchanged the
Witnesses from her with proper Persons from the Buffalo as far
as could be done, which Ship has been detained until now by the
distress of the Colony not affording a Supply of dry Provisions
for her Voyage.   I have, &c.,
                                        WM. BLIGH.

Bligh's
disapprobation
of Short's
general
conduct.

Short, Tetley,
and Lye
ordered to
return to
England.

[Enclosure.]

GENERAL STATEMENT.

General
statement of
the disputes
between Short,
Tetley, and Lye.

ON the 15th November 1806, I received a Letter from Mr. Tetley
1st Lieutenant of the Porpoise, charging Captain Short with improper use of Stores—The Articles of War never read except
once—The Boats Crews kept up at unseasonable Hours, taking
more than his Allowance of Provisions—Behaving in a cruel and
oppressive Manner and making use of unofficerlike language on
the Quarter Deck—And endeavouring to depreciate him in the

* Note 22.

Opinion of the Officers and Ship's Company, and that owing to 1807.
9 Jan. ill usage from Captain Short his Peace of Mind was much broke and his health much injured, Requesting me to take such Steps General statement of the disputes between Short, Tetley, and Lye. as were most conducive to the good of the Service.

On the 19th November or thereabouts, Mr. Lye called on me to complain of Captain Short's usage which I directed him to report in writing.

On the 22nd I received a Letter from Mr. Lye charging Capt'n Short with Unofficerlike and improper behaviour to him and other Officers, which had caused him to be very unhappy and uncomfortable for some time past—Drunkeness—Wasteful Expence of Stores—Expending them unlawfully—Articles of War not read, which had been the Cause of many punishments—The Boats Crews kept up at improper hours and requesting I would take such Steps as to bring Captn. Short to Justice, It being impossible for the Officers of the Ship to live where such flagrant Abuses existed.

On the 9th December, I received another Letter from Mr. Lye that he had been confined a close Prisoner Since the 28th November, and not even allowed to come out of his Cabin to his Meals for Charges he was not acquainted with altho' he wrote for them the 1st December, Yet no Notice was taken of this request; He had written to the Surgeons the 2nd December requesting to be released on Account of his health or otherwise to enclose his Letter to me, Complaining of the Stench of the Family next Cabin to him, but no Notice was taken or enquiry if he was well or not, And therefore requesting my interfering to crush such oppressive treatment.

On the 10th December, on the day I returned from visiting the Harvest, I received a Letter from Captain Short dated the 1st of the same Month informing me for the first time he had confined Mr. Lye on the 28th November for disobedience of his Orders and together with Lieut. Tetley of their behaving with Contempt, talking improperly to the Ship's Company in language tending to make them discontented and to create Mutiny, and requesting an Enquiry to be made.

This Letter was dated the 1st, Altho' not given to me before the Evening of the 10th by Mr. Murphy, Midshipman, whilst I had received Letters from Captn. Short Subsequent to the 1st and this Letter might have been brought to me as well as the others.

In Consequence of this Letter of Captn. Shorts desiring an Enquiry, I gave an Order to Capt'ns King and Houstoun and Lieut. Oxley of the Buffalo to go on board the Porpoise inclosing the foregoing letters for their Guidance.

1807.
9 Jan.

General
statement of
the disputes
between Short,
Tetley, and Lye.

On the 11th the Court sat, And on the next day they reported, with their Minutes of the Enquiry, That Captn. Short had appropriated some Green Baize, Wainscot for Conveniences about the Cabin, And that a false Entry had been made in the Ship's Log Book respecting a Davit having been carried away, which was not; And an Anchor Stock expended said to replace the Davit. The Anchor stock had been Sawed into Boards for Captain Short to replace the Ships Stores of Wainscot which had been used by Captn. Short. That Captain Short had directed the Gunner to expend 2 Musquets, when none were deficient.

That Captain Short had lent the Armourer for some days at the Cape of Good Hope by which the Service was injured by a Carronade being disabled and the Arms in a bad Condition. That also the Boatswains Yeoman was lent to Mr. Fitz in Port Jackson as a Gardener at a time the Ship was refitting.

That the Articles of War had not been read more than twice Since the Ship has been in Commission.

That no Officers' Commissions had been read Except Captain Bligh's and Short's.

That the Boats Crews had been repeatedly kept up after the hour of twelve at Night during the time the Ship was refitting.

That much harsh language has been used by Captain Short to Lieutenant Tetley.

That the Statement of Captn. Short's Drunkeness at the Cape of Good Hope is true by the Boatswain Gunner and Carpenter's Evidence, Independent of Lieut't Tetley's Evidence.

On Captain Short's Charge against Mr. Lye They do not in their Conscience believe that any Censure beyond a Reprimand would be made by a Court Martial, Nor do they conceive that the Charge against Lieut. Tetley and Mr. Lye for treating Captain Short with disrespect and exciting insubordination and Mutiny among the Ships Company is at all proved. Nor can they help pointing out to my Notice the Evidence of the Purser and Surgeon (respecting Lieutenant Tetley's being drunk in his Watch) which they consider entirely shaken—besides which they found the Charge invalidated by the testimony of the Mate of the Watch, Man at the Helm and all the other Evidences questioned in that behalf.

They Submit to me under their present Report how far the Charges against Mr. Lye contains sufficient Grounds for the Confinement he is now in to be tried by a Court Martial which cannot be held in this Country nor can the Prisoner and his Evidences be sent from hence for that purpose without a total hindrance of the Ships Services for want of Officers and Men.

And they finally Submit to my determination whether there be Grounds for a Court Martial on Captn. Short.

1807.
9 Jan.

General
statement of
the disputes
between Short,
Tetley, and Lye.

In Consequence of this Enquiry and a Representation of the Cruelty of shutting Mr. Lye up in his Cabin I gave an Order dated the 13th December to the Surgeons of the Buffalo, of the Colony, And of the New South Wales Corps for them to proceed and state to me the Situation they found Mr. Lye in And they gave Report dated the next day to this Effect:

That they found him confined to a Small Cabin, ill ventilated, and so small as not to admit him to use sufficient Exercise for the preservation of his Health, which, Altho' not very materially impaired at present, Yet that a Continuation of the Confinement in this Climate must eventually prove injurious to his Health, And might produce disease of the most Serious and fatal tendency.

Under all these Circumstances I gave Captn. Short an Order dated the 18th December to liberate Mr. Lye from his Confinement, in which he has been for 3 weeks and to do his Duty until an opportunity occurred to try him by a Court Martial on the Charges he had preferred against him in his Letter dated 1st Decr.

In Consequence of the foregoing Order I rec'd a Letter from Captn. Short in the Evening of the same day endeavouring to obviate the putting my Order into Execution and declaring he could not do duty with Mr. Lye, and requesting him to be kept in Confinement until he could be brought to a Court Martial. To this I replied, that I expected he would consider the Orders he was under as an Answer to this Application.

On the 19th I received another Letter from Captn. Short putting off liberating Mr. Lye under improper Reasons to which I sent him word that he had Orders and I expected he would comply with them.

Accordingly Mr. Lye was liberated.

On the 20th following I received another Letter from Mr. Tetley the first Lieutenant complaining bitterly of Captain Short's Conduct having made him a prisoner to the Ship and telling him he never would quit him till he had answered for the high Charges he had against his life, requesting a Court Martial on Capt. Short according to his Letter of the 15th November last and representing his Situation as truly distressing.

On the 23rd I represented to Captn. Short by Order of this date that as the public Service required it, Officers in this remote Situation could not be kept confined, And therefore Mr. Tetley was to have his Liberty until the Lords Commissioners

1807.
9 Jan.

General
statement of
the disputes
between Short,
Tetley, and Lye.

of the Admiralty Signify their intentions on the Charges he might transmit against Lieut. Tetley.

These Circumstances being ended On Christmas day, two days after, I received a Letter from Captn. Short accusing Lieut. Tetley and Mr. Lye of Drunkeness, Unofficerlike behaviour, and other Charges therein contained. In Consequence of this I wrote to Captain Short Lieut. Tetley and Mr. Lye, and I again gave an Order for a Court of Enquiry, which took place the following day, And in consequence of the said Enquiry representing the State of the Ship truly alarming with Captain Short and his Officers quarelling, that His Majesty's Service as far as related to the Porpoise being useful to the public Duties of the Colony was entirely Suspended by the unfortunate differences which exist on board that Ship between the 2nd Commander, Surgeon and Purser, And first Lieutenant and Master, which might lead me to cause some Change or Separation to take place amongst those Officers and which measure alone could tend to render that Ship fit for public Service.

On the 27th I gave an Order for Mr. Lye to be again liberated, And the next day ordered a Survey on the Stores and Provisions to take place on the 29th instant.

Two days after on the 29th I received another Letter from Lieut. Tetley complaining of a Continuance of Captain Short's Severity and believing his life was not in Safety, Captain Short having prepared Arms loaded and threaten'd he would soon use them.

On the 1st January I received a report of Surveys on the Stores and Provisions remaining on board the Porpoise and gave the following Orders.

1st. To Captn. Short to proceed to England in H. M. Ship Buffalo in Consequence of the determination of the Courts of Enquiry which had been held.

2nd. To Governor King to receive Captain Short in the Buffalo for a passage to England.

3rd. To Lieut. John Putland to act as Commander of the Porpoise until the pleasure of the Lords of the Admiralty be known.

4th. To Lieut. Tetley and Mr. Daniel Lye Master of the Porpoise to hold themselves in readiness to proceed to England in His Majesty's Ship Buffalo in Consequence of the Courts of Enquiry which had been held.

About ten o'Clock I sent Lieut. Putland to take Command of the Porpoise, But at Eleven he returned, Captn. Short having refused to give up the Command of the Ship, Nor would he permit the Commission I had given to be read.

In consequence of this I sent Lieutenant Putland back again with Captain Houstoun of the Buffalo to enforce my Orders. They returned and informed me that Captn. Short had refused to comply as before, Acting in a violent Manner, Swearing by God the Commission should not be read, upon which I sent Captn. Houstoun and Lieut. Putland back with an Order to put Captn. Short under an Arrest and carry my Orders into Execution which was done.

1807.
9 Jan.
——
General
statement of
the disputes
between Short,
Tetley, and Lye.

Concerning Captain Short's Conduct on this occasion I refer to Captn. Houstoun's and Lieut. Putland's Statements.

January 2nd.

This Morning gave Lieut. Putland an Order to allow Captn. Short to be under an Arrest at large to be ready to proceed in the Buffalo and Governor King to· receive Captain Short as a prisoner at Large.

On the next day I sent to Captn. Short, Lieut. Tetley, and Mr. Lye the respective Charges which they had made against each other and they requested their Witnesses accordingly.

On the 7th I received Letters from the Carpenter and Boatswain of the Porpoise stating the deficiency of their Stores being owing to Captain Short ordering them to use but not allowing them to be regularly expended and praying for Relief.

Government House, Sydney, New South Wales, 9th January, 1807.

WM. BLIGH.

———

GOVERNOR BLIGH TO THE RIGHT HON. WILLIAM WINDHAM.

(Despatch No. 1, per H.M.S. Buffalo; acknowledged by Viscount Castlereagh, 31st December, 1807.)

Sir,   Sydney, New South Wales, 25th January, 1807.

On account of the probability of Extra Expences being incurred on the Public Buildings I feel it incumbent on me to inclose the state they were in on my arrival in this Colony.

I have, &c.,

WM. BLIGH.

[Enclosure.]

SITUATION AND DESCRIPTION OF REPAIR OF GOVERNMENT BUILDINGS,* NEW SOUTH WALES, 13TH AUGUST, 1806.

Hawkesbury.—One New Building, intended School, unfinished; One New Granary, with three Floors, one Floor unfinished; Roof and Foundation of Government House totally decayed and untenantable; One Old thatched Store unfit for Service.

Toongabbee Stock Yard and Dairy.—The whole of Government Buildings in a decayed state, quite untenantable, some fallen down.

1807.
25 Jan.

Report on the
general
condition of
public
buildings.

Castle Hill.—One Barn in good repair; One Stone Grainary Floor wants repairing; One New Grainary in an unfinished state; Dwelling and Store Houses wanting Repairs.

Parramatta.—Grainary and Store Houses, the Walls in a decayed State, and the whole in want of new Flooring;

Lumber Yard, Blacksmiths', Carpenters', and Wheelers' Shops in bad repair; Saw-pits and Sheds totally decayed; Government House, Inside Wood-work wants repairs, Out-Houses and Stabling wants great repairs;

Church covered in, but no Pews or anything but a Pulpit, Tower not half built, Walls broke, and will require re-building.

Sydney Stated at large in a separate account.—Store Houses and Grainary in want of New Flooring and Roofing. A New Building intended for Church in an unfinished state, Tower, East end, and twelve feet of the Front Wall in Ruins and Roof unfinished.

RICH'D ROUSE, Superintendant.
THOS. MOORE, Builder.

STATEMENT OF GOVERNMENT BUILDINGS IN SYDNEY, AUGT. 13TH, 1806.

The Master Builder's House wants Plaistering, whitewashing, windows repairing, and part of the Foundation given away.

The Dock Yard—wants Sheds for Boats, and to Work under for Saw-Pits; the Blacksmith Shop and Store Houses and Watchman's Hut wants Plaistering, whitewashing, new Doors and Shutters, rep'g Tiles outside of Staircase, Also New Posts and Railing next the Road.

Wharfinger's Hut—Wants New windows and doors, Plaistering, whitewashing, a new Chimney, and Tileing repaired.

The Coxwain and Boat's Crew's Hut—Wants Plaistering, Whitewashing, Tiles rep'g, a New Fence, Doors, and Windows.

The Gaol.—In good repair, but wants Additional Cells.

The Watchman's Hut.—Nearly Down.

The Lumber Yard.—Wants the Blacksmith's Shop and Shed Whitewash'd, Plaistered, New Doors, Windows, and the Tyling repaired, New Saw-Pitts and Sheds.

The Military Store.—Part of the Walls given away, and wants New Doors, Windows, and the Tileing repaired.

The Granary.—Wants new Flooring, Doors, and Windows, New Shingleing, Stair Case, and Plaistering and Whitewashing, with other Necessary Jobs.

Gov't House and Offices.—Wants New Doors, Windows, window Shutters, lineing and frames, Shingleing, Flooring, whitewashing and Plaistering. All in so rotten a State, wants to be New.

The Judge-Advocate's House.—In good repair; His Office in a bad state—wants to be New.

The Parsonage House.—Wants New doors, Windows, and Fence, Plaistering, Whitewashing, and Tileing repaired.

The Surveyor-Gen'l's House and Offices.—Wants doors and windows, Nearly New whitewashing and Plaister'g; Also new fence

The Old Guard House.—Nearly Down.

The New Do.—Only Wall'd and Roof'd.

The Dry Store.—Wants New Doors, Windows, and Staircase, Plaistering, whitewashing, and repairing the Tiles, also New Flooring.

The Storekeeper's House.—In good repair.

The Superintendant's of the Town Gang House.—Wants new doors and Windows, whitewashing, Plaistering, and Tiles repairing and other woodwork done.

The Exccutioner's Hut.—Wants new doors and window Shutters, Fence and Tiles rep'g, Plaistering, and Whitewashing.

Two Gov't Huts.—Wants Doors, Windows, Tiles, and Fence rep'g, and other wood-work, also Plaistering and whitewashing.

The Sup't of Blacksmith's, the Assistant Engineer, Overseer of Town Gang, and Commissary Clerk.—Wants Windows, doors, Tiles, and fence rep'g and other wood-work, also Plaistering and white-washing.

The Deputy Commissary's House.—Wants New Doors, Window Sashes, Fence, flooring, Whitewashing and Plaistering, a few panes of Glass, other wood-work done; outoffices the same.

Light Horsemen's Barracks and Stable.—Wants new Shingleing, Plaistering, Doors, window-Shutters, and other wood-work.

The Two Salt Provision Stores.—Wants the doors and windows nearly new and other wood-work, Tiles rep'g, Plaistering, white-washing; part of the walls Given way.

The New Church.—The wall at one End down, and the Tower; the roof only half up.

One Wind-mill.—Wants new Plaistering, whitewashing, and rep'g the wood-work.

One New Wind-mill.—Not Finished.

One Old Do. on the fort.—Useless.

The Town Bridge, New.—Part of it down, the other part in a bad State.

The Orphan House.—In good repair; the Offices in a bad state, one Nearly Down.

The Wooden Hospital.—Rotten and decayed; not worth rep'g.

The Other Hospitals.—Wants new Doors, Windows, and shutters, floors Relaying, many panes Glass Broke, whitewashing, and Plaistering, the out-offices some down and others Propt up, also new fence; all the Hospital and Premises in a ruinous State.

The Principal Surgeon's House and Offices.—Wants Plaistering, whitewashing, and Tileing repaired, with some other wood-work done.

Two Assistant Surgeons' Barracks.—Wants new doors and Window Shutters, and other Necessary rep's, Plaistering, and White-washing.

Commiss'y Office.—Wants doors and Windows, nearly New, Plaistering, Whitewash'g, Tileing rep'g, and In General in a very Bad State.

Salt Provision Store.—Wants flooring, doors, windows, and Shingleing, and New Cooperage Yard.

Guard House, Daw's Point.—Wants Plaistering, whitewashing, &c.

Situation of the Military Barracks.

The Surgeon's Barrack.—Wants Nearly new flooring, the Fence part Rotten, Plaistering, Whitewashing, and Tiles rep'g, with wood-work; out-offices in the same state.

Two Captain's and Adj't do.—The same as above.

Military Hospital.—The walls and roof only up.

Five Subalterns' Barracks.—Wants Plaistering, whitewashing, Tileing rep'g, the out-offices the same, and wants nearly all new

1807.
25 Jan.

Report on the general condition of public buildings.

1807.
25 Jan.

Report on the
general
condition of
public
buildings.

doors and Window Shutters; the Pailing at the Back Intirely Gone.

Two Private Barracks.—Wants Plaistering and Whitewashing, the doors and Windows some of them new, and others rep'g.

Three Subaltern's Barracks.—Not finished; the walls and roof only up; Many of the Bricks gone from the Chimney, and part of the Walls also; The roof will require one-third New Tileing, great Numbers being broke and gone; every Part of the Three Buildings are in a ruinous State.

THOS. MOORE, Builder.

RICH'D ROUSE, Superintendent.

GOVERNOR BLIGH TO THE RIGHT HON. WILLIAM WINDHAM.

(Despat^h No. 2, per H.M.S. Buffalo; acknowledged by Viscount Castlereagh, 31st December, 1807.)

Government House, Sydney, New South Wales,

1 Feb.

Report on the
commission
charged for
articles for
barter.

Sir,   1st February, 1807.

The inclosed Documents are in Answer to that part of my Instructions* which directed me to enquire how far 15 per Cent. comes to be charged to the Commissary General for the Superintendance of Sale of Articles for Barter, And which I presume applies only to the Naval Officer as explained by Governor King.   I have, &c.,

WM. BLIGH.

[Enclosure No. 1.]

MEMORANDUM FROM CAPTAIN KING TO GOVERNOR BLIGH.

Information to His Excellency Govr. Bligh respecting the 15 p. Cent.

Memorandum
by King on the
commission
charges.

IT being noticed in an Instruction You have received " that the Articles sent out for Barter are to be disposed of as usual, but I think it proper to call Your Attention to a Charge of 15 p. Cent. to the Commissary General for the Superintendance of Sales of these Goods, it seems to be a very high Allowance and requires Explanation."

As no such Charge was ever made, the allusion appears to be respecting the 15 p. Cent. Mr. Harris is allowed as Collector of the different Duties, Assessments, etc. for the Support of the Orphan Institution And for what is called the Gaol Fund, to which Office is added that of Naval Officer and Treasurer of the Gaol Fund and Superintending the buildings of the Orphan Institution at Sydney, to explain which, it is necessary to state that, As the eventual Receipts, which depend on the Arrival of Ships, might not admit of a fixed Salary being continued to Mr. Harris, It was considered the allowance of 15 per Cent. on the Collection and Receipts would be the most eligible way of recompensing that Officer for his great trouble and Responsibility.

* Note 3.

1807.
1 Feb.

Memorandum
by King on the
commission
charges.

The following Statement shews what the Per Centage has amounted to, One Year with another, since the Commencement of the Institution as extracted from the Proceedings and printed Reports Viz.

Mr. Harris began doing Duty as Naval Officer, Collector of all Fees Assessments and Treasurer of the Gaol Fund, August 21st 1801.

The first Assessment accounted for by Mr. Harris
was on the 1st August 1801 from which time
till the 31st of December 1804 the p. Centage
amounted to £572 13 4½
From 1st January to 31st December 1805 ...... £399 15 9
From 1st January to the 12th August 1806 it
amounted to 38 13 6
                                              _____
                                              £1,011 2 7½

From 21st August 1801 to the 12th August 1806
being 5 Years the Average is £202 4 6

Any Alteration in the Rate of Per Centage, which it may be deemed necessary to make, I am convinced Mr. Harris will readily accede to, as it was not given by his application, but from a persuasion that his Services deserved such a Recompence.

PHILIP GIDLEY KING.

[Enclosure No. 2.]

COMMISSARY PALMER TO GOVERNOR BLIGH.

Sir,   Commissary Office, Sydney, 31st January, 1807.

Commission
received by
commissary
Palmer.

Your Excellency having honored me with an Extract from the Secretary of State's letter to you, calling your Excellency's attention to a charge of 15 pr. Cent. to the Commissary General for the superintendance of sales of the Articles sent out for Barter, and requiring an Explanation thereof, In Answer thereto I beg leave to acquaint your Excellency, that conceiving the Secretary of State means that the above charge is made *by* me, instead of *to* me, I must therefore say that by an Order of Governor King's. dated the 19th August 1802, I was permitted to make a Charge of 5 pr. Cent. on the Amount of the Annual Supplies to be deducted from the profits of such sales, as a compensation for the extra duty and responsibility attendant on the issuing of such Articles; but as Governor King signified by the same order that this benefit was only to arise to me from the sales of the Articles sent by the Perseus and Coromandel for the period of twelve months, I take leave to enclose a Copy of the said Order, and to represent to Your Excellency, that the great

1807.
1 Feb.

Commission
received by
commissary
Palmer.

increase of duties and responsibility of my Office in consequence
of the Articles that are disposed of to the inhabitants and by the
increase of the population and extent of these Territories, I was
induced to memorial the Lords Commissioners of His Majesty's
Treasury stating the above Circumstances and praying that their
Lordships would take the same into their consideration, a Copy
of which memorial was delivered to Governor King, but never
left with their Lordships by my Agent. In such Memorial I
prayed their Lordships to be pleased to permit a Continuation of
the said Allowance of 5 per Cent. upon the Sales of the Articles
to be disposed of for Barter to the inhabitants, I beg leave to
enclose to you a Copy of the same and earnestly hope that as
neither me, or any person employed under me, derive the most
trivial emolument from their situations, Your Excellency will
be pleased to sanction my Application to the Lords Commissioners of the Treasury for the above benefit, that I may be
enabled to reward such persons as may be entrusted in the
disposal of the said Articles by transmitting such memorial to
their Lordships with such remarks as Your Excellency may consider necessary.

I have, &c.,

JNO. PALMER, Commiss'y.

[Enclosure No. 3.]

GOVERNOR KING'S ORDERS TO COMMISSARY PALMER.

Sydney, 10th August, 1802.

YOU are hereby required and directed to receive into your Charge
the Investment of Articles for Barter, arrived by the Coromandel
and Perseus, Transports, and to exchange them for Grain or
Money with such of the Inhabitants as I may grant that indul-
gence to; and in consequence of directions from His Majesty's
Principal Secretary of State for the Colonies, dated the 30th of
January, 1802, you will observe the following Regulations,
Viz.:—

1st.—You are to publish a printed Notice stating the general
Prices of each Article, with an advance of 50 per Cent. on the
prime Cost.

2nd.—To issue no Article without my written Order.

3rd.—Such Articles as are wanted for the Public Use of the
Colony you will expend as such, on receiving my separate Orders
for that purpose, taking proper Receipts for the same.

4th.—You will credit His Majesty's Treasury with the Amount
of the Prime Cost and charges of Articles sold or bartered.

1807.
1 Feb.

Governor
King's orders
re the
government
investments.

5th.—You will deduct 5 per Cent. from the profit of the Sales and Exchanges, for this additional trouble to yourself and the storekeepers charged with the Retail.

6th.—After paying Salaries to the two additional Superintendants of £50 a year each, from the profits arising from the Barter or Payment of the said Investments, you will deliver the value of such overplus Profit arising from the said 50 per Cent., into the hands of the Treasurer of the Orphan Fund twice a Year, i.e., on the 20th of July and 20th day of February, taking the Committee's Receipt for the same as your Voucher.

7th.—You are required to keep a particular and distinct Statement of the Disposal of the several Articles and the Appropriation of the Profits thereof, authentic copies of which you will deliver me half-yearly, to transmit to the Principal Secretary of State for the Colonies, duplicates of which you will forward to the Secretaries of the Treasury and Commissioners for Auditing Public Accounts.

PHILIP GIDLEY KING.

[Enclosure No. 4.]

THE MEMORIAL OF JOHN PALMER.

Commissary
Palmer's
petition for
commission
allowances.

To the Right Honorable the Lords Commissioners of His Majesty's Treasury.

THE Memorial of Mr. John Palmer Commissary of Stores and Provisions for the Colony of New South Wales.

MOST RESPECTFULLY SHEWETH

That your Lordships' Memorialist was appointed Commissary of this Colony in the Year 1790, and he flatters himself the Duties of that Office have been conducted to the satisfaction of your Lordships and for the public Interest.

That by an Order, dated 19th August, 1802, from Governor King, His Excellency was pleased to allow of a charge being made of 5 p. Cent. on the Amount of the Annual Supplies for the extra duty that attended the issuing out of the Investments (now termed Annual Supplies) and particularly those received by the Coromandel and Perseus in barter for Grain, Copper Coin, or other Colonial Currency, to the Officers, Settlers, etc. whom the Governor might grant Orders to receive certain proportions for their domestic uses, which 5 pr. Cent. was to be allowed to your Memorialist on the profit of 50 pr. Cent. that might arise on such sales of Annual Supplies; but His Excellency the Governor having signified that this Allowance was only to continue for twelve Months on what was then disposed of,

1807.
1 Feb.

Commissary
Palmer's
petition for
commission
allowances.

Your Memorialist humbly begs leave to represent to Your Lord-ships that the immense increase of the Duties of his Office, by being under the necessity of keeping Books for the sales of such Goods distinct from all others, and the barter being chiefly effected in Grain, and also the Extra supplies disposed of to Individuals kept separate, renders the Returns more intricate, and to keep such Accounts obliges your Memorialist to employ additional Clerks to assist in those separate duties, and to pay them out of his own private purse.

That the population and extent of the Colony has greatly increased the duties of Your Memorialist's Office, Your Me-morialist most humbly hopes your Lordship will take his Case into consideration and by reason of the great increase of respon-sibility and duty attached to your Memorialist's situation, and as the most trivial emolument does not arise to him or any persons under him, Your Lordships will be pleased to allow the Com-mission of 5 pr. Cent. on all such Investments, or Annual and Extra Supplies, disposed of from the Public Stores for Barter which have or may arrive in this Colony for the above purposes, or to give Your Memorialist such other recompence as to Your Lordships may seem meet, which will enable him to defray the unavoidable expence that he is obliged to incur in employing such persons as Clerks etc. as is necessary for his carrying on the Sd. Duties.

And your Memorialist as in duty bound will ever pray, &c.,

JNO. PALMER, Commiss'y.

GOVERNOR BLIGH TO THE RIGHT HON. WILLIAM WINDHAM.

(Despatch No. 3, per H.M.S. Buffalo; acknowledged by Viscount Castlereagh, 31st December, 1807.)

Government House, Sydney,
Sir,   New South Wales, 1st February, 1807.

Returns and
requisitions
transmitted.

I beg leave to inclose herewith a General Statement of the Inhabitants on the Eastern Coast and out Settlements.

A Statement of Provisions remaining in His Majesty's Stores and also the quantity requisite for a future consumption.

Abstract of the remains of Articles sent out for Barter and a request for a further Supply.

Abstract of the remains of Supplies made up to 12 August 1806 and farther demands made for the Year 1807.

A Demand for Stationary.

I have, &c.,
WM. BLIGH.

[Enclosure No. 1.]

GENERAL STATEMENT of Inhabitants of His Majesty's Settlement on the Eastern Coast and out-Settlements of New South Wales, the 31st December, 1806.

Civil Department Victualled.

Settlements.	Governor and Commander-in-Chief.	Lieut.-Governors (one Lieut.-Col. of N.S.W. Corps) and Commandants.	Aid-du-Camp to His Excellency.	Deputy Judge-Advocate.	Commissary.	Principal Surgeon.	Provost-Marshals.	Chaplains.	Secretary to the Governor-in-Chief.	Surveyor of Lands.	Deputy Commissaries.	Assistant Surgeons.	Boat Builder.	Mineralogist.	Clerk to the Commissary.	Superintendants and Storekeepers.	Women of Civil Department.	Children of Civil, above 10 years.	Children of Civil, above 2 years.	Children of Civil, under 2 years.	Total of Civil Department Victualled.
Sydney	1	1	1	1	1	1	1	1	1	1	1	1	1	1	2	3	12	1	10	4	46
Parramatta	:	:	:	:	:	:	:	1	:	:	1	2	:	:	:	5	7	2	8	4	30
Hawkesbury	:	:	:	:	:	:	:	:	:	:	:	1	:	:	:	1	:	2	2	:	6
Newcastle	:	:	:	:	:	:	:	:	:	:	:	1	:	:	:	1	1	1	:	:	4
Total	1	1	1	1	1	1	1	2	1	1	2	5	1	1	2	10	20	6	20	8	86
Norfolk Island	:	1	:	1	:	:	1	:	:	:	:	1	:	:	:	3	:	:	:	:	7
Hobart Town	:	1	:	1	:	1	:	1	:	1	1	2	:	:	:	6	6	5	2	5	32
Port Dalrymple	:	1	:	:	:	:	:	:	:	:	1	1	:	:	:	3	3	:	:	:	9
Grand Total	1	4	1	3	1	2	2	3	1	2	4	9	1	1	2	22	29	11	22	13	134

1807.
1 Feb.

General statement of inhabitants.

1807.
1 Feb.

General
statement of
inhabitants.

GENERAL STATEMENT of Inhabitants of His Majesty's Settlement, &c.—continued.

Settlements	Major	Captains	Lieutenants	Ensigns	1 Adjutant, 1 Quartermaster, 1 Paymaster	Surgeon	Serjeants	Drummers and Fifers	Privates	Women of Military Department	Children of Military, above 10 years	Children of Military, above 2 years	Children of Military, under 2 years	Total of Military Department Victualled	Loyal Association, Sydney and Parramatta — Captains	Lieutenants	Serjeants	Drummers and Fifers	Rank and File	Total of Loyal Association Victualled	Orphans Victualled from the Stores
Sydney	1	1	:	3	2	1	21	10	314	50	12	113	19	547	1	1	3	2	33	40	11
Parramatta	:	1	1	:	1	:	3	2	77	10	4	33	5	137	1	1	3	2	22	29	10
Hawkesbury	:	:	:	:	:	:	1	:	17	1	1	9	:	29	:	:	:	:	:	:	2
Newcastle	:	:	:	:	:	:	1	:	17	:	:	:	:	18	:	:	:	:	:	:	:
Total	1	2	1	3	3	1	26	12	425	61	17	155	24	781	2	2	6	4	55	69	23
Norfolk Island	:	:	1	:	:	:	1	1	35	:	:	:	:	38	:	:	:	:	:	:	:
Hobart Town	:	1	2	:	:	:	6	2	36	9	:	1	6	63	:	:	:	:	:	:	:
Port Dalrymple	:	1	2	1	:	:	4	2	64	8	1	17	:	100	:	:	:	:	:	:	:
Grand Total	1	4	6	4	3	1	37	17	560	78	18	173	30	982	2	2	6	4	55	69	23

GENERAL STATEMENT of Inhabitants of His Majesty's Settlement, &c.—*continued.*

Settlements	No. of Prisoners, &c., Victualled from the Stores — Men	Women	Children above 10 years	Children above 2 years	Children under 2 years	Total of Prisoners, &c., Victualled	Rations issued — Full	Two-thirds	Half	Quarter	Total No. of Full Rations issued	Total No. of Persons Victualled from the Stores	People not Victualled from the Stores — Men	Women	Children	Total No. not Victualled	Free Settlers and Landholders not Victualled — Men	Women	Total No. of Free Settlers and Landholders not Victualled	Total No. of Souls in the Settlements	Weeks Provisions — Beef and Suet	Pork	Wheat	Sugar as Maize
Sydney	426	53	2	37	13	531	549	130	160	36	724½	1,175												
Parramatta	653	155	:	77	37	922	786	178	118	46	975	1,128												
Hawkesbury	62	6	7	19	2	96	82	18	30	2	109	133												
Newcastle	54	24	:	5	1	84	74	26	5	1	94	106												
Total	1,195	238	9	138	53	1,633	1,491	351	313	85	1,902½	2,542	1,528	733	1,359	3,620	588	412	1,000	7,162	wks. 12	wks. 63 days. 6	wks. 3 days. 3	wks. 26 days. 3
Norfolk Island	154	56	8	100	9	326	199	64	100	9	293	372	195	127	:	322				694	:	wks. 52	:	:
Hobart Town	274	58	11	6	18	367	335	92	31	29	407	466	9	:	:	9				475	:	:	:	:
Port Dalrymple	129	20	:	:	13	162	209	31	31	:	245	271	1	2	2	5				276	:	:	:	:
Grand Total	1,752	372	28	244	93	2,488	2,234	538	453	123	2,847½	3,651	1,733	862	1,361	3,956	588	412	1,000	8,607				

1807.
1 Feb.

General statement of inhabitants.

JNO. PALMER, Commiss'y.

1807.
1 Feb.

Return of
provisions
in stores.

[Enclosure No. 2.]

STATEMENT of Provisions remaining in H. M. Stores at Port Jackson this 31st Decr., 1806; and of those which are required.

Quality.	Quant'y rem'g in Store.	Weekly Issue for 1903 full rations.	No. of Wks. each Species will last at the Full Ration.		Statement of the Quantity of Provisions which will be wanted for the use of the Colony and Settlements for the present Numbers victualled.
			wks	days	
Beef and Suet	lbs. 161033¼	lbs 13321	12	0	The Supply of Salt Pork necessary to be sent so as to arrive here about Jany., 1808, will be a Year's Salt Pork for these Settlements, (Sydney, Parramatta, Hawkesb'y & Newcastle) being 1903 full Rations equal to.... _Pork_
Pork	524716	7612	68	6	At Hobart Town for 405 being the present No. of full rations of Pork....PortDalrymple one Year for 295 do. do. equal to 395,824 lbs / 84,656 " / 55,120 "
Wheat remaining of that purch'd during the year and received in Barter etc.	Bush 241⅞	lbs 19030	⅛		535,600 " N.B. Provided the demand for Salt Pork, sent by the Alexander, dated 1st Novr. 1806, is not complied with.
Maize do do		5709			About 12 Acres of Callavances are ..., and will be ... to pluck about February ..., by which time 12 Acres more will be ..., and will be issued as a ... for Maize etc.
Wheat in Stacks belonging to the Crown, not delivered into Store, estimated at	1200	19030	3	3	The quantity of Wheat that will be required this ?ar to ... the ... ... of ..., ... and ... are unavoidably ... Rations from the Public ..., also to supply the out-
Maize in the public granary do do					Settlements (Port Dalrymple and the Derwent) and likewise to furnish seed for the Ground ... by Government at ... Settlements will be at least 20,000 Bushels, unless the rice ...
Sugar	lbs 18893	7181½	26	3	for by ...or King, ... arrive. 256 acres now planted will be reaped about ... next, the greater part of ... will be required for the Stock to ... to ..., besides ... to ... the
Spirits	galls 1610				Rations of ... there will be required about 7000 Bushels for all the Settlements. For the use of the ... Vessels, etc etc one wanted as a supply is expected by the Sydney that was contracted for by ...or King.

Wheat averaged at 56 lbs pr Bushel

JNO. PALMER, Commiss'y.

[Enclosure No. 3.]

ABSTRACT of the Remains of Annual Supplies sent from England for Barter with the Inhabitants of New South Wales for Grain, Swine's Flesh etc. up to the 31st Decr. 1806 including the Supply p. the Sinclair and the Demand made the 12th August 1806 with a Request for a further Supply for Barter for the Year 1807 supposing that for 1806 being on the Way.

Returns of annual supplies.

[*This was a lengthy return relating to miscellaneous articles of stores. A copy of it will be found in a volume in series II.*]

[Enclosure No. 4.]
[*A copy of this return is not available.*]

[Enclosure No. 5.]
Sydney, New South Wales, Jany., 1807.

DEMAND for Stationary etc. for the use of the Governor's and Commissary's Office at Sydney in New South Wales being a Duplicate Demand of that made on the 12th August last to enable him to supply the different Settlements at Port Dalrymple, Derwent etc.

Requisition for stationery.

		Govrs. Office.
Superfine Royal	Two Reams	
Ordinary Do.	Three Do.	
Foolscap Gilt	One ,,	Two Ream
Do. plain	Eight ,,	Two ,,
Blotting paper	Half ,,	Quarter ,,
Demy fine	Two ,,	Half ,,
Thick post	One ,,	One ,,
Thin Do.	Two ,,	One ,,
Cartridge paper fine for Mess books	Two ,,	Half ,,
Medium	Two ,,	
Quills	Three thousand	One Thousand
Wax	Four lbs.	One lb.
Irish Wafers	Two lb.	One lb.
Penknives	Two Dozen	Four in No.
Memorandum Books	Twelve in No.	
Black Ink Powder	Eight Doz.	Two Dozen
Red Ink Do.	One ,,	Six Papers
Slates	Six in No.	
Slate Pencils	One hundred	
Best Black Lead Do.	One Grose	Three Dozen
Russia Leather	One Skin	
Rough Calf	Six ,,	
Parchment	One Roll	Sixty Skins
Pasteboards	Fifty six lbs.	
India Rubbers, large Bottles	Six in No.	Two Bottles
Ledgers Demy	Two ,,	
Rules Ebony of Sizes	One Doz:	
Narrow Green Ribbon for Dispatches		Six Pieces
Pounce	One lb.	
Tape Red	Six Doz: pieces	Two Doz: pieces
Tin Ruling Pens	Six in No.	
Ink Stands for Offices	Twelve ,,	Two in No.
Letter Books for the Use of the Settlements	Six	Two
Book binder's Tools compleat consist'g of Presses, Letters of sizes, Pallets etc. etc.	One Set	
(Font) Printing Types (the old being worn out, to consist of one Font, small Pica Roman 300 Wt. Italic 50 Wt. 20 lb. Pearl Ash to be careful the Font is compleat	One Set	

App'd.—WM. BLIGH.   JNO. PALMER, Commiss'y.

REQUISITION FOR STATIONERY FOR THE JUDGE-ADVOCATE'S OFFICE.

Requisition for
stationery for
the judge-
advocate's office.

I HAVE the Honor of representing to Your Excellency that since my appointment of Judge Advocate of this Territory, now almost six Years, I have neither Stationary for public service or any allowance whatever on that account. As the duties of my Office has been from Year to Year considerably increasing, and the consequent additional consumption of that Article, I beg leave to request Your Excellency will make the necessary application that Stationary may either be supplied me or that I may receive such a yearly sum as may be thought adequate to purchase it, which has heretofore cost me £20 per Annum.

I must further trouble Your Excellency by observing that if the Statutes at large from 1796 to this period were sent, they would be of great public utility as some penal Acts have passed during that interval which might be particularly useful in this Colony and the trials at the Old Baily and Hicks' Halls* would likewise be very serviceable.

I have, &c.,
RD. ATKINS, J.-A.

Approved with respect to the Books but as to the Stationary I beg leave only to state that I believe the Expence is considerable in his department.

WM. BLIGH.

GOVERNOR BLIGH TO THE RIGHT HON. WILLIAM WINDHAM.

(Despatch No. 4, per H.M.S. Buffalo; acknowledged by Viscount Castlereagh, 31st December, 1807.)

Government House, Sydney,
Sir,   New South Wales, 1st February, 1807.

Proposed land
grants for
Short, Townson,
and Bunker.

By my Letters of the 26th August and 5th November last I had the honor to inform you of applications being made to me by Captain Short Commander of His Majesty's Ship Porpoise under my orders, Mr. Townson and a Mr. Bunker for Land signified to be granted by Mr. Secretary Cooke's Letters to them, and accordingly under that authority I permitted them to look out for the respective tracts they would approve of, when I received directions to locate the same.

Application
of Short for
land grant.

Until the 8th of last Month I had no farther application, when Captain Short after two Naval Courts of Enquiry on Charges made against him by his Officers, and he against them, and had been superceeded in the Command of the Porpoise on the first of the same Month to return home in Order to be tried by a Court Martial, wrote to me a Letter requesting a tract which he pointed

* Note 23.

out, and offered Bills of a Mr. Simeon Lord a resident here, 1807. 1 Feb.
which on no account would I have taken, in payment for Cows.

The conduct of Captain Short has been so irritating, vexatious, Refusal of Short's application.
and oppressive, indeed also so extremely obnoxious to the Colony,
that I directed my Secretary to write to him that as circumstances were changed I had no farther answer to give to his
Letter.

I designed only to have sent Captain Short and his Officers Captain Short sent to England under arrest.
home for their Charges to be legally determined; but he violently
refused to obey my orders to give up the Command of the Ship,
in consequence of which I put him under an Arrest, in which
state he leaves the Country and I have transmitted distinct and
complete documents to my Lords Commissioners of the Admiralty
respecting him, who I trust and hope will not return to disturb,
as he has done, my public and private attention to the good of
this Colony.   I have, &c.,
                                                  WM. BLIGH.

GOVERNOR BLIGH TO THE RIGHT HON. WILLIAM WINDHAM.

(Despatch No. 6, per H.M.S. Buffalo; acknowledged by Viscount
         Castlereagh, 31st December, 1807.)

Sir,   Sydney, New South Wales, 1st February, 1807.

Having directed the Commissary to make a Statement of Expenditure anticipated.
such Sums of Money as may be absolutely necessary to be drawn
for the Support of the Colony I beg leave to enclose the same,
but I assure you, Sir, it shall be lessened by every means in my
power as well as every expenditure of Public Stores; and I have
a hope the general Expence will in a short time be such as to
meet Your Approbation.   I have, &c.,
                                                  WM. BLIGH.

[Enclosure.]

COMMISSARY PALMER TO GOVERNOR BLIGH.

Sir,   Sydney, 1 Feby., 1807.

In consequence of the Inundation last Year which de- Commissary Palmer's statement of the probable expenditure.
stroyed nearly the whole of the Grain at the Hawkesbury and
from the failure of the Crops of Wheat this Year throughout
the Colony, which has caused the price of Grain to be considerably higher than heretofore, I have calculated the quantity of
Grain that will be unavoidably required for the purpose of
victualling the Civil and Military, Prisoners and others who
receive their Rations from the Public Stores, and find that at
least Ten Thousand Bushels of Wheat at 14s. 9d. and Twenty

1807.
1 Feb.

Commissary
Palmer's
statement of
the probable
expenditure.

Thousand Bushels of Maize at Six Shillings which is the least price the Grain can possibly be procured at this Year, and for which purpose there will be a necessity of drawing Bills on His Majesty's Treasury for about the Sum of Twelve Thousand pounds, which, with the Grain we may expect to receive in payment of the Government Debts, will be sufficient for the consumption of Grain for the Current Year; but in the event of the arrival of the Sydney not more than half the quantity of the above mentioned Grain will be required, consequently only half of the above Sum will be wanted, yet I must observe that the Sum of Eight Thousand Nine hundred Pounds will be required to be drawn for, for the purpose of paying for the Four hundred Tons of Rice at Twenty Pounds p. Ton and the Fifteen Tons of Sugar at £60 p. Ton contracted for by Order of Governor King.   I have, &c.,

JOHN PALMER, Commiss'y.

GOVERNOR BLIGH TO THE RIGHT HON. WILLIAM WINDHAM.

(Despatch No. 7, per H.M.S. Buffalo; acknowledged by Viscount Castlereagh, 31st December, 1807.)

Sir,   Sydney, New South Wales, 1st February, 1807.

Reports from
the settlement
at Hobart.
I have the honor to inclose a Copy of Lieutenant Colonel Collins's Letter to me of the 18th October last, with a Statement of the Settlement under his Command.

I have, &c.,
WM. BLIGH.

[Enclosures.]

[*A copy of Lieutenant-Governor Collins' despatch, dated 18th October, 1806, with a general statement of the inhabitants, provisions in store and return of quarterly employment at Hobart, will be found in volume I, series III.*]

GOVERNOR BLIGH TO THE RIGHT HON. WILLIAM WINDHAM.

(Despatch No. 8, per H.M.S. Buffalo; acknowledged by Viscount Castlereagh, 31st December, 1807.)

Sir,   Sydney, New South Wales, 1st February, 1807.

Shipping
returns.
I beg leave to inclose Reports of the Entries and Clearances of Vessels in and from Port Jackson between the 12th of August 1806 and the 31st of December following.

I have, &c.,
WM. BLIGH.

SHIPPING RETURN.

A LIST of Ships and Vessels which have Entered Inwards in the Harbour of Port Jackson, in His Majesty's Territory of New South Wales, Between the 12th Day of August, 1806, and the 31st Day of December following, With the particular Quantity and Quality of the lading of each Vessel.

Time of Entry.	Vessel's Name.	Master's Name.	Number of			Where and when registered.	Where and when built.	Owner's Name.	General Cargo.	From Whence.
			Tons	Guns	Men					
1806.										
20 Aug.	Albion	C. Richardson	362	10	24	Deptford	London	Wilson, Campbell, & Co.	See Appendix A	England.
21 ,,	Alexander	R'd Brooks	278	12	24	Quebec	London	John Locke	Do Do B	Do.
21 Sept.	Arzo	J'n Baden	221	18	26	Foreign	London	Hulletts & Co.	58 Ton Sperm Oil	Coast.
1 Oct.	Aurora	A. Meryck	302	6	25	Metford	Biddeford	D. Sterbeck	44 Do Do 500 S. Skins	Do.
26 ,,	Santa Anna	C. Men	260		14			Prize to the Port a't Bennett — R't Owner.	See Appendix C	Taken, 20 of June, 1806, off St. Bhas.
7 Nov.	Atlanti?	W'm Swain	223	2	22	Prize	London, 1805	Messrs. Enderby	756 Barrels Sperm Oil	Coast.
2 Dec.	King George	W'm ?ly	185		24	Syd.,N.S.W.	Syd., NW	Lord & Co.	55 Ton black Oil, 3,000 S. Skins.	South'd.
4 ,,	Argo	J. Bader	221	18	26	Foreign	London	Hulletts & Co.	90 Ton Sperm Oil	Coast.
29 ,,	Star	J. Wilkinson	119	6	16	Calcutta	?don		14,000 Seal Skins	South'd Islands.

J. HARRIS, Naval Officer.

APPENDIX.

A.—General ?go of the Ship *Albion*: 50 Ton of Salt. 56 Firkins Butter. 80 Boxes ?e. 2 Pnch'n Hams. 60 H'hds Porter. 54 Casks ?d do. 36 and h'lf Chests P. Wine. 17 Do. Sherry. 70 ?es Hollands. 42 Do. Brandy. 9 Do. Cherry. 8 Punch. J. Rum. 6 Do. F. Brandy. 1 Do. Hollds. 17 Crates, 26 Casks Bottles. 4 ?es Stationary. 21 Trunks, 2 Cases, 2 Boxes Haberdashery. 16 Bales and 1 Cask Slops. 15 Boxes and 2 ?ks Hatts. 13 Trunks 2 Casks Shoes. 2 ?es Perfumery. 3 ?es 2 ?ks Sadlery. 5 Casks and 4 Bundles ?ny Ware. 300 Boxes Soap. 9 Boxes ?o Pipes. 25 ?ks Nails. 8 ?ks, 1 Case and 3 ? ?bes Ironmongery. 250 Iron Pots. 8 ?bes roll'd Iron. 30 ? ?bes Iron Hoops. 1 Cask Rivets. 18 ? ?bes Spades. 3 Anvils. 3 Boxes Tin Plates. 6 ?ts Lead. 6 Casks Shot. 2 ?es ?den Pipes. 478 Bars Iron. 3 Anchors. 2 Grapnalls. 3 Casks Paint. 1 Do. Lamp Black. 40 Jars Oil. 26 Kegs Varnish. 6 Cables. 3 Hawsers. 58 ?l Cordage. 3 Casks Line and ?e.

B.—General Cargo of the Ship *Alexander*: 1 Trunk Boots and Shoes. 1 Case Gamblets. 1 Trunk Hosiery. 1 Bale Flannels. 2 Do. Blankets. 3 bales Hardware. 4 Gen. Tool Chests. 8 ?es Cordials. 20 Bolts Canvas. 5 Coil Cordage. 8 ? ?lls ?h and Tar. 40 Cheese. 60 rolls ?o. 50 bags Sugar. 10 bags Coffee. 192 Gall. Rum. 2 H'hds Brandy. 44 Pigs Lead. 12 Do. Sheet Lead. 2 Casks Shot. 40 Bundles Iron Hoops. 40 Gall. Wine.

C.—General Cargo of the Ship *St. Anna*: 303 Boxes ?h. 1,341 Hides Tar. 145 Cedar Planks. 112 Small Do. 48 ?ger Do. 282 pt. Brazil Wood. 375 Stones. 688 Small Do. for Ballast. 54 Hides. Tallow. 3 Packages con'g earthenware Funnels. 2 Boxes Soap. 13 ps. Strip'd Cotton. 24 ?ls.

J. HARRIS, Naval

1807.
1 Feb.

Returns of shipping.

1807.
1 Feb.

Returns of
shipping.

SHIPPING RETURN.

A List of Ships and Vessels which have cleared Outwards from the Harbour of Port Jackson, in His Majesty's territory of New South Wales, between the 12th day of August, 1806, and the 31st day of December following, with the lading of each vessel.

Time of entry.	Vessel's name.	Master's Name.	Tons.	Guns.	Men.	Where and when built.	Where and when registered.	Owner's name.	General Cargo.	Whither bound.	Where bond given.
17 Aug.	Brothers	B. W.h	256	..	20	Nantucket	Nantucket	Obh. Mitchell	700 barrels sperm oil	Coast	Sydney.
21 ,,	Fortune	Hy. M.re	622	20	41	Prize	London	Mestier & Co.	60 tons of coals, 86 pigs of ore, me spars	Bengal	,,
22 ,,	Vulture	Thos. Folger	312	14	30	,,	,,	Mather & Co.	500 barrels sperm oil	Coast	,,
4 Sept.	Britannia	A. Hussey	290	10	27	London	,,	T. Hill	200 tons sperm oil	England	,,
8 ,,	R'd and Mary	Jas. u.as	215	10	24	Dartmouth	,,	Spencer & Co.	Do ,, ,,	Coast	,,
20 ,,	King George	W. Mdy	185	..	24	Sydney	Sydney	Lord & Co.	Ballast	Fishing	,,
29 ,,	.go	J. Baden	221	18	26	..	London	Hulletts & Co.	58 tons sperm oil	..	,,
5 G.	Sinclair	J. H. .ton	610	14	50	.th of England	Hull	Wm. Osbourne	60 tons coals, 3,000 ft. oak.	China	,,
5 ,,	Sophia	Jn. .r	250	..	20	Bordeaux	Prize	Campbell & Co.	Ballast	England	,,
12 ,,	.lon	C. Richardson	362	10	24	.rd	London	,,	,,	Whaling	,,
14 ,,	Elizabeth	E. Bunker	238	2	17	Prize	,,	,,	,,	,,	,,
24 ,,	Aurora	A. Meryck	302	2	26	Mrd	Biddeford	D. Sterbeck	44 tons sperm oil, 500 seal skins	,,	,,
—Nov.	Alexander	Rd. Brooks	278	12	24	.Qec	London	John Locke		England	,,
2 Dec.	Atlantic	Wm. Swain	223	2	22	....	,,	Enderby & Co.	750 barrels sperm oil	Whaling	,,

J. HARRIS, Naval Officer.

1807.
1 Feb.

GOVERNOR BLIGH TO THE RIGHT HON. WILLIAM WINDHAM.

(Despatch No. 9, per H.M.S. Buffalo; acknowledged by Viscount
    Castlereagh, 31st December, 1807.)

Sir,   Government House, Sydney, 1st Feby., 1807.

I beg leave to inclose from Mr. Jamison principal Surgeon Requisition
of the Colony, a demand for Medicines and Surgical Instruments for surgical
which are much wanted; with respect to his other papers I have instruments.
not yet been able to satisfy myself in the propriety of them,
very few Sick having been in the Hospital, but more able Assistants are certainly required.

I have, &c.,
WM. BLIGH.

[Enclosure No. 1.]

SURGEON JAMISON'S RETURN OF THE MEDICAL ESTABLISHMENT.

A LIST of the Medical Gentlemen in the Colony of New South Surgeon
    Wales, with the respective Stations where they are doing report on
    Duty.   the medical
                                                             staff.

Thos. Jamison Esqr. ...	Principal Surgeon Sydney.
Mr. Jas. Thompson	First Assistant, on leave of Absence Mr. Chas. Throsby doing his duty at Kingston, Hunter's River, a distant Settlement.
Mr. D. Wentworth	Second Assistant, at Parramatta.
Mr. Jas. Mileham	Third Assistant, at do.
Mr. John Savage	Fourth Assistant, In Europe under sentence of a Court Martial.
Mr. Jacob Mountgarrett	Acting Assistant Surgeon, Port Dalrymple.
Mr. Jas. Luttrell	do. Sydney.
„ Conolan	do. Norfolk Island.
„ Thos. Arndell	do. Hawkesbury, a Settlement which extends Seventy Miles on the Banks of the River.

Being a Stranger to the intentions of His Majesty's Ministers,
I most humbly beg leave to observe that my motives for making
the present representations are that no blame may be attached
to me hereafter, and here I have to remark that Five of the
Medical Gentlemen now doing duty in this Colony and its
Dependencies are only Acting; should they resign their Colonial
Appointments and retire, as they have not been confirmed, what
will be the situation of those Settlements where they are doing
duty; exclusive of this evil there are Settlements at this moment
destitute of a resident Assistant Surgeon; in my former Letter
I have only wrote for Six additional Assistants, and they would
then have more patients to attend to than any other description

of Surgeons in His Majesty's Service, either by Sea, or Land, after this official communication, I trust no reprehensibility will be attached to him who has the Honor to be with greatest respect, &c.,

THOS. JAMISON,
Sydney, Octr. 20th, 1806.   Principal Surgeon.

[Enclosure No. 2.]
SURGEON JAMISON TO GOVERNOR BLIGH.

Sir,   Sydney, 21st Jany., 1807.

In reply to Your Excellency's Letter of this date, I beg leave to inform you that I wrote for Six additional Assistant Surgeons, but as I am an entire stranger to the intentions of His Majesty's Ministers respecting this Colony, I beg to state for their information that there are three Gentlemen now Acting at remote Settlements, if they are confirmed, and Two others appointed in the room of Messrs. Thompson and Savage (provided those Gentlemen are not returning to this Colony, the former's leave of Absence having a considerable time elapsed). I conceive that Number will be sufficient to discharge the Medical duty of this Colony for the present, at the same time I have to request you will be pleased to transmit my former Letter to His Majesty's Principal Secretary of State for the Colonies Abroad as it contains regulations which I have proposed for the General Hospital—should they meet your approbation I would thank you to give them the Necessary support.

I have, &c.,
THOS. JAMISON,
Principal Surgeon to the Colony.

[Enclosure No. 3.]

[This letter, dated 6th May, 1805, was a duplicate of that transmitted by Governor King in a despatch to under secretary Cooke, dated 22nd May, 1805.]

[Enclosure No. 4.]
SURGEON JAMISON TO GOVERNOR KING.

Sir,   Sydney, May 2nd, 1805.

I beg leave to state to Your Excellency that the Chirurgical Instruments formerly sent out to this Colony, many of them are worn out and otherwise necessarily expended, which renders a further supply necessary. Three Capital sets of Amputating and Trepanning will I conceive be sufficient for the present, and Six complete Setts of Midwifery Instruments, which I wish on the most approved construction; they are very materially wanted, having only one Set in my possession, and none to supply the Out Settlements with.

1807.
1 Feb.

Requisition
for surgical
instruments.

I have, &c.,
Thos. Jamison,
Principal Surgeon.

Appd.—Wm. Bligh.

[Enclosure No. 5.]

Surgeon Jamison to Governor Bligh.

Sir, Sydney, 1st Feby., 1807.

It is with much concern, I state to Your Excellency the distressed state of the General Hospital for want of many essential Medicines, and here it may be necessary to remark, that the Colony requires a much greater supply at the present period than what it formerly did, the Number of Inhabitants at the different Settlements are between Eight and Nine Thousand, and those Settlements are chiefly supplied from hence, which greatly increases the expenditure of Medicine at the General Hospital.

Requisition
for supplies
of medicines.

In February, 1804, I made an Official representation to Governor King, wherein I stated that the Medicines for the use of the Colony were nearly expended, of the esentials there was a material deficience, that a general supply could only obviate the evils that must insue from want of the above Necessary resources, requesting an Official communication of the purport of my Letter to His Majesty's Minister, which would doubtless lead to a removal of the embarrassments I then felt in the discharge of the duties of a Situation, which it was my first ambition to discharge with satisfaction to others and credit to myself.

Since that period no general Supply has been received, a few Medicines came in the William Pitt, they were deficient in quantity as well as of many esential Medicines; under those circumstances, I again feel myself compelled to represent that a great want of almost every kind of Medicines still exists, and I most respectfully beg leave to point out the Absolute necessity of a general Supply, but in order to prevent Government incurring any unnecessary expence by sending out Medicines that are not wanted, I herewith enclose a Schedule of those that are absolutely required, with the quantities I wish of each attached thereto.

Should this measure meet Your Excellency's Approbation, I trust your Official Communication of the tendence of this Letter to His Majesty's Secretary of State for the Colonies will effectually remove the embarrassments I have hitherto so justly complained of.

I have, &c.,
THOS. JAMISON,
Principal Surgeon.

Approved:—WM. BLIGH.

[Enclosure No. 6.]

SURGEON JAMISON TO GOVERNOR BLIGH.

Sir,   Sydney, 1st November, 1806.

On my personal application to Your Excellency for leave to return to Europe, you informed me that it would be necessary to obtain leave from His Majesty's Ministers, I have therefore to request you would be pleased to lay my application for that purpose before the Principal Secretary of State for the Colonies Abroad.

I beg leave to state for the information of His Majesty's Ministers that I have served His Majesty upwards of Twenty Six Years, constantly in actual Service, Eight Years of the above period I served in the Royal Navy, and I have served in this Colony since its first establishment: during the whole of that time I only once applied for leave of Absence.

The dispersed state of my Family and my anxiety of having them under my own protection in this Country, where I am endeavouring to provide a comfortable maintenance for their future support, renders me truly solicitous to obtain leave of Absence to return to Europe for the sole purpose of collecting my scattered Family, and returning hither with them immediately.

In order to prevent any inconveniency arising to the Settlement for the want of Medical Assistance, I will if permitted find a substitute ere I leave the Colony to do my duty during my absence, as this has been permitted in more instances than one I trust there will be no objections made to this.

I have, &c.,
THOS. JAMISON,
Principal Surgeon.

Approved when fit Persons are sent out to hold his Place:
WM. BLIGH.

GOVERNOR BLIGH TO THE RIGHT HON. WILLIAM WINDHAM.

(Despatch No. 5, per H.M.S. Buffalo; acknowledged by Viscount Castlereagh, 31st December, 1807.)

Government House, Sydney,
Sir,   New South Wales, 4th February, 1807.

I have the honor to inclose for your information, a letter *Necessity for the return of* from Lieutenant Colonel Paterson requesting that the Officers *officers on* of the New South Wales Corps who are in England may be *leave, and an augmentation* directed to join their Regiment, and likewise that it may be *of the N.S.W.* augmented in the number of Privates—to this letter I beg leave *Corps.* to draw your attention and to the Returns made to the Secretary of War, the application appearing to me extremely necessary. I also inclose the Lieutenant Colonel's demand for Stationary.

I have, &c.,
WM. BLIGH.

[Enclosure No. 1.]

LIEUTENANT-GOVERNOR PATERSON TO GOVERNOR BLIGH.

Sir,   Sydney, 1st February, 1807.

From the great deficiency at present of Officers for the *Officers on* various duties imposed on the New South Wales Corps under *leave to return.* my Command and the very inadequate number of the Corps in general to perform the Common routine of Duty at Head Quarters and the detached Settlements and outposts, I feel myself bound in duty to request Your Excellency will be pleased to signify in your Official Letter to the Right Honorable the Secretary of State the necessity there exists of an Augmentation to the Military Force of this Colony, and that the Officers belonging to the Regiment in England may be ordered to join. I must *Request for* acquaint Your Excellency that by Letter, dated the 9th of Augt., *an increase in the N.S.W.* 1804, I represented to His Royal Highness the Commander in *Corps.* Chief the inability of the Corps to discharge the various duties to which the situation of this Colony calls His Majesty's Forces, and had His Royal Highness's Answer that an Augmentation should be considered of as early as possible, but that not having taken place except by the Old Men sent out to the Corps from the Royal Veteran Battalion and who are totally unfit for duty in this Colony, I trust I may be excused now urging it again, as highly Conducive to His Majesty's Service.

I have, &c.,
WM. PATERSON,
Lt. Col., N. S. Wales Corps.

1807.
4 Feb.

[Enclosure No. 2.]

LIEUTENANT-GOVERNOR PATERSON TO GOVERNOR BLIGH.

Paterson's
requisition for
stationery.

Sir,   Sydney, 1st Feby., 1807.

As I have not been allowed any Stationary since I took the Command at Port Dalrymple, and as I have been under the necessity of Supplying the Deputy Commissary etc. with that Article, I trust your Excellency will have the goodness to recommend that an adequate supply may be furnished me Annually, or an allowance made me to defray the expence, as well as that which I have already incurred, and which I can but ill afford out of my Salary as Lieut. Governor.

I have, &c.,
WM. PATERSON.

GOVERNOR BLIGH TO THE RIGHT HON. WILLIAM WINDHAM.

(General despatch, per H.M.S. Buffalo; acknowledged by Viscount Castlereagh, 31st December, 1807.)

Government House, Sydney, New South Wales,

7 Feb.   Sir,   7th February, 1807.

I have now the honor to communicate to you the state of this Colony, in addition to my former Despatches in November

Report on the
wheat harvest.

last by the Alexander, since which the Wheat Harvest has been got in, and by a laborious personal examination I have ascertained its produce to be extremely short of what it was first expected. This, together with the Inundation, may be attributed to the Seed last Season being very much damaged by the Moth, to the probability that a part of the Seed which was sown did not vegetate, to the Seed being very scarce (whereby many of the Settlers did not sow much more than half the quantity they would have done on an Acre), and to the Season being wet, so that the Seed in many places rotted in the Ground; these calamitous circumstances are severely felt, and would be alarming but

The maize
harvest.

for the Harvest of Maize, which is now coming on, and will be productive if no Floods take place before it is gathered; nevertheless, both Wheat and Maize will be very scanty to provide Seed and Food until next Year, the smallness of the Maize Crop being owing to there not having been sufficient to Crop the ground.

The wheat
crop.

There were 5,046 Acres of Wheat sown, and its produce I calculate to be 53,198 Bushels, which is ten Bushels per Acre, from whence, deducting 12,000 Bushels for Seed, there remains 41,198 for consumption.

There were 3,120 Acres of Maize planted, which may produce
59,475 Bushels at twenty Bushels per Acre, from whence, deducting 500 Bushels for Seed, there remains 58,975 Bushels for
consumption.

The Wheat and Maize added together make 190,173 Bushels,
which for 8,000 souls gives 13 lbs. per Week for each Person;
this is very little when we consider that the great scarcity of
animal food will cause a greater consumption of Grain, and the
inconsiderate Settlers will use more than is really necessary;
besides what may be wanted for the Shipping and the feeding
of Swine, Poultry, and Cattle, which is the support of the
greatest part of the people. There is no immediate relief to be
expected, except the arrival of the Sydney with four hundred
Tons of Rice, which Governor King sent for last April, and we
are hourly expecting; but Mr. Campbell, a Merchant here, has
my permission to send a Brig to China, by which I hope to have
a small supply of Rice (about Eighty Tons) in the course of
eight months. To enter into farther means to get relief would
not be wise, as it cannot be here in time. We must therefore
struggle through until next Harvest, which will teach the Settlers to be more provident and industrious than by any
admonition whatever; considerable importation would lead to
great indifference, as it would reduce the price of Grain, and
not make it worth their while to grow it; but when they begin
to find a regular market for their Grain, agriculture will be the
chief pursuit both here and at the out-Settlements.

The Harvest thus unproductive has its other consequent evils;
the settler is slow in bringing the Grain to Sale and extravagant
in his Price, which some designing Men are underhand encouraging. I have fixed 14s. 9d. per Bushel as Government
price to those who will supply us, and 15s. for such Wheat as may
be returned into Store as payment for Government Debts; and
have offered Cattle in exchange for Wheat, and am adopting such
means as may be a farther security to our getting a sufficiency
for the consumption of the Persons under Government; but such
a distressed state have I found the Colony in that we are obliged
to get Grain how we can for present use and at a high Price,
having not above 1,200 Bushels unthreshed at Government Farm,
which must be reserved to the last; at present I am sorry to
observe that the little Wheat which is brought to market sells
from 20s. to 24s. per Bushel, but which I hope, when the Settlers
generally begin to thresh, and the Maize Harvest comes in, will
be reduced to the Price which we have offered, and according to
a promise they have made, we shall be better supplied.

1807.
7 Feb.
———
Supplies for the
settlements at
Port Dalrymple
and Hobart.

By the Returns it will be seen that the Derwent and Port Dalrymple were without Grain, but their Crops of Wheat by the accounts I have received were promising and must be now reaped, their wants are for the present relieved, and we are preparing to send Port Dalrymple the further Supplies I have in my power to do, and which could not be done before, because we had not a grain of Wheat to send them, and they will still be in great want if the Supplies already demanded from England by Governor King do not arrive in time.

Condition of
the cattle.

Our Stock of Horned Cattle are doing extremely well, and will in time secure the Country against all want of that kind of Food, and I shall endeavour to increase it by taking, if practicable, some of the Wild Cattle which I have seen in the Cow Pastures.

These fine Animals are increasing fast, and will Stock the country if they are kept free of any molestation by private individuals settling where they are, at present computed to be about Four Thousand; but I think the number overrated. I am given to understand that it was Government's intention they should be undisturbed, and the principle was acted upon

Land grants
at the
Cowpastures.

until Mr. McArthur, in 1805, came from England with an order to occupy Land in the range of those Animals, which Governor King allowed him to do, under some agreement that my Lord Camden was to decide whether he was to remain there, or receive another allotment of Land as an equivalent; on this subject I beg leave, Sir, to refer to Governor King, who can point out, as he has done to me, the bad consequences which will attend giving Grants of Land in that neighbourhood, on the West side of the Nepean, and which he thinks has been done through some miscomprehension of its consequence to the increase of the Wild Herds, connected with the breeding of Sheep, while there is abundance of Land on this side the River, which is very eligible, unless the occupancy was equally allowable to all.

The pastoral
industry.

The Sheep in time will increase in number and quality, both in Carcass and in the Fleece; but the latter is not an object which every one can yet entirely attend to. Herdsmen are scarce, and if a few Individuals were to have all the Servants they pretend should be allowed them to this pursuit, the Agriculturist would want his Labourer, and the Inhabitants Grain for their common consumption.

In general, Animal Food is a greater object to the proprietors of Sheep than the Fleece, as there is an immediate demand for it. When there were a few Thousand Sheep, a more particular attention could be paid to them, and they doubled their numbers in two Years and an Half; but now, being increased to Twenty Thousand and upwards, and not having equal means to take care of them, the increase is not so great, as may be seen by the Returns.

Our utmost exertions must likewise be to Agriculture to supply the Shipping, and the collateral advantages of a Wool Trade will then be supported by competent means.

When my observations on this Country are more matured, I shall think it my duty to submit them to you, Sir; but in the meantime, I take the liberty to recommend the Reverend Mr. Marsden, who now goes Home in the Buffalo, as a Person who can give a proper and just Idea of its Nature and Soil, and any general information, should you require it, having made it his particular study.

It may be proper for me now to inform you, Sir, that besides all the attention which is required to the encouragement of agricultural pursuits and protection of the out-Settlements, there is much for me to do in the Police of the Country (Magistracy not being arrived to that dignity which it should be); in its state of Defence; in repairs and completion of the Public Works and Churches—as stated in the Returns; in regulating Private Buildings and Schools in the Towns; and the watching over the rising generation and impressing upon their minds, by instruction, what has been entirely neglected by their Parents in Moral and Christian Duties; but there are a vast number who have no Parents, the Mothers being dead and their Fathers having left the Country as either Sailors, Soldiers, or Prisoners who became free.

In no Country could there occur more obstacles in gaining these ends, for besides the natural habits of the Prisoner tending to obstruct every attempt, the Settlers are by no means of that character which teaches industry and good-will.

But under all these disadvantages I have the fullest confidence of being able to produce, in due time, some change for the better, and see the Colony assume a more chearing aspect than it does at present.

The Inhabitants are healthy and Marriages increase; in my late Surveys I ascertained the Married Women were 395; Legitimate Children, 807; Natural Children, 1,025.

By my Instructions I am commanded to account for the allowance which has been granted to the Commissary-General of 15 p. cent. that he has hitherto received on the Sale of Articles for

1807.
7 Feb.

Barter; and in answer to which I beg leave to refer to Governor King's and the Commissary's answers thereon, which accompany this despatch, whereby it appears the Per Centage was to the Naval Officer on Monies he received for certain Duties levied for the Orphan School and Gaol Funds.

The spirit traffic.

It is also recommended to me to persevere in the system laid down by Governor King of a rigorous prohibition of any quantity of Spirits without a licence from me for that purpose. This I shall rigidly attend to; it has been a great evil in this Country; but its being used by way of barter has added to its pernicious effects more than by the quantity imported beyond all conception.

The regulation respecting Spirits has been by permits from the Governor to Individuals to receive certain quantities when a Ship arrived, at the market price (about 8 or 9 Shillings p'r Gallon), and allowed to be bartered away at 20s. p'r Gallon by General Orders; but such various ways are adopted that the holder enhances its value from three to five pounds, and even eight has been given by unfortunate People who will not do without it.

The disadvantage of payments in rum.

A Sawyer will cut one hundred feet of Timber for a Bottle of Spirits—value two shillings and sixpence—which he drinks in a few hours; when for the same labour he would charge two Bushels of Wheat, which would furnish Bread for him for two Months; hence those who have got no Liquor to pay their Labourers with are ruined by paying more than they can possibly afford for any kind of labour which they are compelled to hire Men to execute, while those who have Liquor gain an immense advantage.

Bartering of spirits for grain.

At Harvest, or shortly after, those who have got Spirits go or send their Agents to purchase Wheat, and frequently take from the thoughtless Settler two and three Bushels of Wheat for a Bottle of Spirits (which cost the Proprietor only half a Crown), and in the same proportion for any part of his Stock.

On this account principally it is that the Farmers are involved in Debt, and either ruined by the high price of Spirits, or the high price of Labour, which is regulated thereby; while the unprincipled holder of Spirits gets his work done at a cheap rate and amasses considerable property.

A Settler has been known often to give an Acre of Wheat for two Gallons of Spirits, to satisfy his labourer, or for his own use, which would maintain him a whole Year.

These are but few of the evils attending this pernicious Traffic, nevertheless the barter of Spirits has its Advocates; but only those plead in its favor who are ignorant of its effects, or those very few who have imported a large quantity and gain immensely by it.

I have considered this Spirit business in all its bearings, and am come to a determination to prohibit the barter being carried on in any way whatever; it is absolutely necessary to be done to bring labour to a due value and support the farming interest. The importation which has been allowed will be continued, but not in a greater quantity, however less I may reduce it; thus, while the value of the commodity is reduced to a proper standard, the consumption will not be increased, no evil having happened from that cause, but from the limited use of it, by barter. The Licenses for Public-Houses are the same number they have hitherto been, but under certain restrictions and penalties, which will go so far as is practicable to support my intended purpose.

In addition to the reasons already given to prohibit the barter of Spirits, is the strong temptation it holds out to the Settlers and other Inhabitants to erect private Stills, which tend to destroy not only the Grain but the industry and morals of the People. The practice of distillation has been so general that the late Governor found it necessary to prohibit it under certain fines and penalties, and to offer Emancipations, free Pardons, and pecuniary remunerations to those who would give information of Persons employed in this ruinous Work; but the effect has not yet been produced, as this practice still continues in violation of every order and vigilance of the Police. I am aware that prohibiting the barter of Spirits will meet with the marked opposition of those few who have so materially enriched themselves by it.

The part of my Instructions directing my attention to the moral and religious education of the Colony is peculiarly the object of my attention, and everything shall be done for the education of the Children.

We have now all our Artificers employed building the Church of Sydney, which I hope will be completed, or nearly so, in six Months.

The Church at Parramatta will then be our next object, which has been left unfinished to the present day, not a Pew being in it; it will take about five or six months to complete it.

At the Hawkesbury we have turned a large Building into a Church, which will be fitted up while we are proceeding with the others.

The Reverend Mr. Marsden has had no Person to assist him for the last six Years, until just before I arrived, when a Mr. Fulton returned from Norfolk Island to do the duty while he is absent; this Gentleman had the misfortune to be sent to this Country from Ireland in 1798, and since emancipated by Governor King, but holds no Commission; he has done the duty of a Clergyman

1807.
7 Feb.
Prohibition of the bartering of spirits.

Evils of illicit distillation.

Erection of the church at Sydney;

at Parramatta.

Temporary church at the Hawkesbury.

Employment of the Rev. H. Fulton.

1807.
7 Feb.

at Norfolk Island by order of Governor King; his character has been like a moral, good Man, becoming his situation, and has a Wife and three Children.

Necessity for
additional
clergy.

Under this consideration, there will be wanted a Clergyman for Parramatta, the Settlement at the Hawkesbury, Port Dalrymple, and Norfolk Island, if Mr. Fulton should not be continued in his situation.

It will be of great importance that the Clergymen who may be appointed should be married Men.

School teachers
wanted.

With respect to the education of Youth, four respectable Men are wanted for the benefit of the rising generation—these also should be married Men—and a Man and his Wife are necessary for the Orphan School.

Education of
the children.

At present we are doing all in our power to educate the Children, having nearly four hundred of them under tuition in the different parts of the Colony; and I shall use such remuneration to School Masters and Mistresses as will fulfil His Most Gracious Majesty's directions.

Returns and
requisitions
transmitted.

I now forward* by conveyance of the Buffalo, in which Governor King takes his departure, a General Statement of the Inhabitants in the different Settlements under my Government, with an estimate of the time the Provisions remaining at each will last, taken on the 31st December; Abstracts of the Remains and Demands for Provisions, also of Annual and Extra Supplies, and that of Stationary for the use of the Public Offices, of which we are in very great want.

I beg leave farther to state that the Commissary is making up his Accounts to the 31st December last, which will be forwarded by the earliest opportunity.

Returns to be
forwarded
annually.

Governor King has hitherto sent Home every six Months an Abstract of the Receipt and Expenditure of Provisions, Stores, and Annual Supplies; but, from the great increase of business in the Commissary's Department, and the considerable trouble it gives the Governor, and takes him from very momentous concerns of the Colony, I hope my sending them home Yearly will be deemed sufficient: the General State of the Settlements will be sent by every opportunity that offers, and every detail connected therewith.

Captain Short, Commander of His Majesty's Ship Porpoise, being sent home on Charges preferred against him by his Officers

Short's
application for
a land grant.

and he against them, I beg leave to refer you, Sir, to my separate Letter† sent in this despatch concerning his application to me for a Grant of six hundred Acres of Land, and my reasons for refusing him.

* Note 24.   † Note 25.

Lieutenant Colonel Paterson having represented to me the necessity of the Officers of the New South Wales Corps who are in England speedily joining, and of a farther increase to the number of Privates in the Regiment, I beg leave to draw your attention to his Letter* which is sent herewith, as I hope it will meet with your approbation, the Statements of the Corps being sent to the Secretary at War up to this date.

1807.
7 Feb.

The New South
Wales Corps.

In consequence of orders which Colonel Paterson received from His Royal Highness the Commander-in-Chief to send Mr. Cox, the Paymaster of the Corps, home for malversation, he left his Government in tranquillity with Captain Kemp, but he now returns in the Estramina Colonial Schooner, and Mr. Cox in the Buffalo, to answer such Charges as will be brought against him.†

Paymaster Cox
ordered to
England.

I have to apologise for having omitted to state in its proper place that the Commissary computes (in his Letter‡ of this date which accompanies this despatch) there may be a necessity to draw Bills to the amount of twelve thousand pounds for Grain during the present Year; but my attention will be so much to lessen every expence, that nothing but the utmost necessity will force me to draw Bills to such an Amount.

Expenditure
anticipated
by the
commissary.

With the documents already referred to I have the honour to transmit a copy of Lieutenant-Colonel Collins's Letter to me of the 18th October last, with a Statement of the Settlement under his command. An Account of the Entrances and Clearances of Vessels at this place, a Demand from the Colonial Surgeon for Medicines and Surgeon's Instruments, A request from the Judge Advocate to be supplied with the late Statutes§ And a Packet of the *Sydney Gazettes* up to the 1st Instant.

Returns
transmitted.

I reflect with regret that my former dispatches must have occasioned daily expectation of the Buffalo's arrival; but to procure those necessaries she required, as well as the propriety of not sailing till the state of the Country could be known after the Harvest, has delayed her.

Reasons for the
delay in the
sailing of
H.M.S.
Buffalo.

To Governor King I beg leave to refer further information, And have, &c.,

WM. BLIGH.

GOVERNOR BLIGH TO THE RIGHT HON. WILLIAM WINDHAM.

(Despatch per whaler Star.)

Government House, Sydney, New South Wales,
Sir,   19th March, 1807.

19 Mar.

The opportunity, which now offers to enable me to have the honor of communicating with you, is so indirect, and likely

* Note 26.   † Note 27.   ‡ Note 28.   § Note 29.

1807.
19 Mar.

to be so long before the Ship arrives in England, that it induces
me to wait until a more favorable one occurs to transmit to you
duplicates of the Despatches I sent home by the Buffalo, under
the care of Governor King on the 10th of last Month.

Arrival of the
General
Wellesley.

Three days after Governor King sailed, a Ship called the
Wellesly arrived from Prince of Wales's Island with Wheat and
Rice, and has been a serviceable supply. She came here in con-
sequence of the Sydney being lost,* the Ship which Governor
King had sent after the Inundation for Rice to India, and
hearing of the distresses the Colony was in.

Supplies sent
to out-
settlements.

A part of this Supply I have sent to the Derwent, some to Port
Dalrymple, and likewise to Norfolk Island, where also there was
a necessity to send some relief.

Loss of the
Tellicherry.

The Tellicherry, another Ship which sailed about the time the
Sydney did, is also lost*; so that the despatches sent by Governor
King in these Ships will, in all probability, be not forthcoming,
and will render it necessary he should present Copies of them.

Prospects of
the maize
harvest.

I have great satisfaction by informing you that our Maize
Harvest promises to turn out tolerably well; and that the spirits
of the Settlers are great in preparing the Ground for next Year's
Crop. In general, we are improving, and have every hope we

Proposed
insurrection
of convicts.

shall do well, notwithstanding a late attempt to insurrection,
which has been preparing for eighteen Months past, and was to
have been put into execution the day before I arrived, but was
prevented by my appearance off the Coast, and of which Governor
King had an alarm.

No Arms have been found, or any positive overt act been committed, our information leading only to declared plans which
were to be put into execution by the Irish Convicts, headed by
O'Dwyer and some of the Irish State Prisoners, as they are here
called.

It appears that, in order to avoid detection, they determined to
rest their success on seizing the Arms of the loyal Inhabitants;
and in order to effect this, the Irish Servants of the Inhabitants
were on a certain time fixed to massacre their respective Masters,
and the principal Persons of the Colony, and then to possess
themselves of their Arms.

Arrest of the
ringleaders.

Of this determination I continued to have proofs more or less,
when I determined on seizing the Persons represented as the
Ring-leaders, and effected my purpose. O'Dwyer I have put on
board the Porpoise. Byrn, Burke, and some others are in Jail
for Trial, and will be brought forward as soon as our Evidences
are all arranged and prepared.

* Note 30.

1807.
19 Mar.

Under this revolting principle, which has been so long nour- ished and continues to show itself, I must beg leave, Sir, to draw your attention to the state of the New South Wales Corps, which I recommend in the strongest manner to be strengthened accord- ing to Lieutenant-Colonel Paterson's Letter here inclosed, as the distribution of these soldiers are absolutely necessary to keep peace and order; I transmit also an account of how they are disposed of, and request the Officers who are absent may be ordered to join immediately.

The necessity for augmentation of the New South Wales Corps.

It will be of great advantage to have Iron Carriages sent out for the Guns, as specified in former Demands, for besides the wooden ones soon perishing, the Artificers under the Sentence of the Law are now so few that we cannot for some time repair the public works, as, they have been left to go so much to decay. The State of the Ordnance I have the honor to inclose herewith.

Advantages of iron gun carriages.

The Demands sent Home by the Alexander and Buffalo are very necessary, and we are particularly in want of writing Paper, of which there is a great scarcity.

Inclosed are *Gazettes* from the 15th of February to the 15th Instant. I have, &c.,

WM. BLIGH.

[Enclosure No. 1.]

LIEUTENANT-COLONEL PATERSON TO GOVERNOR BLIGH.

Sir, Sydney, 16th March, 1807.

Being now on the Eve of my departure for Port Dal- rymple, I conceive it my Duty, as Commanding Officer of the New South Wales Corps, to mention to Your Excellency the Insufficiency of our Military Forces in this Colony as well as its Dependencies, as stated in my Letter dated the 14th of last February.*

Insufficiency of military forces.

From the very recent alarming Circumstances that have occurred here, I am confident You will see the propriety of this Representation and Your Excellency's recommending to His Majesty's Minister for the Colonies that an Augmentation may be taken into his Consideration and state the urgent Necessity to His Royal Highness the Commander-in-Chief.

Necessity of an augmentation.

.With respect to our Numbers, I need only refer You to the Monthly Returns and to observe that in the Event of being obliged to detach any part of the Military now doing duty at Head-Quarters, how unprotected not only the Government Stores but also the Lives and Property of the Inhabitants would be, and in a constant State of Danger and Alarm.

1807.
19 Mar.

Condition of
the ordnance.

I must also request Your Excellency's Attention with respect to the shattered state of the Gun-Carriages (in consequence of the white Ants), which will always be the Case unless You recommend Iron ones to be sent out; in case an Insurrection ever be attempted there ought to be two Light Field Pieces (called Curricle Guns) at Sydney and the same at Parramatta.

Military force
required.

Having, therefore, offered my Opinion for Your Excellency's Consideration, I beg leave further to observe that the Military Force, adequate for the Safety of this Colony and its Dependencies, ought to be as follows, viz.:—At Head-Quarters, 400; At Parramatta, 200; at the Hawkesbury, 100; At Port Dalrymple, 200; and if any Troops are continued at Norfolk Island, that Port, including Newcastle, The Guards at the Flagstaff and George's Head, 100. From this Statement the Number required in addition to our present Force will be five hundred effective Men.   I have, &c.,

                                        W. PATERSON.

[Enclosure No. 2.]

Distribution
of the New
South Wales
Corps.

DISTRIBUTION of His Majesty's New South Wales Corps, Sydney, 18th March, 1807.

Where Stationed.	Field Officer.	Captains.	Subalterns.	Surgeon.	Assistant Surgeon.	Sergeants.	Drummers.	Rank and File.
Sydney...........................	1	2	3	1	1	17	10	266
So. Head	...	...	...	...	...	...	...	6
Geo. Head	...	...	...	...	...	...	...	4
Parramatta	...	1	1	...	...	4	2	74
Hawkesbury...................	...	...	...	...	...	...	...	14
Cabramatta	...	...	...	...	...	...	...	5
Norfolk Island	...	...	1	...	...	1	2	28
Port Dalrymple	...	1	3	...	....	4	2	63
Newcastle	...	...	...	...	...	1	...	16
Furlough to England........	...	...	...	...	...	...	...	3
Do to India	...	...	...	...	...	...	...	1
Sent to England on Command ...	...	...	...	...	...	1	...	...
Total	1	4	8	1	1	28	16	480

N.B.—The Officers on leave of Absence and those not joined since appointed not included.

                              WM. PATERSON, Lt. Col.

2 Serjts., 1 Corpls., 40 Privates Supernumeraries at Head Quarters not included.

Distribution of His Majesty's New South Wales Corps—*contd.*

1807.
19 Mar.

Distribution
of officers of
the New South
Wales Corps.

Absent Officers.

Colonel Grose	King's leave.
Major Foveaux	do.
Captain Savory ...... ⎱	not joined.
„ Grosser ..... ⎰	
Lieut. Bailey	Resignation given in, Comm'g Officer's Leave of Absence.
„ Anderson	Ditto Do.
Ensign Cressy	Comm'g Officer's leave to England. -
Paymaster Cox	Sent to England in Arrest by Order of His Royal Highness the Commander in Chief.

Officers on Command.

Captn. Kemp .... ⎫	
Lieut. Moore .... ⎬ at Pt. Dalrymple.	
„ Laycock .... ⎭	
Ensign Piper	
Lieut. Piper	at Norfolk Island.
Captn. Abbott .... ⎱ at Parramatta.	
Lieut. Brabyn .... ⎰	

Officers Present.

Lieut. Col. Paterson	
Captn. Johnston	
„ Wilson	Resignation given in Commg. Officer's leave.
Ensign Lawson	
„ Draffen	
„ Laycock	in Arrest and under Sentence of a Gen'l Court Martial.
Lt. and Adjutant Minchin	
Quarter Master Laycock.	in Arrest and under Sentence of Do.
Assistant Surgeon Smith	appointed by the Comm'g Officer to act until His Majesty's Pleasure is known.
Surgeon Harris	

[Enclosure No. 3.]

ABSTRACT.

Return of Ordnance in the Colony of New South Wales, 13th August, 1806.

	Guns.	
	12-Pounders.	6-Pounders.
Mounted at Dawes's Point Battery (but 8 Carriages unfit for Service)	12	2 Iron.
At George's Head Battery (Carriages unfit for Service)	4	Iron.
At Fort Phillip (Dismounted)	..	8 Iron.

1807.
19 Mar.

RETURN of Ordnance in the Colony of New South Wales—*contd.*

Guns.

12-Pounders. 6-Pounders.

Return of
ordnance.

In the Barrack Square (Carriages unfit for
Service) ....   2 Brass Field-
Pieces.

In front of Government House (Carriages unfit.
for Service) ....   2 ditto.

Barrack Square, Parramatta (Carriage unfit
for Service) ....   1 4-pounder, Iron.

W. MINCHIN, Col'l Art'y Officer.

New Carriages for the Field Pieces are making.
Iron Carriages are required for the sixteen 12-Pounders and others.

WM. BLIGH, Governor.

REMARKS ON BATTERIES, MAGAZINE, ETC., ETC.

Report on the
batteries and
magazine.

Fort Phillip.—The Rampart, Merlons and Embrasures of 3
Sides nearly finished.   The outer Wall of the Rampart of the
4th and 5th Sides raised 5 feet.   A Bomb Proof of 14 feet square
completed under one Side, and the Foundation of the 6th Side
nearly Laid.   No Work done since the 16th March 1806.

The Parapet of the Battery at George's Head in a state of
Decay.

The Powder Magazine damp, and unfit to keep Powder in.

The Powder greatly damaged from the damp state of the
Magazine.

W. MINCHIN,
Coll. Arty. Officer and Engr.

SECRETARY MARSDEN TO GOVERNOR BLIGH.

(Per ship Young William.)

21 April.

The question
of procedure
for the court
martial of
marines.

Sir,   21 April, 1807.

Governor King in a Letter to me of the 24 of March, 1806,
transmitted Copies of a Correspondence that had passed between
him and Lieut. Col. Collins of the Royal Marines respecting the
Trial of a Private belonging to the Detachment under his Command at Hobart Town, who had appealed to a General Court
Martial, together with the opinion of Mr. Atkins the Judge
Advocate upon the Subject, stating that he thinks that no Officer
or Private Marine can be Tryed at Sydney unless power should be
Vested in the Governor by my Lords Comrs. of the Admty.
authorizing him to convene such a Court for that purpose; and
having laid the same before their Lordships, I have it in command from them to acquaint You that as Colonel Collins
possessed full power under the Mutiny Act to Try the Man by a

Divisional Court Martial he should not have allowed him to
appeal to a General Court Martial, having no right to make such
Appeal, and that by the Usage of the Services it is only allowed
in Cases concerning pay or Allowances, particularly as Divisional
Courts Martial are now Sworn and have the power of administering Oaths.   I am, &c.,
                                          W. MARSDEN.

1807.
21 April.
—
The question
of procedure
for the court
martial of
marines.

GOVERNOR BLIGH TO THE RIGHT HON. WILLIAM WINDHAM.

(Despatch per ship Duchess of York, *viâ* India.)

Government House, Sydney, New South Wales,
Sir,   6th May, 1807.
      The Ship General Wellesley laden with Wheat and Rice
arriving in this Colony on the 13th of February last (as stated
in my Letter of the 19th of March following) and there then
being an urgent necessity for purchasing as much of those
Articles as possible for the immediate use of His Majesty's Settlements under my care and protection; I have the honor to inform
you, on the Master of the Vessel's agreeing to dispose of the
Wheat and Rice at Twenty Pounds pr. Ton, I gave the Commissary directions to purchase the same agreeable thereto, and to
draw four Sets of Bills on the Right Honorable the Lords Commissioners of His Majesty's Treasury for the payment thereof,
for which I inclose a Voucher, amounting to Four Thousand
Five Hundred and Eighty two Pounds Seventeen Shillings and
Ten Pence; and hope the transaction will be approved of.
                                          I have, &c.,
                                          WM. BLIGH.

6 May.

Purchase of
rice and wheat
ex ship
General
Wellesley.

[Enclosure.]

VOUCHER FOR PURCHASE OF WHEAT AND RICE.

Sydney, New South Wales, 20th March, 1807.

Voucher for
purchase of
wheat and rice.

John Palmer, Esqr. Commissary
to His Majesty's Territory of
New South Wales.

Dr. to Captn. D. Dalrymple of
the Ship General Wellesley.

1807 To 1636 Bags of Wheat 114 tons 16 cwt. 3 qr. 17 lbs. @ £20 pr. Ton	£2,296 18	0¼
— 1624 Bags of Rice 114 tons 5 cwt. 3 qr. 27 lbs. @ Do.	2,285 19	9¾
	£4,582 17 10	

Received this 20th day of March 1807 of Jno. Palmer Esqr.
Commissary Four Setts of Bills of Exchange No. One to No.
Four on the Right Honourable the Lords Commissioners of His

1807.
6 May.
———
Voucher for
purchase of
wheat and rice.

Majesty's Treasury, at Ninety days Sight, in favor of Thomas
Parry Esqr. of Madras, or Order for the Sum of Four Thousand
Five hundred and Eighty two Pounds Seventeen Shillings and
ten Pence Sterling, being Payment for the above Wheat and
Rice delivered into His Majesty's Stores at Sydney between the
16th day of February and the 20th day of March 1807.

For which I have signed five Receipts of this tenor and date.

D. DALRYMPLE.

We the undersigned do hereby certify that the above Wheat
and Rice was purchased on the most moderate Terms.

EDWD. LUTTRELL.

THOS. MOORE.

I do certify that the above Purchase was made by John Palmer
Esqr. Commissary agreeable to my Order.

WM. BLIGH.

Attested: RD. ATKINS, J.-A.

———

GOVERNOR BLIGH TO THE RIGHT HON. WILLIAM WINDHAM.

(Despatch per ship Duchess of York, viâ India.)

Government House, Sydney, New South Wales,

Sir,   6th May, 1807.

Purchases of
grain and wine.
In order to continue securing a sufficiency of Grain for the
Colony and its Dependencies in addition to what has been already
purchased, I have been under the necessity to direct the Commissary to draw Bills on the Right Honorable the Lords Commissioners of His Majesty's Treasury to the amount of Four
Thousand Five Hundred and Seventeen Pounds fourteen Shillings and Ten pence halfpenny, between the 1st of January and
31st of March last, for which I inclose Vouchers; Also the
General Hospital being in great want of Wine for the Sick, and
the Surgeon requesting a Supply, I ordered the Commissary to
purchase a small quantity for that purpose, and to draw for the
Sum of Sixty three Pounds for the payment of the same, agreeable to the Voucher inclosed; and that it may be understood
what is the total Amount of Bills drawn, as likewise for what
purpose, since I have had the honor to take the Command of this
Settlement, I herewith inclose a list of all the transactions, which
I trust and hope Sir will meet with your approbation.

By more direct opportunities I shall have the honor to inform
you particularly the state of the Colony, however I cannot now
omit mentioning that it is considerably improved.

I have, &c.,

WM. BLIGH.

[Enclosure No. 1.]

VOUCHERS FOR PURCHASE OF GRAIN.

Sydney, New South Wales.

WE whose Names or Marks are hereunto Subscribed do hereby acknowledge to have received from John Palmer Esqr. Commissary the Sums expressed against our Names, being payment for Grain purchas'd by him, and delivered into His Majesty's Stores at Sydney, Parramatta and Hawkesbury between the 1st day of January and the 31st of March 1807.

Date.	Names.	Sydney, Parramatta, and Hawkesbury.			Wheat 14/9, Maize 6/-, Barley 7/-, pr. Bush.	Amount.	Signatures.
		Wheat.	Maize.	Barley.			
between 1st Jany. and 31st March, 1807.	Robert Campbell Esqr. & Co.	3926⅞/₄	169⅜/₈	318½/₄	14/9 and 7/-	£ s. d. 3057 18 6	Rob. Campbell.
	Mr. S. Lord	435⅝/₈	....	10	....	324 16 4½	S. Lord
	Thos. Jamison Esqr.	142	....	....	....	104 14 6	Thos. Jamison.
	Matt'w Kearns	177	....	....	....	130 14 9	Matt'w Kearns.
	Mr. Jas. Larra	163	....	....	....	120 4 3	Jas. Larra.
	Mr. D. Bevan	400⅝/₈	15⅝/₈	32⁴/₁₆	....	311 5 1	David Bevan.
	John Harris, Esqr.	235⅞/₈	....	15	....	178 13 1	J. Harris.
		5794⅜/₁₆	185	376⁵/₁₆	....	4228 2 6½	

JNO. PALMER, Commiss'y.

Witness to the above payments:
RD. ATKINS, J.-A.
G. BLAXCELL.

We the Deputy Commissaries and Storekeepers do hereby certify that the quantities of grain expressed under the above Columns have been received by us into His Majesty's Stores.

JAMES SIN, Dep'y My.
JAMES WILSHIRE, Act'g Dep'y Comm'y.
WM. BAKER, Storekeeper.

I certify that the above Grain was purchased by my Order. WM. BLIGH.

1807.
6 May.

Voucher for purchase of grain.

1807.
6 May.

Voucher for
purchase of
grain.

Sydney, New South Wales, March 31st, 1807.

John Palmer Esqr. Commissary

    on Account of Government. .

                    To Messrs. Campbell and Company.   Dr.

To 217 Bags of Rice wt. 14 Ton 9 Cwt. 2 qr. 13 lbs. @
    £20 pr. Ton £289 12 4

Received this thirty first day of March one thousand eight hundred and seven of John Palmer Esqr. Commissary one set of Bills of Exchange on the Right Honorable the Lords Commissioners of His Majesty's Treasury at Ninety Days Sight for the sum of two hundred and eighty nine pounds twelve shillings and four pence being payment for the above Rice purchased for the use of the Colony.

For which We have signed five receipts of this tenor and date.

                          CAMPBELL & Co.

We the undersigned do hereby Certify that the above Rice was purchased on the most moderate terms.

                          THOS. MOORE.

                          RD. ATKINS, J.-A.

I do hereby Certify that the above was purchased by John Palmer Esqr. Commissary Agreeable to my order.

                          WM. BLIGH.

                    [Enclosure No. 2.]

Voucher for
purchase of
wine.

        VOUCHER FOR PURCHASE OF PORT WINE.

        Sydney, New South Wales, 31st March, 1807.

John Palmer Esq. Commissary

On Account of Government   To Messrs. Campbell and Company.

Nov. 19th 1806 Jan. 31st 1807 To Eighteen Dozen of
    Port Wine £63 0 0

Received this Thirty first day of March One Thousand Eight Hundred and Seven of John Palmer Esqre. Commissary One Set of Bills of Exchange On the Right Honorable The Lords Commissioners of His Majesty's Treasury at Ninety days Sight, for the Sum of Sixty Three Pounds being Payment for the above Wine, purchased for the Use of the General Hospital; And for which we have signed five Receipts of this Tenor and Date.

                          CAMPBELL & Co.

We the undersigned do hereby certify that the above Wine was purchased on the most moderate Terms.

                          THOS. MOORE.

                          RD. ATKINS, J.-A.

I do hereby Certify that the above was purchased by John Palmer Esqre. Commissary agreeable to my Orders.

                         ` WM. BLIGH.

[Enclosure No. 3.]

A List of Bills drawn on His Majesty's Treasury by Mr. Commissary Palmer, between the 13th Day of September, 1806, and the 31st March 1807.

N.B.—The Annual Number given in the second Column in Red Ink is in conformity to Lord Hobart's Intimation of beginning each Year with No. 1 for the reason stated in His Lordship's Letter to Governor King the 30th August 1802.

Sydney, New South Wales.

Annual.	Running No.			£ s. d.	
1	1	At Ninety Days sight in favor of Robt. Campbell Esqr.		250 0 0	Payment for freight of the Ship Sophia to Port Dalrymple.
2	2	At Do.	Messrs. Campbell & Co.	259 13 0	for Spirits for the use of the Colony.
1807 1	3	At Do.	Thos. Parry Esqr.	1148 9 0¼	Payment for wheat supp'd the Colony.
2	4	At Do.	Do. ...	1148 9 0	
3	5	At Do.	Do. ...	1142 19 11	Do. Rice.
4	6	At Do.	Do. ...	1142 19 10¾	
5	7	At Do.	Messrs Campbell & Co.	1000 0 0	
6	8	At Do.	Do. ...	1057 18 6	
7	9	At Do.	Do. ...	1000 0 0	Payment for Wheat, Maize
8	10	At Do.	Mr. S. Lord	324 16 4½	and Barley
9	11	At Do.	Thos. Jamison	104 14 6	supp'd the
10	12	At Do.	Matt'w Kearns..........	130 10 9	Colony.
11	13	At Do.	James Larra	120 4 3	
12	14	At Do.	David Bevan...........	311 15 1	
13	15	At Do.	Jno. Harris...............	178 13 1	
14	16	At Do.	Messrs Campbell & Co.	289 12 4	Payment for Rice.
15	17	At Do.	Do. ...	63 0 0	for Wine supplied the Gen'l Hospital.
				9673 5 8½	

Jno. Palmer, Commiss'y.

GOVERNOR BLIGH TO THE RIGHT HON. WILLIAM WINDHAM.

(Despatch per whaler Aurora.)

Government House, Sydney, New South Wales,
Sir, 30th September, 1807.

A Ship called the Aurora intending to sail for England while I am preparing my regular despatches to be sent by the Duke of Portland, a Ship of more security and safe and speedy conveyance, it is incumbent on me, nevertheless, and I feel great satisfaction in so doing, to state the general situation of the Colony, lest any unforeseen accident should prevent the Duke of Portland reaching England.

1807.
30 Sept.

For any omission and shortness of this Despatch I have only to plead the arduous duties I have to perform.

Improvement of the general condition of the colony.

It is an infinite satisfaction to me to say that from the distressed situation, in every respect, in which I found the Colony, it is now rising its head to my utmost expectations. The Public Buildings carry an aspect of their value, and Private Houses the pride of their Inhabitants; poor as they are, yet they are neat, and the Town altogether is become what has not been seen before in this Country.

Industry of the settlers.

In the interior I feel satisfied that the same emulation exists among the Inhabitants; and their Industry materially increasing, great exertions have been made to till the Land, and the ensuing Harvest promises well.

The discontented are checked in their Machinations, while the honest Settler feels himself secure, and the Idler no encouragement.

Conduct of the convicts.

The Convicts are quiet and as orderly as can be expected. Every encouragement is held up to them. The Settlers have a due proportion allotted as Servants; but few of them readily leave off the evil ways they have been accustomed to; their absconding to the woods, however, appears to be barely thought of.

The cost of animal food.

Provisions of Meat kind are scarce and very dear, such as Beef and Pork at one Shilling and ninepence per Pound. It is owing to a few wealthy Persons who have got great Property; but as we are encouraging deserving persons, the benefits Government wish to bestow will become more equally distributed.

Want of many supplies.

What were formerly considered luxuries, and are now become in some degree the necessaries of Life, the Country is entirely bare of, and can only be done away by arrivals with such necessaries. The Whalers and Transports bring scarce anything, and the little they import are sold at several Hundred per. Cent., while they rather distress us at present by their want of Supplies.

Return of the commissariat.

The general Statement, which is inclosed, shows that our Salt Provisions remaining in store will only last thirty-nine weeks for all the Settlements at full ration; from whence, Sir, every judgment may be formed of what is required, when compared with such supplies as may be on the way for the colony and its dependencies.

Despatches acknowledged.

I have the honor to acknowledge the receipt of your despatches* by the Brothers, Young William, and Duke of Portland, and am effectually putting them into execution.

I have, &c.,
WM. BLIGH.

* Note 31.

1807.
30 Sept.

General
statement
of the
inhabitants, etc.

[Enclosure.]

GENERAL STATEMENT of the Inhabitants of His Majesty's Settlements on the Eastern Coast and Out-Settlements of New South Wales, 30th September, 1807.

Settlements.	Governor and Commander-in-Chief.	Lieutenant-Governor.	Commandant.	Deputy Judge-Advocate.	Aid-du-Camp to His Excellency.	Commissary.	Principal Surgeons.	Provost-Marshal.	Chaplain.	Secretary to the Governor-in-Chief.	Surveyor of Lands.	Deputy Commissaries.	Mineralogist.	Boat-builder.	Assistant Surgeons.	Clerks to the Commissary.	Superintendents and Storekeepers.	Beach-Master.	Women of Civil Establishment.	Children of Civil, above 10 years.	Children of Civil, above 2 years.	Children of Civil, under 2 years.	Total of Civil Establishment Victualled.
Sydney	1			1	1	1	1	1	1	1	1	1		1	1	2	5		5	2	5		31
Parramatta												1			2		5		4	2	5	2	21
Hawkesbury															1		1		2	2	1		7
Newcastle			1														1		2		2		6
Hobart Town, 31 March		1		1			1		1		1	1	1		2		8		6	6	2	4	35
Norfolk Island, 17 June			1	1				1*				1†			1		1	1					7
P't Dalrymple, 23 April		1					1					1					2		2		2	3	12
Total	1	2	2	3	1	1	3	2	2	1	2	5	1	1	7	2	23	1	21	12	17	9	119

Civil Establishment Victualled.

* Acting Provost-Marshal.   † Acting Deputy Commissary.

1807.
30 Sept.

General
statement
of the
inhabitants, etc.

GENERAL STATEMENT of the Inhabitants of His Majesty's Settlements, &c.—*continued.*

Settlements.	Major	Captains	Lieutenants	Ensigns	1 Adjutant, 1 Quartermaster, 1 Paymaster.	Surgeon	Serjeants	Drummers and Fifers	Rank and File	Women of Military Establishment	Children of Military, above 10 years	Children of Military, above 2 years	Children of Military, under 2 years	Total of Military Establishment Victualled	Captains	Lieutenants	Serjeants	Drummers and Fifers	Rank and File	Total of Loyal Association Victualled	Orphans Victualled from the Public Store
								Military Establishment Victualled							Loyal Association Victualled						
Sydney	1	1	1	3	2	1	21	10	333	49	4	66	7	499	1	1	3	2	33	40	7
Parramatta	:	1	1	:	1	:	3	2	83	6	4	28	4	133	1	1	3	2	21	28	11
Hawkesbury	:	:	:	:	:	:	1	:	13	1	1	7	:	23	:	:	:	:	:	:	3
Newcastle	:	:	:	:	:	:	1	:	16	:	:	:	:	17	:	:	:	:	:	:	:
Hobart Town, 31 March	:	1	3	:	:	:	6	2	37	9	1	1	8	68	:	:	:	:	:	:	1
Norfolk Island, 17 June	:	:	1	:	:	:	2	2	27	5	:	18	:	55	:	:	:	:	:	:	9
P't Dalrymple, 23 April	:	1	2	1	:	1	6	5	59	6	3	13	11	108	:	:	:	:	:	:	:
Total	1	4	8	4	3	2	40	21	568	76	13	133	30	903	2	2	6	4	54	68	31

GENERAL STATEMENT of the Inhabitants of His Majesty's Settlements—*continued.*

Settlements	No. of Prisoners, Free Men and Settlers Victualled from the Stores — Men	Women	Children above 10 years	Children above 2 years	Children under 2 years	Total of Prisoners, Free Men, and Settlers Victualled	No. of different Rations issued — Full	Two-thirds	Half	Quarter	Total No. of Full Rations issued	Total number Victualled from the Stores	No. of Persons not Victuall'd — Men	Women	Children	Total not Victualled	Free settlers and Land-holders not Victualled — Men	Women	Total Free Settlers and Landholders not Victualled	Total number of Souls in the Settlements	No. of Weeks each Specie will last at the Established Ration — Beef and Pork (wks)	Maize and Flour (wks)	Maize and Sugar as Maize (wks)	Wheat and Rice (wks)
Sydney	498	61	..	31	11	601	898	121	102	18	1,034	1,178	1,778	890	1,565	4,233	588	411	999	7,563	39	5½	57	..
Parramatta	476	123	2	45	22	668	614	141	78	28	754	861	⎱	⎱	⎱	⎱								
Hawkesbury	128	7	..	9	1	145	147	13	17	1	164½	178												
Newcastle	63	21	..	3	3	90	82	21	5	3	100½	113												
Hobart Town, 31 March	276	55	12	14	18	375	343	89	17	30	418½	479	4	..	..	4	4	1	5	488	22½	..	..	46
Norfolk Island, 17 June	134	46	..	38	1	219	172	51	56	1	234½	290	84	93	248	425	101	4	105	820	14	..	10	14
P't Dalrymple, 23 April	112	23	..	2	1	188	192	34	17	15	227	258	..	..	..	..	..	..	..	258	34¾	..	..	16
Total	1,687	336	14	142	57	2,236	2,448	470	292	96	2,932½	3,357	1,866	983	1,813	4,662	693	416	1,109	9,129				

The following Provisions have been sent to the Out Settlements since the several dates expressed against them, Since which times no General Statement has been received from those places, viz:—

⎱ To Hobart Town .... 31 Mar.
⎰ ,, Norfolk Island .... 17 June
⎱ ,, Port Dalrymple .... 23 April

	Beef. lbs.	Pork. lbs.	Sugar. lbs.	Wheat. bushels.	Maize. bushels.	Rice. lbs.
To Hobart Town	..	38,160	561	6,139	..	..
,, Norfolk Island	..	9,540	..	..	200	..
,, Port Dalrymple	33,600	..	..	16,878	500	11,140

JNO. PALMER, Commissary.

1807.
30 Sept.

General statement of the inhabitants, etc.

GOVERNOR BLIGH TO THE RIGHT HON. WILLIAM WINDHAM.

(Despatch marked A, per whaler Aurora.)

Government House, Sydney, New South Wales,
30th September, 1807.

Sir,

Purchase of grain.

Referring to my Letter No. 6 of the 7th of February* and to those of the 6th of May, 1807, I beg leave to acquaint you that Mr. Commissary Palmer drew two sets of Bills of Exchange on the Right Honorable the Lords Commissioners of His Majesty's Treasury on the 30th of June last by my order, one set amounting to Six Hundred and Eighty Eight Pounds Nineteen Shillings and Six Pence in favor of Messrs. Campbell and Company, and the other for Two Hundred and Thirty Seven Pounds Three Shillings and Five Pence Halfpenny in favour of David Bevan, making together the Sum of Nine Hundred and Twenty Six Pounds Two Shillings and Eleven Pence Halfpenny, being for Grain delivered into His Majesty's Stores in this Colony between the 1st of April and the 30th of June 1807 Quarter, and have the honor to inclose a Voucher (No. 5) for the payment thereof.

Return of bills drawn.

Inclosed also is a List of Bills which have been drawn on the Right Honorable the Lords Commissioners of His Majesty's Treasury between the 1st of January 1807 and the present date.

I have, &c.,

WM. BLIGH.

[Enclosure No. 1.]

VOUCHER FOR PURCHASE OF GRAIN.

Voucher for purchase of grain.

WE whose Names are hereunto subscribed do hereby acknowledge to have received from John Palmer Esquire Commissary the Sums expressed against our Names being Payment for Grain purchased by him and delivered into his Majesty's Stores at Sydney Parramatta and Hawkesbury between the 1st day of April and the 30th day of June, 1807.

	Sydney		Parramatta.		Hawkesbury.		Rate per Bushel Wheat 14/9, Maize 6/-	Amount.			Signatures.
	Wheat	Maize	Wheat	Maize	Wheat	Maize		£	s.	d.	
	Bu.	Bu.	Bu.	Bu.	Bu.	Bu.					
Messrs. Campbell & Co.	140 7/8	70 7/8	..	793 1/2	379 7/8	156	..	688	19	6	Campbell & Co.
David Bevan	74	27 1/2	14 1/2	114 7/8	153 1/2	52	..	237	3	5 1/2	David Bevan.
Total Quantity	214 7/8	98 7/8	14 1/2	908 7/8	532 1/2	208	..	926	2	11 1/2	

We the Deputy Commissaries and Storekeepers do hereby certify that the Quantities of Grain expressed under the above Columns have been received by us into His Majesty's Stores.   JAMES WILLIAMSON, Dep'y Comm'y.
WILLIAM BAKER, S. Keeper.
JAMES WILSHIRE, Com'y's Clerk.

Witness to the above payment : RICHARD ATKINS, J.A.
THOS. MOORE.

I do hereby certify that the above Grain was purchased by order.

WM. BLIGH.

* Note 32.

1807.
30 Sept.
Return of
bills drawn.

[Enclosure No. 2.]

A LIST of Bills drawn on His Majesty's Treasury by John Palmer Esquire Commissary between the 1st day of January and the 30th June 1807.

N.B.—The Annual Number given in the second Column in Red Ink is in conformity to Lord Hobart's intimation. of beginning each Year with No. 1 for the reason stated in His Lordship's Letter to Governor King the 30th August 1802.

Sydney, New South Wales.

[This return was a repetition of that forwarded by Governor Bligh as enclosure No. 3 to his despatch dated 6th May, 1807, with the addition of the two following entries.]

16	18	Dated 30th June, 1807	Messrs. Campbell and Co.	688	19	6	Do for Grain for the use of the Colony.
17	19		David Bevan	237	3	5½	
				10,089	15	8	

JNO. PALMER, Commiss'y.

GOVERNOR BLIGH TO THE RIGHT HON. WILLIAM WINDHAM.

(Despatch per whaler Aurora.)

Government House, Sydney, New South Wales,
Sir, 1st October, 1807.

1 Oct.
Departure of
Underwood,
Williams, and
Rawlinson in
the ship
Sydney Cove.

In addition to my Letter of yesterday's date, I consider it necessary to inform You that the following Persons leave this Colony in the Sydney Cove:—

James Underwood formerly a Convict, but now a Trader concerned with a Simeon Lord, and a bad character; also, Francis Williams and Richard Rawlinson who were left here by the Lucy Privateer, and I ordered out of the Colony. These Men, I apprehend, will apply to become Settlers—if they do, I beg leave to request they may not be allowed the indulgence.

I have, &c.,
WM. BLIGH.

GOVERNOR BLIGH TO THE HON. WILLIAM POLE.

(Despatch per transport Duke of Portland.)

30th October, 1807.

30 Oct.

[A copy of this despatch is not available.]

1807.
31 Oct.

GOVERNOR BLIGH TO THE RIGHT HON. WILLIAM WINDHAM.

(Despatch endorsed "General Letter," per transport Duke of
  Portland; acknowledged by Viscount Castlereagh, 15th May,
  1809.)

Government House, Sydney, New South Wales,
Sir,   31st October, 1807.

General
description
of the colony.

In my Despatch of the 7th of February last I had the
honor to assure You of my intentions to transmit for Your information a description of this Colony, as soon as I felt myself competent to do it without material error; and on this task I shall
principally devote this Letter.

Area of the
colony and
of land
occupied.

The inhabited and cultivated part of the Land,* together with
that which is not granted or leased, considering the Sea and the
whole extent of the Hawkesbury River (as far as it is known) to
be its boundaries on the East, North, and West, and an imaginary
East and West line on the South, may be considered to contain
One Thousand Four hundred and Fifty-two square Miles—of
which One Hundred and Forty-Two are granted to Individuals,
One Hundred and Sixty-Two to Government, Thirty-Nine and
an Half as Commons, and Twenty to the Orphan School; therefore, the remains of Land unoccupied is One Thousand and
Eighty-Nine Square Miles, one-third of which is probably not fit
for cultivation.

Water supply.

Within these limits are many Creeks, Springs, and Ponds of
fresh Water. Although not so bountifully supplied as in other
countries, yet the fine River of the Hawkesbury (notwithstanding
the evils attending it by Floods) is a great benefit to that principal part of our Corn Settlement, which, taking in all the
winding, is an extent of more than Sixty Miles.

General
description of
the country.

The Face of the Country is generally very hilly. About Botany
Bay and neighbourhood of George's River it is flatter, with extensive Swamps and the Shores low. The view from any of the
Roads or Hills is extremely confined, owing to every part being
very much covered with Trees of a dark sombre hue, without any
variety of tinge to relieve the Eye. To the westward of the
Green Hills on the Hawkesbury are very high Mountains, and I
have seen some in the North which I consider Forty Leagues
distant. The other part of the Country on this side the River,
westward and southward, is formed in Hills and Dales, waving
like the Sea, their Bases nearly uniting and rising as they advance
towards the high Mountains; to this may be attributed the overflowing of the River during heavy Rains, because they form
receptacles at these times which pour in torrents to empty them-

* Note 33.

selves, independent of any regular Rivers (with which we are 1807. 31 Oct. not yet acquainted) that may fall into the upper part of the General description of the country. Nepean. Northward of the Green Hills is the only extensive Flat we know of, through which the River's course serpentines considerably; the other low grounds may be considered as only borders to the Hills. At the southern extremity of the Nepean, on the West side, lie what are called the Cow Pastures, and come within the foregoing description, the Cattle ranging over and about the hills without any Plains to graze on.

From a high commanding situation, called Grose's Head, my representation of this part of the Country was taken, and from whence I saw no reason to suppose the Country was not accessible in any direction, or the Wild Cattle confined therein.

The best Soil of this Country lies on the West side of the Characteristics of the soil in different districts. Nepean and Hawkesbury, and about the Banks of those Rivers; in most parts it is extremely rich, but in some are rocky projections which are generally of a sandy texture, while the bed of the River consists of Pebbles which are brought by the torrents from the interior of the Country. On the East side of the Nepean to the Sea Shore it is variable, but worst of all near the Coast, where it is very sandy and will produce nothing but Native Shrubs. In this neighbourhood the rocky Land particularly abounds, as likewise along the first part of the Hawkesbury River from the Sea. The intermediate spaces consist of a hungry non-gravelly soil, which, when once broke up does not for many Years recover the natural Grass; of a stiff poor Clay, with an under-strata of Slate, or indurated Clay, between which, in some places, I observed (by digging) that at intervals of nearly three feet were thin stratas of reddish Iron Stone and of Clay mixed with Sand, but still too stiff to work in very dry Weather. The mellow and better parts consist of the same, intermixed with a fine vegetable Mould, which is easily broken up and harrowed.

No Marle, Chalk, or Limestone has been seen. Pure Clay is Deposits of clay. about Sydney, and for the purposes of making Bricks there is abundance in many parts of the Country, tinged more or less with a red colour.

In the material and absolutely essential pursuit of Cultivation Labour required to cultivate the land. the most extreme and arduous labour is bestowed. Trees of great size must first be cut down; the Trunks then being arranged are burnt off, and the Ashes dispersed, before the Ground is hoed and prepared to receive the Grain. This severe labour hoeing must continue in most places while the stumps of the Trees remain in great numbers and lie near to each other; but as I

1807.
31 Oct.

am encouraging the use of the Plough, and granting Oxen to those who desire to purchase them—to work where they can be applied—we hope to see this labour reduced and more work executed.

Impoverished soil.

The actual Cultivators of the Ground in all the old Farms perhaps may just now feel smaller returns than the New Settlers, owing to their having so much longer tilled the parts of the Estates they hold without any intermission. Where the Soil remains good, as on the Banks of the Hawkesbury, or places similarly situated on the sides of the Creeks, this may not be felt; but on the Hills, in the neighbourhood of Sydney and Parramatta, where the Soil is not deep, it must be expected to fail, and other parts of the land must be cleared.

Impossibility of experimental farming.

Experimental farming cannot be pursued in an infant Colony, unless we consider it adopted here by the ignorance of those who possess Grounds and never knew the practical part of Agriculture; most of our Settlers have been of this description; the advancement, therefore, we are to expect is by such general good Rules to lead them to industry as are simple and efficacious.

Necessity for systematic farming.

In order to obtain these ends, the improvement of the impoverished or worn-out Estates must be attended to; certain portions should only be cultivated at proper intervals of time, in order that the strength may be recruited either by natural or artificial means; no more Grain should be sown than the Farmer can keep clear and secure; his Family wants in the Year should be provided; his excess should be capable of being turned into good payments to procure other necessaries, and the independence which every good Man looks forward to and blessed hope tells him to expect.

Improved methods adopted.

To these objects the honest Settler now seems to attend. He is sensible that Ten acres of Grain, cleanly and judiciously sown and reaped, will return him more than Fifteen in the usual slovenly manner that it has been done, besides relieving him from the extra labour which conduced to make him poor; and by this means also his Garden will be timely cropt, and the Potatoes, Pulse, and Vegetables reward him for the time he can allot to this purpose.

Assistance granted by government.

On the part of Government every assistance is given that it sees will accomplish these desirable ends. Prisoner Servants of the Crown are allotted to Settlers according to their industry and capability of maintaining them. Cattle and Stock allowed to all who can purchase them at two-thirds and half the price they can be bought for from private Individuals. This will enable them not only to plough, but to manure and fence in their Grounds, which I have earnestly recommended, and will become a general system in due time.

The Barter of Spirituous Liquors is prohibited, by which means hired labour is become secured more equally to every Man; and the floating Paper Money of an undefined value, besides an unsafe medium, is now obliged to be drawn payable in Sterling— two circumstances which have relieved the Merchant and the honest Man from the designs of the Knave, and prevented the most extraordinary litigations being kept up that ever happened in any Country.

Prohibition of barter in spirits.

Besides English Grain, we have a more staple Crop in Indian Corn, and it can be produced in abundance. It is not liable so much to the blight and other casualties as attend English Grain, and is sold at one-half, and sometimes one-third, of the price of Wheat.

Cultivation of Indian corn.

Government farming is in a certain degree necessary, because it is a check on the price of Grain. We have at present One Hundred and Fifty-One Acres of Wheat and Sixteen of Barley and Oats, besides Two Hundred and Twelve Acres of Ground prepared for Maize, part of which is already planted; and the Crops throughout the Country promise well; the Wheat is now in Ear, and the Weather very seasonable.

Farming by government.

The grazing Ground is in all parts of the Country, but the Grass fails, and the Cattle are very poor four Months in the Year. Some of the natural Grasses make very good Hay; in order to prove this, I have from the neighbourhood of Sydney supplied the Horses and Cows about Government House during the whole Winter, and have now a fine Stack standing, which is the first ever seen in this Country.

Natural hay.

Many artificial Grasses might be brought to us; but I apprehend the Rye and Clover Grass will be of greater advantage than any other. About nine Months since an Acre was sown at the bottom of our Garden, which has flourished in a charming manner; it has been fed upon and cut twice, and is now in fine bloom left for Seed. In low Grounds it will vegetate throughout the Year, but upon the Hills it will not answer so well; however, I have every expectation it will come into general cultivation, and the cultivation at large annually improve. By the Result of the Muster taken in August last, which is herewith enclosed, it will be seen that upwards of Thirteen Thousand Acres were cultivated.

Cultivation of exotic grass.

The Climate is extremely salubrious and temperate; during a short space of the Summer it is very hot, and a few days' hot

The climate.

1807.
31 Oct.

Winds, coming across the Country from the North-West, are scorching and unpleasant, affecting our Fruit and Vegetables.

In the Winter and Spring we have slight Frosts, but after the Month of September they do no injury, and the planting of Maize becomes general.

Mean monthly temperatures.

The monthly medium of the Thermometer at Noon is as follows:—1806: November, 68° to 84°; December, 65° to 103°. 1807: January, 66° to 95°; February, 67° to 84°; March, 66° to 84°; April, 65° to 83°; May, 56° to 77°; June, 52° to 65°; July, 56° to 68°; August, 56° to 75°; September, 59° to 77°; October, 58° to 92°.

Climatic conditions.

With respect to the Winds, they are nearly the same as in all variable Climates, except in duration, when they blow violently, which is by no means so long as in situations more remote from the Equator.

Rainfall.

The Rains are more like those within the Tropics, falling with great violence; but, nevertheless, we have moderate showers advantageous to Agricultural pursuits. Seasons of drought and South-West Winds the Country is sometimes injured by, as likewise by Lightening, which causes blight, fly-moth, and other pernicious insects; but no general calamity do I believe the Colony subject to more than any other Country situated in the same parallels.

Classification of inhabitants.

Under the head of People is to be considered the Convict Prisoner, The Convict who has obtained his freedom, the Free Settler, The Civil Officers of the Crown, and the Military.

Character of the convict class;

It is to be deplored that by far the greater part of the Prisoners remain, after their servitude, the same characters as by their viscious habits they have maintained in their career of life, notwithstanding the rewards and blessings offered to them to do well; but the road to it being honesty and industry is an insurmountable barrier.

of the emancipists.

This melancholy truth has been proved by many of the Emancipations and Free Pardons which have been given; even those who have been raised to some degree of wealth by such means, if happily they leave off thieving, their habits of cheating and knavery seem to be increased by the giving up the other Vice; fair and honorable principle they cannot admit in competition to their habitual reasonings, which make them the most troublesome characters to society and regular government. Not until the next or after Generations can be expected any considerable advance to morality and virtue.

By the leading People of this Class, whose names are Lord, Kable and Underwood, several Masters of Ships have been ruined, the Merchants at home defrauded to a serious amount, and the mercantile interest almost destroyed. With constant litigation and infamous prosecutions in the Courts ·they have been accustomed to be gratified.

The Free Settlers, hitherto, have been in general a thoughtless set of Men, yet, nevertheless, not sparing in their labour to clear their lands; many of them are still addicted to Liquor and disposed to get in debt; while others are becoming cautious in their concerns, and, uniting with acknowledged honest Men, do their utmost to procure domestic tranquility.

Classes of plain sensible farming Men, of moderate expectations, are the most valuable to come here; such as the Blaxlands, who lately came out, become so speculative as to care for nothing but making money; they endeavor to monopolize under a principle of buying as cheap as they can and selling dear. The Blaxlands, in a partnership, seem to turn their minds principally to grazing and selling the Milk of their Cows and Butcher's Meat, which is attended to by Mr. J. Blaxland, in a House at Sydney where he resides, while his brother remains in the Country purchasing Live Stock from those who can be tempted to sell it. The former is very discontented with what Government has granted him, although it is in itself a Fortune. This, with other circumstances, has led me to draw up for my own guidance a plan* I mean to pursue in case Persons come here as Settlers without having the number of Cattle and Servants specified· for their use and benefit—and herewith beg leave to submit it in order that I may be directed to increase or diminish what may be thought proper. On this subject, Sir, I hope to be excused in remarking that as the principle of giving Prisoner Servants is to promote the cultivation of the Land and the wealth of the Employers, and to that end they are to have them for a fixed duration of time of eighteen Months, if the number so allotted exceeds what they demand and can possibly employ, whether it is proper they should benefit by the excess: as, for example, Mr. J. Blaxland is allowed eighty Men (being one to every hundred Acres), for eighteen Months; now as he has at his request taken only Twenty Men, he will have them Six Years, whereby a Settler of this description has a prodigious advantage over the One who has Two Thousand Acres and Twenty Men allowed at the same ratio, eighteen Months, whom he can employ as much to the benefit of the Colony as the other. Again, suppose Mr. J.

Proposed
regulations
for settlers
and the
advantage of
adopting them.

* Note 34.

1807.
31 Oct.

Proposed
regulations
for settlers
ar'd th'e
advantage of
adopting them.

Blaxland to let his Estate, except One Thousand Acres, and takes only ten Men, his whole allowance of Servants will then keep this property in cultivation Twelve Years without any expence for labour, which throws a great damp on the spirit of the other Settlers who come out and cannot have more than eighteen Months of Government labour; as also on those who have been established for some time and are necessitated to pay for such labour as they may require, excepting in cases where Government is able to allow them to take Convicts off the Store, when they have only the expence of victualling and clothing them—and this is an object of importance—as to the Settlers we look principally for a supply of Grain.

Charges against the judge-advocate and principal surgeon.

As to the Civil Officers, I must in point of duty, as in honor, object to Mr. Atkins, the Judge-Advocate, and Mr. Jamison, the Principal Surgeon, who I have permitted to remain in Office on account of not being able to supply their places; but the latter I have dismissed from the office of a Magistrate, because I considered him not an upright Man, and inimical to Government, as likewise connected in improper transactions. With respect to Mr. Atkins, more particularly, he has been accustomed to inebriety; he has been the ridicule of the community; sentences of Death have been pronounced in moments of intoxication; his determination is weak; his opinion floating and infirm; his knowledge of the Law insignificant and subservient to private inclination; and confidential cases of the Crown, where due secrecy is required, he is not to be trusted with.

Emancipists employed as soldiers.

As to the Military, About seventy of the Privates were originally Convicts, and the whole are so very much ingrafted with that order of Persons as in many instances have had a very evil tendency, and is to be feared may lead to serious consequences, more particularly from their improper connection with the Women, by whom they have a number of Children, and which lessens the respect due to the virtuous Mothers and their Families.

Necessity for regular relief of the military.

Considering this to be the case, there is no remedy but by the change of Military duty, a circumstance which can only prevent a fixed Corps becoming a dangerous Militia; while, by the removal of both Officers and Men, it would be a valuable Corps for immediate Service, and that which relieves it be inured and rendered fit for any Climate in its turn, and would be a regular routine of Military duty, and conducive to promotion.

In the description of the Colony to which I am advanced, it appears necessary to notice the administration of Law and Justice.

The Colony is so far improved that the superior people now look with concern on the Civil and Criminal Courts as established by the Patent, and are particularly desirous that the Military may have nothing to do in the Jurisprudence of the Country, either as Magistrates or Jurors; the present Judge-Advocate they consider a very unfit person to correct errors or narrowly to search after the truth; the semblance also to Courts Martial is become irksome.

1807.
31 Oct.

Opposition to the constitution of the law courts.

The Civil Court they think confined to too few members; to both Courts they attach partiality in decision, which to a greater number of Jurors such censure could not be attributable. It appears to me that a mode approximating to the British Forms would be very beneficial and acceptable; how that is to be effected would be presumption in me to point out; but consider it a duty I owe to humanity and justice to pray that the present Judge-Advocate may be immediately superseded by some honorable and judicious Lawyer with a Salary which will make him independent, and other indulgences equal to the most favored Settler.

Suggested reforms in the civil court.

Removal of Atkins advocated.

In order to show what means we have to support a change, I have to observe that there are now One Hundred and Sixty-Six Free Men holding Land who have not come here under the Sentence of the Law, including the Civil Officers, for I consider that the other description of Persons should not be competent to sit in any Court of Justice, nor their Children after them, until a certain period of trial ascertains that they are become fit members of society.

Free immigrants available for jurors.

In a circumstance which lately took place, never was there more villainy attempted to ruin the character of a gentleman than in an attack made on Mr. Gore, the Provost-Marshal. One Underwood who I have had occasion to mention before in this Letter, a Convict a few years back and a bad character, but now raised to some wealth and gone Home in the Sydney Cove, charged him with improperly issuing part of a fifteen-Shilling Bill; and the Gaoler, formerly a Convict, another infamous fellow, charged him with stealing a piece of green-stone not worth Six Pence, but which, with curiosities, was purchased by Mr. Gore; the Justices in error committed him to be tried by the Criminal Court, which acquitted him. Mr. Gore was recommended by Earl Harrington to Lord Castlereagh when Secretary of State; his conduct has been such as to merit my approbation, and he has not lost the confidence placed in him.

Charges against and trial of provost-marshal Gore.

I must now beg leave to state, in concluding this subject, in case any change may be thought proper to be made, that the

1807.
31 Oct.

The governor
to have
absolute
power.

Governor should remain invested with the same power he now holds; he must be determined and firm in his measures, and not subject to any controul here; if he was to be cramped by a Council it would cause great trouble in this Colony.

Progress of
whaling and
sealing.

Our Trade and Manufactures are naturally in a very infant State; the Whale Fishery contributes to the advantage of the English Merchant, and to those persons here who have Craft and can send out people on different parts of the Coast to kill Seals for their Skins, which they sell for a good price, or send Home to their Agents or Consignees.

Trade in
sandal-wood.

The Colonial Vessels are likewise employed in going to the Islands within the limits of the Territory, trading with the Natives for Sandalwood for exportation in transient Ships, which have authority to proceed home by the way of China. Our Exports besides consist only of Grain and Meat, which the Shipping may require, and a few ornamental Woods, which are of little consequence.

Restrictions on
importations.

The Whalers, being confined by their Charters to fishing only, import few of the Articles which would be acceptable; at present, therefore, we have to depend only on an annual Ship or two, as is or may be established, and an occasional Ship belonging to the free Merchants of India, which may be sent hither by permission, or a chance American who may venture to come to this market. By these limitations, and a prohibition on the part of the Colony from trading to the East Indies, it receives very trifling benefits from thence, and suffers great deprivation of necessary supplies.

Colonial
manufactures.

Manufactures are extremely trifling. A small quantity of coarse Linen and Sail-Cloth, with coarse Blanketting, a poor Pottery, and the tanning of Leather are all we have at present, and in consequence our wants are the greater; but it is to be expected that the cultivation of Hemp will hereafter be more considerable, and that Cordage will become a valuable staple and make an ample return. The Flax likewise will be attended to, and the manufacturing it receive all the support that Government can give.

Progress of
brewing.

Brewing is carried on principally with Maize, and the Beer generally drank; but Hops do not at present grow well, and no good succedaneum is yet discovered to answer their use, from which cause the Beer will not keep.

Peach Cyder might be made in large quantities, but we have not yet been able to prevent it from fermenting and becoming sour, which I have attributed to its not being sufficiently racked and cleansed of the pulpy substance of the Fruit. The premium of a Cow, which Government offered last Year to the Person who would produce the two best Hogsheads, may have a good effect.

Salt is now produced in tolerable perfection, and by being cleansed better than formerly cures Meat very well and enables the industrious Fisherman to salt his Fish, and the Merchant to preserve his Seal Skins.

Hereafter we may expect great advantage from Hides and Tallow; from Coals also something may be expected; and these articles will become objects of my earnest consideration, as will every thing which may arise out of unforseen events, as they occur. This leads me to consider when Supplies of Salt Provisions may no longer be required from England. It would be satisfactory if any calculation could be depended on to ascertain this point, but it must so rest on circumstances that any conclusion deduced therefrom would partake of their uncertainty; but I propose reducing the Issues next Year by killing Oxen; in the subsequent Year, if no impolicy of such a measure prevents me, we shall increase the number to be slaughtered; and so proceed on with due precaution to the interest of the general Stock for supplying Settlers and to the advantage of Agriculture. In this particular, Government will, I expect, next Year feel a material saving by the sale of female Stock to the Farmers for Wheat, and thus the common progress will render it less necessary for Government to keep so many Cattle, or grow Grain, as what may be required may be purchased at a moderate price from Individuals; and then, no longer being in need of so many servants, they may be distributed to those who want them, and the Establishment become a certain expence to the Crown, which will admit of further regulations. As to the time when all these things will happen I cannot pledge myself; yet it may be expected within the following six Years, however short of this time we may flatter ourselves to have it accomplished; it will, therefore, be necessary to have Salt Meat sent out until we can see our way with certainty, lest any unforseen accident may happen to the source of our Colonial Supplies.

Prospects of
trade in hide
and tallow
and of
coal-mining.

Local supplies
of animal food.

Female stock
to be bartered
for grain.

Continued
necessity for
shipments of
salt meat.

With regard to the Wild Cattle, we have during the past Winter begun to make use of them by killing some of the outcast Bulls from the Herds and taking a few Calves alive. The next Winter we shall do the same, but as during the Summer the meat cannot be cured the taking of Calves will be our pursuit, in which I hope

experience will teach the Party employed how to be more successful than they have hitherto been.

	£	s.	d.
The expences in killing Nineteen Bulls and One Calf, and taking Eleven Calves alive, including the loss of a Horse,* valued at £100, has been	307	12	10
The Value of the Bulls and Calves	390	12	0
Profit to the Crown	£82	19	2

but the debit of this Account being charged to the utmost, the
profit is virtually more than stated.

By the Wild Cattle is to be understood Animals which no
barrier practicable to be made by us at present can confine, and
no body of Men turn if they want to escape. Gentle means must
be tried, and to this end, in the hilly Country they inhabit, we
mean to entice them by tame Cows, and on the same plan to catch
their Calves. Snares, I fear, will not effect anything to pay for
the expence of catching the few such a plan would produce.
From the nature of Wild Herds, a number of Bulls are driven
away by the superior Animals, and are called Off-casts; these
range the Hills and Valleys by themselves, from five to ten,
fifteen, and twenty in a Herd, and it is such Animals only we
have shot.

As to the Plans of some Individuals, they appear to me to be so
self-interested that no ultimate good would attend them. At all
events, I think it best that Government should for some time
longer keep the concern in their own hands and make some
farther experiments in catching them.

My Letter by the Buffalo† will explain farther on this head, as
likewise on Sheep and Wool; on the latter I cannot help observing
that some wrong impressions were made in England by reports of
the exportation expected from this country. Some of the Ships
which arrived about the time I did had orders to purchase what
was ready, but they found none for Sale.

The Town of Sydney is much improved; but the Church taking
more time to complete than was expected, it will not be ready for
the performance of Divine Service until after Christmas; eight
Bells were first rung on the 29th of May last, which, although too
small, give a chearfulness to the Inhabitants and command attention on the Sabbath day; of this Building I send a Sketch.‡

To His Majesty's most gracious Gift of Plate for the Communion Service, may I be allowed to hope that Coverings for the
Table, Pulpit, and Desk will be added§ to complete this comfortable place of Divine Worship and remove the heathenish
aspect which this place has had heretofore.

* *Marginal note.*—Killed and the rider hurt by an attack of a bull.
† Note 35.   ‡ Note 36.
§ *Marginal note.*—Together with Bible and Prayer Books (*see* note 37).

1807.
31 Oct.

When Governor Philip quitted this Colony he left a memorandum, as may be seen in the Plan of the Town sent herewith,* that no part of Sydney should be leased away, but the whole to be considered the property of Government. In June, 1801, Governor King issued a General Order† that Leases might be granted for five Years; after his departure—and I had begun to make my remarks as circumstances arose—I found several Leases† given and renewed in January, 1806, for fourteen Years, which were eligible and wanted for Government purposes.

Regulations re land in the town of Sydney.

Leases improperly granted.

Lot 77 (not built on)—notwithstanding it belonged to the Church, which was too much confined, Mr. McArthur got a Lease of for fourteen Years, which if he holds will deprive the Inhabitants of a great convenience, as well as the public Place of Worship.

Church lands leased to Macarthur and Lucas.

Lot 93—leased for fourteen Years to one Lucas, within the limits of the Church, as that of Mr. McArthur's.

Lot 8—an extensive Lease of Garden ground contiguous to the Gaol, which should have been for the use of the unfortunate Prisoners contained therein, was renewed to Major Johnston, who lets it out to a private Individual.

Lease to Johnston.

Lot 16 (not built on)—a part of Government Lumber-yard, where the Carpenter's and Smith's Shops are leased for fourteen Years to a Mr. Blaxcell, to our great inconvenience for want of room to carry on the general works and security of the materials; this and the present Lumber-yard were one, and for which the Allotment No. 80 was given in March, 1802, for five Years, with a promise of its renewal until twenty-one Years should expire, whereon are two Windmills and a Bakehouse of considerable value, belonging to Mr. Palmer, in consideration of which the promise was made.

Leases to Blaxcell and Palmer.

Lot 79 (not built on)—leased to a Mr. Harris for fourteen Years, detrimental to the Parade, as Buildings may be required to be erected thereon.

Lease to Harris.

Lot 78 (on which is a Public-house)—leased for fourteen Years; too nearly connected with Government Granaries.

Lot 66—leased to a David Dickinson Mann for fourteen Years in June, 1804; it is close to Government House, and a great annoyance.

Lease to Mann.

Lot 72—leased to Mr. Surgeon Jamison for fourteen Years (not built on), while it is wanted for Government's Boats' Crews, in addition to the one they now have adjoining thereto.

Lease to Jamison.

Lot 15 is a House and Garden, leased to Colonel Paterson for fourteen Years in August, 1804; it has undergone some improvement since Colonel Paterson got it originally from Colonel Grose, and is the most fit place for a Lieutenant-Governor's House.

Lease to Paterson.

* Note 36.   † Note 38.

1807.
31 Oct.

Difficulty in
improving
the town.

I have given these descriptions to show how much Government is confined in any arrangement it may think proper to make for its use or ornament of the Town, and which should have been attended to agreeable to His Majesty's Instructions. Those Persons holding the Lots without any Buildings thereon I have warned that whatever they erect will be at their own risk; and on these heads I beg leave to request instructions.

Villages at
Parramatta
and the
Green Hills.

Parramatta and the Green Hills at the Hawkesbury may be considered as Villages to Sydney, the whole of the Inhabitants getting their livelihood by various ways, carrying on a small traffic with grain and merchandize, and raising poultry and swine; also, at Sydney a number of Persons employ themselves catching Fish for the Market.

The Condition of the Public Buildings at each place on the 13th of August last will appear by the enclosed Statement.

The Out-Settlements of the Derwent and Port Dalrymple I have no personal knowledge of, my presence at Sydney being indispensably necessary.

Reports from
the settlement
at the Derwent.

Lieutenant-Governor Collins's accounts lead me to hope that the Derwent will turn out extremely well; we shall not fail to supply and keep it on a footing with ourselves unless any misfortune happens to our Shipping to prevent it; they will now begin to have resources within themselves as to food and cultivation. The People who go from Norfolk Island will be a valuable acquisition to this Settlement; and a Ship with about One Hundred and Fifty or Two Hundred Convicts, part Artificers, with all necessaries and agricultural implements, would render it a most essential service, and might be divided with Port Dalrymple. As they become acquainted with the Seasons, the inconveniences they have experienced in Agriculture will, it is to be hoped, wear away; and if every Man with good-will puts his shoulder to the Wheel, which it will be his interest to do, they will become of some importance, by supplying Salt Meat, Grain, and other articles which the Country can produce, besides Iron if it becomes an object to work the Ore.

Distress from
want of food
supplies.

This Dependency and Port Dalrymple have no doubt experienced some difficulties; but this part during the time suffered more than either. When I first visited the People, many poor families fed on nothing but a native plant not much unlike our spinage when boiled; while the Derwent and Port Dalrymple had Kangaroo, which here is seldom to be procured.

Law courts and
judge-advocates
for settlements
in Tasmania.

Although I shall speak of Port Dalrymple separately, I may unite it here with the Derwent to request that the Patents for the Civil and Criminal Courts for those places may be sent out

1807.
31 Oct.

by the first opportunity; as the greatest inconvenience arises from not being able to try Offenders, it is an object of great importance; and that two Judge-Advocates of respectable Law abilities, as well as moral qualities, should be sent, one of whom to supersede Mr. Samuel Bate,* who Lieutenant-Governor Collins informs is totally incapable to hold the Office, and otherwise a very improper person; the other to fill the situation at Port Dalrymple.

Law courts and judge-advocates for settlements in Tasmania.

Lieutenant-Governor Paterson's account of Port Dalrymple is very flattering; he describes it to be luxuriant in all its herbage, and that the cattle thrive upon it to his utmost expectation; but he points out a great failure of the Crops occasioned by Frosts, which are very predominant throughout the Year, and a discontent in the few Settlers he has had on that head.

Reports from settlement at Port Dalrymple.

On this Settlement I cannot but express the concern I felt soon after my arrival at finding it not fixed in its Head-Quarters as I had expected. Yorkton had every disadvantage; besides being shut up and inconvenient to Ships in landing their Cargoes except at High water, it is forty Miles distant from Launceston. To this evil followed not only a disjunction of the People, but natural consequences which always attend a small party being divided. In consequence of this I ordered the Surveyor-General down in the month of March with Colonel Paterson, directing him to return with a correct survey and Colonel Paterson's Reports, which I am in daily expectation of, and shall then decide on what is to be done.

During the scarcity which took place at Port Dalrymple the beginning of this Year, Lieutenant Laycock was sent across the Country to the Derwent and found no particular difficulty in accomplishing it, although he took eight days in his journey thither, and six in his return—the direct distance across is about sixty Miles.† This will, of course, become an easy communication, and I think ultimately turn to advantage, whether to the uniting the Settlements or otherwise. For farther elucidation I beg leave to inclose Lieutenant Laycock's Journal.

Overland journey from Launceston to Hobart.

Lieutenant-Governor Paterson having represented to me that a Harbour Master is necessary, in lieu of the former (a Mr. House) who was lost in attempting to reach Port Jackson in an open Boat‡ on service, I beg leave to recommend a Person of that description may be allowed at the rate of fifty Pounds per annum. On the Establishment being formed by Governor King there were three Superintendants appointed, and Mr. House was paid as one of them; but in the present Establishment only two are provided for, corresponding with that of the Derwent.

Harbour-master for Port Dalrymple.

* Note 39.   † Note 40.   ‡ Note 41.

1807.
31 Oct.
Also that he has appointed a Mr. Peter Mills to act as Deputy-Surveyor of Lands, and which I beg leave to request may be confirmed.

Correspondence with Collins and Paterson.

It would, I apprehend, be very unprofitable to trouble You, Sir, with the correspondence with these Dependencies, unless points of information occur or peculiar circumstances arise which render it necessary; but I inclose a Copy of my last Letter to Lieutenant-Governor Paterson dated the 27th of September, and to Lieutenant-Governor Collins dated the 1st Instant, as they give a general idea of the whole.

The last Statements which I have received from the Derwent, Port Dalrymple, and Norfolk Island, as to their Cultivation, Live Stock, and Produce, are also inclosed.

The colonial currency.

I now beg leave to make some observations on the want of Money in this Country for the use of its Inhabitants. Government have kindly allowed Copper Coin to the amount of Two Thousand Five Hundred Pounds to be sent here, and it was thought proper to affix a double value to it, by which means it remains in circulation as Five Thousand. Dollars are more or less in use, according to trade—valued at five Shillings—but mostly hoarded up for sinister purposes. I therefore beg leave to mention as my opinion that, to assist the Copper Coin; if some amount of Silver, such as Shillings, bearing a descriptive mark of this Colony, were sent out—valued at one Shilling and three Pence—which would serve to keep them here, it would be a great convenience without any expence to Government, as on the first outset the total amount sent out may be distributed in place of Bills which will be necessary to be drawn.

The more general use of Money will only come by intercourse with Shipping; yet, for some Years whatever is derived by that means will be secured by speculators, while the stampt Coin will be current.

Evils of the paper currency.

The Paper medium is a great evil to the Poor, although I have made it payable as sterling, because an excessive quantity is put in circulation by particular people, who have no real capital, and if all the Notes now afloat were sent to the Drawers of them there would be almost a general Bankruptcy.

At present Notes are given so low as two Shillings and six Pence, which I propose to do away, it being productive of much inconvenience and fraud; and to enact, as in England, that none are to be drawn for less than Twenty Shillings.

It now remains necessary for me to remark on some circumstances which have taken place.

1807.
31 Oct.
———
Arrival of
H.M.S.
Cornwallis.

On the 12th of April His Majesty's Ship Cornwallis arrived from Madras, commanded by Captain Charles James Johnston,* bound to the Coast of South America on a Cruize, and sailed on the 23rd. We have within these few days had intelligence of him by a Prize† which is now coming up the Harbour. On the 2nd of August, when she left the Cornwallis, they had taken and destroyed fourteen Ships and Vessels; by accounts from Norfolk Island another Prize was wrecked on her way thither; the Crew saved themselves in a Boat, but remain there in a very weak state.

Arrival of the Neva.

On the 15th of June, the Neva, armed Store Ship, belonging to His Imperial Majesty of Russia, arrived from Cronstadt, laden with Stores for the West Coast of America, commanded by Lieutenant Hagemeister‡; she remained here until the 1st of July, and received every supply they wished for, and every respect and attention was shewn to the Imperial Flag.

Trial and punishment of ringleaders of the proposed insurrection.

Referring to my Letter of the 19th of March, stating an Insurrection was on the Eve of breaking out, and that the leading persons were taken up, I have to inform you, Sir, they have since been tried, and the fact, in my opinion, proved, yet they were acquitted—except two, who were sentenced to corporeal punishment; the whole being Prisoners for Life§ I immediately divided the Gang and sent two to each of the Settlements of Norfolk Island, the Derwent, and Port Dalrymple, and kept two here. The two Men who informed of this Conspiracy gave their Evidence so steadily as to induce me to give them Free Pardons,§ and they remain here without any apprehension of being molested by the disaffected Irishmen.

Convicts taken from the colony in merchant ships.

Although the practice of Merchant Ships taking Prisoners from the Colony is much abated, yet it still exists when opportunity offers, notwithstanding the Masters of Ships are, here, under heavy Bonds to prevent it. After the Ships have sailed no proofs can be got of their taking such Convicts away, except by accident, and therefore no punishment can attach to them before they arrive in England. In one instance three Convicts appear to have been taken away in the Argo, by a Letter to Mr. Harris from John Baden, the Master, on his voyage home, stating their being on board. This Ship belongs to the House of Hullets, and was consigned here to Mr. McArthur. As I think this conduct highly reprehensible, and that these Convicts may be landed in England, I feel it my duty to mention the circumstance, in case, Sir, you may please to approve of any regulation being made with the Merchants to prevent such proceedings in future. This

Convicts taken on the Argo.

* Note 42.   † Note 43·   ‡ Note 44.   § Note 45.

Baden likewise informs Mr. Harris that he means to come out with his family as a Settler; should be make application I beg that his request may be refused.

Accounts of the gaol and orphan funds.

By the Accounts of the Gaol and Orphan Funds, which are sent herewith, I have the satisfaction to shew that Mr. Campbell, the most responsible Merchant here, has undertaken the concern at five per Cent. on the Amount.

Importation of a still by Macarthur.

The Distillation of Spirits being prohibited for the best and wisest reasons, everything has been done to prevent such a destructive business being carried on; nevertheless, a defiance has been set up to Government by Mr. McArthur, in importing a Still of sixty Gallons, directed to himself and another of forty Gallons directed to Captain Abbott, of the New South Wales Corps, brought out in the Ship Dart, consigned to Mr. McArthur, as part owner of the said Ship with the House of Hullets and Company, of London. These Stills I ordered into the King's Stores to be sent to the Custom House in London by the safest opportunity. On their being directed to be put on board the Duke of Portland, the Coppers were found in Mr. McArthur's House, from whence, after some objection, they were taken by a young Gentleman, the Naval Officer's Clerk, in consequence of my orders, and shipped with the other parts; but Mr. McArthur, not being satisfied, called the Naval Officer's Clerk before a Bench of Magistrates (the Minutes of which are inclosed) and on which I regret being obliged to shew, by his speech, the inimicability of his mind to Government.*

Proposed erection of a distillery by the Blaxlands.

Under this head of procuring Spirits, whereby a few Individuals would be enriched, it is necessary, Sir, You should be informed that the Mr. Blaxlands have indiscreetly wrote to me requesting to establish a Distillery, and that they would make a part of a Company with any friends I might wish to intimate.

General condition of the colony.

The nature of my Despatches has at this time extended them beyond what will in general be the case; but I hope, Sir, as they are reduced to as small a compass as possible, consistent with your directions that I should inform You fully on the State of the Colony, there will be found nothing said unnecessarily. I shall only repeat that it is allowed to be in a very improved state, and the Inhabitants contented, except a very few who have been in the habit of turning every thing to their own Interest, and have not the full scope allowed them in gratifying their inclinations, particularly in the barter of Spirits, at which the whole country besides are glad in the extreme.

I have, &c.,
WM. BLIGH.

* Note 46.

1807.
31 Oct.

General abstract of the returns of the annual muster.

[Enclosure No. 1.]

ABSTRACT of Acres in Grain, Pulse, &c., in Fallow and Pasture, Alive Stock, The reported Bushels of Wheat and Maize, &c., belonging to Government, Settlers, and others, With the Number of Settlers, &c., in His Majesty's Colony of New South Wales, as appeared at the Muster taken at the different Settlements by His Excellency Governor Bligh, between the 17th and 27th of August, 1807, Showing the Increase and Decrease since the — of August, 1806.

To whom belonging.	Number of Acres in—									Total number of Acres held.	Horses.		Horned Cattle.		Sheep.		Goats.		Swine.		Bushels in hand of			Number of Settlers.
	Wheat.	Maize.	Barley.	Oats.	Beans and Peas.	Potatoes.	Orchard & Garden.	Fallow.	Pastures.		Male.	Female.	Male.	Female.	Male.	Female.	Male.	Female.	Male.	Female.	Wheat.	Maize.	Barley.	
The Crown	151	256	11½	4½	..	100	..	661½	80915	82099½	23	14	1597	1828	345	639	..	..	..	84	2543$\frac{1}{16}$	79	63 $\frac{13}{16}$	..
Military Officers, &c.	48½	71	8	..	..	10½	29¼	1322½	19597	21086¾	37	72	279	375	2657	5275	12	20	60	73	370	55	8	..
Civil Officers, &c. ..	403½	72	68	12¼	6⅝	15⅝	42½	1512	13944½	16077	48	90	332	595	1382	1982	941	62	153	165	1268	87	97	..
Settlers	6082¾	4527¾	779½	112¼	175	265½	413½	4356½	44922½	61635¼	159	210	567	984	4005	8553	587	1375	3762	3617	5179	35	80	..
Individuals not holding Land.	..	..	..	..	..	..	..	..	..	..	22	15	39	47	86	336	63	268	511	585	1579	36	54	..
Total in August, 1807	6685¾	4926¾	867	29	181⅝	391⅝	485¼	7852½	159379	180898½	289	401	2814	3829	8475	16785	1603	1725	4486	4524	10939$\frac{1}{16}$	67972	1702$\frac{13}{16}$	73
Total in August, 1806	6075½	3876½	1003	80	35½	185½	433	9395	145481¼	166565¼	247	305	2203	3083	7914	13543	654	1604	3644	3344	4499	5174	191½	66
Increase	610¼	1050¼	..	49	146⅛	206⅛	52¼	..	13897¾	14333¼	42	96	611	746	561	3242	949	121	842	1180	6440$\frac{1}{16}$	62798	1511$\frac{5}{16}$	57
Decrease	..	..	136	..	..	..	..	1542½	..	..	..	..	..	..	..	..	..	..	..	..	..	..	..	..

[Enclosure No. 1]—*continued.*

RETURN of the Number of Acres of Land sown with the different sorts of Grain, &c., in the Settlement of New South Wales, and the Number of Acres of Pasture and Fallow Land; The Names of the Persons by whom the said Lands are held; The Number of Convicts employed and victualled by Government and by each Individual in the Cultivation thereof, and the Quantity of Live Stock upon each Lot respectively; and also the Number of Settlers in the Colony, together with the Number of Rations issued daily to the Civil and Military Servants of Government, distinguishing the same.

By whom held.	Number of acres in—									Total Number of Acres held.	Horses.	
	Wheat.	Maize.	Barley.	Oats.	Beans & Peas.	Potatoes.	Orchard & Garden.	Fallow.	Pasture.		Male.	Female.
The Crown	151	256	11½	4½	..	100	..	661½	80,915	82,099½	23	14
The Governor..........	10	15	..	..	..	..	1	10	1,309	1,345	..	2
Lieut.-Governor Paterson.	Administering the Government at Port Dalrymple.								100	100*		
Colonel Francis Grose..	Absent on the King's leave, and holds no Ground.											
Lieutenant-Colonel	Lieutenant-Governor.											
Major Josh. Foveaux ..	In England.											
Major George Johnston	16	..	..	..	..	2	4	130	2,682	2,834	7	16
Captains.												
Edward Abbott........	2½	..	..	..	..	..	1½	..	2,027	2,031	2	5
Ralph Wilson.........	..	..	..	..	..	..	..	..	200	200	..	..
Anthony Fenn Kemp ..	..	..	..	..	..	..	..	70	320	390	..	..
John Piper	..	..	..	..	..	..	..	..	..	..	1	7
Lieutenants.												
John Brabyn	..	..	..	..	..	..	¾	100	200	300¾	2	..
William Moore	..	..	..	..	..	..	½	23½	184	208	3	1
William Minchin	..	16	..	..	..	1½	1½	30	334	383	3	3
William Lawson	..	..	..	..	..	..	1	30	330	361	..	6
Cadwallader Draffin....	..	..	..	..	..	..	..	..	..	..	..	..
Ensigns.												
James Mason	..	..	..	..	..	..	..	..	..	..	..	..
William Masters	..	..	..	..	..	..	..	..	..	..	..	..
Archibald Bell	..	..	..	..	..	..	..	..	..	..	..	..
Quar'r-master Thos. Laycock.	..	20	..	..	..	2	3	200	1,430	1,655	3	..
Surgeon John Harris ..	..	..	..	..	..	..	2	275	2,299	2,576	2	..
Paymaster William Cox†	6	20	8	..	..	..	..	54	82	170	1	6
Sydney and Parramatta Loyal Associations— John McArthur, Captain.	14	..	..	..	..	5	14	400	8,100	8,533	13	23
Thomas Moore, Lieuten't.	*Vide* Civil List.											
Richard Atkins, Deputy-Judge-Adv.	..	..	..	..	..	..	1	..	..	1	1	..
John Palmer, Commissary.	223	30	45	3	½	3	6	310	1,672	2,292½	14	17
Will'm Gore, Provost Marshal.	..	..	..	..	..	..	..	..	..	..	..	..
Edm'd Griffin, Secretary	..	..	..	..	..	..	..	..	..	..	..	..
Sam'l Marsden, Chaplain.†	12	..	10	6	½	8	7	500	2,312	2,855½	2	8
Henry Fulton, Clergyman.	..	..	..	..	..	..	..	..	100	100	1	..
Tho's Jamison, Princ'l Surgeon.	50	..	2	2	3	..	3	40	2,200	2,300	3	5
Tho's Arndell..........	60	30	5	¼	2	1	2	..	649¾	750	5	4

* Grant by Gov'r King, and Purchase; Wife and five Daughters in England. †Absent.

[Enclosure No. 1]—*continued.*

1807.
31 Oct.

Returns from the annual muster.

RETURN of the Number of Acres of Land sown, &c.—*continued.*

By whom held.	Number of acres in—									Total Number of Acres held.	Horses.	
	Wheat.	Maize.	Barley.	Oats.	Beans & Peas.	Potatoes.	Orchard & Garden.	Fallow.	Pasture.		Male.	Female.
D'Arcy Wentworth	..	..	..	..	..	..	9	70	1,140	1,219	7	7
James Mileham........	..	..	..	..	..	..	..	..	..	..	..	..
Chas. Grimes, Surveyor-Gen'l.	..	..	..	..	..	..	..	..	..	..	..	..
Augustus Alt, do superann'd.	..	..	..	..	..	..	2	20	248	270	..	..
Tho's Moore	5½	6	..	1	..	½	3½	200	1,703½	1,920	5	1
Ja's Williamson, Dep'y-Commiss'y.	..	..	..	..	..	..	3	130	850	983	2	7
Robert Fitz, do	..	..	..	..	..	..	..	..	..	..	1	6
Ja's Wilshire, Com'y's Clerk.	..	..	..	..	..	..	..	..	..	..	..	..
Will'm Sutton do	5	..	..	..	..	2	1	5	127	140	..	3
John Jamison, Superintend't of Govern't Stock.	..	..	..	..	..	..	..	..	200	200	1	3
Will'm Baker, Storekeeper.	..	..	..	..	⅛	⅛	¼	25½	..	26	1	3
John Gowen, do	..	..	..	..	..	..	..	..	100	100	..	..
Nich's Divine, Superintend't of Convicts.	..	..	..	..	..	..	½	59½	150	210	1	..
Richard Rouse do	10	6	1	..	..	..	¾	..	162¼	180	1	2
Naval Officers.												
Lieut. John Portland*..	..	..	..	..	..	..	..	..	..	..	..	..
Surgeon Edwd. Luttrell†	13	..	1	..	½	½	1	40	344	400	..	1
Captain King†	..	..	..	..	..	..	..	..	..	..	2	7
,, D. Woodriff† ..	..	..	..	..	..	..	..	..	..	1,000‡	..	..
,, Wm. Kent†....	..	..	..	..	..	½	1½	98	1,000	1,200	..	5
Lieut. Jno. Houston† ..	..	..	..	..	..	..	..	..	500	500	..	..
Purser Jno. Sherrard†..	..	..	..	..	..	..	..	..	100	100	..	..
Assistant-Surgeon Jno. Savage.†	25	..	4	..	..	..	1	14	286	330	1	2
Assistant-Surgeon Jno. Thompson.†	..	..	..	..	..	..	..	..	..	..	..	..
Settlers.												
383 Persons, holding various Allotments up to and including 30 acres.	2,078¼	1,461¾	240	28¼	45	89	91¼	700½	1,713½	6,447½	39	40
71 Ditto, from 30 to 50 Acres.	675¾	475½	104	7¾	15½	32½	42	219¼	1,383¾	2,956	12	11
127 Ditto, from 50 to 100 Do.	1,221	998	152¾	26¾	40¼	56¾	89¼	651¾	6,585¾	9,822¼	19	31
80 Ditto, from 100 to 200 Do.	1,158	865½	174¾	16½	50¼	47	99½	673	8,194½	11,279	34	46
20 Ditto, from 200 to 300 Do.	298	247	26	5¼	6½	15¼	17¼	417¾	3,587	4,620	14	22
22 Ditto, from 300 do, and upwards.	651¾	480	82	27¾	17½	25	74¼	1,694¼	23,458	26,510½	41	60
703												
Total held by Settlers	6,685¼	4,926¾	867	129	181⅝	391⅝	485¼	7,852½	159,379	181,898½	267	377

*As a magistrate. † Absent. ‡ This allotment let out and accounted for in settlers' muster.

1807.
31 Oct.

Returns from
the annual
muster.

[Enclosure No. 1]—*continued.*

RETURN of the Number of Acres of Land sown, &c.—*continued.*

By whom held	Horned Cattle			Sheep		Goats		Hogs		Bushels in hand of—		
	Bulls.	Cows.	Oxen.	Male.	Female.	Male.	Female.	Male.	Female.	Wheat.	Maize.	Barley.
The Crown	1057	1,828	540	345	639	..	..	..	84	2,543 1/16	7,049	863 1/3
The Governor	1	20	..	..	30	..	..	..	..	6	..	..
Lieut.-Governor Paterson.	Administering the Government at Port Dalrymple.											
Colonel Francis Grose	Absent on the King's leave, and holds no Ground.											
Lieutenant-Colonel	Lieutenant-Governor.											
Major Josh. Foveaux	In England.											
Major George Johnston	4	61	43	81	170	4	8	5	11	100	..	..
Captains.												
Edward Abbott	..	15	4	150	350	..	..	2	2	10	90	..
Ralph Wilson	..	..	..	..	..	..	..	..	..	..	..	..
Anthony Fenn Kemp	..	7	6	..	..	..	..	..	..	..	..	..
John Piper	..	..	..	..	..	..	..	..	..	..	..	..
Lieutenants.												
John Brabyn	..	1	..	..	..	..	..	2	2	..	..	..
William Moore	..	1	..	..	..	..	..	..	..	..	..	..
William Minchin	2	15	1	11	82	..	..	5	9	40	65	..
William Lawson	3	14	..	50	190	8	12	..	..	..	300	..
Cadwallader Draffin	..	..	..	..	..	..	..	..	..	..	..	..
Ensigns.												
James Mason	..	..	..	..	..	..	..	..	..	..	..	..
William Masters	..	..	..	..	..	..	..	..	..	..	..	..
Archibald Bell	..	..	..	..	..	..	..	..	..	..	..	..
Quar'r-master Thos. Laycock.	4	97	72	237	640	..	..	8	4	50	70	..
Surgeon John Harris	3	40	11	56	200	..	..	5	5	..	20	8
Paymaster William Cox*	4	10	10	72	213	..	..	21	24	20	200	..
Sydney and Parramatta Loyal Associations— John McArthur, Captain.	3	94	108	2,000	3,400	..	..	12	10	150	800	..
Thomas Moore, Lieuten't.	*Vide* Civil List.											
Richard Atkins, Deputy-Judge-Adv.	1	4	1	..	..	..	3	8	5	..	160	..
John Palmer, Commissary.	5	60	48	564	510	..	..	45	36	800	1,200	20
Will'm Gore, Provost Marshal.	..	2	..	..	..	..	..	2	1	20	..	..
Edm'd Griffin, Secretary	..	..	..	..	..	..	..	..	..	..	..	..
Sam'l Marsden, Chaplain.*	2	46	29	302	882	2	6	20	19	..	..	400
Henry Fulton, Clergyman.	..	2	..	30	118	..	..	..	..	3	4	..
Tho's Jamison, Princ'l Surgeon.	3	70	47	..	..	..	2	8	11	200	200	..
Tho's Arndell	1	10	8	50	180	8	12	20	23	60	120	60

* Absent.

[Enclosure No. 1]—*continued.*

RETURN of the Number of Acres of Land sown, &c.—*continued.*

1807.
31 Oct.
Returns from the annual muster.

By whom held.	Horned Cattle.			Sheep.		Goats.		Swine.		Bushels in hand of—		
	Bulls.	Cows.	Oxen.	Male.	Female.	Male.	Female.	Male.	Female.	Wheat.	Maize.	Barley.
D'Arcy Wentworth	1	17	9	40	250	..	..	15	15	20	50	..
James Mileham........	..	..	..	..	..	..	..	..	..	..	..	..
Cha's Grimes, Surveyor-Gen'l.	..	2	..	..	..	..	..	..	..	..	..	..
Augustus Alt, do superann'd.	..	..	..	..	..	1	2	..	2	..	..	..
Tho's Moore	2	33	20	..	..	..	..	1	7	12	100	..
Ja's Williamson, Dep'y-Commiss'y.	1	5	3	120	145	7	11	6	8	7	40	..
Robert Fitz, do	..	3	..	..	..	2	5	1	1	10	30	..
Ja's Wilshire, Com'y's Clerk.	..	2	1	7	35	1	8	1	..	25	100	7
Will'm Sutton do	..	..	..	..	..	..	..	..	..	8	20	..
John Jamison, Superintend't of Govern't Stock.	1	15	7	24	58	..	..	1	3	8	30	..
Will'm Baker, Storekeeper.	..	7	1	..	..	..	..	5	7	16	40	..
John Gowen, do	..	6	..	..	1	..	..	..	..	..	..	..
Nich's Divine, Superintend't of Convicts.	..	..	..	12	8	..	..	1	3	..	..	..
Richard Rouse do	..	11	3	10	25	30	6	9	5	30	260	..
Naval Officers.												
Lieut. John Portland*	..	6	..	..	..	..	2	..	..	..	50	10
Surgeon Edwd. Luttrell†	..	8	7	250	200	6	6	5	..	30	50	10
Captain King†	7	255	100	13	22	4	3	11	8	..	473	..
,, D. Woodrifft ..	..	..	..	..	..	..	..	..	..	..	..	..
,, Wm. Kent† ..	4	19	10	233	128	..	..	3	2	..	20	..
Lieut. Jno. Houston† ..	..	..	..	..	..	..	..	..	..	..	..	..
Purser Jno. Sherrard† .	..	3	..	..	..	..	..	..	..	..	..	..
Assistant-Surgeon Jno. Savage.†	6	9	4	..	..	..	..	5	5	..	..	..
Assistant-Surgeon Jno. Thompson.†	..	..	..	..	..	..	..	..	..	..	..	..
Settlers.												
383 Persons, holding various Allotments up to and including 30 acres.	12	69	33	432	947	156	328	1232	1141	1674	15915	27
71 Ditto, from 30 to 50 Acres.	5	35	11	114	276	95	200	360	381	215	4063	8
127 Ditto, from 50 to 100 Do.	8	69	21	607	1519	73	227	843	790	1050	13729	69
80 Ditto, from 100 to 200 Do.	7	94	65	818	2022	185	389	790	671	969	8630	36
20 Ditto, from 200 to 300 Do.	8	67	27	326	802	42	103	152	129	412	3054	60
22 Ditto, from 300 do, and upwards.	20	650	350	1708	2987	36	128	385	505	859	6954	80
703 Total held by Settlers	1175	3782	1600	8662	17029	660	1461	3989	3938	9141 1/16	63836	1648 1/2 3/4

* As a magistrate.   † Absent.

[Enclosure No. 1]—*continued.*

RETURN of the Number of Acres of Land sown, &c.—*continued.*

By whom held.	Proprietor On	Proprietor Off	Wife On	Wife Off	Concubine On	Concubine Off	Children Legitimate On	Children Legitimate Off	Children Illegitimate On	Children Illegitimate Off	Children's Sexes Legitimate M	Children's Sexes Legitimate F	Children's Sexes Illegitimate M	Children's Sexes Illegitimate F	Convicts On	Convicts Off	Free On	Free Off
The Crown	See Quarterly Employment.																	
The Governor	1	..	..	..	..	..	1	..	..	..	1	..	..	..	15	..	..	2
Lieut.-Governor Paterson.	Administering the Government at Port Dalrymple.																	
Colonel Francis Grose	Absent on the King's leave, and holds no Ground.																	
Lieutenant-Colonel	Lieutenant-Governor.																	
Major-Josh. Foveaux	In England.																	
Major George Johnston	1	..	..	..	..	..	1	..	..	..	6	..	3	3	6	6	..	..
Captains.																		
Edward Abbott	1	..	1	..	..	..	3	..	..	..	2	1	..	..	5	..	2	..
Ralph Wilson	1	..	..	..	..	..	..	..	..	..	..	..	..	..	..	..	..	..
Anthony Fenn Kemp	Absent at Port Dalrymple.																	
John Piper	Commandant at Norfolk Island.																	
Lieutenants.																		
John Brabyn	1	..	1	..	..	..	4	..	..	..	1	3	..	..	1	2	..	..
William Moore	Absent at Port Dalrymple.																	
William Minchin	1	..	1	..	..	..	..	..	..	..	..	..	..	..	2	1	..	1
William Lawson	1	..	..	..	..	..	1	..	..	..	3	..	2	1	1	1	..	..
Cadwallader Draffin	1	..	..	..	..	..	..	..	..	..	..	..	..	..	1	..	..	..
Ensigns.																		
James Mason	1	..	..	..	..	..	..	..	..	..	..	..	..	..	1	..	..	..
William Masters	1	..	..	..	..	..	..	..	..	..	..	..	..	..	1	..	..	..
Archibald Bell	1	..	..	..	..	..	..	..	..	..	..	..	..	..	2	..	..	1
Quar'r-master Thos. Laycock.	1	..	..	..	..	..	1	..	..	..	..	..	..	..	..	5	..	3
Surgeon John Harris	1	..	..	..	..	..	1	..	..	..	..	..	..	..	1	3	..	2
Paymaster William Cox*	..	..	..	..	1	..	..	..	..	..	..	..	..	..	..	8	..	3
Sydney and Parramatta Loyal Associations— John McArthur, Captain.	1	..	1	..	..	..	5	..	..	..	3	2	..	..	..	20	..	10
Thomas Moore, Lieuten't.	*Vide* Civil List.																	
Richard Atkins, Deputy-Judge-Adv.	1	..	1	..	..	..	..	..	..	..	2	..	..	..	4	1	..	1
John Palmer, Commissary.	1	..	1	..	..	..	1	..	..	..	1	..	..	..	..	24	..	26
Will'm Gore, Provost Marshall.	1	..	1	..	..	..	3	..	..	..	3	..	..	..	3	2	..	1
Edm'd Griffin, Secretary	1	..	..	..	..	..	..	..	..	..	..	..	..	..	3	11	..	3
Sam'l Marsden, Chaplain.*	..	..	..	..	..	..	..	..	..	..	..	..	..	..	..	..	..	..
Henry Fulton, Clergyman.	1	..	1	..	..	..	3	..	..	..	1	2	..	..	..	2	1	..
Tho's Jamison, Princ'l Surgeon.	1	..	..	..	1	..	..	..	..	..	..	..	..	..	6	9	..	1
Tho's Arndell	1	..	1	..	..	..	4	2	..	..	2	4	..	..	6	8	..	1

* Absent.

[Enclosure No. 1]—*continued.*

1807.
31 Oct.

RETURN of the Number of Acres of Land sown, &c.—*continued.*

Returns from the annual muster.

By whom held.	Proprietor On.	Proprietor Off.	Wife On.	Wife Off.	Concubine On.	Concubine Off.	Children Legitimate On.	Children Legitimate Off.	Children Illegitimate On.	Children Illegitimate Off.	Sexes Legitimate M.	Sexes Legitimate F.	Sexes Illegitimate M.	Sexes Illegitimate F.	Convicts On.	Convicts Off.	Free On.	Free Off.
D'Arcy Wentworth	1						1									3		2
James Mileham........	1						1			1				1	1			
Cha's Grimes, Surveyor-Gen'l.	1																	
Augustus Alt, do superann'd.		1					1					1				1		
Tho's Moore	1		1												1	4		
Ja's Williamson, Dep'y-Commiss'y.	1			1				1	2					3	1	3		1
Robert Fitz, do			1				1				1				1			2
Ja's Wilshire, Com'y's Clerk.	1			1						1						1		3
Will'm Sutton do	1			1												1		
John Jamison, Superintend't of Govern't Stock.	1			1			2	1					3		1	1		
Will'm Baker, Storekeeper.	1			1											1	2		
John Gowen, do	1															2		
Nich's Divine, Superintend't of Convicts.	1			1												2		
Richard Rouse do	1			1			3	1			3	1			2	1		
Naval Officers.																		
Lieut. John Portland*	1		1												4			
Surgeon Edwd. Luttrell†	1			1				6			3	3			2			
Captain King†																	7	
,, D. Woodrifft.																		
,, Wm. Kent†																	2	1
Lieut. Jno. Houston†																		
Purser Jno. Sherrard†																		
Assistant-Surgeon Jno. Savage.†																		
Assistant-Surgeon Jno. Thompson.†																		
Settlers.																		
383 Persons, holding various Allotments up to and including 30 acres.	28	355	3	110	2	118	2	193	6	128	109	86	65	69	14	68	1	103
71 Ditto, from 30 to 50 Acres.	5	66	2	28		19	7	59		31	30	36	12	9	5	21		32
127 Ditto, from 50 to 100 Do.	9	118	1	54		32		166		52	80	86	34	18	4	79	1	59
80 Ditto, from 100 to 200 Do.	9	71	1	45		15	2	184	3	44	106	80	19	28	10	103	2	63
20 Ditto, from 200 to 300 Do.	1	19	1	13		2	2	54		5	29	27	2	3	2	31	1	28
22 Ditto, from 300 do, and upwards.	4	18	2	9		7	5	25		16	13	17	8	8	51	80		174
703 Total held by Settlers	91	648	20	270	2	201	35	708	9	289	389	353	146	142	158	515	8	524

* As a magistrate.   † Absent.

1807.
31 Oct.

Regulations for
free settlers.

GOVERNOR BLIGH'S Regulations, until Orders to the contrary, in the distribution of Cattle and Servants to persons who come out to New South Wales by Order of the Secretary of State, without any specific quantity being mentioned.

Capital.	Acres.	
£100.	50 to 100.	Two Cows, Two Oxen, Two Ewes, One Sow (to be paid for). To be allowed Two Men, victualled from the Store and clothed for Twelve Months (as p'r Order of Lord Hobart, dated 24th February, 1803), with themselves and families; Also, to take as many men off the Store at their own expence, and to purchase such Stock as Government can conveniently spare.
£300.	100 to 300.	Four Cows, four Oxen, Four Ewes, One Sow (to be paid for). To be allowed Three Men, victualled, &c., And other privileges, as above.
£500.	300 to 500.	Five Cows, Three Oxen, Six Ewes, One Sow (to be paid for). To be allowed Four Men victualled, &c., and other privileges, as above.
£700.	500 to 700.	Six Cows, Four Oxen, Eight Ewes, One Sow (to be paid for). To be allowed Five Men, victualled, &c., and other privileges, as above.
£1,000.	700 to 1,000.	Eight Cows, Four Oxen, Ten Ewes, One Sow (to be paid for). To be allowed Six Men, victualled, &c., and other privileges, as above.
£2,000.	1,000 to 2,000.	Ten Cows, Four Oxen, Twelve Ewes, One Sow (to be paid for). To be allowed Seven Men, victualled, &c., and other privileges, as above.
£3,000.	2,000 to 3,000.	One Bull, Twelve Cows, Four Oxen, Fourteen Ewes, One Sow (to be paid for). To be allowed Ten Men, victualled, &c., and other privileges, as above.
£4,000.	3,000 to 4 000.	One Bull, Fourteen Cows, Four Oxen, Sixteen Ewes, One Sow (to be paid for). To be allowed Thirteen Men, victualled, &c., And other privileges, as above.
£5,000.	4,000 to 5 000.	One Bull, Eighteen Cows, Five Oxen, One Ram, Eighteen Ewes, One Sow (to be paid for). To be allowed Seventeen Men, victualled, &c., And other privileges, as above.
£6,000.	5,000 to 6,000.	One Bull, Twenty Cows, Six Oxen, One Ram, Twenty Ewes, One Sow (to be paid for). To be allowed Twenty Men, victualled, &c., And other privileges, as above.

1807.
31 Oct.

Report on the
condition of
the public
buildings.

[Enclosure No. 3.]

STATEMENT of Government Buildings,* in New South Wales, the 13th August, 1807.

SYDNEY.

Government House	Not repaired.
Offices at Do.	Repaired.
Judge Advocate's House	In good repair.
Do. Office	Rebuilt.
Commissary's Office	Not repaired.
Principal Surgeon's House	Repaired in part.
„ Offices	Repaired.
Clergyman's House	do.
Surveyor General's House	Made tenantable.
The Orphan House	Repaired.
„ Offices	In good repair.
The wood Hospital	Repaired as well as possible.
The other Hospital and Offices	Repaired.
The Master Builder's House	Not repaired.
Assistant Engineer's House	In repair.
Store Keeper's House	In good repair.
Superintendant of Town Gang's House	Not repaired.
Overseer of the Town Gang, and Commissary Clerk's Hut	Repaired.
Superintendant of Blacksmith's Hut..	Not repaired.
Lumber Yard, and Blacksmith's Shop..	Repaired, but too small; wants the ground adjoining to it.
Wharfinger's Hut	Repaired.
The Deputy Commissary's House	do.
Coxswain and Boat's Crew Hut	Repaired, but wants more room.
Dock Yard	All repaired.
The Executioner's Hut	All repaired.
Two Government Huts	Do.
Dry Stores	Partly repaired.
Salt Provision Stores	Two Repaired.
„	One not repaired.
Granary	In complete Repair.
New Church	Nearly finished.
One Stone Wind Mill	Repaired.
One Old Wind Mill	Useless.
One New do.	Finished.
The Gaol	Wants additional cells.
Two Captain and Adjutant's Barracks	Repairing.
Surgeon's Barrack	Not repaired.
Two Assistant Surgeon's Barracks ...	Repaired.
Military Hospital	Complete.
Light Horsemen's Barracks and Stable	Not repaired.
Five Subaltern's Barracks	Repaired.
Three do. do.	In a forward state of being complete.
Two Private's Barracks	Repaired.
Military Stores	Repaired.
Old Guard House	Taken away.
New Guard House	Finished.
Guard House at Dawes Point	Not repaired.

* Note 47.

1807.
31 Oct.

Report on the
condition of
the public
buildings.

HAWKESBURY.

Government House .... Repaired and two new
                                    Rooms added.
The Church, School and Granary ..... Finished.
One Thatched Storehouse .... Out of repair.

TOONGABBE.

The Barn and Dairy .... Repaired.
The other Building in a bad state.

CASTLE HILL.

Stone Granary .... Repaired.
New Granary or Barn .... Finished.
Dwelling house and Storehouse ...... Not repaired.

PARRAMATTA.

Government House .... Not repaired.
         „   Out Offices .... Partly repaired.
Clergyman's house .... In a bad state.
Seven Houses .... Omitted in last Return,
                                    were in a bad State
                                    but are now Repaired.
Officers' and Privates' Barracks ...... In bad Repair.
Light Horseman's Barrack .... Repaired.
New Stabling .... Built.
Church .... Badly built and unfinished.
Granary and Store house .... Partly repaired.
One Wood Granary .... In a bad State.
The New Gaol and Factory .... Badly built and wants re-
                                    pairs.

THOS. MOORE, Ms. Builder.
RICHARD ROUSE, Ms. Carpen'r.

[Enclosure No. 4.]

MEMORANDA of a Journey from Port Dalrymple to the River
Derwent by Lieut. Thomas Laycock.

[Enclosure No. 5.]

LETTER from Governor Bligh to Lieutenant-Governor Paterson,
dated 27th September, 1807.

[Enclosure No. 6.]

LETTER from Governor Bligh to Lieutenant-Governor Collins,
dated 1st October, 1807.

[Enclosure No. 7.]

REPORTS on the Live Stock at the Derwent and Port Dalrymple.

[*Copies of these four enclosures will be found in volume I,
series III.*]

[Enclosure No. 8.]

REPORT of the Muster at Norfolk Island in August, 1807.

[*A copy of this return will be found amongst the Norfolk
Island papers.*]

[Enclosure No. 9.]

The Trustees of the Jail Fund In Account with Robert Campbell Treasurer and Naval Officer appointed on the 2d of May and to receive Five pr. Cent. on all Duties Collected.

Dr.   Cr.

1807		£ s. d.
May 16	To paid for 182 Bushels of Lime for building the Church.	£0 2 0
	" paid Thomas West for Coffins as pr. Order	13 1 0
June 20	" paid John Gowen Storekeeper Salary allowed him for taking charge of the Articles in Store belonging to this Fund from 13th of August to this date.	7 8 8
30	" Balance in my hands at this date and carried to New Account with the Trustees.	1,195 16 8
		£1,225 8 4

1807		£ s. d.
May 29	By Cash from Mr. John Harris late Naval Officer and Collector of Duties for Balance due by him from the 13th of August 1806 to the 31 Decr Last.	498 15 4
"	" Sundry Promisory Notes for Balance due by him from 31 of Decemr last to the 2nd Current for Duties Collected during that period deducting his Commission of 10 pr Cent as pr Account finally Settled this day.	432 3 0
June 30	" Amount of Sales of 25 Cases of Hollands and 173 Gallns of Brandy that remained in Store belonging to the Fund and ordered to be disposed of By His Excelly the Governor.	294 10 0
		£1225 8 4

Sydney, New South Wales, 1st July, 1807.

Rob. Campbell.

1807.
31 Oct.

Balance-sheet of the gaol fund.

Dr. THE Trustees of the Orphan Institution

1806			£	s	d
Decr.	17	To paid William Bateman for washing and shearing the sheep belonging to the Fund	£1	10	0
1807 Janry	31	,, paid Mr. Samuel Marsden for 50 of the 100 Male Sheep agreed to be purchased from him at the Meeting of the Trustees on the 13th of Decemr last.	150	0	0
		,, paid Mr. P. Crook for 3 quarters Schooling of Joseph Barseten	—	19	6
		,, paid for a Cart and Wheat Mill purchased for the use of the Farm at Prospect Hill belonging to the Fund.	17	0	0
February 25		,, paid John Cronin to account of building a Frame of a House on the said Farm	6	0	0
		,, paid John Jones for 13½ lbs of Soap furnished 3rd of June last	—	19	6
		,, paid James Bean for Joiner's Work at the School House ...	6	5	6
		,, paid James Evans Carpenter for putting on the remaining Hip boards on the Roof..	2	0	0
March	7	,, paid H Stroud Balance of his Wages as Master of the School and discharged him by order of the Trustees.	18	15	7
	10	,, paid John Warby for furnishing the Stockeepers with Wheat	3	13	9
		,, paid Mr. Christopher Palmer for Bread and Flour furnished for the Maintenance of the Children to the 22nd of Feby.	84	19	7
	11	,, paid Thomas Rose Overseer of the Stock and Farm at Prospect Hill a quarters Salary on the 9th Currt.	16	5	0
	23	,, paid Matthew Kain for plaisterer's Work to the Wash house at the School	8	0	0
April	20	,, paid Thomas Stubbs for Palisading done at the Garden &c.	14	13	6
May	13	,, paid Thomas Rose to account of erecting the necessary Buildings and Stock Yard on the Farm at Prospect.	20	0	0
	,,	,, paid John Warby for Wheat furnished the Stockeepers	1	16	4½
		,, paid Ann Sandilands Balance of Wages as Cook at the School and discharged her....................................	2	10	0
		,, paid Thomas Bolton balance of his Account for Mason's work done at the School House, &c.	45	12	8
	16	,, paid for Muzzles for the Calves	1	10	0
	25	,, paid Simeon Lord for 560 lbs of Soft Sugar purchased for the use of the children, @ 1s. pr lb.	28	0	0
		,, paid Mr. Samuel Marsden's Attorney for the remainder of the hundred Male Sheep purchased from him.	150	0	0
June	15	,, paid for a Grindstone and Frame for the use of the Farm ...	1	2	0
	25	,, paid Michael Donevan for Wheat supplied to the Stockeepers	3	7	6
		,, paid John Gowen Storekeeper Salary allowed to him for taking charge of the Articles that was in the Store for the use of the School.	4	0	8
	27	,, paid James Deakin for 30 pair of Shoes for the Children...	6	15	0
	29	,, paid Thomas Rose Overseer of Stock a Quarter's Salary...	16	5	0
		,, paid John Cronin for furnishing the Frame of the House at the Farm	1	0	0
		,, paid Thomas Rose for Balance due to him on the Buildings and Stock Yard agreeable to R. Hassal's valuation.	9	8	6
		,, paid William Gough for Shoe Thread, &c.	1	7	0
		,, paid Messrs Campbell & Co for Soap, &c., &c.	18	19	4
		,, paid Mr. Christopher Palmer for Bread and Flour from the 22nd of Feby.	140	12	0
		,, Mr. Commissary Palmer, for Salt Provisions and other furnishing from the Public Store as Pr Account.	252	1	5½
	30	,, My Commission as Treasurer for receiving and paying away Monies £1293 ,, 19 ,, 1½ @ 2 Pr Cent.	25	17	7½
		,, Balance remaining in my hands at this date and carried to the new Account with the Trustees.	232	12	1
		£	1293	19	1½

Sydney, New South Wales, 1st July, 1807.

No. 10.]

In Account with Robert Campbell, Treasurer.

Cr.

Balance-sheet
of the
orphan fund.

1806				
Novr. 18th	By Sundry Promissory Notes received this day from the Reverend Samuel Marsden, Treasurer being the Balance of the Funds belonging to the Institution on the 13th day of August last.	845	1	4
1807				
Febry. 24	Cash from Mr. John Harris Naval Officer and Collector of Duties for the proportion arising to the Fund of the Institution from the said 13th day of August to the 31 of December last deducting his Commission Charg'd at the rate of 10 pr Cent.	53	1	2
May 29	,, Do from Do for proportion of Duties from the 31 of Decemr to the 2nd Currt. when he was removed as Naval Officer deducting his said Commission of 10 pr Cent. as pr Account.	395	16	9
	£	1293	19	1½

ROBT. CAMPBELL.

1807.
31 Oct.

Proceedings of
bench of
magistrates
in suit,
Macarthur v.
Campbell, Jr.

[Enclosure No. 11.]

JOHN MACARTHUR v. ROBERT CAMPBELL, JUN'R.

Report of Proceedings.

24th October, 1807.

Bench of Magistrates: The Judge-Advocate, Major Geo. Johnston,
John Palmer, Esqrs.

MR. CAMPBELL wishes to have the Sense of the Bench how far he
can be considered Incompetent to sit as a Magistrate on the Grounds
of his being an Evidence.

The Bench is of Opinion that, as he is called as an Evidence, he
cannot sit as a Magistrate.

JOHN MCARTHUR, ESQR., being Sworn, Says that the Complaint he
has now to make against Mr. Robert Campbell, Junr., is for that he,
on the 22nd instant, did in an illegal Manner, and contrary to the
Laws of the Realm, take, or cause to be taken away, by the assistance of Several Men, from out of the Dwelling-house in this town
belonging to myself and Mr. Blaxcell, two Copper Boilers, which he
values at £40 Sterling.

MR. ROBERT CAMPBELL, Junr., Says that on the Morning of the
22nd he was ordered by Mr. Robert Campbell, Senior, Naval Officer,
to go to the Bonded Store and Ship on board the D. of Portland two
Stills, with heads and worms compleat. The Bodies of the Stills
(or Coppers) were not to be found in Government Stores; but I was
informed they were in the possession of Mr. Blaxcell. I informed
Mr. Campbell of this Circumstance after having Shipped the Heads
and Worms on board the D. of Portland. Mr. Campbell ordered me
to wait on Mr. McArthur and ask him where the two Bodies of the
Stills were, as Mr. Campbell had the Governor's Orders to take
them away. Mr. McA. particularly asked me if such was the
Gov'r's Order. I informed him that such was his Order to Mr.
Campbell. Mr. McA. then informed me that if I would procure a
receipt from Mr. Campbell he would let me have them, and said
my Receipt would be sufficient. I told him I never took on myself
to give any Receipts in the N.O. Name. I then went to Mr. Campbell, and procured the receipt as contained in No. 1. On my
presenting this Receipt to Mr. McA., he begged leave to differ from
Mr. Campbell, Saying that the words "heads and worms" should be
left out. I again returned to Mr. C., who told me he would give no
other receipt, alledging that it corresponded exactly with the Letter
he wrote Mr. Blaxcell and with his Public Books. On my return
to Mr. McA., he informed me that, Since he could not get a receipt
to his Satisfaction, he would have none, but shewed me where the
Bodies of the Stills were, and that I might take them away at my
own risk. I immediately went and called Cole and the Governor's
Boats Crew, and requested of them to come and carry the Bodies
of the Stills away; in the meantime I saw Mr. Blaxcell standing at
the back door. I asked him if he had any objection for my taking

1807.
31 Oct.

Proceedings of
bench of
magistrates
in suit,
Macarthur v.
Campbell, Jr.

the Boat's Crew into the premises; he answered that he would have nothing to do with it; I might do as I chose; from the strict Orders I had from Mr. Campbell, I immediately ordered them to be carried off and shipped on board the D. of Portland. Says that he had no written Authority.

Mr. McArthur calls JOHN HARRIS, Esq., who, being Sworn :—

Q. by Mr. McA.: Was you not N.O. at the Arrival of the Dart?— *A.* I was.

Q. Did you not receive an Order from the Governor to take the Heads and Worms of two Stills and put them into the Stores?—*A.* There was an Order to that Effect on the 3rd or 4th Bill of Lading written by the Governor, and I had Orders for Mr. Gaven,* the Storekeeper, to receive them into the Stores.

Q. Does it come within Your knowledge that they were so delivered?—*A.* I allways understood that they were till two Months after, when, on the Governor asking me if they were put into the Stores, I sent for Mr. Gaven, the Storekeeper, who told me that he had received the Heads and Worms, but the bodies he had not got. I think he informed me that Mr. Blaxcell had informed him that the Bodies were full of Medicines.

Q. by Bench. At the time the Governor wrote, or gave you an order for the Stills to be put into the stores, Did you understand that it meant the Stills compleat?—*A.* I did.

Q. Were these Stills imported regularly by a Bill of lading, or were they clandestinely imported?—*A.* They were in the Bill of Lading—One Still for Mr. McA., and the other for Capt'n Abbott.

Q. You are a Medical Gentleman, and accustomed to Chemical Operations; is the body of the Still, when the Head and Worm are removed, fitter for the Operation of distilling than any pot or boiler in the Colony?—*A.* No.

ROBERT CAMPBELL, Esqr., Senior, as N.O., Sworn :—

Submits to the Bench the propriety of his being called on as an Evidence by Mr. McA., the Governor having given him an Order to Ship the Stills on board the Duke of Portland.

The Bench, conceiving that Mr. Rob't Campbell, Senior, being responsible for the Acts of his Clerk, is an interested person, consequently is inadmissible as an Evidence.

THOMAS JAMISON, Esqr., Sworn :—

Q. by Mr. McA. Were You not present in the House belonging to myself and Mr. Blaxcell, on the 22nd instant, when Mr. R. C., Jun'r, accompanied by several Men, came there and took from thence two Copper boilers?—*A.* I was at the House occupied by Yourself and Mr. Blaxcell, at the time Mr. R. C., Jun'r, accompanied by several Men, came and took away two Bodies of Stills.

Q. Previous to his taking them, did You not see him offer me a Receipt, to which I objected, Stating that it was incorrect, for that

* Note 48.

1807.
31 Oct.

Proceedings of
bench of
magistrates
in suit,
Macarthur v.
Campbell, Jr.

I had not two Stills with Heads and Worms complete in my possession; and, therefore, as I had only the bodies to deliver up, the
receipt I required was for them alone?—*A.* I saw the receipt offered,
and such a Conversation did pass, or words to that Effect.

Q. Did not Mr. Campbell go out expressing his intention to obtain
the Receipt I required?—*A.* He did; he said he would go to his
uncle and get it altered.

Q. On his return did he not inform me that his uncle would give
no other than the one he had at first presented?—*A.* Yes.

Q. Did I not again refuse to take it?—*A.* Yes.

Q. Did not Mr. R. C. ask if he might take the bodies of the
Stills?—*A.* I think he did.

Q. Did I not reply, " I will show you where the bodies of the
Stills are. You must judge for Yourself of the Sufficiency of Your
authority, for whatever You do is at Your own risk "?—*A.* You said
You would show him where the bodies of the Stills were, and it
must rest with himself how he was to act.

Q. Had the Bodies of the Stills which You saw taken away ever
been used?—*A.* From their Appearance, in my Opinion they never
were.

Q. What do You suppose those two boilers or Bodies of Stills to be
worth in this Colony, supposing them to be appropriated to brewing
or any other domestic purpose?—*A.* I cannot say I am competent to
judge of their Value.

Mr. McA. offers as Evidence the Copy of a Letter written by him
to Robert Campbell, Esq'r., of which the following is a Copy:—

" Sir,   " Sydney, 19th October, 1807.

" Mr. Blaxcell has communicated to me the Contents of a
Letter from You of the 12th instant, relative to two Stills imported
into this Colony in my Ship the Dart, which You state the Governor
has directed are to be Shipped on board the Duke of Portland. In
Answer, I must beg to acquaint His Excellency that I have nothing
to do with the Still belonging to Capt'n Abbott, and that it is my
intention to dispose of my own to some Ship going to India or
China. If that should be objected to, the Head and Worm can be
disposed of as the Governor thinks proper, and I shall appropriate
the Copper to some domestic use.

                                                " I am, &c.,
                                                    " JOHN McARTHUR.

" Robert Campbell, Esq'r., Naval Officer."

to Which Letter I received no Answer; as a proof that the Heads
and Worms of the Stills were delivered into the Government Stores,
I beg leave to produce the Receipt, of which the following is a
Copy:—

                                        " Sydney, 16th April, 1807.

" Received into His Majesty's Stores, at Sydney, from G. Blaxcell, Esqr., Two Heads and two Worms belonging to two Stills.

                                        " JNO. GOWEN, S.K."

Mr. Robert Campbell, Jun'r, calls EDMUND GRIFFIN, Esq'r., His Excellency's Secretary, who being Sworn :—

Q. by Mr. Campbell. Relate to the Court what You know respecting two Stills imported in the Ship Dart?—*A.* On the 8th March last, on which day the Dart arrived, the Master of her was brought on Shore by the N.O. to the Gov'r, when he produced his Invoice and other necessary Papers. On the Governor's examining the Invoice he directed that the Spirits, as usual, were to be taken from the Ship to the Bonded Store, And the two Stills, as appeared in the Invoice compleat were also to be put there, and the Gov'r particularly wrote against the Stills to that Effect, and gave directions to the N.O. that they should be in readiness to send to England by the first Opportunity. About the latter end of March, or some time in April, on some Occasion, Mr. Harris, the then N.O., stated to the Gov'r that the Stills were in the Store except the two bodies (now in question) which he said Mr. McA. said he meant to apply to domestic purposes, at which the Gov'r expressed great Surprise, and told him that he had not complied with his orders, and that he was instantly to see them complied with. Some few days ago the Gov'r told Mr. C., the now N.O., to Ship the Stills on board the D. of Portland, as she was on her return to England, On which I expressed my doubts whether the Governor's Orders had been complied with, with respect to what I have stated as to the Orders given to Mr. Harris, in consequence of his Neglect in March or April; but the Gov'r appeared to have no doubt but that they were in the Stores complete. Mr. Campbell Since told me that I was right in my conjecture, and that the Coppers were at Mr. Blaxcell's, and that he should get them and ship the Stills.

Mr. McA. here objects to that part of Mr. Griffin's Evidence beginning with the words, " Mr. Campbell since told me," &c., because I conceive that the Law requires the best Evidence the Case will admit should allways be produced, and Mr. C., Senior, being present, surely can require no Substitute to communicate what he knows in this Case. Another reason for my objecting is the dangerous and dreadful Consequences to be apprehended (as I conceive) from suffering illegal precedent to be established.

Q. by Mr. McA. Mr. Griffin has stated to the Court that Mr. C., whose Evidence I have not received the benefit of, is N.O. I wish to know whether the Duties of that Gentleman's Office does not require that he should enforce the Governor's regulations and restrictions on all Merchant Ships coming into this Port, and whether it is not thro' him that all duties or fees on Exports and imports are levied?—*A.* I conceive that the Q'n can only be answered in correctness by the General Orders and Regulations on the Subjects of Mr. McA.'s question; therefore, anything that I may give as an Opinion might prove Erroneous.

GEO. DOWLING sworn :—

Q. by Mr. Campbell, Jun'r. You was Naval Officer's Clerk when the Dart arrived?—*A.* I was.

Q. Relate to the Bench what You know concerning two Stills that were imported by that Ship.—*A.* After the Ship was entered, Mr. H.,

1807.
31 Oct.

Proceedings of
bench of
magistrates
in suit,
Macarthur v.
Campbell, Jr.

who was then N.O., went to Gov't House with the Manifest of ye
Cargo. After his return I met him by the Bridge when he showed
me the Manifest, and pointed out a Minute which the Gov'r had
made in his own writing for the two Stills to be put into H.M.
Stores till Opportunity offered of sending them back to England.
Some time afterwards Mr. H. sent me to Mr. Blaxcell's to desire
that the Coppers might be put into the Stores. I was some time
after sent by the Gov'r to Mr. Blaxcell's to order them to the
Stores, and I desired the Storekeeper to receive them.

Q. Did You not go to Mr. Blaxcell's in consequence of Mr. Harris
stating to the Góv'r that the Coppers were not there?—A. The Gov'r
desired me to go.

MR. McARTHUR states that he has produced Evidence to prove to
the Court that two Coppers or Bodies of Stills were taken out of
my house on the 22nd inst. without my Consent. Mr. Griffin, the
Governor's Secretary, has declared in Evidence, that the Gov'r told
Mr. Rob't Campbell, N.O., to take these Bodies of Stills and Ship
them on board the Duke of Portland; by the Acknowledgment of
the respectable Young Gentleman, Mr. R't Campbell, Jun'r, he was
told by his Uncle to execute that command. It would therefore
appear that a British Subject, living in a British Settlement, in
which the British Laws are established by the Royal Patent, has
had his property wrested from him by a Non-accredited Individual,
without any Authority being produced or any other reason being
assigned than that it was the Governor's Order. It is therefore for
you, Gentlemen, to determine whether this be the tenor on which
Englishmen hold their property in N. S. Wales.

The Bench is of Opinion that Mr. Robert Campbell, Junior, was
not authorised to take the Coppers out of Mr. Blaxcell's house, he
not being either a Magistrate or a Naval Officer, Nor did he
receive any Orders from the Governor to that Effect.

GEO. JOHNSTON.
R'D ATKINS.

Mr. Palmer is of Opinion, as Mr. Robert Campbell, Jun'r, acted
under the Orders of Mr. Rob't Campbell, N.O., Sen'r, he is justified
in what he did.   JNO. PALMER.

A true Copy—R'D ATKINS, J.-A.

[No. 1.]

RECEIPT FOR STILLS.

Naval Office, Sydney, 22nd October, 1807.

RECEIVED from Mr. G. Blaxcell, Agent for the Ship Dart, two Stills,
with Heads and Worms, which were entered by that Ship on the
9th March last, addressed for Capt. McArthur and Capt. Abbott,
and allowed to be landed on the express Condition of being sent
to England by the first Ship, and which Stills are now to be shipped
on board the Duke of Portland, by Order of His Excellency the
Governor.

ROB'T CAMPBELL, Naval Officer.

1807.
31 Oct.

Returns of employment of convicts.

[Enclosure No. 12.]

QUARTERLY EMPLOYMENT of Male Convicts Victuall'd and at Public Labour.

1807. Month	Settlement	Agriculture and Stock			Buildings										Boat Builders, etc.			Various Employments												
		Overseers.	Agriculture on Public Account.	Care of Gov't Stock and Grass Cutters.	Brick and Tile Makers.	Bricklayers, Plaisterers and Layers.	Blacksmiths and Labourers.	Shingle, Pale and Lath Splitters.	Brick and Timber Carriages.	Stone Cutters and Layers.	Sawyers and Timber Measurers.	House Carpenters and Labourers.	Painters and Glaziers.	Lime and Charcoal Burners.	Carpenters, Shipwrights and Caulkers.	Labourers, Watchmen and Clerks.	Blacksmiths, Sawyers and Rope Makers.	Making Roads, repairing Bridges and Battery.	Taking Care of Govern't Huts.	Wheelwrights, Millwrights and Labourers.	Basket and Broom Makers.	Flax Dressers, Wool Carders and Weavers.	Millers and Salt Boilers.	Schoolmaster, Bellman and Sexton.	Writers and Clerks.	Coopers, Farriers and Wire Drawers.	Granary, Provision Store and Clerks.	Executioners and Gaolers.	Sadlers and Miners.
June	Sydney	16	…	5	12	10	15	…	20	27	2	25	1	2	6	25	17	4	2	3	2	…	10	3	11	2	9	4	…
	Parramatta	13	…	59	…	4	9	8	15	…	17	7	…	5	…	…	…	…	14	3	2	40	…	1	2	1	6	4	2
	Hawicesbury	…	…	…	…	…	…	6	…	…	…	8	…	…	…	…	…	…	…	…	…	…	…	…	1	…	3	1	…
	Toongabbe	1	10	5	…	…	…	…	…	…	…	…	…	…	…	…	…	…	…	…	…	…	…	…	1	…	…	…	…
	Castle Hill	4	54	14	…	…	2	…	2	…	…	…	…	…	…	…	…	…	1	…	…	…	1	…	1	…	…	…	…
	Total	34	64	83	12	14	26	14	37	27	19	40	1	7	6	25	17	4	17	6	4	40	11	4	16	3	18	9	2

1807.
31 Oct.

Returns of
employment
of convicts.

QUARTERLY EMPLOYMENT—*continued*.

Settlement	General Total	Recapitulate — Servants to Officers etc.	Recapitulate — Various Employments.	Recapitulate — Shipwrights and Boat Builders.	Recapitulate — Artificers etc. Employed in Building.	Recapitulate — Overseers, Stockkeepers & Employed in Agriculture and Grass Cutters.	Servants — Settlers.	Servants — Overseers, Constables Free men doing Government work.	Servants — Non-Commiss'd Officers N.S.W. Corps.	Servants — To Commiss'd Officers Civil and Military Including Superintendants.	Various — Brewery and Sail Makers.	Various — Printers and Book Binders.	Various — Taylors, Shoemakers and Barbers.	Various — Sick and Convalescent.	Various — Attending Hospitals.	Various — Carry Wood and Water for the Guards.	Various — Constables and Watchmen.	Various — Gaol Gang.	Various — Town Gang.	Various — Colonial Vessels.	Various — Government Gardens.	Various — Boats Crews.	Various — Orphan House and Farm.	Various — Blind, Insane and Invalids.	Various — Tanner's Toolhelvers and Thatchers.	Various — Natl, History and Botanist Painters.	Month
Sydney	418	47	188	48	114	21	4	13	:	30	1	2	5	11	9	2	21	27	18	12	5	20	1	2	1	1	June
Parramatta	353	68	153	:	65	72	19	10	:	39	:	:	4	16	7	1	20	2	8	:	3	5	:	9	2	1	
Hawkesbury	28	:	14	:	14	:	:	:	:	:	:	:	:	:	1	1	4	:	:	:	1	2	:	:	:	:	
Toongabbe	20	1	3	:	:	16	:	1	:	:	:	:	:	:	:	:	2	:	:	:	:	:	:	:	:	:	
Cast e Hill	102	2	24	:	4	72	:	2	:	:	:	:	2	5	1	:	9	:	:	:	1	:	:	2	1	:	
Total	926	118	382	48	197	181	23	26	:	69	1	2	11	32	18	4	56	29	26	12	10	27	1	13	4	2	

1807.

QUARTERLY EMPLOYMENT of Female Convicts Victuall'd and at Public Labour.

1807.
31 Oct.

Returns of employment of convicts.

Month.	Settlement.	Woolen & Linen Manufactory.	Spinning & Picking Oakum etc.	Husking Corn & Picking Weeds.	In Care of Govt. Huts.	Sail Makers.	Orphan House & Care of Orphans.	Hospital Nurses.	Midwives.	Sick and Convalescent.	Blind Insane and Invalids.	Government Dairy.	Settlers Wives.	Allowed to Overseers.	Servants to Officers etc.	Women allowed to the N.S.W. Corps.	General Total.
June	Sydney	:	6	3	:	1	:	7	1	1	3	:	:	5	8	:	35
	Parramatta	87	:	:	:	:	3	7	:	11	2	:	:	:	:	:	110
	Hawkesbury	:	:	:	1	:	:	:	:	:	:	:	:	:	:	:	1
	Toongabbe	:	:	:	:	:	:	:	:	:	:	:	:	:	:	:	:
	Castle Hill	:	:	1	1	:	:	:	:	:	:	:	:	1	:	:	3
	Total	87	6	4	2	1	3	14	1	12	5	:	:	6	8	:	149

1807.
31 Oct.

GOVERNOR BLIGH TO THE RIGHT HON. WILLIAM WINDHAM.

(Despatch No. 1, per transport Duke of Portland; acknowledged by
Viscount Castlereagh, 15th May, 1809.)

Government House, Sydney, New South Wales,
Sir,   31st October, 1807.

I have the honor to acknowledge the receipt of your
Despatches of the numbers and dates as stated in the Margin.*

Land grant and
live stock for
John Blaxland.
I felt the strongest desire to comply with your instructions
respecting Mr. John Blaxland. He has received twelve hundred
and ninety acres of land, Sixty Cows, One Bull, Four Oxen, and
Thirty Ewes, with Twenty Men, the proportion he required of
Eighty, the number directed to be allotted to him; the payment
for the Stock to be made by instalments in kind. The remaining
quantity of Land I have ordered to be measured out for him; and
it is to be hoped that, with these great advantages, he will turn
his mind to agricultural pursuits, as well as the grazing of Cattle,
without which the Colony will be but very partially benefited.

Live stock
received by
Gregory
Blaxland.
Mr. Gregory Blaxland having arrived a Year prior to his
brother, received from Governor King Two Bulls, One Ox, and
Seventy-Five Cows, which induced me to grant the great portion
here stated, as it far exceeds, but under that circumstance, what
I considered should have been the case.

Land grant
and live stock
for Bell.
Mr. Bell has received Five Hundred Acres of Land, Four Cows,
and Three Oxen, with other indulgencies, as a Settler.

Land grant
for Kerillac.
On the discharge of M. Huon de Kerillac† from the New South
Wales Corps, I gave directions for his receiving One Hundred
Acres of Land and the usual advantages.

The other Settlers who came by the late Ships have received
the advantages they were to expect and will have every protection.

Before I left England it was understood that no Person was to
come out to live here without express permission; but in the late
Unauthorised
immigrants.
Ships several Persons arrived with no other than orders from the
Transport Office to the Masters of the Ships for their being
victualled during the passage.

Arrival of
convicts.
The Convicts by the Duke of Portland and Sydney Cove
arrived as well as could be expected, and have been allotted to the
different Settlers, to the general advantage of the agricultural
parts of the Colony. Only a few deaths took place in the course
of the Voyage.

Proposed
evacuation of
Norfolk Island.
It is now my duty to reply to your Letter respecting the evacuation of Norfolk Island,‡ and to show my readiness to comply
with the directions therein contained.

The first step that appeared necessary was to communicate with
the Commandant of that place, and, therefore, the moment the

* The margin is blank.   † Note 10.   ‡ Note 49.

Lady Nelson, Armed Tender, could be got ready, which was on
the 5th of last Month, she was despatched with instructions to
Captain Piper on the subject, of which the inclosed is a Copy, Proposed evacuation of
together with a Copy of the directions I had received; she Norfolk Island.
returned here on the 7th Instant, and went again to Norfolk
Island on the 16th to forward the intended evacuation, on the
subject of which I have the satisfaction to state that the Settlers
displayed great willingness, but only two of them have offered to
go to Port Dalrymple.

Lieutenant-Governors Collins and Paterson are apprized of
what is to be done.

It is to be regretted that our means are but small to accom- Want of shipping.
plish this object, having only the Porpoise, besides two trifling
Vessels, the Lady Nelson and Estramina. A smaller Vessel,
called the Resource, is employed between this and Coal River,
and only fit for that purpose.

The Country is bare of agricultural implements, and we have
very few Artificers.

In replying, Sir, to that part of your Letter No. 7, respecting
the information which was to be expected from me connected
with Governor King's despatches, I beg leave to observe that as King's despatches.
only extracts of particular parts of them are in my possession,*
hope my General Letter of the 7th February, 1807, by the Buffalo,
will have conveyed the information required. Such farther
observations as I have been enabled to make and feel necessary
to communicate are contained in my General Letter of this
date.

On the subject of the supplies of Salt Provisions sent out by Salt provisions *ex*
the Duke of Portland and Young William, I beg to inform You Duke of
the Duke of Portland brought only nine Months for victualling Portland and Young
the number of Prisoners in her after their Arrival,—the Young William.
William only 410,576 lbs. of Beef—equal to Twenty one Weeks'
supply for all the Settlements according to the Demand made by
Governor King on the 30th of June, 1805.

But to place our situation in a clear point of view, the Salt Commissariat estimates.
Provisions remaining on the 30th of last Month were calculated
would last at full ration only Thirty nine Weeks for all the
Settlements, as may be seen by the General Statement here
inclosed; from whence, Sir, every judgement may be formed of
what is required, when compared with such supplies as may be
on the way for the Colony and its Dependencies.

For a more minute examination the Commissary's Receipt and
Expence of Provisions is inclosed shewing the Remains, and I

* Note 50.

beg to observe that a great additional expenditure will ensue by the evacuation of Norfolk Island and the number of persons coming out.

Great will be the expence if necessity should require the purchasing of Meat for the subsistence of those who are necessarily victualled from the Public Stores. Owing to the scarcity of Animal Food, Beef and Pork is selling at One Shilling and Nine Pence per pound. I am aware how far I may supply from the Government Herds under such circumstances in case of necessity.

In regard to Colonel Collins's complaint of the distresses he had felt, everything has been done on my part to remove them.

The following Month after I arrived, 12,448 lbs. of Beef, 82,716 lbs. of Pork, 1,000 lbs. of Sugar, with a supply of Articles for Barter, Slop Clothing, and Hospital Necessaries were sent to the Derwent, and on the 2nd of March last a supply of Grain was sent by the Colonial Schooner, Estramina, when the following paragraphs formed a part of my Letter, which are applicable to the present subject.

" By the King George was sent every thing we could spare— our distresses here have been very great—the Poor have neither had Kangaroo to eat or very little of anything else; therefore, while our distresses are equal, I hope the People at the Derwent will bear them with equal fortitude, turn themselves to agriculture, and grow at least as many Potatoes as will serve in lieu of Bread, and not lay such a stress on an article as an absolute necessary of Life, while myriads of People live without it.

" Our greatest exertions have been to get in the Harvest, and to enable us to get grain we have been obliged to send all the Government Thrashers to the different Settlers, by which means I now load the Estramina for you in part with Seed Wheat, and shall look anxiously for her return with the state you are in.

" We have to lament the loss of the Sydney and Tellicherry; the former on the Coast of New Guinea, the latter in the Straits of Apo, so that Supplies expected from them is over, but Mr. Campbell is of opinion his House will, nevertheless, send a Ship here. This account came by the General Wellesley, a Ship from Prince of Wales's Island, which has brought us Rice and some Wheat, in consequence of which the Estramina's lading is completed.

" Both Norfolk Island and Port Dalrymple are in great want; so that to those places likewise I am obliged to send relief, which I hope will be increased by some Ships which may arrive shortly from England, independent of the promising Harvest, which you represented to me coming forward at the Derwent, and must now have been got into stacks.

"The Pork sent from Norfolk Island to Port Dalrymple turned out fine, and by Captain Piper's representation yours was equally so when shipped, and that its turning out otherwise was occasioned by the Storekeeper not keeping the Casks filled up with Pickle. In the stowage of Salt Provisions it is absolutely necessary that the lower Casks are stowed on billets of wood so as to keep their bilges from the ground, for otherwise the weight of the upper ones press all the Pickle out, and the Meat becomes rancid and not fit to eat."

1807.
31 Oct.
———
Extract from
Bligh's letter
to Collins.

Previous to the Estramina's departure from thence the Duchess of York arrived from India with an ample supply of Rice. On the 14th of April a supply of 38,160 lbs. of Pork was sent by the Elizabeth (Whaler), and His Majesty's Ship Porpoise sailed from this on the 10th Instant for the Derwent having on board 63,616 lbs. of Beef, 24,168 lbs. of Pork, a quantity of Maize, and a further supply of Stores, by which the Derwent is now on a par with Port Jackson in respect to Salt Provisions.

Arrival of
the ship
Duchess of
York.

The Estramina sailed on the same day for Port Dalrymple with as much Provisions as she could take, and the Lieutenant-Governor being now in possession of our plans of what is to be done, every thing is in a fair way of succeeding.

Supplies
sent to Port
Dalrymple.

I have likewise informed Lieutenant-Governors Collins and Paterson they must be cautious in sanctioning demands until they have fully considered them, and are convinced of the absolute necessity of such being made, which no doubt will be strictly attended to.   I have, &c.,
                                               WM. BLIGH.

[Enclosure No. 1.]

GOVERNOR BLIGH TO COMMANDANT PIPER.

Government House, Sydney, New South Wales,
Sir,   4th September, 1807.
        I am now preparing to send the Lady Nelson to Norfolk Island, Lieutenant Kent the Commander, by whom you will receive these my dispatches which are of considerable moment, and will require the utmost attention on your part in order that your answer thereto may be clear and concise on every point, that I may unite with you in the completion of a design which will require some wisdom to plan and regularity to execute.

The Lady
Nelson sent to
Norfolk Island.

But in the first place, in reply to your dispatches dated the 17th June last, which I received by His Majesty's Ship Porpoise, I have to inform you we have sent such necessaries as the Lady Nelson will stow and we apprehend you most are in need of: among these are Salt provisions which you will be careful of and

Supplies sent to
Norfolk Island.

1807.
31 Oct.
not use them unless it cannot be avoided; that they may aid us in our ultimate designs, in the execution of which you will see the absolute necessity of looking forward to, and which when effected will have complied with all your other demands.

The salary and status of surgeon Connellan.
In answer to Mr. Connellan* the Island Surgeon's Letter, I see no regular method of doing justice to that Gentleman but by his getting money as his Salary by your Certificate of his having done the duty of Surgeon to your satisfaction and transmitting an authentic Copy of Governor King's letter to you of the 26th February, 1806, respecting him, and the authority which he himself received to hold and act in the situation. By the evacuation of Norfolk Island, to which I have before alluded, on his proceeding to Port Dalrymple he will be authorized to hold a situation, there being a vacancy for a first and Second Assistant Surgeon in the event of these situations not being filled at home, which seems to be implied by the Secretary of State's letter of which I transmit a Copy for your Guidance as likewise Copies of the vote of Parliament for defraying the expences of the Civil Establishment for the last Year.

Instructions re the evacuation of Norfolk Island.
I now come to the most serious part of our consideration, which is the removing of the Inhabitants under your orders to the Derwent and Port Dalrymple, the judicious arrangement of which rests with us to effect, while the remunerations ordered by Government will make up to every Individual for any temporary inconvenience which may be felt in putting His Majesty's Orders into execution.

As I now think it proper to send you Mr. Secretary Windham's letter on this head,† you will be thoroughly acquainted with the whole that is to be done, and you will immediately publish such parts as are necessary for the People to be informed of. I am sure you will not fail to impress on their minds, the propriety of a chearful compliance, and to exhort them to come forward with Spirit to support the intentions of Government, which are solely directed to their good, while on my part they may rely on the most particular care and watchfulness over everything which appertains to their future Interests and Comforts.

You will observe that I am commanded to execute the duty imposed on me with the Colonial Vessels; these are the Porpoise, Lady Nelson, and Estrimena, means not adequate to do much at one time, if they can be spared, for one or more of them must be employed going to Port Dalrymple and the Derwent with provisions, to keep up their necessary supplies. Should it so happen that we employ them together, or either of them, whatever arrangement we make should be as complete as possible—that is,

* Note 51.   † Note 52.

whoever first goes should embark with their absolute necessaries for settling at the place they make choice of, and to avoid as much as possible (by way of exemplification) being like sending Powder in one Ship and Shot in another, whereby if one is lost the other for a length of time becomes of no use.

Another circumstance to guard against is, that no application is to be made to me by any Settler or Person whatever, in order to change the Minister's Commands—every thing must be done as he has directed; and I feel very much satisfied that in the execution of the Service entrusted to you, not only the letter of the Instructions, but the Spirit of them, will be complied with, much to your honor and credit, and which shall not be omitted to be mentioned by me to the Secretary of State when all is done.

I shall anxiously wait for the Lady Nelson's return; but do not send her away until you have thoroughly formed your judgment, whereby it may become the basis of how we are to proceed, and prevent any retrograde movement and injury to the Public.

In your attention to this grand object, nothing will more particularly require your wisdom than the valuation of property, which, from the experience you have had, I am confident will be duly estimated.

Be as correct as you possibly can in the number of Souls that determine to go to the Derwent, and of those who will go to Port Dalrymple, in order that I may inform the respective Lieutenant-Governors thereof, and provide for their maintenance.

Mr. Commissary Palmer will send you an Invoice of the Articles shipped amounting to £673 12s. 3d. He could only send you three Quire of Paper, to which I have added three Quire of my own; altho' I am likely to be in great want of it.

You will not fail to express to Mr. Hibbins, the Deputy Judge-Advocate, the paragraph in the Secretary of State's letter which conveys to him His Majesty's displeasure, and that He has no further occasion for his Services, also that he is not to expect any indulgencies which His Majesty has been pleased to grant to Others. Inclosed is a Letter to Mr. Hibbins from me on the occasion, which you will read and present to him.

I am, &c.,
WM. BLIGH.

[Enclosure No. 2.]

[This was a duplicate copy of the " General Statement of Inhabitants," etc., which was forwarded by Governor Bligh with his despatch to the Right Hon. William Windham, dated 30th September, 1807.]

1807.
31 Oct.
———
Instructions *re* the evacuation of Norfolk Island.

Invoice of stores shipped.

Dismissal of deputy judge-advocate Hibbins.

1807.
31 Oct.

Return of grain
received into
the public
stores.

[Enclosure No. 4.]

ACCOUNT of Grain received into His Majesty's Stores at Sydney,
etc., between the 13th Augt., 1806, and the 12th August, 1807.

	Wheat in Bushels.	Rice in lbs.	Maize in Bushels.	Barley in Bushels.	£	s.	d.
Quantity of Grain received and purchased by Bills on the Treasury	10914⅟₂	288,458	1399₁₅	376₁₅	10,026	15	8
Do by Sale of live Stock	675	..	..	..	504	0	0
Do. Annual and Extra Supplies	1549₁₅	..	1840₁₅	..	1602	15	3
„ in liquidation of Govt. Debts ..	1569₁₇	..	2662₁₅	630₁₅	2227	15	10
„ from Govt. Barns and Stack ...	1727⅟₂	..	1723	..	1704	16	6½
„ as Toll for grinding Grain for Individuals	120₁₅	..	68₁₅	8⅟₂	109	7	8¼
„ for Salt, etc.	8₁₅	..	75	..	24	16	8¼
	16564⅟₂	288458	7768₁₅	1015₁₅	16,200	7	8

			£	s.	d.
13th August, 1806	To amount of Debts due to the Crown		£10,472	0	4
„ „ „	liquidated since Govr. Bligh's Administration ..		3,167	9	10
12th August, 1807	Outstanding Debts remaining to this period ..		7,304	10	6

JNO. PALMER, Commiss'y.

GOVERNOR BLIGH TO THE RIGHT HON. WILLIAM WINDHAM.
(Despatch No. 2, per transport Duke of Portland; acknowledged by
Viscount Castlereagh, 15th May, 1809.)
Government House, Sydney, New South Wales,
Sir,   31st October, 1807.

Misconduct
and suspension
of surgeon
Wentworth.

The extreme misconduct of Mr. Darcy Wentworth, one of
the Assistant Surgeons, in applying Convicts to private labour
whom he received into the Hospital at Parramatta as sick Men,
rendered it absolutely necessary for me to suspend him from his
situation, on the 25th of July last, until His Majesty's Pleasure
is known thereon.

I herewith transmit the Depositions of a Mr. Francis Oakes,
Chief Constable at Parramatta, and John Beldon, an Overseer,
both free Men, of what has recently been done.

Mismanagement
of the hospital
at Parramatta.

Instead of the Hospital being an Assylum for sick Men, and as
soon as they recovered to be returned to Government labour, or
to the poor Settlers from whom they came, it has been a practice
to allow them to remain victualled as Hospital Patients requiring
care, applying their use to private advantage.

Protests of
the settlers.

In my Journeys through the Country the Settlers have stated
to me, in affecting terms, that the Men allowed them by Government constantly framed excuses and got into the Hospital; that
after feeding them for fourteen days (at the expiration of which
time the expence of victualling falls on Government), conformable to the Regulation, they have not been returned to them
upon recovery, by which a heavy loss was sustained on their part,
besides being worn out with fatigue in endeavouring to cultivate
their ground for support—and which appears to me to have been
the case.   I have, &c.,
                                        WM. BLIGH.

1807.
31 Oct.
—
Inquiry into
the conduct
of surgeon
Wentworth.

[Enclosure.]

Sydney, New South Wales, 23rd July, 1807.

QUESTIONS put to Mr. Francis Oakes, Chief Constable at Parramatta, with his Answers thereto, respecting the Conduct of Mr. D'Arcy Wentworth, Assistant Surgeon, and Sworn to before the Judge-Advocate:—

Q. About the 1st of July instant did You receive an order from the Governor to take James McDonald, Larry Killaney, Thomas Steakham, and Michael Downey, four Government Men who were said to be employed at Mr. Wentworth's (Assistant Surgeon to the Hospital) Farm on his own account without permission?—*A.* Yes.

Q. Did You find those Men as reported?—*A.* Yes; and sent them to Castle Hill, because the Men were working for Mr. Wentworth, and I thought they were as capable of working for Government.

Q. Did You Ascertain how long these Men had been working out of the Hospital at Mr. Wentworth's farm on his own private Account?—*A.* Yes; James McDonald, Able Man, sixteen Weeks; Larry Killaney, four Weeks; Thomas Steakham, six Months; Michael Downey, ten days.

Q. Did You find any other Men?—*A.* Yes; James Griffin, working at Mr. Wentworth's Garden; and I, therefore, sent him with the others to work for Government.

Q. Did you observe whether either of these Men were too infirm, and improper persons to be kept at Labour?—*A.* James Griffin seemed to limp a little, but the others seemed able, and particularly James McDonald, who was a stout Man, and fit for any Work. Michael Downey had a cut hand, but it was nearly well, and he was fit to work for Government.

Q. Is the Garden sufficient to give the patients Supplies if duly worked and taken care of?—*A.* I think it is.

Q. Does not the Government allow two able Men to look after it and work it?—*A.* Yes.

Q. Do You know that these Men are frequently taken away from it and worked at Mr. Wentworth's garden?—*A.* Yes; repeatedly. I see them there half their time. They have worked a great deal there. At any rate, they work very little in the Hospital Garden; I don't believe they work more than a day in the Week there.

Q. Do You know of any improper Conduct in the Management of the Persons who have been received into the Hospital besides what You have related?—*A.* Yes. I have known of Men who were patients in the Hospital being let out, and going about Parramatta and the Country doing Mischief, and have been punished and sent to Castle Hill. Many Men have been taken by Wentworth to his Farm and Farmhouse for different purposes ever since he came from Norfolk Island, and he changed them more or less as he found it convenient. Mr. Wentworth lately discharged Francis Horton, after having him four or five Months in his private Employ, while he was deemed a patient for a Sore Thumb, and took Downey (one of the four) in his place. The Hospital, in Regard to Patients being taken out and in, and employed to private labour, has been well known for a length of time. Many of them have been taken before the Magistrates and punished, and returned to Castle Hill from the Hospital.

1807.
31 Oct.

Inquiry into
the conduct
of surgeon
Wentworth.

Q. Have you known labouring Men leave their Masters (Settlers) and, declaring themselves Sick, have been received into the Hospital, and after the poor Settler has fed them a fortnight he lost his Man by their being permitted to work for private purposes?—*A.* Yes.

Q. What are become of the five Men You found with Mr. Wentworth employed in his private purposes?—*A.* James McDonald and Michael Downey are at public Labour; Steakham is in the Hospital; Killaney and Griffin are out-patients.

Q. Have you not heard that Money was given to remain in the Hospital?—*A.* Yes; there is one Wheeler there, who is a prisoner, but acts in delivering the Medicines, and has great Controul; he has certainly received Money to keep the Patients there to avoid Government Labour. About three Weeks ago James Nangle applied to me for a pass to go to the Head Surgeon to see if he could get into the Sydney Hospital, for he had been turned out of the Parramatta Hospital by Wheeler, because he could not give him £2 which Wheeler demanded of him.

Q. What did You conceive the £2 to be given to Wheeler for?—*A.* To be permitted to remain as an Hospital patient as long as he liked, so as to be freed from Government Labour, And I believe there has been a great deal of this Work. As also that this Wheeler practises for himself among the poor people, and as he cannot procure Medicines himself, the Medicines of Government are likely to be used for his private Purposes.

Q. Did You ever receive any Order from His Excellency the Governor to take Men out of the Hospital?—*A.* No, Never. The Men I took were employed to Mr. Wentworth's own purposes.

Q. How were the Men you took from Mr. Wentworth's Farm employed?—*A.* Thomas Steakham, employed in Charge of the Farm House; Mich'l Downey, as a Stockman at the Farm for the Horses; James McDonald, as a Stockman for the Cows; Lawrence Killaney, Servant in the House; and James Griffin working in Mr. Wentworth's private Garden.   FRANCIS OAKES.

Sworn before me this 23rd July, 1807,
                    RICH'D ATKINS, J.-A.

George Beldon, the Overseer of the Gangs at Parramatta, having read to him by the Judge-Advocate the Questions as put to Mr. Francis Oakes, the Chief Constable at that place, with his Answers thereto, he positively Swears that they are true, and within his certain knowledge, he having been at the time the Active person with the said Chief Constable in the Inquiries made therein.

Sworn before me this 23rd July, 1807,   GEORGE BELDON.
                    RICH'D ATKINS, J.-A.

GOVERNOR BLIGH TO THE RIGHT HON. WILLIAM WINDHAM.

(Despatch No. 3, per transport Duke of Portland; acknowledged by Viscount Castlereagh, 15th May, 1809.)

Government House, Sydney, New South Wales,
Sir,.   31st October, 1807.

Proposed land
grant for
Townson.

I beg leave to represent to you that Doctor Townson arrived here in the Duke of Portland, and presented to me a Letter he had received from Sir George Shee, stating that it was your intentions to allott him Two Thousand Acres of Land, with other indulgencies, and I should have authority to grant the same.

I have therefore to assure you, Sir, no instructions have reached me on that head; but in consequence of Sir George Shee's Letter, I have directed Doctor Townson to look out for the quantity of Land, which, together with other Indulgencies he was to expect, I would allow him to hold until I received full instructions, when the whole should be located to him.

His Brother, Captain Townson, and a Mr. Bunker are similarly situated as I have in former Letters represented, and therefore I likewise am to request instructions thereon.

I have, &c.,

WM. BLIGH.

GOVERNOR BLIGH TO THE RIGHT HON. WILLIAM WINDHAM.
(Despatch No. 4, per transport Duke of Portland; acknowledged by Viscount Castlereagh, 15th May, 1809.)
Government House, Sydney, New South Wales,
Sir,   31st October, 1807.

Inclosed I have the honor to send you Abstracts of the Commissary's Accounts from the 13th of August to the 31st of December 1806.   I have, &c.,

WM. BLIGH.

[Enclosures.]

[*These papers will be found in a volume in series II.*]

GOVERNOR BLIGH TO THE RIGHT HON. WILLIAM WINDHAM.
(Despatch, per transport Duke of Portland; acknowledged by Viscount Castlereagh, 15th May, 1809.)
Sir,   Sydney, New South Wales, 31st October, 1807.

Inclosed I have the Honor to transmit the *Sydney Gazettes* from the 8th of February to the 30th of August 1807;

And have, &c.,

WM. BLIGH.

None have been printed since August owing to the great scarcity of Paper.*

GOVERNOR BLIGH TO THE RIGHT HON. WILLIAM WINDHAM.
(Despatch, per transport Duke of Portland; acknowledged by Viscount Castlereagh, 15th May, 1809.)
Government House, Sydney, New South Wales,
Sir,   31st October, 1807.

Enclosed I have the honor to transmit a Report of Entrances and Clearances of Ships and Vessels in and from Port Jackson, from the 1st of January to the 30th of June 1807.

I have, &c.,

WM. BLIGH.

* Note 53.

Margin notes:
1807.
31 Oct.

Proposed land grant for Townson.

Abstracts of a´cou´rts.

Sydney Gazettes.

Shipping returns.

1807.
31 Oct.

Returns of
shipping.

[Enclosure.]

REPORT of Ships and Vessels entered Inwards at the Port of Port Jackson, in His Majesty's Colony of New South Wales, from the 1st of January to the 30th June, 1807, vizt.

When entered.	Name of the Ship.	Master.	Build.	Number of			Built.	Registered.	Names of the Owners.	From whence.
				Tons.	Guns.	Men.				
1807.										
13 Feb.	General Wellesley	D'd Dalrymple	Foreign	400	15	50	Pegue	Madras	Dav'd Dalrymple & Co.	Pulo Penang.
9 Mar.	Durt	Rich'd Smith	,,	189	8	18	....	London	Hulletts & Co.	London.
18 ,,	Hope	Reuben Bromley	American	171	8	26	Connecticut	New York	Fanning & Co.	New York.
4 April	Parramatta	John Glenn	Foreign	102	6	8	....	London	Hulletts & Co.	London.
4 ,,	Brothers	Oliver Russell	,,	252	8	21	....	,,	Hulletts & Blaxland	,,
6 ,,	Dss of York	Austin Forrest	Plantation	192	14	25	Calcutta	Calcutta	Campbell & Hook	Calcutta.
6 ,,	Hannah and Sally	Nath'l Cogswell	American	167	4	11	Dennis Creek	Philadelphia	Nathaniel Cogswell	Rio Janeiro.
8 ,,	Elizabeth	E. Bunker	Foreign	238	2	17	....	London	Campbell & Wilson	The Fiery, off Nw Zealand.
8 ,,	Commerce	Jas. Birnie	Plantation	225	2	23	Newfoundland	,,	James Birnie	Penantipodes.
14 May	Albion	Cuth't Richardson	British	362	10	30	Deptford	,,	Wilson, Campbell, & Page.	The Fiery, off Nw Zealand.
22 June	Sydney Cove	Wm. Edwards	Foreign	282	8	22	Rotterdam	,,	Thos. Wm. Plummer	London.

ROB'T CAMPBELL, Naval Officer.

REPORT of Ships and Vessels cleared Outwards from the Port of Port Jackson in His Majesty's Colony of New South Wales, from the 1st of January to the 30th of June, 1807.

When clear'd.	Name of the Ship.	Master.	Build.	Tons.	Guns.	Men.	Where built.	Registered.	Owner's Name.	Whither bound.	Cargo
1807. 27 Jan.	Harrington	Wm. Campbell	Plantation	180	13	31	Calcutta	Calcutta	Chase & Co.	China	Ballast.
6 Feb.	Commerce	James Birnie	,,	225	2	21	Newf'dland	London	Jas. Birnie	London	150 Casks of Oil, 40 casks of Salted Skins, 12 Tons and 19 cwt. of Brazil wood, 43 Logs and 558 feet of Beef-wood.
9 ,,	Perseverance	Fred'k Lelohf	Colonial	136	2	18	Sydney	Sydney	Campbell & Co.	China	Ballast.
27 ,,	Argo	John Baden	Foreign	221	18	26	....	London	Hulletts & Co.	The Fishery	....
1 Mar.	Elizabeth	J. Walker	,,	102	18	18	Sydney	Sydney	McArthur & Co.	Otaheite	....
1 ,,	King	Jas. Aiken	Colonial	185	18	23	Sydney	,,	Kable & Co.	Fregee Islands.	....
26 ,,		Alex'r Ferguson	Foreign	345	18	56	....	London	Daniel Bennett	On a cruise	....
30 ,,	Star	Jo. Wilkinson	,,	119	6	20	....	....	Ines Birnie	London	14,000 Seal Skins.
2 Apr.	Hope	Reuben Bromley	American	171	8	26	Connectic ut	Philadelphia	Fanning & Co.	South Sea Islands.	....
9 ,,	Dart	Rich'd Smith	Foreign	189	8	18	....	Ldon	Hulletts & Co.	The Fishery	....
20 ,,	Elizabeth	E. Bunker	,,	238	2	17	...	,,	Campbell & Wilson	,,	....
24 ,,	...l Wellsley	D'd Dalrymple	,,	400	14	50	Pegue	...as	D'd Dalrymple & Co.	No Penang	....
6 May	Duchess of York	Austin Forrest	Plantation	192	14	25	...ta	Calcutta	Campbell & Hook	Bengal.	....
26 ,,	Albion	Cuth't Richardson	British	362	10	30	...ord	London	Wilsons, Campbell & Page.	The Fishery	....
11 June	Brothers	Oliver Russell	Foreign	252	8	21	....	,,	Hulletts & Blaxland.	,,	....
13 ,,	Parramatta	John Glenn	,,	102	6	11	....	,,	Hulletts & Co.	Otaheite	....

ROB'T CAMPBELL, Naval Officer.

1807. 31 Oct.

Returns of shipping.

GENERAL CARGOES.

Returns of
cargo.

General Wellsley.—1,767 Bags of Rice, 2,396 of Wheat, 23 Casks and 98 Dozen of Brandy, 20 Casks of Rum, 3 Do. of Arrack, 6 Do. of Gin and 2 Cases of Do. containing in all 4,103½ Galls., 18 Casks of Claret, 17 Cases of Port Wine, 87 Bales and 2 Bags of Tobacco, 16 Bales of Canvass, 37 Boxes of China ware, 6 Chests of Tea, 8 Boxes and 5 Cases of lacquered ware, 1 bale of Baize, 13 Cases of Oilman's Stores, 13 Trunks and 2 Bales of piece Goods.

Dart.—17 Pipes of Brandy, 1,942½ Galls., 3 Pipes and 4 Hhds. of Port wine, 12 Casks of Bottled do., 4 Hhds. of Sherry, 8 Bags of Corks, 6 Casks and 2 Cases of Bullock Harness, 6 Bales and 1 Case of Slops, 5 Pair of Bellows, 5 Vices, 1 Case of Smiths Tools, 2 Casks and 2 Trusses of Cooper's Do., 1 Case of Drugs, 1 Bale of Woolens, 1 Do. of printed Cottons, 1 Box of Millinery, 5 Casks and 2 Cases of Ironmongery, 268 Bars of Iron and 2 Stills, wt. Heads and Worms complete.

Hope.—No Merchandize for Sale here—bound for the South Sea Islands.

Parramatta.—2 Butts of Porter, 2 Casks of Slops, 17 Kegs of Rivets, 5 Bundles of Staves, 14 Casks of Salt and 12 Ton of Bolt and Bar Iron.

Brothers.—90 Blls. of Porter, 100 Firkins Butter, 4 Hhds. Port Wine, 4 packages of Woolen Cloths and Kersimeres, 1 Bale of Slops, 1 Box of Millinery, 1 package of Haberdashery, 7 cwt. of Soap and 9 Cases of Cutlery, Four Butts of Brandy, 1 Pipe of Bottled Wine, 40 Gallons of White Wine, 13 Casks containing Ironmongery, Carpenters Tools, a quantity of Household Furniture, Agricultural Implements, Window Glass etc., 1 Box of Leather and Shoemakers Tools, 2 Cases of Glass ware, 1 Do. of Earthenware, 1 Box of Fire Arms, and a Schooner in frame 59 Tons Burthen with Rigging etc. complete, 25 Tons of Salt, one Barrell of Powder, 2 Chests of Tea and 1 Box of Vermicelli all the private property of Mr. Jo. Blaxland.

Dutchess of York.—65 small Boxes of Tea, 350 Bags of Rice, 2,000 Gunny Bags and 2 Casks of Rum, 234 Galls.

Hanah and Sally.—52 Pipes of Wine, 166 Boxes of Tea, 37 Baskets of Tobacco, 96 Bags and 10 Cases of Sugar, 15 Bags of Corks, 49 Boxes of China, 3 Boxes of Cheese, 1 Trunk and 7 Boxes of Silks and Nankeens and 2 Boxes of Shoes.

Elizabeth.—35 Tons of Sperm Oil.

Commerce.—150 Casks of Oil, 40 Casks of Salted Skins, 12 Tons 19 cwt. of Brazil Wood, 45 Logs and 558 feet of Beef wood, 22,221 Salted and 9,098 dried Seal Skins in Bulk.

Albion.—75 Tons of Sperm Oil.

Sydney Cove.—106 Female Convicts, 47 Coils of Cordage, 10 Anchors, 2 Casks of Blocks, 100 Ash Oars, 22 Barrells of Pitch Tar and Rosin, 4 Punetlets of Paint, 4 pair of Millstones, 10 Cases of Muskets, 1 Case of Musket Balls, 1 Package of Sand Paper, 1 Do. of Razors and 27 Boxes of Candles on account of Government, 1 Box of Stationary and 1 Box of Coopers Tools.

GOVERNOR BLIGH TO THE RIGHT HON. WILLIAM WINDHAM.

(Despatch, per transport Duke of Portland; acknowledged by
Viscount Castlereagh, 15th May, 1809.)

Government House, Sydney, New South Wales,

Sir,   31st October, 1807.

Requisition for
medicines.

    I beg leave to inclose to You the Principal Surgeon Mr. Thomas Jamison's Demand for Medicines which are much wanted, and to submit to Your consideration whether this Gentleman should account for his expence to some Medical Board and pass a regular Account, as I have no possible check on the Department here and he informs me he has never had orders to this effect.

I have, &c.,
WM. BLIGH.

[Enclosure.]

1807.
31 Oct.

A SCHEDULE of such Medicines as are wanted for the Different Settlements of New South Wales Van Dieman's Land and Norfolk Island 1st September 1807.

Requisition for
medicines.

Cort. Perm. Rub.	50 lbs.	Extract Cathart	20 lbs.
Cort. Perm. Flav.	50 lbs.	—— Jalapii	4 lbs.
Pulv. Cort. Perm. flav.	1 cwt.	—— Quassia	5 lbs.
—— —— Rub.	1 cwt.	—— Gentiana	5 lbs.
Kali Vitriolat.	50 lbs.	Flores Chamom.	1 cwt.
Kali Tartarisat.	50 lbs.	Baccinum Juniperii	50 lbs.
Nation Vitriolat.	20 cwt.	Zincum vitriolat	12 lbs.
Nation Tartarisat.	10 lbs.	Cuprium vitriolat	12 lbs.
Magnesia Vitriolat.	1 cwt.	Gum Assafetid	20 lbs.
Ammonia Muriata	25 lbs.	Kali Acetatum	50 lbs.
Aq. Ammonia purae	50 lbs.	Ol. Olive Opt	50 ——
Ammonia Carbonatum	6 lbs.	— Ricini	10 ——
Ferrum Vitriolatum	50 lbs.	Natron	50 lbs.
Acidum Muriaticum	6 lbs.	Kali pp.	30 lbs.
Acidum Nitrosum	6 lbs.	Rad. Gentian.	10 lbs.
Acidum Acetum	2 lbs.	—— Cerp. Vergin	10 lbs.
Cumor Tartari	1 cwt.	—— Scill Ciccat	6 lbs.
Gum Myrrh	10 lbs.	Pulv. Rad. Scill	4 lbs.
Pulv. Gum Myrrh	10 lbs.	Tinct Rad. Scill	10 lbs.
Galls. Alleppo.	10 lbs.	Cum Ammoniacum	10 lbs.
Gum Arabic	1 cwt.	Tinct Benzoini Comp.	4 lbs.
Pulv. Fol. Digit.	20 lbs.	Acetum Commun.	100 ——
Semina Digitalis	1 lb.	—— Distillatum	20 ——
—— Anisi	6 lbs.	Terebinth	2 cwt.
—— Cardamoni	4 lbs.	Ol Terebinth	20 ——
—— Carui	10 lbs.	Bals. Copai	20 lbs.
Cort. Cascarell.	20 lbs.	Tinct Cardamom	5 lbs.
Pulv. Cort. Carcarell.	20 lbs.	Peruvianum	4 lbs.
Caryoph. Aromat.	20 lbs.	Resin flav.	2 cwt.
Mict. Mosch.	30 lbs.	Pix Burgund.	1 cwt.
Cort. Cinnam. Ver.	20 lbs.	Emp. Commun.	40 lbs.
Cort. Winteranus	10 lbs.	—— Adhesii	40 lbs.
Rad. Zingib	20 lbs.	—— Attraheus	80 lbs.
Calomel	50 lbs.	—— Vesicatorum	80 lbs.
Hydrarg Muriat	2 lbs.	—— Sapone	40 lbs.
Cerup Acetatum	50 lbs.	Cerat. Lap. Colam.	4 cwt.
Lionum Quassia	20 lbs.	—— Sapone	50 lbs.
Hydrargyrum	50 lbs.	Ring. risin. flav.	6 cwt.
Flores Benzoini	2 lbs.	Hydrargyrum Nitratum	2 lbs.
Camphora	20 lbs.	—— Calcinatum	4 lbs.
Aloes Socatrin	20 lbs.	Linimentum Saponicum	20 ——
—— Barbadensis	50 lbs.	Sago	10 ——
Pulv. Gum Arabic	1 cwt.	Fordeum Perlate	1 ——
Creta ppt.	1 cwt.	Powder of Arrow Root	1 cwt.
Opium Colat	20 lbs.	Antim. Commun. Pulv.	40 lbs.
Pulv. Rad. Rhei	1 cwt.	Pulv. Febrificy Londoneus	4 lbs.
—— Jalapi	1 cwt.	Pulv. Ipecac Comp.	10 lbs.
—— Ipecac	30 lbs.	Ung. Hydrargy. fatias	50 lbs.
Ether Vitriol	10 lbs.	Confect. Aromat.	20 lbs.
Spt. Vini Rect.	20 —	Confect. Opiat.	20 lbs.
Ol. Lavend. Verum	1 lb.	Pulv. Aromaticus	10 lbs.
Spt. Lavend. Comp.	10 lbs.	Canadin	20 lbs.
Ol. Rosamar Verum	8 oz.	Ether Vitriolic Aquae	6 lbs.
— Menth pip Verum	2 lbs.	Magnesia	10 lbs.
— Anisi Verum	1 lb.	Calcinatum	6 lbs.
— Minth Vulgo	2 lbs.	Cret. Commun.	2 cwt.
— Puligii Verum	1 lb.	Sapo Vinet	20 lbs.
— Cassia Verum	8 oz.	—— Commun.	8 cwt.
Tinct Ferri Muriat.	6 lbs.	Uva Ursi	10 lbs.
—— Rhei	20 lbs.	Cupping Glasses and Scarificater	
—— Jalapii	20 lbs.	Fistulas.	
Ol. Lini Sene Ignii	10 —	Pill Boxes.	
Tinct Senna	10 lbs.	Leather White.	
—— Fol. Digit	20 lbs.	Twine Thread.	
—— Cort. Perm. Comp.	50 lbs.	Paper Wrapping.	
—— Opii	50 lbs.	—— Writing.	
—— Opii Comp.	10 lbs.	Flittering.	
—— Aromat.	10 lbs.	Quills Ink Powder and Wafers.	

A SCHEDULE of such Medicines as are wanted—*continued.*

Glass Funnels.
Tin   Do.
Weights and Scales from 6 lbs.
    to 2 oz.
Glass Measures.
Composition Mortars.
Marble Slabs.
Large Scissors.
Corks Quart Pint and Phials in
    Sorts.
Gallipots.
Machine for impregnating liquid
    with the Carbonic Acid.
A Large Electrical Machine with
    suitable Apparatus for Medi-
    cal Electricity Tinfoil and
    Two Spare Leyden Jars.
One large Beam Scale and
    Weights.
Metallic Bougies.
Lint.
Tow.
Pulv. Stanni ....   6 lbs.
Dolichos. ....   4 lbs.
Cera flav. ....   4 cwt.

Hydrargyrum Sulphur ....   10 lbs.
Conserve Cygnosbat ....   20 lbs.
——————— Rosar. ....   20 lbs.
Sperma Ceti ....   8 lbs.
Liquor Volat C.C. ....   10 lbs.
Hoffman Anod Liquor ....   6 lbs.
Mel Opt. ....   50 lbs.
Pulv. Glychyrrhiza .... 10 lbs.
Alumin. ....   50 lbs.
Cortex Aurant Hyspan. ....   4 lbs.
Cantharis ....   30 lbs.
Radex Contragerva ....   8 lbs.
Elimi Visinae ....   12 lbs.
Gum Gulac ....   20 lbs.
Kali Nitratum ....   30 lbs.
Empl. Lithargyri Hydrargy. ..   10 lbs.
Gum Scamon. ....   2 lbs.
Spt. Æther Nitros ....   8 lbs.
Day Books and Ledgers.
Addenda.
Aq. Ammoniacum cum Calc ...   20 lbs.
Wax Cloath for preserving the
    beds.
50 Iron Cradles for the use of
    the out Settlements.

THOS. JAMISON,
Principal Surgeon.

P.S.—I beg leave to observe His Majesty's Ships on this Station are Supplied with Medicines from the General Hospital by obtaining His Excellency's Order.   THOS. JAMISON,
Approved: WM. BLIGH.   Principal Surgeon.

———————

GOVERNOR BLIGH TO THE RIGHT HON. WILLIAM WINDHAM.

(Despatch, per transport Duke of Portland; acknowledged by
Viscount Castlereagh, 15th May, 1809.)

Sir,   Government House, Sydney, 31st October, 1807.

I have received the inclosed Letter from Mr. Surgeon Jamison requesting leave of absence; but I beg to observe that all our Medical Assistants are not in the Colony.

I have, &c.,
WM. BLIGH.

[Enclosure.]

SURGEON JAMISON TO VISCOUNT CASTLEREAGH.

My Lord,   Sydney, New South Wales, Octr. 16th, 1807.

From the latest accounts I have received from my friends, I find my family affairs much deranged, I therefore most earnestly intreat permission to return to Europe to settle them and bring out my Family, my delay shall be as short as possible, and to prevent any inconvenience arrising to the Medical department, I will procure a Substitute to do my duty during my Absence.

I have, &c.,
THOS. JAMISON, Principal Surgeon.

GOVERNOR BLIGH TO THE RIGHT HON. WILLIAM WINDHAM.

(Despatch, per transport Duke of Portland; acknowledged by
Viscount Castlereagh, 15th May, 1809.)

Sir,   Sydney, New South Wales, 31st Octr., 1807.

My former letter* which I have had the honor to write
will have informed you of the expences of the Colony for the last
year. On this head I have to observe that although the amount
drawn for Grain was Ten Thousand and Twenty six Pounds,
Fifteen Shillings and Eight Pence, our ways and means furnish
Six Thousand One hundred and Seventy three Pounds Twelve
Shillings by which the Grain account was Sixteen Thousand,
Two Hundred Pounds, Seven Shillings and Eight Pence for
consumption as the inclosed Paper will explain.

*Amount
of grain
purchased.*

I now beg leave to inclose the Commissary's Letter to me for
the ensuing twelve months, by which under the calculation he
makes, Twenty one Thousand Pounds may be necessarily drawn
for to supply the Grain for the Colony and its Dependencies.

*Anticipated
expenditure.*

Government's outstanding debts which amounted to Ten
Thousand Four Hundred and Seventy two Pounds and Four
Pence, when I took the Command, have been reduced to Seven
Thousand Three Hundred and four Pounds Ten Shillings and
Six Pence, which by next August we hope to reduce more con-
siderably; And as I admit no new debts to be incurred of any
consequence, our Situation will annually become better.

*Debts due to
government.*

I have, &c.,
WM. BLIGH.

[Enclosure No. 1.]

[A copy of this return is not available.]

[Enclosure No. 2.]

COMMISSARY PALMER TO GOVERNOR BLIGH.

Sir,   Sydney, 17th October, 1807.

I beg leave to represent to your Excellency, that from the
present state of the Stores in these Settlements, and in consequence of the small quantity of Grain cultivated on Account of
Government, considered with the great additional expenditure
of all kinds of Provisions occasioned by the evacuation of Norfolk
Island; the principal part of whose Inhabitants will become
victualled by Government for a certain time, as well as by the
Augmentation which is expected to the Military force here,
Settlers and Wives and families of Prisoners who have and may
be sent out with them, will render it absolutely necessary to purchase about Fifty two thousand Bushels of Grain during the
ensuing year 1808 for which it will be requisite to draw on His

*Anticipated
purchases
of grain
in 1808.*

* Note 54.

1807.
31 Oct.
———
Anticipated
purchases
of grain
in 1808.

Majesty's Treasury for a sum not less than Twenty One thousand pounds; provided that the Wheat can be procured at the price of Ten Shillings per Bushel, and Maize at the price of Five Shillings, agreeable to what was held out to the Settlers last Year as an encouragement for their cultivating their Lands;

I beg permission to apprize Your Excellency that in the above statement I have not calculated upon any Grain that may be received for the present outstanding Debts, nor have I reckoned upon any that may be obtained by Barter for the Supplies sent out by Government, or for any Cattle that may be disposed of for that Article; as I conceive that whatever Grain may be received on these Accounts will be only sufficient to remain on hand to guard against any Accident that may occur by Flood, Blight or otherwise to the present or ensuing Crops; as my so doing is only complying with that part of my Instructions wherein I am directed to keep in Store a Twelve Months supply of Provisions for this Settlement and its Dependencies, and I am now induced to adhere thereto in consequence of the Stores being at this time in such a state of repair as may justify the same as far as it may be prudent considering the destruction made by Weevil etc. to Grain in this Climate.

Supplies of
animal food
necessary.

In the event of no Salt Provisions being sent out from England to this place previous to the expiration of the month of June next, until which time the present remains of Salt Provisions will only last at the present ration for the numbers now victualled in the Settlement; there will be unavoidably a necessity of providing Meat for the subsistance of the Civil, Military, and Prisoners victualled from the Stores, which from the very great scarcity of animal food in the Colony must cause a considerable addition to the Sums necessary to be drawn for, as the average price of all kinds of Meat is not less than One Shilling and ninepence per pound and the want of Salt Provisions will I much fear keep up the same; I beg leave further to observe that heretofore those persons victualled at Norfolk Island were not calculated upon in the demand for Salt provisions for the other Settlements in this Colony, though they are provided for in the present instance; and likewise from the number of Settlers with very large families who have arrived here, as well as the number of Prisoners allowed them as Servants, whilst to these must be added the Wives and Children of Prisoners, Free, who are sent out, and are also required to be maintained:—These considerations will, I hope, induce Your Excellency to see the necessity of providing for these contingencies.

　　　　　　　　　　I have, &c.,
　　　　　　　　　　　　JNO. PALMER, Commiss'y.

GOVERNOR BLIGH TO SIR GEORGE SHEE.   1807.
(Despatch No. 1, per transport Duke of Portland.)   31 Oct.
Government House, Sydney, New South Wales,
Sir,   31st October, 1807.

In answer to your Letter of the 6th of October, 1806, Natives of
concerning two Otaheite Youths sent out from England by the Otaheite.
Brothers, I have the honor to inform you, that, according to
your directions, they have been sent to their Native Country.

I have, &c.,
WM. BLIGH.

GOVERNOR BLIGH TO SIR GEORGE SHEE.
(Despatch No. 2, per transport Duke of Portland.)
Government House, Sydney, New South Wales,
Sir,   31st October, 1807.

I have the honor to acknowledge the receipt of your Letter Despatch
of the 31st of March 1806, inclosing the Estimate of the Charge acknowledged.
of defraying the Civil Establishment of New South Wales from
the 1st of January to the 31st of December 1806.

I have, &c.,
WM. BLIGH.

LORD HAWKESBURY* TO THE COLONIAL GOVERNORS.†
(A circular despatch, per transport Sinclair.)
4th November, 1807.   4 Nov.

INFORMATION having been received that France has taken forcible Letters of
possession of certain Territories and Ports in Italy and in the be issued
Mediterranean and Adriatick Seas, and has subverted their against France
Ancient Government; and erected in the room thereof New and her allies.
Governments; which under her influence are aiding in the
execution of her Hostile Designs against the Property Commerce
and Navigation of His Majesty's Subjects,—His Majesty has
been pleased to order Letters of Marque and Commissions of
Privateers to be granted against the Ships, Goods, and Inhabitants, of the Territories and Ports of Tuscany—The Kingdom of Naples, the Port and Territory of Ragusa and those of
the Islands lately composing the Republick of the Seven Islands,
and all other Ports and Places in the Mediterranean and Adriatick Seas, which are occupied by the Arms of France, or her
Allies. I am therefore to signify to you The King's Commands,
that you instantly cause the same to be made as public as possible
in the .... under your Command in order that His Majesty's

---

* Note 55.
† *Marginal note.*—Circular to the West Indies, America, India, Cape, St. Helena,
New South Wales, Goree.

Subjects may do their utmost in their several stations to make
captures of the Ships belonging to the Ports and Places before-
mentioned.   HAWKESBURY,

       in the absence of Lord Castlereagh.

LORD HAWKESBURY* TO THE COLONIAL GOVERNORS.†
(A circular despatch, per transport Sinclair.)

             Downing Street, 5th Novr., 1807.

ADVICE having been received of an actual Declaration of War by
the Courts of Denmark against Great Britain, I am to signify
to you The King's Command, that you instantly cause the same
to be made as public as possible within........under your........
in order that His Majesty's Subjects may do their utmost in
their several Stations to make captures of the Ships belonging to
Denmark and to destroy its Commerce, for which purpose His
Majesty has been pleased to order Letters of Marque and Commissions of Privateers to be granted in the usual manner.

                    HAWKESBURY,

       in the absence of Lord Castlereagh.

VISCOUNT CASTLEREAGH TO GOVERNOR BLIGH.
(Despatch No. 2, per transport Sinclair.)

Sir,   Downing Street, 30th December, 1807.

     An Application having been made to this office by Lord
Fitzwilliam for a leave of absence for Mr. D'Arcy Wentworth, I
am to desire that he may be permitted to return to this Country
for one year, provided it can be done without inconvenience to
the public service.   I have, &c.,

                    CASTLEREAGH.

VISCOUNT CASTLEREAGH TO GOVERNOR BLIGH.
(Despatch No. 1, per transport Sinclair; acknowledged by Lieutenant-Colonel Foveaux, 6th September, 1808.)

Sir,   Downing Street, 31st December, 1807.

     Your General Letter of the 9th February‡ last was brought
by Capt'n King and received here on the 9th November, and has
been laid before The King.

     Much as I must lament the distress which the Colony has
suffered from the Inundation of the Hawkesbury, and the Care-
lessness of the Colonists in not taking Precautions for securing
their Corn when housed from the danger of Floods, which may
ever be expected in that River, it is a source of much Satisfaction that the produce of the Harvest, though a bad one,

---

* Note 55.
† *Marginal note.*—Circular to the West Indies, America, India, St. Helena, Cape,
New South Wales, Goree.   ‡ Note 56.

together with the Cargoes of Rice which have been ordered, seem sufficient to secure the Colony from anything like Famine; if the Calculation of your Letter be just, the proceeds of the Harvest in Wheat and Maize, joined to the Cargoes of Rice Expected, will produce an allowance of 2 lb. a person for the Colony for very near a year at the calculation of 8,000 inhabitants of all Ages; and I find you have made no Calculation for Potatoes, and which I understand are a certain Crop in the Colony.

With respect to Animal Food, you seem not to be in want; a year's supply was sent from hence in February last, and nearly a like Quantity is now going by the Sinclair and Recovery.

The Price you have fixed for the purchase of Wheat, viz., 14s. 9d. a bushel, is extremely high, though perhaps unavoidable, and, as you state in a subsequent Letter, will oblige the Commissary to draw Bills to the amount of £12,000. These Bills, under the Circumstances of the Calamity which has happened, will, of course, be honored; but the Consideration of such an Expence and of the Danger the Colony has experienced will increase your Exertion to take such measures as will secure it from the Recurrence of an Accident which prudence may certainly prevent. I shall hope, therefore, to hear that the Inhabitants, under your suggestion, have entered into such means of securing their Harvest as to prevent the possibility of such Ruinous Accidents as have lately endangered the Existence of the Colony.

It is impossible for me at this distance to judge of the Inexpediency of the grant to Mr. McArthur of Lands on the Western Side of the Nepean, and what Detriment may arise from limiting the extent of Range in which the Wild Cattle feed. He will, I should hope, readily acquiesce in accepting Lands in another Direction equally profitable for the Feeding of his Flocks, if his occupation of any part of the Cow Pasture should be a real Impediment to the increase of the Cattle; but I would wish to avoid giving any positive Direction for revoking a grant which has been directed to be made with a view of furthering the Spirit of Improvement.

I shall, however, attend to your Suggestion of not directing Lands to be granted in future to the West of the Nepean until I receive your Statement on the subject with such a description of that Quarter of the Country as will satisfy Government that it should not be Settled.

I am to express His Majesty's approbation of the Determination you have adopted to put an End to the Barter of Spirits which appears to have been abused to the great Injury of the Morals of the Colony, and I am to recommend that whatever Regulations you may find it most eligible to establish for the

1807.
31 Dec.

Duties on
spirits.

Sale of Spirits, Yet that you will never admit a free Importation
but preserve the Trade under your entire Controul, and that
you will not fail rigorously to levy the Penalties you shall establish for preventing illegal Import. The Duties upon this Article
will form one of the most material Sources of Revenue, and the
application which is made of them for the support of the Orphan
House ought to be an additional motive to the Settlers to concur
in the policy of levying high Duties on the Article.

The
encouragement
of religion.

I am happy to find that you are so fully engaged in completing
the Churches at Sydney, Parramatta, and the Hawkesbury. Mr.
Marsden has represented the Religious State of the Colony and
laid it also before the Archbishop of Canterbury; And I hope
means will be found to induce a sufficient number of Clergymen
to proceed to New South Wales by the next Ship, or when Mr.
Marsden returns.

Schoolmasters.

I shall also trust that some Schoolmasters, properly qualified,
may be found, who will be induced to proceed at the same period.

The
encouragement
of marriage.

You appear to be sensible of the Importance of promoting the
Increase of Marriages in the Colony; and, undoubtedly, the very
great proportion which appears to exist of illegitimate in comparison with Legitimate Children, leads to the conclusion that a
proper System for advancing this grand object has not been
adopted. From the Circumstances of the Colonists, and the
Numbers that go out leaving their Wives or Husbands in England, and the Disproportion between the Sexes, it must be extremely difficult to remedy the evil complained of; but I have
understood that sufficient Pains have not been taken with respect

Assignment
of female
convicts.

to the Disposal of the Female Convicts on their first arrival in
the Colony, and that they have been indented to improper Persons
in order to ease, as soon as possible, the Expense of supporting
them by Government Rations. The Impolicy of this System is so
obvious that I trust you will not persevere in it, but in every
case endeavour to make the Reformation of the Female Convict
and her regular Settlement by marriage a Consideration superior
to the saving, for any short period, the expense of maintaining
her.

The education
and settlement
of orphans.

In proportion as the Number of Orphans increase, the necessity
augments of providing for their Education, so as to render them
useful and creditable Members of Society; and, with regard to the
Female Orphans, the utmost care should be taken in apprenticing
them and settling them—taking some Security from such Persons
as they may be bound apprentices to for the care of their Religion and Morals, and holding out Encouragement by Grants of
Land to those who marry them, but not suffering such Grants
of Land to be alienated during the Life of the Female Grantee.

Governor King has represented that the Growth of Hemp in the Colony is very luxuriant and the Hemp of the best Staple. As this is an object of Great consequence, I wish you to have a full Experiment and Report made on the Subject, and you will consider whether some Contract might not be entered into for procuring a certain Quantity at a fixed price annually.

1807.
31 Dec.

Proposed cultivation of hemp.

Lieutenant-Governor Foveaux—the Lieutenant-Governor of Norfolk Island—returns in the Sinclair, and carries this Dispatch; And I am to desire that he may proceed to that Island, and that the Establishment of it should be the same as under Gov'r King, unless, in consequence of Mr. Windham's letter, it shall have been previously evacuated.

Return of lieutenant-governor Foveaux.

It is not wished, however, that the Number of Settlers should be there increased; but it seems not adviseable to relinquish an Island so very fertile, and which is so useful in affording Supplies to the South Sea Whalers, and, occasionally, to Port Jackson. I have recommended to Colonel Foveaux particularly to attend to the Culture of the Coffee Plant, which, I believe, he introduced in the Island, and which is now beginning to bear.

Partial reduction of settlement at Norfolk Island.

I shall wish to receive from you the fullest and most detailed Accounts of the Settlements at Port Dalrymple, which, possessing great Advantages, and in its position commanding the Navigation of Bass's Streights, and also in a Soil not only fertile but in many parts clear of Wood, appears also to produce Iron Stone of a very rich Quality; and if that part of the Country also abounds in Lime Stone, this Settlement may be hereafter of considerable Importance. I am on these accounts led to entertain an opinion that the Colony at Port Dalrymple requires your peculiar Attention and to be fully Settled; and I am to desire you will take what means are in your power for ascertaining the productions of its Soil, and especially those which are Mineral.

Advantages of the settlement at Port Dalrymple.

The Settlement of Hobart's Town is represented by Governor King to be at too great a distance for the General Resort of Whalers, and, therefore, not likely soon to become of any material Importance; and if this Information be right, you will not send Settlers there, but retain it as a place where Convicts may be usefully employed till the Utility of forming there a permanent Establishment shall be more fully ascertained. I am, at the same time, to desire you will repeat the caution given by Mr. Windham to Lieut't-Governor Collins, who seems to be inattentive in the Article of Expenditure, and desirous of withdrawing himself upon every occasion from the Superintendance of the Government of New South Wales, and anxious to receive Orders from His Majesty's Ministers alone. You will convince him that he will be made responsible for such charges as he shall

Instructions relating to the settlement at the Derwent.

1807.
31 Dec.

Movements of
the medical
staff.

make which shall not be fully Substantiated and sanctioned by your Approbation. Mr. Savage*—one of the Assistant Surgeons of New South Wales—does not return, having engaged with the East India Company. Mr. D'Arcy Wentworth has received leave to return to England; and I find Mr. Jamieson, the Chief of the Establishment, has prayed for leave to come Home in order to carry out his Family to the Settlement.

Leave of
absence for
surgeon
Jamison.

Under the Circumstances of this application, I cannot refuse allowing you to permit his absence from the Colony, and it must depend upon the Circumstances of your having such a supply of Assistant Surgeons as will not leave the Settlement in want of Medical Attendance. At present I am unable to procure Mates proper to be sent out to the Colony; and I am, therefore, to authorize you to take into the Service such Surgeons or Mates as may visit the Colony in any Ship that comes there, and whom you shall find eligible for Employment.

Land grants
for Townson,
Short, Bunker,
and Fitz.

I am to desire you will carry into Execution the Grants of Land which were promised to Mr. Townson, Captain Short, Mr. Bunker, and Mr. Fitz, the private Recommendation of which you acknowledge to have received, and for which you wait for Official Authority.

The Explanation made by Commissary Palmer respecting the allowance of 15 per Cent., which it was alleged he appropriated to his own use, is fully Satisfactory.

I have, &c.,
CASTLEREAGH.

UNDER SECRETARY COOKE TO GOVERNOR BLIGH.

(Despatch marked " Private," per transport Sinclair; acknowledged by Governor Bligh to Viscount Castlereagh, 31st August, 1808.)

Sir,   Downing Street, 31st December, 1807.

[*The first portion of this despatch is not available.*]

Approval of
Bligh's
administration.

I am to express Lord Castlereagh's approbation of the measures taken by you to relieve the Colony from the late Calamities occasioned by the imprudence of the Colonists in not taking precautions against possible inundations.

I am also to Express his full approbation of the measures you are taking to prevent the barter of Spirits, and His Lordship hopes there is no officer or gentleman or planter in the Colony who will not give you the most cordial assistance in any measures which have a tendency to remedy those evils which the intemperate use of spirits so universally generates.

E. COOKE.

* Note 57.

UNDER SECRETARY COOKE TO GOVERNOR BLIGH.

(Despatch, per transport Sinclair; acknowledged by Lieut.-Colonel Foveaux to Viscount Castlereagh, 6th September, 1808.)

Sir,   Downing Street, 11th Jan., 1808.

Proposals for the export of timber.

I transmit to you by the direction of Lord Castlereagh the copy of a Letter from Mr. Barrow inclosing a Letter from the Commissioners of the Navy, a copy of which is herewith also inclosed:—And I am to desire that you will give every attention in your power to the recommendation of the Navy Board.

I conceive that the Drawings of the Frame Timbers alluded to in the Letter of-the Navy Board are preserved in the Records of the Colony, but your own experience and Knowledge would be sufficient to guide you in framing Directions, should they not have been preserved. This Letter is transmitted by the Sinclair the Proprietor of which has been disappointed of obtaining a License from the East India Company to procure a Return Cargo from India or China, and he may probably be induced to take a Cargo of Timber on very reasonable Terms.

I am, &c.,
E. COOKE.

[Enclosure No. 1.]

MR. JOHN BARROW TO UNDER SECRETARY COOKE.

Sir,   Admiralty Office, 8 January, 1808.

I am commanded by my Lords Commissioners of the Admiralty to send you the enclosed copy of a letter from the Navy Board for Lord Castlereagh's information, Submitting the propriety of the Governor of New South Wales being directed to make a provision of Timber agreeably to the Drawings and Qualities therein mentioned, and to send the same to England by any Ships which may be returning to this Country; and I am to Signify their Lordships' request that he will be pleased to give the necessary orders, as speedily as possible, for the accomplishment of this object, acquainting me, for their Lordships' information with the steps taken on the occasion.

I am, &c.,
JOHN BARROW.

[Enclosure No. 2.]

COMMISSIONERS OF THE NAVY TO THE HON. WILLIAM POLE.

Sir,   Navy Office, 7th Jany., 1808.

The Right Honble. the Lords Commissioners of the Admiralty having by their Secretary's letter of 24th July, 1806, directed us to lose no opportunity consistently with due economy of transporting such Timber, as may be cut and is fit for Ship building from New South Wales to England, by the return of any Ships from that Country; it appears very desirable in order that

1808.
11 Jan.

Proposals for
the export
of timber.

we may take advantage of any occasions, which may offer themselves to transport Such Timber (which opportunities cannot be
otherwise than very uncertain) that a Store of that Article
should be prepared and Kept in the Country ready to ship.

We therefore desire you will please to submit to the Right
Honble. the Lords Commiss'rs of the Admiralty the propriety of
making application to the Secretary of State in order that directions may be given to the Governor of New South Wales to
make a provision of Timber agreeably to the Drawings of the
Frame Timbers of a 98, 74 and 38 Gunship, which were prepared
here and transmitted to John King, under Secretary of State
for this purpose in June, 1802,* and it appears to us, from an
examination of the Specimens of Timber sent home in the Calcutta that the Species Known by the names of the

Stringy Bark	Box and
Iron Bark	Mahogany

are of the most durable quality and may be most advantageously
employed in the construction of His Majesty's Ships. We further propose that the Governor of New South Wales may be
instructed to direct those Species to be Selected in preference to
any other, and shaped into the different Frame pieces alluded to.
It will at the same time be proper that the Governor should be
directed to cause the pieces thus shaped to be piled in such a
manner as will not only give them a degree of seasoning, but at
the same time ensure their preservation; and that he should be
desired to send such quantities of the Timber so selected and
shaped to England by any ships which may be returning to this
Country, when it can be done consistently with due economy.

We are desirous to obtain their Lordships' determination on
this Subject immediately, as we understand the Sinclair Transport is now at Spithead under orders for New South Wales, by
which opportunity it would be very desirable to convey these
instructions to the Governor.   We are, &c.,

                                    W. S. THOMPSON.
                                    H. LEGGE.
                                    R. BARLOW.

VISCOUNT CASTLEREAGH TO GOVERNOR BLIGH.

(Despatch No. 3, per ship Star; acknowledged by Governor Bligh,
10th June, 1809.)

4 Mar.

Permission for
Thomas Kent
to settle.

Sir,   Downing Street, 4th March, 1808.

Mr. Thomas Kent, who has been strongly recommended
to me by Mr. Thornton having applied for permission to go to
Port Dalrymple as a Settler, his request has been acceded to,
and I am to desire you will give him every encouragement to

* Note 58.

which he appears entitled. You will cause a grant of 600 acres to be made out to him in Such Situation as he may fix upon with your approbation subject to the usual Reservations, and you will allow him the use of Six Convicts, which with himself and Servant are to be Victualled from the Government Store for eighteen months. You will also permit to land Six casks of rum, and two of wine, and allow him to purchase from the Government Store eight Cows one Bull and three Oxen for which he is to pay the money on the Spot.

1808.
4 Mar.

Land grant and assistance for Kent.

Mr. Kent engaged to employ in the Settlement from £600 to £1,000, which in the event of his Speculation turning to advantage, he proposes to increase considerably.

I have, &c.,
CASTLEREAGH.

VISCOUNT CASTLEREAGH TO GOVERNOR BLIGH.
(Despatch No. 4, per ship Star.)

Sir, Downing Street, 30th March, 1808.

30 Mar.

Shipment of bay salt.

The Lords Commissioners of the Treasury having in consequence of a recommendation from this Office given directions to the Commissioners of Victualling to Ship 30 tons of Bay Salt for New South Wales to be disposed of by you partly in curing such meat as may belong to the Government, and the remainder by sale to Individuals, I herewith inclose to you a Copy of a Letter that has been received from Mr. Harrison on the subject, together with a copy of the Inclosure therein referred to, by which you will observe that 15 Tons of the said Article have been shipped on board the Recovery, and the same quantity on board the Sinclair, the Prime Cost of which, including the Casks, is £1,187 15s. You will therefore in disposing of any part of the same make such proportionate addition to the cost thereof as you have been directed to make to the several articles sent out to you from this Country for Barter.

I have, &c.,
CASTLEREAGH.

[Enclosure.]
[*A copy of the letter enclosed is not available.*]

VISCOUNT CASTLEREAGH TO GOVERNOR BLIGH.
(Despatch No. 5, per ship Star.)

Sir, Downing Street, 30th March, 1808.

Land grant for John Oxley.

An Application for a Grant of Land in New South Wales having been made by Lieut. John Oxley who has been recommended by Captain King, I am to desire that you will cause to

1808.
30 Mar.
—
Land grant for
John Oxley.

be made out to him in the usual form, and subject to the customary reservations, a Grant of 600 acres near the Nepean,* unless you should find that situation objectionable, and that you will give him every encouragement to which he may appear entitled together with such assistance of convicts as you may be enabled to afford him, consistently with a due attention to the claims of other Individuals.   I have, &c.,

                                    CASTLEREAGH.

VISCOUNT CASTLEREAGH TO GOVERNOR BLIGH.

(Despatch No. 6, per ship Star.)

Sir,   Downing Street, 30th March, 1808.

Medical
attendance on
the military.

I transmit to you herewith the Copy of a Letter that has been received from Mr. Moore, Deputy Secretary at War dated the 3rd instant, together with the Inclosure therein referred to, suggesting the expediency of mutual aid being offered to the Sick Soldiers and others by the Civil and Military Medical Officers employed by Government (as a part of their duty and without extra pay) at New South Wales; and I am to desire that, in furtherance of this Plan, you do give the necessary orders to the Civil Medical Officers under your Government, to attend detachments of troops wherever they may be stationed without a medical Officer.   I have, &c.,

                                    CASTLEREAGH.

[Enclosure.]

[*A copy of the letter enclosed is not available.*]

MAJOR JOHNSTON TO VISCOUNT CASTLEREAGH.†

(Despatch marked A, per whaler Dart.)

Headquarters, Sydney, N. S. Wales,

11 April. My Lord,   11th April, 1808.

The deposition
of Governor
Bligh.

A series of almost incredible circumstances have imposed upon me the distressing task and responsibility of superseding the authority vested in Governor Bligh by His Majesty's Commission, and of assuming the Government of this Colony until His Majesty's Pleasure shall be signified, or until the arrival of an Officer authorized to relieve me in the Command.

Johnston's
reasons for
his action.

Whenever the facts that have influenced me throughout so solemn a transaction shall be laid before my Gracious Sovereign, I humbly trust His Majesty will approve of my conduct, and that it will be apparent I had no alternative but to put Governor Bligh in arrest to prevent an insurrection of the Inhabitants,

* Note 59.   † Note 60.

and to secure him and the persons he confided in from being massacred by the incensed multitude; or, if the Governor had escaped so dreadful an end, and retained his Authority, to see His Majesty's benevolent and paternal Government dishonour'd by cruelties and merciless executions.

The event that I have the honor to report to your Lordship, took place on the 26th of last January, and although such a space of time has since elapsed, I have found it impossible to prepare that arranged detail, and that connected chain of evidence which so uncommon a subject has made it my indispensible duty to transmit to your Lordship.

Why I have been unable to perform this task, I shall as I proceed endeavour to explain, and I respectfully hope that the information and the evidence which I now propose to forward will prove to your Lordship that Governor Bligh has betrayed the high Trust and Confidence reposed in him by his Sovereign, and acted upon a predetermined plan to subvert the Laws of his Country, to terrify and influence the Courts of Justice, and to bereave those persons who had the misfortune to be obnoxious to him of their fortunes, their liberty, and their lives.

In the accomplishment of this plan, one act of oppression was succeeded in a progressive course by a greater, until a general Sensation of alarm and terror prevailed throughout the Settlement. Several inhabitants were dispossessed of their houses, and many others of respectable characters, or who had become opulent by trade, were threatened with the Governor's resentment if they presumed to build upon or alienate their own lands.

These measures, and various other Acts of Violence were projected and supported by the Governor and a junto of unprincipled men, amongst whom it was well known, and has been since proved, the notorious George Crossley, sent to this colony for Perjury, was the principal person, and the one most confided in by the Governor.

Your Lordship will not be surprized that a Government conducted by the Aid of such a Minister, should be hated and detested, as well as feared.

All the inhabitants who were a little advanced in their circumstances beyond the common mass dreaded the approach of the moment when it should become their turn to be sacrificed to the avarice, the resentment, or the fury of the Governor and his friends.

But whilst they were trembling with Apprehension for their own Safety, the eyes of the whole were suddenly turned from the contemplation of the general danger to that of Mr. McArthur, a

1808.
11 April.

gentleman who was many years an Officer in the New South Wales Corps, and who now possesses a large property in this Country.

Alleged
hostility of
Bligh to
Macarthur.

The extent of Mr. McArthur's Estate, the number of his flocks and herds, it had been long seen, had made him extremely obnoxious to Gov'r Bligh. Mr. McArthur, sensible how much he had to dread from the ill-will of an Officer of the Gov'r's well-known character, endeavoured to provide for his security by the most scrupulous circumspection and prudence of conduct. Secluded in a profound retirement on his Estate, and unceasingly engaged in its management and the care and education of his children, his name was never heard of in any public business; but neither caution nor prudence could long shield him from the hostile spirit of the Gov'r. The attack was first commenced upon his reputation, and terminated in the imprisonment of his person in the common Gaol.

After a variety of introductory measures, which your Lordship will find detailed in the copy of the proceedings of a Court of Criminal Judicature, to which I shall hereafter refer, Mr. McArthur surrendered as a Prisoner at its bar on the 25th of last January, charged with two separate misdemeanours. When the Members of the Court had been sworn in, and they were pro-

The trial of
John
Macarthur.

ceeding to swear in Richard Atkins, Esquire, the Judge-Advocate, Mr. McArthur presented a Protest, in which he urged a Variety of objections against that Officer's presiding at his trial. Mr. Atkins endeavoured to prevail upon the Court not to receive or hear the Protest read; but the Members, being of Opinion it ought to be heard, directed Mr. McArthur to proceed. The Judge-Advocate then retired from his chair, and waited until Mr. McArthur had read the protest. When that was done he advanced again, and declared Mr. McArthur should be immediately committed to Gaol. The Court then interfered on behalf of Mr. McArthur, and, after a long altercation, the Judge-Advocate retired from the Court-House, leaving behind him his Papers. These were immediately taken possession of and examined by the Members, and those Papers led to a discovery that the whole plan of the trial had been arranged, and every question prepared that was to be asked thè evidence of the prosecution by the infamous Crossley.

Correspondence
between Bligh
and the
members of
the court.

An immediate correspondence ensued between the Members of the Court and the Governor, in which the Members maintained the propriety of Mr. McArthur's objection to the Judge-Advocate; and the Governor as strenuously insisted upon the Judge-Advocate presiding at the trial.

Whilst this correspondence was carrying on, Mr. McArthur received information from several persons in the Court that a number of armed constables (most of whom were convicts) were parading without the door for the purpose of seizing his person and dragging him to Gaol.

As many of these men were of the most infamous character and entirely devoted to the Provost-Marshal,* who is himself an abandoned and unprincipled person, Mr. McArthur was advised by his friends to appeal to the Court for protection against the danger to which he would be exposed on leaving the Court-House. The Court, considering the appeal to be well founded, transmitted Mr. McArthur's deposition to the Governor, with a letter recommending that the protection Mr. McArthur had required might be given to him; but no answer having been received at four o'clock, the Court remanded Mr. McArthur to his former Bail and adjourned.

The same evening I received a letter from the Governor requesting to see me without delay; but as I was then at my Country house, about four miles from the Town, where I had been confined that day, scarcely able to move and incapable of writing, occasioned by a violent hurt I had received from the oversetting of a Gig, I was under the necessity of returning a verbal answer by the Governor's Orderly, signifying that it would not be in my power to attend him.

The following morning Mr. McArthur was apprehended by a Warrant from the Judge-Advocate and three Magistrates, granted in consequence of a deposition from the Provost-Marshal, who falsely swore that Mr. McArthur had been set at large by the Court of Criminal Judicature, although he had received a notification from the Members previous to their adjournment that Mr. McArthur was remanded to his former Bail.

A very awful impression was made upon the minds of the Inhabitants, as I have been informed, when they saw Mr. McArthur taken to the Gaol; many respectable persons hastened to him; and when the Court assembled at ten o'clock his two Bondsmen presented a copy of the Warrant for his apprehension and a deposition from themselves.

The Court directly wrote to the Governor a letter expressive of their concern, and praying Mr. McArthur might be restored to his Bail. To this letter no answer was given, and the Court having waited until three o'clock adjourned.

When it was known that the Court had broken up without having procured Mr. McArthur's enlargement the agitation of the Town became greatly increased, and information was brought to me at four o'clock by Mr. Harris, Surgeon of the New South

* Note 61.

1808.
11 April.

Members of
the court
charged by
Bligh with
treason.

Wales Corps, that an insurrection of the Inhabitants was to be
feared. In a few minutes after I had received this intelligence
a Dragoon arrived with a letter from the Governor, in which I
was informed that six of the Officers of the New South Wales
Corps had been charged with treasonable practices, and were
summoned to appear before the Governor and the Magistrates at
nine o'clock the next morning. The communication of such
extraordinary measures occasioned temporary forgetfulness of my
bruises, and I immediately set off in a Carriage to the Town.

Arrival of
Johnston at
Sydney.

On my arrival at the Barracks I saw all the Civil and Military
Officers collected, and the most respectable Inhabitants in conversation with them. The common people were also to be seen
in various groups in every street murmuring and loudly complaining, whilst others were watching the movements of Crossley
and the Magistrates, who frequently passed from the Judge-
Advocate's to the Government House. At this Moment it was

Council held
at Government
House.

also known that the Governor was shut up in Council with the
desperate and depraved Crossley; Mr. Palmer, the Commissary;
Mr. Campbell, a Merchant; and Mr. Arndell (the latter three
Magistrates), and that Mr. Gore (the Provost-Marshal) and
Mr. Fulton (the Chaplain) were also at Government House, all
ready to sanction whatever Crossley proposed or the Governor
ordered.

Johnston
requested to
take action.

The Gentlemen who had assembled on my arrival earnestly
entreated me to adopt decisive measures for the Safety of the
Inhabitants and to dispel the great alarm, as it was understood
throughout the Town that the Members of the Court of Criminal
Judicature would be thrown into Gaol; and it was expected, after
such a measure, nothing could limit the excess of the Governor's
cruelties; the Gentleman also warmly urged me to bail Mr.
McArthur, so that he might consult with them on the measures
most proper to recommend at so extraordinary a crisis.

Macarthur
released by
Johnston.

As I had no doubt of the illegality of Mr. McArthur's confine-
ment, I felt no difficulty in acceding to the request, and Mr.
McArthur being released from the gaol directly joined the
Assembly of Officers and Inhabitants who were then at the
Barracks.

Decision to
place Bligh
under arrest.

In a short time after, a letter was presented to me imploring
me instantly to put Governor Bligh in Arrest, and to assume the
Command of the Colony. This letter was also approved of by all
the Officers of the Corps present at Head Quarters; and as the
events I had myself witnessed left me no cause to doubt the
propriety and necessity of complying with this requisition, I
immediately ordered the Corps under Arms, and directed four
Officers to proceed to Government House and summon Governor

Bligh to resign his Authority. The Corps quickly followed, attended by the Civil Officers and a considerable number of respectable Inhabitants.*

The four Officers who had carried the Summons met me at the Governor's door and reported that he was nowhere to be found, nor any information to be obtained of him, although the strongest assurances had been given that his person should be strictly guarded from insult or violence.

After a rigid Search, the Governor, however, was at last discovered in a situation too disgraceful to be mentioned, and which I solemnly declare to your Lordship would have been most gratifying to my feelings had it been possible to have concealed from the Public.

As soon as Governor Bligh made his Appearance, I assured him of his personal Safety and of every attention in my power to offer him.

Whilst the Search was making for Governor Bligh, I was entreated by the Civil Officers and Inhabitants to proclaim Martial Law, and this request meeting my approbation, Martial Law was instantly proclaimed, and continued in force until the next day.

As not a single act of disorder or irregularity was committed during the interesting Scene that I have had the honor to describe to your Lordship, and as the most perfect peace and tranquility were restored throughout the whole Settlement, I published a Proclamation the next morning revoking the Order of the preceding evening and restoring the Civil Government.

I also suspended from their Offices the Judge-Advocate, the Commissary, the Chaplain, and the Provost-Marshal, with all the Magistrates who it appeared had assisted with Crossley to support Governor Bligh in those measures which produced such disgraceful consequences to him and such general alarm and disquietude to the Inhabitants. The same day I filled the vacant Offices by persons who I had every reason to hope would discharge their different duties with fidelity and zeal until His Majesty should be pleased to make other arrangements.

On the evening of the 26th of January, and several succeeding days, Committees were engaged in examining the Judge-Advocate, the Commissary, the Governor's Secretary, Mr. Campbell, Mr. Arndell, Mr. Fulton, and Crossley, from whom many important proofs were obtained of the Governor's intentions and of his confidence in Crossley.

After these examinations were taken, I ordered the Court of Criminal Judicature to assemble that Mr. McArthur might be arraigned on the Indictment that was found amongst the Judge-

* Note 62.

1808.
11 April.

Advocate's Papers, and that the Trial might proceed on the plan Crossley had suggested to ensure his conviction.

Acquittal of Macarthur.

The evidences were examined in the order Crossley had prescribed, and every question asked that he had previously dictated. Your Lordship will discover from the Copy of the trial that Mr. McArthur was acquitted without being put on his defence, and that a complete disclosure was made of the plans which had been deliberately formed for the ruin and destruction of that Gentleman.

The proof of Bligh's guilt.

I respectfully trust this trial and the confessions of the Magistrates and other confidential persons will convince your Lordship of the guilty intentions of Governor Bligh, and how little he regarded the honor of the sacred personage whom he represented, by suffering himself to be guided by a wretch like that man, Crossley, to persecute and oppress His Majesty's Subjects.

Trial and transportation of Crossley.

As soon as Mr. McArthur's trial was concluded, Crossley was brought before the Court,* charged with acting as an Agent or Attorney after having been convicted of Perjury. The Offence being clearly proved, the Court sentenced him to be transported for seven years; and he has been since sent to the Coal-Mines at Newcastle to prevent him from agitating this Settlement again with the contrivance of new villainies.

Trial and imprisonment of Gore.

Mr. Gore, the Provost-Marshal, has also been brought before another Court† of Criminal Judicature, charged with wilful and corrupt Perjury; but, having objected to one of the Members, on the plea of his being prejudiced against him, the Court admitted the objection; and, as he thought proper to refuse giving bail to appear before another Court, he was committed to Gaol until he does give bail, or until a Court can be found in which there shall be no Member to whom he has any objections.

Examination of officers of the commissariat department.

Being convinced that the most shameful abuses had been practised in the expenditure of His Majesty's Stores, and in the distribution of the Public live Stock, I ordered that Mr. Fitz, Deputy-Commissary; Mr. Wiltshire, Mr. Gowen, and Mr. Baker, Storekeepers; Andrew Frazier, a servant of Mr. Commissary Palmer's; and Mr. John Jamieson, Superintendant of Stock, should be examined. The depositions of these persons, although extremely incomplete, will not, I persuade myself, be found inadequate to convince your Lordship of the various frauds that have been committed on the public property, and that His Majesty's interest has not been the first object of consideration with Governor Bligh and Mr. Commissary Palmer.

Deposition of Andrew Thompson.

I would also entreat to lead your Lordship's attention to the deposition of one Andrew Thompson, formerly a convict, the Governor's confidential Manager of an Establishment on the

Banks of the Hawkesbury. This man's confession will, in part, disclose to your Lordship the arrangements made by the Governor for the improvement of his private fortune at the expense of the Crown; and the correspondence of Thompson, found amongst the Governor's papers, will further prove the extensiveness of the plan upon which the Governor intended to proceed.

1808.
11 April.

Bligh's
farming
enterprises.

The Despatch from Lieut.-Colonel Paterson,* which I have now the honor to forward, will apprize your Lordship it is that Officer's intention to leave Port Dalrymple and proceed to this Settlement to relieve me.

Paterson
to relieve
Johnston.

I have requested the Commanding Officer of His Majesty's Ship Porpoise to get ready for sea, in compliance with Lieut.-Colonel Paterson's desire that she might be sent for him; and the ship now only waits for my Despatches.

H.M.S. Porpoise
to be sent to
Port
Dalrymple.

Whether Lieut.-Colonel Paterson is correct in laying claim to this Command, under the existing circumstances of the Colony, I confess myself incompetent to form a decided opinion; but if, as I have understood, Lieut.-Colonel Paterson has a distinct appointment as Lieut.-Governor of Port Dalrymple, and Lieut.-Colonel Foveaux has been appointed by His Majesty Lieut.-Governor of the Territory, I should imagine that Lieut.-Colonel Paterson cannot with propriety quit Port Dalrymple. The Royal Patent for establishing a Civil form of Government in this Colony contains the following Clause:—" And if upon your death or absence out of our said Territory and its Dependencies there be no person upon the place commissioned or appointed by us to be our Lieut.-Governor or Commander-in-Chief of our Said Territory and its Dependencies, Our Will and Pleasure is that the Officer highest in rank who shall be at the time of your death or absence upon service within the same and who shall take the Oaths and subscribe the declaration appointed to be taken and subscribed by you or by the Commander-in-Chief of Our said Territory and its Dependencies, shall take upon him the Administration of the Government and execute Our said Commission and Instructions, and the Several Powers and Authorities therein contained, in the same manner and to all intents and purposes as other Our Governor or Commander-in-Chief should or ought to do in case of your absence until your return, or in all cases until Our further Pleasure be known therein."

The question of
the government
of the colony.

It was in consequence of this Clause that Lieut.-Col. Paterson retained the Command here after the departure of Lieut.-Governor Grose, although he then held only the Rank of Captain in the Army, and Governor King, at the same time, was in the Territory, as Lieut.-Governor of a Dependency,† and a Master and Commander in the Navy.

* Note 65.   † Note 66.

1808.
11 April.

Johnston's
proposed
action.

Forming my opinion from this precedent, and being assured of Lieut.-Col. Foveaux's appointment, I could not conjecture that Lieut.-Col. Paterson would think of leaving his Post at Port Dalrymple, as I apprehend his Supercession, after the arrival of Lieut.-Col. Foveaux, must be certain; but, circumstanced as I am, I had much rather commit an error, by resigning my present command, than expose myself to the slightest suspicion that a single measure I have adopted respecting Governor Bligh has originated in a desire of possessing myself of his Authority, or from any other than the pure motive of promoting the honor of His Majesty's Service, and preserving the tranquility of the Colony.

Johnston's
assumption of
the title of
lieutenant-
governor.

It was from this Motive that I was prevailed upon, at the entreaty of the Officers and the Inhabitants, to assume the Title of Lieut.-Governor, for I must not conceal from Your Lordship that very serious apprehensions were entertained of what might happen if any Officer of the Territory should relieve me before the arrival of Lieut.-Governor Foveaux, or until His Majesty's Pleasure shall be communicated.

Want of
precedents.

If my styling myself Lieut.-Governor be an impropriety, I hope your Lordship will consider the motive, and make allowance for the delicacy and difficulty of a situation where I had no precedent to guide, and no choice but of difficulties. One of the Principal of these has been to determine how, and by what conveyance, Governor Bligh was to be sent to England. His own wish, your Lordship will learn from his letter, was to return in the Command of His Majesty's Ship Porpoise. But to that, it appeared to me, there were almost insurmountable obstacles, for I conceived it would be highly improper to allow him to come out of arrest; and I also knew he had behaved towards the Officers and crew of the Porpoise with such insufferable oppression and inhumanity that the most serious consequences might have arisen if he were permitted to exercise any authority on board her.

The problem
of sending
Bligh to
England.

Symons'
determination
to exhibit
charges
against Bligh.

This information I received from Lieut. Symons (her present acting-commander), who expressed a determination to exhibit charges against Governor Bligh to the Lords of the Admiralty; and, as a preliminary step, he sent two of the Lieutenants to make Depositions respecting some dreadful insults they had received.

The Pegasus
selected to
convey Bligh.

These circumstances, and the possibility that Governor Bligh might touch at one of His Majesty's foreign Settlements and excite injurious opinions of the causes of his supercession, induced me to make choice of the Pegasus, a private Vessel, and to enter into a conditional verbal agreement for his passage, if

the ship should prove in good condition after being surveyed.
But when she had been favourably reported of, her owner, for
some private reasons, considered it expedient to decline the
bargain; and in this dilemma I was necessitated either to send Bligh offered
a passage in
the Dart or
Porpoise.
Governor Bligh Home in the Dart, a South Sea Sealer, or to
give him the option of taking his passage in the Porpoise, on the
conditions that he should pledge his Word of Honor as an Officer
that he would not attempt to assume any Authority, but consider
himself under the restraint of a Military Arrest until he should
receive His Majesty's Commands.

To this he at last acceded, and I made application to the Bligh's
agreement
to sail in
H.M.S.
Porpoise.
Acting Commander of His Majesty's Ship to receive the Governor
on board, and to furnish him with suitable accommodation for
himself and Family.

In endeavouring to make arrangements for this purpose other
obstacles were erected that I had not the power to remove, and
produced a continuance of our correspondence. The Governor's
Letters on this occasion convinced me that neither his past misfortunes nor present humiliating condition had awakened in his
breast a Sense of the advantages which may ever be expected
from a manly and honorable regard to the strict spirit of our
engagements. In truth, my Lord, his whole conduct left me
without doubt that he designed to take the Command of His
Majesty's Ship the moment he put his foot on board her; and
this determined me to send him immediately on board the Dart
unless he unequivocally Subscribed the acknowledgment I required from him. Whilst this point was agitated, Lieut.-Colonel
Paterson's letters arrived in the Harrington from Port Dal-
rymple. The information they contained caused me to deter- Bligh's
departure to be
determined
by Paterson.
mine (as soon as I had ascertained, by a reference to the Public
Papers, that Lieut.-Colonel Paterson had once held the Commission of Lieut.-Governor of the Territory) to postpone Governor Bligh's departure, and to leave it to Lieutenant-Colonel
Paterson to decide in what manner Governor Bligh shall be sent
home.

I am now, my Lord, arrived at the most painful part of my Difficulties
encountered
by Johnston.
task—an explanation of the causes that have prevented me from
preparing a better arranged Statement of the transactions in
which I have been engaged; and it is with deep concern I find
myself obliged to report to your Lordship that the opposition
from those persons from whom I had most reason to expect
support has been one of the principal obstacles I have had to
encounter.

When the Officers and Inhabitants found themselves relieved
from the oppressions of Governor Bligh, the general joy that was

1808.
11 April.

Relief of the
colonists by
Bligh's arrest.

felt displayed itself in rejoicings, bonfires, and illuminations, and in a manifestation of the most perfect unanimity. Even the lowest class of the Prisoners were influenced by the same Sentiments, and for a short time abandoned their habits of plundering. The contemplation of this happy scene more than repaid me for the increase of care, fatigue, and responsibility to which I had submitted for the public benefit; but the unanimity in which I felt so much pleasure I quickly discovered was not to be preserved without a sacrifice of His Majesty's interests, and a departure from the regulations that have been made to check the importation of Spirituous liquors into the Colony.

Attempted
importation
of spirits.

Unfortunately, at the time I took the Command, an American Ship, the Jenny, of Boston, lay in the Port, with five thousand Gallons of Rum and Brandy on board. Many persons were desirous to get permission to purchase this Cargo; but as Governor Bligh had allowed seven thousand Gallons to be landed out of the City of Edinburgh from the Cape of Good Hope, and from an American Brig, which was not then distributed, I thought it my duty to resist every Solicitation; and having received information that Spirits were Smuggling from the American, I ordered her to quit the Port, and sent the Colonial Schooner Estramina to escort her out of sight of land.

The ship Jenny
seized for
smuggling.

On the 13th February, four days after the Jenny sailed, it was reported that she had returned and put into Broken Bay, where she was said to be Smuggling her cargo. Boats were at my request directly armed and sent from the Porpoise with orders to seize the ship if any proof could be obtained of her Smuggling. When the Boats reached the Jenny they found a man from the shore preparing to take a Cask of Spirits, and as there were other strong corroborative proofs that Spirits had been or were prepared to be landed, the Ship was seized and brought back to the Port.

Meeting of
vice-admiralty
court.

I immediately ordered a Vice-Admiralty Court to be Assembled, and Captain Symons, Acting Commander of His Majesty's Ship Porpoise, appointed an Agent to prosecute his claim to the Ship and Cargo as a lawful prize for having violated the Plantation Laws. It appeared in evidence that there was a deficiency of twelve hundred and nine Gallons of the quantity of Spirits which the Jenny entered when she first arrived. But neither that circumstance nor many other strong proofs that an illicit trade had been carried on, were thought sufficient by the Court to warrant her condemnation. The Captain of the American, after giving all the trouble he could, entered a Protest and an Appeal, which will be transmitted with a copy of the Trial by the next Ship that sails from hence; and I am assured that when your

Lordship shall be acquainted with its contents, you will be convinced the condemnation of a Ship for smuggling will not easily be accomplished in New South Wales.

The departure of the Jenny with the remains of her cargo of Spirits was highly disapproved of by many, and the discontent which that event created was much increased by the discovery of my determination to reduce the expenditure of Public Money and Stores, to be extremely circumspect in the distribution of live Stock and Convicts, and not to alienate any lands but on the condition of the Grant being approved by His Majesty's Secretary of State for the Colonies.*

Determined to persevere in this System, and finding I should require the aid of some Gentleman in whose integrity I should have confidence, I requested Mr. McArthur to assist me in the arduous undertaking.

As there was no Office vacant to which I could appoint him, and as it was necessary he should have some public character, I created an Office which has never before existed here, and I appointed him Secretary to the Colony. This unauthorized innovation I trust will not be disapproved, when my peculiar situation is considered, more particularly as it entails no additional expense upon the publick.

My intentions have been so faithfully seconded by the efforts of Mr. McArthur that three hundred persons who were Victualled and clothed by His Majesty when I took the Command now maintain themselves; and many of the most able of these people have been distributed amongst the Settlers to assist in the Cultivation of their lands.

Other comparatively insignificant arrangements have been made, and inquiries into many shameful frauds and abuses, have been commenced in the Department which Mr. McArthur has undertaken to conduct.

But every obstacle that Knavery or cunning could devise has been interposed to distract my attention, and to retard the accomplishment of those necessary objects. So widely extended is the influence of some of the persons who have been engaged in illicit or dishonest practices, that they have contrived to form a combination with several of the better Class, who ought to have held themselves superior to such connexions.

I am concerned to say that the two Mr. Blaxlands, persons who have received such extraordinary encouragement as Settlers, have been among the forwardest and most troublesome of my opposers. These Gentlemen have, unhappily for themselves, formed a connexion with an Inhabitant by the name of Lord, who was once a Convict but now possesses a very extensive

* Note 67.

1808,
11 April.

fortune, or at least the appearance of it, and they have suffered
themselves to be led by this man into a litigation that has drawn
into its vortex several Officers, and proceeded to such lengths
that I have been obliged, although with extreme reluctance, to
order Mr. Grimes (who acted as Judge-Advocate after the suspension of Mr. Atkins) to take my despatches in the Dart, and
Mr. Harris, Surgeon in the New South Wales Corps, to proceed
with their duplicates in the Brothers.

*Grimes and
Harris
ordered to
England.*

Although I have the greatest cause to be dissatisfied with the
part Mr. Grimes has suffered himself ·to be influenced to act,
more particularly when the emergency of public affairs are considered, yet I cannot but hope, from my knowledge of his past
conduct, that his errors have been errors of judgment more than
of design; and I beg to refer your Lordship to Mr. Grimes for
any information you may wish respecting Governor Bligh, with
an entire confidence that he will relate to your Lordship many
important facts.

*Conduct of
Charles Grimes.*

By the Ship Brothers I shall do myself the honor to enter into
a further explanation of my reasons for sending Mr. Grimes and
Mr. Harris with my Despatches; And to provide against the
failure of that Ship, I have requested Mr. McArthur, Junior,
who takes his passage in the Dart with Mr. Grimes, to wait upon
your Lordship as soon as he shall arrive in England.

*Edward
Macarthur to
sail in the Dart.*

After such an unpleasant recital as that which my duty has
imposed upon me respecting the improper conduct of a few Individuals, it is with unfeigned satisfaction that I proceed to
acquaint your Lordship of the contented and happy State in
which all the middle and lower ranks of inhabitants remain;
nor must I omit to report to your Lordship the exemplary and
Soldierlike conduct of the New South Wales Corps, who to their
most perfect obedience and strict discipline, unite the utmost
watchfulness for the preservation of the public peace.

*Conduct of
middle and
lower classes
and military.*

Permit me also to recommend to your Lordship's favourable
notice Mr. Bayly, my private Secretary, who also acts as Provost-
Marshal during the Suspension of Mr. Gore. The zeal and active
exertions of that gentleman has relieved me in a variety of
different Services, and as he has long since given in his resignation to quit the Army, I beg to recommend him for a confirmation of the appointment of Provost-Marshal, under a perfect
conviction that, should His Majesty be pleased to continue him in
that Office, his Services would materially contribute to establish
good order in the Police of this Settlement.

*Recommenda-
tion of Nicholas
Bayly.*

On reviewing the depositions to which I have referred, to
establish the criminality of Governor Bligh, I observe that I have
omitted to notice several representations which were transmitted

*Depositions
relating to
Bligh's guilt.*

to His Royal Highness the Commander-in-Chief last October. 1808.
11 April.
I therefore entreat permission to submit them to your Lordship,
as proofs that neither the Soldier on duty has been screened
against the Violence of Governor Bligh, nor the Soldier in his
cottage from his oppression.

I shall no longer obtrude upon your Lordship on this occasion Johnston's
than to Solicit that whenever the representation of what has self-sacrifice
in taking the
taken place here shall be communicated to my Gracious Sove- command.
reign, your Lordship will have the goodness to offer my humble
assurances that I have sacrificed comparative ease, and have
taken upon myself so great a responsibility rather than submit
to be a witness of His Majesty's sacred name being profaned and
dishonoured by deeds of injustice and violence.

I have, &c.,
GEO. JOHNSTON.

[Enclosure No. 1.]

THE TRIAL OF JOHN MACARTHUR.

PROCEEDINGS of a Court of Criminal Jurisdiction assembled at Proceedings
Sydney, in New South Wales, under the authority of His at the trial
Excellency Governor Bligh's Precept, bearing date the 20th of John
Macarthur.
January, 1808.

Sydney, New South Wales, 25th January, 1808.

Members.—The Judge-Advocate; Capt. Anthony Fenn Kemp,
Lieut. John Brabyn, Lieut. William Moore, Lieut. Thomas Laycock,
Lieut. William Minchin, Lieut. William Lawson, New South Wales
Corps.

THE Precept read and Members sworn by the Judge-Advocate.
John McArthur, Esq., the Prisoner at the Bar, addressed the Court,
praying that he might be allowed to state an objection to Richard
Atkins, Esq., the Judge-Advocate, sitting as Judge on his Trial,
which the Members of the Court, conceiving it but Justice due to
the prisoner, have required his objections to be stated previous to
the Judge-Advocate being sworn. The Prisoner read the Paper
marked A, and solemnly protests against the said Richard Atkins
being allowed to take his seat as Judge on his Trial, for the reasons
therein stated. The Court having taken the same into their mature
and deliberate consideration, are of opinion that the objections set
forth in the Prisoner's Protest are good and lawful objections to
Richard Atkins, Esq., sitting on his Trial, and feeling themselves
bound to state their opinion to His Excellency the Governor on the
Subject, do therefore state as follows:—

Sir, Court-house, 11.15 a.m., 25th January, 1808.

We, the Officers composing the Court of Criminal Jurisdiction
this day assembled, beg leave to state to Your Excellency that a
Right of Challenge, as per paper A, has been demanded by the
Prisoner now before us to Richard Atkins, Esq., sitting as Judge on
his Trial, which we have, after mature and deliberate consideration,
agreed to allow as a good and lawful objection. We, therefore,
submit to Your Excellency to determine on the propriety of appointing another Judge-Advocate to preside on the present Trial. We
further pray Your Excellency's protection in the execution of our

1808.
11 April.

Proceedings
at the trial
of John
Macarthur.

duty, having been grossly insulted and threatened by Richard Atkins, Esq., with a seeming view to deter us in our legal proceedings.

We have, &c.,

Signed by the Members of the Court.

Answer.

Government House, Sydney, 25th January, 1808,

Gentlemen,   Half-past Noon.

In answer to your Letter, just received, I conceive that there could have been no cause of Challenge to the Judge-Advocate, who is the Officer appointed by His Majesty's Patent, and without whose presence there could be no Court.

And I consider that the Judge-Advocate had a right to commit any Person who might commit any gross Insult to him while in his official capacity as Judge of the Court. I do not consider the Court to be formed without the Judge-Advocate, and when legally convened I have no right to interpose any Authority concerning its legal Acts.

I, therefore, can do no otherwise than direct that the Judge-Advocate take his Seat and act as directed by His Majesty's Letters Patent for the constituting the Court of Criminal Jurisdiction, which, being authorised by an Act of Parliament, is as follows:—
"And We further Will, Ordain, and Appoint that the said Court of Criminal Jurisdiction shall consist of Our Judge-Advocate for the Time being, together with such our six Officers of Our Sea and Land Services as Our Governor (or, in case of his Death or Absence, Our Lieutenant-Governor) shall by Precept, issued under his hand and Seal, convene from time to time for that purpose."

I am, &c.,

Directed to the Members by Name.   Wm. Bligh.

From the Court to the Governor.

Sir,   Sydney, 25th January, 1808.

We have had the Honor of Your Excellency's Opinion with respect to the objection made by a Prisoner (John McArthur, Esq.) at our Bar, to the Judge-Advocate. We beg Your Excellency to be assured that we have at all times the utmost deference to any Opinion delivered by Your Excellency; but, in the present case, we cannot, consistent with the Oath we have taken, or with our Consciences, sit with Richard Atkins, Esq., on the Trial of John McArthur, Esq., knowing as we do that the greatest enmity has for these thirteen or fourteen years past existed between the Parties. We pray Your Excellency's further consideration in the present case.   We have, &c.,

Signed by the Members of the Court.

Answer.

Gentlemen,   Sydney, 25th January, 1808, quarter past 2 o'clock.

In reply to your second Letter of this date, I require that you deliver to Mr. William Gore, Provost-Marshal, and Mr. Edmund Griffin, my Secretary, who accompanies him on the occasion, all the Papers that the Judge-Advocate left on the Table, and which were refused to be sent to him by the Constable, and also those which the Prisoner, John McArthur, has read before you, that they may be delivered to the Judge-Advocate, His Majesty's legal Officer.

I am, &c.,

Directed to the Members by Name.   Wm. Bligh.

1808.
11 April.

Proceedings at the trial of John Macarthur.

From the Court in Reply.

Sir,   Court House, Sydney, 25th January, 1808.

We are honored with your Excellency's letter requiring us to deliver to Mr. William Gore, Provost Marshal, and Mr. Edmund Griffin all the Papers the Judge Advocate left on the Table and also those which the Prisoner, John McArthur, Esq., read before us. As it is necessary that we should hold the Papers alluded to by Your Excellency for our own Justification, We beg Your Excellency will be pleased to excuse our giving them up. We are ready to render Your Excellency attested Copies of the whole if you require it.

We have, &c.,
Signed by the Members.

Answer.

Government House, Sydney, 25th January, 1808,
Gentlemen,   Three-quarters past Three o'clock.

I have required the Judge-Advocate's Papers, with those that were read by John McArthur, and I now demand finally your Answer in writing whether you will deliver those papers or not; And I again repeat that you are no Court without the Judge-Advocate.   I am, &c.,
Directed to the Members by Name.   WM. BLIGH.

From the Court in Answer.

Sir,   Sydney, 25th January, 1808.

In Answer to your Excellency's Letter, we beg leave to say that we are ready to furnish Your Excellency with attested Copies of all the Papers required, but the originals we are compelled to keep in justification of our Conduct; Should Your Excellency be pleased, for the furtherance of the Public Service, to appoint another Judge-Advocate for the Trial of John McArthur, Esquire, we are ready to deliver all the Papers to the Person so appointed. The Members of the Court, constituted by Your Excellency's Precept, and sworn in by the Judge-Advocate, beg leave to acquaint you that they have adjourned to wait Your Excellency's further pleasure.

We have, &c.,
Signed by the Members.

Four o'Clock.—The Prisoner, John McArthur, Esq., in a Paper marked B claims the Protection of the Court on the grounds therein stated, a Copy of which the Court feel it necessary to transmit to His Excellency the Governor with the following Letter :—

Sir,   Sydney, 25th January, 1808.

We take the liberty to enclose your Excellency a copy of the deposition made before us as members of the Criminal Court this day assembled, under your Excellency's precept, by John McArthur, Esq., a Prisoner at our Bar and we earnestly entreat that your Excellency will be pleased to order such protection to be given Mr. McArthur as in our humble opinion the nature of· his complaint merits.   We have, &c.,
Signed by the Members.

Four o'Clock P.M.—The Prisoner, John McArthur, Esq., is remanded to his former Bail and Mr. Wm. Gore, the Provost Marshal, acquainted therewith by the Senior Members of the Court.

1808.
11 April.

Proceedings
at the trial
of John
Macarthur.

Five o'Clock p.m.—The Court adjourned till to-morrow morning 10 o'Clock.

10 o'Clock, 26th January, 1808.

THE Court met pursuant to adjournment, and the Prisoner, John McArthur, Esquire, not appearing at the Bar, and the Sureties being called on by the Court to bring forth the Body of the said John McArthur, Esqre., or to forfeit their recognizance, deliver into Court the Deposition marked C. The Court taking the same into consideration, feel themselves bound to record on their minutes that the Testimony therein quoted, and made by Mr. William Gore, the Provost-Marshal, before a Bench of Magistrates (as set forth in the Judge-Advocate's warrant) is False; the Court therefore, on further consideration, think themselves bound to address His Excellency the Governor, as the Executive Authority of the Colony, on the Subject, as follows:—

Sir,   Court-house, Sydney, 26th January, 1808.

We have the Honor to enclose Your Excellency an attested Copy of the address delivered to the Court yesterday by John McArthur, Esquire, a Prisoner at our Bar. The Address we trust will induce Your Excellency to concur in the opinion we have given, that "The Judge-Advocate, Richard Atkins, Esquire, has been challenged on good and lawful grounds, and is ineligible to sit as a Judge in the Cause before us."

We also take the liberty to submit to Your Excellency, that, having taken an Oath "well and truly to try, and a true deliverance make between Our Sovereign Lord the King and the Prisoner at the Bar, and a true Verdict give according to Evidence," that we are bound to proceed to the Trial of John McArthur, Esquire, or to violate our Oath. We therefore pray that Your Excellency will be pleased to nominate some impartial person to execute the Office of Judge-Advocate.

It is with much concern we have learned by the enclosed Deposition made before us by G. Blaxcell, Esqre., and N. Bayly, Esqre., that the Body of John McArthur, Esqre., the Prisoner arraigned before us yesterday, has been forcibly arrested from the Bail which the Court remanded him in, which illegal Act of the Magistrates (grounded on the false Deposition of Mr. William Gore, Provost-Marshal) We beg leave to represent to Your Excellency, is in our opinion calculated to subvert the legal Authority and Independence of the Court of Criminal Jurisdiction constituted in this Colony by His Majesty's Letters Patent, and we therefore pray Your Excellency will discountenance such Magisterial Proceedings, pregnant with the most serious consequences to the Community at large, and that Your Excellency will be pleased to take measures to restore John McArthur, Esq., to his former Bail, that the Court may proceed on his Trial.

We have, &c.,
Signed by the Members.

Three o'Clock.—The Court not being able to obtain an Answer from His Excellency (Altho' by a verbal Message he promised to send one), and having waited since half past Noon, now adjourn till his Excellency's pleasure is known.

Signed by the Members' Order,
A. F. KEMP, J.P.

Copy of a Circular Letter sent to each Member of the Court after their Adjournment.

1808.
11 April.

Proceedings at the trial of John Macarthur.

By His Excellency William Bligh, Esquire, Captain-General and Governor in Chief in and over His Majesty's Territory of New South Wales and its Dependencies, &c., &c.

The Judge-Advocate having presented a Memorial to me, in which you are charged with certain Crimes, You are therefore hereby required to appear before me, at Government House, at nine o'Clock, to-morrow Morning, to answer in the Premises.

Given, &c., this 26th January, 1808.

WM. BLIGH.

To Captain Anthony Fenn Kemp,
 Of His Majesty's New South Wales Corps.
   By Command of His Excellency,
    EDMUND GRIFFIN, Secy.

Compared with the Original by us, of which it is a true Copy.
    A. F. KEMP, J.P.

[Paper marked A.]

To the Members of the Criminal Court.

Papers exhibited at the trial of John Macarthur.

Gentlemen,

 It will, I am convinced, excite your surprize, as I think it must that of every impartial man, to hear that I am brought a Prisoner to this Bar, utterly unacquainted, except from rumours, of the nature of the Accusation against which I am to defend myself.

 Such, however, is the fact; for although I have made three written applications to the Judge-Advocate for a Copy of the Indictment or Information, I have not been able to obtain it.

 In this unprecedented Situation, and having been informed that the charge against me has been founded on certain events, which originated in the illegal and arbitrary conduct of the Judge-Advocate, as exemplified in the Correspondence and Warrants, I did consider it prudent, and a piece of Justice I owed to the Community, to protest against Richard Atkins, Esq., being appointed to sit as a Judge on a Trial wherein he is so much interested, and in which his own Security is so materially involved.

 To prevent unnecessary delay and other consequences that I apprehended, I did, in a Letter to His Excellency Governor Bligh, protest against the Judge-Advocate, and respectfully required that a disinterested person might be appointed to preside at my Trial. To this His Excellency was pleased to answer "That the Law must take its course, as he does not feel himself justified to use any interference with the Executive Power," by which I suppose he meant the Judicial Authority, as I humbly conceive His Excellency's own Power must be the Executive.

 Defeated in this Attempt to obtain what I know to be my lawful Right, my only alternative is to resort to the Members of this Court; and I do so under an entire confidence that whatever I can prove to be my Right, you, as Men of Honor, will grant me.

 To you, then, Gentlemen, I appeal, and now solemnly protest against Richard Atkins, Esq., being allowed to take his seat as one of my Judges at this Trial.

 To support this Protest, my first Objection is because there is a Suit pending betwixt us for the recovery of a Sum of Money that he unjustly withholds, and, as he is screened from the operation of the Law, is to be submitted to His Majesty's Ministers.

1808.
11 April.

Papers
exhibited at
the trial of
John
Macarthur.

My second Objection is because I can prove he has for many years cherished a rancorous inveteracy against me, which has displayed itself in the propagation of malignant falsehoods, and every act of Injustice that can be expected to proceed from a person armed with powers against a man whose life and conduct is, I trust, a public satire on his own.

My third Objection is because I have been long the object of his vindictive malice, in consequence of my having been called as an evidence to support an accusation made against him by John Harris, Esq., that he was a Swindler.

My fourth Objection is because he has associated and combined with that well-known dismembered Limb of the Law, George Crossley (and others of as wicked minds, although not quite so notorious) to accomplish my destruction. In proof of this charge I have Evidence to prove that Crossley has prepared the Information to be produced on this Trial, and has arranged the whole plan of the Evidence, he being considered *eminently* qualified to conduct that part of the business, from his past extensive practice in that particular branch of legal knowledge. I have also Proof in my hand, in the writing of the Veteran Practitioner, Crossley, which will convince the most sceptical Mind that other schemes have been agitated to deprive me of my *Property, Liberty, Honor, and Life.* Here it is, Gentlemen, read it; and after, read the Proceedings of a Bench of Magistrates; and you will see that, for presuming to complain of a most unlawful seizure of my property (which the Judge-Advocate joined in reprobating), it has been determined to ruin me. This precious Document came into my hands, as it were, by the interposition of Divine Providence; it was dropped from the Pocket of Crossley and brought to me; that you may consider it at your leisure I annex a Copy of it, and of the Proceedings of the Bench of Magistrates.

My fifth Objection is because Richard Atkins, Esq., is my Prosecutor in this Trial, and is so deeply interested to procure my Conviction that, should he fail, nothing but the arm of Power can save him from a Criminal Prosecution at this very Bar for his false imprisonment of me.

My sixth and last Objection is founded on his having already pronounced sentence of condemnation against me, as is presumptuously proved (*and can be clearly*) by his declaring that the Bench of Magistrates had the power to punish me by Fine and Imprisonment, thereby clearly demonstrating an intention to deprive me of the benefit of my present Trial.

It will not, I presume, be denied that the Judge-Advocate, from the Constitution of this Court, combines the two characters of Judge and Juror, and that it follows as an indisputable consequence that any Objection which applies to either character is strictly applicable to him. All that therefore remains for me to do is to lay before you the legal Authorities on which I ground my Right of Challenge.

1st. Authority.—"The suspicion of Prejudice may be reasonably inferred against a Juror from the circumstance of his having an interest in the Cause whereby he may be led to wish the condemnation of the Prisoner.

"The prisoner must assign his cause of challenge of the Relevancy or Validity of which the Members are themselves the Judges. The most valid causes of Challenge are—Suspicion of *Malice,* of *Prejudice,* and *infamous Character.*"—*Tytler,* p. 226.

2d. Authority.—" So jealous is the Law of the perfect impartiality of Jurors that it is allowed to be a good cause of Challenge that the Juror has been heard to give his opinion beforehand that the Party is guilty."—*Tytler*, p. 228.

3d. " Two causes of Challenge *impossible to be overruled* are the charge of Corruption or Bribery verified by competent Proof, And Malice or hostile Enmity expressed by *Word* or *Deed*, against the Prisoner. Infamous Character is also a most relevant ground of Challenge."—*Tytler*, p. 227.

4th. " It hath been allowed a good ground of Challenge on the Part of the Prisoner that the Juror hath declared his Opinion beforehand that the Party is guilty."—*Burne's Justice*, 2nd vol., p. 813.

5th. " The Mayor of Hereford was laid by the Heels for sitting in Judgment in a Cause where he himself was Lessor of the Plaintiff in Ejectment, though he by the Charter was sole Judge of the Court."—*Burne*, vol. iii, p. 26.

6th. " In the case of Foxham, Tithing in the County of Wilts, a Justice of the Peace was Surveyor of the Highways, and a matter which concerned his Office coming in question at the Sessions, he joined in making the Order, and his name was put in the Caption. Determined by Lord Chief Justice Holt: it ought not to be, as if an Action be brought by my Lord Chief Justice Trevor, in the Court of Common Pleas, it must be before Edward Neville Knight and his Associates, And not before Thomas Trevor, and it was quashed."—*Burne*, vol. iii, p. 27.

7th. " And the better to remove all cause of suspicion of Partiality, it was wisely provided by the Statutes 4th Edward III, C. 2; 8th Richard II, C. 2; and 33rd Henry VIII, C. 24, That no Judge of Assize shall hold Pleas in any County wherein he was born or inhabits."—*Blackstone's Commentaries*, vol. iii, p. 355.

8th. " Jurors may be challenged for *suspicion* of *bias* or partiality; this may be either a principal challenge, or to the favor. A principal Challenge is such where the Cause assigned carries with it evident marks of suspicion either of Malice or favour; as that he has an *Interest* in the cause, that there is an *Action* depending between him and the Party. These are principal grounds of Challenge, and, if true, cannot be overruled."—*Blackstone*, vol. iii, p. 362.

Gentlemen, It would be an unpardonable waste of your time and an insult to your Understandings to press upon you more Authorities, for these I have submitted are clear to the point. You will now decide, Gentlemen, whether Law and Justice shall finally prevail against the contrivances of George Crossley. You have the eyes of an anxious Public upon you, trembling for the safety of their *Property*, their *Liberty*, and their *Lives*; to you has fallen the lot of deciding a point which perhaps involves the happiness or misery of Millions yet unborn. I conjure you in the name of Almighty God, in whose presence you stand, to consider the *inestimable value* of the precious Deposit with which you are now entrusted.

For my own part, knowing you as I do, I have no apprehensions. I feel assured that neither expectation of reward and favor nor dread of Persecution will influence your decision. It is to the Officers of the New South Wales Corps that the administration of Justice is committed; And who that is just has anything to dread?

Sydney, 25th January, 1808.   JOHN MCARTHUR.

A true Copy compared with the Original by us.

         A. F. KEMP, J.P.

1808.
11 April.

Papers exhibited at the trial of John Macarthur.

COPIES OF PAPERS REFERRED TO IN THE PRECEDING MEMORIAL.

[No. 1 referred to in Document A.]

[1] MR. JOHN MACARTHUR TO JUDGE-ADVOCATE ATKINS.

Sir,   Sydney, 20th January, 1808.

I learn from your Letter of yesterday's date to G. Blaxcell, Esq're, that a Criminal Court is to be assembled on the 25th Inst., before which I am to be brought, and that I have to subpœna my Evidences through the Provost-Marshal.

As I am yet in ignorance of the nature of the accusation you may have to prefer against me to the Court, I presume you will see the necessity of immediately furnishing me with a copy of the intended Indictment or Information, to which, as you, sir, are well aware, I am entitled by Law.   I am, &c.,

JOHN MCARTHUR.

[2] JUDGE-ADVOCATE ATKINS TO MR. JOHN MACARTHUR.

Sir,   20th January, 1808.

As I am certain you are not, by Law, entitled to a Copy of your Indictment or Information, at least in the present Stage of the business, you will excuse my not complying with your request.

I am, &c.,

RD. ATKINS, J.-A.

[3] MR. JOHN MACARTHUR TO JUDGE-ADVOCATE ATKINS.

Sir,   20th January, 1808.

As you say you are certain I am not entitled, by Law, to a copy of the Indictment or Information against me in the present Stage of the business, will you be pleased to acquaint me with the means by which I am to discover what Evidences I shall require to disprove an accusation, the particulars of which it is thought prudent to conceal from me—I say, thought prudent; for, to balance your certainty, Sir, by another, I am certain your refusal to grant my request is illegal, and such as you cannot justify. I therefore, hereby repeat the request.   I am, &c.,

JOHN MCARTHUR.

[4] JUDGE-ADVOCATE ATKINS TO MR. JOHN MACARTHUR.

Sir,   20th January, 1808.

In answer to your second Letter, I have only to refer you to my answer of your first Letter, and to add that your Indictment or Information is not for High Treason.

I am, &c.,

RD. ATKINS, J.-A.

[5] MR. JOHN MACARTHUR TO JUDGE-ADVOCATE ATKINS.

Sir,   \   20th January, 1808.

As you repeat your first answer, and continue to refuse me a copy of the Indictment or Information, I also must repeat my last question, " By what means am I to discover what Evidences I shall require to disprove an Accusation, the particulars of which it is thought prudent to conceal? "

I am thankful for the assurance you have given that I am not to be tried for High Treason, as you well know, Sir, I had too much cause to apprehend it might be intended (that dreadful Crime

having been publicly charged against me by the Provost-Marshal
in the name of His Excellency the Governor) ; But whether I am
to be tried for Treason or a Misdemeanor, with all due deference
to your superior legal knowledge, I maintain that I am entitled to
a copy of the Indictment or Information, in either case; and I take
the liberty to say, if you will condescend to consult your Law
Authorities, that you will discover Trials for Misdemeanors are
never brought on (unless by consent of Parties) until the next
Assizes or Sessions after the Indictment or Information has been
exhibited.   I am, &c.,
                                JOHN MCARTHUR.
A True Copy compared with the Original by us.
                                A. F. KEMP, J.P.

[No. 6] MR. JOHN MACARTHUR TO GOVERNOR BLIGH.

Sir,   Sydney, 22nd January, 1808.
    I have been apprized by a Letter from the Judge-Advocate to
G. Blaxcell, Esq., that I am to be brought before a Criminal Court
on Monday, the 25th Instant, and I have also learnt that the
Members of that Court have been nominated without any notification of Your Excellency's intention to appoint for the time being
a Judge-Advocate to preside at my Trial who is not interested in the
Event. I should, therefore, be wanting in Justice to myself if I
neglected to Protest against Richard Atkins, Esq., being suffered to
sit as the Judge at the impending Trial.
    The reason on which I found my objection is because that
Gentleman is deeply interested to obtain a Verdict against me, in
so much that, should he fail of so doing, he, in the ordinary course
of things, must inevitably descend from the proud Character of a
Prosecutor to the humble and degraded one of a Prisoner, called
upon to defend himself at the very Bar to which he is about to
drag me, for the false imprisonment I have suffered under the
authority of his illegal warrant.
    On this ground it is, Sir, that I do solemnly protest against the
said Richard Atkins. Esq., as a Judge upon my Trial; and, with
all due Deference to your Excellency, that I require, as my lawful
Right, that an impartial Judge may be appointed to discharge the
duties of that sacred Office.   I have, &c.,
                                JOHN MCARTHUR.

[No. 7] SECRETARY GRIFFIN TO MR. JOHN MACARTHUR.

                                Government House,
Sir,   22nd January, 1808.
    His Excellency has directed me to acknowledge the Receipt
of your Letter of yesterday's date, protesting against Richard
Atkins, Esq., Judge-Advocate, as Judge upon your Trial.
    Mr. Atkins being the Judge appointed by His Majesty, and the
only person having the Power to sit as a Judge in the Courts in
this Territory, His Excellency directs me to give you for answer
that the Law must take its course, as He does not feel himself justified to use any interference with the Executive Power as by His
Majesty appointed.   I am, &c.,
                                EDMUND GRIFFIN,
                                    Secretary.

1808.
11 April.

Papers
exhibited at
the trial of
John
Macarthur.

[No. 2 referred to in Document A.]

MR. JOHN MACARTHUR TO GOVERNOR BLIGH.

Sir,   Parramatta, 1st January, 1808.

I did myself the honor to address a Memorial to Your Excellency on the 29th Ultimo, containing the particulars of a Claim I have upon the Judge-Advocate, Richard Atkins, Esq're, for a debt of £82 9s. 5d. that I cannot induce him to pay, and praying that Your Excellency would be pleased in some manner to interpose Your authority in my Behalf, or to cause a Court of Civil Jurisdiction to be Constituted with powers to compel the said Judge-Advocate to Answer my demand according to Law. In reply thereto I yesterday received a Letter from Your Excellency's Secretary, acquainting me that a Court of Civil Jurisdiction is open to take cognizance of all Civil Actions, and that my Memorial will be further answered by the Judge-Advocate.

From this, I understand it is Your Excellency's Opinion that I ought to apply to the present Court of Civil Jurisdiction, of which the person by whom I am aggrieved, is Judge, and to call upon Mr. Atkins to issue a Writ to bring himself before himself to Answer my Complaint.

This, Sir, I hope I shall be excused for saying, would be a proceeding so Novel—would be so extremely opposite to the practice of every Court of Law, and, in my humble Opinion, so entirely inimical to the principles of natural Justice and Equity—that I take the liberty to entreat Your Excellency will be pleased to give my Memorial a reconsideration; for I persuade myself that you will then see the propriety of the request it contains, and that you will be induced to grant me an opportunity of establishing my claim before an impartial and disinterested Tribunal.

I have, &c.,
J. MCARTHUR.

JUDGE-ADVOCATE ATKINS TO MR. JOHN MACARTHUR.

Sir,   10th January, 1808.

Through the favor of His Excellency the Governor, I have been furnished with two Communications of yours—the One under the Shape of a Memorial and the other under that of a letter—on the subject of a Bill drawn by me on my Brother, Lieutenant-Colonel Bowyer, of nigh 15 Years' standing. Sir, that Bill comes to me in a very questionable shape (all its circumstances considered), no protest having yet been produced; but, let that be as it may, I cannot consider it at *present* (under the point of view you now stand, to take your trial at the next Criminal Court) as an Object for discussion. I must, therefore, decline entering on this or any other subject until after that period, our relative Situations not admitting it.

I am, &c.,
RICHD. ATKINS.

P.S.—It never was, nor is it now, my Intention of availing myself of the Statute of Limitations, as my Letters will show.

MR. JOHN MACARTHUR TO GOVERNOR BLIGH.

Sir,   Parramatta, 12th January, 1808.

I take the liberty to enclose you the Copy of a letter I received yesterday from the Judge-Advocate, that I conclude from the manner in which Your Excellency's Name is introduced may be intended as an Answer to the letter I had the Honor to write you on the 1st Inst.

1808.
11 April.

Papers
exhibited at
the trial of
John
Macarthur.

What Mr. Atkins can mean I am unable to conjecture, by saying
the Bill I hold " comes in a very questionable shape (all its Circumstances considered), no protest having yet been produced " ; but
for the satisfaction of Your Excellency I beg leave to state that
when the Bill was first presented for payment it was, on being dishonoured, ·regularly noted, and sent back to this Colony by Capt'n
Brooks. Mr. Atkins, however, instead of shewing any solicitude
to get rid of such a disagreeable testimony, had the address to persuade Capt'n Brookes that if the Bill was again presented to· his
Brother it would be paid ; and to give the greater probability to the
Assurance he wrote a declaration to that effect and signed it officially
as Judge-Advocate. The Bill was, in consequence, taken again to
England, but unhappily met with the same fate it had done at first.

On my return here in 1805 I communicated this unpleasant
event to Mr. Atkins, and I received a written assurance that· the
Bill should soon be paid. More than two Years have expired since
that promise was given, and I am now, in lieu of payment, told
that a Bill drawn near 15 Years cannot be considered " at *present*,"
because I am to take my trial at the next Criminal Court.

If this withholding from me my Money be intended by the Judge-
Advocate as a sort of precurser of a much more severe vengeance that
he is meditating at this threatened Trial, and if your Excellency
should continue to sustain his refusal to pay me by not allowing me
to prove my claim before a disinterested Tribunal, I must submit with
patience ; nor will I any further trouble Your Excellency upon the
Subject until there may be an opportunity to send, with Your
dispatches, a Memorial to His Majesty's Secretary of State for the
Colonies. I have, &c.,

JNO. MCARTHUR.

A True Copy compared with the Original by us.

A. F. KEMP, J.P.

[No. 3 referred to in Document A.]

THE MEMORIAL OF JOHN MACARTHUR.

To William Bligh, Esquire, &c., &c.
MAY it please Your Excellency, The Memorial of John MacArthur,—
Respectfully Sheweth :—

That Richard Atkins, Esq., Judge-Advocate of this Colony,
stands indebted to Your Memorialist in the sum of Eighty-Two
pounds nine Shillings and five pence on account of the principal
and Interest due on a Bill of Exchange, drawn on the 14th February,
1793, by the said Judge-Advocate, on his Brother, General Bowyer,
and which on being presented for payment was refused by the
General in the following remarkable words :—" I will not pay a
Shilling for him." That repeated applications for payment of the
said Bill have been since made to the said Judge-Advocate without
effect.

That on the 21st Inst. Your Memorialist called at the House of
the said Judge-Advocate with intention personally to require his
Money ; but the Judge-Advocate first caused himself to be denied,
and, afterwards finding that Your Memorialist remained in his
Garden, he sent a Servant to say he could not then be spoken with.

That Your Memorialist then left a Memorandum containing the

1808.
11 April.

Papers
exhibited at
the trial of
John
Macarthur.

particulars of his demand, and on the next day he wrote to the Judge-Advocate as follows:—

"Mr. MacArthur will be thankful to Mr. Atkins if he will have the goodness to send him this Morning payment of the Bill which he delivered yesterday for £82 9s. 5d., being the principal and Interest due on Mr. Atkins's draft. in favour of Captain Boyde, drawn near fifteen Years ago."

That the Messenger who took Your Memorialist's note brought back the following Answer —

"Sir,
"I have received your Account of a Bill drawn by me on Sir William Bowyer, so far back as the Year 1793, for £26 6s. Though I am well aware that by the Statute of Limitations I am not legally bound to pay it, yet, Sir, on your producing the Original Bill, together with the Protest, &c., I will pay it, together with the *legal* Interest from the time it was so protested, but not this day.
RICHARD ATKINS."

That Your Memorialist immediately after the receipt of this Letter caused the returned Bill (which is regularly noted for Non-Payment) to be presented to the said Judge-Advocate, when he declared there was a Mistake as to the Sum and interest, but he would be punctual to do what he had before said.

That Seven days have since elapsed. and Your Memorialist has heard nothing further from the said Judge-Advocate, which gave Your Memorialist cause to apprehend that the Judge-Advocate intends to avail himself of the Statute of Limitations, as he has expressly stated in his letter he can if he pleases.

That Your Memorialist being sensible he may have some trouble to set aside such a Plea, humbly submits to Your Excellency's better Judgment the unhappy effects it might produce on the Morals of this Colony if it should appear that a Judge resists the payment of a just Debt, without any other reason to Offer in his Defence than that he chose to take advantage of the Merciful and indulgent spirit of his Creditors.

Your Memorialist humbly trusts that this candid statement of facts will induce Your Excellency to interfere on his Behalf; and, at all events, Your Memorialist respectfully intreats that Your Excellency will be pleased to Constitute a Civil Court of Jurisdiction, with powers to compel the said Judge-Advocate, Rich'd Atkins, to answer Your Memorialist's demand according to law.
JOHN McARTHUR.
Sydney, 29th Decr., 1807.

SECRETARY GRIFFIN TO MR. JOHN MACARTHUR.
Government House,
Sir,   Sydney, 30th December, 1807.
His Excellency directs me to inform you, in Answer to Your Memorial of yesterday's date, that a Court of Civil Jurisdiction is open to take cognizance of all Civil Actions, and that he has communicated Your Memorial to Mr. Atkins, the Judge-Advocate, who will further answer it.   I am, &c.,
EDMUND GRIFFIN,
Secretary.
A True Copy compared with the Original by us.
A. F. KEMP, J.P.

[DEPOSITION REFERRED TO—MARKED B.]

25th January, 1808.

THE prisoner, John McArthur, Esq., now before the Court, claims their protection, he having received information from divers friendly persons that a large Body of Men are Armed with Orders to carry into execution a Warrant from the Judge-Advocate against him for exercising his lawful Right of Challenge against the said Judge-Advocate, and assigning his reasons for it, as he was directed to do by the Court. The Deponent further swears that, from the information he has received, he considers his Life in danger from the unprincipled and atrocious Characters that are combined against him under the direction of the infamous George Crossley; he therefore declines giving any Bail, and entreats the Court will be pleased to put him under the protection of a Military Guard, they being the only persons in whose hands he could consider himself secure.

Papers
exhibited at
the trial of
John
Macarthur.

J. McARTHUR.

A True Copy compared with the Original by us.

A. F. KEMP, J.P.

[Paper marked C.]

DEPOSITIONS OF BLAXCELL AND BAYLY.

To the Court of Criminal Jurisdiction Assembled, Garnham Blaxcell and Nicholas Bayly, Esq'res, do make Oath before this Court that John McArthur, Esq., was this Morning, about nine o'Clock, forcibly wrested from their Charge by two Constables by Virtue of a Warrant of which the following is a Copy, altho' he (the said John McArthur) was delivered in the charge of the said Garnham Blaxcell and Nicholas Bayly Yesterday, when the Court adjourned, by the Officers composing that Court:—

Cumberland, } Whereas Oath hath been made before us this day by
to wit. } William Gore, Esq., Provost-Marshal, that John McArthur, Esq., being surrendered into his Custody in discharge of his Bail, is at large, although he stands charged with certain Misdemeanours in inciting the people to hatred and contempt of the Government, and has escaped out of his Custody contrary to law.

These are, in His Majesty's Name, to require and strictly to charge and command you, and every of you, to take into your Custody the Body of the said John McArthur, and him safely keep and secure in His Majesty's Gaol at Sydney, to answer to all such Misdemeanours, Matters, and Things whereof he stands charged on the information exhibited against him, and him safely keep until he shall be delivered by due course of Law: hereof fail not at your peril.

Given, &c., this 25th January, 1808,—

RICHARD ATKINS.
THOS. ARNDELL.
ROBT. CAMPBELL.
JOHN PALMER.

THE said Garnham Blaxcell and Nicholas Bayly do farther state that they do not consider the person of John McArthur safe, as he was when first put into Gaol delivered in charge of a Constable of notorious bad Character who formerly lived in His House, from whence he was turned away for robbing his Master, and who, as the said Garnham Blaxcell and Nicholas Bayly are informed, was appointed to do this duty although not his regular turn.

1808.
11 April.

Papers
exhibited at
the trial of
John
Macarthur.

The said Garnham Blaxcell and Nicholas Bayly therefore humbly hope that the Court will take such Measures as in their Wisdom may appear to them necessary to restore to them (the said Garnham Blaxcell and Nicholas Bayly) the Body of the said John McArthur, Esq., their Bail Bond not being yet Cancelled.

G. BLAXCELL.
NICHOLAS BAYLY.

Sydney, 26th January, 1808.

A True Copy compared with the Original by us.

A. F. KEMP, J.P.

[Enclosure No. 2.]

SECRETARY GRIFFIN TO MAJOR JOHNSTON.

Government House, Sydney,
Sir,   25th January, 1808, Half past Five o'Clock.

His Excellency under particular public circumstances which have occurred desires me to request you will see him without delay.   I have, &c.,

EDMUND GRIFFIN, Secy.

[Enclosure No. 3.]

DEPOSITION OF PROVOST-MARSHAL.

BENCH of Magistrates:—The Judge-Advocate, Thos. Arndell, John Palmer, Robert Campbell, Esq'res.

Sydney, 25th January, 1808.

WILLIAM GORE, Esq're, Provost-Marshal, being sworn before us, upon his Oath, saith: That John McArthur, Esq're, being under Bail to answer for certain misdemeanors, and having, as this Deponent verily believes, had notice that a Criminal Court would assemble this day, came into the place, together with his Bail, where the Persons intended to compose the said Court were met; and six of the Persons named, with the Judge-Advocate, to compose the said Court, having taken the usual Oath, the said Judge-Advocate not having then taken the Oath, the said John McArthur was, as this Deponent understood and believes, surrendered, the said Members and Judge-Advocate being then in the Room for the purpose of composing the said Court; and this Deponent saith that the said John McArthur, in a paper-writing under his hand, delivered to six of the Persons named in the precept, has stated himself to be a prisoner, and which this Deponent believes to be true; but the said John McArthur is not in Prison, in this Deponent's Custody, in the County Jail or elsewhere; but has refused to give Bail to appear to answer the charges for the misdemeanors with which he stands charged; and this Deponent is informed and believes that the said John McArthur has procured some person or persons unknown, as a Military Guard, to keep him out of this Deponent's Custody. And this Deponent saith he verily believes he may become chargeable for such illegal escape, and prays the Bench of Magistrates to grant him an escape Warrant, or such other protection as the Case may require.

1808.
11 April.

Deposition of
Gore *re*
Macarthur's
alleged
escape.

WM. GORE, Provost-Marshal.

Sworn before us, this 25th day of January, 1808,—

RICHD. ATKINS,   ROBT. CAMPBELL,
THOS. ARNDELL,   JNO. PALMER.

MEMORANDUM by the Members of the Court of Criminal Judicature, made the 26th January, 1808.

IT appearing to the Court of Criminal Judicature now sitting under Authority of His Excellency the Governor's Precept, bearing date the 25th Inst. January, that a Prisoner yesterday brought to the Bar, and remanded to his former Bail, has since that been committed to the Common Gaol of Sydney, forced out of the hands of his Sureties by a Warrant from the Bench of Magistrates, founded on a Deposition made before said Bench by Mr. William Gore, Provost-Marshal, that "The Prisoner (John McArthur, Esq're) was at large, and escaped out of his Custody contrary to Law." We therefore think it a Justice due to the Prisoner to declare that the Deposition so made by Mr. William Gore is false and ill founded and that every legal Step will be resorted to by the Court to bring the Offender to Justice.

Gore charged
with perjury
by members
of the criminal
court.

We are, &c.,
A. F. KEMP, Cap'n N.S.W. Corps.
J. BRABYN, Lieut., N.S.W. Corps.
WM. MOORE, Lieut.
THOS. LAYCOCK, Lieut.
WM. MINCHIN, Lieut.
WM. LAWSON, Lieut.

EXAMINATION of Captain Kemp before a Bench of Magistrates, March 1st, 1808.

Examination
of Anthony
Fenn Kemp.

Questn. 1.—You was a Member of the Court of Criminal Jurisdiction assembled on the 25th January? *Answer.*—I was the Senior Member.

2nd.—Did you on the Evening of that day previous to your Adjournment inform Willm. Gore, Esqre., then Provost Marshal that you had surrendered me* to my Bail? *Answer.*—Before the Court adjourned, I made a particular point of acquainting Mr. Gore, that the Court had remanded the Prisoner John McArthur Esqre. to his former Bail, he signified his assent by making a Bow.

* Note 68.

1808.
11 April.

Examination
of Anthony
Fenn Kemp.

Question by Mr. Gore.—At what time between the meeting and the adjournment of the Court was it that you informed me of the surrender of John McArthur Esqre. to his bail? *Answer.*—To the best of my recollection it was between the hours of Three and four o'Clock.   A. F. KEMP.

Taken before Thos. Jamison and John Blaxland Esqrs. on the above mentioned day.

[Enclosure No. 4.]

GOVERNOR BLIGH TO MAJOR JOHNSTON.

Sir,   Government House, Sydney, 26th January, 1808.

Members of
the court
charged with
treason.

In answer to my Letter of Yesterday, I received a verbal Message by my Orderly from You that you was rendered by illness totally incapable of being at Sydney. I apprehend the same illness will deprive me of Your Assistance at this time; and the Judge-Advocate having laid a Memorial before me against six of your Officers for Practices which he conceives treasonable, I am under the Necessity of summoning them before me, and all the Magistrates have directions to attend at Nine o'Clock tomorrow Morning.

I leave it for you to judge whether Captain Abbott should be directed to attend at Sydney to command the Troops in your Absence.   I am, &c.,

WM. BLIGH.

The memorial
of Richard
Atkins.

COPY MEMORIAL* OF RICHARD ATKINS, ESQUIRE, JUDGE-ADVOCATE.

To His Excellency Governor Bligh, &c.

Sheweth:—

That by a certain Statute made in the 27th Year of His Present Majesty King George the Third, chap. 2, after reciting certain Authorities empowering His Majesty to transport certain Offenders to New South Wales, and that it might be found necessary that a Colony of a Civil Government should be established there, and that a Court of Criminal Jurisdiction should also be established within such place, with Authority to proceed in a more Summary way than are used in England according to the known and Established Laws thereof,—It is Enacted:

That His Majesty had Authority, by Commission under the great seal, to Authorize the person to be appointed Governor of such place to convene from time to time as Occasion might require a Court of Judicature for the Trial and punishment of all outrageous Misbehaviours as if committed within the Realm of

* *Marginal note.*—The rough draft of this memorial written by George Crossley the purport of it known throughout the Town directly after it was written.

1808.
11 April.

The memorial
of Richard
Atkins.

England should be taken in Law to be Treason or Misprision thereof, Felony or Misdemeanour, which Court shall consist of the Judge-Advocate, to be appointed in and for such Place, together with six Officers of His Majesty's forces by Sea or Land, which Court should proceed to try such Offenders respectively before that Court, and cause the Charges against him to be read over, which Charges shall always be reduced into writing, and should be exhibited to the said Court by the Judge-Advocate, and by examining Witnesses upon Oath, to be administered by such Court as well for as against such Offenders respectively, and afterwards adjudging, by the Opinion of the major part of the persons composing such Court, that the party accused is or is not (as the case shall appear to them) Guilty of the Charge, and by pronouncing Judgment therein as upon a Conviction by verdict of death if the Offence be Capital, or of such Corporal Punishment, not extending to Capital punishment, as to the said Court shall seem meet.

And the said Court, it is Enacted, should be a Court of Record, and should have all such powers as by the Laws of England are incident and belonging to a Court of Record.

That His Majesty, in pursuance of the Power given by the said Act, did by His Letters Patent, bearing date the 2nd Day of April, in the 27th Year of his reign, Appoint such Court of Criminal Jurisdiction in this Colony, with the same powers as by the said Act is enacted, and did thereby, amongst other things, will, ordain, and Appoint that the said Court of Criminal Jurisdiction Should consist of His Majesty's Judge-Advocate for the time-being, together with such Six Officers of His Majestie's Sea or Land Service as His said Majestie's Governor should by precept Issued under his hand and Seal convene from time to time for that purpose, and that the same Court should have the powers as by the said Act is in that behalf directed.

That Your Memorialist was appointed by His Majesty his Judge-Advocate in this Colony, and hath been in the Actual exercise of his Office as Judge-Advocate of this Territory for the Term of Seven Years and upwards, and now is in the Actual possession of the said Office of Judge-Advocate.

That some time ago one John McArthur, Esquire, being Charged with Seditious Practices against His Majesty, his Crown, and Dignity, Was put in Arrest, and was admitted to Bail in the Penalty of £1,000, to Answer for the said Offence, and all other Offences, at the then next Criminal Court.

That Your Excellency having been pleased to Issue your precept under your hand and Seal (agreeable to the direction of the Patent) by which Anthony Fen Kemp, Captain in His Majesty's

New South Wales Corps; John Brabyn, William Moore, Thomas Laycock, William Minchin, and William Lawson, lieutenants in the same Corps, were appointed with your Memorialist to compose and become the Members of the said Court of Criminal Jurisdiction, to be held on the twenty fifth day of January Instant, for the trial of all such Offenders as should be brought before the said Court.

That, in Obedience to the said Precept, Your Memorialist caused the said Anth'y Fen Kemp, John Brabyn, William Moore, Thomas Laycock, William Minchin, and W'm Lawson to be Summoned to meet, and as it is the usual Custom for your Memorialist first to administer the Oath to such Six Members, and then for such Six Members to administer the Oath to your Memorialist previous to their being formed into a Court or taking cognizance as a Court of any matter of Charge against any person or persons whatever.

Your Memorialist having Sworn the said Anthony Fen Kemp, John Brabyn, William Moore, Thomas Laycock, William Minchin, and Will'm Lawson, Your Memorialist took the Book to have the Oath administered to himself before those persons, as is usual in such cases, when the said John McArthur made an Interruption and said he had protested against your Memorialist being a member of that Court to sit upon his Trial; whereupon your Memorialist informed the said Six Members that it was no Court without Your Memorialist, and he could not be objected to, as by the Terms of His Majesty's Patent, the Court could not be formed without the Judge-Advocate.

When Mr. Anth'y Fen Kemp said he was no more than a Juryman or one of themselves, and could or should be objected unto, And the said Anth'y Fen Kemp called out to the said Jno. McArthur to read his Objections, and your Memorialist was compelled to remove from his Seat and to hear a great Torrent of Threats and abusive Language read by the said John McArthur to the said persons in a very Violent and outrageous manner, and at the conclusion the said John McArthur Addressed them, in the presence of One thousand persons or more assembled in the Court, and made Use of these, or the like words:—

"Now, Gentlemen, for God's sake, remember You have the Eyes of an expecting public upon you, trembling for the Safety of their Lives, Liberties, and properties."

And, upon Your Memorialist telling the said John McArthur that he would commit him for such his contemptuous Language, the said Anth'y Fen Kemp said to your Memorialist, "You Commit! No, Sir, I will commit you to Gaol"—or used words to that effect.

1808.
11 April.

The memorial
of Richard
Atkins.

That your Memorialist, seeing nothing but confusion likely to ensue by the Conduct of the said Anthony Fen Kemp, John Brabyn, William Moore, Thos. Laycock, William Minchin, and William Lawson, and fearing for his Safety from the great Number of Soldiers with their Side-Arms then in the Court-house, and others who had been Assembled, as your Memorialist believes, Your Memorialist called out that he adjourned the Court, and directed the People to disperse and come away, When the said Anthony Fen Kemp and the other five persons called the people back by saying, "Stay, Stay; tell the people not to go out. We are a Court."

That your Memorialist has since been informed and believes that the s'd John McArthur addressed these parties by saying, "Am I to be cast forth to the Mercy of a Set of Armed Ruffins —the Police"; and said to them that he had received private information from his friends that there was a Set of Armed Ruffins prepared against him when he went out, and requested those Officers to let him have a Military Guard, as in that case they knew they would have something to do to get at him.

And the said John McArthur, then being before brought into Court and surrendered in discharge of his Bail, and in Custody of the Provost-Marshal, was by the said Anthony Fen Kemp, John Brabyn, Willm. Moore, Tho. Laycock, William Minchin, and Wm. Lawson rescued out of the hands of the Civil power and put under the protection of the Military, as Your Memorialist hath heard and believes.

Your Memorialist Shews that a Charge was prepared against the said John McArthur for a certain Misdemeanor in Inciting the people to hatred and Contempt of His Majesty and of the Government as by the Constitution and Law established in this Terri-tory, and for a false and seditious Libel, with intent to incite the People to hatred and Contempt of the Government, and for other High Misdemeanors.

That altho' the said Anthony Fen Kemp, John Brabyn, William Moore, Tho. Laycock, William Minchin, and Wm. Lawson well knew the Charges against the said John McArthur, and that he was under Bail to answer at a Criminal Court for such Offences against His Majesty, his Crown, and Dignity, and that they were to be Members to Sit on that Court, they all dined at a Public dinner with the said John McArthur the day before, and had the Colours of the Regiment of the New South Wales Corps flying all the day, with the Musical Band playing till a late hour.

That your Memorialist, having taken into Court all the Papers and Documents put into your Memorialist's hands by the Gover-

1808.
11 April.

The memorial
of Richard
Atkins.

nor to be exhibited to the Evidence when produced, and also the Information to file of Record, and other papers, the said Anthony Fen Kemp, John Brabyn, William Moore, Thos. Laycock, William Minchin, and William Lawson by this means possessed themselves of those papers and Documents, and, altho' demanded, have refused to deliver them up.

That your memorialist most humbly submits to the Judgment of your Excellency that the Crimes the said Anthony Fen Kemp, John Brabyn, William Moore, Thos. Laycock, William Minchin, and William Lawson have so committed amount to a Usurpation of His Majesty's Government, and tend to Incite or Create Rebellion or other Outrageous treason in the people of this Territory.

And Pray your Excellency to take such Measures in this Case as the Nature thereof, in Your Excellency's Judgment, may require.

And your Memorialist will ever pray, &c.

RICHD. ATKINS.

A true Copy of the original Draft by George Crossley compared by us.

JOHN McARTHUR.

CHAS. THROSBY, J.P.

[Enclosure No. 5.]

MR. JOHN MACARTHUR AND OTHERS* TO MAJOR JOHNSTON.

Sir,   26th January, 1808.

Petition to
Johnston for
the arrest
of Bligh.

The present alarming State of this Colony, in which every Man's Property, Liberty, and Life is endangered, induces us most earnestly to implore you instantly to place Governor Bligh under an Arrest and to assume the Command of the Colony. We pledge ourselves, at a Moment of less Agitation, to come forward to support the Measure with Our Fortunes and Our Lives.

We are, with great respect, Sir,
Your most obedient servants,

By the principal part of the Civil Officers and respectable Inhabitants.

A true Copy compared with the original

R. FITZ, J.P.

[Enclosure No. 6.]

"PROCLAMATION.

Proclamation
by Johnston.

"GEORGE JOHNSTON.

"THE Public Peace being happily and, I trust in Almighty God, permanently established, I hereby proclaim the Cessation of Martial Law.

* Note 69.

"I have this day appointed Magistrates and other Public Functionaries from amongst the most respectable Officers and Inhabitants, which will, I hope, secure the impartial Administration of Justice, according to the Laws of England, as secured to us by the Patent of Our Most Gracious Sovereign.

"Words cannot too strongly convey my Approbation of the Behaviour of the whole Body of the People on the late memorable Event. By their manly, firm, and orderly Conduct they have shown themselves deserving of that Protection which I have felt it was my duty to give them, And which I doubt not they will continue to merit.

"In future no Man shall have just cause to complain of Violence, Injustice, or Oppression; No free Man shall be taken, imprisoned, or deprived of his House, Land, or Liberty, but by the Law; Justice shall be impartially administered, without regard to or respect of Persons; And every Man shall enjoy the Fruits of his Industry in Security.

"Soldiers!

"Your conduct has endeared you to every well-disposed Inhabitant in this Settlement. Persevere in the same honorable Path And you will establish the Credit of the New South Wales Corps on a Basis not to be Shaken.

"God save the King.

"By Command of His Honor the Lieutenant-Governor,

"(Signed) NICHOLAS BAYLY,

"Secretary.

"Head-Quarters, Sydney, 27th January, 1808."

[Enclosure No. 7.*]

COPY OF THE CORRESPONDENCE AND MESSAGES BETWEEN GOVERNOR BLIGH AND LIEUTENANT-GOVERNOR JOHNSTON.

[A] *Major Johnston to Governor Bligh.*

Sir, Head-quarters, 26th January, 1808.

I am called upon to execute a most painful duty. You are charged by the respectable Inhabitants of Crimes that render you unfit to exercise the Supreme Authority another Moment in this Colony; and in that Charge all the Officers under my command have joined.

I therefore require you, in His Majesty's sacred Name, to resign your Authority, and to Submit to the Arrest which I hereby place you under, by the advice of all my Officers, and by the advice of every respectable Inhabitant in the Town of Sydney.

I am, &c.,

GEORGE JOHNSTON,

Major commanding N.S.W. Corps.

1808.
11 April.
Proclamation by Johnston.

Bligh summoned to resign by Johnston.

Orders for the
examination of
the papers of
Bligh;

[B] *Major Johnston to Officers.*

Sydney, 28th January, 1808.

You are hereby directed to examine all the Papers belonging to William Bligh, Esq., And to detain all papers that in any way relate to the Public Concerns of this Colony and its Dependencies; all other papers you are to return him. You are to acquaint him that during your Examination of those papers He may be present and have any Friend or other persons also present he may choose to appoint.

You are afterwards to proceed to the examination of the papers of Richard Atkins, Esqr., and those of John Palmer, Esquire, and you are to detain every paper belonging to those Gentlemen, which are in any Shape connected with the Public Concerns of the Colony.   GEORGE JOHNSTON,

Lieutenant-Governor.

To Capt. Ed. Abbott, Thos. Jamison, Esq., Garnham Blaxcell, Esq., Nicholas Bayly, Esq.

[C] *Governor Bligh to Major Johnston.*

Government House, Sydney,

Sir, ·   28th January, 1808.

By frequent private communications with His Majesty's Principal Secretary of State for the Colonies before I left England, I was ordered to inquire into particular circumstances, to which I have made Answers; and an application being made to me to give up the Public Papers of the Colony by a Committee from you, I think it due to my consequence and Situation, under the Consideration before Stated, to object to give up a particular Book and a few particular Papers to any person except yourself, Sealed.   I am, &c.,

WM. BLIGH.

[D] *Major Johnston's Order.*

Sydney, 28th January, 1808.

I HEREBY Command you to proceed to the Execution of my Orders, as expressed on the other side of this paper.

GEORGE JOHNSTON,

Lieutenant-Governor.

To Captain Ed. Abbott, Thos. Jamison, Esq., Garnham Blaxcell, Esq., Nicholas Bayly, Esq.

[E] *Mr. Nicholas Bayly to Governor Bligh.*

Sydney, 28th January, 1808.

I AM directed by His Honor the Lieut.-Governor to acquaint you that the late Magistrates and other persons (who it is proved you were in the habit of consulting) have been examined on Oath before Committees· constituted under the Lieut.-Governor's Authority; that, from the Confessions of those Persons, it appears that you have been Acting upon a Settled Plan to subvert the Laws, to terrify and influence the Courts of Justice, and to deprive every person who had the misfortune to be obnoxious to you of their Property, Liberty, and Lives. The Lieutenant-Governor, feeling that an Offence of such Magnitude must be productive of the most serious consequences, is impelled by Sentiments of Humanity to give you this early notice that you may consider and seriously reflect on the measures which may be necessary for your Justification.

His Honor has further directed me to assure you that as soon as the examinations are complete, you shall be furnished with a Copy, and that, if you think proper, all the Evidences shall be re-examined in your presence, and be directed to answer any questions you like to propose to them. His Honor has also desired me to assure you that it will give him the greatest satisfaction to contribute by every means in his power to the Alleviation of the distress of your present Situation, and to the comfort and accommodation of you and your Family.

NICHOLAS BAYLY,
Secretary.

[F] *Mr. Nicholas Bayly to Governor Bligh.*

Note.—Governor Bligh having expressed some apprehensions that an Investigation of his conduct was to take place in this Country, the following Message was sent in explanation:—

Sydney, 29th January, 1808.

I AM directed by His Honor the Lieutenant-Governor to acquaint you, Sir, that the Message I delivered Yesterday was only intended to apprise you that the Confession of the late Magistrates (combined with other evidence) would occasion an accusation of the most serious kind to be preferred to His Majesty's Government against you, of which His Honor was induced, by Sentiments of humanity, to give you the earliest Notice; And that, as you appeared to Misunderstand his meaning, and to think an enquiry was to take place in this Country on your Past Conduct, His Honor was solicitous to correct such a Mistaken belief.

His Honor also directs me to State that he shall feel himself under the necessity of declining to receive any addresses from you unless they are directed to him as Lieutenant-Governor of this Territory.

NICHOLAS BAYLY.

Margin notes:
1808. 11 April.
Charges preferred against Bligh.
Bligh to be permitted to cross-examine evidence.
No inquiry into Bligh's conduct to be held in the Colony.

1808.
11 April.

[G] *Mr. Nicholas Bayly to Governor Bligh.*

29th January, 1808.

Method to be adopted for the maintenance of Bligh's household.

I AM directed by His Honor the Lieutenant-Governor to acquaint you that whatever supply of Live Stock you may require for the Subsistence of your Family shall be immediately furnished from the public Herds and Flocks, as usual; that, if you chuse to retain your present establishment of Servants, their Rations shall continue to be issued from the Public Stores. His Honor has further directed me to state to you, Sir, that receipts will be required for every Article issued on your Account; that a Charge will be made for the same at the Current Market Prices; and that, when you leave the Colony, an Account will be made up and transmitted to His Majesty's Ministers, that they may determine whether such Stock, Provisions, and Stores are or are not to be paid for by you. His Honor has also directed me to State that the Exigencies of the Public Service oblige him to reduce your establishment of Horses to five, and His Honor requests that you will direct such to be selected as you most approve.

NICHOLAS BAYLY.

[H] *Lieutenant Lawson to Governor Bligh.*

Copy of a Message to Governor Bligh.

Bligh to be permitted to receive visitors.

HIS Honor the Lieutenant Governor has directed me to wait on You, Sir, and to inform you that all the papers which appear to have been in Your Possession having been given up, any persons that you may be desirous of consulting have liberty to visit you.

WM. LAWSON,
Aide-de-Camp to the Lieut. Governor.

[I] *Governor Bligh to Mr. Nicholas Bayly.*

Government House, Sydney, 31st January, 1808.

Memorandum of papers seized.

GOVERNOR BLIGH requests a Copy of the list of Papers which have been taken from Government House from him. Mr. Griffin, his Secretary, who lives at Lieut. Moore's, can Copy them as agreed by Mr. Bayly and Mr. Blaxcell, if Lieutenant-Governor Johnston approves of it.

Governor Bligh will also be obliged to Mr. Bayly for the written Messages which he was so polite to say he would send, and which he took away by mistake the 28th Instant.

Bligh's compliance with Johnston's arrangements.

Governor Bligh will comply with Lieutenant-Governor Johnston's directions respecting the Horses, Servants, and Provisions, and requests Mr. Bayly to inform the Lieutenant-Governor of it.

[J] *Mr. Nicholas Bayly to Governor Bligh.*

1st February, 1808.

I AM directed by His Honor the Lieutenant-Governor to wait The tomb of captain Putland. on you, Sir, and to say that if you have determined on any Plan of finishing the Tomb of your late Son-in-Law,* Captain Putland, or, if you have not, and are desirous to consult with any of the Artificers upon the Subject, they shall be immediately ordered to wait upon you, and to proceed to the execution of your Wishes. His Honor thinks it will be proper that an estimate may be made of the Expence, which will be transmitted with other Accounts, for His Majesty's Ministers to decide whether the Tomb is to be finished at your Expence or that of the Public.

N. BAYLY,
Secretary.

[K] *Governor Bligh to Major Johnston.*

Sir,   Government House, Sydney, 1st February, 1808.

Being Captain of His Majesty's ship Porpoise (now absent Bligh's naval status. from Port Jackson on Service), by virtue of a Commission from the Right Honorable the Lords Commissioners of the Admiralty, of the 13th November, 1805, and, by a Subsequent Order of their Lordships, dated 27th February, 1807, required and directed to hoist and wear a Broad Pendant, which constitutes the Rank of Commodore, I have to state the same for your information, in order that I might be permitted to prepare to Sail for England as soon after her Arrival as Possible.

I am, &c.,
WM. BLIGH.

[L] *Mr. Nicholas Bayly to Governor Bligh.*

Sir,   Head-quarters, Sydney, 1st February, 1808.

I have it in Command from His Honor the Lieutenant- Bligh to be sent to England in arrest on a private ship. Governor to acquaint you, in Answer to your Letter of this day, that the causes of your supercession are of so Serious a Nature that your Arrest will be continued until His Majesty's pleasure shall be known, and that every exertion is making to facilitate your departure from hence for England. His Honor has also directed me to acquaint you that it is his intentions to send you Home by a Private Ship, and that every necessary accommodation shall be provided for you and your Family.

I have, &c.,
NICHOLAS BAYLY,
Secretary.

* Note 71.

[M] *Governor Bligh to Major Johnston.*

Sir,   Government House, Sydney, 2nd February, 1808.

I have to acknowledge the receipt of your Secretary's Letter of Yesterday's date, in Consequence of my Letter to you of the same date; but as I do not consider it a sufficient Justification for me to my Lords Commissioners of the Admiralty for my not proceeding to England in His Majesty's Ship Porpoise, I think it proper to transmit for your further information a Copy of their Lordships Commission, constituting and appointing me Captain of His Majesty's Ship Porpoise, and of their Lordships' Orders directing me to hoist and wear a Broad Pendant (alluded to in my Letter of Yesterday's date), which you will observe have not the most distant reference to my Situation as Governor of His Majesty's Territory of New South Wales, in which I consider myself under an Arrest until I arrive in England, and His Majesty's Pleasure is known.   I am, &c.,

WM. BLIGH.

[N] *Mr. Nicholas Bayly to Governor Bligh.*

Sir,   Headquarters, Sydney, 2nd February, 1808.

Bligh not to
be permitted
to sail in the
Porpoise.

I am commanded by His Honor the Lieutenant-Governor to acknowledge the receipt of your Letter of Yesterday's date, with its enclosures, No. 1 and No. 2.

I am further commanded to acquaint you that His Honor feels great concern at being obliged to decline complying with any wish of yours, but that he cannot permit you, Sir, to return to England in His Majesty's Ship, the Porpoise, without acting contrary to his own Sence of what his duty requires.

I have, &c.,

N. BAYLY,
Secretary.

[O] *Mr. Nicholas Bayly to Governor Bligh.*

Sydney, 5th February, 1808.

I AM directed by His Honor the Lieutenant-Governor to apprize you that he cannot allow you to hold any communication with the Officers and Seamen of His Majesty's Ship Porpoise, and that He shall consider any attempt to do so, either by Letter or otherwise, as a Breach of your Arrest.   N. BAYLY,
Secretary.

[P] *Mr. Nicholas Bayly to Governor Bligh.*

Sydney, 8th February, 1808.

HIS Honor the Lieutenant-Governor has directed me, Sir, to inform you that he intends to send Dispatches to His Majesty's

Ministers by the Ship Dart, and that she will Sail in Ten days; 1808.\
11 April. that, if you are desirous to send any Letters by her, either publick or private, they shall be put into the Dispatch Box; and, if you Despatches to be sent by the Dart. wish it, the Box shall be Sealed in your presence with your own Seal. N. BAYLY,
Secretary.

[Q] *Mr. Nicholas Bayly to Governor Bligh.*

Sydney, 11th February, 1808.

I AM ordered by His Honor the Lieutenant-Governor to inform Bligh to be sent to England in the Pegasus. you, Sir, that he has agreed for the Cabin of the Pegasus and 20 ton of Freight, intending to send you to England in that Vessel; That the Cabin shall be fitted up in any manner you think proper to point out; and that you may be enabled to arrange your Accommodations to your own wishes, His Honor has desired me to present you with a Plan of the Cabin as it is now divided; That a Survey will be immediately ordered on the Ship; and, if you desire it, a Boat shall attend to take you on board, that you may examine her Yourself, and determine if anything be wanting which can be supplied to Contribute to the Safety and comfort of your voyage.

If any of the Servants you may select to accompany you are Bligh's attendants to accompany him. Prisoners, or if there be any Medical person you may like to attend you, their Emancipations will be given to them, Subject to the approval of the Secretary of State. The Lieutenant-Governor will be thankful if you will come to some decision respecting the completion of the Tomb of your late Son-in-Law.

NICHOLAS BAYLY,
Secretary.

[R] *Governor Bligh to Major Johnston.*

Sir, Government House, Sydney, 11th February, 1808.

In Answer to your Message by Mr. Bayly this Morning, Bligh's objections to sailing in the Pegasus. stating that you had agreed for the Cabin of the Pegasus and 20 tons of Freight in Order to Convey me to England in that Vessel, and that accommodation should be fitted to my wishes and everything supplied to contribute to the safety and comfort of my Voyage, I trust the Objections I now make will be very maturely considered, to the Safety of my life, and that I may not, with my Family and Friends, be sent in the above Ship to perform a Voyage of the greatest danger through the tempestuous Weather which is ever, during the Winter Season, from hence round Cape Horn, and where we can find no Port to get relief; to which I

Bligh's
objections to
sailing in
the Pegasus.

must add the distresses that will attend an affectionate Daughter, who is to accompany me in a very Weak and low State, and who is constantly confined and sick at sea.

My objections to the Pegasus, under the impressions of the very long Voyage I have to perform, are that I consider her too small and too weak for my Safety and accomodation. If she was of a Sufficient Burthen I should then be under the necessity of objecting to her, as her Iron fastenings are insecure; her Bottom not sufficiently tight; her Iron Work, from the great age of the Ship, may be in a decayed State and not sufficient; her Sheathing green Wood, and that she will be dangerously leaky; that her Pumps will not keep her free; that her Rigging, from long wear in a hot Climate, is perished and will not support the Masts in long and continued Storms now to be met with; and that I do not consider her well found in either Sails, Anchors, or Cables.

Bligh's
suggested
alternatives.

Under such calamitous expectations, founded on Sound and great experience, I have to call your attention how the whole may be avoided, and I trust to your entire Satisfaction, without loss of time, increase of expence, or hindrance to the Public Service, and which I must state to obviate any supposed necessity of my proceeding in the said Ship Pegasus.

Several Ships will arrive here next Month; these Ships (Whalers) are all Copper-bottomed, and well-found, and on their arrival will in a few days be ready to sail for England.

Bligh willing
to embark
in one of
Campbell's
ships.

I may here also observe that Mr. Campbell's Ship, the Albion, is soon expected, and should you approve of my desire to leave in that Ship, the expence may be left for the decision of His Majesty's Ministers. The Alexander (Brooks) is hourly expected from England, and should she arrive previous to the Albion, Mr. Campbell will also engage that she shall sail with me Home, with every exertion after her arrival, on the same terms.

To this I must likewise beg you will consider that it will be some time before my Papers in your Possession will be ready for me, and my Affairs settled, to conclude which I will not lose a Moment in executing.

With regard to the Medical Assistants and the Servants you have been so good as to offer me, I have to request a Short time to deliberate who I may name for that purpose.

I am, &c.,
Wm. Bligh.

[S] *Mr. Nicholas Bayly to Governor Bligh.*

Sir,   Sydney, 19th March, 1808.

I am Commanded by His Honor, the Lieut'-Governor, to inform you that the Objections expressed in your Letter of the

11th Ult'o against the Pegasus occas'd him to defer making any conclusive Agreement for the hire of that Vessel until her repairs should be completed, and he should be enabled, by the report of experienced Officers and Ship Carpenters, to form a Correct Opinion of her Condition.

A Survey has in Consequence been held upon her, and a favourable report has been made; but, as circumstances have arisen which have induced her Owners to decline freighting her to Government, The Lieut'-Gov'r has directed me to enclose a Copy of the order and report of survey that you may be satisfied he never entertained a thought of sending you home in an insecure Ship.

I am further ordered to express the L't-Governor's great regret that none of the Ships have arrived what you appear to have expected this month, and to inform you that as the Winter Season is advancing he considers himself obliged to hasten your departure.

You are aware, Sir, that the choice of means to carry this measure into effect is extremely circumscribed, and that there is no Ship in this port on board which you and your Family can be comfortably accommodated, except His Majesty's Ship Porpoise.

The Accompanying Copy of a Letter to the Acting Commander of His Majesty's Ship, and that of his Reply will convince you that there are insuperable objections to your going on board the Porpoise, unless at your own particular request, and under a Solemn engagement on your Word of Honor as an Officer that you will not attempt to assume any Command, and that you will consider yourself in Arrest until His Majesty's pleasure shall be signified on your late supercession. On these Conditions being acquiesced in, the Lieutenant-Governor has Commanded me to inform you that a requisition shall be made to Captain Symons to receive you and your Family on board, and to proceed to England; but, should you think it proper or prudent to reject this arrangement, much as the Lieu't-Governor will regret separating you from your Family, and being obliged to put you on board a Vessel in which he cannot procure you Suitable accommodations, Yet a sense of duty, arising from a regard to the welfare of the Colony and the honor of His Majesty's Service, leaves him no choice but that of sending you Home in the Ship Dart, now ready to Sail.

I have, &c.,
N. BAYLY,
Secretary.

1808.
11 April.

Orders for the
survey of the
ship Pegasus.

[T] *Order of Survey.*

Copy of the Order and report of Survey referred to in the
above Letter.

By His Honor George Johnston, Esqr.,
Lieutenant-Governor of the Territory
of New South Wales, &c., &c., &c.

WHEREAS I have deemed it expedient for the good of His
Majesty's Service to engage with the Owner of the Ship Pegasus
for a certain Portion of Tonnage of that Ship from hence to
England, provided upon a due Examination of her State and
Condition, she is found capable of performing that Service.

You are therefore hereby required and directed to repair on
board the said Ship Pegasus, and there take a Strict and Careful
Survey, on her Hull Masts, Rigging and Sails, and report to me
from under your hands the exact State in which they appear to
be; taking particular care to examine the Soundness and tight-
ness of her bottom (which has recently been Sheathed), the
Security of her Iron fastenings Timbers and Upper Works
whether her rigging is in good and fit State, her Masts Sound,
and Sails in sufficient quantity and good repair—and whether the
said Ship Pegasus is in all respects capable of performing a
voyage to England with Safety.

You will also examine and report the State of her Ground
Tackle, noticing any and what Articles she may appear to be in
want of And finally to take this Survey, with Care Accuracy, and
impartiality and to make Oath to the Truth of your Report.

Given under my hand at Sydney in the Territory afores'd
this 18th day of February 1808.

GEO. JOHNSTON.

To
Jas. Symons, Esqr., Commander H.M.S. Porpoise;
Mr. Roger Best, Carpenter;
Mr. Russell, Master of the Brothers;
Mr. Smith, Master of the Dart;
Mr. Bunker, late Master of the Eliz'h.

[U] *Survey of the ship Pegasus.*

PURSUANT to an Order from His Honor George Johnston Esquire
Lieutenant Governor of the Territory of New South Wales,
&c., &c.

WE the undersigned persons have this day repaired on board the
Ship Pegasus and there taken a Strict and careful Survey of the
Ships Hull, Masts, Rigging and Sails, Anchors and Cables

together with her Yards, and other Spars, and do find them as follows (vizt) :—

That the Ship's Hull, Timbers and Iron fastenings are good, that she makes no Water, her Bottom and Sheathing are good, Masts and Yards good and sufficient in number; her Lower Top Mast and running Rigging Sails, two Cables, one Hawser, and one Anchor, are in good State wanting the following Articles to proceed on so long a Voyage (vizt) Two Anchors, One 13 Cwt., the other between 2 and 5 Cwt. One 6 or 7 Inch Hawser, One Main Stay Sail, One Jib, One Fore Top Mast Stay Sail, One Mizen Course, and two Steps for the Fore and Main Masts.

And we are of Opinion that the Ship is in every respect (if furnished with the above Articles) capable of performing the voyage to England with the greatest Safety, And we do declare that we have taken this Survey, with such care and equity that we are willing (if required) to make Oath to the impartiality of our Proceedings.

Given under our hands on board the said Ship Pegasus, Sydney Cove, New South Wales, this 2nd day of March, 1808.

J. SYMONS, Commander of H.M.S. Porpoise;
R. BEST, Carpenter of   do.;
O. RUSSELL, Master of the Brothers;
RICH'D SMITH, Master of the Dart;
E. BUNKER, late Master of the Elizabeth.

Sworn before me this 5th March 1808
C. GRIMES, Acting J.-Ad.

Sails on board in good repair belonging to the Pegasus (vizt)
One New Main Sail—Two Fore Sails—Two fore top Sails—One Main Top Sail—One Mizen Top Sail—One Main Top Gal't Sail—One Fore do. do.—One Mizen do. do.—One Jibb—One Mizen—One Fore Top Mast Stay Sail—One middle Stay Sail—One Main T. Mast Stay Sail—One Mizen do. do.—One lower Steering Sail—One Main Top Mast do.—One Main Top—One fore Top Mast do. Gal. do.

[V] *Major Johnston to Lieutenant Symons.*

Sir,   Headquarters, Sydney, 16th March, 1808.

The disappointments I have experienced in my endeavours to procure a passage to England with suitable accommodations for the late Governor and his Family, have left me no alternative but that of requesting you will be pleased to inform me whether the rules and Regulations of the Naval Service will admit of your receiving him on board His Majesty's Ship Porpoise, for

1808.
11 April.

Proposal to
send Bligh
under arrest
on the Porpoise.
the purpose of conveying him to England in Arrest; And if you should be of Opinion that you can receive him on board, I shall be thankful if you will have the goodness to acquaint me with what accommodations can be spared.

I am, &c.,

GEORGE JOHNSTON.

[W] *Lieutenant Symons to Major Johnston.*

Sir,   H.M.S. Porpoise, 16th March, 1808.

Symons to
receive Bligh
as first captain.
In Answer to your letter of this day's date, I have to inform you that when Capt. Bligh comes on board His Majesty's Ship Porpoise I must consider him as first Captain, and I am ready to receive him when you may think proper.

I further beg leave to inform you that half the Commander's Accommodation belongs to him.

I have, &c.,

J. SYMONS.

[X] *Governor Bligh to Major Johnston.*

Sir,   Government House, Sydney, 12th February, 1808.

The proposed
completion of
Putland's tomb.
In Answer to your written Message of the 1st Instant by Mr. Bayly, that if I had determined on any Plan of finishing the Tomb of my late Son-in-law,* Captain Putland, or if I had not and was desirous to consult with any of the Artificers upon the Subject they should be immediately ordered to wait upon me and to proceed to the execution of my wishes, and that the expense should be transmitted with other Accounts for His Majesty's Ministers to decide whether the Tomb is to be finished at the public or my private expence, I have to express my thanks for this Offer; but as Mrs. Putland is extremely anxious that the Body should be sent to England to his Friends, I have to request that the vault may only be covered over, and a flat stone put thereon until an Opportunity offers to comply with Mrs. Putland's wishes.

The Place where the Body lies I had Contrived to be a Part of a large Vault (of which Mr. Divine, the Superintendant, has a Plan) for the Family use of all Governors who might require it.

I am, &c.,

WM. BLIGH.

[Y] *Mr. Nicholas Bayly to Principal Surgeon Jamison.†*

Sir,   Sydney, 12th February, 1808.

Bligh's charges
against
Jamison.
In consequence of your Letter of the 10th Inst., I was directed by His Honor, the Lieutenant-Governor, to require from the late Governor a Specification of the Offences you had com-

* Note 71.   † Note 72.

mitted to occasion your dismissal from the Office of Magistrate, and to draw down upon you the severe Accusation contained in his Letter of the 31st October, 1807, to His Majesty's Secretary of State. His Honor has this day received in reply a Letter from the late Governor, wherein he begs leave to refer to the decision of His Majesty's Ministers.

His Honor has directed me to assure you that it affords him particular Pleasure to declare that he conceives your dismissal from the Magistracy is only to be attributed to your having attended him as a Friend on that day to Witness an Interesting Conversation on Public Business.

And His Honor has also directed me to recommend that you do not give Yourself any further trouble upon the Subject, because in his Judgment no stronger Testimony of the Integrity of your Life can be produced than the Silence of your Accuser when called upon to come forward and Justify his extraordinary attack upon your reputation. I am, &c.,

NICHOLAS BAYLY,
Secretary.

1808.
11 April.

Bligh's charges against Jamison.

Johnston's opinion *re* Jamison's dismissal from the magistracy.

[Z] *Mr. Nicholas Bayly to Governor Bligh.*

Sydney, 13th February, 1808.

I AM directed by His Honor the Lieutenant-Governor to inform you, Sir, that your wishes respecting the Tomb of your late Son-in-Law shall be minutely complied with. I am also directed to acquaint you, Sir, that fair Copies of many of the Confessions and Examinations concerning your late Government are prepared and ready to be sent to you, which will be done as soon as they have been compared with the Originals and properly attested. His Honor therefore wishes that your Secretary should attend at the Barrack of his Aid-du-Camp at 10 o'Clock this Morning that the business may be immediately proceeded upon.

N. BAYLY,
Secretary.

Copies of papers to be submitted to Bligh.

[AA] *Governor Bligh to Major Johnston.*

Sir, Government House, Sydney, 13th February, 1808.

I have to acknowledge the receipt of your written Message by Mr. Bayly this Morning, stating that fair Copies of many of the Examinations concerning my late Governm't are prepared and ready to be sent to me, which will be done as soon as they have been compared with the Originals and properly attested; and You therefore wish my Secretary sh'd attend at the Barrack of your Aid de camp at 10 o'Clock this Morning, that this Business may be immediately proceeded upon.

Bligh's refusal to accept copies of the examinations.

1808.
11 April.

In Answer to which I must beg to inform you, that I cannot receive any Papers in this Country, relative to my late Government, to which the above mentioned Message alludes.

I am, &c.,

WM. BLIGH.

[BB] *Governor Bligh to Major Johnston.*

Sir,   Government House, Sydney, 17th February, 1808.

Witnesses
required by
Bligh in
England.
On the other side I send you a list of Persons that will be necessary for me to have sent to England, and have to request that you will be pleased to take the requisite Steps for providing them with a Passage accordingly.   I am, &c.,

WM. BLIGH.

Richard Atkins, Esq.	Late Judge-Advocate.
Thomas Arndell ⎫	
Robert Campbell ⎪	
John Palmer ⎬	Late Magistrates.
James Williamson ⎭	
Mr. William Gore	Late Provost-Marshal.
Mr. Edmund Griffin	My Secretary.
Rev'd Henry Fulton	Late Chaplain.
Mr. James Wiltshire	Commiss'y's Clerk.
Mr. Nich's Divine ⎫	
Mr. R'd Rouse ⎬.......	Superintendants.
Mr. Fra's Oakes ⎭	
Mr. Andrew Thompson	Chief Constable at Hawkesbury.

[CC] *Mr. Nicholas Bayly to Governor Bligh.*

19th February, 1808.

Johnston's
refusal to
order the
witnesses to
proceed to
England.
I AM directed by His Honor the Lieut.-Governor, in Answer to your Letter of the 17th Inst., to say that he has no Authority to interfere with any of the persons you have named as necessary to attend you to England, except those who have His Majesty's Commission, and that he should not consider himself justified even to order them, unless for very sufficient and satisfactory reasons assigned by you. If, however, any of those persons should Chuse voluntarily to attend you, His Honor will use every effort, consistent with Economy, to procure them a Passage.

I have shown the Bill to His Honor, given in for Stone Mason's Work, who is of Opinion that it is a gross imposition, and ought not in the slightest degree to be attended to.

NICHOLAS BAYLY.

[DD] *Governor Bligh to Major Johnston.*

Sir,   Government House, Sydney, 20th March, 1808.

I have received by your Orders from Mr. Bayly, your Secretary, a Letter of Yesterday's date, enclosing a Copy of a

Letter written by you to James Symons, Esquire, addressed, Acting-Commander of His Majesty's Ship Porpoise, dated 16th Instant, and his Answer thereto.

You State that I am aware that the Choice of means to carry me Home are extremely circumscribed, and that there is no Ship in this Port on board of which me and my Family can be comfortably accommodated, except His Majesty's Ship Porpoise, and the accompanying Letter to the Acting-Commander of His Majesty's Ship, and his reply, will convince me that there are insuperable objections to my going on board the Porpoise, unless at my own particular request, and under a Solemn engagement, on my Word of honor as an Officer, that I will not attempt to assume any Command, and that I will consider myself in Arrest until His Majesty's Pleasure shall be signified on my late Super-cession. That on these Conditions being acquiesced in, You inform me that a requisition shall be made to Capt. Symons to receive me and my Family on board, and to proceed to England; but should I think it proper or prudent to reject this Arrangement, much as you will regret separating me from my Family, and being obliged to put me on board a Vessel in which you cannot procure me suitable Accommodation, Yet a sense of duty arising from a regard to the Welfare of the Colony, and the honor of His Majesty's Service, leaves you no choice but that of sending me Home in the Ship Dart now ready to Sail.

In your Letter to the said James Symons, Esq., addressed, Acting-Commander of His Majesty's Ship Porpoise, you request he will be pleased to inform you whether the Rules and regulations of the Naval Service will admit of his receiving me on board for the Purpose of carrying me to England in Arrest, and that you will be thankful if he will acquaint you what accommodation can be spared.

In Answer to which Mr. Symons' Letter is as follows:—

Sir,   H.M.S. Porpoise, 16 March, 1808.

In Answer to your Letter of this date I have to inform you that when Captn. Bligh comes on board the Porpoise I must consider him as First Captain; and am ready to receive him when you may think proper—I further beg leave to inform you that half the Commander's accommodation belongs to him and I have, &c.,

J. SYMONS.

In reply, I have to refer you to my former Letters of the 1st, 2nd, and 13th of February, with their respective inclosures, which Clearly point out that I laid an undoubted Claim to the Command of the Porpoise, and which claim I still make. With respect to your requiring my Word of Honor as an Officer that

1808.
11 April.

Bligh's claim
to the command
of the Porpoise.

I will not attempt to assume any Command here, and that I will consider myself in Arrest until His Majesty's Pleasure be signified on my late Supercession, I pledge myself to do; but with regard to His Majesty's Ship Porpoise, I, in the Name of His Majesty, and in the Name of the Lord High Admiral, or Commissioners for executing the Office of Lord High Admiral of Great Britain, do most solemnly and positively demand to be put in Possession of her, that I may return to England with my Family and Friends according to the Dignity of my Rank and Station.

Illegality of
Symons'
command.

I have, in order that you might be acquainted with my Naval Authority, communicated to you the Power I possess; by the Documents alluded to, you will see that Actg.-Lieutenant Symons has illegally appointed himself Acting-Commander of his Commanding Officer's Ship, and does not wear his distinguishing Flag; and I must further observe that unless it is hoisted again by me, the whole Officers and Ship's Company will be involved in ruin by supporting such a transaction with their Acting-Lieutenant, who only commanded them in the execution of a particular Service by my Order.

Bligh willing
to sail in
command of
the Porpoise.

If, therefore, I understand you right, you do not intend to take any Authority upon you to prevent my Commanding His Majesty's Ship, as on my proceeding on board to that effect it will be a further sacred pledge of my Appearance in England, and will prevent you, Sir, from separating me from my Family, which can only be done by force, and then His Majesty's Government will Judge of the Violence of such an Act—An Act which they will readily declare as an Insult to the British Nation, and likewise to humanity, when they find that the Dart is a poor, small, wretched Vessel of 197 Tons burthen, with only one Deck, deeply Laden with Salted skins, and no adequate Accommodation.   I am, &c.,

WM. BLIGH.

[EE] *Mr. Nicholas Bayly to Governor Bligh.*

Sir,   21st March, 1808.

Johnston's
refusal of
Bligh's
proposal.

I am Ordered by His Honor the Lieutenant-Governor to Acquaint you that Your Letter of yesterday's date shall be transmitted to His Majesty's Ministers with such other Public Papers as may enable them to form a just Opinion of the Measures which have been adopted towards you, both before and since your supercession. I am further, Sir, directed to inform you that unless you think proper to comply with the Conditions prescribed in my letter of the 19th Instant, You cannot be permitted to take your

Passage on board His Majesty's Ship Porpoise—that you will be expected to prepare yourself immediately to Embark on board the Dart.

NICHOLAS BAYLY,
Secretary.

[FF] *Governor Bligh to Major Johnston.*

Sir, Government House, Sydney, 22nd March, 1808.

As by your Letter of Yesterday You have positively refused me the Command of His Majesty's Ship Porpoise, I have nothing further to observe than as I refuse to go in the Dart I must proceed in the Fox, a Brig belonging to Mr. Campbell.

I am, &c.,
WM. BLIGH.

Bligh's refusal to sail in the Dart.

[GG] *Mr. Nicholas Bayly to Governor Bligh.*

Sir, Headquarters, Sydney, 22nd March, 1808.

I am Commanded by His Honor the Lieutenant-Governor to inform you, he remarks with the greatest concern that his endeavours to do everything in his power to secure a Comfortable accommodation for you and Your Family on your Passage to England seems to have produced no effect upon your mind.

I am further Commanded to acquaint you that, although you say You "must proceed in the Fox, a Brig belonging to Mr. Campbell," it will not be permitted, for reasons that will be explained to His Majesty's Ministers; and that, unless you think proper to take your Passage on board His Majesty's Ship Porpoise on the Conditions that have been explained, You will be required to embark on board the Dart on the 1st April.

N. BAYLY,
Secretary.

Johnston's decision re Bligh's passage.

[HH] *Governor Bligh to Major Johnston.*

Sir, Government House, Sydney, 23rd March, 1808.

I have received your Secretary's Letter of Yesterday's date in which I am informed that, although I said in my Letter to you of the same date I must proceed in the Fox, a Brig belonging to Mr. Campbell, it will not be permitted for reasons that will be explained to His Majesty's Ministers, and that unless I think proper to take my Passage on board His Majesty's Ship Porpoise on the Conditions that have been explained, I shall be required to embark on board the Dart on the 1st of April.

In reply to which I am under the necessity of requesting to be informed if by the word "' required " it is meant that I shall be

Bligh asks if Johnston will force him to sail in the Dart.

1808.
11 April.
forced to embark on board the Dart. As you expressed great regret in your Letter of the 19th Instant that none of the Vessels had arrived which I alluded to in mine of the 11th Ultimo, I was induced to propose the Fox, that had just arrived.

I am, &c.,
WM. BLIGH.

[II] *Mr. Nicholas Bayly to Governor Bligh.*

Sir,   Sydney, 24th March, 1808.

Johnston's previous indication of the use of force.

I am Commanded by His Honor the Lieutenant-Governor to inform you, in Answer to your Letter of Yesterday's date, that it has been his unceasing Study, ever since you were put in Arrest, to avoid saying or doing anything towards you at which the most scrupulous delicacy could take offence; and that when he caused it to be signified that you would be required to embark on board the Dart, he naturally concluded you must have understood that, if the requisition was not complied with, it would be most certainly enforced.

I am further Commanded to acquaint you that enquiries have been made respecting the Fox, and the result has not removed His Honor's objections to your embarking in that Vessel.

Johnston's final decision.

In Answer to your Observations that His Honor had expressed great regret that none of the Vessels had arrived which were alluded to in your Letter of the 11th Ult., I am directed to refer you to that Letter as an Evidence that the Fox cannot be considered as one of the Vessels which you signified was to be expected in the Month. But that you may not be led into an unavailing controversy on Words, I am Commanded distinctly to State again, that you will be expected to embark on board the Dart on the 1st of April, unless you shall prefer taking your Passage in His Majesty's ship Porpoise on the Conditions already proposed.

As the time fixed for the Sailing of the Dart is so short, your immediate answer is expected.

I have, &c.,
N. BAYLY,
Secretary.

[JJ] *Governor Bligh to Major Johnston.*

Sir,   Government House, Sydney, 24th March, 1808.

Recapitulation of Bayly's letter.

I have to acknowledge the receipt of your Secretary's Letter of this day's date, stating that he is commanded by you to inform me, in Answer to my Letter of Yesterday's date, that it has been Your increasing study, ever since I was put in Arrest, to avoid saying or doing anything towards me at which the most scrupulous delicacy could take offence; and that when you caused it to be signified that I should be required to embark on board the Dart, You Naturally concluded I must have understood that if the requisition was not complied with it would most certainly be enforced; Also, that he is further Commanded to acquaint me that enquiries have been made respecting the Fox, and that the result has not removed Your objections to my embarking in that vessel; That in answer to my observation that you had expressed great regret that none of the Vessels had arrived which were alluded to in my Letter of the 11th Ultimo, he is directed to refer me to that Letter as an Evidence that the Fox cannot be considered as one of the Vessels which I signified was to be expected in this Month; but that I may not be led into an unavailing Controversy on Words, he is commanded distinctly to State again that I shall be expected to embark on board the Dart on the 1st ot April, unless I shall prefer taking my Passage in His Majesty's Ship Porpoise on the Conditions already proposed, and that as the time fixed for the sailing of the Dart is so short my immediate answer is expected.

In reply thereto, I therefore acquaint you that the Dart being the only Vessel offered besides His Majesty's Ship Porpoise, and having very sufficient and Satisfactory reasons for objecting to proceed in that vessel, as I shall make appear to His Majesty's Ministers and my Lords Commissioners of the Admiralty, I do on that account only agree to take my Passage in His Majesty's Ship Porpoise, on the Conditions prescribed in your Secretary's Letter of the 19th Inst. I am, &c.,

WM. BLIGH.

[KK] *Mr. Nicholas Bayly to Governor Bligh.*

Sydney, 24th March, 1808.

I AM directed by His Honor the Lieut.-Governor to request information of the Names of the Persons you propose to embark with you on board His Majesty's Ship Porpoise.

I have, &c.,

NICHOLAS BAYLY,
Secretary.

[LL] *Governor Bligh to Major Johnston.*

Sir, Government House, Sydney, 25th March, 1808.

In Answer to Mr. Bayly, your Secretary's, letter to me this Evening, stating that he was directed by you to request information of the Names of the persons I propose to embark with me on board the Porpoise, I have to inform you they are as

1808.
11 April.

Witnesses to
embark with
Bligh on the
Porpoise.

follows:—Mr. Atkins, Judge-Advocate; Mr. Campbell, Mr. Palmer, Mr. Arndell, Mr. Williamson, Magistrates; Rever'd Mr. Fulton, Chaplain; Mr. Gore, Provost-Marshal; Mr. Fras. Oakes, Mr. R'd Rouse, Mr. Nichs. Divine, Mr. Andrew Thompson, Mr. Jas. Wiltshire, Mr. Geo. Crossley, George Dowling, and Mr. Edward Griffin, my Secretary.

Servants
required by
Bligh on the
Porpoise.

With respect to Servants, who I acknowledge you offered me in your Message of the 11th Ulto., as well as any Medical Assistance —which is now supplied by my Surgeon of the Porpoise—subject to the Secretary of State's directions, in case it should be necessary, I have to request to be allowed for Mrs. Putland, one Woman Servant—not yet determined on; George Jubb, my Steward—a deserving Person, who has had and continues in the Charge of all my Property; Henry Trotman, Cook and Baker, and John Webb, Convicts.   I am, &c.,
                                                WM. BLIGH.

P.S.—Had I gone Home in a private Ship, Mr. O'Connor was the person I should have applied for as Medical Assistant.

[MM] *Mr. Nicholas Bayly to Governor Bligh.*

Sir,   Sydney, 25th March, 1808.

Crossley to go
to England as
a prisoner.

I am ordered by His Honor the Lieutenant Governor, in reply to your Letter of this date, containing the return of persons you wish to take to England, to refer you to my Letter of the 19th February, and further to acquaint you, as George Crossley, a Convict, is added to the Number named in your letter of the 17th of Feb'y, he shall be allowed to attend you, but as a prisoner, Subject to return to this Colony to serve out what period may remain unexpired of the Sentence he is now suffering under.

Conditional
emancipations
for Bligh's
servants.

The Prisoner Servants You have selected will also have Conditional Emancipations made out, Subject to the approval or disapproval of the Secretary of State.*
                                          I am, &c.,
                                            N. BAYLY,
                                                Secretary.

[NN] *Governor Bligh to Major Johnston.*

Sir,   Government House, Sydney, 27th March, 1808.

Rations for
passengers on
the Porpoise.

I have to request you will inform me what Ration of Provision will be allowed to each person who may embark with me on board His Majesty's Ship Porpoise.
                                          I am, &c.,
                                            WM. BLIGH.

* Note 73.

[OO] *Governor Bligh to Major Johnston.*

Sir,   Government House, Sydney, 28th March, 1808.

In order that proper arrangement may be made for my accommodation in His Majesty's Ship Porpoise, both in my Cabin, State Room and Store Room, in order to receive my Stores and Necessaries; I have to request, you will allow me communication with her, or the Carpenter to come to me to receive directions what to do.   I am, &c.,

WM. BLIGH.

Bligh's request for permission to give orders to the carpenter.

In Consequence of the foregoing Letter the Carpenter was sent to Governor Bligh.

[PP] *Governor Bligh to Major Johnston.*

Sir,   Government House, Sydney, 28th March, 1808.

I have to request to be informed when I may expect all the Books and papers, public and private, which were taken from me by a Committee appointed by you for that purpose, on the 28th January, and of which an Account was taken, will be returned to me (excepting the Public Registers and Indents of Prisoners); also my Commission as Governor of His Majesty's Territory of New South Wales and its dependencies, and that of Vice-Admiral of the same.   I am, &c.,

WM. BLIGH.

Bligh's request for the return of his papers.

[QQ] *Mr. Nicholas Bayly to Governor Bligh.*

Sydney, 29th March, 1808.

I AM directed by His Honor the Lieut. Governor to inform you, Sir, that the delay of an Answer to your Letter of the 27th and your two Letters of the 28th has been occasioned by some difficulties that have arisen respecting your Accommodation on board His Majesty's Ship Porpoise, and which his Honor laments he has not been able to settle as he could have wished. A Copy of this Correspondence is now preparing and will be sent to you as soon as possible with Specific Answers to the Several points on which you have required information in your three Letters.

I am, &c.,

N. BAYLY, Secy.

Reasons for non-reply to Bligh's letters.

[RR] *Mr. Nicholas Bayly to Governor Bligh.*

Sir,   29th March, 1808.

I am Ordered by His Honor the Lieutenant-Governor to inform you, in reply to your three Letters of the 27th and 28th Inst., that he proposes to victual the persons who may attend you

The victualling of Bligh's servants.

1808.
11 April.

to England on a two-thirds Ration equally to what he under-
stands is the rule of the Service; but if you desire that a larger
allowance may be given to them, it will be readily complied with
on the condition of your holding yourself responsible to Gov't for
the Expense.

The carpenter to wait on Bligh for orders.

W. Moore, the Master Carpenter, has had orders to attend
you to receive your instructions for fitting up your accommodations on board His Majesty's Ship Porpoise in any manner
you may like, and the accompanying correspondence will explain
how much the Lieutenant-Governor has endeavoured to obtain
the whole Cabin for your Use.

Such Books and papers as the Lieut.-Governor does not consider it needful to retain will be sent to you on Friday Morning.

I have, &c.,

NICHOLAS BAYLY,

Secretary.

[SS] *Major Johnston to Lieutenant Symons.*

Sir,   25th March, 1808.

Bligh's proposed voyage to England in H.M.S. Porpoise.

You will herewith receive the Copies of a Correspondence
which has been held with the late Governor, William Bligh, Esq.,
relative to his return to England. From that Correspondence you
will learn that he has voluntarily Chosen to take his Passage on
board His Majesty's Ship Porpoise, now under your Command,
in preference to taking his Passage in the Ship Dart. This has
been acceded to by me, on the express conditions that he shall
enter into a Solemn Engagement, on his Word of Honor as an
Officer, that he will not attempt to assume any Command, and
that he will consider himself in Arrest until His Majesty's
pleasure shall be signified respecting his late supercession.

The necessity of making this arrangement for the return of the
late Governor to England will also be explained by the accompanying Letters; it is, therefore, only requisite for me now to
represent to you that the good of His Majesty's Service requires
he should immediately leave this Colony, and to request that you
will, on that Consideration, be pleased to receive him and his
Family on board the Porpoise.

A return of the persons the late Governor may intend to take
with him shall be immediately procured, and be transmitted to
you, that you may make arrangements for his and their comfortable Accommodation.

Whatever assistance you may require for the Speedy equip-
ment of His Majesty's Ship shall be directly supplied; and my

own knowledge of your zeal and past Active exertions in forward- 1808.
11 April.
ing the Public Service, leaves me without doubt that you will be
ready for Sea in a Week. I am, &c.,

GEO. JOHNSTON.

[TT] *Lieutenant Symons to Major Johnston.*

His Majesty's ship Porpoise,
Sir, Sydney Cove, 26th March, 1808.

In answer to your Letter of Yesterday's date, requesting
me to receive Capt'n Bligh on board His Majesty's Ship Porpoise,
I have to inform you that I am at any time ready to receive Symons to
surrender
command
to Bligh.
him; and I must again repeat that on Capt'n Bligh's coming on
board His Majesty's Ship Porpoise I must receive his Orders,
and will give up half the Accommodation appropriated for the
Commander, any other comfortable accommodations for Passengers will be impossible, as the Nature of the Service will not
allow any alteration of her Cabins.

I further beg leave to inform you, If the Weather is favourable, and with every exertion, the Ship may be got ready for a
voyage to England in fourteen days. , I have, &c.,

J. SYMONS.

[UU] *Major Johnston to Lieutenant Symons.*

Sir, Headquarters, Sydney, 26th March, 1808.

I have the honor to acknowledge the receipt of your letter
of this day's date in Answer to my Application to you to receive
W'm Bligh, Esq., and his Family on board His M. Ship Porpoise.

If you refer to the Conditions on which he is permitted to take Bligh's
agreement *re*
his voyage on
the Porpoise.
his Passage in His Majesty's Ship, I think no doubt can be enter-
tained of so Solemn an engagement being rigidly observed by any
Officer who holds the Ship's Commission, should it, however,
prove otherwise, I conceive you can be Subject to no responsibility if you conform in every respect to the rules and regulations
of your own Service, of which, as I have no competent knowledge,
I do not presume to offer an Opinion.

You will receive with this a return of the persons named by Passengers to
travel on the
Porpoise.
the late Governor to accompany him to England, and I earnestly
recommend that you will make every arrangement in your Power
for their accommodation. I have also to request you will have the
goodness to allot a Cabin for Lieut. Minchin, who goes Home
with my despatches. I beg leave to repeat that whatever assistance you may require in getting ready for Sea shall be instantly
supplied, and I sincerely hope you will be ready within the time
you have Specified.

GEO. JOHNSTON.

1808.
11 April.

[VV] *Lieutenant Symons to Major Johnston.*

His Majesty's ship Porpoise,

Sir,   Sydney Cove, 26th March, 1808.

Limited
accommodation
on the Porpoise.
I have to acknowledge the receipt of your Letter of this date, inclosing a list of Passengers required by Captain Bligh to be accommodated on board His Majesty's Ship Porpoise. I have already intimated my readiness to divide the Apartments allotted for the Commander of that Ship with Capt'n Bligh, and I shall be enabled to furnish Three Cabins, one of which I will appropriate for Lieut. Minchin; but any other accommodations for Officers, Gentlemen, or Families will be totally out of my Power.

I must request to be furnished with Carpenter and the Materials to fit up Captain Bligh's Cabin in the way he may wish.   I have, &c.,

J. SYMONS.

[WW] *Major Johnston to Lieutenant Symons.*

Sir,   27th March, 1808.

Request for
explanation of
Symons' letter.
I beg to be informed whether I am to understand by your Letter of Yesterday's date that you cannot receive any persons on board His Majesty's Ship Porpoise except such as can be accommodated in the Apartments You propose to allot for the use of the late Governor, and in the Cabins (three) which you say you will be enabled to furnish.

If you will have the goodness to make a regular demand for the Mechanics and the different Materials you may want it shall be immediately complied with.

GEO. JOHNSTON.

[XX] *Lieutenant Symons to Major Johnston.*

His Majesty's Ship Porpoise,

Sir,   Sydney Cove, 27th March, 1808.

Accommodation
on the Porpoise.
In Answer to your Letter of this day's date, I meant to inform you in my Letter of Yesterday's date that there cannot Possibly be any accommodations but the half of the Commander's Cabin, and three Cabins before the Gun-Room that are Comfortable for Gentlemen; but I can receive about twenty or thirty other persons to hang their hammocks amongst the Ship Company.

Alterations
possible.
I have to request the Master Carpenter may be sent on board H.M.S. Porpoise, and I will point out the Spaces that can be Spared to erect the three Cabins, and every Assistance shall be given on my part to forward your wishes. A Circumstance

occurred Yesterday of the Master being taken out of the Ship 1808.
11 April. for debt, should he be unable, from that Circumstance, not to proceed on the voyage, there will be another Spare Cabin; and I will endeavour to manage Matters that the Midshipman may mess with the Warrant Officers, which, if I should be able to accomplish, will enable me to make accommod'n for another Gentleman.

Probable
additional
accommodation.

I have, &c.,
J. Symons.

[YY] *Major Johnston to Lieutenant Symons.*

Sir,   Headquarters, Sydney, 27th March, 1808.

I have ordered Mr. Moore, the Master Carpenter, to attend you to-morrow morning at daylight, or at any other hour you may think proper to appoint, for the purpose of making the Space that you propose to allot for the late Governor and his Family, and for Lieut't Minchin, on board His Majesty's Ship Porpoise.

The carpenter
to wait on
Symons for
orders.

But before you come to a final determination upon the Subject, permit me to express my regret that no more than one-half the Commander's Cabin can be given up; and to recommend that you will have the goodness to consider whether it may not be practicable to make some arrangement which may enable you to give the late Gov'r more than one-half the Cabin for himself and his Daughter.

Cabins for
Bligh and
Mrs. Putland.

I am, &c.,
Geo. Johnston.

[ZZ] *Major Johnston to Lieutenant Symons.*

Sir,   Headquarters, Sydney, 29th March, 1808.

I have to request you will have the goodness to send me an Official Answer to my last Letter respecting the Accommodation of the late Governor.

Johnston's
request for a
reply from
Symons.

Permit me, at the same time, to recommend to your Consideration whether it might not be a pleasing circumstance to His Majesty's Government in England if you were to offer the whole Cabin.

I am, &c.,
Geo. Johnston.

[AAA] *Lieutenant Symons to Major Johnston.*

His Majesty's Ship Porpoise,

Sir,   Sydney Cove, 29th March, 1808.

I should have answered your official Letter of 27th had I conceived it required one, but I had previously determined to allot two-thirds instead of half the Cabin of the Porpoise for Capt'n Bligh's accommodations, and I have given such directions to the Master-Carpenter; and it is not consistent with the nature

Accommodation
for Bligh on
the Porpoise.

of the Service for me to,dispossess any of the other Officers of their Appartments, which must be the Case if I give up my own altogether.   I have, &c.,
                                                        J. SYMONS.

[BBB] *Governor Bligh to Major Johnston.*

Sir,   Government House, Sydney, 29th March, 1808.

Bligh's claim
to entire use of
commander's
cabin.

I have received your Letter of this day's date with a Copy of the Correspondence You have had with Acting Lieutenant James Symons for the Accommodation to be made commodious according to my Rank and Station the Cabin to be for my entire use—I observe how much you are anxious that this should be done, and Agreeable to your Orders Mr. Moore the Master Carpenter will call on me to Morrow by which means every thing will be easily regulated; but Lieutenant Symons can have no part of my Cabin.

I will be answerable for the quantity of Provisions at whole Allowance for the Passengers who may accompany me.
                                                        I am, &c.,
                                                        WM. BLIGH.

In Consequence of the foregoing Letter Mr. Moore the Master Carpenter waited on Governor Bligh.

[CCC] *Governor Bligh to Major Johnston.*

Sir,   Government House, Sydney, 29th March, 1808.

Bligh's orders
for Kent to
command the
Porpoise.

I am under an Arrest by your Orders, with further injunctions that if I communicate with the Officers of His Majesty's Ship Porpoise, it will be considered as a Breach of the said Arrest. The Lady Nelson is now arrived with Lieutenant Kent. I therefore, under the Authority of the Naval Commissions I hold, Inclose to you a Letter to Lieutenant Kent, who is the legal First Lieutenant of the Porpoise, which Letter I request, in the name of My Lords Commissioners of the Admiralty, may be delivered, it containing my Warrant to him to command His Majesty's Ship Porpoise.   I am, &c.,
                                                        WM. BLIGH.

[DDD] *Mr. Nicholas Bayly to Governor Bligh.*

Sydney, 30th March, 1808.

Conditions
imposed on the
transmission of
Bligh's orders
to Kent.

I AM directed by His Honor the Lieutenant-Governor to wait upon you, Sir, and acquaint you that after considering your Letter of this day's date (inclosing an Order to Lieutenant W'm Kent to take upon himself the command of His Majesty's Ship

1808.
11 April.

Porpoise) that His Honor will cause that Order to be forwarded to Lieutenant Kent provided you think it proper to subscribe the following Conditions:—

Conditions imposed on the transmission of Bligh's orders to Kent.

First: that you will not hereafter attempt to plead your hav'g been permitted to give Lieut't Kent an Order to assume the Command of His Majesty's Ship Porpoise as a Precedent which can justify you in giving any future Orders respecting His Majesty's Ship until His Majesty's Pleasure shall be known.

Secondly: That you will write to Lieutenant Kent a Letter (to be transmitted to him by His Honor the Lieutenant-Governor) wherein you shall pledge your Word of Honor as an Officer that you will not, after your embarkation on board His Majesty's Ship Porpoise, assume any Command or consider yourself in the said Ship otherwise than as a Passenger, Subject to the restraint of the Military Arrest in which you have been placed by His Honor the Lieutenant-Governor.

NICHOLAS BAYLY,
Secretary.

[EEE] *Governor Bligh to Major Johnston.*

Sir,   Government House, Sydney, 30th March, 1808.

I have received your written Message by Your Secretary, Mr. Bayly, of this day's date. My Zeal for the Public Service, and a point of Honor to you, Sir, induced me to send Lieut. Kent's Commission as Commander of His Majesty's Ship the Porpoise to your Care, to be transmitted to him. I also inform you I cannot enter into any further Conditions than I have already agreed to.   I am, &c.,

Bligh's refusal to accept further conditions.

WM. BLIGH.

[FFF] *Mr. Nicholas Bayly to Governor Bligh.*

Sydney, 30th March, 1808.

HIS HONOR the Lieutenant-Governor desires that you may be apprised of His Intentions as early as possible, has directed me to wait upon you for the purpose of communicating that he has determined on your taking your Passage to England in the Dart, the reasons for which will be fully explained to you to-Morrow Morning.   N. BAYLY,

Johnston's orders for Bligh to sail in the Dart.

Secretary.

[GGG] *Mr. Nicholas Bayly to Governor Bligh.*

Sir,   Sydney, 31st March, 1808.

I am directed by His Honor the Lieutenant Governor to acquaint you, in explanation to the reasons that have made him

1808.
11 April.

Reasons for
compelling
Bligh to sail
in the Dart.

determined to send you to England in the Ship Dart, that he
conceives your refusal to sign the Conditions communicated to
you in my Message of Yesterday as a Clear indication that you
must have it in contemplation to evade or disregard the obligation imposed on you in my Letter of the 19th Inst. as follows:—
"You will be convinced that there are insuperable objections to
your going on board the Porpoise unless at your own particular
request, and under a Solemn engagement, on your Word of
Honor as an Officer, that you will not attempt to assume any
Command, and that you will consider yourself in Arrest until
His Majesty's Pleasure shall be signified on your Supercession.
On those Conditions being acquiesced in, the Lieutenant-
Governor has commanded me to inform you that a requisition
shall be made to Capt. Symons to receive you and your Family
on board, and to proceed to England,"—which Obligation you
have absolutely pledged yourself to conform to in your Letter of
the 24th, wherein you State that "the Dart being the only Vessel
offered besides His Majesty's Ship Porpoise, and having very
Sufficient and Satisfactory reasons for objecting to proceed in that
Vessel, as I shall make appear to His Majesty's Ministers and My
Lords Commissioners of the Admiralty, I do, on that Account
only, agree to take my Passage in His Majesty's Ship Porpoise
on the Conditions prescribed by you in your Secretary's letter
of the 19th Inst."

His Honor is further confirmed in his Opinion of your intentions from my relation of the Conversation I had the honor to
hold with you last night, wherein, no doubt, you will recollect
you declared in the most pointed manner that you would take
the Command of the Porpoise as soon as you went on board. In
communicating this Conversation to the Lieutenant-Governor I
did not omit to repeat the Arguments you urged in defence of
the resolution you had formed; but the Lieutenant-Governor, so
far from being convinced by those Arguments, is decidedly of
Opinion that no obligation can be so binding on an Officer as his
Parole of Honor, and that any attempt to evade such a Pledge is
disgraceful to the Party and degrading to His Majesty's Service.

I am further directed to express the Lieutenant-Governor's
deep concern at being obliged to make such remarks upon any
part of the Conduct of an Officer so circumstanced as Yourself,
and that nothing but a desire to prevent his own intentions from
being misrepresented could have induced him to enter into this
Explanation.   I have, &c.,

NICH. BAYLY,
Secretary.

[HHH] *Governor Bligh to Major Johnston.*

Sir,   Government House, Sydney, 31st March, 1808.

I have this day rece'd a letter from your Secretary, Mr. Bayly, stating it to be written by your directions as an explanation of the reasons that have made you determine to send me to England in the Ship Dart, which shall be duly presented to His Majesty's Ministers. The language he has been pleased to use is not that which will be Justified, and it is peculiarly to be noticed under my present Situation, while it is necessary to say your reasoning is wrong and not founded on the whole of the Case.

Bligh's retort to Johnston.

My letter of last night informed you that I could not enter into any further Conditions than I had before agreed to, those I still pledge myself to abide by, and the Letters respecting which will speak for themselves; but last night Mr. Bayly seemed to have such doubt that I declared it could not possibly be supposed that the Arrest I was under by you should deprive me of fighting His Majesty's Ship Porpoise with any Enemy's Ships I might meet, and which has no connection with that Arrest. My right is to be allowed to go home in His Majesty's Ship Porpoise. I have appointed a Commander, whose duty will rest with himself, and he is bound to account for me, living or dead, to My Lords Commissioners of the Admiralty, stating the Arrest to which I was to Answer.

Bligh's explanation of his remarks to Bayly.

I imagine it is from your not being acquainted with the Naval Service that you required me to write the Letter you did to Lieut. Kent; but to add to the information I had before given you, I sent by your Secretary the Naval Article of War, which I suppose you can have no power to counteract. As Captain, therefore, of His Majesty's Ship Porpoise, and Commodore commanding His Majesty's Ships and Vessels in these Seas, I do again request to go on board the Porpoise, where proper accommodations can be fitted up for the Officer who attends me officially from you, and with whom I engage to present myself to the first General Officer he finds it his duty to attend on when we arrive in England.   I am, &c.,

Bligh's decision.

WM. BLIGH.

[III] *Mr. Nicholas Bayly to Governor Bligh.*

Sir,   Headquarters, Sydney, 1st April, 1808.

I am directed by His Honor the Lieut.-Governor, in reply to your Letter of Yesterday, delivered this Morning, to say that he neither can nor will be led into a Controversial correspondence on Matters of Opinion. You must be sensible, Sir, that the Lieut.-Governor's anxiety to send you home in His Majesty's

Refusal of controversial correspondence.

1803.
11 April.

Explanation
of Johnston's
motives.

Ship Porpoise originated in a sincere desire to secure You suitable Accommodations, and not to Separate you from your Family. This, however, His Honor was aware could not be allowed without either permitting you to take the Command of the Porpoise or obtaining from you a Solemn Pledge that you would not attempt to assume any Command on board her, but consider yourself as a Prisoner under the restraint of the Arrest in which it has been found expedient to place you.

Bligh to be
forced to sail
in the Dart
unless he agrees
to Johnston's
terms.

To this Condition, Sir, You did conform in the most unqualified manner in your Letter of the 24th of March; and when you were called upon to confirm this compliance by writing such a Letter as might Justify the Officer who should receive you as a Prisoner on board His Majesty's Ship, you absolutely refused so to do, and demonstrated by such refusal that it was your intention to take the Command. Surely, Sir, it will not be denied that such a design, if carried into effect, would be a breach of your engagement. I am, therefore, directed by His Honor the Lieutenant-Governor once more explicitly to inform you that unless you sign the Conditions prescribed you will be required (and if needful obliged) to embark on board the Ship Dart on Sunday Morning, where the best accommodation will be provided that vessel can afford for you and any Gentlemen you may think proper to take with you.

N. BAYLY,
Secretary.

[JJJ] *Mr. Nicholas Bayly to Governor Bligh.*

Headquarters, Sydney, 1st April, 1808.

Discovery of
Paterson's
appointment as
lieutenant-
governor.

I AM directed by His Honor the Lieut.-Governor to announce to you, Sir, that the Government Papers were searched this Morning, in consequence of a rumour that a Communication had been made in the Year 1801 from His Majesty's Secretary of State of the Appointment of Lieut.-Colonel Paterson to the Office of Lieut.-Gov'r of this Territory, and that the Document so spoken of has been found.

Bligh's
departure to
be delayed
until the
arrival of
Paterson.

This Circumstance has impressed on the Lieut.-Gov'r the necessity of referring to the Consideration of His Honor Lieut.-Gov'r Paterson all the cir's'ces connected with, or relating to, the restraint that has been imposed upon you, and has induced him to determine upon immediately despatching His Majesty's Ship Porpoise to Port Dalrymple for the purpose of bringing Lieut.-Gov'r Paterson to this Settlement, that he may decide on the measures proper to be adopted towards you in the present Crisis.

Actuated by the same Motives which have uniformly influenced his conduct, His Honor has embraced the earliest Moment to

acquaint you of His Intentions, and to inform you that your
departure from hence will be delayed until the arrival of Lieut.-
Gov'r Paterson. NICHOLAS BAYLY.

[KKK] *Mr. Nicholas Bayly to Governor Bligh.*

Sir, 13th April, 1808.

I am directed by His Honor the Lieutenant-Governor to Proposed
acquaint You that the Dart will sail early to-morrow Morning, departure of the Dart with
and that any Despatches You may wish to send shall be taken despatches.
Charge of this Evening by Mr. Grimes, or any other person on
Board the Dart you may chuse. I am, &c.,

N. BAYLY,
Secretary.

[To the above a verbal answer was given that there were no
letters to send.]

[Enclosure No. 8.]

COPY OF GENERAL ORDERS. Johnston's
orders *re*
[A.]

26th January, 1808.

THE present alarming state of the Colony having induced the Prin- Martial law.
cipal Inhabitants to call upon me to interpose the Military Power
for their relief, and to place His Excellency Governor Bligh in
Arrest, I have, with the advice of my Officers, considered it necessary, for the good of His Majesty's Service, to comply with their
request. I do, therefore, hereby Proclaim Martial Law in this
Colony, to which all Persons are commanded to Submit, until
measures can be adopted for the restoration of the Civil Law on a
permanent Foundation.

By Command of His Honor the Lieu't-Governor.

NICHOLAS BAYLY, Secretary.

[B.]*

Head-quarters, 27th January, 1808.

RICHARD ATKINS, Esquire, Judge-Advocate, is suspended from that Suspension
Office. of Atkins.

Edward Abbott, Esquire, is appointed Judge-Advocate during his Civil
suspension. appointments
and suspensions.
Anthony Fenn Kemp, Esq., John Harris, Esq., Thos. Jamison,
Esq., Charles Grimes, Esq., William Minchin, Esq., Garnham Blaxcell, Esqre., John Blaxland, Esqre., and Archibald Bell, Esqre., are
appointed Magistrates, and those persons who heretofore performed
the duties of that Office are to consider themselves dismissed.

Lieutenant Lawson is appointed Aid-de-Camp to His Honor the
Lieutenant-Governor.

Nicholas Bayly, Esqre., is appointed Secretary to His Honor the
Lieu't-Governor, and to be Provost-Martial during the suspension
of William Gore, Esqre., who is hereby Suspended from his office.

John Palmer, Commissary, is suspended from that Office; and
James Williamson, Esqre., is directed to take upon himself the
charge of His Majesty's Stores, and act as Commissary during his
suspension.

* Note 74.

1808.
11 April.

Johnston's
orders *re*
Civil
appointments
and suspensions.

Robert Campbell, Esqre., is dismissed from the Offices of Treasurer to the Public Funds, Naval Officer, and Collector of the Taxes,
and he is hereby directed to balance his accounts and to deliver
them to His Honor the Lieutenant-Governor.

Thomas Jamison, Esq., is appointed Naval Officer.

By Command of His Honor the Lieutenant-Governor.

NICHOLAS BAYLY, Secretary.

[C.]

28th January, 1808.

Changes of
gaoler and
constable.

MR. DANIEL McKAY is appointed Gaoler of the County Gaol in this
Town, in the place of Mr. Barnaby Riley, who has resigned.

Mr. Francis Oakes, Chief Constable at Parramatta, is dismissed
from that Office, and Mr. Barnaby Riley is appointed Chief Constable of that Town and the Districts connected with it.

[D.]

Sydney, 30th January, 1808.

Civil
appointments.

CAPTAIN ABBOTT, having requested to decline the appointment of
Acting Judge-Advocate, his Nomination to that Office is revoked, and
Charles Grimes, Esq're, is appointed to act as Judge-Advocate
during the Suspension of Richard Atkins, Esq're.

The Reverend Henry Fulton is suspended from discharging, in
future, the Office of Chaplain in this Colony.

Attendance at
thanksgiving
service.

The Officers, Civil and Military, are ordered to attend Divine
Worship on Sunday next at the New Church ; and any well-disposed
Inhabitant is requested to be present to join in thanks to Almighty
God for his merciful interposition in their favor, by relieving
them, without bloodshed, from the awful situation in which they
stood before the memorable 26th Instant.

Assembling
of criminal
court.

A Criminal Court of Jurisdiction will assemble at Sydney on
Tuesday next, the 2nd of February, for the Trial of such offenders
as may be brought before it ; The Court to consist of the Acting
Judge-Advocate and Six Officers of the New South Wales Corps.

[E.]

31st January, 1808.

Survey of the
public stores.

THE following Gentlemen are ordered to an immediate Survey
of all the Stores and Provisions in His Majesty's Stores :—Garnham
Blaxcell, Esquire ; John Blaxland, Esquire ; Mr. Thomas Laycock ;
Mr. Thomas Moore, Builder ; Captain Ebor Bunker ; and Mr. James
Williamson, Acting Commissary.

Mr. Commissary Palmer is directed to attend the Survey, and,
when it is completed, to sign the report.

[F.]

2nd February, 1808.

Civil
appointment.

MR. ANDREW THOMPSON is dismissed from his Situation as Constable
at the Hawkesbury, and Mr. Richard Fitzgerald is appointed to
that Office.

[G.]

3rd February, 1808.

Abbott's
status as a
magistrate.

BY the Appointment of Edward Abbott, Esq're, on the 27th January
to act as Judge-Advocate, he was created a Magistrate ; but, as He
has declined accepting that Office, it may be necessary to explain
that he is still a Magistrate, and to be respected accordingly.

[H.]

6th February, 1808.

1808.
11 April.

THE Deputy Commissary, Mr. Fitz, is hereby ordered to collect the Debts owing to Government, for which Service he will be allowed a remuneration of 2½ per Cent.; all Persons who stand indebted to the Government are requested to pay their Debts immediately.

Johnston's orders re Debts due to government.

[I.]

7th February, 1808.

JAMES SYMONS, Esq're, Commander of His Majesty's Ship Porpoise, is appointed a Magistrate, and is to be respected as such.

Civil appointment.

Officers and all other Persons who may have occasion to make applications to the Lieutenant-Governor relative to their private Concerns are directed to communicate their business by a written memorandum, and the Lieut.-Governor forbids any verbal request being made to him except on Public affairs.

Applications to Johnston.

If the Officers and respectable Inhabitants are desirous to purchase a moderate Supply of Spirits for their Domestic uses, the Lieutenant-Governor will readily grant them permission; But it is at the same time to be understood that the former orders respecting the Importation and Landing of Spirits are still in full force, and that a rigid observance of them is required.

Purchase of spirits.

The Lieutenant-Governor feels confident that no Officer will so far forget himself as to abuse the indulgence allowed him as to attempt to obtain Spirits clandestinely; but that his intentions on this subject may be known, the Lieutenant-Governor hereby promises that if any person in trust shall be detected by a Soldier in illicit practices, the Soldier shall be rewarded for the discovery with a discharge, a Farm, and other indulgencies; If by a Prisoner, he shall receive an unconditional emancipation, and be provided with a Passage to England.

Rewards for discovery of illicit traffic.

[J.]

8th February, 1808.

THE present state of His Majesty's Stores renders it necessary to reduce the Ration of Salt Meat to two pounds to each Man. The Ration of the Women and Children to be reduced in proportion in lieu of the two Pounds taken off. The Officers, Civil and Military, and the Troops are to receive Three pounds and a half of Fresh Beef; The Convicts are to receive Six Pounds of Wheat in addition to the present quantity issued to them.

Reduction in ration of meat.

The Commissary will direct the deputy Commissaries and Store-Keepers to issue the Soldiers' Ration as follows:—On Saturdays, two Pounds of fresh Beef and two Pounds of Pork; on Thursdays, One pound and a half of Fresh Beef.

Issue of rations.

[K.]

10th February, 1808.

A COURT of Civil Jurisdiction will assemble on Monday, the 15th Instant, composed of. the Acting Judge-Advocate, Charles Grimes, Esq're; Mr. Thomas Laycock, and Mr. Thomas Moore.

Assembling of civil court.

A General Court-Martial will assemble on Wednesday, the 17th Instant. Officers for that duty:—Captain Anthony Fenn Kemp, President; Lieutenant William Moore, Lieut. Thomas Laycock, Lieut. William Lawson, Lieut. C. Draffin.

Assembling of court martial.

1808.
11 April.

Johnston's
orders *re*
Appointment of
Blaxcell as
auctioneer.

It having been represented to the Lieut.-Governor how Satisfactory it would be to the Inhabitants if a Gentleman of respectability were to be appointed to do the duty of Auctioneer, Garnham
Blaxcell, Esquire, is hereby appointed Vendue Master, as Auctioneer
to the Colony, and all other Persons are forbidden from acting in
that capacity.

[L.]

11th February, 1808.

Civil
appointment.

DAVID LANGLEY, Superintendent of the Government Blacksmiths,
is dismissed.

Thomas Hodges is appointed Superintendent of the Government
Blacksmiths, in the Room of David Langley.

[M.]

12th February, 1808.

Appointment
of Macarthur
as secretary to
the colony.

JOHN MCARTHUR, Esq're is appointed a Magistrate and Secretary
to the Colony. It is to be understood that no Salary or Emolument
can be attached to either of these Appointments. All Public Letters
relative to the Civil Department, are in future to be addressed to
the Colonial Secretary.

Muster at the
Hawkesbury.

A Muster will be taken on Wednesday at the Hawkesbury of all
Persons victualled at that Settlement by Government.

[N.]

17th February, 1808.

Members of the
civil court.

IT having been represented to the Lieut.-Governor that Mr. Moore,
Master Builder, cannot discharge the duty of a Member of a Civil
Court without neglecting his other duties, the Acting Judge-Advocate
has been directed to draw for another Member, and that lot having
fallen upon John Blaxland, Esq're, he is hereby ordered to Sitt as
a Member.

[O.]

18th February, 1808.

Honourable
acquittal of
Wentworth by
court martial.

ALTHOUGH the Lieutenant-Governor perfectly approves of the Sentiments expressed by the Court-Martial respecting the charge against
Mr. D'Arcy Wentworth, His Honor declines, under the existing
circumstances, to insert more of it in the General Orders than that
part which expresses that the Prisoner is not Guilty on the first
charge or second charge, and do therefore Honorably acquit him.

The Court-Martial is dissolved, and Mr. D'Arcy Wentworth is to
return to his duty.

[P.]

19th February, 1808.

Assembling of
vice-admiralty
court.

A VICE Admiralty Court will assemble on Saturday the 20th Inst.
composed of the following persons :—Edward Abbott, Esqr., Judge-
Advocate ; Charles Grimes, Esqr., Registrar ; Members : James Wil-
liamson, Esqr., acting Commissary ; Mr. Richard Smith, Mariner
and Master of the Dart, Sealer ; Mr. Simon Pattison, Mariner and
Master of the City of Edinburgh ; Mr. Oliver Russel, Mariner and
Master of the Brothers, Sealer ; Mr. Eber Bunker, Planter, late
Master of the Elizabeth, Whaler ; John Blaxland, Esqr., Planter ;
Gregory Blaxland, Esqr., Planter ; Nicholas Bayly, Esqr., Marshal of
the Court. Mr. William Sherwin is appointed to do duty, as Store
Keeper at Parramatta.

Commutation of
death sentence.

Samuel Cooley, under Sentence of death, is pardoned on condition
of his serving as a Convict for Life.

[Q.]

22nd February, 1808.

1808.
11 April.

CHARLES GRIMES, Esq're, is appointed Notary Public to the Colony. The following Persons John Williams, Daniel McAlones, David Gibson, Thomas Bray, Thomas Haywood, John Cole, James Taylor, John Moorley, Richard Wright, having been found guilty* of Piracy and Sentenced to die by a Court of Vice Admiralty, His Honor the Lieut. Governor has pardoned them, on Condition of their Serving as Convicts for Life.

Johnston's orders re Commutation of death sentence.

[R.]

23rd February, 1808.

A MUSTER will be taken of all the Men, Women, and Children— except the Military—victualled from His Majesty's Stores at Sydney, on Thursday, the 25th Inst., and those victualled at Parramatta on Saturday, the 27th Inst. The Muster will commence at ten O'Clock on Thursday Morning, at the House of G. Blaxcell, Esq're, and at Government House, Parramatta, on Saturday Morning, at ten O'Clock.

General muster.

Charles Throsby, Esq're, is appointed Magistrate for Newcastle and the parts adjacent; and he is to be obeyed and respected accordingly.

Appointment of magistrate at Newcastle.

[S.]

24th February, 1808.

THE Lieutenant-Governor having purchased Six hundred Gallons of Spirits for the Supply of the Non-Commissioned Officers and Privates of the Corps, the same will be issued to them in the Quantity of one Gill to each Man per day, for which they will be charged at the rate of Six Shillings and ninepence per Gallon, The first serving to commence on Monday, the 29th Instant.

Issue of spirits to the military.

The present distressed state of the Corps for necessaries, which cannot be purchased from any private Individuals in the Colony, has induced the Lieut.-Governor to order 450 Duck Frocks may be supplied from His Majesty's Stores to make each Non-Commissioned Officer and Private a pair of Pantaloons.

Issue of clothing to the military.

The Acting-Commissary will therefore immediately issue 450 Frocks, for which the Officers Paying Companies will pay the acting Commissary the Established price.

[T.]

1st March, 1808.

WILLIAM LAWSON, Esquire, is appointed a Magistrate for the County of Cumberland. He is to be obeyed and respected as such.

Appointment of Lawson as magistrate.

[U.]

3rd March, 1808.

THE Lieutenant-Governor cannot too strongly express his approbation of the disinterested offer made by the Loyal Sydney Association to serve without claiming any Rations from Government; and he assures them that he will never loose an opportunity to do anything in his power to promote their welfare, or to give them a compensation for the Patriotic Sacrifice which they have made in a manner so honorable to themselves.

Free service of the Sydney association.

Lieutenant Thomas Moore is promoted to the Rank of Captain and Commandant, vice Rich'd Atkins, Esq.

Promotion of Moore.

The Acting Commissary will cease in future to serve Rations to the Loyal Sydney Association.

Rations for the Sydney association.

* Note 75.

1808.
11 April.

Johnston's
orders re
All Complaints are to be made before the Magistrate for the Week every Morning at Ten o'Clock, except on Tuesdays and Saturdays, on which days a full Brevet will assemble.

[V.]

5th March, 1808.

Assembling of
criminal court.
A COURT of Criminal Judicature will assemble on Tuesday the 8th Instant of the following Officers:—Captain James Symons, Royal Navy; Captain Edward Abbott, New S. W. Corps; Lieut. William Ellison, R.N.; Lieut. Joseph Short, R.N.; Lieut. Cadwallader Draffin, N.S.W. Corps; Ensign Archibald Bell, N.S.W. Corps.

[W.]

7th March, 1808.

Postponement
of meeting of
criminal court.
THE Court of Criminal Judicature ordered to assemble on Tuesday, the 8th Instant, will not assemble until further Orders, in consequence of the indisposition of Captain Abbott, one of the Members.

Issue of clothing
to the military.
The Acting-Commissary will issue from His Majesty's Stores to the Quarter Master Serjeant of the New South Wales Corps the two hundred Shirts remaining in the Store, and two hundred and fifty Duck Frocks for the use of the Non-Commissioned Officers and Privates. The acting-Commissary will charge the usual Price for the Shirts and Frocks, which are to be paid for by the Officers paying Companies.

Suspension of
duty on coal.
His Honor, the Lieutenant-Governor, taking into consideration the high price of Fuel and the distress of the Poor Inhabitants for that Indispensible necessary of Life, hereby directs that all duties upon Coals shall cease from this day, and that no other charge shall be made upon Coals at Newcastle than ten shillings per Ton, which is to be considered as a *price paid* to defray the expence of receiving them from the mines.

[X.]

16th March, 1808.

Applications
for stores.
PERSONS wanting to obtain Supplies from His Majesty's Stores on their Private account are to apply to the Lieu't-Governor on Mondays before ten o'Clock in the Morning; any applications made at any other times will not be attended to.

[Y.]

[*A copy of a general order, marked thus, is not available.*]

[Z.]

23rd March, 1808.

Resignation of
Blaxland as
magistrate.
JOHN BLAXLAND, Esquire, having requested to resign his Situation as a Magistrate, in consequence of his intending to leave this Colony, his resignation has been accepted.

The same cause having induced Mr. Blaxland to apply to be relieved from Sitting as a Member of the Court of Civil Jurisdiction and Mr. Thomas Laycock being, from a Severe illness, incapable of Sitting.

Constitution of
civil court.
Mr. Blaxland and Mr. Laycock are to be relieved from that duty. Mr. R. W. Wrather and Mr. William Emmett are appointed to be Members of the Court of Civil Jurisdiction, which is to assemble to-morrow, the 24th Instant.

[AA.]

[*A copy of a general order, marked thus, is not available.*]

[BB.]

3rd April, 1808.

WHEREAS Oliver Russel, Master of the Ship Brothers, and Robert Daniels, acting Chief Mate of the Said Ship, were on Wednesday the 30th day of March last past convicted of the crime of Perjury by the Court of Criminal Jurisdiction,* then Sitting and Sentenced (Under the Authority of an act of 2d Geo. 2d) to be transported for Seven Years; and whereas it appears the said Oliver Russell and Robert Daniels were never indicted in due form of Law before the said Court for the said Crime of Perjury, nor allowed the means of Justification to which they were by Law entitled—His Honor the Lieutenant Governor, actuated by an anxious desire to preserve the Rights and Liberties of Englishmen inviolate, and to convince Strangers resorting to this Colony, that they have nothing to apprehend from the oppression of power, from whence soever proceeding, Hereby annuls and declares Invalid the Sentence of Transportation pronounced against the said Oliver Russell and Robert Daniels, and restores them to all the Rights and privilidges they were possessed of before the aforesaid Sentence was pronounced.

[CC.]

'   5th April, 1808.

His Honor the Lieu't-Governor has been pleased to approve and accept of the resignation of Charles Grimes, Esq're, as Acting Judge-Advocate.

His Honor has further to signify that he has no further occasion for the Services of Charles Grimes, John Harris, and James Symons, Esquires, as Magistrates.

The additional charges on the Importation of Cedar from Newcastle having totally destroyed the Trade in that Article, it is hereby directed that in future no further charge shall be made on Cedar upon account of Government than three half-pence per superficial Foot.

[Enclosure No. 9.]

27th January, 1808. Examination of Richard Atkins, Esquire, taken before us this day, Cap'n Ant'y Fenn Kemp, Lieut. Lawson, Chas. Grimes and G. Blaxcell, Esqrs.

Q. Were you present at a Bench of Magistrates—and there sitting as a magistrate—when Capt'n McArthur brought forward a charge against Mr. Rob't Campbell, jun., for having illegally taken from the dwelling-house at Sydney, then and at present occupied by Mr. Blaxcell, two copper boilers, or bodies of stills?—*A.* I was.

Q. From the circumstances that appeared in the course of this investig'n, and for reasons which appeared to the Bench during the examination, did you not, as one of the magistrates, give it as your opinion that the seizure of the boilers—or stills—was irregular and illegal on the part of Mr. Rob't Campbell, junr.?—*A.* I did.

Q. Upon waiting upon Gov. Bligh (as we understand is usual) with the proceedings of the Bench of Magistrates, did not the Governor express his disapprobation as to your decision; and if he

* Note 76.

1808.
11 April.

Examination of
Richard Atkins.

did, what was the language he made use of?—*A*. To this question Mr. Atkins answers: That, agreeable to the usual practice of the Judge-Advocate producing to His Excellency the Governor the proceedings of the Bench of Magistrates, he went up, accompanied by Mr. Palmer, Mr. Campbell, and Mr. Gore (the Provost-Marshal). That being introduced into the Governor's presence he read, according to custom, the proceedings of the Bench upon that occasion. I will not take upon myself to say whether or not the Governor expressed by words his disapprobation, but from appearances my feelings told me that he did. A conversation and observations from Mr. Campbell, Mr. Palmer, and Mr. Gore took place, in which they expressed their strong disapprobation of the opinion I had given, and that it appeared to me I was the butt of their sarcasm on that occasion. That His Excellency the Gov'r then said, " Never mind it; it will do."

Q. Did not Mr. Crossley prepare a memorial accusing the officers composing the Criminal Court of treasonable practices?—*A*. He did; and for the truth I refer to the papers now in the possession of Lieu't Lawson.

Q. Has not Gov'r Bligh, to your own knowledge and in your presence, consulted Geo. Crossley what steps were to be taken against the officers composing the Court of Criminal Judicature after you had quitted your seat as Judge-Advocate; and if so, what was Crossley's opinion?—*A*. Upon my quitting the Court I proceeded to Government House, accomp'nd, to the best of my recollection, by Mr. Campbell, Mr. Palmer, and Mr. Griffin. We went up to the Governor's office, and there I either found Mr. Crossley or Crossley entered a few minutes afterwards. That it then became very naturally the topic of conversation what was necessary to be done upon the occasion alluded to. Various opinions were given upon so momentous a subject and Crossley's opinion was often resorted to. It is impossible for me to express the exact words Crossley said upon that occasion, but the tendency of them was thus: " That it was his opinion that as six members of the Criminal Court had taken upon themselves to adjudicate without the Judge-Advocate, that it was a treasonable offence." In corroboration of what I have now asserted, I beg leave to refer again to the papers in the possession of Lieu't Lawson, where that opinion will be confirmed in Crossley's own handwriting.

Q. What was the opinion of the gentlemen assembled at Government House, provided the officers attended the summons and had been found guilty of the treasonable practices they were accused of?—*A*. I find some difficulty in answering this question. It plainly appears that by a letter* written by Gov. Bligh to Major Johnston, the Commanding Officer·of the New South Wales Corps, intimating to him that he had ordered six officers in his Corps to appear before him and the Bench of Magistrates, the result of those gentlemen's appearance and the investigation that would naturally have taken place would have been their guide as to the complexion of the crime they might or might not have been guilty of; but it was upon talking the matter over, I gave my opinion that the most that could have been done was to make it a bailable offence. I do further declare upon the oath that I have taken that in my opinion it ought not to have been a subject of investigation at that time.

Q. Do you as a law officer conceive a Bench of Magistrates competent to judge of an offence of that nature—meaning treasonable

* Note 77.

practices?—*A.* I think that a Bench of Magistrates can take cognizance of any crime whatever so far as to justify them to commit for any offences whatever, but not to decide on the guilt or acquittal of those persons, which must be left to the decision of a superior Court.

Mr. Atkins's candid offer to disclose every improper measure that he has been forced to sanction, from being completely under the influence of the Governor, and that he has been obliged to do things officially altogether repugnant to his better sense, and entirely to keep his situation, being a dependant man, made him act as he did or has. Mr. Atkins states that when he received a letter from Messrs. Blaxcell and Bayly, offering to give bail to any amount for the person of Mr. McArthur, in the presence of the Governor, Campbell, Fulton, Gore, Palmer, and Crossley, that Mr. Atkins felt inclined to give an answer, but Geo. Crossley said, " Let no answer be given."

Mr. Atkins states that he never saw the letter to the Governor from the Court accusing Mr. Gore of direct perjury.

Q. Does it not come to your knowledge that Mr. Gore has said, " That there is a conspiracy against the Gov'r of which Mr. McArthur is at the head "?—*A.* I answer that Mr. Gore has frequently intimated to the Governor that there was a party forming against him ; but that I never heard him say that Mr. McA. was at the head, as far as my recollection serves me.

Mr. Atkins declares that Geo. Crossley informed him that there had been an indictment drawn out by him against Mr. McA. respecting two stills imported by him (Mr. McA.) in the Dart, and that he (Crossley) had persuaded the Governor not to act upon it at that time ; but that upon the last business taking place, the Governor had insisted that, contrary to his (Crossley's) opinion, and likewise contrary to mine, when Crossley informed me a few days back that the Governor insisted that that charge should make the first comp't in the intended information.

Mr. Atkins declares that the whole of the questions to be asked the seven witnesses against Mr. McArthur were written and framed by Geo. Crossley, and that among the papers now in Lieut. Lawson's possession, the several questions to be put to the different witnesses are in the handwriting of Mr. Griffin, the Gov'rs Sec'y ; and I further declare that not a single question was framed by me, but that the whole was the composition of Crossley ; and I further declare that prior to Crossley reading me those questions he informed me that he had read them to the Governor, and they were approved by him.

Mr. Atkins says that Mr. Palmer applied to him in the presence of Crossley, and said that he wished to have a copy of the questions to be asked him that he might be enabled to answer them ; and, addressing himself to Crossley, said, " You promised me a copy." Crossley answered, " You shall have them immediately," or to that effect, which conversation took place in Mr. Atkins' house.

RICH'D ATKINS.

28th Jany., 1808. *Mr. Atkins' examination cont'd.* *Q.* Has not the Governor at different times endeavoured to influence your opinion in civil causes before you prior to the Court giving their decision?—*A.* He has frequently, and has frequently told me that he was the lawgiver in this colony, and woe be unto any man who dared disobey him, for his order was equal, or of the same effect, as the laws of England.

1808.
11 April.

Examination of
Richard Atkins.

Q. You have performed the duty of Judge-Advocate for many years in this colony;—was it not always the custom previous to Governor Bligh's taking the command that the members chosen upon the Civil Court were elected by ballot?—*A.* It was my usual practice to put down upon papers the names of such gentlemen who were eligible to sit as members of the Civil Court, which list was submitted to Gov'r King. The names were then placed in a hat, and the two first drawn were the members ordered on that duty.

Q. What method, in choosing members for Civil Courts, has been adopted by Gov. Bligh?—*A.* He chose them himself. I generally gave a list, and the Governor pointed out two.

RICH'D ATKINS.

A true Copy compared with the Original by us.

A. F. KEMP, J.P.
CHAS. THROSBY, J.P.

[Enclosure No. 10.]

Examination of
John Palmer.

THE EXAMINATION of John Palmer, Esq.:—

Q. How long have you been appointed by Gov'r Bligh to act as a magistrate?—*A.* About five or six months.

Q. During that period, have you not frequently met at Government House with other magistrates to take into consideration different matters relative to the colony?—*A.* Yes.

Q. In deliberations of the above nature, has not George Crossley been frequently present and consulted?—*A.* Yes, he has in points of law, as he was supposed to be better acquainted with them than any other person.

Q. Shortly after the decision of a Bench of Magistrates respecting two stills, did you ever hear that an information or indictment was to be preferred against Mr. McArthur?—*A.* I did not hear anything about it till very lately.

Q. Do you recollect going to Hawkesbury to take the last muster?—*A.* Yes.

Q. Did you not at that time assemble the magistrates together in consequence of an information given by George Crossley respecting Cap'n McArthur, which you had forwarded to the Governor, and which had been returned to you for that purpose?—*A.* Yes.

Q. Have the goodness to state what was the nature of the information, to the best of your recollection?—*A.* I cannot now charge my memory with it.

Q. Do you positively say, upon your oath, that you have not the smallest recollection of any proceed'g that took place on that occasion?—*A.* I recollect that Mr. Badgery, Mr. Pitt, and Mr. Hobby were called.

Q. By whom were they called?—*A.* By me and Mr. Arndell respecting Cap'n McArthur.

Q. Was George Crossley present?—*A.* He was present when Mr. Pitt was called.

Q. Was George Crossley sworn at the time he appeared before you?—*A.* Yes; he was the first person sworn.

Q. What was he sworn to?—*A.* To the best of my recollection to some conversation which had passed between him and Mr. Pitt.

Q. Did you not, previous to the examination of the above persons, think or believe the charges you understood Crossley was going to exhibit respecting Capt'n McArthur were of a serious nature?—*A.* No; I did not.

1808.
11 April.

Examination of
John Palmer.

Q. Who first made the communication which caused you and Mr. Arndell to assemble concerning Capt'n McArthur?—*A.* Mr. Crossley, to the best of my recollection.

Q. Was it verbal or in writing?—*A.* I think it was in writing.

Q. Previous to you and Mr. Arndell's assembling, had you any communication with the Governor concerning it?—*A.* Yes.

Q. How came that communication to be made to you?—*A.* By my enclosing Crossley's letter to the Governor to know if I should take any notice of it.

Q. You state in part of your evidence that Crossley was sworn to some conversation between him and Mr. Pitt;—was that conversation of the same nature as the information contained in George Crossley's letter to you?—*A.* I suppose it must have been, but I cannot recollect.

Q. Was the evidence of all those that were examined tending to the same purport?—*A.* I suppose so.

Q. Did the information given on oath by George Crossley, and the evidence given by Mr. Pitt, Hobby, and Badgery agree?—*A.* I do not think they did, to the best of my recollection.

Q. As the evidence of George Crossley and the witnesses you think did not agree, as a magistrate sworn to do justice between all parties, why did you not commit Crossley?—*A.* I did not know I had the power to do it, nor did I think it necessary. I sent the documents to the Governor for his inspection.

Q. By whom were the depositions of Crossley, Badgery, Pitt, and Hobby, taken?—*A.* I do not recollect; I might have taken them myself.

Q. Did you, at the time of taking the above depositions, think Capt'n McArthur obnoxious to the Government of the colony?—*A.* No; I did not.

Q. Was you not a member of a Bench of Magistrates when Capt'n McArthur was committed to take his trial at a Criminal Court?—*A.* Yes.

Q. In consequence thereof, does it come to your knowledge that any information or indictment has been prepared against Mr. McArthur?—*A.* I do not know.

Q. Did you ever hear or know of such a thing being in agitation; and, if so, from whom?—*A.* I have, but cannot speak positively from whom.

Q. Do you say upon your oath that you cannot bring to your recollection any one individual from whom you have heard it?—*A.* I cannot at this moment.

Q. Did you never hear Mr. Campbell mention it?—*A.* I might, but cannot speak positively.

Q. Did you never hear Gov'r Bligh, Mr. Gore, or Mr. Griffin mention the circumstance?—*A.* I might, but cannot speak positively.

Q. Have you not been subpœned to attend a Criminal Court on Mr. McArthur's trial on behalf of the prosecution?—*A.* Yes.

Q. Have you ever seen certain questions, or heard them read from a written paper, that you understood were to be asked you in the course of your examination?—*A.* Yes, I think I have, but did not pay any attention to them.

Q. Who were they shown to you by?—*A.* I think by George Crossley.

Q. Where did Crossley show you those questions, and who was present?—*A.* At my own house, and no person present that I remember.

Q. Did Mr. Atkins never speak to you concerning them?—*A.* He might; but I cannot charge my memory.

Q. Was you sent for yesterday to Government House as a magistrate?—*A.* Yes, I suppose so.

Q. What time was you sent for?—*A.* Overnight; the Governor had directed me to be there by 8 o'clock in the morning.

Q. Was there, in the course of the morning, a meeting or consultation with the magistrates besides yourself on any particular business?—*A.* Yes, there was.

Q. During the different periods you was present as a magistrate at the consultations, mention the names of every person who was likewise present?—*A.* Mr. Campbell, the Governor, Mr. Griffin, Mr. Fulton, Mr. Gore, Mr. Atkins, George Crossley, occasionally in and out of the room.

Q. Was you present when any letter or letters was sent by the Criminal Court to the Governor?—*A.* I do not know; if I was it was not above one.

Q. When that one letter came did you read it or hear it read, and what remarks were made upon it?—*A.* I do not remember.

Q. For what purpose did Mr. Campbell leave the meeting or consultation at Government House to go to George Crossley?—I understood he went to see if Mr. Atkins's memorial was done.

Q. Did you hear Mr. Atkins's memorial read, and who was in the room at the time?—*A.* The Governor; all the magistrates, Mr. Fulton, Mr. Gore, and, I believe, George Crossley.

Q. After the memorial was read, what measures were recommended by the magistrates and George Crossley to be adopted respecting the members composing the Criminal Court?—*A.* To summon them to appear before the Governor the next morning at 9 o'clock.

Q. Did not George Crossley say that those officers were guilty of treasonable practises?—*A.* I cannot positively say; but I think he did, or words to that effect.

Q. Did not the Judge-Advocate, Mr. Campbell, Mr. Arndell, and yourself concur in opinion that the officers were guilty of treasonable practices?—*A.* They concurred in the opinion of the propriety of sending notices to the officers.

Q. Were not those officers to have been committed to prison for detaining the papers brought into Court the day before by the Judge-Advocate?—*A.* Not that I recollect.

Q. If those officers had appeared before the magistrates and not have given what they, the magistrates, might have considered a satisfactory reason for detaining those papers, from the conversation which took place on that subject between the magistrates, what was to have been done with the officers?—*A.* I cannot say.

Q. Was you not one of the magistrates before whom Mr. Gore, the Provost-Marshal, made oath that Capt'n McArthur had escaped from his custody, and in consequence signed his committal to the county gaol?—*A.,* Yes, I was.

Q. At what place did you sign the warrant—at the Judge-Advocate's office or at Government House?—*A.* At Government House.

Q. Was Governor Bligh present at the time, or in any way made acquainted with the oath Mr. Gore had taken, and the purport of the warrant?—*A.* The Governor was backwards and forwards in the room, and therefore cannot say.

JNO. PALMER.

A true Copy compared with the Original by us.

A. F. KEMP, J.P.
CHAS. THROSBY, J.P.

[Enclosure No. 11.]

EXAMINATION of Mr. Griffin, the Governor's Secretary, taken before Capt. Anthony Fenn Kemp, Lieutenant Lawson, and Mr. Grimes, 26th January, 1808:—

Q. Were you ever present whenever any consultations respecting Mr. McArthur's stills were agitated, and who were present; and do you know of any indictment being prepared by George Crossley previous to the one exhibited to the Criminal Court respecting the stills?—*A.* Yes; and the indictment was drawn out, by the Governor's desire, by George Crossley, and I have frequently sent messages to Divine's by the order of the Governor to see if Crossley was there.

Q. Who were present when the Governor consulted George Crossley besides yourself?—*A.* I cannot recollect.

Q. Did you ever send to George Crossley to meet you at Wooloomoolo by the Governor's order?—*A.* Yes, I did.

Q. For what purpose was George Crossley sent for by you?—*A.* To make his remarks on the speech made the day before by Mr. McArthur at the Bench of Magistrates and the proceedings in general, for the information of the Governor.

Q. Did he make any remarks, and what became of them?—*A.* He did; they were taken by me to the Governor, and shewn him, and some time after taken to the Hawkesbury by me and given to George Crossley by order of the Governor, with the proceedings of the Bench of Magistrates, for the purpose of framing an indictment against Mr. McArthur.

Q. Was that indictment framed?—*A.* It was, and sent to me some time after, with a letter accompanying it.

Q. What was the reason the indictment was not acted upon?—*A.* I cannot tell, not being present, that I recollect, at any consultations respecting it, but the Governor directed it to be laid bye.

Q. Do you know why Geo. Crossley was consulted by the Governor on Mr. McArthur's business, in preference to Mr. Atkins, the Judge-Advocate?—*A.* Because he was thought to understand the forms of law best.

Q. Do you know if the Governor was acquainted with any animosity subsisting between Mr. McArthur and George Crossley at the time, or with Mr. Atkins, the Judge-Advocate?—*A.* I do recollect Mr. Atkins shewing the Governor a letter from himself to Mr. McArthur in 1796,* accusing Mr. McArthur of improper transactions, of which letter I took a copy; also another letter from Mr. Atkins to Governor King, some years back, stating Mr. McArthur being the cause of many unpleasant things in this colony.*

Q. Was any person present with the Governor when Geo. Crossley was consulted by him how far Mr. McArthur could be punished for

* Note 78.

his speech before the Bench of Magistrates respecting the seizure of his stills?—*A.* At several times Messrs. Palmer, Campbell, and Atkins were present.

Q. Do you recollect what punishment George Crossley gave his opinion could be inflicted?—*A.* If proved, fine and imprisonment.

Q. Have you been present at any time within these few days when Geo. Crossley was consulted by the Governor respecting the Criminal Court, or the officers then sitting, and who were present? —*A.* I was. Messrs. Fulton, Atkins, Campbell, Palmer, and Gore were present, and, I believe, Mr. Arndell.

Q. What was their determination?—*A.* The Governor determined patiently to let the members proceed, and see what steps they would take.

Q. Was that Crossley's advice?—*A.* I think it was.

Q. Do you know why Mr. Gore, the Provost-Marshal, quitted the Criminal Court and ordered all the constables away?—*A.* Because the Judge-Advocate quitted the Court.

Q. Were all the persons abovementioned at the Government House when the first letter came to the Governor from the Court? —I believe they were.

Q. Was the letter read to the above persons?—*A.* It was read in their presence.

Q. Who gave any opinion on that letter, and what were their opinions?—I gave an opinion that the extract of the patent should be sent, and a reference to the General Orders; but before I gave that opinion I saw the Governor's written one, which was corrected by Geo. Crossley, and, after the alteration, was sent to the Court, approved by the whole.

Q. On the answer to the above letter from the Court (the gentlemen abovementioned still being in consultation at the Government House), what steps were proposed to the second letter from the Court?—*A.* The Governor, not conceiving the Court to be complete without the Judge-Advocate, directed Mr. Campbell to write to that effect, which the Governor signed; all the persons present approved of the answer after being written. There was much conversation, and George Crossley was present and approved of it, and particularly myself. It will more particularly appear by reference to the letters.

Q. Were any steps proposed, should the Court still persist to sit as a Court after receiving the above letter?—*A.* Mr. Campbell and Geo. Crossley, with the Governor and myself, proposed sending to demand the papers left by the Judge-Advocate from the Court, and the Governor particularly concurred, as I did myself. I do not recollect any other steps being proposed; but · after the Judge-Advocate gave a memorial to the Gov'r (which he understood had been framed by Geo. Crossley and Mr. Atkins), accusing the members of the Court of being guilty of treasonable practices, it was then the Governor's determination to order the officers before himself without delay, and Geo. Crossley recommended a summons to be sent, in the first place, to the whole as a body, but afterwards individually. I myself strongly objected to the opinion of Geo. Crossley to the Governor, wishing the Governor to give an order from himself to require the attendance of the six officers. The Governor agreed in my opinion, on which I immediately began the preamble by putting the Governor's titles on a sheet of paper when

Geo. Crossley, standing by me, wrote in pencil the substance of an order which I altered, and the Governor approved of the alterations, and the orders so altered were sent requiring their attendance at 9 o'clock the following morning instead of immediately.

Q. What steps were proposed should the officers attend the above orders?—*A.* The Governor proposed having all the magistrates present, when the Judge-Advocate's memorial should be read to those officers by me. The Governor asked Geo. Crossley's opinion what steps could be taken against them. Geo. Crossley's opinion was that no steps could be taken if the officers persisted in their being a constituted Court; but it was difficult for him in so novel a case to give an opinion what should be done; but the Governor, with the advice of the magistrates, would be able to come to some determination, and should it be proved that they were an unlawful assembly they might be committed, but be liable to bail, by Act of Parliament, on which Mr. Gore proposed, in concurrence with Geo. Crossley, that a summons should be directed to him by the magistrates as Provost-Marshal to bring the bodies of the six officers composing the Criminal Court then sitting before the Governor and the magistrates immediately, and was not objected to by any person but myself; but after much conversation I carried my point by having the order sent by the Governor, which Mr. Gore afterwards thought better than the summons. Geo. Crossley particularly told the Governor that when the officers appeared before him he would be able to judge, with the advice of the magistrates, what steps could be taken.

Q. What observations were made by the assembly (Crossley and the gentlemen at Gov't House) to the last letter written by the Criminal Court, accusing Mr. Gore of direct perjury, on account of which Mr. McArthur's person was taken from their protection and put into goal?—*A.* The Gov'r determined not to give an answer to that or the former letter sent by the six officers to him that day in consequence, as I understood, of their last letter the preceding day, stating that they had adjourned until the Governor's pleasure might be known; and I particularly pointed out to the Governor that if the six officers were considered a Court the preceding day in consequence of their statement, that the letters should not be answered, not having signified his pleasure, agreeable to their statement. Mr. Gore laughed at the idea of his being accused of perjury, and said to me, " Mr. Griffin, you was present the two last times I was in Court; did you hear any such conservation?" I replied, " I did not "; but that the last time, as he was going away with the letter from the officers, Capt. Kemp called him and said, " Mr. Gore, you will officially say to the Governor that the Court is adjourned until his pleasure is known," but that I did not hear that Mr. McArthur was ordered to his original bail, and in opposition to which I said, " How could it be the case when the officers had the preceding day enclosed an attested copy of an affidavit, taken before them, by Jno. McArthur, Esq're, in which, amongst other things, was sworn that he declined going on the bail which he had been brought before the Court by?" Mr. Gore agreed with me, and on Geo. Crossley giving his opinion that Mr. Gore could bring a civil action against the officers so accusing him, he determined to take that step. The Governor appeared to me to think that he could not, even after bringing the officers before himself and the magis-

1808.
11 April.
Examination of
Edmund Griffin.
trates, be able to do anything against them; but the Courts must be
suspended and all proceedings go through the magistrates until the
Governor heard from England.

Q. Has it not come within the Governor's knowledge that Crossley
has been convicted of corrupt and wilful perjury, for which crime
he was sent to this country?—A. I suppose it has, by common report.

Q. Has it not come within the Governor's knowledge that Crossley's conduct has been notorious during his residence in this
country?—A. I do not know if the Governor is acquainted with it,
but I have heard it spoken of.

Q. Do you know of any correspondence to the Governor direct or
through you with Geo. Crossley?—A. I have mentioned one letter to
myself, and he has two or three times written to me saying that he
was at Sydney, and I once saw a short letter to the Gov'r from
Crossley on the subject of an Act of Parliament, to the best of my
recollection.

Q. Do you know that the Governor has frequently sent express for
Crossley to consult him on public business?—A. He has been sent for.
27th Jany., 1808.   EDMUND GRIFFIN.

A true Copy compared with the Original by us.
                                         A. F. KEMP, J.P.
                                         CHAS. THROSBY, J.P.

[Enclosure No. 12.]

Examination of
Robert
Campbell.
EXAMINATION of Mr. Robert Campbell, taken before Capt'n An-
thony Fenn Kemp, Lieut't Lawson, Mr. Grimes, and Mr.
Blaxland, January 26th, 1808:—

Q. Were you ever present whenever any consultations respecting
Mr. McArthur's stills were agitated, and who were present; and do
you know of any indictment being prepared by George Crossley
previous to the one exhibited to the Criminal Court respecting the
stills*?—A. I was sent for, as Naval Officer, by note from the Governor, to bring certain documents respecting those stills, and the
Parramatta schooner, which, I believe, was for the purpose of
framing an indictment against Mr. McArthur. I was present when
the indictment was brought to Mr. Griffin, and read by Mr. Griffin
to the Governor. No comments were made by either party, and I
don't know why the indictment was not acted upon, nor do I recollect if ever the subject was agitated in the presence of the Governor
by George Crossley; but I know the indictment was framed by
George Crossley.

Q. Do you know if the Governor was acquainted with any animosity subsisting between Mr. McArthur and George Crossley at the
time, or with Mr. Atkins, the Judge-Advocate?—A. When the Governor received a letter from Mr. McArthur, and Mr. Atkins was sent
for, he related the whole of their quarrel to the Governor respecting
a bill of Mr. Bond's.

Q. Have you been present at any time within these few days
when George Crossley was consulted by the Governor respecting
the Criminal Court, or the officers then sitting, and who were
present?—A. Yes, I was; in company with Messrs. Palmer, Atkins,
Gore, and Griffin, and Mr. Fulton.

Q. What was your determination respecting the members?—A.
Mr. Atkins related what had passed to the Governor, which the
Governor minuted down himself, and George Crossley, in his
presence, impressed on the mind of the Governor that there could

* Note 79.

be no Court if the Judge-Advocate was not present, in which Mr. Atkins strongly concurred, and that the Judge-Advocate could not be displaced.

Q. What was the Governor's determination respecting the Court? —*A.* Patiently to let the members proceed, and see how they would act, agreeable to the advice of George Crossley.

Q. Do you not conceive that George Crossley was the principal adviser to the Governor respecting the Criminal Court?—*A.* Yes; I do.

Q. Were any steps proposed to the Governor should the Court still persist to sit as a Court, after receiving a letter from the Governor? *A.* It was proposed to send to demand the papers left by the Judge-Advocate in the Court.

Q. Did you ever see any memorial against the officers of the Criminal Court from the Judge-Advocate?*—*A.* Yes, I did; it was read and presented to the Governor, and the Judge-Advocate was sworn to the contents of it by all the magistrates present. The Governor quitted the room with George Crossley, and returned with a written paper; and, on its being read, George Crossley recommended to the Governor to summons, through the Provost-Marshal, all the officers composing the Court before him and the magistrates immediately. Mr. Campbell proposed milder measures, by sending for the officers to attend himself.

Q. Who dictated the order to be sent for the attendance of the officers?—*A.* George Crossley wrote it in pencil, and it was altered by Mr. Griffin, at the wish of several persons present, to the shape it was sent in.

Q. What was to be the mode of proceedings if the officers attended the order?—*A.* The memorial from the Judge-Advocate was to be read to them, and certain questions put to them, but what they were he does not know; but he understood, if they did not comply with the Governor's requisition, that the Commanding Officer was to be directed to put them under a military arrest. That the magistrates, with the Governor, were to be assembled for the purpose of investigating the accusation made against the officers of the Court by the Judge-Advocate; and, if proved that they had acted treasonably, they were to be committed to jail; or, should they be committed on suspicion of treason only, that the offence was bailable.

Q. What observations were made by Crossley and the gentlemen assembled at Government House to the last letter written by the Criminal Court, accusing Mr. Gore of direct perjury, on which account Mr. McArthur's person was taken from their protection and put into jail?—*A.* It was a general opinion that no answer should be given to the letter, Mr. Atkins being then preparing an accusation against the Court, and George Crossley was absent with Mr. Atkins at Divine's house drawing out the Judge-Advocate's memorial.

Q. Does it come within your knowledge that the Governor is acquainted with the crime for which George Crossley was sent to this country, and that the Governor must be acquainted with Crossley's improper conduct during his residence in this country?— *A.* I conceive the Governor must have heard of it from report, but cannot positively say so.   ROBERT CAMPBELL.

A true Copy compared with the Original by us.

A. F. KEMP, J.P.
CHAS. THROSBY, J.P.

* Note 80.

1808.
11 April.

Examination
of Thomas
Arndell.

[Enclosure No. 13.]

THE EXAMINATION of Thos. Arndell, Esq., Magistrate at Hawkesbury, taken this 26th January, 1808:—

Q. Did you, about the time of the last muster, receive a letter from Governor Bligh to examine certain witnesses on oath respecting some treasonable and seditious words said to be spoken by Mr. MacArthur?—*A.* I did, in conjunction with Mr. Palmer.

Q. And who did you examine in consequence of such letter?—*A.* Geo. Crossley, Mr. Hobby, Mr. Pitt, and James Badgery.

Q. What was their testimony on this occasion?—*A.* The testimony of George Crossley went to prove that he had heard Mr. Pitt say that Badgery had told him Mr. MacArthur had expressed in his presence certain defamatory words relative to the Government of this colony; but upon the examination of the other witnesses, it clearly appeared the whole of Crossley's evidence was false and illfounded, and that no words had ever been made use of by Mr. MacArthur in any way applicable to what had been asserted by Crossley.

Q. Did you and Mr. Palmer, after finishing the depositions, forward them to the Governor for his examination?—*A.* Yes; they were taken by Mr. Palmer for that purpose.

Q. To-day, when you were sent for to Government House as a magistrate, was George Crossley in the room with the Governor when you entered?—*A.* Yes; he was.

Q. Who was in the room at that time besides the Governor and George Crossley?—*A.* The Judge-Advocate, Mr. Campbell, and Mr. Palmer.

Q. During the time you sat there as a magistrate, was George Crossley consulted by the Governor as to the measures to be taken with the officers composing the Criminal Court?—*A.* Yes; he was.

Q. What steps or measures did Crossley advise to be taken in this business, and did he not say the officers were guilty of treasonable practices?—*A.* Crossley said they were guilty of treasonable practices, and advised steps to be taken against the officers.

Q. Did the Judge-Advocate, Mr. Campbell, Mr. Palmer, and yourself concur in the opinion of Crossley?—*A.* Yes.

Q. It was then generally understood that the officers guilty of the above charges were to have been ordered before a Bench of Magistrates to-morrow, and there to have been committed to prison for detaining the papers brought into Court the day before by the Judge-Advocate?—*A.* Yes.   THOS. ARNDELL.

A true Copy compared with the Original by us.

A. F. KEMP, J.P.
CHAS. THROSBY, J.P.

[Enclosure No. 14.]

Examination of
the Reverend
Henry Fulton.

EXAMINATION of Reverend Mr. Fulton:—

Q. Has not Geo. Crossley, within these few days, been in the habit of being consulted by the Governor concerning the Criminal Court?—*A.* Yes.

Q. Did you not see all the letters addressed from the Court to the Governor, and relate your opinions concerning them?—*A.* It was thought by the Governor and Crossley and himself that another Judge-Advocate could not be appointed, unless he was temporarily suspended or legally deprived of his commission.

1808.
11 April.

Examination of
the Reverend
Henry Fulton.

Q. Do you think it consistent with justice, or the honor of His Majesty's Government, that any man should be screen'd from the payment of his debts?—*A.* No; certainly not.

Q. Do you think, if any man claimed a debt of the Judge-Advocate, that he should be deprived of his commission to enable the person to commence a prosecution for the recovery of it?—*A.* I have heard in those cases the Judge-Advocate would be suspended.

Q. If the Judge-Advocate would be suspended because a debt was claimed from him, on what ground did you give your opinion that he could not be suspended for a criminal act charged against him by the Court?—*A.* Because I did not think the Court was complete.

Q. Do you think it consistent with justice or equity that a man who is accused of enormous crimes by a prisoner, which crimes the prisoner produces incontrovertable evidence to prove, ought to be allowed afterwards to sit as a judge on his trial?—*A.* I never heard that the allegations of a prisoner ever set aside a judge of the Court.

Q. Have you not, within the space of a few weeks, told Mr. Jamieson, at Parramatta, that Mr. McArthur would receive a sentence of fine and imprisonment?—*A.* I believe I said it was probable he would, if convicted.

Q. Did not Mr. Jamieson reply, " For shame, Mr. Fulton ! Would you imprison a man with a wife and family "?—*A.* I do not recollect.

Q. You were of opinion that the officers of the Criminal Court should be committed to gaol?—*A.* I candidly acknowledge I was.

Q. After the memorial of the Judge-Advocate's, composed by Geo. Crossley, was read, what was the determination of the Governor and magistrates, and others, assembled at Government House?—*A.* If it appeared from ignorance they had proceeded in the way they had, they could not be committed; but if it appeared from their answers that they clearly comprehended the nature of their crime, they were to be committed. That was Crossley's opinion.

Q. Was it Crossley's opinion that, if the officers persisted in being a constituted Court, on coming before the Governor and magistrates, according to the orders, " that no steps could be taken against them "?—*A.* I do not recollect.

Q. Was any place determined on for conducting the Courts of Justice, should the six officers be committed?—*A.* I did not hear any.

Q. In consequence of Mr. McArthur being committed to gaol, was it not the determination of the magistrates, with the Governor at their head, to bring the prisoner before them—meaning Mr. McArthur—and try him for the charges exhibited against him, and pass sentence upon him?—*A.* I understood that Mr. McArthur was to remain in gaol till there was sufficient officers to try him.

HENRY FULTON.

A true Copy compared with the Original by us.

A. F. KEMP, J.P.
CHAS. THROSBY, J.P.

[Enclosure No. 15.]

GEORGE CROSSLEY'S EXAMINATION.

Examination
of George
Crossley.

26th January, 1808.

GEORGE CROSSLEY being duly sworn, deposeth that he has been these three or four years employed by Mr. Atkins, the Judge-Advocate, to give his private law opinion on many occasions; that he was applied to either by the Governor or the Judge-Advocate to draw

1808.
11 April.

Examination
of George
Crossley.

up an information against Mr. McArthur, respecting a charge made
against Mr. Robert Campbell, jun'r, by Mr. McArthur, wherein Mr.
McArthur had made use of inflamatory language, according to the
Governor's opinion; the deponent gave his opinion that the language,
being spoken before magistrates, could not operate against Mr.
McArthur, and he believes the information was not acted on from
that opinion; the deponent further declares that he was sent for
by the Judge-Advocate, on the subject of a written message sent
by Mr. McArthur to the Judge-Advocate, on the subject of a warrant
sent to bring his person, on the complaint of some seamen belonging
to the Parramatta schooner, to draw up an indictment against John
McArthur, Esq're; he drew it up and delivered it to the Judge-
Advocate; that the deponent drew up this day a memorial for the
Judge-Advocate, stating that the six officers sitting on a Criminal
Court were conducting themselves irregularly so as to create
rebellion in the colony, to be delivered by the Judge-Advocate to the
Governor, and that the Governor furnished the deponent with the
copies of letters, which passed between the officers of the Criminal
Court and himself, for the purpose of correcting the memorial of
the Judge-Advocate; that he was employed by Mr. Gore in a late
trial; that Mr. Gore took him to the Governor's to obtain his permission to plead for him; that he was employed in private by the
Judge-Advocate against Mr. Gore, in an action against him by James
Underwood, to draw up the indictment; the deponent has received
from the Government within these four months, one cow and two
bullocks, to be paid for in wheat, at the rate of twenty-eight pounds
for the cow, and the same for the bullocks, as he believes; that he
got between eighty and ninety pigs at 5d. per lb. alive, and the
sucking pigs at 4s. each, to be paid for in wheat, lately.

Q. Have you had any private conversation with the Governor
to-day?—A. I have been at the Government House to-day with the
Governor, and been advising with him respecting the Criminal
Court, then sitting, who would not dissolve by his direction.

Q. Did the Governor consult you how the officers composing the
Criminal Court could be punished?—A. He did; and I recommended
moderate measures—by recommending the Major to be sent for, or
the officer next in command.

Q. Did you know the contents of the letters or summons written
to the officers composing the Criminal Court this day?—A. I did.*

Q. Did you know the contents of the letter written to Major
Johnston this evening, accusing the officers of treason?—A. I did.

Q. Was you consulted on the propriety of that letter?—A. I saw
no impropriety in it.

Q. Was you present at Sydney on the day the magistrates met to
consult on the seizure of the bodies of stills, the property of J.
McArthur, Esq're?—A. I was in the Court during the trial.

Q. Was you not sent for to Wallomoolo the next day to be
consulted how Mr. McArthur could be punished for the language
made use of before the magistrates?—A. I was sent for to look at
the proceedings taken before the Bench, and to advise how far they
were proper.

Q. Who sent for you?—A. The message came in the Governor's
name.

Q. Who was present?—A. Mr. Griffin the Governor's Secretary,
and Mr. Palmer.

* Note 81.

Q. Did the Governor consult you on the subject at any time?—*A.* I think it was by the Governor's desire; I was to give my opinion in writing.

Q. Has it not been determined by the Governor in your presence that Mr. McArthur should be punished by pillory and imprisonment, or·flogging?—*A.* No.

Q. Did you not receive an assurance that you should be appointed to act in some legal capacity at the Court which assembled on the 25th inst.?—*A.* No.

Q. Did you not boast that if the officers objected to your coming into Court to assist the Judge-Advocate, that the Governor would take their commission from them?—*A.* No.

Q. Did you not tell James Larra so, or words to that effect?—*A.* No; I said to somebody that if the Governor gave me an authority, under the seal of the colony, I thought the Court would be very bold to object.

Q. Did you receive a written authority from the Governor to plead in any Court?—*A.* I did, in the case of Mr. Gore.

Q. Have you been bred to the law?—*A.* I have.

Q. What punishment has the law ordained on any attorney who has been convicted of perjury, that shall afterwards become an agent, or be concerned in any suit pending before any court of justice?—*A.* None after a pardon, or in this country at any time.

GEO. CROSSLEY.

Sworn before me, 26th Jany, 1808—C. GRIMES, J.-A.

A true Copy compared with the Original by us.

A. F. KEMP, J.P.
CHAS. THROSBY, J.P.

[Enclosure No. 16.]

PROCEEDINGS AT THE TRIAL OF JOHN MACARTHUR.

PROCEEDINGS of a Court of Criminal Jurisdiction, held by virtue of a Precept under the hand and seal of His Honor George Johnston. Esquire, Lieutenant-Governor in and over His Majesty's Territory of New South Wales and its Dependencies, 2nd February. 1808.

The Acting Judge-Advocate, Capt. Ant'y F. Kemp, Lieut. Thos. Laycock, Lieut. Wm. Minchin, Lieut. W. Moore, Lieut. Wm. Lawson, Lieut. C. Draffin, members.

John McArthur, Esquire, placed at the Bar, and the following Indictment read:—

New South Wales, } Charles Grimes, Esquire, Acting Deputy
Cumberland, to wit. } Judge-Advocate to our Sovereign Lord the
King, and acting as Judge-Advocate, lawfully appointed by George Johnston, Esquire, Lieutenant-Governor of His Majesty's Territory called New South Wales, on behalf of our said Lord the King, delivers of Record of the Court of our said Lord the King of Criminal Jurisdiction, the said Court being held at Sydney, in the County of Cumberland, in the Territory aforesaid, on the Second day of February One thousand Eight hundred and Eight, and then and there informeth the said Court and giveth the said Court to understand that John McArthur, late of Parramatta, in the County of Cumberland, in the Territory of New South Wales, Esquire, is charged to be guilty of certain charges and offences contained in the subjoined Indictment prepared by Richard Atkins, Esquire, the Judge-Advocate, and laid before the Court of Criminal

Jurisdiction assembled the twenty-fifth day of January last, in answer
to which Indictment the said John McArthur did appear before the
said Court of Criminal Jurisdiction, and was arraigned at its bar,
the Acting Judge-Advocate therefore prays that the said John
McArthur may plead in answer to the said Charge prepared by the
Judge-Advocate, Richard Atkins, Esquire, and take his Trial thereupon according to due course of law.

New South Wales ⎱ RICHARD ATKINS ESQUIRE Deputy Judge
Cumberland (to wit) ⎰ Advocate to our Sovereign Lord the King
and Acting as Judge Advocate lawfully
appointed of our said Lord the King in and for His Majesty's
Territory called New South Wales in the county of Cumberland on
behalf of our said Lord the King delivers of record of the Court of
our said Lord the King of Criminal Jurisdiction the said Court
being held at Sydney in the County of Cumberland in the Territory
aforesaid in the twenty fifth day of January one thousand eight
hundred and eight and then and there informeth the said Court
and giveth the said Court to understand That John McArthur late
of Sydney in the County of Cumberland in the Territory of New
South Wales Esquire is charged to be guilty of the Charges and
Offences hereinafter mentioned and prays that the said John
McArthur may plead in Answer to the said Charges and take his
Trial thereupon in due course of Law and the said Charges so
delivered of record and recorded in the said Court having been
reduced into writing according to the direction of the Letters
Patent were in due form of Law read over to the said John
McArthur in the words or to the effect as followeth (that is to say)

Cumberland (to wit) Richard Atkins Esquire Judge Advocate of
our Lord the King informeth the court of Criminal Jurisdiction in
and for the same Territory of New South Wales and charges John
McArthur late of Sydney in the County of Cumberland Esquire
with the hereinafter mentioned Misdemeanors and Outrageous
Offences (that is to say) for that the said John McArthur not
regarding the Laws and Statutes of this Realm of England or the
Orders and Regulations of the Colony made agreeable to the Same
did unlawfully without the Licence and consent of the Governor of
this Territory for that purpose first had and obtained unlawfully
import or cause and procure to be imported or brought into this
Territory in a certain Ship or Vessel called the Dart of which said
Ship or Vessel the said John McArthur was Owner reputed owner
or part owner two certain Stills Articles of Merchandize or Utensils
called Stills used for distilling of Spirituous Liquors which said
Utensils are not lawful to be in the possession of any private
person in the Colony without such Licence or consent first had and
Obtained. That William Bligh Esq. Governor in Chief of this
Territory having had Notice that such unlawful Merchandize (to
wit) the said Stills were on board the said Ship or Vessels afterwards (to wit) on the eighth day of March One thousand eight
hundred and seven to prevent the same being unlawfully used in
this Territory ordered and directed that the same Stills should be
sent back to England by the first opportunity but that in the
mean time the said Stills might be landed from the same Ship or
Vessel the Dart upon Condition that the same should be put into
His Majesty's public Store there to be kept until another Ship or
Vessel should arrive in Port Jackson that would receive the said
Stills on board to be exported to England in confirmation of the

said Order or direction on that Occasion given. That the said John McArthur not regarding the Laws of this Realm or the ordinances or Regulations of the Territory made in that respect or the directions of the said Governor given conformable to those Laws did in contempt and violation of the same and in breach of the Condition on which the said Governor had given permission for the said Stills to be landed from the said Ship or Vessel the Dart in order to be deposited in the said Public Store and in contempt and violation of the Laws in force against having in the Possession of any person private or unlawful Stills contrary to Law and the Ordinances and Regulations of this Territory in that behalf made, he the said John McArthur did wrongfully and unlawfully take out of the said Vessel the Dart the bodies of the said Stills and did cause the same to be unlawfully removed to the house of him the said John McArthur in Sydney aforesaid in the County aforesaid and then and there unlawfully kept the same in his own possession and refused and neglected to deposit the same in the said public Store agreeable to the Order and directions given as a Condition on which the said Stills were allowed to be landed out of the said Ship or Vessel the Dart as aforesaid and the said John McArthur having after Notice refused or neglected to perform such Condition in contempt of the Laws and regulations used in this Territory and the Laws of the Realm that the said Jno. McArthur having unlawfully kept the said Bodies of Stills out of the said Public Stores from thence until the twenty second day of October One thousand eight hundred and seven aforesaid, the same Governor was pleased to order and direct that the said Stills and every part of them should be put on board a certain other Ship or Vessel called the Duke of Portland the said last mentioned Ship or Vessel the Duke of Portland then lying in Sydney Cove outward bound for England or some port in England, That one Robert Campbell the Younger being lawfully authorized to put the said Stills on board, and to take the Bodies of the same from the house of the said John McArthur, and then and there with the heads and Worms to Ship them on board the said Ship or Vessel the Duke of Portland for the purpose of their being conveyed in that last mentioned Ship to England agreeable to the Conditions on which they were first allowed to be removed out of the said Ship or Vessel the Dart, he the said Robert Campbell on the twenty second day of October aforesaid in the Year afores'd at Sydney aforesaid in the County aforesaid in obedience to the order and direction of the said Governor in order to put the said Bodies of Stills with the heads and Worms on board the said last mentioned Ship or Vessel the Duke of Portland the said John McArthur being minded and intending in that respect to oppose and hinder the lawful executive power of the Governor of this Territory and to obstruct and hinder the due Administration of the Laws of the Realm and Justice of the country as by Law duly Authorized and being minded and intending unlawfully to bring the Governor and Government of the Territory into disrespect, hatred and Contempt of the people of this Colony and unlawfully to libel and falsely to calumniate the said William Bligh Esquire the said Governor in Chief of this Territory of and concerning the Administration of Justice in the same Territory and of and concerning the Acts and Orders of the same Governor in the said Government the said John McArthur with design to Speak and publish divers libellous and Outrageous unlawful words in the presence and hearing of divers good and worthy

1808.
11 April.

Proceedings at the trial of John Macarthur.

Subjects (to wit) the words and Sentences hereinafter mentioned he the said John McArthur did falsely and unlawfully cause the said Robt. Campbell the Younger (afterwards to wit) on the twenty fourth day of October One thousand eight hundred and seven to be brought before Richd. Atkins Esq. and other His Majesty's Justices at Sydney when the said John McArthur in order unjustly to raise the attention of the people of this Territory and to cause them to assemble on pretence of hearing the said untrue allegation of the said Jno. McArthur against the said Robt. Campbell the Younger but in fact to speak the unlawful words of the Governor and Government in the hearing of those people did falsely on the said twenty fourth day of October One thousand eight hundred and seven aforesaid at Sydney aforesaid among other things alledge that the said Robert Campbell the Younger "did on the twenty second day of October aforesaid take away by the assistance of several Men out of the Dwelling house in the Town of Sydney belonging to him the said John McArthur and Mr. Blaxcell (meaning one Garnham Blaxcell) two Copper Boilers value forty pounds Sterling" and in course of the said unlawful charge there being divers persons to the Number of One hundred or thereabouts then and there assembled under pretence of hearing the said unlawful charge against the said Robert Campbell the Younger he the said John McArthur did among others use the following false and unlawful words or Arguments intending seditiously to inflame the Minds of those people against the Governor and Government of this Territory of New South Wales, and to bring the Governor and Government of the Territory into hatred and Contempt of the people with an unlawful and Seditious intent to libel the Acts of the Governor in the Government did then and there on the same twenty fourth day of October aforesaid in the Year last aforesaid at Sydney aforesaid in the County of Cumberland aforesaid in the presence and hearing of divers good and worthy Subjects then and there assembled to the number of One hundred or More, he the said John McArthur did falsely wickedly and libellously seditiously and maliciously with intent to incite those people to hatred and Contempt of the said Governor and Government for the Acts of the said Governor in his Government of this Territory falsely say declare and publish these false and Libellous Words or Words and Sentences to the meaning purport and effect as follows (that is to say) ." I have produced Evidence to prove to the Court that two Coppers or Bodies of Stills were taken out of my house on the twenty-second instant (meaning the twenty-second of October aforesaid) without my Consent. Mr. Griffin, the Governor's Secretary, has declared in Evidence that the Governor (meaning the said William Bligh, Esq.) told Mr. Robert Campbell. Naval Officer (meaning one Robert Campbell, Esq., a Justice of Peace for the said County of Cumberland and acting as Naval Officer in Port Jackson in the said County of Cumberland) to take those bodies of Stills and Ship them on board the Duke of Portland (meaning the said Ship or Vessel, the Duke of Portland) by the acknowledgment of the respectable young Gentleman, Mr. Robert Campbell, Junior. he was told by his Uncle to execute that Command; it would therefore appear that a British Subject, living in a British Settlement in which the British Laws are established by the Royal Patent, has had his property wrested from him by a non-accredited individual, without any Authority being produced or any other reason being assigned than that it was the Governor's order.

It is therefore for you, Gentlemen, to determine whether this be the tenor on which Englishmen hold their property in New South Wales "—which said false, scandalous, libellous, wicked, seditious, and unlawful words were then and there wickedly and unlawfully intended to libel the Governor and Government of this Territory and to bring the Governor and the Acts of the Governor in the execution of the Government into Contempt, disgrace, and hatred of the people, and to incite the people to hatred and contempt of the Governor of the same Territory, to the evil example of all others in the like cases offending in contempt of our said Lord the King, and his laws and in contempt of the Governor and Government of this Territory, contrary to the form of the Statute and against the peace of our said Lord the King, his Crown, and Dignity.

1808.
11 April.

Proceedings at the trial of John Macarthur.

And the said Richard Atkins Esq. Judge Advocate of our said Lord the King in and for the Territory of New South Wales aforesaid on behalf of our said Lord the King informeth and giveth the said Court of Criminal Jurisdiction further to understand and be informed That the said John McArthur, late of Sydney aforesaid in the County of Cumberland aforesaid, Esq., being a person of evil mind and disposition and of dishonest Conversation and being minded and desirous to raise dissatisfaction and discontent in the people of this Colony against the Constitutional Government of the same and to raise hatred and Contempt and dissatisfaction against His Excellency Wm. Bligh Esq., the now Governor in Chief of the same Territory, and its Dependencies and to raise discontent, ill will, hatred, and mistrust in the Minds of the people against other the Officers of Justice in this same Territory of New South Wales as by His said Majesty appointed and by legal Authority authorized to execute the Laws of the Colony in the County of Cumberland aforesaid, He the said John McArthur unlawfully wrongfully deceitfully and unjustly devising and intending to create discontent in the Minds of the people and to incite the people of this Colony in the County of Cumberland afores'd to hatred and Contempt of the Government according to the Laws and Constitution established on the seventh day of December One thousand eight hundred and seven at Sydney aforesaid in the County of Cumberland aforesaid did with intent to raise dissatisfaction in the Master Mates and Crew of a certain Ship or Vessel of which the said John McArthur was Owner part Owner or reputed Owner called the Parramatta Schooner then lying in Sydney Cove in the County of Cumberland aforesaid did write or cause to be written and to be delivered to one John Glen (he the said John Glen being then Master or Commander of the said Ship or Vessel the Parramatta Schooner) a certain false and Libellous defamatory Letter to the purport and effect as follows (that is to say)

" Sir,   " Sydney, New South Wales, 7th December, 1807.
     " In Consequence of the illegal and extraordinary Conduct of the Naval Officer, Robert Campbell, Esq're, in retaining the Schooner Parramatta's Papers and preventing her from entry (altho' the return of the Papers has been repeatedly required and the entry of the Schooner solicited), I must consider myself as virtually dispossessed of her. This is therefore to give you, the Mate and Seamen of the said Schooner, Notice, which you will make known to them, that I have abandoned the said Schooner, and that neither you nor them are henceforward to look to me for Pay or provisions.

I have also to require that you will wait upon the said Robert
Campbell, Esquire, Naval Officer, accompanied by sufficient Witnesses, and that you do deliver to him a Copy of this Letter,
signifying at the same time that you are ready and desirous to give
him an Inventory of the Schooner's Stores, Provisions, and Cargo
before you leave her.　　　　　　　　　　" I am, &c,.

" To Mr. John Glen,　　　　　　　　　　　" JOHN McARTHUR.
　　　　Master of the Parramatta Schooner, Sydney Cove."

which said Letter was then and there falsely and deceiptfully meant
and intended to raise dissatisf'n in the Minds of the Master Mates
and Crew of the said Ship or Vessel and to incite and cause discontent and disobedience in the Seamen and other the Crew of the
said Vessel the Parramatta Schooner and to cause them to come on
Shore from the said Vessel in an unlawful manner in breach and
violation of the rules and regulations of this Territory as by Law
established and to Stir up and create disorder and tumult amongst
the Officers and Crew of the said Vessel to the disturbance of the
peace and that after receipt of the said Letter the said John Glen,
the Master, the Mates and Crew of the said Vessel the Parramatta
Schooner came on Shore in breach and Violation of the Colonial
Regulations in that behalf made for keeping peace and good order
in the Territory and the said John Glen afterwards (to wit) on
the fourteenth day of Decemr. afores'd at Sydney aforesaid in the
Year last aforesaid in the County aforesaid being on the occasion
of coming on Shore in Violation of the Port Orders before the said
Judge Advocate with the Ship's Crew or the greater part of them
put to Answer why he had unlawfully abandoned the said Ship or
Vessel and Why he had suffered the Seamen to come on Shore when
he the said John Glen and other the Crew of the said Vessel the
Parramatta Schooner on Oath charged the said John McArthur as
being the occasion of their so doing, and the said John Glen
delivered a Copy of the said Letter abovementioned Signed by the
said John McArthur as a reason for his so acting, and the said
John McArthur was thereupon by Letter from the said Judge
Advocate among other things required and summoned to attend
before the said Judge Advocate at Sydney aforesaid on the then
next day at ten o'Clock in the forenoon to shew cause for such his
Conduct therein but the said John McArthur did not attend but
refused or neglected so to do, and thereupon wrote a Letter on
Service addressed to Richd. Atkins, Esqr. Judge Advocate to the
purport and effect as follows:—

　" Sir,　　　　　　　　　" Parramatta, 14th December, 1807.
　　" I am to acknowledge the receipt of your Letter of this date,
acquainting me that the Master, Mates, and Crew of the Schooner,
Parramatta, have violated the Colonial Regulations by coming, unauthorised. on Shore, and that they in their Justification say I have
deprived them of their usual Allowance of Provisions, for which
Conduct you require me to come to Sydney to-morrow and shew
cause.　I have only in reply to say that you were many days ago
informed that I had declined any further interference with the
Schooner, in consequence of the illegal conduct of the Naval Officer
in refusing to enter the Vessel and retaining her papers, notwithstanding I had made repeated Applications that they might be
restored.　So circumstanced, I could no longer think of submitting
to the Expence of paying and victualling the Officers and Crew of a
vessel over which I had no control; but previously to my declining

to do so, my intentions were officially made known to the Naval Officer. What Steps he has since taken respecting the Schooner and her people I am yet to learn; but as he has had two Police Officers on board in charge of her, it is reasonable to suppose they are directed to prevent irregularities, And therefore I beg leave to refer you to the Naval Officer for what further information you may require upon the Subject.

"I am, Sir, Your H'ble Servant,
"John McArthur."

which said last mentioned Letter is unlawfully calculated for delay and to oppose the lawful orders of the Colony in respect of Vessels coming into this Port here, and to bring the Governor and Govern't of the Territory into disrespect and hatred and contempt and afterwards (to wit) on the fifteenth day of December aforesaid in the Year aforesaid at Sydney aforesaid in the County aforesaid the said Judge Advocate did in his Office of a Justice of the Peace in and for this Territory in form of Law make a Warrant under his hand and Seal and directed the same to one Francis Oakes, Chief Constable at Parramatta to be executed according to Law by which said Warrant after reciting that Complaint had been made before him on Oath that John McArthur Esq. the Owner of the Schooner Parramatta then lying in this port (meaning Port Jackson) had unlawfully stopped the provisions of the Master Mates and Crew of the said Schooner whereby the said Master Mates and Crew had violated the Colonial Regulations by coming unauthorized on Shore And Whereas the said Judge Advocate did by his Official Letter bearing date the fourteenth day of December require the said John McArthur to appear before him on the fifteenth day of December at Ten o'Clock in the forenoon of the same day And Whereas the said John McArthur did not appear at the time aforesaid or since, the said Francis Oakes was by the said Warrant in His Majesty's Name commanded to bring the said John McArthur before the said Judge Advocate and other His Majesty's Justices on Wednesday then next, the sixteenth of the same instant December at 10 o'Clock of the same day to Answer in the premises and thereof fail not, which said in part recited Warrant afterwards (to wit) on the same day and Year last aforesaid at Sydney aforesaid in the County aforesaid was delivered to the said Francis Oakes the Chief Constable aforesaid to be executed according to the exigency and direction of the same therein contained and afterwards (to wit) on the same day and Year last aforesaid at Sydney aforesaid in the County aforesaid the said Francis Oakes went with the said Warrant to the house of the said John McArthur and then and there shewed the said John McArthur the said Warrant under the hand and Seal of the said Richd. Atkins Esq. the Judge Advocate (he the said Rd. Atkins having full power and lawful Authority to grant such Warrant) and the said Francis Oakes told the said Jno. McArthur that he, the said Francis Oakes was to bring the said Jno. McArthur down to Sydney and the said John McArthur having read the said Warrant and taken a Copy of the same said to the said Francis Oakes these false libellous wrongful seditious and unlawful words in Contempt of the Laws of the Realm and of the Authority of the said Judge Advocate in his Office of Judge Advocate in Contempt of the executive power of the Government in him vested by Virtue of his Office "You may tell the persons directing that Warrant (meaning His Excellency Willm.

1808.
11 April.
————
Proceedings at
the trial of John
Macarthur.

Bligh Esquire Governor and the said Judge Advocate) that I (meaning himself the said John McArthur) will never submit to it (meaning the said Warrant) until I (again meaning himself the said John McArthur) am forced for I (again meaning himself the said John McArthur) treat it (meaning the said Warrant) with Scorn and Contempt as I (meaning himself the said John McArthur) do the persons who has sent it (meaning the Govern'r and Judge Advocate) ; had the person who directed it (meaning the said Judge Advocate) served it instead of you (meaning the said Francis Oakes) I (meaning himself the said John McArthur) would have spurned them from my presence " and the said John McArthur then and there told the said Francis Oakes that if he came a second time to come well Armed, for he (meaning himself the said Jno. McArthur) never would submit till blood was shed (meaning that the said John McArthur would resist the lawful Officers in the execution of their duty in arresting him on said Warrant by force of Arms) and the said John McArthur then and there represented the Gov. as a Tyrant and said they (meaning the Governor and Naval Officer) had robbed him of Ten thousand pounds and the said Jno. McArthur then and there told the said Francis Oakes he would not submit to the Warrant (meaning the aforesaid Warrant the said Francis Oakes then in Order had to Arrest the said Jno. McArthur upon) and the said Jno. McArthur called the Governor (meaning the said Wm. Bligh Esq. Governor in Chief of this Territory) a Tyrant (meaning in his Government of this Territory) and said he (meaning the said John McArthur) would not submit to any such Tyrannical power (thereby meaning and falsely alledging that the Governor in the Executive power of the Government of this Territory acted unlawfully and ruled by Tyrannical power contrary to the Law and Constitution of this Realm), And the said John McArthur having taken a Copy of the same Warrant so shewn him as afores'd by the said Francis Oakes he the said John McArthur wrote on a piece of Paper certain words and then took a Copy of the words he had so written for him to keep, when the said Fras. Oakes having no other person with him to assist in the execution of the said Warrant, said to the said John McArthur " shall I wait on you in the Morning, Sir " in reply to which the said John McArthur said take this paper (meaning the Paper he the said John McArthur had before written and took a Copy of the words of as aforesaid to keep) and You (meaning the said Francis Oakes) will have no blame (meaning that such paper would excuse or indemnify the said Francis Oakes for not taking the said John McArthur into Custody by virtue of the said in part recited Warrant) and the said John McArthur then and there delivered to the said Francis Oakes the said paper so by him as aforesaid written which said paper contained (in writing) the false, scandalous, Seditious, Libel and unlawful defamatory words following (that is to say) " Mr. Oakes, You will inform the persons who sent you here with the Warrant You have now shown me and given me a Copy of, that I never will submit to the horrid tyranny that is attempted until I am forced, that I consider it with Scorn and Contempt as I do the persons who have directed it to be executed. John McArthur, Parramatta, 15th Decr., 1807," and the said John McA. then and there said to the said Francis Oakes these false, scandalous, malicious, defamatory, seditious words (that is to say), Mr. Oakes be careful of yourself, I (meaning himself the said John McArthur) don't blame you (meaning the said Fras.

1808.
11 April.

Proceedings at
the trial of John
Macarthur.

Oakes) but they (meaning the said Governor, Judge Advocate and other Officers in power for the Government of the Territory) have made you the unhappy Instrument to accomplish their own ends (meaning thereby to intimidate the said Francis Oakes in his Office of Constable in executing the said Warrant, and also meaning that the Governor, Judge Advocate and other Officers of the Government were Acting in an Unlawful manner and for illicit purposes) which said false, scandalous, inflammatory, seditious, wicked and deceiptful words and writings so as aforesaid used and published by the said John McArthur as aforesaid were then and there (to wit) on the same fifteenth day of December aforesaid at Sydney aforesaid in the County of Cumberland aforesaid unlawfully and maliciously intended by the sd. John McArthur falsely and seditiously to incite the people of this Territory to the hatred and Contempt of our said Lord the King in his Government in this Territory and to bring the Governor, Judge Advocate and other Officers having the executive power of the Laws of the Government and the Governor of the Territory as by Law established into contempt and disgrace and hatred of the people to the evil example of all others in like cases offending contrary to the form of the Statute in such case made and provided in contempt of our said Lord the King and his Laws and against the peace of our said Lord the King his Crown and Dignity.

And the said Richd. Atkins Judge Advocate of our said Lord the King in and for the Territory of New South Wales aforesaid of our said Lord the King informeth and giveth the said Court of Criminal Jurisdiction further to understand and be informed that the said John McArthur, late of Sydney aforesaid, in the county of Cumberland aforesaid, Esq. being a Malicious and Seditious Man and of a depraved Mind and wicked and diabolical disposition and deceiptfully wickedly and maliciously contriving and abetting against Wm. Bligh, Esq., His Majesty's Governor in Chief of the Territory of New South Wales aforesaid and maliciously contriving and abetting against Richd. Atkins, Esqre. His Majesty's Deputy Judge Advocate in and for the Territory of New South Wales and other Officers of the same Territory by His Majesty lawfully appointed and duly Authorized by the laws of this Realm to administer Justice according to the Laws and Constitution of that part of Great Britain called England and to vilify and represent the said Wm. Bligh Esq. and others as unjust Officers and Ministers and little fit to be used and entrusted by our said Lord the King in the weighty Affairs of this Territory of New South Wales and to bring the said Wm. Bligh, Esqre., the said Governor in Chief and other Officers of Government (as much as in him the said John McArthur lay) into an ill opinion hatred and Contempt of His Majesty's liege Subjects and to represent the said Governor in Chief and other the Officers as Corrupt persons and to bring them into great Scandal infamy and hatred with all the liege Subjects of our said Lord the King, he the said Judge Advocate having lawfully made a Warrant under his hand and Seal the said Richd. Atkins, Esq. being a Justice of the Peace, by Virtue of his Office, in and over the Territory of New South Wales and having lawful and competent Authority to make such Warrant against the said John McArthur, by which same Warrant, one Francis Oakes (the said Francis Oakes being then and there Chief Constable of the Town of Parramatta in the Territory aforesaid) was for the reasons therein set forth

1808.
11 April.

Proceedings at
the trial of John
Macarthur.

in His Majesty's Name commanded to bring the said John McArthur before the sd. Judge Advocate and other His Majesty's Justices on Wednesday then next the sixteenth day of December aforesaid at ten o'Clock of the same day to Answer in the premises in the said Warrant alledged and the said Francis Oakes going to Arrest the said John McArthur by virtue of and under colour of the same Warrant for the Offences therein mentioned and having permitted a Copy of the same Warrant to be taken by the said Jno. McArthur he the said Jno. McArthur did among other things say, declare, write and publish divers false, scurrilous, feigned, scandalous, Seditious and Malicious Words in Substance and effect that he the said John McArthur would not submit to the said Warrant (meaning the said Warrant above in part recited) until he was forced, and the said John McArthur said to the said Francis Oakes "You may tell the persons directing that Warrant (meaning the said Richd. Atkins, Esq., the Judge Advocate afores'd) that he the said John McArthur never would submit unto it until he was forced" (meaning that he would resist the execution of the said Warrant on his person by force) that he, the said John McArthur treated it (meaning the said Warrant) with scorn and contempt, as he, the said John McArthur, did the persons (meaning the said Governor in Chief and Judge Advocate) who had sent it, that had the persons who directed it served it instead of the said Fras. Oakes, he the said John McArthur would have spurned them (meaning the said Governor in Chief and Judge Advocate) from his presence, and the said John McArthur then and there said that if he the said Francis Oakes came a Second time (meaning if he came again to execute the said Warrant) to come well armed for he (the said John McArthur) never would Submit till Blood was shed (meaning that the said John McArthur would resist the execution of the said Warrant on his person by force of Arms) And the said John McArthur then and there represented the Governor (to wit) the said Wm. Bligh Esqr. Governor in Chief of this Territory, as a Tyrant and said they (meaning the said Governor and other Officers of the Government) had robbed him (meaning the sd. John McArthur) of Ten thousand pounds, and the said John McArthur said that he would not submit to the Warrant (meaning the Warrant the said Fras. Oakes had to Arrest him upon) but the said John McArthur said let them alone (meaning the said Wm. Bligh Esq. the Governor Judge Advocate and other Officers of Justice in the Colony) they (meaning the aforesaid Officers) would soon make a rope to hang themselves and the said Jno. McArthur then and there called the Governor (that is to say Wm. Bligh Esqr.) a Tyrant and said he (the said John McArthur) would not submit to any such tyrranical power (meaning that the said Wm. Bligh and other the Officers of Governmt.) in the execution of the Government of this Territory acted by unlawful and tyrannical power And the said John McArthur then and there wrote and Subscribed a certain false scandalous and libellous paper writing and then and there did cause to be written and published the same paper writing in these or the like words: "Mr. Oakes (meaning the said Fras. Oakes) You will inform the persons who sent you here with the Warrant you have now shown and given me a Copy of that I never will submit to the horrid tyranny that is attempted until I am forced; that I consider it with Scorn and Contempt as I do the persons who have directed it to be executed. John McArthur, Parramatta, 15th Decr., 1807," to the great scandal and infamy of the said Wm. Bligh Esq. Governor in Chief of our said Lord the King in and over His Majesty's Territory called New South Wales, and also to the great scandal and infamy of the said Richd. Atkins Esq. the Judge Advocate of our said Lord the King in and over the said Territory and other the Officers having lawful Authority to Administer Justice in the same Territory in contempt of our said Lord the King and his Laws, to the evil and pernicious example of all others in the like case offending and against the peace of our said Lord the King his Crown and Dignity.

1808.
11 April.
——
Proceedings at
the trial of John
Macarthur.

Plea—Not Guilty.

RICHARD ATKINS, Esq., sworn :—

Question from Mr. Atkins, the late Judge-Advocate, to the Members of the Court.—Whether I am bound to answer any questions that may be put to me that has reference to my late official Office as Judge-Advocate of this Territory, under His Majesty's Sign Manual? The Court are of opinion that you are bound to answer the questions proposed to you.

Question from Court.—Are the papers, specified in the following List, the same as left by you in the Court of Criminal Judicature, on the 25th of January last, and detained by the Officers composing that Court? :—List of papers :—Indictment; List of questions to support the indictment; Proceedings of a Bench of Magistrates; Warrant, dated 15th December, 1807; Warrant under which the Prisoner was apprehended; Proceedings of a Bench of Magistrates on Prisoner's Commitment; Paper delivered by the Constable— said to be delivered by the Prisoner; Letter, 14th December, 1807; Letter, answer from the Prisoner, 14th December, 1807; Letter, protesting against the Judge-Advocate, to the Governor, with the Governor's answer; Notice of Trial; Bail Bond; Judge-Advocate's determination to record Sentence of Guilty; Mode of punishing the prisoner; Deposition of Francis Oakes, 16th December.—*A.* They are.

Q. Are you ready to come forward to prosecute John McArthur, Esq., on the Indictment framed by you and which You have heard read?—*A.* I am not.

Q. State your reasons.—*A.* The reasons that I give are the following: That the information which I instituted against John McArthur, Esq., and which has now been read, and to which the said John McArthur, Esq., has pleaded not guilty, I did not in my individual Capacity as Richard Atkins, Esq., but in my public one as holding His Majesty's Commission; I therefore conceive that my Official Duty is for the present completely finished, consequently cannot stand forth as the Prosecutor of John McArthur, Esq.; but in any other Capacity I have no objection to answer any questions that may be put to me, and are relevant to the Subject.

Q. Was the Indictment against John McArthur, Esq., framed by you as Judge-Advocate?—*A.* It was to have been exhibited by me as Judge-Advocate, and I do apprehend that his Office does not exclude him from the advantages arising from the superior knowledge of any man that may be more conversant in the object upon which the Judge-Advocate consulted him than he (the Judge-Advocate) was.

Q. Were not the Evidences on behalf of the Crown furnished by you or any other person with your knowledge with a list of Questions to be asked them before the Court?—*A.* The Evidences were not furnished by me, neither was a single question contained in the following list before the Court, and which I intended to ask the respective Evidences on the part of the Crown, framed by me.

LIST OF QUESTIONS.

[Here followed a list of the questions,* which were intended for the examinations of Edmund Griffin, Robert Campbell, Jr., John Harris, Robert Campbell, John Palmer, John Glen and Francis Oakes, all of which were used in the examination of the said witnesses in this trial with the exception of the following:—]

JOHN HARRIS, ESQRE.

Questn. 1. Were you not the Naval Officer in this Port when the Ship the Dart arrived in March last?

2. Did you or not at that time receive orders from the Gov. to see that two Stills that were imported in that Ship were put into the King's Stores for Safe keeping?

3. Was or not the Condition of landing those Stills that they should be so deposited in the Store until an Opportunity offered to send them to England and were the Bodies of those Stills put into the Store agreeable to the Condition of that Permission to land or not?

4. How long might it be after the order given to have them put into the Store that it came to your knowledge that the Bodies of them were taken to Mr. McArthur's or any other house?

5. Upon it being discovered that the Bodies of these two Stills had been removed to Mr. McArthur's house and that Contrary to the Condition on which they were allowed to be landed from the Vessel did you or not cause any Application to be made to Mr. McA. to have them brought to the King's Store or not?

6. Is it not the Custom of this Colony for known persons to execute the orders of the Governor without any Warrant in writing for that purpose and did you ever know any Question made of the legality of an Order given by the Governor verbally being quest'd because it was not in Writing and has it not been the Custom for every Gov. to give verbal orders in cases like that under inquiry?

7. You have many Years acted as a Justice of the Peace in this Territory and as such are acquainted with the Statutes and local orders of the Colony, do you think it consistent with those laws that a private person without the licence of the Governor has any right to have in his possession Utensils to distil Spirituous Liquors in this Colony, and has it not always been the Custom to seize and destroy such utensils whenever found, declare all you know on this occasion, and explain what has been the Usage and law in practice in respect of private Stills in this Colony as you know or believe.

8. Has it not been the usual Custom in this port in cases of particular Ships to place Constables or other Officers on board to prevent the Cargo being Smugled on Shore or landed without permiss'n or any Goods being put out of the Ship without a permit or order for that purpose being first obtained?

MR. FRANCIS OAKES.

Quest. 1st. You are the Chief Constable of the Town of Parramatta look upon the paper writing now produced and shewn to you and say if you did not receive that Warrant with orders to Arrest the Pris'r as therein mentioned.

2. When you received that Warrant did you apply to any person to know how you should act and to whom declare?

* Note 82.

1808.
11 April.

Proceedings at
the trial of John
Macarthur.

3. You are well known to the Pris'r to be the Chief Constable at Parramatta are you not?

4. Did you or not go to the House of the Pris'r and did you see him?

5. Did you or not tell him you had orders to take him to Sydney under that Warrant?

6. Did you shew him that Warrant and did you not suffer him to take a Copy of it?

7. After you had shewn this Warrant to the Pris'r and let him take a Copy of it, had you any Conversation with him?

8. In the course of that conversation when speaking on public duty did the Pris'r say to you "You may tell the persons directing that Warrant that I never will submit unto it, until I am forced for I treat it with Scorn and Contempt as I do the persons who have sent it, had the persons who directed it served it instead of you, I would have spurned them from my presence" or such or the like words?

9. Then you say that the Pris'r did use such or the like words.

10. As you understood at the time who did the Pris'r mean by the persons directing that warrant?

11. Can you say as to your belief who the Pris'r meant when he said "I treat it with scorn and contempt as I do the persons who have sent it"?

12. Did or not the Pris'r tell you that if you came a second time to come well Armed for he never would submit until blood was shed?

13. By the Pris'r saying he would not submit until Blood was Shed did you not understand that he meant to resist the Officers in the execution of the Warrant by force of Arms?

14. Did or not the Pris'r say to you that the Gov. was a Tyrant?

15. Did he not mean His Excellency Gov. Bligh the Gov. in Chief of this Territory?

16. Did he not say they had robbed him of £10,000 and if he did who did you understand he meant had robbed him of that sum?

17. Did or not the said Jno. McArthur say to you that the Gov. was a Tyrant and that he wd. not submit to any such Tyrannical power?

18. By saying the Gov. was a Tyrant did he not mean Gov. Bligh?

19. By saying he would not submit to any such Tyrannical Power did you or not understand him to mean that Gov. Bligh in the Executive power of the Govt. of this Territory acted unlawfully and ruled by Tyrannical power and contrary to the Law and Constitution or what else did he mean?

20. After Mr. McA. had taken a Copy of the Warrant you had ag't him did he or not write upon a piece of Paper some words and then take a Copy of what he had written to keep, and if he did did he not say to you take this paper and you will have no blame?

21. Did he not then deliver you the Paper he had so before written and taken a Copy of?

22. Look upon the paper now produced and say if that is the paper so wrote in your presence, and after having taken a Copy of it, delivered it to you.

23. Previous to your having this paper delivered to you did you not say to the Pris'r shall I wait on you in the Morning, Sir, and was not that paper given as a reply to that Question?

24. You had no Assistants with you, had you or not?

25. Then you say that the paper which the Pris'r wrote in your presence and took a Copy of and some short time after delivered it saying if you took that paper you would have no blame?

26. Did or not the Pris'r after this say to you these or the like words " Mr. Oakes be careful of yourself I don't blame you but they have made you the unhappy Instrument to accomplish their own Ends "?

27. Can you Say who the Pris'r meant by " they have made you the unhappy Instrument to accomplish their Ends " was it or not as you understood Gov. Bligh the Judge Advocate and other officers?

28. Did you understand that the Pris'r meant to insinuate that the Gov. and other Officers were Acting in an unlawful manner, and for unlawful purposes?

29. Did the Pris'r or not say " let them alone they will soon make a rope to hang themselves " if you did whom did he mean by they as you understood?

The Prisoner's Examinateing Mr. Atkins :—

Q. Was not the Indictment or information framed by Geo. Crossley, a person sent into this Country as a Convict under the Sentence of the Law for Perjury?—A. It was framed by Geo. Crossley, and who, I believe, was sent into this Colony for the crime as stated in the question.

Q. Did you receive the information so prepared by George Crossley because you approved of its contents or because you were commanded so to do by the Governor?—A. In consequence of having received directions to prosecute Mr. McArthur, he having been committed for Trial by a Bench of Magistrates; and knowing the very great difficulty that I laboured under in not having had what is called a legal education, and feeling it a matter of a most momentous nature, I wrote a letter to Mr. Crossley, directed to him at the Hawkesbury, but before I had sealed it I heard Mr. Crossley was down at Sydney, but I sent the Letter to Mr. Devine's, where he usually sleeps, purporting that he (Crossley) being better versed in such a business, that I should be obliged by his assistance, and that I was sure the Gov'r would be equally so. When I saw Crossley, he told me that Mr. Divine had written to him, desiring his immediate Attendance. Some short time after Crossley brought me the Information in his own handwriting, of which the one before the Court is a Copy. I wished to make some immaterial alteration, which was objected to by Crossley.

Q. What caused you to be sure that the Governor would be pleased by Crossley's interference?—A. Because the Governor had before employed Crossley on a similar occasion, and had been in the custom of consulting Crossley on law business.

Q. State to the Court on what particular occasion the late Governor did employ Crossley to draw up an information or Indictment? —A. The information against O'Dwyer and others, which was for misprision of Treason or intending to disturb the Peace of the Colony, and the questions on that Trial were framed by Crossley.

Q. Was he not employed or consulted in drawing up an information against the late Provost-Marshal?—A. He was both employed and consulted by the Governor on that business.

Q. Was he (Crossley) not employed as an Advocate for the Provost-Marshal on his Trial, and did not the Governor order the Criminal Court who tried the late Provost-Marshal to admit Crossley into that Court as an Advocate?—*A.* He (Crossley) was ordered by the Governor, to the best of my belief, to act as Advocate or Friend for Mr. Gore on his Trial, and he was admitted as such the first day only under the direction of the Court that no question was to be put to him, but by the prisoner (Mr. Gore), to whom he might suggest any question that he (Crossley) might think necessary to his justification.

Q. Then you mean to say that Crossley was first employed to prepare the Accusation against the late Provost-Marshal, and afterwards to convince the Court that the Accusation was good for nothing?—*A.* It certainly appears so by my Answers.

Q. Were you induced to give it as your opinion that Crossley could be admitted to advocate any cause in a Court of Justice because you really thought so or because you was obliged to give that opinion from the terror you was under from the threats of the Governor?—*A.* It certainly was my opinion that Geo. Crossley, notwithstanding he had been found guilty of Perjury, that his having received a free Pardon under the Seal of this Colony, as well as having expiated his Offence by having served the term of his Transportation, that he was in the Eye of the Law a new man, and was as competent, and ought to be considered as possessed of the rights of a Citizen, as any other Person, and that was my reason to give it my opinion that he was competent; but upon looking further into the Statutes at large, and more particularly an Act, but in whose reign I do not this moment recollect, but the tendency of which was that if any Attorney, Councillor, Agent, or any other person connected with the Law, after having been so convicted, should come into any Court to plead in any cause before that Court, it was competent for the said Court, after having enquired in a Summary way, the Court could transport such person for seven years. In consequence of which I did alter my original opinion during the Trial of Mr. Gore.

Q. As you knew it was Criminal for any Attorney who had been convicted of Perjury to practise as an Attorney or Agent in any suit at Law, what induced you to consent to Crossley being employed as an agent to prepare the information which now causes me to stand in the degraded and humiliating condition of a Criminal at the Bar of this Court?—*A.* You will give me leave to make a pointed distinction between a Person coming into a Court as Attorney or Agent and that of a person knowing his abilities as a private individual and possessed of that knowledge which I found myself deficient in. I therefore did not consult him as an Attorney or Agent, but as an Individual possessed of such knowledge as I required.

Q. Do you mean to say that a man who is employed to do another's business is not his agent?—*A.* I certainly do mean to say that he is not, and for this reason: As the word Agent in the Eye of the Law, for if any gentleman of any condition was possessed of knowledge which I wished to acquire and I did obtain it, the general acceptation in point of Law could not be applied to such person from whom I obtained such information.

Q. If I understood your evidence right, you have not only declared that you consulted Geo. Crossley and acted upon his Opinion, but that you did absolutely employ him to draw up the Information against me, and which Information so prepared by Crossley I am now obliged to defend myself against. I therefore repeat again:

Did you not know it was improper to employ any such character in performing so solemn an Instrument as that of an Accusation against a Gentleman of Honor and Character, which accusation it appears from a paper in your own handwriting was intended to overwhelm him with Disgrace and Misery, and to expose him to a punishment worse than Death—a Public and Disgraceful exposure in the Pillory?—A. I did consult Geo. Crossley for the purpose of obtaining every Information he could give me upon the object of my then Attention, and I did conceive that the most useful manner in which he could give me that knowledge was by drawing up that Information in the technical Terms of the Law, of which, as I said before, I felt a deficiency. I request that that paper, alluded to in the question, may be produced, that I may be enabled to make such remarks upon it that may satisfy the Court that it was not for sinister purposes alluded to in the question. The Paper read as follows :—

" If any one by writing, printing, preaching, or other speaking shall use any Words or Sentence to incite the People to hatred and contempt of the King or of the Government and Constitution of this Realm, he shall incur the punishment of a high Misdemeanour—that is, Fine, Imprisonment, and Pillory; and for a second offence he is subject to a similar punishment or transportation for seven years, at the discretion of the Court." " But a prosecution for a Misdemeanour under this Act must be brought within Six months; and this Statute shall not affect any prosecution for the same crimes by Common Law, unless a prosecution be previously commenced under the Statute. This Statute is to continue in force until the end of the next Session of Parliament after the demise of the Crown. 36 Geo. III, c 7."

I answer that having asked Geo. Crossley under what Act he conceived the Crime with which McArthur was charged would come, he told me that it was the 36 Geo. III, c 7. Knowing as I did that I was not possessed of that Act I asked him what could be done for the want of it, conceiving that it might be called for; Crossley told me that it would have been better if the Act had been in the Colony, but as it was not he told me that Mr. Lord had the last edition of *Blackstone's Commentaries.* I should find a note subjoined by Mr. Christian, the Editor of that last Edition, which said note quoted that part of the said Act applicable to the Case. I sent for it and extracted what appears before the Court in my handwriting, and I believe that it will be admitted that it was my duty, as Judge-Advocate, to make myself Master of the Law, that in the event Mr. McA. had been found Guilty, to give the necessary information to the Court, that they might apply all or any part, in their discretion, and that it could not be, nor can it be considered without forcing the Intent of that Paper to be viewed in any other point than that I have stated, or prejudging the Case. I further say that let a man be Guilty of such 'and such Offences, which has nothing to say whatever to the point on which he is consulted; and as I believed that there was no other person in the Colony so competent to give it as Crossley, I was under the necessity of applying to a bad Character for that information which, if I could have got from an honest man, I would not have applied to Crossley.

Q. Do you, or do you not, know that it was unlawful to employ Geo. Crossley in the way you have?—A. To which I answer that perhaps as Judge-Advocate, and as a Law Officer, it would have been much better to have been guided by my own Judgment than to have had recourse to any other persons; but as I did not abide by that, I conceive it no further improper than because Mr. Crossley was a bad Character; and it is no uncommon thing for even Judges in England to take the opinion of Solicitors, Councillors, or Attorneys without enquiring the Characters of the Persons applied to.

Q. Do you mean to say it is no uncommon thing for a Judge in England to take the private Opinion of an Attorney who has been convicted and publicly punished for Perjury?—A. I believe that a Judge will not ask the opinion of any person in Public, and who they ask in private is more than I can answer to.

Q. I have endeav'rd by all the means my humble abilities can suggest to me to obtain a direct answer to a plain question, and I now beg to submit to the Court the propriety of their deciding whether Mr. Atkins shall answer to the Question: Did he, or did he not, know that it was unlawful to employ such a Character as Geo. Crossley in preparing such an Instrument as the Information on which I am now tried?—A. I do not think it unlawful, but improper.

The Prisoner requests Mr. Atkins's Letter to him, informing him of the irregularity of the Officers and Crew of the Parramatta, Schooner, may be read—which was read as follows:—

"Sir,   "14th December, 1807.
"I have it in Command from His Excellency the Governor to acquaint you that the Master, Mates, and Crew of the Schooner Parramatta, of which you are Owner, have violated the Colonial Regulations by coming unauthorised on shore, and that in their justification they say you have deprived them of their usual Allowance of Provisions, and that they have no means of subsistence on board your Schooner. In consequence of such their representations I request your Attendance at Sydney to-morrow morning, at 10 o'Clock to shew cause for such your Conduct.
                                          "I am, &c.,
"John McArthur, Esq., Parramatta."   "RD. ATKINS, J.-A.

Q. Was this the first Complaint that you received of the same kind from the Officers and Seamen of the Parramatta, Schooner?—A. I think it was. I was sent for up to Government House, and from information that the Governor had received (I believe from Mr. Campbell) that Mr. McA. had stopped the Wages and Provisions of the Officers and Crew of the Parramatta, Schooner, I was desired by the Governor to send for the Master, Mates, and Crew of the said Schooner and take their depositions on that head; I did so, and the following is the Deposition taken:—

                                          "14th December, 1807.
"Mr. John Glen, Master of the Parramatta, being required to state his reasons why he has abandoned the Command of said Ship, and why he suffers the sailors to come on shore, delivers the accompanying paper as his reason for so doing; that in consequence he went to Mr. Rob't Campbell, the Naval Officer, and delivered to him a Copy of the said Letter, before witnesses, who told him that he would acknowledge he had got a copy of the same, but had no Answer to give; that as soon as he had left Mr. Campbell he went to Government House for the purpose of showing the Letter to the Governor, who refused receiving it. That he then went on board

and read said Letter to the men and sealed up the hold. Says that since that period—the 8th Inst.—he has not received any Provisions whatever from his Owner, Mr. McA., and that since that period he has considered himself as divested of all Command over the said Vessel and Crew, nor has he exercised any since that time.

" JNO. GLEN."

" Mr. John Graves, Chief Officer of said Ship, says that he was present on board the Parramatta at the time Mr. Glen read Mr. McArthur's Letter to the Ship's Crew; that in consequence he left the Vessel and has since that time received no provisions from her or from his Owner, nor has he exercised any Command whatever over the Crew.   " JOHN GRAVES."

" George Brown, John Knight, Christopher Shelto, George Piercy, and Alexander Lincoln, John Thomas and John Marks, sailors belonging to the Schooner the Parramatta, respectively say: That since the 8th Inst. they have done no duty on board the said Ship; neither have they received any provisions; that they have since that time generally been on shore, but usually slept on board.

<table>
<tr><td></td><td>" GEO. BROWN (his x mark).</td></tr>
<tr><td></td><td>" JOHN KNIGHT (his x mark).</td></tr>
<tr><td>" Sworn before me, this</td><td>" CHRIST'ER SHELTO (his x mark).</td></tr>
<tr><td>14th December, 1807,—</td><td>" GEO. PIERCY (his x mark).</td></tr>
<tr><td>RD. ATKINS, J.-A.</td><td>" ALEXR. LINCOLN (his x mark).</td></tr>
<tr><td></td><td>" JOHN THOMAS.</td></tr>
<tr><td></td><td>" JOHN MARKS (his x mark)."</td></tr>
</table>

In consequence of that Deposition I wrote the Letter.*

Q. Were you directed by the Governor to write the Letter?—A. I will not positively say that I was or was not, but that I was desired by the Governor to take the Depositions and act upon them.

The Prisoner requests the Letter to be read, in Answer to the one of the 14th of December, which was read as follows:—

[Here followed a copy of the letter from John Macarthur to Richard Atkins, dated 14th December, 1807, which was also included in the indictment.]

Q. At the time you rece'd the above Letter, did you not know that the Naval Officer had refused to enter the Vessel or to allow her Cargo to be landed?—A. Mr. Campbell informed me that he had done so—Mr. Campbell, the then Naval Officer.

Q. Did you not also know that the Naval Officer had possession of the Schooner's Register and all her Papers, and that he refused to give them up, although repeatedly pressed so to do?—A. I have no doubt that he was in possession of all the Papers, and that he had refused to give them up.

Q. As it appears that the Schooner's Cargo could not be landed because Entry was refused, and it is certain she could not go to Sea without her papers, was it right to call upon me to be answerable for the conduct of Officers and Seamen belonging to a Vessel over which I had no control?—A. I thought it was right.

Q. How long would you have considered me bound to be answerable for the Conduct of the Officers and the Crew of the Schooner if her papers had never been restored or she been permitted to enter?—A. So long as the Crew had no means of living on board, or until something was settled respecting the Schooner.

* Note 83.

1808.
11 April.
Proceedings at
the trial of John
Macarthur.

Q. Then it was to be understood that if the late Governor and the Naval Officer had thought proper never to settle the matter in dispute respecting the Schooner, I should have been for ever bound to pay, victual, and to be answerable for the Conduct of her Officers and Crew?—*A.* If the Governor or Naval Officer, or either of them, did an illegal Act, an action would lay and they must answer it.

Q. Do you mean to say that if I had brought an Action against the Naval Officer, and that he had urged in his justification that he had acted by the Orders of the late Governor, that you, under the then existing state of things, would have presumed to allow me to enter an Action?—*A.* To that I answer that if Mr. McArthur had come to me and said I want to enter an Action against Mr. Campbell for £10,000, the Action or Writ would not have been refused him; but when the cause came to be heard and was at issue, I cannot take upon myself to say what the Decision of the Judge-Advocate and the two Members would have been, or what plea Mr. Campbell would have set up. I would not have refused to enter an action against Mr. Campbell as Naval Officer.

Q. Did you not know that the Schooner had been removed from a place of safety in the Cove and taken by order of the Naval Officer or Governor into one so exposed that she was in the greatest danger of drifting on Shore?—*A.* I did not.

Q. Do you not know that it is the duty of the Master of any Vessel immediately to make a Protest in behalf of himself, his Owners, and the Underwriters concerned whenever he shall conceive that he has been illegally treated?—*A.* I dare say it is.

Q. Is not making a Protest the first Legal preparatory step to the commencement of a Civil Action?—*A.* I do not know that it is.

Q. Were you not the Notary Public of this Colony?—*A.* Governor King appointed me to that Office.

Q. Did not the Master of the Parramatta Schooner, accompanied by myself and Mr. Blaxcell, present a Protest to you?—*A.* He did.

Q. Did you not at first refuse to note that Protest?—*A.* I did.

Q. Did I not request you to acquaint yourself with its Contents?—*A.* I think you did.

Q. Did you not then read the Protest and require some hours to consider whether you should note it or not?—*A.* I think I did.

Q. Did you not return the Protest, refusing to have anything to do with it?—*A.* I returned the Protest with my Compliments, and begged leave to decline receiving it.

Q. Did you not first consult the Governor, and ask him whether you should or should not discharge the Duty of your Office?—*A.* I carried the Protest up to the Governor to know if I should receive it or to that effect; but I must observe that it was no more than my usual Practice to do when the Executive Government was in any manner concerned.

Q. Did you consult the executive Authority in those cases because you thought it was right, or because you was afraid had you done otherwise that you would have been ill-treated?—*A.* If I had taken it without the Governor's consent, I should, I have no doubt, have been reprobated by him, and should have incurred his Displeasure.

Q. Has the late Governor ever expressed his displeasure to you for acting in a manner that you knew to be right, in indecent and outrageous Invectives?—*A.* He certainly has expressed his Displeasure in a manner that has hurt my feelings.

Q. State to the Court the most improper Expression that you recollect he has ever made use of to you on such an Occasion?—*A.* I have received very abusive language from him, but cannot call it to mind.

Q. Has he never told you, and at the same time shaking his fist in your face, " Sir, you have two Opinions, have you—a Public Opinion and a Private Opinion "?—*A.* I think he did make use of the Gesture and Words.

Q. Did he never call you a Wretch or Villain?—*A.* Never to my recollection.

Q. Did he never so operate on your feelings by his threats and by his violence as to induce you to declare that if you knew His Excellency's Opinion you would take care to make your own conform to it?—*A.* Such a circumstance is not within my Recollection; but I might have said that in trifling things I would give way rather than have words with him.

Q. Have you not, through fear of his Vengeance, been induced to give Opinions and to decide on Causes contrary to what you know to be just?—*A.* I do not think it a proper Question, therefore decline answering it.

Q. Did you never alter an Opinion which you had given as Judge of the Civil Court by Order of the Governor?—*A.* I cannot call it to mind.

Q. Do you think it impossible that you did so?—*A.* I do not think it likely that I did so.

Q. You have heard the Letter of the 14th Decr. read ;—Did you not, in consequence of the receipt of that Letter, issue the following Warrant for the apprehension of my Person. *Warrant read, as follows* :—

" New South Wales : Whereas Complaint hath been made before me upon Oath that John McArthur, Esq., the Owner of the Schooner Parramatta, now lying in this Port, hath (illegally) stopped the provisions of the Master, Mates, and Crew of the said Schooner, whereby the said Master, Mates, and Crew have violated the Colonial Regulation by coming unauthorized on shore; And whereas I did by my Official Letter, bearing date the 14th day of this Instant Dec'r, require the said Mr. McArthur to appear before me on the 15th day of this Instant Dec'r, at ten o'Clock of the forenoon of the same day; And whereas the said John McArthur hath not appeared at the time aforesaid nor since, these are therefore, in His Majesty's name, to Command you to bring the said Jno. McArthur before me and other His Majesty's Justices on Wednesday next, the 16th Inst. Dec'r, at ten o'Clock of the same day, to answer in the premises; and hereof fail not.

" Given under my Hand and Seal, at Sydney, this 15th day of December, 1807.   " RICHD. ATKINS, J.-A.

" Mr. Francis Oakes, Chief Constable, Parramatta."

—*A.* I did.

Q. Did you issue that Warrant by order of the Governor?—*A.* No; but with the Approbation of the Governor.

Q. Under the Authority of what Law or Statute did you issue that Warrant?—*A.* I conceived that I issued that Warrant for a contempt of not obeying the official Summons I sent.

Q. What Summons do you allude to?—*A.* The Letter* I wrote to you on the 14th Dec.

* Note 83.

1808.
11 April.

Proceedings at
the trial of John
Macarthur.

Q. Do you not know that the law requires a Summons should be directed to a Constable, Commanding him to serve it, and do you not know that a sealed Letter is no Summons?—*A.* I do know that a sealed Letter is no Summons in Law; and if my politeness to Mr. McArthur has brought me into an error, I think it ought not to be taken advantage of.

Q. Do you not think, when you talk of Politeness, that Politeness and Justice required you should have taken Legal Measures; if you thought your letter not properly attended to, that you should have issued a Summons and not a Warrant, which was to drag a Gentleman from the bosom of his family at a late hour of the night?—*A.* I conceived Mr. McArthur would have taken that Letter as I meant it—a Summons; therefore, it not being attended to, I did issue a Warrant.

Q. Do you conceive that because you chuse to disregard Legal Forms all other persons are bound to conform to your Practice?—*A.* I certainly do not.

Adjourned to 9 o'Clock to-morrow morning.

3rd February.—Court met pursuant to Adjournment. The Prisoner continued to cross-examine Mr. Atkins.

RICHARD ATKINS, Esqr., Sworn :—

The Prisoner requested the Warrant,* dated 15th December, may be read, which was read accordingly.

Q. Did you think the Cause assigned in that Warrant sufficient justification to order the Arrest of my Person?—*A.* I did, in conseq'ce of supposing my Official Letter had the full effect of a Summons, and conceiving that Letter was treated with Contempt, was the cause of my issuing the Warrant.

Q. Do you not know that when two or more Magistrates are assembled in Sessions that they are a Court of Record, and possess more ample powers than any single Magistrates; and do you not know that it is declared in *Burns's Justice* "that the Sessions cannot award an Attachment for Contempt in not complying with their orders"?—*A.* I know of no such Court in this colony as a Court of Sessions; all Judicial Proceedings in this Colony have been guided by the Patent, and it there expresses that the Courts of Civil and Criminal Jurisdiction shall be Courts of Record. I believe no attachment of the person can issue from a Court of Sessions in England.

Q. Do you not know that it is declared in *Addington's Penal Statutes* that no Justice of the Peace can meddle with any matters except some Statute gives them power, and none by Common Law?—*A.* I do not recollect that Addington mentions it. I have not been in the habit of consulting law books, but on such cases to obtain information as were at the time under my consideration.

Q. Can you produce any Statute or Law Authority to justify the apprehension of my person for not choosing to comply with the request, or order, communicated in a Sealed Letter?—*A.* I cannot.

Q. Do you not know that it is declared by Burn "that if a Magistrate issue a Warrant, wherein he hath no Jurisdiction, or in a matter wherein he hath no Cognizance, the Officer ought not to

* Note 84.

execute such Warrant; for if a Justice send a Warrant to a Constable to take up one for slander or the like, the Justice hath no Jurisdiction in such cases, and the Constable ought to refuse the execution of it "?—*A*. I dare say I have read it, and have no doubt it is as stated by Mr. McArthur.

Q. What steps did you take after being informed that that Warrant had not been executed?—*A*. Mr. Oakes came to me in the morning to my Office, about 6 o'Clock in the Morning, 16th December, and acquainted me with the Circumstances that did occur in the Execution of that Warrant on Mr. McArthur at Parramatta. Mr. Oakes informed me that he had received my Warrant and that in consequence that he had gone to Capt. Abbott to mention that he had such a Warrant; that after that he went to Mr. McArthur's house and found him in bed; he (Oakes) rapped at the window, on which Mr. McArthur got up, and, on Mr. Oakes entering the House, informed Mr. McA. that he had a Warrant against him. Mr. McArthur requested to look at it and Oakes gave it to him, and I think said a Copy was taken by Mr. Han'l McArthur; that Mr. McA. flew into a violent passion and said he never would submit to it, and he stated also that Mr. McArthur said he never would submit to such horrid Tyranny; that Mr. McArthur wrote the following Paper :—

" Mr. Uakes,—You will inform the Persons who sent you here with the Warrant you have now shewn me, and given me a Copy of, that I never will submit to the horrid Tyranny that is attempted until I am forced; that I consider it with Scorn and Contempt, as I do the persons who have directed it to be executed.

" Parramatta, 15th December, 1807.   " J. McARTHUR.·'

Which being read, Mr. McArthur acknowledges to be the Paper he wrote and gave to Mr. Oakes. I further state that Mr. Oakes informed me that he had said to Mr. McA., " Shall I wait on you in the Morning, Sir? " Mr. McA. replied, " Keep that Paper, for that will be your justification," or to that effect; and that Mr. McA. further said, " Leave them alone; they will soon find a Rope to hang themselves," or words to that effect. Oakes then went away from Mr. McA., and came down the next morning and related what I have before stated, on which· I went up to Government House and asked for the Governor. They informed me he was not stirring, on which I went away, and was sent for in about half an hour. I related to the Governor what Oakes had told me, and showed the Governor the Paper, on which the Governor ordered me to convene a Bench of Magistrates, which I did, and they met. The following Paper being read is their proceedings thereon :—

BENCH OF MAGISTRATES.

The Judge-Advocate; Major Geo. Johnston; Robt. Campbell, John Palmer, Esquires.

                                        " 16th December, 1807.

" MR. FRANCIS OAKES, Chief Constable at Parramatta, came this day before us, and deposed on oath that in consequence of a Warrant from the Judge-Advocate to him directed, he went to the house of John McArthur, Esq., and presented to him the said Warrant; that after his having read it, he fell into a great rage, and said he would not submit to it until he was forced; and said, ' You may tell the Person that he treated it with Scorn and Contempt as he did the Persons that sent it,' and said that if the

1808.
11 April.

Proceedings at
the trial of John
Macarthur.

Persons directing that Warrant had served it instead of him (the Deponent) he would have spurned them from his presence; and Deponent further says that the said Jno. McA. declared in his presence that if he came a second time to come well armed, for that he would never submit until there was blood shed. The said John McA. averred that he had been robbed of £10,000; that he did not consider he had committed a Criminal Act; and that he would not go, but said, 'Let them alone; they will soon make a Rope to hang themselves.' " FRANCIS OAKES.

" Sworn before us, this 16th December, 1807,—
" RD. ATKINS,
" GEO. JOHNSTON,
" ROB'T CAMPBELL,
" JNO. PALMER."

Mr. Oakes further says that he saw John McArthur, Esq., write the Paper.*

The Court was then cleared, and after much Conversation respecting the business before them, they were of Opinion that as I had issued the first Warrant it would be better for me to issue the Second, which I did, and the following is a Copy which was read :—

" New South Wales: Whereas on the 15th day of December, in the Year of our Lord 1807, I issued my Warrant. directed to Mr. Francis Oakes, Chief Constable at Parramatta, authorizing him to bring before me John McArthur, Esq., to answer in the Premises; And Whereas the said Francis Oakes came this day before a Bench of Magistrates, the Judge-Advocate, Major Geo. Johnston, Robert Campbell, and John Palmer, Esq'res, Justices assigned to keep the Peace being present, and deposed on Oath that the said John McArthur had refused to obey the said Warrant, but treated it in the most contemptuous and disrespectful manner; these are therefore to authorise and require you to take into your Custody the Body of the said John McArthur, Esq., and him safely lodge in His Majesty's Jail until he shall be discharged by due Course of Law;—for which this shall be your Authority.

" Given under my Hand and Seal at Sydney, this 16th day of December, in the Year of our Lord 1807.

" RICHARD ATKINS, J.-A.

" To Mr. John Redman, Chief Constable at Sydney; Mr. Francis Oakes, Chief Constable at Parramatta; and all other His Majesty's Peace Officers and all others whom it may concern."

I delivered the Warrant into the hands of the persons to whom it is directed and they went away. In a short time they returned and said they could not find Mr. McArthur. Some little time after, Mr. Gore, the Provost-Marshal, came and acquainted me that Mr McArthur was at Mr. Grimes's, the Surveyor-General. This being communicated to Redman or Oakes, either by me or Mr. Gore, in consequence of which they went to Mr. Grimes's House, and, I suppose, found Mr. McArthur there, for he (Mr. McArthur) was almost immediately brought before me, In consequence as they (Redman and Oakes) informed me that Mr. McArthur wished to be brought before a Magistrate, and Mr. McA. was by me admitted to bail to appear before a Bench of Magistrates as on the next

* Note 84.

morning. A Bench of Magistrates was, in consequence, convened for the next morning. The following Paper being read to the Court is their proceedings thereon :—

FULL BENCH OF MAGISTRATES.

The Judge-Advocate ; Major Geo. Johnston ; Capt. Ed. Abbott ; Robt. Campbell, John Palmer, Esquires.

"17th December, 1807.

" THE Bail of John McArthur, Esq., having brought him into Court, and the Bench was going to proceed when Mr. McArthur objected to Mr. Campbell sitting as a Magistrate on this Investigation, stating, among other reasons, that his improper conduct as Naval Officer has been the cause of the present business, and that he had Notice given him that it was his intention to institute an Action against him for £10,000, and that for these reasons he considered Mr. Campbell as an interested person, therefore objects to him.

" On the Bench being cleared Two of the Magistrates were of opinion that the Objections against Mr. Campbell sitting were sufficient, and two Magistrates were of a contrary Opinion.

" On the Court being opened, and the Opinion of the Bench read, Mr. McArthur, after having addressed the Bench in a few words, waived his Objections against Mr. Campbell's sitting ; but Mr. Campbell declined taking his Seat, and the Bench proceeded.

" Mr. Gore, the Provost-Marshal, came into Court and delivered the following Messages from the Governor to the Judge-Advocate : ' His Excellency the Governor-in-Chief is debarred the opportunity of consulting with the Judge-Advocate, the only Law Officer of the Crown in this Territory ; he has directed me to submit to the Judge-Advocate, now sitting in Court, whether the affair now investigating before the Bench—it being a matter not of Property but a charge of a Criminal Nature—whether a Member of the Bench can be excepted against as incompetent, from interested motives, to sit as a Member thereof.'*

" Mr. Francis Oakes, Chief Constable at Parramatta, sworn, says that he received a Warrant from the Judge-Advocate for the purpose of bringing John McArthur before him, in consequence of which he went to the house of Mr. McArthur and served it on him. Mr. McArthur asked him to let him look at it, which he did. After having read it he fell into a great Rage and said, ' You may tell the persons directing that Warrant that I never will submit unto it until I am forced, for I treat it with Scorn and Contempt, as I do the persons who have sent it.' He further said : ' Had the person who directed it served it instead of you he would have spurned them from his presence.' He further said, ' that if I came a second time to come well armed, for he never would submit till blood was shed.' He further said : ' That he had been robbed of £10,000, and that he had not committed any Criminal Act, and that he would not submit to the Warrant ; but let them alone, they will soon make a Rope to hang themselves.' He likewise mentioned the Governor's Name with a great deal of disrespect. The Paper† being shewn him, he says he saw Mr. McArthur write that paper, which he afterwards delivered to him.

"FRANCIS OAKES.

* *Note in the original.*—This message answered by letter to His Excellency the Governor, but not copied in the proceedings.   † Note 84.

"Mr. McArthur being asked if he has anything to say, states: 'That he stands before you, Gentlemen, as a Prisoner under the Authority of a Warrant from the Judge-Advocate.' Mr. McArthur proceeding to call in question the legality of the Judge-Advocate's Warrant, the Bench stopped him, not considering it an Object for their Consideration.

1808.
11 April.

Proceedings at the trial of John Macarthur.

"Mr. McArthur stands committed for a Criminal Court.

> "RD. ATKINS.
> "GEO. JOHNSTON.
> "ED. ABBOTT.
> "JNO. PALMER."

Bail given.

In consequence of such Committal Mr. McArthur was admitted to Bail to appear before the next Criminal Court.

Questions from the Pris'r to Mr. Atkins. When you went to the Government House to inform the Governor of what I had said respecting your first Warrant, did you take Oakes with you, or was he sent for?—*A.* He was sent for to Government House, and he came.

Q. What occasioned the late Governor and yourself, with Oakes, to go out of Government House and to walk on the high Ground behind?—*A.* To prevent any Person hearing what was said.

Q. Was not Oakes's Story put into a state of arrangement during this walk, as it was to be told before the Bench of Magistrates ordered to assemble?—*A.* It was not. Oakes related his story to the late Governor, the Governor asked him some questions respecting the business, and Oakes was desired to attend the Bench of Magistrates and relate what he knew and had stated to the Governor.

Q. Was the late Governor civil and kind in his manner to Mr. Oakes?—*A.* He was.

Q. It appears from the Proceedings of the Bench of Magistrates who committed me for Trial that Mr. Campbell voluntarily declined sitting after being objected to by me;—Do you think he did so because he thought he had no right to sit or because he was ashamed to sit after the remarks I had made on his attempting it?—*A.* I must confess that I was surprised that on Mr. McArthur making the first objection to him that he did not decline sitting; and I gave him an opportunity by saying, I think, "What do you say, Mr. Campbell?" but he made no Reply, and the Court was cleared, and on the opening of the Court Mr. McArthur then addressed the Court on the impropriety of Mr. Campbell sitting; but Mr. McArthur waived his objection, when Mr. Campbell declined sitting, and the Bench proceeded.

Q. Do you remember that when Mr. Gore, the Prov't-Marshal, came before the Bench of Magistrates and delivered a Message requiring the immediate attendance of the Judge-Advocate on the Governor, that he, amongst other things, said " that he was directed by the Governor to accuse me of an overt Act of high Treason," and my requesting that part of the Message might be taken down?—*A.* I well recollect Mr. Gore, the P.M., delivering a Message to that effect.

Q. Do you remember that when I was brought before the Bench of Magistrates on the 17th Dec'r that you declared the Bench had power either to commit me for Trial or to punish me at their discretion, either by Fine or Imprisonment?—*A.* Such an Assertion is not within my recollection.

1808.
11 April.
Proceedings at
the trial of John
Macarthur.

Q. Previous to the Bench assembling, had you not a firm reliance that two Members of the Bench—namely, Messrs. Palmer and Campbell—would coincide in your Opinion as to the manner I was to be treated?—*A.* I firmly believe, from the Observations that I have made on those Gentlemen as Magistrates, that they would in most cases—but I will not take upon myself in all—give their opinion in a manner most congenial to the late Governor's opinion.

Q. After my Commitment you have stated that Geo. Crossley prepared the Information now exhibited against me;—did he do that with the Approbation or by the desire of the Governor?—*A.* Crossley told me he did.

Q. Have you not been obliged to govern yourself by the Opinion of Crossley in every step which has been taken since my Commitment until the late Governor was happily superceded?—*A.* Crossley's Opinion as to the mode of proceeding did govern me to the extent stated.

Q. Was the Paper now before the Court, containing questions to be asked, the Evidences in support of this Prosecution drawn up by you or by Crossley?—*A.* Not a single question was drawn up by me, but the whole by Crossley; and I recollect that Mr. Palmer, one of the Witnesses, in my presence asked Geo. Crossley for the Copy of the Questions to be asked him, which he (Crossley) had promised to furnish him with. Crossley replied he should have them in the course of an hour.

The following Paper the Prisoner requested might be read, which was read as follows, viz. :—

"25th January, 1808.

"The King } Court of Criminal Jurisdiction.—It is ordered by
v. } the Court that unless the Defendant plead to
John McArthur. } issue, on or before Eleven o'Clock, on the Twenty-sixth Day of this instant January, Judgment of Guilty be recorded in this Cause.

"By the Court,   R.A., J.-A."

Q. State to the Court, was that Paper prepared by You or Geo. Crossley?—*A.* I copied it from a Paper prepared by Geo. Crossley.

Q. To what purpose was it intended to be applied?—*A.* That, in the event of Mr. McArthur refusing to plead, that Judgment of Conviction should be entered upon Record agreeable to the Statute.

Q. Why was it expected that I should refuse to plead?—*A.* It was a matter of doubt, suspecting that Mr. McA. would object to me as Judge of the Court, and should his objections have been overruled by the Court, Mr. McA. might not have pleaded; and then Judgment might have been entered on Record agreeable to the Statute.

Q. Did you expect that if I had objected to you as a Judge in my cause, that the Court would have overruled the Objection; and if you did, did you expect that they would have been governed in their Opinion by fear of Consequences?—*A.* I am sensible that, whatever Opinion they might have given on that occasion, that they would not have been biassed by fear of Consequences, but would have been actuated by the dictates of their own Ideas.

Q. You have repeatedly declared that the first Comp't in the information relating to the affair of the Stills was introduced contrary to your Opinion?—*A.* When Mr. Crossley brought me the Information in his own handwriting, he informed me that the first Comp't was grafted from an Information which he had drawn up some time back by the desire of the late Governor, and which I

1808.
11 April.

Proceedings at
the trial of John
Macarthur.

knew nothing of, and that it was expressly the Governor's direction to him, though contrary to his Ideas, that that should make the first Comp't in the present Information.

The Prisoner requests the Proceedings of a Bench of Magistrates of the 24th Oct'r, 1807, may be read, which was read as follows, viz. :—

[*Here followed a copy of the proceedings in the suit of John Macarthur v. Robert Campbell, Jr.; a duplicate of those forwarded as enclosure numbered 11 to Governor Bligh's general despatch to the Right. Hon. William Windham, dated 31st October, 1807.*]

Q. Did you take the above Proceedings up to the late Governor that day?—*A.* I did.

Q. Did you not meet me in the Street that Evening and tell me that you had been grossly abused for having done your Duty?—*A.* I cannot recollect it.

Q. Were you not grossly abused at Government House when you took up the Proceedings of the Bench?—*A.* When I went with the Proceedings to Gov't House I was accompanied by Messrs. Campbell, Palmer, and Gore; upon going into the room where the Governor was, accompanied by those Gentlemen, I began, as usual, to read the Proceedings. After having read the whole, the Governor did not say anything, but as far as looks would go, appeared to me to be highly dissatisfied. A Conversation then took place between Messrs. Campbell, Palmer, and Gore, and Mr. Griffin, in which I appeared to be the butt of their Obloquy and Sarcasm for the opinion I had given on those Proceedings; this continued for near half an hour; at last the Governor said, "Never mind it; this will do"; the expression was said in such a way as clearly indicated to me the dissatisfaction of the Governor to the Opinion I had given on that occasion, and that I did on that Evening and since mention to several persons that " my feelings were never more hurt than they were on that day." I thought I had been bullied and browbeaten by those persons.

Q. Do you remember meeting me in the Street a few days previous to the 24th October, and having said that I was not aware of the hundredth part of the Wickedness going forward in the Government House?—*A.* I will not take upon myself to say that I made use of those express words; but I remember opening myself very freely to Mr. McArthur at that time, and I have no doubt that I did express my high Dissatisfaction at what was going on at Government House.

Q. Previous to the Assembling of the Criminal Court on the 25th of January last, did I not make repeated written Applications to you for a Copy of the Information on which I am now prosecuted on?—*A.* I received three Letters on that Subject from Mr. McArthur, and my reason for refusing to give it was because Mr. Crossley had informed me that by Law he was not entitled to it until he had pleaded to it.

Q. Has not the late Governor declared in your presence that his Will should be the Law, and woe be to him that dared to oppose it, or words to that effect?—*A.* He has.

Mr. Atkins's Depositions—which he acknowledges to be correct—the Prisoner requests may be ent'd in the Minutes—which are as follows :—

[*A copy of the deposition of Judge-Advocate Atkins was also forwarded as enclosure No. 9 in this despatch.*]

Q. from the Court to Mr. Atkins.—Have you reason to suppose that Mr. Campbell is acquainted with the questions he was to be asked on Mr. McArthur's Trial?—*A.* I cannot speak to my own knowledge; but Mr. Crossley informed me that he was going down to Mr. Campbell to show them to him.

Mr. Edmund Griffin being sworn :—

There being fifteen Questions found in the Papers left by Mr. Atkins in the Court on the 25th January in the handwriting of Mr. Griffin, the Governor's Secretary, which questions Mr. Atkins intended to ask this Evidence on the present Trial, the Court asked them in their original Order.

Q. 1. Was you or not present on the 8th day of March, 1807, or at any other and what time, when the Master of the Ship or Vessel the Dart came to Gov't House with Mr. Harris, the then Naval Officer, or with any other and what person, to make a Report to the Governor of the Arrival of that Vessel, with the Manifests or accounts of the Cargo?—*A.* I was.

Q. 2. Upon his delivery to the Governor, or any and what other Person, the Accounts of that Vessel's Cargo, did it or not appear there were two Stills on board; and if yea,* Did or not the Governor direct that those Stills should be deposited in one, and which, of His Majesty's Stores, to be there Safely kept until an opportunity happened that they might be sent back to England, or what directions were then made with respect to those Stills being suffered to be landed. and on what Conditions?—*A.* Upon Mr. Harris, who was the then Naval Officer, with the Master of the Vessel producing the Ship's Papers, it appeared on one of the papers that there were two Stills on board the Vessel, and I think that Mr. Harris particularly pointed them out: the late Governor expressed much surprise at it, and desired that they should be put into the bonded Store, on which Conditions they were allowed to be landed, and directed Mr. Harris to have them in readiness to be sent back to England.

Q. 3. Then you say that the Governor's permission to let those Stills be landed was only on the Condition that they should be put out of the Ship into one of the King's Stores to be kept safe until they could be sent back to England?—*A.* I did understand so.

Q. 4. Those directions were given by the Governor in your Presence to Mr. Harris, the then Naval Officer,—were they or not?—*A.* They were.

Q. 5. Did you at any time after, and when, hear Mr. Harris tell the Gov'r that the Bodies of those Stills were at Mr. McArthur's house and not in the Store?—*A.* I heard Mr. Harris tell the Governor so, some time the latter end of March or April.

Q. 6. What did the Gov'r direct Mr. Harris to do on the receipt of such an Account, or what Orders did he give?—*A.* The Governor directed Mr. Harris to comply with his original Orders that the Stills as invoiced should be lodged in the bonded Store.

Q. 7. Was you present in the Month of Oct. last, or at any other time, when the Governor gave a direction to Rob't Campbell, Esq., the now Naval Officer, to have those Stills taken from the Store and sent on board the Ship or Vessel the Duke of Portland?—*A.* I was present when those directions were given at the time Stated.

Q. 8. Was or not the Vessel the Duke of Portland at that time laying in Sydney Cove, and in a short time expected to depart on her Voyage to England, or how else?—*A.* She was laying in the Cove and expected to sail for England.

* Note 85.

1808.
11 April.
Proceedings at
the trial of John
Macarthur.

Q. 9. Upon it being at this time discovered that the Bodies of those two Stills were not put into the King's Store, according to the condition they were suffered to be landed upon, what Orders did the Governor, or any other person, to your knowledge, give on that occasion?—*A.* The late Governor directed Mr. Campbell, the Naval Officer, should Ship the Stills compleat.

Q. 10. Do you in any ways know the handwriting of the Prisoner (John McArthur, Esq); and if yea, look upon the Paper writing now produced and shewn to you, and say if it is or not the handwriting of the Prisoner, as you know or believe. Letter read as follows:—

" Sir,   " Sydney, 19th October, 1807.
" Mr. Blaxcell has communicated to me the Contents of a Letter from you of the 12th Inst., relative to two Stills imported into this Colony in my Ship the Dart, which you State the Governor has directed are to be shipped on board the Duke of Portland.

" In Answer, I must beg you to acquaint the Governor that I have nothing to do with the Still belonging to Capt. Abbott, and that it is my intention to dispose of my own to some Ship going to India or China. If that sh'd be objected to, the head and worm can be disposed of as His Excellency thinks proper, and I shall appropriate the Copper to some domestic use.

                                              " I am, etc.,
" Robert Campbell, Esq.   " JOHN McARTHUR."

A. Letter produced (as above), To the best of my knowledge is Mr. McArthur's handwriting.

Q. 11. It not only appears by this Letter that the Prisoner was Owner of the Ship the Dart—as he calls it my Ship the Dart;—do you or not know by any other and what way that the Prisoner was the Owner of that Vessel or not?—*A.* I have no doubt Mr. McArthur was an Owner of the Ship Dart.

Q. 12. Did you hear the Prisoner make a Speech, or address, which at his request was taken down by the Judge-Advocate; and if yea, look upon the Paper Writing now produced to you, and say if those are or are not the words then and there pronounced by Mr. McArthur or not: declare?—

[*Here followed a copy* of Macarthur's address (attested by Richard Atkins, J.-A.) to the court in his suit against Campbell, jr.*]

A. Yes.

Q. 13. Do you or not believe and understand by these words, and the manner in which Mr. McA. used them, that this Speech was made to incite hatred and ill-will to the Governor and Government of this Territory in the minds of the People there assembled, or how otherwise?—*A.* After leaving the Court, I expressed myself on my return to Government House to the Governor and several Gentlemen assembled there that I did conceive Mr. McArthur had spoken a very inflammatory Speech, and that it appeared to me to have a tendency to incite hatred and ill-will against the Governor and Government of this Territory.

Q. 14. Does it or not appear to you by the Words then used that the Speech was calculated to inflame the minds of the bye-standers against the executive Power of the Government, and to insinuate to the People that the rights and property of the individuals were unlawfully infringed upon by the Governor and those in the Authority of the Government, or how else?—*A.* It did so appear to me.

* Note 86.

1808.
11 April.
Proceedings at
the trial of John
Macarthur.

Q. 15. Is it not Customary for the Governor to give his directions verbally in matters like those enquired of?—*A.* The Governor always gives his orders to the Naval Officer verbally, to the best of my recollection.

The Prisoner, being asked what questions he has to propose to this Witness, asks:—

Q. Are you not in the habit of being consulted by the late Governor and of giving your Opinion on most subjects of Public business to him?—*A.* I have been.

Q. Did the Governor on important business frequently follow your Advice?—*A.* Yes, in some instances.

Q. How old are you?—*A.* Twenty-one in September next.

Q. On the Oath you have taken, did you not know that the Bodies of the Stills remained in my possession from the time that they were landed until the time they were forcibly taken away?—*A.* I did not know they were in Mr. McA.'s possession until I heard it from Mr. Harris, some time in March or April.

Q. As you heard the Bodies of the Stills were in my possession in March or April, did you not know that they remained there until they were seized?—*A.* In Oct., when the late Governor gave the Naval Officer (Mr. Campbell) directions about the Stills, I expressed my doubts that Mr. Harris had put them in the Bonded Store.

Q. You have stated that you thought the Speech I made to the Bench of Magistrates respecting the unlawful Seizures of the Bodies of those Stills was an inflammatory one, and that it appeared to you to carry hatred and ill-will to the Governor and Government of this Territory;—Pray, Sir, were you born in England or Turkey?—*A.* I was born and educated in England.

Q. Now, Sir, as you have acted as Counsel to the Governor, are you not acquainted that the property of an Englishman cannot be taken from him without lawful Authority in writing?—*A.* I do not know the Law sufficient to answer it.

Q. Do you not know that these Coppers were taken from me without any Authority in writing?—*A.* I really believe there was none.

Q. Has it never occurred to you that such a seizure of property and such a mode of Proceeding was more likely to incite hatred and ill-will against the Gov'r than anything I could say or do?—*A.* No, never in the most distant manner, except that I suppose Mr. McArthur would not like it.

Q. How did you know I would not like it?—*A.* I supposed so, the Stills having been brought into the Colony, and the Gov'r ordering them out again.

Q. Did you not know that these Stills were regularly entered in the Custom House at London, and that they were fairly and openly brought into this Colony; and do you not know that the Manifests from the Custom House contained a Specification that two Stills made part of the Cargo of the Dart?—*A.* The two Stills did appear on one of the Ship Dart's Public Papers; by that paper the Stills did appear to be brought openly into this Colony.

Q. Do you not know that the Heads and Worms of both Stills were readily given up to the Governor's order and lodged in the Public Stores?—*A.* I did know, from Mr. Harris's report, in March or April, that the Heads and Worms were given up directly and sent into the Public Stores, but that Mr. McA. said that he would keep

1808.
11 April.

Proceedings at
the trial of John
Macarthur.

the boilers—they were full of Medicines, which came packed from England, in them—and after their being emptied he would employ them for domestic purposes.

Q. Can, you State to the Court what made the late Governor so particularly anxious to get those Stills out of the Colony?—*A.* The Governor conceived they were illegally imported, and that he would send them to the Commissioners of the Customs.

Q. On the Oath you have taken, did you never hear anything of a Plan of carrying on a Public Distillery, under the firm of Palmer, Campbell, and Co., or either of those persons?—*A.* Never heard such a thing hinted at.

Q. You have stated that the Governor frequently gives verbal Orders—not written ones?—*A.* To the Naval Officer.

Q. Does he not frequently give verbal Orders to other persons?—*A.* Yes.

Q. Have you never heard the Governor assign a reason for declining on a variety of occasions to give written Orders, and declining on many others to give written Answers?—*A.* I cannot charge my recollection.

Q. Have you never heard him tell persons, at their peril, never to give any written messages he might send them with?—*A.* I cannot charge my recollection.

The following Paragraph being read from the Copy of the Governor's public Letter to the Secretary of State, by the Duke of Portland :—

"The Distillation of Spirits being prohibited for the best and wisest reasons, everything has been done to prevent such a destructive business being carried on; nevertheless a Defiance has been set up to Government by Mr. McArthur in importing a Still of sixty Gallons, directed to himself, and another of forty Gallons directed to Capt. Abbott, of the New South Wales Corps, brought out in the Ship Dart, consigned to Mr. McArthur as part Owner of the said Ship with the House of Hulletts and Company, of London. These Stills I ordered into the King's Stores to be sent to the Custom House, in London, by the safest opportunity. On their being directed to be shipped on board the Duke of Portland the Coppers were found in Mr. McArthur's house, from whence, after some objection, they were taken by a young gentleman (the Naval Officer's clerk) in consequence of my orders, and shipped with the other parts; but Mr. McArthur, not being satisfied, called the Naval Officer's Clerk before a Bench of Magistrates (the Minutes of which are enclosed) and on which I regret being obliged to shew by his Speech the inimicability of his mind to Government, *and particularly in renewing a remembrance of a Person who has been the disturber of the tranquillity of the Colony.*"*

The Prisoner requires the Evidence to state why this erasure was made?—*A.* The Governor, on comparing the Copy, desired it to be left out without assigning any particular reason; but I think the Governor thought it too severe.

Q. By what Act do you divine the Governor's thoughts?—*A.* I do not pretend to any such Act.

The Prisoner having closed his Cross-Examination of this Witness on the part of the Crown, wished to defer the Examination on his own part until he had made his Defence, which was overruled by

* The pen had been drawn through the words printed in italics (*see* note 87).

1808.
11 April.

Proceedings at
the trial of John
Macarthur.

the Court, who are of opinion that Mr. Griffin should now be examined fully.

Court adjourned until 8 o'clock to-morrow morning.

4th February, 1808. The Court met, pursuant to adjournment.

MR. EDMUND GRIFFIN, Sworn:—

Q. from the Prisoner. I am charged with endeavouring to excite hatred and ill-will in the minds of the inhabitants of this Colony against the Governor and Government of this Territory, and you have been brought forward to support that Charge. It is now my purpose to call upon you to prove that I am an innocent and falsely accused man. I therefore ask you whether you ever witnessed any Act of mine which displayed a determination on my part to commit so enormous an offence?—*A.* It does not come within my knowledge; only the act of making a Speech before a Bench of Magistrates, which I conceived to be inflammatory.

Q. There is the Speech* alluded to—Point out the part that you conceived inflammatory?—*A.* That part, " It would therefore appear, &c.," and from the very particular manner the Speech was delivered to the bye-Standers.

Q. Do you not know that my property was taken from me?—*A.* I know that the two Bodies of the Stills were taken from your house.

Q. What Office does the Person hold in the Colony that took them?—*A.* The Person that took them was, I believe, Mr. Robt. Campbell, Junior, and he was Clerk, as I understood and know, to Mr. Rt. Campbell, Magistrate and Naval Officer.

Q. What Authority had that person for seizing these Copper boilers?—*A.* I believe he had the Naval Officer's verbal Orders.

Q. Did you ever hear or ever read of any man being Criminally prosecuted for going before a Bench of Magistrates and Complaining that his property was wrested from him by a non-accredited individual, who had no authority to show to justify such a deed of violence?—*A.* I do not recollect ever having read or heard of such an Act.

Q. Did you ever hear of any man being dragged as a Criminal to the Bar of a Court of Justice for calling upon the Magistracy of the Country to decide whether his property could be so taken from him with impunity to the Offender?—*A.* No, I never did.

Q. Do you not know that the Law allows every man to complain to the Magistracy of any injustice he may conceive he may have suffered?—*A.* I have always understood that every Individual has that right.

Q. What more then have I done, and upon what ground do you defend your Declaration that I intended to excite Hatred and ill-will in the minds of the People against the Governor and Government of this Territory?—*A.* I have no other ground than having been present and heard it, and it is my Opinion.

Q. When you came as a Spectator of the Proceedings of that Bench of Magistrates, can you on your Oath say that you came with an honest, impartial, and unprejudiced mind?—*A.* I cannot say that I was unprejudiced against Mr. McArthur from everything I had heard.

Q. You have frequently seen me at Government House in apparent habits of familiar intimacy with the late Governor?—*A.* No more familiar than any other Gent'm that visits Government House.

Q. Have you not frequently seen me Breakfast, Dine, and Sup at Government House on the same day?—*A.* I cannot charge my recol-

* Note 86.

1808.
11 April.

Proceedings at
the trial of John
Macarthur.

lection if on the same day; but I have frequently seen Mr. McArthur Breakfast, Dine, and Sup there.

Q. Do you not know that the Governor has more than once lamented that he had not a spare Bed in the house to accommodate me or any part of my Family when down at Sydney?—*A.* Yes.

Q. When you have seen me at Government House, have I not always been respectful and attentive to the late Governor?—*A.* It always appeared so to me.

Q. Have you not always seen the Governor polite and attentive to me?—*A.* Yes.

Q. Do you not know that during this apparent friendly intercourse that the Governor was taking measures, both by his Speeches and his Letters, to distress and ruin me?—*A.* No, I do not.

Q. Did you never hear the Governor give any Opinion of me during that time?—*A.* I cannot charge my recollection.

Q. Did you never hear the Gov'r speak of me before he came here?—*A.* I do not recollect.

Q. Do you not know that he had determined, before he came here, to obstruct me in my pursuits?—*A.* No, I do not.

Q. Have you never heard any reason assigned for my ceasing to visit at Government House?—*A.* No. I heard the Governor say one time, on his coming from Parramatta, that Mrs. McA. paid a visit at the Gover'nt House there, when she apologised for Mr. McA. not calling on account of ill-health, on which the Governor said to Mrs. McA. that he w'd call on Mr. McA. He did so, and Mr. McA. came in from riding while he was there, and Mrs. McA. informed the Governor he had just been riding round his Farm. The Governor expressed his surprise at seeing Mr. McA. so well, having been informed the day before by Mrs. McArthur that he kept his room. Mr. McA. told the Gov'r that that was the first time of his going out since his illness, and that Mrs. McArthur seemed confused. The Governor said he thought it was done that Mr. McA. might have to say that the Gov'r had called on him and that he would not return the Visit, since which time Mr. McA. has not been at Gov't House.

Q. Were you present as Secretary to the Governor in the Court of Appeal when a Suit of mine was brought forward against And. Thompson?*—*A.* I was.

Q. When that Court adjourned the first time, had I been heard in support of my Appeal, or in answer to a paper given in by the respondent?—*A.* No.

Q. Did you not afterwards furnish me with a Copy of the respondent's Paper?—*A.* I did at your request.

Q. When the Court of Appeal was opened did I not present a Paper to the Governor, stating it was an answer to the Respondents? —*A.* Yes.

Q. Did not the Governor refuse to receive it?—*A.* Yes.

Q. Did he not instantly direct you to read his Award against me, without ever having heard me utter a word in support of my Plea?—*A.* Yes, he did.

Q. Have I ever been in Government House since that day?—*A.* To the best of my recollection, you never have.

Q. During the time the *Sydney Gazettes* were published, was not the Proof Sheet always brought to Gov't House to be corrected and approved?—*A.* Yes.

* Note 88.

Q. In the *Gazette* which was published the week before the Governor pronounced Judgment against me, was there not a Paragraph which completely corresponded with, and appeared calculated to justify, the Governor's decision. *Gazette produced, and read as follows :—*

. " 5th July, 1807.

" THE extraordinary Fluctuations that have taken place in the Price of Wheat since the Flood in March, 1806, have given rise to many Litigations, which a little sincerity might have superceded. It is generally known that when Grain was plentiful nearly all Bargains made at the Agricultural Settlements were for the produce of the Ground at the Store prices. The amount in cash was divided into Bushels, and Notes issued, rating Wheat at its then present maximum—which seldom exceeded 7s. 6d. per Bushel, though now at 28s. to 30s. Losing sight then of the Value of the Commodity in exchange for which these Notes had been exacted, and the specific terms of the Contract are conscientiously demanded, without any consideration of the excessive Loss which must evidently fall upon an unfortunate Debtor who, to cover an original demand of £50, must necessarily expend £200. How conscience can reconcile the Requisition must be referred to those who are interested in the event of such Transactions.

" It is a happy reflection, however, that Disputes of this nature are no longer permitted to arise from an indiscretion in the mode of granting Notes of Hand. By referring to His Excell'y's General Order of 1st November, 1806,* and the Proclamation published on the 3rd of January last,* we find a remedy to an evil which many have to lament the pressure of. In the Public Ordinances above quoted we beg to remind the public it is enacted ' that all outstanding notes, payable in Copper Coin or Colonial Currency, are to be considered as Sterling Money, and the amount sued for as if the term Copper Coin or Colonial Currency had not been expressed ; and further, that all Checks and Promissory Notes shall be drawn payable in Sterling Money, in consequence of the undefined manner in which Notes have hitherto been given, and the many evils and Litigations which have resulted therefrom in the Colony.' It is not only the Duty but the interest of every well-meaning man to pay strict obedience to a Regulation, the design of which is to abolish the Chicanery to which the inaccuracy of these Instruments gave rise. Grain was once considered as a Legal Tender for a Debt contracted, and was, therefore, one Species of Colonial Currency. It is evidently dangerous, however, for an individual to bind himself in the payment of any specific number of Bushels of any Article to which unforeseen events may give even . a tenfold value—and Shylock still insists upon his Bond. The Orders admit not of misconstruction ; the Sterling value of the Note when drawn, in justice should be demanded, whatever be the mode of payment, and any excess upon that just demand is 'unquestionably an invasion of another's rights "?—*A.* I recollect the Paragraph alluded to by Mr. McArthur.

Q. On the day after the Governor pronounced his decision in the Court of Appeal, was not another *Gazette* published containing a Paragraph completely applicable to my suit? *The Gazette produced (12th July) Vizt :—*

EXTRACT.

" IN cases respecting Wheat-Notes, wherein the present holder is not the person to whom a Note was originally granted, is it not an

* Note 89.

insult to common Justice that he should require a greater consideration for it than he had himself allowed?

"This question is suggested in the idea that if A. receive from B. a
Note of Hand (drawn payable to the latter by C.) for twenty Bushels
of Wheat—it then being at 8s.—he must of consequence have taken
such Note in consideration of the Sterling sum of £8 at the most.
Then, if A. retain possession of the Note until Wheat became five
times as valuable as it was when he received it, and then insists upon
the sum of twenty Bushels, whether does he sue for £8 or £40; and if
any Sum that exceeds his first and only equitable Claim, upon what
principle of Equity can he pretend to justify it?"—*A.* I recollect
the paragraph.

Q. Do you remember in the following *Gazettes* the Publication
of two Letters under the signature of "An Oculist"?—*A.* Yes.

EXTRACT from the *Sydney Gazette* of the 26th of July, 1807.

"To the Editor of the 'Sydney Gazette.'

" Sir,—Every lover of truth must be pleased at the impartiality
of your excellent Publication; but much as I admire your luminous
style of reasoning and the logical precision of your Arguments in
general, I confess they failed of their usual effect in the Lecture you
favoured us with in your last paper on A., B., C.

" Permit me to continue the Case you have assumed, and to suppose C. holds an Obligation drawn by A., when Wheat was at 8s.
per Bushel, to deliver a certain quantity to B. or Bearer, and that
before the Obligation is discharged it falls to 5s., could C. demand
either from A. or B. the difference in value occasioned by such a
depression of the Price? If not, it appears that the literal Tenor of
every Engagement ought to be fulfilled, and that specific Contracts
must be sacred and binding, as it surely will not be denied that if
the holder of an Obligation is to bear the loss when the commodity
he has bargained for falls in its Value, he ought not to be deprived
of the benefit of its rise.—Your constant reader,

"AN OCULIST."

" P.S.—I think your honest Zeal has animated you rather too
much in your Paper of the 5th Inst., and the interest I feel for the
success of your useful labours induces me to recommend you to
abstain as much as possible from calling Names, for, altho' well-
informed, liberal people are sensible of the powerful effects of that
Practice, there are many narrow minds with whom it may do you
injury."

" To the observation of 'An Oculist,' the Publisher begs leave to
reply that, unconscious as he is of any Superiority in his style of
reasoning, yet he has by no means an Inclination to doubt the sincerity of the very flattering Encomium with which so well-informed
a Correspondent has been pleased to honor him.*

" That the manner in which the 'Oculist' has continued the
quoted proposition is at once precise and logical, the judicious
reader doubtless will pronounce; but how far his reasoning may be
considered to preponderate must be submitted to the Public Opinion.

" Before he presumes to offer an objection to the above Statement
of the case between the parties A., B., and C., the Publisher respectfully refers the reader to his observations on the subject of Wheat
Notes contained in the *Gazette* of the 5th and 11th of the present
Month, wherein he presumes not to oppose the fulfilment of specific

* Note 90.

Contracts, but to warn the Individual against entering into engagements that might be attended with consequences fatal to his interests.   He considered it a well-known fact that the Notes floating about the different Settlements were made payable in Grain, because it was, with little exception, the only mode of payment which the Settler had, and ought therefore rather to be considered as a security for the payment of a specific sum than as a specific Contract for furnishing the number of Bushels expressed. In the one case, the holder of a Note for twenty Bushels, granted to him under a presumption that 8s. per Bushel would be the Market Price when due, upon the receipt of £8 in money could not be a loser, since that was in the first instance the very extent of his demands. That circumstances may induce him to give a preference to the mode of payment expressed must be admitted, as may a portion of inconvenience likewise from the incapacity of the Drawer to comply with the strict Letter of the Note.

" In reversing the picture, the Publisher requests the ' Oculist's ' attention to the doleful condition of a Drawer, who, to satisfy an actual demand of £8 originally, must from the most direful necessity, produced by the most disastrous of Events, procure by Purchase what Providence had deprived him of, and that at a period too, when instead of 8s., the Market Price was advanced to £4 Sterling per Bushel.

" In answer to the Query—Supposing a depression in the price to have taken place?—he begs to observe, that in engagements of this kind, men generally look forward to natural events, and that as no such depression could happen unexpectedly, it was in every man's power to guard against its consequences ; but now, unhappily, the case was different, the rise was rapid and not gradual, Distress and Consternation were universal. It was a dreadful reverse, which none but the Supreme could have averted, and against which man had not the power to provide. Upon reference to the Papers above alluded to, the ' Oculist ' will perceive that the publisher was not so immoderate as to presume a wish that his poor opinions should be accepted as a Lawful Standard.   To conscience did he appeal, and if his opinions were erroneous, he trusts they are not unreasonable.

" To the Charge contained in the Postscript, he is at a loss to reply, as he never has in any instance so far departed from a principle of justice as to have recourse to Personal Animadversion or reflection, and he considers the ' Oculist ' to be in possession of too liberal a mind seriously to suppose him capable of so manifest a breach of Duty and good Manners."

EXTRACT from the *Sydney Gazette* of the 2d of August, 1807.

" *To the Printer of the ' Sydney Gazette.'*

" Mr. Editor,—If I disapproved of your representations and reasoning on the subject of Wheat-Notes previous to the Publication of my Letter, my disapprobation is not diminished by the reply that accompanied it, for you still persevere in what now appears to me a studied attempt to mislead and confound the Public opinion.

" I have nothing to do with the persons who you say persecuted the unfortunate sufferers from the Flood at the Hawkesbury, and endeavoured to compel them to expend £200 to discharge an obligation originally not worth £50. For the Credit of the Colony, I hope no circumstance of the kind has happened, and as far as my own

1808.
11 April.

Proceedings at
the trial of John
Macarthur.

knowledge extends, I must say, I know of no instance of such obduracy; but on the contrary, of many wherein the holders of Contracts have humanely postponed their demands to the present Year.

" In your Paper of the 5th and 12th Ult., you assert that ' the Sterling Value of the Note (meaning Wheat-Notes) when drawn in justice, should be demanded, whatever be the mode of Payment; and any excess upon that just demand is unquestionably an invasion of another's right; and that to demand more for such a Note than the original value given ' is an insult to common justice.'

" An endeavour to propagate such Doctrines excited my attention, and was the cause of your being troubled with my Sentiments. The spirit of what I am desirous to maintain is, that if I, this Year, agree and pay for a certain quantity of Wheat to be delivered next Season, I have an indisputable right to demand its delivery, however it may rise in price; because, let it fall ever so low, I am obliged to receive the Wheat without any compensation for its diminished value.

" Should it, however, be the will of Providence to afflict this Colony again, and to cause a large portion of our Crops to be destroyed, I must indeed be insensible to every feeling of humanity, were the person with whom I have contracted amongst the sufferers, if I did not commiserate his distress. But is the same forbearance to be expected by every Individual that I may have dealings with? Am I to forego my right with the man who has escaped the Calamity, and only resists my claim that he may sell his Wheat at a tenfold price, or employ it in some profitable Speculation? Or if I do not comply with such a demand, am I to be stigmatised with ' exacting,' with insensibility to the feelings of ' Conscience,' with the opprobrious epithet of ' Shylock,' with being ' an invader of another's rights,' ' an insulter of common justice.'

" To use such Language upon any occasion is in truth, Mr. Editor, ' a manifest breach of Duty and good Manners '; and what is infinitely more reprehensible, the pernicious Doctrine with which you have contrived to work up these invectives, is calculated to produce no less an effect than that of destroying all confidence in our mutual dealings with each other, and to banish integrity and good faith from our Society.

" Before I conclude, allow me to correct an Error you have entertained, respecting my expectations of the effect my Letter would produce. Be assured, I never indulged an Idea that my reasoning, however logical, however just, would ' preponderate ' against the force of any opinion you have avowed."

" AN OCULIST."

Q. What sensation did those Letters produce upon the Governor and yourself?—A. I do not recollect any particular sensation they produced, or any remark being made upon them; but I recollect the Printer's answers were said by the Governor to be well written.

Q. Did you never hear the Governor say who he supposed the " Oculist " to be—yes or no?—A. I do not recollect that I did.

Q. Did you never hear him denounce vengeance against the Author?—A. No; I do not recollect.

Q. Do you not know that I have never been paid the money awarded to me in the Court of Appeal of which I have been speaking?—A. I knew it was not paid some time since, but not now.

Q. Did you not send me in a Bill of £5 odd for Fees in the Court of Appeal?—*A.* Yes.

Q. Did I not send you back a Draft on the Provost-Marshal for the amount, accompanied by an advice underneath, in which I desired the P.-M. to pay your demand and to remit me the Balance of what might remain due on the Sums the late Governor had awarded me?—*A.* You did.

Q. Did you not send me back that Draft with an indorsement on the back that it was refused payment for want of effects?—*A.* I did.

Q. Did I not immediately send the Money, and obt'n'd your Receipt?—*A.* Yes.

Q. Did you not then feel that I had appealed to the Governor for the recovery of a just Debt, and all the justice I had got was a refusal to be heard in support of my Plea and £5 odd money out of pocket?—*A.* No, I did not.

Q. Did you not know, Sir, that a Verdict had been given by the Governor in my favour for £35; did you not know that I had not received a farthing of it, although many months had expired; and did you not know that I had been obliged to pay you £5 odd Fees?— *A.* I knew the Verdict was given in favour of Mr. McA.; the Provost-Marshal told him the money was not paid, and the £5 odd money was paid me for Fees.

Q. As Secretary in the Court of Appeal, knowing these circumstances, was it not your duty to have informed the Gov'r that such a dreadful stain was cast upon the Justice of this Government?—*A.* I do not conceive I am obliged to answer any questions that may criminate myself—not that I conceive this to be one. I told Mr. Gore, the P.-M., that I conceived he ought to have put the Verdict in effect. Mr. Gore did not conceive he had, until applied to by the parties; but on my advice he got attested Copies of the Award from me, saying he would execute it.

Q. Did you never tell the Governor this circumstance?—*A.* I think I did, some time afterw'ds.

Q. What did he say?—*A.* I do not recollect what he said, or if he said anything.

Q. Did he give you no Orders?—*A.* None that I recollect.

Q. You have seen Geo. Crossley, the well-known perjured and pilloried Attorney, frequently at Government House?—*A.* I have.

Q. Do you know whether the Gov'r consulted him on points of great conseq'nce respecting the Government of this Country?—*A.* Yes.

Q. Did he not consult Geo. Crossley and follow his advice by sending a Letter to His Honor, the Lieut.-Governor, accusing the Officers composing the Criminal Court, which assembled on the 25th January, of Treasonable Practices? *Letter read as follows:*—

" Government House, Sydney,
" Sir,   " 26th January, 1808.
     " In answer to my Letter of yesterday, I received a verbal message by my Orderly from you that you was rendered by illness totally incapable of being at Sydney. I apprehend the same illness will deprive me of your assistance at this time; and the Judge-Advocate having laid a Memorial before me against Six of your Officers for practices which he conceives Treasonable, I am under the necessity of summoning them before me, and all the Magistrates have directions to attend at Nine o'Clock to-morrow morning.

1808.
11 April.

Proceedings at
the trial of John
Macarthur.

" I leave it for you to judge whether Capt. Abbott sh'd be directed to attend at Sydney to command the Troops in your absence.   " I am, &c.,
" To Major Johnston,   " WM. BLIGH.
        " Commanding His Majesty's New South Wales Corps."

A. I wrote such a Letter by the Governor's direction from the Governor's own handwriting; but I suppose the Governor did consult Crossley, as the Governor and Crossley were in an adjoining room, and the Governor brought that Letter in his own handwriting.

Q. Did not Crossley draw up the Information which I am now defending myself against by Order of the late Governor?—*A.* The Governor sent an order for Crossley for that purpose; but when Crossley came down he produced a Letter from the Judge-Advocate, requesting him to draw out such an Indictment or Information which the Governor approved of, saying that he had sent to Mr. Crossley to see how far the information drawn by Crossley would agree with that drawn by the Judge-Advocate, and the Governor approved of Crossley's proceeding to draw out an Information, and directed him to do it.

Q. Did not Geo. Crossley write all the questions which the Judge-Advocate was to ask the Evidences to support this Prosecution?—*A.* Yes.

Q. You also copied them?—*A.* Yes.

Q. Did you ever rehearse or repeat your Answers to these questions before the late Governor?—*A.* I did repeat the purport of what I could answer to those questions to the Governor.

Q. Were you present at Gov't House on the 24th October, when the Judge-Advocate brought the proceedings of the Bench of Magistrates to the late Governor?—*A.* Yes.

Q. Was not the Judge-A.'s opinion on that Bench very much found fault with?—*A.* Yes.

Q. Who found fault with it?—*A.* I believe I did myself, and the Gov'r too.

Q. In what manner was he found fault with?—*A.* I do not recollect the particular manner in which he was found fault with.

Q. Would you not have been very much hurt if you had been spoken to in the same Language that you used to the J.-A. on that occasion?—*A.* I think I should.

Q. Was it not determined between that day and the 1st of the following month that the Judge-Advocate should be punished for his opinion by a representation to Government against him?—*A.* No, it was not; the representation was determined on before.

Q. Has not the Judge-Advocate been terrified by the Threats and Violence used towards him at Government House into a declaration that he would take care that his opinions should always agree with the Governor's—or words to that effect?—*A.* I do not know.

Q. Have you ever heard that he has been opprobriously abused by the Governor?—*A.* Yes.

Q. In what language?—*A.* I do not recollect the particular language.

Q. As you have declared you have repeatedly given your Opinion to the Gov'r, did your humanity ever induce you to point out to him the indecency of abusing an old man of 60 years of age,* who filled the first Law Office in the Colony?—*A.* I never did give my opinion on that head as I recollect.

* Note 91.

1808.
11 April.

Proceedings at
the trial of John
Macarthur.

Q. As you have stated that my words and manner before the Bench of Magistrates was in your opinion calculated to excite the hatred of the People against His Majesty's Government, did it never occur to you that degrading and abusing the only Judge in the Colony was more likely to bring the Government into contempt than any words or looks of mine?—*A.* No; it never did occur to me.

Q. On the 25th October, the day following that on which my complaint was made before the Bench, did you not go to Woola-moolla, by order of the Gov'r, to consult with Crossley on the best means to pursue to punish me for having made that complaint?—*A.* I did go to Wallamalla, by order of the Gov'r for Crossley to make his remarks, which he did in writing, stating it was indictable, and an Indictment or Information was drawn up by Crossley.

Q. I suppose you went to Wallamalla because it is in a remote situation, and there was a better chance that your meeting with Crossley might be kept secret?—*A.* No; a message was first sent to Mr. Devine's; but Crossley being at Wallamalla, I went down there.

Q. Who was present at the Consultation?—*A.* Mr. Palmer, myself, and Crossley.

Q. In consequence of this Consultation, it was determined to draw out an Indictment against me, which Indictment or Information now stands as the first comp't in the information before the Court, does it not?—*A.* To the best of my recollection it does.

Q. What was the cause that this first part of the Information was laid by?—*A.* I do not recollect the cause, but it was so determined by the Governor.

Q. As you found it was not to be brought forward, had you not the curiosity to enquire why it was preserved?—*A.* No.

Q. At what time was it determined that this Paper should be brought forward again?—*A.* At the time Oakes made a complaint.

Q. Were the Warrants that were issued against me issued in consequence of any orders or directions from the Gov'r?—*A.* It does not come within my knowledge.

Q. When the information was received at Government House in what manner I had treated the first Warrant, was there not a great deal of joy and exultation?—*A.* None, that I recollect.

Q. Did you feel no particular satisfaction?—*A.* No.

Q. Was the punishment that was to be inflicted upon me never talked of?—*A.* I think I recollect Crossley telling the Governor what the Punishment would be if the charges were proved.

Q. Was it never suggested that it would be necessary to send me out of the Colony?—*A.* I have frequently heard the Gov'r speak on that subject, but never say that it would be absolutely necessary, or that it would be done. I have heard, but from whom I do not recollect, that there was an idea that Mr. McA. would make his escape from the Colony and not stand his Trial.

Q. How long is it since you first heard the Gov'r talk of sending me out of the Colony?—*A.* Prior to the issuing of the Warrants and since.

Q. Was it not intended to favor me with a little Fine and Imprisonment before they sent me away?—*A.* It was intended, if you had been convicted before the Court, and that they had awarded a sentence of Fine and Imprisonment, that that Sentence sh'd have been put in execution, as I suppose.

Q. Did you never hear the Pillory spoken of?—*A.* I have heard that you w'd be subject to that Punishment. Crossley said it.

1808.
11 April.

Proceedings at
the trial of John
Macarthur.

Q. Was it not also thought a little flogging would be beneficial?—*A.* I do not recollect any such thing.

Q. Do you know the principal cause of the Governor's dislike to me?—*A.* No, I do not; but I have heard the Gov'r say that it was extraord'ry that a gent. of Mr. McA.'s property could not live quiet, and that he thought Mr. McA.'s general conduct very improper.

Q. How long ago is it since you heard the Gov'r say so?—*A.* Before the business of the Stills.

Q. What proof of disquietude had I shown before the business of the Stills?—*A.* I do not know. I do not myself recollect any.

Q. I suppose had I submitted quietly to the unlawful seizure of my property and the Illegal Arrest of my person, I sh'd have passed with the Gov'r as a quiet, good sort of Man?—*A.* I cannot say.

Q. Did you never hear the Gov'r express a dislike to my possessing so large a Property in the Colony?—*A.* No; but the Gov'r in general terms had expressed his disapprobation of large Tracts of Land being given to Individuals, as to Mr. McArthur, Blaxland, &c.

Q. When it was found that the Officers who were appointed to sit on the Criminal Court on the 25th Jan'y would not allow Mr. Atkins to sit as Judge of the Court, what did the Gov'r determine to do with me?—*A.* The Governor appeared undetermined what to do before Mr. Gore's Deposition was taken, after which it was determined to keep the Pris'r in Jail until delivered by due course of Law.

Q. When it was determined to charge the Officers of the Criminal Court with Treasonable Practices, was it not also determined to charge me with the same?—*A.* Not to my knowledge.

Q. Was the Memorial charging the Officers with Treasonable Practices drawn up by Crossley?—*A.* I believe it was, and copied by Mr. Atkins's Clerk, and signed by Mr. Atkins, and sworn to at Government House, in the Governor's presence, before Messrs. Campbell, Palmer, Arndell, and Williamson.

Q. Was it not then determined, if the Officers did not submit to the will of the Governor, that the Criminal Court sh'd be set aside altogether and the Magistrates be invested with the Criminal Court's power?—*A.* No; but what I understood was, that what crimes could be taken cognizance of by the Magistrates would be; but in Criminal Cases they were to lay over until the Governor should hear from England.

Q. Have you never heard it said at Government House that I wanted to be the Oliver Cromwell of this Country?—*A.* Yes, I have; but do not recollect when or whether the Gov'r was present, or who said it.

Q. You have stated in your Evidence this day that you are in the confidence of the Governor; that you frequently give your opinion to him; that you have heard me accused of being a troublesome man—of being desirous of becoming the Oliver Cromwell in this Country;—now state what instances you know of troublesomeness, of Criminal or Bloody Ambition, which I have ever been Guilty of?—*A.* I cannot state any, or know of any.

Q. Do you know that I have ever attempted, directly or indirectly, by flattery, entertainments, or other sinister means, to form a Party in this Country against the late Gov'r?—*A.* I cannot say that I do know of any.

Q. Do you know of a single Act of Injustice that I have ever committed against any human being?—*A.* I cannot say that I do.

MR. ROBERT CAMPBELL, junior, sworn:—

[*This evidence was a repetition of that given by the same witness in the suit Macarthur v. Robert Campbell, Jr., a copy of which was forwarded as enclosure numbered 11 to Governor Bligh's general despatch to the Right Hon. William Windham, dated 31st October, 1807. This witness was not cross-examined by Mr. Macarthur.*]

ROBERT CAMPBELL, Esquire, sworn:—

The Nineteen Questions intended to have been asked Mr. Campbell by the late Judge-Advocate, the Court are of Opinion should be asked in their Original Form.

Q. 1. Did you or not, in the month of Oct. last, or at any other and what time, receive directions from His Excellency the Gov'r to have two Stills that had been brought into this Colony in the Ship or Vessel the Dart put on board the Ship or Vessel the Duke of Portland, to be sent in that Ship to England; and if yea, please to state what these orders were, and what you did in respect of those orders?—*A.* About the 10th Oct. the late Gov'r gave me verbal orders to go to the King's Stores and see that two Stills were lodged there, and, as I understood, were landed from the Dart, to be shipped on board the Duke of Portland. I think on or about the 12th of Oct. I wrote a Letter to Mr. Blaxcell mentioning the circumstance; about five or six days afterw'ds I received a Letter addressed to me as Naval Officer, the contents of which I communicated to the late Governor. He then told me that he could not comply with Mr. McA.'s request, for it was on the condition of the Stills being sent to England by the first Ship that he had allowed them to be landed, and inforced his former orders.

Q. 2. Was you or not present on the 24th Oct. last when the Pris'n'r made a charge against Mr. R't Campbell, the younger, for taking the bodies of these Stills out of his Dwelling-House a few days before; and if yea, did not the said R't Campbell, Jun., act in that matter by your Orders, and how many people might be assembled at that place on that occasion, as you believe?—*A.* Mr. Robert Campbell, Junr., acted by my orders in conseq'nce of the orders I received from the late Gov'r. I was present at the Bench of Magistrates on 24th Oct. I believe there might be Sixty or Seventy Persons present.

Q. 3. Did you hear the Pris'r make an Address or Speech on that occasion; and if yea, look upon the paper* now produced and say if those are or are not the words, or the tenor and purport of the words, used by him on that occasion: declare?—*A.* To the best of my recollection, those were the words spoken by Mr. McA., or to that effect.

Q. 4. Do you or not believe and understand by the words and the manner which the Pris'r used when he spoke those words, that that address was calculated by the Pris'r to excite hatred and illwill to the Governor and Gov't of this Territory in the minds of the people that were assembled on that occasion, or how else: declare?—*A.* It is a matter of opinion, but I certainly considered the Language inflammatory.

Q. 5. Does it not appear to you by the words "It would, therefore, appear that a British Subject, living in a British Settlement in which the British Laws are established by the Royal Patent,

* Note 92.

had had his property wrested from him by a non-accredited Individual, without any authority being produced or any other reason
being assigned than that it was the Governor's orders," that the
Pris'r by such assertion meant to inflame the minds of the People
to hatred and contempt of the Governor and Govt', and to assert
that the Governor's orders were contrary to the known Laws of
the Land: declare?—A. I have always conceived that the Governor
of this Territory could always give such Orders as he thought
proper, though repugnant to the known Laws of the Land, and I
know it has been done; but what were Mr. McA.'s motives in
making that Speech is impossible for me to say.

*1808.
11 April.*

Proceedings at
the trial of John
Macarthur.

Q. 6. Does it not appear to you by the words used by Mr. McA.
in that speech: "It is, therefore, for you Gent'm'n to determine
whether this be the tenor on which Englishmen hold their property
in New South Wales," that he meant to incite the Byestanders to
hatred and contempt of the Government and those entrusted with
the Executive Power of the Gov't, by insinuating that the property of Individuals was unlawfully taken, &c., thereby Libels
the Gov'r and Gov't, or how else?—A. I suppose that Mr. McA.,
when he made that speech, did conceive that it was unlawful to
have his property sent out of this Colony in the Duke of Portland. (Here read that part of the Patent* "our present and
all our future Governors and Lieut.-Governors, and our Judge-
Advocate for the time being shall be Justices of the Peace within
the said place or Settlement. And that all and every such Justice
and Justices of the Peace shall have the same power to keep the
Peace, Arrest, take Bail, bind to good behaviour, suppress and
punish Riots, and to do all other matters and things with respect
to the Inhabitants residing or being in the place and Settlement
aforesaid as Justices of the Peace have within that part of Great
Britain called England, within their respective Jurisdictions.")

Q. 7. The Court knows that every Justice of the Peace has a Right
by Law to order unlawful Stills to be seized, and do you or do you not
know it is so?—A. I have always understood that Stills were prohibited in this Colony, and that the Justices had the power to seize them.

Q. 8. Is it not the custom in this Colony for known persons to
execute the orders of the Governor without any Warrant in writing
for that purpose; and did you ever know any question made of the
Legality of an Order given verbally by the Governor of it being
illegal because it was not in writing before this cause of the Pris'r
in Oct. last: declare?—A. I know of no instance; I have always
rec'd my orders as Naval Officer verbally.

Q. 9. Is it not the custom for the Governor to give his directions
verbally in matters like that now inquired of or not?—A. Answered
before.

Q. 10. In or about the month of Nov'r last, did or did not the
Vessel the Parramatta Schooner arrive in this Port; and, if so, was
or not one John Glen the Master, and the Pris'r, John McArthur,
Esq., the Owner or part Owner?—A. Yes; there was such a Vessel,
commanded by John Glen, and Mr. McA. was part Owner.

Q. 11. Did or not that same Vessel sail from this Port on or
about the month of June last?—A. Yes.

Q. 12. Upon that vessel's returning here, was or not a charge
made against the Masters and Owners, or some of them, with
having suffered one John Hoare, a Prisoner under conviction in this

* Note 93.

Colony, to escape in that Vessel, and was not such accusation under some legal investigation after the return of the Ship?—*A.* Yes.

Q. 13. Was or not one or more Constables, by order, and whose order, in the month of November or December last, put'on board that Vessel; and, if so, was it not given in charge to such Constables and other Officers that they were placed there to prevent the Cargo or any part of it being smuggled on shore, or landed, or put out of the Ship without the usual permission?—*A.* Constables were sent on board by order of the Police Officer, and I understand for the sole purpose of preventing any part of the Cargo being landed until permission was given.

Q. 14. Is it not usual and customary in this Port to put any and what Constables or other Officers on board Vessels to prevent smuggling, or having the Cargo or any part of it landed without legal permission?—*A.* It is customary to send a Military Guard. This is the first instance where Constables have been sent in charge, to my knowledge.

Q. 15. In a .Letter, purporting to be written by the Prisoner to John Glen, in which letter the Pris'r charges you with a refusal to enter the Vessel the Parramatta Schooner, and other matters, and in the same Letter he desires Glen will give you a Copy of that Letter before a legal Witness; did you receive from Mr. Glen any such Copy?—*A.* I did.

Q. 16. Was not your reason for denying the Schooner to be entered because John Hoare, a Prisoner, had escaped in her from this Colony, and the Masters and Owners had refused to give the security to pay the penalty of their Bond if recovered by Law?—*A.* I received orders from the Governor not to enter the Schooner Parramatta; but wish to refer to my Letter-Book, which is now in the possession of His Honor the Lieut.-Governor.

Q. 17. That Suit being now depending, and security given to abide the event of an appeal, has not the Vessel since been entered and the Papers returned?—*A.* Yes, except the Register, all Registers being ordered to be kept in the possession of the Naval Officer until the Vessels got their clearance, which is the custom, as I understood, in other Ports.

Q. 18. Then the Bond, being as well for the Master and Owners as the Vessel and its Cargo, were engaged to perform the condition when security was given that what was recovered by Law if, in the event of the suit the recovery of the Penalty of the Bond should be affirmed, the Papers were restored and the Vessel entered in due course; was it so or not?—*A.* The necessary Bonds were given as required, and the Vessel was entered.

Q. 19. Is not that Letter of which you had a Copy, said to be written by the Prisoner to Mr. Glen, the Master of that Vessel, and by him directed to be read to the Ship's Crew, in your belief, calculated to create dissatisfaction in the minds of those people with respect to the administration of Justice in this Colony?—*A.* I rather think the letter was written for the purpose of making the Naval Officer responsible for the damage the Owners might receive by the detention of the Schooner, rather than influence the minds of the Crew against the Government.

Q. from the Court. Do you know by whom the above questions were framed?—*A.* I saw them in the handwriting of Crossley. He brought them to my house, for the purpose of shewing them to me, on the 18th ulto.

Questions from the Prisoner :—

Q. It seems the questions you have answered were shewn to you some time ago, in the handwriting of the well-known perjured and pilloried Attorney, Geo. Crossley;—have you ever, to him or to any other person, recited the Answers, or the purport of the Answers, you intended to give to those questions?—*A.* I never recollect having done so to any person.

Q. Do you consider it consistent with the honor of a Magistrate, and the integrity of a British Merchant, to receive any Information from such a character, relative to a prosecution on which you knew you were to be called as an Evidence?

Mr. Campbell declines answering the question. The Court cleared. The Court are of opinion that he is not obliged to pronounce a Judgment to his own Actions.

Q. In your answer to the 1st Question, you have stated that you rec'd a Letter from me in Answer to one of yours respecting two Stills; that Letter I wish to be produced (*letter produced and read**) ;—did you answer that Letter?—*A.* I did not.

Q. Is it not usual when Letters are written to Official Persons, and when the Letter expressly requires an answer, that either a written or verbal one sh'd be given?—*A.* Certainly it is customary; but I was ordered by the late Governor not to answer that Letter.

Q. Did the Governor assign his reasons for not allowing you to answer that Letter?—*A.* The Governor said those Stills were allowed to be landed from the Dart on the express condition of their being sent to England in the first Ship, and that no request of keeping any part of them could be complied with, and inforced his former orders.

Q. Did you communicate this determination of the late Governor to me; but did you not, without any explanation, send your Nephew to my house to bring the bodies of the Stills away?—*A.* No; I did not communicate the Gov's determination, and sent to order the Bodies of the Stills away.

Q. When you sent your Nephew to the King's Stores did he not find the Heads and Worms of those Stills in the King's Stores?—*A.* Yes.

Q. When I required a Receipt for the two Bodies which were in my possession, why did you insist upon my taking the following receipt, which expresses two Bodies, Heads, and Worms complete; and why did you refuse to give me a Receipt for the Bodies I declared myself ready to give up? *Receipt produced and read, as follows* :—

"Naval Office, Sydney, 22nd October, 1807.
"RECEIVED from Mr. G. Blaxcell, Agent for the Ship Dart, two Stills, with Heads and Worms, which were entered by that Ship on the 9th March last, addressed for Capt. McArthur and Capt. Abbott, and allowed to be landed on the express condition of being sent to England by the first Ship, and which Stills are now to be shipped on board the Duke of Portland, by order of His Excellency the Governor.
"ROB'T CAMPBELL, Nav. Officer."

A. As the orders given by the late Gov'r to me were to ship the Stills complete, I did not conceive it necessary to give but one Receipt.

Q. You have admitted that you rec'd the Heads and Worms from the King's Stores; it is also admitted that I had no part but the bodies in my possession; would you, if you was to receive an Anchor

* Note 94.

from a Blacksmith and a Cable from a Rope-Maker, refuse to give a receipt to each person because the Cable and Anchor are appendages to each other?—*A.* I would not.

Q. Upon what principle, then, did you insist upon my taking a receipt by which it would have appeared that I had two unlawful Implements in my possession, and which effect there can be no doubt that receipt was intended to effect to my prejudice in the minds of His Majesty's Ministers?—*A.* I declare I had no other motive than conceiving them to be one property.

Q. On the Oath you have taken, did you not know that the late Gov'r intended to make a representation to His Majesty's Ministers respecting those Stills?—*A.* I never knew it, from my own knowledge, but suppose all goods ordered away from the Colony by the Gov'r must be accompanied by a Certificate.

Q. You have declared that you considered the words I used before the Bench of Magistrates, before whom I complained of the seizure of those Coppers, was inflammatory; declare what words I used on that occasion you consider so? (*Speech produced.*)*—*A.* The general tenor from " in which the British Laws, &c."

Q. You have acted as a Magistrate in this Colony, and do you not know that your Oath as a Magistrate required you to protect every man in the quiet possession of his property?—*A.* I have always acted to the best of my Judgment and agreeable to the Oath that I have taken.

Q. Have you never in your Magisterial Capacity been governed by the opinions of Geo. Crossley and the orders of the late Gov'r, in opposition to what your Oath and y'r conscience pointed out to you to be the right?—*A.* I cannot answer this question, it having a tendency to criminate myself.

Court adjourned till Half-past Eight o'Clock to-morrow (5th February).

The Court met pursuant to adjournment.

ROBERT CAMPBELL, Esq., sworn:—

The Prisoner being desirous not to proceed further in the Examination of this Evidence, but to submit to his own consideration the propriety of detailing to the Court all he knows of the events which has caused this trial.

Mr. Campbell details all the circumstances, as follows:—I was sent for by note from the Gov'r, as Naval Officer, to bring certain Documents respecting the Stills and the Parramatta Schooner, which I believe was for the purpose of framing an Indictment against Mr. McArthur. I was present when the Indictment was brought to Mr. Griffin and read by him to the Gov'r. No comments were made by either party, and I do not know why the Indictment was not acted upon, nor do I recollect if ever the subject was agitated in the presence of the Gov'r by Geo. Crossley; but I know the Indictment was framed by Crossley, when the Gov'r rec'd a letter from Mr. McA. respecting Mr. Atkins. Mr. Atkins was sent for, and he related to the Gov'r the whole of the quarrel that had taken place respecting a Bill of Mr. Bond's between himself and Mr. McA.† I have been present within these few days with other Gent'm when Geo. Crossley was consulted by the Gov'r respecting the Criminal Court and the Officers then sitting. Mr. Atkins at that time related to the Gov'r what had passed in the Court, which the Gov'r minuted down himself, and Crossley impressed on the Govr's mind that it could not be a Court without the Judge-Advocate, in which opinion Mr. Atkins strongly

* Note 86.   † Note 95.

1808.
11 April.

Proceedings at
the trial of John
Macarthur.

concurred, and that the Judge-Advocate could not be displaced. It was, by the advice of Crossley, determined patiently to let the Court proceed and see how they would act. Crossley was the principal Adviser to the Gov'r. It was determined also to send and demand the Papers left in the Court by the Judge-Advocate. I heard a Memorial* from the Judge-Ad., accusing the Six Officers of the Criminal Court of Treasonable Practices, read to the Gov'r in the presence of all the Magistrates. The Gov'r then quitted the room with Crossley, and returned with a written paper, and on its being read, Crossley recommended the Gov'r to summon by the Provost-Marshal all the Officers composing the Court before him and the Magistrates immediately; but I proposed milder measures, by the Gov'r sending to desire their attendance on himself only. Crossley wrote an order in pencil, and it was altered by Mr. Griffin to the shape it was sent in.† It was proposed, sh'd the Officers attend, that the Memorial from the Judge-Ad. should be read to them and certain questions put to them, but what they were I do not know; but I understood, if they did not comply with the Govr's requisitions, that the Commanding Officer was to be directed to put them under Military Arrest, and that the Magistrates, with the Gov'r, were to be assembled to investigate the accusation made against the Officers of the Court by the Judge-Ad., and if proved that they had acted Treasonably, they were to be committed to Jail; or should they be committed on suspicion of Treason only, that the offence was bailable. On the receipt of the letter from the Court to the Gov'r accusing Mr. Gore, the P.-M., of direct and wilful Perjury, it was the general opinion of the Gentlemen at Gov't House that no answer be given, Mr. Atkins and Crossley being then away preparing an accusation against the Officers. The Gov'r must have heard from report the crime for which Crossley was sent to this Country.

JOHN PALMER, Esquire, sworn :—

Fourteen Questions asked by the Court, which were prepared in the handwriting of Edmund Griffin, Esq., Secretary to the Gov'r.

Q. 1. You have been many years an officer in this Territory; is it not customary for the Gov'r to give his directions by verbal orders, and has not that been the general custom in the time of every Governor of this Colony, as you know or believe?—A. I have in general had written orders—sometimes verbal ones.

Q. 2. You was present on the 24th October last, when a charge was exhibited by Jno. McArthur, Esq., against Mr. R't Campbell, Jun'r, by which Mr. McA. alledged that Mr. Campbell had taken out of his dwelling-house unlawfully two Copper Boilers, value £40;—was it or not so?—A. I was present.

Q. 3. This charge being made against Mr. Campbell as for a Crime had caused a great many people to assemble;—how many people, in your opinion, were there present and assembled as you know or believe?—A. From Sixty to One hundred Persons.

Q. 4. You, being one of the Justices met on that occasion, was of opinion there was no foundation for the Charge, was you or not?—A. I was.

Q. 5. Upon that occasion Mr. McA. made a speech, which was taken down at his request by the Judge-Ad.; did he or not, and if yea, as you heard those words, look upon the paper writing now produced,‡ and say if the same be not a Copy of the same words, as taken down by the J.-A., and the identical words used by the

Pris'r on that occasion, and before the People then and there assembled: declare?—*A.* The Paper produced, it is the same as taken at the time.

Q. 6. Then you heard the Pris'r rehearse those or the like words in the hearing of the people, and saw the Judge-Ad. write them, as he then produced and spoke them,—did you or not?—*A.* Yes.

Q. 7. By the way which Mr. McA. pronounced the words and the words of themselves, did you or not understand the Pris'r meant to incite the People to hatred and contempt of the Gov't and Constitution and the Gov'r of this Territory?—*A.* I conceived that the words and the manner in which they were delivered had a tendency to do so.

Q. 8. Is not Mr. Rob't Campbell, Jun'r, a person well known in this Colony as a person in the confidential employ of Rob't Campbell, Esq., a Justice of Peace and Naval Officer; and in your opinion did not Mr. McA. well know him previous to the 24th October last?—*A.* I suppose so.

Q. 9.* Do you not believe that the Pris'r made that Charge against Mr. Rob't Campbell, Jun'r, with design to collect a great number of people that he might make in their hearing such sort of representation of and concerning the Gov'r and Gov't as he did, and to incite the people to contempt of the Gov't, or how else?—*A.* I cannot say what Mr. McA.'s intentions might have been.

Q. 10. Has not the Pris'r always been a discontented person, as you have understood, in the time of every Gov'r that has been here, or how else?—*A.* I do conceive that Mr. McA. has been a discontented person under every Government in this Colony.

Q. 11. Do you know the handwriting of the Pris'r; and if yea, look upon the Paper Writing now produced,† and say if the same be or not the proper Handwriting of the Pris'r, as you know or believe?—*A.* I believe it to be his handwriting.

Q. 12. Do you know the handwriting of Rich'd Atkins, Esq., Judge-Ad.; and if yea, look upon the Paper Writing, now produced,‡ is not that a Warrant under his hand and Seal, and how else, as you know or believe?—*A.* It is a Warrant under his hand and seal. Paper produced vizt:—

[*Here followed a copy of the warrant; also printed on page 310.*]

Q. 13. Is not Mr. Fra's Oakes, to whom that Warrant is directed, Chief Constable at Parramatta?—*A.* He was at that time.

Q. 14. Look upon the Paper Writing now produced and shewn† ; say if that is or not the handwriting of the Pris'r, as you know or believe?—*A.* (*The Paper produced*) I believe it is.

Q. from the Court. Was you not furnished with a Copy of the questions now asked you on the part of the Crown by Geo. Crossley ? —*A.* I think I was; I thought little of them and destroyed them.

Q. Did you not apply personally to Crossley to give you a copy?— *A.* I cannot take upon myself to say if I did or not.

The Prisoner's Cross-Examination of this Evidence:—

Q. Have you ever recited to the Gov'r. to Geo. Crossley, or any other person the answers you intended to give to the questions, of which you rec'd a Copy from Geo. Crossley, and to which questions you have now answered?—*A.* To the Gov'r, no; to Geo. Crossley I had some conversation about them; but to no other person, because I conceived when I came on my Oath I might think very differently.

* Note 97.   † Note 98.   ‡ Note 99.

1808.
11 April.

Proceedings at
the trial of John
Macarthur.

Q. Are the answers you have now given the same as you would have given had the late Governor retained his Authority?—*A.* Yes.

Q. You have given it as your opinion that Mr. Rob't Campbell, Junr., did nothing illegal in taking the Copper Bodies of two Stills from my house without a written authority—did you form that opinion from evidence when you sat on the Bench, or did you not declare the same opinion before you heard a single evidence in support of my complaint?—*A.* I declared it from the evidence I heard on the Bench, and never thought of it before, that I recollect.

Q. You have said that a large assembly of People was collected together at the Court-House when I made my complaint;—do you know that those people were collected by my contrivance, or at my desire?—*A.* I do not know anything about it.

Q. Do you not think that they were rather collected by an anxious desire to hear whether the Magistrates would support the late Gov'r in ordering the private property of Individuals to be wrested from them?—*A.* I never gave it a thought at all.

Q. You have said that you understood by the words I uttered before the Bench of Magistrates, and by my manner and looks, that you think I intended to inflame the minds of the People against the late Gov'r?—*A.* I think the words and manner had that tendency; the Speech produced, I think the whole of it, had that tendency.

Q. Can you point out no particular expression in that Speech which appears to you to have that tendency?—*A.* No, but the whole.

Q. Was that part inflammatory in which I say that two Coppers—or Bodies of Stills—were taken out of my house on the 22nd Inst. without my consent?—*A.* I have before answered that the whole, in my opinion, was inflammatory.

Q. Were you not sitting as a Magistrate in the discharge of your Magisterial duty when I uttered what you conceived to be an inflammatory speech;—did you, or did you not, take any steps to punish me for the demonstration of such seditious intentions?—*A.* I was sitting as a Magistrate. There was no steps taken by me for the punishment of Mr. McA.

Q. Do you not know that your Oath as a Magistrate required you to leave nothing undone in your power to bring any man to justice who sh'd endeavour to excite the people to a breach of the Peace, either by inflammatory speeches or otherwise?—*A.* Yes.

Q. How then do you excuse such a manifest breach of your duty, to which you were bound by your Oath?—*A.* I merely give it as a matter of opinion. Had I been certain Mr. McA. had those intentions I should have given it my opinion that he should be committed.

Q. You have sworn that you consider me to have been always a discontented character under every Gov'r;—was I discontented under the Government of Gov'r Phillip?—*A.* I thought so.

Q. State one particular instance of discontent which you know?—*A.* Mr. McA. was discontented at Gov'r Phillip not allowing him to keep a Cask or two of Spirits, which Gov'r Phillip had ordered me to put into the Store.

Q. Do you not know that the Cask or two of Spirits to which you allude was the property of the present L't-Gov., and purchased from the Royal Admiral for the supply of the Regiment, by order of Major Grose?—*A.* No, I do not. It is so long ago I cannot speak to it.

Q. When you came to me with a message from Gov'r Phillip, desiring that this Cask of Spirits might be given up, did I not tell you that I had nothing to do with it; that it was lodged in the Regimental Store, of which I had the Charge; but that I would accompany you to Gov't House and explain the circumstance?—*A.* It is so long ago that I cannot recollect.

Q. Did you not accompany me to Gov't House; and when we were introduced to the presence of Gov'r Phillip did he not, in a violent passion, refuse to hear a word, and declare that he would instantly put me under Arrest?—*A.* I do not recollect; perhaps I might.

Q. Did I not reply: " Sir, you may please yourself. You are the first Officer that ever threatened me with an Arrest; and I give you my word of Honor, if I am put in Arrest, I shall require a full and sufficient explanation of the cause before I consent to sit quietly down under such a Disgrace "?—*A.* I do not recollect being present at such a Conversation.

.*Q.* Did I not immediately retire, and having given you the Key of the Regimental Store, did you not cause a Legar of Brandy to be rolled from thence and put into the Public Store?—*A.* I do not recollect it.

Q. Was not that Cask of Spirits given up the day after to Major Johnston, the Proprietor of it, by order of Governor Phillip?—*A.* It might; I cannot say.

Q. Do you not know that from the violent language used to me that night by Gov'r Phillip, I ever after refused to sit at his table?— *A.* I have already said I do not recollect being present at any conversation with Mr. McA. and Gov'r Phillip.

.*Q.* Was I discontented under Major Grose, who succeeded Gov'r Phillip in the command?—*A.* I did not suppose an Officer would be discontented with the Commander of the Regiment, and did not mean to include Major Grose or L't-Col. Paterson amongst the Governors.

Q. Was I discontented under Gov'r Hunter?—*A.* I have always understood so.

Q. Do you know of any personal altercation or difference which took place between myself and Gov'r Hunter?—*A.* No; I do not recollect particularly.

Q. Do you not know that I had the Management of the greater part of the Public Concerns, and was entirely in his confidence, until, in an unfortunate moment, I unwisely advised him to be cautious of the Expenditure of Public Money, and not to suffer thousands of Bushels of Grains to be bought and put into the Public Stores to rot and perish?—*A.* No, I know nothing of it.

Q. Do you not know that I did give him some advice relative to the Expenditure of Public Money, and that from that moment he became so estranged from me, and acted in all points so contrary to my advice, that I found it incumbent on me to resign all further interference in the Public Affairs, assigning as a reason, by letter, that a due regard to my honor and character obliged me to do so?— *A.* No.

Q. Was I discontented under Gov'r King;—can you state any particular instance?—*A.* You was discontented under Gov'r King, or you would not have been sent out of the Colony in the manner you was.

Q. Did not the difference which existed between me and Gov'r King originate in his attempting to screen a man from the punishment a Criminal Court had sentenced him to for assaulting Capt. Abbott, and threatening to assault me because we took the necessary steps to recover from his hands the plundered effects of a deceased brother Officer*?—*A.* I cannot say what it originated in. I was not in the confidence of Gov'r King.

1808.
11 April.

Proceedings at the trial of John Macarthur.

Q. Was not our differences further increased by his putting me into an ignominious Arrest for meeting a person who had challenged me, and by his refusing to bring me before a Court-Martial to justify my conduct, and by his sending me a Prisoner to England, and taking every means in his power to deprive me of an opportunity of proving how greatly I had been calumniated, injured, and oppressed?—*A.* Yes, I suppose they might.

Q. Have you never, Sir, been discontented with Gov'r King? [Mr. Palmer refused to answer the above question. The Court cleared on the propriety of it. Are of opinion that he must answer it in the Affirmative or Negative, unless he states it will criminate himself.]—*A.* Yes.

Q. Has Gov'r King never called you a Traitor?—*A.* Yes, in a state of Frenzy.

Q. Have I been discontented under the late Gov'r Bligh?—*A.* Yes, I think so.

Q. Can you state any particular instance of my discontent?—*A.* It is my opinion.

Q. Can you say whether any personal difference or altercation has ever taken place between myself and Gov'r Bligh?—*A.* Not that I know of.

Q. As you have been in habits of strict intimacy with the late Governor, and have been generally understood to be one of the principal Advisers of his measures, is it not likely, if any such altercation should have taken place, that he would have informed you?—*A.* I cannot say.

Q. Do you not know that the late Gov'r and his Family were in the habits of Social Intimacy with me and mine for many months after his arrival here?—*A.* I have known part of the Family to visit.

Q. Does it not come within your knowledge that the late Gov'r, his Daughter, and his late Son-in-Law were frequently entertained at my house?—*A.* I have heard so, but never saw them.

Q. Have you never heard the late Gov'r express a great dislike to me?—*A.* I never heard the late Gov'r express a dislike to any person whatever that I recollect.

Q. Have you not been in the late Gov'r's confidence?—*A.* I believe I was.

Q. Have you never heard the late Gov'r declare his intention to send me out of this Country?—*A.* Never in my life that I recollect, and believe it very foreign to his thoughts.

Q. Are you not acquainted that I have never visited at Gov't House since the late Gov'r decided against me in a Cause of Appeal without allowing me to offer a word in support of my plea?—*A.* I know nothing about it.

Q. Have you never heard it talked of in the Gov'r's presence how or in what manner my Commercial and Agricultural Pursuits might be interrupted?—*A.* No, never to my knowledge.

Q. Then you have never heard him speak with disapprobation of me?—*A.* In a small degree I may, but not seriously.

Q. Have you never been directed by the late Gov'r to do anything injurious to me?—*A.* Never.

* Note 100.

1808.
11 April.

Proceedings at
the trial of John
Macarthur.

Q. Were you not directed by the late Gov'r to sit as a Magistrate in conjunction with Mr. Arndell and examine Geo. Crossley on Oath relative to any matters he chose to accuse me of?—*A.* No.

Q. Did you not examine Geo. Crossley on Oath respecting certain Seditious Expressions, and did you not allow him to swear that he had heard two other persons—namely, Messrs. Hobby and Pitt—declare that I had uttered Seditious Expressions?—*A.* All I recollect of the business is that Geo. Crossley was put on his Oath respecting what he (Crossley) said that Mr. Pitt had said. The Papers are forthcoming, and I have not thought of the business since till lately.

Q. Did you not know that the Law admits of no hearsay Evidence, and that it rejects with Horror all those who have been proved to be perjured?—*A.* Yes.

Q. Did you examine Mr. Hobby?—*A.* Yes.

Q. Did he contradict Crossley's Testimony?—*A.* I cannot recollect, I thought it a matter of so little moment.

Q. Did you examine Mr. Pitt?—*A.* Yes; a few questions were asked him, which was the reason that Crossley was put on his Oath.

Q. Did not Mr. Pitt contradict the Charges of Crossley, and in y'r presence call Crossley a perjured old Villain?—*A.* He did, until Crossley was put upon his Oath, when Pitt acknowledged in part the charges.

Q. If it sh'd appear on produc'g those Minutes that Crossley's testimony was completely contradicted by Mr. Hobby, and in most parts by Mr. Pitt, are you prepared to give a reason why you did not immed't'ly commit Crossley for Perjury, and for having formed a Criminal Conspiracy against me?—*A.* I did not consider it a matter of any moment, but put the proceedings into my pocket, as I was going to Sydney the next day, and showed it to the Governor.

Q. from the Court. Did you not relate every circumstance to the Gov'r of what took place at the Hawkesbury between yourself, Crossley, Hobby, and Pitt; and if you did, relate them to the Court, and the Gov'r's opinion?—*A.* I did not, nor did the Gov'r give any opinion.

The Cross-Ex'm of this Ev'ce on the part of the Crown from the Court and Prisoner is here closed.

Questions from the Prisoner to this Witness in support of his Defence:—

Q. You have been many years in the practice of taking the advice of G. Crossley?—*A.* On my own private affairs chiefly.

Q. Were you not a Member of a Bench of Magistrates assembled on the 24th October, and did I not bring before that Bench a complaint against Mr. Robert Campbell, Jun'r, for unlawfully taking two Copper Boilers, which I valued at £40 St'g, from my house?—*A.* Yes.

Q. Did not the majority of that Bench decide that the taking of those Coppers was not authorized?—*A.* Yes.

Q. I have been accused of making a Seditious and Inflammatory Speech before that Bench;—did you as a Magistrate sitting on it propose that I sh'd be either committed or in any other way punished for the words spoken on that occasion?—*A.* No, I did not.

Q. When the Bench broke up, did you go to Gov't House?—*A.* I think I did.

1808.
11 April.

Proceedings at
the trial of John
Macarthur.

Q. Did you make any representation to the Gov'r of what passed at the Bench?—*A*. I do not recollect I did.

Q. Were you present when the Judge-Adv'c'e took the Proceed'gs to the Gov'r?—*A*. I cannot take upon myself to say; I cannot recollect; I might have been.

Q. Were you present at the Gov'm't House that day when the Judge-Advocate was very violently abused and found fault with for the Opinion he had given on the Bench?—*A*. Not that I remember.

Q. Do you not remember that you did find great fault with the Judge-Advocate for his Opinion?—*A*. No, I do not indeed; I hardly suppose myself equal to do it.

Q. Did you never consult with any person how and in what manner I could be punished for the words I had uttered to the Bench?—*A*. Never, to my recollection.

Q. Was not George Crossley sent for to your house the following day, 25th October, to meet you and the late Gov'r's Secretary; and did -he not come there, and was he not asked to give his opinion how or in what manner I could be punished?—*A*. I do not know if Crossley was sent for. He came there. Crossley was not asked any questions in my presence. I went out of the room and left him with Mr. Griffin.

Q. Were you not inf'd by Mr. Griffin of the business on which Crossley was sent for?—*A*. I can't recollect what the business was.

Q. Do you not know that Geo. Crossley gave it as his opinion that day at your house that the words I had uttered before the Bench of Magistrates the preceeding day were indictable, and might be punished by Fine and Imprisonment?—*A*. He might have said so, for he talked a great deal; but I do not recollect it.

Q. What was the cause of Crossley being sent for to your house?—*A*. I do not recollect his being sent for.

Q. Did you not meet Mr. Griffin that morning between yours and the Government House, and did he not tell you he wanted Crossley; did you not reply, " I will soon bring him or send for him "; and did you not soon after return to y'r own house and Crossley quickly follow?—*A*. I met Mr. Griffin, and soon after ret'd to my own house and saw Mr. Crossley there. Whether he came before me or after I cannot say; I do not recollect. Mr. Griffin said he wanted Crossley. I do not remember the conversation about Crossley. Mr. Griffin might have asked me about Crossley, but cannot charge my memory.

Q. Do you not know that Crossley drew up an Indictm't which forms the first comp't which I read on opening your Ev'ce?—*A*. I have heard so; I never saw it or heard it read until in Court, to the best of my recollection.

Q. Who did you hear it from?—*A*. I cannot say who. I heard Crossley say he had been busy with Mr. Atkins about an Indictment.

Q. Did the late Gov'r never consult you whether it would be advisable then to prosecute me for what I had said at the Bench of Magistrates, or whether it would be more prudent to reserve it as a rod in pickle?—*A*. No, he never did.

Q. Did you go to Gov't House on the morning of the 16th December, the day on which you attended a Bench of Magistrates to hear the accusation of the Constable Oakes against me?—*A*. I go there every morning.

Q. Did the Gov'r inform you that morning what Oakes had accused me of, or did he consult you in what manner I sh'd be

1808.
11 April.

Proceedings at
the trial of John
Macarthur.

proceeded against?—*A*. I think the Gov'r told me what Oakes had
said; but did not consult me what was to be done.

Q. When you attended the Bench of Magistrates that day to assist
in examining Oakes, did you think, from the Ev'ce he gave, that I
deserved to be apprehended?—*A.* I did.

Q. If you thought I deserved to be apprehended, why did you
refuse to join the Judge-Advocate in signing that Warrant which
was issued from the Bench, and only signed by the Judge-Advocate?
—*A.* Because it was the Judge-Advocate's opinion that it was all
that was necess'y, and the opinion of the whole.

Q. You attended the Bench on the 17th December, the day on
which I was brought a Prisoner before it?—*A.* Yes, I believe so.

Q. Did you go to the Govt. House in the morning before you
attended the Bench?—*A.* I might or might not; cannot recollect.

Q. Did you not determine, with y'r Brother-in-law, Mr. Campbell,
another Member of that Bench, that it w'd be prudent not to bring
me to any Trial, but to fine and Imprison me by the authority of the
Bench; and were you not satisfied that the J.-A. w'd be afraid to
oppose y'r opinions, and, therefore, to jail I must go?—*A.* No; nor
had I any conversation with my Brother-in-Law about Mr.
McArthur.

Q. Did I not object to Mr. Campbell sitting on that Bench,
assigning as a reason that he was an interested person; and did you
not strenuously contend that he should sit?—*A.* Mr. McArthur did
object to Mr. Campbell, and I thought Mr. Campbell ought to sit;
but do not recollect being strenuous about it.

Q. On the Oath you have taken, can you say that you came into
the Court-house with an honest, impartial, and unprejudiced mind?
—*A.* Yes, I can.

Q. Can you swear that you were actuated neither by rancour,
animosity, or a preconcerted plan, to disgrace me in the Eyes of
the World, and to ruin and distress a numerous, innocent, and
inoffending Family?—*A.* Yes, I do from my heart; and I say
further that I have felt very sorry for Mr. McArthur's Family.

Q. Have you never been present at Gov't House when Geo.
Crossley was there?—*A.* Yes, I have.

Q. Have you never been present with the late Gov'r when he has
consulted him?—*A.* No, I do not recollect any particular consultation; I have heard the Gov'r ask his opinion on points of Law.

Q. Did you never recommend Crossley to the Gov'r as a good
sort of man?—*A.* I have said that he is not so bad as he is pointed
out. I never knew him to deceive me in anything I had to do with
him in his opinion.

Q. Were you present at Gov't House the greater part of the 25tu
and 26th January?—*A.* Yes, I was.

Q. Were you consulted those days by the Gov'r how it w'd be
proper to proceed with me and the Criminal Court then assembled?
—*A.* I do not recollect any particular consultation that day. I was
backward and forward in the Office.

Q. Did you not consult honest Geo. Crossley these two days?—*A.*
No, I did not.

Q. Did you not go down to Mr. Divine's house to hurry him in
drawing up the Memorial and other Papers w'h he was preparing
for the Judge-Advocate to sign?—*A.* No, I did not.

Court adjourned till 9 o'clock to-morrow morning.

1808.
11 April.

Proceedings at
the trial of John
Macarthur.

6th Feb'y, Court met pursuant to adjournment.

JOHN GLEN sworn :—

The Eighteen Questions intended to have been asked by the late Judge-Advocate, it is the opinion of the Court shall be asked in their original order.

Q. 1. Was you or not Master of the Parramatta Schooner?—*A.* I was.

Q. 2. Is or not John McArthur, Esq., a part Owner of that Vessel?—*A.* He is.

Q. 3. After you sailed from this Port, in or about June last, or at any other time when you got to sea, was or not one John Hoare, a Prisoner who had escaped from this Territory, found on board or not?—*A.* He was.

Q. 4. That John Hoare afterwards got away from your Ship—did he or not?—*A.* Yes.

Q. 5. On your return to this Colony in Nov'r last, some investigation into that matter of the escape of John Hoare was made the subject of Inquiry,—was it or not?—*A.* Yes at Gov't House. I was examined on oath before the late Governor, the Judge-Advocate. and Naval Officer respecting the voyage in general and John Hoare being on board.

Q. 6. And upon that the Court of Civil Jurisdiction gave a Verdict against you; but there is an Appeal depending, is there not?—*A.* Yes there was, and an Appeal is now pending.

Q. 7. Did you receive any Letter from the Prisoner, dated the 7th Dec'r last; and if yea, is the following Paper a copy of it?

[*Here followed a copy of the letter from Mr. Macarthur to Mr. Glen, dated 7th December, 1807; see page 295.*]

A. It is a copy of it.

Q. 8. Did you not communicate the contents of this Letter to the Mates and Crew of the Vessel the Parramatta Schooner?—*A.* I did.

Q. 9. Did you make the application to Robert Campbell, Esq., Naval Officer, as directed by that letter?—*A.* I did.

Q. 10. Upon your communicating the contents of this letter to the Ship's Crew, did they or not consider themselves much hurt, in a distant Port from England, to be left without support?—*A.* They did.

Q. 11. Did not you and all or some of the ship's company, in conseq'ce, come on shore; and if yea, was not you on that occasion before the Judge-Advocate?—*A.* Yes.

Q. 12. Was you not told by that Officer that by the Crew coming on shore you had violated the Colonial Regulations?—*A.* I was.

Q. 13. Did not you and them make Oath of the occasion being because of that letter, and did you or not shew the same letter and give the copy as an excuse for such your conduct, or how else?—*A.* I did.

Q. 14. In consequence of what you or the Crew said, is it within y'r know'ge that the J.-A. wrote to the Prisoner and required him to attend and show cause for his conduct, or have you heard it from the Prisoner?—*A.* I heard it from the Judge that he had wrote to Mr. McArthur.

Q. 15. Look upon the Paper now produced* and shown to you;— is it the handwriting of the Prisoner; and say if the two Police Officers mentioned to be on board were placed there for any other purpose but to prevent anything going out of the Vessel without a legal permit, or how else?—*A.* I believe it to be the handwriting of Mr. McArthur; and I understood that the Police Officers were put on board the Schooner to prevent anything being landed from

* Note 101.

her, and to prevent any intercourse with the shore, or any illegal proceedings. The day following my Exam'n at Gov't House I received permission from the Gov'r to come on shore.

Q. 16. As you are a seafaring man, did you ever know of one of the Owners in a distant Country making an attempt to discharge the Master, Mates, and Crew from an English Vessel; and do you think such conduct is consistent with justice or not?—*A.* I did not consider myself discharged. I waited on the Naval Officer to deliver the copy of the letter, as I was directed by my Owner. The Naval Officer said he acknowledged the receipt of the letter, but had no answer to give. I waited on Mr. McA. after leaving the Naval Officer, who desired me to wait upon the Governor to show him the letter and see if he would give me redress. I did go to Gov't House. I met His Excellency at the back door, and delivered the letter to him that I received from my Owner, Jno. McA., Esq're. The Governor asked me who I was. I told him my name, on which he gave me the letter back without opening it, and told me, for a Scoundrel to be gone; that he knew nothing about me or my Owners either—saying, clenching his fist and stamping with his foot, " Damn you, Sir, I will teach you to take away Prisoners from this Colony, you Scoundrel "; he said, " If ever I catch you on my premises again "—then stopped and ordered me to be gone.

Q. 17. Do you not consider Mr. McA. answerable for the damages you may have sustained by reason of such conduct, if neither you nor the Ship's company had acted in such way to the Owners as to make such conduct necessary?—*A.* There was no damage sustained by me or the Ship's company.

Q. 18. Was you and all the Ship's Crew discharged from this Vessel?—*A.* No.

Cross Questioned by the Prisoner :—

Q. When you arrived, did you not come to Anchor at the head of the Cove in a place of safety?—*A.* Yes, I did.

Q. Did not some person shortly after come off, and after having taken possession of the Vessel, did they not cause her anchor to be weighed, and removed the Schooner into a dangerous situation done by the Naval Officer's order?—*A.* The Gov'r's Coxswain ordered the pilot to weigh the anchor again, and remove the Schooner opposite the Naval Officer's Stores, outside the Porpoise.

Q. Did you not lay in that situation several days in great danger, and were you not once nearly on shore?—*A.* She was in a state of danger, and I had informed the Naval Officer that she had not anchors sufficient to hold her in the situation she had been moved to. She was near going on shore.

Q. You have said that two Police Officers were put in charge of the Vessel soon after your arrival; state whether you was not obliged also to give up all your Ship's papers, comprising your Registers, your Licenses, Port Clearances, and, in short, every paper that could show either yours or your Owner's title to the Vessel?—*A.* Yes.

Q. Did you not after that frequently apply to the Naval Officer to enter the Vessel, and did he not always refuse?—*A.* I did, and was always refused.

Q. Did you not, after being refused entry, repeatedly apply that your papers might be returned, and were they not refused?—*A.* Yes.

1808.
11 April.

Proceedings at
the trial of John
Macarthur.

Q. When you informed me of this, did I not tell you that as the Vessel was refused entry, and thereby prevented landing her Cargo, that as your papers were refused, and the Vessel consequently prevented sailing to another Port, and as the Naval Officer had two Police Officers on board of her, I considered myself as completely dispossessed—that you must therefore apply to the Naval Officer for directions what you was to do with yourself, Officers, and Crew? —*A.* Yes.

Q. Did I not, in consequence of that, give you the Letter,* and desire you to leave a Copy with the Naval Officer?—*A.* You did.

Q. Had you not plenty of provisions on board—both Bread and Meat?—*A.* Yes.

Q. The reason why you did not use those Provisions was because, as the Vessel's Stores and Cargo were given up to the Naval Officer, you thought it necessary to have his instructions before you used any more of them. When the Mates and some of the Seamen of the Parramatta went to state their situation to the Naval Officer, and required his instructions, did he not threaten to kick them from his door?—*A.* I did not think it proper to use any provisions until I knew whose directions I was to be under; and I was told the Naval Officer had threatened to kick the Mates and Seamen when they went to require his directions.

Q. Have you, your Officers, or any part of your Crew, ever been confined, tried, or punished for breaking the Colonial Regulations, altho' I am here a Prisoner at the Bar, charged with having caused you so to do?—*A.* No.

FRANCIS OAKES, sworn —

Says on the 15th day Dec'r last I rec'd a Warrant from the Judge-Advocate, R'd Atkins, Esq., wherein I was directed to bring to Sydney, on the 16th, John McArthur, Esq., to appear before the Judge-Advocate, among other of His Majesty's Justices of the Peace. I being well aware that it was a delicate piece of business, I called on Capt. Abbott, a Justice of the Peace—under whose particular directions I had been for a considerable time—and informed him of the business, and shewed him the Warrant, and asked him, as it was specified in the Warrant for me to bring Jno. McA. to Sydney, whether it was necessary for me to go personally with him. Capt. Abbott replied and said he did not conceive it was, and gave me directions to go to Mr. McA. and present the·Warrant. He dared to say that he would comply with it, and that I might go down to Sydney as if I was going on my own business—only to see that Mr. McA. made his appearance, agreeable to the directions of the Warrant. Under these directions I went to Mr. McA.'s house and inf'd one of his servants—who was in the Kitchen—that I wanted to see Mr. McA. on some particular business. The Servant went and informed Mr. McA., in consequence of w'h Mr. McA. came to the back door of the house. I informed him that I had just recd. a Warrant from R'd Atkins the J.-A., wherein I was directed to bring him to Sydney to-morrow, 16th. He asked me to give him the Warrant, which I did, and he politely asked me into the Parlour; he ordered me a chair to sit down, and made me a Glass of Grog. During the same time he was perusing the Warrant, and said that it was an illegal thing, and requested me to take it to Capt. Abbott for him to back it. After saying a great deal, in consequence of the Warrant being presented, desired pen, ink, and

* Note 102.

1808.
11 April.

Proceedings at
the trial of John
Macarthur.

paper might be given me that I might write down what he had said,
which I declined to do, in consequence of w'h Mr. McA. took a pen
and wrote the Note—which being produced before the Court* is the
same or to the same effect. I remarked it was a disagreeable
business and hoped he would not be angry with me. He gave me
that paper as a justification that I had done my duty in serving the
Warrant, and with great reluctance I took it off the table, asking
him if it was his will that I sh'd take it. Mr. McA. replied, " By all
means." I asked him if I should wait on him in the Morning. I
do not recollect him making any reply; in consequence of w'h I
came away with the paper.* I went to Capt. Abbott a second time,
who I found in bed. I requested the Servant in the Kitchen to
inform Capt. Abbott that Mr. McArthur would not comply with the
Warrant, and that I had waited on him (Capt. Abbott) for directions how to proceed. Capt. Abbott, I believe, did not get up; but
I went to the window and informed him that Mr. McA. had given
me his written objections why he w'd not comply with the Warrant,
and I informed Capt. Abbott verbally of the substance of it, and
asked his advice how I s'd proceed. He replied and said that he
did not think the Warrant was sufficient to use violence. I then
asked him if I had better to proceed on to Sydney in the morning.
He told me I had. I then made application to him for the Parramatta Boat. He informed me that it was at Sydney, and that I had
better set off early in the morning. Under those directions I left
Capt. Abbott's Yard. In going home, Mr. Edward McArthur overtook me and said that his father w'd go to Sydney, and requested
the written paper again. I told him to deliver my compl'ts to his
father; that I could not deliver it with propriety; but that if he
complied with the Warrant I perhaps would not present it. In the
morning I went to Sydney. I went to Mr. Atkins's Office and
presented the paper that Mr. McA. had given me. Mr. Atkins
desired me to wait until he had seen the Gov'r. Some short time
after I was sent for to Gov't House and requested by Mr. Atkins
to relate to the Gov'r and himself what I had passed, w'h I did,
and was as I have stated to this Court. The Gov'r seemed to blame
me that I had not brought Mr. McA. down. On the same day I
was brought before a Bench of Magistrates to give Ev'ce on the
business, which I did. After my Ev'ce resp'ng the paper was gone
thro', I informed the Bench that Mr. McA. had s'd at the time I
first presented the Warrant at his house that " had the Person who
issued that Warrant served it instead of me he w'd have spurned
him from his presence," or words to that effect; and that Mr.
McArthur at the same time said, after cautioning me what I was
about, that " if I came a second time to enforce the Warrant to
come well Armed, that he never would submit till Blood was shed."
Mr. McArthur further remarked at the same time that he had been
robbed of £10,000, but said, "Let them alone; they will soon make
a Rope to hang themselves." He said the Gov'r and them had
robbed him.

Q. Relate the Conversation that passed several days after between
the Gov'r and yourself?—A. There were certain questions put by
the Gov'r, and I gave certain answers. I cannot recollect the
particulars.

Q. State to the best of your recollection the purport of the questions that the Gov'r put to you?—A. The Gov'r said that it was
necessary to explain some questions that he had got to put to me.

* Note 103.

The purport of them was the questions that were taken from the Depositions taken by the Judge-Ad. on the 16th. One question was to this effect: "What did Mr. McA. mean when he said he treated the Warrant with scorn and contempt, as he did the persons who issued it?" I told the Gov'r that I supposed he meant Mr. Atkins and himself.

Q. Was Mr. Atkins present when you had the above conversation with the Gov'r?—*A.* No.

Q. Was Geo. Crossley present?—*A.* No; he came upstairs to the Gov'r just after the questions and answers were concluded.

Q. Did Crossley put any questions to you, or had you any conversations with him on that subject?—*A.* He did not at that time put any questions. I asked him if I was warranted in breaking open Mr. Blaxcell's door, and he said I had done nothing but my duty. Crossley never put any questions to me, or ever took anything down in writing from me.

Q. Was you ever sworn in as Constable?—*A.* No.

Q. Did any conversation pass between you and the Gov'r wherein Mr. McA. was concerned but that which you have now stated to the Court?—*A.* I did state the circumstance of Mr. Hannibal McArthur taking a copy of the Warrant, and Mr. E. McA. going for Mr. Bayly. I was asked who I conceived Mr. McA. meant when he said, "Let them alone; they will soon make a Rope to hang themselves"; and I answered I supposed he must mean every Officer in Power.

Q. You have stated to this Court that a conversation passed between you and the Gov'r at the time alluded to which you do not think prudent to mention;—what was that Conversation?—*A.* The conversation that passed as related in my last answer, and some other questions that I cannot recollect.

Q. Did or not the Pris'r say to you that the Gov'r was a Tyrant?—*A.* I do not recollect he did.

Q. Did you ever tell the Gov'r that the Pris'r had said that he, the Gov'r, was a Tyrant?—*A.* I told the Gov'r that Mr. McArthur represented him as a Tyrant, which opinion I formed from the paper delivered by Mr. McA. to me; but what I said to the Gov'r I did not say on oath.

Cross-examined by the Prisoner:—

Q. You have stated in your Ev'ce that you are not a sworn-in Constable; did you not come to my house at Parramatta on the ev'g of the 15th December for the purpose of apprehending me, under the authority of a Warrant from the Judge-Advocate?—*A.* I came to serve one.

Q. Did you serve that Warrant?—*A.* I served it, so far as giving it into the hands of Mr. McA.

Q. Did you lay your hand on my person and require me to submit to your authority?—*A.* No.

Q. You say I gave you a Glass of Grog and offered you a chair, and you have recited the whole of my conversation;—pray did you say nothing?—*A.* You gave me a Glass of Grog and offered me a chair. I have not recited the whole of the conversation, but the particulars. I did say something.

Q. Did you not say that it was the common conversation of the place how shamefully the Naval Officer had behaved in stopping the Parramatta Schooner and her Cargo?—*A.* I do not recollect anything of the kind.

Q. Did you not say that the whole Country cried out against such arbitrary proceedings?—*A.* I do not recollect it.

Q. Did you not say that you knew the Warrant which you had brought was an illegal one; and, let the consequ'ces be what they would, that you w'd not serve it?—*A.* No; I never considered the Warrant illegal I conceived I had served.

Q. Did I not say. "Oakes, you are a poor Man; you may give Offence. Go to Capt. Abbott, tell him I will not obey this illegal Warrant, and get his Instructions how you shall act"?—*A.* Mr. McA. said it·was an illegal Warrant, and requested me to take it to Capt. Abbott to back it.

Q. Did you not reply, "I know it is of no use to take it to Capt. Abbott. I know he will not have anything to do with it"?—*A.* No.

Q. Why did you not immed't'ly take it to him when you found he w'd not obey it?—*A.* I did immed't'ly take it to Capt. Abbott.

Q. Did I not, immed't'ly after I told you "I will not obey this Warrant," and desired you to go to Capt. Abbott's, sit down and write the paper produced to the Court?*—*A.* Yes.

Q. Did you not receive this paper as a justifi't'n of yourself and as a full and complete answer to the Judge-Ad:?—*A.* I did.

Q. Whilst I was copying this Paper, did you not say you was glad to have it, because it would prevent you making any mistake in repeating my words?—*A.* No.

Q. Did you not say, "Do you think I can be hurt, Sir, for not serving this Warrant, for I w'd on no acc't insult a Gentleman like you by taking him out of his house at this hour of the Night"?—*A.* I don't recollect.

Q. Do you not remember I said, "Oakes,-this Warrant can only be meant as an insult to me, and most probably they will be angry with you for disappointing their expectations; but you may tell them in your excuse that I am a sort of Gentleman you do not much like forcing into anything, and that if they send you with another Warrant they had better provide you with an Armed Force, for I looked in a desperate ill-humour"?—*A.* No.

Q. Did you not reply, "I will tell them that I will take care not to expose my Life to danger, for I think there will be Blood Shed"? *A.* No.

Q. During the whole time that you were at my house, did I treat you with any unkindness or incivility?—*A.* No, but to the contrary.

Q. You have declared in y'r Ev'ce that my Son overtook you on your return home, and requested you in my name to return the written paper I had given you, w'h you refused, and by w'h ev'ce it appears as if I had been desirous to retract the answer I had sent to the Judge-Advocate. Now, I ask you, on your Oath, whether my Nephew† did not tell you the next morning that that message was never authorized by me, but sent by Mr. Bayly without my know-l'dge?—*A.* Yes.

Q. Then, why did you conceal that Cir'ce from the C'rt but with an intention to make me appear like one of the pusilanimous Tribe you had enlisted yourself amongst?—*A.* I did not see it necessary.

Q. Did you not tell Mr. Crook and Mr. Hassall, on your return from my house on the 15th Dec'r, that I had been very ill-used, or words to that effect?—*A.* No.

1808.
11 April.

Proceedings at
the trial of John
Macarthur.

Q. What did you tell them?—*A.* I did not tell them anything particular.

Q. Did you not tell Capt. Abbott that I was very ill-used. or words to that effect?—*A.* I do not recollect.

Q. When you came to Sydney the next morn'g. did you go to the Governor or the Judge-Ad. first?—*A.* I went to the Judge-Ad.

Q. How long after that was it that you went to the Gov'r?—*A.* Between eight and nine o'Clock.

Q. Where did you see the Gov'r?—*A.* In the Garden.

Q. Who was with him?—*A.* Mr. Atkins.

Q. You then showed him the paper, did you?—*A.* No; I had given it to Mr. Atkins before.

Q. Did the Gov'r talk much to you about what had passed the preceding ev'g?—*A.* No great deal.

Q. Did you continue in the Garden all the while you was with the Gov'r?—*A.* In the Garden, and from thence to the field at the back of the House.

Q. I suppose you went into that private situation, recollecting the old proverb that " Walls have ears "?—*A.* I do not know the Gov'r's reason.

Q. You rec'd a Warrant to apprehend me that day, did you not?—*A.* Yes.

Q. How many Armed Men accompanied you when you went to execute that Warrant?—*A.* Three, with Sticks or Cutlasses.

Q. Do you, upon y'r Oath, mean to say that you do not know that two of these men were armed with Cutlasses?—*A.* I believe two of them had Cutlasses.

Q. When you went to apprehend me on this Warrant, did you not go through the open rooms of Mr. Blaxcell's house in search of me?—*A.* Yes.

Q. Did not Mr. Blaxcell assure you I was not there?—*A.* Yes.

Q. Did you not go to a locked door of Mr. Blaxcell's and break it open, exclaiming, " We are no Children "?—*A.* After Mr. Blaxcell and his Lady were requested to open it and refused, it was bursted open.

Q. Did you find me there?—*A.* No.

Q. Where did you find me?—*A.* At Mr. Grimes's, sitting Publicly in Company with sev'l other Gent'm.

Q. When you produced the Warrant, did I resist it with any violence?—*A.* No; but you said you w'd not comply with it, desiring the Gentl'm to take notice that he was taken against his will.

Q. Did you go to Gov't House after you had apprehended me?—*A.* I cannot recollect.

Q. Did you get nothing that day from the Gov'r?—*A.* I do not recollect I did.

Q. Did you get no Spirits out of the Store that day?—*A.* I do not recollect.

Q. How many Gallons did you get as your Share amongst the Constables?—*A.* I got ten Gallons as a Superintendent.

Q. Was not your Share always Five Gallons before?—*A.* Sometimes Five, sometimes Ten, as other Superintendents.

Q. Was not the quantity of Spirits to be issued on that occasion left to Cap't Abbott, the Magistrate at Parramatta. and did he not put y'r name down for Five Gallons only?—*A.* Yes; but in consequence of my name being down in the List of Supt's I rec'd the same as them.

Q. How often have you been at Gov't House since I was apprehended to be consulted on the Ev'ce you was to give on my trial?—
A. Once.

Q. How often have you seen Crossley since?—*A.* Never on Mr.
McArthur's business.

Q. Has Crossley never shewn you or any other person the questions you were to be asked on this Trial?—*A.* Never.

Q. As you have acknow'dg'd that you told the Gov'r that I had
represented him to be a Tyrant, had you no other reason for so
saying than the opinion you formed on the written paper I gave
you?—*A.* No.

Q. How do you justify yourself in the presence of God and man
for being the cause of my standing at this Bar to defend myself
against an accusation of calling the Gov'r a Tyrant and a Robber,
when you acknowl'dge you never heard me utter such words?—*A.*
I do not think that is the cause of your being brought here.

The Evidence on the part of the Crown being closed, the Court
are of opinion that the Prisoner need not make any Defence.

FINDING OF THE COURT.

The Court are of Opinion that no one of the Charges of which you
are arraigned before this Court have been proved; that the Speech
you made before the Bench of Magistrates was not seditious or
stronger language than an unauthorized seizure of your property
might warrant, or they would have taken cognizance of it; and
that the Warrant issued against your Person on the 15th Dec'r has
been proved to the satisfaction of the Court to have been illegally
issued and served; and that the Paper writing you delivered to
Oakes, an unsworn Constable, you were defensible in. We therefore
Unanimously and Fully Acquit you of all the Charges laid in the
Information against you, and you are hereby discharged.

                              C. GRIMES, Acting Judge-Advocate.
A true Copy compared with the Original.
                                        JOHN McARTHUR, J.P.
                                        CHARLES THROSBY, J.P.

[Enclosure No. 17.]

THE EXAMINATION of Mr. Robert Fitz, Deputy Commissary:—

New South Wales.
27th Jany., 1808.

Q. You have been a Deputy Commissary in this Colony about 17
Months?—*A.* Yes.

Q. During which time (until within a few weeks) you attended
on Duty at the Commissary's Office?—*A.* Yes.

Q. Relate what you know as to the appropriation of His Majesty's
Stores?—*A.* Governor Bligh has regularly been supplied with Cloathing for all his Servants, and for which I believe no charge is made
in the Books of the Office. The Governor has also been supplied
with Spirits from the Bonded Store, and at one time took for his
use a quantity of Port wine, and a few days prior ordered wine to be
purchased from Mr. Campbell at £3 10s. per Dozen for the use of
the General Hospital.

Q. What quantity of Port wine, as you suppose, was taken by
the Governor?—*A.* As far as I can judge, about a Pipe.

1808.
11 April.

Examination of
Robert Fitz.

Q. What quantity of Wine was purchased of Mr. Campbell?—*A.* I cannot recollect the quantity, but what was purchased was paid for by a bill on His Majesty's Treasury.

Q. Has Mr. Palmer, the Commissary, been in the habit of issuing articles from the King's Stores without previously obtaining the Governor's Permission for that purpose?—*A.* He has.

Q. Does it come within your knowledge that Articles have been sent from the Stores to the Hawkesbury, where they have been appropriated to the private use of Governor Bligh?—*A.* Yes; but having been at Hawkesbury only a week I cannot speak to any more than a quantity of Nails.

Q. What number of Convicts are victualled from the Public Stores belonging to Governor Bligh's farm at the Hawkesbury?—*A.* Upwards of 20. I believe 27 besides Captain Putland's men.

Q. What Quantity of Spirits has there been lately sent up to the Hawkesbury to be issued to the Settlers under your directions?—*A.* 1,040 Gallons by Gauge, which yielded 1,047 by issue.

Q. How was it distributed, and how was it paid for?—*A.* It was distributed in stipulated quantities by the Governor's Order, and paid for by Wheat turned into Store, The Receipts being first signed by the Storekeeper, and then given to me.

Q. Does it come within your knowledge that other Hospital Necessaries, exclusive of the Port wine, as well as different kinds of Goods sent out by Government for Barter, have been taken by Governor Bligh, and appropriated to his private purposes?—*A.* I know of a quantity of curled hair, as well as Candles, Duck, and other Articles, as it was always customary to comply with all Orders sent by the Governor for the Issue of Stores.

Q. Do you know of a quantity of Oil having been purchased by Mr. Commissary Palmer of his Brother-in-Law, Mr. Campbell, for the public use, and what price was paid for it per Gallon?—*A.* I cannot speak as to the quantity, but what has hitherto been paid for was at 4s. Per Gallon.

Q. At the time Mr. Palmer was giving 4s. per Gallon for Oil, does it not come within your knowledge that he could have purchased it elsewhere at 2s. 6d.?—*A.* Mr. Lord has informed me that he offered Oil at that Price.

Q. Does Mr. Palmer still continue to take Oil from Mr. Campbell as he wants it for Public use?—*A.* Yes.

Q. Has Mr. Palmer to your knowledge any share in the Oil which he gets from Mr. Campbell?—*A.* I have heard that he has.

Q. Do you issue Stores at Hawkesbury by your own Authority, or do you receive Orders for that purpose from the resident Magistrate?—*A.* I receive Orders from the Magistrate.

R. FITZ, Dy. Commiss'y.

Taken before Wm. Minchin, Robert Townson, Nicholas Bayly, G. Blaxcell.

[Enclosure No. 18.]

Examination
of James
Wilshire.

THE EXAMINATION of James Wilshire, Deputy Commissary:— Sydney, New South Wales, 26 Jany., 1808.

Q. Up to what Period have you given in to Governor Bligh The Return of Expenditure of Grain and Provisions in your Charge, and the Quantity of each Article remaining?—*A.* I cannot tell without referring to my Books; but I believe it is three weeks or a month since I gave the Governor my Return.

Q. Has not Mr. Commissary Palmer taken from you Stores at various times—Wheat, Flour, and Maize—which to your knowledge has been converted to his own private purposes as a Baker?—*A.* Yes, he has.

Q. You say he has taken Grain and Flour at different times; but, it is to be presumed, not without an intention of replacing it; Does he. therefore, at this time stand indebted to the Store in any quantity of the above Articles?—*A.* To the best of my recollection, he owes the Stores 100 Bushels of Wheat, about 2,000 lbs. of Flour, and 100 Bushels of Maize; but it can be more correctly ascertained by referring to my Books.

Q. Does it come within your knowledge that Mr. Commissary Palmer has been in the habit of directing Maize to be received into His Majesty's Stores, and ordering the same to be noted in the Books as Wheat received, charging One Bushel of Wheat for two Bushels of Maize?—*A.* Mr. Palmer at one time standing indebted to the Stores between Two and Three Hundred Bushels of Wheat, said he had a quantity of Maize which he would turn into the Stores, two for one—that is, meaning Two Bushels of Maize for One Bushel of Wheat. He put a Quantity of Maize into the Stores at that time; but, from Information which I conceive he received of this transaction being known, he directed me to give him Credit for the Maize, and afterwards made good the Wheat for which he then stood indebted.

Q. What was the Price paid for Maize received into the Stores at the time Mr. Palmer turned in the above quantity?—*A.* Six Shillings Per Bushel.

Q. What was the Price of Wheat?—*A.* Fourteen Shillings and nine Pence Per Bushel.

JAMES WILSHIRE, Actg. Dep. Commissary.

Taken before A. F. Kemp, Wm. Minchin, Wm. Lawson, G. Blaxcell.

[Enclosure No. 19.]

EXAMINATION of Mr. John Gowen, Superintendent of Stores:— New South Wales, 28th Jany., 1808.

Q. Are all Orders for the Issue of any Stores directed to you?— *A.* After being countersigned by Mr. Palmer.

Q. Do the orders state how the Articles are to be paid for?—*A.* Generally.

Q. Has Mr. Palmer Since Governor Bligh's Command received any Articles from you?—*A.* Mr. Gowen produces a List of the Articles issued to Mr. Palmer for which he has received his Verbal orders, who said He would at a future period give him the Governor's order; also two Boxes of Candles which he does not know if entered.

Q. Do you know if the Articles in the List have been paid for?— *A.* They have not been paid for nor are they entered in the Day-Book.

Q. Has Mr. Palmer not received any other Articles from the Stores under your charge?—*A.* None without being regularly entered.

Q. Has Charles Thompson received any Articles since Governor Bligh's command from your Stores, and by whose order?—*A.* He has received considerable quantities, both in his own name and others, by orders Signed by Governor Bligh, and countersigned by Mr. Palmer, that the articles so delivered have been paid for either in Wheat Receipts, or Copper Coin on delivery.

Q. Do you know that Charles Thompson is in the constant habit of retailing the Articles he has received from the Stores at a great Advance?—*A.* Charles Thompson keeps a Public Shop, but the Deponent never was in it, but by common report has heard he does Sell Such Articles.

Q. Who have received the Boxes of Candles from the Stores?—*A.* The officers only.

Q. Has not Andrew Thompson received Stores on the Public Account by the Governor's order?—*A.* He has, in large quantities.

Q. Is it not customary to Send all articles for the Public Use to the Commissary or Storekeeper having charge of distant Public Stores?—*A.* Since Governor Bligh's Command, Articles have been sent to Individuals and not to the Commissary or Storekeeper either at Parramatta or Hawkesbury, which mode was never practiced by any former Governor.

Q. Have you ever received Mr. Palmer's or any other private Notes in Payment for Articles delivered from the Stores you have the charge of?—*A.* I have received private Notes and keep them until I have an order from the Commissary (sometimes verbally from Holmes, the Office-Keeper) for Sums of Money when he takes the Person's receipt for the Sum so delivered, and charges in my Accounts to the Commissary.

Q. Have you not received more of Mr. Palmer's Notes than any other Persons?—*A.* I have, by the particular direction of Mr. Palmer, received his Notes in preference.

Q. Has not Thomas Abbott, dealer, received quantities of Stores from you, and by whose order, and how paid for?—*A.* Thomas Abbott has received Articles from me; most of the orders were signed by the Commissary, Mr. Palmer only expressing that they were to be charged to Mr. Palmer's Account.

Q. Do you within your knowledge know that Thomas Abbott sells the Articles he has received from the Public Stores openly in his Shop?—*A.* I never was in Thomas Abbott's Shop, but have heard he does.

Q. Has Mr. Campbell received any Articles from the dry Stores. by whose order, and how paid for?—*A.* Mr. Campbell has received 312 Yards of Canvas by Mr. Palmer's verbal order only in Dec'r, 1806, expressing that it was to be replaced the first Supplies; it has not been returned, nor entered in the Day-Book.

Sworn before me: C. GRIMES, J.P.   JNO. GOWEN.

A true Copy compared with the Original.

A. F. KEMP, J.P.
CHAS. THROSBY, J.P.

[Enclosure No. 20.]

EXAMINATION of Mr. William Baker, Storekeeper of His Majesty's Stores at the River Hawkesbury, before A. F. Kemp, William Minchin, and C. Grimes, Esqres., 30th January, 1808.

Cumberland to wit.

Q. Are you the Storekeeper at the Hawkesbury?—*A.* I am.

Q. What Receipts do you give for Stores sent under your charge? —*A.* A List is sent by the Commissary, and I give a Receipt on the delivery.

Side notes:

1808.
11 April.

Examination of John Gowen.

Examination of William Baker.

1808.
11 April.

Examination
of William
Baker.

Q. In what manner is Grain received into your Stores?—*A.* I give Receipts for all Grain I receive, which Receipts are taken to the Commissary's Office; and should the Persons be indebted to the Government the amount is placed to their Credit, but does not know how the persons are paid should they not be indebted to the Crown.

Q. Has there been any Irregularities in your Department in the expenditure of Public Grain under your Charge?—*A.* About three months since, when the Stores were not open for the General Receipt of Indian Corn, I was directed personally by Governor Bligh, in the presence of the Commissary, to receive the Indian Corn which had been grown on a purchased Farm of Gov'r Bligh's on the Hawkesbury River, and directed by the Governor to make out Receipts for the Grain so taken into the Stores in the name of Andrew Thompson, and that since that Period the Deponent has issued weekly from the Stores Eight Bushels of Maize for the private use of Governor Bligh's farm; and the Governor in the presence of Mr. Palmer (the Commissary) ordered me to expend the Corn so issued in my Public Returns as issued for the use of Government Stock; another irregularity, about four or five months since, was that the Deponent was verbally ordered by Mr. Palmer, the Commissary, to issue to his (Mr. Palmer's) Overseer of his Farm at the Hawkesbury twelve Bed Ticks for the purpose of making Bags for carrying Grain, saying, "you know how to expend them." The Bed Ticks were issued and not entered in the Issue Book of the Store.

Mr. Baker further states that from 27th August, 1807, the Period that Governor Bligh purchased Tyler Farm at the Hawkesbury, thirty-three men have been victualled from the Public Stores, and one Woman, who were employed on the Governor's Farm. That when called on at the General Muster about Ten weeks since, as usual, to answer for the number of Persons victualled, he was designed by the Commissary (Mr. Palmer) not to take any notice of Governor Bligh's Servants, and Fifteen of the number were accounted for by Andrew Thompson, The Governor's Bailiff or Overseer of his Farm, and principal Constable at the Hawkesbury, as employed in the Camp Gang, which Gang are supposed to be working for the sole advantage of the Crown. There are now victualled Six Men on the Farm of the late Captain John Putland from the Stores at the Hawkesbury.

WM. BAKER.

Q. Did you at any time receive payment for Grain from Mr. Commissary Palmer which was not put in the Public Stores?—*A.* Previous to Mr. Palmer's leaving the Colony for England, Mr. Palmer was indebted to the Deponent £53 Sterlg., and Mr. Palmer directed a Receipt for Grain put into the Public Stores (but does not recollect in whose name) to be made out by one of the Clerks. The Deponent is to his own knowledge certain that the Grain was never put into any Public Store, and the Deponent did receive the Receipt as payment of the above Sum of Fifty-three Pounds Sterling.

WM. BAKER.

A true Copy compared with the Original.

A. F. KEMP, J.P.
CHAS. THROSBY, J.P.

[Enclosure No. 21.]

1808.
11 April.

Examination
of Andrew
Frazier.

ANDREW FRAZIER being duly Sworn answers to the following Questions:—

Q. You are the Baker belonging to Mr. Palmer, the Commissary?—A. I am; but the Bakehouse business is conducted in the name of Christopher Palmer.

Q. Have you ever received ' Grain from the Public Stores and baked it either into Biscuit or Bread, and by what sort of Order did you receive such Grain from the Public Stores?—A. I have received Grain very often from the Public Stores, by Order of my Master, Mr. Commissary Palmer, sometimes expressing the particular Service for which the Grain is to be expended—and sometimes for the Government use.

Q. Are you certain all the Grain you have so received by the several Orders has been absolutely expended on Public Services in its kind?—A. When I receive Wheat from the Public Stores for the purpose of baking into Biscuit for the Colonial Vessels, or any other Public Service, I am directed and do mix, by order of my Master, Mr. Commissary Palmer, a certain proportion of Maize or Barley, the Private Property of Mr. Palmer, and issue for the Government use a quantity of Biscuit equal to the weight the Wheat would have produced; this has been the Custom since Governor Bligh's Command; but during the Government of Governor King, I always received the different kind of Grain of which I made Public biscuit from the Stores, in the proportion I made such Bread.

Q. Is not the Wheat you receive from the Public Stores, if baken without any mixture, of more value than the Biscuit or Bread you issue on the Public Account?—A. It is.

Q. Is not the Grain which you bake into Biscuit or Bread for Public Services ground at the Public Expence, and are you not paid a certain Sum of money Per Cwt. for your Labour in making such Grain into Bread?—A. Seven Shillings and Sixpence Per Cwt. is allowed and paid for in Grain from the Public Stores at the Current Price; the Grain is always made into Flour at the Public Expence.

his
ANDREW   X   FRAZIER.
mark

A true Copy compared with the Original.

A. F. KEMP, J.P.
CHAS. THROSBY, J.P.

[Enclosure No. 22.]

EXAMINATION of Mr. John Jamieson, Superintendent of Stock, taken before A. F. Kemp, C. Grimes, and John Blaxland, Esqres., and Lieutenant Lawson.

Examination of
John Jamieson.

New South Wales,
28 Jany., 1808.

Q. What Orders have you received to deliver Cattle to Individuals, by Governor Bligh, as a Present?—A. Mrs. Putland, two Cows; Mr. Williamson, one Cow; Mrs. Fitz, one Cow; Mr. Fulton, One Cow (not expressed if a present or not); George Crossley, one Cow and one Bullock (not expressed, as usual, if a present, or to be paid for); Mrs. Gore, One Cow.

1808.
11 April.

Examination of
John Jamieson.

Q. What number of Cattle or Stock of any kind have you delivered by Governor Bligh's Order for his own private use or advantage?— *A.* Twenty Cows. and twenty Calves by their sides, consisting— Males 5, and Females 15; One Bull, Thirty Ewes, and thirty Lambs (the Lambs—Males, 15; Females, 15), Six Sows in Pig, and one Boar; Six Sows went to Governor Bligh's Farm without Mr. Jamieson's knowledge, which Sows were likewise in Pig. On Mr. Jamieson's making inquiry from the Overseer who had charge of the Pigs, why he delivered the Six Sows without his direction, was informed that an Order had been sent by Mr. Palmer, the Commissary, for their delivery. Mr. Jamieson conceives that his having taken notice of the irregularity in his department was the cause of the Six Sows being returned to Castle Hill (from whence they were taken), but in bad Condition; they left the Government Drove in Pig, and, after being absent Six or Seven weeks, they were returned not in Pig. Mr. Jamieson, to the best of his belief, conceives the Six Sows that were returned, on their being taken from the Government Drove, must have been within about a week of the time of farrowing. Mr. Jamieson further states that, some Months after his having chosen and sent the twenty Cows and Calves to Governor Bligh's Farm, the Governor went to the Hawkesbury and saw his Cows. The Governor, some weeks after his return from the Hawkesbury, expressed a dislike to Seven or Eight of the Cows chosen by Mr. Jamieson, and said he would give him an Order to exchange them. About a fortnight after the above Conversation, Andrew Thompson, the Governor's Overseer to his Farm, came to Mr. Jamieson with a verbal message to know when it would be convenient for him to exchange the Eight Cows Governor Bligh had disapproved of? Mr. Jamieson had selected seven only, immediately after his Conversation with the Governor, of the best Cows in the Government Herds, and had given directions to the Drover to deliver them to any person who came in the Governor's name. Eight Cows were driven by Andrew Thompson to the Government Herd, and, Mr. Jamieson having only selected Seven Cows, Thompson remained until an Order was brought from Mr. Jamieson to deliver the Eighth, in which Order Jamieson directed the herdsman to give a Cow equal to those he had selected, which were the best in the Herds. Mr. Jamieson has never since received the written Order promised by Governor Bligh, nor were the Calves belonging to the Eight Cows returned with them. Mr. Jamieson states that a difficulty was suggested by Mr. Palmer, how the twenty Calves and thirty Lambs were to be accounted for in the Public Returns, for the Calves and Lambs had been entered. On consulting how the deficiency could be accounted for, the accounts being then going Home, it was determined that the next twenty Calves and thirty Lambs which might fall should not be entered in the Returns, which would make it appear that Governor Bligh had only received twenty Cows and thirty Ewes.

Q. What quantity of Sheep, Hogs, or Bullocks have you delivered weekly for the domestic use of the Government House?—*A.* Mr. Jamieson cannot from recollection state, but he makes Public Returns. One Bullock is constantly killed every week, but sometimes two—the Returns state the particulars; twenty Wethers are sent at a time, which usually last about five or six weeks; until within about two Months there was a Sow heavy in Pig sent down weekly. Mr. Jamieson has often been surprized how Sows so heavy in pig could be destroyed at a time when Pigs were so scarce—so many having been destroyed by the unfortunate Flood at the Hawkesbury, and which made their destruction of the utmost consequence to the Colony.

JNO. JAMIESON.

Q. What quantity of Pigs are now under your charge belonging to Government?—A. There are nine.

Q. What has been done with the others?—A. I was informed, about Six weeks since, by the Overseer at Castle Hill, that Mr. Williamson, the Deputy Commissary, had been at Castle Hill to value all the Government Pigs. On receiving the Information, Mr. Jamieson questioned Mr. Williamson about the Transaction, who informed him that he had been directed by Letter from the Commissary, Mr. Palmer, to go and value all the Pigs belonging to Government; and, to the best of Mr. Jamieson's knowledge, Mr. Williamson informed him he had valued them at from 5d. to 7d. Per lb. About a fortnight after receiving this Information, one of his Overseers of the Public Stock came and informed Mr. Jamieson that George Crossley was at Castle Hill, and the Superintendant, Knight, was weighing the Pigs and branding them; that the Pigs were driven away either that Evening or the following Morning. Mr. Jamieson gave a discharge the week following for the 89 Pigs in the Public Returns to George Crossley, though he never received (as was usual on the location of all Public Stock) any Order or Message whatever.

JNO. JAMIESON.

A true Copy compared with the Original.

A. F. KEMP, J.P.
CHAS. THROSBY, J.P.

[Enclosure No. 23.]

DEPOSITION of Andrew Thompson before J. Jamieson and C. Grimes, Esqres., being duly sworn, Deposeth to the Questions asked him.

New South Wales,
26 Jany., 1808.

Q. Have you the management of the Public business at the Hawkesbury—A. I have, under Mr. Arndell. There are above an hundred Men victualled by Government. There are from twenty to thirty Men employed on Governor Bligh's Farm; there has been thirty victualled by the Crown. There are seven at Captain Putland's Farm now. I have drawn various supplies for Governor Bligh's Farm from the Public Stores. I have the account. I have drawn quantities of Stores on my own account from the Public Stores, which are paid for, and I have credit, I believe, with the Commissary. I have the charge of Governor Bligh's Private Concerns at the Hawkesbury.* Twenty Cows with Calves were drawn from the Public Herds on account of Governor Bligh, and Eight Cows heavy in Calf on account of Captain and Mrs. Putland. Seven or eight of the Cows without their Calves were returned to the Government Herds, and an equal number drawn in Calf on Governor Bligh's Account. There were twelve of the best Sows in Pig drawn from the Government drove at Castle Hill, and a Boar, and thinks (but can ascertain it by his returns) that Six were returned after

* Note 106.

Pigging, without their young ones, to Castle Hill; that they were fed by Grain or refuse Grain from the Public Stores, and driven into the Woods in the day time on account of Governor Bligh; that there were Pigs afterwards received both from Sydney and Castle Hill, said to belong to Governor Bligh. There has been a large quantity of Cedar received on account of the Public and Governor Bligh; that I have had a quantity of Cedar from the Mountains on my own account without duty by Permission from the Governor. Part of the Cedar has been appropriated to building Pews in the Church at Hawkesbury. The Pew marked No. 1 is built for the Governor. Andrew Thompson's name is marked on Pew No. 2. The Magistrates Pew will come in about No. 14. The Pew marked No. 2 was built by the Public Labourers and in part by the Public Timber. I manage the Governor's dairy Concerns at the Hawkesbury and dispose of his Milk at 10d. Per Quart. I take Grain in payment for the Milk, which Grain I have on hand. I have about Seventy or Eighty Pounds Sterling worth of Grain on account of Milk belonging to Governor Bligh. I have put into the Stores about two thousand Bushels of Grain within these twelve Months on my own account, but will give an exact return. I have about thirty Convicts in my employ, most of them good Men. I picked them when I had an opportunity. I drew One hundred and ten Gallons of Prize Spirits by Governor Bligh's permission, about two months ago, for which I am to pay about 8s. Per Gallon, and have sold it in small quantities at from 18s. to 20s. Per Bottle. I have received during the last Twelve months about Three hundred Gallons exclusive of the Prize Spirits. I have never had any Colonial distilled Spirits to my knowledge in my House, within this last twelve months, or had any sold on my account. George Crossley has informed me he was consulted by the Governor. George Crossley has informed me that the Charge against Mr. McArthur was liable to be punished by Fine, Imprisonment, or Pillory, but that he thought it would not reach the Pillory in this Colony. Since the Criminal Court has been sitting, Geo. Crossley has spoken about the Judge-Advocate leaving his Seat, and said that they were not a Court without the Judge-Advocate. I have been consulted by the Governor on Public Affairs and some things of little consequence about the Officers. That I have been on very good terms with the Governor. I have heard that the Governor has said that he preferred sitting down with an Hawkesbury Settler than an Officer, and is not certain Governor Bligh did not tell him so. The Governor has about Seventy or Eighty Sheep on his Farm, originally drawn from the Public Flocks. The Governor has a Shed on his Farm of about Two hundred feet long, weather-boarded and shingled, with a Barn of Brick 50 ft. by 18, a Brick House about 50 by 14 feet containing three Rooms, and there is another House of nearly the same dimensions now building; all the Buildings were completed by the Labourers of the Crown. I imagine the Buildings would cost an Individual upwards of a Thousand Pounds; but I can give a nearer Estimate. Nine Oxen were generally employed, fed by Grain from the Public Store. James Simpson has had two Men fed by the Crown, from nearly the time that Governor Bligh purchased his Farm, one as a Settler and the other as a Constable, that I passed my Note for the purchase of the Farm, £100, which was to be paid me from the Produce of Governor Bligh's Farm put into the Store. I hold Governor Bligh's Memorandum to that effect. I

have no particular Instructions from Governor Bligh about his
Farm, but I have been informed by Governor Bligh that the Stock
and Articles drawn from the Store were to be paid for, and he
wished everything to be fair and Honorable.

1808.
11 April.
Deposition of
Andrew
Thompson.

AND'W THOMPSON.

A true Copy compared with the Original.

A. F. KEMP, J.P.
CHAS. THROSBY, J.P.

[Enclosure No. 24.*]

[1] MR. ANDREW THOMPSON TO GOVERNOR BLIGH.

Sir,   Hawkesbury, 16th October, 1807.

Correspondence
and returns
relating to
Bligh's farm.

I beg leave to inform your Excellency that I went into
Toongabbee Yards and exchanged eight of the inferior Cows,
with the Bull, and obtained good and sufficient ones in their room,
which will fully Answer the purpose and make a great difference
and advantage in your Excellency's Flock, which, from pasturage
and attention, will be one of the best in the Colony to their
Number, the Cows being now again all in Calf; also, all the other
Stock is in a prosperous State, as per returns inclosed. I did not
get up your Excellency's Pigs from Castle Hill, as one of them
had just farrowed and could not travel, but will on Monday next.
We are planting the Maize to the best advantage by manuring
all the upper lands, &c., which will be done in a day or two, when
we will turn our prompt attention towards the Buildings and Inclosures until Harvest, that will shortly come on, as all your
Excellency's Wheat in the Upper lands is now in Ear, which,
with the General Crops in this Extensive Settlement, has every
appearance of giving a plenteous and joyful Harvest to make
the People happy under your Excellency's Auspicious and benign
Government, the Beauty and Gratification of which would be
highly enhanced should your Excellency, amidst your many and
important Duties, be pleased to visit our ample plains in the full
fruition of Harvest.

I beg leave with the most profound respect to subscribe myself
Sir, Your Excellency's, &c.,

AND'W THOMPSON.

17th October, 9 o'clock p.m.

P.S.—I open this on the receipt of your Excellency's to inform
you, if you please, that I delivered you the transfer of Simpson's
Estate, and that your Excellency put it, with other Papers, I
think, into a Desk on the Bill Room Table upstairs, and has no
other papers of consequence relative to Estates up here except
the inclosed agreement of the Overseers, which I had kept with
a design of settling with him myself, if pleased. He is a very
serviceable, attentive, Active Man at present on these Estates. I

* Note 106.

1808.
11 April.
Correspondence
and returns
relating to
Bligh's farm.
will take the liberty of waiting on your Excellency in a Week's time with the little curiosities, &c. I have taken the Liberty of sending a few, just caught, live fresh-Water Fish, hearing Captain Putland had a desire for such, and would be glad to send more at any time if acceptable.

I am, Sir, your Excellency's Devoted, &c.,

AND'W THOMPSON.

A true Copy compared with the Original by us.

JOHN MCARTHUR, J.P.
CHAS. THROSBY, J.P.

[2] COPY OF MEMORANDUM IN GOV. BLIGH'S HANDWRITING 1807.

	Dr.			Cr.		
	£	s.	d.	£	s.	d.
January 1st to purchase Money for 146 Acres of Thomas Tyler	150	0	0			

By Articles found at the Farm as Follows :—
One Iron Pot, One Axe, One Spade, One Shovel, One Grubbing Hoe, Two Hoes, One Old Bucket.

To Articles furnished as follows :—
One Bucket, One Iron Pot, Two Spades, Six Hoes, Four Scythes, One Brush Hook, One Maul and 2 Wedges, One Mill and one Sieve berr'd Thompson, One Padlock One File Do. Do., 10,000 Nails of Sorts, Two Axes New, 40 Boards, 3 Pieces of Quartering.
April 18th : 1 Bull, 28 Cows, 5 Bull Calves, 15 Heiffer Do., 9 Working Bullocks, 6 Breeding Sows.

May 27th By Sale of 93½ Bushels @ 6s. 112 Dolls 1s. £28 1 0

A true Copy compared with the Original by us.

JOHN MCARTHUR, J.P.
CHAS. THROSBY, J.P.

[3] A GENERAL ACCOUNT of labour done at His Excellency's Farm, Stock, Tools &c. up to August 22nd 1807 as pr. Sundry returns.

	A.	R.	P.
Wheat sewed chipped and Harrowed in	40	0	0
Brush, Corn, Stalks, &c. cut and bruised off	37	3	0
Breaking up ....\..............	37	3	0
Timber fell	14	2	0
Burned off	4	0	0
Fell and burned off, dead Trees left standing and Bodies of others left lying on	28	0	0
Breaking up New Ground and chipping it again ..	2	1	0

Pulled Husked and delivered of Maize 84 Bushel. Repaired Two Houses and a Barn. One House Built, Weather-Boarded, Floored and Shingled, with Chimney, Doors, Window Shutters &c. &c. com-

1808.
11 April.

Correspondence
and returns
relating to
Bligh's farm.

pleat. A Large shed for Stock 120 feet long, part Weather boarded and Shingled. Made three Ladders and split and drew in 4,000 pailing. Getting and carrying Home Posts, Railing, Timber for Sawyers, &c. &c. A Paddock Fence, with Posts and Railing, and One Railed Yard 14 Rod Square. Two Large Pailed Yards, with Styes, Pens, &c. done with pailing, put up and nailed compleat. Split and carried Home 24,600 Shingles. Sawyers Work done of Scantling Boards and Battins, 6,556 feet.

Bricks made and burned 25,000
Bricks made and not burned 21,000
                                              _____
                                    Total 46.000

Live Stock received from Parramatta.

Cows	20	Stock received from Parramatta for Captain Putland
Bull	1	
Heiffer Calves encrease here	2	
Heiffer Calves received ...	15	Cows 8
Bull Calves received	5	14 Jany. 1 Cow and Calf 2
Working Bullocks	9	Encrease here Bull Calves 2
His Excellency's horned Cattle .... Total	52	Capt. Putland's Horned Cattle .... Total 12

Live Stock Continued—From Sydney.

Received from Parramatta		Goats Female 2
Female Sheep	46	Breeding Sows 3
Male Do.	14	Young Pigs Male 1
Young Lambs encrease here Male	5	Do. Do. Female 1
Do. Do. Female	14	
	79	7

Received from Castle Hill.

Breeding Sows	12	Fowls rec'd from Mr. A.T.
Boar	1	5 Young Hens and 1 Cock 6
Young Pigs encrease here Male	30	1 Turkey Hen and Cock .
Do. Do. Female	20	2 Geese and a Gander ..
		2 Ducks and a Drake ... 2
	63	14

Totals Horned Cattle 64
       Sheep 79
       Goats 2
       Swine 68
                   _____
                   163 Head

Fowles Ducks, Geese and Turkies 14

A true Copy compared with the Original before us.

JOHN McARTHUR, J.P.
CHAS. THROSBY, J.P.

1808.
11 April.

Correspondence
and returns
relating to
Bligh's farm.

Tools &c. Received pr. Mr. A. T.

2 Cross Cut Saws, 1 Pitt Saw, 1 Hand Saw, 3 Wedges and 1 Maul,
3 Froes, 13 Hoes, 3 Grubbing Hoes, 7 Axes, 3 Brush Hooks, 5 Spades
and Shovels, 4 Scythes Worn out, 4 Files Do., 1 Do. borrowed of
Mr. Thompson, 2 Mills 1 borrowed of Do., 2 Seives, 1 Fork, 1 Rake,
1 Padlock borrowed of Mr. A. T., 4 Buckets, 6 Buckets Worn out,
12 Yds. Canvas made into 5 Bags, 3 Ladders, 1 Grinding Stone,
2 Pr. of Handcuffs, 2 Wheel Barrows, 5 Iron Pots, 5 Casks,
12 Blankets issued to Government Men, 33 Yds. Grey Cloth for
Blanketting Do. Do., 1 Cart and Harness for Bullock with Iron
Axletree Iron Traces and Collar compleat, 1 Brick Makers Bench
Stock and Moulds, 1 Timber Carriage, 6 Bois and Traces, 2 Broad
Axes, 2 Adzes, 4 Tommy Hawks, 2 Augurs, 1 Harrow, 6,000 Nails in
hand and all the rest used, 17 Gimlets, 3 Hammers, 18 Planes of
different sizes and Moulds, 2 Plough or Phillister Do., 6 Jack trying
or smoothing Plains, 1 Guage, 1 Draw Knife, 1 Pr. Compass, 10
Chizzels of different sizes, 9 Gouges Do. Do., 2 Hammers, 6 Pieces
of Old Rope for Bullocks Tethers Timber Carriages &c. &c. &c.
A true Copy compared with the Original before us.

JOHN McARTHUR, J.P.
CHAS. THROSBY, J.P.

[4] MR. ANDREW THOMPSON TO GOVERNOR BLIGH.

Hawkesbury, 19th December, 1807.
May it please Your Excellency,
As the Harvest is now finished, and near the end of the
year, and your Excellency unfortunately unable to come up to see
the Progress made on your Estate, I take the Liberty to enclose a
Kind of general agregate Statement of improvements and a fuller
description of Cattle, with their Names, &c., that your Excellency
might know and be convinced that your Estate and Stock was
making every possible profitable progress and Improvement that
could be made; and without troubling your Excellency's Attention from the important Duties of your high and dignified
Situation elsewhere required, humbly begging leave to assure and
point out to your Excellency that I ever have and will use every
means in my Power (and I trust none could or would do it
better) towards the Improvement of the Estate and Stock, which
will prove to the fullest Advantage, as I pointed out to your
Excellency, in a Year or two more, As I hope now plainly
appears from what I have done this first Season as a beginning
only, and all things are now in a regular train; The Male Stock
of all kinds coming on in fat and high Order for marketing to
good Advantage; the Crops of Wheat now secured, and that of
Corn growing; the Good Buildings, inclosures, and improvements
enhances the value of the Plantation according to their Value;
the produce of the Dairy now about Seven Pounds Sterling per

1808.
11 April.

Correspondence
and returns
relating to
Bligh's farm.

Week; and the great increase of stock, under care and attention, is of great Value; but of such things I can as opportunity offers point out more plainly hereafter on the Spot.

I have taken the Liberty to make a kind of private Testimony inclosed wherein I would hold myself responsible in every Shape and bound in my own Person and Property that there has, nor shall be, no error, impropriety, debt, or incumbrance on the Management of your Excellency's Estate; with a desire to Show that everything was done only with a genuine desire to serve and please your Excellency, having ever felt the most grateful Pleasure and satisfaction in being able to render myself in the smallest degree serviceable or acceptable in your sight, and nothing could cause Me more compunction and grief than the Idea of having offended your Excellency.

I beg leave, with the most profound Gratitude and respect, to Subscribe myself, sir, Yours, &c.,

AND'W THOMPSON.

A true Copy compared with the Original by us.

JOHN McARTHUR, J.P.
CHAS. THROSBY, J.P.

[5] EXTRACTED from Private Ledger.

Hawkesbury, 19th December, 1807.

Weekly account with W. Walker, of Milk delivered from His Excellency's Dairy. N.B.—Walker to have the Brick House, &c., rent free, for selling this and Mr. Thompson's other Milk, from this 4th of October, 1807.

				£	s.	d.
From October 4th to the 11th,	84	Quarts at 10d. per Quart		3	0	10
11th to the 19th,	93	Do.		3	17	6
19th to the 26th,	100	Do.		4	3	4
26th to Nov'r 1,	135	Do.		5	12	6
From November 1 to the 9th,	150	Do.		6	3	0
9th to the 16th,	152	Do.		6	6	8
16th to the 23rd,	168	Do.		7	0	0
23rd to the 30th,	181	Do.		7	10	10
30th to Dec'r 7,	187	Do.		7	15	10
From December 7 to the 14th,	191	Do.		7	19	2

Total Cash in hand for His Excellency on this Account is 60 0 10

PRIVATE Remarks and true calculations on His Excellency's farming concerns, Stock and Estate, here.

The fat Weathers and Weather Lambs, the Barrow Swine that will be fat for killing, when butchered and sold to the best Advantage for Grain, as my own, instead of allowing such extortionate profit to the Butcher, will save the poor People more, and bring about Six pounds each on average. Sheep and Lambs, admits of a

1808.
11 April.

Correspondence
and returns
relating to
Bligh's farm.

certain calculation for a return of Cash at the end of the ensuing Quarter, by said Grain, with the Farms' produce, &c., being put into Store, about to the following Amount, viz.,—

24 Wedders and Lambs and 5 Swine, at about £6, is £174 0 0
The Crop of Wheat now secured in two Stacks; and 12 Acres, part of the Crop of Maize that will be ripe then 250 0 0
Cash now in hand up to the 14th Inst., as per Dairy Account, not including this Week 60 0 10
And considering about £7 per Week for Milk up to the 31st March, the end of the Quarter, when the Cost Bills of this place is consolidated, being 15 Weeks, will be ....:.................................. 105 0 0

Total Cash to be realised this Season on the trivial things without reducing the Principles, which will remain worth £3,678, Established Stock, &c. 589 0 10

It is to be hoped His Excellency will pardon the Liberty of these private hints, and should they not be approved of, any other directions will be very carefully obeyed by His Excellency's Devoted Servant,

ANDREW THOMPSON.

A true Copy compared with the Original by us.
JOHN MCARTHUR, J.P.
CHAS. THROSBY, J.P.

[6] DECLARATION OF ANDREW THOMPSON.

Hawkesbury, 19th December, 1807.

HAVING undertaken the Management of an Estate here for His Excellency Gov'r Bligh, purchased last Season from Tyler and Simpson, with the grand design of showing what great Improvements and Progress could be made on Farming and Colonial Estates here, Season by Season, under strict attention and industry, proper plans, and good Management, and by such a Noble, laudible, and public example in a Chief Governor (as shown by the King of Great Britain Himself), has had its desired effects to convince and excite all descriptions of People to that Spirit of Adventure and persevering Industry which ultimately give a people happiness, plenty, and Independence. And whereas His Excellency has been pleased to trust this little Patriotic Experiment on Colonial Farming to my Charge, I do hereby certify and declare that the whole is according to the Statement given in, and has been managed without impropriety or known Error, And that there is no Debt, charge, or encumbrance standing or to pay of or belonging to the Management of this Estate of any nature or kind whatsoever up to this, as I shall answer for the same in my Character, Person, and Property in time past or to come, so long as I may have the Management thereof, as Witness my Hand, voluntarily signed, place, and date as above.   AND'W THOMPSON.

A true Copy compared with the Original by us.
A. F. KEMP, J.P.
CHAS. THROSBY, J.P.

1808.
11 April.

Correspondence
and returns
relating to
Bligh's farm.

[7] SOME OBSERVATIONS on His Excellency's Farm for the ensuing Year:—

Tyler's Farm, although eligibly and pleasantly situated, has only about 14 Acres of good land now fit or ready to grow Grain without manuring the poor lands, which never pays or yields so well as the fertile plains (and would beg leave to make a proposition on that head if His Excellency is not displeased therewith). And this next Year's produce of said Farm, on computing 15 Bushels of Wheat per Acre at 10s. per Bushel is £105 0 0
The House and improvements intended and set on foot
    for this Year will be worth and enhance the Value
    of this Estate to 400 0 0

       Total present and apparent Advantage this Year £505 0 0

Further certain advantages to be gained on it, viz., was there Six Breeding Cows, Two Mares, and Fifty Ewes placed here, as the land is good Pasturage, and a large common (the same by it), they would no doubt, from the directions, care, and attention that should be shewn them, breed almost every one, which would be then, Say, Nine Calves, breed without expense, to value £30 each 270 0 0
Also, say, 45 lambs increasing, no expense till worth
    £2 each 90 0 0
Two foals in same way would in due time give 200 0 0

     The Total profit next Year would be £1,065 0 0

N.B.—But it may be observed that a common Farmer who has to pay for everything would by no means have such profits.

Andrew Thompson would name a Plan for laying in this Stock and some other proposals for promoting His Excellency's and Captain Putland's Interest in this Business, in which He has had so much experience of Farming, if allowed that Confidence in which he would sooner lose his Existence than do anything willingly to forfeit it.

A true Copy compared with the Original by us.

                 A. F. KEMP, J.P.
                 CHAS. THROSBY, J.P.

[8] MR. ANDREW THOMPSON TO GOVERNOR BLIGH.

Sir,   Hawkesbury, 30th June, 1807.

    I take the liberty to inform your Excellency that Mr. Jamison spoke to Me at Parramatta about getting your Excellency's Sheep up here, with their last Lambs, before they yeaned again; saying it might not perhaps appear so well to have their numbers trebled in the Government Stock, and if your Excellency pleases to send up the Sheep left at Government House in Sydney by the Bearer to Govt. Flock at Toongabbee, Mr. Jamison will there give Me your Excellency's full Number of Good Sheep, and their last years Lambs: where I will attend to receive, and

1808.
11 April.
———
Correspondence
and returns
relating to
Bligh's farm.

see them safe brought out to Your Excellency's Farm: and
every care shall be taken of them, with all other of Your Excellency's Stock and concerns up here; by Sir

Your Excellency's, &c.,

AND'W THOMPSON.

A true Copy compared with the Original by us.

A. F. KEMP, J.P.
CHAS. THROSBY, J.P.

[9] RETURN of Stock Improvements, etc. at His Excellency's
Farm 19 Decr. 1807.

Cows.	Colour and Description.	Names.
1	Black with Small Horns	Violet
2	Red with Short Horns	Daisy
3	Black with White Belly ....!........	Snake
4	Brown with White Belly	Squirrel
5	Mouse Colour White Belly	White Flanks
6	Black with a Star in the Forehead	Star
7	Black with the Horn tips Cut	Black Bird
8	Black and White	White Recoup
9	Black and White	Magpye
10	Black large and Stout Made	All Black
11	Black with White Back and Legs	White Stockings
12	Red and White	Broad Horns
13	Red and Sharp Horns	Cherry
14	Black with Off Flank White	Blacky
15	Black with the Horn Tips cut	Comely
16	Red with White Back no Horns	Nutt
17	Red with long High Horns	Primrose
18	Brown with Short Horns	China
19	Brown with White Belly	Fox
20	Black with White Back	Slouch
21	Brindle no Horns	Polly
22	Brown with White Spots no Horns	Betsy

Rec'd these last 2 from Sydney since last Return and One year
Old Heiffer all sick and Weakly.

LIST and Description of Heiffers.

Year Old Heiffers.	Colour and Description.	Names.
1	Black and White	Young White Rump
2	Black	Brown Nose
3	Black with a Grey Spot on her Back ..	Grey Back
4	Brown	Young Mouse
5	Brown with White Belly	Rat
6	Red	Ginger
7	Black and White	Beauty
8	Black with White Back	Young Slouch
9	Brown	Sandy
10	Red and White Spotted	Young Nutt
11	Brown	Browny

1808.
11 April.

Correspondence
and returns
relating to
Bligh's farm.

LIST and Description of Heiffers—*continued.*

Year Old Heiffers.	*Colour and Description.*	*Names.*
12	Red and White Belly	Young Cherry
13	Speckled Red and White	Cuckow
14	Brindled	White Back
15	Red and White	Young Squirrel
16	Red Brindled with no Horns from Sydney	Young Polly (sick)

Year Old Bullocks.	*Colour and Description.*	*Names.*
1	Black	Johnny
2	Brown	Young Fox
3	Black	Young Tippoo
4	Black	Weasel
5	Red	Bottony
6	Red with Bent Horns, A Young Bull	Timmy

Encrease here 6 Male Calves
             6 Female Calves
Working Bullocks 10

	Totals.
Cows	22
Year-old Heiffers	16
Bull	1
Working bullocks	10
Encrease here	6 Male Calves
Do. Do.	6 Female Do.
Total	66 Horned Cattle

last Return, 61; Encrease since, five, Including the three received from Sydney.

Sheep.

Ewes	46	
Wethers	14	Fat
Encrease { Male Lambs	10	Fat
here { Female Do.	19	
Total	89	Sheep

Fowls, &c., &c.

Five Hens and One Cock ..	6	One Gander and two Geese .	3
Encrease fifteen Chickens ..	15	One Drake and two Ducks .	3
One Turkey Hen and Cock .	2		
		Total	29

Swine.

Breeding Sows	9	Increase here:—Sow-Slips ..	20	
Boar	1	Do.	Barrow-Slips 30	
From C. Hills Barrows	5	Do.	Suckling ... 20	
From Do. Barrow-Slips	4			
From Do. Sow-Slips ...	4	Total	93	

Increase since the last Return, 10.

1808.
11 April.

Correspondence
and returns
relating to
Bligh's farm.

RETURN of Captain Putland's Stock at His Excellency's Farm
December 19th 1807.

Cows.	Colour and Description.	Names.
1	White with Black Spots	Fanny
2	Black with White Breast	Upright
3	Grised	Grey
4	Black and White	Magpye
5	Red and White with Wide Horns	Whitesides
6	Black with Sharp Horns	Stately
7	Black with White Breast	Smith
8	Black with tips of Horns cut	White Boots
9	Black with Sharp Horns	White Tail

Male Calves encrease here 5 Female Do. 2.
Received Male Cult 1   Total 17 Horned Cattle.

Swine.		Goats.
Breeding Sows	3	Female 2 Total
Male Slip	1	
Female Do.	1	

Total 5 Swine

N.B.—The whole of the Cattle, Sheep, Swine, &c., are marked
except the young Calves and Suckling Pigs.

His Excellency's Cattle are marked on the near Horn and Hip
with the Initials of His Name Viz. W.B. The Sheep and Pigs on
the Near side or hip Do.

And

Captain Putlands with P. on the off Horn and Hip. Pigs on the
off side.

One Brick Building (as out Offices) 54 feet long 15 Wide and
9 High Containing Kitchen, Servants Room and Court House,
Kitchen flagged Window and door Frames Roofed but not Shingled;
One Brick Barn 50 feet long 18 feet Wide and 13 feet High, Wall
plates tie Beams and Rafters up, but not Shingled.

One Shed 200 F. long Weather boarded and nearly shingled containing at the End Two Rooms for Stock Men &c. as Guards, with
Double Brick Chimney Doors, Windows, &c. compleat, about the
Centre a House for the Overseer to live in with Dairy, Store Room
&c., this has also a Brick Chimney paved Floor with Doors Windows
&c. compleat, also an open part for Milking in, another for the
Sheep &c. with Pens for Calves, Styes for Pigs, Pailed and Nailed
at top and bottom with Convenient Gates, Doors &c.

A Six railed Fence forming different Paddocks or enclosures for
Stock, well Nailed and Battened at each Joining post, containing
about fifteen Acres.

Six Pailed Yards Viz. a Barnyard 100 Feet Square, a Pigyard 80
feet Square with Sheep Yard. Milking Yard House Yard and Stock
Yard, All Nailed at Top and bottom with convenient Gates and
fastenings to and from each other occasionally.

A true Copy compared with the Original by us.

A. F. KEMP, J.P.
CHAS. THROSBY, J.P.

1808.
11 April.

Correspondence and returns relating to Bligh's farm.

[10] Mr. Andrew Thompson to Governor Bligh.

Sir,   Hawkesbury, 26th March, 1807.
    I beg leave to inform your Excellency that when Mr. Knight came up yesterday about changing the Freshmen at Your Farm (which shall be done) I was out with five Men and an Overseer at Captain Putland's Farm; where I set them to work and fully surveyed it, and which I hope to improve to his Satisfaction and Interest; it being a very fine Estate; but in my humble Opinion wants a small addition of (I believe) vacant Land to make it more compleat, that I will if you please explain when I come down to Your Excellency; there also wants an adjustment of Governor King's Boundary* as his Overseer, contrary to the Opinion of the other Men there, claims a very eligible Space of Land on Captain Putland's lower side line, which can however be easily decided by Jas. Main,† who measured both Farms—I hope your Excellency will be pleased to observe by the enclosed returns that every attention is paid to your own Estate; which, in Improvements and produce, will I am certain give Your Excellency every satisfaction and profit; and more so in my humble Opinion should you be pleased to approve of some further plans which I will take the Liberty of waiting on your Excellency shortly to explain, and with due submission to your Excellency's great Wisdom, an attention to Farming and improvement, which the Sovereign was pleased to practise at Home, might not be unworthy of his Grand Representative here, as an example for all others, exciting them to that in which the riches and prosperity of States must depend—Craving your Excellency's Pardon for this Liberty and digression I beg leave with all due respect to subscribe myself
                            Your Excellency's, &c.,
                                    Andrew Thompson.
A true Copy compared with the Original by us.
                            A. F. Kemp, J.P.
                            Chas. Throsby, J.P.

[11] Mr. Andrew Thompson to Governor Bligh.
Sir,   Hawkesbury, May 27th, 1807.
    Agreeable to your Excellency's desire, I take the Liberty to enclose a list of such respectable Free Settlers (from England) as wishes to have a Man off the Stores when they are to spare.
    Inclosed also is returns of Stock and labour at your Excellency's Farm up to the end of last Week; everything is going on well, and there is now, with the addition of a little new Cultivated Ground, upwards of Eighteen Acres sowed with Wheat which looks very well. There will be a very great increase of

* Note 107.   † Note 108.

1808.
11 April.

Correspondence
and returns
relating to
Bligh's farm.

Swine shortly, considering there was only Six to breed from; but
would be very glad of an Order to Mr. Knight for Six more such,
as they would be all one trouble to take care of and a double
advantage to your Excellency. I would also beg leave again to
hint the benefit of the Flock of Ewes when you might have
leisure to give Order for them, and I would come into Toongabbe to choose and bring them safe out. Sincerely begging
leave gratefully to assure your Excellency that every exertion
shall be used in my part to promote your Excellency's wishes
and real Interest in every Shape, of which I hope in due time
to give the fullest proofs, I have took the liberty of sending One
hundred and twelve Dollars, and 1s. the price of 93½ Bushels of
nett Maize @ 6s. per Bushel of yours put in Store to my Name,
in a little Box with the Vouchers in it, not telling the Bearer
what he carried, as the lure of Money however trifling often ex-
cites peculation in this Country. I hope Your Excellency will
pardon at this Moment my not waiting on you, being very busy
in saving the Wheat seed after those seasonable Rains as well as
the people in general up here, the Season being far advanced and
the labour much retarded by the former dry weather; but now,
bless God and Your Excellency's gracious governance, there is
every happy appearance of Extensive and Ample Crops of Wheat
for the ensuing Season.

I am gratefully thankful to your Excellency for your justice
and goodness respecting the insinuations made against My
Character in telling you that I was then concerned in distilling,
To which I again beg leave to pledge My life and property *is
false,* defying any Person in existence to prove that I ever spoke
or Acted against Your Excellency's Order on this head since the
day it was published up to the present moment. But your Excellency is or will no doubt be convinced that the Slander of this
Country would deprive you of honest Men if your Excellency's
just Wisdom and penetration did not counteract such destructive
Plans.

I beg leave, with all due respect, to subscribe myself, sir,
Your Excellency's, &c.,
AND'W THOMPSON.

A true Copy compared with the Original by us.
A. F. KEMP, J.P.
CHAS. THROSBY, J.P.

[Sub-enclosure.]

Bricks made and burned for the above buildings and
others to be built, used and unused 105,000
Scantling Boards and Battins saved for do. and others
to be done, used and unused 14,954

Timber fell, burned off &c. .... 120 Acres
New Ground broke up and planted and Old do. broke
  up and planted with Maize .... 18 Do.
Grubbed up Trees Roots &c. for Garden ground .... 3 Do.
Chipped and hilled Maize .... 18 Do.
Built in the Barn Yard two Staddles, on which are built two
  Stacks of Wheat and thatched compleat.

N.B.—Much time taken up with Stock etc. also in getting and bringing home Timber for Sawyers and Fences made and to be made. ANDREW THOMPSON.

1808.
11 April.
Correspondence and returns relating to Bligh's farm.

[12] MR. ANDREW THOMPSON TO GOVERNOR BLIGH.

Sir, Hawkesbury, 1st January, 1808.

From a fidelity and strong attachment to your Excellency, which nothing can shake or alienate, I took the liberty of properly putting forward with the greatest Energy amongst the respectable People here and other parts of the Country this inclosed address, which I named some time ago as designed to strengthen your Excellency's Government and confound the Enemies thereof, by thus Evincing to the World the popularity and high Estimation in which it is held by all the respectable Inhabitants of this Colony. And deeming it necessary that your Excellency might know fully, In Order to receive and Act upon it so fully as your Wisdom might see fit, when fully signed and delivered through the Hands of the Resident Magistrate here, who will be solicited by the People to deliver the same to your Excellency about Monday next, which will then, I humbly hope, prove to your Excellency the full and Loyal adherence of these Settlements to your Person and Government. In this please to Pardon my forward Zeal, and the liberty of this Private Letter from, Sir,

Your Excellency's faithful, &c.,
AND'W THOMPSON.

Address from settlers to Bligh.

P.S.—Everything at your Excellency's Farm is going on well, the particulars of which and some other private matters I will, if Opportunity offers, explain faithfully and fully to your Excellency by word of Mouth only, having no greater gratification or ambition in the World than essentially serving your Excellency. A.T.

[Sub-enclosure.]

SETTLERS' ADDRESS TO GOVERNOR BLIGH.

New South Wales, 1st January, 1808.

May it please Your Excellency,

We, the undersigned, Free and Principal Proprietors of Landed Property, and Inhabitants of the rising and extensive Colony of New South Wales, beg leave, on the beginning of another Year, to approach Your Excellency and express the fullest and unfeigned Sense of Gratitude for the Manifold, Great, and Essential Blessings and Benefits we freely continue to enjoy from Your Excellency's Arduous, Just, Determined, and Salutary Government over us, happily evinced by the present plenteous and flourishing State of this Country, rapidly growing in Population, Opulence, and all Improvements calculated by a Wise and Patriotic Government to make a large Colony of People happy and rich in all their internal Resources. And, while enjoying such inexpressible Benefits from Year to Year under Your Excellency's Auspicious and benign Government, We feel and hold ourselves gratefully bound, at the risque of Our Lives and Properties, at all times, as liege Subjects, to support the same, And ever prove ourselves worthy of a continuation of your Protection, Attention, and Encouragement during Your Excellency's gracious Government over us, which may God long continue. Yet, although Your Excellency's unwearied Zeal for the Public Welfare is so fully exhibited and its effects so sensibly felt by all Ranks of People, and that there are no inconveniences under which we labour that You would not redress, were it in your Power—which we doubt in these two Cases are not, else they had been remedied by your Wisdom ere this—And therefore humbly solicit Your Excellency, in your goodness, that, from your local knowledge and general observations—should you not deem it improper—to make representation to His Majesty in Council that he might be graciously pleased to allow such privilege of Trade to their Country Vessels and themselves as other Colonies have, And that the Law might be administered by Trial by Jury of the People, as in England. Although elaborate explanations might be made on these Subjects, and the greatest difference shewn, from the time the Regulations were appointed for securing a small Colony of Prisoners planted on these Shores, compared with the extensive rising Greatness and Enterprising Spirit of the Colonists over which Your Excellency now happily Governs; But these discussions to You would be needless, as Your Excellency, in your extensive researches, has minutely examined the whole Country, its Maritime and Inland Trade, Stock, Agriculture, Manufactures, Arts, and Resources, and its Inhabitants, House by House; Therefore, we rest our Welfare and desires in the fullest Confidence for You, in your Wisdom and Goodness, to direct. And, praying a long continuance of Your Excellency's Happy and benign Government,

We* remain, sir, &c.

A true Copy compared with the Original by us.

A. F. KEMP, J.P.
CHAS. THROSBY, J.P.

* Note 109.

[Enclosure No. 25.]

1808.
11 April.

OFFICERS AND SETTLERS* TO MAJOR JOHNSTON.

Sir,   Sydney, New South Wales, 27th January, 1808.

We, the undersigned, beg leave to offer you our most
grateful thanks for your manly and honorable interposition to
rescue us from an Order of things that threatened the destruction
of all which Men can hold dear. We hail you, Sir, as the Pro-
tector of our Property, Liberty, Lives, and Reputation.

In this Moment of joyful exultation we must not, however, be
unmindful of our future Security, and with a view to the arrival
in this Colony of any Officer superior to yourself in Rank, before
His Majesty's Gracious Pleasure shall be known respecting the
Supercession of Governor Bligh, We take the liberty respectfully
to represent that we think you ought (before you resign the
Command) to stipulate that that Officer shall confirm the
measures you have wisely adopted for the Public Security and
for the Honor of His Majesty's Government.

With great respect, &c.

ED. ABBOTT, J.P.   ARCH'D BELL, J.P.
J. HARRIS, J.P.   G. BLAXCELL, J.P.
WM. MINCHIN, J.P.   C. GRIMES, J.P.
THOS. JAMISON, J.P.   JOHN MCARTHUR.

[Enclosure No. 26.]

DEPOSITION OF ACTING-LIEUTENANT ELLISON.

Sydney, New South Wales, 7th March, 1808.

ACTING-LIEUTENANT WILLIAM ELLISON belonging to His Majesty's
Ship Porpoise voluntarily deposeth that on the 25th day of
April He was sent for with Mr. Joseph Short, Master's Mate, to
Government House by William Bligh Esqre. first Captain of
His Majesty's Ship Porpoise and late Governor of this Territory
for the purpose of making certain Depositions respecting the
Sailing of the General Wellesly; that Mr. Short proceeded to
make his deposition before the said William Bligh Esquire, and
that whilst he was so engaged the Said William Bligh Esqre.
did utter a torrent of reproaches and shocking abuse against
Mr. Joseph Short. That having compleated his Deposition Mr.
Short retired from the Room when this Deponent likewise proceeded to make his deposition, and was Assailed by the Said
William Bligh Esqre. in like manner. That amongst other
words uttered, the said William Bligh Esqre. did declare that this
Deponent and the officers of His Majesty's Ship Porpoise were
"a parcel of nefarious Scoundrels and a disgrace to His Majesty's
Service." This deponent further maketh Oath that whenever

*Note 110.

Letter of thanks
to Johnston.

Request for
future security.

Deposition of
William Ellison
re Bligh's
abusive conduct.

he has had occasion to wait upon the Said William Bligh Esqre. on Duty, he has always used Deponent in a most unofficerlike and ungentlemanlike manner. WM. ELLISON.

Sworn before me

JOHN McARTHUR, J.P.

A true Copy compared with the Original.

R. FITZ, J.P.

[Enclosure No. 27.]

Deposition of
Joseph Short
re Bligh's
abusive conduct.

DEPOSITION OF ACTING-LIEUTENANT SHORT.

Sydney, New South Wales, 8th March, 1808.

ACTING-LIEUTENANT JOSEPH SHORT belonging to His Majesty's Ship Porpoise, voluntarily deposeth that on the 25th day of April he attended at Government House by order of William Bligh Esquire, First Captain of His Majesty's Ship the Porpoise, and late Governor of this Territory, for the purpose of making a certain Deposition, respecting the Sailing of the Ship General Wellesly, That this deponent was then Master's Mate of the Porpoise, and that when he was admitted into the presence of the said William Bligh Esquire, Acting-Lieut. William Ellison also accompanied him. That during the time this depon't was making the aforesaid Deposition, the said William Bligh Esqr. uttered the most opprobrious abuse against this Deponent and amongst other words did say That he was a damned Cowardly rascal, or fellow, and that he had behaved in a most Unofficer-like manner. That his behaviour has subjected him to receive Corporal Punishment. JOSH. SHORT.

Sworn before me one of His Majesty's Justices of the Peace for the Territory the day and Year above written.

JOHN McARTHUR, J.P.

A true Copy compared with the Original.

R. FITZ, J.P.

[Enclosure No. 28.]

[Two papers marked No. 1.]

Memorial of
John Blaxland.

[A] THE MEMORIAL OF MR. JOHN BLAXLAND.

To His Honor George Johnston, Esqre., Lieutenant-Governor of New South Wales, &c., &c., &c.

THE Memorial of John Blaxland part and managing Owner in this Port of the Ship Brothers.

Sydney, 3rd March, 1808.

Most respectfully sets forth

That your Memorialist having had divers causes to disapprove of the Conduct of Oliver Russel the present Master of the Ship Brothers and having yesterday ordered him to deliver up

the Ship and Cargo on the annexed Charges—and his Non Com- 1808.
11 April.
pliance compels Memorialist to request Your Honor will be
pleased to order an Investigation of the said charges, and on Memorial of
John Blaxland.
what Authority he presumes to resist Memorialist's Orders, as
Memorialist cannot after being in possession of the facts stated,
in Justice to the other Owners concerned with himself, suffer
him to take so valuable a Cargo out of this Port.

I am, &c.,
JOHN BLAXLAND.

Notice.

BEING about to Leave this Colony for Eighteen Months, I have John Blaxland's
attorneys to
pay his
promissory
notes.
arranged with Simeon Lord and Gregory Blaxland to Pay and
Receive all or any of my Promissory Notes, at any Time the
Holders may choose to present them for Payment; and for the
Satisfaction of the Holders Mr. Lord has approved this Notice.

Approved: S. LORD. JOHN BLAXLAND.
Sydney, March 16, 1808.

Criminal Charges.

Charges made
by John
Blaxland
against Russell.

1st Selling a Spar at the Cape of Good Hope the property of the
Owners of the Ship Brothers.

2d Ordering 4 lbs. of Meat per day to be charged to the Ship's
Account which was sent to his Acquaintance (Castle).

3d Sending on shore a quantity of Paint, Paint Oil, Spirits of
Turpentine, Cheese, Sugar, Butter, Decanters, Plates and a
Dish water-Bason and Jug, the Property of the Owners.

4th Sending on Shore Half a Bushel of Split Pease to Parramatta
the property of the Owners.

5th Sending on Shore about 20 Gallons of Spirits the property of
the Owners.

Civil Charges.

1st Expressing when off Saldanah Bay that if the Ship would not
carry the Sail then set she should drag it.

2d After arriving in this Port subjecting the Ship to seizure
and the Owners to the forfeiture of the Bonds entered into
by smugling Rum on Shore the property of the Ship, and
selling it to Thomas Ivory.

3d For suspending from his duty the Chief Mate and after his
arrival not reporting him or bringing him to trial, consequently conniving at his Misconduct if Guilty.

4th For not obeying his Orders in neglecting to land sufficient
Men for the purpose of Sealing to the great injury of the
Concern and afterwards not leaving a Gang of Men on the
Islands agreeable to his Instructions.

1808.
11 April.

Charges made
by John
Blaxland
against Russell.

Fraud.

1st Making a false report of the State of the Salt provisions in
the Ship after arriving in this Port.

2d. For threatening to injure Memorialist 400 or 500 Pounds if
in his power after his arrival in England.

Contempt.

For improper Conduct during the Passage and disobedience of
Orders and Instructions, whereby the Owners have sustained damage to a considerable Amount.

[B] MR. JOHN MACARTHUR TO MR. JOHN BLAXLAND.

Sir,   Head Quarters, Sydney, 3rd March, 1808.

John Blaxland
to produce his
authority for
making claims.

I am commanded by His Honor the Lieut. Governor to
require that you do transmit to me the Authority upon which
you found your Claim to an Investigation of the Conduct of
Mr. Oliver Russell Master of the Brothers.

I am also to acquaint you that a reference to the General
Orders will enable you to discern that all applications respecting
the private affairs of Individuals are to be addressed to me.

I am, &c.,
JNO. MCARTHUR,
Secy. to the Colony.

[No. 2] MR. JOHN BLAXLAND TO MAJOR JOHNSTON.

Sir,   Sydney, 3 March, 1808.

I am much concerned by a letter just delivered to me from
Mr. McArthur that Your Honor doubts my having any Authority
on the Ship Brothers.

Macarthur
charged with
prejudice.

I must avail myself of the indulgence you are kind enough to
grant me, that of applying to you in this respect, as Mr. McArthur
is concerned in the same house and therefore liable to be prejudiced against me.

Blaxland's
rights to
make charges.

I have shewn to Mr. Grimes part of my papers, who will I am
satisfied tell you that I have a right to scrutinize into Oliver
Russell's Conduct as Màster of the Ship Brothers, and that that
claim is founded on having paìd a large sum of money for a
Share of the Ship in consequence of which I claim the protection
of the laws in support of my property, and from the late fortunate
change which has taken place, I make no doubt but that Your
Honor will see impartial Justice administered.

I am, &c.,
JOHN BLAXLAND.

[No. 3] MR. JOHN MACARTHUR TO MR. JOHN BLAXLAND.

Sir,   Head Quarters, Sydney, 4th March, 1808.

Johnston's reply *per* Macarthur.

I am ordered by His Honor the Lieutenant Governor to acquaint you that he felt the greatest Surprize at the receipt of your Second letter of yesterday's date, after you had received so explicit a notification that all applications relative to private business were to be addressed to me.

His Honor desirous however to persuade himself that you have committed this Irregularity a second time from inadvertence, has directed me to explain that the authority upon which you found your Claim to an investigation of the conduct of Mr. Oliver Russell, was required, not because His Honor doubted your having such authority, but because the production of such powers was necessary to justify the interference you solicited.

You are, therefore, Sir, to understand that whenever you shall be pleased to transmit the proofs of your authority over Mr. Russell, they will be examined with the most serious attention, or should you prefer any other mode of bringing forward your claims, His Honor hopes it cannot be necessary to assure you that the ordinary and established Courts of Justice are open for the legal redress of all grievances.

I am further directed to acquaint you, that if you should ever feel that you have just ground of Complaint against me, for acting with prejudice, or for being guilty of any other impropriety, His Honor will be always ready to attend to your representations. Altho' at the same time His Honor commands me to apprize you, that he will not permit wanton attacks to be made with impunity upon a public Officer, who has no other reward for his services, than what arises from the consciousness of intending to do everything in his power for the advancement of the happiness, the prosperity and the Security of the Colony,

I am, &c.,
JOHN MCARTHUR, Secretary to the Colony.

[No. 4] MR. JOHN BLAXLAND TO MAJOR JOHNSTON.

Sir,   Sydney, 4th March, 1808.

By a letter which I received this morning written by Mr. McArthur at the desire of Your Honour, I am sorry that it should be supposed I could wish to disobey any Orders you have directed to be observed. At the same time I must appeal to Your Honor's usual liberality that you would not direct any one to unfold his private concerns when there might be a chance of its being injurious to him.

Blaxland's appeal to Johnston.

Having before stated my sentiments in that respect I trust that Your Honor will exculpate me from wishing to make any attack on the character of Mr. McArthur.

I remain, &c.,
.JOHN BLAXLAND.

[No. 5] MR. JOHN BLAXLAND TO MR. JOHN MACARTHUR.

Sir, Sydney, 10th March, 1808.

Blaxland's petition.

As Secretary to the Colony I enclose you a Petition with the accompanying Papers and have likewise sent you Park on Insurance having referred to several parts which I think applicable in the present case, particularly page 182.

As the Dart will soon sail I must write to Messrs. Hullett and Co. requesting them to make a further Insurance on the Cargo of the Ship Brothers, which must be done at a higher premium after the very imprudent conduct of the master (if effected at all) and I hope as a friend of theirs, and being concerned in the same house, you will see the necessity of my removing him from the Command, and that you will lay the papers before His Honor the Lieutenant Governor.

I am, &c.,
JOHN BLAXLAND,
Part and Managing Owner of the Ship
Brothers in this Port.

COPIES of Accompanying Papers mentioned in the last Letter and referred to in the petition following.

Viz. (*Paper marked No. 1*).

Blaxland's letter of dismissal to Russell.

Copy of a Letter to Captn. Russell dated 2d March, 1808.

I AM induced for the benefit of the other Owners concerned with myself to dismiss you from the Command of the Ship Brothers, and I do desire you to give up the Command accordingly, As I do not after what has happened conceive it safe to trust the Ship to England under your Care—should you refuse to comply with my desires on this business, I shall proceed against you on the following charges.

[*Here followed a copy of Mr. Blaxland's charges against Captain Russell; see page 377.*]

(*Paper marked No. 2.*)

Captain Russell to Mr. John Blaxland.

Sir, Sydney Cove, 2d March, 1808.

Russell's acknowledgment of letter.

I received your letter of the 2d. Inst. requesting me to give up the command of the Ship Brothers of London now lying at Anchor in Sydney Cove—In answer to which I am sorry to say in doing Justice to my Employers in England I cannot submit to any such Order—therefore take such steps as you think proper and act accordingly.   Respectfully yours,

O. RUSSELL,

Commander Ship Brothers.

(*Paper marked No. 3.*)

Partnership Agreement of Messrs. T. and J. Hullett and J. Blaxland.

MEMORANDUM of an Agreement entered into on the 20th June 1806, Between the undersigned Persons, who hereby mutually covenant and agree with each other as follows:—

1st. The Undersigned agree to become joint Adventurers in the purchase and outfit of a Vessel, and in the Cargo to be carried by her to Port Jackson in New South Wales, after landing which She is to proceed on the Fishery in the South Seas.

2d. All the Undersigned agree to hold Shares in the Said Ship and Cargo in proportion to the Amount set opposite to their respective Signatures hereto.

3d. Messrs. Hulletts Brothers and Co. of London are to be the Agents of this Concern in *England,* as soon as they can find a Ship fit for their purpose they are to purchase her, and to call on the Undersigned for immediate Payment of the Prime Cost of the Ship in proportion to their respective Shares.

4th. The Vessel to be registered in the names of the said Parties and to be fitted for Sea and manned by Hullett Brothers and Co. with all convenient Speed.

5th. The Undersigned are to pay the remainder of their Subscriptions as the money may be wanted, on receiving seven days' notice to that Effect from Hullett Brothers and Co.

6th. Whatever money may remain after the outfit of the Ship is to be laid out in a Cargo.

7th. When the Cargo is on board, and the Ship ready for Sailing, the Accounts are to be made up, and respectively to be examined, approved and signed by the Concerned.

8th. Mr. Blaxland (one of the Undersigned Parties) is to take his Passage on board this Vessel—to the Settlement of New South Wales—He is to be allowed the Passage for himself and family, but to lay in provisions at his own expence and also to pay for any extraordinary accomodations which he may desire, beyond those usually found in a Ship.

1808.
11 April.

Partnership
agreement
between
Messrs. Hullett
and John
Blaxland.

9th. He is to be allowed the necessary room in the Vessel to take out such Stores and Effects for his own Use, as he may think fit, but not to exceed fifty Tons, and he is to pay for Freight at the Rate of Eight Pounds p'r Ton of Forty Cubic Feet measurement, To Hullett Brothers and Co. for the benefit of the joint concern, which Money is to be paid before the sailing of the Vessel and also to be laid out in Goods for the Cargo.

10th. Mr. Blaxland during the Voyage outwards, during his Stay at New South Wales, and during the time that the Ship is Whaling, is to have the management and direction of the said Ship, as far as respects the sale of the Cargo and the course the Vessel shall take for the purpose of Whaling, and to Superintend and direct the repairs and victualling after his arrival at Port Jackson and during the time she may put in there; for the expence of which he is to account with Hullett Brothers and Co.

11th. Mr. Blaxland may during the voyage put into the Cape of Good Hope as may hereafter be determined on—and there Barter and sell any part of the Cargo. Immediately after arrival at Port Jackson, he is to land the Cargo and dispose of it, so that the Ship may proceed with convenient Speed on the Fishery —Mr. Blaxland is to remit the Net Proceeds in Government Bills, as soon as possible to Hullett Brothers and Co. who are to account for the same with the concerned, at the Ratio of their respective Interests—It is however to be understood that Mr. Blaxland is to remit the nett Proceeds of the Cargo, but in case *Mr. Blaxland should deem it more advantageous to Barter any part of the Cargo for Oil or Seal Skins; or to purchase the same with any part of the Nett Proceeds he may do so and consign these Goods on freight by the first Vessel.* The return Cargo of the Ship whether it may consist of the produce of her own fishing, or of Goods purchased for account of the Owners is to be consigned to Hullett Brothers and Co. Mr. Blaxland is to be allowed a Commission of five p'r Cent. on the Amount of the Outward Cargo, and in like manner Hullett Brothers and Co. are to charge a Commission of Two and a half p'r Cent. on the Sum expended for the purchase, Outfit &c. of the Ship and for the Cost of the Cargo as likewise for the Sale of the Goods sent by any other Ship, as returns for any part of the outward Cargo: and One per Cent. additional for their Guarantee if the return Cargo should be sold on credit.

This Agreement to extend to all Subsequent Voyages which the Ship may make for account of the concerned.

Proper Accounts are to be kept by Hullett Brothers and Co. of all Sums paid and received by them on account of the Concern which Accounts shall be open to the Inspection of all parties interested therein, or their authorized Agents as often as any of them may require it, so as for every one to be informed at all times of the State of the Accounts.

1808.
11 April.

Partnership agreement between Messrs. Hullett and John Blaxland.

In case any of the Parties should be desirous of withdrawing from the Concern or become Insolvent, the remaining parties shall have the right of taking such share or Shares at such value, as shall be settled by two indifferent persons.

It is further agreed that in Case any of the Parties hereto *shall neglect* or *refuse to comply* with the Conditions above Specified, Such party or parties shall forfeit to the remaining Persons concerned, the Sums already advanced by them.

As it is intended, to take out a Shallop to be employed in those Seas for catching Seals and Sea Elephants, this Shallop is to be fitted out and manned and victualled by Mr. Blaxland who is to charge all his Expences and five p'r Cent. Commission thereon, and to send to Messrs. Hullett Brothers and Co. on Freight all the Seal Skins and Oil which the Shallop may procure He is likewise to be allowed Two and a half p'r Cent. on the Nett proceeds of these Goods in London as a Compensation for his trouble in preserving and reshipping them.

JOHN BLAXLAND .... £2,500.
THOMAS HULLETT ⎫ ... £2,500.
JOHN HULLETT ⎭

(Paper marked No. 4.)

Mr. John Blaxland's Instructions to Captain Russell.

Instructions to Oliver Russell.

EXTRACT of a Paragraph in Capn. Russell's Instructions when he went on his sealing Voyage from Mr. John Blaxland.

" But should you be fortunate and find any place where you can land your Men with Salt and Provisions sufficient to procure your Cargo, then I wish you to return direct with the Ship touching at the Bay of Islands for Potatoes and Spars, which will help to pay as well as any other Kind of Merchandize to be sold here for the good of the voyage. When the Ship shall be refitted and supplied with more provisions and Salt to return and take the Cargo of Skins on board and proceed direct for England."

Extract from Mr. John Blaxland's Accounts.

Extract from John Blaxland's accounts.

EXTRACT from Mr. John Blaxland's account current with the Hulletts Brothers and Comp'y signed by him where it appears that he has £4,000 in the Ship Schooner and Investment. September 22d 1806 To his share in the Adventure New South Wales including Ship Cargo and the Schooner Antipodes £4,000.

1808.
11 April.

John Blaxland's
memorial to
the bench of
magistrates.

(*Paper marked No. 5.*)

Mr. John Blaxland to the Honble. Bench of Magistrates.

HOWEVER repugnant it may be to my feelings to bring Mr. Oliver Russell before you on such serious charges, as I am at present obligated to do, Yet I feel it a duty I owe the other Owners as well as to myself after such an unprecedented and insolent defiance, and refusal to deliver up to me the Ship and Cargo, the property of me and the other Owners, which are solely under my management and direction while in this Port—GENTLEMEN, I beg leave to state the first Cause of my entering into the Concern—On my application to Messrs. Hulletts Brothers and Co. while in England for a passage in one of their Ships to this Colony, they proposed to me that I should be concerned with them in a Ship to be purchased to come out here on a Sealing or Whaling Voyage, in which Ship I might have a passage for myself and family with every accomodation I might wish to which I acquiesced, the Brothers was purchased and I became an Owner —Accordingly it was then agreed I should have the sole management of her and her Cargo, together with the Schooner called the Antipodes, that was brought out in frame on board the said Ship Brothers and as a part of the said concern for the general Benefit—I accordingly proceeded and during our passage and stay at the Cape of Good Hope the said Mr. Oliver Russell conducted himself in such an improper manner, that soon after my arrival in this port, I was determined to supersede him in his Command, and one day went on board accompanied by Mr. Lord informed him of his improper Conduct and that he had made me and the other Owners liable for the Bond, if not the Ship to confiscation from his selling and aiding to smuggle the Ship's Spirits: but on his promising to conduct himself properly and to pay implicit obedience to my future Orders, as well as the improbability of my getting a good master in this Port, I was induced to look over his Misconduct if I should not have any other occasion to find fault, but to my utter Astonishment I found on his return, that he had in the most daring manner and contrary to his Orders and to the great Injury of the other Owners been to Norfolk Island and purchased at a most exorbitant price a quantity of Salt Pork and Bread instead of returning to this Port, refitting and going back to the Islands and proceeding from thence direct to England, besides the loss of not less than 20,000 Skins that might have been preserved and the Ship now at St. Helena on her Passage instead of being in this Harbour.

There are a number of Circumstances more I could bring forward, but trust I have sufficiently elucidated the business without unnecessarily taking up the time of the members comprising the Bench.

1808.
11 April.

John Blaxland's memorial to the bench of magistrates.

There are a number of charges which will appear on the examination before the Honble. Bench of Magistrates now convened more than I would take up their time to state here, which I trust will be fully sufficient to convince the Members that I have only acted conformable to my duty in the Situation. I have been placed here by the rest of the Owners to bring them forward and not from any motive of private resentment or prejudice to Captain Russell.

JOHN BLAXLAND.

(Attached to the foregoing.)

Mr. Lord,

Please to deliver to the bearer one Gallon of Paint Oil and twelve pounds of white lead being a verbal Order from John Blaxland Esqr.

You will oblige   Your Humble Serv't,

O. RUSSELL.

(A second Paper marked No. 5.)

PROCEEDINGS OF A BENCH OF MAGISTRATES.

Proceedings of the bench of magistrates in the case of Blaxland v. Russell.

Present: Thomas Jamison, James Symons, John Harris, Willm. Minchin, Esqrs.

New South Wales, 5th March, 1808.

JOHN BLAXLAND Esqr. came before Bench and stated certain grievances against Captain Russell of the Ship Brothers as P'r Memorial and requests that the Ship's Register and Articles should be laid before the Bench—The Ship's Articles and Register produced—By the latter of which it appears that Mr. Blaxland is part Owner of the Ship Brothers—also by the 10th Article of a private agreement made between the Owners of the said Ship, it appears that " Mr. Blaxland during the voyage outwards, during her Stay at New South Wales, and during the time the Ship is Whaling is to have the management and direction of the said Ship as far as respects the Sale of the Cargo, and the course the vessel shall take for the purpose of Whaling, and to superintend, and direct the repairs and victualling after her arrival in Port Jackson, and during the time she may put in there, for the expence of which he is to account with Hullett Brothers and Co."

The Bench are of opinion that Mr. Blaxland may proceed to substantiate any criminal Charge (that has happened in this Port) against Captain Russell.

Charge 1st. Sending on Shore a Quantity of Paint Oil, Spirit of Turpentine, Cheese, Sugar, Butter &c.

MR. S. LORD Sworn :—

Q. Did you not hear Mr. Oliver Russel ask me for some Paint belonging to the Ship Brothers, and did I not refuse him saying

1808.
11 April.

Proceedings of
the bench of
magistrates in
the case of
Blaxland v.
Russell.

" that I would suffer nothing to go belonging to the concern for
private Uses, but I would let him have some of my own " which I
brought out for my own use?

Answer. Yes, I did.

Q. Did I not tell you to let Oliver Russel have some of my own
paint?

A. Yes you did; and here is an order of Mr. Russel's selling a
quantity of Rum, the Property of the Ship Brothers to Thos.
Ivory.

A.* Some time after the arrival of the Ship in this Port, it came
to my knowledge that Thomas Ivory had got a quantity of Spirits
from the Brothers. I sent for Ivory who informed me he had 24
Gallons, but that he had a Permit for 4 Gallons of it; that I afterwards went on board with Mr. Blaxland, when Mr. Russel acknowledged, that he had sold the Rum to Ivory, but that he had taken
it in lieu of some of his own that had been made use of for the
Ship which he had purchased in England.

Q. Did you not go on board the Brothers with me after her return
into this Port the 2d Time and speaking of the Salted provisions
of the Ship did not Mr. Oliver Russel say that he had but one
Cask or that the last Cask was broached " or words to that effect "?

A. Yes he did, and said that he had sent Captn. Smith a Cask of
Pork and Mr. Moody another.

FREDERICK HAZLEBURG, late Chief Officer of the Ship Brothers
sworn :—

Q. Did not Mr. Oliver Russel on his arrival in this Port, sell to
a person of the name of Ivory, a Kilderkin of the Ship's Spirits,
wrapped round with two Hammocks, and stowed in a Hogshead of
the Ship's porter, so as to prevent its being discovered?

A. Yes.

Q. You know it to be the Ship's Rum?

A. Yes there was no other in the Ship to my knowledge.

Q. Did you receive the two hammocks back again from Ivory?

A. Yes I did.

Q. Did the Kilderkin ever come back again?

A. Not to my knowledge.

Q. Did not Captain Russel order you to send to Parramatta half
a bushel of Split Pease, the property of the Owners?

A. Yes, I did send 16 Quarts.

Q. Did you not send half a Keg of white Paint, by order of
Captn. Russel on shore, to his House at this place, and a quantity
of Paint Oil, Spirits of Turpentine, Loaf Sugar, Cheese, Hams,
Butter, Decanters, Tumblers, Plates and a Dish, Water Bason and
Jug the property of the Ship?

A. Yes, I sent half a Keg of white paint and the best part of a
loaf of Sugar, but cannot speak to the other articles.

Q. Did you ever know of any Glass or Crockery Ware ever being
purchased for the Ship by any other person than the owners?

A. The Owners paid for them.

RICHARD HOUSEGOE, Steward of the Brothers, sworn :—

Q. Relate what you know of Captain Russel's sending articles
from the Ship Brothers to the house of Elizabeth Guest?

A. I know that Capn. Russel did send one Cheese 6 lb. Butter,
half a dozen Plates, some small qnty. of Paint Oil, 2 Tumblers and
2 Goblets, a Ham and one Wash hand Bason and Jug.

* Note 111.

1808.
11 April.

Proceedings of
the bench of
magistrates in
the case of
Blaxland v.
Russell.

FREDK. RICHESTER, Ship's Cook, sworn :—

Q. Did you not carry some paint, and several things from the Brothers to the house of Elizabeth Guest?

A. I did carry about a pint of black paint, 2 Stone bottles, but I do not know what they contained, and some dirty Cloaths.

THOS. IVORY sworn :—

Q. Did you not receive from Captn. Russel of the Ship Brothers, a quantity of Rum, in a Cask bound round with 2 Hammocks, and put into a hogshead with Porter, belonging to the Ship Brothers, and landed as Porter?

Ivory submits the Question to the Bench how far it will be proper for him to give an answer to a question that may in some measure criminate himself having been acquainted by Mr. Lord, that he had been purchasing Ship's Stores?

The Bench are of an Opinion that he should not answer this question.

Q. Was you not in the Cabin, and saw some Rum put into a Cask, and that Cask wrapped round with two Hammocks and put into a Hogshead and afterwards filled up with bottled Porter?

A. I saw no Rum in the Cabin, but what was in the Decanters but saw some Porter started out of Bottles into a Hogshead.

Q. On your Oath do you not know that there was Rum in that Cask?

A. Yes.

I submit this Question to the Bench—The Bench are of Opinion that it may be answered by him.

Q. Had you not prior to that, purchased a Hogshead of Porter from Captn. Russel?

A. I had purchased a bottle of Porter contained in a Hogshead.

HENRY PURDY sworn :—

Q. Did you not see some Rum put into a Cask, and that Cask wrapped round with two Hammocks and put into a Hogshead filled with bottled ———*?

A. No I did not.

Q. Where was you when a man of the name of Ivory was in the Cabin with Captn. Russel and a Cask sent on Shore out of the Cabin?

A. I was at work in the Steerage, when Ivory was in the Cabin with Captn. Russel, and when a Cask came out of the Cabin, and I handed in two Hammocks but I do not know what became of the Cask; whether it went out of the Ship or not.

JAMES ANDERSON sworn :—

Q. Did you not carry a Trunk with some Glass ware and other Articles to the House of Elizth. Guest from the Ship Brothers?

A. I did carry a Box from the hospital Wharf to the house of Elizabeth Guest but what it contained I know not.

The Bench having maturely considered on the evidence which has been brought forward against Mr. Oliver Russel on the 3 Charges (under the head of Criminal Charges) are fully of opinion that there is not sufficient grounds to justify his being committed for criminal Trial (on such charges) do therefore discharge him.

THOMAS JAMISON.   WM. MINCHIN.
J. SYMONS.   J. HARRIS.

* Blank in the copy available.

(*Inclosed in No. 5.*)

The Petition of John Blaxland to Major Johnston.

THE humble Petition of John Blaxland Esqr., Part and Managing owner of the Ship Brothers.

Most respectfully sheweth,—That Your Memorialist on the 2d day of March wrote to Mr. Oliver Russel Master of the Ship Brothers ordering him immediately to deliver up the Ship and Cargo to your Memorialist, as he, your Memorialist, could not suffer him any longer to command her after his repeated misconduct as will appear by Paper No. 1 it will be found by his answer No. 2 that he puts Memorialist at defiance and refuses to comply with his Orders, in consequence of which Memorialist was obliged to apply to Your Honor to order such investigation as you might deem meet as per Memorial of the 3d Instant.

On Saturday the 5th Instant a Bench of Magistrates met to investigate the charges preferred by your Memorialist against Captain Russel, where he still persisted that Memorialist had no Authority to call him to account or suspend him from the Command, although it appeared by the Register and Memorialist's agreement with the Owners that Memorialist was, and is, not only authorized but bound under penalty of forfeiting his share of the concern in the said Ship Brothers should he not act for the general benefit of all parties during the Ship's stay at New South Wales as by the paper No. 3 as well as the different Extracts No. 4—It will also appear by the proceedings of the Bench of Magistrates No. 5 that, Your Memorialist was only allowed to call evidence on three charges considered as Criminal, and committed in this Port—Memorialist conceives that according to Law he ought to have been allowed to prove all the other charges that in any degree appeared fraudulent; but Memorialist trusts that on perusing the proceedings Your Honor will be convinced that the charges are not frivolous or unfounded but of serious matter in as much as they come under the denomination of Barratary as will clearly be proved by Park's Marine Insurances under the head of Barratary Pages 30 @ 32, 82 @ 91, 182 and Appendix No. 1 upon Policies which Book Memorialist has sent Your Honor with the different references to the present subject, conceiving that by them there will no doubt remain of the legality of his request and of the necessity there is for him on behalf of the rest of the Owners as well as himself to pursue this method to indemnify all parties against the Insurers should any Accident or Loss happen to the Ship for want of Your Memorialist's attention in removing from the Command of that Ship a Man whose conduct he has every reason to disapprove and the risk of whose future behaviour would entirely rest on Your

Memorialist should any accident happen after being in possession of the facts he has such undoubted proof that the Captain's deviations from his Instructions is Barratry and it is clear from *that part** of the Paragraph No. 4 of his Instructions instead of obeying them; when he had landed his Gang at the Bounty Islands he immediately proceeded to Norfolk Island, where he was not certain of getting Supplies nor even an Harbor to anchor in, and it will also appear by the Log Book, he was six days longer than he might have made this Harbor in where he was certain of obtaining Supplies and on his return to the Bounty Islands, after taking his Skins on board might have proceeded direct to England with a greater number than he now has, besides having provided for the Gangs to have remained, where they might have procured Twenty thousand Skins more as well as saved at least two months of his passage to England; but instead of which he went to Norfolk Island and run the Owners to upwards of £700 expences the greatest part of which might have been saved had he come here. On his arrival here he declared he had but one Cask of Salt meat on board tho' it appeared on survey he had eleven or thirteen.

1808.
11 April.
———
Petition of
John Blaxland
to Johnston.

When at the Cape of Good Hope, altho' Your Memorialist was there, he disposed of a Spar the property of the Ship, and ordered four pound of Meat to be sent to a friend of his at that place named Castle every day, and to be charged as if sent to the Ship; after being accused of such proceedings before the late Governor on his arrival at this Port *said,* that the Spar was his property, given him by the Ship's Husband before he left England and desired the Mates if called upon to say so, and caused the Chief Mate to add'en the Log Book after having been accused, entered as if, at the time it was landed which will appear by reference, as well as be proved by the Mate's affidavit, if required, the said Spar appearing in the Schedule of the Ship's Stores; and he has even in *this Port,* after being refused, sent on shore for his own private purpose Spirits, Porter, Paint Oil, Paint Spirits of Turpentine &c. &c.; it also appears in his Log Book a Ham and Cheese was sold here for the purpose of purchasing Sugar although your Memorialist was on the Spot to supply him with every necessary wanted. There is also deficient from the Cargo a firkin of Butter which was brought out as part of the Investment and two Whale Lines; exclusive of his conniving at the Mate's sending on Shore for their use, Spirits, Molasses, Cheese, Butter, Fish and Canvas, as well as subjecting the Ship to seizure and the Owners to the Bond by smugling the before mentioned Spirits.

* These words in italics were erased in the original.

As Memorialist considers that if he had no other than that of *part* Owner (which appears by Register) that would be sufficient, as Mr. Russel can certainly be considered no more than a Servant, and if agrieved may sue for damages but not retain Memorialist's property.

If Your Memorialist was inclined to bring a civil Action against the said Mr. Oliver Russel he is prevented, by being himself a Member of the Civil Court; but should another be appointed in his room for that purpose, the Ship might be detained and Your Memorialist no nearer from the interposition of appeals, but he cannot have objection to Mr. Russel's proceeding to England in the Ship Brothers as a passenger, and to the examination of any evidence that may attend to his advantage hereafter, Your Memorialist being allowed the same indulgence.

Your Memorialist could adduce many more charges to convince Your Honor of the necessity of this application, but does not wish to intrude further on your time, trusting Your Honor will take it into Your mature consideration, and grant Your Memorialist's request, by giving him authority to displace Mr. Russel from being Commander of the Ship Brothers, for the advantage of himself and the other Owners, for which Your Memorialist will be ever bound to pray.

Sydney, New South Wales, 10th March, 1808.

JOHN BLAXLAND,
Part and Managing Owner in this Port
of the Ship Brothers.

(Attached to No. 5.)

MR. JOHN MACARTHUR TO MR. JOHN BLAXLAND.

Sir,   Head Quarters, Sydney, 14th March, 1808.

Johnston's
refusal to
interfere
between
Blaxland
and Russell.

I have laid your papers before His Honor the Lieutenant Governor with the Law Authority you referred to in support of your Claim to be authorized to dispossess Mr. Russell of the Command of the Brothers, And I am directed to acquaint you that His Honor is convinced he has no power to interfere in such a business.   I am, &c.,

JNO. MCARTHUR,
Secretary to the Colony.

[No. 6] MR. JOHN BLAXLAND TO MR. JOHN MACARTHUR.

Sir,   Sydney, 15th March, 1808.

I have to acknowledge the receipt of your letter of yesterday's date in answer to my Memorial of the 10th Inst. and I am sorry His Honor the Lieut. Governor has not power to protect me and the other Owners in England in removing Mr. Oliver Russell from the Command of the Ship Brothers after being in possession of such facts as stated in Memorial.

You will be pleased to state to his Honor the Lieutenant Governor that I am compelled to protest against the Master and all others it may concern and proceed to England in the Ship Brothers accompanied by Captn. Scott and Mr. Hasselberg to protect our property.

Blaxland's protest.

I am, &c.,
JOHN BLAXLAND, Managing Owner.

[No. 7] MR. JOHN MACARTHUR TO MR. JOHN BLAXLAND.

Sir,   Head Quarters, Sydney, 16th March, 1808.

I am directed by His Honor the Lieut. Governor to desire information whether he is to understand your letter of Yesterday as intended to express a complaint that you have not received all the protection from His Majesty's Government to which the Laws entitle every man; or whether any interference has taken place which has prevented you from bringing any matter in dispute between you and Mr. Oliver Russel before the established Courts of law; I am also directed to enquire whether the Protest you signify you are compelled to make against the Master of the Brothers and all others it may concern be intended to have any reference to the official Correspondence you have lately held with Government respecting the Concern of that Ship, and if it be so intended, that you will explicitly communicate what are the reasons which induce you to consider such a Protest necessary.

Blaxland to explain his letter.

I am, &c.,
JOHN MCARTHUR,
Secretary to the Colony.

[No. 8] MR. JOHN BLAXLAND TO MR. JOHN MACARTHUR.

Sir,   Sydney, 16th March, 1808.

I have to acknowledge the receipt of your Letter of this day's date and I must beg leave to refer His Honor the Lieutenant Governor to the documents already in his possession.

But I find it my duty on account of the Underwriters and the other Owners to protest against Oliver Russel's Conduct, and it appears customary in all protests to add, to all whom it may concern, but how far it may concern those documents I cannot venture to say.

Reasons for protest.

I am, &c.,
JOHN BLAXLAND.

1808.
11 April.

[No. 9] MR. JOHN BLAXLAND TO MR. JOHN MACARTHUR.

Sir,   Sydney, 17th March, 1808.

Blaxland's
resignation
as magistrate
and member of
civil court.
Having arranged my business to leave this Colony in the Ship Brothers I must beg you will inform His Honor the Lieutenant Governor that I request he will accept my resignation as a Magistrate and that I wish him to appoint another Member for the Civil Court.   I am, &c.,

JOHN BLAXLAND.

(Attached to No. 9.)
MR. JOHN MACARTHUR TO MR. JOHN BLAXLAND.

Sir,   Head Quarters, Sydney, 17th March, 1808.

Blaxland to be
detained until
civil causes
pending are
settled.
I have laid your letter before His Honor the Lieut. Governor, who has directed me to acquaint you that he has accepted the resignation of your situation as a Magistrate; but that he cannot, without violating the laws, sanction your quitting the Colony, until the whole of the causes now pending before the Court of Civil Jurisdiction (of which you are a Member) are decided upon, Unless any of the Parties who have commenced Actions shall voluntarily consent to withdraw them.

I am, &c.,

J. MCARTHUR, Sec. to the Colony.

[No. 10] MR. JOHN BLAXLAND TO MR. JOHN MACARTHUR.

Sir,   Sydney, 18th March, 1808.

Blaxland
determined to
sail in the
whaler
Brothers.
I have to acknowledge your letter of yesterday's date in answer to His Honor the Lieut. Governor wherein he accepts my resignation as a Magistrate but says he cannot permit my leaving the Colony without violating the Laws, my being a member of the Civil Court. As there is no Cause pending that has been in any shape heard, any other eligible person surely can fill that Situation, for would all the Actions be invalid if from illness or death I was unable to attend—And Your Honor having suffered Mr. Moore and Mr. Harris to be changed I cannot see how my being so can be in any shape injurious to the parties concerned—But the absolute necessity of my returning to England in the Ship Brothers for the safety of the property of the other Owners as well as my own leaves me no other alternative, unless I am detained in the Colony a Prisoner.

I am, &c.,

JOHN BLAXLAND.

[No. 11] MR. JOHN MACARTHUR TO MR. JOHN BLAXLAND.

Sir,   Head Quarters, Sydney, 18th March, 1808.

If you will have the goodness to refer to the letter I addressed to you yesterday, you will discover that instead of informing you His Honor the Lieut. Governor "cannot permit your leaving the Colony" I have stated that His Honor "cannot without violating the Laws *sanction* your leaving the Colony" and as it is possible you may on calm reflection discover that your mistake has led you into a Train of extremely erroneous reasoning, I have taken the liberty to suggest this circumstance being well assured that one error frequently leads to a greater, and entertaining a hope that this well intended caution may induce you to depend more upon your own unbiassed judgement in the steps you may adopt than upon the advice of any person you can at this time have an opportunity to consult.

1808.
11 April.
———
Blaxland's
misinterpreta-
tion of letter.

I am, &c.,

Jno. McArthur, Secy. to the Colony.

[No. 12] Mr. John Blaxland to Mr. John Macarthur.

Sir,   Sydney, 18th March, 1808.

In answer to your letter of this evening after thanking you for your caution I have again to request you to inform His Honor the Lieutenant Governor of my determination to quit the Colony for a short period and proceed to England in the Ship Brothers of which I am a part Owner for the security of my property, if not prevented by unforseen circumstances.

Blaxland's
determination
to sail in the
Brothers.

I am, &c.,

John Blaxland.

[No. 13] Mr. Charles Grimes to Mr. John Macarthur.

Sir,   Sydney, 19 March, 1808.

I have this day received a letter from Mr. Jno. Blaxland purporting that he is called to England immediately on very important business—therefore wishes to decline sitting as a Member of the present Civil Court—and requesting that I would inform His Honor the Lieut. Governor of the Circumstances, so that a proper person may be appointed in his room—How far it may be correct I confess I have not sufficient legal knowledge to determine, but as no cause pending before the Court has been entered upon—nor any process issued—when the other Member was not present—I have respectfully to submit to the Lieut. Governor—that I do not see any bad consequences that can arise from another eligible person being appointed.

Grimes' opinion
on resignation
of Blaxland
from civil
court.

I am, &c., &c.,

C. Grimes, A'g J.-Ad.

[No. 14] Mr. John Macarthur to Mr. Charles Grimes.

Sir,   Head Quarters, Sydney, 23d March, 1808.

I am directed by His Honor the Lieut. Governor to acquaint you, that in consequence of your representation, that

1808.
11 April.

Blaxland's
resignation
accepted.

Mr. Blaxland may without impropriety be withdrawn as a Member of the Court of Civil Jurisdiction, you may signify to that Gentleman that his request is complied with.

I am further ordered to desire that you will give in a List of eligible Persons that another member may be drawn for.

I am, &c.,

JOHN MCARTHUR,
Secretary to the Colony.

[No. 15] MR. JOHN BLAXLAND TO MAJOR JOHNSTON.

Sir,   Sydney, 31st March, 1808.

Victualling of
Otaheitians on
the Brothers.

I have enclosed for your Honor's Information an account of the provisions expended on board the Brothers by two Otaheitans while on their passage from England.

Having sent you a letter* from the Secretary of State's Office on the Subject, and the Ship Brothers being about to return I will thank your Honor to give Directions accordingly.

I am, &c.,

J. BLAXLAND.

[No. 16] MR. JOHN BLAXLAND TO MAJOR JOHNSTON.

Sir,   Sydney, 1st April, 1808.

Papers retained
by Russell.

Agreeable to your Honor's desire I write to you stating that I have demanded of Oliver Russel, now a Convict,† the Papers belonging to the Ship Brothers and that he has not sent them.

I hope Your Honor will be pleased to direct that they may be given up as I am fearful they may be made away with.

I am, &c.,

JOHN BLAXLAND.

[No. 17] MR. JOHN BLAXLAND TO MAJOR JOHNSTON.

Sir,   Sydney, 2nd April, 1808.

I wrote to Your Honor yesterday through Mr. McArthur, requesting to have the papers belonging to the Ship Brothers given up as Oliver Russel is now a Convict, to which Letter I have not yet got an answer; and as I am fearful of their being destroyed, I have to request you will give your directions accordingly.   I am, &c.,

JOHN BLAXLAND.

[No. 18] MR. JOHN MACARTHUR TO MR. JOHN BLAXLAND.

Sir,   Head Quarters, Sydney, 2d April, 1808.

Papers retained
by the Crown.

I am directed by His Honor the Lieut. Governor to acquaint you that the papers of the Brothers are in the hands of

* Note 112.   † Note 113.

Government, where they will be taken care of until a determination can be formed on the extraordinary case of Mr. Russel.
                    I am, &c.,
                        JOHN McARTHUR, Secy. to the Colony.

[No. 19] MR. JOHN BLAXLAND TO MR. JOHN MACARTHUR.

Sir,   Sydney, 2d April, 1808.
        I have this instant received a Letter through you from Johnston's
His Honor the Lieut. Governor informing me that the papers previous
of the Ship Brothers are in the hands of Government where they interfere.
will be taken care of until a determination can be formed on
the extraordinary case of Mr. Russel—I must refer him to His
Honor's Letter in answer to my Memorial of the 14th of March
where he informs me he is convinced he has no power to interfere
with such business.
        Oliver Russel having been convicted of wilful and corrupt Hazelburg
Perjury and sentenced to seven Years Transportation* I have Blaxland to
found it expedient for the benefit of all concerned to appoint command the
Mr. Hazelburg to the command of that ship and as I expect she Brothers.
will be ready for sea on or about Tuesday next I have to request
the papers may be forwarded to me on Monday or I shall be
under the unpleasant necessity of throwing the Ship and Cargo
on His Honor's hands, she having already been detained more
than seven days from the misconduct of the late Master.
                    I am, &c.,
                        JOHN BLAXLAND,
            Part and managing Owner of the Ship Brothers.

[No. 20] MR. JOHN BLAXLAND TO MAJOR JOHNSTON.

Sir,   Sydney, 2d April, 1808.
        On looking over my papers I find Your Honor has not Victualling of
answered my Letter of the 31st of March requesting you will Otaheitians on
furnish me with the provisions expended on board the Ship the Brothers.
Brothers by two Otaheitans while on their passage from England,
Mr. Windham's Letter† having been sent to you on the Subject,
I have only to ask whether Your Honor will comply with my
request.   I am, &c.,
                        JOHN BLAXLAND.

[No. 21] MR. JOHN BLAXLAND TO MAJOR JOHNSTON.

Sir,   Sydney, 4th April, 1808.
        Having this Instant been informed by Mr. Hazelburg who Command of
is the legal Commander of the Ship Brothers that Oliver Russel, the Brothers
Robert Daniels, George Howe, and one of the Mates of the Ship Russell.
Dart have gone on board of the said Ship of which I am part .

* Note 113.   † Note 112.

1808.
11 April.
———
Command of
the Brothers
re-assumed by
Russell.

and managing Owner in this Colony and called the people aft and read a paper to them and declared he was authorised by it, and that he had Your Honor's Orders to take the command of the said Ship, and has since ordered the people not to obey Mr. Hazelburg as he was Captain of the Ship, and he now actually has possession of that Ship by force of Arms, together with George Howe, Robert Daniels and the said Mate of the Dart, and which act I consider an act of Piracy,—if Your Honor has not given any such Orders in which case I request to be immediately informed or shall I be under the necessity of applying to Captn. Symons of His Majesty's Ship Porpoise to attack her— But in the event of Your Honor's having authorised him to take the Command I have to request that he may be immediately apprehended for wilful and corrupt perjury against myself Mr. Lord and Mr. G. Blaxland of which I now complain and am ready to substantiate; at the same time allow me to say that I look to you for the Ship's papers as stated in Your Possession by Your Honor's Letter through your Secretary of Yesterday's date.

I am, &c.,
JOHN BLAXLAND.

(Attached to No. 21.)
MR. JOHN HOLDEN* TO MR. JOHN BLAXLAND.

Sir,   Head Quarters, Sydney, 4th April, 1808.

Acknowledg-
ment of letters.

I am directed by Mr. John McArthur Esqre to acknowledge the receipt of your letter of the 31st March, your One of the 1st Instant, your three of the 2d Instant and your one of the 3d Instant.   I am, &c.,
JOHN HOLDEN.

[No. 22] MR. JOHN BLAXLAND TO MAJOR JOHNSTON.

Sir,   Sydney, 4th April, 1808.

Blaxland's
request for
confirmation
of letter.

I have this morning received a letter dated Head Quarters, Sydney, 4th April, 1808, Saying I am directed by John McArthur Esqr. to acknowledge the receipt of your letter of the 31st March, your One of the 1st Instant, your three of the 2d Instant, and your One of the 3d Instant, signed John Holden Clerk, and directed to me on His Majesty's Service.

I have to request your Honor will be pleased to inform me whether I am to consider that as àn answer to those letters to enable me to pursue such measures for the security of my property as the law directs—or that man's Signature as Official not having seen his name in the General Orders.†

I am, &c.,
JOHN BLAXLAND,
Part and managing Owner of the Ship Brothers in this Port.

* Note 114.   † Note 115.

DEPOSITION OF CAPTAIN KEMP.

1808.
11 April.
———
Deposition of
Anthony Fenn
Kemp *re*
alleged plot to
assassinate
Macarthur.

Cumberland To wit. DEPOSITION of Anthony Fenn Kemp Esqre. taken on oath before me, One of His Majesty's Justices of the Peace in and for the said County, at Parramatta this Twenty seventh day of March in the Year of Our Lord One Thousand Eight Hundred and eight.

DEPONENT being duly sworn deposes, that Mr. Greg'y Blaxland came to his house on the evening of the Twenty fourth Inst. between the hours of Eight and Nine, and said he had something particular to communicate to him, that Deponent asked him what it was, that he replied, that it was of so serious a nature that he could not mention it to him in the house fearing it might be overheard, and requested Deponent to walk with him in front of the House, that Deponent went out with him, and Mr. Blaxland then desired, that what he was going to acquaint him with might be Kept secret, fearing the consequence that might ensue, if it was known he was the Informer; Deponent promised he would not divulge anything he (Mr. Blaxland) would tell him, upon which Mr. Blaxland told the Deponent that there was a Plan laid at the Hawkesbury to assassinate Mr. McArthur, and that there were people employed, who would willingly sacrifice their lives to accomplish it, that Deponent said he thought it was impossible, that Mr. Blaxland replied there were a number of Hawkesbury Settlers at Sydney, and that there would be a great number there shortly, and told deponent that Mr. McArthur had used him and his Brother very ill in interfering with their Shipping concerns, but that he could not bear the Idea of murder being committed, that Mr. Blaxland then wished Deponent good night, and went away—Deponent states that Mr. Blaxland appeared to him much confused when he gave him the above information, but from what cause Deponent cannot tell.

ANTHONY FENN KEMP.

Taken and sworn before me
    the day and Year above written
            WM. MINCHIN, J.P.

[Enclosure No. 29.]

CORRESPONDENCE WITH CHARLES GRIMES, ESQUIRE, ACTING JUDGE-ADVOCATE.

[1] *Mr. Nicholas Bayly to Mr. Charles Grimes.*

Sir,   Head Quarters, Sydney, 1st April, 1808.
    His Honor the Lieutenant Governor On Examining the minutes of the Court of Criminal Jurisdiction, which you pre-

1808.
11 April.

Conviction and
sentence of
Russell and
Daniels for
perjury.

sented to him yesterday, finds that Mr. Oliver Russel, Master of
the Ship Brothers and Mr. Robert Daniels the Chief Mate, who
came before the Court—One as a Prosecutor and the other as
Evidence, have been convicted of Perjury* and Sentenced to seven
years Transportation and that after Sentence was passed the
Court strongly recommended both to the Lieut. Governor's
Clemency. The circumstances, under which this conviction took
place, And the recommendation which followed it, has excited
the Lieut. Governor's most earnest attention; and has induced
him to require you, as Judge of the Court, to point out on what
part of the Evidence the guilt of these two persons was established; and what reasons operated on the minds of the Court to
recommend them to mercy, if they were satisfied of their having
committed so abominable a crime.   His Honor the Lieut.
Governor also requires to be informed why these persons were not
after their Conviction ordered into Custody, as it appears from
the Testimony of the Gaoler that you, Sir, directed them to be
at large. Your immediate Answer is expected.

I am, &c.,
NICHOLAS BAYLY, Secy.

[2] Mr. Charles Grimes to Major Johnston.

Sir,   Sydney, New South Wales, 1st April, 1808.

In answer to your Secretary's Letter of this day's date I
respectfully beg leave to observe that you know me to be no
Lawyer—therefore incompetent to give a Law opinion. I took
solemn Oath to give Sentence according to the Evidence brought
before me—and I now avow that the Sentence I wrote and wherein the particular Instance is expressed, on which it was given
against Oliver Russell, and Robert Daniels (and which I had the
honor to lay before you, and now respectfully return for your
Inspection), was, and is my Opinion, and was the Opinion of the
majority of the Court. And the punishment was awarded from
the Act of 2d Geo. 2d Chap. 25.

In answer to that part of your Secretary's Letter requiring
that I should give the reasons that operated on the minds of the
Court to recommend them to your Clemency, I must respectfully
beg leave to observe, that I do not feel myself obliged to divulge
my private opinion or the private Opinion of the Members—I
received the opinion of the Majority of the Members, which I
read to them.

In answer to that part of the Letter respecting the prisoners
being at large—I did desire the Jailor, as far as I recollect, not
to confine them until your pleasure was known, telling him at

* Note 113.

1808.
11 April.

the same time that they could not get away—if it is an Error it shall never occur again—And if it is your pleasure, which I now request to know, they shall be instantly placed in Jail.

I have, &c.,

C. GRIMES, Actg. J.-Ad.

[3] *Mr. Nicholas Bayly to Mr. Charles Grimes.*

Sir,   Head Quarters, Sydney, 2d April, 1808.

I am directed by His Honor the Lieut't Governor to inform you in answer to your Letter of the 2d Instant, that he has referred to the Statute of the 2d. George 2d under the Authority of which you have stated, that Russel and Robert Daniels were convicted of perjury and sentenced to seven Years Transportation.

By that Statute it is plain, that persons charged with perjury must be tried by Indictment, I am therefore directed to desire that you will acquaint the Lieut. Governor whether Russel and Daniels were indicted, and if they were that you will transmit the Indictment. That you will also state whether when Russell and Daniels were suddenly transferred from the condition of a Prosecutor, and an Evidence, into that of Prisoners, the Court took a new Oath, a just Verdict to give, and a true deliverance to make betw. our Sovereign Lord the King, and the Prisoners at the Bar? because if they did not, it would appear that Russell and Daniels have been convicted of perjury, and sentenced to Seven Years Transportation, without the Court ever taking the usual Oath to do them justice.

I am, &c.,

NICHOLAS BAYLY, Secy.

Irregularities in procedure of the court.

[4] *Verbal Notice of Resignation by Mr. Charles Grimes.*

AFTER the Letter No. 3 was written, Mr. Grimes called upon the Lieut. Governor, and expressed his wish to resign the situation of Acting Judge Advocate. The Lieutenant Governor acceded to his Wish, on condition that he should decide all the suits for which writs had been issued—and desirous to conciliate the hostile Spirit displayed by this Gentleman and his Friends, thanked him for having undertaken the Office.

Resignation of Grimes as judge-advocate.

[5] *Mr. Charles Grimes to Major Johnston.*

Sir,   Sydney, 3d April, 1808.

I yesterday received your permission to resign my Situation of Acting Judge Advocate. And have this morning been informed that you wish me to finish the causes pending in the Civil Court for which processes have actually been issued.

Grimes' willingness to finish causes pending in civil court.

1808.
11 April.
———
Grimes'
willingness to
finish causes
pending in
civil court.

I shall at all time feel particularly happy, in contributing all in my power for the public Service; and will readily do it—and hope to complete the whole within the week when I shall have every paper ready to make over to my Successor.

I have, &c.,
C. GRIMES.

[6] *Mr. Charles Grimes to Major Johnston.*

Sir,   Sydney, New South Wales, 3d April, 1808.

Grimes' opinion
on the sentence
of Russell and
Daniels.

In my personal conversation with Your Honor this morning, you thanked me for what I had done as Judge Advocate and I must acknowledge the receipt of Your Secretary's Letter after that conversation has surprized me—I have only to remark that what I did as Judge Advocate, And a Member of the late Criminal Court—I must now repeat I conceived to be correct—and must again refer you to the Proceedings for the reasons why that Court sentenced Oliver Russell and Robert Daniels to be transported for seven Years. I must also retract the offer I made

Refusal to act
as judge-
advocate.

of doing any more duty as Judge Advocate conceiving that every Action of mine may be misconstrued.   I have, &c.,

C. GRIMES.

[7] *Mr. Nicholas Bayly to Mr. Charles Grimes.*

Head Quarters, Sydney, 4th April, 1808.

Grimes to
decide all
causes pending
in the civil
court.

I AM directed by His Honor the Lieut. Governor in answer to your letter of yesterday to say that you appear to have misunderstood the tendency of the conversation when His Honor returned you his thanks—that expression of Approbation, Sir, related only to your undertaking to discharge the Duties of Judge Advocate; not to the manner in which those Duties have been executed. I am further directed to acquaint you that it is expected you will decide all the Civil Causes for which you have issued Processes or you will be held responsible for the consequences.   I am, &c.,

NICHOLAS BAYLY, Secy.

[8] *Mr. Nicholas Bayly to Mr. Charles Grimes.*

Sir,   Head Quarters, Sydney, 4th April, 1808.

Grimes'
absence from
sittings
of the civil
court.

I am directed by His Honor the Lieut. Governor to acquaint you that I have this Instant received Information from the two Members of the Civil Court of Jurisdiction, that they have attended their Duty at the Room where the Court usually assembles, and that in consequence of your not being present, they have been obliged to adjourn without proceeding to Busi-

1808.
11 April.

ness. I am therefore ordered to require that you will immediately assign your reasons for this apparent neglect and disobedience of His Honor's Orders of this day.

I am, &c.,

NICHOLAS BAYLY, Secy.

[9] *Messrs. Wrather and Emmett to Mr. John Macarthur.*

Sir,   Monday Morning, 4th April, '08·

Pursuant to the appointment of the Judge Advocate we attended the Civil Court this morning at ten o'Clock and waited 2 or 3 hours without meeting the Judge Advocate. We sent to enquire whether it was Mr. Grimes' intention of sitting or no, And as we can get no decided Answer, we were induced to represent it to you, in consideration of the expence and hardships this delay subjects many who are at the expence of maintaining their necessary Evidences—many of them from the remotest parts of the Settlement. We shall therefore take the liberty of waiting on you for your Sentiments and directions, and remain

Sir, &c.,

WRATHER AND EMMETT.

Difficulties created by Grimes' action.

[10] *Mr. Charles Grimes to Major Johnston.*

Sir,   Sydney, New South Wales, 4th April, 1808.

In answer to Your Secretary's Letter of this day's date, however painful it may be to my feelings, after having been accused by Mr. McArthur, as Colonial Secretary in Your Honor's presence, of not taking down the Evidence of the last Criminal Court correct, and told by him that Oliver Russell should enter an action against me, and that he would supply him with money for that purpose.

And having likewise received a public Censure by the Proclamation of yesterday* for my Conduct as a Member of the late Criminal Court, from which circumstances I fear Persons having Suits before any Court of which I am a Member will not feel satisfied that Justice is done them. Likewise there is another reason for my declining entering into the causes now pending and for which processes have been issued before the present Court of Civil Judicature—fearing I may be liable to Prosecution for Irregularity. The Processes excepting a few (which I have no objection to hear provided the Parties are satisfied) having been issued under the sanction of different Members, than those who now compose the Court—and there is a Precedent in the case of Mr. Tough of one Member only quitting his seat of a new Precept being issued to form another Court—but having made a

Reasons for Grimes' absence from sitting of civil court.

promise which you still expect me to perform I will hear all the
Processes which are now issued—provided you conceive there is
no irregularity and that I shall not be liable to a prosecution
for it.   I have, &c.,
                                              C. GRIMES.

[11] Mr. Nicholas Bayly to Mr. Charles Grimes.

Sir,   Head Quarters, Sydney, 4th April, 1808.

Grimes to
embark on the
Dart with
despatches to
England.

I am directed by His Honor the Lieut. Governor to
acquaint you, that the Exigencies of His Majesty's Service and
the peculiar Situation of this Colony make it indispensibly necessary that an Officer well acquainted with the causes which have
occasioned the Supercession of Governor Bligh should take home
his dispatches to His Majesty's Ministers, that if anything therein
should appear doubtful or not sufficiently explained, they may be
enabled immediately to obtain the Information required.

The Lieutenant Governor has in consequence made choice of
you, Sir, for that Service, satisfied that no person can be more
competent to give such explanation, than one of those who have
called upon him to assume the command, and pledged their lives
and fortunes to support the measure.

You are therefore immediately to prepare yourself to embark
on board the Dart where a passage is provided for you.
                                       I am, &c.,
                                  NICHOLAS BAYLY, Secy.

[12] Mr. Charles Grimes to Major Johnston.

Sir,   Sydney, New South Wales, 4th April, 1808.

Grimes willing
to sail in the
Dart.

In answer to your Secretary's Letter of this day's date, I
have to inform your Honor that I am ready at all times to forward any Service you may require of me—but must request to be
informed the latest hour that the Dart is expected to sail—and I
will be ready.   I have, &c.,
                                              C. GRIMES.

[13] Mr. Nicholas Bayly to Mr. Charles Grimes.

Sir,   Head Quarters, Sydney, 5th April, 1808.

Misconstruction
of conversation
by Grimes.

I am directed by His Honor the Lieut. Governor in reply
to your letter of yesterday wherein you say, "however painful
it may be to my feelings after having been accused by Mr.
McArthur, as Colonial Secretary in Your Honor's presence of
not taking down the Evidence of the last Criminal Court correct,
and told by him that Oliver Russell should enter an action against
me and that he would supply him with money for that purpose,"
to inform you that the whole representation of that conversation

is incorrect, and that Mr. McArthur instead of saying what you aver, officially informed you, that there lay on the Table a Petition* from Oliver Russell and Robert Daniels, wherein you were accused *by them* of recording the transactions of the Criminal Court different from the Truth; and that they were prepared to prove that instead of confining the Evidence to the Offence the Court was assembled to try, it appeared to be your principal Object to suffer irrelavent matter to be brought forward, entirely calculated to cast a Stain upon Mr. McArthur's Character—that this if true was in his opinion such an unjustifiable and dishonorable step, he was determined to exert himself to the utmost to.call you to account for your Conduct before the Court of Kings Bench, and that he would expend his last Guinea rather than Justice should be perverted with impunity.

1808.
11 April.

Statements in petition from Russell and Daniels.

I am, &c.,

NICHOLAS BAYLY, Secy.

[*A copy of Major Johnston's proclamation, dated 3rd April, 1808 (see page 277), was transmitted with this enclosure.*]

[Enclosure No. 30.]

THE FOLLOWING STATEMENTS were transmitted to His Royal Highness the Commander in Chief last October, but not sworn to at the time.

Statements relating to Bligh's treatment of the military.

William Blakemore's Statement.

11th April, 1808.

IN March last His Excellency Governor Bligh came to me and enquired if the Hut opposite my own dwelling was mine? I answered, Yes. His Excellency asked why I had not his liberty to build it. I told His Excellency that it was built two Years before he came to the Colony. He then asked who gave me liberty to build it. I answered, Major Johnston. His Excellency then damned Major Johnston and Major Paterson too; he did not care a damn for them; no person should have two Houses and others go without.

WM. BLAKEMORE.

The above Statement Sworn to before me, One of His Majesty's Justices of the Peace, this 11th day of April, 1808.

WM. MINCHIN, J.P.

Sergeant Johns' Statement.

I WAS one morning in the month of November last on the Battery Guard at Dawes' Point. His Excellency Governor Bligh came there, and after looking at the men he asked for their Arms one after the other, and having wrenched the flints out, he threw them on the ground, and said in a passion that the men were not fit to have Arms, and they were a disgraceful Set and no use, and said a good deal more in the same way.

BENJ'N JOHNS, Serj't.

The above Statement Sworn to before me, One of His Majesty's Justices of the Peace, this 11th day of April, 1808.

WM. MINCHIN, J.P.

* Note 117.

1808.
11 April.

Statements
relating to
Bligh's
treatment of
the military.

Statement of Sergeant-Major Whittle.

HIS Excellency Governor Bligh sent for me one Sunday morning
in consequence of Drummer Whittle going out to shoot some
Pidgeons (which the Owner Mr. Bevan gave him permission to do),
and after talking a good deal to the Boy, he severely reprimanded
me, for what he had done, and told me to beware, for it was like
the other depredations committed by the New South Wales Corps,
and said a great deal more.

THOS. WHITTLE, Sergt.-Major.

The above Statement sworn to before me, one of His Majesty's
Justices of the Peace, this 11th day of April, 1808.

WM. MINCHIN, J.P.

Joseph Bramwell's Statement.

SOME Months ago, coming from the Bush with my Horse and Cart,
I saw His Excellency Governor Bligh coming on horseback along
the road. I immediately drew my Cart as far out of the Road as
the Ditch would permit me, and stood up in my Cart and saluted
His Excellency as he passed by; he was in a violent passion, and
abused me with the appellation of tremendous B-gg-r, Wretch, &c.,
and on being told that I was a Soldier, he ordered the Horseman
to take me to Government House, when remaining some time there,
Mrs. Putland came to the door, and told me I must take care in
future never to meet the Governor on the road with my Cart.

his
JOSEPH X BRAMWELL.
mark

The above Statement sworn to before me, One of His Majesty's
Justices of the Peace, this 11th day of April, 1808.

WM. MINCHIN, J.P.

Serjeant-Major Whittle's Statement.

HIS Excellency Governor Bligh, on passing by my house the middle
of last December, stopt and asked whose house it was, on hearing
which I came out, saluted him, and informed him that it was mine.
He then asked me how I got it. I answered that I had exchanged
another House (which cost me a great deal of money) for it. He
then asked me how I held it. I informed him that I held by Lease,
of which Six or Seven Years were yet unexpired. His Excell'y
immediately replied, in a violent passion, that neither House or
Ground should be mine; that it was his, but that I might remove
the Materials of the House off the Ground as soon as I pleased, for
that I should not have the Ground, and this he repeated several
times as he rode off. In consequence of which I made my House
and Ground over to my Commanding Officer in order, if possible,
to save it for my young family (six Children). I further declare
that the said House and Ground is worth to me Six Hundred
Pounds.   THOS. WHITTLE, Serjeant-Major.

Sworn before me this 11th day of April, 1808.

WM. MINCHIN, J.P.

Adjutant Minchin's Statement.

Sydney, 30th September, 1807.

ON Sunday last, the 27th Inst., shortly after Divine Service, I
received a Message from H.E. Governor Bligh to attend him at

Government House, which I immediately obeyed, when I was informed by His Excellency "that several of the Soldiers of the Corps had behaved in a most shameful Manner in Church during the Service, by laughing and making faces at his Daughter, so much so that she was obliged to quit the Church; that he followed her into an adjoining Room, and, on learning from her the cause of her distress, he returned to the Church; that the vile wretches had the audacity to stare and laugh at him also; that when the Service was ended he took Lieut. Draffin and Ensign Bell with him to where the Soldiers sat, and pointed out to them and to the Drill Serjeant the Men who had conducted themselves improperly; he then retired from Church," with the whole of which he directed me to acquaint the Commanding Officer.

1808.
11 April.

Bligh's
complaint of
the conduct of
soldiers in
church.

On Monday morning the Governor again sent for me to know whether I had made enquiry into the cause of the Conduct of the wretches who had behaved so ill in the Church.

I acquainted His Excellency that, from all I could learn—and that I had it from the best information—the cause of the Men's laughing, whom His Excellency noticed, was an arch Drummer, having observed a hole in another's Cap, he picked up a feather and put into it, and the other Men having some time afterwards observed it, they involuntarily laughed, and, fearful of being seen by His Excellency or the Officers in Church, they had looked over each other's Shoulders towards his Seat. I at the same time begged to assure His Excellency that I did not think there was a Man in the Regiment who would offer the smallest Offence to him or Mrs. Putland. His Excellency here got warm, and observed to me that the excuse was a patched-up Story of the wretches, and swore that if any one dared to offer him an Insult that he would have the villain's head off; that they might as well say the Drummer had put a feather into a Man's A—e, and that they had laughed at it.

He then desired to be informed how many Men there were in the Regiment who had been Convicts. I answered about 70, but that they were in general the best Men we had, to which His Excellency replied that the creatures he saw in Church looked more like Jail-birds than anything else, On which I asked His Excellency if he had any further Commands; he answered none, but desired me to tell Major Johnston that he expected to see him.

WM. MINCHIN, Adj't, N.S.W. Corps.

Sworn before me this 11th April, 1808.

[No signature.]

MAJOR JOHNSTON TO VISCOUNT CASTLEREAGH.

(Despatch per whaler Dart.)

Headquarters, Sydney, New South Wales,
My Lord,   12th April, 1808.

It is with great regret I trouble Your Lordship with a report of another disagreeable Circumstance.

In my letter of the 11th I had the honor to inform Your Lordship that His Majesty's Ship Porpoise was ready to proceed to Port Dalrymple to bring Lieut.-Colonel Paterson to this Settlement.

1808.
12 April.

Appointment
of Kent as
commander
of H.M.S.
Porpoise.

I had no sooner finished my Despatch to Your Lordship than I received the accompanying letter from James Symons, Esq're, then Acting Commander of the Porpoise, and I learnt from unquestionable authority he meant to proceed to Sea without my Despatches to Lieut.-Colonel Paterson. As such an act must have extremely disconcerted Lieut.-Colonel Paterson, and have created some confusion at Port Dalrymple, I considered it for the advantage of His Majesty's Service to send for Lieut. William Kent, and to deliver to him the Warrant from Commodore Bligh appointing him Acting Commander of the Porpoise, an appointment Your Lordship will find accounted for in the Document No. 7 referred to in my letter A.*

I also wrote to Capt'n Symons to apprise him of my determination, and the next day Captain Kent took the Command of His Majesty's ship. This management, I respectfully hope, will receive Your Lordship's approbation, as it was resorted to for no other reason than to secure Lieut.-Colonel Paterson from the embarrassment he must naturally have felt if the Porpoise had arrived at Port Dalrymple without any Despatches from this Settlement.

I expect to have my Letters ready for the Porpoise by the 16th Instant.

I have, &c.,
GEO. JOHNSTON.

[Enclosure No. 1.]

LIEUTENANT SYMONS TO MAJOR JOHNSTON.

Sir,   His Majesty's Ship Porpoise, 12th April, 1808.

Symons'
proposed
sailing for Port
Dalrymple.

I beg leave to acquaint you that His Majesty's Ship Porpoise, under my Command, is ready for Sea, and I purpose sailing as soon as the Wind is favourable, to conform to the request of Lieutenant-Governor Paterson, which I received through you. All the Stores are on board, and I have to request your Letters may be forwarded to me as soon as possible. Have been perfectly ready these six days past, and only waiting for your Despatches.

I have, &c.,
J. SYMONS.

[Enclosure No. 2.]

MAJOR JOHNSTON TO LIEUTENANT SYMONS.

Sir,   12th April.

Kent appointed
to command
H.M.S.
Porpoise.

I have to acknowledge the receipt of your Letter of this date, wherein you inform me You purpose sailing as soon as the Wind is favourable. In Answer to which I find it necessary to acquaint You that I have this Evening transmitted to Lieutenant

* Note 118.

1808.
12 April.

Kent appointed
to command
H.M.S.
Porpoise.

William Kent a Warrant from Commodore Bligh to take the Command of His Majesty's Ship Porpoise, and that I hereby release you from every engagement or promise you have made to me not to receive any Orders from Commodore Bligh.

I am, &c.,

GEO. JOHNSTON.

MAJOR JOHNSTON TO VISCOUNT CASTLEREAGH.

(Despatch per whaler Dart.)

Headquarters, Sydney, New South Wales,
My Lord,   12th April, 1808.

Almost the first object of my attention after the event which I have had the honor to report to Your Lordship was the state of His Majesty's Stores.

As I was convinced from personal observation of the Frauds and Abuses practiced in the Commissary's Department, I ordered the Papers in that Office to be secured, and an immediate Survey to be taken of every kind of Store and every description of Provisions remaining.

That Survey, and a careful examination of the Books, will soon enable me, I hope, to transmit to Your Lordship satisfactory information on every subject connected with that Department.

Being aware that large quantities of Grain had been drawn from the Stores on the plea of its being baked into Biscuit for the Colonial Craft by the Commissary, who is engaged in an extensive baking concern, I required from him a Return of the Flour, Meal, and Wheat received by him from His Majesty's Stores between the 13th August, 1806, and 26th January, 1808; but instead of furnishing the Return (although the requisition has been frequently repeated) the Commissary thought proper to make evasive excuses and to treat my Authority with contempt by absolutely refusing to send the required information.

There now remains in His Majesty's Stores only Two hundred and forty-eight Tierces of Beef and Three hundred and ten Tierces of Pork. From this quantity I have determined to send Four hundred Tierces to the Derwent, to enable Lieut.-Gov'r Collins to issue a full Ration of Provisions to the Inhabitants, and to abolish the practice of hunting for their subsistence, instead of being employed in Agriculture and in those labours necessary for the permanent establishment and welfare of that Society.

That I might carry this plan into effect without injury to this Settlement, I have reduced the Ration of Salted Meat issued here

1808.
12 April.

Issue of fresh
in lieu of
salt meat.

to one-half, and have issued to the Officers of the Civil and Military Department and the Soldiers three pounds and a half of fresh Beef in lieu of the reduced quantity of Salted Meat, and to the Prisoners Six Pounds of Wheat. By this arrangement the Prisoners have a Ration quite as sufficient for their support as the established one and altogether as acceptable to themselves.

Advantages of
issuing grain.

The Agriculture of the Country will also be encouraged by the encreased consumption of Grain, and a very considerable saving will accrue from the difference of the expence, as the additional Six pounds of Wheat only costs One Shilling, and the Two pounds of Pork that is reduced, when every expence on its importation is calculated, would have cost, I imagine, at least Two Shillings and Sixpence.

Report on the
public live
stock.

I have the honor to transmit Your Lordship a Report of Survey of the Public Live Stock, from which you will discover that this valuable property is in a very deplorable Condition, and has been fast degenerating in consequence of improper management. So little attention has been paid to them, that when Mr. John Jamieson, the person who has had the principal charge, was called upon for a return of the different kinds, it appeared he had no Books, and had never taken the trouble to inform himself of the state of the Herds. His practice was to return the encrease of Years as Calves, and by his last return there appears to be 2,540 Calves and only 760 Cows. That a more perfect knowledge might be obtained of the state of the Cattle, I directed Mr. Fitz, Deputy Commissary, to superintend their arrangement, and that the Breeding Cows and Calves, the Heifers, the Oxen, and the Steers might be formed into Herds, in which each kind might be kept apart. But in proceeding to the execu-

Dismissal of
Jamieson and
appointment
of Hume.

tion of this duty, he was so much opposed by the Superintendant (Jamieson), who positively refused to give the least assistance, and behaved with such insolence in other respects, that I have been obliged to dismiss him from his Office, and to appoint Mr. Andrew Hume, to succeed him. I must, however, respectfully endeavour to impress upon Your Lordship that this encreasing and highly valuable property well deserves that a man of Character, Knowledge, and Respectable condition in Life should be appointed with an adequate Salary for conducting it. At present I propose to make Mr. Hume accountable to Mr. Fitz, and to give that Gentleman some compensation for the labour of occasionally visiting and inspecting the whole Stock.

Conceiving that a moderate distribution of Cows amongst the steadiest of the Settlers and Inhabitants will be of great Public utility (as it is indisputable they improve more under the management of Individuals when they become their private property than when herded in large numbers with only the care of Convicts, who have no interest in them), I have promised to dispose of Three hundred Cows and a few Working Oxen at £28 per head, to be paid for immediately in Grain, and the Cattle to be received with the usual restriction as to Killing or selling them.

By these means all the Grain wanted by Government this Year *for this Settlement* will be provided, and I shall be relieved from the necessity of drawing Bills for its purchase on His Majesty's Treasury. These measures for the reduction of the expences of the Colony, and the improvement of the Cattle, will, I respectfully hope, be approved of by Your Lordship, and I persuade myself the steps I have pursued to facilitate the evacuation of Norfolk Island will also receive Your Lordship's approbation.

Having discovered from Mr. Windham's Despatch of the 30th December, 1806, the solicitude of Government to accomplish that object without additional expence, I considered it my duty to lose no opportunity of giving effect to the Orders of Government. Under this impression, I have made a Contract with the Master and Supercargo of the City of Edinburgh, a ship of Five Hundred and twenty-six Tons burthen to proceed to Norfolk Island, and to take as many of its Settlers, Stock, &c., to the Derwent as she can carry, for which Service she is to be paid in Timber.

I shall take care to provide a sufficient quantity to pay the full amount of her Freight, and the whole will be procured without the expence of an extra Guinea.

The accompanying return of Public property alienated to individuals since I have taken the Command, will inform Your Lordship that I have not been lavish in its distribution, nor regardless of the trust which uncontrollable Circumstances has placed in my hands.

I presume Your Lordship will have received before this many complaints from the Gentlemen who have come out as Settlers under the immediate sanction of Lord Camden, Your Lordship, and Mr. Windham, of the little attention they have obtained, and from some, of the total disappointment of their hopes and expectations. It became an immediate object of my care to acquaint myself with the Orders that have been sent out for the establishment of these Gentlemen, and I have already proceeded to shew my attention to Commands that I feel are entitled to the respectful Obedience of whoever may Administer the Government of this Colony, by distributing Servants, permitting them

1808.
12 April.

Encouragement
of free settlers.

to choose their Land, and by assurances of Live Stock, and every other indulgence promised them by His Majesty's Secretary of State. At the head of this description of persons stands Mr. John Blaxland, and his Correspondence* with me on the subject of his Claims will show Your Lordship the principle on which I propose to act.

I have great satisfaction in reporting to Your Lordship that we have had a plentiful Wheat Harvest, and that the maize now ripe is the most abundant Crop ever seen in the settlement.

Enclosures to
despatches.

On observing the imperfect and incorrect manner in which the Documents accompanying my Despatches are Copied,† I feel most sensibly the necessity of apologising to Your Lordship for transmitting them in such a state, but I trust Your Lordship will take into consideration the hurry in which they have been made up, and the many avocations that have completely occupied the whole time of the few persons from whom I could command assistance.   I have, &c.,

GEO. JOHNSTON.

[Enclosure No. 1.]

CORRESPONDENCE WITH COMMISSARY PALMER.

[1] *Mr. John Macarthur to Commissary Palmer.*

Sir,   Head Quarters, Sydney, 18th March, 1808.

Palmer
requested
to submit
returns.

I am directed by His Honor the Lieutenant Governor to request you will furnish him with a return of the quantity of Flour Meal and Wheat you received from his Majesty's Stores for the purpose of making biscuit for Government between the 13th August 1806 and 26th January 1808 and the quantity of Biscuit you returned in consequence thereof.

I am, &c.,

JOHN MCARTHUR, Secretary to the Colony.

[2] *Mr. John Macarthur to Commissary Palmer.*

Sir,   Head Quarters, 31st March, 1808.

His Honor the Lieut't Governor not having received the return of the quantity of Flour Meal and Wheat you received from His Majesty's Stores for the purpose of making Biscuit for Government between the 13th August 1806 and 26th January 1808 and the quantity of Biscuit you returned in consequence thereof, as required in my letter to you of the 18th Instant, I am directed to request you will furnish the Return in the course of the day.   I am, &c.,

JOHN MCARTHUR, Secretary to the Colony.

* Note 119.   † Note 120.

[3] *Major Johnston to Commissary Palmer.*

Sir,   Head Quarters, Sydney, 1st April, 1808.

Two Letters have been written to you by the Secretary of the Colony requiring you in my name to furnish an account of the Flour, Meal and Wheat received by you from His Majesty's Stores, for the purpose of making Biscuit for Government, between the 13th August, 1806, and 26th January, 1808, and no answer having been given thereto, I do hereby direct and order you to furnish the return immediately and to account for your past neglect and disobedience.

I am, &c.,
GEO. JOHNSTON.

[4] *Commissary Palmer to Major Johnston.*

Sir,   Sydney, 1st April, 1808.

I received your Letter this morning, informing me that two Letters had been wrote by the Secretary of the Colony requesting in your name that I would furnish an Account of the Flour, Meal and Wheat, received by me from His Majesty's Stores for the purpose of making Biscuit for Government between the 13th August 1806, and 26th January 1808, and stating no answer had been given thereto.

In reply to which I beg to acquaint Your Honor, that I waited on you the next Morning, after receiving the first letter, and gave my reasons for not answering Mr. McArthur, which I conceived were satisfactory, but as you are pleased now to order me to furnish the return immediately and to account for my past neglect and disobedience; I think it proper in justification to myself bearing His Majesty's Commission as Commissary to state my reasons for not complying with Mr. McArthur's two letters.

In the first place I am not in possession of a single Book or paper to enable me to make any accounts out whatever, in the next place I consider myself not bound to furnish Mr. McArthur with any Accounts at all, nor am I, agreeable to the Instructions I have received from the Right Honorable the Lords Commissioners of His Majesty's Treasury, compelled to obey any Orders or Directions I may receive from any other person than the Governor, or the Officer commanding for the time being.

Lastly, being deprived of my Situation as Commissary, I do not conceive I can be called upon to render any Specific Account until I have an Opportunity of justifying and explaining the whole of them to the Lords of the Treasury to whom I hold myself responsible.   I have, &c.,
JNO. PALMER.

[5] *Mr. John Macarthur to Mr. James Williamson.*

Palmer to have
access to all
necessary
books.

Sir,   Head Quarters, Sydney, 6th April, 1808.

His Honor the Lieut't Governor has directed me to inform you that Mr. Palmer may have access to any of the Books
he may desire, to enable him to make up the Accounts of the
Treasurer of the Orphan Fund, And likewise such Accounts as
may be necessary for him to make a Return of the Wheat, Meal
and Flour, drawn by him from the Public Stores, of which you
will be pleased to inform him.

I am, &c.,

JOHN McARTHUR, Secretary to the Colony.

[6] *Mr. James Williamson to Mr. John Macarthur.*

Sir,   Commissary's Office, Sydney, 6th April, 1808.

The enclosed is a Copy of the Answer I received from
Mr. Palmer to the letter which you was directed by His Honor
the Lieutenant Governor to write to me on Service this Morning.

I am, &c.,

JAMES WILLIAMSON, Actg. Commissary.

*[Enclosed in No. 6] Commissary Palmer to Mr. James
Williamson.*

Sir,   Sydney, 6th April, 1808.

I have to acquaint you in answer to your letter of this
morning, that until the whole of my Books and Papers, that
were taken from me, are returned, I cannot make up any accounts
whatever; when they are returned, I will make up such Accounts
as respect the Orphan School and Settlers. The Accounts of the
Treasury will be made up by me and delivered to the Lords
Commissioners of the Treasury, to whom only I can account.

I am, &c.,

JNO. PALMER.

[7] *Mr. John Macarthur to Commissary Palmer.*

Sir,   Head Quarters, Sydney, 6th April, 1808.

I am directed by His Honor the Lieut't Governor to inform you that Mr. Williamson the Acting Commissary has
received Orders to give you Access to any of the Books in the
Commissary's Department which may enable you to make up a
return of the Flour Meal and Wheat, you have received from His
Majesty's Stores for the purpose of making Biscuit for Government, and the quantity of Biscuit you have returned on Account
thereof between the 13th day of August, 1806, and the 26th
Jany., 1808.

Mr. Williamson is also directed to give you access to such Books as may enable you to make up the Account of the Treasurer of the Orphan Fund—His Honor has further directed me to require in his name that the Return of Flour, Meal, Wheat and Biscuit, and the Treasurer of the Orphan Fund's Account may be immediately transmitted to me.

I am, &c.,

JOHN McARTHUR, Secretary to the Colony.

[8] *Commissary Palmer to Major Johnston.*

Sir, Sydney, the 6th April, 1808.

I have received a letter from Mr. McArthur saying that Mr. Williamson the Acting Commissary has received Orders to give me access to any of the Books in the Commissary's department which may enable me to make up certain Accounts. I beg to say that I have already stated, if my Books and Papers which were taken from me were delivered back into my Charge (which I now demand) I should then be able to make up my Accounts with the Orphan School and the Settlers, all other accounts whatever I consider myself only answerable to the Lords of the Treasury for, and am determined to render no other accounts to Mr. McArthur or any other Person in this Colony. And I further say that I cannot be called upon by you for any Accounts whatever, that took place during His Excellency Govr. Bligh's Government.

I have, &c.,

JNO. PALMER.

[9] *Mr. John Macarthur to Commissary Palmer.*

Sir, Head Quarters, Sydney, 6th April, 1808.

I am directed by His Honor the Lieutenant Governor to acquaint you in answer to your letter of this date, that it shall be transmitted (together with your other letters upon the same subject) to His Majesty's Ministers, as evidence that you have thought it necessary to add insolence, contempt, and disobedience of the Lieut't Governor's Authority to the other offences you have committed.

I am further directed to acquaint you that as soon as the Ships have sailed, immediate measures will be resorted to, which, it is hoped, may bring you into a more temperate frame of mind.

I am, &c.,

JOHN McARTHUR, Secy. to the Colony.

1808.
12 April.

[Enclosure No. 2.]

Estimated
remains of salt
provisions
in store.

RETURNS OF THE COMMISSARIAT DEPARTMENT.

THE supposed Remains of Salt Provisions in His Majesty's Stores at Sydney, Parramatta, and Hawkesbury, taken from the Deputy Commissary's and Storekeepers' Returns, including the issue of the 9th April, 1808.

Settlement.	Beef Lbs.	Pork Lbs.
Sydney	68,209	98,185
Parramatta	7,312	998
Hawkesbury	7,951	....
	83,472	99,183

N.B.—Total remains of Beef 83,472 or 248 Tierces.
    Do.   Do.   Pork 99,183 or 310 Do.

Provisions sent
to Hobart
and Port
Dalrymple.

STATEMENT of Provisions sent to His Majesty's Settlements at the River Derwent and Port Dalrymple between the 26th January and 12th April 1808.

Settlement.	Beef. lbs.	Pork. lbs.	Wheat. Bushels.	Barley. Bushels.	Spirits. Gallons.
River Derwent	2,080	3,180	1,700	..	...
Port Dalrymple ...	....	....	1,550	79	125
Total	2,080	3,180	3,250	79	125

N.B.—The above includes One Thousand Bushels of Wheat, now ready to be sent in the Governor Hunter, Schooner.

JAMES WILLIAMSON, Act'g Commissary.

[Enclosure No. 3.]

REPORT OF SURVEY OF LIVE STOCK.

Sir,   20th February, 1808.

Report on the
public live
stock.

Agreeable to your Honor's Order of the 15th Instant We have Surveyed the Government Stock and make the following Report.

The Government Black Cattle being Herded together in too great Numbers, We conceive it would be highly advantageous to separate them into smaller Herds. A Great Part of them are kept in Situations where the Feed is of an inferior quality and insufficient for such great Numbers, And the Dairy Cows appear over milked.

They would be further benefitted if the large Steers were separated from the Breeding Cows, and the Young Stock from the Old, particularly the young Heifers from the Bulls, until a proper period; as the Young Stock Breeding too soon appears to us the cause of the degeneracy so apparent in many of the Younger part of Particular Herds. Heifers, in our Opinion should not have Calves until three Years Old, they would also be essentially improved by introducing Bulls of a Superior Breed.

The Government Horses appear to us of very inferior kind.

The Government Sheep appear many of them small and sickly 1808.
12 April. which will always be the case if the Ewe Lambs are permitted to Breed before they are of a proper Age. Or the Old Ewes Report on the public live stock. more than once in the Year or after they are too old.

J. HARRIS.
JOHN BLAXLAND.
G. BLAXLAND.

[Enclosure No. 4.]

RETURN of Government Stock for 13th February, 1808. Expence, Return of government stock. Decrease, and Remains to 20th February, 1808.

Place where Kept—Increase and Decrease.	Cattle.					Horses.				Sheep.				
	Bulls.	Cows.	Bull Calves.	Cow Calves.	Oxen.	Males.	Mares.	Fillies.	Colts.	Rams.	Ewes.	Wethers.	Ewe Lambs.	Wether Lambs.
Parramatta	7	72	180	159	62*	14	8	8	10	6	198	178	41	144
Increase	..	..	..	..	..	..	..	..	..	..	..	..	..	..
Toongabbe	4	165	266	438	..	..	..	..	..	..	..	..	..	..
Increase	..	..	3	2	..	..	..	..	..	..	..	..	..	..
Castle Hill	2	45	93	102	48	..	..	..	..	..	177	..	256	7
Increase	..	..	..	..	..	..	..	..	..	..	..	..	..	..
Seven Hills	7	469	696	583	..	..	..	..	..	..	..	..	..	..
Increase	..	..	5	4	..	..	..	..	..	..	..	..	..	..
Sydney	..	9	6	3	70	..	..	..	..	..	..	..	..	..
Increase	..	.	..	..	..	..	..	..	..	..	..	..	..	..
Total of Increase.	20	760	1,249	1,291	579	14	8	8	10	6	375	178	297	151
Decrease by Accident	..	..	..	..	..	..	..	..	..	..	..	..	..	..
Supplied the Stores.	..	..	..	..	3	..	..	..	..	..	..	..	..	..
Government House.	..	..	..	..	..	..	..	..	..	..	..	..	..	..
Bartered for Grain..	..	..	..	..	..	..	..	..	..	..	..	..	..	..
Granted to Settlers, &c.	..	..	..	..	..	..	..	..	..	..	..	..	..	..
Total of Decrease.	..	..	..	..	3	..	..	..	..	..	..	..	..	..
Total of Remains.	20	760	1,249	1,291	576	14	8	8	10	6	375	178	297	151

* Remarks: Sent three Oxen to Sydney for Slaughter.

Swine.

Place Where.	Breeding Sows.	Female Slips.	Hogs.	Sucklings.	How disposed of.
Hawkesbury	....	....	....	....	....
Toongabbe	....	....	....	....	....
Castle Hill	...	....	9	....	....

[Enclosure No. 5.]

CHARTER PARTY OF THE SHIP CITY OF EDINBURGH.

THIS CHARTER PARTY Indented made concluded and Agreed upon this twenty fourth day of February in the Year of our Lord One thousand eight hundred and eight by and between Simeon Patteson, Master of the good Ship City of Edinburgh, Burthen five hundred and twenty six Registered Tons, and Alexander Berry* Supercargo of the said Ship on the one part, and George Johnston Esquire, Lieutenant Governor of the Territory of New South Wales, on the part and behalf of His Majesty of the other part, in manner and form following (that is to say) The said Simeon Patteson and Alexander Berry, for and in behalf of themselves and all and every the part owners of the said Ship or Vessel, Have Granted, and to Hire, and to freight Letten; and by these presents Do grant Hire, freight and Let the said Ship City of Edinburgh to the said Lieutenant Governor to Sail from this port to Norfolk Island, and from thence to the Derwent, and from the Derwent back to this port, and to receive on board, all such Stores, Provisions, Settlers or other persons, and all such Live Stock, as the said Lieutenant Governor shall think proper to embark, or send on board from hence, or as the Commandant of Norfolk Island shall think proper to send on board from the said Island, And the said Simeon Patteson and Alexander Berry on behalf as aforesaid, Do further Contract and agree to proceed with all possible dispatch from hence to Norfolk Island, and on their arrival, to be aiding and assisting by their Boats and by all other ways and means in their Power to hasten and facilitate the Embarkation of such Stores, Provisions, Settlers, Prisoners, or other persons, and all such Live Stock, as the Commandant may deem it for the good of His Majesty's Service to send on board, and after receiving the said Stores, Provisions, Settlers, Prisoners and Live Stock, and the Despatches of the Commandant of Norfolk Island, that they will proceed with the said Ship the City of Edinburgh to the Derwent and on their arrival at that Place that they will be aiding and assisting with their Boats &c. &c. and by all other ways and means which they can command for the Landing of the said Stores, Provisions, Settlers, Prisoners and Live Stock, And it is hereby understood and agreed by and between the Parties to these presents that a person who shall be appointed by the Lieutenant Governor as an Agent for and on behalf of Government, shall have the Superintendence and direction of all such Stores, Provisions, Settlers, Prisoners, and Live Stock, and whose directions relative to the same shall be attended to by the said Simeon

* Note 121.

Patteson and Alexander Berry, And they do further agree that
they will use all Possible Care for the preservation and safe
keeping of all such Stores Provisions, and Live Stock as they
may receive on board. And that they will do everything in their
Power for the Accomodation of such Settlers, Prisoners, or
other Persons, as may be embarked on board the said Ship, and
that whilst such persons may remain on board, that they will
cause them to be treated with all possible Care and humanity,
And they the said Simeon Patteson, and Alexander Berry Do
further covenant and Agree that they will take on board Fifty
Tons of Water, before they do depart from hence, for the supply
of the persons and Live Stock, which they may receive on board
the said Ship. The said Simeon Patteson and Alexander Berry
do also Covenant and agree that after they have Landed the said
Stores, Provisions, Settlers, and Prisoners and all such live
Stock, they will receive Lieutenant Governor Collins's Dispatches
on board, and return with all possible Expedition to this port,
And on the other part it is hereby agreed that the said George
Johnston Esq., Lieutenant Governor as aforesaid, shall Pay or
cause to be paid unto the said Simeon Patteson and Alexander
Berry twenty three Shillings Freight per Ton per Month (that
is to say) for five hundred and twenty six Tons, the registered
Tonnage of the said Ship in manner following: Sawed Timber
and Wood of the Dimensions and Prices specified in the under-
written Schedule shall be delivered at the Water side (as hereafter mentioned) to the said Simeon Patteson and Alexander
Berry to the full Amount of the freight of the said Ship, for and
during the time she shall have been employed in the Service of
Government which said Freight shall commence from the day on
which she shall sail from hence on her intended Voyage to Norfolk Island, and shall continue until the day after her arrival in
this Port; That such part of the Timber to be so paid as can be
procured without detaining the said Ship by Lieutenant Governor
Collins at the Derwent shall be delivered to the said Simeon
Patteson and Alexander Berry at Hobart Town, or at any other
place at the water Side, which may be more convenient at the
said Settlement in part Payment of the said Freight, And that
a Spar Deck shall be erected at the expence of Government for
the accomodation of the Settlers, Prisoners, and other Persons to
be embarked as aforesaid, the Materials of which are to be taken
in further part Payment of the said Freight, at the price fixed
in the said Schedule, And that the remainder shall be delivered
at the Dock Yard or places adjacent in the Cove of the Town of
Sydney, And for the better Security and due performance of
this Agreement it is hereby Covenanted that if either of the

1808.
12 April.

Charter party
of the ship City
of Edinburgh.

1808.
12 April.

Charter party
of the ship City
of Edinburgh.
subscribing Parties shall fail strictly to perform the Conditions
which it contains he or they shall forfeit the Sum of Two
Thousand Pounds Sterling to the party aggrieved. In Witness
whereof the said Parties to these presents have hereunto set their
hands and Seals the day and Year first above written.

SIMEON PATTESON (L.S.).
ALEXR. BERRY   (L.S.).
GEO. JOHNSTON   (L.S.).

Sealed and Delivered (where no Stamps are used) in the
presence of

WILLIAM LAWSON.
CADW'R DRAFFIN.

Schedule referred to.

Schedule of
prices of timber.
PRICES of Timber and Sawing to be supplied by Government on
Account of Freight as per foregoing Charterparty.

Cedar Logs Four Pence per superficial Foot;
Logs of Common Timber for Beams, Nine pence per Cubic Foot;
Sawed Scantling (side and Edge to be measured) Twenty five
Shillings per hundred;
Flooring Boards Sixteen Shillings per hundred;
Sawing Beams, Sixteen Shillings per hundred four sides to be
measured;
Sawing Cedar—Inch Boards, Ten Shillings per hundred net
Measurement;
All Cedar Boards above one Inch thick, side and edge to be
measured—all the Timber to be good and Merchantable
according to the usage of the Colony.

SIMEON PATTESON.
ALEXR. BERRY.
GEO. JOHNSTON.

[Enclosure No. 6.]

Return of
public property
alienated.
RETURN of Public property alienated to Individuals from the
26th January to the 12th April, 1808.

ONE hundred Acres of land granted to Adjutant Minchin in the
vicinity of George's River, subject to the approval of His
Majesty's Secretary of State for the Colonies.
Two town allotments Leased for fourteen Years.
One Do.   Do.   Lease renewed for fourteen Years.
One Cow given as a reward for the discovery of a Still agree-
ably to the Orders of Governor King on that head.

GEO. JOHNSTON.

[1] MR. JOHN BLAXLAND TO MAJOR JOHNSTON.

1808.
12 April.

Agreement
with Messrs.
Blaxland
unfulfilled.

Sir,   Sydney, 11th February, 1808.

I beg leave respectfully to represent that having entered into certain engagements with His Majesty's Ministers previous to my leaving England which was communicated to the late Governor Bligh by Letters entrusted to my charge and which I delivered soon after my Arrival, I must beg leave to refer your Honor to see them, See the enclosed Papers*—1, 2, 3, 4 and I trust you will not withhold that from me which was the only inducement for my leaving a good business in England and being at the great expence of removing my family thus far.

I have only had 1,290 Acres of Land granted and as the Land is to be chosen by myself I trust you will suffer me to take some in and about the Swamps in the Neighbourhood of Botany Bay and some by Georges River—It is stipulated that I am to have 80 Convicts for 18 Months but I have never been able to gett more than twenty three and many of those incapable of Labour, See Paper No. 5. The late Governor in his Letter to the Secretary of State says I did not ask for more than twenty, which is not correct, as he complained of his inability of sparing more, but said I should have them, when in his Power to comply with their Instructions.

With regard to the Cattle, a reference to the public Papers will convince you, Sir, that no one part has been complied with, as my Brother with half the Capital got seventy eight and as those papers will shew I have only obtained Sixty four.

My Brother has 2,000 Acres of land yet due to him, he is desirous to take in the neighbourhood of the Swamps near Botany Bay which I respectfully hope you will see no objection to, as the Land will require a large Capital to make fit for any thing.

By the list I have enclosed you, therein will see my Brother and myself have several men unfit for labour, which we hope and trust you will have the goodness to exchange.

I am, &c.,

JOHN BLAXLAND.

[2] MR. JOHN MACARTHUR TO MR. JOHN BLAXLAND.

Sir,   29th February, 1808.

His Honor the Lieutenant Governor has taken your letter of the 11th inst. and its accompanying documents into consideration, and having found your claim correspond with the Instructions of H. M. Ministers, His Honor has commanded me to acquaint you, that there will be no objection to your Brother and you having the residue of your Land in any unappropriated

Terms of
agreement with
Messrs.
Blaxland to
be fulfilled.

* Note 122.

1808.
12 April.

tract.—that your full number of Servants shall be granted to you, whenever the Circumstances of the Colony will allow it, and

Terms of
agreement with
Messrs.
Blaxland to
be fulfilled.

that you shall receive Ninety two Head of Cattle, under the usual restrictive Clauses respecting their alienation, at £28 per Head—the manner of paying for which is to be left to the decision of H. M. Ministers—whose Orders thereon are to be considered conclusive.

I am also further directed to acquaint you, that if any of the Men you now have are incapable of labour, they may be returned.

J. McARTHUR, Secretary to the Colony.

GOVERNOR BLIGH TO VISCOUNT CASTLEREAGH.

(Despatch per whaler the Brothers; acknowledged by Viscount Castlereagh, 15th May, 1809.)

Government House, Sydney, New South Wales,

30 April.

My Lord,   30th April, 1808.

Previous
despatches.

[1]* My last Dispatches by the Duke of Portland on the 30th of October† will have communicated very favourable accounts of the Colony and its welfare, continued, to the infinite satisfaction of every good person, until the 26th of January.

Prosperous
condition of
the colony.

[2] The Country became well cultivated, the Settlers and Landholders had a Market for whatever their labours produced, and confidence in each other was bringing about every good that was expected. Their Industry was recompensed with a good harvest, and to add to this the convicts were become reconciled and contented in their Situations as Servants, feeling no oppression or wanton punishment.

Suppression of
monopolies.

[3] When Ships arrived, the usual impositions were oppressed, the necessaries which they introduced were open to every one's purchase, and by this means the numerous people in the Country had opportunities to relieve their wants without being so much subject to the wicked monopolising persons who heretofore had been making themselves rich on the Vitals of the Poor.

Address from
settlers.

[4] On the first day of the year, under an impression of what I had done for them, I received a dutiful Address,‡ signed by nearly nine hundred persons, which never was known in this Country before; but to this Address it is to be observed that John McArthur, Edward McArthur, Hannibal McArthur, Garnham Blaxcell, John Blaxland, Gregòry Blaxland, Captain Townson, Doctor Townson, Charles Grimes, Surgeon Jamison, Nicholas Bayly, and D'Arcy Wentworth's names, and some others, are not

Discontent of
certain persons.

affixed, or any of the Military Officers. These persons, checked in the enormous practice of bartering Spirits, which had principally been the almost ruin of the Colony, became privately discontented; and the Arch Fiend, John McArthur, so inflamed their

* Note 123.   † Note 124.   ‡ Note 125.

·minds as to make them dissatisfied with Government, and tricked
them into misfortunes, even to his own advantage, which they
now, at too late a period, acknowledge, in addition to the iniquity
he has led them of Treason and Rebellion to the State.

[5] This McArthur began his career with endeavours to delude
the Settlers and Landholders, but who execrated him for the
attempt, as they had always done. He then opposed the Civil
Magistracy, and bid defiance to all law and Colonial Regulations; and, after all, under the pretext of great benefits which
would arise to the Military, he, with a Mr. Nicholas Bayly,
seduced Major Johnston and all the Officers and Privates of the
New South Wales Corps from their duty and allegiance into
open Rebellion against me, His Majesty's Representative and
Governor-in-Chief of the Colony, and the whole Civil Power and
Magistracy.

[6] This Rebellious Act was done so suddenly that in about
five minutes from the time we first knew of it, Government
House was surrounded with Troops, Major Johnston having
brought up in battle array above three hundred men under Martial
Law, loaded with Ball, to attack and seize my person and a few
friends, some of whom were Magistrates, that had been at dinner
with me. Their Colours were spread, and they marched to the
tune of the "British Grenadiers"; and, to render the spectacle
more terrific to the Townspeople, the Field Artillery on the
Parade was presented against the House where I became arrested,
and had five Centinels placed over me, and the Civil Magistrates were put under an arrest in their own houses.

[7] In order to detail some things explanatory of the conduct
of the designing persons connected with the Rebellion of the
New South Wales Corps, it is proper I should at least show the
recent circumstances which took place antecedent to their treasonable attack on my· person and the confinement which I still
.remain under. To go farther back would fill a volume in explaining the wickedness of McArthur and Bayly and their ad- Bligh's opinion
of Macarthur's
evil influence.
herents; the former stands sufficiently notorious in all the
Accounts which have been sent to Your Lordship's Office since
the Colony began, and whose very breath is sufficient to contaminate a multitude, and who has been a disturber of Public
Society and a venemous Serpent to His Majesty's Governors.
He has hitherto overcome them with his artifice; but under the
dignity and firmness I have pursued, he has been obliged to add
low and illiberal falsehoods and a most cowardly force of Arms.
As to the latter, I believe he stands dismissed from the New South
Wales Corps for improper conduct,* and of notoriety likewise in
your Lordship's Office.

* Note 126.

1808.
30 April.

Regulations for
preventing the
escape of
convicts.

[8] From the frequent desertions of the Convicts it was necessary to make a Colonial Regulation that the Masters of Ships
and Vessels should give a Bond of eight hundred pounds, with
fifty pounds each, not to take away such characters when they
sailed from the Port. Mr. McArthur and his partner, Mr. Blaxcell, became bondsmen on a vessel called the Parramatta, belonging to Mr. McArthur, and the Vessel sailed for Otaheite.

Escape of
John Hoare in
the schooner
Parramatta.

[9] A suspicion arose that a John Hoare had absented himself,
and on the return of the Schooner we found he had been
secreted on board and allowed to escape from Otaheite in a ship
called the General Wellesley, bound to India.* In consequence
of this the Naval Officer sued for the Amount of the Bond in the
Civil Court, and on the 14th of December last it was determined
that the Bond was forfeited. On this decision Mr. McArthur was
very illiberal and abusive. He refused to have anything to do

Macarthur's
abandonment of
the Parramatta.

further with the Vessel, or to pay or victual the Master or Crew,
and they were turned on shore. Shortly after they petitioned me
for redress, and I directed the Judge-Advocate to enquire legally
into the transactions, who immediately wrote to McArthur a
polite letter to appear and explain why those men were thrown
on the Public without support.

[10] The next morning the Judge-Advocate received a letter
from McArthur which contemptuously referred him to the Naval
Officer, and refused to attend or give any explanation. The
Judge-Advocate therefore issued a Warrant to Mr. Oakes, the

Serving of
warrant for
the arrest of
Macarthur.

Chief Constable, to bring McArthur from Parramatta the next
day to appear before him, and Oakes accordingly arrested
McArthur, who nevertheless refused to obey, and warned him if
he came again to come well armed, as some blood should be spilt
before he would submit, and then wrote a Paper and delivered
it to Oakes, saying it might save him some trouble. Oakes
remonstrated, and said, " Sir, I will call in the morning; you will
then have time to consider." " No," McArthur replied, " Take
it now," which he did, and returned without McArthur, but who,
nevertheless, some time after followed Oakes to Sydney—who
had delivered the Paper he had received to the Judge-Advocate.
The Paper contained as follows:—

" You will inform the Persons who sent you here with the Warrant you have now shown to me, and given me a copy of, that
I never will submit to the horrid tyranny that is attempted until
I am forced; that I consider it with Scorn and Contempt, as I do
the persons who have directed it to be executed.

" (Signed)   J. McArthur."

[11] The Judge-Advocate, on receiving this written Paper,
called together Major Johnston, Mr. Palmer, and Mr. Campbell,

* Note 127.

as Magistrates, who all agreed that Mr. Judge-Advocate Atkins should enforce the Warrant he had issued as a Magistrate, and seize McArthur. He did so by directing another Warrant to the Chief Constable and others, who arrested McArthur and took him before the Judge-Advocate, who admitted him to Bail to appear before a full Bench of Magistrates the next day (Thursday, the 17th).

1808.
30 April.

Arrest of
Macarthur
on a second
warrant.

[12] Accordingly, the Magistrates, Major Johnston, Captain Abbott, Mr. Palmer, Mr. Campbell, and the Judge-Advocate met. When McArthur came before them he objected to Mr. Campbell sitting, in his usual impertinent and irritating language. Mr. Campbell did not sit, but the others proceeded to business, and committed McArthur for Trial before a Criminal Court, but admitted him to Bail for his appearance.

[13] On the morning of the 21st December, the Factory at Parramatta was burnt down; it had been set on fire by a quantity of rubbish of the Flax under the Shed, which surrounds the Yard, and speedily communicated to the Outside of the Building, which it destroyed. The Gaol, being connected with this building, was with difficulty saved.

[14] It appeared that this violent outrage had been committed through design, yet with the utmost enquiries we have not been able to find out the perpetrators of the deed.

[15] On Tuesday, the 29th, while McArthur was under an arrest of Bail to be tried by a Criminal Court, I received a Memorial from him against the Judge-Advocate on account of a Bill drawn fifteen years ago upon General Bowyer. It appeared that this bill was for £26 6s., and was drawn the 4th February, 1793. McArthur had now made it amount to £82 9s. 5d.; and Judge-Advocate Atkins declared he had never heard anything about it until ten days before, and the Bill had received no regular protest, although McArthur, in his Memorial to me, stated that it had been regularly protested. I referred this business, however, to Mr. Atkins, who promised to settle the Bill. McArthur requested that, in order to enable him to arrest Mr. Atkins and sue him for the debt, I would suspend him for the time; and this Suspension appeared to be the object he had in view to enable him to plead it more powerfully as a reason why he should not sit on his Trial in the ensuing Criminal Court.

[16] On the 4th January, 1808, Captain Putland, of His Majesty's Ship Porpoise, died. He was my Son-in-law, and on the 7th was buried near the Church* with all Military Honors— the Officers and all the New South Wales Corps attended the Procession—Major Johnston as one of the Chief Mourners.

* Note 71.

1808.
30 April.

Probable
motives for
the transfer
of Abbott to
duty at Sydney.

[17] On the 11th I discovered that Arrangements had been made some time before for Captain Abbott, the Commandant of the Troops at Parramatta, to exchange duties with Captain Kemp at Sydney. Abbott was a Magistrate, and it was supposed he would be continued such at Sydney, and that Kemp would be appointed at Parramatta in his place. By this change their plan was to have a preponderancy in the Benches of Justices. As this arrangement was without my knowledge, it was an incorrectness in Major Johnston, who ought to have communicated it to me in the first instance. However, I settled it in the following manner:—I allowed the change to take place; but as we wanted no additional Magistrate at Sydney, Captain Abbott's Services in that capacity were no longer necessary; and I appointed Mr. Williamson, a Deputy Commissary of long standing in the Colony, a Magistrate at Parramatta. Mr. McArthur also came down to live at Sydney about this time.

Arrival of ships
with cargoes
of spirits.

[18] On the 12th a Ship, called the City of Edinburgh, arrived from the Cape of Good Hope, laden with about twenty-two thousand gallons of Spirits—a leaky Ship, which rendered it necessary for her to discharge her cargo immediately; but as the quantity of wine and spirits seemed enormous, I ordered it into Store until I could consider what quantity ought to be distributed; and this precaution was the more necessary as two American Ships, the Jenny (Captain Dorr), and the Eliza (Captain Corry), were in the Harbour, whom I had been under the necessity of restricting from issuing their Spirits, but had permitted them to dispose of their wine and merchandise they had before the City of Edinburgh arrived.

Macarthur's
endeavours to
placate the
military.

[19] These circumstances existing, McArthur began to influence the minds of the New South Wales Corps, by promising them large quantities of wine at a very low price, which he foresaw I would be under the necessity of preventing; and also by attempting to erect an enclosure round Ground whereon was a Public Well adjoining to the Church, which I prevented him taking possession of until the will of His Majesty's Minister should be known, although he had got a lease* of it from Governor King [but which was given in a very hasty manner as soon as the Fortune arrived—a Ship which sailed in company with us from England—and announced my near approach].† I was led to this determination from a conviction of the great inconvenience which would arise to the Public by encroaching on the little ground that belonged to the Church for uses applicable to it, while he maliciously circulated a report that he was to be deprived of the benefit of his lease; and what rendered it probable was that, by his beginning to enclose the Ground, I was under the

* Note 128.   † Note 123.

necessity of publicly putting a stop to his work, which he had secured to accomplish suddenly by hiring a number of men of the New South Wales Corps. I had offered him a compensation for this ground to its full amount in or about the Town which was not already secured for Government, or occupied by an Individual. It must not be forgotten that during this time McArthur was under an arrest to be tried by a Criminal Court.

[20] Major Johnston came on the 22nd and informed me that he and his Officers had agreed to institute a Mess, where they should dine together every Twenty-fourth day of the Month, and requested at the same time a Permit from me for a Pipe of Wine from the City of Edinburgh as a Present for that Mess—which request I granted.

[21] They dined together on the 24th for the first time in one of the Barracks, before the door of which they planted their Regimental Colours; and the music played till about nine or ten o'clock. Of this Party—besides the Military Officers—were (as I was informed by Mr. Atkins, the Judge-Advocate), Mr. Bayly, Surgeon Jamison, Dr. Townson, Mr. Grimes, Surveyor-General; Mr. Mileham, Assistant Surgeon; Mr. John and Gregory Blaxland, Settlers; Mr. Garnham Blaxcell, Merchant; Mr. Hannibal McArthur, Mr. Edward McArthur, and his father, Mr. John McArthur—who was to be tried by a Criminal Court the next day. This extraordinary meeting, where six of the Members of that Court, were collected with the Prisoner whom they were to try, seemed to indicate sedition; but no person then conceived of it otherwise than a trick of theirs to intimidate and insult the Government.

[22] On the Morning of the 25th, the Judge-Advocate and the other Members of the Court met. The Judge-Advocate read the Precept and administered the Oaths to the six Members. The Prisoner then desired they would proceed no further until they permitted him to read a Protest, which he held in his hand, against the Judge-Advocate, Richard Atkins, Esq., sitting on his Trial. The Judge-Advocate said it was inadmissable. Captain Kemp and Lieutenant Lawson insisted he should be permitted to read it, in which the other four Members acquiesced, and Captain Kemp refused to administer the Oath to Mr. Atkins. On this an altercation arose, Mr. Atkins insisting they could be no Court without him. However, McArthur proceeded to read what he called a Protest, which was a violent invective against Mr. Atkins. The chief objections which it contained were, that he (Mr. Atkins) was in his debt, of infamous character, and had hostile enmity against him (McArthur). The Judge-Advocate then arose and said he would commit the Prisoner, for it was a

Meeting of
criminal court
for the trial of
Macarthur.

most illegal proceeding in the Court to permit by violence such a Paper to be read against him, and in the Prisoner to read it before he (the Judge-Advocate) was sworn in; and he represented to me that, besides the Scurrilous matter it contained, Mr. McArthur delivered it with emphasis, tone of voice, and gesture which was calculated to excite the disrespect and indignation of the Surrounding multitude against His Majesty's Judge-Advocate.

[23] Captain Kemp, Lieutenant Minchin, and Lieutenant Lawson said the Judge-Advocate should not commit McArthur; and Captain Kemp added that he would commit him (the Judge-Advocate).

[24] The Judge-Advocate, on being refused to sit, quitted the House, loudly calling out there was no Court, and sent back the Constable to bring the Public Documents which he had prepared and made ready for the prosecution; but the Six Members refused to give him up the Papers, and he came to report the case to me, saying that he had been treated extremely ill, and looked for my protection in supporting the Law and Justice, which the Colony called for. *Vide* full Statement.*

Civil officers'
opinion on the
meeting of the
criminal court.

[25] Mr. Campbell and Mr. Palmer, Justices of the Peace; Mr. Griffin, my Secretary; Mr. Fulton, Clergyman; and Mr. Gore, Provost-Marshal, were present, and heard and saw all that passed, and certified to me that Mr. Judge-Advocate Atkins had done all he could do, and that the tumultuous conduct of Captain Anthony Fenn Kemp, Lieutenant John Brabyn, Lieutenant William Moore, Lieutenant Thomas Laycock, Lieutenant William Minchin, and Lieutenant William Lawson, obliged Mr. Atkins to retire.

[26] Letters passed immediately from the refractory Members to me, requiring another Judge-Advocate. In reply to this, I declared them to be no Court, and that the Judge-Advocate could not be superseded; for both they and the Prisoner contended for

Right of
challenge not
permitted by
the patent.

a right of challenging, although the Patent expressly declares that the Court shall be composed of His Majesty's Judge-Advocate and such Six Officers of His Forces, either by Sea or land, as the Governor shall direct. [27] Many inconveniences would arise if the Governor attended to every representation of a Prisoner, or of the Members of a Court, in suspending the Judge-Advocate; and, though it were granted that the Governor might use his discretion in suspending him on such occasions, yet it seems quite unreasonable that he should be compelled to do it, as the Patent gives the Members of the Court no such power. If the right of challenge was admitted, there would not, in cases innumerable, be a sufficiency of Officers to

* Note 129.

form a Legal Court in the Colony, which the Patent seems wisely to provide for. [28] Here I demanded the Public Papers of the Trial, which they refused.

[29] They now wrote to me for a Military Guard for Mr. McArthur, and enclosed an Affidavit of his, made before them, signed by all their Names, stating that he heard he was to be taken by a large body of armed men, who had orders to carry into execution a Warrant from the Judge-Advocate for executing his lawful right of Challenge against the said Judge-Advocate and assigning his reasons for it, as he was directed to do by the Court; that he considered his life in danger from the unprincipled and atrocious characters combined against him, under the direction of the infamous George Crossley; and that he therefore declined giving any Bail, and entreated the Court would be pleased to put him under the protection of a Military Guard, they being the only persons in whose hands he could consider himself secure. [30] This deposition, which refuses to give Bail, and the consequent demand of the Six Members, seems to have been made by preconcerted measures, in order to intimidate the Civil Power, which Power (for there was no other) is unlawfully called a body of armed men of atrocious and unprincipled characters. I must also observe that the Judge-Advocate had issued no such Warrant as that alluded to in the affidavit, and that the assertion is not founded in truth, but appears to have been invented in order to give a plausible pretence to his declining giving any Bail; for he knew while the Trial pended he could not be admitted to Bail but by the will of the Prosecutor, under a Bond to the Provost-Marshal, which prosecutor was Mr. Atkins, whom he had so villified a few hours before.

[31] It is worthy of observation that Mr. McArthur used every endeavour to win over Mr. George Crossley to assist him in his defence, even by waylaying him in his journey to Sydney, where he came by the Solicitation of the Judge-Advocate, Mr. Atkins, to assist him in drawing up the Indictment against McArthur on the part of the Crown; but when McArthur found that he could have no influence over Crossley, he endeavoured to injure him, first by attributing to him such situations as he did not hold, and secondly, by his influence over the Military Officers, procured a Sentence of Transportation to the Coal-Mines for seven years against him for giving this Assistance to Government.

[32] On my demanding a second time the Public Papers of the Prosecution to be delivered up to His Majesty's Judge-Advocate, the Six Members answered that they could not deliver up the Original, but I should have copies of them, and that they would adjourn until my pleasure was known.

1808.
30 April.

Johnston
summoned to
an interview
by Bligh.

[33] The Civil Power appearing to be in a precarious State, I now wrote to Major Johnston, who was living at his Country house, about four miles from his Barracks, and had not come into Town the whole day, requesting to see him on public business of importance, to which he returned a verbal answer by the Trooper (Thornby) whom I had sent, that he was too ill to come, having the evening before fallen out of his chaise on his return from the public dinner.

Escape warrant
issued against
Macarthur.

[34] Mr. Gore, the Provost-Marshal, now came to declare that McArthur was out of his Custody, having refused to give Bail. I therefore referred it to the Judge-Advocate and the Magistrates, who determined that Mr. Gore should make the necessary oath that his Prisoner (McArthur) was out of his Custody, which he did, and they granted an Escape Warrant to take McArthur up.

Arrest of
Macarthur.

[35] On this being done, the Magistrates were called upon to meet again the next morning, being Tuesday, the 26th, when McArthur was arrested and sent to Gaol by virtue of the Warrant issued the night before. A few hours afterwards the Six Officers met again, without any order or direction from me, and wrote two letters; one of which was inclosing the objections of McArthur to the Judge-Advocate's sitting; the other accusing Mr. Gore of Perjury for having sworn McArthur was not in his Custody, and requiring another Judge-Advocate to be appointed. I returned no answer.

Meeting of
magistrates at
government
house.

[36] According to appointment, the Magistrates, Mr. Atkins, Mr. Palmer, and Mr. Campbell met at Government House in the Morning, together with Mr. Gore, Provost-Martial, Mr. Griffin, my Secretary, and Mr. Fulton, Clergyman, a little before the six Officers assembled in the Court House. In the course of the day they were joined by Mr. Arndell and Mr. Williamson, Magis-

Atkins'
memorial
to Bligh.

trates, at which time Mr. Atkins presented a Memorial* to me, stating his Situation as Judge-Advocate bearing His Majesty's Commission; that he had been ill-used and degraded; that the Six Members refused to swear him in; that the Prisoner McArthur had been and was on terms of intimacy with the Soldiers and Officers; that he heard he had dined with them the Sunday preceding at the Mess; that McArthur's language had been inflammatory to a great degree; that, under all these circumstances, did pray that I would not remove him from his situation, and that the said Six Officers might be summoned before me to answer for their crimes, which to him appeared treasonable.

[37] This Memorial having been read in my presence, and in the presence of all the Magistrates, and sworn to by Mr. Atkins I ordered a Summons to be sent to each of the Six Military

* Note 130.

Officers to appear before me the following morning at nine
o'clock, as it was at this time too late to proceed on this business,
that they might answer to the said Memorial of the Judge-
Advocate's. I also ordered the Magistrates to attend at the time
appointed, and wrote to Major Johnston again, suggesting, if he
was not able to be at Sydney at this examination, the propriety of
Captain Abbott's being sent for to come from Parramatta to take
command of the Troops. The Trooper Messenger, whose name
was Tollis, and carried this letter, soon returned, and said the
Major desired him to inform me that he was so ill as to be unable
to write, but that he *would get a person to write an answer in the
evening.*

[38] Things being so far arranged, Mr. Campbell, Mr.
Palmer, Mr. Arndell, and Mr. Williamson retired to dine with
me some time after five o'clock. About Sunset we heard that Mr.
McArthur was liberated from the Gaol by Major Johnston's
Order in writing, as follows :—

" To the Keeper of His Majesty's Gaol at Sydney.

"You are hereby required and directed immediately to
deliver into the Custody of Garnham Blaxcell and Nicholas
Bayly, Esqrs., the body of John McArthur, Esq., who was committed by Warrant, dated the 25th Inst., signed by Richard
Atkins, Thomas Arndell, Robert Campbell, and John Palmer,
Esquires, it having been represented to me by the Officers composing the Court of Criminal Judicature that the Bail-Bond
entered into by the said Garnham Blaxcell and Nicholas Bayly
remains in full force. Herein fail not, as you will answer the
contrary at your Peril.

" Given under my hand and Seal at Sydney, New South
        Wales, the twenty-sixth of January, 1808.
                        " GEO. JOHNSTON, J.P.,
        " Lieut.-Governor, and Major commanding N.S.W. Corps."

[39] Besides the unlawfulness of this Order, which was issued
before they put me under an arrest, and which was a usurpation
of my authority, the circumstances stated in it are untrue; for
as soon as the Bailsmen brought the Prisoner before the Judge-
Advocate and the Six Members to whom the Precept was read,
their Bond became Null and Void, and the Prisoner could not
again, before the trial was terminated, be at large on Bail without
the consent of the Prosecutor, and a fresh Bail-Bond being given
to the Provost-Marshal. It is true Captain Kemp swore that he
told Mr. Gore, the Provost-Marshal, that he delivered him up to
his *former Bail,* but Mr. Gore asserts, and my Secretary, who
accompanied him, swore, that he heard no such thing, and that he

1808.
30 April.

did not think it possible that Captain Kemp could have thus expressed himself without his knowledge; indeed, if Captain Kemp had said so, such an expression could not have bound his former Bails Men.

March of
military to
government
house.

[40] Immediately followed an operation of the Main Guard at our Gates priming and loading with Ball cartridges, and the whole body of Troops began to march from the Barracks, led on by Major Johnston, the Band playing the "British Grenadiers," and colours flying. [The intention of those troops may in some manner be known by the enclosed paper from a respectable settler.]* In five minutes the whole House was surrounded by an Armed Force, consisting of between three or four hundred men, all loaded with Ball cartridges, the Officers attending in their proper places. Without ceremony they broke into all parts of the

Arrest of
magistrates and
civil officers.

house (even into the Ladies' room) and arrested all the Magistrates, Mr. Gore, Provost-Marshal, Mr. Fulton, the Clergyman, and Mr. Griffin, my Secretary. Thus the Civil Power was annihilated, and the Colony in the hands of the Military, guided by McArthur and Bayly. Nothing but calamity upon calamity was to be expected, even Massacre and secret Murder. [41] I had only just time to retire upstairs to prevent giving myself up, and to see if anything could be done for the restoration of my

Arrest of
Bligh.

Authority; but they soon found me in a back room, and a daring set of Ruffians under arms [headed by Serjeant-Major Whittle],† intoxicated by spirituous liquors, which was given them for the purpose, and threatening to plunge their bayonets into me if I resisted, seized me. I was now obliged to go below, where I found the rooms filled with Soldiers, and presently Lieutenant Moore came forward and presented me with a letter from Major Johnston, a Copy of which follows:—

[Here followed a copy of the letter marked A in enclosure No. 7 to Major Johnston's despatch, dated 11th April, 1808 (see page 241), but signed as follows:—]

"I am, &c.,

"Geo. Johnston,

"Acting Lieu't-Gov. and Major commanding N.S.W. Corps.
"To William Bligh, Esq., F.R.S., &c., &c., &c."

[42] I had just read this infamous and rebellious Letter when I received a Message from this Lieutenant Moore that the Major wished to see me in the adjoining room. When I went I found

Johnston's
speech to Bligh
in the presence
of insurrec-
tionaries.

him at the head of his armed men, and in the presence of Doctor Townson, John and Gregory Blaxland, Garnham Blaxcell, Charles Grimes, Surgeon Jamison, Nicholas Bayly, Hannibal McArthur, and Edward McArthur; he pronounced a Speech similar to the

* Note 131.   † Note 123.

letter before stated. I was now directed to have no communi- 1808.
30 April.
cation with any person whom I had been accustomed to see as a
Friend; even my Secretary, Mr. Griffin, was ordered from me Examination of
Edmund
Griffin.
and was hurried before a Committee—Martial Law having been
proclaimed—and, in the midst of Terror, interrogated respecting
my conduct and concerns as Governor. Of this Committee
McArthur was a Member, and said to Mr. Griffin on the occasion,
" Never was a revolution so completely effected, and with so much
order and regularity." He ridiculed Mr. Griffin's Youth, laughed,
sneered, and did and said everything to disturb his mind, so that
he afterwards knew not what he said from the state he was
thrown into by irregular questions which were put to him, and
the browbeating he suffered, besides expecting every moment to
be murdered.

[43] Dr. Townson, Mr. Grimes, Surgeon Jamison, Mr. Blaxcell, Seizure of
Bligh's papers.
and Mr. John Blaxland, rummaged all the rooms upstairs for my
Public and Private Papers, which they secured and locked up in
my Office. Doctor Townson and Mr. Grimes were particularly
clamorous and indecent in demanding my Keys from John Dunn,
my Servant, and in knocking my Drawers and Cabinet about,
swearing at him that he knew well where the Governor kept all
his private Papers.

[44] On my retiring I saved the Papers containing the
Accounts of yesterday's proceedings, but all those of to-day were
secured by the Rebels. When they had thus far proceeded, five Sentinels
placed at
government
house.
Centinels were placed over the House, in and out of doors, and I
was left with only my Daughter and Mrs. Palmer about nine
o'clock at night.

[45] I have pursued my account with as little digression as
possible, that the proceedings may be the more distinct; but it is
now necessary to observe that the Law was not Martial in this
Colony; and that in Defence of the Law and Civil Power, and Seizure of
Bligh under
civil law.
the Liberty of the Subject, I have been seized while I was acting
as the Representative of Our Most Gracious King, and in an
exemplary manner, at the risk of my life, supporting the independence of the loyal and honest Subjects of this remote Colony
according to our Patent and the Laws of England.

[46] But the Arrest states that this was done by the Officers of The
participation of
officers in the
insurrection.
the New South Wales Corps and respectable Inhabitants of
Sydney. Surely, if the latter had been so disposed, there could be
no excuse for the former, who were particularly placed here and
regularly paid for the Support of His Majesty's Government in
this Territory, and not for the subversion of it. The Settlers in
the Colony, amounting to some hundreds, ought to have been
consulted, if they thought it could have sheltered them from

1808.
30 April.

punishment for such a traitorous and rebellious Act; but the fact is, that when the Troops marched from the Barracks not more than six or seven names* had been affixed to the Paper

Signatures to address obtained by armed force.

which exhorted them to commit this crime; while the whole of those who subscribed their names afterwards declare they did it at the point of the bayonet, which declaration Wentworth made three days afterwards. Constables were sent to that part of the Town called the Rocks, and the other parts, to drive people to subscribe their names to this Paper to Major Johnston, after the Act of Rebellion was done; and emissaries were sent with Papers through the interior of the Colony for the same purpose. The Paper just alluded to I have procured a copy of; it was written at the moment by McArthur himself, and is as follows:—

Address to Johnston.

[47] [*Here followed a copy of the letter forwarded as en-closure No. 5 to Major Johnston's despatch, dated 11th April, 1808 (see page 240), but signed as follows:—*]

"We are, &c.,

" JNO. MCARTHUR.	THOS. MOORE.
" JOHN BLAXLAND.	THOS. LAYCOCK.
" JAMES MILEHAM.	JOHN GOWEN.
" S. LORD.	N. DIVINE.
" G. BLAXLAND.	WM. BAKER.
" D. WENTWORTH.	JAS. WILSHIRE.
" N. BAYLY."	

And by upwards of one hundred other Inhabitants of all descriptions, some of which are the worst class of life.

Services of the secretary to Bligh.

[48] When I was arrested I desired of Mr. Johnston that my Secretary might be continued with me, to which he replied: "I see no objection, provided it be approved of by the Inhabitants"; but Mr. Nicholas Bayly said he thought it was improper, but that he would go and ask. He then went out to McArthur, who kept in the rear of the Line of the Troops, and returned immediately, saying it could not be admitted, for McArthur and Bayly were the high Inquisitors. [Simeon Lord, Henry Kable, Eber Bunker, D'Arcy Wentworth, and some others were also with the troops.]†

Communication with the interior prevented by the insurrectionaries.

[49] Every precaution was used by the Rebels to prevent any communication with the interior of the Colony. Guards were set on the road to Parramatta, and no one suffered to pass. Orders were stuck up by Captain Abbott at Parramatta that no communication was to be held with me, as Major Johnston had put me under an arrest and assumed the Government. Oakes, the Chief Constable, who had fled from Sydney, went to Captain Abbott on his arrival at Parramatta and told him the Governor was put under an arrest. "Very well," replied Captain Abbott, " it must be for the better."

* Note 132.   † Note 123.

1808.
30 April.

[50] Besides the seizure of all my Private Instructions, Letter-books, and Papers, the Judge-Advocate's and Commissary's Papers and accounts were likewise taken possession of, and Centinels placed over them, and all these Documents are still kept from me and them.

Seizure of books and papers.

[51] When we now consider the changes of Stations of Captains Abbott and Kemp; McArthur's committing himself by writing a contemptuous Paper; his coming down to live at Sydney; and other circumstances which I have detailed, as well as some which I have not mentioned, which took place before, such as declaring to Mr. Fulton the soldiery would not have the Prohibition of bartering Spirits, and that such measures would not be suffered were there fifty men of Spirit in the Colony; and as going about the Country telling some of the Settlers that I governed very ill, and that he was determined to go Home and have me recalled, that he might prosecute me; [also his making a seditious speech before a Bench of Magistrates and a great number of persons whom he contrived to assemble to hear a pretended impeachment against a Mr. Robert Campbell, junior, for stealing two copper boilers, although Mr. Robert Campbell only executed the Naval Officer's and my orders in carrying the bodies of two stills out of his (McArthur's) yard and putting them on board the Duke of Portland to be returned to England, from whence they were imported without permission*];—I say, when we consider these things, it will appear that this subversion of His Majesty's Government was effected in consequence of a settled plan of McArthur's, and not by a mere accident arising from the business of his Trial.

Subversion of government was a plan settled by Macarthur.

[52] The crime of Major Johnston and all his Officers is not to be considered as lessened by the wicked artifice of McArthur. No; it will hereafter be proved that they had at the moment an imaginary expectation they could hold the Colony in their own hands, for there were agreements† signed that they would not give up their Authority on the arrival of a Superior Officer unless he agreed to their measures until His Majesty's pleasure were known; and they persuaded themselves also that the whole Executive Authority would rest with themselves, and having no check, they would soon secure wealth. At all events, they would have about eighteen months before anything could be done from England to thwart their designs, and this they hoped to prevent by representations which they might frame against me, their Governor. [53] "Until His Majesty's pleasure was known" is an artful phrase they have made use of in order to cloak themselves under an appearance of a consciousness that they acted according to right principles.

The culpability of Johnston and his officers.

1808.
30 April.

Profits made
by the barter
of spirits.

[54] It is inconceivable what money has been made by some people, through the means of bartering Spirituous Liquors, and the sufferings of the multitude on that account. Beef and Mutton is now selling at eighteenpence per lb.; therefore, if a person has Liquor which he procures at eight shillings per Gallon, he can dispose of it for forty Shillings in Barter for such Meat; and, therefore, with a Gallon of this Liquor he can purchase twenty-six and two-thirds of meat; whereas a person who could not procure Liquor can only go to market with his eight shillings with which he can only buy five pounds and one-third. From this we may see how the people at large must suffer who cannot procure Spirituous Liquors, and the immense gain those have who can get them. A few Individuals have had permission to procure large quantities by one influence or another at very low rates, and afterwards disposed of it up to as high as eight hundred per cent. profit; but these evils were now done away, to the great satisfaction of the people of the Colony except the Individuals alluded to, at the head of whom is McArthur and the Officers; but I need not enter farther into this Business, which has been fully explained in my dispatch by the Buffalo of the 7th Feb'y, 1807, and as I have delineated the characters of the People whom I have to deal with in my Dispatch by the Duke of Portland.

My next Dispatch shall be followed up from this clause in as full a manner as hitherto; but I am now under the necessity to relate the transactions which have followed the 26th in a Summary way in order to embrace an opportunity which presents itself, a gleam of Hope having arisen to me to communicate with your Lordship with certainty by a Ship called the Brothers through private means. I was strongly inclined to write by a

Reasons for
sending no
despatches by
the Dart.

Ship called the Dart which sailed a few days ago, but on reflecting that she was in the interest of McArthur, and that Charles Grimes, the Surveyor-General, and McArthur's Son went passengers in her, both deeply implicated in the Rebellion, I was constrained to forbear, being assured that through the vigilance of my enemies my Dispatches would be relanded and never sent Home. I was the more ready to believe this, knowing the infamous transaction of their keeping Governor King's Dispatches on the occasion of troubles he had in this Country, and the Box which had contained them was only delivered at Your Lordship's Office filled with old paper.* These Dispatches were concerning McArthur, and we may therefore judge who was interested in the machination. The Duplicate of them was transmitted by a Captain McKellar in a small vessel, but who has been lost; afterwards a third set was sent, which, owing to the few opportunities

* Note 134.

of writing to England, did not reach your Lordship's Office before McArthur arrived in England, and, from the false representations he made, had gained his ends.

His Majesty's Ship Porpoise was absent on the duty of evacuating Norfolk Island. She returned a few days after the 26th, and Acting Lieutenant James Symons, who commanded her, joined the Rebel Party, accepting an appointment as Magistrate, and gave himself a Commission as Acting Commander without ever communicating with me, while I was prevented from having any transaction with the Ship; so that, in addition to their other treasonable Acts, they annexed that of striking my Broad Pendant, and of taking away my Ship, which by every means in my power I have been endeavouring to regain without effect. On the 29th of March the Lady Nelson Tender arrived from the same Duty the Porpoise had been on, commanded by Acting Lieutenant Kent. This Officer immediately waited on me before he could be prevented, and, conceiving a favourable opinion of him, I immediately sent a Commission to him to take Command of the Porpoise; but I was obliged to do it through Major Johnston, the present self-appointed Lieutenant Governor; however, Lieutenant Kent did not take Command of the Porpoise till the 12th Instant, and to my great surprize he sailed on the 18th for Port Dalrymple to fetch up Lieutenant-Colonel Paterson, and I have since heard nothing of him.

On the 27th Committees were formed, and continued Sitting several days, before whom all the Magistrates and those who were considered as having been intimate at Government House were brought and examined concerning my administration and intentions. Every wicked artifice as well as threats were used to force affirmative answers to all such questions as their diabolical minds could propose, and some of them were brought to such agitation from a fear of their lives that they knew not what they said or did, trembling under Martial Law and the tyranny which existed. The Committees were composed of McArthur, Bayly, Blaxcell, Mr. Grimes, Captain Kemp, Lieutenant Minchin, Lieutenant Lawson, Lieutenant Draffin, Doctor Townson, and Mr. John Blaxland. On the following day Mr. Bayly, the self-created Lieutenant-Governor's Secretary, accompanied by Captain Abbott, Mr. Jamieson, the principal Surgeon, and Mr. Garnham Blaxcell, came to Government House, and in a very Robesperian manner he read and delivered a Paper to me of which the following is a copy:—

[*Here followed a copy of the letter, marked E, in enclosure No. 7 to Major Johnston's despatch, dated 11th April, 1808 (see page 242), with the omission of the words, " and other persons," in the second line.*]

1808.
30 April.

A true copy of the Message delivered to Captain Wm. Bligh, late Governor of His Majesty's Territory, by Order of His Honor the Lieutenant-Governor.

Bligh's
repudiation
of Johnston's
authority.

This daring Outrage of depriving me of my Government, where my Person was sacred, and reading a charge of this nature, so diabolically false, roused my indignation, and I denied their Authority in any proceeding not authorised by myself, as to my King and Country only would I be answerable for any act of

Removal of
Bligh's papers
and books.

mine in this Colony. At this time my Papers, Books, and Private Instructions, which were locked up on the Evening of the 26th, were ordered to be examined, and with the Great Seal of the Colony were taken away. My Books, containing Copies of Letters to and from the Secretary of State, together with my Private Instructions, I objected to give up to the Committee that were appointed. On this a written Order was brought from Major Johnston commanding them to put his Orders into execution. I therefore had nothing left but to seal the Books and Papers alluded to, and they took them with the others.

Grimes
appointed
judge-advocate
by Johnston.

Charles Grimes, the Surveyor-General, was about this time appointed Judge-Advocate, Criminal and Civil Courts were constituted, and also a Court of Vice-Admiralty. The first Criminal

Trial and
acquittal of
Macarthur.

Court was for the Trial of McArthur, by which he was acquitted of the Charges that were to have been exhibited against him by Mr. Atkins, on which occasion some of the Privates of the New South Wales Corps, led by their Serjeant-Major, Whittle, assembled as a Mob, and in a chair on a stage carried him in triumph round the Town of Sydney. Magistrates were appointed

Magistrates
appointed by
Johnston.

instead of those who had acted under me; these were, Captain Abbott, Captain Kemp, Lieutenant Minchin, Lieutenant Lawson, Ensign Bell, and Mr. John Harris, Surgeon of the New South Wales Corps, Mr. Thomas Jamison, Principal Surgeon, Mr. Garnham Blaxcell, and Mr. John Blaxland, and some little time after McArthur was appointed a Magistrate and Colonial Secre-

Civil officers
appointed by
Johnston.

tary; N. Bayly, Provost-Marshal in place of Mr. Gore, whom they have persecuted in a violent manner. At last he denied their Authority and Government altogether; and refusing to give Bail they committed him to Gaol, where he now remains in a Cell, and Blaxcell, the Licensed Auctioneer, in the room of a Mr. Bevan, who had held the Situation for a length of time by Appointment from Governor King. Mr. Williamson superceded Mr. Palmer as Commissary, and Jamison, the Principal Surgeon, was appointed Naval Officer in the place of Mr. Campbell.

Many acts of injustice and irregularity have been committed in the Courts; even my Letter-Books, containing copies of my letters to the Secretary of State, were publicly read by McArthur and others, and my Private Instructions—that part respecting America—was read in the presence of American Masters of Ships during the time of the Trial of one of them for Smuggling. The copy of my Despatch sent in October last by the Duke of Portland, wherein I felt it my duty to give a description of the Colony and characters of certain persons, was communicated to all the Officers, in order to excite them to hatred of my proceedings, and to show I was no friend to them.

Among the numerous alarming and terrific Reports and Orders that were given out every day, at a time when the Soldiers and Townspeople were filled with Spirituous Liquors, the Bellman was ordered to cry publicly through the Streets that a Meeting would be held at the Church at eight o'clock at Night. At the hour appointed the Church was crowded with Soldiers and the disaffected party, with McArthur at their head, who made a Speech on the happy change of affairs, and the advantage that all present would derive therefrom. He then expatiated on my Administration, and called me and my Magistrates bloodthirsty Wretches and Villains, who wished to drink his blood, and made use of other seditious expressions, which he closed with this observation: that although he had suffered much from it, yet he *hoped no harm would happen to me or the Magistrates.*

Blaxcell, assisted by Bayly and Lord, proposed that a Sword should be voted to Major Johnston, not under the value of one hundred guineas, for the wise and salutary measures which he had adopted to suppress the Tyranny which ruled this Country; that an Address of thanks might be presented to the New South Wales Corps for their *spirited* and *manly* conduct on the 26th of January; and an Address of thanks to John McArthur, Esquire, as having been *chiefly* instrumental in bringing about the happy change which took place on that day, and likewise that a *Delegate* might be appointed to be sent to England,* to which Office McArthur was appointed, and a Subscription was proposed and set on foot to defray his expences.

John Blaxland proposed that a Service of Plate should be voted for the use of the Mess of the Officers of the New South Wales Corps for their spirited and patriotic conduct.

There were present at this Meeting John McArthur, Garnham Blaxcell, Nicholas Bayly, John Blaxland, D'Arcy Wentworth, Lieutenant William Minchin, Simeon Lord, and other persons of their Party.

* Note 135.

1808.
30 April.

Factions created
amongst the
insurrec-
tionaries.

On this Assembly I shall just observe that the Party is now
divided and subdivided, and all of them have withdrawn their
Subscription, and McArthur refuses to go to England.

These divisions have been attended with consequent effects.
They have begun to reproach each other, trembling for fear of
the event; some of the Magistrates have given up their places;
the Judge-Advocate Grimes gave up his, and they can now barely
form a Bench.

Disapproval of
Collins and
Paterson.

It now appears that, under all their iniquities, their apprehensions are increased by the accounts they have received from
Colonels Collins and Paterson, who have expressed their highest
indignation at their proceedings, the latter of whom I learn has
determined to come here.

Pleas of
ignorance.

Their conduct they now wish and endeavour to palliate by
asserting they never knew Colonel Paterson bore a Commission
as Lieutenant-Governor of the Territory; that if they had they
would not have gone so far as they had done; but that now, seeing
their errors, they had come to a determination to await the
Lieutenant-Colonel's arrival to judge of the propriety of the
restraint they had put me under, and in what manner I am to
proceed to England. This determination was announced to me
by the following written message, when they had been threatening
to send me away in the Dart, and which I resisted.

[*Here followed a copy of the letter marked JJJ in enclosure
No. 7 to Major Johnston's despatch, dated 11th April, 1808; see
page 270.*]

Previous
announcements
of Paterson's
appointment.

It is only necessary to observe on the foregoing that Lieutenant-
Colonel's appointment as Lieutenant-Governor of the Territory
has been thoroughly made known by Public Orders on that
account, and annually noted in the Almanacks,* by which no
doubt can be entertained of their having known it and of their
art of fabricating an untruth.

I returned no answer, or have I had any communication
farther with them.

Settlers
favourable
to Bligh.

In this manner the case now stands, and I am anxiously looking
for the event, an event of some moment, as the Settlers are in a
very enraged state of Mind at the indignity I suffer through my
arrest. Their want of Arms has prevented much bloodshed, and
the precaution of disarming them, which was adopted to prevent
any bad consequence in the Interior by the Prisoners rising,
whereby the Military became of greater power, has by this means
acted against us, and enabled them to act with greater confidence.

Among the Acts of these Rebels some things seem to have been
carried on with peculiar art and design. They have deprived me,
and continue to keep possession, of all my Books and Papers, so

* Note 136.

that I have nothing but my memory to assist me. The Commissary's Papers are also in their possession, and by that means they
have got a power of making any representations they please
without any present means of having their falsehoods exposed. I
have been led to this conclusion by a friend procuring me the
copy of some Affidavits which it is said are transmitted to your
Lordship. The falsehood and meanness of these documents will
appear from one specimen of an Affidavit said to be made by one
Fitz, a Deputy Commissary, a creature of McArthur's and one of
the Rebellious Party, wherein it is asserted that Governor Bligh
received from the Bonded Stores one Pipe of Port Wine for his
own use, and that he (Governor Bligh) ordered a quantity of
Wine to be purchased from Mr. Campbell, at the rate of three
pounds per dozen, for the use of the General Hospital, which wine
was appropriated to his (Governor Bligh's) own use. The Commissary's accounts will show that before my arrival there had been
a quantity of Port Wine sent out for Barter, and which was
distributed to the Officers in pipes and cases. Governor King,
expecting to be relieved, reserved one Pipe for his Successor in
case of Accidents, and on my arrival he directed it to be charged
to my account, which the Commissary did. With respect to the
Wine purchased from Mr. Campbell by the Commissary, it took
place long after my arrival, from a demand made by the Surgeon
of the Hospital, and he received it from the Commissary, who
took his receipt for it. This circumstance I have taken notice of,
in order that your Lordship may be aware of the misrepresentation these people may make to you, sensible that your Lordship
will oppose to them, on any reflections you make, your confidence
in the honor and dignity of my character, whose conduct has, by
justice and humanity, brought the Colony to a very advanced
State compared with what it has been before.

The Conduct of Major Johnston and his Party will be found
very reprehensible, from what I have heard, with respect to
Government concerns. They have issued the Stores wantonly
and improperly to their private purposes. They have sold a large
ten-oared Boat which was kept for the Governor's use. They are
giving away and disposing of Government Cattle to their own
Party. They have renewed and given Leases of several places
in the Town; they are employing in their private concerns Artificers and Labourers and Government Cattle; they have let out
the Government Brew-house, Factory, and Government Garden
at Parramatta; and have turned off the Store a number of de-
crepid and infirm People, besides the worst of Convicts, who are
now committing depredations on the Public, and are the dread
of every person; and McArthur has dismissed Mr. John Jamieson,

1808.
30 April.

Seizure of
Bligh's and
Palmer's papers
to prevent
exposure of
falsehoods.

Bligh's
contradiction
of Fitz's
affidavit.

Mal-
administration
of Johnston
and his party.

Mal-
administration
of Johnston
and his party.

Public property
issued to
Macarthur.

Bligh's desire
to return to
England.

Suggested trial
of Grimes,
E. Macarthur,
Minchin, and
Marlborough.

Employment
of H.M.S.
Porpoise.

the Superintendent of Government Stock, on account of his
having refused to remove the Herds to Broken Bay, where there
is scarcely anything but rocks and barren ground, in order that
his own might have the entire range of Government Ground in
the neighbourhood of Parramatta. Everything they think of is
done to supply the want of Public Credit, and to impress an
Idea that the Colony can be supported at less expence than
hitherto. They have even sold from the Store three pairs of
Mill-Stones which were intended to be sent to the Out-Settlements, and McArthur has taken two pair of them to himself, as
likewise thirty Stand of Arms, which there is no doubt were sent
in the Parramatta to barter for Pork in the South Sea, and their
Vessels have been fitted out with the Canvass and Sails of His
Majesty's Ships.

How all these evils will end, and a restoration of peace take
place in the Colony, it is impossible for me to say until Colonel
Paterson arrives; but it is my duty to represent that I think it
absolutely necessary I should return Home to show what must be
effected for its Security.

I shall now beg leave to conclude this Dispatch with requesting
of your Lordship that the two of the Rebels, Charles Grimes and
Edward McArthur, who have gone home in the Dart, and Lieutenant Minchin, of the New South Wales Corps, with his Servant,
Marlborough,* who proceed in the Ship I now write by, may be
secured in order to be tried in due time.

I have omitted to mention that I have had no opportunity of
Communicating with the Out-Settlements; but the Ship Rose,
Brooks Master, which arrived on the 14th Instant from England,
touching at the Derwent in her way hither, brought a Secret
letter from Lieutenant-Governor Collins,† a Copy of which I beg
leave to enclose for your Lordship's information.

I have, &c.,
WM. BLIGH.

GOVERNOR BLIGH TO THE HON. WILLIAM POLE.

(Despatch per whaler the Brothers.)

Government House, Sydney,
Sir,   New South Wales, 30th April, 1808.

I have to acquaint you, for the information of My Lords
Commissioners of the Admiralty, that since my last despatch to
their Lordships by the Duke of Portland on the 30th of October
last, to the 26th of January, His Majesty's Ship Porpoise has been
employed in the Evacuation of Norfolk Island. Their Lordships
will have been informed of my appointing Lieutenant John Put-

* Note 137.   † Note 138.

land to be Acting Commander of His Majesty's Ship Porpoise, 1808.
30 April. who, until extreme ill-health from a decline, was a valuable Assistant to me. He died on Shore while the Porpoise was at Death of
Putland. Sea under the charge of Acting Lieutenant James Symons, on the 4th of January. On the 26th of January the New South Arrest of Bligh. Wales Corps rose in Rebellion against me and the Civil Power, and have deprived me of all Authority, constituted others in our place, by the power of the Corps (above three hundred Men) surrounding my House and putting me under an Arrest. A few days after the Porpoise arrived, when in place of Acting Lieu- Rebel party
joined by
Symons. tenant James Symons forcing his way to me, he joined the Rebel Party, and Major Johnston, the Commandant, directed that all communication should be prevented between me and His Majesty's Ship, and Acting Lieutenant James Symons appointed himself Commander of the Porpoise, and more strongly united himself with the Rebels.

On the 29th March, the Lady Nelson, Tender to the Porpoise, arrived from the same service she had been on, and Acting Lieutenant Kent waiting on me before any one knew of it, and Kent appointed
commander of
the Porpoise. he apparently knowing his duty as an Officer, I appointed him as Acting Commander of the Porpoise, whereby Acting Lieutenant Symons became superceded, and by this means I thus far secured the possession of His Majesty's Ship; but as further communi- cations were interrupted, I can only say that the Porpoise sailed Sailing of
H.M.S.
Porpoise for
Port
Dalrymple. with Lieutenant Kent to Port Dalrymple, as I hear, to bring up Lieutenant-Colonel Paterson, Lieutenant-Governor of the Terri- tory, to this place (by directions from Major Johnston, the self- appointed Lieutenant-Governor), to whom the Rebels say they will refer everything they have transacted.

Thus I have done all I can to secure His Majesty's Ship, besides positive demands to the Rebel Chief to give her up to me, showing that ruin must fall on those on board of her if it is not complied with.

In restoring this Colony to a state of great comfort and im- Bligh's
determination
to restore the
civil power. provement, as well as happiness to all the good People in it, and supporting the Civil Government, I have been rebelliously de- prived of my Authority and in a Cowardly and dastardly manner. I have defended it at the risk of my Life; and I will, if possible, return Home with the Ship I command, that my representations may give it security and prevent it becoming a nest of Buc- chaneers.

The oppressions which the industrious Settlers have undergone are beyond description, and a disturbing Character, one John Macarthur
the virtual
governor. McArthur, who has made himself rich on their vitals, is virtually now the Governor of the Colony.

1808.
30 April.

Possibilities of
the despatch
being stolen.

All my Books and Public and Private Papers have been taken from me, and I have nothing but my Memory to guide me.

Whether this will ever reach their Lordships is a doubt, or I either, for it is highly probable my despatches will be landed and destroyed after they have applied them to their purpose, and if private murder can be effected, there are persons here who will perpetrate the deed for a Bottle of Spirituous Liquor; but my whole security is in the affection of the Settlers and Landholders, who to the amount of nine hundred sent me a dutiful Address on the first day of this Year. The opportunity I have is by the Brothers, Russell Master; in her is sent Home a Lieutenant Minchin, of the New South Wales Corps, and his Servant Marlborough, deeply implicated in the Rebellion, which makes the safety of my despatch more uncertain.

I have now only to refer their Lordships to His Majesty's Secretary of State for the Colonies for further information, assuring them of every endeavour on my part to support the Honor and Dignity of my situation.

I have, &c.,
WM. BLIGH.

MAJOR JOHNSTON TO VISCOUNT CASTLEREAGH.

(Despatch per whaler the Brothers.)

Head Quarters, Sydney, New South Wales,
My Lord,   30th April, 1808.

Bligh's charges
against
Jamison.

I have the honor to transmit to Your Lordship the Copy of a Correspondence that has been occasioned by the Accusation preferred against Thomas Jamison Esqr. Principal Surgeon, by Governor Bligh in his letter* to Mr. Windham by the Duke of Portland.

Court martial
on Wentworth.

I have also the honor to forward a Copy of a Court Martial held on Mr. D'Arcy Wentworth at his own request. And I have the pleasure to report to Your Lordship that Mr. Wentworth is now discharging his duty; which he does, and has always performed, in a manner highly reputable to himself and beneficial to the Settlement.   I have, &c.,
GEO. JOHNSTON.

[Enclosure No. 1.]

[1] A COPY of a letter from Nicholas Bayly Secretary to Thomas Jamison Esqr. Principal Surgeon.

Sir,   Head Quarters, 6th February, 1808.

On examining the public papers found at Government House, a letter was found containing a Paragraph which appears

* Note 139.

1808.
30 April.

Charges made
by Bligh
against
Jamison.

to have been intended to produce an injurious effect against you on the minds of Government, His Honor the Lieutenant Governor not considering it right that any Man should be accused of an offence without being allowed an opportunity to justify himself has directed me to enclose you a Copy of the Extract, that you may take such measures for your defence as you may think proper. NICHOLAS BAYLY, Secretary.

A COPY of an Extract from a letter written by the late Governor to the Secretary of State by the Duke of Portland dated 31st October 1807 enclosed in the above.

" As to the Civil Officers I must in point of Duty as in Honor Object to Mr. Atkins the Judge-Advocate, and Mr. Jamison Principal Surgeon, who I have permitted to remain in Office, on account of not being able to supply their places, but the latter I have dismissed from the office of a Magistrate, because I considered him, not an upright Man, and inimical to Government as likewise connected in improper transactions."

Head Quarters, 6th February, 1808.

A true Copy: NICHOLAS BAYLY, Secretary.

[2] A COPY of a letter from Thomas Jamison Esqr., Principal Surgeon, to His Honor Major George Johnston.

Sir, Sydney, 10th February, 1808.

I have to acknowledge the receipt of your Honor's letter, enclosing an Extract of a letter written by the late Governor to the Secretary of State, dated the 31st October, 1807.

As I consider the charges contained in the Extract Groundless and Malicious, calculated to ruin me secretly in the Eyes of His Majesty's Ministers, I have to request you will be pleased to order a General Court-Martial to Investigate my Conduct, and give me an opportunity of Vindicating my injured reputation.

Jamison's
request for a
court martial.

I have further to request you will take the necessary steps to direct the late Governor to come forward to substantiate any Charges he may have to prefer against me.

I have, &c.,
THOMAS JAMISON,
Principal Surgeon.

[3] A COPY of a letter from Nicholas Bayly, Secretary, to Thomas Jamison Esqr. Principal Surgeon.

Sir, Sydney, 12th February, 1808.

In consequence of your letter of the 10th Inst. I was directed by His Honor the Lieutenant Governor to require from

1808.
30 April.

Bligh's refusal
to state
charges.

the late Governor a specification of the offences you had committed to occasion your dismissal from the office of Magistrate, and to draw down upon you the severe accusations contained in his letter of the 31st October, 1807, to His Majesty's Secretary of State, His Honor has this day received in reply a letter from the late Governor, wherein he begs leave to refer to the Decision of His Majesty's Ministers, His Honor has directed me to assure

Johnston's
confidence
in Jamison.

you that it affords him particular pleasure to declare that he conceives your dismissal from the Magistracy on the 22nd September is only to be attributed to your having attended him as a friend on that day to witness an Interesting conversation on public business.

And His Honor has also directed me to recommend that you do not give yourself any further trouble upon the subject because in his Judgment, no stronger testimony of the Integrity of your life can be produced, than the silence of your Accuser when called upon to come forward and justify his Extraordinary attack upon your Reputation.

I am, &c.,
NICHOLAS BAYLY, Secretary.

[A] A COPY of a letter from Nicholas Bayly Secretary to William Bligh Esqre.

Sir,   Sydney, 11th February, 1808.

Bligh
requested
to submit
particulars
of charges.

I am directed by His Honor the Lieutenant Governor to annex a Copy of a letter from Thomas Jamison Esqr. Principal Surgeon, relative to the accusations you have preferred against him, in your public letter to the Secretary of State by the Duke of Portland, and requiring that he may be brought to a General Court Martial for the Vindication of his injured Reputation.

His Honor has in consequence desired me to request that you will be pleased to specify what offences Mr. Jamison has committed, and, to inform you, that when he is acquainted with the particulars of your Charges, you will be at liberty to proceed to the proof of them in any manner you most approve.

I have, &c.,
N. BAYLY, Secretary.

[B] EXTRACT of a letter from William Bligh Esqr. dated the 12th February in answer to the letter marked A.

Bligh's refusal
to submit
charges.

"IN reply to which I have only to observe, that the private communication of my letter to the Secretary of State respecting Mr. Jamison, I must beg leave to refer to the Decision of His Majesty's Ministers to whom that Gentleman can apply."

[4] A COPY of a letter from Thomas Jamison Esqr., Principal Surgeon, to His Honor Major George Johnston.

1808.
30 April.

Sir,   Sydney, 14th February, 1808.

I have to acknowledge the receipt of your letter of the 12th Ins't, with the enclosures, and I am much concerned to learn that the late Governor declines coming forward to prove his Allegations against me before a General Court-Martial, feeling conscious of not deserving such censure. It is particularly gratifying to me to find you acquit me, and that you attribute my dismissal from the Office of Magistrate to the cause of attending as a friend to witness an Interesting conversation, and the enclosed letter from the late Governor a few hours after that event strongly warrants the Conclusion.

I shall, under these circumstances, let the matter drop in this Country, trusting I shall be enabled at a future Period to prove the rectitude of my conduct to His Majesty's Ministers.

I have, &c.,
THOMAS JAMISON, Principal Surgeon.

Jamison's regret that no court martial can be held.

[Sub-enclosure.]

A COPY of the letter of dismissal from the Office of Magistrate alluded to in the above from Edmund Griffin, Secretary, to Thomas Jamison, Esq'r'.

Removal of Jamison from magistracy.

Sir,   Government House, Sydney, 22nd September, 1807.

I am commanded by His Excellency to inform you that he has no further occasion for your Services as a Magistrate.

I am, &c.,
EDMUND GRIFFIN, Secretary.

[5] SURGEON JAMISON TO MAJOR JOHNSTON.

Sir,   Sydney, 12th March, 1808.

Although I derived much satisfaction from the letter of the 12th February, which you directed your Secretary to write me, I deem it further necessary, in order to justify my Character (so dear to me) to Government, to use all the means in my power to accomplish that purpose, on which account I beg leave to trespass once more upon you.

Jamison's desire to clear his character.

I have, Sir, too high an opinion of the honor and probity of His Majesty's Ministers to fancy for a moment they would be influenced to do or believe anything injurious to the reputation of an Officer without first affording him the opportunity of replying; still, Sir, a representation conveyed to them, in a public letter from the Governor of a Colony, of so strong and serious a nature as that made by Governor Bligh against me, I confess myself a little alarmed lest it should impress His Majesty's Ministers'

1808.
30 April.

Jamison's
desire to clear
his character.

minds with distrust as to my honor and allegiance. No doubt they do not suspect the Validity of the representation, as they are not in the habit of receiving false and malicious insinuations from Governors against any of His Majesty's Servants.

Had I been guilty of the crimes imputed to me, why did not the Governor bring me to trial; this he knew would not answer his purpose, as, before Men of honor, the innocent have nothing to fear; but my accuser chose to pursue a method more secret, from which it was impossible for me to fend, because I was ignorant of any accusation. I trust his insidious attack, intended to ruin my reputation, will fall on his own guilty Shoulders.

I have now, Sir, to request you will be so good to transmit this letter to His Majesty's Principal Secretary of State for the Colonies with the enclosed correspondence which I have had the honor of holding with you on the present subject; that, I hope, and such other testimony as I shall apply for in England from the Gentlemen I have had the honor of serving under in this Colony (from the time the Colony was first settled), will, I trust, exonerate me from the Vile charges I am so unjustly accused of. At the same time, I trust His Majesty will be graciously pleased to afford me the means of obtaining that justice which His Majesty is at all times so ready to grant to Officers embarked in the Service of the Crown.   I have, &c.,

THOS. JAMISON,
Principal Surgeon.

[Enclosure No. 2.]

COURT MARTIAL ON D'ARCY WENTWORTH.

New South Wales, 17th February, 1808.

Proceedings of
court martial
for the trial of
D'Arcy
Wentworth.

PROCEEDINGS of a General Court-Martial, held by Virtue of a Warrant under the hand and Seal of His Honor George Johnston, Esquire, Lieutenant-Governor of His Majesty's Territory of New South Wales, &c., &c., &c.

Captain Anthony Fenn Kemp, President; Lieut. Will. Moore, Lieut. Wm. Lawson, Lieut. Thos. Laycock, Lieut. C. Draffin, Members: Charles Grimes, Esq'r., Deputy Judge-Advo'te.

THE several Warrants appointing the President, Members of the Court, and Deputy Judge-Advocate being read, and the Members and Judge-Advocate being sworn,—

D'Arcy Wentworth, Esquire, Assistant Surgeon in New South Wales, brought before the Court, and the following Charges exhibited against him by Charles Grimes, Esquire, Deputy Judge-Advocate:—

1st. In employing Servants of the Crown who were entrusted to his Care in labour on his own Grounds, and in taking Charge of his own Stock.

2ndly. In employing for his private Emolument Settlers' Servants who have been sent into the Hospital Sick, to the great loss and

1808.
30 April.

Proceedings of
court martial
for the trial of
D'Arcy
Wentworth.

Injury of their Masters, and thereby subjecting Government to an heavy Expence for the Maintenance of the Men so improperly kept on the Sick or Convalescent Lists.

Plea—Not guilty.

Letter from the Judge-Advocate to William Bligh, Esq'r., dated 16th of February, 1808, and William Bligh, Esquire's, Answer to Lieutenant-Governor Johnston, read to the Court:—

"His Honor the Lieutenant-Governor has directed me to transmit to You the Copy of the Charges against Mr. D'Arcy Wentworth, and at the same time to acquaint You that His Honor wishes to know if there is any person You may wish to appoint as Prosecutor before the General Court-Martial to be held to-morrow; or, if there is any particular Manner in which You are desirous that the prosecution should be conducted. "Charles Grimes."

"Sir, "Government House, Sydney, 16th February, 1808.

"I have this day received a Letter from Mr. Charles Grimes, Acting Judge-Advocate, enclosing a Copy of Charges against Mr. D'Arcy Wentworth, stating that His Honor The Lieut.-Governor had directed him to transmit to me the same, and at the same time to acquaint me that His Honor wishes to know if there is any person I may wish to appoint as prosecutor before the General Court-Martial to be held to-morrow, or if there is any particular Manner in which I am desirous that the Prosecution should be conducted.

"In reply to which I have only to refer you to my Letter of the 10th instant, and to inform You that I cannot enter into any such Circumstances until I return to England, and where I can only assign reasons for any Act of mine in this Colony.

"I am, &c.,
"Wm. Bligh."

Edmund Griffin, Secretary to the late Governor Bligh, Sworn, And the Letter, with the accompanying Depositions of Oakes and Beldon, from Governor Bligh to the Right Honorable William Windham, sent by the Duke of Portland, read.

[*A copy of these two depositions were forwarded by Governor Bligh with his despatch, dated 31st October, 1807, and numbered 2.*]

Q. from the Prosecutor. Are the Letter and Depositions produced true Copies of those sent to England by the Ship Duke of Portland? —*A.* They are.

Q. by the Prisoner to the Evidence. Did You overhear the late Governor mentioning any Settler's Name who had complained of my having detained their Men in the Hospital improperly, Or has any person ever accused me to You officially?—*A.* I cannot recollect, But no Person has complained officially to me.

Q. Did I not officially apply thro' You to Governor Bligh, on or about the 18th of April last, to be allowed to take two Government Servants off the public Stores; And, if I did, what reasons did I assign for doing so?—*A.* I recollect an Application to take two Men off the Store to take Care of Your Horses.

Q. On being refused my request, did I not beg You again to state to the Governor "that having no Servant allowed me by Government, that it would be impossible for me to carry on the duties of my Office Unless he would allow me to have two Men off the Store to take Care of my horses, which I used for Government purposes"? —*A.* Yes.

1808.
30 April.

Proceedings of
court martial
for the trial of
D'Arcy
Wentworth.

Q. On being refused a second time, did I not beg You to tell the Governor that it would be impossible for me to attend the Sick at Castle Hill as I was ordered by the Principal Surgeon, and that I should be compelled to order the Sick of every description into the Hospital at Parramatta?—*A.* You did.

FRANCIS OAKES, late Chief Constable, Sworn :—

States to the Court the irregularities committed by Mr. Wentworth, as Assistant Surgeon, in employing Convalescents to his own private Purposes. A few days prior to Mr. Wentworth's suspension I was directed by the late Governor by Letter to go to Mr. Wentworth's Premises, and take four Men that were employed by him without permission. I went to Mr. Wentworth's house and found two Men, and sent a Constable to Mr. Wentworth's farm, who took two other Men; But one of the men specified in the Governor's Letter was out with Mr. Wentworth's Cattle, and came and gave himself up in the Evening. I was directed by the Governor's Letter to get an Account of the Number of days that the Men I found on Mr. Wentworth's premises had been employed; Also to send the Men found to Government Labour at Castle Hill. I found five Men, and sent them to Castle Hill, and reported the next day in Writing the Men's Names, and the time they had been employed, which is as stated in the Deposition.

Q. by the President. Did You acquaint Capt'n Abbott, the Officer in Command, and Magistrate at Parramatta, with the Orders that You had received from the late Governor?—*A.* I believe I did. I shewed him the Letter.

Q. from the Prisoner. In Your Depositions before Mr. Atkins, You have related many other irregularities which happened in the Hospital at Parramatta;—Can you point out a Single person from whom Money was taken to get Admittance into the Hospital, or any person who was discharged thro' the influence of Wheeler, the Clerk of the Dispensatory?—*A.* I was informed by a Man of the Name of Nangle, who applied to me for a pass to go to Sydney to the Principal Surgeon, that he had been turned out of the Hospital because he would not give Wheeler, the Clerk, the Sum of two pounds.

Q. Do You know of any person taken into or discharged from the Hospital improperly since I had the Charge?—*A.* No.

Q. Can You mention the Name of any Settler's Servant who was received into the Hospital and detained there from improper Motives during the time that I had the Charge?—*A.* No.

Q. Can You inform the Court of any person let out of the Hospital to go about the Country doing Mischief since I had the Charge, and who has been punished and sent to Castle Hill for the Offence?—*A.* No.

Q. What Authority had You to say that Wheeler had a great influence over me, and that he made use of the Public Medicines for his own private purposes?—*A.* I do not believe I did say so. I do not think he has any Influence on Mr. Wentworth, or that he does make use of the public Medicines for his own purposes.

Q. Do You know that I employed the Hospital Gardeners in my own private Garden, except in their own time?—*A.* Yes.

Q. Was the Hospital Garden, at the time I was put under Arrest, not in good Order?—*A.* No.

Q. Did You ever hear that I had neglected to attend the Sick during the time I had Charge of the Parramatta Hospital?—*A.* No.

1808.
30 April.

Proceedings of court martial for the trial of D'Arcy Wentworth.

Q. by the President. As You knew Mr. Wentworth was intirely unacquainted with the Depositions You had made against him before the Governor and the Judge-Advocate, I ask You upon Your Oath, did any person enjoin You to Secrecy that you should not divulge the Deposition You had made?—*A.* No.

Q. Where were the Depositions taken against Mr. Wentworth, and who was present?—*A.* At Government House, in the presence of the Governor, the Judge-Advocate, and Mr. Griffin, the Governor's Secretary.

Q. Did You ever disclose to any person the questions you had been asked by the late Governor; if not, what were Your reasons for keeping them Secret?—*A.* I never did disclose them to any person. I had no reason for keeping them Secret.

Q. Did it not appear to You that the questions asked by the Governor were for the purpose of injuring Mr. Wentworth, if he had employed Men improperly?—*A.* Yes.

Q. You have said that many Men have been taken from the Hospital by Mr. Wentworth and employed about his Farm and Farm-house for different purposes ever since he came from Norfolk Island;—State Your reasons for the Assertion?—*A.* There have been Men; Francis Horton and Lawrence Killaney have been employed on his Farm very often.

Q. When Lawrence Killaney was brought by You before the Magistrates for being absent from the Hospital, and had been working at Mr. Wentworth's Farm, what was the decision of the Magistrates?—*A.* The Magistrates were of Opinion that it was improper that the Hospital Patients should be working about the Country and that they would put a Stop to it.

Q. Did You ever receive private Instructions to look after the Hospitals during Mr. Wentworth's having Charge?—*A.* Yes, repeatedly, from the Magistrates, but no particular ones during the time Mr. Wentworth had Charge.

Q. from the Court. How long have You been Chief Constable at Parramatta?—*A.* Above two Years.

Q. Is it not customary for Individuals to employ Servants of the Crown after they have done their Government Labour?—*A.* Yes.

Q. Were not the two Gardeners allowed to the Hospital at liberty, with the permission of the Surgeon, to go to work for themselves when the Garden was in good Order?—*A.* Yes.

Q. Is it not common to give the Servants of the Crown a task?—*A.* Yes.

GEORGE BELDON sworn:—

Q. from the Prosecutor. Do You know of Mr. Wentworth, the Assistant Surgeon, employing the Hospital Patients to his own private Advantage during the time he had charge of the Parramatta Hospital?—*A.* I know that Mr. Wentworth had four Men employed—two at his House and two at his Farm—and had been employed some time at labor for his Advantage, Thomas Stakeham and Michael Dowling at his Farm and James McDonald and Lawrence Killaney about his House. I informed Rouse, the Superintendent, how these Men were employed, and Rouse informed the late Governor and the Men were taken from Mr. Wentworth and sent to Castle Hill to public Labour. Francis Horton had been employed by Mr. Wentworth, but was discharged after being three

1808.
30 April.

Proceedings of
court martial
for the trial of
D'Arcy
Wentworth.

Months at Mr. Wentworth's Farm on the Wound of his hand being well. James Griffin was employed two days about Mr. Wentworth's House, tho' on the Hospital List.

Q. You have been long the Camp Overseer;—is it not customary for the Person who has charge of the Hospital to employ the Convalescent Patients in doing any light work about his Barrack or Garden?—A. Yes.

Q. Has Mr. Wentworth made use of the Convalescent patients otherwise than has been customary for other Assistant Surgeons at Parramatta during the Six Years You have been an Overseer?—A. No.

Q. Where were the Depositions You took against Mr. Wentworth taken, and in whose presence?—A. I was sent for some time in July last by the late Governor to the Government House at Sydney; the Governor and Judge-Advocate were present; the Governor asked me about the Men taken from Mr. Wentworth. Some Questions were asked me by the Judge-Advocate—Some that I could Answer and some that I could not—And I told the Judge-Advocate that I could not Answer some; that the Judge-Advocate would have read all the Questions, but the late Governor told the Judge-Advocate that there was not any occasion. About two Months after a Paper was given for me to sign by Mr. Griffin, the Governor's Secretary, at Parramatta; But the Contents I do not know, not being able to read; but some part was read by Mr. Griffin, but not the whole, as I saw more writing on other Sheets of Paper. Mr. Oakes was present when I signed the Paper presented by Mr. Griffin.

Q. from the Prisoner. How long was it after the Men were taken from my Charge that three of them were sent in by the Superintendant at Castle Hill to the Hospital?—A. They were sent in a few days after.

The Evidence on the part of the Prosecution being closed, the Prisoner enters on his Defence:—

Gentlemen,   Sydney, 17th February, 1808.

When I reflect upon the great disgrace which I have suffered in the Eyes of the Colony in being so improperly suspended from my Situation after Seventeen Years faithful Services, It is with unspeakable pleasure that I am this day allowed to vindicate my Conduct before a Court of Honorable Men, who I am confident will decide upon my Case with impartiality and Justice. But notwithstanding the numerous Injuries and Acts of Injustice which I have experienced from the late Governor, I am induced, by a Consideration of the Melancholy Situation to which he has reduced himself by his own Misconduct, to refrain from attempting to explain the Motives by which he was actuated in his very extraordinary Conduct towards me.

I shall therefore content myself with disproving the whole of the Charges he has so unjustly preferred against me to His Majesty's Secretary of State, and which, Gentlemen, I have the supreme happiness of assuring You I will do to your entire Satisfaction.

D. WENTWORTH,
Ass't Surgeon.

THOMAS JAMISON, Esquire, Principal Surgeon, called by the Prisoner and Sworn:—

Q. by Prisoner. Did I, in or about the 18th April last, represent to You that I had been refused by the late Governor Bligh to have two

Government Servants allowed me off the Stores to take care of two
of my own Horses that I found necessary to keep to carry on my
Duty?—*A.* I recollect the representation perfectly, but cannot say
if on that day.

1808.
30 April.

Proceedings of
court martial
for the trial of
D'Arcy
Wentworth.

Q. Did You not wait on the late Governor in Consequence of my
Representation, and what Answer did you receive?—*A.* I did, and
the Governor informed me that You should not have a Servant off
the Stores.

Q. Did I not receive Orders from You to visit the Sick at Castle
Hill once a Week, or oftener if necessary?—*A.* I received such
directions to that Effect officially from the Governor and communicated them by Letter to You.

Q. Did I not represent to You the hardship of being refused to
get Servants off the Store, when the Governor even allowed my
Predecessor, Mr. Mileham, to make use of the Convalescent Patients
for his domestic purposes?—*A.* I remember the Observation being
made by You, and said that if Mr. Mileham had been sanctioned
by Governor Bligh there could be no impropriety in Your doing
the same.

Q. Did You at any time after this Conversation give me either
written or verbal Orders not to employ the convalescent Patients in
any way I thought proper?—*A.* No.

JAMES MILEHAM, Esquire, Assistant Surgeon, Sworn :—

Q. by the Prisoner. State to the Court what public Situation You
held in Parramatta on the 14th April last?—*A.* Doing the Duty of
Assistant Surgeon and in Charge of the hospital.

Q. Was You not under the Necessity of visiting the Sick at Castle
Hill, distant Nine Miles, and several other distant places, and was
You not obliged to use your own Horses for that duty?—*A.* I was.

Q. Did not the late Governor Bligh allow You to employ the
Convalescent Patients under Your Care as You thought proper for
Your domestic Purposes?—*A.* On the Governor's first visiting the
Hospital under my Charge I made him acquainted that I employed
certain Patients who were Convalescents for my private Convenience, which the Governor approved of by saying, " He wished to
make my Situation respectable."

Q. Has it not been the Practice since You have been doing the
duty as Assistant Surgeon for Yourself and the Principal Surgeon,
under every Governor, to employ the Convalescent Patients in any
Way You thought proper, with the knowledge of the Governors?—
A. Yes.

Q. Did you not, during the time the Colony was much distressed
for Provision, and You had the Charge of the Hospital, allow some
Convalescent patients to come to my House; if so, what were Your
Motives for so doing?—*A.* I did allow some Convalescent Patients
to go to do light Work for You to obtain some provisions, they not
having sufficient Allowance from my Hospital.

Q. Do you not know that I often Employ the Hospital Gardeners
in their own time, and that I always pay them for their Labour?—
A. I do, and have been present when You have paid them.

RICH'D ROUSE, Superintendent, Sworn :—

Q. by the Prisoner. During the time I have had Charge of the
Hospital at Parramatta, and You have had the direction of the
public Yard, have I ever improperly kept any Government Servant

1808.
30 April.
———
Proceedings of
court martial
for the trial of
D'Arcy
Wentworth.

in the Hospital list, or refused to take anyone into the Hospital who was a fit Object belonging to Your Department?—*A*. No; not one.

GEORGE MEALMAKER, Superintendent of Weaving Flax and Wool, Sworn:—

Q. During the time you have acted as Superintendant, while I had charge of the Parramatta Hospital, do You know of any instance of my having kept any Man or Woman under Your direction longer in the Hospital list than was necessary, or ever refused to take a proper Object into the Hospital?—*A*. I do not.

Court adjourned till 9 o'Clock to-morrow, 18th February.
Court Met.

RICHARD ATKINS, Esquire, late Judge-Advocate, Sworn:—

Q. by Prisoner. Was You enjoined to Secrecy by the late Governor about the Depositions taken by You from Oakes and Beldon against me?—*A*. I was, sometime subsequent to Mr. Wentworth's Court-Martial. I was sent for by the Governor, I think, about ten o'Clock in the Morning; he took me into a small Office, and told me there were some depositions which he wished me to Swear Oakes and Beldon to, and sent for Oakes first. I read the questions to Oakes, which to the best of my recollection were in the hand Writing of the Governor's Secretary, and the written Answers, which Oakes said were correct, and I swore him to them. After which Beldon was sent for, when I read the whole of the questions and the Answers signed by Oakes to him, and Beldon said the whole of them were correct, and I believe Beldon signed them.

Q. Have I not been frequently in the habit of attending You as a Medical Man, and have I not at all times been attentive to You?—*A*. No Man could have been more attentive to me as a Medical Man.

Q. from the Court: Was either Oakes or Beldon, at the time the Depositions were made against Mr. Wentworth, enjoined to. Secrecy by the late Governor?—*A*. I do not know; it appeared to me that it was done with Secrecy.

Q. Is it not consistent with Equity, when Depositions are taken against any person, to make the person accused acquainted with them?—*A*. No doubt; but, being enjoined to Secrecy by the Governor, I did not feel myself warrantable in giving the Information to Mr. Wentworth.

The Prisoner calls on the President and the Judge-Advocate to speak to his Conduct as a Medical Man for many Years back.

CAPTAIN KEMP, the President, States he has known Mr. Wentworth thirteen Years, and has always considered him particularly attentive to his duty, and correct in his Conduct as an Officer.

The JUDGE-ADVOCATE States he has known the prisoner upwards of Seventeen Years, and that he has in every instance within his knowledge conducted himself as a Medical Man and Officer with the strictest Propriety.

The Court, having maturely and deliberately considered the Evidence for and against the Prisoner, as well as what he had to offer in his defence, is of Opinion that the Prisoner is not guilty on the first Charge or Second Charge, and do, therefore, honorably acquit him. The Court, adverting to what has appeared in Evidence in the Course of this Trial, feel themselves called on by a Sense of

Duty to express their pointed disapprobation of the Novel and unprecedented Measure of taking private Depositions against an Officer, to be transmitted to His Majesty's Ministers, without allowing the party accused an Opportunity to defend himself.

1808.
30 April.

Proceedings of court martial for the trial of D'Arcy Wentworth.

ANTHONY FENN KEMP,
Capt'n and President.

MAJOR JOHNSTON TO VISCOUNT CASTLEREAGH.

(Despatch per whaler the Brothers.)

Headquarters, New South Wales,
My Lord,   30th April, 1808.
      This Despatch will be forwarded by the ship Brothers, with Duplicates (as compleat as the time and other circumstances have admitted) of the Despatch I had the honor to transmit for Your Lordship by the ship Dart.

I am now anxiously expecting the arrival of Lieutenant-Colonel Foveaux, of whose intended departure from England I have received information by the Rose, a private ship.

Arrival of Foveaux expected.

Lieutenant-Colonel Paterson may also be soon expected from Port Dalrymple, His Majesty's Ship Porpoise having sailed from hence on the 19th Instant for the purpose of bringing him from that Settlement.

Probable early arrival of Paterson.

On the arrival of either of those Officers I shall lay before him all the Evidences of Governor Bligh's guilty Conduct, and I hope some plan will then be adopted to facilitate his departure for England.

I feel great pleasure that it is in my power to repeat to Your Lordship assurances of the general tranquil state of the Colony, notwithstanding the active tho' secret endeavours of some discontented persons and incendiaries to disturb and alarm the ignorant and remote Settlers.

Tranquillity of the colony.

I had the honor to inform Your Lordship, in my Despatch of the 11th Instant, that the two Mr. Blaxlands had displayed a disposition to be extremely troublesome, and the voluminous enclosures that accompany this Letter will, I hope, convince Your Lordship that I have not preferred an unfounded accusation.

Difficulties created by John and Gregory Blaxland.

The Gentlemen were no sooner relieved from the terror they had felt, in consequence of the threats, violence, and oppression of Governor Bligh, than they became troublesomely importunate to divert my attention from the most urgent Public business to the immediate consideration of their private affairs.

Desirous to conciliate all Classes as far as might be consistent with the observance of my superior duties, and being also sensible

1808.
30 April.

Claims of the
Blaxlands
favourably
considered.

that Your Lordship's agreement with the Mr. Blaxlands had not
been fulfilled by Governor Bligh, I took an early opportunity to
learn the nature of their real Claims, and having satisfied myself
of their extent, I gave them a positive assurance of my intention
to do them justice by a prompt obedience of Your Lordship's and
Mr. Windham's Orders respecting their Lands, Cattle, and
Servants.

Almost any other men under such encouraging circumstances
would have been contented and grateful; but these Gentlemen
have become more restless and dissatisfied from indulgence, and
their disregard of propriety of conduct seems to have increased in
proportion as they have felt their just rights and privileges were
no longer in danger of being violated.

. It would be an improper trespass upon Your Lordship's time
were I to trouble you with anything more than a general detail
of their Conduct.

Dispute
between
John Blaxland
and Russell.

When they considered themselves certain that their agreement
would be literally fulfilled, they made a personal application to
Mr. McArthur, Secretary to the Colony, to obtain my sanction of
their forcibly turning the Master of the Ship Brothers on shore.
On enquiry, it appeared that Mr. John Blaxland holds a share of
one moiety of the Vessel, and that Messrs. Hulletts Brothers & Co.,
of London, were the Owners of the other part; that the latter are
also the Ship's Husbands, and possess, by virtue of their mutual
agreement, the power of appointing a Captain and Officers to the
ship. As the Captain had made a most successful voyage, having
procured nearly Forty Thousand Seal-Skins, with which he only
waited for a small supply of Provisions to return to England, Mr.
McArthur earnestly advised Mr. Blaxland not to make an attempt
that would detain the ship in Port at a heavy expense, and certainly terminate in the disappointment of his expectations; for,
on an investigation of Mr. Blaxland's authority over the Vessel,
it appeared to be very Circumscribed.

Blaxland's
charges against
Macarthur.

Reasonable and disinterested as was this advice, Mr. Blaxland
rejected it without regard to consequences; and Mr. McArthur,
because he declined to become an auxiliary in an act that he
considered indefensible, was attacked by every species of Calumny,
and indirectly accused of endeavouring to frustrate Mr. Blaxland's wishes from interested motives.

Blaxland's
request for
an inquiry.

Under the influence of a most irritable temper, and Stimu-
lated by an Inhabitant of the name of Lord, who was once a
Convict and now appears to have formed a kind of Partnership
with the Mr. Blaxlands; the elder brother sent me a Memorial,
requesting an investigation of the conduct of the Master of the

Brothers on certain Charges that were annexed; But being
desired to lay before me the authority upon which he founded
his claim to such an investigation, he at first evaded the request,
and at last intreated to be excused from unfolding his private
Concerns.

Mr. Blaxland then laid a Copy of the Memorial and Charges* he
had sent to me before a Bench of Magistrates, who appear to have
examined his complaint, and all the Evidence he thought proper
to produce, with great patience and attention, and to have dismissed his Charges as insufficient to justify any further proceedings against the Master of the Brothers.

Not satisfied with this decision, Mr. Blaxland next transmitted
me a Copy of the Proceedings of the Magistrates, with a Petition
that I would give him authority to turn the Master out of the
ship; and because I declined to comply, I and Mr. McArthur have
been threatened with Protests and prosecutions, and Mr.
McArthur, whose advice it has been supposed I have followed,
with Assassination.*

These threats have been considered by myself and Mr.
McArthur as undeserving notice, and the Mr. Blaxlands and Mr.
Lord finding I was not to be provoked by their improper conduct,
at last thought it advisable to go on board the ship Brothers, and
to commit an Assault on the Master.

When the Master made his complaint to me, I directed him to
the Magistrates, and they very properly referred the Accusation
to be decided upon by a Court of Criminal Jurisdiction. The
Court being assembled, the Trial commenced, and in the midst of
the Proceedings the Majority, without Indictment, Trial, or the
observance of any principle but a most ungovernable prejudice,
Sentenced the Prosecutor and his Chief Mate (who was an Evidence) to Seven Years' transportation for Perjury, and, at the
same time that they found them guilty of so abominable an
Offence, recommended them to Mercy. Mr. Blaxland, Junior, was
found guilty of the Assault, and fined Five Pounds—the elder
Mr. Blaxland and his Partner, Mr. Lord, were acquitted.

Trial of the
Blaxlands and
Lord by
criminal court.

Russell and
Daniels
convicted
of perjury.

The Master, Mr. Russell, was considered, after the Sentence of
Transportation, as dispossessed of the Command of his ship, and
Mr. Blaxland, having accomplished the object for which he had
so long contended, directed another person to go on board as
Captain.

When the results of this Trial were reported to me, and I
examined the minutes, and heard of the extraordinary manner in
which the Trial had been conducted, I directed Mr. Grimes,* the
Acting Judge-Advocate, to point out the particular Evidence on

* Note 140.

1808.
30 April.

which the Conviction of Perjury had been founded, and to state
the reasons of the Court for recommending the Offenders to
Mercy.

Grimes' refusal
to discuss the
sentence of
the court.

Mr. Grimes returned an evasive answer to the first part, and
sheltered himself under an excuse that he did not consider himself obliged to divulge the private Opinions of the Majority of the
Members. But, My Lord, I am running imperceptibly into a
detail that would be almost endless, and into conclusions many
of which are, from the nature of the subject, unavoidably conjectural. I will, therefore, beg to refer Your Lordship to the
Official Papers it has occasioned, and I respectfully hope, when

Russell and
Daniels
liberated by
Johnston.

the whole are considered, my relieving the unfortunate Mr. Russel
and his Mate from the consequences of a Sentence they certainly
did not deserve, will be approved. Had Mr. Russel been tried a
second time, I know not what might have resulted, for there are
abundance of Evidences to be found here who will swear anything; and I am concerned to report to Your Lordship that there
are a few persons in the Colony who are more influenced by Mr.
Lord and his associates than by a regard to justice, or by a desire
to support me in the detection and punishment of Frauds or other
Crimes.

Russell to
return to
England.

The Condition on which Mr. Russell returns to England is that
he shall abide by Your Lordship's Orders or forfeit Two Thousand
Pounds. Mr. Russell is a plain, uneducated Seaman; but if
Your Lordship should be pleased to examine him, I think he will
be capable of explaining Mr. Blaxland's motives for desiring to
turn him out of his Ship.

The Trial and Proceedings against Mr. Russell, unimportant as
they must appear to Your Lordship, have been made the vehicle

Opposition of
certain officers
to Johnston.

of much mischief, and have been used as a mask under which a
few Officers have displayed a vexatious opposition to my Government. As I saw no means of relief in the present Circumstances
of the Colony but by sending the most active away, I ordered Mr.
Grimes to take my Despatches in the Dart, and directed Mr.
Harris, Surgeon of the New South Wales Corps, to hold himself
in readiness to proceed in the Brothers. My Correspondence with
the latter Officer* will in part explain to Your Lordship the spirit
that has prevailed, and I lament that a severe illness which now
confines Mr. Harris to his bed prevents his taking his Passage in
the Brothers, and will for a time deprive Your Lordship of that
information which he states is never likely to be known but from
himself. As I was unsuccessful in my endeavours to prevail upon
Mr. Harris to explain this secret; and could not but see that
some discontent still prevailed, I wrote to all the Officers* of the

* Note 141.

1808.
30 Apr'l.

Colony in the way I thought most likely to draw forth the desired information; but in this attempt I was also entirely disappointed by their answer.

Mr. Harris being incapable of taking home my Despatches, I have selected Lieut. Minchin for that Service, as an Officer who is well acquainted with the violence, Oppression, and Tyranny of Gov'r Bligh, and from his perfect knowledge of the present state of the Colony, altogether as well qualified as Mr. Harris to give Your Lordship any information that may be required.

Minchin to carry despatches to England.

The most serious difficulty I have now to surmount is the want of an Officer to Act as Judge-Advocate, and as it is of great importance to the Welfare and Peace of the Settlement that the Office should be filled by a person of Talents and integrity, I shall, if it be possible, forbear from appointing anyone until the arrival of Lieut.-Colonel Foveaux, who, it is to be hoped, may bring an Officer of that description, to whom a temporary appointment might not be unacceptable.

Want of a judge-advocate.

It has been a subject of serious regret that I have not been able, by every exertion, to get the Papers Copied which are referred to in my Duplicate Despatch A; but I hope the safe arrival of the Originals will make them unnecessary.

Duplicates of enclosures.

I propose to forward complete Triplicates by the Rose, a private Ship, that I am informed Sails for England in a Month, and by that conveyance I shall transmit Returns of the state of this and the other Settlements. I have, &c.,

GEO. JOHNSTON.

Triplicates to be transmitted.

[Enclosure No. 1.]

THE PROTEST OF JOHN BLAXLAND.

Protest of John Blaxland.

NEW SOUTH WALES.

BY THIS PUBLIC INSTRUMENT OF PROTEST, Be it known unto all Men who shall see these Presents that on the Twenty sixth Day of March in the Year of Our Lord One Thousand Eight Hundred and Eight, Before me Charles Grimes Esqre., His Majesty's Acting Judge Advocate and Notary Public for this Territory, personally appeared John Blaxland Esqre. part and managing Owner of the Ship Brothers, of the Port of London, whilst in this Port, who claimeth a Right on Behalf of himself and his Partners in England, and all other Parties and Persons concerned, or that it may in any wise concern to protest, and DOTH accordingly on Behalf of himself and the other Owners of the said Ship, or all and every or any others it may in any wise concern, solemnly PROTEST against Mr. Oliver Russell, Master of the said Ship, now riding at Anchor in Sydney Cove Port

1808.
30 April.

Protest of
John Blaxland.

Jackson in this Territory, with a Cargo of Thirty Eight Thousand fine Salted Fur Seal Skins on Board her, of the reputed
Value of Thirty Thousand Pounds Sterling and upwards, together
with the said Ship underwrote for the Sum of Seven Thousand
Five Hundred and Fifty Pounds Sterling for the Voyage, and
against all or any other Person or Persons that may in any wise
appear liable for any Damages or any Part thereof, by reason
of his or their interfering or unlawfully refusing to interfere,
or in any wise advising or aiding the said Oliver Russell that
may have in any wise effected, or that may in any wise hereafter
effect the said Ship and Cargo, or Deponent, or the other Owners,
or any Person or Persons in any wise interested directly or
indirectly, touching the Premises, Now be it known to all whom
it may concern or appertain in any wise that the said Oliver
Russell has been guilty of innumerable Acts of sufficient Consequence to justify Deponent on Behalf of himself and his Partners,
to supersede him in the Command of the said Ship, and to cause
him to be conveyed to England to answer for such Acts, and for
that Purpose, Deponent on the second Day of this Instant March,
wrote to the said Oliver Russell a Letter, requiring him to give
up the Command of the said Ship, on the pain of being prosecuted on the Charges therein stated, and at that Time known
to Deponent, as will appear by Papers No. 1 and 2 accompanying
this Protest—The said Oliver Russel having persisted, and still
persists in keeping Command of the said Ship, necessitated
Deponent to apply to His Honor the Lieut. Governor of this
Territory for legal Authority to supersede and bring to Justice
the said Oliver Russell, as by attested Copies (regularly numbered) of a Correspondence between the said Deponent and John
McArthur Esqre. called Colonial Secretary, will appear—
amongst which Papers and Documents No. 8 it will appear, that
Deponent brought some of the said Charges before Thomas
Jamison, John Harris, William Minchin Esquires and Captain
James Symmonds all Commissioned Magistrates in this Territory, not being allowed to adduce Evidence in Support of all the
Charges exhibited—but Deponent conceiving that the Law extended, and that there were Courts competent to try any Offences
whether committed in this Territory or elsewhere, did a second
time petition His Honor The Lieutenant Governor, as will appear
by Paper No. 9 and wherein Deponent pointed out, that it was
possible for him to bring Charges before a Civil Court for the
Reasons therein stated; and from the Answer received to that
Petition Deponent made Application to Charles Grimes Esqre.
Acting Judge Advocate as Law Officer of this Colony, as will
appear by Papers Nos. 20 and 21.

1808.
30 April

Protest of
John Blaxla

And Deponent further declares, that the said Oliver Russel has been Guilty of various Acts, which come under the Appellation of Barratry, as stated in the accompanying Correspondence, together with the several Matters and Things herein after mentioned Viz.

1st. That the said Oliver Russell has since his arrival in this Colony, altered the Log Book of the said Ship, respecting the Transactions on Board the said Ship at the Cape of Good Hope.

2nd. That the said Oliver Russell has disobeyed the Instructions given him for his proceeding during his Sealing Voyage, greatly to the Injury of the Owners; particularly by running to Norfolk Island and incurring an unnecessary Expense instead of returning to Port Jackson.

3rd. That the said Oliver Russell in open Defiance of Deponent threatened to draw Bills on the Keel of the said Ship to settle his own Accounts, as will appear by Copies of Papers marked alphabetically from Letter A. to P.

4th. That the said Oliver Russell has refused a Passage in the said Ship to one of the Officers belonging to the Concern, by which an unnecessary Expense must be incurred to the Owners, giving for his Reason "that the Person he refused was a Principal Evidence against him."

5th. That the said Oliver Russell has threatened to injure Deponent in his Concern, in the said Ship, to the Amount of Four or Five Hundred Pounds Sterling, to do which according to the Share Deponent holds, he must at least incur an unnecessary Expense to the said Ship of Fourteen or Fifteen Hundred Pounds Sterling.

6th. That the said Oliver Russell has traduced Deponent's Character at Norfolk Island.

7th. That the said Oliver Russell has refused to take Two Thousand Seal Skins on Board the said Ship, belonging to the Schooner Antipode; after having requested a Survey to be taken by Proper Persons to ascertain if the said Ship was fit to carry them, and the Report was made that she was fit.

8th. That the said Oliver Russell when Deponent went on Board the said Ship accompanied by his Carpenter to settle about his Accommodation on His Passage to England, as he thinks it necessary to go for the Protection of his Property, the said Oliver Russell insulted him, and threatened to put him in Irons during the Passage, and even at that time to turn him over the side of the Ship, and since has made a false Accusation on Oath to bring Deponent to a Criminal Trial, and positively refused to receive him on Board but as a Passenger, and not even as such unless he paid him down the Sum of Two Hundred Pounds Sterling for his Passage, and then to ship as a Passenger only.

9th. That the said Oliver Russell did on his Return to this Port from his Sealing Voyage make a false Return of the Provisions on Board the said Ship.

10th. That the said Oliver Russell during his Sealing Voyage put his Chief Officer under an Arrest, without reporting it to Deponent on his Arrival, or bringing him to Trial according to his Articles.

11th. That the said Oliver Russell in open Defiance of Deponent's Orders, declared he will ship a second Officer, who has been turned out of the Ship City of Edinburgh now lying in this Cove for bad Conduct, and further declared that he will carry his late Chief Officer home in Irons.

And from all the aforesaid Reasons, and various Circumstances Deponent DOTH most solemnly PROTEST against the said Oliver Russell proceeding to England or elsewhere in the said Ship Brothers as Master, in which Ship as Managing Owner in this Colony Deponent is so materially concerned; and against the said John McArthur Esqre. for in any wise interfering, in offering to advance the said Oliver Russell Money, and as he has declared given him the best of Advice, who at that Time was officially corresponding with Deponent and against all and every Person or Persons it may in any wise concern, reserving to himself or any of the Parties interested or concerned, the Power and Privilege of a Free Subject of His Majesty's Dominions to take such Means to obtain Relief and Redress in the Premises as he they or any of them shall be directed and advised by Counsel learned in the Law for that Purpose and doth hereby present this Instrument declaratory of his Intent and Purpose to the said Charles Grimes Esqre. Notary Public, whom he the said Deponent requests to receive, and to administer to him the usual Oath taken or subscribed on such or the like Occasion.

In Testimony of the Truth of the aforesaid Deponent hath subscribed his Name—This done, and Protested, at Sydney in New South Wales on the Day and Year above written.

JOHN BLAXLAND,
Part Owner of the Ship Brothers.

Sworn before me at Sydney in New South Wales, this 26th day of March, 1808.   C. GRIMES, Ag. J.-A.

Witness present: JNO. OBEE.

True Copy of the Original: C. GRIMES, Ag. J.-A.

1808.
30 April.

[Enclosure No. 2.]

PROCEEDINGS AT THE TRIAL OF JOHN AND GREGORY BLAXLAND AND
SIMEON LORD.

Proceedings at
the trial of
John and
Gregory
Blaxland and
Simeon Lord.

New South Wales ⎱ PROCEEDINGS of a Court of Criminal Judicature
28th March 1808. ⎰ held by virtue of a Precept under the Hand and
Seal of George Johnston, Esquire, Lieutenant
Governor of his Majesty's Territory of New
South Wales &c. &c. &c.

The Acting Judge Advocate.

Captain James Symons ⎫
Lieut. Will. Moore   ⎬ Members.
Lieut. C. Draffin   ⎭

⎧ Lieut. Jno. Brabyn
⎨ Lieut. Thos. Laycock
⎩ Ensign A. Bell

Precept read, and Court Sworn.

John Blaxland, Gregory Blaxland, Esquires, and Mr. Simeon
Lord Brought to the Bar (the following) Indictment read :—

" New South Wales ⎫ John Blaxland, Esquire; Gregory Blaxland,
County of   ⎬ Esquire; and Mr. Simeon Lord, Merchant,
Cumberland.   ⎭ Severally stand charged that they on the
nineteenth day of March One Thousand eight
hundred and eight in the forty eighth Year of the Reign of our
Sovereign Lord George the third with force and Arms on board the
Ship Brothers, then lying in Sydney Cove in the County aforesaid,
in and upon one Oliver Russell, Master of the Said Ship Brothers
in the Peace of God and our Said Lord the King, then and there
being did make an Assault on the Person of the Said Oliver Russell
to the great damage of the Said Oliver Russell, and against the
Peace of our Said Lord the King His Crown and Dignity."

Plea not Guilty.

MR. OLIVER RUSSELL Sworn, Produced the (following) Papers
No. 2 and 3 *read.*

" NEW SOUTH WALES. Before the Honorable Court of Criminal
Jurisdiction.

On the Prosecution of Captain Oliver Russell
against
Mr. John Blaxland, Mr. Gregory Blaxland, and Simeon Lord,

Gentlemen,

I beg leave to address you and to represent that on Saturday
the 19th instant I was in command of my own Ship ; when between
two and three in the Afternoon of that day, the above named
Parties came on Board, and Mr. John Blaxland, a part Owner,
informed me that he had brought his Carpenter on board to view
the accomodations he was to have in his Passage to England. On
the approach of the Parties, I waited on the Gang way in Person.
I received them with respect, and they were introduced on the
Quarter Deck ; when Mr. J. Blaxland talked on the Subject of his
accomodations :—I told him in Answer to his request of occupying
the Cabin and my Sleeping Room, that I would expect, if He did So,
to be paid for the Same. Gentlemen—from the mild conduct I have
pursued—I could hardly expect the *violent, outrageous,* and *unwarrantable* Assault that ensued by Mr. Gregory Blaxland, Seconded
by Mr. J. Blaxland, and aided, Abetted, and Assisted by Simeon

1808.
30 April.

Proceedings at
the trial of
John and
Gregory
Blaxland and
Simeon Lord.

Lord—Now, Gentlemen, as it is necessary to describe the nature of this Assault I will do it in distinct words to be Substantiated by proof; and, I trust, that prefering a Criminal prosecution to a Civil action for damages will clearly evince that my motives were not of a pecuniary nature, but merely a determined resolution to resist So unwarrantable an Assault upon my Person, when on board of my own Ship, which, according to the Law, is my Castle; and in consequence of the Steps, Language, Outrage, Assault, and unjustifiable conduct pursued by the Persons now before you, had I acted as the Law would justify, the consequences would have been dreadful; and I ought in justice to myself to have acted with that Self preservation which allows the most powerful Resistance.

Gentlemen—It is not my intention to animadvert upon the Testimony given before you; Because that painful Task I confidently Trust will be performed by yourselves; And in order to avoid Prolixity, and Circumlocution, and in the undoubted faith of this Arduous undertaking being performed by you, I will commence with Stating to this honorable Court, that a Man's life and Person is to be protected against Assault and Batteries, and every violence either by desperate or common Invaders.

The Law particularly expresses "That if any Person in Anger lift, or Strick his Arm and merely offer to Strike another, or menace any one with Staff or Weapon, it is a Trespass and assault in Law; and, if a Man threatens to Beat another Person, or lye in wait to do it,—If the other is hindered in his business, and receives loss thereby, Action lies for the Injury."— Lamb B: I, 22 aff. P.C. 603.

Now, Gentlemen, it will appear to you in Proof, that this wanton Assault, this outrageous act, this violent Breach of Peace, was committed under and by direction of a Justice assigned to Keep the Peace, and to prevent any breaches of it;—How far his conduct will escape the discrimination of the Law, You, Gentlemen, will best determine, and, Gentlemen, you will further find, that one of the parties, Mr. Gregory Blaxland, who first commenced the affray accosted me in the most opprobrious Language, and then collared me, for a pretended Insult offered to His Brother, Mr. John Blaxland; as Magistrate he, Mr. John Blaxland, also collared me, regardless of the Oath he had taken as a Magistrate, as a Conservator of the Peace, and the duty he owed to Society, as Evidence will prove to you. Gentlemen, I have not the temerity to Sport or attempt to trifle with the Court; nor have I a wish to trespass on your time unnecessarily; But from the before cited case, I have no doubt, under the Proof to be adduced, that Lord will be found to be the principal aggressor.

Gentlemen, I beg leave further to recite to you by Law Authority— "That any injury whatsoever (be it ever so Small) being actually done to the Person of a Man, in angry or avengeful Manner, or rude or insolent manner, as by Spitting in his face, or any ways touching him in Anger, or violently jostling him are Batteries in the Eye of the Law."—I. Hawk: P.C. 263-4.

From this very particular Act, Gentlemen, and the Proofs to be adduced to substantiate the charge, There is not the smallest doubt but that the Parties before you as Defendants will be found Guilty— as they are all Men of opulence; and, if they had not known better, had it in their power to be better advised.

1808.
30 April.

Proceedings at
the trial of
John and
Gregory
Blaxland and
Simeon Lord.

Now, Gentlemen, I further crave leave to observe That for an Assault, "The wrong doer is Subject both to an Action at the Suit of the Party, wherein he shall render damages; and also to an Indictment at the Suit of the King; wherein he shall be fined according to the Heinousness of the offence."—I. Hawkins 263.

On this Statute, Gentlemen, I am conscious that from the Strength of evidence to be adduced in Support of the Prosecution, the charge will be substantiated manifestly and incontrovertibly; and I will refer with Submission to the 6th G. 2d. C. 23 S. 17 wherein the whole of this business is explained; And the Punishment for Such an offence annexed: and in order to be correct, I will refer to I. Hawk, 133; Where it is particularly expressed, that every Battery includes an Assault, But for the Satisfaction of your minds, I will refer Submissively to 3 Salkeld 46. You will also find that a person is justifiable in every possible means of resistance, when an Assault and Battery of another is effected, or attempted, by Threat, Menace, or Assault; or attempt to beat him from his lawful Watercourse or highway.

From what has been stated. Gentlemen, You will naturally admit that I acted with So much deliberation and Calmness on the day of Assault, as to exclude every presumption of impropriety on My Side, and consequently, to preclude the Possibility of a Plea in justification of the Defendants' Conduct, from provocation, or any other Cause. Many Men in my Situation would have acted far otherwise and the first Law of nature strengthened, Admitted, and confirmed by the British Laws, would have justified every Means of resistance upon my part—And had a fatal consequence unhappily insued the Prosecutor would have been Saved harmless by the Law; But how different the consequences to the Defendants.

It is an established Maxim, Supported on the Authority of Blackstone 3—12—0 that any Person going into the House of another, and will not leave it, That the Owner is Justifiable in turning Such Persons out; Here, Gentlemen, it becomes necessary to claim Your attention, when you find, that as a lawful Commander of the Ship Brothers, that, that Ship is my Castle, where every Infringement, where every outrage, that malice could invent or Strength and Power effect, was committed on my Person, in direct violation of what Law prescribes, and a Conservator of the Peace ought rather to Prohibit than promote.

Gentlemen, Pardon my presumption, when I observe, that I trust I have not inserted one Single tittle, but what will be clearly proved to your Satisfaction.

Now, Gentlemen, I will crave permission to lay before you the particular Purposes, and the ground on which the whole of this business hinges. It originates from the Machinations of my Chief Officer Mr. Hazleburg, and I have not the smallest doubt it will appear to you the most wanton Persecution that was ever Sett on foot: Because the Magistrate. Mr. John Blaxland, as part Owner, instead of supporting me in the Execution of my duty as Commander of the Ship Brothers has thought proper to encourage that Officer in Acts that are really too disgraceful for a man Supporting the name of a Magistrate to take Cognizance of: Inasmuch as the Said John Blaxland has encouraged and Cherished that Officer to Answer certain private motives he may have entertained; and that Such officer had rendered himself far from trustworthy by His misconduct on board the Vessel under my command. But to explain,

1808.
30 April.

Proceedings at
the trial of
John and
Gregory
Blaxland and
Simeon Lord.

Gentlemen, the repeated acts of misconduct exhibited by Mr. Hazel-burg both ashore and afloat, and which can and will be Satis-factorily proved by Evidence, caused me to confine him, which step I did not take until the Ship's Safety was absolutely at Stake. On one occasion (amongst many others) he in a state of inebriety Set the Vessel on fire—On many occasions he has exhibited Similar tokens of disregard and Intoxication, He has likewise repeatedly endangered the Ship's Safety by acts of misconduct which have called loudly for my Censure, as from a reference to my Log Book will fully and explicitly appear.

Gentlemen, do you not consider as Men of Honor that I as Commander of that Ship and as a Man of Integrity had a right So to dispose of Mr. Hazelburg as to prevent his further endanger-ing the Vessel? Surely! and had not Mr. John Blaxland thought otherwise, perhaps this violent Aggression never would have pressed on your attention—In every act respecting Hazelburg, Mr. John Blaxland has evinced the Strongest attachment to a man who had in So many instances proved himself unworthy of the Situation of an Officer on board—What could be the cause of this—could he continue in his Situation so dangerous a Man? considering likewise that Mr. Blaxland as Owner and resident Agent in this Colony, should have been convinced of the necessity which induced me to Suspend him from the duty of an Officer; Altho' I nevertheless extended him every former Indulgence.

Gentlemen, there is nothing more or less than a undeserved, tho' rooted Enmity on the part of Mr. John Blaxland that has caused him to act in this highly improper manner; and he has uniformly evinced a determination to Support that Man, and to render him Subservient to his Private Views against the Prosecutor, whose removal from his command, and ultimate destruction are unhappily the objects of Mr. John Blaxland's inclination.

Gentlemen, I beg leave to call your attention to a Letter from Mr. John Blaxland, the then Magistrate, dated 2d March 1808 and of which the following is a Verbatim Transcript.

" Sir,

" In consequence of your repeated misconduct, I am induced, for the benefit of the other Owners concerned with myself to dismiss you from the Command of the Ship Brothers, and I do desire you to give up the Command accordingly as I do not after what has happened conceive it safe to trust the Ship to England under your care—Should you refuse to comply with my desires on this business I shall proceed against you on the following charges :—

[Here followed a copy of the twelve charges made against Oliver Russell (see page 377), with the addition of the following fifth civil charge.]

" 5· For leaving the Sealing Ground with Salt Sufficient to have cured 3,000 Skins, and having plenty of Provisions Water and Wood in the Ship.   " JOHN BLAXLAND.
" Sydney, 2d March, 1808.
" Mr. Oliver Russell, Commander of the Ship Brothers."

After the Perusal of this Letter, it would be almost unnecessary to trespass on your time or Patience by a recital of circumstances corresponding with this—By which you will find, that the utmost Threats, menaces, and every oppression has been attempted to be practised against me—From this Letter it must appear, That unless I would give up the Possession of the Ship under my Command, I

1808.
30 April.

Proceedings at
the trial of
John and
Gregory
Blaxland and
Simeon Lord.

would be tried, first for 5 Criminal charges stated in the foregoing Letter, 5 Charges to be exhibited by Civil Actions, two charges for Fraud, and at least one for contempt to Mr. John Blaxland.

Gentlemen, on a perusal of this Original Letter, I am truly confident that all the Paint and Oil in the 3rd Charge will not be Sufficient to give this Letter that black complexion with which it was intended. Here the Cloven Foot is discovered. Criminal Charges were to be exhibited, because It was the determination of Mr. John Blaxland to dispossess me of the Command of the Ship Brothers for purposes justifiable to his own mind; And, Gentlemen, you will discover, that provided I had complied with that threatening Letter, he was well disposed to drop those Criminal accusations, which was tantamount to compound Felony.

On the Civil Charges very little comment is required for this reason, If Mr. John Blaxland had effected his purposes by condemning me before a Criminal Court, a Civil Court would not be required: But Self Sufficient, and acting with his Coadjutor, Simeon Lord, thought he could not invent too many actions against an innocent injured Man,—Mr. John Blaxland, not satisfied with the 1st Criminal Charge, or the 2d by Civil Actions, intermixes a third by *way of Fraud*. How consistent those charges may appear to you, Gentlemen, is not for me to determine—On the 4th charge of Mr. John Blaxland in this Letter I was to have been tried for contempt and disobedience of orders during the Passage; Here, Gentlemen, appears the strongest inconsistency that Artifice and Cunning could invent; Because Mr. John Blaxland ought, if any case he had to shew, to exhibit Such cause on my Arrival in this Colony. But it appears, that the Letter was written under Magisterial Authority, and that he exercised his authority as a Magistrate on board the Ship Brothers whither it extended not; and if it did, it Surely is a Principle of British Justice, that in his own Cause no Man Shall be a Magistrate.

Gentlemen, it must be obvious to Your discernment, that I have the most Serious Complaint that Law can point out against all the Parties, as common Invaders under Colour of Magisterial Authority; and that the Act has been perpetrated by a Magistrate, who over acted his Authority, and two Coadjutors who derived their Sanction from an illegal Power, and confirmed the act of imperious and premeditated oppression and Injustice which in a Magistrate are not less punishable than in any other man—but surely the reverse, as it was incumbent upon him to protect the Subject rather than invade his liberties.

Gentlemen, it is admitted a legal Maxim, that the intention of a crime must be constituted by Some accompanying Acts under Such intentions and by the threats held out to me it will appear in the clearest light by adverting to the Letter No. 3, I am threatened with numerous Charges Criminal as well as civil—all which are calculated to stab my reputation, and procure my ruin, But this Instrument may prove much more consequential than my Persecutors are aware of.

I beg leave to state to you Gentlemen, that in order to complete my destruction, Mr. John Blaxland employed the Printer to prepare Public Notices for the express purpose of overwhelming me in all the misery and distress he or his associates could invent; and in order to convince you of that intention, I beg leave here to recite the Notice So drawn up and prepared by Mr. John Blaxland; and

1808.
30 April.

Proceedings at
the trial of
John and
Gregory
Blaxland and
Simeon Lord.

which is in the following Words: "Notice—Whereas Mr. Oliver
Russell, Master of the Ship Brothers, has by Letter bearing date
the 18th Instant, threatened to draw Bills of Exchange on the
Credit of the Said Ship, of which I am part Owner and acting
Agent in this Colony.—This is to caution the Public against receiving
or negociating any such Bills, or any other Bills drawn on the
account of the Said Ship, without my approbation as they will be
protested in England.   " (Signed)   JOHN BLAXLAND."

Now, Gentlemen, let me impress your minds with the consequences attendant on So glaring and daring a Notice. Has it not
been calculated and intended to depreciate my Character, and to
all intents and purposes ruin my credit, Can it for a moment be
Supposed that any responsible Individual in the Colony would
advance me one Single Shilling. No. It could scarcely be believed.
But the intention is clear. It was determined right or wrong to
dispossess me of the Còmmand of the Ship Brothers. When found
impracticable by exhibited Criminal Charges, It was then plotted
that no debts would be paid by the Owner, and consequently that I
must be immured in the dreary confines of a Gaol which would give
the last grand Seal to their intentions.

It is further to be observed that such Public Printed Notice is a
complete Libel, and must evidently tend to render manifest the
Union of effort that has been employed to my Injury By Mr. John
Blaxland and the other Defendants ultimately to Stamp upon the
Transaction that has given rise to this Prosecution, its full and
Specific Import, as being the effect of premeditated malice, garnished
with all the Circumstances of Perfidy and oppression.

Confident that from my Profession in Life I could not be considered as experienced or at all conversant with the routine of
legal procedure, and that it consequently behoved me in Justice to
myself to employ a Person whose capacity herein was more extended, I made my Election of Such Person who was immediately
Subpoena'd by the Defendants, with no other obvious intention
than to deprive me of his assistance certainly, every Man who considers himself in dangerous circumstances may be excused for
endeavouring to avoid his danger. But strange as it may appear,
Gentlemen, when I have submitted to this one Essay of Chicanery,
and had made election of a second Person, as my Assistant before
this Honorable Court, Scarcely had we exchanged a Sentence on the
business, before a Subpoena was likewise Served on him at the
Defendants' Summons; and this Second act was certainly convincing, that the Perversion of Justice was more the Defendants'
object than the Evidence of the Parties.

Gentlemen, I vouch to prove all I have asserted; and I am conscious that your exalted Sentiments of honor. Truth, and Justice
will by an impartial verdict Secure the Safety of a Commander
against The future Attacks of a Body of interested Persons who
have conspired to destroy him; and at the Same time, by Such an
Instance of your Justice convince the World. that Rank and
affluence are alike incapable of influencing Gentlemen, who are Men
of Honour by Character and Profession; that you are capable of dispensing with every relative Consideration of Circumstances between
Man and Man, and that the exalted Criminal who dares infract his
Country's Laws, Shall at the Same time draw upon him their disgust,
and leave only to your most revered Consideration, the measure of
Punishment which ought in Justice to await the Crime.

1808.
30 April.

Proceedings at the trial of John and Gregory Blaxland and Simeon Lord.

Gentlemen, You are well informed that in preference to Indictment at the Suit of the King, I might by Civil Actions have Sued for Pecuniary compensation for the Injury I complain of. And I trust, Gentlemen, that the mode I have adopted will Sufficiently evince my disinterestedness, and confirm my Declaration, that it is for the love of Justice I prosecute.

That Mr. John Blaxland is a part Owner of the Ship Brothers (under my Command) I am ready to acknowledge as He likewise must do that I have ever respected him as such While it was nevertheless incumbent on me to consider myself as Commander of that Ship, and by no means open to any controul exceeding that of an Agent—as I do not know Mr. John Blaxland himself in any other relative Capacity—Whereas my Instructions which are fully comprehensive, vest in me Such powers that are far Superior to any that can be claimed by virtue of any Agency whatever—Mr. Gregory Blaxland, and His Coadjutor Mr. Lord, have in this instance likewise taken false refuge; and will I trust as non-accreditted Persons, acting without any Species of authoritative right, receive Such Judgement as, in Your impartiallity shall be esteemed their due.

Gentlemen, Permit me to offer to your impartial View the unaccountable conceptions which Mr. John Blaxland must have entertained of the Powers vested in the Sacred Commission of a Magistrate; as a Conservator of the Peace, that Gentleman was empowered by every means within the extent of his ability to preserve the Peace, and to Summon every legal aid in his Support therein, but how far perverted have his notions been! in his own behalf, it was his fond belief, that he could exercise his Powers in every Situation, without considering some little change of Process, necessary to be observed on Ship board and on Shore. But this Magistrate, considering the Authority derived from his Commission as paramount to any other Species of authority, with a Temerity approaching turpitude itself placing himself at the Head of two Persons, who had not even been admitted into the Sydney Watch, in a daring tempestuous Manner, laid violent hands on the astonished Prosecutor, While Simeon Lord, like the renowned Bobadil, danced round him with a brandished Cane.

Gentlemen, I shall no further trespass on your Patience than to state to you, among other Practices, The Evidence for the Prosecution will leave no doubt on your minds that Mr. John Blaxland notwithstanding his Worshipful Authority has either directly or indirectly endeavoured to influence the testimony of the Seamen of the Ship Brothers, by the exhibition of threats on the one part, and of promises upon the other. He has likewise, by virtue of his own authority procured a Survey to be made of the Ship Brothers, which is little short of a violation of a right vested in the Lieutenant Governor only; and committed innumerable other extravagancies, which prevent the possibility, as the Prosecutor must conceive, of His escaping Justice except upon the plea of Lunacy; for a previous Survey had actually been taken by order of the Lieutenant Governor, without whose authority it became a violent Trespass on decorum and contempt of the first Authority—Gentlemen, I will also prove to you that the very moment previous to the Commission of this outrage upon my Person on board my Ship I had received the Defendants in the most polite and hospitable manner, but that they, intent upon the mischief, used every opprobrium in order to irritate

1808.
30 April.

Proceedings at
the trial of
John and
Gregory
Blaxland and
Simeon Lord.

my temper and give colour to their design; that the Defendant,
Lord, who had no business on board that Ship, had the contumacy
to apply the Epithets of Thief, Rogue, and Damned Cowardly
Scoundrel to the Prosecutor; that the Prosecutor's Teeth were
threatened to be driven down his Throat by Gregory Blaxland;
that both the Defendants (Blaxlands) attacked and violently pushed
and drove him from the Mizen Mast to the taff rail while the
Prosecutor was in momentary expectation of a Salute from the
impending bludgen of Mr. Lord—That the Defendant John Blaxland,
commanded the Ship's Company to leave their duty wherever they
might be stationed, and come forward in order to assist him in
binding the *Villain Russell*; but that the People, who bore evidence
to the illiberal deportment of the Defendant, John Blaxland, declined
complying with that order, by reason of their utter disapprobation
of his Conduct and their extreme concern for the Prosecutor. That
upon the Evening of Thursday the 17th instant the Defendant John
Blaxland, was applied to by some of the Seamen for Money on
account, and received for answer that he would be on board the
next day to take possession of the Ship; when he would Summon
the Ship's Company aft, and if they *Sided* with him and *obeyed
Such orders as he would then give*, they might have *whatever
Money they might want* : But upon their non-compliance, they should
not have any Money; and moreover, *that he would stop their Wages
in Great Britain.* That Simeon Lord did actually declare that "if
Justice was administered in New South Wales, the prosecutor
would be hanged" and that He was in other respects not only
privy to the assault, but the most opprobrious of the Assailants,
and in fact too a very principal in the act itself in promoting,
encouraging, aiding and abetting therein and at the same time
blinding with his heterogenous Concequence a number of legal
precedents to Justify their unwarrantable acts; That the Prosecutor, after having in the first instance hospitally received the
Defendants without any Species of Provocation Submitted to their
Invectives, and with a degree of Patience Scarcely to be imitated,
Chose rather to put his trust in the Laws of his Country, than
to Suffer any momentary Impulse to get the better of his Tem-
perance; and that after all these Injuries So cool and so deliberate
was the Prosecutor in his own Acts that after this very unfriendly
treatment, he had received from the Defendants—he ordered a
Boat to be manned for their accomodation when they were ready
to go on Shore—That the Defendant, John Blaxland, had actually
attempted to excite the Ship's Company to Mutiny, by declaring to
some of them that in consequence of their obedience to his orders
should they be sent to Gaol, he would Support them there, and go
hither with them himself.

Gentlemen, as Prosecutor in this Serious Charge against the
Defendants, I have exhibited my Complaint to your impartial View.
The Circumstances of the Case I have thus respectfully laid before
you. As Englishmen, I know you Enemies to oppression, as Men
of Honor, I know you susceptible of those Superior feelings which
do credit to a British Juror. From your impartial Verdict I expect
redress for a most grievous attack upon my priviledges in Society;
to the Evidence I am now to adduce I rest the merits of the Case.

Most respectfully, &c.,

Sydney, 28th March, 1808.   OLIVER RUSSELL.

To The Honorable Court of Criminal Jurisdiction, &c., &c., &c.

1808.
30 April.

Proceedings at
the trial of
John and
Gregory
Blaxland and
Simeon Lord.

Mr. Oliver Russell respectfully begs leave to State to this Honorable Court—that he hath Occasion for the Assistance of Some Person more conversant than himself with the routine of legal Procedure to aid him in Support of this Prosecution; and did therefore make Election of a Person to whom he confided all the relative Circumstances of his Case: But that in order to deprive him of Such necessary assistance, the Person to whom he herein alludes has been Subpoena'd to give Testimony on the Defendants' Side. That Supposing himself of necessity obliged to dispense with Such Assistance, he did make application to a Second, and he has also been Subpoena'd, with no other possible view than to preclude the possibility of the Prosecutor's conducting his complaint in legal form. He therefore beggeth leave to urge it as a Maxim of British Law, that an Agent cannot be examined against his principal because he is bound to keep his Secrets; Secondly that the Defendants cannot of right demand that their Evidence should be examined apart, But crave it as an indulgence which the Court may grant, an Application, which in the present instance would be highly injurious to the Ends of Public Justice. The Prosecutor therefore Prays that he may be permitted Such Assistance, and that if the Testimony of such Assistant be really necessary to the Defendants' Case, the Prosecutor may likewise have the Priviledge of his Evidence, and that he may be admitted as His first Evidence before this Honorable Court Albeit that the Defendants may have the benefit of their Cross Examination and the Prosecutor have the benefit of his assistance afterwards.

Most respectfully, &c.,

March 28th, 1808.   OLIVER RUSSELL.

Q. by Deft. Lord. At what time and place was it that I shook my Stick over your Head; and demanded as you say whether you would comply with Mr. Jno. Blaxland's request to accomodate him with what accomodation he wished—as he was part Owner and Super Cargo and would go home Commander of the Ship?

A. On the afternoon of the 19th Inst. on the Quarter Deck after being Seized by the two Mr. Blaxlands and forced against the Fife Rail you stood before me with a lifted Stick and repeated the words as before Stated and threatened on my non compliance to cut me down or knock me down.

Q. Who was present?

A. Mr. Daniels acting Chief Officer, James Roof Cooper, the Carpenter, The Cabin Boy, and Eliz. Guest.

Q. Was Jno. Goodsold nearer than the Carpenter or Cooper?

A. I did not see him at that time.

Q. Was it before or after Eliz. Guest came out of the Cabin.

A. She was standing on the Cabin Gang way ladder.

Q. Was Henry Purdie the Cabin Boy on Deck at the time?

A. He was standing in the Gang way with Eliz. Guest.

Q. Where was Mr. Daniels standing at the time?

A. Endeavouring to extricate me from the two Mr. Blaxlands.

Q. Did you not when Mr. John Blaxland and myself came on board the Brothers with Captains Bunker and Smith to Survey the Ship Brothers to ascertain if she could carry more Skins inform Mr. Blaxland that if He would lett you know who was going to England with him you would prepare accordingly.

1808.
30 April.

Proceedings at
the trial of
John and
Gregory
Blaxland and
Simeon Lord. ·

A. I did.

Q. Did you make any terms for the accomodation he might want?

A. No.

Q. Was there any conversation about what Sum was to be paid?

A. No.

Q. Was there not an allowance made for a certain quantity of Water to be put on board for the use of four Persons who were to accompany Mr. Blaxland to England—at the time of the Survey?

A. There was room reserved for Water for extra Passengers and Stock.

Q. Did not Mr. J. Blaxland on coming on board on the 19th ask you why you would not receive the Skins on Board according to the Report of Survey?

A. No.

Q. Did you not ask Mr. J. Blaxland what Cabin he did want?

A. No.

Q. Did not Mr. J. Blaxland point out to you that he wished to have the Cabin on the Starboard Side—and did you not reply that if he had that Cabin and half the great Cabin he should pay for it and then to go home as a Passenger and further that unless he behaved properly you would confine him to his Cabin and if after that He continued to behave ill you would put him in Irons?

A. The Starboard Cabin was pointed out and I informed Mr. Blaxland that if He had that and half the great Cabin He should pay for it—and that He should go as Passenger only—I made use of no threats.

Q. Was you asked what you wanted for the State Room—and that as He could mess with you he did not wish the great Cabin to be divided?

A. I do not recollect the Conversation.

Q. Did you not before Mr. Ellison came on board say you would be paid £200 down before Mr. Blaxland came on board and that he might have half the great Cabin?

A. I recollect such Conversation taking place after Mr. Ellison came on Board—but do not recollect any Conversation on the Subject prior.

Q. Was you not immediately informed that Mr. Blaxland would not comply with your terms—and that he required you to point out his accomodation as part Owner—that he might set his Carpenter to work—and that if there was anything to be paid for his Passage it should be Settled with the Owner in England?

A. I do not recollect any such conversation.

Q. Did you not then Say—that I suppose you are come to tie me to my Cabin and take my Ship from me as you threatened to Mr. Daniels Yesterday? .

A. Such Words might have passed—as I was informed by Mr. Daniels that such threats had been made.

Q. Did you not on Mr. Blaxland and myself denying making use of any threats to Mr. Daniels call us both Liars and Say that you would prove it?

A. No.

Q. Was not Mr. Daniels called from the Cabin and asked if Mr. Blaxland or myself had made use of any threats of tying you and · did not Mr. Daniels deny having given you such information?

A. Yes.

1808.
30 April.

Proceedings at
the trial of
John and
Gregory
Blaxland and
Simeon Lord.

Q. Was you not immediately informed of the Words made use of to Mr. Daniels Vizt. that Mr. Blaxland had said if Captain Russell continued to behave as improperly as He had done—that he should take all legal means in his Mr. J. Blaxland's power to confine him to his Cabin and take him home a Prisoner; and that if He could not get Authority—that he should (as Owner) appoint another Captain to that Ship before the Judge Advocate which he Mr. Blaxland considered he had Authority to do without consulting any Person?

A. No.

Q. Did you not reply to Lord I like to hear Gun fart " and that I wish I had a Billy Goat to Beat Mr. J. Blaxland " go home and sell your Milk and Cabbage and not interfere with my Ship making use of violent Guistures at the time by striking the Companion and Boom with a Rope?

A. The conversation did take place—and in concequence of abusive Language made use of to me—the threat of the Billy Goat I cannot recollect but it might have happened.

Q. Was it not in concequence of the above Language that Mr. Gregory Blaxland said that they had come on board to ask civil Questions and that they expected civil Answers—and not abuse?

A. No.

Q. Did you not immediately advance as if going into the Cabin, or to meet Gregory Blaxland and did not Jno. Blaxland step in between you to prevent any quarrel?

A. Mr. Gregory Blaxland advanced to me and took me by the Shoulder and shoved me back on the Fife Rail—when Mr. Jno. Blaxland caught hold on my other Shoulder.

Q. Did I (Lord) on Mr. Daniels going up to rescue Capt. Russell say that they were not going to hurt Mr. Russell but to prevent his going into the Cabin to fetch Arms?

A. I do not recollect.

Q. Was it at the time Mr. Daniels came up to you and the two Blaxlands had hold on you that I lifted up my Stick and threatened to cut or knock you down, and made use of the Conversation you have before Sworn to?

A. Yes.

Q. Was Eliz. Guest standing on the Cabin Gang way at that time?

A. Yes.

Q. Did I not sit on the Starboard Railing or Stand close to the Mizen Shrouds from the time that the words ensued ·between Gregory Blaxland and you and that you was collared until Eliz. Guest came out of the Cabin and attempted to scratch Jno. Blaxland?

A. No.

Q. Did I not on Eliz. Guest coming out of the Cabin and laying hold of Jno. Blaxland quit my situation on the side of the Ship and advance to her and raise my Stick at her, and tell her she had no business there and called her a damned Bitch?

A. No.

Q. Did you not desire her to be gone and on doing So did I not return to the Side of the Ship?

A. No.

Q. Was I not close to the Side of the Ship when the two Blaxlands lett you go on condition of your getting no fire Arms?

A. You was sitting on the Fife Rail.

1808.
30 April.

Proceedings at
the trial of
John and
Gregory
Blaxland and
Simeon Lord.

Q. Did you not go into the Cabin and bring up a Stick and Eliz. Guest follow you on deck to prevent you making use of it and did you not say on your return to the Deck that you had brought a Stick as Mr. Lord had one and you had nothing else to defend yourself with?

A. I did bring up a Stick—and Said I had as much right to wear a Stick as any Person on board as I was Comm'r of the Ship and that S. Lord replied You are a damned Coward or you would make use of it.—I do not recollect if Eliz. Guest followed—but Soon after I ordered her below.

Q. On your Saying that you had nothing but a Stick to defend yourself with did I not offer you my Stick to keep during my Stay if you was affraid of it—say that I knew better than make use of it on board the Ship?

A. You offered me your Stick—but I declined receiving it Saying I had a Stick of my own and knew how to make use of it when I thought proper.

Q. Did you make any complaint to Lieut. Ellison when he came on Board of your having been Assaulted?

A. I do not recollect making any complaint to Lieut. Ellison.

Q. Did not Mr. Gregory Blaxland on Mr. Ellison coming on board say that he had taken the liberty of sending for him to keep peace and be present until his Brother asked Captain Russell some civil questions as they could get nothing but abuse: instead of civil Answers?

A. Conversation to that purpose took place.

Q. Why did you not at that time complain to Lieut. Ellison of your having been assaulted, instead of taking us into the Cabin to settle about the terms of Mr. J. Blaxland's Passage?

A. I thought it would be more regular to make a complaint before a Magistrate on Shore.

Q. Did Mr. J. Blaxland at any time that he was on board say that he was a Magistrate, or that he was acting as a Magistrate that day meaning 19th Inst.?

A. No.

Q. Did you not on my going over the Ship's Side desire me if I ever came on Board your Ship again to leave my Stick on Shore, and did I not offer to leave it then with you, until the Ship Sailed if you was affraid of it?

A. I desired you to leave your Stick on Shore if you ever came on board my Ship—you replied you was in the Habit of wearing a Stick and was ready to meet me at any time on Shore—but you did not offer to leave it on board.

Q. Did you not on my offering you my Stick Say that you had one of your Own, and that you would make use of it when you mett me on Shore?

A. No.

Q. Did you not before you went to complain to the Magistrates See John McArthur Esqre. and receive advice to make an Affidavit to that effect—that you did?

A. I did See Mr. McArthur and believe he advised me to go to the Magistrate's to make a complaint (the following is a Copy).

" Captain Russell of the Ship Brothers came before the Bench and complained that John Blaxland Esqre. Mr. Gregory Blaxland and Mr. Simeon Lord came on board the Brothers this Day and after using very provoking Language Mr. Gregory Blaxland Seized him by the Collar on the left Side when Mr. John Blaxland seized him on the other Side whilst Mr. S. Lord Shook a Stick over his head and demanded whether he would comply with their request to furnish Mr. J. Blaxland with what accomodations he wished as He was Owner Supercargoe and would go home Commander of the Ship —That Captain Russell requesting to be liberated was let at large on conditions of not making use of any Fire Arms, on any pretence whatever—with much other violent Language.

1808.
30 April.

Proceedings at the trial of John and Gregory Blaxland and Simeon Lord.

" Sworn before us this 19th March 1808 and 22d do.
" (Signed)   J. HARRIS.
" Oliver Russell."   " THOS. JAMISON.

Q. Was the Letter produced dictated by Mr. McArthur Vizt. :—
" Mr. Blaxland.
" Sir,
" I received your Letter the 2d Inst. Requesting me to give up the Command of the Ship Brothers of London now lying at Anchor in Sydney Cove. In Answer to which I am Sorry to Say: in doing Justice to my Employers in England I cannot Submit to any Such order; therefore take such Steps as you think proper and act accordingly.   ·   " Respectfully Yours,
" O. RUSSELL, Commander Ship Brothers.
" Sydney Cove, 2d March, 1808."

A. No.
Q. Did Mr. McArthur advise you to write the Memorial produced?
A. No.
Q. Do you Swear that neither the Letter or Memorial above alluded to were dictated or advised to be sent by Mr. McArthur?
Court cleared at the request of the Prosecutor on the propriety of Answering the above Question.
The Court are of opinion that you " *have already answered that question Separately—therefore see no reason why you should not answer the present one* "*—must Answer the question having Answered the Question Separately before.
A. No.
Q. Was the Letter No. 5 advised to be written by Mr. McArthur?
A. No.
Q. Did you not receive from Mr. McArthur (thro' Capt. Smith) message how to act before the Bench of Magistrates when bro't forward on the charges exhibited by Mr. Blaxland?
A. No.
Q. Did not Captain Smith send a Note to you when the Bench of Magistrates were Sitting before your Trial came on?
A. Yes and I went out to him.
Q. Did Captain Smith leave you and return again before you went into the Bench?
A. I do not recollect.
Q. Was the conversation you had with Captain Smith relative to the business coming on before the Bench?
A. Yes.
Q. Did he make use of Mr. McArthur's Name recommending you what to Say?
A. No, to the best of my recollection.

* In the original the words in italics were scored through.

1808.
30 April·

Proceedings at
the trial of
John and
Gregory
Blaxland and
Simeon Lord.

Q. You mean positively to Swear that you received no advice from Mr. McArthur thro' Captain Smith at that time or since respecting the business between yourself and Mr. Jno. Blaxland?

A. To the best of my Recollection—never.

Q. Letter marked E. Produced Vizt.

" Sir,

" I request you will have the goodness to accept the enclosed Bills as I insist they are Ship accounts, and nothing relative to my private concerns; therefore as part Owner and Agent of the Ship Brothers—you will honor the Bills or I shall be under the disagreable necessity of drawing to that amount prior to leaving the Colony—the amount is £89 14s. 0d.

" I am, Sir,

" John Blaxland, Esqre., " Your Obe't Serv't,

" Sydney, 17th March, 1808. " O. RUSSELL.

" P.S.—An Answer as Soon as convenient is required.—O.R."

Q. Was you advised to write that Letter by Mr. McArthur and to enclose to Mr. Blaxland receipts from the Seamen for Money advanced by you—as if advanced by Mr. Jno. Blaxland?

A. No.

Q. Did not Mr. McArthur offer to furnish you with money *to pay those Receipts** if Mr. Blaxland on your writing to him *would not** and enclosing the receipts; refused to advance it?

*A. Mr. McArthur offered to advance me Money on my own Acc't on my application which money I meant to appropriate in part payment of the Sums advanced to the Seamen—and to pay my private Debts, and I informed Mr. McArthur that I should be detained if the Money was not paid.**

A. Yes.

Q. Did you write the Letter marked† after being offered by Mr. McArthur to have any Money advanced?

A. Yes.

Q. Was you not positively refused to employ Persons to get Wood charged in the above Letter?

A. Yes.

Q. Was you not advised by Some Persons from the time that Mr. Blaxland was on board at the Survey—and the 19th Instant to demand Money from him for his Passage in the Brothers.

A. No.

Q. Are not you and all the Officers and Crew on lays or Shares of what the Brothers may earn during her Voyage from the time she left Port Jackson?

A. Yes.

Q. Are you intitled to a greater Share than your lay of Money received for Passengers?

A. Yes it is the custom that the Master and Owner divide it.

Q. Have you a right to any part of the Passage Money before the Ship arrives in England?

A. It is customary to pay the money before the Ship Sails.

Q. Have you any authority to demand from· the Principal Owner and Agent who you admit as such £200—before you will receive him on board as a Passenger in this Port?

A. No.

* In the original the words in italics were scored through.
† *Marginal note.—See* No. 8.

1808.
30 April.

Proceedings at
the trial of
John and
Gregory
Blaxland and
Simeon Lord.

Q. What was your reason for demanding the 200£ from Mr. Blaxland when he came on board by your own Agreement with his Carpenter to make the Alterations he wished—and to Say that you would not receive him as an Owner but as a Passenger only?

A. I demanded the £200 for giving up my Sleeping place and half the Cabin—I never said I would not receive him as an Owner.

Q. Did you at the time of the Second Survey make any objections to Captain Scotts doing the duty as Mate—as you did not like Mr. Hazelburg doing duty again, as the Owner must pay Scott wages untill he returned to England?

A. I did not object taking Scott as 2d Officer.

Q. Is the Letter produced your writing Vizt.

" Sir,

" In regard to the Survey held on board the Brothers the 12th of February I admit the remainder part of the Stores which are Seven Whale Lines ought to have been sent on Shore, but not knowing whether they would be accepted as the other Stores lay in the Boat 36 Hours on Shore with a Guard from the Ship before any Person would receive them—then I got grossly abused from Simeon Lord for sending them.

" And as for your Second Survey I deem it not legal as it was not an order from the present Governor.—but be that as it May I was not sent to New South Wales—after Oil or Skins taken by any Ship or Crew except the Brothers—and as you have a Copy of my Sailing Instructions, from the Gentlemen that appointed me Commander of the Ship Brothers (read them) where I am specially ordered to procure a full Cargo of Spermaceti Oil and Seals Skins—therefore as you wish to make it appear that I have not done my Endeavour relative to that order, I request you to furnish the Ship with a quantity of Salt and Provisions that I may Cruise two Months longer on the Coast, That I may gett what you call a full Cargo thence to proceed to England.

" Concerning Captain Scott I can never think of taking him to England in the capacity of an Officer and even he is not a Safe Person to be in a Ship in any Shape whatever unless better guarded than the Brothers—You will recollect some days prior to our Arrival at Saldana Bay when he done his utmost to seduce the People to Mutiny even took them abaft on the Quarter Deck and requested to know what course the Ship was steered and at the Same time said he had bro't a Man to bear Witness—and further Said if they were all of his Mind he would immediately go into the Cabin and put a Stop to it—and before I will ever take him on Board the Brothers I must report him to the Governor and in course the truth will come to light. " I am, &c., &c.,

" John Blaxland, Esqre., " O. RUSSELL.

" Sydney, 18 March, 1808."

A. Yes.

Court adjourned till 9 OClock Tomorrow Morning.
29th Court met.

MR. OLIVER RUSSELL Sworn—Paper marked No. 7 Produced by the Prosecutor read (Vizt.) :—

To The Honorable Court of Criminal Jurisdiction.

Gentlemen,

From the number of irrelevances that have already been obtruded upon your Patience—I am thoroughly at a loss to imagine

1808.
30 April.
Proceedings at
the trial of
John and
Gregory
Blaxland and
Simeon Lord.

upon what Grounds the Defendants propose to Sett up a Justifying Plea : If it be their design to defend themselves against the Prosecutor's challenge of Assault by torturing his Evidence with nugatory Interrogatories purposely contrived to entangle them in what the Defendants may afterwards expound to be contradictory assertions, permit me to pray Of this most honorable Court that both the Prosecutor and the Defendants may by your decree be bound to adhere to the matters now before the Court, without being permitted to protract the event by the Introduction of any matter that May be considered foreign to the charge exhibited.

Gentlemen—An Indictment has been prefered against the Defendants : I have given testimony upon the matter of complaint and have likewise been obligated to make Answers to questions perfectly indiferent—and I therefore crave to be permitted to proceed therein without interruption agreable to the Indictm't. The Defendants have already endeavoured by an enquiry perfectly Foreign to the Subject to bewilder the Evidence upon a plain and Simple fact, it is very far from my wish Gentlemen that a Single circumstance should go unravelled that can in any wise benefit the Defendants— But as the ends of Justice only bring me forward, I crave your countenance and trust that I may be So far protected as to be defended from . Insult before this Honorable Court—I have not offered myself an Evidence in my own Cause—I presented a Statement of my Grievances, and prepared to prove upon the Evidence. I humbly contend Gentlemen that the Defendant Mr. Lord has no Authority by Law to Question me beyond the extent of my charge on which the Indictment is framed. And I Sincerely trust you will permit me to proceed with proof to Establish the Assault for which the Defendants stand at your Barr under such charge.

Gentlemen,

I do not come forward as a turgid Prosecutor, intent upon any Man's destruction—I only crave Protection of the Laws, If my charge be substantiated Your Verdict will be my future Security— for conscious every Man must be that thus Secured the Defendants will be convinced that they have erred and thenceforth relinquish every Effort to my Prejudice.

Most respectfully, &c.,

29th March, 1808.   OLIVER RUSSELL.

Court cleared on the propriety of the Prayer.—Are of opinion that they are ready to hear your evidence to prove all the grievances you state you are prepared to bring forward in your Statement of Yesterday.

M. J. Blaxland. Q. Did you not call me a Liar on board the Brothers when I denyed the Conversation that you Said passed between Mr. Daniels and myself a day or two prior to my going on board?

A. No.

Q. You have Sworn that I said I would go home Commander, Supercargo and Owner as you know I have no Knowledge of Navigation how could you Suppose it Possible that I should make use of Such expressions?

A. You did make use of the above expressions.

Q. Who was present when I made use of those expressions?

A. Mr. Gregory Blaxland and Mr. Lord in the Ship's Cabin.

Q. Was Mr. Ellison present?

A. No.

Q. You said you did not call me a Liar but that you called Mr. Lord a Liar?

A. Yes.

Q. Was it before or after Mr. Daniels was called out of the Cabin that you called Mr. Lord a Liar?

A. I do not recollect.

Q. Was it not in concequence of that abuse that I went between you and my Brother to prevent any irregularity?

A. No.

Q. You have sworn that my Brother and myself held you till you complied with our request?

A. Yes.

Q. What was the request?

A. That I would not make use of Fire Arms and in concequence of my making that Promise you released me.

Q. How long did we hold you?

A. About five minutes.

Q. Was any other violence offered you or any other request made to you than that you should not go below to gett Arms?

A. Yes while you and your Brother held me, Mr. S. Lord requested that I would comply with J. Blaxland's request to give up my Sleeping Cabin and half the great Cabin.

Q. You have sworn that Mr. S. Lord at the time he made the above request held a Stick over your head, demanding that you should comply with my request?

A. Yes.

Q. Was anything said about a Stick until you brought one up on the Deck?

A. No.

Q. Did you send for Lieut. Ellison?

A. No.

Q. Was not Lieut. Ellison in the Cabin all the time we three *Persons** were there?

A. I do not recollect.

Q. Was it not on the Deck before Mr. Ellison came on board that you called Mr. Lord a Liar?

A. Yes.

The Court cleared on the Shameful prevarication of Mr. Oliver Russell—The Court do not conceive it amounts to direct and Wilful Perjury.

From Mr. Blaxland. Q. Did not Mr. Lord immediately Answer that you must not call me a Liar in any place but the Quarter deck or before a Bench of Magistrates or words to that effect?

A. I do not recollect.

Q. You have stated before the Magistrates of this Colony that you had no knowledge of me for Six Weeks after you had the Command of the Ship Brothers?

A. Declines Answering the above Question—waved by the Defendant.

Q. Did not Mr. McArthur inform you before the Bench of Magistrates when we were committed, that if you had taken his good

1808.
30 April.

Proceedings at
the trial of
John and
Gregory
Blaxland and
Simeon Lord.

* This word in italics was scored through in the original.

1808.
30 April.

Proceedings at
the trial of
John and
Gregory
Blaxland and
Simeon Lord.

advice you would not have written that threatening Letter—stating
you must have recourse to the Keel of the Ship (Vizt.) :—

" Sir,
    " I beg you will send an Answer to my request this Morning
in regard of the Bills which were presented of Money advanced to
people on board, on Ship account, and if you will not honor them
I positively declare they must be paid—therefore should be sorry to
be compelled to have recourse to the Keel, *Likewise the Bill for the
Wood.*   " Yours respectfully,
" Sydney, 18th March, 1808.   " (Signed)   O. RUSSELL.
    " (Directed) John Blaxland, Esqre., Sydney."

A. Words to that Effect did pass.

Q. Have you not already Sworn that you had never received any
Advice from Mr. McArthur, either from himself or thro' Capt.
Smith or otherwise?

Prosecutor Objects to Answer the above Question on the ground
that it will criminate himself.

Q. Have you not been often at Mr. McArthur's House consulting
him Since you was accused of improper conduct by me particularly
on 5th March?

Prosecutor Declines Answering the above Question on the ground
that it will criminate himself.

Q. Did you not tell Mr. Glanville late Mate of the City of Edinburgh who you was going to Ship as 2d Mate of the Brothers that
you was going to give up the Command of the Ship on the 1st or 2d
of March and that you desired him to apply to me for employment?

A. I never told Mr. Glanville that I should give up the Ship, and
I do not recollect desiring him to go to Mr. Blaxland.

Q. Have you any other instructions from Hullett and Brothers
as Commander of the Brothers than those of the 11th and 22nd of
September, 1806?

A. I received one Instruction from the Hulletts, and a Copy said
to be from them of another which I received at Sea from Mr. J.
Blaxland and I did not See the Original.

Q. Had you conducted Yourself improperly in England, would not
Hullett and Brothers have turned you out of the Ship Brothers?

A. Yes.

Q. Provided they were in this Colony could they do the Same?

A. No.

Q. What is the reason you resist my Authority as you acknowledge that I am the managing Owner and Agent in this Colony?

A. You not having authority to dispossess me of my Command
of the Brothers.

From the Court Q. Have you authority to refuse giving a Passage
to the Principal Owner and Agent in this Colony in the Ship
Brothers for the purpose of going to England with his own property?

A. No, nor never did, except that I demanded £200 as Passage
Money or that I was ready to Submit it to Arbitration.

Q. Had you the Power to turn Mr. Blaxland out of the Ship on
your Arrival here supposing that he did not chuse to go on Shore?

A. Yes.

Q. How was Mr. Blaxland received on board the Brothers in
England?

A. As part Owner and Passenger.

1808.
30 April.

Proceedings at
the trial of
John and
Gregory
Blaxland and
Simeon Lord.

From Mr. J. Blaxland Q. Did I not on my refusing to pay £200 for the accomodation you offered me desired that you would point out some Place for me that my Carpenter might fit up?

A. No.

Q. Why did you not bring Mr. Hazelburg forward to the charges you had confined him for—on your Arrival in this Harbour as Hazelburg requested himself in writing—and myself verbally?

A. I shipped Mr. Hazelburg in England; I thought it proper to take him back there to have him tried for his misconduct.

Q. Was it not in this Port that you found the Ship on fire—by Mr. Hazelburg's neglect as you have stated also Some of the Charges you alledge against him were committed here?

A. The Ship being on Fire was in this Port.

Q. Why was you going to Ship a Second Officer when Messrs. Hazelburg and Scott were here Officers belonging to the Concern and I had informed you that it was necessary they should go home?

A. Mr. Hazelburgh was under Arrest and I did not think Scott capable of doing duty as Chief Officer—nor would I receive him as an Officer, but do not recollect refusing to receive Scott as a Passenger.

ROBERT DANIELS Sworn—acting Chief Officer:—

By Prosecutor Q. Was you on board the Brothers when the Defendants came on board, relate what passed?

A. I was between Decks when they came on board and about a quarter of an hour after—I was called by Mr. Lord to come on Deck, on coming up I found the Captain and the Defendants talking loudly but do not recollect the particular Words—I was asked by Mr. J. Blaxland if I had informed the Captain that he (meaning J. Blaxland) was coming on board the Ship to tie the Captain—I informed Mr. Blaxland that I had told the Captain that he was coming to put him under an Arrest—Words ensued between the Defendants and the Captain from his abusing the Defendants and Mr. G. Blaxland told the Captain that He would knock his teeth down his throat—The Captain Said He (Mr. G. Blaxland) had no business with it—when Mr. G. Blaxland said that he (Capt. Russell) had insulted his Brother and he would take up his cause—when Mr. G. Blaxland advanced towards the Captain and collared him on one Side, and at the Same instant Mr. J. Blaxland caught the Captain by the Collar—I then went up to endeavour to part them and caught the Captain by one Collar and Mr. J. Blaxland by the Arm desiring them to lett go which they did and the Captain attempting to go down the Cabin Ladder the two Mr. Blaxlands stepped between the Capt: and the Gang way to prevent him—and made the Captain promise not to get Fire Arms—during all which time Simeon Lord was leaning on the quarter Rail—from which Situation he did not move, but I saw him lift his Stick but not in a threatening manner but why he did it I do not know—I was between the Captain and Mr. Lord with my back towards Lord nor did I hear Lord say anything—I was not apprehensive of Lords meaning to use any violence—On Captain Russell promising not to get fire Arms he was admitted to go down and brought up a Stick; at the time the two Blaxlands had hold of the Captain, Eliz. Guest and the Cabin Boy were at the bottom of the Companion Ladder, but could See on the Deck—The Cooper was at the brick of the Quarter Deck all the time; Eliz. Guest before the

1808.
30 April.

Proceedings at
the trial of
John and
Gregory
Blaxland and
Simeon Lord.

two Blaxlands lett the Captain go came on Deck and screamed
when Lord asked what business She had there, and his Stick was
lifted—he was angry and advanced a pace nearer to Eliz. Guest but
further from the parties Scuffling, and called her a damned Bitch
but I did not See Lord attempt to Strike her or any body else—or
threaten to strike any Body and had he made a blow I was the
nearest Person; on Captain Russell coming on Deck with a Stick he
said He had as much right to wear a Stick as any Person on board, as
long as He commanded, to which no reply was made by any Person
—about five minutes after Mr. Ellison came on board; what passed
I do not know, being forward with the People but after walking a
short time they all went into the Cabin and I was not in the Cabin
at all—neither of the Blaxlands or Lord went into the Cabin before
Mr. Ellison came on board. On Mr. Lord going away I was over the
side, Captain Russell desired him if ever He came on board again
to leave his Stick—when Lord offered to leave it at that time with
him, until the Ship Sailed if He was affraid of it.

Court adjourned till 9 o'Clock Tomorrow.

30th March 1808 Court met.

ROBERT DANIELS Sworn :—

From Prosecutor Q. Did not the two Blaxlands push me violently
from the Mizen Mast to the Fife Rail?

A. Yes.

Q. Did either of the Prisoners say that I was Thief Rogue or
Scoundrel?

A. Mr. Lord called you a Thief and said he could prove it which
happened after the Captain brought his Stick up.

Q. Did Captain Russell during the time the Prisoners were
aboard give any Offence to them?

A. Yes—by desiring Mr. J. Blaxland to go home and Sell his
Pigs, and sell His Milk and butter; which happened when I was
on the Main deck.

Q. Did you hear Mr. J. Blaxland tell me that he could confine
me to my Cabin, and that he would go home himself Master or
Commander of the Ship?

A. No.

Q. Did Mr. J. Blaxland at the time the Prisoners were on Board
on the 19th call the Ship's Company aft to seize the Captain?

A. Mr. Jno. Blaxland called the Ship's Company forward to assist
which happened after the Capt: brought up his Stick; but there
was no quarrelling between the Parties at the time—no words
were made use of to seize the Captain.

Q. Did the Captain at any time threaten the Prisoners to make
use of Fire Arms?

A. No.

Q. On hearing that the Prisoners were coming on Board—did you
say to the Captain they were coming?

A. I said " Now we shall have it " Supposing that from what I
heard Mr. Blaxland say the day before that there would be words
between the Captain and him.

From Prisoners Q. Was you at Lord's House on the 18th instant
respecting the Ship's business when Mr. J. Blaxland and Lord told
you of many acts Captain Russell was accused of and which you
Said you never heard of before?

A. Yes.

1808.
30 April.

Proceedings at
the trial of
John and
Gregory
Blaxland and
Simeon Lord.

Q. Did We not inform you that if He (Capt: R.) did not behave better that Mr. J. Blaxland would be obliged to take every legal means to get authority to supercede him, but if he could not get authority that he should be under the necessity of giving the Command to the Mate or Some other Person by laying regular Papers before the Judge Advocate, and carry the Capt: a Prisoner to England, which Steps ought to have been taken before,—or words to the Same meaning?

A. Mr. John Blaxland said he had tried all he could to Supercede Capt. Russell without effect but that he would himself come on Board the next day and see who was to be Master of the Ship and that he should bring his Carpenter with him.

Q. Did not Capt: Russell after you denied Mr. Blaxland having Said that he was coming on Board to *tie* Capt: Russell call him (Mr. Blaxland) a Liar—or was it before?

A. I never heard Capt: Russell call Mr. J. Blaxland a Liar.

Q. Did Captain Russell before you came on Deck at the time you were Shaving call any Persons Liars?

A. No.

Q. Was not you called up to prove that we had not Said we would tie Captain Russell in his Cabin?

A. Yes.

Q. Did you not tell Capt: R: after denying that Mr. J. Blaxland had threatened to tie Capt: R: that you had informed Capt: R: that Mr. Blaxland would come on board to put him under an Arrest?

A. Yes.

Q. Did not Capt: R: desire Mr. J. Blaxland to go home and Sell his Milk and Cabbages—and say that He wished he had a Billy Goat to beat him—at the same time passionately beating the Boom with a Rope?

A. I heard all the Conversation about the Billy Goat.

Q. Did not this conversation happen before Mr. G. Blaxland laid hold of the Captain and after Mr. G. Blaxland Said to Captain R. that they came to ask civil Questions and expected Civil Answers?

A. Yes.

From Mr. Jn. Blaxland Q. Do you positively Swear that I held hold of the Collar of Cap: Russell's Coat?

A. You had hold of the Coat above the elbow.

Q. Did I go between Captain Russell and my Brother to prevent their fighting when Capt: R. Said he would go down and Soon Settle it?

A. No.

JOHN RICHARDSON, Carpenter of the Brothers, Sworn:—

From the Prosecutor Q. Was you on board on the 19th Inst. when the three Prisoners came on Board and what Passed?

A. Yes when the Prisoners came on board they were wellcomed by the Captain, and Mr. J. Blaxland told him that he was come with his Carpenter to fit up his accomodation and on being asked by the Capt: what part of the Ship he wanted, pointed out the Starboard Cabin, then occupied by the Captain, and being still further questioned by the Capt: where he would live—replied He did not care—that the Captain offered to Mess with him in the great Cabin—the Captain desired to know what Mr. Blaxland would give him for his Cabin and was answered that he would give him

1808.
30 April.

Proceedings at
the trial of
John and
Gregory
Blaxland and
Simeon Lord.

nothing, being the principal Owner, and insisted on having that Cabin and that He would go home in the Ship, Capt. Russell did not say a Word to Mr. G: Blaxland when he Gregory Blaxland called Capt. Russell a Puppy, and went immediately to Capt. R. and collared him and Mr. J. Blaxland immediately advanced and caught R. by the other Collar, on Captain Russels being pushed by the Blaxlands near Simeon Lord—who was leaning on the quarter Rail and on Capt. Russell being within about two feet of him—and fronting him—he lifted his Stick—in a passionate manner, and shook it three times over the Captain's head—Saying that if Capt. Russell had had Justice done him—He would have been Transported as Soon as He was himself. Captain Russell requested the Blaxlands to lett him go—which they did and on the Captain attempting to go below Mr. G. Blaxland asked him if he was going to gett Fire Arms, and the Captain said No, but on coming up with a Stick the Captain said He had as much right to carry a Stick having a Command as other Persons, who have no command. Soon after the Captain came on Deck—Mr. J. Blaxland called the Ship's Company forward—and the Captain desired them to keep to their duty, on the Men not coming forward Mr. J. Blaxland said that He would not Answer another Shilling for them and that He would Protest against their Wages at the Same time He, Mr. Blaxland, Sent a Boat for the Lieut. of the Porpoise—on the Lieutenants coming on board, Mr. J. Blaxland the Captain and Lieut. Ellison and the Carpenter went into the Cabin, and Mr. G. Blaxland and Mr. Lord remained on deck—about ten Minutes after Capt. Russell came on Deck by himself and a few minutes after him Mr. John Blaxland Mr. Ellison and the Carpenter also came on deck; a short time after the Party went away, and on Mr. Lord getting over the side of the Ship Capt. Russell told Mr. Lord that he must not bring a Stick again on board to insult him if He did Captain Russell would find one himself, Lord replied I always carry a Stick to guard myself and if you will come on Shore in an Hour—I shall be in the Road.

Q. Did you hear Captain Russell make use of the word Billy Goat?

A. No.

Q. When Mr. G. Blaxland laid violent hold of Captain R: did Mr. J. Blaxland interpose to prevent him?

A. No.

Q. Did Captain Russell raise His Hand to strike the Persons who had hold of him?

A. No.

Q. Did Captain Russell by word or action give any offence whatever to Mr. G. Blaxland before they collared him?

A. No.

Q. Did you hear Mr. Lord tell Captain Russell that He was a Thief, Rogue or Scoundrel?

A. No.

Q. Did you hear Mr. Lord tell Captain Russell that he would knock down or cut him down if He did not comply with Mr. J. Blaxland's demand?

A. No.

Q. Did you apply for Money on your own Account on or about the 16th Inst. to Mr. J. Blaxland?

A. Yes and was refused.

1808.
30 April.

Proceedings at
the trial of
John and
Gregory
Blaxland and
Simeon Lord.

From the Court: *Q.* Who was present at the time the Blaxlands collared and kept hold of Captain Russell?

A. The Cooper, Jno. Goodsold, Eliz. Guest; Robt. Daniels the Chief Officer came from the Cabin after the Blaxlands had collared the Captain but did not go near them except by passing them—and going forward before the Main Mast—if the Mate had touched the Captain or Blaxlands—I must have seen him—as I never quitted the Deck.

Q. Who called Mr. Daniels up from the Cabin?
A. I did not hear him called from below.

Q. Did you hear him called on the Quarter deck and who by?
A. He was called aft by Mr. J. Blaxland when walking before the Main Mast and was questioned by Mr. J. Blaxland.

Q. Did Eliz. Guest remain at the bottom of the Ladder or did she come out of the Cabin directly?
A. She came out of the Cabin.

Court cleared on the Prevarication of the Evidences.

CAPT. RUSSELL Sworn:—

From the Court Q. Did Mr. Daniels at the time Mr. Blaxland had hold of you come near or touch you or either of the Blaxlands—or endeavour to extricate you?
A. Yes.

Q. Did Mr. Gregory Blaxland and Mr. Lord go into the Cabin or remain on Deck at the time Lieut. Ellison and Mr. John Blaxland went with you into the Cabin?
A. They went into the Cabin.

JOHN GOODSOLD Sworn:—

From the Court: *Q.* Did you on the 19th Instant when the Prisoners at the Bar were on board and the two Blaxlands had hold of Captain Russell See Robt. Daniels the acting Chief Officer on the Quarter Deck and what did he do?
A. Mr. Daniels was not on the Quarter Deck during the whole time that the Blaxlands had hold of Capt. Russell.

Q. Did Mr. G. Blaxland and S. Lord go into the Cabin after Lieut. Ellison came on board—or did they remain on the Quarter Deck all the time?
A. Mr. G. Blaxland ordered me down; the Capt., Mr. J. Blaxland, Lieut. Ellison and myself went down and about a minute after Mr. G. Blaxland and Lord followed and Staid all the time.

JAMES ROOP, Cooper of the Brothers, Sworn:—

From the Court Q. Did you see Mr. Daniels the acting Chief Officer on the Quarter Deck of the Brothers on the 19th Inst. when the two Mr. Blaxlands now Prisoners at the Bar had hold of Captain Russell on the Quarter Deck and what did he Say or do?
A. Mr. Daniels was called by Mr. Blaxland—he did not touch or go near the two Blaxlands during time they had hold of Captain Russell; and was not during the whole time they had hold of Captain Russell on the Quarter Deck.

ALEXANDER Low Sworn (a Seaman of the Brothers):—

Q. Did you see the Prisoners at the Bar on board the Ship Brothers on the 19th Inst. and did you see the two Blaxlands all

1808.
30 April.

Proceedings at
the trial of
John and
Gregory
Blaxland and
Simeon Lord.

the time they had hold of Captain Russell on the Quarter Deck—
and who was present or interfered with the party Scuffling?

A. I was present and Saw the Blaxlands from the time they had
hold of Captain Russell—to the time they lett him go and no person
interfered.

Q. Was Mr. Daniels on the Quarter Deck during the time the two
Blaxlands lett Capt. Russell go?

A. No.

The Court called on ELIZ. GUEST Sworn —

Q. Did you see the two Mr. Blaxlands when they had hold of
Captain Russell on board the Brothers on the 19th Inst. and did
you See any Person attempt to rescue Capt. Russell from them?

A. I did see the two Blaxlands when they had hold of Captain
Russell, and no Person but myself attempted to rescue him.

Q. Was Mr. Daniels on the Quarter Deck at the time they had
hold of Captain Russell? .

A. I did not see Mr. Daniels on the Quarter Deck until after
Captain Russell was released.

HENRY PURDIE (Cabin Boy) Sworn:—

From the Court Q. Was Mr. Daniels the Chief Officer on the
Quarter Deck of the Brothers at the time the two Mr. Blaxlands
had hold of the Captain, or did he release the Captain from them?

A. I saw the Blaxlands lay hold of Captain Russell and lett him
go—Mr. Daniels was forward at each time they had hold of the
Captain nor did I see any Person go near them.

The Court cleared on the Perjury of Captain Russell and Robert
Daniels; are of opinion that the Perjury is clearly proved particularly in the instance of Daniels not being on the Quarter Deck
during the Affray between Captain Russell and the two Blaxlands—
And Sentence Oliver Russell and Robert Daniels to be transported
for Seven Years, but Strongly recommend both to the clemency of
the Governor.

Prior to the Court being cleared Mr. Oliver Russell Strongly
expressed the unfortunate situation in which he was involved and
wished to withdraw the Indictment.

Court adjourned till ½ Past 10: O'Clock Tomorrow.

31st March 1808 Court met.

The Prisoners asked if they wished to Cross examine the last
Evidences—wave the Examination.

Mr. Gregory Blaxland admits the Assault, and calls John Goodsold to prove that it was not maliciously intended.

JOHN GOODSOLD Sworn, Asked by the Prisoner Mr. G. Blaxland to
relate the . circumstances attending the Affray between him and
Mr. Russell on the 19th Inst. states that Mr. J. Blaxland and
Capt. Russell had Words—and on Capt. R. calling Mr. J. Blaxland
a Liar and a fool, Mr. Gregory Blaxland went up to Capt. Russell
and caught him by the Collar, but do not know what he said when
Mr. J. Blaxland caught hold of the Captain also, and held him until
Capt. Russell promised he would not get Fire Arms—Mr. J. Blaxland when he went up to Captain Russell appeared to go for the
purpose of parting his Brother and Captain Russell by saying
" Psha " and endeavouring to pacify them; Mr. Russell, from the
Prisoners first coming on Board and talking with Capt. Russell,
had a Rope in his hand with which he continued violently to Beat

different Parts of the Ship—On Mr. John Blaxland asking what accomodation he was to receive on board Capt. Russell replied according to Your behaviour as a Passenger and said if he did not behave well he would put him in Irons—Mr. Gregory Blaxland did not speak but civilly to Capt. Russell before he caught hold of him.

1808.
30 April.

Proceedings at the trial of John and Gregory Blaxland and Simeon Lord.

MR. GREGORY BLAXLAND in his Defence

Pleads the irritation of his Spirits on hearing his Brother who was an Owner of the Ship and himself also naturally interested—so grossly abused by the Master Capt. Russell particularly, as His Brother had given him notice to give up the Command of the Ship for misconduct and throughs himself on the Mercy of the Court.

MR. JNO. BLAXLAND pleads in his Defence that He laid hold of Captain Russell to prevent his Brother and Capt. Russell coming to Blows or any mischief arriving particularly from Captain Russell having Said He would go below and Soon Settle it—conceiving at the time he meant to fetch Fire Arms.

MR. S. LORD in his Defence—conceiving no charge has been proved against him trusts the Court will acquit him and conceive it to be a malicious Prosecution if not a conspiracy to ruin him.

The Court are of Opinion that Mr. Gregory Blaxland has acted very incorrect, but that he was Provoked to it by the ill Language of Captain Russell—but fine him Five Pounds Lawful Money of Great Britain.

The Court are of Opinion that Mr. John Blaxland is not Guilty—but laid hold of Captain Russell from motives to prevent any ill consequences.

The Court are of Opinion that the Assault or Threats have not been proved in any instance against Mr. Simeon Lord—and do therefore acquit him.

C. GRIMES, Acting J.-Advocate.

[Enclosure No. 3.]
MR. JOHN BLAXLAND TO MAJOR JOHNSTON.

Sir,   Sydney, 7th April, 1808.

Mr. Lord being informed by Mr. Bayly the Provost Marshal, that there being no Judge Advocate he cannot receive instructions to Subpoena any Witnesses, I have requested Your Honor will give directions for the following persons to be made legally acquainted that they will be wanted to attend on the Trial of Oliver Russel,* at the next Criminal Court.   I am, &c.,

JOHN BLAXLAND.

Witnesses required for the trial of Russell.

Witnesses wanted by John Blaxland on the Trial of Oliver Russel at the next Criminal Court:—Lieut. Ellison, Lieut. Moore, Lieut. Draffin, Lieut. Laycock, Gregory Blaxland, Simeon Lord, John Goodsolde.

[Enclosure No. 4.]
MR. SIMEON LORD TO MR. NICHOLAS BAYLY.

Sir,   Sydney, 6th April, 1808.

Not knowing who will be appointed Judge Advocate, I request of you as Provost Marshall to·cause the following persons

* Note 142.

1808.
30 April.

Witnesses
required for
the trial of
Russell.

to be subpoena'd as Witnesses on the Trial of Mr. Oliver Russel committed to take his Trial for Perjury.   I am, &c.,

.   S. LORD.

John Blaxland, Esqre., Greg'y Blaxland, Esqre., Robert Daniels, James Rufe, Cooper, Ship Brothers; Henry Purdy, Cabin Boy Do.; John Goodsolde, Sydney, &c.; Eliz'th Guest, Sydney.

[Enclosure No. 5.]

MR. SIMEON LORD TO MAJOR JOHNSTON.

Sydney, 7th April, 1808.

May it please Your Honor,

The enclosed is a Copy of a letter I sent to Nichs. Bayly Esqre. Provost Marshal requesting him to cause the persons therein named to be subpoena'd to attend on the Trial of Mr. Oliver Russel; but he has informed me that he cannot receive any Instructions of that nature but thro' the Judge Advocate, and not knowing who will be appointed to that important Office, I hope Your Honor will be pleased to order some person to acquaint them legally, that their attendance is required or to subpoena them.   I am, &c.,

S. LORD.

[Enclosure No. 6.]

MR. JOHN BLAXLAND TO MR. JOHN MACARTHUR.

Sir,   Sydney, 13th April, 1808.

Copies of
public papers.

As the pressure of business is so very severe I would not have asked the smallest favor of you could I have obtained the Papers without, but it certainly appears strange that you should Keep Papers belonging to Public transactions without those persons having access to them to whom they particularly relate.

I am, &c.,

JOHN BLAXLAND.

NOTE.—On the day when Mr. McArthur was making up the Despatches to go by the Dart, Mr. Blaxland requested the Copy of the proceedings of a Bench of Magistrates. Mr. Blaxland's clerk was allowed to Copy them, but on Mr. McArthur's declining to Attest the Copy as correct, until he should have leisure to examine it, this Letter was sent to him.

[Enclosure No. 7.]

Protest of
John Blaxland.

THE PROTEST OF JOHN BLAXLAND.*

NEW SOUTH WALES.

County of
Cumberland
to wit.

BY THIS PUBLIC INSTRUMENT OF PROTEST Be it known unto all Men who shall see these Presents that on the Eleventh Day of April in the Year of Our Lord One Thousand Eight Hundred and Eight Before me Charles Grimes Esquire Notary Public for the Territory of New South Wales aforesaid personally appeared

* Note 143.

1808.
30 April.

Protest of
John Blaxland.

John Blaxland of Sydney Esqre. Part and Managing Owner of the Ship Brothers of the Port of London whilst in this Port (Port Jackson) who claimeth a Right on Behalf of himself and the other Owners of the said Ship, the Underwriters and all and every other Person or Persons it may in any wise concern to protest and doth accordingly solemnly make this second PROTEST or Extension of Protest against Mr. Oliver Russell late Master of the said Ship, Major George Johnston now administering the Office of Governor as Lieutenant Governor, as Governor or otherwise of the Territory of New South Wales aforesaid and against John McArthur Esqre. now acting in the nominal Office of Colonial Secretary, as Secretary or otherwise and also against Lieutenant William Minchin, Lieutenant William Lawson, John Harris, Thomas Jamison and Garnham Blaxcell Esquires all commissioned Magistrates to keep the Peace for the said County or any or either of them inasmuch as the said Oliver Russell did on the Twenty Eighth Day of March last cause Deponent together with his Brother Gregory Blaxland Esqre. and Mr. Simeon Lord Merchant to be indicted and tried for what he called an Assault but in the Course of the Trial and Proceedings the said Oliver Russell and Robert Daniels one of his Witnesses were found Guilty of Wilful and Corrupt Perjury and sentenced to Seven Years Transportation as will appear by the attested Copy marked A. No. 1 accompanying this Instrument of Protest in Consequence of which Deponent appointed Frederick Hasselburgh Chief Mate of the said Ship to the command of her and demanded of the said Oliver Russell the said Ship's Register and other papers as will appear by Papers No. 1 and 2 accompanying this Instrument of Protest but not receiving them or any Answer Deponent wrote to His Honor Major George Johnston Governor as aforesaid thro' the said John McArthur Esqre. Colonial Secretary complaining and requesting of His Honor to order the said Register and Papers to be delivered to him See No. 3 and 4 and Answer No. 5 by which Deponent considered the said Ship to have been taken out of his Hands but in Order to prevent any Misunderstanding Deponent wrote the Original of Paper No. 6 and the Time limited for the Papers being restored in No. 6 not being expired and Information being given Deponent that a Proclamation was printing reversing the Proceedings of the Criminal Court against the said Oliver Russell and Robert Daniels and that the said Oliver Russell was going on board the said Ship that Afternoon being that of Sunday the 3rd of this Instant April, and that if the said Oliver Russell was resisted in taking the Command it would be enforced; In consequence of this Intelligence, Deponent wrote a Letter to Captn. James

Symmons of His Majesty's Ship Porpoise see Copy No. 7 but before this letter reached him and on Mr. Hasselburgh's Return on Board the said Ship who had Directions not to suffer the said Oliver Russell or any other Person to come on Board her the said Oliver Russell together with George Howe, an emancipated Convict, Robert Daniels, and one of the Mates of the Ship Dart went on Board the sd. Ship Brothers and called the Ship's Crew aft when the said George Howe read a Paper which Deponent believes to be the Proclamation above alluded to, and when the said Oliver Russell declared that he had the Command of the sd. ship Brothers, ordered the Crew to obey him and excited them to mutiny against the said Mr. Hasselburgh, who Deponent had authorized to command her—upon which Deponent wrote a Letter (No. 8 Copy) to His Honor Major Johnston Governor as aforesaid complaining of this Outrage and accusing the said Oliver Russell of Wilful and Corrupt Perjuries that he had been Guilty of (exclusive of that Perjury of w'ch he was convicted, sentenced to be transported for, and afterwards pardoned by Proclamation). On the 4th of this Inst. April Deponent received a Letter (Copy No. 9) and being astonished at its Contents, deponent wrote another Letter (No. 10 Copy) but received no Answer—that Deponent and the said Mr. Simeon Lord applied to the Magistrates and gave Information on their Oaths against the Said Oliver Russell for Perjury.

The Deponent also and the said Mr. Frederick Hasselburgh gave Information on Oath against the said Oliver Russell, George Howe, Robert Daniels and the Mate of the Ship Dart for their having piratically taken the said Ship Brothers and Deponent further deposed upon Oath that the said' Oliver Russell did feloniously take the sd. Ship's (Brothers) Papers out of her and lodge them in the Hands of Government without Deponent's knowledge or Consent when the Bench of Magistrates then sitting appointed the next Day to bring the said Oliver Russell to answer the Charges before a full Bench, but prior to his coming on Shore to appear before the said Bench a Guard of Soldiers was sent on Board the said Ship Brothers as Deponent was informed at the Request of the said Oliver Russell to prevent any Person Deponent might send to get possession of the said Ship Brothers—the said Bench consisted of the before named Lieutenant Will'm Minchin, Lieutenant William Lawson, John Harris, Thomas Jamison and Garnham Blaxcell, Esquires, Magistrates as aforesaid, who ordered the said Oliver Russell to find Bail for his Appearance at the next Court of Criminal Judicature to answer the Charges of Perjury exhibited against him but they refused to take Cognizance of the Charges of

Piracy and Outrage committed by the said Oliver Russell, George
Howe, Robert Daniels and the Mate of the Ship Dart or of the
said Oliver Russell having taken the Papers heretofore alluded
to out of the said Ship Brothers.

Deponent on the 4th of this Instant received Copy of an
Official Letter No. 11 directed to John Harris Esqre. wherein it
appears a Passage has been provided for him in the said Ship
Brothers of which Ship Deponent is part and managing Owner
in this Colony and w'ch Passage was provided for the said John
Harris Esqre. without Deponent's Consent or Knowledge; all of
which Proceedings Deponent considers contrary to Law and that
the said Ship Brothers and Cargo has been violently and arbi-
trarily taken out of Deponent's Hands by those and numerous
other Acts.

And Deponent therefore doth make this Protest against any,
everyone, or all of the Parties concerned relative to the said Ship
Brothers and Cargo for any or all Damages Detention or Losses
that may accrue in any wise whatsoever by Reason the before
Statement as well as any or all the Expenses and Damages
Deponent may accrue from Loss of Time, Detention of his
Passage to England as well to prosecute the former Protest as
this; and Deponent is deprived of such Passage in the said Ship
Brothers nor durst he go on Board her thro' Fear of some Evil
Consequences happening to him whilst the said Oliver Russel is
on Board.

Against all of which Acts of any or all of the Parties Deponent
doth most solemnly Protest and doth hereby present this Instrument declaratory in his Intent and Purpose to the said Charles
Grimes Esqre. Notary Public whom he the said Deponent requests
to receive and to administer to him the usual Oath taken or subscribed to on such or the like Occasion.

In Testimony of the Truth of the aforesaid Deponent hath
subscribed his name—This done and protested at Sydney in New
South Wales on the Day and Year above written.

JOHN BLAXLAND.

Sworn before me: C. GRIMES, Notary Publick.

[Enclosure No. 8.]

THE MEMORIAL OF JOHN BLAXLAND.

Sydney, New South Wales, 19th April, 1808.

THE Memorial of John Blaxland to Major Johnston, Esqre.,
Lieut.-Governor, &c., &c., &c.,

Most respectfully sets forth,

That although Your Memorialist has verbally informed
you that he has regularly protested against Oliver Russell for

1808.
30 April.

Protest of
John Blaxland.

Memorial of
John Blaxland
to Johnston.

several Acts of Misconduct, and also against Your Honor, John McArthur, Colonial Secretary, and the five Magistrates who refused to take cognizance of the charges exhibited against the said Oliver Russell, George Howe, Robert Daniels, and one of the Mates of the Ship Dart by Memorialist and Frederick Haselburg on Oath, and complained of to Your Honor by letter on the 3rd Inst. yet, your Memorialist deems it necessary thus Officially to inform you that he has transmitted those Protests to England, accompanied by all the Correspondence and Documents relating to those transactions.

However Your Memorialist may feel himself exhonorated from any loss or blame yet he feels it his duty again to inform Your Honor that he has received a letter from Messrs. Hullets which would justify him had he no other authority to supersede Oliver Russell in the Command of that Ship after he had been guilty of one improper act, much less so many as would have been inevitably proved against him, had he had an opportunity.

He is also informed that the Seal Skins of the quality of those on board the Brothers are now selling on an average from 15/ to 20/ Shillings each, and which might have been near England at this time, instead of lying here eating up the Provisions that ought to have been for his passage.

Your Memorialist respectfully hopes that Your Honor will seriously take these circumstances into your consideration as well as allow him the opportunity of proving the Charge of Perjury against Oliver Russell that he is now held to Bail for. At the same time Your Memorialist wishes to assure Your Honor that he makes this statement from no wish in any way to give Offence but for the purpose of exonorating himself from any blame as well as to apprise you of the immense loss and Damages that must follow from the detention of that Ship, and the expences of your Memorialist's passage with Captn. Scott and Frederick Haselburg to England in another Vessel together with the loss that must be sustained by the Antipode Schooner having a Boat and other Stores that could be spared from the Brothers.

I am, &c.,

JOHN BLAXLAND.

[Enclosure No. 9.]

THE PETITION OF JOHN BLAXLAND.

To His Honor Lieutenant Governor Johnston, &c., &c., &c.

THE humble Petition of John Blaxland sheweth that he received a letter from Oliver Russel of yesterday's date with the Copy of an answer to a Petition* of Oliver Russels on the 18th instant from John McArthur Esqr. Colonial Secretary, by which it

* Note 144.

appears Your Honor has consented to Oliver Russel's departure from this Colony he entering into a Bond* of Two Thousand Pounds to deliver himself up to His Majesty's Government on his arrival in England.

However reluctantly your Petitioner may feel in entering into the merits of the conduct of Oliver Russel, or his not receiving any answer to his former Letters and Memorial, together with the other Documents relative to the ship Brothers by which he considers himself exhonorated from all or any loss or damage that has, or may happen, Yet, he feels it a duty he owes to himself as a British Subject, and the others concerned with him, to crave leave in the most respectful manner to state what he considers the legal objections to Oliver Russel's departure from this Colony before he has been Acquitted, or found guilty of the various Charges exhibited against him, vizt:

Because your Petitioner has paid four Thousand pounds for a share in the Ship Brothers, and from his Agreement is obliged to act as managing Owner for that Concern in this Colony, and from Oliver Russel's improper Conduct, he did order him to give up the Command of that Ship and has since given the same to the Chief Mate, and which charges were complained of to Your Honor at the time and some of them were proved before a Bench of Magistrates on the 5th of March last as well as being now under Bail for Wilful and Corrupt Perjury an accusation of Piracy and robbing the said ship of her papers, while a Prisoner, and before then threatning to draw Bills on the Keel of the ship for money to pay his own private accounts with, and since having committed an Outrage on some of the Crew of the said ship; threatning to Shoot and Murder others, who came forward to complain and Swear their lives against him, so as your Honor was, as your Petitioner was informed, obliged to send a Guard on board to prevent serious Consequences, together with several other Charges of a Criminal nature that have never been taken cognizance of, all of which the Patent of this Colony for establishing Courts of Justice in it have provided for, and the Witnesses were then present, at the time he was held to Bail; there were a sufficient number of Officers that certainly could not be prejudiced against him, but altho' your Petitioner can have nothing to say about the New South Wales Corps, yet for their honor and the Cause so lately embarked in together with Your honor's Proclamation,* Your Petitioner most respectfully hopes that Your Honor will not suffer such an insinuation to go abroad that it is possible such men of known Integrity could be at all prejudiced against any person brought before them for trial much more Oliver Russel in whose fate they could not be

* Note 145.

1808.
30 April.

Petition of
John Blaxland
to Johnston.

interested, and from Your Honor's Proclamation of the 3rd
Instant they must have seen the impropriety had they acted from
prejudice; but exclusive of these reasons it cannot be a moment
doubted that any person in the situation of Oliver Russel would
not give anything short of their lives to escape from trial of such
Crimes as he must be sensible of the guilt of; and more
especially when he will have an opportunity of getting rid of the
principal Witnesses by having them Pressed, or leaving them
behind in this or some other Port, nor can it be supposed likely
he would carry the Ship to a part where he must give himself up
for so serious a trial as that of Perjury; nor does your Petitioner
consider that any Court in England would take cognizance of
Charges exhibited against him here, they having so wisely by the
Patent provided for Criminal and other trials in this Country;
and how is it possible that Petitioner can procure the Evidence
necessary to be given in England, or who is to pay the Expences
of such Witnesses provided they could be procured. Surely your
honor will not sanction his departure from this Colony before
trial from any suggestions of his, or his advisers, and your
Petitioner most ardently craves that he may be brought to such;
not only for the Charges he is under Bail for, but all and other
such ones as may be brought against him, that any Court in this
Territory is competent to Try—And Your Petitioner will humbly
pray.

JOHN BLAXLAND.

Sydney, 23rd April, 1808.

[Enclosure No. 10.]

THE MEMORIAL OF SIMEON LORD.

Memorial of
Simeon Lord
to Johnston.

To His Honor George Johnston, Esqre., Lieutenant-Governor,
&c., &c.

THE Humble Memorial of Simeon Lord of Sydney Merchant.

Most respectfully sheweth,

That Memorialist was brought to Trial before a Criminal
Court for an alledged Assault on one Oliver Russel who was
found guilty of Perjury in endeavouring to support that charge,
and also in various other Instances; on which Accusation, Mem'st
was acquitted; and in consequence of Your Honor's Proclamation
of the 3rd Instant, Mem'st applied on the 4th instant to the
Magistrates* to Commit the said Oliver Russel for Trial on specific
Charges on Oath for Wilful and Corrupt Perjury who, being
ordered to find Bail on the 5th instant accordingly did on the 7th
instant following, when Mem'st applied to the Provost Marshal,
and afterwards to Your Honor, requesting the Witnesses might

* Note 142.

be regularly subpoenaed to attend such Trial, and which Request Mem'st had no doubt was complied with, until he saw on the 22nd Inst. a Copy of a letter from John McArthur Esqre. to the said Oliver Russel, of which the following is a Copy:—

"Sir, "Head Quarters, 21st April, 1808.

"I am commanded by His Honor the Lieut. Governor to acquaint you that he has taken Your Petition, dated the 18th instant, into consideration, and that combining the reasons you have assigned for being anxious to sail for England with the valuable Cargo of the Brothers, and the total impossibility there is of bringing you to trial in the Colony for want of a sufficient number of officers who can be considered by you disinterested, His Honor is induced to comply with the Prayer of the Petition, and to sanction your departure on the Conditions you have proposed—a Bond shall therefore be drawn up immediately by which you will be engaged to surrender yourself on your arrival in England to His Majesty's Government and to abide by their Orders or to Forfeit Two thousand Pounds.

"If you call at this office tomorrow morning at 12 O'Clock, the Bond will be prepared, and when you have executed it, your Bonds to appear before the next Court of Criminal Jurisdiction shall be returned. "I am, &c.,

"JOHN MCARTHUR,

"Mr. Oliver Russell." "Secretary to the Colony.

In consequence of which Letter, Mem'st craves leave to offer for Your Honor's Consideration the following Reasons why the said Oliver Russell should not be suffered to depart from this Colony before he is either Acquitted or found Guilty of the Charges alledged and exhibited against him.

1st. Because the Patent for establishing Courts of Justice in this Colony has sufficiently provided for taking Cognizance of and bringing to Justice Persons accused of any Offences or Crimes against the Laws.

2ndly. Because the Crime, Oliver Russell is now under Bail for, was Committed in this Colony, and the Prosecutor and Evidences are on the spot, and it is not Clear to Mem'st that if the said Oliver Russell was even to be brought before a Court in England, such Court could or would take Cognizance of the Crime now against him, as the Laws have wisely provided means of trying Offences here.

3rdly. Because the said Oliver Russel's Plea of there not being a sufficient number of disinterested Officers in the Colony to try him is unfounded, as at, and since the time of his being held to Bail, there was a sufficient number of Officers here who were not Members of the Court by which he was found Guilty of Wilful and Corrupt Perjury, namely Captn. Edwd. Abbott, Captn. A. F. Kemp, Lieut. Wm. Minchin, Lieut. Wm. Lawson, Lieut. Kent, and Lieut. Ellison, and Mem'st hopes Your Honor will not suffer so vile a suggestion to be spread abroad as that any Officer of the New South Wales Corps could or would be guilty of forswearing himself, as your Mem'st is of opinion it would be little short of, if such a poor subterfuge as that could be admitted, as certainly every Member of a Court Swears well and truly to try every Charge brought before him, and an Impartial Verdict give according to Evidence.

4thly. Because, from Your Honor's high sense of Honor, you will see impartial Justice administered to all descriptions of people without Respect to Persons; Your Honor's Proclamations* of the 27th Jany. last, and of the 3rd instant, as well as the reasons there were for Your Honor taking the Reins of Government, fully convince Mem'st that you will not leave it in the power of any of His Majesty's Subjects to complain of any unequal distribution of Justice; and Mem'st humbly submits that the said Oliver Russell ought to be tried for the heinous Crime of Perjury now against him, as well as your Mem'st was tried on the unfounded Charge of an alledged Assault.

5thly. Because it is impossible for Mem'st to leave his Concerns in this Colony which are not less than £30,000 Stg. to proceed to England to prosecute for an Offence, which the Laws of England and the Patent of this Colony have provided for to be tried here; nor could Mem'st procure the Witnesses who are now here to attend in England.

Lastly. Mem'st conceives that any Person under Bail for a Crime of such nature would in order to evade Justice offer any Kind of Bond in his power, that he might escape from Trial, nor can your Mem'st comprehend that Your Honor can for a single moment suppose that the said Oliver Russell would take the Ship Brothers to England under every Circumstance Your Honor is apprised of.

Mem'st well knowing and conscious of Your Honor's good Intentions to duly administer Justice to all His Majesty's Subjects under Your Command emboldens him to solicit your protection, and notwithstanding the infamous suggestions of the said Oliver Russell and his Advisers, Mem'st hopes he may have an opportunity of bringing him to Justice as an Example to all others Guilty of such or the like Offences.

And Y'r Mem'st will ever Pray, &c., &c.

S. LORD.

Sydney, New South Wales, 25th April, 1808.

* Note 145.

[Enclosure No. 11.]

The Memorial of Oliver Russell.

To His Honor George Johnston, Esquire, Lieutenant Governor, &c., &c.

The humble Memorial of Mr. Oliver Russell in behalf of himself and Mr. Robert Daniels.

Most Respectfully Sheweth,

That upon Monday the 28th of March, 1808, Memorialist did appear before a Court of Criminal Jurisdiction upon Indictment to prosecute John Blaxland and Gregory Blaxland, Esquires, and Mr. Simeon Lord, a Merchant, for an Assault committed by them jointly against Memorialist on board the Ship Brothers then and now lying in this Port, and of which the Memorialist was the Commander.

That the Memorialist being Sworn an Evidence for the King was put upon Cross Examination by the Defendants above named, during which a great many questions were put to Memorialist which were totally irrelevant for the due Elucidation of the Complaint set forth in the Indictment but which he was nevertheless commanded by the Court to Answer, altho' the Memorialist (then the Prosecutor) Was of Opinion that most of the said Questions were proposed to him to bewilder him in delivering such Evidence and ultimately to ensnare him for sinister Purposes.

That in the course of the proceedings had upon the said Trial, it appeared to Your Honor's Memorialist (and in that Supposition he then was and still is abetted not only by the General Rule of Evidence enjoined to be adopted in all similar Cases, but also by the unfortunate result of it to him) that a Strong bias was evident in the manner that Evidence was obtained, received and recorded by the Court, who certainly derived their Authority from the Laws of the Parent state and Your Honor's Precept, and should have consequently adhered to the due rule of Evidence warranted and pointed out by Law.—And after the hearing of that cause before that Honorable Court for two days sitting and part of a third, with that adherence to the Rule of Examination of Witnesses, and of Your Memorialist (the then prosecutor) above animadverted upon, The Court on the said third day of that Trial, thought proper, upon part of the Testimony given by Memorialist to declare it as their Opinion that the same was wilful and corrupt Perjury, And that that Crime was committed by him with Circumstances of strong Aggravation which called for Exemplary Punishment.

That on the said 3rd day, one John Richardson was called on by the Prosecutor to depose to certain facts, and having given his

Testimony to the Court, *The prosecutor* was immediately after-wards converted by that Tribunal into an *Evidence*, and that against himself. And being about to be resworn in that latter Capacity, He Strongly objected thereto upon Principles of Law and Justice, which must be obvious to the most moderate Capacity, Namely that no Man can be legally called upon to Self-criminate. This Objection, however well founded, was overuled by Order of the Court And he in consequence was compelled to reply to such Interrogatories as were then proposed to him, without even the qualifying option of so replying to the best of his belief or Recollection; for in such terms the Court refused to receive that Evidence; And thus entangled in a Net work, composed with great Ingenuity by his adversaries, the Court considered his Replies as above Stated to Amount to Perjury.

Your Memorialist humbly begs leave to state to Your Honor That by Statute 23 G. 2 cap: II s. 3 The Judge of Assize (sitting the Court, or within 24 hours after) may direct any Witness, if there shall appear to him a reasonable Cause, to be *prosecuted* for Perjury. And by Stat: 2. G. 2 c. 25 which Act is made perpetual by the 9th of the same Reign c: 18 The Crime of Perjury is made Punishable by Transportation for 7 Years.— That by I Hawkins 172 " The false Oath alledged should be proved to be taken with some degree of deliberation, for if upon the whole Circumstances of the Case It shall appear probable that it was owing rather to the Weakness than to the perverse-ness of the party, as where it was occasioned by Surprise or Inadvertency or a Mistake of the true state of the question, it cannot but be hard to make it Amount to voluntary and corrupt Perjury."

How far this legal doctrine applies in the case of Your Honor's Memorialist, the true Statement thereof will shew And if any doubt can exist in this Territory as to the legal Mode of Trial for that Crime being attainable only by Indictment—See 2 Hawk: 433.

That notwithstanding the above recited authorities Your Honor's Memorialist was charged by that Honorable Court *instanter* with being a Culprit who had incurred the Penalties of Perjury, and was immediately put upon his Trial for such alledged Offence, Thus transgressing every priviledge preserved by the British Constitution by the Common and Statute Law, of Opportunity of self defence, and in the very teeth of a positive Act of Parliament, which it was the Court's duty strictly to adhere to—Nor is there in this or any similar Case any discretionary or dispensing Power under any Circumstance

whatever vested in any expositor of that Law, from the Lord
Chief Justice of England to His Majesty's Judge Advocate of
the Territory of New South Wales, including both these dignified
Characters, But to literally pronounce it when violated.

Memorialist does not deny but that the Evidence by him given,
and written by the Court (wherein the Charge of Perjury was
grounded) might be legally received in Substantiation of *that
Charge* when put upon his Trial for the same; but such Trial
should be instituted by Indictment according to the Authorities
above quoted such being the invariable legal Rule, thereby giving
the Party charged *that* Opportunity which the Law secures him,
of preparing due defence by Production and Examination of
Witnesses, and obtaining upon demand thereof a Copy of that
Indictment, if conceived necessary to that Defence. Instead
however of adhering to this legal Rule, The Honorable Court
thought proper to adopt a Summary Mode in which Memorialist
conceives they were not justified by Law.

Thus then, was your Honor's Memorialist brought forward as
a Culprit who had violated the Law And under Sanction of the
Execution whereof he was sentenced to be deprived of his liberty
for Seven Years! His protecting Shelter being thus turned
into an Engine of extreme Adversity and unwarrantable Injury
to him—The Honorable Court however in its Clemency was
pleased, upon passing that Sentence to accompany it with the
alleviating Assurance, that they would recommend Memorialist
to Your Honor's lenity.

Under such Recommendation however, he does not fly for
refuge to Your Honor, Whose lenity and Strict Principles of
Justice, and admissible Compassion, Are too fully impressed
upon Your Honor's Memorialist in Common with all those who
have the Honor and sufficient discernment to appreciate Your
Character to render such recommendation necessary, however
well intended, And he therefore comes forward with not only
a Claim upon Your Commiseration, but upon Your Honor's
Justice, as a British Subject illegally convicted under your
Government to see that Justice and Right be done him, attempered
with that benevolent Condescension, in effectuating this favor
which characterises the breast of humanity.

That an *Arrest* or at least a *Suspension of Judgment* was
ardently solicited by Your Honor's Memorialist, when about to be
pronounced, which was peremptorily refused by the Honorable
Court, Altho' in innumerable Similar Cases Where the proceedings are adhered to with the most scrupulous legality, in the
British Courts of Jurisprudence, the Indulgence is granted, most
generally from one Term to the other In Order, obviously to

afford Scope to the Prisoner, to offer intermediately such exculpatory or mitigating Evidence as may induce the lesser punishment prescribed by the Law to be inflicted upon him; and not by an indeliberate Judgment be precipitated into a Gulph, whereby he is deprived, not only of the natural Rights of a subject, But also by such imputed Crime rendered incompetent to come forward in Protection of his Person or Property as a legal Witness: And Memorialist has further to lament, that the Civil privation, consequent to this Sentence, involves the forfeiture of a trust to him committed, whereto much Confidence and Responsability are Attached, namely, the Command of the Ship Brothers of London now lying in this Port, whereof he was Master, under the appointment of Messrs. Hullett Brothers and Co. (of which latter description Mr. John Blaxland is) And Your Honor's Memorialist cannot hesitate to assert, that the various vexations and obstructions thrown in his way by Messrs. Blaxland and Lord, are acted upon from a concerted principle of obtaining the exclusive possession and Command of that Ship. To the extreme injury of Memorialist and his Employers in Great Britain, in which they have too well succeeded Unless such Machinations are rendered abortive by Your Honor's interposing Power on behalf of your humble Memorialist.

That as Evidence of the flagrant Irregularities and undue Influence used in the Examination and Management of the Witnesses produced on the Trial of Messrs. Blaxland and Lord on the prosecution of Your Memorialist, the following Brief Statement thereof is submitted, irrefragably proving as he apprehends that had he been put upon his trial in the Usual Manner, thereby being permitted a regular Arrangement of defence, Evidence, so contradictory, and so obtained, would be rejected in Proof of that Charge as adduced by his Opponents And that those produced on his behalf would have attained his complete Acquittal.

That upon the first day of the said Trial, Memorialist's Examination was wholly occupied by the Examination of One of the Defendants, to Wit, Simeon Lord.

That upon the day following, namely Tuesday the 29th the Memorialist did again appear in Court to prosecute his said Complaint and had to Answer to certain Interrogatories prepared by another of the Defendants to Wit Mr. Jno. Blaxland—which said Interrogatories were of the most part a repetition of the former; save only that they were differently couched, and artfully contrived to surprise the Memorialist into replies that might admit a prevaricatory Construction.

1808.
30 April.

Memorial of
Oliver Russell
to Johnston.

That the Memorialist finding as he had much reason to apprehend, that his destruction was the Ardent Object of the Defendants, Blaxlands and Lord, and at length dreading the Vortex that he plainly perceived to be ingeniously contrived for him, Did Solemnly refuse to give Answer to any further Interrogations;—And at the instance of the Acting Judge Advocate, who demanded that no other refusal would be received as admissible, but the dread that Memorialist's Answer would tend to criminate himself, Was actually compelled to take Shelter even under that distressing plea; Which Memorialist conceives it was the Judge Advocate's duty to defend him from, as he was an Evidence for the Crown, And had no real Interest in the prosecution.

That upon the said 29th of March, Memorialist's Examination was nearly concluded, when the Court Cleared And upon reopening the Memorialist (and then Prosecutor) was informed by the Acting Judge Advocate that Shameful Prevarication had been made use of by Memorialist, but that fortunately for Memorialist, it did not extend to Wilful and corrupt Perjury! Whereupon Mr. Blaxland resumed his Cross Examination of Memorialist.

That the said Mr. John Blaxland, one of the Defendants, then produced certain papers relative to Memorialist's Ship Concerns; And at length terminated his Interrogatories; that being the 2d day of Trial, after which Memorialist could not consider himself liable to be resworn, but to remain before the Court as Prosecutor for the King.

That Mr. Robert Daniels, Acting Chief Officer of the said Ship Brothers, was then called upon by Memorialist, and in the course of his Examination gave Evidence in behalf of the Prosecution; And after having so done, the same was read over to him by the Acting Judge Advocate Who at the same time desired him to point out any Impropriety therein, that it might be then corrected, as after *that* day it would not be in his Power to do so; When the said Robert Daniels said the whole of his Assertions were correct.

That on the following Morning (30 March) the Memorialist proceeded to the Examination of that Evidence.

That after having finished the Examination of the said Robert Daniels for the Crown, in the Course of which the Memorialist was much interrupted, one of the Defendants (Lord) proceeded to his Cross Examination, followed by that of Mr. John Blaxland.

The next Evidence called upon was John Richardson, the Ship's Carpenter, who very positively and collectedly proved the assault committed on Your Memorialist.

That on his Cross Examination he admits that Daniels came up at the time of the Scuffle—that the Defendants had hold of Your Memorialist *at that time*—that Daniels passed them and walked before the Mainmast &c. as hereafter will appear.

That among other Errors in stating the testimony upon the Records of the Court, the following Omissions recur to the Memorialist as material to be laid before your Honor:—

Question from S. Lord to Captain Russel: Did you not after going on Shore and before you went to the Magistrates, go to Capt. John McArthur and receive Advice to go and make an Affidavit to that effect?

A. Instead of going to a Magistrate or Bench of Magistrates I went to the Lieutenant Governor Johnston to lodge my Complaint, and Mr. McArthur was present &c.

Q. Did Capt. McArthur advise you to lodge the Complaint?

A. He was present when I lodged it, and I believe he did advise me to do so, as he told me I had come to the wrong place, and I believe I did.*

Mr. Daniels in his general Statement says, that Mr. John Blaxland had mentioned it to him, that he had tried every means (against Capt. Russell) but could not get Justice.

Question from Lord to Capt. Russell: Did you not (among other Things) say to John Blaxland he might go home and Sell his Milk and Cabbages &c.?

A. I was first grossly insulted by John Blaxland and Simeon Lord—I told John Blaxland he had better go and sell his Milk and Cabbages, and feed his Pigs, than come on board as Commander of that Vessel on his threatening me with Transportation, and saying I should be hanged and that I was a Coward and a Villain.*

That Memorialist in his Examination also said that one of the Defendants (S. Lord) had upbraided him as a thief, Rogue, Vagabond &c.

The Question upon which the Charge was grounded against him is as follows:—

"'Did Mr. Daniels Your Chief Officer touch, *or* come near, *or* endeavour to extricate you from the Blaxlands when they collared You?

Answer.—"Yes."—Which several Clauses being disjunctive, the very coming near of Daniels (which has been substantiated by almost every Witness) and perfectly admitted by the Defendants Lord and Blaxlands, is a palpable Justification of the Answer *Yes*—And Yet, Memorialist hath, upon negative and contradictory inadmissible and tortured Testimony, been convicted of the Crime of Perjury, wilful and Corrupt.

* Note 146.

1808.
30 April.
———
Memorial of
Oliver Russell
to Johnston.

The Evidence of Richardson saith—that when the Blaxlands had hold of the Captain Daniels *passed them,* and walked before the Main Mast, from which it is obvious he must have been *near* them.

John Goodsould saith—*" I did not see him near them at that time "* which does not amount to an exclusion of his being near them, and is consequently nugatory.

James Rolfe saith *" I did not see Daniels there at all* Mr. Blaxland called him up but he did not remain "*—nor was it at the time of the Scuffle how was he certain whether it was before or after.

Which testimony is highly contradictory of the former two, and surely ought not to have been admitted on a Charge of any kind.

Alexander Low saith, *I did not see Daniels on the quarter deck I was at* Work *and did not see the whole transaction,* he (Daniels) *might have been on deck without my seeing him.*

Elizabeth Guest Saith " I did not see Mr. Daniels there, he might be there, but I did not see him," and

Henry Purdy a boy deposed somewhat to the same Effect.

That in confirmation of the Averment made by Memorialist relative to the admission of Injustice of the Sentence passed against Memorialist and Mr. Robert Daniels, Memorialist begs leave to lay before your Honor certain quotations from the Cross Examination of Memorialist and the said Daniels by Messrs. Lord and Blaxlands; namely, *Quest. from Mr. John Blaxland to Daniels :* Had I hold of Capt. Russell's Collar?

A. I cannot say his Collar but it was here abouts (afterwards made out by the Court to be) above the Elbow.

Quest. from Mr. Lord to Memorialist :—Did not I say to Mr. Daniels on his coming up to rescue Capt. Russell, " that it was not intended to hurt Captain Russell, but only to prevent his going into the Cabin for fire-arms " ?

That in addition to the Circumstances herein above recited Your Memorialist hath personally to Complain of the denial of Priviledges which every British Subject upon Trial hath a lawful right to claim.

That the matter upon which the Crime of Perjury was alledged, was by the Cross Examination by the Defendants thus directly admitted to be true. Notwithstanding that 6 Persons, who were evidently taken by Surprise, had otherwise declared, with a provision that Mr. Daniels might have been present at the place mentioned, but that they did not see him, which the Memorialist conceives to be omitted on the face of the Court proceedings; whereof Memorialist hath grievously to com-

1808.
30 April.

Memorial of
Oliver Russell
to Johnston.

plain of prejudice from the Error in the said proceedings; and
moreover that the said Evidence, tho' negative in itself was made
absolute by the Court for surely the very Nature of the Evidence
was a prohibition to any thing Affirmative; as several Persons
might be in one Room and after a lapse of time find it difficult
even at a temperate Moment to call to remembrance who those
Persons were; whereas Memorialist contends the Evidence aforesaid were taken by Surprise and being unexpectedly challenged
upon a collateral Circumstance only, and not upon the material
fact, under the strongest Influence of terror and Affright partly
produced by the impressive manner of Swearing in Persons who
by their own acknowledgement had never taken an Oath before,
upon whose testimony a strong contradiction to the fair and
admitted Testimony of Memorialist and Mr. Robert Daniels
aforesaid was immediately implied; and the Cross Examination
of either of whom Memorialist was palpably refused, Altho' as
it since appeared, he was under a Nominal Indictment for perjury; Which numerous respectable Evidences then were and now
are ready to disprove; but of which favorable Circumstance
Memorialist could not then avail himself, by reason that time
was not permitted him to call upon such Evidence, nor even
upon the Evidence of any of the by Standers, or in any way to
arrange any Species of defence against an Accusation as unexpected as unjust; And of the Injustice of which Memorialist
supposed no Person in Court could plead Ignorance from the
general tenor of the Evidence; and which being represented and
argued to the Court in behalf of Memorialist, So Simple but yet
so palpable an Objection was overruled upon a Principle that the
odds in number of Evidence were six to two, without Consideration of the distinction in point of credibility; Whereupon
Memorialist, conscious that the Defendants themselves would
and must have given Evidence in his favor, did most respectfully
submit to the Honorable Court a wish to abandon the Prosecution
against the Defendants in *toto,* as the only alternative that
remained to him in Order to benefit by their Evidence; Whereas
this request was likewise overruled, by reason that the prosecution *must* be proceeded in; that as Prisoners at the Bar of
Justice, their Evidence to the perjury alledged was inadmissible,
and the more especially as even their bare acknowledgement in
favor of Memorialist would be also an acknowledgement of the
Fact for which they stood indicted. That in reply to this,
Memorialist prayed the Court that the Investigation of his
alledged Offence might be postponed* until the trial of Assault
should be concluded, in Order that he might receive the benefit
of the Defendants' testimony, which likewise was overruled, upon

* Note 147.

a principle that so *flagitious* an Offence as that imputed to Memorialist and Mr. Daniels must be immediately attended to, and punish'd in an exemplary way.

That from the foregoing Premises faithfully laid down to Your Honor, Memorialist respectfully submits the following deductions as warranted by the legal authorities hereinbefore quoted (the only ones extant) that the trial and Conviction of Memorialist is *ab origine* repugnant to the Laws, being illegally instituted and informally prosecuted.

That under the whole of the preceding Statement, Your Honor's Memorialist supplicates your interposition by rectifying these Errors in such Manner as your Honor shall Judge expedient for his Relief: And he most respectfully Concludes this long Intrusion upon Your Time and Condescension by obtruding thereon an Observation by that venerated Commentator on the British Laws, Mr. Justice Blackstone. Vol. 3 p. 390.

" Where the facts are complicated and intricate, the Evidence of great length and variety—and sometimes contradicting each other—and where the Nature of the dispute very frequently introduces nice questions and Subtilties of Law either party may be surprised by a piece of Evidence which (had he known of its production) he could have explained or answered; or may be puzzled by a legal doubt which a little Recollection would have solved."

That there must be a virtual tho' not expressed controuling Power vested by the Constitution of the Patent of this Colony in your Honor for preserving the Criminal as well as Civil Law inviolate, which latter resort comes before Your Honor by Appeal, by a discretionary Exercise thereof in that respect, without recurring to an extension of Mercy but Merely Annulling any illegal Sentence *prima facie*, must be a certain consequence of those Powers impliedly delegated by the Crown to the Governor of this Colony. For even should Your Honor be disposed to Pardon Your Memorialist from the Sentence of Perjury, Yet such Pardon cannot restore him to his Civil Rights by rendering him a Competent legal Evidence, the Effects of such Sentence remain in *Statu quo* as to restoration to that right unless by Writ of Error (inadmissable here), or by Act of Parliament unattainable here, the same shall be reversed and rendered completely null. But as the Sentence, under which Your Honor's Memorialist thus illegally and ignominiously labours, cannot operate to his prejudice in any point of view beyond the limits of this Territory, he ardently supplicates that Your Honor will eradicate the same therein, as well on his own behalf as that of Mr. Robert Daniels; by which he will be restored to the Command of his Ship, the Services of an honest and deserving Officer: Both of whom shall ever recollect with heartfelt Gratitude that they are indebted, TO HIS HONOR MAJOR GEORGE JOHNSTON, HIS MAJESTY's Lieutenant Governor of New South Wales, for a Boon so invaluable as a restoration to liberty from a thaldrom so imminent.   OLIVER RUSSELL.

Port Jackson, 1st April, 1808.

APPENDIX to the Memorial of Mr. Oliver Russell in behalf of Memorialist and Mr. Robert Daniels.

To His Honor George Johnston, Esquire, His Majesty's Lieutenant Governor, &c., &c.

May it please Your Honor,

Your Honor's Memorialist believing that the Error in the Judgement pronounced against himself and Mr. Robert Daniels, and of which his Memorial very respectfully Complaineth, proceeded from misinterpretation by the Court of the words of the Statute of 2d Geo. 2d C. 25 s. 2, which enacteth,

" That besides the punishment to be inflicted by Law for so great Crimes, it shall be lawful for the Court or Judge before whom any person shall be *convicted* of Wilful and Corrupt Perjury, or subornation of Perjury to order such person to be sent to some house of Correction, for a time not exceeding 7 Years, there to be kept to hard labour during the time; otherwise to be transported for a term not exceeding 7 Years as the Court shall think proper; Therefore Judgement shall be given, that the person convicted shall be committed or Transported accordingly; besides such punishment as shall be adjudged to be inflicted on such person agreeable to the Laws in being, and if Transportation be directed, the same shall be executed in such manner as is provided by Law for Transportation of Felons—and if any person so committed or Transported shall voluntarily escape or break prison, or return from Transportation before the Expiration of the time, such person, being lawfully convicted, shall suffer Death as a Felon; and shall be tried for such Felony in the Country where he so escaped, or where he shall be apprehended."

Upon the Words of the said Statute Your Honor's Memorialist begs leave respectfully to Observe that the Clause contained therein stating—" That it shall be lawful for the Court or Judge before whom any person shall be *convicted* of Wilful and Corrupt Perjury &c." has in the case submitted to Your Honor been misapplied by the Court; which has not at the same time taken into Consideration the strict necessity which the law imposes that every Conviction shall be legal, and that it is altogether

1808.
30 April.
—
Memorial of
Oliver Russell
to Johnston.

repugnant to the Genius of Our excellent Legislature to proceed to a Conviction before the Party under accusation shall have undergone Commitment, shall have been regularly indicted on the Statute; shall consequently be put upon his Plea, and be permitted to defend himself as well by the Examination of Evidence, as by every other mode allowed in general Cases.

Your Honor's Memorialist likewise begs leave to advert to I Hawk P.C. c. 69 s. 22 "that no false Oath within the Statute which doth not give some person a just cause of Complaint, therefore if the thing sworn be true, tho' it be not known by him who swears it to be so the Oath is not within the Statute; because it gives no just Cause of Complaint to the other party, who would take advantage of the other's want of Evidence to prove the truth; from the same ground, no false Oath can be within the Statute unless the party against whom it was sworn suffer some disadvantage by it." To Convict a Man of Perjury, a probable evidence is not enough, but the Evidence must be strong and Clear.

And upon a reference to the most eminent law authorities the Error of proceeding against Your Honor's Memorialist except by Indictment will very obviously be discovered; for in 2d of Hawk. 287, it is said, "It seems that the Court will not ordinarily at the prayer of the Defendant grant a *Certiorari* for the Removal of an *Indictment* of Perjury." *And again* in 2 Hawk. 258, "The Court generally will not quash an *Indictment* for a Crime of so enormous a Nature as Perjury, for insufficiency in the caption or body of it, but will oblige the Defendant either to *plead* or *demur* to it." By the 23rd of Geo. 2 cap. II s. 3 "the Judge may direct any Witness (if there shall appear to him a reasonable Cause) to be prosecuted for Perjury &c. which prosecution shall be conducted without expence to the party injured."

From the foregoing Authorities, and doubtless from many others which the Memorialist hath not lain before Your Honor, but which are equally cogent and decisive, on the *necessity* of a prisoners being in a uniform way *indicted* on the Statute for the Offence of Perjury, Your Honor's Memorialist doubts not that the irregularity of the procedure adopted by the Court will appear, from its total departure from every such received Authority; and the Memorialist therefore rests his Case to Your Honor's high and Sacred Regard to the just and impartial dispensation of the Laws, as well without prejudice as innovation.

Most respectfully subscribed, and Attached to the Memorial of

OLIVER RUSSELL.

Port Jackson, 2nd April, 1808.

1808.
30 April.

Proceedings
of bench of
magistrates on
the prosecution
of Russell
for perjury.

[Enclosure No. 12.]

PROCEEDINGS OF A BENCH OF MAGISTRATES.

John Harris
James Symons
William Minchin
William Lawson
} Esquires

4th April, 1808.

John Blaxland Esqre. came before the Bench and complained that he had received Information that Several things are now missing belonging the Ship Brothers which he has reason to believe are now at the House of Oliver Russell, and Prays that a Search Warrant may be issued for their recovery.

*John Housegoe Sworn, says that he has frequently seen Oliver Russell cut Canvas belonging to the Ship and that he has every reason to suspect that it is in the House of Oliver Russell.**

FREDERICK HAZELBURG came before the Bench, and made the following Deposition (Vizt.) :—

"Mr. Frederick Hazelburg, Commander of the Ship Brothers, comes before the Bench of Magistrates to make Oath that Yesterday being Sunday the third Instant that Oliver Russell, Robert Daniels, George Howe and one of the Mates of the Ship Dart, did come on Board the Ship Brothers, and called the Men Aft and read to them a Paper and declared he had the Command of the Ship, and thereby excited the Ship's Company to Mutiny and took from him (Frederick Hazelburg) the Said Ship without any authority or orders from the Managing Owner in this Port—John Blaxland, and the Deponent farther declares that after he had received instructions to keep possession nor to suffer the said Oliver Russel to give any orders or the People to obey him, the said Oliver Russell ordered him to quit the Quarter Deck, and this Deponent further Saith that he has received further written instructions from the said John Blaxland to take on board some Seal Skins and to get the Ship in readiness for Sea but this Deponent declares that he dare not attempt to go on Board to put such orders in force for fear of the said Oliver Russell and Robert Daniels having excited the Ship's Company to mutiny together with George Howe and the Mate of the Dart.

" FREDK. HASSELBURG."

Also came before us JOHN BLAXLAND who deposes that he is part and managing Owner in this Colony of the Ship Brothers and that in concequence of Oliver Russell having been transported for Seven Years he did give the Command of the Ship Brothers to Frederick Hazelburg and that he has not nor ever will give Oliver Russell any authority to resume the Command again, but he considers it a violation of the Laws and his property, and that he is ready to prove that he is guilty of wilful and corrupt Perjury in his Oath whereby he was committed to be tried by a Criminal Court, and repeatedly so on the Proceedings on that Trial; and from the Letter from John McArthur Esqre. of the 2d of April it appears he has robbed the Ship of the Papers and lodged them in the hands of Government.

JOHN BLAXLAND.

MR. SIMEON LORD Sworn States to the Bench that Mr. Oliver Russell has been guilty of wilfull and corrupt Perjury by which he

* The words in italics are scored through in the original.

the said Simeon Lord was brought before a Criminal Court and tried for an Assault and also at the Same Court he has frequently Sworn falsities to his prejudice and therefore Prays that he may be allowed an opportunity of proving the Same before a Criminal Court.

S. LORD.

Refered to a full Bench of Magistrates tomorrow.

J. HARRIS.
J. SYMONS.
WM. MINCHIN.
WM. LAWSON.

1808.
30 April.

Proceedings of bench of magistrates on the prosecution of Russell for perjury.

BENCH OF MAGISTRATES.*

Thomas Jamison ⎫
Will. Minchin   ⎪
Garnham Blaxcell ⎬ Esquires
Willm. Lawson   ⎪
John Harris   ⎭

5th April, 1808.

MR. OLIVER RUSSELL brought before the Bench and the Depositions of Yesterday read to him—that were taken against him.

Mr. Lord and Mr. Blaxland called upon to inform the Bench in what instance Oliver Russell was guilty of Perjury as Stated in their Oath Yesterday.

The 1st Charge by Mr. Lord Vizt. that Simeon Lord came on Board the Brothers this day and after using very†

Charge the 1st by Mr. Lord:

Whilst Mr. Lord shook his Stick over his head and demanded whether he would comply with their request to furnish Mr. John Blaxland with what accomodation he wished as He was Owner, Supercargo, and would go home commander of the Ship.

Mr. Oliver Russell not being to be found—The Bench adjourns till to Morrow 9 oClock.

WM. MINCHIN.
G. BLAXCELL.
WM. LAWSON.

Bench met: William Lawson ⎫ Esquires.
Garnham Blaxcell ⎭

7th April, 1808.

MR. OLIVER RUSSELL comes before the Bench and gives in the following Paper, Vizt.:

" To the Honorable the Bench of Magistrates.

" Gentlemen,

" I humbly supplicate your interposition in rescuing an unoffending Man from one of the most determined and Palpably determined Schemes of Persecution that Malice and imposture could Possibly devise against him—To your exalted Sentiments of honor and humanity I already have to acknowledge the Sincerest obligation: before you I have been challenged with Offences calculated to Strip me of character in Society, and to deprive me of my command of a Ship now in this Port (to Wit the Ship Brothers of London) with a large and valuable Cargo now on Board upon which Cargo I have a certain claim, of which my pursuers seem determined to exert every odious effort to deprive me of.

" For this inhuman purpose Gentlemen, a List of charges Some of which were as infamous as others were contemptible—did Mr. J. Blaxland who is intangled in a Mercantile House in this Colony,

* Note 148.   † The words in italics are ruled through in the original.

1808.
30 April.

Proceedings
of bench of
magistrates on
the prosecution
of Russell
for perjury.

whose interests are in no wise connected with those of my Owners
(to Wit Messrs. Hullett Brothers and Company a very respectable
House in London) exhibit against me; but of all which I was
acquitted before an Honorable Bench of Magistrates convened on
the 5th day of March last* past to investigate Such vexatious and
complicated charges, Failing in the Object proposed by my Persecutors (Messrs. Simeon Lord and John and Gregory Blaxland
Esqres.) I was afterwards Assaulted by them, when on board my
Vessel, and instead of opposing violence to my Assailants, I considered it right to appeal for Justice to the Law—Before a Court
of Criminal Jurisdiction my complaint was heard, and the proceedings thereupon you are acquainted with.

"This Trial, Gentlemen, was concluded on the 30th Day of March
and upon the 5th day of this present Month was I Summonsed to
attend an Hon'able Bench of Magistrates at the Suit as I believe
of Mr. John Blaxland and Mr. Simeon Lord, who had apparently
canvased all the innumerable interrogatories put to myself and
others upon the Trial aforesaid in order to ground certain Complaints of Perjury upon whatever might in any way be termed
contradictory, without materially affecting the Case before the Court
or not without consideration of the express Words of the *3rd Institute 167* "For if it be not material tho' it be false it is no Perjury,
because it concerneth not the Point in issue and therefore is in effect
extrajudicial," Surely, Gentlemen, it cannot be considered as
material to the point in Issue, which was a matter of Assault
clearly Substantiated—whether Henry Purdie stood at the time
upon the first or Second Step of a Ladder; It was not a circumstance with which an Evidence could be Supposed Strictly to charge
his Memory, The Deponent could not at all be interested in the
Answer; and therefore it could not be either Wilful or corrupt; The
other charges are no less extrajudicial, as not applying to the Strict
fact of the Assault, as Set forth in the Indictment. Gentlemen, in
circumstantial Evidence not immediately affecting the grand Subject
of Prosecution, how rarely do you find two Evidences exactly
correspond, The smallest prevalency of doubt may occasion some
difference of reply; and how doleful would be the condition of a
Witness, were he at the moment of Examination to suppose that
inevitable Prosecution was to be the effect of Such his Examination
and what honest Man durst at any time to bring a Prosecution for
an injury, while he labours beneath the apprehension that the
Persons accused were to be permitted to prepare a vortex for his
destruction.

"Gentlemen, the Law is happily on my Side—To that Law
impartially dispensed by you, do I humbly appeal for help in the
hour of extreme oppression.

"Gentlemen, I was upon the 5th Instant Summonsed before a
Bench of Magistrates upon various charges of Perjury, but against
the Verbal order of Commitment I hereby beg humbly to object.

"1st.—That the 3rd of Blackstone 126 containeth an objection,
namely, 'That in Prosecution for Felony it is usual to deny a copy
of the Indictment, when there is any the least probable cause to
found such Prosecution upon, For it would be very great discourage-
ment to the Public Justice of the Kingdom if Prosecutors, who had
a tolerable ground of Suspicion, were liable to be sued at Law,
whenever their Indictments miscarried.'

* Note 149.

"But an action on the Case for a *malicious* Prosecution may be founded on an Indictment, whereon no acquittal can be had. My complaint against the Parties was not declared to have been sett up in malice,—being proved in fact, and one of the Defendants was convicted notwithstanding that the examination of his Evidence was in the Prosecutor's absence, which is also prohibited by Law.

"It is therefore clear Gentlemen that it was the duty of the Judge if he considered the Prosecution as of Malice—to order the Parties a Copy of the Indictment that they might have Sued by *Action of Damages* for Pecuniary recompense—but this not appearing, and the Judge not having ordered such copy of Indictment to the Defendants, they had no possible mode of redress hereafter, if even they had been brought forward of Malice instead of the fair and Justifiable Grounds on which they were Prosecuted.

"2ndly.—Gentlemen, I humbly object to any Single matter taken on record by that Court of Criminal Jurisdiction being received as Evidence in any Judicial proceeding whatsoever. By reason that the Proceedings were illegal, and that the whole are annulled and made absolutely void thereby, as the Law hath or rather leaveth not the Power to Select particular parts of a Proceeding; but if any part be vitiated, the *whole must fall contaminate*. This Objection, Gentlemen, I feel sufficient to ground and firmly stand upon, But I now beg leave.

"3rdly.—To shew Gentlemen, that to an Honorable Bench of Magistrates the Crime of Perjury alledged to have been committed before a Judge cannot be cognizable for nothing done in a Superior Court can be recognized by any Court or Sessions that hath inferior Jurisdiction; and upon this ground, I likewise Stand with deference to your Superior information.

"4thly.—I humbly refer this Honorable Bench to the authority of Mr. Hawkins, as celebrated as revered—whereby it will appear in Q. 40, that Justices of the Peace hath no Jurisdiction over Perjury at the Common Law—And

5thly.—I humbly appeal to the 23rd of Geo: 2: Cap: II s. 3— whether any private individual have any right to complain of Perjury committed before a Judge, who is alone to determine of Perjuries committed before himself, and to command thereupon within a limitted Space of 24 Hours, which is evidently done to prevent designing men from harrassing an Evidence with vexatious prosecutions upon matters which they could not be supposed to understand, and I say, Gentlemen, that as the Judge hath not in Court ordered the Defendants to have a Copy of their Indictment, that irregularity rests with him alone, and their Appeal before the Honorable Bench was tantamount to an impeachment of the Judge whose irregularity (if so it be) must by Law save the Prosecutor harmless; as the above Statute—by a clause of Limitation confineth the order of Prosecution to 24 Hours—and this complaint was in Six Days after brought, and not by the Judge at all—but by parties interested in the Event, who cannot give Evidence at all.

"Gentlemen, I stand upon my Country's Laws. As Englishmen, a suppliant Stranger craves your Protection by the preservation of those Laws inviolate. You must See, Gentlemen, that my persecutors are interested in my ruin; and I will make their very infamous designs yet more apparent by referring you to a Letter addressed to me by one of the Parties,* whereby he is by *Statute* exposed to Penal durance, upon two Several counts, the first for

1808.
30 April.

Proceedings of bench of magistrates on the prosecution of Russell for perjury.

* Note 150.

1808.
30 April.

Proceedings
of bench of
magistrates on
the prosecution
of Russell
for perjury.

sending a Letter threatening Prosecution, Unless certain terms are complied with, and the 2d Stipulating for the compromise of Felonies.

" Gentlemen, I have not an immediate inclination to prosecute the Person I allude to, tho' in my hands I possess the indubitable Means and thus it is that he rewards my Lenity and Forbearance.

" Gentlemen, My activity in procuring a valuable Cargo for my Owners is a strong presumption of my fidelity; and had Mr. Jno. Blaxland wished to have been considered equally attached to the interests of a House, in which He declares himself interested, Surely he could not for many Weeks past have endeavoured to throw insurmountable impediments in the way of my departure, conscious as at the same time he must be, that every day of my detention exposes my Freight to certain Hazard. Gentlemen, in any matter of complaint relative to the Ship Brothers Mr. John Blaxland hath no controul over me, As resident Agent he was to perform a certain duty, that was not to interfere with my Command, but his Object has been to benefit the House that he is connected with in this Colony at the expense of My Owners, Messrs. Hullett Brothers and Company of London, in whose behalf as well as my own I very respectfully solicit your impartial interference.

" Signed respectfully,
" OLIVER RUSSELL."

Mr. John Blaxland and Mr. Simeon Lord being requested to inform the Bench at what time they first attended to make Oath to the Perjury committed by Oliver Russell—state that the Proclamation issued by His Honor the Lieutenant Governor was made known on the Afternoon of Sunday. the 3rd Inst., and that they gave in their Deposition to a Bench of Magistrates on Monday Morning the 5th Instant.

We have very maturely weighed the circumstances of this very extraordinary case of Oliver Russell against whom Oath has been made by Messrs. Blaxland and Lord of his having committed wilful and corrupt Perjury, and as the Opinion of a full Bench of Magistrates on the 5th instant was unanimous as to Mr. Russell's finding Bail to take his Trial at the next Criminal Court for such offence and from the Testimony of Mr. J. Blaxland and Lord that they exhibited their complaint within twenty four Hours after the Sentence of the Criminal Court had been annulled by a Proclamation of His Honor the Lieutenant Governor—We are of Opinion that the said Oliver Russell shall find Bail for his appearance to take his Trial at the Criminal Court upon the Charges exhibited against him by the said Lord and Blaxland.

G. BLAXCELL.
WM. LAWSON.

BAIL BOND FOR OLIVER RUSSELL.

CUMBERLAND
TO WIT. } Be it remembered that on the Seventh Day of April in the Forty-eighth Year of the Reign of our Sovereign Lord George the Third, Oliver Russell, Mariner, Robert Sidaway and George Howe came before us Garnham Blaxcell and William Lawson, Esquires, two of His Majesty's Justices of the Peace in and for the said County, and Severally acknowledged themselves to owe our Sovereign Lord the King, that is to say the Said Oliver Russell in One Hundred Pounds, and Robert Sidaway and George Howe Fifty Pounds each of good and Lawful Money of

Great Britain, each, to be respectively Levied of their Lands and
tenements goods and Chattels if the said Oliver Russell shall make
default in the Performance of the condition subjoined—

Proceedings
of bench of
magistrates on
the prosecution
of Russell
for perjury.

. The condition of this Recognizance is such, that if the above
bounden Oliver Russell shall appear to take his Trial at the next
Criminal Court of Jurisdiction on a charge of Perjury, then this
Recognizance to be void and of none effect or otherwise to remain
in full force and Virtue.

OLIVER RUSSELL.
R. SIDAWAY.
GEORGE HOWE.

Taken and acknowledged the day and Year above Written
before us :—WILLIAM LAWSON.
G. BLAXCELL.

[Enclosure No. 13.]

THE HUMBLE MEMORIAL OF OLIVER RUSSELL

Master of the Ship Brothers, of London

UNTO His Honor George Johnston, Esquire, Lieutenant-Governor
in and over His Majesty's Territory of New South Wales
and its Dependencies, &c., &c., &c.

Respectfully Sayeth,

That your Honor's Memorialist was relieved by your
Honor's Proclamation* bearing date the third day of April, 1808,
from a Sentence of Transportation for Seven Years pronounced
against Memorialist by and before a Court of Criminal Jurisdiction upon the thirtieth day of the Previous March, the proceedings of which said Court. did to your Honor's Wisdom and
great love of Justice appear to have been illegal, and contrary to
the Laws by which the British Constitution is supported and the
Subjects' Rights defended.

That the Proceedings of the said Court were unimpartially
and incorrectly Recorded by the Acting Deputy Judge Advocate,
whose mind was obviously influenced by prejudice against Your
Honor's Memorialist, and did therefore omit such parts of Memorialist's Testimony, given before the said Court as would have
tended to the Advantage of his Charge or complaint against the
Defendants, and furthermore by the general incorrectness of the
said Acting Deputy Judge Advocate in recording the Evidence by
Memorialist so given, it was manifest to Memorialist that it was
in contemplation of the said Acting Deputy Judge Advocate to
give colour to a pretended charge of prevarication against Memorialist and at length to charge him with the heinous crime
of Perjury and to pass Sentence against Memorialist for the said
alledged Crime without permitting him the Power of Defence.

* Note 145.

1808.
30 April.

Memorial of
Oliver Russell
to Johnston.

That your Honor's Memorialist were upon Tuesday the 5th Day of April summoned to appear before a Bench of Magistrates at the Citation of Simeon Lord, who is denominated a Merchant, and who resideth in the Town of Sydney in this Territory of New South Wales in and over which Your Honor doth happily Rule as His Majesty's Lieutenant Governor; That one John Blaxland Esqre. who is a part Owner and Resident Agent for the Ship Brothers aforesaid did in concert with the Said Simeon Lord appear before the said Bench of Magistrates and there and then exhibit in conjunction with the said Lord certain new accusations of Perjury against Memorialist which were by them alledged to have been committed by Memorialist before the Court of Criminal Jurisdiction aforesaid; upon the incorrectness of the Manner in which the Evidence taken before whom has been recorded by the Acting Deputy Judge Advocate, the Memorialist respectfully refereth Your Honor to two Depositions hereunto subjoined, confident as Memorialist likewise is that many other Persons are now willing to depose to the same Effect.

That upon the Corporal Oaths of the said Lord and Jno. Blaxland, Esqre. Your Honor's Memorialist was ordered to find Bail to Answer to the said alledged Accusations before a Court of Criminal Jurisdiction; and for which Proceedings of the said Bench Memorialist respectfully refereth Your Honor to the written reports taken by the said Bench bearing date the 5th day of the present April and upon the 6th and 7th likewise of the said Month, That Memorialist was thus said to be under commitment notwithstanding that Memorialist did to the said Bench offer Lawfull objections to his said commitment, which was and is expressly contrary to an Act of Parliament passed in the 23rd Year of the Reign of King George the 2d Chapter the II Section 3 which enacteth:

That the Judge of Assize (Sitting the Court or within 24 Hours after) may direct any Witness if there shall appear to him a reasonable cause to be *Prosecuted* for Perjury; and may assign the party injured, or other Person undertaking such Prosecution Counsel, who are to do their duty Gratis and Such Prosecution so directed shall be carried on without any Duty or Fees whatsoever and the Clerk of Assize or other proper Officer of the Court shall give gratis to the Party injured, or Prosecuted, a Certificate of the same being directed, together with the names . of the Counsel assigned him, which Certificate shall be sufficient Proof of such Prosecution being directed—provided that no such direction or Certificate shall be given on the Trial.

" And the party prejudiced by the Perjury shall not be admitted to prove the Perjury " saith L. Raymond 396.

1808.
30 April.

Memorial of
Oliver Russell
to Johnston.

That Memorialist did humbly state unto the said Bench of Magistrates the foregoing Act of King George the Second as one of His objections to the Act of Commitment, which was upon the 7th Day of April confirmed, and Your Honor's Memorialist was held to bail in the sum of £200 to wit himself and two Sureties in £50 each, That the Memorialist humbly referreth Your Honor to the proceedings of the said Bench already Quoted for the several objections by him so stated as aforesaid.

That by the Said Act of King George the Second the discretional Power of Commitment is vested in the Judge alone whom the Law hath wisely deemed to be the proper and only Person to alledge the Crime of Perjury before himself committed Wilfully and corruptly, and to direct Prosecution thereupon, For it surely did unto our great and Venerable Law givers appear and seem that malicious prosecutions for the imputed Crime of Perjury would inevitably be consequent to every complaint by Action or Indictment were the Parties accused countenanced by Law in setting up mischievous Allegations against the accuser, Complainant or his Witness's; and so eventually would the Claims of Justice be defeated, and effectually repelled, by reason that it would be dangerous in any One to Prosecute or to give Evidence before a Court of Justice, But that by the said Act it hath fortunately been otherwise provided and decreed; inasmuch as that the discretional Power of allegation is thereby vested in the Judge alone, and that even his Authority herein is by a clause of limitation especially restricted to the space of 24 Hours after the Sitting of the Court, and also, that a Certificate of Challenge must be issued from the Clerk of Assize *or other Proper Officer*—Whereas that no such Certificate hath been granted issued or Produced, That the interval between the Sitting of the said Court, and the exhibition of the aforesaid Charges upon which commitment hath been declared was five whole days instead of 24 Hours; That the said Charges have not been and were not sett up by order of the Judge; who as Memorialist declareth hath by an illegal Sentence himself offended against the Law, and thereby rendered Null and void the whole of the proceedings whereupon the Accusations so alleged against Memorialist as aforesaid have been maliciously sett up by the said Lord and Blaxland, who are Persons interested in the complaint, who were under Indictment and were Prosecuted by Memorialist for an Assault of which the Brother of one of the Parties (to Wit, Mr. Gregory Blaxland) was convicted and therefore Malice is much more than presumable, and that Whereas they are in all respects whatsoever notoriously known to be interested Per-

1808.
30 April.

Memorial of
Oliver Russell
to Johnston.

sons, and the above Quotation lain before your Honor from Lord
Raymond doth expressly say that a party prejudiced by the
Perjury shall not be permitted to prove the Perjury.

That the said Lord and John Blaxland, Esqre. are known to
have endeavoured in various ways to divest your Honor's Memorialist of the Command of his aforesaid Ship, and among other
their adopted Means have instituted against him numerous
grievous and vexatious charges and Accusations, Criminal as
well as Civil, which were dismissed by the Magistrates before
whom those complaints were made—That the Crew of the aforesaid Ship Brothers have been excited to disaffection towards your
Honor's Memorialist by secret Agents individuously Employed
against him, altho' that Memorialist hath heretofore ever enjoyed
the perfect good will towards him of the said Crew, as he hath
every reason to be well assured that he is happily in the Possession
of the full and implicit confidence of His Owners in London, to
Wit Messrs. Hullett Brothers and Co., who are known to be a
very respectable Mercantile House; and that from the conduct
of the said John Blaxland Esqre. before a Bench of Magistrates
it was unfortunately found necessary to determine upon the
Merits of a Complaint Set up against his said Crew or part of
them upon Saturday the 16th of this Present April, it was more
than presumable that the said John Blaxland, Esqre. had in a
great measure abetted such disaffection in order by such undue
means to endeavour to effect the Accomplishment of his design
of divesting your Honor's Memorialist of his Charge and Command of His said Ship. He the said John Blaxland, Esqre.
having of his own free will as Memorialist believeth, come forward before the said Bench accompanied by the said Lord with
intent to vindicate Memorialist's Said Seamen, and to defend
them against Memorialist's just Complaint as their Lawful
Commander.

That so numerous and divers have been the Acts and devices,
concerted by the said Lord and Jno. Blaxland, Esqre. and
attempted to be effected and enforced against him, The Memorialist who is a Solitary Stranger in this Colony, and hath no
dependence, no single Hope of Protection and Defence against
the Wickedness of his Persecutors, But in Your Honor's impartial Love of Justice and great Benevolence of Disposition,
which benignant Attributes so truly dignify Your Honor's most
exalted Character.

That your Honor's Memorialist hereby complaineth to your
Honor of Prejudice industriously implanted in the Public Mind
against Memorialist by the Artifices of his said joint Persecutors,
Lord and Jno. Blaxland, Esqre. the former of whom, although

to all appearance illiterally reared and educated, and once a
Seven Years Transport in this Colony, and in the most mean
and humble habits, is by the Public Voice declared to be a
common Barrater, and the other a Gentleman under influence of
the Evil Counsels of the former, forgetful of every sense of duty
to his Brother Owners and himself, and who regardless of the
interest of Memorialist's Owners in London, hath engaged and so
intricately intangled himself within the interested Schemes of
his Seducer, as now openly and avowedly to abet the plans of
Ruin formed against Your Honor's Memorialist and against the
Welfare of his said Owners in London by endeavouring to wrest
from Your Honor's Memorialist his charge and Command aforesaid, and by thus transfering the said charge in all Moral
Probability likewise to effect a Transfer of His Said Ship's
consignment to some Agent of the said Lords either in London,
or elsewhere, she having now on Board a large and valuable Cargo
of 38,000 Seal Skins on board, of which Memorialist is per
Agreement entitled to one twelfth Share.

That your Honor's Memorialist respectfully Prayeth your
Honor to receive under your high consideration the Danger and
great Risque of damage to which his said Cargo must by longer
detention be exposed, and the concequent necessity that he should
as soon as possible proceed to England with his said Freight in
which he is no less interested than his said respectable Owners—
That your Honor will likewise be pleased to take under consideration the evident malignity of his Pursuers, and that under
all the foregoing circumstances relative to his very hard and
distressing Case, and the more especially the dread which Your
Honor's Memorialist hath of prejudice obtaining in the Minds of
those who might by your Honor's precept be appointed to try the
merits of the Charges thus unlawfully instituted ag't Memorialist—Your Honor will be graciously pleased to admit
Memorialist to an Extent of Bail himself in the Sum of two
thousand Pounds (his share in the said Cargo being upon moderate Computation of much greater value) Whereby Your Honor's
Memorialist may be held to Bail in the amount aforesaid upon
his Arrival in England to render himself up to His Majesty's
Government to any charge or Charges that shall or may be there
exhibited against him.

And in grateful Remembrance of Such Your Honor's goodness
and impartiallity Your Honor's Memorialist as in duty Bound
will ever Pray.

OLIVER RUSSELL.

Sydney, in New South Wales, 18th April, 1808.

Russell's bond
for his
appearance
in London to
answer the
charge of
perjury.

[Enclosure No. 14.]

NEW SOUTH WALES. { KNOW ALL MEN by these Presents That I Oliver Russell, Master of the Ship Brothers of the Port of London, now lying in this Port, Am held and firmly bound to His Majesty's Principal Secretary of State for the War Department and Colonies for the time being in the Penal Sum of Two thousand Pounds of lawful Money of Great Britain to be paid to His Majesty's said Secretary of State or his certain Attorney, for which Payment well and truly to be made, I bind myself my Heirs Executors and Administrators firmly by these Presents Sealed with my Seal, Dated at Sydney New South Wales, the twenty eighth day of April in the forty eighth year of the Reign of our Sovereign Lord George the third by the Grace of God of the United Kingdom of Great Britain and Ireland, King, defender of the faith, and in the Year of our Lord, One thousand and eight hundred and eight.

THE CONDITION of this Obligation is such, that if the above bounden Oliver Russell shall within one Week after his Arrival in the Port of London surrender himself to His Majesty's Principal Secretary of State for the War Department and Colonies and enter into such further Obligation as may be then required from him, to Answer to the Charge of Perjury (for which Crime he at present stands Committed for Trial, on the Oaths of Mr. John Blaxland and Mr. Simeon Lord) either in England or in this Country as His Majesty's said Principal Secretary of State shall be Pleased to direct, then this Obligation shall be void and of none effect—or else shall be and remain in full force and Virtue.   OLIVER RUSSELL.

Signed Sealed and Delivered (where no Stamps are Used) in the Presence of   JOHN MCARTHUR.
                    D. D. MANN.

[Enclosure No. 15.]

CORRESPONDENCE WITH JOHN HARRIS, ESQUIRE, SURGEON.

[1] *Mr. Nicholas Bayly to Surgeon Harris.*

Sir,   Head Quarters, Sydney, 4th April, 1808.

An officer to
be sent with
despatches to
England.

I am directed by His Honor the Lieut. Governor to acquaint you that the Exigencies of His Majesty's Service, and the peculiar situation of this Colony, make it indispensibly necessary that an Officer well acquainted with the causes which have occasioned the supercession of Governor Bligh should take home his dispatches to His Majesty's Ministers, that if anything therein should appear doubtful, or not sufficiently explained, they may be enabled immediately to obtain the Information required.

The Lieutenant Governor has in consequence made choice of you, Sir, for that Service, satisfied that no person can be more competent to give such explanation, than one of those who have called upon him to assume the Command, and pledged their lives and fortunes to support the measure.

You are therefore immediately to prepare yourself to embark on board the Brothers, where a passage is provided for you.

I am, &c.,

NICHOLAS BAYLY, Secy.

1808.
30 April.

Harris to embark on the Brothers with despatches.

[2] *Surgeon Harris to Major Johnston.*

Sir, Sydney, 5th April, 1808.

As His Majesty's Service requires my attendance in England, I beg to assure you that I am ready to embark on board the *Brothers* whenever she may be ready to sail, or you may require me. And I trust I shall be able to explain to His Majesty's Ministers many things which otherwise might never have reached them.

I have, &c.,

J. HARRIS.

Harris' willingness to report to the secretary of state.

P.S.—Having some private concerns to arrange previous to embarkation may I beg you will be pleased to excuse my attendance on Regimental Duties.

[3] *Mr. Nicholas Bayly to Surgeon Harris.*

Sir, Head Quarters, Sydney, 5th April, 1808.

I am directed by His Honor the Lieutenant Governor to acknowledge the receipt of your Letter of this day, declaring your readiness to embark on board the Brothers, and that you trust you shall be able to explain to His Majesty's Ministers many things which otherwise might never have reached them; As this latter declaration implies either that you are in possession of some information unknown to the Lieut. Governor, or to insinuate that you have a charge to make against him, or some Persons now employed in official Situations, His Honor has directed me to require that you immediately transmit an explicit explanation upon this obscure Observation.

I am, Sir, &c.,

NICHOLAS BAYLY, Secy.

Harris requested to explain obscurities in his letter.

[4] *Surgeon Harris to Major Johnston.*

Sir, Sydney, 5th April, 1808.

I have to acknowledge the receipt of your Secretary's Letter of this date; In answer thereto I have to inform you, that

1808.
30 April.

it is very probable I may be in possession of many transactions which may not have come to your knowledge; and if I am, I shall consider it my duty to inform His Majesty's Ministers thereof.

I have, &c.,

J. HARRIS.

[5] *Major Johnston to Surgeon Harris.*

Sir,   Head Quarters, Sydney, 7th April, 1808.

Harris to make a full report in England.

As you are to take my Dispatches to England, it is proper I should apprise you as early as possible, that it is my Intention to refer His Majesty's Ministers to you, for such Information as you possess respecting the Tyranny and Oppressions of Governor Bligh over the Officers, Soldiers and Inhabitants of this Settlement.

You will naturally explain your own reasons for joining with the Officers and Inhabitants in calling upon me to assume the Command, and to put Governor Bligh in arrest; And I particularly recommend to you, not to neglect making known " those things to His Majesty's Ministers which might never have reached them " but for your Return to England.

I am, Sir, &c.,

GEO. JOHNSTON.

[Enclosure No. 16.]

[1] MAJOR JOHNSTON TO OFFICERS.

Gentlemen,   Headquarters, Sydney, 26th April, 1808.

Discontent of officers with Macarthur.

I have observed the discontent which has for some time prevailed amongst a few Officers with the greatest concern; and as I have unquestionable Evidence that this discontent has entirely arisen from the confidence I have reposed in Mr. McArthur, Secretary to the Colony, I have now assembled all of you together who are doing duty at Head Quarters, and have sent a Copy of this Letter to the detached Posts, that those Officers who have anything to alledge against that Gentleman may come forward and distinctly state in writing what it is they have to Charge him with.

Johnston willing to hear complaints.

If he has committed any Offence, it is not my intention to shut my Ears against the proof of it. If anything improper in his Conduct can be made appear, he shall be immediately dismissed from his Office. And I hope some of you Gentlemen will have Public Spirit sufficient to supply his place, and to perform the laborious duties Mr. McArthur now discharges without reward or emolument.

To preserve the peace of the Settlement, and to promote the prosperity and Honor of His Majesty's Government are my only objects, and I am confident that those objects cannot be secured but by the annihilation of the party spirit that has unfortunately too much prevailed, almost ever since the day when You all urged me to assume the Government, and pledged your words of Honor to support me in the measure. How far a desire to deprive me of the services of Mr. McArthur at such a crisis as the present can be considered as an observance of that promise, it will rest with those Gentlemen who are adverse to him to explain. For my own part, I think no Officer will aver that Mr. McArthur has not fulfilled his share of that solemn engagement; That he has not devoted himself with unremitting assiduity to the Public affairs; That he has not exposed himself to reproach and obloquy by his exertions to detect the frauds and oppressions of the late Governor; Or that he has not faithfully done everything in his power to carry my wishes into effect for the reduction of the expenditure of Public Money, and to prevent the improper distribution of the Public Servants and Property.

1808.
30 April.
Prevalence of party feeling.

Johnston's defence of Macarthur.

But perhaps these are his Offences. If so, let me assure you that he has only obeyed my Orders, and that, had he acted differently, I should have been as ready to withdraw my Confidence from him as I know some of you are desirous that I should.*

I am, &c.,
GEO. JOHNSTON.

To Captain Edward Abbott, Captain A. F. Kemp, John Harris, Esq're, Surgeon; Lieut. John Brabyn, Lieut. William Moore, Lieut. Thomas Laycock, Lieut. and Adjt. Wm. Minchin, Lieut. William Lawson, Lieut. Cadwallader Draffin, Ensign Archibald Bell, New South Wales Corps; Captain Thomas Moore, Sydney Association; Thomas Jamison, Esq're, Principal Surgeon; James Williamson, Esq're, Acting Commissary; Nicholas Bayly, Esq're, Acting Provost-Marshal; Mr. Fitz, Deputy Commissary; Mr. D. Wentworth, Assistant Surgeon; Mr. James Mileham, Assist't Surgeon; Garnham Blaxcell, Esqr., J.P.

[2] OFFICERS TO MAJOR JOHNSTON.

Sydney, 26th April, 1808.

THE undersigned Officers having Assembled by order of His Honor the Lieutenant Governor to give their Sentiments on a letter which His Honor laid before them, Are Unanimously of Opinion that they do not feel themselves justified, nor would they presume to call in question the right or propriety of his consulting any person he may think proper, either publicly or privately, and that they shall at all times feel much pleasure in

Officers' refusal to impugn Johnston's administration.

* Note 151.

1808.
30 April.

obeying His orders, which is all they consider they have to dó as Officers serving under him.

Ed. Abbott, Capt. N.S.W. Corps.	James Williamson, Act'g Com'ry.
Anth'y Fenn Kemp, Capt'n.	R. Fitz, D'y Com'ry.
Wm. Moore, Lieut.	Nicholas Bayly, Act'g P.-M.
Thos. Laycock, Lt.	G. Blaxcell, J.P.
Wm. Lawson, Lieut.	Wm. Minchin, Lieut. & Adjt.
Cadw'r Draffin, Lieut.	N.S.W. Corps.
Thos. Moore, C.L. Assoc'n.	D. Wentworth.

UNDER SECRETARY COOKE TO GOVERNOR BLIGH.
(Despatch per ship Æolus.)

5 May.

Assignment
of convicts
transported in
the Speke.

Sir,   Downing Street, 5th May, 1808.

I have received Lord Castlereagh's directions to transmit to you herewith the Copy of a Letter I have received from Mr. Beckett, Under Secretary of State for the Home Department dated 29th Ultimo, together with the assignment of the Convicts who have been embarked on board the Speke for the Settlement under your Government. You will observe that the term "life" against Jane Rafty alias Holden and Élizabeth Lloyd has been written upon an erasure.   I have, &c.,   E. COOKE.

[Enclosures.]
[Copies of these are not available.]

UNDER SECRETARY COOKE TO GOVERNOR BLIGH.
7th June, 1808.
[A copy of this despatch is not available.]

GOVERNOR BLIGH TO VISCOUNT CASTLEREAGH.*
(Despatch per ship Rose; acknowledged by Viscount Castlereagh,
15th May, 1809.)

30 June.

Proclamation
of martial law
by Johnston.

My Lord,   30th June, 1808.
  *   *   *   *   *   *   *   *

55. I have already said that Martial Law was proclaimed; it was done in the following words:—

" GEORGE JOHNSTON.

" THE present alarming State of the Colony having induced the principal Inhabitants to call upon me to interpose the Military Power for their relief, and to place His Excellency Governor Bligh in arrest, I have, with the advice of my Officers, considered it necessary, for the good of His Majesty's Service, to comply with their request. I do, therefore, hereby proclaim Martial Law in this Colony, to which all Persons are commanded to submit, until measures can be adopted for the restoration of the Civil Law on a permanent foundation.

" By Command of His Honor the Lieu't-Governor,

" (Signed) NICHOLAS BAYLY, Secretary.

" Head-Quarters, 26th January, 1808."

* Note 152.

56. I have only to observe on this Proclamation that the Colony was in a most tranquil state, and the Inhabitants happy—except McArthur and his Party, who was alarmed at the issue of his trial, and seemed uneasy that he could not be above all Law.

57. The next day a General Order, as I was informed, was published, as follows:—

[*Here followed a copy of the general order, dated 27th January, 1808; see page 271.*]

58. A little after this the following Proclamation was published:—

[*Here followed a copy of the proclamation, dated 27th January, 1808; see page 240.*]

59. This Proclamation was followed up with a salute of Twenty-one Guns from Dawes' Point, and the Standard of Great Britain was hoisted. The Troops fired three Vollies from the Parade.

60. On that and several succeeding days, Committees again met, before whom all the Magistrates and those who were considered as having been intimate at Government House were brought and examined concerning my administration and intentions. Every wicked artifice, as well as threats, were used to force affirmative answers to all such questions as their diabolical minds could propose, and some of them were brought to such agitation from a fear of their lives that they knew not what they said or did, trembling under the tyranny which was existing.

61. These Committees were composed of McArthur, Bayly, Blaxcell, Grimes, Jamison (Surgeon), Captain Kemp, Lieutenant Minchin, Lieutenant Lawson, Lieutenant Draffin, Doctor Townson, and Jno. Blaxland.

62. There were likewise Benches of Magistrates ordered, and they began to arrest many Persons who were considered loyally attached to my Government, and the most threatening messages were sent to others.

63. Agents were sent about the Town of Sydney, who, by threats and promises, induced the greatest part of the Inhabitants to illuminate their Houses and make Bonfires on that and the following Night; and a scene of drunkenness, even among the Troops as well as the People in the Town, gave apprehension for the safety of Government House, from whence my Arms had been taken by Lieut. Moore through the orders of Major Johnston.

64. On the Morning of the 28th, a Committtee, composed of Mr. Nicholas Bayly, Captain Edward Abbott, Thomas Jamison (Principal Surgeon), and Mr. Garnham Blaxcell, came to me;

1808.
30 June.

and Bayly, in a very Robespierrean manner, read and delivered the following charge:—

Charges to be made against Bligh.

[*Here followed a copy of the letter dated 28th January, 1808, which was also forwarded by Major Johnston with his despatch dated 11th April, 1808; see E, page 242.*]

Refusal to acknowledge Johnston's authority.

65. The daring impudence of reading a Charge of this nature, added to the outrage of depriving me of my Government, increased my indignation. I denied their authority in every proceeding not authorised by myself, and told them that only to my King and Country would I be answerable for any act of mine in this Colony.

Bligh's defence of his regulations.

66. With respect to my subverting the Laws, it rests upon the local Regulations I have made. Those, it can be proved, have been the most salutary, and conformable to my Instructions from His Majesty's Ministers; it is true they gave umbrage to a certain description of Men because they tended to put an end to monopoly, and encouraged the industrious Man to rise above his common level, which former practices prevented.

Administration of justice.

66.* As to intimidating and influencing the Courts of Justice, many in the Colony can bear testimony that I never interfered in their concerns; every complaint made to me was referred to them and the Magistrates. To the Judge-Advocate I have shewn my disapprobation when Justice was disgracefully delayed and other instances of partiality occurred which he was chiefly the cause of. At such times I only shewed my Authority by admonitions and strict Justice.

Relations with private citizens.

67. In regard to the third part of the Charge, no Person ever became obnoxious to me unless by a breach of the Laws which it was my duty to see duly executed. A certain description of Men (the present Usurpers) thought great Offences might be committed by them with impunity, and an equality of distributive Justice was called by them a settled plan of depriving them of liberty, property, and their lives. Where there was a likelihood of amendment in any unfortunate Person my attention was ever drawn to that object, and this line of humane conduct has been productive of a great deal of good, and been exemplified the last Year in the reduction of crimes and punishments, to the great comfort of every one.

Examination of Bligh's papers ordered by Johnston.

68. Immediately after my declaration, before mentioned, the Committee produced a written Order, which they received from Major Johnston, as follows, and was read by Mr. Bayly:—

"Sydney, 28th January, 1808.

" You are hereby directed to examine all the Papers belonging to William Bligh, Esq., and to detain all Papers that in any way relate to the public concerns of this Colony and its Depen-

* Note 153.

dencies; all other Papers you are to return him. You are to acquaint him that during your examination of those Papers he may be present and have any Friend or other Persons also present he may choose to appoint.

1808.
30 June.
———
Examination of
Bligh's papers
ordered by
Johnston.

" (Signed) GEORGE JOHNSTON,
" L't-Governor.

" To Capt. Ed. Abbott, Thos. Jamison, Esq., Garnham Blaxcell, Esq., Nicholas Bayly, Esq."

69. To this Order I objected, as also to the acknowledging Major Johnston as Lieutenant-Governor, when Capt. Abbott and the other Members of the Committee replied that my objections were useless—that they had received Orders and would therefore execute them.

70. My Papers and Letter Books, my Private Instructions, the Great Seal of the Colony, and my Commissions, which had been seized and locked up the night of my confinement, under a guard of two Centinels, were now taken possession of; but I insisted on keeping my private Letter Books, in which were entered Copies of my Letters to and from the Secretary of State, and a duplicate of my last despatches (which lay prepared for the first opportunity of sending off) and I sealed them up. On this occasion, that respect might be shown to these Books and Papers, I wrote as follows:—

Seizure of Bligh's papers.

" Sir, " Government House, Sydney, 28th January, 1808.

" By frequent private communications with His Majesty's Principal Secretary of State for the Colonies before I left England, I was ordered to enquire into particular circumstances, to which I have made answers; and an application being made to me to give up the public Papers of the Colony, by a Committee from You, I think it due to my consequence and situation, under the consideration before stated, to object to give up particular Books and particular Papers to any Person except yourself, sealed.

Certain books and papers to be delivered to Johnston under seal.

" I am, Sir, your obedient humble Servant,

" To Major Johnston." " (Signed) WM. BLIGH.

71. In consequence of this Letter Mr. Bayly returned and read to me the following Order which he had received :—

Johnston enforces his orders.

" Sydney, 28th January, 1808.

" I hereby command you to proceed to the execution of my Orders, as expressed on the other side of this Paper.*

" (Signed) GEORGE JOHNSTON,
" L't-Governor.

" To Captain Edw'd Abbott, Thos. Jamison, Esq., Garnham Blaxcell, Esq., Nicholas Bayly, Esq."

* *Marginal note.*—This Order was written on the back of the one preceeding.

1808.
30 June.
And farther, His Honor the Lieutenant-Governor had directed him to state that he should feel himself under the necessity of declining to receive any addresses from me unless they were directed to him as Lieutenant-Governor to this Country, which Order was signed " Nicholas Bayly, Secretary," and addressed " William Bligh, Esq."

Johnston desires to be addressed as lieut.-governor.

Seizure of the great seal.

72. At the departure of the Committee I again objected to their taking away the Great Seal of the Colony, but Mr. Bayly declared that they could now command it; it was needless for me to make any opposition. A part of the Papers were only taken away this day, and the remainder locked up as before, with two Centinels at the Door.

Further removal of papers.

73. The following morning the same Committee came again, and took away another assortment of Papers, public and private. Many of them were secret Letters, containing private information concerning the affairs of the Colony.

Bligh's farm at the Hawkesbury.

74. All the Land upon the material parts of the Banks of the Hawkesbury being granted away to Individuals, except a small spot in which Government House stood, and the extent of that Settlement rendering it necessary to have a resting-Place in my journeys, as well as to render it easier for the Settlers to have access to me, I directed the Rev'd Samuel Marsden to purchase a small Place* eligible for my purpose, which he did of a Person returning to England for one hundred and fifty Pounds of my own money at the rate of a Pound per Acre, and to which I added by purchase an adjoining piece of about one hundred Acres for one hundred Pounds. In the cultivation of a part of this spot, I also wished to prove by example to the Settlers that a few Acres properly taken care of would produce as much as a great many by their modes of farming, whereby considerable time and labour would be saved for other valuable concerns. The private Accounts of this Farm, which had been sent to me by the Person who took care of it, and were in my private Desk, this Committee seized. Although I received them a considerable time before, yet the public concerns of the Colony did not give me time to peruse them.

Protests against seizure of papers.

75. Messrs. Palmer, Campbell, and my Secretary, friends of Government, were present at the seizure of all the Papers, and remonstrated against the unlawfulness of taking them away; but the Committee answered they were the only competent judges of what ought to be done, and Captain Abbott told my Secretary he was very impertinent in dictating to them.

Missing papers.

76. Among the Papers of the proceedings concerning the six Officers, the two Letters from them on the 26th and the Judge-Advocate's Memorial† to me were missing. I therefore desired

* Note 106.   † Note 154.

the Judge-Advocate might be sent to. Mr. Surgeon Jamison was appointed to go accordingly; but Mr. Atkins denied having the Memorial, saying he had only the rough Copy, which the Committee directed to be delivered to the Lieutenant-Governor.

77. To add to other insults, I received a written Message from Major Johnston by Mr. Bayly, stating that rations should be continued from the public Store to my Servants, and live Stock from the public Herds and Flocks for my Family, and that Receipts would be required from me for every Article issued on my Account, that a Charge might be made for the same at the current market prices; that when I was to leave the Colony an Account would be made up and transmitted to His Majesty's Ministers that they might determine whether such Stock, Provisions, and Stores were or were not to be paid for by me; and farther, that he must reduce my establishment of Horses to five. Soon after, another Message was delivered to me, that in case I chose a Tombstone to be erected over the Remains of the late Captain Putland (my Son-in-law) it would be done and the expense transmitted Home to know if I was to be charged with it. I had designed and executed a part of a Mausoleum which I intended for the reception of the Remains of Governors who might die in this Colony; it was near the Church, and in the finished part of the Vault Capt. Putland's Remains had been deposited.

78. On the 30th of January, the Committee came again and took away another assortment of Papers, and, locking up my Office, the Centinels were taken away and my friends were allowed to see me. Rebellious Courts of Justice were going on,* and my Book, containing Copies of Letters to the Secretary of State, sent for, and paragraphs read to elucidate my conduct and designs, as likewise to irritate the minds of the Officers and People. That the People might be attached to the rebellious Party, they promised numerous Licenses, Cows, and other Stock out of Government Herds and Flocks, while they were sending Memorials into the Country; and by these promises and threats they induced a number of poor Persons to sign them, which are the kind of documents they have to give a color of consistency to their rebellious proceedings.

79. The serious part of my duty which I had orders to execute in evacuating Norfolk Island caused His Majesty's Ship Porpoise to be now absent, but expected every day to arrive; the object of securing this Ship on her return became of great consequence to me, for the Officers of her (particularly Acting-

<table>
<tr><td>1808.
30 June.</td></tr>
<tr><td>Victualling of Bligh's household.</td></tr>
<tr><td>Erection of captain Putland's tombstone.</td></tr>
<tr><td>Attempts to alienate the people from Bligh.</td></tr>
<tr><td>Bligh's endeavour to obtain command of H.M.S. Porpoise.</td></tr>
</table>

* *Marginal note.*—To the time of this Despatch being closed they have executed seven Persons (*see* note 155).

1808.
30 June.

Bligh's
endeavour
to obtain
command of
H.M.S.
Porpoise.

Lieutenant Symonds who had the Command of her on account
of the sickness and death of Captain Putland and Acting-
Lieutenant - Ellison having been here during the time of His
Majesty's Ship Buffalo) were very intimately connected with the
rebellious Party in all their practices. On-this concern I wrote
to Major Johnston, and demanded that she should be given up to
me on her return; that in the meantime I might make the necessary preparations for her fitting out; this I urged by Letters
showing the distinction between my situation as Governor and
Commodore on this station; but my endeavours proved unsuccessful, as by two Letters from him he refused my having again
the Command of the Porpoise, as it was his intention to send me
home in a Merchant Ship.

Removal of
Bligh's broad
pendant.

80. My Broad Pendant was flying in the Estramina, a Government Colonial Schooner, but it was hauled down in consequence
of Major Johnston's Order to the Master of her the day after my
confinement—a Copy of which I inclose.

Symons' union
with the
rebel party.

81. On the 4th of February the Porpoise arrived, and Acting-
Lieutenant James Symons, who commanded her, did not hoist my
Broad Pendant, but joined with the rebel Party, accepted an
Appointment as a Magistrate from them,. and gave himself a
Commission as Acting-Commander, without ever communicating
with me, or sending the public Dispatches which he had received
at Norfolk Island and the Derwent; at the same time I was prevented from having any communication with him by the following written Message from Major Johnston :—

"Sydney, 4th February, 1808.

Bligh's
communication
with the
Porpoise
prohibited.

"His Honor Lieutenant-Governor Johnston has commanded me
to acquaint you that he cannot allow you to hold any communication with the Officers of His Majesty's Ship Porpoise, and that
he shall consider any attempt to do so, either by Letter or otherwise, as a breach of your arrest.

"(Signed)   NICHOLAS BAYLY, Secretary."

Proposals for
Bligh's voyage
to England.

82. From this period various Letters passed tending to deprive
me of any hopes to regain my Ship, and threats that I should be
sent away first in one and then in another Merchant Ship, in
which neither convenience nor my.personal safety could be at all
expected, and which I resisted. After this they began to make
offers that I might go in the Porpoise on terms my honor would
not admit of, such as resigning my Command to a rebellious and
self-made Commander, and who dishonorably had made a requisition to Major Johnston, as Lieutenant-Governor, to demand of
me all the Orders that had been received from the Admiralty
concerning the Ship.

83. An armed Vessel, with Letters of Marque, having arrived from the Cape of Good Hope, called The Fox, I required to get out of my confinement into her; this produced a Letter stating that unless I agreed to go in the Porpoise, on their conditions, I should be *required* to embark (with any one Person I might choose to attend me) in the Dart in a few days; this was a poor miserable Vessel with only one Deck, deeply loaded with salted Skins, and in the interest of McArthur. I then wrote to Major Johnston to know if by the word "*required*" he meant that force would be applied, who answered in the affirmative; upon which other difficulties occurred, which were controverted between me and them, when the Lady Nelson, Tender, which had been employed on the same service as the Porpoise, arrived on the 29th March.

1808.
30 June.
———
Proposals for
Bligh's voyage
to England.

84. This Vessel was commanded by Acting-Lieutenant Kent, properly first Lieutenant of the Porpoise, who immediately waited on me before he could be prevented. I therefore, conceiving a favorable opinion of him, and hoping by this means to get the Command of the Porpoise—at all events, to turn out Lieutenant Symons—sent him a Commission; but, as I was prohibited from communicating with her Officers, I was obliged to do it through Major Johnston, who refused to deliver it unless I, by Letter to Lieutenant Kent, signified that I would give up my authority over that Ship until we arrived in England. This I refused, and some Letters passed between us concerning it. At length, on the 1st of April, they sent the following written Message:—

Kent appointed
commander of
the Porpoise
by Bligh.

[*Here followed a copy of the letter from Mr. Nicholas Bayly to Governor Bligh, dated 1st April, 1808; see page 269.*]

85. I have only to observe on the foregoing that Lieutenant Colonel Paterson's appointment as Lieutenant-Governor of the Territory had been thoroughly made known by public Orders on that account, and annually noted in the Almanacs,* by which no doubt can be ascertained of their having known it, and of their art in fabricating an untruth.

Previous
knowledge of
Paterson's
appointment as
lieut.-governor.

86. A few days after I received this message, Major Johnston delivered to Lieutenant Kent the Commission I had sent him to take command of the Porpoise, which he accordingly did.

Delivery of
Bligh's
commission
to Kent.

87. As soon as this became known to me, I procured two friends to throw themselves in Captain Kent's way, and to impress on his mind that now, being legally appointed, he was to separate himself from any intimacy with the Rebels, and keeping his Ship in good order, never to lose sight of me or suffer any insult to be offered to my Person and dignity or obey any orders from the present Usurpers, which he promised faithfully to do. Notwith-

Orders secretly
conveyed
to Kent.

* Note 136.

1808.
30 June.

standing this, on the 19th of April, he sailed, and I was told it
was to bring up Lieutenant Governor Paterson from Port Dalrymple.

Reasons for
Paterson's
non-arrival
at Sydney.

88. Captain Kent returned on the 26th of May without bringing up Lieutenant Governor Paterson or me any Message or
Letter from him. It is reported that the cause of Colonel Paterson not coming up was my remaining in the Colony; and as he
knew that without my death or absence he could not legally
assume the reins of Government, he thought it too dangerous to
attempt to restore my authority, as he considered all the Officers
of the Corps were concerned in the rebellion. By report, too, I
find the Porpoise has been aground, and is in so leaky a state
as to require to be hove down and have two new lower Masts.

89. Notwithstanding the messages I had sent to Captain Kent
he became a Member of their Criminal Court.

Macarthur and
Bayly in
virtual
command.

90. It will appear from what I have related of the transactions
of the 26th of January that McArthur and Bayly had the chief
consular command at the Government House on that Evening.
At the time of McArthur's liberation from Gaol he said, in the
hearing of Ryley, the Gaolor, "now the last card is played."
When he parted from the Government House and went to the
Parade he enquired for Mr. Gore (the Provost-Marshal), and on
being told that he had been taken to his own House he said,
"send him to Gaol immediately"; and it was done accordingly.

Macarthur's
influence over
Johnston.

91. It now became evident McArthur was, privately, the
director of every measure, and that he had unbounded influence
over Major Johnston; but that he might exercise his power in a
more public manner, it was necessary he should take some official
situation. In order to enable him to do this it was thought proper
he should be acquitted of the crimes with which he had been

Trial of
Macarthur.

charged. Major Johnston, therefore, by his Precept convened a
Criminal Court on the 2nd of February, the members of which
were Charles Grimes, their Judge-Advocate, Captain Anthony
Fenn Kemp, Lieutenant William Moore, Lieutenant Thomas
Laycock, Lieutenant William Minchin, Lieutenant William Law-
son, and Lieutenant Cadwallader Draffin, to try John McArthur,
Esq., on the Indictment preferred against him by Judge-Advocate
Atkins.

Methods of
conducting
the trial.

92. The loyal Persons who would have attended at this trial
were subpœnaed as Witnesses merely to keep them out of Court,
for few of them were examined, and any other Persons of whom
they had any suspicion were literally turned out of Court. But
it was easy to foresee what would be the event of this trial, when
the Persons who sat as judges had contributed their joint efforts
in perpetrating the Crime to which the charges laid against him

were only an incitement. As they by their actions approved of 1808.
30 June.
overthrowing His Majesty's Government, his offences would, of
course, to them appear meritorious. Through the whole it Methods of
conducting
the trial.
appeared they were trying the Governor and that McArthur, in-
stead of being Prisoner at their Bar, directed the prosecution,
for he brought forward my Letter-Book—which contained my
correspondence with the Secretary of State—out of which he
read such passages as suited his designs, and audaciously brow-
beat and interrogated my Secretary to divulge all conversations
he might have heard me enter into, in which he was supported
by the lawless members of that Tribunal, who at last acquitted Acquittal of
Macarthur.
him on the Evening of 6th of February. Immediately after, a
great number of Soldiers assembled as a mob, and with Sergeant-
Major Whittle at their head carried McArthur in a chair fixed Rejoicings of
Macarthur's
adherents.
on a Stage which they bore on their shoulders in triumph, with
loud huzzars, round a part of the Town of Sydney. His Majesty's
Ship Porpoise, then under Acting-Lieutenant Symons's command, gave three cheers. Late in the Evening McArthur's
Agents and those of the New South Wales Corps, by allurements
and threats, produced a general illumination, the Bells rang in
the Church Steeple, and eleven Guns were fired in an adjoining
Cove, as I believe, on board the Schooner Parramatta, belonging
to McArthur.

93. As the Reverend Henry Fulton showed a public and pointed Suspension of
Rev. Henry
Fulton.
disapprobation of their measures on the Evening of the 26th of
January, and when examined before their Committee showed no
disposition to yield to them, orders were issued, thro' Major
Johnston, that he should consider himself as suspended from his
Office as Chaplain. McArthur, as Ordinary, introduced a prayer
for Major Johnston, styling him the Lieutenant-Governor, into
the liturgy—the same as that formerly used for the Viceroy
of Ireland. Crook, a missionary, was appointed to perform
Divine Service on Sundays, and to baptise; and Charles Grimes, Introduction of
civil marriage.
Surveyor-General, Captain Anthony Fenn Kemp, and Ensign
Archibald Bell were ordered to perform the ceremony of marriage.*

94. A General Order was issued that all Officers should go to Holding of a
thanksgiving
service.
Church on Sunday, the 31st of January, and it was expected that
every well-disposed Person would attend to return thanks to
Almighty God for their deliverance on the memorable 26th of
January; in consequence of which the New South Wales Corps
went to Church with their Officers, in military order, under Arms
and Colors flying. Major Johnston, McArthur, and all the junto,
with their Ladies, accompanied them.

1808.
30 June.

Public meeting
held in the
church.

95. Among the numerous alarming and terrific reports and orders that were given out every day, on Monday, the 8th of February, in the Morning, at a time when the Soldiers and Towns People were filled with Spirituous Liquor, the Bellman was ordered to cry through the Streets that a Meeting would be held in the Church at eight O'Clock at Night. At the hour appointed the Church was crowded with Soldiers and the disaffected Party, of whom the chief were Lieutenant William Minchin, Lieutenant William Lawson, Mr. D'Arcy Wentworth, Edward McArthur, Gregory Blaxland, Lieutenant William Moore, Surgeon John Harris of the New South Wales Corps, Thomas Jamison (Principal Surgeon), Doctor Townson, Isaac Nicholls, Henry Kable: besides these were Nicholas Bayly and Garnham Blaxcell, who, assisted by Simeon Lord, proposed that a

A sword and
address to be
presented to
Johnston.

Sword should be voted to Major Johnston, not under the value of one hundred Guineas, for the wise and salutary measures which he had adopted to suppress the tyranny which ruled this Country, and with it an Address of thanks for his manly and spirited con-

Addresses of
thanks to the
N.S.W. Corps
and Macarthur.

duct on the 26th of January; that an Address of thanks should be presented to the New South Wales Corps for their spirited and manly conduct on the same day; that an Address of thanks might also be presented by the Inhabitants of the Town of Sydney to John McArthur, Esquire, as having been chiefly instrumental in bringing about the happy change which took place on that

A delegate
to be sent to
England.

day; and likewise that a *Delegate* might be appointed to be sent to England to state to His Majesty's Ministers those grievances the Inhabitants of this Colony laboured under during the administration of Governor Bligh and to pray redress.

96. They then asked who should be appointed; some insignificant Person said John McArthur, and he was accordingly sent for. He immediately came, and in very studied language

Macarthur's
charges against
Bligh and his
adherents.

described what he called the injuries which he had received from His Excellency Governor Bligh and the Bench of Magistrates, telling the People that they then beheld a Man who had nearly fallen a victim to a band of bloody-minded and bloodthirsty butchers, villains who wanted to drink his blood, and farther using the most scurrilous language against the Governor and Bench of Magistrates, comparing them to nothing less than a parcel of Assassins. He said that Plans, the most diabolical, had been laid with such damnable craft that they could not have failed to overwhelm him in total ruin and destruction had it not been for the timely interposition of divine providence in rescuing him from the malice of his Enemies, at the same time using such pathetic tones and gestures as he thought would most affect and delude the People who were around him. He farther stated that, notwithstanding the injuries he had received from the Governor and Magistrates, *yet he did not wish a hair of their heads to be injured.* He then concluded by thanking the Populace for the Honor they conferred on him by appointing him their Delegate, and said, however repugnant it was to his wishes to embark for England at that time, and notwithstanding his want of capacity to fulfil the arduous task imposed on him, yet in gratitude to his friends he would devote the last hour of his existence to their service, would immediately settle his affairs, proceed to England, and lay before His Majesty's Ministers the very heavy grievances under which the Inhabitants of these Settlements laboured during His Excellency Governor Bligh's administration that they might be redressed.

1808.
30 June.

Macarthur's
acceptance of
the position
of delegate.

97. Mr. Garnham Blaxcell then arose and proposed that a subscription should be opened for the purpose of defraying their Delegate John McArthur's expences in proceeding to England and accomplishing his undertaking. On this Mr. John Blaxland stood up and proposed that a Service of Plate should be presented by the Inhabitants to the Officers of the New South Wales Corps, for the use of their Mess, as a testimony of their gratitude and respect for their very spirited, manly, and patriotic conduct on the ever memorable 26th of January, 1808.

Subscription
opened to defray
Macarthur's
expenses.

98. In consequence of Mr. Blaxcell's proposal, a subscription was opened and, as I am informed, the following Persons voted the sums as here expressed against their names, and at the same time signed a Paper—of which the enclosed is a Copy*:—

	£	s.	d.		£	s.	d.
Lord, Kable, and Underwood	500	0	0	Rosetta Marsh	20	0	0
				Mary Skinner	10	0	0
Nicholas Bayly	100	0	0	Edward Wills	30	0	0
John Blaxland ... ⎱ Gregory Blaxland ⎰	200	0	0	Dan'l McKay	10	0	0
				William Evans	5	5	0
Garnham Blaxcell ..	100	0	0	John Redman	10	0	0
Eber Bunker	20	0	0	John Gowen	10	0	0
Elizabeth Driver ...	30	0	0				
Isaac Nicholls	50	0	0		£1,095	5	0

99. Lord, Kable and Underwood, together with the nine last named Persons, except John Gowen who was a Marine, are of low character and came out as Convicts. Isaac Nicholls was on the 13th of June 1802 reprieved from Sentence of Death which had been passed on him for a Crime committed in this Colony. Lord, Kable and Underwood are partners in trade; but Underwood at this time was on his passage to England.

Description of
subscribers.

100. Notwithstanding this subscription, report says that not a farthing has been realised, and it seems to be confirmed, for McArthur disgusted the principals and became afraid of going to

Subscribers'
dislike of
Macarthur.

* Note 157.

1808.
30 June.

England, as it will appear hereafter, by his putting himself into Office. The Night ended in a great scene of drunkenness, during which, although some horrid Act was every hour expected to happen, yet it did not take place, notwithstanding McArthur indirectly recommended it to the People, and the time was so propitious to his Plans.

Bligh's charges against Wentworth.

101. It will appear in my Despatches by the Duke of Portland that I suspended Mr. D'Arcy Wentworth, Assistant Surgeon, and gave my reasons for so doing. The Rebels who had seized my Papers and read my representation concerning him, sent him a Copy, and in order to clear him of the accusation there contained contrived that he should be tried on those Charges by a Court-Martial. On this occasion Major Johnston applied to me on the 9th of February to know if I had any other Evidence besides Oakes and Beldon, whom they discovered by my Papers to have given me the private information I had concerning him. To this I replied that my Letter to His Majesty's Secretary of State con-

Court martial on Wentworth.

tained the Charges I preferred against him; nevertheless, they presumed to bring him to a Court-Martial, acquitted him, and Major Johnston restored him to his situation.

Bligh's charges against Jamison.

102. In a similar manner they extracted out of my Despatches what I had represented against Mr. Thomas Jamison, Principal Surgeon, and sending it to him, they also wished to bring him to trial, and wrote to me requesting that I would be pleased to specify what offence Mr. Jamison had committed, and that when he was acquainted with the particulars of my Charges, I should be at liberty to proceed to the proof of them in any manner I might most approve. In reply to this, I observed that the private communication of my Letter to the Secretary of State respecting Mr. Jamison I referred to the decision of His Majesty's Ministers, to whom he might apply.

103. On or about the 15th of February a printed Order was Stuck up to this effect:—

Macarthur appointed secretary to the colony.

" John McArthur, Esq., is appointed Secretary to the Colony and a Magistrate, and all applications are to be made to him. It is to be observed that no emolument is attached to either situation.

" By Command of His Honor the Lieutenant-Governor.

" (Signed)   NICHOLAS BAYLY,

" Secretary."

As a proof of this, I enclose the first *Sydney Gazette* published under their authority May the 13th 1808.

104. This declaration is truly insulting when we consider the conduct of McArthur and Major Johnston, who is only his instrument. By this appointment McArthur has become the sole

manager of the Colony; he has given every lucrative situation to his creatures; he has issued the Stores wantonly to his own and their private purposes; has given away and disposed of Government Cattle to persons greatly in his debt, so that the profits of them will finally return to himself; he has received and given away several Leases of places in the Town to his party; he is employing in his own and their private concerns, Artificers, Labourers, and Government Cattle; he has let out Government Factory; he has even sold from the Store three pair of Mill-stones which I intended for the Out-Settlements, and taken two pair of them to himself, as likewise thirty Stand of Arms, which there is no doubt have been sent in the Parramatta, his Schooner, to barter for Pork in the South Sea; and his and their Vessels have been fitted out with Anchors, Cables, Canvas, Sails, and other Articles necessary for His Majesty's Ships and Vessels here. He has dismissed Mr. John Jamieson, Superintendant of Government Stock, as appears by his (Mr. Jamieson's) Letter,* on account of his having refused to remove the Government Herds to Broken Bay, where there is scarcely anything but Rocks and barren Ground, in order that his own Cattle might have the entire range of Government Ground in the neighbourhood of Parramatta. As a further insult to Government, he has sold a large ten-oared Boat, which had been kept for the Governor's use, and has let out the Garden of Government House at Parramatta, by which the Governor's Table was in part supplied, and the Premises are become degraded. He will, perhaps, state for Major Johnston that this is all done to procure money for public uses, as no one will take their Bills; but there would have been no occasion for this ruinous system had I been in power, and therefore it is an highly additional offence to the subversion of His Majesty's Government. McArthur has issued many Licenses for selling Spirituous Liquors to Persons, some of whom are well known to sell Spirits for him and his Party. The worst of Characters have erected Signs to denote their authority for vending those Liquors, among whom a ferocious and merciless Gaoler, Daniel McKay (who was reinstated in that office, from which, out of motives of humanity, he had been dismissed) erected one having on one side an Highland Officer emblematic of Major Johnston, with one foot on a Snake and his Sword through it, to whom a Female Figure is in the attitude of presenting a Cap of Liberty; on the reverse of this is printed, in large characters, "the ever memorable 26th of January, 1808." In the House of one John Driver is painted, on one side of his Hall, in large Characters, "Success to Major George Johnston; may he live for ever! our Deliverer and the Suppressor of

* Note 158.

Margin notes:

1808.
30 June.

Macarthur the actual administrator.

Appropriation of public stores by Macarthur.

Dismissal of Jamieson by Macarthur.

Issue of spirit licenses by Macarthur.

Sign-boards on licensed houses.

Sign-boards on
licensed houses.

Tyrants." One John Reddington, a disaffected Irishman, has the Sign of the Harp without the Crown; and one W'm Evans, formerly a Servant of McArthur and Blaxcell's, and since the 26th January, appointed their Provost-Marshal's Bailiff, has erected a Sign representing King Charles the Second in the Oak on one side, and on the other is painted, in large characters, "the ever memorable 26th Jan'y, 1808."

105. I have already mentioned (in paragraph 18) that the American Ship, Jenny (Captain Dorr), was in the Harbour, and that I could not permit her to sell any Spirits. She sailed on the

The ship Jenny
ordered to leave
Port Jackson.

8th of February for China, but was so suddenly sent out of the Port,. on a pretended suspicion of smuggling, that she could not stow her Cargo, in consequence of which was obliged to put into Broken Bay. This had no sooner become known than McArthur

The Jenny
seized as prize
to H.M.S.
Porpoise.

asserted she had returned to smuggle, and persuaded Acting-Lieutenant Symons to seize her as a Prize for the Porpoise— which he did—and brought her back here on the 16th. On the

Meeting of
vice-admiralty
court.

22nd a Court of Vice-Admiralty was held, by a Precept from Major Johnston, as here enclosed,* to decide the case, of which Captain Abbott was Judge, Chas. Grimes, Register, Nicholas Bayly, Marshal, and Garnham Blaxcell, the Partner in Trade with McArthur, acted as Agent for the Prosecutor, Symons. In the course of the Trial an altercation arose between Mr. Blaxcell and Captain Abbott, on account of which the former left the Court and McArthur took his place and brought with him my private Instructions from His Majesty's Ministers, reading aloud such parts of these Instructions as related to the importation of Spirits into the Colony; and also read that part which related to the Americans with respect to Trade, and thereby impressing on the American Masters and Men an Idea of the intentions of His Majesty's Government being unfavorable to them. After all, the Ship and Cargo were restored to Captain Dorr, who, feeling himself much injured, has appealed to the High Court of Admiralty, and left it with his Agent to be sent to England. The inclosed Information* has been sent to me, and I beg leave to recommend it to Your Lordship's perusal, as it is a fair description of the Characters it notices, and shows that Major Johnston and other Officers of the New South Wales Corps had used every underhand means to smuggle the whole of the Spirits from this

Importation
of wine and
spirits.

Ship previous to the 26th of January. Since that time there has been imported here 48,710 Gallons of Wine and 12,650 Gallons of Spirits, to the manifest injury of the Colony.

106. Among the extraordinary circumstances which have taken place under the present ruling power, it is conducive to general information to mention that a Brig, called the Harrington,

* Note 159.

William Campbell, Master, which arrived on the 30th March, and 1808. 30 June.
was equipped and ready for Sea (lying a little without the Cove) Seizure of the
was taken possession of and her Crew turned on Shore by a brig Harrington
Prisoner called Stewart (a determined Man, who had frequently by convicts.
endeavoured to leave the Colony in òpen Boats, and in consequence was put to labour in the Gaol gang, but after my confinement was liberated) and about forty other Convicts, who carried
her to Sea on the 16th of May and have not since been heard of.*
This was a well-known Vessel, which I found here on my arrival
in the Colony, for she had been detained by Governor King for
piratically taking two Spanish Vessels on the Coast of Peru. I
brought out orders for her release and she was given up accordingly, and sailed on the 28th of January, 1807. During her
detention the House of Chace, Chinnery and Company in India,
to which she belonged, failed; and it appears, since her arrival
this time, on the 30th of March, that the Master, instead of
having proceeded to the Port of Madras for the benefit of the
Creditors, connected himself with McArthur and proceeded to the Macarthur's trading alliance
Fiji Islands for a Cargo of Sandal-Wood, and from thence to with William
China, where he procured a valuable Cargo in exchange; but as Campbell.
he there could not clear out for this Colony, he sailed to Malacca
for that purpose and brought the Cargo to McArthur since my
confinement. McArthur well knew, under these circumstances
(particularly not having gone to her lawful Owners), had the
Brig returned here while I had the power of acting, she would not
have been permitted to land her Cargo. One would almost pronounce as a certainty from this circumstance that McArthur had
calculated the exact time when the Government would be subverted, for the additional purpose of bringing on ʻillegal communications with the East Indies.

107. I have said before (in the 34th paragraph) that, on the Gore imprisoned
Night of the 25th of January, Mr. Wm. Gore, the Provost- by Macarthur on a charge
Marshal, made Oath that McArthur was out of his custody; it of perjury.
was in consequence of a pretence of this Oath being false that he
was ordered to Gaol by McArthur on the Night of the 26th. As
this was done without any examination before a Bench of their
Justices or committal, he was afterwards liberated, and on the
1st of March was summoned before Mr. Jamison, Principal Sur- Gore committed
geon, and John Blaxland, Settler, who committed him to be tried by magistrates for trial.
by a Criminal Court for wilful and corrupt Perjury.† He gave
Bail, and on the 21st of March was brought before their Court, Trial of Gore.
consisting of Charles Grimes (Judge-Advocate), James Symons
(acting Lieutenant and self-created Acting Commander of the
Porpoise), Captain Edward Abbott, Acting Second Lieutenant
William Ellison, of the Porpoise, Lieutenant William Moore,

* Note 160.   † Note 161.

1808.
30 June.
Lieutenant Thos. Laycock, and Lieutenant Cadwallader Draffin,
when he denied their Authority as being convened by the Precept
of Major Johnston, who could have no Authority to issue a
Precept without the Death or Absence of the Governor; they
Postponement
of Gore's trial.
then put off his Trial; but as he knew the Charge was groundless,
and that they only wished to harass him by it, he would not again
give Bail. On this they committed him to a Cell of the common
Gaol, from whence many an unfortunate creature had been
dragged to the Gallows. Here he lay until the 30th of May, and
then, without giving him any previous notice to summons his
Witnesses, as they had done before, they suddenly brought him
to their Court House, which was a Military Barrack. After some
Trial and
conviction of
Gore.
time, the Court met, consisting of Captain Anthony Fenn Kemp
(their Judge-Advocate), William Kent (Acting Commander of
the Porpoise), Capt. Edward Abbott, Lieutenant William Moore,
Lieutenant Thos. Laycock, Lieutenant William Lawson, and
Lieutenant Cadwallader Draffin, all of the New South Wales
Corps. The Judge-Advocate read the Indictment. Mr. Gore
denied their Authority and refused to plead. The Court was then
cleared, and on its reopening their Judge-Advocate pronounced
sentence of Transportation for seven Years, and he was sent to
the Coal River at Newcastle on the Evening of the 4th of June,
the Anniversary of the Birth of Our Most Gracious King,
leaving behind him his affectionate Wife and four fine Children,
the eldest of whom is about eight Years of Age, wholly dependant
on his friends for support. Thus they have treated a loyal
Officer of the Crown who had always done his duty with attention
and great humanity.

Gore's protest
and intended
defence.
108. For the farther illustration of this outrageous Act, I
recommend to Your Lordship's particular Attention the inclosed
Copy of Mr. Gore's Protest on the 27th of March, and of the
Defence he intended to have made on that day had they proceeded
on his Trial, together with Copies of his Letters to me of the 31st
of May and 2nd of June.

Hayes sent to
Newcastle for
condemning the
insurrection.
109. Sir Henry Brown Hayes, a person under sentence of
transportation, who had been living in a retired manner on a
little Estate about seven miles from Sydney, and who seldom
came into Town, being in the habits of conversing with the
Officers, and having expressed his loyalty and disapprobation of
their measures, asserting they would be capitally punished for
their traitorous Acts, was likewise sent to the Coal Mines. Thus,
in terrorem, the Usurpers held up punishment to those who dared
to speak in favor of my administration against their treasonable
practices; and notwithstanding the illegality of their Courts, they
have condemned many Persons and executed seven.*

* Note 155.

1808.
30 June.

The case of
Oliver Russell
and Daniels.

110. On the 30th of March, Oliver Russell, Master of the Ship Brothers, while conducting a prosecution before their Court of Criminal Jurisdiction, consisting of Charles Grimes, as Judge-Advocate, Lieutenant James Symons (self-created acting Commander of the Porpoise), Lieutenant William Moore, Lieutenant John Brabyn, Lieutenant Thomas Laycock, Lieutenant Cadwallader Draffin, and Ensign Archibald Bell, against John Blaxland, Gregory Blaxland, and Simeon Lord, for assaulting him on board his Ship, received, together with his Mate, a Sentence of transportation during seven Years for what they called perjury in their Evidence. He and his Mate were liberated from this Sentence three days afterwards by a Proclamation (a Copy of which I here enclose, authorised by Major Johnston, and signed " John McArthur, Colonial Secretary," on the ground of informality and illegality. On this Proclamation being issued, their Magistrates, Surgeon John Harris, Surgeon Jamison, Charles Grimes (Surveyor), Lieutenant James Symons, and Garnham Blaxcell (the Partner of McArthur in Trade), summoned Russell and his Mate before them, when Harris, who was the Rival of McArthur, having the strongest party on the Bench, committed them for Trial at the next Criminal Court. On this, McArthur and Major Johnston dismissed Charles Grimes as Magistrate and Judge-Advocate, and Harris and Symons from the Magistracy, and Jamison, from some reasons unknown, no longer continued to act, and the proceedings against Russell and his Mate were then dropt. Russell went home as Master of his Ship, taking with him Lieutenant William Minchin (and his Servant, Marlborough), of the New South Wales Corps, who, it is said, carried with him duplicate dispatches from McArthur and Major Johnston of those which Grimes and Edward McArthur had carried with them in the Dart—all actually implicated in the Rebellion. By the Brothers I wrote hastily a Dispatch, dated the 30th April, Mr. Campbell having thought of the means of its getting safe to Your Lordship, by directing it to Mr. Wilson, Merchant, in Fenchurch Street, under a Cover as Bills of Exchange.

Method of
sending Bligh's
despatches.

111. Among the acts of these Persons, some things seem to have been carried on with peculiar art and design; their having deprived me and continuing to keep possession of all my Books and Papers put me in a situation in which I have nothing but my memory to assist me; and as they have the Commissary's Papers also in their possession, they can make any representation they please without any present means in Mr. Palmer's power of proving their falsehoods. I have been led to this conclusion by a friend procuring a Copy of an Affidavit,* which it is said is transmitted to Your Lordship; the falsehood and meanness of this

Detention of
public books
and Papers.

* Note 162.

Bligh charged
with mis-
appropriation of
public stores.

document is manifest; it appears to be made by Mr. Fitz, Deputy Commissary, a creature of McArthur's, and one of the rebellious party; it asserts, " that Governor Bligh received from the bonded Store one Pipe of Port Wine for his own private use, and that he (Governor Bligh) ordered a quantity of Wine to be purchased from Mr. Campbell at the rate of three pounds per dozen for the use of the General Hospital, which Wine was appropriated to his (Governor Bligh's) own use." The Commissary's Accounts will show that before my arrival there had been a quantity of Port Wine sent out for Barter which was distributed to the Officers in Pipes and Cases. Governor King, expecting to be relieved, reserved one Pipe for his Successor, in case of accident, and on my arrival he directed it to be charged to my Account, which the Commissary did. With respect to the Wine purchased from Mr. Campbell by the Commissary it took place long after my arrival, from a Demand made by the Surgeon of the Hospital, Mr. Jamison, who received it and gave his Receipt. These circumstances I have taken notice of in order that Your Lordship may be aware of the misrepresentations these persons may make to You, sensible that Your Lordship will oppose to them, in any reflections You make, Your confidence in the honor and dignity of my character and conduct, who, by justice and humanity, had brought the Colony to a flourishing state, compared with what it was before.

Addresses to
Johnston ante
dated by Fitz.

Signatures
obtained by
fear.

112. Mr. Fitz, whom I have just mentioned, is living at the Hawkesbury, where he has been very assiduous in the Service of McArthur and Major Johnston, particularly in framing Addresses to the latter, which he ante-dates, approving in the highest manner of Major Johnston's conduct and reprobating mine. I here enclose a Copy of one of these Addresses which I have obtained, and was carried about for Subscribers immediately after the 26th of January—a time of terror; as also the Copy of a Letter I received from Mr. Arndell, one of the Subscribers, expressive of the state of his mind at the time of signing it. He imposes on the credulity of the poor Settlers, and influences some to sign them; he has received a comparatively large proportion and choice selection of Cattle from the Government Herds since the 26th of January, a part of which, as it is reported, is a present; the remainder, or the whole, he will be enabled to pay for in Wheat and Maize procured from the Settlers by Spirituous Liquors, which he pays away to them in barter at an enormous price.

113. I hope no misfortune may have happened to my Dispatch by the Duke of Portland,* as it contains very material information to Your Lordship respecting the Colony, and my plans put into

* Note 163.

execution respecting the Evacuation of Norfolk Island. We had 1808.
30 June. began on this work, and it was going on so uniformly and gradually, with only the Porpoise, Lady Nelson, and Estramina, The evacuation of Norfolk as did away every disagreeable sensation which lay on the minds Island. of the People, who saw the necessity of leaving their habitations, which they had been so long accustomed to; but after my arrest the work ceased until the City of Edinburgh, taken up for that purpose, sailed on the 26th of May.

114. The Vessels I employed were to return here regularly Bligh's every Voyage they made; so that I had it in my power to regulate arrangements for the and send the necessary supplies, so far as I was able, for the evacuation. numbers each Vessel took, and prevent any difficulties arising at the Derwent; but these precautions have not now been taken, and I very much fear that, employing so large a Ship at this season of the Year as the City of Edinburgh to take so great a number of persons at once to the Derwent, will cause much difficulty and distress, as it is almost impossible that Colonel Collins will be able to provide for their security and health. This Officer, I The insurrection understand, has publickly disavowed the authority of the present repudiated Rulers, and I beg leave to inclose Copies of two private Letters by Collins. from him, the last of which is dated since my arrest, and the other on the day it took place. Both the Derwent and Port Dalrymple Settlements were in a state of improvement and advancing with this part of the Territory, but the unparalleled act of rebellion which has taken place is a very great check to them, and will, I fear, increase the public debt. Had the Colony gone on in the way it was proceeding, every poor Man would have paid his debt this year; but what a melancholy reverse is now! they will still remain embarrassed and require indulgence. At Terrorism practised by present not a Person dares to speak, and their fears and anxieties the military. are kept up by the Soldiery, who give out as a cant phrase, "the Color of my Cloth," whenever it is required of them to say by what authority they make any demand or do anything improper to other classes of persons. These Troops are now kept in a pampered manner, while the poor prisoner is in nearly a starving condition; and the friends of Government inform me that, to a certainty, the Inhabitants lament in silence they cannot show Loyalty of their loyalty and affection through a fear of their lives. If I settlers to Bligh. stood in need of a defence, I need not make a better of my government having been satisfactory than this, and the affectionate and dutiful Address presented to me on the first day of this Year. I was confident of being the Instrument of conferring prosperity and happiness on this Colony, and altho' I could not expect these blessings speedily to take place, yet had I had time they would have been effected; nevertheless, this rebellion, while

1808.
30 June.

Probable
results of the
rebellion.

it is apparently against all good, will, I have a firm belief, ultimately operate in its favour. In a few Years these people would
have made themselves formidable in opposition, and required a
great armament to have subdued them; but now such regulations
can be made as will ensure their lasting obedience. The Civil
Power will require to be put on a firm.basis, regulated by proper
Law Officers, and the Military to be distinct and frequently exchanged for other Troops; to this, when the few turbulent persons
such as McArthur, who particularly aspires to the Government,
and has even a Military Orderly to attend him and Light Horsemen when he rides into the Country, are made an example of,
all will be well.

115. When, in my Despatch of the 31st of October last, I spoke
of the New South Wales Corps, little did I think, My Lord, that
the principal reason I urged in support of my position—its becoming a *dangerous Militia*—would have so soon been exemplified.

116. Having received no information from Major Johnston as
to his intentions respecting me, in consequence of the return of
His Majesty's Ship Porpoise from Port Dalrymple, on the 26th
of last month (paragraph 88), I wrote a Letter to him on the
18th Instant, stating I had been in daily expectation of receiving
some notice from him respecting Lieutenant-Governor Paterson,
on whom, he had before written to me, his future plans depended.

Expected
arrival of
Foveaux.

After some days he answered that he had deferred coming to any
determination until the arrival of Lieu't-Colonel Foveaux, who
was daily expected, as a Ship (called the Cumberland) from England, which arrived here on the 22nd, had brought an account
that he was on his Voyage hither. Report states that Lieutenant-
Colonel Foveaux was in the Lady Sinclair and had another Ship
with him, called the Recovery, and that they had about two
hundred Troops on board.

117. I feel great regret at the length of this Despatch, but the
remoteness of the Colony and this momentous occasion require
that nothing should be omitted which can any way develope the
designs of these Persons. The extraordinary Hydra of New

Macarthur's
character.

South Wales, differing only from the mythological description
of that Serpent by affixing six of his Heads on the Shoulders of
others he had prepared for them, induces me to add still farther
some marks of his character. Before I took command of the
colony, great ill-will had subsisted between the Government, the
Military Officers, and this McArthur; with the Settlers and
people he was the most hated person it is possible to conceive.

Addresses
presented
to Bligh.

The first Address (No. 18) presented to me was signed by Major
Johnston "for the Military," Mr. Atkins "for the Civil," and
McArthur "for the free Inhabitants," expressing their affection

and loyalty. I received it as such, and published it. Shortly after I was surprised by receiving two Addresses—one from the Hawkesbury (No. 19) and the other (No. 20) from Sydney— disavowing their having any knowledge of an Address under the signature of McArthur, a person whom they reprobated and considered unfit to communicate their sentiments on such an occasion. In order to promote harmony and good-will, and cause all rancour to cease, I did not publish these oppositions, but on the contrary, recommended, and I thought effected, a reconciliation among the People to give another trial of the Person they so openly disapproved of; they did this with great good nature to the Hydra I have represented, and not one but himself could have committed such offences in return as he has been guilty of—a Man who had received such Gifts from Government as he has, and might have lived in affluence and comfort, if he had possessed a good disposition. Beside the Addresses I have here alluded to I also inclose the Copy of one from the Settlers to Major Johnston, showing to that moment their disapprobation of McArthur's principles and conduct (No. 21); a Copy of one said to have been transmitted to Lieutenant-Governor Paterson by the Porpoise (No. 22), showing their disapprobation of my confinement, of the confusion that reigns in the Colony, of McArthur being at the head of affairs, and promising the Lieutenant-Governor their support in placing them again under the protection of the King and the Laws; and a Copy of one from the loyal Settlers at Baulkham Hills, who came out as free Settlers from England (No. 23), intended to have been presented to Lieutenant-Governor Paterson on his arrival, promising their support in giving full satisfaction to me and to the Government of our Most Gracious Sovereign in this Colony, for the gross insults and injury done in the arrest of my Person, whom they revered, and expressing their confidence in him that he would take prompt and effective means to secure the principals in this most unjustifiable transaction; also a Copy of one to him to the same effect from some of the loyal Settlers at the Hawkesbury, who likewise came out as free settlers (No. 24). I further inclose two grateful Addresses to me from the Settlers—the one on account of the encouragement I gave to the cultivation of Grain (No. 25), and the other on the suppression of an intended Insurrection at the beginning of last year, requesting the ring-leaders to be disposed of so as to prevent future troubles (No. 26). The Chief of this conspiracy, Dwyer, who was banished to Norfolk Island, and was to have been kept at the Derwent, has been sent for by the present Rulers—an extraordinary circumstance, for which no reason can be assigned, unless they propose by their

1808.
30 June.

Addresses presented to Bligh.

Addresses of settlers to Johnston and Paterson.

Addresses of settlers to Bligh.

1808.
30 June.

indulgence to him to induce him hereafter to unite with his old party in an opposition to Government should they feel his assistance necessary.

118. I shall now conclude with observing to Your Lordship that I am ignorant of what their real intentions are with respect to myself. I am still kept a Prisoner to this House under various pretences, as I have already stated, by their Centinels, one of whom, when I walk in my Garden, always follows me at a short distance.   I remain, &c.,

Bligh kept a prisoner in government house.

WM. BLIGH.

[Enclosure No. 1.]

ADDRESS OF SETTLERS TO GOVERNOR BLIGH.

New South Wales, January ye 1st, 1808.

Address of settlers to Bligh.

May it please your Excellency,

[Here followed a copy of the address forwarded by Major Johnston to Viscount Castlereagh in his despatch, dated 11th April, 1808, as a sub-enclosure to number 12 in the enclosure numbered 24.]   We remain, Sir,

Your Excellency's truly devoted, Respectful and most Obedient Humble Servants,

[Signed by 830 persons.]

[Richard Atkins, J.A., Robert Campbell, J.P., Thomas Arndell, J.P., John Palmer, J.P., Thomas Hobby, John Harris, E. Bunker, Henry Fulton, Asst. Chaplain, Wm. Gore, Provost-Marshal, Thomas Moore, James Williamson, Rowland Hassal, R. Fitz, William Sutton, N. Divine, Andrew Thompson, George Crossley, Lazarus Graves, Chas. Dailey, Thomas Thorsby, Samuel Terry, Geo. Mealmaker, Thomas Halfpenny, Wm. Emmett, Martin Mason, Rebecca Cox, Thos. Matcham Pitt, Isaac Cornwell, Wm. Chapman, Wm. Rouse, Joseph Stubbs, Saml. Gatehouse, Robt. Allen, Geo. Cox, Wm. Aspinall, Robt. Shrieves, Edward Cox, John Bowman, Jas. Blackman, John Dight, &c., &c.]

[Enclosure No. 2.]

ESCAPE OF CONVICT IN THE SCHOONER PARRAMATTA.

Public Notice.

27th June, 1807.

Public notice re the escape of John Hoare.

WHEREAS John Hoare, a Convict for Life, has absented himself from the Gang in which he was employed at Sydney, and is supposed to have left this Colony in a Vessel called the Parramatta, these are to direct and require all persons who can give information respecting the said John Hoare having absconded in manner aforesaid, to give the earliest intelligence to the Judge-Advocate; in failure whereof they will Subject themselves to be considered,

and will be prosecuted as aiding and assisting the said John
Hoare to escape as aforesaid from this his place of confinement,
to which he was sentenced by Law. And if the Said John Hoare
shall still be in this Colony, all manner of persons are strictly
charged to deliver him up to the Civil Power, on pain of being
prosecuted for harbouring or concealing the said Convict; and
any person so delivering him up as aforesaid shall receive a
reward of ten guineas.

By Command of His Excellency,

RD. ATKINS,

Judge-Advocate.

AFFIDAVIT OF MR. JAMES ELDER.

COUNTY OF CUMBERLAND ⎱ James Elder, Missionary of the Island
TO WIT ⎰ of Taheite, one of the Society Islands
in the Pacific Ocean, came before me,
One of His Majesty's Justices of the Peace for Said County, on
the twenty sixth day of July in the year of Our Lord 1808, and
made Oath on the Holy Evangelists, that on or about the month
of August last, John Jefferson, Justice of the Peace for that
Island wrote a letter on His Majesty's Service to John Glenn,
Master of the Schooner Parramatta, charging him to take care
of John Hoare, a Convict, and bring him back to Port Jackson
from whence he had escaped; and some time after, he (Elder)
and Cummings, now the Master of the Dundee, told Glenn that
Hoare was hidden on board the General Wellesley, and desired
that he would Search for him, but Glenn did not search, and he
is convinced Hoare went away in the Wellesley.

JAMES ELDER.

Sworn before me this 20th day of July, 1808,

JNO. PALMER, J.P.

[Enclosure No. 3.]

THE TRIAL OF JOHN MACARTHUR.*

MEMORANDUM of the Proceedings of the Criminal Court assembled
Monday, the 25th day of January, 1808, about ¼ past 10 o'clock.

Members:

The Judge-Advocate.

Capt. A. F. Kemp.	Lieut. Jno. Brabyn.
Lieut. Wm. Moore.	Lieut. Thos. Laycock.
Lieut. Wm. Minchin.	Lieut. Wm. Lawson.

The Judge Advocate having sworn the Members in, Mr. McArthur,
a Prisoner at the Bar, began by saying that he protested against
Richard Atkins, Esquire, sitting as Judge. The Judge Advocate
replied that there could be no Court until the Judge Advocate was
sworn in, and he applied to Captain Kemp, as Senior Member, so to
be sworn in agreeable to the established practice of Criminal Courts

* Note 164.

1808.
30 June.

Memorandum of
the proceedings
at the trial of
Macarthur.

in this Colony, which Captain Kemp refused to do, and said that he would hear Mr. McArthur's reasons, and Lieut. Lawson immediately repeated, " We will hear him "; on which the Judge Advocate again repeated that there could be no Court until he (the Judge Advocate) was sworn in, and as it was their determination to hear Mr. McArthur that he (the Judge Advocate) should retire from his Seat, which he did; They then suffered Mr. McArthur to proceed, which he did in a strain of personal and public invective addressing himself to the Six Members, as well as to the Public in General, in a very peculiar manner. After Mr. McArthur had finished, the Judge Advocate rose from the Bench, to which he had retired, and addressed himself to Mr. McArthur, saying that, as Judge of Record and Judge Advocate and Magistrate of this Territory, he would issue a Warrant and commit him to His Majesty's Gaol. Mr. McArthur then claimed the Protection of the Six Members, and Capt. Kemp particularly said that he would commit the Judge Advocate. Mr. Atkins then said, " You commit me, Sir." " I would, Sir," said Captain Kemp. Mr. Atkins then replied that the Court was adjourned, which they took no notice of, but desired Mr. McArthur to remain. Captain Kemp said also, on Mr. McArthur being desired to remain, " We will protect you." Captain Kemp further said, addressing himself to the Judge Advocate, " You are no more than a Juryman, and have no more power than one of us." After the Judge Advocate had taken his hat, and was at the outside of the Bar, he again told them that the Court was adjourned, and further ordered the Court to be cleared. The Judge Advocate desires a Constable to bring his Papers. The Constable returned, and gave him for answer that the Members refused to give them up, saying that they were Public Papers, but they gave the desk belonging to the Judge Advocate on which the Papers were lying, while they kept all the Public documents of the Crown.

At ¾ past eleven, the following letter was received :—

Sir,   Sydney, 25th January, 1808.

We the Officers composing the Criminal Court of Jurisdiction, appointed by Your Excellency, beg leave to state to you that a Right of Challenge to the Judge Advocate, Richard Atkins, Esq., has been demanded by the Prisoner, John McArthur, Esq., which we as a Court, after mature and deliberate consideration, have agreed to allow as a good and lawful objection. We, therefore, submit to your Excellency to determine on the propriety of appointing another Judge Advocate to preside in the present Trial. We further pray Your Excellency's protection in the execution of our Duty, having been grossly insulted and threatened by Richard Atkins, Esq., with a•seeming view to deter us in our legal proceedings.   We have, &c.,

Signed : A. F. KEMP, Capt. New S. Wales Corps,
         J. BRABYN, Lieut.   Do.
         WM. MOORE, Lieut.   Do.
         THOS. LAYCOCK, Lieut.   Do.
         WM. MINCHIN, Lieut.   Do.
         WM. LAWSON, Lieut.   Do.

Addressed :
    " On His Majesty's Service,"
        His Excellency Governor Bligh, etc., etc.

In consequence of the above I wrote the following letter, and sent it by Mr. Gore, Provost Marshal (and Officer of the Court) to Captain Kemp and others that signed the foregoing—accompanied by Ensign Bell, who brought it.

1808.
30 June.

Memorandum of
the proceedings
at the trial of
Macarthur.

Government House, Sydney, 25th January, 1808,
Gentlemen,   half past Noon.

In answer to your letter, just received, I conceive that there could have been no cause of Challenge to the Judge-Advocate, who is the Officer appointed by His Majesty's Patent,.and without whose presence there can be no Court,

And I consider that the Judge-Advocate had a right to commit any person who might commit any gross Insult to him while he was in his Official Capacity as Judge of the Court. I do not consider the Court to be formed without the Judge-Advocate, and when legally convened I have no right to interpose any Authority concerning its legal Acts.

I, therefore, can do no otherwise than direct that the Judge-Advocate take his Seat and act as directed by His Majesty's Letters Patent for the constituting the Court of Criminal Jurisdiction, which, being authorised by an Act of Parliament, is as follows:—

" And We further Will, Ordain, and Appoint that the said Court of Criminal Jurisdiction shall consist of Our Judge-Advocate for the time being, together with such Six Officers of Our Sea and Land Service as Our Governor (or, in case of his Death or Absence, Our Lieutenant-Governor) shall by Precept, issued under his Hand and Seal, convene from time to time for that purpose.

I am, &c.,
WM. BLIGH.

To

Captain Anthony Fenn Kemp ⎤
Lieutenant John Brabyn   ⎪
Lieutenant Wm. Moore   ⎪   Of His Majesty's
Lieutenant Thos. Laycock   ⎬   New South Wales Corps.
Lieutenant Wm. Minchin   ⎪
Lieutenant Wm. Lawson   ⎦

Sir,   Sydney, 25 January, 1808.

We have had the honor of your Excellency's Opinion with respect to the objection made by a Prisoner (John McArthur Esq.) to the Judge Advocate in answer to our letter to your Excellency on the Subject.

We beg your Excellency to be assured that we have at all times the utmost deference to any opinion delivered by your Excellency; but in the present case, we cannot consistent with the Oath we have taken, or our consciences, sit with Richard Atkins, Esqr., in the Trial of John McArthur, Esq., well knowing the hostile enmity which has existed between them for these last thirteen or fourteen years. We therefore pray your Excellency's further consideration on the Subject.   We have, &c.,

ANTHY. FENN KEMP,	Capt. N.S.W. Corps.	
J. BRABYN,	Lieut.	Do.
WM. MOORE,	Do.	Do.
THOS. LAYCOCK,	Do.	Do.
WM. MINCHIN,	Do.	Do.
WM. LAWSON,	Do.	Do.

His Excellency Governor Bligh.

1808.
30 June.

Memorandum of
the proceedings
at the trial of
Macarthur.

Government House, Sydney, 25th January, 1808,

Gentlemen,   Quarter past 2 o'clock.

In reply to your Second letter of this date I require that you deliver to Mr. William Gore, Provost Marshal, and Mr. Edmund Griffin, my Secretary, who accompanies him on the occasion, all the Papers that the Judge Advocate left on the Table, and which were refused to be sent to him by the Constable, and also those which the Prisoner John McArthur has read before you, that they may be delivered to the Judge Advocate His Majesty's legal Officer.

I am, &c.,

WM. BLIGH.

To

Captain Anthony Fenn Kemp ⎫
Lieutenant John Brabyn   ⎪
Lieutenant Wm. Moore   ⎬   Of His Majesty's
Lieutenant Thos. Laycock   ⎪ New South Wales Corps.
Lieutenant Wm. Minchin   ⎪
Lieutenant Wm. Lawson   ⎭

At this time a Report was brought that Major Johnston was taken Speechless, and Doctor Jamison and Harris were sent for out at his Country House 4 Miles from Town. Soon after another report was spread that he had been bled and was much better.

At ½ past three Mr. Gore and Mr. Griffin returned with replies to the last letter, as follows :—

Sir,   Sydney, 25 January, 1808.

We take the liberty of enclosing to your Excellency a copy of the Deposition made before us as Members of the Criminal Court, this day assembled, under Your Excellency's Precept, by John McArthur, Esqr., Prisoner at the Bar.

We earnestly entreat your Excellency will be pleased to order such protection to be given Mr. McArthur as in our humble opinion the nature of the complaint stated by him before us merits.

We beg leave to assure Your Excellency that it is not without the most heartfelt Sorrow that we have been eye witnesses this day of the Laws having been grossly violated by Richard Atkins, Esqr., the Judge Advocate, in threatening before the Sacred Tribunal of a Criminal Court to commit John McArthur, Esqr., the prisoner at the Bar, who was pleading his own Cause by the Court's Order, to Gaol as a common Felon.

We have, &c.,

ANTHY. FENN KEMP, Capt. N.S.W. Corps.
J. BRABYN,   Lieut.   Do.
WM. MOORE,   Do.   Do.
THOS. LAYCOCK,   Do.   Do.
WM. MINCHIN,   Do.   Do.
WM. LAWSON,   Do.   Do.

His Excellency Governor Bligh.

The Prisoner, John McArthur, Esqr., now before the Court, claims their protection he having received information from divers friendly persons that a large body of men are armed with orders to carry into execution a Warrant from the Judge Advocate against him

for exercising his lawful Right of Challenge against the Said Judge
Advocate, and assigning his reasons for it, as he was directed to do
by the Court. The Deponent further Swears that from the information he has received he considers his life in danger from the unprincipled and atrocious Characters that are combined against him
under the direction of the infamous George Crossley, he therefore
declines giving any Bail, and entreats the Court will be pleased to
put him under the protection of a Military Guard, they being the
only persons in whose hands he could consider himself Secure.

J. McArthur.

1808.
30 June.

Memorandum of
the proceedings
at the trial of
Macarthur.

Sworn before the Court of Criminal Jurisdiction this 25th day
of January, 1808.

Signed by the aforesaid Officers.

Sir,   Sydney, 25th January, 1808.

We are honored with Your Excellency's letter requiring of us
to deliver to Mr. Gore and Mr. Edmund Griffin all the Papers the
Judge Advocate left on the Table, and also those of the Prisoner,
John McArthur, Esqr., read before us;

With all due Submission to Your Excellency's Commands, we
beg leave to state that we are not defensible in giving up the Papers
alluded to to any person unless your Excellency thinks proper to
appoint another Judge Advocate to proceed on the Trial of John
McArthur, Esqr.

We have, &c.,

Anthy. Fenn Kemp,	Capt.	N.S.W. Corps.
J. Brabyn,	Lieut.	Do.
Wm. Moore,	Do.	Do.
Thos. Laycock,	Do.	Do.
Wm. Minchin,	Do.	Do.
Wm. Lawson,	Do.	Do.

In answer to the foregoing, the following letter was sent:—

Government House, Sydney, 25th January, 1808,

Gentlemen,   Three quarters past Three o'clock.

I have required the Judge Advocate's Papers, with those that
were read by John McArthur, and I now demand finally your
answer in writing whether you will deliver those Papers or not,
and I again repeat that you are no Court without the Judge
Advocate.

I am, &c.,
Wm. Bligh.

To

Captn. Anthony Fenn Kemp
Lieut. John Brabyn
Lieut. Wm. Moore   Of His Majesty's
Lieut. Thos. Laycock   New South Wales Corps
Lieut. Wm. Minchin
Lieut. Wm. Lawson

This letter was sent by Mr. Gore and Mr. Griffin to those addressed.
The Affidavit was sent back to have the copy of the Attestation
added to it.

1808.
30 June.
Memorandum of
the proceedings
at the trial of
Macarthur.

At 5 o'clock Mr. Gore and.Mr. Griffin returned with the following Letter, and the Affidavit above mentioned Signed by the whole of those to whom the above letter is addressed.

Sir,   Sydney, 25th January, 1808.

In answer to your Excellency's letter, we beg leave to Say that we are ready to furnish your Excellency with an attested copy of all the Papers required, but the originals we are compelled to Keep in justification of our conduct, or should your Excellency be pleased for the furtherance of the Public Service to appoint a Judge Advocate for the trial of Mr. McArthur we are ready to deliver them up to the person so appointed. The Court constituted by Your Excellency's Precept, and sworn in by the Judge Advocate, beg leave to acquaint you they have adjourned to wait your Excellency's further pleasure.

We have, &c.,

A. F. KEMP,	Capt. N.S.W. Corps.	
J. BRABYN,	Lieut.	Do.
WM. MOORE,	Do.	Do.
THOS. LAYCOCK,	Do.	Do.
WM. MINCHIN,	Do.	Do.
WM. LAWSON,	Do.	Do.

Immediately after this I wrote the following letter to Major Johnston :—

Government House, Sydney, 25th January, 1808,

Sir,   half past 5 o'Clock.

His Excellency under particular public Circumstances desires me to request you will see him without delay.

I have, &c.,
EDMUND GRIFFIN.

In the place of any Letter being written in answer to my above Letter, Thomas Thornby, one of my Bodyguard, who carried it, returned and said :—" Major Johnston's compliments to Mr. Griffin. That he was sorry that he could not write an Answer to him to the Note he had received ; That he was dangerously Ill, and it would endanger his Life to come to Camp ; his right Arm was tied up, and he said he has been bled." Thus ended this Proceeding. The Papers of the following day, the 26th January, were seized.

WM. BLIGH.

CIRCULAR LETTER SENT TO EACH MEMBER OF THE COURT AFTER ADJOURNMENT.

THE Judge Advocate having presented a Memorial to me, in which You are charged with certain Crimes, you are therefore hereby required to appear before me at Government House, at Nine o'Clock to-morrow Morning to answer in the Premises.

Given under my Hand and Seal at Government House, Sydney, this 26th day of January, 1808.

WM. BLIGH.

[Enclosure No. 4.]

AFFIDAVIT OF GEORGE SUTTOR.

I, GEORGE SUTTOR, free settler at Baulkham Hills, being in Sydney on 26th January, 1808, and seeing the Greater part of the New South Wales Corps under Arms with fixed Bayonets, marching down from the Barracks, I hastened among others to know the cause; and was informed that they were going to arrest the Governor; and on proceeding a short way with them, I distinctly heard Serjeant Major Whittle make use of these expressions, "Men, I hope you will do your duty, and don't spare them." The men replied, "Never fear us." And some person from the opposite Side cried out, "Hush! hush!" I think it was John McArthur Esqr. The Serjeant Major Whittle also said, "Children, go out of the way, for some of you I expect will be killed."

GEO. SUTTOR.

Sworn before me this 4th day of June, 1808,

JNO. PALMER, J.P.

[Enclosure No. 5.]

GENERAL ORDER.

MAJOR JOHNSTON having arrested His Excellency Governor Bligh, and having taken upon himself the charge of the Government, no orders are to be obeyed unless they come from him.

By Order of Major Johnston.

EDWARD ABBOTT,
Captain Commanding, Parramatta.
Martial Law is proclaimed.

[Enclosure No. 6.]

MAJOR JOHNSTON TO JOHN APSEY.

BY His Honor George Johnston, Esq'r., Lieutenant-Governor of His Majesty's Territory of New South Wales and its Dependencies, &c., &c., &c.

You are hereby required and directed to haul down the Broad Pendant now flying on board the Colonial Schooner Estramina, lying at anchor in this Harbour under your Command, for which this shall be your Authority.

Given under my Hand, at Head-Quarters, Sydney, New South Wales, this 27th day of January, 1808.

GEO. JOHNSTON.

To Mr. John Apsey,
Commander of the Schooner Estramina.

1808.
30 June.

Agreement
to defray
Macarthur's
expenses to
England, and
presentations
to Johnston
and officers.

[Enclosure No. 7.]

Copy of an Agreement* entered into on a Subscription being voted
to defray the expences of Mr. McArthur's proceeding to
England as a *Delegate,* and to present a Sword to Major
Johnston, and a Service of Plate to the Officers who composed the Criminal Court on the Trial of McArthur.

At a most respectable Meeting of the Inhabitants of the Town
of Sydney, convened on Monday, the eighth day of February,
1808, several propositions were made, and unanimously agreed to,
in order to carry into effect the Resolution they so cheerfully
acquiesced in for the general benefit of every Individual in the
Colony, by a representation to Parliament of the various grievances they have for a length of time laboured under, and more
particularly so under the Administration of Governor Bligh, it
was found expedient the raising, by voluntary Subscription, a
sum of money adequate to defray the Expences of John McArthur,
Esqr., who was nominated the fit Representative of this Colony to
lay before His Majesty's Ministers in England Such circumstances as have transpired to the detriment of the Commerce,
Welfare, Peace, and Advancement of this Place, and to pray
that His Majesty will be pleased to make such alterations in the
mode of Government as may tend to the Advantage, Peace,
Prosperity, and Happiness of this Community; as also for the
purpose of defraying the expences of a Sword to be presented
to His Honor Lieutenant-Governor Johnston, and a Present of
Plate to the Officers composing the Criminal Court on the Trial
of John McArthur, Esqr. We, the Undersigned, do most willingly
Subscribe the respective Sums against our Names expressed, for
the above laudable purposes; and as it is necessary, for the proper
management and appropriation of the Sums received for such
intentions, that a Committee consisting of such Members as the
majority of the Subscribers may think proper to appoint, to conduct the same, and to see that the Money is applied solely to
the purposes intended by us.

	£	s.	d.		£	s.	d.
Lord, Kable, and Un-				Isaac Nichols	50	0	0
derwood	500	0	0	Rosetta Marsh	20	0	0
Nicholas Bayly	100	0	0	Mary Skinner	10	0	0
Jno. and Greg'y Blax-				Edward Wills	30	0	0
land	200	.	0	Daniel McKay	10	0	0
Garnham Blaxcell ..	100		0	William Evans	5	5	0
Eber Bunker	20	0	0	John Redman	10	0	0
Elizabeth Driver ...	30	0	0	John Gowen	10	0	0

* Note 165.

[Enclosure No. 8.]

JOHN JAMIESON TO GOVERNOR BLIGH.

Sir,   Parramatta, 28th April, 1808.

The late presumptuous and unprecedented Act against your Person, which ought to have been deemed as Sacred as His Majesty's, was by none more disapproved of than myself; at the same time I thought it my duty to continue in my Situation for the good of the Public until I saw how things were likely to be Settled, as it was generally supposed that the Freeholders of Land throughout the Colony would rise in your behalf for the purpose of reinstating you in your lawful authority, of which they are all sensible of your being so very unjustly deprived. But their efforts, as yet, has proved impracticable—not for the want of good will, but the want of means. When I found Mr. McArthur wanted the whole of Government Stock to be removed to Broken Bay, amongst rocks and barren ground, to the great detriment of the Cattle, that he might have the whole range of land where they now graze for his own Stock to run in, I remonstrated against his proceedings, knowing that I held my situation for the preservation of the Stock instead of its destruction. As I could not act under Mr. McArthur and Mr. Fitz, Deputy-Commissary, to do justice to the Government Cattle that has been so many years under my charge, which has both been my pleasure and my duty to improve it, with real concern I now see them neglected, and under the care of a very worthless man*; but trust I shall not have that mortification longer. I thought it my duty to shew John Palmer, Esq., Commissary, the whole of the Correspondence that had passed on the Business between Major Johnston, Mr. McArthur, and myself, which shall be faithfully transmitted to your Excellency whenever it may be your pleasure to peruse it, by which means you will see that I have never deviated from my duty, either to your Excellency or the Public. I sincerely wish that Colonel Paterson was arrived to put an end to the Anarchy, Injustice, and Tyranny, which at present prevails in Defiance of all Law and Justice.

JNO. JAMIESON,
Principal Supt. of Government Stock.

P.S.—I shall trust to your Excellency to lay this letter before His Majesty's Ministers, after having served the Public faithfully for Sixteen years.

* Note 166.

[Enclosure No. 9.]

MAJOR JOHNSTON TO CHARLES GRIMES, REGISTER.

Johnston's
warrant for
summoning a
vice-admiralty
court.

BY His Honor George Johnston Esquire Lieutenant Governor of His Majesty's Territory called New South Wales.

WHEREAS His Majesty by especial Commission under the Great Seal of the High Court of Admiralty of England, bearing date the 12th day of April in the year of Our Lord 1787, hath been graciously pleased to ordain, constitute and appoint the Captain General and Governor in Chief in and over the said Territory called New South Wales to be Vice Admiral, Commissary and Deputy in the Office of Vice Admiralty in the said Territory and its Dependencies, to take cognizance of and proceed in all Cases within the Maritime Jurisdiction of the Vice Admiralty of the said Territory, and Whereas, by Virtue of Such Power and Authority, I have constituted and appointed Captain Edward Abbott of the New South Wales Corps to be President and Judge in a Court of Vice Admiralty which is to be holden and assembled for the purpose aforesaid on Saturday the 20th day of February. Now I, the Said George Johnston, do by these Presents nominate and appoint Captain Edward Abbott, James Williamson Acting Commissary, Richard Smith Master of the Dart, Simeon Patterson Master of the City of Edinburgh, Oliver Russell Master of the Brothers, Mr. Ebor Bunker, Planter, Mr. John Blaxland Planter, and Mr. Gregory Blaxland Planter, to compose and constitute such Court of which the Said Edward Abbott is to be President as aforesaid for the Purposes hereinbefore mentioned, and which Said Persons severally and respectively you Charles Grimes Esqr., Register in the Said Court of Vice Admiralty, are to cause to be hereby Summoned to attend and hold Such Court at 10 o'clock on the Said Saturday at Sydney aforesaid. For which this shall be your Warrant.

Given under my Hand and Seal this 19th day of February, 1808, at Sydney as aforesaid.

GEORGE JOHNSTON (L.G.).

[Enclosure No. 10.]

MR. ROBERT CAMPBELL'S REPORT ON THE SPIRIT TRAFFIC.

Robert
Campbell's
report on the
landing of
spirits from the
ship Jenny.

ON Monday afternoon the 7th of February, Mr. David Bevan informed me that two days before Governor Bligh was arrested, the Major authorized several Officers to get Spirits out of the American Ship Jenny, Captain Dorr, and that it was done at Twelve o'clock at night and carried round to Cockle Bay. That on Thursday the 3rd of February, Captain Kemp sent an order on board for one hundred Gallons of Brandy to be carried to Parramatta and it was delivered in Mr. Dorr's absence by the Supercargo; the following morning Mr. Laycock informed the Major of this circumstance, and which was the cause of the Ship being so precipitately ordered away. That the last Spirits was not paid for when the Ship sailed, having been Settled by a Bill of Captain Kemp's which Mr. Bevan is to get consolidated and remit the Amount to Mr. Franceur by the Eliza.

1808.
30 June.
———
Robert Campbell's report on the landing of spirits from the ship Jenny.

On the 17th of February, after Captain Dorr had been brought back with his ship to Sydney, he related to me the following circumstances.

On the night of the Illumination, the 28th January, Serjeant Major Whittle came to him at Mr. Bevan's, where he lodged, and wanted Two Pipes of Brandy to keep up the Night, for payment of which he offered a Paymaster's Note of £173 14s. 9d., and said that he was sent by Mr. Minchin for that purpose. Captain Dorr positively refused, and went on board his ship to give strict orders to allow no Spirits to go over the side, and returned on shore; but some time after Whittle went on board, and with the Serjeant of the Guard went into Mr. Franceur's cabin, where he was asleep, and informed him he was come by order for two casks of spirits, and that there was the payment—throwing into his Cot the before mentioned Pay Note. The Spirits were then put into the Boat and carried round to Cockle Bay.

That about three weeks after his Arrival (2nd November 1807) Kemp drove him out to the Major's, who they found with Lawson; and that the Major said he was glad to see him, and asked him to sit down. That he was afterwards asked if he had got leave to land his spirits, and on Kemp observing "Do you not intend to Smuggle?" the Major said "By God, the Governor must look very sharp otherwise we will take it from you in spite of him." Captain Dorr observed, that he had given his word to Governor Bligh, and that the object was so trifling he would run no risks. That the general topic of conversation was respecting Spirits, and that in General Grose's time the Officers were allowed to go on board of Ships when they pleased, and purchase a cask or two from the Americans from three to four Shillings per gallon, and sell it afterwards for two and three pounds; that in those times the Officers could live, cultivate their Farms, and make money, but at present they could do nothing but barely exist.

That the Officers of the Porpoise when at the Derwent, commanded by Lieutenant Symons, received from the American

1808.
30 June.

Robert
Campbell's
report on the
landing of
spirits from the
ship Jenny.

Ship Topaz, belonging to the same merchants as Captain Dorr, upwards of Eight hundred gallons of Rum, and one hundred and fifty of Gin, that about three hundred was only on account of the Ship, for which Bills were drawn on the Victualling Board, and the remainder was purchased by the Officers on their own private account, and afterwards Sold by them at two and three pounds per gallon.

Extract from Captain Dorr's letter to me.of the 22nd March, 1808.

" In your time, I have not only been called upon, but pressed against my inclination by the Officers of the New South Wales Corps to enter into illicit practices against the Rules and Regulations of the Colony. Upon the Suspicion of such practices you well know I have lately been brought before a Vice Admiralty Court held for that purpose; and what is more Surprizing, by the same Man, Lieutenant Governor Johnston, who gave his free permission to the Officers under him to undertake the smuggling of my Spirits on shore, when William Bligh Esq. was Governor, and only wished that his name might not be mentioned. Captain Kemp came to me one day, while at dinner with Mr. Bevan and other Gentlemen, to take me out in his Chaise to Major Johnston's Seat. I went with him, and found the Major at home, and after being there a little time they took a walk in the garden, and were there for some time. Captain Kemp and myself returned to Sydney, and he informed me that he had been talking with the Major respecting my Spirits, and said that the Major had given his permission, but wished that his name might not be brought in question.

" I have since that been repeatedly called upon by the Gentlemen Officers to undertake the business, and I have as repeatedly denied them. Lieutenant Lawson, now the Lieutenant Governor's Aid-de-camp, came on board the ship just after our arrival, solely for that purpose, saying it could be done with the greatest Safety, and everything he could possibly say to carry it into effect but my answer was No, for I had no such intention; and in that manner I have been continually harrassed by those Gentlemen Officers, and men employed under them, to undertake the Smuggling of Spirits; the temptation offered and such frequent applications would be almost impossible for any man to withhold.

" Mr. John McArthur and Garnham Blaxcell, the two Gentlemen that pretended to adhere, at my trial, so strictly to the Rules and Regulations of this Colony, and the private Instructions

from the Secretary of State to His Excellency Governor Bligh,
have forgot I presume, that they were ready in his Governor
Bligh's time to take and Smuggle from Captain Corry of the
American Brig Eliza now here, all his Spirits at Twenty Shillings a Gallon, which Captain Corry informed me was the case."

ROBT. CAMPBELL.

Sydney, March 31st, 1808.

[Enclosure No. 11.]

THE PROTEST OF PROVOST-MARSHAL GORE.*

Gentlemen,

Holding my Commission as the Provost Marshal of this
Territory, under His Majesty's Sign Manual and countersigned
by one of His Majesty's Secretaries of State, I contend it to be
my duty, and corresponding with my Allegiance to my Gracious
Sovereign to deny your Jurisdiction as a Court, and therefore
your incompetency to try me, for according to Blackstone page
267, " All Jurisdictions of Courts are either mediately or immediately derived from the Crown, their proceedings run generally
in the King's name, they pass under His Seal, and are executed
by His Officers." And the Act of Parliament, on which the
Patent for establishing a Court of Criminal Jurisdiction in this
Territory is founded, has provided that in case of the death of
the Governor or of his Absence from the Territory, then the
Lieutenant Governor or the Officer next in Command is empowered to take upon himself the administration of the Country;
but in this case the Governor is not dead, neither is he absent
from the Colony, the consequence therefore, is that as His
Majesty has not delegated His Authority to any other Individual
in this Territory at present in the exercise of such Authority, to
issue a precept for the purpose of convening a Court of Criminal
Jurisdiction; that no authority whatsoever exists in any person
or Body of men in this Country to convene and institute any
Court of Criminal Jurisdiction, nor can such Court so convened
and constituted have any existence in Law; but if the Governor
even was absent the Law has made no provision for the present
case, not taking into its view that any man, or Body of men,
would attempt to depose, as it does not allow His Majesty's
Governors to be deposed from their Authority on any pretence
whatsoever, by the People over whom His Majesty has placed
them as His Governors.

Admitting however, that you were a lawfully convened and
constituted Court, you cannot, I assert, conscientiously discharge
the Sacred duty with which the Law would have entrusted you, it

* Note 161.

1808.
30 June.

Gore's protest
against the
jurisdiction
of the criminal
court.

being my undoubted privilege as a British Subject to exercise my Right of Challenge, which I do peremptorily on the following unanswerable grounds; that the Justices who committed me, and the Members before whom I am called, have an Interest direct, immediate and consequential in my conviction, inasmuch that they have contributed their united efforts to subvert His Majesty's Government in this Territory, of which I was an accredited Member:—That I am obnoxious to the Persons who have assumed the administration is clear and decisive; and it is equally certain that every means which Injustice can devise will be employed to vilify my character, in order to justify their own conduct to His Majesty's Ministers.

I, therefore, for the aforesaid strong and imperious reasons, do most solemnly protest against being put on my Trial before you, and beg you: First, on the ground of your not possessing Jurisdiction; Secondly, on the ground of your having in your Individual and Collective capacities palpable Interest in my disgrace as a public Officer; Thirdly that it would be against the allegiance and fidelity I owe to my revered King; and lastly, on the ground that it would be in a direct opposition to that Obedience which my Commission enjoins me to act with towards His Majesty's Governor of this Territory. Therefore these are my reasons for now applying, and I hereby do apply to the present Acting Deputy Judge Advocate of this Territory, in his official Capacity, to take such measures as are legal and proper to remove my Trial before His Majesty's Court of King's Bench in England, it being the only Court before which, to the best of my belief and Knowledge, I can, in the present Situation have a fair and impartial trial

Before I conclude, allow me, Gentlemen, to observe, that I am actuated by no motives of disrespect towards you, I am only contending against your Authority, and for my own right as a British Subject and as a British Civil Officer, who by Virtue of his Office being immediately under the protection of and amenable to His Majesty's Court of King's Bench, claims his unalienable right of going before that Superior Court, from which he confidently expects to obtain a full, a free, and an impartial Trial.

I, likewise, Gentlemen, beg leave to deprecate the intention of using any language which may be calculated to irritate your minds, as I have merely expressed myself in such terms and manner as I imagined shall have, with the least degree of acrimony, a tendency to repel the base ungenerous and unfounded

Offence with which I am charged, and to promote the fullest and most impartial discription of its merits and demerits before the most proper Court.

1808.
30 June.

Gore's protest against the jurisdiction of the criminal court.

21st March, 1808. WM. GORE.

Read by Mr. Gore and afterwards delivered to the Acting Deputy Judge Advocate on the 21st of March, 1808, when Six Officers were assembled with him for the purpose of holding a Criminal Court.

[Enclosure No. 12.]

PROVOST-MARSHAL GORE'S INTENDED DEFENCE.

Gentlemen,

I am indicted for having committed wilful and corrupt Perjury, and I am now on my Trial. I shall occupy as little of your time as is consistent with the duty I owe to myself, to my family, to my character, and to public Justice.

Proposed defence of William Gore before the criminal court.

In the first place, I shall ground my defence on a denial of the Jurisdiction of the Six Members who were convened by His Excellency Governor Bligh's Precept, for the purpose of their constituting a Court of Criminal Jurisdiction; for as they refused to swear His Majesty's Judge-Advocate a Member of such intended Court, they never had existence as a Court, they being defective of their principal Member as prescribed by Law; and in Law it is laid down as an irrevocable Maxim, that when an Act of Parliament designates or marks out the specific number of persons who shall act, preside, or are to adjudicate in any Judicial Proceedings, it shall never consist of less or fewer than such designated number; and the Act of Parliament on which the Patent for establishing Courts of Criminal Jurisdiction in this country is founded, declares in specific terms that such Courts shall consist of Six Officers of His Majesty's Sea and land Forces, and of His Majesty's Judge-Advocate for the time being, it follows, *a fortiori,* that such Six Members possessed no legal authority to take the Prisoner out of my Custody, and to render him to his former Bail. Should it nevertheless be insisted that they were invested with such Authority, I, however, object to the determination, it being a point on which, if any possible doubt can exist in the minds of dispassionate men, cannot be decided here, and must be referred to His Majesty's Ministers for their instructions respecting it.

I contend they were not vested with such Authority, for when the Prisoner appeared with his Bondmen at the Bar of the Court before which he was to be tried, the Bond became null and void, his former Bail were no longer responsible for him, they

1808.
30 June.

Proposed
defence of
William Gore
before the
criminal court.

were free from the Condition and obligation of the Bond, and the Prisoner was then in my Custody; and if the Court afterwards, on application from the Prisoner or his Counsel, was inclined to indulge him with Bail, it could not be granted without the consent of the Prosecutor or his Counsel; but even in that case the new Bail Bond should have been given to me, for I alone was answerable for the Prisoner's appearance when he once came with his Bail into Court; but the Prosecutor or his Counsel were not applied to for their consent—no fresh Bond was exacted from them or given to me. I was not their Officer, they had no legal existence as a Court, and my duty directed me to disclaim their authority.

If, however, they were a Court, I have now proved without a chance of being refuted, that they could not re-deliver the Prisoner to his former Bail, as he was then in my Custody, and he or his Bondsmen did not express a desire to enter a new Recognizance to me. I therefore still considered him in my custody, from whence, when he withdrew himself, he was in Law guilty of an Escape, and by Virtue of my Office I was armed with full and sufficient authority to pursue and re-take him; but Governor Bligh, from his uniform disposition that the Law should be literally complied with, desired my authority should be supported by an Escape Warrant, which was granted unto me under the Signatures of four Justices; however, before such Warrant was granted, my Deposition that the Prisoner, Mr. McArthur, was not then in my custody, or in any other Custody that I knew of, was necessary. I therefore made an Affidavit of its truth—I was then, and I am still justified by the Law—and the Fact, which I shall prove by Evidence, and from the most incontestible Authorities. Even allowing, for Argument's sake, that the Six Members had legal authority to deliver the Prisoner, without a Bond, to his former Bail, I acted legally, because I positively swear that I never knew he was delivered to his former Bail; and as to my assent by a *Nod* or a *Bow,* I did not understand that a delivery of the Prisoner to Bail was the purport of Captain Kemp's address to me; but to admit a *Nod* or a *Bow* as Evidence in a Court of Justice would, I make no doubt, be deemed a novel, a ridiculous, and too dangerous a precedent for, in Law, to convict a man of perjury. A probable evidence is not enough, but it must be a strong and clear Evidence. A Bow or a Nod has not even the strength of probability; they are at best merely conjectural, and are so wholly undefinable as to allow of all persons, according to their various interests and pursuits, to attach what meaning they please to them; but, Gentlemen, it would be an abuse and a waste of your time, and an imposition on your understandings, to delay you longer on this Subject. I shall, therefore, only observe that in Law they cannot be admitted as proof against me.

1808.
30 June.

Proposed
defence of
William Gore
before the
criminal court.

With respect to Captain Kemp's testimony,* I most solemnly swear that I never heard him express himself to the effect he has sworn, and against his Oath is the direct evidence of Mr. Griffin. And besides, it being physically impossible, by any Evidence, however strong, to prove that I heard the words so sworn to by Captain Kemp, as spoken by him to me, I humbly submit to you, Gentlemen, that I have not sworn a false Oath, nor am I guilty of Wilful and Corrupt Perjury; for, according to Hawkins, 172, though I might be in error I was not, however, guilty of Perjury, wilful or corrupt, because "when a person even swears falsely, if he mistook the true state of the question, it is not Perjury." But, Gentlemen, although I have deliberated to this moment on the Oath I have taken so far back as the 25th of January, I am still firmly persuaded, and convinced that I was not in error, for the Prisoner, Mr. McArthur, was not in my Custody, nor in any custody that I know of at the time I made a deposition to that effect; but he could not be in custody of any other person, without his executing a Legal Bond to me.

Lastly, Gentlemen, as in Civil Cases I am answerable to the Party injured, so in Criminal matters to the Crown. Had I, of my own mere descretion, any right or the authority to permit the Prisoner, Mr. McArthur, to be delivered to his former Bail without observing even the formality of a Bond? Would I not have exposed myself to a Prosecution at the Suit of the Crown? And would I not be indebted to the lenity and forbearance of His Excellency Governor Bligh if he did not instantly, on the affair coming to his Knowledge, place me under an Arrest, and call a Court-Martial on me if my Offence were a Military one; or would he not, put the question in any point of view you choose, have suspended me for incapacity, for a shameful neglect of my Duty, and for a breach of his Orders? This last is a more convincing argument than I have yet used of the folly, of the absurdity, and of the wickedness of the Prosecution that has been instituted against me; it is a certain and positive proof that the design of the Prosecutor has originated in motives dishonourable to himself as a Man, and in every respect repugnant to the principles of common Sense and common honesty. Permit me, Gentlemen, to ask you where is the Officer of the Crown who would venture on so hazardous an enterprise as the execution of this duty, if for the performance of it he was threatened with a prosecution, intended ultimately to affect his life, his character, and his honor? And if every ignorant and discontented caviller

* Note 167.

and ruler against the Government was not only secretly encouraged but openly supported in instituting such vexatious, harrassing, and unfounded prosecutions?

Let me again, Gentlemen, call your attention to the last argument I have adduced, and ask you, Had I pleaded ignorance to Governor Bligh that such a Bond was necessary to be executed to me, would not His Majesty's Ministers, on the matter being reported to them, approve of my suspension and deservedly deprive me of my Appointment for incapacity; and if from motives of Interest or Favor I had consented to the Prisoner's returning to his former Bail, would I not meritedly, in the eyes of His Majesty's Ministers, and of all faithful and honest Servants of the Crown, incur the base censure of a venal Officer, too corrupt to hold an honorable Commission?

[Enclosure No. 13.]

[A] PROVOST-MARSHAL GORE TO GOVERNOR BLIGH.

Sir,   Cells, Sydney Jail, N.S.W., 31st May, 1808.

Gore's account
of the
proceedings
at his trial.

I presume you have already been informed of the additional unprecedented outrage and atrocious violation of the Laws of England, that a Body of persons styling themselves a Court of Criminal Jurisdiction has perpetrated against the person of a British Subject and of a British Officer who has the honor of holding a Commission under His Majesty's Sign Manual, by dragging me yesterday from the Dungeon in which they have cruelly and illegally immured me since the twenty-first of last March, before them, without the least warning, without a minute's notice, when the infamous Kemp, who acted as Judge-Advocate on the occasion, read an Indictment charging me with having committed wilful and corrupt Perjury, and asked me, "Are you guilty or not guilty?" "I have a few observations to make; I believe I have them in my hat." "We do not wish you to say anything; We do not wish you to speak; are you guilty or not guilty?" "I deny your Jurisdiction." "We are not to be harangued by you, Mr. Gore; We are not come here for you to harangue us." "I will not plead; I deny your jurisdiction." "It is not for you to deny our jurisdiction; I will pass sentence on you if you will not plead." "You are an Unlawful Assembly, and illegally constituted; the most disgraceful, the most rigorous sentence you can pronounce on me I shall receive as the greatest Honor you can confer on me; I shall not acknowledge your Authority; I deny your jurisdiction." *Captain Abbott*: "Mr. Gore, you can challenge any Member—you can challenge any Member." "No, possessing my fealty and my allegiance to my King, I deny your jurisdiction; I will not plead—for you are an unlawful Assembly." *Captain Kemp*: "Clear the Court; Clear the Court." The Court having been opened again, after a lapse of about Twenty minutes, Kemp said: "We have recorded that you have refused to plead." "I have; I do." "And we have Sentenced you to be transported for seven years." "You have conferred on me the greatest Honor you are capable of conferring—the only Honor I could receive from such Men. Loyalty and Treason could not unite; Treason and Loyalty could not associate, could not agree." *Kemp*: "Take him away; take him off; take him away; take him away."

The preceding is an accurate Statement of the iniquitous Proceedings of yesterday; they certainly afford the most unanswerable comment on the enormities our Despots commit, under the influence of desperation and the hope and expectation of future immunity and pardon, and the best refutation of the Calumnies and false accusations with which they have assailed and uniformly endeavoured to circumvent and destroy my character, since my arrival in this Country. I trust, Sir, that as far as it was in my power I have done my Duty—that I have acquitted myself as a faithful Servant of the Crown and as a loyal and firm Officer. Be assured, Sir, that the personal danger I encounter and the Sacrifice of my liberty are but minor considerations in my breast. My life I would willingly risk in the maintenance of the dignity and Authority of my venerated Sovereign and of his Virtuous and much injured Representative. Favor and respect from such men as my debased persecutors are would, believe me, be considered by me as my greatest dishonor. As it is whispered to me that I may be taken by surprize tomorrow Morning and sent to the Coal River, from which it would appear that these fellows are desirous of preventing me from going to England, for the reasons I have heretofore mentioned, pardon my entreating you to state to His Majesty's Ministers the unhappy condition of my poor family—the forlorn, the unmerited, and the miserable Situation to which my dear and amiable wife, and my tender, my darling infants, are reduced by the veriest miscreants in existence, surely cannot fail to interest His Majesty's Ministers in their behalf, particularly as I am apprehensive, with great reason, that an attempt may be made on my life. To you, Sir, as their Advocate, and to the justice and magnanimity of His Majesty's Ministers, I commit them in the hour of the most unheard-of calamities and oppressions. I fondly flatter myself that our Great and Beneficent King would (if I was to lose my life through the Villainy of our enemies), upon a proper representation, consider them worthy and deserving his Royal protection and consideration.

Marginal notes:
1808. 30 June.

Gore's account of the proceedings at his trial.

Treatment received by Gore from the officers.

Gore's anxiety regarding his family.

1808.
30 June.

Gore's farewell
to Bligh.

Should I not have an opportunity of having the honor and
satisfaction of a personal interview with you before your departure from this ill-fated Country, I now, Sir, take my leave of you,
and beg your acceptance of my sincerest thanks and acknowledgments for the great kindness and attention you have evinced
towards my family and myself. I wish you and Mrs. Putland
every happiness, and I pray for your (indeed, I do not doubt it)
complete triumph over your enemies. Enemies, have I said?—
an Enemy is an honorable character;—your cowardly defamers,
the lawless assassins of every honest, every honorable, and every
independent principle. May God bless and protect you!

I have, &c.,

WILLIAM GORE.

[B] PROVOST-MARSHAL GORE TO GOVERNOR BLIGH.

Sir,   Cells, Sydney Jail, N.S.W., 2nd June, 1808.

Additional
details relating
to Gore's trial.

From the agitation my mind has undergone, I inadver-
tently omitted, in my Letter of the 31st of May, to tell you that,
when I was taken by four constables from the Cell in which I
am incarcerated, on Monday, the 30th of May, I was conducted by
them to the Military Barracks (it was then precisely 25 minutes
after 12 o'clock), where I was ordered to be kept until two o'clock
(the Court, as I was informed, being adjourned to that hour) as
a Show and Spectacle for the derision and amusement of the Soldiers, one Constable keeping constantly by my side on the Parade,
and the Chief Constable occasionally attending and walking on
the other side whenever he observed McArthur approaching to
and coming on the Parade.

The Barrack being at length opened, which they called the
Court-House, and the persons assembled who were to compose the
Court, it is now, Sir, for you to judge how great must have been
my Surprise on seeing the identical Captain Kemp presiding as
Judge-Advocate who, on the 25th of last January, acted so
conspicuous a part by threatening to commit His Majesty's
Judge-Advocate to Jail, and who at length turned him out of
Court—the very Monster who volunteered as a Witness to swear,
before Jamison and Blaxland, two of his self-created fellow-
Justices, that I was Guilty of the pretended Crime (for which he
was actually sitting in judgment on me), with which the Traitor,
McArthur, had charged me—for Kemp had sworn, on the first of
March, before the above two persons, that "I heard him tell me
that the Court would return McArthur to his former Bail, as *I
bowed to him at the time of his telling me so.*"

Lieutenants Moore, Laycock, and Lawson, who had likewise
been subpœnaed as witnesses against me in this cause, and Cap-

tain Abbott also, who allowed the Validity of a Challenge I made
to him on the 21st of March, in this very Cause, too, were all
Members of the Court—or, rather, of this traitorous Assembly;
they, of course, prejudged me, for they had long before declared
themselves ready to swear to my Guilt. This base Stratagem
was artfully planned by them, in order to discredit my testimony
hereafter, by levelling (what they imagine) a fatal blow against
my reputation; but, although I must suffer great hardship by
their barefaced violation of all the rules of justice and decorum,
they have, however, fallen themselves into the pit they dug for
me—for, in fact, they had no intention of trying me on the
30th of May; they were fully satisfied of the too palpable injustice of keeping me locked up in a dungeon, and they saw that
the Public began to observe it, and to express themselves freely
on the Subject—notwithstanding which they considered it prudent to continue me in prison with so infamous a charge hanging
over me. But, in proportion as their preconcerted injustice
appeared more evident, they became more Solicitous to remove
from themselves the blame and odium of my Confinement on so
false a charge by making a Show and a deluding display of their
moderation and affected Clemency in granting and acquiescing
in the propriety of the Challenges which, in the Vanity and folly
of their hearts, they flattered themselves I would make; and, had
I fallen into their snare, there not being any other Officers in
the Country who could try me, they would then propose to me
to give Bail, and, on my refusal, they would have re-committed
me to Gaol. Thus the purpose of their iniquitous designs would,
in a great measure, have been effected. However, as my seclusion
from Society, within the walls of a prison, had not as yet broken
down my Spirit, nor the power with which they had so traitor-
ously invested themselves had intimidated me, their project, deep
and artfully laid as it had been, was frustrated, and, by my denial
of their jurisdiction, they have been precipitated into the per-
petration of the foulest and most flagitious enormity and offence
against the Laws of the Realm and the Rights and Liberty of the
Subject; And their having debarred me the indulgence of offering a few observations to them precludes them from the suspicion
even of intended impartiality, and stamps their injustice with
the rankest inconsistency. I have, &c.,

WILLIAM GORE.

[Enclosure No. 14.]

PROCLAMATION.
WHEREAS Oliver Russell, Master of the Ship Brothers, and Robert
Daniels, Acting Chief Mate of the said Ship, were on Wednesday,

1808.
30 June.

Proclamation
of the pardon
of Russell
and Daniels.

the 30th day of March last past, convicted of the Crime of Perjury by the Court of Criminal Jurisdiction then Sitting, and
Sentenced (By an Act under the Authority of 2'd Geo' 2'd) to
be transported for Seven Years; and whereas it appears the said
Oliver Russell and Robert Daniels were never indicted in due
form of Law before the said Court for the said Crime of Perjury, nor allowed the means of Justification to which they were
by Law entitled, His Honor the Lieutenant-Governor, actuated
by an anxious desire to preserve the Rights of Englishmen inviolate, and to convince Strangers resorting to this Colony that
they have nothing to apprehend from the Oppression of Power,
from whencesoever proceeding, Hereby Annuls and declares
Invalid the Sentence of Transportation pronounced against the
said Oliver Russell and Robert Daniels, and restores them to all
the Rights and Priviledges they were possessed of before the
aforesaid Sentence was pronounced.

God Save the King.

By command of His Honor the Lieutenant Governor.
JOHN McARTHUR, Colonial Secretary.
Sydney, 3rd April, 1808.

[Enclosure No. 15.]
[A] MR. JOHN BRENAN TO MR. ANDREW THOMPSON.
Dear Sir,　　　　　Mary Mount, Hawkesbury, 28th April, 1808.

　　　Mr. Arndell informed me you wished to have a Copy of
the Letter addressed to Major Johnston which I was unfortunately concerned in by going amongst the Settlers to get their
Signatures* thereto, and for which I sincerely repent in my duplicity in taking the advice of others in doing which I ought not
to have done. I am happy to have it to send you and herein
enclosed.　　　　　　　　　　　　　　I am, &c.,
JNO. BRENAN.

[B] ADDRESS OF SETTLERS TO MAJOR JOHNSTON.
To His Honor George Johnston, Esqr., Lieutenant-Governor of
the Colony of New South Wales.
　　Sir,
　　　　Impressed with the highest Sense of the Obligation due to
you for having come forward at this momentous crisis to extricate the Loyal Inhabitants of the Colony from that dread and
horror which the recent arbitrary measures had caused—
Measures which, if pursued as they hitherto have been, must have
ultimately proved destructive to this infant State, as well as
injurious to the finances of the Mother Country, and which tend
to destroy those rights so dear to every Englishman.

* Note 168.

We presume to address you in the most unfeigned manner, earnestly hoping. you will accept our grateful acknowledgments, unadorned by any fulsome language. The Oppressions which we have lately undergone had nearly blunted those feelings which as Men we ought to have cherished; but, anxious for the Welfare of our Families, and to avert those Calamities which would have inevitably attended those persons who might have refused to sign a recent Address, many of us therein reluctantly praised those Proceedings which in our hearts we could but condemn. Now that we could freely express the Sentiments of our Minds, we gladly beg to assure you that we are ready to support you with our lives and properties, conscious that every Act of your Administration would meet His Majesty's approbation.

We cannot in language sufficiently praise the meritorious services of the New South Wales Corps on this memorable occasion.

[Signed by sixty-six persons.]

[Robert Fitz, Thos. Hobby, John Brenan, Benj'n Carver, William Mason, James Badgery, James M. Pitt, James Richards, John Benn, George Hall, Thos. Arndell, Thomas Biggers, Andrew Hume, Thomas Dargin, Law'ce May, Wm. Baker, S.K., Wm. Faithful, Josh. Cunningham, James Cox, *and 47 others.*]

[Enclosure No. 16.]
THOMAS ARNDELL TO SECRETARY GRIFFIN.

Sir,   Sydney, 11th April, 1808.

I signed a Paper a few days subsequent to the 26th January, expressing my disapprobation of a Paper which I signed not long before, which Paper contained thanks to Governor Bligh for his kindness to the People and good Government of them. I now most solemnly declare that I signed the Paper subsequent to the 26th January through fear, and without so much as knowing the Contents at the time I signed it. It might have contained more than I have expressed, but I don't know what they are.*   I am, &c.,

THOMAS ARNDELL.

[Enclosure No. 17.]
[A] LIEUTENANT-GOVERNOR COLLINS TO GOVERNOR BLIGH.

26th January, 1808.

[A copy of this despatch will be found in volume I, series III.]

[B] LIEUTENANT-GOVERNOR COLLINS TO GOVERNOR BLIGH.

Dear Sir,   Hobart Town, 4th April, 1808.

It was with the utmost concern I heard by a letter from Major Johnston of the unprecedented attack made by that Officer

* Note 168.

1808.
30 June.

Address of settlers to Johnston.

Arndell's signature obtained through fear.

1808.
30 June.

Collins'
disapproval of
Bligh's arrest.

upon your person and Government on the 26th January last. Of the circumstances which led to this desperate and illegal proceedings I am only generally informed, nor can I deem them such as to warrant such a dereliction from the duty and subordination which were due to you as the Representative of Our Sovereign in this part of his Dominions. Had not Major Johnstone's Signature been to the letter in which he officially informed me of the violent and highly responsible Measure he had resorted to, I never could have believed that any Officer bearing the King's Commission would have dared to have advanced one Step towards overthrowing the Executive Authority of the Government which he was bound to protect and support.

Feeling as I do upon this unhappy business, I beg you to be assured it never can meet with my approval or countenance, and I at this moment particularly regret the loss of your advice and opinion upon many points respecting the Norfolk Island Settlers, whereby His Majesty's Service may eventually be injured.

Allow me, Sir, to offer my condolence to Yourself and Mrs. Putland on the melancholy event which has lately taken place in your family, and to express my Sincere wishes for your safe and speedy arrival in England, where a certain triumph over your few enemies will undoubtedly attend you, and what I trust will be a greater and more permanent Satisfaction, His Majesty's approbation of your conduct in the execution of the high Commission with which he had invested you.

It would give me the greatest pleasure to be honoured with the Knowledge from yourself that you are in health, and that no further indignity has been offered to your person.

I remain, with every wish for your welfare, and sentiments of respect,   Yours, &c.,
                                            DAVID COLLINS.

[Enclosure No. 18.]

ADDRESS TO GOVERNOR BLIGH.

Address of
welcome to
Governor
Bligh.

To His Excellency William Bligh, Esquire, Captain-General and Governor-in-Chief in and over His Majesty's Territory of New South Wales and its Dependencies, &c.

May it please Your Excellency,—   14th August, 1806.

The Officers, Civil and Military, with the Free Inhabitants of this Colony, beg leave respectfully to offer their sincere congratulations to Your Excellency upon your Appointment to this Government, and to express their happiness at your safe Arrival.

They trust that Your Excellency will not entertain unfavourable opinions of the fertility and natural Resources of the Country from the unfortunate Scarcity which the late Inundations have occasioned; for be assured, Sir, you will find the Country, under the ordinary dispensations of Providence, neither wanting in fertility nor barren of resources; but on the contrary, capable of maintaining its Inhabitants in plenty, and of becoming, with moderate encouragement, a Colony of considerable importance to Great Britain.

1808.
30 June.
———
Address of
welcome to
Governor
Bligh.

We have an undoubting confidence that Your Excellency, by a just, moderate, firm, and wise Government, will promote the happiness of all who deserve it; and we feel animated by a pleasing hope that, under your Excellency's Auspices, Agriculture will flourish, and Commerce increase, whilst enjoying as far as Circumstances will admit the Constitutional Rights of British Subjects, we shall in due time rise above our present comparative state of insignificance, and by our example prove to the World what great exertions Mankind will make when properly incited to exercise their natural Powers.

We intreat Your Excellency to believe that, anxious as we are for the improvement of Agriculture and the extension of Commerce (the two great sources of Population, Civilization, and Morality), we are perfectly Sensible they alone are not sufficient to secure the Welfare of our Infant Establishment, but that it is the indispensable duty of us all to combine with our endeavours to accomplish these objects a reverential regard to the Laws, and a cheerful acquiescence in such Measures as Your Excellency may adopt to improve the true interest of the Colony.

Convinced that our prosperity and happiness will be the great objects of your Excellency's care, we earnestly hope your Excellency will find your Administration productive of real and permanent satisfaction, and honour to yourself.

> GEORGE JOHNSTON, for the Military ⎫
> RICHARD ATKINS, for the Civil ⎬ Inhabitants.
> JOHN MCARTHUR, for the Free ⎭

GOVERNOR BLIGH'S ANSWER.
Government House, Sydney,
Gentlemen, 14th August, 1806.

I accept your Congratulations and Address with very great satisfaction; and am happy in believing I am not less honoured with your confidence than I feel a disposition and determination to promote the welfare of this infant Colony, the Government of which Our Most Gracious King has committed to my charge, united with you, his dutiful and loyal Subjects, in your respective situations of trust and confidence.

Bligh's reply
to the address
of welcome.

It will be a heartfelt satisfaction to His Majesty and His Government to learn from your Address that the Country settled

1808.
30 June.

Bligh's reply
to the address
of welcome.

under his benign Influence is capable of ample returns to the
industrious Settler and Merchant, under due Exertions, Regulations, and Encouragement; to the ends of which I draw very
happy conclusions by your dutiful Representation, determining
to support a reverential regard to the Laws, and inculcating a
true sense of Religion and Morality.

Your confidence in me, I trust, will tend to realise the benefits
you look to. I have met you with great affection, and shall watch
over your cares and interests to the utmost of my power, to render
Society a blessing, and the Colony flourishing.

I have, &c.,
WM. BLIGH.

[Enclosure No. 19.]

HAWKESBURY SETTLERS' ADDRESS, 1806.

Address of
welcome from
settlers at the
Hawkesbury to
Governor
Bligh.

To His Excellency, Wm. Bligh, Esq., Captain-General and
Governor-in-Chief in and over His Majesty's Territory of
New South Wales, &c., &c.

THE Address of the Settlers, Landholders, and Cultivators of
Land, and other Principal Inhabitants of Hawkesbury, whose
names are hereunto written.

We congratulate your Excellency on your safe arrival in this
Territory, and we think ourselves happy to express thanks to our
most gracious Sovereign for the attention His Royal Majesty
has shown to the people of this Colony in appointing a person of
your Excellency's superior understanding, knowledge, and ability
to the Government of this Country.

We consider ourselves the more fortunate in this at a time
when the Country is labouring under the greatest calamity in
being brought to the near approach of a Famine; to avert its
advances at this period can only be attained by Your Excellency's superior circumspection and wisdom.

We state, with the deepest concern, the occasion of this
threatened calamity to be (in some degree) by the Great Flood
which it pleased Divine Providence to send in March last, the
rise of the water being near ten feet perpendicular height greater
than had been in this Colony since it was first inhabited by
Europeans.

This disaster happened at a time when the Landholders, Settlers, and Cultivators were struggling to overcome a still greater
difficulty occasioned by the oppressions before in practice by a
mistaken policy in oppressing the Merchants and Inhabitants
in general by sending from this Port ships that arrived with
merchandize, of Necessaries and Comforts, by not suffering them
to land their goods for sale, although the Colony was in the
greatest want of the Articles they brought.

In having for many years past reduced the price of Grain and other Articles, the produce of agriculture, to so low a price that the produce of the land would not pay the Grower the Expenses of Cultivation, to the general ruin of the Settler, and by not paying for such Commodities in money, or such Bills as would enable the Settlers to purchase Articles of Necessity at a ready-money price, so that before this unfortunate Flood (which gave the finishing Stroke to the distresses of the Inhabitants), the Settlers were in general in that impoverished State that, exclusive of the great length of time it may take to restore the Colony, a sum of £200,000 would scarcely restore it to the State it was when Governor Hunter left the Colony in 1800.

1808.
30 June.
—
Address of welcome from settlers at the Hawkesbury to Governor Bligh.

We look up to your Excellency in Wisdom to put in practice such means as may be for the Salvation, honor, and interest of the Colony, and for averting the approach of Famine and distress to its Inhabitants—

By restoring the Freedom of Trade.

By permitting Commodities to be bought and sold at a fair open Market (by all the Inhabitants).

By preventing that painful Monopoly and Extortion heretofore practised.

By protecting the Merchant and Trader in their properties, and the People in general in their Rights, Privileges, Liberties, and Professions, as by Law established.

By suffering the Laws of this Realm to take their due course in matters of property without control.

That Justice be administered by the Courts authorized by His Majesty, according to the known Law of the Land.

By causing payment to be made in such Money or Government Orders as will pass current in the purchase of every Article of Merchandize without Drawback or Discount.

We most respectfully assure your Excellency we are ready on all occasions to lay down our Lives and Fortunes for the protection and support of Your Excellency in the good Government, Welfare, and Prosperity of the Colony, and to comply with every recommendation your Excellency may in wisdom propose for the Government of this Territory.

We look up to the time when it may please His Majesty to authorize in such a manner as his justice may deem meet a Legal Authority to make Local Laws for the Government of the Colony.

We subscribe this Address, the loyal People, Settlers, Landholders, Cultivators, and other Principal Inhabitants of Hawkesbury and parts adjacent.

We, the Free Inhabitants who subscribe this Address, request Messrs. John Bowman, Matthew John Gibbons, George Crossley,

1808.
30 June.

Address of
welcome from
settlers at the
Hawkesbury to
Governor
Bligh.

William Cummings, and T. M. Pitt, or any of them, as our
Deputies (in our names) to present this Address, and, at the same
time, to represent the Infringement made on our Rights, Privileges, and Liberties by John McArthur, Esq., who appears by the
*Sydney Gazette** to have signed " For the Inhabitants " without
our previous knowledge, consent or authority, public or private.

[*Among the 244 names, nearly one-half are signed with a
cross. Some names may be given*:—Edward Reynolds, Andrew
Johnston, William Waring, John Austin, Jane Rose, Lazarus
Graves, Tho's M. Pitt, R'd Hayman, W'm Hancey, W'm Rouse,
Edward Pugh, John O'Hara, R'd Allwright, Tho's Biggers,
Adam Bell, Sam'l Griffiths, Mich'l Connolly, George Crossley,
W'm Mason, James Dunn, James Badgery, W'm Cummings, R'd
Tuckwell, Matth' J. Gibbons, H. T. Stockfish, Andrew Hume,
Tho's Appledore, Israel Rayner, John Bowman, W'm Bowman,
Sarah Stubbs, James Lowry, W'm Slaughter,. James Dunlop.]

In compliance with the general wishes of the Settlers and other
free Inhabitants at Hawkesbury and parts adjacent, we are
deputed to have the Honor of presenting their address to your
Excellency.

And they require us in their names to represent, Altho' they
approve of the Address to your Excellency which appear'd in the
Sydney Gazette on the 17th of August Instant, and had they been
previously applied to for the purpose, would have given it their
assent;

Yet they consider the Act of John McArthur, Esq., in signing
for them " the Free Inhabitants," without previous application
or authority, public or private, to be such an invasion of their
Rights and Privileges as British Subjects as to call for their
pointed animadversion, and authorize us to say that had a Public
Meeting been held they would by no means have authorized Mr.
McArthur to have signed such Address to Governor King as
appears in the Second Paper.*

JOHN BOWMAN.   MATTHEW GIBBONS.
WILLIAM CUMMINGS.   THOMAS MATCHAM PITT.
GEORGE CROSSLEY.

[Enclosure No. 20.]

SYDNEY SETTLERS' ADDRESS TO GOVERNOR BLIGH.

Address of
welcome from
settlers at
Sydney to
Governor
Bligh.

AN Address to His Excellency Wm. Bligh, Esq., Captain-General
and Governor-in-Chief in and over His Majesty's Territory
of New South Wales and its Dependencies, &c., &c.

May it please Your Excellency,—   22nd September, 1806.

We, the Free Inhabitants of Sydney, in the Territory of
New South Wales, Collectively and Individually, respectively

* Note 169.

1808.
30 June.

Address of
welcome from
settlers at
Sydney to
Governor
Bligh.

beg leave to offer our unfeigned Congratulations to Your Excellency upon your Appointment to this Government, and to express our happiness at your safe and long-wished-for arrival.

We have an undoubted confidence that Your Excellency, by a just, Firm, and wise Government, will promote the happiness of all who deserve it, and we trust that no false impressions to the prejudice of any of the Subjects over whom you are to rule will best weigh in your Excellency's mind; but we entreat you to, and doubt not but you will, govern us with an impartial hand, and do honor to the high and important Trust Our Most Gracious King has been pleased to depute to your Charge; and we feel animated by a pleasing hope that, under your Excellency's Auspices, Agriculture will flourish, Commerce increase, and we as British Subjects enjoy our Country's Constitutional Rights; and let us assure Your Excellency that we are well aware that it is the indispensable duty of us all to hold a reverential regard to the Laws under which we have been brought up, and to cheerfully acquiesce in such Measures as Your Excellency may adopt for the good of the Colony and the true Interest and happiness of all descriptions of its Inhabitants.

We, with every due submission to your Excellency, beg to state our ignorance of the former Addresses which appeared in the *Sydney Gazette**—one to the late Governor King and the other to Your Excellency—at the foot of which appears the name of John McArthur, Esq., for the Free Inhabitants; nor do we hesitate in saying that it never was our intention to address the former; and that we consider such addresses being signed for us by a person undeputed and unauthorised as an Infringement on our Rights and Privileges, as well as being contrary to justice and equity; and as it is not our General Voice, we proclaim it to be (in our opinion) highly unconstitutional, as well as he, the said John McArthur's, taking a liberty that we never have allowed, nor can or will sanction; and we beg to observe that had we deputed anyone, John McArthur would not have been chosen by us, we considering him an unfit person to step forward upon such an occasion, as we may chiefly attribute the rise in the price of Mutton to his withholding the large flock of Wethers he now has to make such price as he may choose to demand.

Convinced that our prosperity and happiness will be the great objects of your Excellency's care, We earnestly hope your Excellency will find your Administration productive of real and permanent Satisfaction and honor to yourself; and we, the Free Inhabitants, most sacredly assure your Excellency that we will, at the hazard of our lives and property, protect and support you

* Note 169.

1808.
30 June.

Address of
welcome from
settlers at
Sydney to
Governor
Bligh.

in the due Administration of Justice, and conduct ourselves as loyal Subjects to our Much Beloved Sovereign as long as we shall live.

[*Among the 135 names are*: S'm Lord, Ja's Jno. Grant, Jesse Mulcock, George Guest, Wm. Regan,. Isaac Nelson, John Shea, James Ball, Thomas Burgess, Thomas Bradley, Henry Shaffrey, Joseph Prosser, Aaron Burt, Michael Geary, James Aitken, Wm. Roberts, John Sparrow, Ab. Whitehouse, D. D. Mann, Adam Riley, George Gordon, Francis Cox, Henry H. Neale, John Lyster, Thomas Stubbs, Joseph Stubbs, Thomas Hartmann, &c.]

Sir,   Sydney, Sept. 22nd, 1806.

The principal Inhabitants having requested me to deliver their Address to Your Excellency and to act as their Representative on the Occasion, I, with every deference,.beg to lay the same before you and to answer for them in any matter relative thereto your Excellency may wish to be informed.

I have, &c.,

S. LORD.

[Enclosure No. 21.]

SETTLERS TO MAJOR JOHNSTON.

Sir,   11th April, 1808.

We, the undersigned Freeholders and Cultivators of Land in the County of Cumberland, in His Majesty's Territory of New South Wales, are impressed with surprize and alarm to see John McArthur, Esq., hold the Office of Colonial Secretary; And we believe that, under colour of discharging the duty of that Office, the said John McArthur has violated the Law, violated public faith, and trampled on the most Sacred and Constitutional Rights of British Subjects.

John McArthur does not hold the above-mentioned Office by Commission from the King; and as the Inhabitants of this Colony have no Confidence in the said John McArthur, he having without any Authority from them, assumed to himself the Office of our Representative, and in our name presented an Address, which we have already disavowed, and declared our Sentiments that John McArthur is the Last Man we would depute to represent us in any case whatever.

We believe John McArthur has been the Scourge of this Colony by fomenting quarrels between His Majesty's Officers, Servants, and Subjects; his monopoly and extortion have been highly injurious to the Inhabitants of every description.

We most earnestly pray that the said John McArthur may be removed from the said Office of Colonial Secretary, from all other Offices, and from all Public Councils and interference with the Government of this Colony.

1808.
30 June.

And that you may be pleased to lay this, our most earnest request, before His Majesty's Lieutenant-Governor Paterson, that, if he see meet, it may be transmitted to His Majesty's Ministers.

Settlers' protest aga'nst Macarthur as colonial secretary.

. We feel the most lively sense of Gratitude towards those Officers and Gentlemen who have endeavoured to support the Laws, and protect His Majesty's Subjects from the illegal and unconstitutional measures pursued by the said John McArthur, as Colonial Secretary, and with the most sincere respect subscribe ourselves. We are, &c.,

[No names.]

CERTIFICATE OF MR. THOMAS ARNDELL.

I THOMAS ARNDELL, ESQUIRE, who came into the Colony at its first formation, as a Commissioned Officer, and for thirteen years since retired to my own Estates from that Public Service by His Majesty's special permission on an Annuity during life for past Services, and have since held the Situation of Principal Magistrate of the extensive Agricultural Settlements in the Interior, vizt, Hawkesbury, Richmond, Nepean, Portland, &c., Do hereby certify that the People since His Majesty's Governor was dispossessed, have been altogether prohibited the privilege of Petitioning or representing the Grievances they laboured under, owing to the influence and allowed Measures which has been adopted by a Mr. John McArthur called the Secretary to the Colony. And I do Vouch that this is one of the Papers, the annexed requisition Signed by Six Principals of a District (according to the Regulation) which, with those of other Districts was refused, denouncing Vengeance to the Applicants, for their requesting the Rights and Privileges allowed by the Laws of the Realm to the Suffering Subjects.

Settlers refused the right to petition against grievances.

Sydney, 11th April, 1808. THOS. ARNDELL.

[Enclosure No. 22.]

SETTLERS TO LIEUTENANT-GOVERNOR PATERSON.

To His Honor William Paterson Esq. His Majesty's Lieutenant-Governor in and over the Territory of New South Wales and its Dependencies.

Address of settlers to lieut.-governor Paterson.

Sir, 18th April, 1808.

We the undersigned Freeholders most earnestly wish, and anxiously hope for your Honor's speedy and safe Arrival at Head Quarters, to take upon you the re-establishment of His Majesty's Government, and to restore tranquility in this Colony.

1808.
30 June.

Address of
settlers to
lieut.-governor
Paterson.

The particular State of the Colony is truly alarming to every Man of observation and reflection.

His Majesty's Governor-in-Chief a *Prisoner*; Public Officers appointed by His Majesty, Magistrates and other Officers, legally appointed, all removed; also five of the Magistrates created by the now ruling power, who acted with impartiality, and justly opposed the present measures, dismissed or resigned; their Acting Judge-Advocate sent home; the Civil and Criminal Courts annulled; the independent and impartial judgment of the Officers who composed them publicly censured and condemned by Proclamation of the 3rd Instant*; the Superintendant of the Police (John Harris, Esqr.) also under Orders to leave the Colony, whose departure we might have much reason to regret, and whom we request you will be pleased to retain as a principal Man, now holding the confidence of the People and supporting their Rights.

The whole Government appears to be put into the hands of John McArthur, Esqr., who seems a- very improper person, he having been a turbulent and troublesome Character, constantly quarrelling with His Majesty's Governors, and other principal Officers, from Governor Phillip to Governor Bligh; and we believe him to be the principal agitator and promoter of the present alarming and calamitous state of the Colony.

We solemnly declare that we had no fore-knowledge, act, or part of the strong measures taken on the 26th day of January last. We protest against the means adopted to obtain Signatures to a Paper carried round to sanction what was done on that day—threatening Individuals with imprisonment; to be sent out of the Colony by the first Ships, and that they would be marked Men who refused to sign it; that many of the most worthless and abandoned members of society have subscribed that Address, and even Prisoners in Gaol.

We pledge ourselves, on your Arrival, to give you our support at every hazard that is dear to Man, in restoring the Government and placing us again under the protection of the King and the Laws.

We beg leave to subscribe Ourselves, with the most profound respect—   Your Honor's, &c.,

Thomas Arndell, John Baylis, Caleb Wilson, Edward Reynolds, John Bowman, Martin Mason, Andrew Thompson, James Davison, John Howe, John Turnbull, Andrew Johnston, James Mein, John Johnston, Law'ce May, George Hall, Matthew Lock, John Tibbutt, Paul Bushel, Henry Baldwin, John Jamieson (Principal Sup'dt of Gov't Stock), Thomas Abbott, and several others.

* Note 170.

[Enclosure No. 23.]

MESSRS. SUTTOR AND McDOUGALL TO MR. ROB'T CAMPBELL.

Sir, Baulkham Hills, 6th May, 1808.

We have sent down the inclosed Address, which is ex- pressive of our sentiments, and, if approved, we beg of you to present, or, if you think better, we will come down for that purpose. In that case shall request the favor of the earliest intelligence of the Colonel's arrival.

Address to be
presented to
Paterson on
his arrival.

We are, &c.,
GEO. SUTTOR,
AND'W McDOUGALL.

[Sub-enclosure.]

ADDRESS OF SETTLERS TO LIEUTENANT-GOVERNOR PATERSON.

To His Honor Lieutenant-Governor Paterson,—

Address of
welcome to
Paterson.

Permit us, Sir, to congratulate You on your safe arrival at Head Quarters. It is with the most heartfelt satisfaction that the People of this Colony hear the pleasing intelligence; for to You they look up for the re-establishment of that Law and Order which the most extraordinary and violent interposition has so recently deprived them of, and substituted in its room Anarchy, Confusion, and the most unjustifiable Oppression.

We, therefore, deem it the duty of every honest and well-meaning Man, to step forward and make known his real Sentiments at the present Crisis. And we pledge ourselves to be ready to give you every information and support in our power in order that full satisfaction and justice may be given to the Governor (whom we highly revere) and Government of our Most Gracious Sovereign in this Colony, for the gross insult and injury done them, in the Person of His Excellency Governor Bligh, to whom we are most zealously attached.

Therefore, Sir, from your known Loyalty to His Majesty's Person and Government, we cannot but feel the most confident reliance that You will take prompt and effectual means to secure the principals in this most unjustifiable transaction. In so doing you will have, not only the good will, but the highest esteem of every unbiassed and deserving Character in this Colony, joined with the just applause and support of the British Empire.

We have, &c.,

GEO. SUTTOR.	THOS. HARDY.
AND'W McDOUGALL.	WILL'M HANCEY.
JOHN SMITH.	MICH'L HANCEY.
JOHN HILLAS.	

1808.
30 June.

Address of
settlers to
Paterson.

[Enclosure No. 24.]

SETTLERS' ADDRESS TO LIEUTENANT-GOVERNOR PATERSON.

To His Honor William Paterson, Esquire, His Majesty's Lieutenant-Governor, &c., &c.,—

Sir,   Hawkesbury, 1st May, 1808.
        Permit us to express Ourselves with the freedom of British
Subjects, who are deeply interested in the future prosperity of
this Colony. We have embarked our all, and look forward to
improvement, that our Children may reap the benefit of our
industry. With pleasure we saw the Colony reviving from the
most melancholy calamity, the streams of justice purified, Crimes
of the deepest dye prevented, discipline established, a system of
monopoly and extortion in some measure suppressed, that had
been long and severely felt by us and our families, nearly to the
deprivation of every comfort; as our hopes were beginning to
revive, and prospects heighten, we were suddenly alarmed, on
the 26th day of January last, at His Excellency Governor Bligh
being arrested and confined a close Prisoner in his own House;
the Judge-Advocate, Provost-Martial, and other public Officers
appointed by the King, and holding his Commission, arrested or
removed; and every legal Magistrate in the Colony struck out of
the Commission of the Peace, and others appointed; a body of
Men heated with Wine going from House to House, threatening
and menacing His Majesty's loyal Subjects with imprisonment,
to be sent out of the Colony, and deprived of all indulgencies
from Government, and that they would be marked Men who
refused to sign a treasonable and seditious Paper to sanction
what had been done on that day. We are alarmed at the informa-
tions of the most worthless and abandoned Prisoners for Life
being taken on Oath to accuse their Masters, and that in the
absence of the accused; the Masters taken from their families
on such information, and told that they need not apply for
protection, for they shall have none. We disavow and protest
against the above measures, as the highest insult to the King, in
the Person of His Representative, Governor Bligh; the highest
outrage and contempt to the British Government and the Laws,
highly injurious to the honor of the British Nation in this
Colony, and to all regular Government, subordination, and discipline so necessary in this Colony. Placing the most implicit
confidence in your Loyalty to the King, your honour and experience as an Officer, your virtue and impartial justice as a
private Gentleman, We rejoice at your arrival at this momentous
and alarming Crisis; it is to You we look with hope for deliverance from the oppression, alarm, and terror we have laboured

under for some Months past; and we pledge ourselves to give 1808. 30 June.
you every support and information in our power to enable you to
re-establish His Majesty's Government in the Person of His Address of settlers to Paterson.
Representative, Governor Bligh, whom we have reason to adore
for that protection and justice we have experienced under his
firm and steady Government, the want of which has been highly
injurious to us and our families when He arrived as Governor
in this Colony. And we most earnestly pray that you will place
us again under the protection of the King and the Laws. Permit
us to subscribe ourselves, sir, &c.,

MARTIN MASON.	JAMES DAVISON.
RICH'D ROUSE.	ANDREW JOHNSTON.
JOHN BOWMAN.	JOHN HOWE.
J. W. LEWIN.	JOHN JOHNSTON.
DAVID LANGLEY.	JAMES MEIN.
CALEB WILSON.	JOHN TURNBULL.

[Enclosure No. 25.]

ADDRESS OF HAWKESBURY SETTLERS TO GOVERNOR BLIGH. Address of settlers at the Hawkesbury to Governor Bligh.

Hawkesbury, New South Wales, 29th January, 1807.

To His Excellency William Bligh, Esq., F.R.S., Captain-General
and Commander-in-Chief in and over His Majesty's Territory of New South Wales and its Dependencies, &c.

May it please your Excellency,—

We, the undersigned, Holders of Landed Estates and
Principal Inhabitants of the Hawkesbury, Portland, Richmond,
and Nepean Settlements, and other adjacent places in this
Colony,

Beg leave most respectfully to return our Grateful thanks for
the unbounded attention, Labors, and pains Your Excellency in
your great Wisdom has ever manifested towards us, and the
general Welfare and prosperity of this extensive Colony at large,
in the dreadful Crisis of General Calamity in which you found
it.

And we, from the highest Sense of Gratitude and Public Duty,
beg leave to assure your Excellency, while enjoying our Native
Laws and Liberty and living under a just and Benign Government, we will be ready at all times, at the risque of our Lives
and Property, lawfully to support the same; and willing to antici-
pate Your Excellency's just and humane wishes for the public
relief, We have subscribed all the Grain we can possibly spare
from our own support to be carried to the Public Stores at your
stipulated price, rejecting far greater prices in money which we
could receive from the present Market Sale; and we hope the

1808.
30 June.
———
Address of
settlers at the
Hawkesbury to
Governor
Bligh.

quantity subscribed (with more than probably may be spared)
will furnish Your Excellency with means for the present Year's
Support without reverting to the ruinous necessity of Importation, which Your Excellency in your Wisdom and Penetration so
justly sees and sets forth. And as these fertile Settlements has·
ever furnished a Superabundance of Food, which is evident
from the low prices it sold at, and the Great Surplus and Quantities annually spoiled, wasted, and wilfully destroyed; and we
doubt not, under the blessing of God and your wise measures,
that the Produce of our Lands next season will again be more
than abundantly sufficient for the fullest support of the whole
Territory, and in which case We will as readily supply such
Quantities as Your Excellency may require at your fixed price
of next season, and every endeavour to show ourselves worthy
of your Encouragement and Protection, praying for your Prosperity and a long continuance of your just and Benign Government.

[*Signed by 156 persons.*]

[Thomas Arndell, Thos. Hobby, Lazarus Graves, Joseph Kers-
well, Andrew Thompson, George Crossley, Robt. Martin, Owen
Tierney, Edward Pugh, John Dight, Robt. Campbell, Lawrence
May, Patrick Connolly, Rich. Allwright, Chas. Palmer, John
Palmer, Elizabeth Burne, Thos. Matcham Pitt, Rebecca Cox,.
George Hall, Paul Randall, William Addy, Wm. Cummings,.
Wm. Field, Wm. Rouse, M. Everingham, Henry Stockfish, Thos.
Appledore, *and 128 others.*]

[Enclosure No. 26.] ·

SECOND ADDRESS FROM HAWKESBURY SETTLERS TO GOVERNOR BLIGH.

Hawkesbury, 25th February, 1807. ·

May it please Your Excellency,

· We, the Holders of Landed Estates, Public Officers, and
the Principal Inhabitants of the extensive Settlements of the
Hawkesbury, Portland, Richmond, and Nepean, and parts adjacent in New South Wales,

Beg leave to return our sincere thanks for your wise and unwearied Solicitude over the Public Welfare at all times, in your
arduous, dignified, and important Station, over such extensive
Colonies, now rising again from late Calamities unto happiness.
and opulence, under a just, equitable, and gracious Government, which we, imprest with the strongest desire to support
with our Lives, as also a bounden duty in all loyal Subjects,
have willingly, according to Your Excellency's Order, enrolled
our names for the Defence of the Country, in which we will
readily participate at all times of need, but sincerely hope that.

your Excellency, in your wisdom, by judging from the real and
presumptive proofs exhibited in this Country now and for many
years past by those disaffected People, of their relentless and
incorrigible spirit of Rebellion, Murder, and Atrocity, keeping
liege Subjects in constant alarm, that you will be graciously
pleased to dispose of the Ringleaders and Principals so as to
prevent future Conspiracy amongst them, and to restore public
Tranquility, which blessing of peace and happiness may Your
Excellency long continue to give and enjoy in your gracious
Government over us, is the earnest prayer of Your Excellency's
devoted, &c.

1808.
30 June.

Address of
settlers at the
Hawkesbury to
Governor
Bligh.

[*Signed by 546 persons.*]

[Thomas Arndell, James Cox, And'w Thompson, Tho's Dargen,
Phillip Tully, Henry Trethaway, Bishop Thompson, Thomas
Hobby, G. W. Evans, William Baker, Samuel Ker, Samuel
Solomon, Jonathan Griffiths, John Westgarth, *and 532
others.*]

To His Excellency Wm. Bligh, Esq., F.R.S.,
Captain-General and Commander-in-Chief, &c., &c.

GOVERNOR BLIGH TO VISCOUNT CASTLEREAGH.

(Despatch marked "Secret," per ship Rose; acknowledged by
Viscount Castlereagh, 15th May, 1809.)

Government House, Sydney,

My Lord,   New South Wales, 30th June, 1808.

The Despatch which accompanies this Letter contains the
substance of one which I hastily wrote and sent by the Brothers
on the 30th April but more fully detailing the enormity of
the rebellion of the New South Wales Corps against me, their
Captain-General and Governor-in-Chief, and the Civil Power of
this Colony, together with other circumstances which have come
to my knowledge in the course of this interval under my unparalleled situation.

Despatch
detailing
Bligh's arrest.

A Ship called the Dart sailed from hence a fortnight before
the Brothers; but that Ship was so much in the interest of
McArthur, and Charles Grimes, the Judge-Advocate of their
Criminal Courts, and McArthur's Son, both deeply implicated in
the rebellion, going passengers in her, that I was constrained to
forbear writing by her, being assured that, through the vigilance
of our Enemies, my Despatches would have been secretly relanded
and given to the Rebels. I was the more ready to believe this,
knowing the infamous transaction of Governor King's despatches
on the occasion of troubles he had in this Colony with McArthur,
being stolen, and when the Box which had contained them was
delivered at Your Lordship's Office filled with old Paper.*

Reasons for not
sending
despatch by
the Dart.

* Note 134.

1808.
30 June.

Despatch
forwarded
secretly to
England.

As the Brothers took Home Lieutenant Minchin, of the Corps, and his Servant, called Marlborough, two noted characters in the rebellion, I had some doubts of writing by her; but I got Mr. Campbell to convey my Despatch by the Master as a Packet of merchantile Accounts and Bills of Exchange, and for which he got a Receipt. I have made many reflections on the criminality of the messengers sent home by Major Johnston, and I trust that the act of bearing the Rebels' Despatches will cause their imprisonment, in order, at least, to answer for their rebellious conduct in this Colony, if not for their arraignment on their arrival in England.

Charges made
against Bligh.

The supporters and abettors of the rebellion, as they now are cr may hereafter be found, will, I am fully confident, be brought to a most serious · and immediate Trial. Their Charges against me I consider barely deserving my notice; but the factious and rebellious manner of making them is a public concern to this Colony. I might give many proofs of my judgment and zeal for its welfare, of which for sixteen months they had been reaping the fruits, but I forbear, as it would be departing from my character. Where I am materially accused, there I shall be ready to produce a defence of my conduct; but that must be on a complaint of the People and not of such Rebels.

Anticipations
re Macarthur's
line of defence.

I have no doubt, my Lord, that you will have Memorials drawn up by McArthur expressive of my severity, and perhaps incompetency to govern, expressing the cause of integrity, innocence, and abilities on his side; but he has certainly inveighled the New South Wales Corps and some poor thoughtless creatures to get into his debt (from a lust of spirituous Liquors), and thereby becoming dependant on him, they lose their liberty by a Gaol, or become his immediate Vassals, and do as he directs them. I am far from thinking that if the Corps felt themselves aggrieved they were not entitled to lay their case before His Majesty; but they cannot be competent judges of my duty, and therefore, under the high Authority by which I held my Government, their guilt is the greater in taking it from me. Added to this, they have induced persons by threats or promises to sign to the rebellious act after it was perpetrated, thereby subjecting these poor people to a Trial for an offence of which they had no knowledge beforehand. But it will not escape Your Lordship's observation that I

Settlers'
confidence
in Bligh.

am among Convicts, emancipated Persons, and Settlers from England, and on an aggregate computation nearly ten thousand Souls, and yet nothing but good-will and confidence in me have appeared but in the Military Officers, McArthur, Bayly, and a few interested individuals. Under no Government which I might have had the honor to hold, would I have allowed to my person unbecoming familiarities or disputation; but it was peculiarly 1808.
30 June. my duty to support such dignity in this Colony, in order to my being considered an Individual in whom honor and the interests of the State were preserved, and justice and moral duties were exemplified. This has been a great shock to the Persons I have *Causes of rebellion.* noticed in the rebellion, who, through ambition, rapacity, and an unwarrantable desire to acquire wealth in an instant (which few can or ought to possess), aiming only to be rich by the poverty of others, without the merit of any social duties to their neighbours, together with habits of disrespect and many insults to their former Governors, have brought to issue in good time what is to be the remedy to so malignant and contagious a disease.

The Military and Navy, from their long stay in the Colony, *Officers contaminated by local conditions.* get sadly taken up in Convict connections which produce loose principles and debaucheries, to the great infringement and detriment of moral Society; it has likewise caused neglect equal to a dereliction of their duty; and when Officers of Army or Navy become Settlers, or enter into pursuits out of their line, they blend their private concerns with their public Service, and become opposers to the Governor's measures, instead of defending them as they otherwise would do if they confined themselves to their respective Ranks and Stations. It is, therefore, highly advisable *Necessity for periodical relief of military.* to remove the Troops at certain periods—it is absolutely necessary to the success and stability of the Colony—for these people already think they should have the government in their own hands; and such as McArthur consider themselves aggrieved that *Influence of Macarthur.* appointments should be sent out from England, while, in his Idea, all places of trust and confidence should be given to Persons who are resident in the Colony. Under this incendiary way of acting, he has produced all the mischief which has happened; and, like being intoxicated with hopes of having power, he has already shewn his expectations of rising to entire controul and authority. At this time it would effectually destroy the very principles of amnesty on which industrious persons look to the oblivion of all past offences, and where, as the Recorder of Bombay has lately declared in his Sentence on a Criminal, they may venture to hope for a Life of tranquility and usefulness, and even for the possibility of acquiring esteem.

Besides the changing of the Military, there should be two *Periodical relief of men-of-war on the station.* Vessels of War here, to be relieved in turn every three Years; the greatest benefit would result from this system, both as to the order of the Community and the Shipping, and enable the Governor to send Home at a moment an account of any transaction which the Public Service might require.

1808.
30 June.

Proposed
separation of
civil and
military powers.

Another part of the task which seems necessary to the welfare of the Colony, is to keep the Military distinct from the Civil Power and Courts of Justice; it is that which is the wish of the People, and will prevent the sudden growth of private Fortunes by the Barter of Spirits and monopolizing of Grain; will cause the Settlement to be supplied with Men more moderate, or less eager in the pursuit of wealth, and who will have a lasting attachment to it.

Bligh's
suggestions
for the trial
of the officers.

I beg leave, My Lord, under an impression that you may expect some opinion of mine as to the most effectual and ready means of bringing these people to an account, to offer with the greatest deference to Your Lordship's consideration, in the first instance, to remove the New South Wales Corps into the Ships in which other Troops may be sent out to supply their places; and secondly, to have a Commission of Law Officers ready to judge of the whole transaction: removing them to England would be the means of losing very material Evidence, and in that case it will be absolutely requisite for some eminent Gentlemen of the Law to come here to select the Witnesses who are the most necessary. Nothing so serious can be confided to Mr. Atkins, who has evinced his weakness by endeavouring to get appointed as Judge-Advocate with the present Rulers, but who have thrown him off, to his very great disgrace.

Necessity for
selection and
protection of
witnesses
against the
rebels.

A consideration of importance which appears also to me, is, how far Witnesses may be allowed to be produced on the side of the Rebels, because in such a Country as this, on their part, the greatest subornation will take place. Convicts have been allowed to appear as Witnesses in particular Cases; but under the present consideration, where rebellion may be a part of their tenets, perhaps agreeable to Justice they may be objected to. If the New South Wales Corps is deprived of doing the Settlers and others any mischief, I am confidently assured they will all come forward to express loyalty and affection, and as may be seen by their Addresses; therefore the Armament which may be thought necessary to send out is only such as to act against the Troops. I recommend that the Ships should all rendezvous at the Derwent, where they will be informed of the state of the Colony by Lieutenant-Governor Collins, and from thence proceed together here. It may be advisable to lay an embargo on all Vessels they

Possible
contamination
of relieving
troops.

find here. Your Lordship can barely have a conception of the present Rulers, for I do assure You they would, if they procured a communication with any Troops which came against them, prevent their acting conformably to their orders, notwithstanding the utmost vigilance and determination of the Officers. I am deprived of all power, and peculiarly watched and guarded.

I farther beg leave to submit to Your Lordship's consideration
what will be necessary to be done with those Persons who have
received, from the present Rulers, the Cattle of Government and
His Majesty's Stores of all kinds; perhaps, according to the
possessors' characters, and the way they paid for or acquired
them, may guide this proceeding, as the worst Characters have
got this property into their possession. All the public acts by
Deeds, and Grants of Land, and Leases, I apprehend may be done
away by a proclamation to that effect, under the crime of rebellion when they were granted.

As Money can be procured here sufficient to pay the Troops, it
would be a most desirable thing for them to be paid in cash,
whereby their pay would give them a most satisfactory advantage. At present a Soldier, in order to get a little money, takes
up some kind of Slops, Merchandize, or Liquor, from his Officers,
which he sells for less than it cost him, and the consequence is
that every 24th day of the Month he has little to receive. By this
means the Paymaster's Notes, that become consolidated in Bills
drawn for the amount, remain in the Officers' hands, which are
disposed of at an advance of about fifteen per Cent., or more, to
the loss of the Soldier, besides that which he sustained on the
sale of the Merchandize which he had procured to give him a
little ready money.

During the course of my Government no Memorial has been
presented against any measure; on the contrary, highly approving
of what I had done, and I conceived that cordiality subsisted
between Major Johnston, his Officers, and myself; the Corps, in
general, seemed extremely pleased with the attention which was
shewn to them; and it surpassed my expectation that, in a Colony
where so much bickering had taken place, any harmony could
have been so soon produced; but all Persons appeared to me
becoming happy and contented until the public Enemy, McArthur,
began his secret machinations. Major Johnston's political illness, and not coming to me when sent for, although he was
capable of commanding the Troops in the Rebellion, deprives
him of the benefit of any excuse.

I have every confidence, My Lord, of your approbation of my
conduct, and that Your Lordship will lay my Case before my
King and Country, that His Majesty may be graciously pleased
to send me relief, and shew to this new World that obedience
is the first duty which is due from them.

I am, &c.,

WM. BLIGH.

1808.
30 June.

VISCOUNT CASTLEREAGH TO GOVERNOR BLIGH.

(Despatch No. 7, per transport Duke of Portland.)

Sir,   Downing Street, 30th June, 1808.

Recommenda-
tion of Rev. H.
Fulton to Bligh. I transmit to you herewith the Copy of a letter and of its Inclosures that I have received from the Archbishop of Canterbury, relative to the Revd. Henry Fulton, who is acting as Assistant Chaplain at Port Jackson, and who requests to be appointed by Commission* to that Situation, in order that he may not be superseded; and I am to desire that you will treat Mr. Fulton with such degree of favour as his Conduct since his Arrival in New South Wales may appear to deserve.

I have, &c.,

CASTLEREAGH.

[Enclosure No. 1.]

THE BISHOP OF DERRY TO THE ARCHBISHOP OF CANTERBURY.

My Lord,   .   Londonderry, 5th August, 1807.

I take the liberty of enclosing a Letter to Your Grace which I lately received from Port Jackson. The Writer of it was for some time a Beneficed Clergyman in the Diocese of Killaloe; he owed his situation to me for his exemplary Conduct as a Clergyman; that situation, however, he forfeited by connecting himself with the disaffected in the Year '98. He confessed his Crime, and agreed to transport himself for Life to Botany Bay.†

Since that time I have not heard of him till I received his Letter, except that his Friends declared that his confession was extorted by fear of a species of torture at that time too common.

I shall not presume to request your Grace's agreeing to his request; but from my opinion of him prior to the transaction which caus'd his Banishment from Ireland, I would almost venture to pledge myself his future conduct. He is a very well-informed Man, and had been peculiarly zealous in the discharge of his duties as a Clergyman.   I have, &c.,

WM. DERRY.

[Enclosure No. 2.]

REV. HENRY FULTON TO THE BISHOP OF DERRY

My Lord,   Sydney, Port Jackson, 1st September, 1806.

Services of
Fulton in
the colony. Ten months after my arrival at Port Jackson Governor King gave me a conditional emancipation, and afterwards employed me for some as assistant Chaplain to this part of the Colony, then sent me to Norfolk Island where I performed the duties of Chaplain. For this he some years gave me bills on His Majestie's Treasury for 5s. per day, Some years 7s. 6d., and one year £96 for the year. He this year gave me a free pardon for what he was pleased to call my exemplary behaviour as a

* Note 171.   † Note 172.

protestant Clergyman. He has ordered me to Port Jackson this year to do the duties of the principal Chaplain who goes to England along with him, for he is relieved by Governor Wm. Bligh. I have no commission as assistant Chaplain, and therefore may be superseded. If your Lordship would procure this commission for me by an application to His Grace of Canterbury it would add to the many great favours which I have received from your Lordship. I am emboldened to ask this favour from your Lordship by my experience of your Lordship's goodness, and the many remarkable instances of attention which I received from your Lordship. Your Lordship is the only person to whom I ever applied myself on this subject. I do not know what my friends may have done. I ought to have mentioned that the Governor drew on the treasury for £182 10s. one year, or at the rate of 10s. per day. Whether your Lordship will comply with this request or not, be assured that at this time the least mark of your Lordship's attention would be considered as one of the happiest occurrences in my life,—Your Lordship's often obliged, and very humble Son and Servant,

1808.
30 June.

Fulton's request for a commission as chaplain.

HENRY FULTON.

VISCOUNT CASTLEREAGH TO GOVERNOR BLIGH.

(Despatch No. 8, per transport Duke of Portland.)

Sir,   Downing Street, 30th June, 1808.

An Application having been made to me in favour of a Widow Woman named Sarah Bentley, who accompanied her husband a few years ago to New South Wales, whither he was transported for theft: I am to desire that you will endeavour to procure a passage to this Country for her and her Children 4 in Number by the first opportunity, and in case they are destitute that you should give directions for their being victualled for the voyage.   I have, &c.,

Orders for the return of Sarah Bentley and children.

CASTLEREAGH.

VISCOUNT CASTLEREAGH TO GOVERNOR BLIGH.

(Despatch No. 9, per transport Duke of Portland.)

Sir,   Downing Street, 30th June, 1808.

I herewith transmit to you an application from Lady Louisa Conolly in behalf of John Moore, now a Convict in New South Wales, together with his Petition to Lady Louisa, recommended by Mr. Wilson, late Chaplain in the New South Wales Corps: I am to desire that you will take this case into your Consideration and if the Conduct of the Prisoner since his

Proposed pardon for John Moore.

1808.
30 June.

Proposed
pardon for
John Moore.

Arrival in New South Wales should have been such as to entitle
him to indulgence, that you will grant him a free Pardon and
allow him to take the first opportunity of returning to Ireland.

I have, &c.,

CASTLEREAGH.

[Enclosures.]

[Copies of these papers are not available.]

GOVERNOR BLIGH TO THE HON. WILLIAM POLE.

(Despatch per ship Rose.)

Government House, Sydney, New South Wales,

1 July.

Removal of
Bligh's broad
pendant by
Johnston's
orders.

Sir,   1st July, 1808.

I beg leave to represent to You for the information of My
Lords Commissioners of the Admiralty, that during the absence
of His Majesty's Ship Porpoise in January last, I ordered my
Broad Pendant to be hoisted on board a Government Colonial
Schooner called the Estramina; but on the 27th of January, the
day after the usurpation of the Government by Major Johnston,
he sent a written Order to Mr. Apsey, Master of her, to haul it
down, which he did, a Copy of this Order has lately been sent to
me from Mr. Apsey, and I inclose it for their Lordships' information.   I have, &c.,

WM. BLIGH.

[Enclosure.]

*[A copy of this order was also forwarded as enclosure No. 6 to
Governor Bligh's despatch to Viscount Castlereagh, dated 30th
June, 1808.]*

VISCOUNT CASTLEREAGH TO GOVERNOR BLIGH.

(Despatch No. 10, per transport Duke of Portland.)

18 July.

Land grant
for paymaster
Mell.

Sir,   Downing Street, 18th July, 1808.

Mr. Mell who proceeds by the present opportunity to
New South Wales as Paymaster of the New South Wales Corps
having applied for a Grant of Land, I am to desire that you will
cause to be made out to him in the usual Form and subject to
the Customary Reservations a Grant of 300 Acres and that you
will give him such Assistance of Convicts and Stock on the
principle laid down in your Plan transmitted in Dispatch of the
31st Octr. last as you may be enabled to afford him consistently
with a due Attention to the Claims of other Individuals.

Mr. Mell has been strongly recommended by Sir James Cock-
burn and I trust will be found to merit any Attentions you may
have the Goodness to shew him.   I have, &c.,

CASTLEREAGH.

MAJOR JOHNSTON TO VISCOUNT CASTLEREAGH.

(Despatch per ship Rose.)

Head Quarters, Sydney, New South Wales,

My Lord,   31st July, 1808.

Herewith I have the honor to transmit to your Lordship Commissary's account. a duplicate of the acting Commissary's Account Current, with the Lords Commissioners of His Majesty's Treasury for the period I held the Command of this Colony, with his respective Vouchers in support of the sums it has been necessary to draw for the publick services.

A reference to the Commissary's accounts will satisfy Your Lordship that the purchase of Grain for the Supply of the Southern Settlements has occasioned an expense nearly equal to the whole amount for which I have had occasion to draw.

I have, &c.,

GEO. JOHNSTON.

[Enclosures.]

[Copies of these accounts will be found in a volume in series II.]

ESTIMATE of the probable Amount for which it will be requisite Estimated to draw Bills upon His Majesty's Treasury to defray the amount of bills to be drawn Expences incurred in this Settlement from the 26th January for January to the 31st July 1808—in which is included £1,656 12s. for the purchase of Grain sent to Port Dalrymple and the Derwent.

For 1,550 Bushels of Wheat at 10s. per Bushel sent to Port Dalrymple	£775	0	0
For 79 Bushels of Barley at 8s. per Bushel sent to Port Dalrymple	31	12	0
For 1,700 Bushels of Wheat at 10s. per Bushel sent to the Derwent	850	0	0
For the purchase of Grain &c. for the Supply of this Settlement, the Returns and Vouchers for which have not yet been obtained from the Acting Commissary	2,000	0	0
	£3,656	12	0

EXTRACT of a letter from Lt. Governor Collins to George Johnston, Esqr., dated Hobartown, Van Diemen's land, 11th June, 1808.

"I HAVE the Satisfaction of Stating that I have now upwards Supplies of of twelve Months grain in His Majesty's Stores, And therefore grain at the Derwent. hope this information will reach you in time to prevent your fulfilling your intention of Sending me any further Supply of wheat for the present.

1808.
31 July.
———
Shipment of
beef and pork.
" The Beef and pork by the City of Edinburgh will also place
me much at my ease with respect to wet provisions, And I can
not but feel sensible of your Attention to our Situation Since
you have had the direction of the Government at Port Jackson."

GOVERNOR BLIGH TO VISCOUNT CASTLEREAGH.

(Despatch per ship Rose; acknowledged by Viscount Castlereagh,
15th May, 1809.)

Government House, Sydney,
My Lord,   New South Wales, 31st August, 1808.

31 Aug.
Transmission
of despatches.
1st. This is the first opportunity I have had of communicating with your Lordship since the sailing of the Ship Brothers
in April last. I have been greatly embarrassed by not having any
Person by whom I could send home my Despatches; the friends
about me, on whom I can depend, are so few that I cannot dispense with their assistance in my present situation; but Captain
Brooks, of the Ship Rose, belonging to the House of Messrs.
Campbell and Wilson, I am assured, will faithfully carry these to
Your Lordship's Office, and under that confidence I shall commit
them to his care. The accompanying Dispatch is closed to the
30th June, and from that time this is continued.

Arrival of the
transport
Recovery.
2nd. On the 24th of last Month the Recovery Transport arrived
with Troops under the orders of Captain Cummings, who paid not
the least attention to me; but the daily expectation of Lieutenant-
Expected
arrival of
Foveaux.
Colonel Foveaux's arrival gave me hopes of a satisfactory change
in affairs, and I had, to effect that purpose, prepared my Secretary, Mr. Palmer, Commissary, and Mr. Fulton, Chaplain, to be
the first Persons to wait on him; and, in order that Your Lordship may be informed of what has passed between Colonel
Foveaux and myself, I inclose the Correspondence.

Arrival of
Foveaux.
3rd. He arrived in the Sinclair on the 28th, and the Gentlemen
got off to the Ship in good time; but the Master, whose name is
Jackson, refused to admit them on board; however, they delivered
my introductory Note (No. 1) to Lieutenant-Colonel Foveaux,
and brought me an answer from him (No. 2), that " he had the
honor to acknowledge the receipt of His Excellency Governor
Bligh's Note, and, although very unwell, would wait on him as
soon as possible." Major Johnston, McArthur, and others soon
got on board, and remained the day. I, therefore, the next
Bligh's demand
to be reinstated.
Morning, sent the same Gentlemen as before, with an Order to
Lieutenant-Colonel Foveaux (No. 3) to use his utmost endeavours to restore me to my Authority, and they to represent
the opinions of the Loyal People of the Colony. The same day
he waited on·me, accompanied by Mr. Finucane, his Secretary,

and presented a written Paper, which he called his final determination on the consideration of my Order to him, stating that
he considered it beyond his Authority to reinstate me in the
Government. On my asking him if he meant to persist in such
an opinion, and his replying he was determined to do so, I
returned him his Paper and desired he would communicate its
contents by Letter, which he did by No. 4, addressed to William
Bligh, Esq., &c., &c.

4th. By Lieut.-Colonel Foveaux I had the honor to receive a
letter from Mr. Cooke of the 31st December, 1807, which gave me
infinite satisfaction, as it expressed Your Lordship's approbation
of my conduct in the measures I was taking to prevent the Barter
of Spirits, and your hopes that there would be no Officer, or
Gentleman, or Planter in the Colony, who would not give me
the most cordial assistance in any measure which had a tendency
to remedy those Evils which the intemperate use of Spirits so
universally generates. Had not the word "Private" been
written on this Letter, I should not have got it, for all public
documents, although directed to me, are taken possession of as
belonging to the concerns of the Colony; besides the guilt of
this act, it is a most afflicting circumstance to know that these
Persons should be in possession of any of Your Lordship's
Despatches.

5th. Mr. Cooke's Letter informed me also that Lieut.-Colonel
Foveaux was to proceed to Norfolk Island, if not evacuated.
Had I been in power, the partial evacuation might not have
prevented Your Lordship's designs being put into execution,
but Lieut.-Colonel Foveaux seemed to think it not proper to
proceed on this duty.

6th. On the 31st* the *Gazette* announced Lieutenant-Colonel
Foveaux's assuming the administration of the Government; but
no notice was taken of McArthur, as Colonial Secretary, with
whom, however, it is known Lieutenant-Colonel Foveaux is on
terms of great intimacy.

7th. The very great Supplies which Your Lordship has caused
to be sent out in the Sinclair and Recovery would have made
the People rejoice, and firmly fixed the Colony in affluence; but
the loyal Persons are not allowed to expect any benefits; and
Lieutenant-Colonel Foveaux has dared to offer threats of indignity to my person, as may be seen by his Letter (No. 23).
The offence was my sending for an Overseer to fill up a chasm
in the Road which prevented my Daughter's Carriage passing.

8th. By all the information I can obtain, the Colonists are
becoming more and more wretched. They had prepared
Addresses to Lieut.-Colonel Foveaux, praying he would restore

1808.
31 Aug.

Foveaux's
refusal to
reinstate Bligh.

Despatch
received from
under secretary
Cooke.

Proposed
movements
of Foveaux.

Assumption of
the government
by Foveaux.

Supplies
received from
England.

* Note 173.

1808.
31 Aug.
———
Addresses to
Foveaux.
the Government to its former state, but before they got to
Sydney he had announced his having taken the Command of the
Colony, which deterred them from proceeding any farther,
especially as the Civil Court, constituted by Major Johnston's
Precept, which had adjourned previous to Lieut.-Colonel
Foveaux's arrival, was ordered to re-assemble, and which cer-
tainly indicated that he approved of the former measures.

Bligh's
treatment by
Foveaux.
9th. With respect to myself, I remain a Prisoner, with three
Centinels over me, as I have been since the 26th January; but
Lieutenant-Colonel Foveaux has allowed the Officers of the Porpoise to call on me, although he has positively refused to allow
of my embarking unless on conditions of being a Prisoner, which
I have reprobated, as may be seen by Letters from No. 6 to 12—
indeed, I have refused to admit of any conditions; yet Your
Lordship will observe, by Lieutenant-Colonel Foveaux's Letter of
the 26th Instant (No. 29), it is questioned whether I mean to
leave the Colony, as if I was at full liberty so to do, whereas it is
on condition of my going as a Prisoner. The Porpoise is still
under repair.

Bligh's appeal
to Paterson.
10th. Very great fluctuations appears in the minds of the
present Rulers; the Estramina is sent to Port Dalrymple, and by
her I wrote to Lieutenant-Governor Paterson (as herewith inclosed) to use his utmost endeavours to suppress the Mutiny of
the New South Wales Corps under his Command that I might
proceed in the Government of the Colony. We may expect the
Vessel to return in six weeks. Thus these Persons are tearing the
Colony to pieces and endangering its very existence.

Bligh's report of
his position
to India.
11th. On the 20th Instant a Brig called the Eagle sailed for
Calcutta. I embraced the opportunity of writing to Lord Minto
and Sir Edward Pellew on the subject of my confinement and the
deplorable state of the Colony, submitting to their consideration
how far they could send me relief until advice should be received
from England. This Vessel belongs to Messrs. Campbell and
Company's house in India, and through them I got the
Despatches secretly conveyed on board. All I write is done in a
most secret manner, as I am threatened with close confinement,
and perhaps the Gaol, in order to shorten my existence, but that
Providence which has hitherto protected me still bears me up to
bring about its wise purposes.

Orders of
Foveaux re
advocates in
the law courts.
12th. The *Gazette* of the 28th Instant, which is herewith inclosed, contains an order* of Lieutenant-Colonel Foveaux, by
which it would appear that Counsellors and Advocates who were
formerly Prisoners had been admitted into the Courts of this
Country by His Majesty's Governors. I cannot see why such
Orders were issued, unless by sending the *Gazette* to England it

* Note 174.

could be expected to impress an Idea on the minds of His Majesty's Ministers that such things existed; but neither Counsellors nor Advocates were ever allowed to plead openly; the Settlers and Officers in general employed them to draw up their Cases, and even Lieutenant-Colonel Foveaux, I am informed, has consulted them.

1808.
31 Aug.

Orders of
Foveaux re
advocates in
the law courts.

13th. I shall conclude by observing to Your Lordship, in addition to what I have said in my Despatch of the 30th of June (paragraphs 78 and 92) respecting my Letters to the Secretary of State being read in their Courts to elucidate my conduct and designs, as well as to inflame the minds of the People, that extracts are likewise taken and distributed, for some friend of Government has sent a Copy of a few of them, which I here inclose, and it appears were found with Simeon Lord.

I have, &c.,

WM. BLIGH.

COPY OF CORRESPONDENCE BETWEEN GOVERNOR BLIGH AND LIEUT.-COLONEL FOVEAUX from 28th July to the 31st August, 1808, including some Orders and Letters concerning the Porpoise.

[Enclosure No. 1.]

GOVERNOR BLIGH TO LIEUTENANT-COLONEL FOVEAUX.

[On His Majesty's Service.]

Government House, 28th July, 1808.

GOVERNOR BLIGH presents his Compliments to Colonel Foveaux, and has sent his Secretary, Mr. Griffin, and his Friends, Mr. Palmer and Mr. Fulton, to wait on him to request a private communication.

[Enclosure No. 2.]

LIEUTENANT-COLONEL FOVEAUX TO GOVERNOR BLIGH.

On board the Sinclair, 28th July, 1808.

LIEUTENANT-COLONEL FOVEAUX has the honor to acknowledge the receipt of His Excellency Governor Bligh's Note, and, although very unwell, will wait on him as soon as possible.

[Enclosure No. 3.]

GOVERNOR BLIGH TO LIEUTENANT-COLONEL FOVEAUX.

By His Excellency William Bligh, Esquire, &c., &c.

HAVING been unwarrantably confined, and my Government wrested and taken out of my hands on the 26th of January last, when the Colony was in a most tranquil and high state of Improvement, I yesterday sent, in order to state the same for your information, Mr. Commissary Palmer, Mr. Griffin, my Secretary,

Bligh's orders
to Foveaux to
reinstate him.

1808.
31 Aug.

Bligh's orders
to Foveaux to
reinstate him.

and the Rev'd Mr. Fulton, to wait on you. As they were refused
by the Master of the Ship to be admitted on board, and having
heard that Major Johnston, Mr. John MacArthur, and other
Persons were afterwards admitted, I now send them again to
represent my situation and the opinion of the loyal people of this
Colony, and do hereby request that they may have permission
to see you, and that you use your utmost endeavours to reinstate
me in my Government as representative of our Most Gracious
Sovereign and as Captain-General and Governor-in-Chief.

Given under my hand, etc., this 29th day of July, 1808.

WM. BLIGH.

[Enclosure No. 4.]

LIEUTENANT-COLONEL FOVEAUX TO GOVERNOR BLIGH.

On Board the Sinclair,
Sir,   Port Jackson, 29th July, 1808.

Refusal of
Foveaux to
reinstate Bligh.
In reply to your communication of this day's date, delivered to me by Mr. Griffin, I have to observe that as the
Government has been upwards of Six months out of your hands,
and as the affair has been submitted to His Majesty's Ministers,
who alone are competent to decide, I cannot take it upon myself
to judge between you and the Officer whom I find in the actual
command of the Colony.

Untill the decision of His Majesty's Ministers shall be received, I conceive it to be beyond my authority to reinstate you
in the Government, and it only remains for me to adopt such
measures as I deem to be most effectual for the preservation of
the public tranquility, the security of Public and private property, and to follow, in the discharge of the arduous duties imposed upon me, a System of the strictest economy and the most
impartial justice between persons of every description.

I have, &c.,
J. FOVEAUX.

[Enclosure No. 5.]

GOVERNOR BLIGH TO CAPTAIN KENT.

Bligh's orders
for the hoisting
of his broad
pendant on
H.M.S.
Porpoise.
By William Bligh, Esq., Commodore commanding His Majesty's
Ships and Vessels employed in the South Pacific Ocean.

WHEREAS, on the 30th Nov'r last, I received an Order from my
Lords Commissioners of the Admiralty, dated the 27th February,
1807, to hoist and wear a Broad Pendant on board His Majesty's
Ship Porpoise, or such Ship as might be on the Station (a Copy
of which you will receive herewith), I immediately hoisted it on
board His Majesty's Colonial Schooner Estramina (as the Porpoise was then detached on a particular Service, and as no

Man-of-War was in the harbour of Port Jackson) on board of which Vessel it continued flying until the 27th January last, when it was hauled down by the directions of Major Johnston, commanding Officer of the New South Wales Corps, who the day before confined me and usurped the Government of this Colony; and whereas the said Major Johnston prevented me from having any communication with His Majesty's Ship Porpoise on her return on the 4th February, and continued to act in such manner up to this day (except, through his hands, allowing me to convey an acting Commission to you), when Lieut't-Colonel Foveaux being arrived, has granted you permission to communicate with me. You are, therefore, hereby required and directed to hoist and wear my Broad Pendant on board His Majesty's Ship Porpoise, entering me on the Ship's Books as Commodore; and you are to enter Mr. Edmund Griffin as my Secretary, on a separate supernumerary List.

1808.
31 Aug.
Bligh's orders for the hoisting of his broad pendant on H.M.S. Porpoise.

Given, etc., this 30th day of July, 1808.

WM. BLIGH.

[Enclosure No. 6.]

GOVERNOR BLIGH TO LIEUTENANT-COLONEL FOVEAUX.

Sir, Government House, Sydney, 1st August, 1808.

As by your Letter of the 29th Ult'o you have declined reinstating me in my Government, and as by your Proclamation of the 30th,* published in a *Gazette* of yesterday, you have taken upon yourself the Government of this Colony, I request to know whether you intend to keep me a Prisoner here.

Bligh's request to know if he is to be kept a prisoner.

I am, &c.,
WM. BLIGH.

[Enclosure No. 7.]

LIEUTENANT-COLONEL FOVEAUX TO GOVERNOR BLIGH.

Sir, Headquarters, 2nd August, 1808.

In answer to your Letter of yesterday's date, I beg leave to acquaint you that I have no objection to your proceeding to England as soon as you think proper, either in the Porpoise, which I mean to send Home as soon as she shall be ready for Sea, or in any other Vessel more agreeable to yourself in which suitable accommodation can be procured. I have, &c.,

Bligh to be allowed to sail for England.

J. FOVEAUX.

[Enclosure No. 8.]

GOVERNOR BLIGH TO CAPTAIN KENT.

By William Bligh, Esq., &c.

You are hereby required and directed to fit out His Majesty's Ship Porpoise with the utmost dispatch, for the purpose of my

H.M.S. Porpoise to be refitted.

proceeding to England as soon as possible, and you are to take
care that she be completed with Provisions, Stores, and necessaries of all kinds for eight months.

Given, etc., this 3rd day of August, 1808.

WM. BLIGH.

[Enclosure No. 9.]

GOVERNOR BLIGH TO LIEUTENANT-COLONEL FOVEAUX.

Sir,   Government House, Sydney, 3rd August, 1808.

Foveaux
informed of
Bligh's orders
to Kent.
In reply to your Letter of the 2nd Instant, in answer to my
Letter of the day before, requesting to know if you meant to keep
me a Prisoner here, stating that you had no objection to my pro-.
ceeding to England as I thought proper, either in the Porpoise or
in any other Vessel more agreeable to myself in which suitable
accommodation can be procured,—I have to inform you that I
have given orders to Captain Kent to get His Majesty's Ship
Porpoise in readiness for Sea to receive myself and family, to
proceed Home without delay.   I am, &c.,

WM. BLIGH.

[Enclosure No. 10.]

LIEUTENANT-COLONEL FOVEAUX TO GOVERNOR BLIGH.

Sir,   Headquarters, 4th August, 1808.

Conditions
imposed on
Bligh's
departure.
I beg to state to you that I have no objection to your
proceeding to England in His Majesty's Ship Porpoise; but it
must be clearly understood by you that you are to consider yourself bound by the conditions to which you acceded previous to
my arrival, on obtaining Major Johnston's consent to embark in
that Vessel.

Upon any other terms I am determined not to permit you to
leave the Colony while the Command rests with me.

I have, &c.,

J. FOVEAUX.

[Enclosure No. 11.]

GOVERNOR BLIGH TO LIEUTENANT-COLONEL FOVEAUX.

Sir,   Government House, Sydney, 4th August, 1808.

I have received your Letter of this day stating that you
have no objection to my proceeding to England in His Majesty's
Ship Porpoise; but it must be clearly understood by me that I am
to consider myself bound by the conditions to which I acceded,
previous to your arrival, on obtaining Major Johnston's consent
to embark in that Vessel; And that upon any other terms you
are determined not to permit me to leave the Colony while the
Command rests with you.

In reply thereto, I inform you that I will not enter into any 1808.
31 Aug.
conditions whatever, except returning to England immediately
in Command of His Majesty's Ship Porpoise, bearing my Broad Bligh's refusal
to accept any
conditions.
Pendant, which is at the peril of any one to tarnish or deprive
me of.

Major Johnston closed all conditions and determinations of
what was to be done with regard to the confinement I was put
under, referring to Lieut.-Gov'r Paterson, and next to yourself,
to decide on the measures as soon as either might arrive. It now
rests with you, only, to grant or refuse my proceeding in the
Porpoise as before stated.

I am, &c.,
Wm. Bligh.

[Enclosure No. 12.]

Lieutenant-Colonel Foveaux to Governor Bligh.

Sir, Headquarters, 6th August, 1808.

I have already stated to you, in my Letter of the 4th inst.,
the only conditions on which I can consent to your embarking
for England.

Should you have any communication to make to Lieut't-Gov'r Paterson to
be consulted.
Paterson, I beg leave to inform you that I have ordered a
Colonial Vessel to be got ready which will proceed to Port
Dalrymple in the course of Two or Three days.

I have, &c.,
J. Foveaux.

[Enclosure No. 13.]

Governor Bligh to Lieutenant-Colonel Foveaux.

Sir, Government House, Sydney, 8th August, 1808.

On the 28th of March last I made application to Major Bligh's demand
for the return
of his books
and papers.
Johnston for my Commissions and all my Books and papers
which had been taken from me to be delivered up into my possession. In answer to this, the next day I was informed by Letter
that on the following Friday such Books and papers as he did
not consider it needful to retain would be sent to me. This not
being fulfilled, I sent my Secretary to Major Johnston to repeat
my demand on the 8th May, in answer to which two days after I
received the following Letter:—

Sir, Head Quarters, Sydney, 10th May, 1808.

I am ordered by His Honor The Lieut. Governor to
acquaint you in answer to the application made by Mr. Griffin
that as Lieut. Colonel Paterson and Lieut. Colonel Foveaux are
daily expected to arrive, the Lt. Governor considers it proper to

Bligh's demand
for the return
of his books
and papers.

defer coming to a determination respecting the return of any
papers belonging to you that are now in his possession.

I have, &c.,

WILLIAM LAWSON, Aid de Camp.

You now being here, I am, by His Majesty's appointment as
Captain-General and Governor-in-Chief, called upon to repeat
the purport of the Correspondence, and particularly in His
Majesty's name to call upon you to put me in possession of the
Commission with which he invested me, His instructions under
the sign Manual and those of the Right Honorable Viscount
Castlereagh, His Majesty's Principal Secretary of State for the
Colonies, my Letter Books of all kinds, and my Book of my
decisions on appeals, together with all other papers I have been
so dispossessed of.   I am, &c.,

WM. BLIGH.

[Enclosure No. 14.]

LIEUTENANT-COLONEL FOVEAUX TO GOVERNOR BLIGH.

Sir,   Headquarters, 9th August, 1808.

I have referred your Letter of yesterday to Major Johnston who is at present some distance from Head Quarters.

I annex a Copy of my Letter to him on that subject, and shall
loose no time in communicating to you his answer.

I have, &c.,

J. FOVEAUX.

[Enclosure No. 15.]

LIEUTENANT-COLONEL FOVEAUX TO MAJOR JOHNSTON.

Sir,   Headquarters, 9th August, 1808.

I herewith transmit you a Copy of a Letter received
yesterday from Capt. Bligh, requiring his Commission, books,
papers, &c., to be returned to him.

As I am determined not to interfere in the measures you have
thought it expedient to adopt respecting Capt. Bligh's suspension
from the Government previous to my arrival in the Colony, I
must leave it entirely to your judgment how far his request can
be complied with.   I have, &c.,

J. FOVEAUX.

[Enclosure No. 16.]

LIEUTENANT-COLONEL FOVEAUX TO GOVERNOR BLIGH.

Sir,   Headquarters, 9th August, 1808.

I was much surprised at receiving a Verbal Message this
Morning by a person calling himself a Gardner, intimating that
he had been desired by you to inform me that no more vegetables
were to be sent for my use from the Government Garden. I beg

to remind you that the Garden is maintained at a very heavy
expence, entirely defrayed by Government, and after a sufficient quantity of its produce is provided for your Table (for which I Disposal of vegetables from have given my permission) you can have no pretence on any the government account to interfere in the distribution of the remainder.

I have further to add that I shall in future take no notice of any communication you may find it necessary to make to me unless it be delivered in writing.   I have, &c.,

J. FOVEAUX.

[Enclosure No. 17.]

GOVERNOR BLIGH TO LIEUTENANT-COLONEL FOVEAUX.

Sir,   Government House, Sydney, 9th August, 1808.

In answer to your Letter of this day's date respecting the Depletion of the Government Garden, I have to acquaint you that Thomas Alford, government garden. the Government Gardner, having reported that the Roots and Vegetables were taken in such quantities out of the Garden as would not leave a sufficiency for the use of the House, I told him no one was to have any without his representing it to me, except Colonel Foveaux, to whom I desired him to represent the want of Glass for the Pine-Apple Plants.   I am, &c.,

WM. BLIGH.

[Enclosure No. 18.]

SECRETARY GRIFFIN TO MR. J. FINUCANE.

Sir,   Government House, Sydney, 10th August, 1808.

Thomas Allen, one of the Labourers in the Garden be- Removal of a longing to this House, having been taken away this day by the labourer from Overseer of the working Gang, I am directed by His Excellency the garden. Governor Bligh to request that you will be pleased to inform me if the Overseer had authority for so doing.

I am, &c.,

EDMUND GRIFFIN.

[Enclosure No. 19.]

MR. J. FINUCANE TO SECRETARY GRIFFIN.

11th August, 1808.

MR. FINUCANE's compliments to Mr. Griffin.   Begs leave to Cause of acquaint him that he finds Allen was ordered by Colonel Foveaux removal of labourer. from the Government Garden, it having been represented that a man could be spared from thence to assist in unloading the Vessels lately arrived with Supplies from England.

Mr. Finucane will esteem it a favor if Mr. Griffin will let him have a Copy of Capt. Bligh's communication to Colonel Foveaux, of the 29th of last month, requiring to be reinstated in the Government.

1808.
31 Aug.
In the hurry of landing, Mr. F. has mislaid the original, and as it is necessary to send a copy of it to Lieut.-Governor Paterson by the Estramina, which will sail to-morrow, he takes the liberty of requesting Mr. Griffin will let him have one.

[Enclosure No. 20.].

SECRETARY GRIFFIN TO MR. J. FINUCANE.

Government House, 11th August, 1808.

Copy of
Bligh's orders.
MR. GRIFFIN's Compliments to Mr. Finucane, incloses a Copy of His Excellency the Governor's order of the 29th Ulto. to Lieut.-Colonel Foveaux to reinstate him in his Government, as requested by Mr. Finucane in his Note of this morning.

[Enclosure No. 21.]

LIEUTENANT-COLONEL FOVEAUX TO GOVERNOR BLIGH.

Sir,   Headquarters, 15th August, 1808.

Stationery for
the public
service.
Captain Jackson having mentioned to me that you have claimed a Case of Stationery as your private property which came out in the Sinclair, I beg to acquaint you that I know of none, except one, which has been sent to my Quarters, directed from the Commissary-General's for the Governor's Office here, which being evidently intended for the Public Service, I must decline giving up.   I have, &c.,

J. FOVEAUX.

[Enclosure No. 22.]

GOVERNOR BLIGH TO LIEUTENANT-COLONEL FOVEAUX.

Sir,   )   Government House, Sydney, 15th August, 1808.

Bligh's claim
to the
stationery.
In reply to your Letter of this day's date, I have to observe that I made a particular request for Stationary for my use, and therefore have no doubt that the case in Question was sent as directed in consequence; but as you decline giving it up to me, I must put up with the Inconvenience.

I must also remark that such Paper as has been sent out heretofore for the general use of His Majesty's Service was always directed to the Commissary's Office; and I understand that a case of Stationary so directed, of a much larger size than the one alluded to, has been received by the said Ship.

I am, &c.,

WM. BLIGH.

[Enclosure No. 23.]

LIEUTENANT-COLONEL FOVEAUX TO GOVERNOR BLIGH.

Sir,   Headquarters, 15th August, 1808.

Some of the overseers having reported to me that you have thought proper to give them orders respecting the execution of parts of their duty, I must acquaint you that should you do so again I shall be under the necessity of taking some very effectual method of preventing any interference on your part in anything whatever relative to the affairs of this Colony.

1808.
31 Aug.

Bligh's orders to overseers.

I have, &c.,
J. FOVEAUX.

[Enclosure No. 24.]

GOVERNOR BLIGH TO LIEUTENANT-COLONEL FOVEAUX.

Sir,   Government House, Sydney, 23rd August, 1808.

Referring to your Letter of the 9th Instant, I have to request to be informed when I may receive an answer to my Letter of the 8th, respecting my Papers being delivered up to me.

The question of Bligh's papers.

I am, &c.,
WM. BLIGH.

[Enclosure No. 25.]

LIEUTENANT-COLONEL FOVEAUX TO GOVERNOR BLIGH.

Sir,   Headquarters, 23rd August, 1808.

I have sent a Copy of your Letter of this day to Major Johnston, with a request that he would give an immediate answer to the requisition contained in your Letter of the 8th inst.

Foveaux's apology for delay in reply.

Had I not imagined that his answer had been conveyed directly to yourself, I should not have suffered such a length of time to elapse without letting you hear from me on that subject.

I have, &c.,
J. FOVEAUX.

MR. J. FINUCANE TO MAJOR JOHNSTON.

Sir,   Head Quarters, 23rd Augt., 1808.

I am directed by Lt. Govr. Foveaux to transmit you a Copy of a Letter this moment received from Capt. Bligh together with the answer thereto and to request your immediate attention to the subject of it.   I have, &c.,
JAMES FINUCANE.

[Enclosure No. 26.]

CAPTAIN KENT TO COMMODORE BLIGH.

Sir,   His Majesty's Ship Porpoise, 25th August, 1808.

In consequence of application having been made to me to sit as member of the Court of Criminal Jurisdiction, and you having in your orders of the 26th of August, 1806, Ordered that Two Commissioned Officers of His Majesty's Ship Porpoise should attend as Members on application being made by the Judge-Advocate,—I therefore wish to know if those Orders are to be complied with, that I may be at liberty to sit as the Law directs.   I am, &c.,

The question of Kent sitting in the criminal court.

WM. KENT.

SECRETARY GRIFFIN TO CAPTAIN KENT.

Kent to sit
in courts
summoned
by Bligh.

Sir,   Government House, Sydney, 25th August, 1808.

In answer to your Letter of this morning, I am commanded
by His Excellency Governor Bligh, Commodore commanding His
Majesty's Ships and Vessels here, to say that when you see his
Signature to any Precept for a Criminal Court, then you are to
obey his Orders of the 26th August, 1806.

I am, &c.,
EDMUND GRIFFIN.

[Enclosure No. 27.]

LIEUTENANT-COLONEL FOVEAUX TO GOVERNOR BLIGH.

Sir,   Headquarters, 25th August, 1808.

Confirmation of
Bligh's orders
requested by
Foveaux.

Enclosed I send you a Copy of a Letter from Capt. Kent
to the acting Judge-Advocate, informing him that he had received
an order from you not to attend a Criminal Court unless your
signature was to the Precept.

I request to know whether the information communicated by
Capt. Kent be correct.   I have, &c.,
J. FOVEAUX.

CAPTAIN KENT TO CAPTAIN KEMP.

Sir,   25th August, 1808.

Kent's
inability to sit
on the criminal
court.

Having seen the precept for attending a Court of Criminal
Jurisdiction as one of the Members, I have to inform you that, in
consequence of having received an Order from Commodore Bligh
of this day's date, ordering me not to attend the Court of Criminal
Judicature without his Signature is to the Precept, I have therefore to inform you I cannot attend.   I am, &c.,
WM. KENT.

[Enclosure No. 28.]

GOVERNOR BLIGH TO LIEUTENANT-COLONEL FOVEAUX.

Sir,   Government House, Sydney, 25th August, 1808.

Bligh's
explanation
of his orders.

In answer to your Letter of to-day, I inform you that
Capt. Kent wrote to me to know if I would sanction his sitting as
a Member on a Criminal Court, agreeable to my orders of the
26th August, 1806. I wrote to him that when he saw my Signature to a Precept for a Criminal Court, he was to obey my
orders of that date; but I gave him no orders not to sit on a
Criminal Court.

The subject is at his own discretion.   I am, &c.,
WM. BLIGH.

[Enclosure No. 29.]

LIEUTENANT-COLONEL FOVEAUX TO GOVERNOR BLIGH.

Sir,   Headquarters, 26th August, 1808.

I send you a Copy of Major Johnston's reply to the requi- Bligh's papers
to be detained
sition made by you in your Letter of the 8th inst. for the restitu- until Paterson's
tion of your papers, &c. arrival.

For my own part, I wish to decline interfering until the arrival
of Lt.-Gov'r Paterson, or until I receive a notification of his
intention, unless, previous to either, it be your design to leave the
Colony, in which case I must adopt measures to obtain copies of
such as may be necessary for carrying on the public business.

I have, &c.,
J. FOVEAUX.

[Enclosure in above.]

MAJOR JOHNSTON TO LIEUTENANT-COLONEL FOVEAUX.

Sir,   25th August, 1808.

As I considered most of the papers which were taken from
Government House necessary to the administration of the
Government of the Colony, I declined coming to any determination respecting their return until the arrival of Lt.-Gov'r Paterson
or yourself, of which Captain Bligh was apprized on the 28th of
May; But, as you have relieved me in the Command, I am ready,
as I signified to you on your arrival, to deliver all the papers
whenever you should be pleased to receive them.

I have, &c.,
GEO. JOHNSTON.

[Enclosure A.]

GOVERNOR BLIGH TO LIEUTENANT-GOVERNOR PATERSON.

Sir,   Government House, Sydney, 8th August, 1808.

Lieutenant-Co'l. Foveaux having informed me that he Bligh's report
intends sending a Colonial Vessel to Port Dalrymple, I embrace of his arrest
to Paterson.
it as the first opportunity I have had to inform you that, on the
26th January last, Major Johnston, together with his Officers and
New South Wales Corps under his command, aided by Mr.
McArthur, Bayly, and others, did, without any remonstrance, put
me in confinement within the premises of Government House,
where I remain at this moment. A Committee seized all my
Letter-Books, Book of Appeals, my Commission appointing me
Captain-General and Governor-in-Chief, my Vice-Admiralty
Commission, My Instructions under the sign-Manual, together
with those from My Lord Castlereagh, Principal Secretary of
State for the Colonies, All my Papers—many of which were

1808.
31 Aug.
private—and the Great Seal of the Colony. At that time the Country was in Peace and happiness, and the Settlers—as they are now—highly satisfied with my administration.

Bligh's demand
to be reinstated
by Paterson.
On this unpar'lled occasion I call upon You, as Lieutenant-Colonel of His Majesty's New South Wales Corps, and Lieut.-Governor of the Territory, to use your utmost endeavours to suppress this Mutiny of the Corps under your command, that I may proceed in the Government of the Colony according to the powers delegated to me by our Gracious Sovereign.

It remains with me to state that I will enter into no conditions; but I am disposed to inform you that, as Captain-General and Governor-in-Chief, all the Troops are bound to obey me, and that no Person whatever could lawfully deprive me of my Government unless by orders in due form from the King, or from him to whom he should delegate his Power, Death or absence being the only cases where the Governor's power and Authority can cease, He being the King's immediate representative.

I have had no controul over His Majesty's Ship Porpoise; but heard that you had requested her to be sent down for you, and that she went in consequence. Since Lieut.-Colonel Foveaux's arrival, the Officers have been permitted to call on me.

I am, &c.,
WM. BLIGH.

[Enclosure B.]

Extract from
Bligh's despatch
re conduct of
emancipists.
EXTRACT of a Letter written by William Bligh, Esqr. (late Governor), to His Majesty's Principal Secretary of State, dated 31st October, 1807.

IT is to be deplored that the greater part of the Prisoners remain after their Servitude the same Characters, as by their vicious habits they have maintained in their Career of Life, notwithstanding the Rewards and Blessings offered to them to do well; but the Road to it, being Honesty and Industry, is an insurmountable Barrier.

This melancholy Truth has been proved by many of the Emancipations and Free Pardons which have been given; even those who have been raised to some degree of wealth by such means, if happily they leave off thieving, their habits of cheating and Knavery seem to be encreased by the giving up the other Vice—fair and honorable Principal they cannot admit in competition to their habitual Reasonings, which make them the most troublesome characters to Society and regular Government—not until the next or after Generations can be expected any considerable Advance to Morality and Virtue.

By the leading People of this Class whose Names are Lord, Kable, and Underwood, several Masters of Ships have been ruined; the Merchants at home defrauded to a serious Amount; and the Mercantile Interest almost destroyed. With constant Litigations and infamous Prosecutions in the Courts they have been accustomed to be gratified.

1808.
31 Aug.

Extract from Bligh's despatch re conduct of emancipists.

A True Copy: JOHN McARTHUR, Secretary to the Colony.

***

GOVERNOR BLIGH TO VISCOUNT CASTLEREAGH.

(Despatch per ship Rose; acknowledged by Viscount Castlereagh, 15th May, 1809.)

Government House, Sydney, New South Wales,
My Lord,   31st August, 1808.

Mr. Commissary Palmer having represented to me the losses which Government have sustained since the 26th January last, and the improper management of the present Rulers, I beg leave to inclose his Letter for Your Lordship's information.

Palmer's report on Johnston's administration.

I have, &c.,
WM. BLIGH.

[Enclosure.]

COMMISSARY PALMER TO GOVERNOR BLIGH.

Sir,   Sydney, New South Wales, 31st August, 1808.

I beg leave to state to Your Excellency in what manner I have been treated by Major George Johnston, of the New South Wales Corps, and those acting under him. About 7 O'Clock in the Evening of the 26th Jan'y last, He (the Major), with the Corps under him, marched from the Barracks to the Government House and put Your Excellency in Confinement; 'tis needless for me, I presume, to comment further on that head, Your Excellency being in full possession of every transaction that took place there.

The arrest of Bligh.

This act so atrocious in its nature, and for which the law both Military and Civil has provided such high penalties could not have been perpetrated by Men possessing such properties and comforts as many of them had, unless prompted by the wildest frensy. The friends of Government and of the Mother Country feel the most pungent sorrow that a person in Your Excellency's exalted station should be treated with such indignity. They perceive the security of the lives and liberties of themselves and families and of every honest and loyal Man destroyed—they perceive their properties in danger, and every thing dear to Man rendered precarious by such a daring and unparalleled outrage, they feel for yourself and regret that disinterestedness rigid integrity and honor should be so cruelly persecuted.

1808.
31 Aug.

Arrest of
Palmer and
seizure of his
papers.
Immediately after this transaction they surrounded my Office, and not only seized upon the whole of my Public and private Books and Papers, but also ordered the Keys of the Stores to be given up, and I was told by Adj't Minchin to consider myself under an Arrest; they then put seals on the doors of the Office, and placed a Centinel at each door. A few days after Mr. Bayley, Mr. John Blaxland, and Mr. Garnham Blaxcell broke the Seals of the Office, and ordered my Desk to be opened, and took there-from such papers as they thought proper; they then seized my Ledgers, Books, and other Papers, and gave them into the Charge of a Serjeant and Centinels to take to Major Johnston's Barracks, in order to be deposited there, where they remained until the

Return of
papers after
arrival of
Foveaux.
11th instant (a few days after the Arrival of Lieut't-Col'l Foveaux), when they were returned to me. I further beg leave to state that a Mr. McArthur was appointed Colonial Secretary, a Situation never before known in the Colony, nor was ever permitted by Authority. Soon after he came to Act in that Situation he took from Major Johnston three Government Ledgers, and had them removed to his House, where they remained until I received them with the other papers.

Effects of the
seizure of
Palmer's books.
I have to remark, not only the extreme hardship I laboured under for the want of my Books, &c., but also the loss Government sustained by their detention, as it precluded me from making up my Accounts or receiving any debts due from Individuals to Government. I had been busily employed, prior to the seizure of my Books, &c., in arranging and making, not only my Accounts, required to be made up by the Auditor's Office, but also every Account to the 31st December, 1807. I have to remark to Your Excellency the reason of my Accounts not being closed sooner was owing to the want of Stationary, there being very little in the Colony to be procured, and that at such an extravagant price that I purchased as little as I could possibly do with, being in dayly expectation of receiving a supply from England. I beg leave further to observe that if such change had not taken place the outstanding Debts due to Government from Individuals would have been nearly paid, as well as the Stores filled with Grain, for Your Excellency is well aware that during the last Muster every Settler and other Individual indebted to Government was restricted from disposing of their Grain at the then ensuing Harvest, until they had paid their debts, but as they found no demand was made upon them after the Change took place, the greatest part of them immediately disposed of their Grain to the great detriment of Government—and Your Excellency will admit that very few of those debts can now be got in until next Harvest.

Thus far I have thought proper to relate to you the manner of 1808. 31 Aug. the first procedure of this self-created Government, and shall proceed to state to Your Excellency for your information what has been transacting since relative to my department. A few days Administration of the commissariat under Johnston. after my suspension a Survey was ordered on the Provisions, Stores, &c., remaining in the Stores, and a Report was not made thereon for several Months afterwards, nor have I as yet received a Copy of such report. Immediately on their receiving the Keys of the Stores, and even before a Survey took place, they began to Issue Articles from the Store, and continued until the Stores were nearly drained.

One instance I beg leave to state: McArthur and Blaxcell Issue of public stores to Macarthur, Blaxcell, and Kable. received two p'rs of Mill-Stones (French Burrs), and Henry Kable another p'r, as also the former thirty Stand of new Arms, no doubt for the express purpose of Barter, as they were put on board, as I am well informed, the Parramatta Schooner, bound to the South Seas as a Sealer. The Stones were fixed in a Mill of theirs. The Colony has suffered greatly by the disposal of these Stones, as they were intended to have been sent by You to the Infant Settlements in order to grind their Grain, and which they are much in want of. It is not only their receiving out of the Stores the things abovementioned, but also they have received a large Quantity of Cordage, Iron, Canvas, Sails, and Slops to supply their Vessels, &c., and besides various other things never intended to be disposed of, having been sent out for the express purpose of His Majesty's Vessels, and for other Government purposes. The Officers of the New South Wales Corps, McArthur, Issue of stores to the military and others. Blaxcell, Nichols, &c., were drawing dayly Articles from the Stores; some of them, as I before stated, were valuable to Government, and had not a supply been recently received, the Colony must have felt it severely, as the Soldiers received Trowsers, Frocks, Shirts, &c., which were sent out for the Clothing of the Prisoners, and drained the Stores of every necessary Article. The Prisoners could not, or did not, receive more than a part of what they otherwise might have had, and were entitled to; thus the Prisoners were almost left naked; again, McArthur, having the sole management of all affairs relative to the Colony, taking upon himself the ordering every matter belonging to Government, has been disposing of several Hundred Head of Cattle, chiefly to the Military and their Distribution of government cattle by Macarthur. favorites, and some to Settlers for Grain, many of whom will never have it in their power to pay, being neither persons of property at present, nor of any likelyhood of ever being so. Besides, from the first of his self-appointed situation he has been

1808.
31 Aug
Mutton bartered
by Macarthur.
delivering into the Stores at Parramatta several Hundred Pounds
of Mutton weekly, some of which was of a very bad quality, and
receiving out of the Stores here fresh as well as Salt Meat in
lieu of part thereof.

The Factory, which was a great benefit to the Colony, he took
from Government, and got the same into his own and his Emissaries hands in order to work up his Wool; by this cunning and
Art he has not only turned his Mutton into Store, the greater
part of which was very old and poor, which caused a great discontent among those who received their rations from the Store at
Tyranny of
Macarthur.
Parramatta; but such was his tyranny that upon any complaint
being made he not only used severe threats of oppression but did
actually send the persons to hard labour, or the Coal River, there
to work in the Mines. One Instance of his tyrannical disposition
amongst the many: taking the advantage of my Ledgers not being
closed, He ordered a debt List to be made out, and, because one
of my Clerks told him that he could not make out the same
correct, nor could any person without my assistance, as he did
not know what Credit was to be given to many persons, nor
having the Settlement of the same, he reviled and loaded him
with every vile Epithet imaginable, and ordered him to be sent
to the Coal River if he did not immediately set about making out
such list, which he was obliged to do, and such List he now
detains in his possession—for what purpose I know not. One
other instance of the sinister views of McArthur I beg leave to
Distribution of
bonded spirits
by Macarthur.
state: A Quantity of Spirits was bonded in the Stores, which
was at two different times disposed of to the Military Officers,
and a few of the Civil, which they sold afterwards to Individuals
at the rate of £3 and £3 5s. p'r Gallon; there being a quantity
of Wine and Porter disposed of also to his favorite Banditti, the
Casks wherein the same was contained were received by him and
Blaxcell into the Stores, and One Gallon of Spirits granted by
his permit to the Individual returning the same in; what became of those Casks is a mystery, as few or none of them has
been converted to Government purposes; but the greater part, if
I am well informed, were filled with Salt, Flour, &c., and put on
board their Vessels for their private trade. One other remark I
beg leave to make is that, in order to keep the Military quiet,
and induce them to praise the change of Government, they having
Alteration of
the military
ration.
Seven Pounds of fresh Beef at Sydney, and at Parramatta
Seven Pounds of fresh mutton, served to them Weekly as a
Ration, besides an additional Quantity of Grain, whereas the
Prisoners only received Two Pounds of Pork or Three and half
Pounds of Beef. I only mention this to show You the Vil-
lainous and tyrannical part they acted, for in times of scarcity it

is well known, in every former Governor's time, that the Soldiers
and Prisoners were on the same Ration; but this was done, as
they feared a revolt would take place, to secure their affections,
and attach them more strongly to their rebellious party; but that Effect of the
is not the worst, if we look to the consequence of their killing slaughter of
public stock.
8 or 10 Bullocks a Week for these sixteen Weeks or upwards,
which has not only lessened Government Herds greatly, but also
deprived the industrious Settler of receiving them for payment in
order to till their Ground, as I know it was your intention so
to assist the Settlers in their agricultural pursuits, and thereby
enable them to get forward with the tillage of their Land, and
lessen the price of Grain.

The Articles received out of the Stores in Major Johnston's Administration
time have been procured without any order or permission from commissariat
the Acting Commissary, but mearly by that of the Majors or in favour of
Macarthur and
McArthurs, and that they were to be paid for on delivery, but his favourites.
they thought proper to waive that, and several hundred of Pounds
remain unpaid in his time, but this is done mearly to serve their
favourites, very few indeed of the Settlers could receive any
thing in the Major's time except it was their favourites—As there
are several other Instances of the vile Intentions of this rebellious Party, but having written some short time ago to the Right
Hon'ble the Lords Commissioners of His Majesty's Treasury—
Inclosed I have the Honor to lay before You a Copy* thereof
wherein You will perceive I have stated several things, which I
presume is unnecessary to state in Yours at this time—It would
fill a Volume to renumerate every base stratagem carried on by
this McArthur and his Emissaries, and their various subterfuges
practised by them to Individuals in the Colony—What they could
not get by fair means to answer their purpose, they resorted to
menaces and threats, and by that means extorted confessions
from them quite false, for the People at one time were so
fearful of offending them that they durst not give a denial, but
advanced things that were totally void of foundation, not only
that they having embarked largely in every species of Trade
Barter and Monopoly, and Blaxcell, McArthur's Mercantile
partner, being appointed Auctioneer it gave them a large Scope
to get into their hands Articles of every description, as also the
ready Money or Grain Receipts which they received Copper
Coin out of the Store for, and by that means still had a greater
power to crush the Settlers and other Individuals.

It may not be thought improper to remark that such was the Autocratic
infamy of McArthur, in order to Answer his own views no doubt powers
exercised by
and arrogate to himself as much power as possible, Issued an Macarthur.
order for all outstanding Grain Receipts to be brought into him,

* Note 176.

1808.
31 Aug.

Autocratic
powers
exercised by
Macarthur.

and he would adopt a mode of payment. Such a measure was never before known in any part where a Commissary was, as he only was responsible for the payments, but in short this self created Colonial Secretary was Lieut. Governor, Commissary and every thing else, in fact every person was under his controul and direction and seemed to tremble even at his Nod. Such was his pride and ambition that he not only had an Orderly Serjeant to attend his door but a Cunstable also which intimidated the people so much when there on business, as to make them assert untruths rather than feel the severity of his lash, especially at such a time when the Minds of the People were much inflamed against their proceedings, and which he well knew to be the case, therefore used every Act of tyranny to keep them under. No person whatever except himself is in possession of any Grain Receipts for Cows disposed of, nor the Numbers sold, as he attended the sale and delivery of them himself, and instead of the Acting Commissary being in possession of any Stock returns or Grain returned in for Cattle in Order to ballance his Accounts, the same are kept by McArthur from him, and I make no doubt with some sinister view or other; as a proof of this when Mr.

Accounts for
sale of public
cattle.

Wilshire was appointed Acting Commissary by Col. Foveaux, he requested to know what Grain had been put in by the purchasers of Cattle at a public Vendue, wherein Mr. Blaxcell, McArthur's Mercantile partner, was Auctioneer. As no returns had ever appeared at the Commissary's Office, Mr. Blaxcell refer'd the same to McArthur, who conscious of doing wrong and fearful of a discovery, which would be attended with the worse consequences not only to them, but the party—Blaxcell caused an advertisement to be inserted in the *Sydney Gazette* (11th Septr.) calling upon every Person who had purchased Cattle at that Sale to forthwith settle the same otherwise measures would be resorted to to compel them as the time allowed them for payment had long

Decrease in
government
stock by
slaughter
and sales.

expired. I mentioned before that there were 8 or 10 fine large Bullocks killed Weekly in order to be Issued to the Officers and Troops, the whole as near as I can learn making upward of 280 Head—and the Cows disposed of to Individuals are *120*, exclusive of *40 and 37*, what they stiled *Old Cows of the Bengal Breed,* sold by Auction for Maize, the decrease of Government Stock in a little better than Six Months will stand thus.

Killed at the Store upwards of ..... 280 fat Bullocks
Disposed of for Wheat .... 120 Cows, the greater part
            of those were Choice
            Cows selected by McAr-
            thur for his favourites.
At Sale by Public Auction .... 77 Cows Bengal Breed
              477 Head

Besides a great Number given to Favourite Individuals which are to be returned in kind, the Number I have not been able to learn—Now if Your Excellency will be pleased to look at the manner the Cattle has been disposed of, to whom, and the Numbers each has received, it will be a convincing proof the loss not only Government has suffered in the first place, as also the loss sustained to the Industrious Settlers, which I am well satisfied was your wish and desire to protect, in preference to those, who may be only stiled Hawkers, Pedlars, &c., and living entirely upon the vitals of the Settlers, by disposing to them Articles, which may be stiled Luxuries, and thereby getting into their hands, Grain &c. which prevents them from turning it into Store to pay off their Government Debts.

1808, 31 Au^g.

Effects of the traffic in cattle.

The Idea of disposing of Cattle to Individuals for Grain was one of Your Excellency's wise and well adopted plans for encouragement of Industry, long before the Revolution took place, and even Books were kept at my Office for the insertion of Names, and the Number of Cows each Individual wished to have, but Your Excellency did not mean to suffer any person to have more than One or two each, and only to those who might be thought deserving of encouragement; the reverse of disposing of them by McArthur is now the Case; he has not only suffered Individuals who have got large Stock of their own to receive Cows even from 8 to 16 Head each, but also upon Credit, for by the following Statement such will appear:—

Method of bartering cattle adopted by Bligh.

Disposal of cattle by Macarthur.

	Wheat Bushels.	Maize Bushels
120 Cows disposed of at 56 Bushels of Wheat for Each Amounts to	6,720	——
77 Cows Sale by Auction about	——	7,000
Out of the above Quantity there has been received only	3,874	1,621
Deficiency due to Government	2,846	5,379

Now Your Excellency will please to observe that these Cows were to be paid for before delivery, and I dare say that few Individuals did so, but the favourites got them on Credit, and if I am rightly informed many of them never càn or will be able to pay—the distribution of them was as villainous as could be, and what never would have been allowed had Your Excellency been acting in Your Government, for I may venture to say that no person in the Colony would have received from Your Hands an Order to receive any thing like the Number as I shall state to you, the reason is very obvious for it prevented the Settlers who Your Excellency might have thought proper to give En-

Credit allowed to certain purchasers.

1808.
31 Aug.

Favoured
recipients of
government
cattle.

couragement to from receiving a Cow or two, which to many would have been a great Comfort and relief in affording nourishment to themselves and Families. I now beg leave to state to Your Excellency a few of the Names amongst the many that have received Cows for payment.

Mr. Fitz, Deputy Commissy.	10 Not Settled for.
Mr. Blaxcell (McArthur's partner)	14 do.
Lieut. Lawson	16, 2 only Settled for.
Fitzgerald, formerly a Prisoner, now appointed Cunstable at the Hawkesbury ..	7 . do.
Isaac Nichols, formerly a Prisoner	12 Not settled for.
Ratigan, Dealer for the Officers of the New South Ws. Corps	8, 4 paid for.
Saml. Terry, formerly a Prisoner	4, 2 only Settled for,

Cattle sold but
not paid for.

besides many more from 3 to four each, not settled for, therefore as far as I am able to learn out of the 120 Cows disposed of, and of the 77 sold by public Auction there appears now to be accounted for to Government upwards of 100 Head of Cattle, and 'tis not likely that any of them or at least the greater part of them can be paid for before next Harvest and I am afraid many never will.

Probable
increase of
stock disposed
of.-

If those Cows had been remaining in Government Herds and not disposed of till next Harvest in all probability Governm't. would have had an increase of nearly 100 more, as many of them selected for the favourite party were heavy in Calf and in fact I am told several of them even Calved before they got them home.

Appropriation
of fresh meat
by Macarthur.

I have further to remark to Your Excellency the large Quantities of Fresh Beef McArthur received from the Stores, sometimes 60 lbs., 80 lbs., and as far as 137 lbs. Weekly, exclusive of a proportion of Tripe, Hearts, Offal, &c., and I myself never received more than 7 lbs. He has endeavoured by every subtle means whatever to demand and receive ten times the Quantity any other person had of every Species, and by his Vile, Artful,. tyrannick, and oppressive manner, no person was at liberty to Notice it, as he took care to get such Books where Entries were made of the same into his own .hands and by that means prevented even the Acting Commissary himself to check him;. however, to a Stranger it would be a convincing proof of some base underhand dealing about to be practised by him in the Sequestration of the Books or Returns from the different Stores, as well as from the Storekeepers' Returns, as it totally put it out of the Power of any person except his chosen few to make any discovery of his vile Intentions.

The vile machinations of McArthur and the good he has
rendered the Colony, will be seen by Your Excellency in the
following Statement:—

1803.
31 Aug.

Value of stock
and stores
disposed of by
Macarthur.

	£	s.	d.
Cows disposed of as before stated, 197 in No.	5,516	0	0
Bullocks killed at the public Store, 280 Head	7,840	0	0
Exclusive of Cattle given to different People, to be paid in kind and as Gifts	....		
	£13,356	0	0
Grain returned in for the above	2,342	5	0
Leave a Ballance	£11,013	15	0
Articles Issued from the Store, exclusive of Government purposes	2,374	10	11½
Various purchases made	1,690	3	2
	£4,064	14	1½

Grain received for payment of Articles	£175	0	0			
Copper Coin received	524	6	6			
				699	6	6
Ballance				£3,365	7	7½

Therefore in the above rough Calculation Your Excellency will
percéive that instead of Government debts being lessened there
appears an increase to be added of £3,365 7s. 7½d. exclusive of the
Cattle Account as above stated, and I am fully convinced had
Your Excellency been Acting in Your Government, the greatest
part of the Old debts would have been paid, and the Settlers and
others would have been much better satisfied as the wise mode
adopted by Your Excellency precluded them from running in debt
to Government or receiving any Articles from the Store before
payment was actually made. One thing further I wish to advert
to, Your Excellency, and that is respecting my suspension. I
have never had any Specific Charge or reason assigned for the
same except vague report; and what charges they have or might
have to alledge against me, I am at a loss to know, for I can
assure Your Excellency I have never in the execution of my
duty as Commissary, which I have now held for upwards of
Eighteen Years past, and never had the most trivial charge or
complaint alledged against me; and had it not been for the party
Spirit of Rebels, not even the slightest Charge whatever would
have been thought of, for I can safely say that I never swerv'd
from the path of rectitude, but always had the Interest of the
Colony at Heart as well as the different Settlements, and I am
fully convinced in my own Mind that I have always made it my
chiefest Study to assist the Industrious Settler and promote
their Interest, conceiving it to be for the Material Interest of

Increase in
amount of debts
due to
government.

Suspension
of Palmer
without specific
reason.

1808.
31 Aug.

the Government, as well as the advancement of the Colony. I
could submit many things more to Your Excellency but trust
what I have suggested will be deem'd sufficient for thé present,

Palmer's
request for
submission of
report to
England.

and should it meet with Your Approbation I have to solicit Your
Excellency's laying the same with the Inclosures before the Right
Hon'ble the Lords Commissioners of His Majesty's Treasury or
the Secretary of State for their perusal with such observations
as Your Excellency may think proper for the more fully eluci-
dating the same.   I have, &c.,
                                        JNO. PALMER, Commiss'y.

[Sub-enclosure No. 1.]

MR. JOHN JAMIESON TO COMMISSARY PALMER.

Sir,   Parramatta, 20th July, 1808.

Deterioration of
the public stock
under
Macarthur's
administration.

You may think it very extraordinary that I have never
wrote you Officially, since I refused to act under the directions
of *Mr. McArthur.* I was only looking on for a while to see what
would be the issue of their driving and removing the Cattle to
all parts of the Country. It is well known to yourself, and every
Person in the Colony, that when the shameful Transaction took
place, respecting His Excellency Governor Bligh, that Government Stock of all kinds were then in the best State:—However,
since that Period they are sadly changed for the Worse, many
dead, others mutilated through neglect. The Stockmen well
know the Characters of their Superintendants Messrs. McArthur,
Fitz, and Hume, with whom they can take any Liberty to the
great detriment of His Majesty's Service and the destruction of
the Cattle. This was what I plainly foresaw would be the Case
from the orders that were given respecting the Stock by Major
Johnstone and Mr. McArthur: they seem to aim at nothing but
its total ruin and the destruction of the Colony. As I was conscious I eat His Majesty's Bread to do justice to the Public, I
could not therefore hold my situation any longer, as to follow
their Orders was an inevitable injury to the Public Interest:—
the Stock is some Thousands of Pounds worse since they took
possession.

Distribution of
the public stock
by Macarthur.

But what will surprise you most is the unwarrantable distri-
bution of them amongst the Officers, the Non-Commissioned
Officers of the New South Wales Corps, and other Individuals;
Officers that have never raised a Single Bushel of Wheat in the
Colony, and sorry I am to say some of the Officers in Your Own
Department have followed their pernicious Example. The Officers
that have received them got from Six to Ten and Seventeen
Cows, besides Bullocks; for which it is *said,* they are to pay in
Grain. In the following way they obtain *Spirits* to what Amount
they please, which they sell from five Hundred to a Thousand

Per Cent. for Grain to the unthinking Settlers who have been deprived ·from procuring a single Drop by any other Channel, since the unfortunate day of the unjust Arrest of His Excellency Governor Bligh. There are also many of the most undeserving Characters that received Cattle; the Serjeants had One, two, and three Cows each; The Serjeant Major I am told had five on account of his having been very Serviceable. I cannot forbear mentioning Mr. Fitz (Deputy Commissary) who has been so officious in the Cause, Mr. McArthur has rewarded him with *Seventeen Picked Cows*, and some Bullocks; and yet it is well known, that he has not the means to pay for them, With every other Indulgence that it is in his power to give:—And other useful Creatures of Mr. McArthur's have received the same Indulgence, and many of the disloyal Settlers, who have been very forward in supporting their Measures. But the most respectful are still Loyal to His Excellency Governor Bligh and will support him with their Lives and Properties.

I still consider myself in His Majesty's Service and shall deem it an honour to do my Duty as soon as His Excellency Governor Bligh is re-established in his Lawful Authority. I hope, Sir, that you will lay this before His Excellency, I trust that His Majesty's Ministers will do me Justice, and reward me for my Sixteen Years faithful Services to the Public, which can be testified by His Excellency Governor Phillips, and all the succeeding Governors to the time of His Excellency Governor Bligh.

I am, &c.,

JOHN JAMIESON,

Principal Superintendant of Government Stock.

[Sub-enclosure No. 2.]

COMMISSARY PALMER TO THE SECRETARIES TO THE TREASURY.

Gentlemen, Sydney, New South Wales, 29th April, 1808.

I beg leave to state to you for the information of the Right Honorable the Lords Commissioners of His Majesty's Treasury, that on the 26th of January last the New South Wales Corps with Major Johnstone at their head Marched from the Barracks to Government House where they immediately surrounded it, and put the Governor in Arrest and placed five Sentrys over him: They then seized on the whole of his public and private Papers: At the same time they took possession of my Office together with the Public Stores under my Charge, and ordered me to give up the Keys of the Stores, Adjutant Minchin at the same time telling me I was to consider myself under an Arrest. The Judge Advocate's Office was taken possession of in like manner; Since which Time I have never been suffered to have a single Book or Paper belonging to my Department, the

Margin notes:

1808. 31 Aug.

Cattle received by non-commissioned officers.

Cattle issued to Fitz.

Jamieson's loyalty to Bligh.

The arrest of Governor Bligh.

Seizure of public officers and papers.

1808.
31 Aug.

whole of them having been taken to Major Johnstone's Barrack, although I have several times required and demanded them.

Incomplete
survey of stores
taken.

It is true there was a Survey of the Stores and Provisions taken, yet the report of Survey has not been Signed or the Charge of Provisions and Stores regularly taken from me, although this violent Act of Rebellion took place better than three Months since.

Coercive
measures
adopted by the
rebel party.

I now beg to observe that the most Infamous and Villainous Plans have been adopted by the Self appointed Lieutenant Governor, with the assistance of Messrs. McArthur, Baily and others of the Rebellious Party, that ever could have been thought of; by their going about the Country and endeavouring by every artful means in their Power to extort Affidavits from all descriptions of Persons that would alledge any thing against the Governor or those that were attached to the Government. Many of these Affidavits have come to my knowledge some of which are against myself. As an Instance I think it proper to state that

Charges made
by Baker
against Palmer.

a Person named Baker deposed that prior to Mr. Palmer's leaving this Colony, he came to him, and ordered him to write a receipt for Wheat returned into His Majesty's Stores amounting to the Sum of Fifty three Pounds, which receipt he paid him for a Debt of the like Sum, he Mr. Palmer owed him, Mr. Baker, on a Private Account: And Mr. Baker further deposed, that the said Wheat for the Receipt given was never put into His Majesty's Stores. It appears very extraordinary that this Baker should come forward after a Period of Twelve Years to accuse me of an Act, which if it had taken place, he must have been equally Guilty from what he has Sworn to—The only way that I can account for his having taken such Affidavit, that Persons have been employed for the purpose of traducing my Character, and as he has been for some Years given to Drink, he has been persuaded to come forward against me, they conceiving from the length of time he has served under me as Storekeeper, it would have great Weight: Although at the same time I do not believe he could have known what he had been swearing to, having

Affidavit
repudiated
by Baker.

declared in the presence of several People that he never had taken such an Affidavit, and that he was ready to make Oath to the same whenever called upon, and he further said that he never knew me to do anything improper while he had served under me.

Charges made
by Fitz against
Bligh.

Another Instance is, that a Mr. Fitz, a Deputy Commissary who came from England lately, has deposed that Governor Bligh did receive from the Bonded Stores One Pipe of Wine, and that he Governor Bligh Ordered a quantity of Wine to be purchased from Mr. Campbell at the Rate of £3 P'r Dozen for the use of the General Hospital, which Wine was appropriated to his (Governor Bligh's) own use.

This Deposition is founded on what is base and false. There was a Pipe of Wine, *Out* of a considerable Number sent out for Barter, which Governor King, prior to the arrival of Governor Bligh, Ordered me to reserve for him:—I did so, and carried it to the charge of Governor Bligh. The Wine that was purchased from Mr. Campbell was supplied to the Hospital from his Stores, and never was received by any Person but Mr. Jamieson, the Principal Surgeon.

I have mentioned those two Affidavits to shew the Minds and dispositions of the infamous Characters that have taken a part against the Government with the Military:—And I do most solemnly declare that the rebellious Steps that have been taken against the just and firm Governor Bligh, and those attached to him, have been unprovoked and without his having given the least cause of Complaint on their part: And I am fully convinced it will appear so, whenever the Business is Investigated. My Books and Papers as Commissary are withheld from me, although Major Johnstone has told me more than Once, that they were not making use of them, and that he would see about it to-morrow when I might have them. This is all the Answer I can get from him, so that you will be pleased to inform their Lord-ships, that it is totally out of my power to make up any accounts whatever. From every thing I can Learn the most improper uses are now making of the Cloathing and Stores. Mr. McArthur has received for his own private use two Pair of Mill Stones, and Thirty Stand of Arms; the Arms are no doubt sent for Barter (in the Parramatta Schooner belonging to him) to the South Seas. He has likewise received Sails, Canvas, and a Variety of Other Articles, which were reserved by Governor Bligh for particular Services. All the Slop Clothing, consisting of Shirts, Frocks, and Trousers, that were sent out for the use of the Prisoners have been taken for the Soldiers so that the Prisoners have not any of those Articles to wear. I should have been more full in giving you an Account of what has taken place, but am fearful I shall not be able to get this Letter conveyed by the present Opportunity.   I have, &c.,

JNO. PALMER, Com'y.

GOVERNOR BLIGH TO THE HON. WILLIAM POLE.
(Despatch per ship Rose.)
Government House, Sydney, New South Wales,
Sir,   31st August, 1808.
I have the honor to write to You for the information of my Lords Commissioners of the Admiralty, and I beg leave to refer you to my despatch of the 30th of last April as being immediately connected with my present Letter.

1808.
31 Aug.

After I had appointed Lieut. William Kent as Acting Commander of the Porpoise on the 29th of March, he sailed, as then related, for Port Dalrymple on the 19th of April without any orders from me, although I sent my Secretary and the Master of

Kent
cautioned by
Bligh to avoid
the rebel party.

the Rose, Mr. Richard Brooks, to impress on his mind that it was necessary to separate himself from the Rebels, and keeping his Ship in good order, never to lose sight of me or suffer any insult to be offered to my Person and dignity, or obey any orders from the Usurpers.

On the 26th of May Captain Kent returned from Port Dalrymple without Lieutenant Governor Paterson, neither did I receive any

Prohibition
of Bligh's
intercourse
with the
Porpoise.

Letters, or had I any communication with him, all intercourse between me and the Officers of the Porpoise being prohibited; and notwithstanding the message I had sent to him before he sailed, and warned him to keep away from the Rebels, he on the 30th of May became a Member of their Criminal Court* which while it sat condemned to Death and Transportation several Persons.

H.M.S.
Porpoise
damaged at
Port
Dalrymple.

In coming out of Port Dalrymple, the Porpoise got on a Rock, and received so much damage as required her to be hove down. Her Fore and Main Masts were in such a bad state as to require new, and her Tops were also reported to be decayed. On the execution of these duties they have been employed, and are now beginning to rig.

Until the 30th of July I knew nothing of His Majesty's Ship but by observing her through my Spy Glass. At that time

Arrival of
Foveaux.

Lieutenant Colonel Foveaux arrived with an augmentation of Men to the New South Wales Corps, and from him Captain Kent had permission to wait on me. I then gave him a written Order

Kent ordered to
bear Bligh's
broad pendant.

to bear my Broad Pendant in conformity to their Lordships' Order of the 27th of February, 1807; but it had been flying from the 26th of May in consequence of a verbal notification to him previous to his sailing for Port Dalrymple. On my asking Captain Kent where Lieut. Symons was, he informed me, that on

Status of
Symons.

his taking the Command of the Ship Lieutenant Symons left her, and was marked on the Books superseded, as he considered him to have been Commander of the Porpoise. The impropriety of this conduct I told Captn. Kent would be represented to their Lordships, as I had no immediate power to correct it.

I am still a Prisoner, and under such an unparelleled situation, I hope their Lordships will see that I have done my utmost to

Bligh's
attempts to
obtain command
of the Porpoise.

secure His Majesty's Ship. For their farther information I beg leave to inclose such Correspondence as I have had concerning my getting more fully the command of her. I also beg leave to inclose Copies of Letters respecting Captain Kent sitting on a Criminal Court under the present usurped Government.

* Note 177.

The Colony is in a very impoverished and forlorn state, and
now entirely under the Military and McArthur; every Person
except them, is broken spirited, and Agriculture very much
neglected, relief from England is the only comfort they look to.

The Rebels appear to have had much fluctuation in their
opinions how to act; it is now said to rest with Lieut. Governor
Paterson, to whom Lieutenant Colonel Foveaux has sent the
Estramina Colonial Schooner.

I am under much difficulty in sending home my despatches,
having no particular Person to whom I can intrust them, but
the Master of the Ship Rose; the friends about me are so few
that I cannot dispense with their services.

I herewith transmit the State and Conditions of His Majesty's
Ship Porpoise on the 30th of July and this Instant; and under
the fullest confidence that I shall have every relief sent to me,

I have, &c.,
Wm. Bligh.

[Enclosure No. 1.]

[*This comprised copies of the letters, numbered 5, 6, 7, 8, 9, 10,
and 11, which were enclosed in Governor Bligh's despatch to
Viscount Castlereagh, dated 31st August, 1808.*]

[Enclosure No. 2.]

[*This consisted of copies of the letters numbered 26, 27, and
28, enclosed in the same despatch.*]

[Enclosure No. 3.]

[*Copies of the returns relating to H.M.S. Porpoise are not
available.*]

Governor Bligh to Viscount Castlereagh.

(Despatch per ship Rose; acknowledged by Viscount Castlereagh,
15th May, 1809.)

Government House, Sydney, New South Wales,

My Lord,   1st September, 1808.

Inclosed are the Reports from the Naval Officer's department of the arrivals and departures of Ships, together with an
Abstract of Duties collected, and General Statement of the
Orphan and Gaol Funds on the 31st December last, including
Mr. Campbell's Letter, stating the amount of the Cash to be
£2,091 16s. 6d., less £68 19s. 6d., which he paid into the hands of
the Usurpers when they compelled him to give up his trust.
These circumspect Accounts, in part, show what order the
affairs of this Colony were arriving at.

I have, &c.,
Wm. Bligh.

1808.
1 Sept.

Return of
shipping:
inwards.

[Enclosure No. 1.]

SHIPPING RETURN.

REPORT of Ships and Vessels entered Inwards from the Port of Port Jackson in His Majesty's Colony of New South Wales, from the first day of July to the 31st December, 1807.

When enter'd.	Name of the Ship.	Master.	Build.	Tons.	Guns.	Men.	Where Built.	Registered.	Name of the Owners.	From whence.	Cargo.
7 July	Young William (Isle of Portland)	Will'm Watson	Foreign	252	8	22	Rotterdam	London	Daniel Bennett	London	*
27 "	Grand Sachem	John Clark Spence	"	523	18	39	Bourdeaux		"		†
11 Sept.	Aurora	Coffin	American	250	18	22	Newbury	Newbury	Benjamin Roach	Whale Fish'ry	140 Ton of Oil.
14 "	Elizabeth	Mick	British	300	18	24	Milford	Milford	Daniel Sterbeck	"	130
16 "	Invisible	E. Bunker	Foreign	238	2	10	London	London	Campbell & Wilson	"	60
21 "	Albion	Rob't Turnbull	"	351	10	28	Deptford		Daniel Bennett	"	138
22 "	Ferrett	Ch. Richardson	British	362	10	24			Wilson, Campbell, & Page	"	50
26 Oct.	Duchess of York	Philip Son	Plantation	208	10	25	Calcutta	Calcutta	Daniel Bennett	Fegee Islands	100
2 Nov.	Jenny	Austin Forrest	American	192	14	25	New York	Boston	Campbell & Hook	Boston	65 ton of Sandal-wood.
12 "	Pegasus	Will'm Dorr, jun.	Prize to His Majesty's Ship Cornwallis.	205	6	14			John Dorr ... Capt. Johnston	Coast of Peru	† §
9 Dec.	Eliza	E. Hill Correy	American	185	3	10	Providence	Providence	Brown & Ives	Buenos Ayres	‖
17 "	Iphigenia	Seth Smith, jun.	"	270	10	50	Salem	Boston	John Dorr	The Fishery	A ...ity Seal-Skins.
18 "	Parramatta	John Glenn	Foreign	102	3	10		London	Hulletts & Co.	Otahaite	65 Casks of Pork.

* Provisions for Government, 3 Cases ... Glass, 2 Firkins of ... Merchandize for Dr. Townson, 7 ...ks of Ironmongery, 3 Do of Glass, and Earthenware, 4 ...ges of ... for Ensign Bell 1 Cask of ...s, 1 Bale of Haberdashery, and 2 Casks of Spirits 238 Gs for the Master.

† Female ...ks and ... Stores. 4 ...ks and 9 Bls of Spirits 496 ...ls, 1 ... and 2 Bales of ...

‡ 46 ; ...ls of Pork 127 Kids and Farrells of ..., 44 Bls of ... 13 Pipes of Brisket, 10 ...ks of Hams and Bacon 48 half Bls of Tongues, 60 ...s, 1 Package of Haberdashery, 6 ... 97 Do of Cyder, 19 Bls of Vinegar, 52 Kegs of ...o, 5 Boxes of Spanish Liquorice, 10 Chests of Tea, 6 ; ...ls of not permitted to be ...ded. ...r ...ks, 37 Bls and 4 Tierces of ...rm and Port Wine, 30 Hhds of Rum, 11 Pipes and 2 half Do of Brandy

§ 163 Bags of Sugar, 195 Bags of Rice, 2 Coils of Cordage, 12 Hides, 301 Jars and 5 ...ks of Spirits 4970 G...

47 ; ...ls and 10 Kids of Beef, 1 Cask of Salt Fish, 13 Kegs of ...to, 10 Casks of Ale, 19 ...ls Cordage, 10 ... er Casks of Sherry and Lisbon Wine, 7 Pipes of Teneriffe, and 2 Boxes of ...ut, 14 Pipes of Spirits ...ks Linseed Oil, 39 ...er Casks Repairs, but ...els to be ...ad in ...ms of His ...elly ...or Bligh's ...mit. ...id to be landed on account of the Vessel requiring

Naval Office, Sydney, 31st December, 1807.

ROBT. CAMPBELL, Naval Officer.

[Enclosure No. 1]—*continued.*

SHIPPING RETURN.

REPORT of Ships and Vessels cleared Outwards from the Port of Port Jackson in His Majesty's Colony of New South Wales, from the first day of July to the 31st December, 1807.

When clear'd	Name of the Ship	Master	Build.	Tons.	Guns.	Men.	Where Built.	Registered.	Name of the Owners.	Where bound.	Cargo
10 July	St. Anna	Will'm Moody	Foreign	220	..	20	(Spanish)	Prize	Lord, Kable, & Underw'd,	The Seal Fishery,	& The Seal Fishery, and to proceed to London.
25 ,,	Hannah & Sally	Nath'l Cogswell	American	167	4	11	Dennis Creek.	Philadel-ph'a.	Nath'l Cogswell	Canton	19,300 Seal-Skins.
12 Sep.	Young William	Will'm Watson	Foreign	327	8	30	Bourdeaux	London	Daniel Bennett	The Fishery	....
26 ,,	Grand Sachem	Coffin Whippey	American	250	..	22	Newbury	Newburry	Benj'n Roach	,,	....
26 ,,	Indispensible	Rob't Turnbull	Foreign	351	10	28	....	London	Daniel Bennett	,,	....
10 Oct.	Aurora	And'w Meryck	British	300	..	34	....	Milford	D'l Sterbeck and others.	Milford	130 Ton of Oil, and 292 Salted Seal Skins.
20 ,,	Ferrett	Philip Skelton	,,	208	10	25	....	London	Daniel Bennett	The Fishery	....
20 ,,	Albion	Cuth't Richardson.	,,	362	10	24	Deptford	,,	Wilson, Campbell, & Page.	,,	....
24 ,,	Sydney Cove	Will'm Edwards	Foreign	282	8	22	Rotterdam	,,	Thos. Wm. Plummer.	London	161 Casks of Oil and salted Seal-Skins. In Bulk, 22,074 Skins, 12 Tons 19 Cwt. of Brazil Wood, 37 Logs of Beef-Wood, and a quantity of Plank.
7 Nov.	Elizabeth	Alex'r Bodie	,,	238	2	24	....	,,	Campbell & Wilson	The Fishery	635 Casks of Oil, 16 Do. of salted Seal-Skins. In Bulk, 6,254 Skins, 18 Logs of She-Oak, 2 Stills with Worms and Heads, as p'r Certificate.
7 ,,	Duke of Port-land.	Jo. Clark Spence	,,	523	18	39	....	,,	Daniel Bennett	London	
24 ,,	Duchess of York.	Austin Forrest	Plantation	195	14	40	Calcutta	Calcutta	Campbell & Hook	Canton	Ballast.
19 Dec.	Amethyst	Seth Smith, jn.	American	270	10	50	Salem	Boston	John Dorr	The Seal Fishery	....

Naval Office, Sydney, 31st December, 1807.

ROBT. CAMPBELL, Naval Officer.

1808.
1 Sept.

Return of shipping: outwards.

1808.
1 Sept.

Return of duties and shipping dues collected.

[Enclosure No. 2.]

ABSTRACT of Duties and Fees of Entry received on Ships and Vessels at Sydney, New South Wales, from the 2d of May to 31st of December, 1807.

Date	Names of the Ships	Entry (£ s. d.)	Wharfage (£ s. d.)	Duties (£ s. d.)	Total (£ s. d.)	Orphan's Proportion (£ s. d.)	Jail Fund (£ s. d.)
1807.							
May 14	Albion	2 0 0			2 0 0	2 0 0	
June 22	Sydney Cove	4 2 0	15 9 0		19 11 0	19 11 0	
July 7	Young William	4 2 0	0 1 0	17 17 0	22 0 0	4 3 0	17 17 0
July 27	Duke of Portland	4 2 0	1 3 6	7 5 6	12 11 0	5 5 6	7 5 6
Septemr. 11	Grand Sachem	6 7 0			6 7 0	6 7 0	
" 14	Aurora	4 2 0			4 2 0	4 2 0	
" 16	Elizabeth	2 0 0	5 18 0		7 18 0	7 18 0	
" 16	Indispensible	4 2 0			4 2 0	4 2 0	
" 21	Albion	2 0 0	5 5 6		7 5 6	7 5 6	
" 22	Ferrett	4 2 0	4 13 0		8 15 0	8 15 0	
October 26	Duchess of York	4 2 0	5 16 6	181 19 0	204 2 6	178 11 0	25 11 6
Novemr. 2	Jenny	6 7 0	16 19 0	325 10 0	344 9 6	18 19 6	325 10 0
" 12	Pegasus	2 0 6	4 6 0	162 14 4	173 7 4	105 2 4	68 5 0
Decemr. 9	Eliza	6 7 0			5 6 0	5 6 0	
" 17	Amethyst	5 6 0	1 12 6		3 12 6	3 12 6	
" 18	Parramatta	2 0 0		29 17 0	59 8 0	59 8 0	
" 31	Colonial Vessels as pr. Entry Book	29 11 0					
		£92 12 6	71 4 0	725 2 10	888 19 4	444 10 4	444 9 0
	Deduct Naval Officer's Commission 5 Pr. Cent.				44 8 10	22 4 6	22 4 4
					£844 10 6	422 5 10	422 4 8

Naval Office, Sydney, 31st December, 1807.

ROBT. CAMPBELL, Naval Offr.

1808.
1 Sept.

Details of
abstract of
duties and
shipping dues.

[Enclosure No. 2]—*continued.*

EXPLANATION of the Fees and Duties as express'd in the within Abstract Vizt.

Description	£ s. d.	Description	£ s. d.
Ship *Albion* as a Whaler	£2 0 0	*Grand Sachem.*	
		Entry as a foreign Ship	£6 7 0
Sydney Cove.			
Fees of Entry	4 2 6	*Aurora.*	
Wharfage on the following Articles exported for London—		Entry	4 2 0
161 Casks of Oil and Skins at 6d.	4 0 6		
2,074 Skins in Bulk	6 12 4½	*Indispensible.*	
67 Logs of Beef Wood	0 18 6	Entry	4 2 0
12 Tons 19 of Brazil Wood	3 17 7½		
	19 11 0	*Elizabeth.*	
		Entry	2 0 0
		Wharfage on 238 Casks of Oil exported by the Duke of Portland	5 18 0
Young William.			7 18 0
Entry	4 2 0	*Albion.*	
Duty on 2 Casks of Spirits issued from the Bonded Store 238 Galls. at 1s. 6d. ..	17 17 0	Dues of Entry	2 0 0
Wharfage on Do.	0 1 0	Wharfage on 211 Casks of Oil exported by the Portland	5 5 6
	22 0 0		56
Duke of Portland.		*Ferrett.*	
Entry	4 2 0	Entry and Wharfage on 196 Casks Do. ..	8 15 0
Duty on 496 Galls. of Spirits H. M. Ship P., 399 no Duty is paid 97 at 1s. 6d.	7 5 6	*Duchess of York.*	
Wharfage on 47 Packages	1 3 6	Entry ..	4 2 0
	12 11 0		

1808.
1 Sept.

Details of
abstract of
duties and
shipping dues.

[Enclosure No. 2]—continued.

EXPLANATION of the Fees and Duties, &c.—continued.

Jenny.

Entry as a foreign Ship	£6	7	0
Ad Valorem Duty on Invoices 8,910 Dollars at 5 pr. cent.	111	7	6
Wharfago on 633 Packages	15	16	6
Duty on 622 Galls. of Wine at 9d.	23	6	6
Do. on 30 Gs. of Spirits allowed to be landed for the use of the tain and Supercargo 1s. 6d.	2	5	0.
Export Duty on 18 Ton of Sandal Wood imported by King, Colonial Vessel	45	0	0
	204	2	6

Pegasus (Prize).

Entry	2	0	6
Duty on 4,970 Spirits less 430 Gal. to Govt. and to Porpoise 4,340 at 1s. 6d.	325	10	0
Wharfage on 678 Packages at 6d.	16	19	0
	344	9	6

Eliza.

Entry as a foreign Ship	6	7	0
Ad Valorem Duty on Invoices £1,419 8s. 6¼d.	70	19	4
Duty on 1,820 Gs. of Wine	68	5	0
Wharfage on 172 Packages	4	6	0
Export Duty on 9 Tons 8 Cwts of Sandal Wood imported by the Elizabeth, Colonial Vessel	23	10	0
	173	7	4

Amethyst.

Entry as foreign wt. no Trade	£5	6	0

Parramatta.

Entry	2	0	0
Wharfage on 65 Casks Pork	1	12	6
	3	12	6

Colonial Vessels, Vizt.

Entry of 59 Vessels from Hawkesbury wt. 1,693 Bushels of Wheat and 20,577 of Maize at 2s. each is	5	18	0
Of 18 Do. from Broken and Botany Bay with 5,327 Bs. of Lime	1	16	0
Of 16 Vessels from Newcastle with 107 Ton of Coals, and 36,754 Superficial feet of Cedar at 5s.	4	0	0
Of 2 Vessels from the Fegee Islands wt. 248 Ton of Sandal Wood, 1 ton of Coir for making Rope and 3 Casks of Hogs Lard	0	10	0
Of 1 Vessel from Otahaitee wt. 55 Casks of Pork	0	5	0
Of 5 Vessels from the Fishery and Norfolk Islands, importing 29 Ton of Oil 11,304 Seal Skins, 31 Boxes of Soap and 24 Casks of Pork	1	5	0
Duties on Oils and Cedar from Newcastle imported by the for 115 Vessels	29	17	0
	15	17	0
	59	8	0

Rob. Campbell, Naval Offr.

[Enclosure No. 2]—*continued.*

STATE of the Funds arising from the Entrys and Duties on Ships, fines levied, &c., &c., at the 31st day of December, 1807, vizt:

Balance on the Treasurer's Account with the Trustees of the Orphan Institution for their proportion ..	£269	0	0
Balance on the Treasurer's Account with the Trustees of the Jail Fund	1,822	16	6
	£2,091	16	6

N.B.—The exportation Duty on 291 Tons of Sandal Wood, being the remainder of the Quantity imported from the Fegee Islands last Year and not yet exported will make an additional Fund of £727 10s., being at the rate of £2 10s. pr. Ton when shipt.

ROB. CAMPBELL, Treasurer.

Sydney, New South Wales, 31st Decem'r, 1807.

[Enclosure No. 3.]

MR. ROBERT CAMPBELL TO GOVERNOR BLIGH.

Sir, Sydney, 11 March, 1808.

I conceive it my duty to inclose your Excell'y the Report of the Arrivals and Departures of Ships, from the 1st of July to the 31st of Decemb'r last, an Abstract of the Duties collected by me as Naval Officer from the date of my Appointment with a general state of the remaining Funds amounting to £2,091 16s. 6d. exclusive of the Duty that would arise on the exportation of the Sandal Wood imported last Year; and of this sum there was expended when your Excellency was dispossessed of your just and beneficient government on the 26 of January by Major Johnston and other usurpers, £68 19s. 6d., and as I was publickly dismissed on the subsequent day, the Accounts and Money were ordered to be transferred to Mr. Thomas Jamieson who was appointed Naval Officer and Collector of Duties in my room.

I have, &c.,
ROB. CAMPBELL.

LIEUTENANT-COLONEL FOVEAUX TO VISCOUNT CASTLEREAGH.

(Despatch marked A, per ship Rose.)

My Lord, Sydney, Port Jackson, 4th September, 1808.

The despatches transmitted from hence by Major John-ston in May and June last by the Ships Dart and Brothers* will have apprized your Lordship of the change which has been made

* Note 178.

1808.
4 Sept.

in the Government of this Country, and will enable your Lordship to conceive my Surprize and concern at finding myself call'd upon at the moment of my arrival to assume the Command of the Colony, under circumstances so very unexpected and embarassing.

Foveaux
informed of
Bligh's arrest.

On approaching the harbour on the 28th of July, it was reported to me that Governor Bligh was in a state of Arrest, and in a few minutes after I received this information a letter was delivered to me from the Governor, in which he desired an interview at Government House.

The astonishment I felt at the report of the Governor's Arrest was increased on observing that, in naming the persons he had deputed to wait upon me, he had spoken of a Mr. Fulton (a man whom I had known in Norfolk Island in the condition of an emancipated convict) as his friend; and this circumstance

Justification
of arrest of
Bligh.

strongly tended to confirm the information I had at first received —that the Governor had been chiefly guided by persons of that Class, in following whose advice, it has been since proved to me, he had so violated private property, and had so tyrannized over the colonists, that nothing but his removal from the Government could have prevented an insurrection, with all its attendant miseries.

When my arrival was announced to Major Johnston, he waited on me on board the Sinclair, and having briefly reported the State of the Colony, and the circumstances which induced him to assume the Command, he submitted to me copies of his letters to your Lordship, with their numerous inclosures.

Johnston's
reports to
Foveaux.

When I had examined them, and made every enquiry from those persons whom I knew to be most capable of giving me correct information, and on whose word, from my knowledge of their characters and veracity, I could place every confidence, My

Foveaux's
decision.

Mind was fully satisfied of the unavoidable necessity of the measures which had been taken, and that I had no choice left me but to maintain the Government in the way it was resigned into my hands.

On the following morning the same persons who had before waited on me from the Governor came on board, and delivered to

Bligh's
demand to be
reinstated.

me a written Requisition from him to use every means in my power to reinstate him in the Government; But as I had by this time received the most convincing evidence of the abhorrence in which he is held, and that he had not only oppressed the Colonists by the most unheard-of means; but, in the execution of a plan to improve his own fortune, had sacrificed the interests of Govern-

1808.
4 Sept.

ment by a wasteful expenditure of the Public Stores, and the most glaring appropriation of the Live Stock and labourers of the Crown to his own private purposes, I resolved on seeing him, and explicitly communicating my determination not to comply with his request.

On my landing (on the 29th of July), I was met by the whole body of Officers, Civil and Military, and the principal inhabitants with the exception of a few who have been pointed out in Major Johnston's Letters as the promoters of the disorders of violences which were committed under the Government of Captain Bligh.

Foveaux's
reception in
the colony.

Immediately after, I waited on the Governor at Government House, and on our Meeting presented him with a paper containing my Resolution not to interfere with his suspension, which, having read, he requested that it might be put in the form of a letter, and after a general and uninteresting conversation, we parted.

Refusal to
reinstate Bligh.

Having referred to Lord Hobart's Instructions,* dated 24th June, 1803, I assumed the Command of the Colony as Acting Lieutenant-Governor, in the absence of Lieutenant-Governor Paterson, which I signified by a Proclamation, and at the same time I made arrangements to despatch the Colonial Vessel Estramina to Port Dalrymple to report my arrival and the steps I had taken.

Command
assumed by
Foveaux.

A few days unavoidably passed in preparing the Vessel for sea, and adverse winds prevented her proceeding on her voyage till the 21st of August.

Reports sent
to Paterson.

I have the honor to enclose your Lordship a copy of my letter by the Estramina, by which you will more fully learn my opinion with regard to the State of the Colony previous to my arrival, and the general sentiments which prevail amongst all classes of the people at the time of my taking Command.

Your Lordship will have naturally entertained an expectation from the letters of Major Johnston, wherein he reported his intention to dispatch His Majesty's Ship Porpoise to Port Dalrymple, in compliance with Lieutenant-Governor Paterson's Order, that I should find the latter in the Command of the Colony; But I have to lament that an erroneous report which had reached him of my holding the Appointment of Lieutenant-Governor of the Territory, operated so forcibly on his mind as to prevent him from leaving Port Dalrymple, as is explained in the enclosed letter.

Causes of
Paterson's
remaining
at Port
Dalrymple.

Your Lordship will also learn from my letter to Lieut.-Governor Paterson, that the Porpoise unfortunately struck the ground and

The disposal
of H.M.S.
Porpoise.

was very materially injured at Port Dalrymple when sent thither for the Lieutenant-Governor, and that when her repairs are completed, great difficulties are to be apprehended respecting her future disposal, Governor Bligh continuing to manifest a resolution to perplex the public service by every artifice in his power, and by obliging the acting-Commander of that Vessel, by His order, to pay no attention to the requisitions I have found it necessary to make.

General report
on Johnston's
administration.

The short time I have in the Settlement, and the variety of urgent and unpleasant matters which have pressed upon my attention, have prevented me from preparing returns of the State of the Colony; but it is with much pleasure, I assure your Lordship, that a System of the strictest economy has been observed ever since the suspension of Governor Bligh's Authority, and that the utmost attention has been paid to supply the Dependant Settlements of Port Dalrymple and the Derwent; insomuch that Lieut. Governor Paterson has reported the former to be in the possession of provisions for 12 months, and Lieut. Governor Collins has requested that no more might be sent to him, as he wanted sufficient Storehouses to contain them.

Expenditure
incurred by
Johnston.

I have every reason to believe that the whole amount of the expences incurred during the Command of Major Johnston, for which it will be needful to draw Bills on His Majesty's Treasury, will not exceed £4,000.

But though it has been that Officer's particular wish to close his Public Accounts to forward by this Conveyance, so many obstacles have been created in the Commissary's Office that it has been found impossible to get them made up.

Confirmation
of Fitz's
appointment
by Foveaux.

Having found Mr. Fitz one of the Deputy Commissarys appointed by Major Johnston to adopt means for the preservation and improvement of the Government Herds of Cattle, which have been in a state of the greatest confusion and rapidly declining, I have confirmed the appointment, and have ordered him to be entirely employed in the management of that very important concern, which now requires an increased degree of care from the neglect which it suffered under the direction of Superintendant Jamison.

Dismissal of
Andrew Hume.

A person by the name of Hume, who succeeded the former Superintendant, has proved so unworthy by indications of dishonesty as his predecessor was from inattention, and he, therefore, has also been dismissed.

This circumstance has considerably augmented the labours of Mr. Fitz, and placed him under the necessity of often travelling

from one extremity of this Settlement to the other, for which, as 1808.
4 Sept.
it also puts him to a great expence, I have promised to allow him
a compensation of ten shillings per day, to be paid in Cattle, the Remuneration allowed to Fitz.
produce of the herds, at £28 each.

The integrity and diligence of Mr. Fitz makes me feel confident that the public interest will derive great advantages from
this management, and I respectfully hope that as no real
additional expense will be incurred it will receive your Lordship's approbation.

I enclose a return of the present State of the Cattle, and as the Returns of live stock.
herds are now all properly divided, and the animals of different
kinds separated from each other, it may be expected that their
increase will be great and their condition much improved.

It will be satisfactory to your Lordship to learn that grain of
every kind is now in the greatest abundance thro'out the Settlement, and that the growing crops bear the most promising Prospects of harvest.
appearance.

I have not as yet had time to remove from headquarters, but I
am informed there is an immense quantity of Maize lying Absorption of surplus grain.
unhoused and perishing, the owners setting but little Value upon
it for want of a Market. This is an evil which cannot but prove
a great check upon industry, and will, I fear, be a long time
before it can be obviated; But as the rearing and feeding of
Hogs will occasion a great consumption of corn, I intend to
offer 1s. per pound for Swines' flesh for the use of His Majesty's
Stores, which by increasing the demand for grain, will tend to
encourage the cultivation, and thereby promote the interest of
the Colony.

I also intend to offer the same price for beef and mutton, for Beef and mutton to be purchased by government.
unless the grazier can find a certain market for his produce, the
Colony will yet be many years dependent on Great Britain for a
large portion necessary for the supply of its inhabitants.

When this price has operated to increase the quantity equal to
the demand, there will be a competition amongst the breeders,
and that competition will naturally produce abundance in the
Market at a reduced price.

The judicious exchange which has been made by Major John- Cattle bartered for grain by Johnston.
ston of the aged and refuse cattle from the Government herds has
obtained a Supply of near 12,000 bushels of Wheat and Maize,
and engagements have been made for the receipt of as much more
upon the same terms as will abundantly Supply this Settlement
for the remainder of the present year. Twenty-eight pounds per
head has been the price fix'd on the Cattle, and the wheat taken

1808.
4 Sept.

in exchange from the Settlers has been received at ten Shillings, and the Maize at five Shillings per Bushel. A great saving of Salt Provisions has also arisen from supplying the Civil and Military Establishments with fresh beef.

Commissariat
returns to be
prepared.

Complete returns will, I hope, be got ready previous to the arrival of Lieut.-Governor Paterson, of every receipt and expenditure that has taken place in His Majesty's Stores; and if unexpected circumstances should detain the Lieut.-Governor at Port Dalrymple, they shall, when made out, be transmitted to your Lordship, with the survey of remains of provisions and Stores which was taken on the suspension of Mr. Palmer.

At the same time that I assure your Lordship that no exertion of mine shall be wanting to enforce the performance of this necessary duty, I am concerned to represent that it will be obtained with difficulty, because the greater part of the persons employ'd in the Commissary's Office are not to be depended upon, the whole being averse to the economical system that has been introduced, and anxious to be restored to the enjoyment of their former enormous perquisites.

Allegations of
abuses in the
commissariat
department.

It appears that from the commencement of Captain Bligh's Government the public property has been made a prey of by the lowest assistants in Mr. Palmer's Office, who, closely following the example set them by their Superiors, have carried their depredations to a surprising extent, which they have accomplish'd with the greatest artifice and success; and, altho' the fact is unquestionable, it would be impossible, in the peculiar situation of the Colony, to find persons more honestly disposed to fill their places should their removal be attempted.

However, as I am convinced that unless some striking example be made, the abuses introduced by Mr. Palmer can never be effectually eradicated, I am determined to turn my attention to that particular object, in the hope of devising means to ensure the public conviction of some of the principal delinquents in that Department.

Litigation to be
discouraged.

Another equally important consideration will be in what manner to correct the pernicious effects which have arisen from Governor Bligh's encouragement of a class of persons who have most successfully employ'd themselves in promoting a spirit of litigation in the Colony under the guidance and example of the notorious George Crossley.

Suits pending
before the civil
court.

There are at least one thousand Suits now pending before the Court of Civil Judicature, which may be expected to give rise to numerous appeals, and these will be render'd so intricate by artful statements, supported by false oaths, that it will be almost impossible to discover the truth; and such great uncertainty prevails that people of character, whose claims are just, often prefer sacrificing their property to encountering the difficulties and delays of a legal process, or to be exposed to the horrible calumnies which the wretches who have been suffered to officiate as lawyers never fail to invent, and prepare evidence to support.

1808.
4 Sept.

As a preliminary to the reform of this monstrous abuse, I have considered it adviseable to forbid any person from interfering without proper authority in the Management of causes pending before the Court.

Advocates to be approved.

Before I terminate this Subject, it is incumbent on me to acquaint your Lordship that, although Major Johnston did not intend to appoint an Acting Judge-Advocate until the arrival of the Lieutenant-Governor or myself, the urgent State of the affairs of the Colony obliged him to depart from this Resolution, and to name Captain Kemp, of the New South Wales Corps, to perform the duties of that Office.

Appointment of Kemp as judge-advocate by Johnston.

That Officer accepted the Appointment with great reluctance, and with the positive assurance that he should be relieved from it whenever a proper person could be found to succeed him.

At the first Criminal Court which assembled after Captain Kemp's Appointment, Mr. Gore, the suspended Provost-Marshal, was, in the ordinary course of business, brought up for tryal on a charge of Perjury perfer'd against him by the Officers of the Court accused by Governor Bligh of treasonable practices (the particulars of which have been detailed to your Lordship in Major Johnston's letter of the 11th of April last).

Trial of Gore for perjury.

Mr. Gore having contumaciously disputed the legality of the Court, and refused to plead to the Indictment, there remained no alternative but to pass the Sentence of the Law upon him, which was that he should be transported for the term of Seven Years, in consequence of which he was sent to the Coal River by Major Johnston.

A moderate Volume would not be sufficient to contain a Statement of the Frauds and Offences committed by this man since the first moment of his arrival in the Colony; And, altho' his character of atrocities were perfectly known to Governor Bligh, and persons whom he had swindled frequently solicited redress, he was suffer'd to trespass with impunity upon the laws, and to indulge himself in the most expensive habits at the cost of the unfortunate people whom he plundered and insulted.

Charges made against Gore.

It is with the utmost satisfaction I am enabled to confirm to your Lordship the high character which all former Governors have justly given of the good conduct and strict discipline of the

1808.
4 Sept.

Approbation
of the New
South Wales
Corps.

New South Wales Corps, and that I can assure you, with the utmost truth, that their claim to approbation has not been in the slightest degree shaken by the late events which have agitated the Colony—a circumstance the more remarkable when the exasperating conduct and intemperate language used by Governor Bligh towards them on a Variety of Occasions is consider'd.

Want of proper barracks.

After the length of time the Colony has been established, it will, perhaps, surprise your Lordship to learn that there are not barracks enough for more than half the strength of the Regiment, and that what are built are unprovided with the usual furniture, and have neither Kitchens nor cooking places, nor, in fact, any of the accommodations requisite for the comfort or convenience of the Officers or Soldiers; and that they are without any fence or enclosure, and, consequently, there is no other Security to prevent the men from mixing with the Convicts than their own good inclinations and sense of propriety.

Reinforcements quartered in a granary.

The reinforcements which arrived in the Sinclair and Recovery I have been obliged to quarter in one of the Granaries, and, altho' the building is almost indispensable for the purpose for which it was constructed, yet the Soldiers must continue to occupy it until some addition can be made to the Barracks, which, from want of Artificers and properly qualified Superintendants, will be a work of much difficulty, and will require a considerable time to execute.

Erection of storehouse at Parramatta.

At present the principal Artificers are employ'd in erecting a substantial stone Storehouse at Parramatta, the old one having entirely fallen into ruin. Much inconvenience and expence has been hitherto sustained by building the Stores at a distance from the waterside. The new Store now building is situated so close to the water that boats of burden can approach it and receive and discharge their Cargoes with the greatest ease, and without the expence of any additional labourers.

Exchange of land with Macarthur.

Government having no land possessing this advantage of situation are indebted to Mr. McArthur for the Grant of an Acre and a half, which will be sufficient for a very extensive range of buildings, and for which he has declined accepting any other equivalent than a piece of Land of equal extent in the vicinity of this town.*

Storehouses to be erected at Sydney.

Great labour and cost will be prevented by having the whole of the Public Stores contiguous to the water. I shall, therefore, make immediate arrangements to commence buildings on a similar plan at this place; and if, for want of time, it should be out of my power to complete them, I shall endeavour to impress upon my Successor in command the advantages which will be derived

* Note 180.

from stores so situated; at present they are at such a distance
from the Wharf that a large number of men are almost constantly
employ'd in removing provisions; and when there are Ships to
discharge of their cargoes, every other necessary work is unavoidably suspended to prevent them coming on demurrage.

This despatch will be delivered to your Lordship by Captain Despatch
Symons, of the Royal Navy, whose knowledge of the Colony and entrusted to
Symons on the
of Governor Bligh's Violence and Oppression particularly qualifies Rose.
him to explain any points on which your Lordship may desire
further information; the Governor, aware of this, has exerted
himself to prevent Capt'n Symons's return to England, and has
received much assistance from Messrs. Campbell & Co., part
owners of the Rose, who are entirely under his influence, and are
besides anxious on their own accounts to prevent any one from
having a passage in that Vessel to whom I could entrust my
Despatches with the least confidence of their being safely delivered.   I have, &c.,
                                              J. FOVEAUX.

[Enclosures Nos. 1, 2, and 3.]

*[These consisted of the letters and order forwarded as en-
closures numbered 1, 3 and 4 to Governor Bligh's despatch to
Viscount Castlereagh, dated 31st August, 1808.]*

[Enclosure No. 4.]

EXTRACT of a Letter from the Secretary of State to Lieutenant- Instructions to
    Colonel Foveaux, dated Downing-street, 24th June, 1803.   Foveaux to
act as lieut.-
You will perceive that it is His Majesty's Pleasure that Lieu- governor.
tenant-Colonel Paterson should proceed to the proposed Colony,
and that you should return to Head Quarters, where you will, in
Colonel Paterson's absence, execute the duties of Lieutenant-
Governor, as you will continue to enjoy the Appointment you
have hitherto received in Norfolk Island.

                                              HOBART.

[Enclosure No. 5.]
PROCLAMATION.

JOSEPH FOVEAUX,   Sydney, 30th July, 1808.

As the Government of this Colony has been upwards of six Foveaux's
months out of the hands of William Bligh, Esquire, and as the reasons for
refusal to
circumstances attending his suspension have been fully sub- reinstate Bligh.
mitted to His Majesty's Ministers, who alone are competent to
decide, Lieutenant-Governor Foveaux conceives it to be beyond
his Authority to judge between Captain Bligh and the Officer
whom he found in the actual command of the Colony.

1808.
4 Sept.

Policy to be
adopted by
Foveaux.

In assuming the Administration of the Government until His Majesty's pleasure shall be known, Lieutenant-Governor Foveaux is determined to adopt such measures as he deems to be most effectual for the preservation of the public tranquillity and the Security of public and private property; and to follow, in the discharge of the arduous duties imposed upon him, a system of the strictest œconomy and the most impartial justice between persons of every description.

Finucane
appointed
secretary to
Foveaux.

All reports, communications, and other correspondences relating to public business are to be transmitted to James Finucane, Esquire, who is appointed Secretary to Lieutenant-Governor Foveaux.

God Save 'the King!

By Command of His Honor the Lieutenant-Governor.

JAMES FINUCANE, Secretary.

[Enclosure No. 6.]

LIEUT.-COLONEL FOVEAUX TO LIEUT.-GOVERNOR PATERSON.

Sir,   Sydney, 16th August, 1808.

I have the honor to report to you that I arrived here on the 28th of last month, and on the following day landed and assumed the Command of the Colony, having been directed by the Secretary of State (an extract* of whose letter I annex) to execute the duties of Lieutenant-Governor during your absence.

Command
assumed by
Foveaux.

Inquiry into
the causes of
Bligh's arrest.

Having found the late Governor (Captain Bligh) in a State of Arrest, I endeavoured to inform myself of the causes which led to his being so, by enquiries from every description of persons whose information was mostly likely to enable me to form a judgment of the truth; and altho' these enquiries have discovered to me that a great difference of opinion has prevailed amongst the Officers, as well as amongst the other principal inhabitants, on many points since that event took place, yet the whole were and still continue unanimous in their Sentiments of the absolute necessity of suspending Captain Bligh from the Government as the only means of preventing an insurrection.

It appears that Captain Bligh has been principally advised by George Crossley, Messrs. Campbell, Palmer, and Fulton; and it is generally believed that they intended to have established a monopoly of the Public Stores and revenues of the Colony at the expense of the interests of Government as well as of every individual unconnected with themselves. In the prosecution of

Allegations of
conspiracy
against Palmer
and others.

* Note 179.

their plans they have gone such lengths, by violating private property and infringing personal liberty, as to occasion universal terror amongst all classes of people from the highest to the most obscure; and this apprehension still prevails to such a degree, that I saw no choice left but to maintain the Government in the way I found it, until I shall either be relieved by your arrival or shall receive the Orders of His Majesty's Ministers.

*1808.
4 Sept.*

Decision to continue the suspension of Bligh.

The accompanying correspondence,* which has taken place between Captain Bligh and myself, will inform you how extremely desirous he is of being reinstated in the Government, although nothing can be more certain that his own destruction, as well as that of any person who might attempt to restore him, would be the inevitable result of such a step.

Bligh's desire to be reinstated.

I lament that there is no Vessel here at present except the Estramina by which I can forward this dispatch, the Porpoise being under repair for the damages she received when she struck the ground at Port Dalrymple, and, from all the information I can collect, she will require near two months to fit her for sea. And even when ready, I cannot depend upon her being at my disposal, as Captain Kent professes himself to be entirely under the control of Captain Bligh, whom he expresses a wish to receive on board, and whose orders alone, as his Commanding Officer, he seems determined to obey.

Repairs to H.M.S. Porpoise.

You will observe that Captain Bligh has declared his intention of proceeding to England in the Porpoise, and has issued his orders for the necessary arrangements for that purpose to Captain Kent, which orders he has hitherto thought proper to obey. But as Captain Bligh is in a State of Arrest, there appears to me to be great inconsistency in suffering him to exercise any authority whatever; yet I find myself unable to devise a safe method of preventing it, from the apprehension of improperly interfering with the regulations of the Naval Service.

Bligh's orders to Kent.

From all these circumstances, it must be evident how anxious I feel to be released from the embarrassments which press upon me, either by your arrival or by receiving the Instructions of His Majesty's Ministers for my future guidance, most particularly with respect to the disposal of Captain Bligh, should he not really mean to carry into effect the intention he has expressed of going to England in the Porpoise.

Foveaux's desire to be relieved.

It is incumbent on me to assure you that I have already per- fectly satisfied myself that Captain Bligh has been acting on a settled plan to destroy and ruin the better Class of Inhabitants, and that Major Johnston is in possession of incontrovertable proofs of his being guided in the most important concerns of the

Foveaux convinced of Bligh's guilt.

* Note 181.

1808.
4 Sept.

Colony by the advice of Crossley, your knowledge of whom will enable you to judge in what a dreadful State the whole Settlement must have been involved previous to the change which Major Johnston was called upon to effect.

Necessity for
immediate
decision.

Should your health, or any other circumstance, prevent your taking a passage in the Estramina, I feel it my duty to impress upon you that the interests of this Colony require that some settled plan should be immediately adopted for its Government, and that a determination should be formed (whatever established regulations it may interfere with) to hasten the departure of Captain Bligh, as, from the intriguing disposition of him and his partizans, the public mind will continue unsettled, and perturbed as long as he is suffered to remain in the Colony.

Instructions
relating to
settlements at
Hobart and
Port
Dalrymple.

. I enclose you an extract of Lord Castlereagh's letter of the 31st of December* last, relative to the affairs of the Settlements at Port Dalrymple and the Derwent, by which you will learn the views of Government respecting the latter, and their expectation that the most economical System shall be pursued by Lieut.-Governor Collins, and that he shall have the sanction of the Officer in Command here for every material arrangement he may find it necessary to make for carrying on the Public Service.

Should you not take your passage in the Estramina, I have to request you will be pleased to order her to return here immediately, as it will be necessary to despatch her as soon as possible to Norfolk Island.   I have, &c.,

J. FOVEAUX.

[Enclosure No. 7.]

MAJOR JOHNSTON TO LIEUTENANT-GOVERNOR PATERSON.

Headquarters, Sydney, New South Wales,
Sir,   18th April, 1808.

I have to acknowledge the receipt of Your dispatch of the 12th Ultimo, by the Harrington.

The arrival of the Porpoise at Port Dalrymple will evince my

Paterson's
status as
lieut.-governor.

readiness to resign the Government of this Territory to You as its Lieutenant-Governor; And I beg You to be assured that had I entertained an idea that the Commission you received in 1802 had not been Superseded by your Appointment to a distant dependency, and by the Nomination of a Successor to You as Lieutenant-Governor of the Territory, I should have certainly solicited your return to Head Quarters at the time I reported the Change which I have been called to make.

The Accompanying Extract from my Letter to Lord Castlereagh by the Dart, will more properly explain the motives that

* Note 182.

have governed my Conduct in the arduous part Circumstances have called upon me to perform; And I hope you will be convinced how entirely unnecessary the Arrangements were, which You have considered it prudent to make with private individuals to secure Yourself a Conveyance to Port Jackson. 1808.
4 Sept.

It was my intention to transmit You by the Porpoise a Copy of my Letter to the Secretary of State, and of the Inclosures it contained, that were sent by the Dart on the 17th Instant; but the speedy departure of the Brothers and the short time I am informed the Rose is to stay here (by both which Ships You must see the necessity of my writing) has made it impossible. Inability to
transmit
duplicates of
despatches.

I therefore shall not attempt to give You any detail of what has occurred since the 26th of January, because an imperfect One would more tend to perplex than to inform You.

I shall cause every necessary paper to be prepared against your Arrival, and I shall do myself the Honor to wait on You on board the Porpoise with them, that You may have it in Your power to form a correct Opinion of what has been done, and in some degree to determine respecting the future disposal of Governor Bligh, who, I lament to say, I had it not in my power to send out of the Colony, before the receipt of Your Letter by the Harrington, for want of a Ship that could accomodate him and his Family, And from obstacles of his own creating which have prevented him from going on Board the Porpoise. Full papers to
be submitted
to Paterson.

Your dispatches to the Commander-in-Chief and to Lord Castlereagh have been forwarded by the Dart.

All the Stores we have it in our power to Supply have been sent, with One Thousand Bushels of Wheat and Seventy-Nine Bushels of Barley; the latter, I imagine, must be acceptable for Seed. Shipment of
stores to Port
Dalrymple.

I am, &c.,
GEORGE JOHNSTON.

[Enclosure No. 8.]

LIEUTENANT-GOVERNOR PATERSON TO MAJOR JOHNSTON.

Port Dalrymple, Van Dieman's Land,

Sir, 14th May, 1808.

In acknowledging the receipt of Your despatch of the 18th Ult'o by His Majesty's Ship Porpoise with a small Supply of Provisions and Stores, I have to express my satisfaction at Your attention to my desire, and regret that I was not in possession earlier of the reasons that actuated You in forwarding me, in January last, Your Information of the Important Change in the Government at Port Jackson by such a Conveyance as rendered Paterson's
satisfaction
at Johnston's
explanation.

1808.
4 Sept.

my passage by its return impossible, stating at the same time my
reasons in making any reference to a private channel to procure
such Conveyance, arose from the apprehension of a possibility
that in so extraordinary a Crisis other employments might have
taken place for the Government Vessels, that the Porpoise might
be on her passage to England, or that other Changes equally
unexpected and equally affecting my peculiar Situation might
have ensued. I must, however, at the same time also add that it
did appear to me somewhat wanting of explanation why, at a
moment of such serious suspension of the Supreme power, and
from such Causes as have actuated it, it did not immediately
occur to require the presence and the Assistance in so unprecedented a juncture, of the Officer who by such Suspension
unquestionably from two evident reasons became the Chief in
Command; and altho' I am persuaded Your Experience in the
Service, Your regard for the real Interests of the Territory, and
Your Judgment in the steps consequent on the necessity of their
support at so alarming a period, could not have been exceeded
by any efforts of mine, yet it did, and does yet, appear to me,
that no option was left to either of us, that You, only temporarily
holding the Command until I could take it, did not depend on
our Individual choice, but that it followed and became evident
from the very nature of the Circumstance itself.

I am, however, gratified, from the explanation of Your Last,
at seeing the belief I had entertained confirmed, that the Conduct
You have pursued in the Instance in question has arisen from
opinion of its propriety, although I may differ on the basis of
such Opinion, and for which difference I shall state my reasons,
which are briefly that I have always believed, when required by
His Majesty's Ministers to leave the Head Quarters of the Government, it was in the Capacity of the Lieutenant-Governor of the
Territory to act from the experience it might be supposed I had
acquired in the temporary direction of an experiment of which
success was doubtful, and my Orders from the late Governor
King on the occasion are expressly addressed to me as such
"Lieut.-Governor of the Territory"; but I have never conceived
that my having been pointed out to be employed for the time
being on an extra and arduous duty, because my Offices during
the presence of the Governor could be dispensed with at Head
Quarters, could in any manner imply a supercession of my
priority of Command in the Case of His death or absence from
his Government; nor have I ever judged it either the Intention
of His Majesty that it has been so expressed by His Ministers, or
that it is in any point of view possible or consistent with the

Johnston's
delay in
sending for
Paterson.

Paterson's
difference of
opinion with
Johnston.

King's Service, that I should be placed under the Controul of a
Junior Officer. On the contrary, it has always appeared to me
that the same reasons which induced my being fixed on to fulfil
His Majesty's Intentions at Port Dalrymple must operate abso-
lutely in the necessity of my taking the Command of the Mother
Settlement in any accidental case of Interregnum in its regular
Government until an Officer appointed to the Duty by the
Crown should arrive, after the Ministers have received Informa-
tion of the Interreign.

Your Intimation of the Nomination of a Successor to me as the
Lieutenant-Governor, that such Nomination also Supersedes my
duty to take the Command agreeable to the Words of the Patent
" As the Officer highest in Rank," and the Statement that my
Successor was daily expected, has determined me, however, to
wait the event of the precise nature of his Commission being so
speedily made known, as my state of health renders the probability of my having early to return to this Settlement at the
present Season of serious consideration; for however I am convinced it cannot have been foreseen at home that it was likely
any Appointment given to Lieutenant-Colonel Foveaux should
place him in the Command of His Senior Officer, Yet, should
there at the same time arrive a Separate Commission ordering
me to remain in the direction of this small Settlement I shall
feel it necessary to chearfully obey it, hoping that a representation of my most singular Situation may immediately effect a
Change favourable to my Years and length of Service.

I have therefore stated my Intention to Captain Kent of not
embracing the opportunity of the Porpoise being at present in the
Harbour, but that I shall wait until I have such further Information as may correctly guide my Conduct; and I have to request
that You will (should You be still in the Command), by the
earliest possible opportunity, place me in possession of the first
Intelligence you may receive from England, that at this important moment no time may be lost in my concluding on a Subject
so materially affecting us both, and the Territory at large.

I am fully aware of the very arduous and constant occupation
that must have devolved on You, and that You can yet have had
but time to complete Your several dispatches to England; but,
trusting the Cause of my not having yet received them may have
in some measure subsided, I beg also to request You will favour
me with the Copies of the Papers You mention, not doubting but
You must apprehend my anxiety to be Acquainted with the whole
of the particulars involved in the Deposition of the late Governor.

I have, &c.,

WM. PATERSON.

1808.
4 Sept.

Accounts for
purchase of
provisions.

[Enclosure No. 9.]

THE Right Honorable the Lords Commissioners of His Majesty's Treasury in Account Current with James Williamson Esquire Acting Commissary of Stores and Provisions in His Majesty's Territory of New South Wales.

Dr.		£	s.	d.	Cr.		£	s.	d.
1808. Between the 31st July & 2nd Sept.	To Amount of Grain purchased from Individuals as per Voucher A	154	0	0	1808. Septr. 2nd.	By Two sets Bills drawn in favor of the following persons as per Vouchers. Orders and Receipts. Vizt.			
						No. 1 Bill in favor of Thomas Jamison Esqr. as per Voucher A Order and Receipt No. 1......	154	0	0
	,, Amount of Fresh Mutton from John McArthur Esqr. as per Voucher B.	125	7	0					
						No. 2 Bill in favor of John McArthur Esquire as per Voucher B Order and Receipt No. 2	125	7	0
		279	7	0			279	7	0

Approved: J. FOVEAUX.

Sworn before me this 2nd Sept., 1808: RICHD. ATKINS, J.A.

JAMES WILLIAMSON, Actg. Comy.

[Enclosure No. 10.]

LIEUTENANT-COLONEL FOVEAUX'S WARRANT TO ACTING-COMMISSARY WILLIAMSON.

1808.
4 Sept.
—
Foveaux's
warrant for
payment of
accounts.

BY His Honor Joseph Foveaux, Esquire, Lieut.-Governor of His Majesty's Territory of New South Wales, &c., &c.

YOU are hereby Ordered and directed to draw two Sets of Bills (No. 1 and 2) of Exchange on the Right Honorable the Lords Commissioners of His Majesty's Treasury, No. 1 in favor of Thomas Jamison Esquire, or Order, for the sum of One hundred and fifty four pounds Sterling, and No. 2 in favor of John McArthur Esquire or Order for the sum of One hundred and twenty five pounds Seven Shillings Sterling being to liquidate Receipts given in payment for two hundred and sixty Nine Bushels Wheat at ten Shillings per Bushel Seventy Eight Bushels Maize at five shillings per Bushel and two thousand five hundred and Seven pounds Mutton at One Shilling per pound purchased by my Orders for the purpose of Victualling those necessarily supported by the Crown between the 31st July and the present date.

Given under my Hand at Head Quarters, Sydney, this 2d Septr., 1808.

J. FOVEAUX.

[*Enclosure No. 11 will be found on page 640.*]

[Enclosure No. 12.]

ACTING-COMMISSARY WILLIAMSON TO LIEUTENANT-COLONEL FOVEAUX.

Sir, Commissary's Office, Sydney, Septemr. 2d, 1808.

I have the Honour to Acquaint You that the under-mentioned Quantities of Wheat, Maize and Animal Food have been purchased by your Orders from Settlers and others between the 31st July and the present date—Vizt. Two hundred and sixty nine Bushels Wheat, at Ten Shillings P'r Bushel, Seventy eight Bushels Maize at five shillings Per Bushel and two thousand five hundred and seven pounds Mutton at One Shilling Per Pound for the purpose of issuing Weekly as a Ration to those Victualled from the Public Stores at the different Settlements in this Colony. And that there are now Receipts delivered in for the said Wheat Maize and Mutton Amounting to Two hundred and Seventy nine pounds Seven shillings which were given in payment for the above and are ready for being liquidated by Bills on His Majesty's Treasury if it meets your approbation.

I have, &c.,

JAMES WILLIAMSON, Actg. Comy.

1808.
4 Sept.

Return of
live stock.

[Enclosure No. 11.]

A RETURN of Government Stock, and actual Numbers remaining on the 25th August, 1808.

Where kept.	Bulls.	Cows and Calves.	Cows in Calf.	Heifers.	Bull Calves.	Cow Calves.	Steers.	Work'g Oxen.	Fatten'g Oxen.	Total.	Stallions.	Geldings.	Mares.	Fillies.	Horse Foals.	Total.	Rams.	Breed'g Ewes.	Young Ewes.	Wethers.	Ewe Lambs.	Ram Lambs.	Total.
							Horned Cattle.					Horses.						Sheep.					
Parramatta								56		56	1					1	4			185			189
Toongabble	3		98		13	14				128			2		1	3							
Seven Hills	3		235		305	323	321		100	1,287													
Half-Way Pond			14	374	11	5				404													
Race Ground	6		138		15	5				164													
Castle Hill	2		137	13	10	10		17		189		1	9	7	7	24		333	134	145	30	27	669
Prospect Creek	2	370							296	668													
Devil's Back			4		1		328			333													
Connors', Kiss'g Point					2					2													
Sydney		20						67		87		13				13							
Lent to diff't persons								33		33		3				3							
Total	16	390	626	387	357	357	649	173	396	3,351	1	17	11	7	8	44	4	333	134	330	30	27	858

1808.
6 Sept.

LIEUTENANT-COLONEL FOVEAUX TO VISCOUNT CASTLEREAGH.

(Despatch marked B, per ship Rose.)

My Lord,   . Sydney, Port Jackson, 6th September, 1808.

In answer to your Lordship's dispatch of the 31st De- Impossibility of protection of crops at the Hawkesbury from floods. cember, 1807, Addressed to Governor Bligh, I am concerned to state that it is my fixed opinion that no precautions can be taken which will effectually secure the crops on the farms of the Hawkesbury from the consequences of the periodical floods which overflow its banks; And whilst our principal agricultural exertions are confin'd to that part, it is much to be fear'd that the distress's experienced by the Colonists in the year 1806 will frequently recur.

By referring to the chart of the country Your Lordship may discover that the principle part of the Settlers are established on small allotments of land, the whole of which are subject to be overflown, and that they consequently have no means of housing their grain in any Situation of Security.

On inquiring into the state of the wild cattle, I have not been The problem of the wild cattle. able to learn that any arrangements which have hitherto been made for taming them, or turning them, when slaughtered, to advantage, have been successful; And the genuine opinion entertained here is that they never can be productive of any essential benefit, but on the contrary afford a temptation to desperate and depraved convicts to establish themselves in the Mountains without the reach of controul, when the wild herds will supply a neverfailing source of Subsistence.

On this account I am of opinion that it is desirable that the Proposals for settlement of the Cowpastures. lands to the Westward of the Nepean should be settled as soon as possible by people of character, whose establishment may tend to prevent a banditti from resorting to the Mountains, and who, from their vicinity to the cattle, may perhaps devise some plan by which they may be made useful.

The accompanying return of Spirits which have been permitted Return of spirits landed. to be landed in this Settlement by Major Johnstone and myself is the best proof that I can submit to your Lordship of the attention which has been paid to enforce the established restrictions on their importation.

The whole of the Spirits which I have allowed to be landed Distribution of spirits to licensed publicans. have been distributed among the licensed publicans (who amount to 112, and pay a considerable annual tax for their licenses) at such prices as they could agree upon with the importers; And the quantity so distributed did not exceed ten gallons to each person.

It is proper, however, Your Lordship should be apprized that, in defiance of every precaution, there are numberless private Stills in the country, and that very large quantities of Spirits are

1808.
6 Sept.

Smuggling
and illicit
distilling.

unquestionably clandestinely imported, by which Means a class of persons, Many of whom ought never to have been raised beyond the condition of labourers, have amass'd large properties in the country; And truth impels me to declare that I know of no consequence which has arisen from the existing restrictions except that of Making the gentleman and the Man of character, who would blush at being detected in an illicit transaction, the tributaries of the daring and unprincipled Smuggler and distiller.

Maintenance
of the orphan
school.

I shall endeavour to maintain the Orphan School upon the plan introduced by Governor King, Altho', from the want of a proper person to intrust with the direction of the children, unavoidable abuses and irregularities will arise.

Erection of
churches.

I found the church* at the Hawkesbury completed, and that at Sydney so much so that public worship is now performed in it.

Impossibility
of reforming
female convicts.

It would be highly satisfactory could I give your Lordship any cause to hope that the morals of the female part of the convicts were likely to be reform'd; but I am concern'd to represent that the general loose and dissolute characters of the Settlers and their Servants—amongst whom the women are principally distributed—are more likely to confirm them in the practice of vice than to contribute to their amendment.

Cultivation
of hemp.

I shall endeavour to prevail upon the most industrious cultivators to sow what hemp seed they can procure. The quantity, however, will be very inconsiderable, as the whole of the seed sent from England when Governor Bligh came out proved to be entirely spoil'd, And most of the small stock of good Seed which Government possess'd was distributed by the Governor amongst people whose lands were not calculated for its growth, or who have paid no attention to its culture.

The
evacuation of
Norfolk Island.

Major Johnston's despatches by the Dart and Brothers will have acquainted Your Lordship that the evacuation of Norfolk Island has been too far carried into execution to admit of any arrangement for its re-establishment untill His Majesty's pleasure be known.

Relative
advantages of
Hobart and
Port
Dalrymple.

As I have at present no knowledge of the comparative excellence of the two Settlements of Port Dalrymple and the Derwent, Your Lordship will excuse my offering an opinion upon the subject, But any information that may be required respecting their harbours can be given to your Lordship by Captain Symons of the Royal Navy, who from frequent voyages to them in the execution of his professional duty is perfectly acquainted with them both.

I have avail'd. myself of the Rose's touching at the Derwent to transmit an extract of that part of Your Lordship's letter relative to the affairs of that Settlement to Lieut. Governor Collins, And I trust Your Lordship will approve of the Step I have deem'd it

* Note 183.

expedient to take in writing to the house of Messrs. Campbell and Hook to prevent their fulfilling a contract* which I heard by accident that Lieut. Governor Collins had entered with them for the supply of several hundred head of small Bengal cattle at a very heavy expence, of which no notification whatever was made to this Government.

Experience having proved that the delicate constitutions of cattle bred in India are very unfitted to resist the inclemencies of a country situated in a high latitude, and that on their first importation great Mortality amongst them would unavoidably ensue, I am intirely at a loss to conjecture Lieut. Governor Collins's motive for taking upon himself the responsibility of incurring so heavy an expence, as he must have been aware that the herds at Port Dalrymple, from which he could obtain supplies, are in a flourishing State, and that if further additions to the breeding stock at Van Diemen's land were requisite, they could be obtained here from the public herds, already seasoned to the climate, and of an infinitely superior kind to any he could expect from India, without any additional expence to Government.

The distress'd State of the Colony for medical aid, and the expression of Your Lordship's wish to provide such as could be obtain'd in this country, has induced me to appoint Mr. Wm. Redfern† to act as an Assistant Surgeon. As his skill and ability in his profession are unquestionable, and his conduct has been such as to deserve particular approbation, I beg to solicit for his confirmation.

I found all the gentlemen to whom grants of lands had been recommended by Your Lordship Already in possession of them, except Mr. John Blaxland, who has express'd himself dissatisfied with the arrangements made on his behalf by Major Johnston; but, as He returns to England in the Rose, I conceive any explanation or interference on my part unnecessary.

I have, &c.,
J. FOVEAUX.

[Enclosure No. 13.‡]

A RETURN of Spirituous Liquors imported by permission of Lieutenant-Governor Foveaux, from the 1st of August, 1808, to 6th of September following.

From What Vessel imported.	Number of Gallons.	How Distributed.
Sinclair	919	} Issued to 111 Licensed Persons.
Recovery........................	232	
Total	1,151	

THOS. JAMISON, Naval Officer.

* Note 184.   † Note 185.   ‡ Note 186.

Side notes:
1808. 6 Sept
Cancellation of contract for importing cattle.
Collins' action inexplicable.
Appointment of Redfern as assistant surgeon.
Return of spirits landed ex Sinclair and Recovery.

1808.
6 Sept.

Return of
spirits landed
ex Harrington,
Eagle, and
Rose.

A RETURN of Spirituous Liquors imported by Permission of Major Johnston, from the 27th of January, 1808, to the 31st of July following.

From What Vessel Imported.	Number of Gallons.	How Distributed.
Harrington......................	320½	Capt'n Campbell & Mr. Davidson.
Eagle	530	Government.
Rose .... {	526	Government.
	1,706½	Officers, Civil & Military, & others.
Total	3,083	

THOS. JAMISON, Naval Officer.

[Enclosure No. 14.]

LIEUTENANT-COLONEL FOVEAUX TO LIEUTENANT-GOVERNOR
COLLINS.

Sir,   Sydney, Port Jackson, 8th September, 1808.

I have the Honor to inform you that I arrived here on the
29th of July, and assumed the Command of the Colony in
obedience to Orders from the Secretary of State to act as Lieutenant-Governor during the absence of Lieut.-Governor Paterson.

The Inclosed Extract from Lord Castlereagh's dispatch, dated
31st December, 1807, will acquaint you that it is the intention of
His Majesty's Government that You shou'd obtain the sanction of
the Governor, or Officer in Command here, for any expences you
may incur for the Settlement at the Derwent, and I hope the
Supplies of Provisions sent You by Major Johnston will prevent
the necessity of any immediate reference on that head.

Having heard by accident that You had entered into an extensive Contract with the House of Messrs. Campbell and Hook for
the purpose of obtaining several Hundred Head of Bengal Cattle,
of which no intimation whatever had been given to this Government, and having ascertained by an Application to Messrs.
Campbell & Co., that such a Contract had absolutely been made, I
considered it my duty to write to them before it was possible for
them to send any Communication to India on the Subject; but
whether the expression of my Sentiments of the impolicy and
disadvantage of the Contract to Government will deter them from
executing it, I am unacquainted.

You must be sensible that any number of Horned Cattle from
India will on their first arrival require the assistance of a great
many Men, and as, from Your Own representation, you have not
any to spare (and there is no prospect of Your receiving a reinforcement from hence until more Convicts shall be sent from

England) the Importation of such a Cargo of Cattle at the 1808.
6 Sept. Derwent must very much increase the difficulties of which You complain.

And it is almost an absolute certainty that without proper Assistance the greater part of the Cattle would fall victims to the severity of a Climate to which they are unaccustomed.

Should it hereafter be considered advisable by You to encrease Cattle available at Sydney. the Number of Cattle on Van Dieman's Land by the Importation of more Breeding Stock, ample Supplies can be obtained from hence on Your applying for them, without any additional Expence to Government, hardy in Constitution, seasoned to the Climate, and infinitely better in Quality than any that can be procured from the East Indies.   I have, &c.,

J. FOVEAUX.

[Enclosure No. 15.]

LIEUTENANT-COLONEL FOVEAUX TO MESSRS. CAMPBELL AND HOOK.

Gentlemen,   Head Quarters, Sydney, 15th August, 1808.

Major Johnston having handed over to me the correspon- Campbell and Hook notified of Foveaux's disapproval of contract. dence relative to the contract entered into between you and Lieut. Governor Collins for supplying the Settlement of Hobartstown with five hundred Bengal cows and other cattle, I beg to inform you that any extraordinary expences incurr'd by that Settlement will not be approved by His Majesty's Government, unless previously sanctioned by the officer in command here, on which head particular instructions have been brought out by myself.

Considering the introduction of so large a number of Bengal Cattle to be altogether unnecessary, and that no sufficient reason can be assigned to justify the extraordinary expence of such an importation, I think it needful to acquaint you that it is my intention to take the earliest opportunity of conveying to His Majesty's Ministers my total disapprobation of such a Measure.

I am, &c.,

J. FOVEAUX.

[Enclosure No. 16.]

CONTRACT FOR THE IMPORTATION OF CATTLE. Contract made by Collins for the importation of cattle.

A CONTRACT having been entered into Between Robert Campbell Esquire of Sydney Merchant of the One Part, and David Collins Esquire Lieutenant Governor of His Majesty's Settlement at Hobart Town Van dieman's Land on the Other Part, for the purpose of supplying the said Settlement with Three Hundred of Cattle and other Articles therein specified, which Cattle and other Articles were to arrive at the said Settlement on or before the first day of. April One Thousand Eight Hundred and Eight, but unforeseen Circumstances having prevented the completion of the aforesaid Contract a part whereof only having been

1808.
6 Sept.

Contract made
by Collins for
the importation
of cattle.

dispatched from India and delivered in the said Settlement, and the same reasons still existing for wishing a supply of Cattle.

It is hereby consented to by the said Lieutenant Governor, that the part of the said Contract yet remaining to be fulfilled, that is to say the Importation of Three Hundred Head of breeding Cows is to be considered as still in force and extending the Term limited for their arrival unto the first day of May One Thousand Eight Hundred and Nine.

And in pursuance of the above Consent it is hereby covenanted, concluded and agreed upon this fourteenth day of June in the Year of Our Lord One Thousand Eight Hundred and Eight at Hobart Town Van dieman's Land between the said Lieutenant Governor Collins and Charles Hook Esquire, a partner in the House of Messrs. Campbell and Hook of Calcutta Merchants, for himself and the said Messrs. Campbells, that there shall be put on board a Ship or Ships Five Hundred Cows whose age shall not exceed four, or under two Years, One Stallion whose age shall not exceed four Years, and six draught Bullocks, all which said Cattle shall be Consigned to the said Lieutenant Governor David Collins or the Lieutenant Governor for the time being, such as may arrive in a Merchantable state to be paid for by Bills on His Majesty's Treasury at the following prices (Vizt.) for each Cow landed and delivered at Hobart Town Twenty six pounds, for each Calf which may be Calved on the passage, and landed and delivered as above Five pounds—for one Stallion .... and for each draught Bullock so landed ....

And the said Charles Hook for himself and the above mentioned Messrs. Campbell covenants and agrees with the said Lieutenant Governor David Collins, that the said Cows, Stallion and draught Bullocks shall be delivered in this Settlement (danger of the Seas and capture of the Enemy excepted) on or before the first day of May, One Thousand Eight Hundred and Nine; in failure of which He the said Charles Hook Esquire bindeth himself and the said Messrs. Campbells to the said Lieutenant Governor David Collins or the Lieutenant Governor for the time being in the Penal sum of One Thousand Pounds of lawful Money of Great Britain to be recovered and paid by these presents. In witness thereof the Parties to this Agreement have hereunto set their Hands and Seals this day and Year first above Written.   DAVID COLLINS.
                                         C. HOOK.

Signed, Sealed and delivered (where Stamps are not used) in the Presence of
               WM. COLLINS.

[Enclosure No. 17.]

CERTIFICATE OF EXAMINATION OF WILLIAM REDFERN.*

WE whose Names are hereunto subscribed do hereby certify that Certificate of We have examined Mr. William Redfern touching his Skill in examination of Wm. Redfern. Medicine and Surgery, and the other necessary collateral Branches of Medical Literature, and that We find him qualified to exercise the Profession of a Surgeon &c. And consequently to fill the Situation of an Assistant Surgeon in any Department of His Majesty's Service.

Given under Our Hands at Sydney in New South Wales this first day of September, 1808.

THOS. JAMISON, Principal Surgeon.

J. HARRIS, Surgeon, New So. Wales Corps.

WM. BOHAN, Assistant Surgeon New South Wales Corps.

LIEUTENANT-COLONEL FOVEAUX TO VISCOUNT CASTLEREAGH.

(Despatch marked C, per ship Rose.)

My Lord,   Sydney, Port Jackson, 6th September, 1808.

In reference to that part of my letter (A) relative to the Opposition to opposition attempted to be given by Messrs. Campbell & Co. to despatches in my dispatches being conveyed to England by Capt'n Symonds, I the ship Rose. beg leave to enclose for Your Lordship's perusal copies of the correspondence which took place with the Supercargo of the Rose on that occasion.

From these your Lordship will perceive that the Rose has navi- Infringement gated to the Eastward of the Cape of Good Hope without produc- Co'n'pany's ing a license from the East India Company or a clearance from charter. the Custom-house of London, a circumstance which excited my particular attention from its having been intimated to Me in England that she had taken from thence upwards of Eight thousand gallons of Spirits.

As I have the strongest reason to believe that the house of Security given Messrs. Campbell has made arrangements for a very extensive Campbell. importation of Spirits into this colony, I have deem'd it incumbent upon Me to oblige them to enter into a bond of four thousand pounds that they will Account to the Satisfaction of Your Lordship for any irregularity they May have committed, a reference which, I hope, will confine the Speculations of that house in future within limits prescribed by Law and the orders of His Majesty's Government.

I have, &c.,

J. FOVEAUX.

* Note 185.

1808.
6 Sept.

[Enclosure No. 18.*]

[1] JAMES FINUCANE TO RICHARD BROOKES.

Sir, Sydney, Headquarters, 31st August, 1808.

Symons to
carry
despatches *per*
the Rose.

Captain Symmonds, of the Royal Navy, having requested the necessary steps may be taken to secure him a passage in the Rose, agreeably to the Provision made on that head by Act of Parliament; And it being also of the utmost importance to His Majesty's Service that the Public Despatches to the Secretary of State should be taken Home by an Officer,—I am directed by Lieutenant-Governor Foveaux to require that You do give Orders to the Commander of the Ship Rose to receive Captain Symmonds on Board her, for which the usual Allowance will be paid by Government on Your arrival in England.

I am, &c.,

JAMES FINUCANE,
Secretary.

COPY of an Answer from Mr. Brookes, Supercargo of the Ship Rose, to a requisition from Lieut.-Governor Foveaux to receive Capt. Symmonds, of the Royal Navy, on Board, and provide him with a passage to England, as Bearer of the dispatches to Government.

Sir, Sydney, 1st September, 1808.

Brookes'
refusal to
accommodate
Symons.

I receiv'd Your Letter of the 30th August. In Answer thereto I have to observe that it's not in my power to take Mr. Symmonds, of the Royal Navy, on Board the Rose.

Any Public Despatches the Lieut.-Governor shou'd think proper to send by me I shall feel a pleasure in delivering.

I am, &c.,

RICH'D BROOKES.

[2] JAMES FINUCANE TO RICHARD BROOKES.

Sir, Sydney, 1st September, 1808.

Despatches to be
conveyed only
by an officer.

The Circumstance of Your having demanded a Bond of £500 from Mr. John Blaxland that he would take home no Letters in the Rose, and the close and intimate relation which is known to exist between Captain Bligh and Messrs. Campbell & Co., part Owners of that Ship, together with the great solicitude which the former has shown to prevent every respectable person leaving the Colony who can give Evidence of the real state of its Affairs, induces Lieut.-Governor Foveaux to entertain an Opinion that his dispatches can only be safe in the Charge of an Officer.

I am, therefore, directed to acquaint You that he will not sacrifice the good of the Service and the public future welfare of this

* Note 186.

Colony to a mere punctilio, nor will he patiently submit to a vexatious opposition to a request which he is satisfied never could have been refused but for sinister reasons.

You will, therefore, determine either to receive Capt'n Symmonds on Board or to prepare Yourself not to expect any future forbearance with respect to the Ship Rose.

I am, &c.,
JAMES FINUCANE.

[3] JAMES FINUCANE TO RICHARD BROOKES.

Sir, Headquarters, Sydney, 1st September, 1808.

As Lieut.-Governor Foveaux has discovered from Your Correspondence that the Rose left England without a Licence from the Hon'ble East India Company to Navigate to the Eastward of the Cape of Good Hope, and without entering into the Bond prescribed by Act of Parliament for securing the Company's privileges from being invaded, I am directed to enquire whether that Licence has been forwarded to you by the last Arrivals from England. I am, &c.,

Demand for the
license of the
ship Rose.

JAMES FINUCANE,
Secretary.

[4] RICHARD BROOKES TO JAMES FINUCANE.

Sir, Ship Rose, Sydney Cove, 2nd September, 1808.

I am at a loss to comprehend the meaning of the following Paragraph in Your Letter of Yesterday's date:—" You will therefore determine either to receive Capt'n Symmonds on Board, or to prepare yourself not to expect any further forbearance with respect to the Ship Rose."

I request being informed if His Honor Lieut.-Governor Foveaux intends to prevent the Ship Rose, now ready for Sea, from proceeding to England with the Cargo of Oil and Skins permitted to be Shipped on Board of her the 26th July last, agreeable to Lieut.-Governor Johnston's permission, Countersigned by the Naval Officer. I am, &c.,

R'D BROOKES.

[5] RICHARD BROOKES TO JAMES FINUCANE.

Sir, Ship Rose, Sydney Cove, 2nd September, 1808.

In Answer to your Letter of Yesterday's date, I am to inform you that the Hon'ble East India Company's Licence for the Ship Rose was to be forwarded to St. Helena, where she is to touch for Convoy on her present Voyage.

Papers of the
Rose in proper
form.

I think it a duty incumbent on me to State, for the Information of His Honor Lieut.-Governor Foveaux, that no Cargo

1808.
6 Sept.

would have been received on Board that Ship, nor any Clearance granted from the Custom-house at the Port of London, unless the Bonds which You allude to had been duly executed.

I am, &c.,

RICH'D BROOKES.

[6] JAMES FINUCANE TO RICHARD BROOKES.

Sir,   Head Quarters, Sydney, 2nd September, 1808.

The ship Rose to be seized as an illicit trader.

I am directed by Lieut.-Governor Foveaux to Acquaint You, in Answer to Your two Letters of this day, that from the Circumstance of the Rose having come into those Seas on a Trading Voyage, and having Imported into the Colony a large quantity of Spirituous Liquors, without producing any Clearance from the Port of London, or any Licence from the East India Company, he considers it his duty not to suffer so mysterious a transaction to pass without investigation.

Desirous to effect this by the most moderate means in his power, he had determined to Commission Capt'n Symmonds to explain the Affair to Government; but as You have thought proper to refuse that Officer a Passage in the Rose (altho' expressly required for the furtherance of His Majesty's Service), I am directed by the Lieut.-Governor to Acquaint you that he feels himself compelled to determine on seizing the Rose as an illicit Trader, and to detain her in this Port until he shall receive Instructions from England.

I am, &c.,

JAMES FINUCANE,

Secretary.

[7] RICHARD BROOKES TO JAMES FINUCANE.

Sir,   Sydney, 3rd September, 1808.

Consent of Brookes to Foveaux's demands.

Referring to Your Letter of Yesterday, and the Ship Rose having been since taken possession of by Thomas Jamison, Esq., Naval Officer, with a party of Soldiers, I beg leave to State, for the consideration of His Honor Lieut.-Governor Foveaux, that when I requested in my Letter of Yesterday to be informed if he intended to prevent the Rose from Sailing, it was done with no other view than to enable me to determine whether I should put myself to much inconvenience by taking Mr. Symmonds, or subject the Ship to detention; and being conscious of my own rectitude of Conduct, and that the Owners of that Ship have been duly Licensed by the Hon'ble Court of Directors of the East India Company to Navigate in those Seas, and that the quantity of Spirits was lawfully Shipped and regularly suffered to be Landed at this Port and the Derwent, I am ready to give such Security

as His Honor may require for my abiding by the decision of His
Majesty's Ministers, and will receive Capt'n Symmonds on Board
agreeable to your Letter of the 31st Ulto. in order that the Ship
may be permitted to proceed on her Voyage to England.

I am, &c.,
RICH'D BROOKES.

[8] JAMES FINUCANE TO RICHARD BROOKES.

Sir,   Headquarters, 3rd September, 1808.

I am directed by Lieut.-Governor Foveaux to Acquaint
You that he has received with much satisfaction the notification
of Your Intention to take Capt'n Symmonds on board the Rose,
it being infinitely more pleasing to him that the Circumstance of
the Rose navigating in those Seas without producing a Clearance
from the Custom House of London, or a License from the East
India Company, should be decided on in England than that the
Ship and Cargo should be detained here. You will therefore
receive no further interruption to proceeding on your Voyage.

Permission for the Rose to sail for England.

I am further Ordered to apprise You that the Serjeant of the
Guard on Board the Rose has reported some highly disrespectful
expressions which You uttered yesterday against the present
Government of the Colony.

Caution to Brookes re his conduct.

And I am directed to recommend to You more caution in
future, as a repetition of such language wou'd most probably
be productive of unpleasant Consequences.

I am, &c.,
JAMES FINUCANE,
Secretary.

LICENSE TO BE GRANTED TO THE ROSE BY THE EAST INDIA COMPANY.

Sir,   East India House, 13th August, 1807.

The Court of Directors of the East India Company have
considered your request that a License may be granted the Ship
Rose to proceed on a Voyage from London to Monte Video and
New South Wales with Colonial Stores, consisting of Foreign
Wines, Porter, Woollen Cloth, Cottons, Linens, Ironmongery,
Hats, Shoes, &c., on a Bond being entered into for the said
Stores being Landed in New South Wales; and further, that
leave may be granted for the said Ship to bring a Cargo of Oil,
Seal-Skins, and Wool, the produce of New South Wales, from
thence to London; and I have to acquaint You that the Court
have permitted You to Ship the Stores above-mentioned on the
Terms stated in your Memorial, and they have also resolved that
You be granted a License for the Rose to bring back a Cargo of

License to be granted to the ship Rose.

1808.
6 Sept.

License to be
granted to the
ship Rose.

Oil, Seal-Skins, and Wool, the produce of New South Wales, but not to lade back with any Articles the growth or produce of any other place within the Company's limits. I am, &c.,.

W. RAMSAY,
Secretary.

I do hereby Certify that the foregoing is a True Copy from the Original.   RICH'D BROOKES, Supercargo Ship Rose.

BOND ENTERED INTO BY RICHARD BROOKES.

Bond of
Richard Brookes
to appear in
England.

KNOW All Men by these presents that I, Richard Brookes, Supercargo of the Ship Rose, of London (now in Sydney Cove in the Territory of New South Wales) am held and firmly bound unto the Right Hon. Robert Stewart, commonly called Viscount Castlereagh, One of His Majesty's Principal Secretary's of State for the Colonies and War Department, or to the Secretary of State for the Colonies and War Department for the time being, in the penal Sum of Four Thousand Pounds of lawful British Money, to be paid by the said Richard Brookes or his certain Attorney, his Heirs, Executors, Administrators, or Assigns, For which payment well and truly to be made I bind myself, my Heirs, Executors, Administrators, and Assigns firmly by these presents.

Now Whereas the Said Ship Rose, of London, has Imported into this Colony a Cargo consisting of Spirituous Liquors, Wines, and other Merchandize without having any Port Clearance on Board from the Officers of His Majesty's Customs in London, And the said Ship Rose has been Navigated into those Seas being within the limits of the East India Company without any License or other Authority to shew for so doing except the annexed Letter from the East India Company's Secretary, in which it is to be observed no Spirituous Liquors are mentioned.

The Condition of this Obligation is such that if the within bounden Richard Brookes shall, within One Month after his arrival in England, explain in a satisfactory manner the above-recited circumstance to the Right Honorable Robert Stewart, commonly called Viscount Castlereagh, One of His Majesty's Principal Secretary's of State for the Colonies, or to the Principal Secretary of State for the Colonies for the time being, then this Obligation shall be void and of none effect, or else shall be and remain in full force and Virtue.

Sealed with my Seal, dated this twelfth day of September, in the Year of Our Lord One Thousand Eight Hundred and Eight.

RICH'D BROOKES.

Sealed and delivered in presence of:

WM. KENT.
J. STOAN.

LIEUTENANT-COLONEL FOVEAUX TO VISCOUNT CASTLEREAGH.

(Despatch marked D, per ship Rose.)

My Lord,   Sydney, Port Jackson, 6th September, 1808.

The present distress'd state of the Colony for labourers Shipment of particularly Mechanics who could give the least assistance in timber unavailable preparing timber for the purposes of ship building, as required through want by the Navy board in their letter to your Lordship of the 8th of of labour. January last,* makes it intirely impracticable to prepare a cargo for the Sinclair, and untill a reinforcement of Convicts shall arrive, I fear it will not be possible to get ready such a quantity of wood as might be considered an object in England.

Your Lordship however may be Assured that I shall not neglect ascertaining by what means so important an Object is most likely to be accomplished, and that I shall embrace the earliest opportunity of carrying the orders of Government into execution.   I have, &c.,
                                                        J. FOVEAUX.

LIEUTENANT-COLONEL FOVEAUX TO VISCOUNT CASTLEREAGH.

(Despatch marked E, per ship Rose.)

My Lord,   Sydney, Port Jackson, 8th September, 1808.   8 Sept.

I have the honor to acquaint your Lordship that in conse- Williamson quence of the inquiries which I reported (in my letter A) it was arrest for my intention to commence into the abuses in the Commissary's irregularities in department, satisfactory proof has been obtained of the Acting his department. Commissary Williamson having applied provisions from His Majesty's Stores to his private use, I have therefore placed him under Arrest, And have Ordered a general Court Martial to assemble on the 12th inst. for his tryal on the enclosed charges.

I have, &c.,
                                                        J. FOVEAUX.

[Enclosure No. 19.†]

CHARGES prefer'd against James Williamson Esqre. Deputy Com- Charges missary, And late Acting Commissary of Stores and pro- preferred against James visions, by order of His Honor Lieut. Governor Joseph Williamson. Foveaux.

1st. For having embezzled fresh and salted provisions and Maize from His Majesty's Stores between the 27th of January, 1808, And the 1st of September of the same year during which period he had the charge of His Majesty's Stores, as Acting Commissary.

* Note 187.   † Note 186.

1808.
8 Sept.

Charges
preferred
against James
Williamson.

2nd. For having within the same period directed the then acting Store Keeper Mr. James Wilshire to make a false entry of the weights of beef slaughter'd in His Majesty's Stores.

3rd. For having himself within the same period made false entries of the weights of beef slaughter'd in His Majesty's Stores.

Sydney, 5th Septr., 1808.

GOVERNOR BLIGH TO VISCOUNT CASTLEREAGH.

(Despatch per ship Rose; acknowledged by Viscount Castlereagh, 15th May, 1809.)

Government House, Sydney,

10 Sept.

Symons' return
without Bligh's
leave.

John Blaxland's
return to
England.

My Lord,   New South Wales, 10th September, 1808.

Since my Despatch of the 31st Ultimo I have been much surprised to find that the present Lieutenant-Governor has obliged Captain Brooks of the Rose to take home Acting Lieutenant James Symons, belonging to the Lady Nelson, Tender to the Porpoise, in defiance of all propriety and decorum, Lieutenant Symons having no authority from me to proceed, as he is deeply implicated in Mutiny and other offences.

Mr. John Blaxland also, who assisted in dispossessing me of my Government, is also allowed to leave the Colony, notwithstanding my remonstrance; and conceiving them both highly culpable, I enclose the Correspondence I have had on that subject, requesting Your Lordship will be pleased to judge whether they should be detained or not on their arrival in England.

I have, &c.,

WM. BLIGH.

[Enclosure No. 30.*]

GOVERNOR BLIGH TO LIEUTENANT-COLONEL FOVEAUX.

Sir,   Government House, Sydney, 1st September, 1808.

Bligh's demand
for the
detention of
Symons and
Blaxland.

Being informed that Acting Lieutenant James Symons is about to leave the Colony for England, I have to inform you he is an Officer in His Majesty's Naval Service under my Command, and concerned with the persons who dispossessed me of my Government. I therefore call upon you, in the name of my King and Country, to prevent the said Act'g-Lieutenant James Symons quitting this Territory until His Majesty's Pleasure be known.

And whereas Mr. John Blaxland, who assisted in dispossessing me of my Government, is, as I am informed, about to depart this Territory, I have likewise to call upon you to direct that he may be kept in the Colony until His Majesty's Pleasure be known.

I am, &c.,

WM. BLIGH.

* Note 186.

[Enclosure No. 31.]

LIEUTENANT-COLONEL FOVEAUX TO GOVERNOR BLIGH.

Sir,　　　　　　　　　Headquarters, 1st September, 1808.

Conceiving the return of Capt. James Symons to England
with my dispatches to be most essential to the good of the Service,
you may be assured that I shall persevere in my determination to
send him Home in the Rose.

Respecting Mr. John Blaxland, I beg to acquaint you that as
I know of no offence he has committed which can authorize his
detention either in this Colony or elsewhere, I must decline imposing any restraint upon him.

I have, &c.,
J. FOVEAUX.

Foveaux's
refusal to
detain Symons
and Blaxland.

[Enclosure No. 32.]

LIEUTENANT-COLONEL FOVEAUX TO GOVERNOR BLIGH.

Sir,　　　　　　　　　Headquarters, 1st September, 1808.

As you have been apprized by me of my intention of
sending Capt. Symonds to England as the Bearer of my dispatches to His Majesty's Government, I have to request information from you whether the order transmitted to that Officer by
Capt. Kent to repair on board the Lady Nelson was given with
your Sanction.　　　　　　　I have, &c.,
J. FOVEAUX.

Kent's orders
to Symons.

[Enclosure No. 33.]

GOVERNOR BLIGH TO LIEUTENANT-COLONEL FOVEAUX.

Sir,　　　Government House, Sydney, 1st September, 1808.

The Laws and Regulations of His Majesty's Naval Service
are as peculiar as their consequence is great. They will admit of
no Officer on shore, of what Rank soever he may be out of the
Naval Service, to interfere with it. If, therefore, you, Sir, take
the Naval department under your consideration and controul, I,
as a Prisoner, cannot prevent it. Whatever Captain Kent has
done, I suppose is from a General Order, in answer to his Letter
of the 29th Ulto., which I wrote yesterday, saying that the Officers
of the Porpoise must be according to the Establishment, which no
Naval Officer can change but by orders from the Admiralty. To
this, too, I have to inform you that Captain Kent, as Commander
of the Porpoise, has all the interior management of the Ship,
agreeable to a particular order from My Lords Commissioners
of the Admiralty.　　　　　　　I am, &c.,
WM. BLIGH.

Bligh's refusal
to allow
Foveaux's
interference in
naval matters.

1808.
10 Sept.

GOVERNOR BLIGH TO THE HON. WILLIAM POLE.

(Despatch per ship Rose.)

Government House, Sydney,

Sir,   New South Wales, 10th Septr., 1808.

Mutinous
conduct of
Symons.

In my Letter of the 30th of April last I mentioned to You for the information of My Lords Commissioners of the Admiralty that Acting Lieutenant James Symons had united with the Rebels here, and created himself Commander of the Porpoise. Since the appointment of Lieutenant Kent by me to the Command of the Porpoise, I find that Lieutenant Symons has so connected himself with Lieutenant-Colonel Foveaux that he has engaged to carry home his Despatches in the Rose without any permission from me or discharge from the Service. Of Lieutenant Symons's situation with respect to the Porpoise, their Lordships will be informed by the inclosed Orders given by me to Lieutenant Symons, marked A.

Bligh's orders *re*
naval officers.

During the time in which intercourse between me and the Officers of the Porpoise was prohibited, Lieutenant Ellison, by the order of Captain Kent at the request of Major Johnston, left the Porpoise and took the Command of the Lady Nelson Tender. In Consequence of this, Captain Kent wrote to me to know how he was to act with respect to him, the Vessel, and Lieutenant James Symons—in reply to which I sent him orders that Lieutenant Ellison and every Officer of His Majesty's Ship Porpoise must occupy their respective situations agreeable to the Establishment. It appears from the Correspondence (marked B) between Captain Kent and Lieutenant Symons, that the latter asserts he was discharged from the Porpoise, which assertion is not correct; for although he was superseded in the Command, he was not discharged from the Ship, and Captain Kent ought to have kept him on the Ship's Books. My situation as a Prisoner prevents my taking any farther steps at present to detain him, which it was the duty of Captain Kent to have done; but I submit to their Lordships, how he should be treated on his arrival in England, who was a Mutineer, Deserter, a Rebel Magistrate, and Member of their Criminal Courts.

Correspondence
with Foveaux *re*
naval matters.

The Inclosure, marked C, I take the Liberty to submit to their Lordships for their farther information on the subject, it being a correspondence between me and Lieutenant Colonel Foveaux, by which I endeavoured to detain Lieutenant Symons, and to show Lieutenant Colonel Foveaux he had no right to interfere with the Naval Service.

On the 15th August, I had an opportunity of writing to Sir Edward Pellew by a Ship bound to Calcutta, stating my situation,

and submitting to his consideration how far he could send me
assistance. I have, &c.,

WM. BLIGH.

[Enclosure A.]

GOVERNOR BLIGH'S ORDERS TO LIEUTENANT SYMONS.

By William Bligh, Esquire, Captain of His Majesty's Ship Porpoise, and Senior Officer of His Majesty's Ships and Vessels employed on the Coast of New South Wales, &c., &c., &c.

You are hereby required and directed, as the changeable and peculiar circumstances of the Public Duty of this Colony require it, to proceed on board His Majesty's Ship Porpoise, and there take upon You the charge and command of first Lieutenant of that Ship, in the absence of Lieutenant Kent now in His Majesty's Armed Tender Lady Nelson on duty, strictly charging and commanding all the Officers and Company of the said Ship subordinate to You, to behave themselves jointly and severally, in their respective Employments, with all due Respect and Obedience unto You their said first Lieutenant; and you to be obedient to your Captain or any other your superior Officer, complying with such Orders as they may give for the good of His Majesty's Service: And for so doing this shall be your Order.

Given under my hand, etc., this 17th day of May, 1807.

WM. BLIGH.

By William Bligh, Esquire, etc., etc.
WHEREAS Captain Putland has been found totally incapable of proceeding to Sea, on account of extreme ill-health, by Survey of the fifth Instant:

You are therefore hereby required and directed to proceed with His Majesty's Ship Porpoise to the Derwent, where you are to deliver the Provisions and Stores which have been shipped on board her for that purpose, together with my Despatches for Lieutenant Governor Collins; and you are to return to Port Jackson with the utmost despatch.

Given under my Hand, etc., this 8th day of October, 1807.

WM. BLIGH.

By William Bligh, Esquire, etc., etc.
CAPTAIN PUTLAND continuing in a state of total incapacity to do his Duty, and proceed to Sea in His Majesty's Ship Porpoise,

You are hereby required and directed to proceed to get the Ship ready for Sea with the utmost despatch, and having so done report to me in order to receive further directions.

Given under my Hand, etc., 19th November, 1807.

WM. BLIGH.

1808.
10 Sept.

Governor
Bligh's orders
to James
Symons.

By William Bligh, Esquire, etc., etc.
You now being equipped for Sea, You are hereby required and
directed to proceed with His Majesty's Ship Porpoise (her Captain being unfit to embark) to Norfolk Island, and there delivering my Despatches to Captain Piper, the Commandant, You will
receive on board such Settlers, together with their Families, live
and dead Stock, or Stores, as he may point out to you to embark
for the Derwent. Such Stores as the Commissary has sent on
board you are to deliver also to Captain Piper, except one hundred
Bushels of Seed Barley, which are intended for the Derwent, to
which place you are to proceed when Captain Piper, the Commandant, has finally agreed with You on the concerns you are to
undertake, and approves of your departure.

On your arrival at the Derwent you will inform Lieutenant-
Governor Collins of your proceedings, and request him to receive
the Persons and things you have without delay; and having so
done you will return hither with the utmost dispatch.

As the duty which you have to fulfil is the complete evacuation
of Norfolk Island, I have to enjoin you to keep up the utmost
cordiality with the Commandant and the Lieutenant Governors of
the Derwent and Port Dalrymple, cheerfully consulting with
them, and representing what you can accomplish in the number
of Souls, with their necessaries, you can take on board the Ship.
And that nothing may occur to delay the duty alluded to, you
have my permission and orders to take down any and all Bulkheads which you may see will give you more room for Stowage,
and carry a greater number of People, taking care to preserve
such Bulkheads in order that they may be put up again when it
becomes necessary. And for so doing this shall be your Order.

Given, etc., 25th November, 1807.

WM. BLIGH.

[Enclosure B.]

[1] CAPTAIN KENT TO COMMODORE BLIGH.

His Majesty's Ship Porpoise, Sydney Cove,
Sir,   29th Augt., 1808.

The position
of lieutenant
Ellison.

In consequence of a Letter dated the 27th Inst. which I
have received from Lieut. Ellison of His Majesty's Ship Porpoise under my Command (a Copy of which I have herewith
inclosed) whom I had ordered to take charge of His Majesty's
armed Tender Lady Nelson to proceed to the Hawkesbury at the
request of Lieut. Governor Johnston, desiring me to inform
him into whose charge he was now to resign the Stores and
Provisions belonging to the said Tender in order that he may

receive such receipts and Documents as he had given when he took charge of her, and as I had received your Verbal Order that Lieut. Ellison on his arrival should join His Majesty's said Ship Porpoise I have to request you will·please to inform me if he is to return on board the Porpoise or that it is your wish he should remain on board the Nelson in Case she should be immediately wanted for the good of His Majesty's Service.

1808.
10 Sept.

The position
of lieutenant
Ellison.

I have, &c.,
WM. KENT.

[2] LIEUTENANT ELLISON TO CAPTAIN KENT.

His Majesty's Armed Tender Lady Nelson,
Sir,   Sydney Cove, 27th Augt., 1808.

I beg leave to acquaint you that the Lady Nelson under my Command is unloaded and is ready to proceed on any Service you may wish to send her.

Ellison's
request for
instructions.

But as I understand that you have received orders from His Excellency Governor Bligh for my immediate return on board His Majesty's Ship Porpoise under your Command,

I particularly beg leave to be informed unto whose charge I am to resign the Stores and provisions belonging to the Lady Nelson in order that I may obtain such receipts and documents for my own Security and for the Good of His Majesty's Service.

I have further to request that you will furnish me with such orders as you may think proper for my return on board His Majesty's Ship Porpoise.   I have, &c.,

WM. ELLISON.

[3] SECRETARY GRIFFIN TO CAPTAIN KENT.

Sir,   Government House, Sydney, 31st August, 1808.

In answer to your Letter of the 29th Instant, I am commanded by His Excellency Commodore Bligh to observe to you, That Lieut. Ellison and every Officer of His Majesty's Ship Porpoise must occupy their respective situations agreeable to the Establishment.

Officers to take
positions
accord'n, to
establishment.

With respect to any Provisions or Stores that may be at any time on board the Lady Nelson, you will be acquainted by His Excellency's Order of the 4th Sept., 1806, to Capt. Short that the Warrant Officers will be held responsible for them, A Copy of the above mentioned order I am directed to inclose.

His Excellency, also, Commands me to observe that he is prevented from having any thing to do with the Government of the Colony.   I am, &c.,

EDMUND GRIFFIN.

1808.
10 Sept.

[4] CAPTAIN KENT TO COMMODORE BLIGH.

His Majesty's Ship Porpoise, Sydney Cove,

Sir,   Port Jackson, 3d Septemr., 1808.

The question of Symons' discharge.

I have the honor to inclose you a Copy of my Letter to Mr. James Symons, together with a Copy of his answer wherein he refers me to the Ship's Books for his discharge.

From the Lady Nelson's Books he is discharged into those of His Majesty's Ship Porpoise but it was by his own Orders, and on the Porpoise's Books he is discharged superceded.

I therefore beg that you will be pleased to give me such instructions as you may judge proper on the occasion so that Lieut. Ellison may obtain proper receipts for the Stores, in Order that he may join His Majesty's Ship Porpoise.

I am, &c.,

WM. KENT.

[5] CAPTAIN KENT TO MR. JAMES SYMONS.

His Majesty's Ship Porpoise, Sydney Cove,

Sir,   Port Jackson, 1st Sept., 1808.

Symons ordered to take command of the Lady Nelson.

I have to inform you that this day I have received a Letter from Commodore William Bligh, ordering all Officers to repair on board to their respective Situations; he likewise enclosed in his Letter to me an order that was given to Capt. Short to bear you and fourteen Men in the Lady Nelson, Armed Tender, to His Majesty's Ship Porpoise, as supernumeraries for wages and Victuals.

I have therefore to request you will join His Majesty's armed Tender Lady Nelson and assume the Command which Lieut. Ellison will deliver up to you, he being ordered to join His Majesty's Ship Porpoise you giving him proper receipts for the Stores.   I am, &c.,

WM. KENT.

[6] MR. JAMES SYMONS TO CAPTAIN KENT.

Sir,   Sydney, 1st September, 1808.

Symons' claim to his discharge.

I have to acknowledge the receipt of your letter of this day's date and beg leave to refer you to the Books of His Majesty's Ship Porpoise wherein you will see that I am discharged from His Majesty's Armed Tender Lady Nelson and likewise His Majesty's Ship Porpoise.

I have further to acquaint you that I have engaged to take His Honor Lieut. Governor Foveaux's Dispatches to England and shall be happy to carry any you may have to send to the Admiralty.   I have, &c.,

J. SYMONS.

[7] SECRETARY GRIFFIN TO CAPTAIN KENT.

Sir,   Government House, Sydney, 3rd September, 1808.

In answer to your Letter of this day's date I am com- No discharge manded by His Excellency Commodore Bligh to refer you to his made by Bligh of the 31st Ulto. in addition to which I am ordered to inform you that he has given no orders for the discharge of any Officer, Seaman or Marine since the 27th of May, 1807; and His Excellency directs me to observe, that the management of the Ship's Books and interior Regulations of the Ship, you are accountable for to The Right Hon'ble the Lords Commissioners of the Admiralty.   I am, &c.,

EDMUND GRIFFIN.

[Enclosure C.]

[This included copies of the correspondence between Governor Correspondence *Bligh and Lieutenant-Colonel Foveaux, which were also for-* and Foveaux. *warded as enclosures numbered 30, 31, 32 and 33 to Governor* *Bligh's despatch to Viscount Castlereagh, dated 10th September,* *1808.]*

———

LIEUTENANT-COLONEL FOVEAUX TO ————.*
(Despatch per ship Rose.)

Dear Sir,   Sydney, Port Jackson, 10th September, 1808.

I arrived here on the 28th of July, and was naturally Arrival of much astonished and concern'd at the Situation in which I found colony. the Colony plunged by the extraordinary conduct of Captain Bligh.

Before I landed, I made every possible inquiry into the circumstances attending the change that had been made in the government, and the result produced a profound conviction in my mind Justification of that nothing but that change could have saved the colony from a Bligh's arrest. general insurrection with all its inevitable horrors; And that any attempt to replace the government in the hands from whence it had been removed, would have been attended with circumstances no less dreadful and certain.

Since I have had the command I have omitted no opportunity Charges of ascertaining the truth of the heaviest of the numerous charges against Bligh. prefer'd against the Governor (for to investigate the whole would be the work of years), And I do not hesitate to declare that he has appear'd to me, thro'out his whole administration, to have acted upon a settled system of enriching himself, and a few of his necessary agents, at the expence of the interests of His Majesty's government, and of the people entrusted to his command; And that in the prosecution of his plans he has been guilty of the most oppressive and often wanton attacks on private property and personal liberty, as well as the most flagrant waste and shameful misapplication of the public stores and revenues of the colony.

* Note 188.

1808.
10 Sept.
The chief of his council was the noted George Crossley, a convict of the most abandon'd character, whom, as well as others of the same class, he publickly and avowedly consulted in the most important concerns of his government.

Foveaux
impugns the
truth of
Bligh's reports.
Whatever representations Captain Bligh may have sent home respecting his removal from power will, I am convinced, be found as little intitled to credit as almost all the information which he officially transmitted to Ministers on the situation and interests of the colony at large, or on the conduct and characters of many of the individuals on whom he had occasion to report.

Justification
of Johnston's
actions.
Should an investigation be order'd to take place in this country, which I think desirable, as the only measure that can ascertain the truth beyond the possibility of doubt, I will forfeit my existence if the verdict of an impartial tribunal will not completely justify the Measures which Major Johnston was call'd upon to adopt.

Foveaux's
opinion of
Bligh.
Captain Bligh has notified to me that he meant to proceed to England in the Porpoise, but I have every reason to be certain he entertains no such intention. As no change whatever was made in his domestic concerns in consequence of his suspension, he remains in possession of Government House, with all the advantages attach'd to it; And while he is suffer'd to live luxuriously at a heavy expence to the public, he will be in no hurry to relinquish his enjoyments; besides, I am convinced he has not nerve enough to face the enquiries which on his arrival in England will doubtless take place into his conduct.

He has endeavoured to throw every possible obstacle in the way of the public business; but I have given him to understand that in the execution of my duty I am neither to be impeded nor intimidated.

I have been so short a time in this country, and have been so occupied in making a thousand arrangements which could not be postpon'd, that I have not as yet received the reports necessary to furnish me with information accurate enough to enter into a detail'd account to the Secretary of State of the Situation of the colony. My own observations however enable me to assure you,
Condition of
the public
buildings.
that the public buildings are in a state of deplorable decay and delapidation—so much so, that I am decidedly of opinion that most of them must be rebuilt. Nothing seems to have been attended to but the improvements at Government House, the surrounding grounds, and at Captain Bligh's private farms, where nearly all the best of the public Servants have been employ'd at an enormous charge to the Crown, and to the total neglect of the most essential works of the colony.

He has likewise occupied many of the public labourers for a
considerable time in erecting and ornamenting a residence for
one of the several prostitutes whom (notwithstanding his constant professions of religion and morality) he was in the habit
of maintaining.

The church at Sydney is the only public work which received a
small, and but a very small, share of his attention; And in this,
considerable progress had been made previous to his arrival, And
since his suspension it has been very nearly completed.

As Captain Bligh's public letter of the 31st of October last
will apprize you of his intention of depriving the holders of
several leases and grants of their property, I feel myself obliged
most strongly to urge to you the impolicy of such interference.
The Governor made no scruple on many occasions in direct violation of every right, to dispossess people of their ground, destroy
their improvements, and pull down their houses without any
justifiable pretence, and apparently thro' a mere wanton desire of
annoyance, as much of the ground on which houses stood that
have been pull'd down, still remains unappropriated to any purpose whatever; and it was a constant and familiar expression of
his, when any of the injured persons complain'd, "It is all my
own." The consequence was that no man looked upon his property as secure, altho' guaranteed to him by the strictest forms of
the Law, or the most solemn assurances of the Government, and
the improvement of the colony, either in building or in agriculture, must have been totally obstructed had so ruinous a system
been persever'd in. And while upon this Subject, I think it due
to the real interests of the colony to declare my opinion that
grants should be made to those persons who have expended large
sums of money in the erection of houses, a few of which in the
town of Sydney would not, I assure you, disgrace the most
fashionable Square in London, and have cost the proprietors
several thousand pounds, altho' built upon leases of very limited
extent, the renewal of which must totally depend upon the will
of the future Governors.

Whilst this System continues, it cannot fail to operate against
the improvement of the town; and altho' I cannot but disapprove
of the character of many of the persons now holding the most
eligible leases, yet I am of opinion that they ought to receive
grants, as I am sure the uncertainty of their tenures will in
future deter others from hazarding the expense of undertaking
such substantial buildings.

The caution contained in Lord Castlereagh's last letter (31st
Dec'r, 1807), relative to Colonel Collins' conduct, particularly
with regard to the expenses of the settlement he commands, I

1808.
10 Sept.

have taken care to forward to him, and I can assure you that never was a lecture on public economy more truly necessary on any occasion than on that of the establishment of Hobarts-town.

Collins' contract for importation of cattle.

Colonel Collins, without any reference or notification to this Government, lately enter'd into a contract with the house of Messrs. Campbell & Hook, of this place, to supply his settlement with five hundred Bengal Cows and other cattle, which would probably cost Government near Twenty thousand pounds, altho' he could be abundantly supplied with cattle from Port Dalrymple, and we have here an infinitely larger Number than we can take care of, already season'd to the climate, and, therefore, able to withstand the inclemency of Van Dieman's Land, which is known from experience would prove fatal to many of the delicate breed of Bengal cows, upwards of two hundred which were on a former occasion landed from India at Port Dalrymple having died.

If I am to judge of Colonel Collins's want of men, by his own representations he has already sufficient engagements without encumbering himself with large herds of cattle, which require many experienced hands to attend to them, for unless they, or indeed any kind of cattle, are well taken care of, the encrease of numbers beyond a certain point will rather diminish than augment the means of subsistence of the settlement.

Foveaux's endeavour to cancel the contract.

As the vessel intended to transport them from India did not sail from hence untill the 20th of last month, I thought it my duty to do everything in my power to prevent so useless and extravagant a contract from being carried into effect, and a copy of my letter to Messieurs Campbell & Hook upon that subject accompanies my public dispatch.

I must confess, however, that I am hopeless of its producing the desired effect, as, in addition to the advantages to be derived from the contract, there will be other contingent benefits to an amount not easily to be calculated, which will induce the parties concerned to run considerable risk rather than sacrifice the prospect.

You may form a pretty accurate conception from whence these advantages are to arise, when you are informed of the circumstances attending the speculations of the Rose to this colony.

Prohibition of the importation of spirits.

Notwithstanding Governor Bligh's possitive prohibition of the importation of spirits at any of the dependent settlements (unless the ship first touched here, and obtained his permission), and the ruin which appear'd inevitable to any adventurer who should presume to infringe his orders, The Rose, a private ship, avowedly owned by the house of Messrs. Campbell and Hook, put into the

Derwent on her voyage from England, and landed several thousand gallons of spirits, which have since been disposed of amongst
the unfortunate Settlers from Norfolk Island, who, having no Spirits landed
from the Rose
at the Derwent.
other means of making the purchase, were indulged with permission to sell their little stock of salted pork to the Government, at
the expense of one Shilling and ninepence per pound.

Thus were these unhappy people furnished with the means of
indulging in dissipation and drunkeness for a few days, and
deprived of the means of subsistence for years. I must now beg
to repeat an opinion, which I have already often urged at your
office, that the excessive restraints which have been imposed upon
the importation of spirituous liquors have very powerfully contributed to heighten the desire of the colonists to possess them, and
have absolutely encreased the evils which they were intended to
diminish.

But I despair of lessening the force of the impressions which
have been made on the minds of Government upon this Subject,
and I am sensible I shall find few inclined to admit the truth of
facts, which in one week's observation of this colony would be
clearly obvious to a mind of your discernment.

As only a limitted quantity of spirits, infinitely short of the
demand, is allow'd to be imported, its common circulating value
fluctuates from two to three pounds Sterling per gallon. Three-
fourths of the whole quantity fall into the hands of persons in the
employment of Government, or are obtained by the inhabitants of
the town at an average price of about twelve shillings, and are
again distributed by them at the advanced price amongst the
Settlers and labourers who live in the interior of the country.
These people, sensible that a threefold proportion of the reward
of their industry is extorted from them, eagerly engage in smuggling and distilling, and in nineteen cases out of twenty they do
so with success. The numerous orders which have been given
upon the Subject, And the rewards offer'd to informers may
occasion a belief that neither smuggling nor distilling are very
common; but I can assure you that the reverse is the truth, nor
is it possible to prevent it in a country so thinly inhabited, and
in which the whole of the population consider themselves
oppress'd and injured by the existing regulations.

The persons who derived the greatest advantage from the trade
in Spirits, under the Government of Captain Bligh, were Mr. Participation
of Campbell,
Palmer, and
Thompson in
the spirit
traffic.
Commissary Palmer and Mr. Campbell, both of whom have
houses so situated that they can land any quantity without
observation. It has also been found that an overseer of Captain
Bligh's, by the name of Thompson, was permitted to land a considerable quantity of spirits, near 200 Gallons, and this at a time

1808.
10 Sept.

when the officers were refused a gallon, and were known to be reduced to the necessity of drinking water only.

Crossley charged with illicit distilling.

The notorious Crossley was also a favor'd object; but he appears to have directed his attention principally to distilling, as two stills were found hidden in his garden a few days after the arrest of his friend the Governor.

The Strange events which have occur'd in this country, and the consequent embarrassments which have ensued, will, I trust, point out to you the absolute necessity of sending some person as

A new governor and judge-advocate wanted.

Governor (should one not already have been appointed) possess'd of talents and integrity enough to remedy the evils entail'd on the colony by the System which has hitherto been acted upon in its government; and next in importance to the Governor, I must mention the Situation of Judge-Advocate, which should be immediately fill'd by a person of character and knowledge of the law, with such a salary as would induce a person of that description to accept it, and would place him above the necessity of stooping to unbecoming means of Seeking a remuneration adequate to the trouble of the office, and enable him to live with a suitable degree of respectability in a country where even the most common necessaries of life are not to be procured unless at a most enormous expense.

Special instructions required for governors.

I cannot help suggesting to you the prudence of giving particular instructions to the Governors of all these settlements respecting the management and disposal of the Stores and government Stock of cattle, and the distribution of the convict labourers of the Gov't, which, I fear, have hitherto been look'd upon as meant rather for the convenience and emolument of individuals than for the good of the public, or the Service of the Crown. It is indeed my opinion that the public herds should be distributed amongst the settlers, as the expense of attending to them is infinitely greater than any benefit which Government can expect to derive from them.

Condition of settlers from Norfolk Island at the Derwent.

Notwithstanding the unreasonable length of this letter, I must trespass a moment longer to mention to you the deplorable state of the unfortunate Settlers from Norfolk Island, who have been forced to quit their establishments and proceed to the Derwent, without having been allow'd sufficient time to prepare for their removal, agreeable to what I know to have been your humane intention.

Cap'n Symons, of the Navy, whom I send to England in the Rose with my dispatches, will be able to give you every information upon this, or any other Subject connected with the affairs of this Colony.   I have, &c.,

J. FOVEAUX.

(Despatch per ship Rose.)

Government House, Sydney,
Dear Sir,   11th September, 1808.

Lieutenant-Colonel Foveaux, on his arrival here, delivered Acknowledg-
me your letter of the 31st of December, and I have now an despatch.
opportunity by the Rose, Rich'd Brooks, Master, to send home
my Dispatches. In this letter I only take up my pen to thank
you for your good wishes towards me.

With respect to Captain Short, I do not see how I am impli- The case of
cated in any unkindness, or want of attention; if my statements
had been considered, as well as his, they would have proved his
turbulent disposition, and that he would not allow me to be on
any footing with him but constant disputation; this, however, I
should have submitted to, on my own part; but Governor King,
and the Court of Inquiry, found that no person could live under
Captain Short's Command; and the Charges of his Officers were
such that the public service obliged me to send him Home, or I
should have been highly censurable. I cannot doubt of Governor
King having represented all this; yet I am surprised that he has
allowed of some representations which he and His Officers might
have refuted, and to this I attribute the extraordinary letter*
written by the members of the Court-Martial in Captain Short's
favour, but whose decision I by no means call in question.

As to Mr. Fitz and his family, I know of no disagreement in the Relations
passage out; on the contrary, they dined with me frequently every and Fitz.
Week, and we were particularly kind to them and their little
Boy, who we made a pet of; and when we arrived they were asked
to our House with great attention, the services which were
immediately necessary were granted, and Mrs. Fitz was made
as comfortable as the other Ladies. The desire you was pleased
to express in his favour should have been amply attended to. I
only wanted a little time to look about me, and after the first
grant of land which I gave him, I would have followed it up with
others, without any Cause of jealousy from other Persons. But
I was sorry to find that he soon became under obligations to
McArthur, and was accordingly obliged to submit to his Wishes.

My coming out to this Country was from the purest Motives, Bligh's
and have done justice to every individual in it, which all well- of relief.
disposed persons acknowledge. Under a full confidence of having
justice done to me I shall wait with resignation for relief.

Believe me, &c.,
WM. BLIGH.

* Note 189.

1808.
13 Sept.

LIEUTENANT-COLONEL FOVEAUX TO VISCOUNT CASTLEREAGH.

(Despatch marked F, per ship Rose.)

My Lord,   Sydney, Port Jackson, 13th September, 1808.

Copies of the
Sydney Gazette.

I have the honor to transmit your Lordship the *Sydney Gazettes* from the period of their republication* to the 11th instant.   I have, &c.,

J. FOVEAUX.

GOVERNOR BLIGH TO THE HON. WILLIAM POLE.

(Despatch per ship Rose.)

Government House, Sydney,

15 Sept.   Sir,   New South Wales, 15th Sept., 1808.

Brookes in
charge of
Bligh's
despatches.

The Bearer Captain Richard Brooks will deliver to you my dispatches; and will be ready to give you every information he can respecting the State of this Colony.   I have, &c.,

WM. BLIGH.

VISCOUNT CASTLEREAGH TO GOVERNOR BLIGH.

(Despatch No. 11, per transport Experiment.)

16 Sept.   Sir,   Downing Street, 16th September, 1808.

Authority for
Underwood to
become a
settler.

Mr. Underwood who some time ago received Mr. Windham's Permission to proceed to New South Wales to establish himself with his Family as a Free Settler having represented to me that you had not received such Sanction as you conceived to be necessary for allowing him to avail himself of the permission abovementioned, I am to desire you will permit the said Mr. Underwood and his Family to settle in such part of the Territories under your Command as he shall prefer and I trust he will by his general Good Conduct entitle himself to your protection and Encouragement which in such Case I request you will extend to him.   I have, &c.,

CASTLEREAGH.

VISCOUNT CASTLEREAGH TO LIEUTENANT-GOVERNOR PATERSON.

(Despatch per transport Experiment.)

8 Oct.   Sir,   Downing Street, 8th October, 1808.

Convict labour
for Marsden's
farm.

The Reverend Mr. Marsden has stated to me his Apprehensions lest his Property should have received Injury during the late Commotion in New South Wales; I am therefore to desire that his Overseer may receive the same Assistance by the Allowance of Labourers as he was receiving before the Commotion took Place.   I have, &c.,

CASTLEREAGH.

* *Marginal note.*—No. 228 to No. 245 incl. (*see* note 190).

LIEUTENANT-COLONEL FOVEAUX TO UNDER SECRETARY COOKE.
(A private letter per transport Sinclair.)

Dear Sir,   Sydney, Port Jackson, 21st October, 1808.

As the Sinclair sails from hence this day, I avail myself Sailing of the Sinclair.
of the opportunity she offers of writing to you, but as I look upon
it as a very precarious one, I have not thought it prudent to trust
a public letter by it, nor even to Communicate as much at length
to you, as I would by a more certain conveyance.

After the departure of the Rose, Governor Bligh, taking advan- Bligh assumes
tage of the permission I gave him to see the officers of the Por- command of
poise, assumed the command of her, and prevented her and the the Porpoise.
Colonial vessels from rendering any Service whatever to the
Colony, and took every step in his power to impede and embarrass the business of the public, in consequence of which I was
under the disagreeable tho' absolute necessity of forbidding (on
the 17th of last Month) any further intercourse between him and
the officers of the Porpoise, since which event that vessel, as well
as the Lady Nelson, has been restored to the Service of the
Colony, for which alone they are stationed here.

In answer to a letter which I wrote on the 14th of last month Bligh's refusal
to Governor Bligh, requesting to know when he meant to proceed to leave the
to England, as he stated to Me (on the 3'd of August last) he colony.
intended to do without delay, He informed me that he had no
intention whatever of leaving the Colony. This I always sus-
pected, as I stated to you in my last letter.

As I have received authentic information that he was exerting Necessity for
every Means in his power to inflame the Minds of the Settlers by proposed
sending emissaries amongst them, who promised in his name that restraint on
in the event of his restoration to the Government he would make Bligh.
them rich and happy, I thought it my duty to inform him that if
he persevered in his attempts to disturb the public peace, I would
send him to England by the first opportunity, and until such
opportunity should occur I would remove him from Government
house and be obliged to impose some additional restraint on his
person. These threats, and preventing his communicating with
the Porpoise, have render'd him quiet, and he has given me no
further trouble. He remains at Government house, enjoying the
same advantages as when I wrote to you by the Rose.

The Estramina, which I sent to Port Dalrymple immediately Paterson's
after my arrival here to convey Colonel Paterson hither, return'd reasons for not
on the 12th instant without him. He assigns the bad State of his returning to
health and the want of proper accomodation in that vessel as the headquarters.
cause of his not having come to Headquarters, and requires that
the Porpoise may again be sent for him. I have accordingly
requested her Commanding officer to proceed with her to Port

1808.
21 Oct.

Dalrymple, and she is expected to Sail in four or five days, the damages she received when before dispatch'd for Colonel Paterson being now nearly repair'd.

Want of supplies at Hobart.

Having learn'd by the Estramina that Colonel Collins's settlement was much distress'd for provisions, from the circumstance of the City of Edinburgh not having arrived there (on the 16th of Sept'r) with the ample supplies sent from hence, and with the remainder of the Settlers, &c., from Norfolk Island, it was my intention to have dispatch'd a vessel to their relief; but this has been render'd unnecessary, as, by a Ship which arrived here a few days since from Norfolk Island, I find that the City of Edinburgh had sail'd from thence on the 9th of Sept'r, and consequently her Arrival at the Derwent may be expected before that of any vessel which I could now dispatch for that Settlement.

A small settlement to be maintained at Norfolk Island.

On the 30th September there remain'd on Norfolk Island Two hundred and fifty persons of every description, Eight horses, Twenty-one ass's, Seventy-two horn'd cattle, and three thousand and five sheep. As it appears that Government are anxious about the cultivation of the Coffee plant, I have directed that a small party shall remain (until I receive your further instructions) to attend to it, and also to look after the Stock, which at present we have no Means of removing, For the Men-of-War hitherto stationed here are not adapted to that purpose, and are really of no benefit whatever to the public, altho' maintain'd at a most enormous expense. And the Colonial Vessels, which alone are requisite for the Service of this colony, are much too small for that and many other duties they are wanted for.

Necessity for colonial government vessels.

I therefore most strongly recommend that no ship of the former description shall at all be kept here, and that two of the latter, of a proper construction (about 200 tons burden), and to be consider'd as entirely Colonial, shall be sent from England.

Price offered by government for meat.

In my letter A* to the Secretary of State, by the Rose, I, by Mistake, Mentioned one shilling per pound as the price I intended to offer for Meat to be received into the Stores. The price offer'd has been Nine pence for all kinds of Animal food (without the heads or feet), and a quantity equal to my expectation has been already received.

Supplies of grain in store.

My Letter A by the Rose has informed the Secretary of State that we have a Sufficient quantity of grain in Store to serve untill the produce of the ensuing harvest shall be saved, And I am happy to inform you that the growing crops wear a most luxurious appearance. We have nothing therefore to dread except the overflowing of the Hawkesbury, a calamity which would inevitably expose the Colony to the horrors of famine, as was the case in the spring of 1806.

* Note 191.

I expect to see the walls of the New Stone granary erecting at Paramatta completed in a fortnight.

I have commenc'd a substantial brick Barrack, 180 feet in length and two Stories high,* in addition to the old one here; a measure render'd indispensible from the encreased numbers of the Corps by the reinforcements arrived in the Sinclair and Recovery and by those expected in the Ships now on their passage from England.

Erection of barracks.

The dependent Settlements are much distressed for want of convicts, And we have none to send them, as we can with much difficulty find a sufficient Number of hands to carry on the most essential of the public works.

More convicts wanted.

A Vessel call'd the Star arrived here from England on the 10th inst., by which I learn that the Speke, transport for this colony, parted in Latitude 9° N. to proceed to the Cape of Good Hope.

Arrival of the ship Star.

When the Rose sail'd from hence a General Court Martial was sitting for the tryal of Mr. Williamson, a Deputy Commissary, and who acted as Principle Commissary from the period of Mr. Palmer's Suspension untill placed by Me under Arrest.

Court martial on James Williamson.

The proceedings† of the Court Martial (altho' but a very slight Specimen of the knavery of our Commissariat was laid before it) will convince you of the necessity of sending out some Men of Character and Common honesty to fill the Situations of that very important department.   I have, &c.,
                                        J. FOVEAUX.

By the Albion whaler, which is expected to sail from hence direct for England in about three weeks, I shall send my public letters &c.

GOVERNOR BLIGH TO VISCOUNT CASTLEREAGH.

(Despatch marked No. 1, per whaler Albion.)

Government House, Sydney,
My Lord,   New South Wales, 28th October, 1808.

28 Oct.

1st. I have now the honor of writing to your Lordship, in continuation of my Despatches by the Rose, Richard Brooks Master, in September last,‡ since which I have been annoyed by Letters or threats, although still in confinement, and have no other expectation until I receive relief from England, and am able to reassume my Power and Authority, than a repetition of such insults. The insolence, wickedness, and duplicity of the principal Rebels exceed all description. The People see, with

Insults and threats received by Bligh.

* Note 192.   † Note 193.   ‡ Note 194.

1808.
28 Oct.
great concern, how much the Colony is injured, Government plundered, and beggary making hasty strides to their utter ruin, by being deprived of their common advantages, and a settled plan of prosecutions, which deprive those who are in debt of all

Administration of justice.
they have. The Benches of Magistrates and Courts of Justice are mockeries of what they represent, and since my Despatch of the 30th of June five Persons have suffered Death; nevertheless the People are obliged to submit under the most afflicting considerations. They have no Money in circulation, all is doubt, the barter of Spirits is going on, and Money is realized in the hands of the principal Rebels. Such is their art, impudence, and im-

Trading methods adopted by principal rebels.
portunity, that they constrain some Persons by threats and promises to purchase the property from them which they have monopolized from Shipping; others they allure to get into their debt by promises of no hasty payment being required. If they show any reluctance, it is done away by assurances of profit which they will acquire, and if that does not effect the purpose, they are warned of such displeasure as induces them to submit to all their terms, and Debtor and Creditor is established. This being done, the laws of necessity are pleaded for Settling Accounts. Capiases are issued, and executions follow, and the unfortunate Debtor is obliged to sell all he has or go to Gaol; to avoid the latter all is brought to public auction, when it is so contrived that few bidders dare appear, and the whole falls into the hands of those merciless Creditors and Rebels at half its price, and frequently much less. In these transactions, during the present state of things, a remarkable character, beside the Credi-

Provost-marshal appointed by the new government.
tor, is conspicuous; this is the Provost-Marshal,* appointed after the Rebellion, to which he is devoted, and whose unprincipled mind divests him of all charity. Whenever the day of reckoning comes, such a scene of crimes of some of the leading Persons will be developed as will be truly astonishing. It will require great foresight and precaution to prevent the People from committing the most violent acts of resentment.

Removal of settlers from Norfolk Island.
2nd. Concerning the poor Settlers of Norfolk Island, I am not well informed, but report states them to be discontented; the plan of Major Johnston and McArthur of employing the City of Edinburgh to carry them to the Derwent was not approved of; she sailed from hence as far back as the 26th of May, left Norfolk Island on the 9th of September, leaving only about two hundred Persons, including the Military, on the Island, since which we have heard nothing of her.† This was the infamous Ship which sold and distributed her Liquors to McArthur and his Emissaries at the time of the Insurrection.

* Note 195.   † Note 196.

3rd. The Harvest here, I am informed has a tolerably good appearance, but probably will not be very sufficient for next Year's consumption, because a less quantity of Seed was put into the Ground than was last Year.

4th. It is said that the present Rulers pride themselves much in not drawing Bills on the Treasury, when the fact is no Person will receive them; but of this, after all, will be found very calamitous to the State, and of considerable expence beyond that which would have been absolutely necessary under regular Government; also, such a waste of Cattle has taken place as will be very detrimental to Agriculture, besides weakening the power of the Governor, to whom Settlers look for advantages, and are cheered in their pursuits by his bounty and rewards.

5th. My last Despatches to Your Lordship were scarcely made up when Lieutenant-Colonel Foveaux began a fresh Correspondence in order to place me in some farther difficulty, at the whole of which I have felt the utmost indignation, and I inclose it, in continuation of his former Letters.* It behoved me to use such methods as to discover what their real intentions were, and they appear to be chiefly aimed at inducing me to go Home as a Prisoner at my own request, that it should not appear they were turning me out of the Colony. The next object was to get me away before any relief could arrive from England, whereby they flattered themselves they would succeed the better in their Cause; and lastly, if I took the Porpoise, they would have an unprecedented example of a Flag Officer confined in his Ship where his Flag was flying. Having now failed to circumvent me, they again deprived me of any communication with the Ship, and Captain Kent, her Acting Commander, has consented to it, and is intimate with Lieutenant-Colonel Foveaux, whose Letter of the 17th of September (No. 38) concludes with unwarrantable threats, which I treated with the contempt they deserved.

6th. Your Lordship will please to recollect I informed You of the Estramina being sent to Port Dalrymple to bring up Lieutenant-Governor Paterson. She returned on the 12th Instant without him, and I heard no more until the 18th, when Lieutenant-Colonel Foveaux wrote to me (No. 39) stating that Lieutenant-Governor Paterson had written to me, that unless I proceeded to England I must go to Parramatta House that he might reside here to carry on the affairs of the Colony; and Lieutenant-Colonel Foveaux adds that he had written to Captain Kent to proceed to Port Dalrymple to bring up the Lieutenant-Governor, and that I must make my arrangements as soon as possible. To this very seditious request I replied by No. 40 that

1808.
28 Oct.

Bligh's refusal to leave government house.

I would not quit my House or Premises—they were mine until His Majesty should be pleased to remove me from them, being His Representative, and likewise a British Flag Officer, whose Flag it was at the peril of any Man to remove out of my sight; that I had received no Letter from Lieutenant-Governor Paterson.

Paterson's correspondence.

7th. On the next day I received No. 41, with Copies of two Letters* which had been sent to Lieutenant-Colonel Foveaux by Lieutenant-Governor Paterson, who had intimated to him that the original of that dated the 29th of Sept'r had been sent to me by the Estramina, but which appears not to have been so, unless it has been intercepted; in that case this artifice has deprived me of it. I have made no reply to such a curious compound, but I think that Lieutenant-Governor Paterson has artfully been drawn from the line of his duty, and prevented from doing his utmost to bring his Corps to obedience. In this extraordinary Copy of his Letter, it appears that he has received intimation of a determination to oppose him if he did not side with them in their measures; some very threatening Letter has therefore been sent to convince him of this, and it is conformable to the information I have given in paragraph 52 of my Despatch dated the 30th of June. The directions for removing me from Government House; his advice to me to return home; his diffidence in describing if he erred that it would not be through design; and, after all, taking the side of the Corps without seeing me, is what he must

Paterson's delay in assuming the government.

account for. Since the 26th of January last, six opportunities had offered direct from Port Dalrymple, by either of which he might have come here—Viz't, the Speedwell Schooner, which carried him intelligence of the Rebellion a few days after my confinement, from the Rebels themselves; the Brig Harrington, which touched there on her way from India; the Brig Perseverance, also which returned by that Port on her way hither from China; the Favourite, in her way from India; His Majesty's Ship Porpoise, in May last, which went to him for that purpose; and the Estramina Schooner.

H.M.S. Porpoise to be sent to Port Dalrymple.

8th. On the 25th Instant, I received a Letter (No. 42) from Lieutenant-Colonel Foveaux informing me that, at Lieutenant-Governor Paterson's requisition, His Majesty's Ship Porpoise was to sail for Port Dalrymple on Sunday next, and that, if I wished to make any communication to that Officer, he would transmit it. I replied to the Lieutenant-Colonel that I was surprised at Lieutenant-Governor Paterson's requisition, as he knew me to be Commodore on this Station, and was equally astonished at the compliance of Captain Kent; and that, from my imprison-

* Note 198.

ment, and my communication being stopt with him, I had to request he would inform him that it was my orders he did not leave the Cove; to this Lieutenant-Colonel Foveaux replied (No. 44) that the Porpoise would sail as he had already informed me.

9th. Thus, again, His Majesty's Ship is taken from me to bring H.M.S. up a Lieutenant-Governor who openly has avowed his taking the Porpoise removed from side of his rebellious and mutinous Corps, in which, also, her Bligh's control. Acting Commander has joined, and must of consequence take upon himself to strike my Broad Pendant, in defiance of my Orders and the Rules of our Service. In the last Voyage she was nearly lost, and I have my fears in this. This wanton insult is the greater as there is the Lady Nelson and the Estramina— Colonial Schooner—now lying in the Cove.

10th. About this time I allow myself to imagine that Your Relief Lordship will have been informed of all that has been done here. expected by Bligh from A Ship called the Speke I soon expect from England, which England. probably will be the last before relief arrives; whatever despatches are sent by her I shall be deprived of, as the Rebels are peculiarly solicitous about answers to my Despatches sent by the Duke of Portland. Your Lordship, I am confident, will judge of what my feelings will be to know those Despatches get into their hands.

11th. I send these Despatches by Mr. Charles Cockerill, in the Despatch to Ship Albion. I have no idea when another opportunity may be sent in the Albion. occur by which I can again have the honor of writing to Your Lordship; it will probably be a long time, as there is no Ship on the Fisheries which is expected to sail for eight or ten Months.

I have, &c.,

WM. BLIGH.

[Enclosure No. 34.*]

LIEUTENANT-COLONEL FOVEAUX TO GOVERNOR BLIGH.

Sir,   Headquarters, Sydney, 14th September, 1808.

The very large demands which have been made upon the Bligh's Public Stores for the use of His Majesty's Ship Porpoise, make proposed departure in me anxious to be informed when she may be expected to be ready the Porpoise. for Sea, and when ready whether it be your intention to proceed to England in her without delay, as signified by You in your Letter to me of the 3rd of August last.

I have, &c.,

J. FOVEAUX.

* Note 186.

[Enclosure No. 35.]

GOVERNOR BLIGH TO LIEUTENANT-COLONEL FOVEAUX.

Bligh's request
for an
explanation.

Sir,　　　　　Government House, Sydney, 14th September, 1808.

As I have received Letters from you dated the 4th and 6th of August, which differ in their purport with mine of the 3rd, your Letter of to-day does not allow me to comprehend what you mean about my return to England. It is, therefore, necessary for me to know whether You mean that I am to enter into any conditions.　　　　　　　　　　　　　　　I am, &c.,

　　　　　　　　　　　　　　　　　　　　WM. BLIGH.

[Enclosure No. 36.]

LIEUTENANT-COLONEL FOVEAUX TO GOVERNOR BLIGH.

Sir,　　　　　　Headquarters, Sydney, 15th September, 1808.

Concessions
granted to
Bligh by
Foveaux.

When You represented to me on my arrival in the Colony that You were prevented holding any communication with the Officers of His Majesty's Ship Porpoise, I was induced to remove the restriction You complained of, hoping that by your being allowed to see her Acting Commander it might facilitate her repairs, and thereby afford You the means of sooner returning to England.

But I never entertained the slightest idea that you would, under existing circumstances, attempt to assume any Command in this Colony. In this, however, I have had the mortification to be disappointed, and instead of finding the repairs and depar-

Difficulties
created by
Bligh.

ture of the Porpoise hastened, the difficulties which before existed respecting her have been increased by the Steps You have taken to prevent her Acting Commander from complying with my requisitions.

Alternatives
offered to
Bligh.

In this state it is impossible I can suffer things to remain any longer without disregard to the Welfare of His Majesty's Service, And therefore I feel myself obliged to submit to your choice, either to prepare Yourself to embark in the Porpoise as soon as she can be got ready, and to return in her immediately to England, or to forbear from attempting to exercise any Command by giving orders or otherwise whilst you remain here.

Pledges given
by Bligh.

If you shall determine to proceed to England in the Porpoise, it does not appear to me that I can propose any conditions which can be more binding on You than the pledge You have already given (and from which you have never been released) that You will consider yourself under Arrest until His Majesty's Pleasure shall be known.

Should that pledge be forgotten or violated after your departure from hence, you alone will be responsible.

I have, &c.,

J. FOVEAUX.

[Enclosure No. 37.]

GOVERNOR BLIGH TO LIEUTENANT-COLONEL FOVEAUX.

Sir,   Government House, Sydney, 16th September, 1808.

In reply to your Letter of Yesterday, I have to inform You that it is my intention to remain in the Colony until His Majesty's Pleasure shall be known. His Majesty's Ship Porpoise has Captain Kent to command her; and if you deprive me of commanding with him, I in my present situation cannot prevent it.

Bligh's decision to remain in the colony.

I am, &c.,

WM. BLIGH.

[Enclosure No. 38.]

LIEUTENANT-COLONEL FOVEAUX TO GOVERNOR BLIGH.

Sir,   Headquarters, Sydney, 17th September, 1808.

The intention You expressed yesterday of remaining in the Colony until His Majesty's pleasure be known, and the intimation contained in your Letter of the 3rd of August of your having given orders to get the Porpoise ready to proceed Home with Yourself and family without delay, are so completely contradictory and surprizing, that (when I consider them and reflect on the interruptions and confusion You have caused by your Orders since You have been permitted to communicate with Captain Kent) I can not admit a doubt but it is your design to do everything in your power to impede His Majesty's Service and to disturb the peace of the Colony, by weakening the confidence of people in inferior situations as to the power of the present Government to protect them.

Bligh's inconsistency and opposition to Foveaux.

For these reasons, should circumstances prevent Lieutenant-Governor Paterson from relieving me in the Command, I feel it will be my duty to take the first opportunity which shall present of sending You to England.

Foveaux to send Bligh to England.

As I am satisfied that no other consequences can possibly result from Your being permitted to have further intercourse with the Officers of His Majesty's Ship Porpoise than an increase of difficulties and the retardment of the King's Service on points materially affecting the order and Welfare of this Colony, I must desire that you will in future forbear from issuing any orders to, and from any kind of official communication with Captain Kent, or any other Officer or person belonging to His Majesty's Ship Porpoise.

Prohibition of Bligh's intercourse with the Porpoise.

1808.
28 Oct.
Your Compliance with this will relieve me from the unpleasant task of removing You from Government House, or of imposing additional restraint on your Person.   I have, &c.,

J. FOVEAUX.

[Enclosure No. 39.]

LIEUTENANT-COLONEL FOVEAUX TO GOVERNOR BLIGH.

Sir,   Headquarters, Sydney, 18th October, 1808.

Bligh to vacate government house for the use of Paterson.

By Lieutenant-Governor Paterson's Letter to me of the 29th of last Month, received by the Estramina, he acquainted me that he has written to You to inform You " that unless you proceed to England it will be necessary that You should remove to the Government House at Parramatta, that the Government House at Sydney may be ready for his reception to enable him to carry on the very anxious duties of the Offices become incumbent on him by the interregnum that has been occasioned," and he desires that should you not have left the Colony that I should cause proper steps to be taken for your removal by the period I may have reason to expect his arrival.

As I have applied to Captain Kent for His Majesty's Ship Porpoise to proceed immediately to Port Dalrymple for the purpose of conveying Lieutenant-Governor Paterson to Head Quarters, I have to request (in compliance to his desire) that You will make arrangements, with as little delay as possible, for the removal of Yourself and Family to the Government House at Parramatta, unless it be your intention to leave the Colony previous to the time that Lieutenant-Governor Paterson's arrival may be looked for.

Should it be your determination to go to Parramatta, I shall give directions for every assistance being rendered you in the removal of your establishment, and for having the House and Garden prepared for your reception.   I have, &c.,

J. FOVEAUX.

[Enclosure No. 40.]

GOVERNOR BLIGH TO LIEUTENANT-COLONEL FOVEAUX.

Sir,   Government House, Sydney, 18th October, 1808.

Bligh's refusal to leave government house.

I have just received your Letter of to-day, in answer to which I inform you that I will not quit my House or Premises. They are mine until His Majesty is pleased to remove me from them, being His Representative, and likewise a British Flag Officer, whose Flag it is at the Peril of any Man to remove out of my sight.

I have not received any Letter from Lieutenant-Governor Paterson.   I am, &c.,

WM. BLIGH.

[Enclosure No. 41.]

LIEUTENANT-COLONEL FOVEAUX TO GOVERNOR BLIGH.

Sir,   Headquarters, Sydney, 19th October, 1808.

Enclosed I beg leave to enclose You Copies of two Letters transmitted to me by Lieut.-Governor Paterson, who intimated to me that the original of that dated the 29th of September was conveyed to You by the Estramina.

Correspondence with Paterson.

I have, &c.,
J. FOVEAUX.

[Sub-enclosure No. 1.]

[*This was a copy of Governor Bligh's letter to Lieutenant-Governor Paterson, dated 8th August, 1808, which was also forwarded as enclosure A to Governor Bligh's despatch to Viscount Castlereagh, dated 31st August, 1808.*]

[Sub-enclosure No. 2.]

LIEUTENANT-GOVERNOR PATERSON TO GOVERNOR BLIGH.

Port Dalrymple, Van Dieman's Land,
Sir,   29th September, 1808.

Your Communication of the 8th Inst.* I duly received by the Estramina Schooner, and I must express I have been surprised that You should have deferred it so considerable an interim as has elapsed between the 26th Jan'y and the 8th August (the date), two Opportunities having presented themselves—Viz't, by the Speedwell and by His Majesty's Ship Porpoise—your silence by which conveyance causes me much astonishment, as it must have consequently occurred to You that the adventitious Suspension of your Authority, from whatever Cause proceeding, devolved it in the same moment, without his having an Option, on your immediate Successor in the Command of His Majesty's Forces then within the Limits of the Territory, as your Lieutenant, to whom, I cannot help observing, it appears to me it would not have been imprudent to have instantly referred and possessed of every information in your power, to enable him the better to judge of the nature and of the Causes of the Critical displacement of Your Authority.

Bligh's delay in communicating the facts of his arrest to Paterson.

I must, at the same time, assure You that the call you make on me after this elapse was unnecessary, for could I have seen the possibility of restoring Your Authority without the Orders of His Majesty's Ministers—or indeed, previous to my receiving them—with safety to the Colony, I should not have waited for your demanding what I should have felt compelled to perform the instant I was acquainted with the occurrences that have hap-

Bligh's appeal to Paterson for support.

* Note 199.

1808.
28 Oct.

pened. Nor, I trust, should I have forgotten myself so far as to have presumed to have exacted Conditions from him, whose duty it must have been, the instant he revived Supreme Command, to have conformed to no Stipulations but those of my Superiors; but I can not, in justice to you, conceal that the Causes which have been represented to me as the inducement of the Arrest you urge me to release You from are of an import— and, at the same time, such serious consequences are stated to me may be apprehended should this Step be taken—that I cannot conscientiously wish an Act which can do no possible good until intelligence is received from England, and may be productive of evils my life cannot counterballance.

Paterson's decision to await orders from England.

It has further been represented to me that your departure from the Colony has alone been protracted by Yourself; but I beg to submit to your judgement that your own interests require an immediate presence before those who only can now decide on your conduct, and on the Steps that have been pursued, their Causes and Consequences; and I must add, I feel persuaded that the Peace and Interests of the Settlement over which You have presided equally demands you to hasten your departure, for remaining, as unforeseen circumstances have situated You, can be productive of no good effect to the Community, and prevents the agitation subsiding that has ensued, unavoidably, from an event of so uncommon a nature.

Paterson's reasons for Bligh's return to England.

I have but to add that, in the conduct I myself pursue, in the very intricate situation I am placed, if I am thought to have err'd, it will have proceeded from a deficiency of Judgement and not an absence of intention to Act for the Honor and the Welfare of His Majesty's Service.

Causes that I have explained to the Right Hon'ble the Secretary of State have hitherto prevented my appearing at Port Jackson; but I am now preparing to leave my present Command by a Vessel for which I have written with this opportunity to convey me to Sydney, where I shall take upon me the temporary Administration of the Government until I am possessed of directions for my further Guidance; and, should you not have left the Country before the period I may be expected to arrive, I have been necessitated to apprise Lieut't-Governor Foveaux that it will become unavoidable that you should remove to the Government House at Parramatta, that I may be enabled to carry on the business of the Colony at the Government House of the Head Quarters.

Paterson to assume the temporary administration.

I have, &c.,
,WM. PATERSON.

[Enclosure No. 42.]

LIEUTENANT-COLONEL FOVEAUX TO GOVERNOR BLIGH.

Sir,　　　　　　　　Headquarters, 25th October, 1808.

I beg leave to acquaint You that, in compliance with H.M.S. Lieut.-Governor Paterson's requisition, His Majesty's Ship Por- poise will sail on Sunday next for Port Dalrymple.

Should you wish to make any communication to that Officer, I shall transmit such Letters as you may think proper to send.

I have, &c.,
J. FOVEAUX.

H.M.S. Porpoise to sail for Port Dalrymple.

[Enclosure No. 43.]

GOVERNOR BLIGH TO LIEUTENANT-COLONEL FOVEAUX.

Sir,　　　Government House, Sydney, 25th October, 1808.

I am much surprised to find that Lieutenant-Governor Paterson has made the requisition mentioned in your Letter of this Morning, as he knew me to be Commodore on this Station, and equally astonished at the compliance of Captain Kent. From my imprisonment and my communication being stopt with him, I have to request You will inform him that it is my orders that he does not leave this Cove.　　　　I am, &c.,
WM. BLIGH.

Interference with Bligh's naval command.

[Enclosure No. 44.]

LIEUTENANT-COLONEL FOVEAUX TO GOVERNOR BLIGH.

Sir,　　　　　　　Headquarters, 26th October, 1808.

In answer to your Letter of yesterday, I have to acquaint You that the Porpoise will sail for Port Dalrymple on Sunday next (as I have already informed You) for the purpose of con- veying Lieut.-Governor Paterson to Head Quarters.

I have, &c.,
J. FOVEAUX.

H.M.S. Porpoise to carry Paterson to Sydney.

GOVERNOR BLIGH TO VISCOUNT CASTLEREAGH.

(Despatch No. 2, per whaler Albion.)

Government House, Sydney,
My Lord,　　　　　New South Wales, 28th October, 1808.

In consequence of a seditious Advertisement in the Rebel *Gazette* of the 25th Ultimo (which I enclose) by Lieu't-Colonel Foveaux, I received the enclosed Papers from Mr. Campbell, who in my time was Naval Officer. The Sandal-Wood has been procured with old Iron, made into a kind of Chisels, and Nails, Beads, and Trinkets of any kind, and on very fair principles, which the Estimate shows. I put a Duty of £2 10s. per Ton on

Importation of and duty on sandal-wood.

Importation of
and duty on
sandal-wood.

exportation, which was paid by the Purchaser, and not at all felt
by the Merchant. I valued the Sandal-Wood at only £50 per Ton,
while it sold here for about £70, on an average, to Vessels going
to China.   I remain, &c.,
                                              WM. BLIGH.

[Enclosure No. 1.]
GOVERNMENT AND GENERAL ORDER.
Headquarters, Sydney, 24th September, 1808.

Abolition of
the duty on
sandal-wood.

THE duty laid by order of Governor Bligh on the shipping of
Sandal-Wood is not in future to be levied; but the exporters of
that article are to be required to enter into security for the
payment of it, should the imposition of such duty be sanctioned
by His Majesty's Ministers, for whose instructions on that head
Lieutenant-Governor Foveaux means to apply by the earliest
opportunity.

Such sums as have hitherto been paid on account of said duty
are to be returned by the Naval Officer to the persons who paid
them, on their giving security for the repayment should they be
hereafter called upon for that purpose, in consequence of the
continuance of the duty being approved of by the Government in
England.

By Command of His Honor the Lieutenant Governor.

JAMES FINUCANE, Secretary.

[Enclosure No. 2.]
MR. ROBERT CAMPBELL TO GOVERNOR BLIGH.

Sir,   Sydney, 26th September, 1808.

Campbell's
opinion on
the duty on
sandal-wood.

On reading the General Order of Yesterday respecting the
duty on sandal-wood, I cannot refrain expressing my indignation
at the Art and Chicanery that has been attempted by the Persons
who usurped your Excellency's Government, to place the salutary
and wise Regulations you had enacted for the general benefit and
Welfare of the Colony in an unfavourable point of view, no doubt
with an intention of deluding the Public to answer sinister purposes; permit me to inclose your Excellency an Estimate of the
Cost and Charges of a Colonial Ship or Vessel on a Sandal-Wood
Voyage, which is done on principles the rascality and deceit practiced here cannot refute.

As this duty was only to be paid when the Article came to be
exported, it could not operate against the Inhabitants, not even
those who had experienced so very lucrative a trade in procuring
Sandal-Wood, as the Duty was paid by the Purchaser, and who
have paid a much greater price than Fifty Pounds p'r Ton, the
Value that had been rated when the Exportation Duty of Fifty
Shillings p'r Ton was first enacted.   I have, &c.,
                                              ROB'T CAMPBELL.

[Enclosure No. 3.]

1808.
28 Oct.

Estimate of the Cost, Expences, and Outfit of a Colonial Vessel proceeding on a Voyage to the Feejee Islands for Sandal-Wood, &c.

Estimated cost of trading voyage to Fiji.

	£	s.	d.
Value of the Vessel fitted for Sea, with Boatswain, Carpenter, and Gunner's Stores	2,000	0	0

Monthly Wages, viz.:—

Master	£15
Chief Mate	8
Second Do.	6
Carpenter	6
Boatswain	5
15 Seamen @ £4	60

	£	s.	d.
£100 per Month for 6 Months is	600	0	0

Provisions and Trade.

		£	s.	d.		£	s.	d.
26 Weeks at 1 lb. Pork pr. Man pr. Day, is 3,640 lb. at 1s. 6d.		273	0	0				
26 Weeks Bread per Man, is 3,640 lbs. @ 36s. per Cwt.		58	10	0				
Flour, 520 lb. @ 6d.		13	0	0				
Sugar, 520 lb. @ 1s.		26	0	0				
Spirits, ½ Gill daily per Man, 45 Galls. @ 15s.		33	15	0				
Trade		200	0	0				
						604	5	0
Premium of Insurance on £3,000 (Sea Risk) @ 5 per Cent.						150	0	0
Total Amount						£3,354	5	0

Cr.

	£	s.	d.
Suppose 130 Tons of Sandal-Wood, being the Average of Four Cargoes already received, at £50 per Ton..	6,500	0	0
Deduct the Cost of the Vessel and outfit with sailing Expences agreeable to the above estimate	3,354	5	0
	3,145	15	0
Add the Value of the Vessel on her return	1,200	0	0
Net Profit on investing a Capital of £3,354 5s. in Six Months	£4,345	15	0

Estimated profits from a cargo of sandal-wood.

Rob't Campbell.

Mem.—The Estimate of Duties to be paid on Sandal-Wood was made on Fifty Pounds per Ton, whereas it has been sold here by the Proprietors considerably higher.

1808.
28 Oct.

GOVERNOR BLIGH TO THE HON. WILLIAM POLE.

(Despatch per whaler Albion.)

Government House, Sydney,

Sir,   New South Wales, 28th October, 1808.

Previous
despatches.

    The last Dispatches which I had the honor to write to you
for the information of My Lords Commissioners of the Admiralty were dated the 1st July, 31st August, and 10th of September,
and sent by Mr. Richard Brooks of the Rose, to whose care they
were particularly confided, together with a duplicate of my letter
of the 30th of April To the arrival of Lieutenant Colonel Foveaux
(who has declared himself as Lieutenant Governor of the Colony).

Correspondence
with Foveaux.

I had been troubled with many designing, artful, and some insulting Letters which seemed intended, as those do which I have
received since from Lieut. Colonel Foveaux, to place me in some
farther difficulty. To the 6th of August their Lordships are now
in possession of these letters; and I suppose I should not again
have been troubled with any more of them but on the 14th
September Lieutenant Colonel Foveaux renewed his correspondence under the auspices of McArthur, in order to entrap
me to consent to return home in the Porpoise without any
command, notwithstanding my having expressed great indignation at his presuming to interfere with my Naval authority.
The correspondence I beg leave to inclose, by which their Lordships will observe the artfulness, ignorance and insolence of
these Usurpers of Government, which they have acquired through
Treason and Mutiny. To the Spirit of such principles their
Lordships will likewise see they are threatening me with a Jail,
as my existence is a terror to them; I think, however they will

Prohibition of
intercourse
with H.M.S.
Porpoise.

not dare to do that, altho' they have again deprived me of any
communication with my Ship on board of which My Broad
Pendant is still flying, and I am informed that Captain Kent
has received a Letter to comply with the restrictions I am placed
under, which I apprehend is the case, as he has not called on
me since.

Departure of the
Lady Nelson.

On the 22nd Ulto. I observed the Lady Nelson Tender to sail
out of the Harbour, of Her destination and Captain Kent's
motives for permitting her to depart I expect he will inform
their Lordships. He has been fully apprised by me of his Duty,
but I cannot find that he has once demanded my Person out of
the hands of this rebellious Soldiary, or rather the officers of
the New South Wales Corps.

    In my Dispatch of the 31st August, I mentioned that the
Estramina Schooner was sent for Lieutenant Governor Paterson;

she returned on the 12th Instant without him. He wrote up to
Lieutenant Colonel Foveaux, and it appears by Copies of two
letters inclosed to me from the Lieutenant Colonel that he has H.M.S.
Porpoise to be
sent to Port
Dalrymple for
Paterson.
joined their party, and written for His Majesty's Ship Porpoise
to go down for him, which requisition had been made to Captain
Kent. I immediately wrote to Lt. Col. Foveaux and told him, it
was at the Peril of any Man to remove the Flag which was
flying out of my sight. Affairs thus stood until the 25th Instant
when I received another Letter from the Lieutenant Col. informing me that His Majesty's Ship Porpoise would sail for
Port Dalrymple on the following Sunday. I immediately replied
that I was surprised at Lieutenant Governor Paterson's requisition as he knew me to be Commodore on this Station, and
I was equally astonished with the compliance of Captain Kent,
and that from my confinement and my communication being
stopt with him, I had to request he would inform him that it was
my Orders he did not leave the Cove Yet it is persisted in This
correspondence is contained in No. 2 which is enclosed.

Thus again it appears that His Majesty's Ship is taken from
my command to bring up a Lieutenant Governor who openly
avowed his taking the side of his rebellious and mutinous Corps,
in which also her Acting Commander has joined, as he has fired
a Gun and made the Signal for Sailing, and must in consequence take upon himself to strike my Broad Pendant in defiance
of my orders and the rules of our service. This wanton insult is
the greater, as there is the Lady Nelson and a fine Schooner
called the Estramina now lying in the Cove.

Under every confidence of their Lordships' support,

I have, &c.,

WM. BLIGH.

[Enclosures Nos. 1 and 2.]

[*Copies of this correspondence were also forwarded as enclosures numbered 34, 35, 36, 37, 38, 42, 43 and 44 to Governor
Bligh's despatch to Viscount Castlereagh, dated 28th October,
1808.*]

GOVERNOR BLIGH TO VISCOUNT CASTLEREAGH.

(Despatch per whaler Albion.)

Government House, Sydney.

My Lord,   New South Wales, 4th Novr., 1808.

Mr. Commissary Palmer by his enquiries into the conduct
of the Rebel Party has discovered great frauds in their transactions with Government Property. To point out a small part

of their iniquity he has sent the inclosed Letter, which I beg
leave to submit for Your Lordship's inspection, as it shows the
labour we shall have to correct all these abuses when I have it in
my power to resume my Government.

·I have, &c.,
WM. BLIGH.

[Enclosure.]

COMMISSARY PALMER TO GOVERNOR BLIGH.

Sir,　　　　　　　　　　　　　　Sydney, 4th November, 1808.

In addition to the letter I did myself the honor of laying
before Your Excellency, of the 31st August last,* I have to offer a
few further remarks.

The gross impositions carried on by the persons now in office,
to engross not only Grain, but also every other article, is beyond
conception; there are several instances of their purchasing Grain
from the Settlers and others at so low a rate as 2s. 6d. and 3s. p'r
Bushel (and has been frequently sold by execution on their effects
at 1s. 6d.), and paying for it in Spirits at £2 10s. and £3 p'r
Gallon; This they turn into store, and receive for it Articles from
the Store, or Cattle from the Government Stock. The advantages
arising to the purchaser of Cattle will appear as follows:—

	£	s.	d.
Government price for an Ox, or Cow	28	0	0
By 112 Bushels Maize at 5s., the price given by Government	28	0	0
112 Bushels of Maize, purchased from Individuals at 3s. p'r Bus'h	16	16	0
6¾ Gallons of Spirits, to pay for the same at £2 10s. p'r Gallon, is	16	16	0
Profit arising on the 112 Bushels of Maize, 2s. p'r Bushel, the difference between the sum paid and the sum allowed by Government	11	4	0
Do. from the 6¾ Gallons of Spirits	12	15	0
Total gain on the above	23	19	0

By the above statement it appears that the purchaser has the
Cow for £4 1s., and a clear profit of £23 19s. So much for barter
of Spirits for Grain, &c. The Settlers by this means are deprived
of pay'g their Government Debt, or putting Grain into Store.
Several of them have, upon application for that purpose, been
refused, owing to the Artifice of their Agents up the Country.
Fitz may be classed as one of the first, and one of the busiest of
the party. The situations he now holds, and the close Intimacy
subsisting between McArthur and Blaxcell, rather enforces the
People to let him have Grain at any price; and, being their
principal Agent, he is supplied by them with Spirits, Tea, Sugar,

* Note 200.

&c., in Order to pay for it. Thus Your Excellency will please to 1808.
4 Nov. observe all the Grain falls into the Hands of a few. Thus far Methods adopted to monopolise grain supplies. the Settlers are deprived of the Indulgencies they might have otherwise have had, either of receiving Articles from the Store, or Cattle, had they been permitted to put it in the Stores on their own Accounts.

The Quantity of Cattle received by Mr. Fitz is great, and Disposal of public live stock. scarce one of them paid for; indeed, the greatest part disposed of since the 26th January are still unsettled, so that the loss to Government will be immense; and Fitz, having taken upon himself the Superintendence of the Stock, can be of no Service to Government as Deputy-Commissary, and I am well persuaded in my own mind that his acceptance of the same arises from some sinister View to serve the Party and himself in the selection of Stock, and 'tis very evident that the sale of Cattle must have been made mearly as a Cloak, for the greatest part of the Cattle sold were old and very poor, and fell into the hands of McArthur, Blaxcell, Lawson, and a few others at a very low price, and were by them returned back to Government Stock; for what purpose they were permitted so to do needs no Comment, Fitz being the grand Selector.

One thing I cannot help remarking of McArthur and his Col- Malpractices permitted in the issue of stores. leagues : they received Articles from the Store to fit up and furnish their Houses, and issued as for Government use, and never meant to be charged against them. However, conscious of their having acted improperly, or fearful that Government might hear of it and cause an enquiry to be made, they have now requested Bills to be made out, and the Articles that stood charged as for Government use to be altered, and to stand as a charge against themselves. It is singular that this did not strike them before, as many of the Articles have been Issued so long ago as February last, and they well knew that they were issued from the Stores to answer their own private purposes, and, at the same time, knew they were Charged to Government.

It is a matter of astonishment to me, and I make no doubt Fresh beef issued to Johnston. will also be to Your Excellency when you are informed of the Quantity of Fresh Beef received by Major Johnston from the 26th Jan'y to the 30th July (viz.) Beef 1,268 lbs., and 4,562½ lbs. of Offal as P'r Inclosed Account, fearful of an Investigation he like Mr. McArthur has ordered a Bill to be made out and I suppose means to pay a part of the same.

Such infamy practised by this Selected party is really won- Discontent amongst the settlers. derful and the Inhabitants in general seem now awake to it and murmur greatly at their proceedings, finding dayly that the

1808.
4 Nov.

Discontent
amongst the
settlers.

Colony gets worse and worse, and no encouragement or indulgences whatever is given to any person, except to the Party themselves, or their few favorites, as nothing can be had except what comes through their Hands. Spirits seems to be the only mode of payment hitherto resorted to.

Payment of
claims in
spirits.

As the Limeburners and every person who have any Claims upon Government gets paid in that way, even the Freight of Vessels are paid in that manner—Nichols who seems to be the favorite has received Spirits twice on that account, and even

Informal
payments
made to
Isaac Nichols.

made a Charge for Freight of Provisions and Stores to the Coal River, an Instance never before known or suffered, as the Carriage of Provisions &c. thither was always thought by the Owners of Vessels and Boats an Indulgence, as it saved their procuring Ballast, and he has received payment for Freight when Government Col. Vessels has been in Ballast, and going to the same Port and such has been the alacrity us'd by him in getting his Vessel loaded or unloaded, that even Artificers or Mechanics have been taken from public duty to assist, and have had her ready for Sea again in the course of a day or two when the Government Vessels have been a Week or more, so that his Vessel is mostly at Sea and principally employed by Government on Freight—the only reason that can be assigned for this Man receiving such Indulgencies may be this—he was particularly active at the time of the deposing Your Excellency, and by Subtile Artifice procuring Signatures to the address handed about by the rebellious party.

I have further to observe the nefarious practices carried on by the party to keep as much as possible the Soldiers in favor—

Favours given
to military.

They have caused the whole of their Women and Children to be Victualled from the Public Stores, and Kable from a hint drop'd him by one of their Party suffered the Serjeants to receive from his proportion of Spirits allowed him by Genl. Order, One Gallon each at prime Cost.

Macarthur's
alleged
suppression
of evidence.

Such Still and I may add ever will be the consciousness of McArthur's Villainy, and afraid of his dark and diabolical designs being brought to light, has interested himself so far as to get his late Orderly when Colonial Secretary, Serjt. Hughes, sent to Port Dalrymple fearful of his reporting to Col. Paterson his transactions while in office, and I am informed from a Person that saw Hughes on board His Majesty's Ship Porpoise that it was very much against his wish to go down, having a small Family he knew no reason why he should be sent, except by his speaking freely to McArthur respecting a Cow he promised him from Government for his services as orderly to him.

I believe Your Excellency knew of a Ship called the Pegasus being sent after Captain Campbell's Brig Harrington and fitted out by Government. The Outfit, Stores &c. were to be returned or charged—They were as well as Provisions given in Charge to Mr. Symons, what Account he has rendered I know not, but this I can say, nothing of any consequence has been returned into Store—the deficiency amounts to about £870—exclusive of 6 weeks Provisions put on board for 71 Persons and 50 Gallons of Spirits.

1808.
4 Nov.

Expenses of the voyage of the Pegasus in pursuit of the Harrington.

In the former part of my letter I mentioned the Number of Cattle disposed of but had omitted to state the Number of Oxen lent, which has since come to my knowledge, therefore now think proper to shew Your Excellency the Names of the Persons receiving Cattle for payment as well as Oxen lent (Viz.).

Cattle disposed of and lent.

Fitz	42	Cows disposed of	6	lent
Lawson	18	,, do.	7	do.
Fitzgerald	10	,, do.	5	do.
Blaxcell	24	,, do.	10	do.
J. Blaxland	32	,, do.	16	do.
G. Blaxland	38	,, do.	22	do.
Nichols	17	,, do.	6	do.
McArthur	11	,, do.	—	do.
Capt. Kemp	24	,, do.	14	do.

besides a Number of others from 2 to 6 each by those means Your Excellency will see how much Government Stock is reduced and by what means. The mode of disposal of them is unprecedented, and if I mistake not or am rightly informed, part of those Oxen so lent to the above persons are let out to hire by them to Individuals—The exact Account of Stock at present I cannot get at, for instead of the Superintendant of Stock making a Weekly Return as heretofore usual to the Commissary's Office, not one Single Return has been made except One jumbled together (and that altered in many respects by Fitz) which no person can understand but themselves. I need not point out to Your Excellency the reason of this vile procedure, as I dare say You will agree with me in Opinion that their illicit transactions are so *dark* and *glaring,* they are afraid of the same being brought to *light,* nor do I suppose the Returns will ever appear in their true state but be moddelled afresh to Answer their own Ends, whenever they are obliged to return them in—McArthur and Fitz has the chief management of Stock returns, as well as the Grain, and two such adepts in Villainy, they could not be in better hands—but I trust a future time will develope all and shew their transactions in their true Colours.

Returns of stock not available.

I have, &c.,
JNO. PALMER, Commissary.

1808.
4 Nov.

Return of
beef and offal
issued to
Johnston.

[Sub-enclosure.]

AN Account of Beef and Offal consisting of Tallow, Hearts, and
Tongues, &c., drawn from His Majesty's Store, Sydney, by
Major Johnston from 13th February to 23rd July, 1808,
Inclusive.

1808.	No. of Bullocks Killed.	No. lbs. Beef.	of lbs. Offal.	
February 13th	3	89	83	N.B.—The One hundred and
,, 20th	3	70½	114½	Sixty One pounds of Beef is
,, 27th	3	75	84	deducted' from the Amount,
March 5th	3	78	84	One Thousand two hundred
,, 12th	3	59½	101	and Sixty-Eight Pounds, as
,, 19th	3	67½	155	allowed him for his Weekly
,, 26th	3	77	144	Ration at Seven Pounds per
April 2nd	3	63	152½	Week.
,, 9th	3	57	124	
,, 16th	3	25	151	The Beef sold in the Market, at
,, 23rd	3	50½	133	I believe 1/6 per pound, most
,, 30th	5	76	195	of the time he drew this Beef
May 7th	5	51	271	the Offal would have brought
,, 14th	5	61	196	a much greater price for making
,, 21st	5	47½	245	Candles and Soap these Arti-
,, 28th	6	51½	230½	cles being very scarce in the
June 4th	7	48½	257	Country. English Candles and
,, 11th	7	33	256	Soap sold from 2/6 to 3/6 per
,, 18th	7	16½	242	lb. about this time.
,, 25th	7	34½	205	
July 2nd	7	48	243	
,, 9th	7	47	267	
,, 16th	9	16	300	
,, 23rd	8	25½	359	
	118	1268 161	4562½	@ 1/6 £342 3 9 Total to be carried to Account.
		1107 lbs.		@ 1/3 69 3 9
				£411 7 6

GOVERNOR BLIGH TO VISCOUNT CASTLEREAGH.

(Despatch per whaler Albion.)

Government House, Sydney,
New South Wales, 7th Novr., 1808.

7 Nov.

Departure of
H.M.S.
Porpoise for
Port
Dalrymple.

My Lord,

In consequence of the Ship Albion not sailing on the
28th Ultimo, I have the opportunity to inform Your Lordship
that His Majesty's Ship Porpoise sailed on the 1st Instant for

Port Dalrymple to bring up Lieutenant Governor Paterson, not‑ 1808.
7 Nov. withstanding my opposition as stated in my Letter of the 28th Ultimo, No. 1.

Departure of
H.M.S.
Porpoise for
Port
Dalrymple.

I have nothing of consequence farther to communicate to Your Lordship, and have, &c.,

WM. BLIGH.

GOVERNOR BLIGH TO THE HON. WILLIAM POLE.

(Despatch per whaler Albion.)

Government House, Sydney,

Sir, New South Wales, 7th Novr., 1808.

The accompanying Despatches were closed on the 28th Departure of
Kent in H.M.S.
Porpoise. Ultimo, but the Ship being detained I have the honor to write again to acquaint You for the information of my Lords Commissioners of the Admiralty that on the 1st Instant Captain Kent took His Majesty's Ship to Sea without my permission, leaving the Lady Nelson, Tender, and Estramina, Colonial Schooner, in the Cove, but neither of them bearing my Broad Pendant, although Lieutenant Ellison of the Porpoise is left in Command of the former.

A Mr. Charles Cockerill in the Ship Albion will have the charge of these Despatches to deliver to You.

I have, &c.,
WM. BLIGH.

GOVERNOR BLIGH TO UNDER SECRETARY COOKE.

(Despatch per whaler Albion.)

Government House, Sydney,

Sir, New South Wales, 8th Novr., 1808.   8 Nov.

The Bearer Mr. Cockerill I have deputed to take my Delivery of
Bligh's
despatches. Dispatches to you as soon as the Albion anchors in any Port of Great Britain. He may be able to give you information on particular circumstances, but he was not here on the 26th January.

The Master Mr. Richardson who has charge of the Dispatches, 'till the Ship arrives, has my orders to suffer no delay to take place in their being delivered.

I have, &c.,
WM. BLIGH.

Lt. Col. Foveaux has taken all my Stationary, and I am reduced at present to this miserable paper.

1808.
8 Nov.

GOVERNOR BLIGH TO UNDER SECRETARY COOKE.

(A private letter per whaler Albion.)

Government House, Sydney,

Dear Sir,   New South Wales, 8th November, 1808.

Bligh's
compliments
to Cooke.

To my Dispatches which will come under your inspection I have only to express my sincere wish that you may enjoy good health, and to acquaint you of my having written by the Rose, Richard Brooks Master, in September last.

I am perfectly, and with great esteem I beg leave to subscribe myself, &c.,

WM. BLIGH.

LIEUTENANT-COLONEL FOVEAUX TO VISCOUNT CASTLEREAGH.

(Despatch marked A, per whaler Albion.)

9 Nov.

Despatches by
the Albion.

My Lord,   Sydney, Port Jackson, 9th November, 1808.

The departure of the Albion whaler for England affords me an opportunity of communicating with your Lordship, which I avail myself of, with so great a degree of mistrust that I do not think it prudent even to commit to her conveyance the duplicates of my dispatches to your Lordship by the Rose.*

Want of
confidence in
Messrs.
Campbell & Co.

This distrust arises from the Albion being partly the property and entirely under the controul of Messrs. Campbell and Co. of this place, who, as your Lordship has been informed by my letter of the 4th of September last, took every Measure in their power to prevent my dispatches to your Lordship from being convey'd to England in the Rose, And who have on the present occasion refused to allow the Master of the Albion to accomodate two officers with a passage to England, agreeable to a requisition made by me for that purpose; And my want of confidence is naturally encreased from the circumstance of its being well ascertained that very few of such letters as have heretofore been entrusted to ships from this colony under the influence or Management of Messrs. Campbell & Co. have ever reached the hands of those persons to whom they were directed in England.

Supplies of
grain
available.

I am, therefore, under the necessity of confining myself at present to some very general remarks upon the affairs of the Colony, and it gives me much pleasure to commence with acquainting Your Lordship that the Stores contain a sufficient quantity of grain to serve until the produce of the ensuing harvest shall be saved, which, from the appearance of the growing crops, promises to be uncommonly abundant.

Price offered by
government
for meat.

I beg leave to correct a Mistake in my letter (A) of the 4th of September to Your Lordship, by the Rose; I mentioned one Shilling per pound as the price I meant to offer for meat to be

* Note 201.

taken into His Majesty's Stores, the price offer'd has been nine pence, And a quantity (chiefly Swine's flesh) equal to my expectation, has already been received.

I expect that the walls of the New Stone granary at Paramatta Granary at Parramatta. will be completed in less than a fortnight.

I have commenced and made very considerable progress in the Erection of erection of a substantial brick barrack,* one hundred and eighty barracks. feet in length, And two stories high, in addition to the old one, a measure become indispensible from the increased strength of the New South Wales Corps by the reinforcements which arrived in the Sinclair and the Recovery, and by those expected in the Ships now on their passage from England.

The completion of the new Barrack will, however, by no Means afford adequate accomodation for the number of the Corps stationed at Head Quarters, and the present distress'd state of the colony for Government Mechanics and labourers puts it out of my power to carry on a further extension of the new or even to accomplish the necessary repairs of the old one. The troops must, therefore, still continue in a great degree exposed to the inconveniences described to your Lordship in My letter (A) of the fourth of September.

The Estramina, Schooner, which I sent to Port Dalrymple immediately after my arrival here, to convey Lieutenant-Governor Paterson hither, returned on the 12th of last Month without him. He assigns the bad state of his health and the want of Reasons for sufficient accomodation in the Estramina as the causes of his not Paterson's delay in having come to headquarters, And requires that His Majesty's returning Ship Porpoise may again be sent for him. As the damages to Sydney. sustained by that vessel when before dispatched on the same Service were completed, I applied to her Acting Commander, Captain Kent, to proceed with her to Port Dalrymple, And She accordingly sail'd from hence on the 31st Ultimo.

I beg leave to enclose for Your Lordship's perusal, a copy of Correspondence Lieut. Governor Paterson's letter to me (with its enclosures) by with Paterson. the Estramina, And of Mine to him by the Porpoise.

These papers will Acquaint Your Lordship of Captain Bligh's determination of remaining in this colony untill His Majesty's pleasure shall be known.

I have transmitted the proceedings of the general Court Martial Court martial by which the late Acting Commissary Mr. Williamson has been on James Williamson. tried, to The Judge Advocate General, to whom (after he has received His Majesty's decision thereon) I beg leave to refer your Lordship for the Sentence pass'd by the Court.

I have to observe that the order given by Governor King (which is annex'd to the proceedings of the Court) and men-

* Note 192.

1808.
9 Nov.
———
Williamson's
claim to the
issue of fresh
meat.

tioned by Mr. Williamson in his defence, as authorizing the Store Keeper to issue a certain portion of fresh beef for the use of the Commissary, was given at a time when it was usual to Kill a bullock only occasionally and at very considerable intervals, and could never have been intended to convey a right to every Succeeding Commissary to appropriate to himself the same quantity from every bullock to be kill'd when the rations of meat served to the whole Civil and Military establishments consisted solely of fresh beef, and when consequently not less than eight or ten bullocks on an average were slaughter'd every week, as was the case during the period that Mr. Williamson was in charge of the Stores, And when he took for himself more than double the Weight mentioned in Governor King's letter. And I think it further necessary to apprize Your Lordship that immediately after my taking the Command of the Colony, I gave a particular and possitive order to Mr. Williamson that no person whatever was, on any pretence, to draw from the Stores a greater quantity of provisions than the ration allowed by His Majesty's regulation, And I understand that a similar injunction was given him by Major Johnston My predecessor in the Command.

I make no doubt but that a reference to Governor King respecting the order produced by Mr. Williamson (as well as of other matters attending the tryal, which may require explanation) will convince Your Lordship that My opinion upon that subject is not ill founded.

Necessity for
the appointment
of an expert
commissary.

Altho' I had it in my power to lay before the Court Martial but a very trifling specimen of the immense frauds committed in the Commissariat, I trust enough has transpired to convince your Lordship of the absolute necessity of sending some person of integrity, experience and respectability to preside over a department of such peculiar importance to the interests of His Majesty's government in this colony, and of providing him with assistants from England possess'd of common honesty and diligence (a description of Men not to be found in this Country) to fill the Subordinate Situations of Store Keepers and Clarks.

Arrival of the
brig Star.

The Brig Star arrived here from England on the 10th of last Month, and her Master has reported to me that the Speke Transport for this Colony parted in Latitude 9° North, to proceed to the Cape of Good Hope.   I have, &c.,

J. FOVEAUX.

[Enclosure No. 1.]

LIEUTENANT-GOVERNOR PATERSON TO LIEUT.-COLONEL FOVEAUX.

Sir,   Launceston, Port Dalrymple, 29th September, 1808.

Your dispatch of the 16th Ult'o* has afforded me a satisfaction to perceive You have Acted with a deliberation equal to

* Note 202.

1808.
9 Nov.

the firmness I had anticipated you wou'd exercise in the most Critical state you have found the Public Affairs.

Paterson's regret for delay in returning to Sydney.

You will doubtless have been Acquainted with the reasons that have prevented your finding myself at Port Jackson, and altho' retrospection is fruitless, I now regret that any representation shou'd for a moment have suspended the resolution I had formed from the Opinion I entertained that my duty to repair there was absolute; but from the intimation transmitted to me of your being Appointed my Successor in the Lieutenant-Governorship of the Territory, I judged it prudent to wait your daily expected Arrival.

Paterson's severe illness.

Since the departure of His Majesty's Ship Porpoise my Constitution has undergone a Trial I had given up all hopes of surviving, and that has left me debilitated beyond any attack I have before known; indeed, so much so, that altho' I am not unaware of the pressing necessity of my presence at Sydney, yet I feel I shou'd, by venturing on a Passage in the Estramina, be criminally rushing in my destruction.

I have therefore return'd her as early as Circumstances wou'd allow, that no time may be lost in a Vessel of larger burthen being sent, in which I may venture to once more repair to the Head-Quarters of the regiment I have the Honor to Command in New South Wales, with some shadow of hope of reaching them.

Bligh's restoration inadvisable.

The Contents of the 2d, 3d, and 8th Paragraphs of your Dispatch relating to the late Governor Bligh impress me fully with the Conviction that by any Power in it to attempt his restoration to Command wou'd be dangerous to the safety of the Territory, and that no Authority but that of His Majesty's Ministers can now extricate the Colony from the state the unforeseen events occurring have placed it in.

Paterson's advice to Bligh to sail for England.

In Answer to the first Communication I have receiv'd from Captain Bligh since his Arrest, I have stated to him my apprehension that he will be meeting the wishes of his Superiors if he repairs to England as instantly as possible, where alone the Approval or disapprobation of his Conduct, or of the steps that have Annulled his Authority, can further affect him.

Bligh to vacate government house at Sydney.

By my dispatch you will also learn I have inform'd that Officer, unless he does so proceed, it will be necessary he shou'd remove to the Government House at Parramatta, that the Government House at Sydney may be ready for my reception, to enable me to properly Carry on the very anxious duties of the Offices become incumbent on me by the Interreign that has been occasioned. And I have to beg that You will (shou'd he not have left the Colony) Cause the proper steps to be taken for his removal by the period you may have reason to expect my Arrival.

1808.
9 Nov.

The control of
the naval
service.

The delicacy you have exercised with respect to interfering with the Naval Service, from an apprehension of the Step you might take not being strictly Conformant to its regulations, I cannot but much approve, expressing at the same time my own inability to form a Conclusion that can safely decide the line to be adopted in so singular an instance, although I must add it appears to me that His Majesty's Ship Porpoise having been sent out for the Service of the Settlement, she must consequently be at the Controul of the director of it for the time being.

Necessity for
Bligh leaving
the colony.

It wou'd be here, further, at such a Moment, improperly withholding from You an Opinion of which the nature of Your decisive Communication alone requires my explicit avowal,— that, as the Country is now Situated, I see the absolute necessity of the late Governor quitting the Colony, if the removal from the Inhabitants of any Cause of further agitation is exclusively Considered; indeed, I fully believe the Ministers will be of Opinion so much time shou'd not have elapsed as has been lost by the obstacles which, it appears, have protracted his Departure; and it seems to me, from every point of view in which I have seriously Contemplated the Subject, that it shou'd have been desired by this Officer himself, as immediately as possible after his Authority had been rendered void, from whatever Cause his Cessation proceeded; but I am at the same time persuaded, You will be aware, how difficult it must be for me to form any decisive Conclusion of the further Arrangements necessary, in the Instance, while I am so distant from the Capitol, where, on my Arrival, shou'd your own judgment not have removed the necessity, they will become the first Subject of my determinations; and if Captain Bligh, in the intermediate time, has not

Employment
of H.M.S.
Porpoise.

expressed his unequivocal intention of Sailing as early as His Majesty's Ship Porpoise is ready for Sea, I have to beg You will represent to Capt. Kent that it is my request this Vessel shou'd again Sail for Port Dalrymple to Carry me to Head Quarters, provided she is (as I have reason to suppose must be the Case) prepared for the Voyage by the time my Dispatch reaches you; for, notwithstanding it becomes to us difficult to resolve how far the disposition of this Vessel is Subject to the entire discretion of the Officer who has the Supreme responsibility and Charge of the Territory, for the protection and benefit of which she must have been sent, yet it is a duty, at all events, to prevent the possibility of any blame of her not contributing to such Objects devolving on Ourselves by our not having pointed out the means; and, indeed, I must add that unless Captain Kent considers himself restricted by his Subjection to the Orders of Captain Bligh,

I have the most perfect reliance on his meeting Our wishes with 1808.
9 Nov.
the alacrity that gave me so much pleasure in April last.

Shou'd there, however, be any obstacles to the Porpoise sailing Vessel to be
chartered if
Porpoise not
available.
for this purpose directly, it will become absolutely necessary, and
I must Authorise you, as speedily as possible to take up any
Vessel adapted that may be in the Harbour; and shou'd you not,
from any Cause, Conclude on the Terms of the Voyage yourself,
I see no plan to be pursued more equitable, or that must be more
satisfactory in so particular a Case to His Majesty's Ministers,
than to leave them to a decision conformant to the method I
proposed with the Master of the Brig Harrington, in March last,
my Memorandum of which I enclose; and as a necessity exists Stores to be sent
to Port
Dalrymple.
of Cloathing and Stores of every description being immediately
sent to this Settlement, as well as the propriety of a Supply of
Salt Meat, as by the period I may expect an Arrival there will be
only four Months' rations in the Colony, the Expense that may
be occasioned will be materially Counterballanced by the Sum it
will save in the Opportunity afforded of sending these Supplies.

An Overland Dispatch from Colonel Collins having Apprized Despatches
to England.
me of the means of Communicating direct with the Secretary of
State, I have been unavoidably necessitated to detain the Estramina longer than I had intended, to enable the forwarding many
necessary Papers to His Lordship.

I have now only to Conclude by observing that whatever steps Paterson's
request for
Foveaux's
advice.
are taken in the Interim of being acquainted with the Sentiments
of His Majesty's Ministers, they must be so replete with important Consequences, and require such serious Consideration,
that I feel I shall be in need of a Conjunction of all the Assistance that can be afforded me, and I have a gratification in looking
forward to the Benefit I must receive by your having Arrived in
so urgent a Moment.   I have, &c.,
                                        WM. PATERSON.

[Enclosure No. 2.]

LIEUT.-COLONEL FOVEAUX TO LIEUTENANT-GOVERNOR PATERSON.

(Despatch marked No. 3.)

Sir,   Sydney, Port Jackson, 27th October, 1808.

I have to acknowledge the receipt of your letter of 29th of H.M.S.
Porpoise to be
sent for
Paterson.
Sept'r by the Estramina, and to acquaint you that, in Compliance
with your desire, I immediately applied to Capt'n Kent, Commander of His Majesty's Ship Porpoise, to proceed to Port
Dalrymple, for the purpose of conveying you from thence to
Head Quarters, who willingly acquiesced in the request and lost
no time in getting his Ship ready for that Service.

1808.
9 Nov.

Bligh's
decision to
remain at
government
house.

The annexed Copy of my correspondence with Capt'n Bligh will apprize you of his intention of remaining in this colony untill His Majesty's pleasure shall be known, and of his determination not to relinquish the Government house at Sydney, Altho' required by me, in obedience to your instructions, to remove to Paramatta.

Paterson's
correspondence.

You will also learn that he denies having received any letter from you, as intimated to me in your despatch; But, that he may be informed of your Sentiments respecting his delay in this country, and of your desire that he may leave the Government house, for your accommodation, I have sent him the paper which you enclosed me, purporting to be a copy of a letter from you to him, dated the 29th of Sept'r, the original of which, you gave me to understand, was conveyed to him by the Estramina.

Stores shipped
in H.M.S.
Porpoise.

. I have sent in the Porpoise agreeable to your requisition a Supply of Stores and provisions for the Settlement, and of regimental Cloathing for the detachment of the New South Wales Corps, But as the investment Stores are intended solely for the officers, Settlers, &c., I have thought it expedient to defer making any distribution for Port Dalrymple untill your arrival a delay which can be attended with no inconvenience, as frequent opportunities will occur of sending down Supplies in the colonial trading vessels at a very trifling expense to Government.

Quarters for
Paterson at
Sydney.

As the quarters occupied by me in the Barracks since I have had the Command of the Colony are in an excellent state of repair, and have received considerable additions and improvements since you resided in them, and next to Government house, afford the best accomodations that can be procured for you, I shall have them ready for your reception; And shall myself, previous to your arrival, make Arrangements for removing to Parramatta, or wherever else I can find a suitable habitation.

The letters you have transmitted me for England I shall forward by the Albion Whaler which I am informed will sail in the course of a week.

Brabyn
ordered to Port
Dalrymple.

As you have express'd a wish to have another officer And there being no Captain who can possibly be dispensed with at Head Quarters I have order'd Lieutenant Brabyn to proceed to Port Dalrymple he being the Senior Lieutenant of the Corps and the official notification of his promotion to a company being expected by the first communication from England.

Want of
commissariat
officers.

The late Acting Commissary, Mr. Williamson, being under arrest and suspended from his office untill the Sentence of a general Court Martial, by which he has been tried for embezzlement, shall be approved of by His Majesty, Mr. Wilshire being appointed to fill his Situation, And Mr. Fitz being employ'd on another very important duty, it is totally out of my power to 1808.
9 Nov. send Any person belonging to the Commissary's department from hence to act at Port Dalrymple during the intended absence of Mr. Riley.

With regard to sending down the number of convicts you require, I have to assure you that it is impossible to spare a Man from this Settlement, as we have been so distress'd for labourers as to be obliged to hire Soldiers to thrash the Government wheat, and I fear we shall be considerably embarrass'd for hands sufficient to save the produce of the ensuing harvest on the Government farms. I have, &c.,

Insufficiency of convict labour.

J. FOVEAUX.

LIEUTENANT-COLONEL FOVEAUX TO VISCOUNT CASTLEREAGH.

(Despatch marked B, per whaler Albion.)

My Lord, Sydney, Port Jackson, 9th November, 1808.

I have the honor to acquaint your Lordship that after my dispatches were sent on board the Albion this Morning, The City of Edinburgh, which was charter'd by Major Johnston to remove the Settlers from Norfolk Island to The Derwent arrived here from the latter Settlement.

Arrival of the City of Edinburgh.

I beg leave to transmit your Lordship copies of Lieut. Governor Collins's letters to me with their enclosures, by which you will learn the very distress'd Situation of the Settlers from Norfolk Island, And I lament that it is altogether out of my power to contribute to their relief by affording them a Supply of convicts, as I find considerable difficulty in collecting a sufficient number of Mechanics or labourers to carry on the most essential of the public Works.

Despatches received from Collins.

I also enclose for Your Lordship's information a return of the persons remaining at Norfolk Island on the 30th of September last with the Stock belonging to Government and to Individuals.

Lieut. Governor Collins having represented to me that his settlement is in want of a Supply of every discription of Stores, except provisions, I shall lose no time in dispatching a colonial vessel with as large a proportion as can be spared of the Government and investment goods which arrived in the Sinclair, and of which I have not as yet commenced the distribution.

Stores to be sent to Hobart.

Although Lt. Governor Collins acknowledges my intimation to him of the step I had taken to prevent the fulfilment of his expensive and unnecessary contract with Messrs. Campbell and Hook for Supplying the Settlement with Cattle from Bengal (as stated in my letter B. of the 4th of September) he does not complain that any inconvenience is likely to result from my interference, And had he entertained any such apprehension, it must

The contract with Campbell and Hook.

1808.
9 Nov.

Stock available for Hobart.

have been removed by the offer which Lieut. Governor Paterson has informed me he made to drive to the Derwent half the Stock of cattle at present at Port Dalrymple, And by my notification that he could be provided with any number he may require from hence, whenever he thought proper to apply for them, without any cost whatever to Government and almost without the risque of danger or delay. I have, &c.,

J. FOVEAUX.

[Enclosures Nos. 1, 2, 3, and 4.]

[*These consisted of letters from Lieutenant-Governor Collins, with their enclosures, copies of which will be found in volume I, series III.*]

[Enclosure No. 5.]

[*This return from Norfolk Island will be found amongst the papers relating to the settlement at that dependency.*]

LIEUTENANT-COLONEL FOVEAUX TO UNDER SECRETARY CHAPMAN.

(A private letter per whaler Albion.)

Dear Sir, Sydney, Port Jackson, 9th November, 1808.

By the Albion, which will sail in a few hours, I send you a duplicate of my private letter of the 6th of September by the Rose.

Embarrassment caused by Paterson's indecision.

To the information contained in it, and in My despatches to The Secretary of State, I have little more to add than that I feel myself placed in a most embarrassing and disagreeable Situation by the indecisive conduct of Colonel Paterson, who seems extremely reluctant to leave Port Dalrymple, And yet wishes to be thought altogether as anxious to repair to where he must be conscious his duty calls him.

Abuses at Hobart.

However Strong my Suspicions had before been of the little attention paid at the dependent Settlements to anything but individual interests, they are now more than reallized, And the Arrival of the City of Edinburgh this afternoon from the Derwent has afforded me the most possitive conviction that a System of the most unexampled profusion, waste, and fraud, with respect both to Money and Stores, has been carried on, almost without the affectation of concealment or sense of shame.

Maladministration of Collins.

Colonel Collins, notwithstanding the immense and scarcely credible sums he has drawn for, has not, since the establishment of the Settlement, erected even a shed sufficient to secure the public Stores from the plunder of thieves or shelter them from the inclemency of the weather; and the large Supplies of Stores and implements which he brought from England and which he 1808.
9 Nov. has received from hence, seem to have been converted to no purpose whatever of utility either to the Crown or the Colony.

The System of Government at Port Dalrymple seems to be Model'd upon the same plan as that of the Derwent.

After this Statement, I look upon it as unnecessary to repeat Necessity for appointment the suggestion I took the liberty of offering in my private letter of good of the 6th Sept'r,* respecting the Selection of Men of talents and administrators. integrity for the Government of these Settlements, should it be the expectation of Ministers that England is to derive Any benefit from them to compensate for their expense.

The Brig Star arrived here on the 10th of last Month. I have Importation of spirits in the permitted about 600 Gallons of Rum and Brandy, imported in her brig Star. from England, to be landed, One-half of which I have allowed the proprietors—Messrs. Lord and Kable—who are very extensively engaged in shipping concerns, to appropriate to their own uses, and the remainder has been distributed amongst the officers of the Civil and Military establishments in the proportion of Six Gallons to each.

The harvest promises a most plentiful Supply of grain. As soon as it shall have been saved, I intend to make a distribution Proposed barter of horned cattle amongst the Settlers in exchange for wheat for of cattle. the use of Government, which will Materially reduce the expenses of the ensuing year; And that of the present year, I am happy to inform you, will amount to a sum extremely inconsiderable when compared with the expenditure of preceding Years.

I have, &c.,
J. Foveaux.

LIEUTENANT-COLONEL FOVEAUX TO JUDGE-ADVOCATE GENERAL.

(Despatch per whaler Albion.)

(?) November, 1808.

[A copy of this despatch, enclosing a copy of the proceedings of the court martial on acting commissary Williamson, is not available.]

GOVERNOR BLIGH TO VISCOUNT CASTLEREAGH.

(Despatch per whaler Albion.)

Government House, Sydney,

My Lord,   New South Wales, 12th November, 1808.   12 Nov.

Since closing my Despatches for the Albion, the City of Arrival of the City of Edinburgh has arrived after an absence of twenty-four Weeks. It Edinburgh.

* Note 188.

1808.
12 Nov.

Settlers
removed from
Norfolk Island.
is reported that she carried twenty eight families, amounting to
two hundred and fifty Souls, to the Derwent, where she left them
in a state of wretchedness, almost naked, and has left two hundred and ninety on Norfolk Island. I hope a correct Account
may be transmitted by Lieutenant-Colonel Foveaux, but I have
to observe on whatever it may be, that it is an increase of evils
which never would have attended my Administration.

Lands granted
by Johnston
and Foveaux.
To support the principles of the late Rulers, among other
cunning arts which they have devised to lead the unwary into
their snares, and shew their Authority, is their bold and determined way of giving Grants of Land to certain Persons who they
believe can be secured in their interests. This extraordinary act
is not only rebellious, but insulting; and I find it is used up to
this moment in order to make as many proselytes as they can to
defend them. It varies, however, in one instance, for Major
Johnston has given two thousand Acres to his Son, who, of
course, required no such stimulation to support his Father. I do
not know that the Great Seal has been put to these Grants of
delinquency; but I beg leave to inclose a List which has come to
light this day by a report of the Deputy Surveyor, and there is
little doubt of its being enlarged. Under Your Lordship's directions to me these things will be readily settled the instant I
reassume my Authority, and the People are confident of support.
All Supplies of Stationary being taken from me, I am under the
necessity of writing on what I can get, and hope your Lordship
will admit of this apology.

I have, &c.,

WM. BLIGH.

[Enclosure.]

Return of
lands granted.
ACCOUNT of Land* given away by Major Johnston and Lieutenant Colonel Foveaux up to 8th November, 1808, as far as
can be known at present.

Major Johnston.

Lieut. Lawson	Five Hundred Acres at the foot of the Blue Mountains.
George Johnston (Major Johnston's Son).	Two Thousand Acres including Emu Island, bound by the Range of Mountains and the River Nepean.
Lieut. Minchin	One Hundred Acres at George's River.
Lieut. Moore	Eighty-three Acres near Long Cove.
Ensign Bell	Six Hundred Acres at Richmond.
Mr. Fitz	Six Hundred Acres, and Six Hundred Acres for Captain Short of His Majesty's Ship Porpoise.
Capt. Kemp, the present Judge-Advocate.	Five Hundred Acres.

* Note 203.

Lieutenant-Colonel Foveaux.

—— Faithful .... One Thousand Acres at the back of
                        Canterbury.
Mr. Jas. Wilshire .... Five Hundred Acres adjoining the
                        above.
One of Mrs. Pitt's Daughters Five Hundred Acres.

LIEUTENANT-COLONEL FOVEAUX TO VISCOUNT CASTLEREAGH.

(Despatch per H.M.S. Porpoise.*)

My Lord,   Sydney, New South Wales, 31st December, 1808.

I have the honor to acquaint Your Lordship that the undermentioned Quantities of Grain and Animal Food were purchased by my Order between the 31st July and 31st December, 1808, for the purpose of victualling those necessarily supported at the Expense of the Crown in this Colony:—

Vizt.

Voucher A ..	269	Bushels of Wheat at 10/	£134	10	0
	78	Bushels of Maize 5/	19	10	0
„ B ..	2,507	Pounds of Mutton 1/	125	7	0
„ No. 1 ..	1,745	Pounds of Mutton 1/	87	5	0
„ 2 ..	59	Bushels of Wheat 10/	29	10	0
	378	Bushels of Maize 5/	94	10	0
„ 3 ..	39,795½	Pounds of Animal Food /9d. ..	1,492	6	7½
„ 4 ..	645$\frac{18}{16}$	Bushels of Wheat 10/	322	16	3
	674	Bushels of Maize 5/	168	10	0
	400	Bushels of Barley 7/	140	0	0
„ 8 ..	11,547	Pounds of Salted Pork 1/	577	7	0

And having deemed it expedient to freight one of the Colonial Vessels with Stores and Provisions for the use of the Settlement at the Derwent; and also to purchase a Quantity of Rice and Sugar for the use of the General Hospital in this Settlement, I have to inform Your Lordship the following Expenses have been incurred consequent thereon in addition to the above amount for Provisions. Vizt.

Voucher No. 5 To Freight of the Venus Schooner	£120	0	0
„ Purchase of 24 Canvas Bags	12	0	0
6 „ Purchase of Rice for the Gen. Hospital	28	0	0
7 „ Purchase of Sugar for Do.	93	2	6

	£3,444	14	4½

And the Acting Commissaries having applied to me by Letter for leave to draw Bills on His Majesty's Treasury to liquidate

* Note 204.

these Expenses, I therefore ordered them to draw the following in favor of the undermentioned persons:—

Vizt.

				£	s.	d.
2nd September 1808	No.	1	Thomas Jamison	154	0	0
do.		2	John McArthur	125	7	0
31 December	„	No. 1	do. do.	87	5	0
„ do.	„	2	Thomas Jamison	124	0	0
„ do.	„	3	Rob. Campbell	374	17	9
„ do.	„	4	Neville Butler	173	11	3
„ do.	„	5	James Larra	167	15	3
„ do.	„	6	Garnham Blaxcell	132	0	0
„ do.	„	7	William Redfern	100	0	0
„ do.	„	8	do. do.	100	0	0
„ do.	„	9	do. do.	200	0	0
„ do.	„	10	do. do.	177	7	0
„ do.	„	11	Thomas Jamison	121	2	6
„ do.	„	12	do. do.	205	14	3

Total Amount of Bills drawn	2,243	0	0
Balance on account of outstanding Receipts..	1,201	14	4½
	£3,444	14	4½

I beg leave to state to your Lordship that the Vouchers for the whole of the Expenses incurred during the periods I had the honor of Administering the Government of the Colony are inclosed herewith, and will be drawn for at a future period.

I have, &c.,

J. FOVEAUX.

[Enclosures.]

[Copies of these vouchers with full accounts will be found in a volume in series II.]

COMMENTARY.

COMMENTARY

DESPATCHES.

AUGUST, 1806—DECEMBER, 1808.

Note 1, page 1.

Governor Bligh's Commission.

THIS commission is printed from a copy which is preserved in the office of the state governor at Sydney. This copy is not divided into paragraphs. On comparison of this commission with those of governors Phillip, Hunter, and King (*see* page 1 *et seq.*, 513 *et seq.*, volume I, and page 384 *et seq.*, volume III), it will be observed that each is a copy of the other, with the exception of very minor alterations in text and spelling, and the insertion of the preliminary clauses, which were rendered necessary by the revocation of the preceding commission, in all commissions except that of Governor Phillip. In the commission granted to Governor Bligh by the admiralty, he was granted the privilege of flying a broad pendant, which was not possessed by his predecessor, Governor King.

Note 2, page 14.

Townships.

The word "township" had a specific meaning differing from that commonly used at the present day. It consisted of an aggregation of settlers in a defined area, and usually contained one or more collections of houses known as "towns." The township, whose area was frequently as much as 20,000 or 30,000 acres, roughly corresponds to the modern "shire."

Note 3, page 15.

Also page 100.

Additional Instructions to Governor Bligh.

A comparison of the royal instructions issued to Governor Bligh (*see* page 8 *et seq.*) with those issued to Governor King (*see* page 391 *et seq.*, volume III) will show that they are identical except for the omission in the former of the clause in the latter numbered 6, which related to the cultivation of flax. Governor King's instructions were also a repetition of those issued to Governor Hunter. Notwithstanding all the shortcomings that were alleged against the administrations of Bligh's two predecessors, it was not considered advisable to alter or amplify the royal instructions to Bligh. Verbal conversations at the colonial department and this letter from Viscount Castlereagh contained all the specific directions which were deemed necessary by the secretary of state to achieve numerous reforms.

Note 4, pages 17 and 70.

Lord Buckinghamshire.

Lord Hobart, the former secretary of state for war and the colonies, had succeeded his father as the fourth Earl of Buckinghamshire in November, 1804.

Note 5, page 24.

I propose sailing . . . to arrive in England about the latter end of April.

Governor King did not sail from Port Jackson in H.M.S. *Buffalo* until the 10th of February, 1807, six months after the arrival of Governor Bligh. The causes of the delay were King's ill-health and anxieties regarding the impoverished condition of the commissariat in the colony, which might have necessitated the employment of the *Buffalo* in a voyage to procure provisions.

Note 6, page 26.

Ships.

In the return of shipping (*see* page 114), no ships were entered outwards on the 26th of August and 7th of September, but the date of the outward clearance did not always correspond with the actual date of sailing, as a ship was detained sometimes by adverse weather. The ships referred to by Governor Bligh were the *Britannia* and probably the *Richard and Mary.* The despatches, dated 26th August (*see* pages 19 and 21), were sent in the former vessel, and duplicates were forwarded probably by the latter.

Note 7, page 34.

Also page 35.

The discovery of a Shoal.

This discovery was either a re-discovery of Middleton reef or the actual discovery of the Elizabeth or Seringapatam reef. Middleton reef had been discovered and named by lieutenant Shortland in July, 1788, but its existence was regarded as doubtful, when subsequent search, in the schooner *Francis* and in the armed tender *Supply*, failed to locate it. The west elbow is in lat. 29° 27′ 40″ S., and long. 159° 3′ 38″ E. Elizabeth reef is in lat. 29° 55′ 30″ S., and long. 159° 2′ E.; its discovery has been usually assigned to the ships *Claudine* and *Marquis of Hastings* in the year 1820. It is possible that Elizabeth reef was identical with the reef discovered in 1788 (*see* note 82, volume I). The crew of the *Britannia* thought that they were wrecked on Middleton reef.

The original draft of the protest of the ship *Britannia* is preserved amongst the records of the supreme court at Sydney, and is dated September, 1806.

Note 8, page 48.

Fiscull.

The fiscull or fiscal was a collector of customs and revenues in the establishment at the Cape of Good Hope.

Note 9, page 55.

Also page 80.

A Court Martial on Captain Short.

Joseph Short was tried by a court martial after his arrival in England on charges preferred against him by lieutenant Tetley. He was honorably acquitted. The hardships of his position were brought under the notice of the admiralty (*see* note 189) by the members of the court, and shortly afterwards he was employed with the Sea Fencibles. It was alleged in England that the trial had arisen from the disputes between Governor Bligh and himself (*see* note 22). In reply to these allegations, Tetley made a sworn statement that he had not been instigated by Bligh in making his charges.

Note 10, page 55.

Also page 182.

G. L. M. Huon de Kerillac.

No land grant was recorded as issued by Governor Bligh in consequence of these orders from the secretary of state. On the 8th of August, 1809, lieutenant-governor Paterson granted 400 acres in the district of Minto to Gabriel Louis Marie Huon de Kerillian, and this grant was confirmed under the name of Kerillian by Governor Macquarie on the 1st of January, 1810. On the last date, Macquarie granted him also 100 acres in the district of Bankstown; this is probably the grant referred to by Governor Bligh, which had not been completed *in propria forma.* On the 25th of August, 1812, a grant of 30 acres at George's River was issued to G. L. M. H. de Kerillan. Thus there are four different spellings of the same name in official documents.

Note 11, page 70.

Your instructions.

There was no alteration by the inclusion of additional matter in the King's instructions (*see* page 8 *et seq.*) given to Governor Bligh from those given to Governor King. In a letter, dated 20th November, 1805 (*see* page 15 *et seq.*), Viscount Castlereagh conveyed further directions to Governor Bligh which were important in character for the development of the colony.

Note 12, page 72.

A Despatch . . . . dated 20th July, 1805.

The despatch referred to was addressed to under secretary Cooke (*see* page 539, volume V); as also the despatch, dated 8th September, 1805 (*see* page 552 *et seq.*, volume V).

Note 13, page 72.

A plan delivered in by Lieutenant Governor Foveaux as the General Rule for your proceedings.

Lieutenant-governor Foveaux's "observations" will be found on page 74 *et seq.*, and page 78 *et seq.*

Note 14, page 80.

Military, Septr. 8.

Governor King forwarded a despatch, marked "Military" and dated 20th July, 1805 (*see* page 524 *et seq.*, volume V), with his despatches, numbered 1, 2, 3, 4, and 5, bearing the same date. The reference is undoubtedly to a duplicate of this despatch, dated 8th September. Governor Bligh's letters of the 15th of March and 1st of April, 1806, were written on board the transport *Sinclair* when at sea, and the letter of the 30th of May on H.M.S. *Porpoise* when in Simon's Bay at the Cape of Good Hope. These despatches detailed the differences which had arisen between captain Short and himself on the voyage to New South Wales (*see* note 22).

Note 15, page 81.
The Report of His Majesty's Law Officers.

The reports of Messrs. Nicholl, Perceval and Gibbs were enclosed with
Viscount Castlereagh's despatch to Governor King, dated 21st November,
1805 (*see* volume V, page 625 *et seq.*).

Note 16, page 81.
Capt. King's Conduct etc.

The reference was to Governor King's action in refusing permission for
the landing of the spirits imported on the brig *Eagle,* which had been
reported by King in his despatches, dated 30th April and 20th July, 1805
(*see* pages 429 and 531 *et seq.,* volume V).

Note 17, page 81.
Governor King's letter of ————.

The proceedings of the court martial on assistant surgeon Savage were
transmitted by Governor King to Sir Charles Morgan, the judge-advocate
general, with his despatch, dated 20th July, 1805 (*see* page 549, volume V),
and the decision thereon was communicated to Governor King by the Right
Hon. Nathaniel Bond, Morgan's successor, in a despatch, dated 24th April,
1806 (*see* page 712, volume V). There were only brief references in the
despatches to the colonial department, dated 20th July, 1805 (*see* pages
524 and 543, volume V), and copies of the proceedings were not transmitted
with them. It is probable that the report referred to as enclosed with this
despatch, dated 30th December, 1806, was a copy of the Right Hon.
Nathaniel Bond's letter to the Duke of York, dated 24th April, 1806 (*see*
page 712, volume V).

Note 18, page 82.
In January, 1805, Governor King it appears informed the Secretary of State.

The reference was to the fourth paragraph of the despatch to Lord
Hobart, dated 8th January, 1805, and numbered 11 (*see* page 258, volume V).

Note 19, page 83.
Two Ships . . . . as stated in the margin.

The two ships were the transports *Tellicherry* and *William Pitt,* which
arrived at Port Jackson on the 18th of February and 14th of April, 1806.
The provisions shipped were detailed in a despatch from the victualling
board, dated 10th June, 1805 (*see* page 484, volume V).

Note 20, page 84.
My general letter.

The general letter was dated 9th January, 1807 (*see* page 91 *et seq.*).
It is clear that either the despatch dated 2nd January or the general letter
is misdated.

Note 21, page 86.
Lieutenant John Putland.

John Putland was the son-in-law of Governor Bligh, and had fought under
Nelson at the battle of the Nile. He arrived in the colony as lieutenant
on H.M.S. *Porpoise* under the command of Joseph Short. He commanded

the *Porpoise* for nine months in 1807, until he became ill and was relieved by James Symons. After lingering for some weeks, Putland died of consumption on the 4th of January, 1808, and was buried three days later with full military honours near the site of St. Phillip's church.

Note 22, page 92.
My former Despatches.

The despatches were dated 15th March, 1st April, and 30th May, 1806, and were addressed to secretary Marsden. The first two were written on board the transport *Sinclair,* when at sea, and the third on board H.M.S. *Porpoise,* when in Simon's Bay at the Cape of Good Hope. They detailed the differences which arose between Governor Bligh and Joseph Short during the voyage. These were chiefly of a minor nature. Short protested against the flying of Bligh's broad pendant from the *Sinclair.* Short contended that the *Sinclair* was under his command, and gave J. H. Jackson, the master, sailing orders. When Bligh altered the course of the *Sinclair,* Short signalled to keep the course laid down. This order was ignored, and Short fired a shot across the *Sinclair's* bows and another astern of her. Further disputes arose over the prize money on a Danish ship captured on the 14th May, 1806, and over Short's refusal to muster Bligh on the books of H.M.S. *Porpoise.* (See the Right Hon. W. Windham's criticism on these disputes, page 80.)

Note 23, page 110.
The trials at the Old Baily and Hicks' Halls.

The papers, requisitioned by Richard Atkins in this letter, have been described in note 196, volume III.

Note 24, page 126.
I now forward.

These returns consisted of the enclosures to the despatch, dated 1st February, 1807, and numbered 3 (*see* page 104 *et seq.*).

Note 25, page 126.
My separate Letter.

The letter was dated 1st February, 1807, and numbered 4 (*see* page 110 *et seq.*). Following the usual practice of the period, Governor Bligh regarded the despatches, dated 25th January, 1st and 4th February, as enclosures to his " general " despatch, dated 7th February.

Note 26, pages 127 and 129.
His Letter.
My Letter dated the 14th of last February.

The copy of the letter from lieutenant-governor Paterson relating to the augmentation of the New South Wales Corps was dated 1st February, 1807, and was forwarded by Governor Bligh with his despatch, dated 4th February, 1807, and numbered 5 (*see* page 119).

Note 27, page 127.

Mr. Cox . . . . to answer such charges as will be brought against him.
Mr. William Cox had been suspended from the office of paymaster to the New South Wales Corps in April, 1803. The causes of his suspension were

detailed by Governor King in a despatch, dated 9th May, 1803 (*see* page 166 and also note 52, volume IV). His estate was sequestrated and placed in the hands of trustees (*see* page 541 *et seq.* and also note 136, volume IV).

Note 28, page 127.
His Letter of this date which accompanies this despatch.

Commissary Palmer's letter was forwarded as an enclosure to the subordinate despatch, numbered 6, and dated 1st February (*see* page 111).

Note 29, page 127.
A copy of Lieutenant Colonel Collins's Letter . . . . the late Statutes.

Lieutenant-colonel Collins' letter was forwarded with the despatch numbered 7 (*see* page 112), the returns of shipping with the despatch numbered 8 (*see* page 112 *et seq.*), the requisition for medicines and surgical instruments with the despatch numbered 9 (*see* pages 116 and 117), and the judge-advocate's requisition with the despatch numbered 3 (*see* page 110). All these despatches, dated 1st February, 1807, were subordinate to the " general " despatch, dated 7th February, 1807.

Note 30, page 128.
The Sydney being lost.
The Tellicherry . . . . is also lost.

The *Sydney,* a ship of 900 tons, was chartered (*see* page 699 *et seq.,* volume V) by Governor King to procure a cargo of provisions for the colony. She cleared for Calcutta on the 14th of April, 1806, and during the outward voyage was wrecked on a reef off the coast of New Guinea. All her crew were saved, and arrived at Calcutta *viâ* Penang on the 9th of October, 1806.

The *Tellicherry,* a ship of 468 tons, cleared for China on the 6th of April, 1806, with the object of procuring a cargo of rice for the settlement (*see* page 708, volume V). She was wrecked in the straits of Apo, on the coast of Laconia, and the crew succeeded in reaching Manilla, P.I., in the ship's boats. From there, they embarked for Canton, where they arrived on the 1st of August, 1806.

Note 31, page 138.
Your despatches by the Brothers, Young William and Duke of Portland.

These despatches were dated 6th April, 4th May, 20th May, 2nd June, 27th June, 31st July, 18th September, 6th December, 18th December (5), 30th December (2), 1806, and January, 1807. They will be found on pages 694, 712, 714, 715, 718, and 760 in volume V, and pages 24, 39, 55, 56, 57, 70, 80, and 81 in this volume. The despatches carried in the *Young William* were duplicates of those carried in the *Duke of Portland.* The ship *Brothers* arrived in Port Jackson on the 4th of April, the *Young William* on the 7th of July, and the *Duke of Portland* on the 27th of July, 1807.

Note 32, page 142.
My Letter No. 6 of the 7th of February.

The letter, numbered 6, was dated the 1st of February in the copy transmitted to England (*see* page 111). It was a subordinate letter to Governor Bligh's " general " despatch, dated 7th February, 1807.

Note 33, page 144.

The inhabited and cultivated part of the Land.

The lands described by Governor Bligh in this despatch are those included within the modern county of Cumberland, with the exclusion of the extreme southern part between North Menangle and Appin·on the west and the sea coast on the east. The inhabited portion included also the grants to Messrs. Macarthur and Davidson in the neighbourhood of Menangle within the modern county of Camden, and the grants within the modern county of Cook on the northern and western banks of the Hawkesbury between the Grose and Colo rivers. The lands alienated to individuals may be classified into five groups according to locality: from Woolloomooloo bay westward on both sides of the Parramatta river and thence to Prospect and Toongabbe; the alluvial lands on both sides of the Hawkesbury river from the junction of the Grose to the junction of the Colo river; on both banks of George's river from the site of the modern town of Liverpool to the junction of Harris creek; on the eastern bank of the Nepean river from a point about two miles south of the present railway bridge to its junction with the Grose river; and on the banks of South creek from the junction of Kemp's creek to the settlement at the Hawkesbury. The lands reserved for public purposes have been described in note 174, volume III, and the location of the commons in note 113, volume IV, and in note 30, volume V. The grants for the benefit of the orphan institution have been described in note 14, volume V.

Note 34, page 149.

A Plan.

This plan or series of regulations will be found on page 168. It was approved subsequently by the secretary of state.

Note 35, page 154.

My Letter by the Buffalo.

The despatch referred to was dated 7th February, 1807 (*see* page 120 *et seq.*).

Note 36, pages 154 and 155.

A Sketch.

The Plan of the Town sent herewith.

These enclosures will be found in the volume of charts and plans.

Note 37, page 154.

Together with Bible and Prayer Books.

In a letter, dated 7th February, 1803, to the lords commissioners of the treasury, Lord Hobart requested that instructions should be given to the agent for the colony to purchase, " for the settlements established and to be established in New South Wales," tablets for the altars at Port Phillip and Port Jackson, church plate of silver for each, and prayer books and bibles for each. In his despatch, numbered 11, and dated 1st March, 1804 (*see* page 551, volume IV), Governor King acknowledged the receipt, *per* H.M.S. *Calcutta*, of the tablets and communion plate. A bible, prayer book, and communion service were brought out also in the first fleet, and these were in use in the church at Sydney. The necessity for this further requisition by Governor Bligh is not clear.

The story of land tenure in the city of Sydney is complex and interesting. Prior to his departure in 1792, Governor Phillip had caused a map of the town to be prepared by surveyor Alt. At the same time, a line was traced from the mouth of the stream flowing into Woolloomooloo bay to the head of Darling harbour. Phillip informed his successor, lieutenant-governor Grose, that this line was to be regarded as the boundary of the town in that direction, and on the 2nd of December, 1792, he signed a memorandum stating: " It is the orders of Government that no Ground within the Boundary line is ever granted or let on Lease and all houses within the Boundary line are and are to remain the property of the Crown." Some doubt is thrown on the accuracy of this date by the fact that the same date is attached on the map to a note relating to the boundary line. In this note, Phillip used the words " of this the Lieutenant Governor *was informed before I left the Country* "; as Phillip sailed on the transport *Atlantic* on the 11th December, 1792, the use of the words in italics, if written on the 2nd of December, 1792, is incomprehensible. The problem is further complicated by the fact that on the 8th of December, 1792, Phillip granted four leases within this boundary line. One of these leases, 100 feet by 200 feet on the north side of High-street (now George-street), issued to Phillip Schaffer for a term of fourteen years, was resumed by Governor Hunter by purchase for the crown on the 21st of March, 1798. If the dating of his order is accurate, it is difficult to understand why Phillip himself should ignore it six days later.

The practice of granting leases in the town of Sydney, commenced but discountenanced by Phillip, was continued by his successors, and in the plan of Sydney by surveyor Charles Grimes, dated May, 1800, thirty seven allotments are shown in private possession, which were held under various tenures.

Governor King, by a general order, dated 11th June, 1801 (*see* page 255, volume III), regulated the tenure by enacting that crown lands and buildings might be leased for a term not exceeding five years, provided they were not required for public purposes. King, like his predecessor Phillip, abrogated his own order, and sanctioned several leases for a period of fourteen years within the town of Sydney.

In the plan of the town, prepared by surveyor James Meehan by order of Governor Bligh and dated 31st October, 1807, ninety-nine allotments are delineated which were leased to private individuals. In this map, the northerly extremity of the boundary line is moved about nine hundred feet east of its location by surveyor Alt in 1792, thereby including a new sector within the town of Sydney.

Governor Bligh probably intended to re-inforce the regulation of Governor Phillip prohibiting leases within the boundary line, but his deposition by major Johnston prevented any action being taken.

At the same time as he defined the southern boundary of the town, Governor Phillip caused a ditch to be dug, commencing at the northern end of the town boundary at Woolloomooloo, and following an irregular line with an aggregate north-westerly direction to the modern site of the hotel Metropole. All the land lying to the north of this ditch as far as the waters of Port Jackson was reserved for the use of government house, then situated at the present corner of Bridge and Phillip streets. Within this area, several leases had been granted, and houses had been erected by permission of

Phillip's successors. On the 23rd of July, 1807, Governor Bligh ordered all occupants of houses in the neighbourhood of government house to vacate and remove their dwellings on or before the 1st of November following.

Of the leases mentioned by Governor Bligh, lots 77 and 93 lay close to St. Phillip's church on the south-east and west sides; lot 8 on the eastern side of George-street opposite Essex-street; lot 16 at the southern corner of George and Bridge streets extending east to the Tank stream; lot 79 on the northern side of Margaret-street between George and York streets and adjoining lot 77; lot 78 was leased to Robert Sidaway and lay between Margaret and Jamieson streets adjoining lot 79; lot 66 was situated near the site of the hotel Metropole; lot 72 at the site of the offices of the taxation commissioners; lot 15 on the western side of George-street, opposite Bridge-street, and adjoining lots 77, 78, and 79.

Note 39, page 157.
Samuel Bate.

Samuel Bate had been appointed deputy judge-advocate for the settlement at Port Phillip by warrant, dated 15th January, 1804, *vice* Benjamin Barbauld, the first appointee, who had refused to sail for the settlement. When Bate arrived, lieutenant-governor Collins had removed the settlement from Port Phillip to the Derwent river, and Bate took up the duties of his office at Hobart. He was not superseded as Governor Bligh suggested, and was confirmed in his office by Governor Macquarie.

Note 40, page 157.
The direct distance across is about sixty miles.

Governor Bligh underestimated the distance between Launceston and Hobart by about forty miles. Lieutenant Laycock experienced no difficulties in his exploration. Leaving Launceston, he crossed the South Esk river above its junction with the Lake river, and followed the eastern banks of that and the Macquarie rivers for about seven miles. Taking a southerly course, he ascended the mountains in the neighbourhood of Mount Kingston and Miller's Bluff. Passing these, he travelled south, touching the eastern side of Lake Sorell, which he discovered. From the lake, his journey was uneventful, until he reached the banks of the Derwent river, a little above New Norfolk. Leaving the river to avoid the hills, he travelled eastward for about seven miles, when he returned to the banks and followed the river to Herdsman's cove. From this bay he travelled by boat to Hobart.

Note 41, page 157.
Mr. House, who was lost in attempting to reach Port Jackson in an open Boat.

William House had acted as harbour master at Port Dalrymple. In February, 1807, when all the provisions at the settlement had been expended and the inhabitants were living on a precarious supply obtained by hunting, he had been sent in a long-boat with four hands to carry a despatch to Governor Bligh, reporting the reduced state of the colony. He never reached Port Jackson. He left a wife and three young children.

Note 42, page 159.
Captain Charles James Johnston.

Charles James Johnston was a cousin of major George Johnston. He commanded the frigate *Cornwallis* on her cruize for making reprizals against enemy shipping.

Note 43, page 159.
A Prize.

This was the ship *Pegasus*, which arrived in Port Jackson with a prize crew on board under the command of Thomas Graham. She was consigned by captain Johnston to John Harris and Edmund Griffin, and was condemned as a lawful prize at a vice-admiralty court on the 24th of January, 1808. She carried a cargo of rice, sugar, and spirits from Peru.

Note 44, page 159.
Lieutenant Hagemeister.

The *Neva*, laden with stores, called at Port Jackson on her voyage to the Russian settlement on the island of Kadjack on the north-west coast of America. She was a vessel of nearly 400 tons burthen, and carried 14 guns. She had sailed from Cronstadt on the 2nd of November, 1806. This was her second voyage in southern seas. On her first voyage, in company with the *Nadegada*, she had been expected to call at Port Jackson during the year 1804 (*see* page 306, volume IV).

Note 45, page 159.
The whole being Prisoners for Life.
The two Men who informed . . .. Free Pardons.

The circumstances surrounding the transportation of Michael Dwyer, John Mernagh, Hugh Byrne, Martin Burke, and Arthur Devlin and their subsequent trial for treasonable practices have been detailed in note 203, volume V. The two men pardoned were Dominic McCurry and Daniel Gready. Their two pardons were dated 4th of June, 1807, and these were the only emancipations granted by Governor Bligh during his administration.

Note 46, page 160.
The inimicability of his mind to Government.

In the copy of this paragraph (*see* page 321), which was produced at the second trial of John Macarthur, it is curious that an additional sentence was added, and the pen was then drawn through it.

Note 47, pages 97 and 169.
Government Buildings.

The master builder's house occupied the site of the Mariners' church.

The dockyard was the adjoining allotment on the east side of George-street, and extended as far south as the offices of the taxation commissioners.

The gaol was situated on the west side of George-street at the corner of Essex-street.

The lumber-yard lay on the east side of George-street, commencing about fifty feet south of the Bridge-street corner.

The granary was built on the west side of George-street, near the corner of Jamieson-street.

Government house was situated at the corner of Bridge and Phillip streets.

The commissary's office and the judge-advocate's, chaplain's, and surveyor's houses were built in a row from east to west on the south side of Bridge-street on the sites occupied by the education and lands offices.

The dry store stood near the south-eastern corner of the customs house building.

The salt provision stores adjoined the granary on the west side of George-street.

The new church was St. Phillip's church.

The town bridge was in Bridge-street over the Tank stream, a few feet west of Pitt-street.

The orphan house was built on the allotment at the northern corner of George and Bridge streets.

The general hospital lay on the west side of George-street, opposite the southern end of the dockyard.

The surgeons' houses were built adjoining the hospital on the north side.

The officers' barracks were erected on the northern side of Margaret-street and the western side of York-street, near the corner of these two streets.

The soldiers' barracks were a continuation of the officers' barracks on the west side of York-street.

The military hospital was built behind the southern end of the soldiers' barracks.

Note 48, page 175.

Mr. Gaven.

This is an error probably made by the transcriber of the original proceedings. The storekeeper's name was John Gowen.

Note 49, page 182.

Your Letter respecting the evacuation of Norfolk Island.

This was the despatch numbered 6, and dated 30th December, 1806 (*see* page 70).

Note 50, page 183.

I beg leave to observe that as only extracts of particular parts of them are in my possession.

This statement by Governor Bligh casts an interesting sidelight on the mystery surrounding the absence from government house, Sydney, of contemporary copies of despatches. to England and the original despatches from England in the period antecedent to the administration of Governor Macquarie. With the exception of certain papers recently received from England, the records preserved in the office of his Excellency the State Governor begin with a volume, labelled 1800-1806, containing longhand copies of miscellaneous despatches and letters received from England belonging to that period, but no section is complete. This volume is not contemporary with the period, as it is written on paper watermarked 1821. At the reverse of this book, there are copies of a letter from Lord Sydney to the governor of New South Wales (dated 6th April, 1787), additional instructions to Governor Phillip, a warrant for using the great seal, two letters dated 1799, one letter dated 31st October, 1804, one letter dated 31st July, 1805, and the estimates for the year 1805. This volume was written up at a date subsequent to the year 1821, but it is not known from what material. The next volume, in order of date, begins with copies of despatches from England, dated 1809, which were received by Governor Macquarie in 1810, and from this last year the series of despatches to and from England are practically complete except for the enclosures.

Governor King preserved copies of most despatches to and from England in several large letter-books, which contained also copies of many enclosures. These volumes are extant, and most likely they were the only copies kept by the governor. That they were taken by him as his private property, when he vacated office, is proved by Bligh's statement. It is probable that the same practice was followed by King's predecessors, Phillip, Grose, Paterson, and Hunter, and also by his successor, Bligh, when he regained possession of his papers from the insurrectionaries after the arrival of Governor Macquarie. Some additional proof of the probability of this practice may be derived from the fact of the acquisition by the government of New South Wales in recent years of a volume containing copies of despatches during the administration of lieutenant-governor Grose.

Note 51, page 186.

Mr. Connellan.

John Connellan had arrived in the colony as assistant surgeon on the transport *Tellicherry* from Ireland, with letters of recommendation from secretary A. Marsden (*see* page 550, volume V). He had been appointed acting surgeon at Norfolk Island in February, 1806, in consequence of the vacancy created by the absence on leave of assistant surgeon James Thomson, and by the suspension of assistant surgeon Savage.

Note 52, page 186.

Mr. Secretary Windham's letter on this head.

This was the despatch, numbered 6, and dated 30th December, 1806 (*see* page 70 *et seq.*).

Note 53, page 191.

None have been printed since August owing to the great scarcity of Paper.

The scarcity of paper was one of the difficulties with which George Howe, the printer of the *Sydney Gazette*, had to contend from the commencement of publication. All kinds of paper were used, including light brown paper. The scarcity became acute in September, 1806. On the 7th of September, the issue was printed on a single sheet of paper, and all issues from the 21st of the same month to the 30th of August, 1807, were printed in like manner. During this period, the size of the sheet varied considerably, and on the last-mentioned date the publication was discontinued. Prior to the issue dated 7th September, the size of the paper had been four pages of post folio.

Note 54, page 197.

My former letter.

This was the despatch, numbered 6, and dated 1st February, 1807 (*see* page 111 *et seq.*).

Note 55, pages 199 and 200.

Lord Hawkesbury.

Robert Banks Jenkinson, by courtesy Lord Hawkesbury, had been appointed secretary of state for the home department on the 25th of March, 1807. In December, 1808, he succeeded his father as the second Earl of Liverpool.

Note 56, page 200.

Your General Letter of the 9th February.

The copy of this despatch, which is preserved in the public record office, London, is dated 7th February, 1807 (*see* page 120 *et seq.*).

Note 57, page 204.

Mr. Savage.

Assistant surgeon John Savage arrived in the colony *per* H.M.S. *Glatton* on the 11th of March, 1803. He was a *protégé* of Edward Jenner, and, associated with surgeons Jamison and Harris, had introduced vaccination in the colony (*see* note 227, volume IV). He was tried by court martial in June, 1805 (*see* page 712, volume V), and returned to England on the whaler *Ferrett.*

Note 58, page 206.

Transmitted to John King . . . . in June, 1802.

The following letter was sent to under secretary King by the commissioners of the navy in June, 1802:—

Sir,   Navy Office, 11th June, 1802.

In Answer to your Letter of the 5th April last, we transmit to you herewith Drawings of the Frame Timbers of a 98, 74 and 38 Gunship, with proper Dimensions and necessary Information for the purpose of providing the Timber at New South Wales; And desire you will be pleased to lay the same before the Right Honble. Lord Pelham for his Lordship's giving such Directions thereon to Governor King as he may think proper.

We are, &c.,

A. S. HAMMOND.
J. HENSLOW.
B. TUCKER.

Note 59, page 208.

A Grant of 600 acres near the Nepean.

This despatch was not received by Governor Bligh. Lieutenant-governor Paterson issued a grant, dated 21st February, 1809, of one thousand acres to John Oxley in the parish of Narellan. The land was described as " bounded on the south-west side by the Nepean River, commencing at the Crossing Place near the Old Government Hut." This hut was situated at the site of the modern bridge at Camden. " On the south-east side " the land was bounded by the Cowpasture-road. The grant was named Kirkham, and by this name a part of the property is still known.

Note 60, page 208.

Major Johnston to Viscount Castlereagh.

Governor Bligh, in his evidence at the court martial on Johnston, insinuated that John Macarthur was the real author of this despatch. Under previous administrations, the secretary to the governor frequently wrote the official despatches, and the governor merely directed the subject-matter to be included. If Macarthur's duties in the new office of secretary to the colony included those of the old office of secretary to the governor, it is not improbable that he was the author. The despatch as a whole is a studied and biassed exposition of the facts in favour of the insurrectionaries, and is more like a composition by Macarthur than by Johnston. An original copy of this despatch is preserved in the office of the chief secretary at Sydney, and in that copy the division into paragraphs is slightly different, and the enclosures are numbered in different order (*see* note 70).

Note 61, page 211.

The Provost Marshal.

William Gore had received his commission from Viscount Castlereagh on the recommendation of the Earl of Harrington. He arrived in the colony on the 6th of August, 1806, with Governor Bligh. He soon became involved in disputes with Bligh's opponents, and had been tried and honourably acquitted by the criminal court in 1807 on a charge of improperly issuing part of a fifteen shilling bill and stealing a piece of greenstone.

Note 62, page 213.

The Corps quickly followed, attended by the Civil Officers and a considerable number of respectable inhabitants.

This statement is clearly inaccurate, and was probably intended to mislead the secretary of state. Of the principal civil officers, the judge-advocate, the commissary, the provost-marshal, the acting chaplain, the principal superintendent of stock, and the naval officer and collector of taxes were loyal to Governor Bligh. Charles Grimes, the surveyor-general, Thomas Jamison, the principal surgeon, and James Mileham, assistant surgeon, took the side of the insurrectionaries. As recorded in note 69, Charles Grimes admitted signing the requisition to major Johnston after the arrest, and it is probable that John Macarthur, John and Gregory Blaxland, James Mileham, and Simeon Lord were the only non-combatants who marched with the military to government house, with the exception of those attracted by curiosity, as stated by George Suttor (*see* page 549).

Note 63, page 214.

Crossley was brought before the Court, charged with acting as an Agent or Attorney after having been convicted of Perjury.

The details of the original conviction, sentence, and transportation of George Crossley will be found in note 130, volume IV. He acted as adviser to William Gore, when the latter was tried by the criminal court in 1807, but was not allowed to plead before the court. He had practised as an attorney prior to his transportation, and after his arrival in the colony his professional knowledge was frequently made use of by the colonists in their legal business. Thereby he rendered himself liable to a sentence of transportation under the statute, which disbarred for ever from practice an attorney who had been convicted of perjury.

Note 64, page 214.

Mr. Gore . . . . has also been brought before another Court.

William Gore appeared before the criminal court on the 28th of March, 1808. He objected to James Symons and Ellison on the grounds that they held no rank, or, if any, that of midshipman in the navy; and to Edward Abbott on the ground that he had prejudged the case. William Gore's account of his second appearance before the insurrectionary court will be found on page 560.

Note 65, page 215.

The Despatch from Lieut. Colonel Paterson.

This despatch is not recorded in the list of enclosures transmitted to Viscount Castlereagh. The despatch was as follows:—

LIEUTENANT-GOVERNOR PATERSON TO MAJOR JOHNSTON.

Sir,   Port Dalrymple, Van Dieman's Land, 12th March, 1808.

I have to acknowledge the receipt of your Dispatch of the 2nd Ulto., acquainting me with the change you state you have conceived it necessary to make in the Government at Port Jackson.

Removed from the possibility of being able to offer an opinion, or judge of the momentous events you relate, I can only express my hope that the Steps you have subsequently taken, and are now pursuing, may prove for the benefit of His Majesty's Service; and I have only to add that, however I would wish to avoid the necessity such unforeseen causes peremptorily impose, there remains to me no conduct to pursue but the one I have explained to His Majesty's Minister, in my Dispatch to him of this day, it is my intention to adopt, for my perseverance in which I consider my future Character, and the enjoyment of His Majesty's countenance, at Stake.

I therefore have to beg you will, as immediately as possible, cause to be despatched to me a Vessel of sufficient Capacity to convey myself and Family to the Head Quarters of the Regiment I have the Honor to command in New South Wales, and of the Government of these His Majesty's Territories, which I should particularly wish to be His Majesty's Ship the *Porpoise*; but, if circumstances absolutely prevent her coming, I would wish to have chartered any Vessel adapted that may be or should arrive in the Harbour, for the payment of which I will draw Bills on the Treasury.

By the opportunity of the Vessel you may send for the purpose I point out, such Supplies as are immediately wanted for the use of this Settlement can be conveyed, which I would recommend you to give directions should be the case, more particularly clothing, about three months dry provisions for 250 Rations, an augmentation to the detachment, and a small addition to the number of prisoners. I mention these, as another means may not present itself before the expiration of the Winter.

I have enclosed a letter to Captain Symons, should you judge such necessary to send him.

I think it necessary to further state that I do not at present purpose making any particular change in the arrangement you have formed at Sydney until I may hear from His Majesty's Ministers.

I have, &c.,
W. PATERSON.

P.S.—I have omitted to state that I have acquainted the Duke of York of my intentions, enclosing His Royal Highness a copy of my Dispatch to yourself and to the Minister.

I have further omitted to state that, although from the experience I have myself hitherto had of your public conduct, I have not any reason to suppose you will neglect to fulfil my requisition of immediately despatching a Vessel; yet, as I conceive I shall be unable to justify myself to the Crown if I neglect to provide against all possibilities of a prevention of my taking the command at Sydney, I have directed my Agent at Port Jackson, in the event of your not forwarding me a conveyance within one month from your receipt of my present dispatch, to take up, at the expence of the Crown, any Vessel he can procure; and should no arrival capable of transporting me hence take place in three months from this date, I shall, concluding I am not to expect one from Port Jackson, despatch an Officer to the Settlement at the Derwent, to charter round the first Ship, in the name of His Majesty, that may come in.—W.P.

Note 66, page 215.
As Lieut.-Governor of a Dependency.

Major Johnston was in error with regard to the relative positions of the lieutenant-governors. Francis Grose and William Paterson had been appointed lieutenant-governors of the territory, whereas Philip Gidley King and Joseph Foveaux were appointed lieutenant-governors of Norfolk Island, and David Collins lieutenant-governor, first, of Port Phillip, and, later, of Hobart. The last three appointees were subject to the jurisdiction of the government at Sydney. When, in 1803, Paterson was detached to take command of the settlement at Port Dalrymple, he retained his status as lieutenant-governor of the territory. In the same year, 1803, the reduction of the establishment at Norfolk Island was ordered, and Joseph Foveaüx was instructed to return to Sydney and "in Colonel Paterson's absence, to execute the duties of Lieutenant Governor" (*see* page 631). It is clear that there was no doubt as to Paterson's status as lieutenant-governor on the establishment at Port Jackson.

Note 67, page 219.

On the condition of the Grant being approved by His Majesty's Secretary of State for the Colonies.

In his administration of land grants, major Johnston was circumspect, and he by no means assumed the full powers conferred by letters patent on the administrator of the colony. The grants issued by him indicate that he regarded his government as temporary and limited in powers. All his grants were qualified by the clause that each was issued "on the express condition of being subject ·to the approbation of His Majesty's Ministers and in case of their disapproval is to be considered null and void."

Johnston made twelve grants of a total area of 6,814 acres. They were:—

(1)	2nd April,Wm. Minchin	100 acres.	(7)	19th July, Archibald Bell	500 acres.
(2)	16th May, Wm. Moore	84 ,,	(8)	19th July, Robert Fitz	600 ,,
(3)	23rd July, D'Arcy Wentworth	270 ,,	(9)	19th July, Robert Fitz	600 ,,
(4)	8th July,George Johnston, Jr.	2,000 ,,	(10)	19th July, Dorothy Merchant.	60 ,,
(5)	9th July, John Townson	1,950 ,,	(11)	19th July, Aaron Byrne......	100 ,,
(6)	9th July, John Townson	50 ,,	(12)	19th July, Wm. Lawson......	500 ,,

Of these grantees, the secretary of state intended to give orders for grants of 1,000 acres to John Townson (*see* page 21), and of an undetermined area to Robert Fitz (*see* page 204), and had given orders for grants of 500 acres to Archibald Bell (*see* page 39), and of 50 acres to Dorothy Merchant (*see* pages 25 and 39). · Governor Bligh had not made any of these grants, and Johnston fulfilled simply the official instructions or intentions in six of his grants with the qualification that he gave an additional 1,000 acres to Townson and 10 acres to Mrs. Merchant.

The subsequent history of these grants is interesting. The grant numbered 9 was exchanged by lieutenant-governor Paterson in June, 1809, for a corresponding area in the same district (Upper Nelson) in which the grant numbered 8 was situated. The grants numbered 3, 7, 8, 10, 11, 12, and the exchanged grant for 9, were confirmed by Governor Macquarie by new grants, dated 1st January, 1810, and those numbered 5 and 6 by new grants, dated 11th April, 1810.

The grants to Minchin, Moore, and Johnston, junior, were disallowed by Governor Macquarie.

Adverse criticism of Johnston's issue of land grants is confined practically to the 2,000 acres granted at Emu Plains to his son, George Johnston, and the 500 acres to William Lawson, which, being on the western side of the Nepean river, were contrary to previous practice adopted in that neighbourhood.

Note 68, page 235.

You had surrendered me to my Bail.

It is clear from this question that this examination was conducted by John Macarthur, and probably formed part of · the magisterial inquiry prior to the trial of William Gore by the court of criminal jurisdiction on the 21st of March.

Note 69, page 240.
Mr. John Macarthur and Others.
The original of this letter was presented by the family of major Johnston to the government of New South Wales, and is now preserved in the national art gallery, Sydney. The signatures were:—

John Macarthur
John Blaxland
James Mileham
Simeon Lord
Gregory Blaxland
James Badgery
Nicholas Bayly
Garnham Blaxcell
Thomas Jamison
Charles Grimes
Thomas Hobbs
D'Arcy Wentworth
Thomas Laycock
Thomas Moore
Robert Townson
Isaac Nichols
William Evans
Jesse Mulcock
John Reddington
William Baker
William Jenkins
Nathaniel Lucas
Henry Kable
Henry Sykes
Robert Sidaway
Augustus Alt
Henry Williams
David Bevan
James Larra
Edward Hills
J. W. Lewin
W. Blake
George Hughes
Thomas Hughes
R. Fitzgerald
Thomas Abbott
John Connell
William Baker
Nicholas Divine
William Stewart
John Apsey
Richard Cheers
Thomas Jones
Martin Short
Thomas Broadhurst
Donald Moore
Ralph Stowe
George Bowers (?)
Abraham Moore
John Pawley
George Guest

William Grosvenor
Nathaniel Lloyd
William English
J. Sutton
William Ross
David Batty
William Wale
T. Boulton
Richard Tuckwell
John O'Hearne
Thomas Lawrence
James Parrott
William George
Valentine Wood
Matthew Kearns
John Lyster
Thomas Casey
William Hatney
Thomas Jennings
James Hardwick
John Graham
John White
Joseph Underwood
Henry James Purcell
Daniel Cubitt
Reuben Uther
James John Grant
Samuel Terry
John Waldron
I. Nelson
Samuel Foster
Thomas Allwright
George Phillips
Thomas Broughton
Joseph Hodges
Joseph Ward
James Wilshire
John Gowen
William Thorn
James Evans
Robert Traves
James Vanderoom
William Fielder
John Driver
William Bennett
Richard Robinson
John Thorley
John Griffiths
Owen Connor
Hugh McEvoy

William Davis
John Hughes
William Beggs
J. Collingwood
Thomas Brown
Cornelius Hennings
Richard Oldham
Joseph Morton
Patrick Marman
William Watkins
William Hennis
Jeremiah Cavanaugh
John Griffiths
Francis Cox
Robert Lack
William Holness
Robert Brown
Thomas Hartman
William Blue
Thomas Legg
Thomas Parsonage (?)
Matthew Elkin
Thomas Moxon
John Davis
Richard Wade
John Ever (?)
John Anson
L. Jones
Richard Palmer
Abraham Levy
Daniel Deicon
George Connoway
John Richardson
Joseph Flood
John Hanslip (?)
Edward Smith
Absolom West
Charles Williams
Thomas Becker
Charles Walker
John Wilks
James Mackay
Charles Evans
Patrick Drovy
Richard Harding
Henry Yeates
Jonathan Green
James Wild
George Cooke
Andrew Frazer.

The body of this letter is in the handwriting of John Macarthur, but the date and subscription are in an unknown hand. Most of the one hundred and fifty-one signatures were added to the document after major Johnston had taken action and deposed Governor Bligh. Charles Grimes, the surveyor, admitted in evidence at the court martial on Johnston that he signed after the event, and it is probable that John Macarthur, John and Gregory Blaxland, James Mileham, and Simeon Lord were the only signatories prior to Johnston's march on government house, provided that John Harris' statement (quoted in note 132) is not correct, and that the entire document was not prepared after the arrest was accomplished.

Note 70, page 241.

Enclosure No. 7.

In the copies of this despatch and its enclosures, which are preserved in the chief secretary's office, Sydney, this correspondence is referred to as enclosure No. 25. Also the letter marked A is made into a separate enclosure, numbered 6, and the enclosure, numbered 6 on page 240, is numbered 7. Enclosure No. 8 (*see* page 271) is omitted, and the enclosures numbered 9 to 25 (*see* page 277 *et seq.*) are re-numbered 8 to 24. In the copy of this correspondence forming enclosure No. 7, the letters are numbered and not lettered, the paper marked B being numbered 1, the letter marked Y is omitted, leaving sixty-two numbered letters and papers, and the following letter is added as No. 63 :—

LIEUTENANT LAWSON TO GOVERNOR BLIGH.

Sir,   10th May, 1808.
    I am ordered by His Honor the Lieutenant-Governor to acquaint you, in Answer to the Application made by Mr. Griffin, that as Lieut.-Colonel Paterson and Lieut.-Colonel Foveaux are daily expected to arrive, the Lieutenant-Governor considers it proper to defer coming to a determination respecting the return of any papers belonging to you that are now in his Possession.   I have, &c.,
                                               WM. LAWSON.

In this enclosure, most of the letters to Governor Bligh were addressed to "Wm. Bligh, Esq.," subsequent to his deposition, and the letters to major Johnston, subsequent to the 29th of January, to "Lieutenant Governor Johnston."

Note 71, page 245.

Also pages 252 and 423.

The Tomb of your late Son-in-Law.

John Putland was buried in a vault which was built in the grounds of St. Phillip's church.

Note 72, page 252.

Mr. Nicholas Bayly to Principal Surgeon Jamison.

This letter is not preserved amongst the copies of this series of correspondence which are filed in the office of the chief secretary at Sydney. From its subject-matter, it belongs to the correspondence which was forwarded as enclosure numbered 1 by major Johnston in his despatch, dated 30th April, 1808 (*see* page 442), and it is practically a literal copy of the letter numbered 3 in that enclosure. The inclusion of this letter in this series as sent to England is probably an example of "the imperfect and incorrect manner in which the Documents accompanying my Despatches are Copied" (*see* note 120).

Note 73, page 260.

Conditional Emancipations . . . Subject to the approval or disapproval of the Secretary of State.

During his administration, major Johnston granted only one pardon which was recorded in the register of pardons. This warrant was dated 18th June, 1808, and was issued to a female convict on the recommendation of lieutenant Lord. In all his land grants (*see* note 67), major Johnston made them subject to the approval of the secretary of state, but in the abstract of this pardon no such limitation is recorded.

Note 74, page 271.

B.

Of those appointed by major Johnston within twenty-four hours of the arrest of Governor Bligh, Edward Abbott, A. F. Kemp, John Harris, William Minchin, Archibald Bell, and William Lawson were on the active list and Nicholas Bayly on the retired list of the New South Wales Corps; Garnham Blaxcell was a partner of John Macarthur, who had retired from the corps; John Blaxland was a firebrand, who in a few weeks was as antagonistic to Johnston as he was to Bligh; Thomas Jamison, who had been removed from the magistracy by Bligh, was principal surgeon; Charles Grimes, who in a few weeks allied himself with Blaxland's party against Johnston, was surveyor-general; and James Williamson, who was suspended subsequently for embezzlement by lieutenant-colonel Foveaux, was deputy commissary. The new administration was placed in this way in the hands of the military and a few obvious malcontents.

Note 75, page 275.

Found guilty of piracy . . . . the Lieut. Governor has pardoned them.

In those cases in which the governor or administrator exercised the royal prerogative and commuted a death sentence passed by the law courts, it was the practice for a warrant of pardon to be executed and registered in the secretary's office. Major Johnston did not continue this practice. No reprieves are registered for these nine men, nor for the man and woman sentenced to death at the criminal court on the 13th of June, who were also pardoned by Johnston. The act of piracy was committed by the seizure of the *Marcia*, a colonial vessel of 26 tons belonging to Henry Kable and Co.

Note 76, page 277.

Convicted of the crime of Perjury by the Court of Criminal Jurisdiction.

The particulars of the conviction of Oliver Russell and Robert Daniels for perjury, without indictment, will be found in the proceedings at the trial of John and Gregory Blaxland and Simeon Lord (*see* page 484).

Note 77, page 278.

A letter written by Governor Bligh to Major Johnston.

This letter was dated 26th January, 1808 (*see* page 236).

Note 78, page 283.

A letter from himself to Mr. McArthur in 1796.

Another letter . . . . stating Mr. McArthur being the cause of many unpleasant things in this colony.

The first letter was as follows:—

Sir,   August, 1796.

The repugnance I feel at descending to an Epistolary or any other Altercation with a Man of your principles can only be surmounted by the gratification that naturally results to a Man of Honour in delineating even by paper the deformity of an opposite Character; and where can I find a subject like yourself?—A Man, the baseness of whose heart even imagination, however warm, can hardly portray. To enter into contact with such a Being might become contagious; but, however, on this occasion I will not decline giving my unequivocal Sentiments of so worthless a member of Society.

That your Charges, or, as you now term them, Assertions, against me were founded upon the most ignoble motives, such as Malice, Revenge, &c., is incontestably proved by your meanly abandoning them, after positively pledging yourself to support them by "Proof oral and written." What must your Sense of Shame be when you, a Goliath of Honour and Veracity, should resort to a subtifuge at which the meanest Convict might blush, by skulking from substantial meaning and screening yourself by a jingle of words from that manly perseverance which should mark the Character of a Man professing as you do. The Quibble between charges and assertions is of too flimsy a Texture to require a comment. It is only worthy of a dastardly Coward like yourself. Your original meanness and despicable littleness pervades your every Action. It shows the cloven foot. Return to your original nothing; we know what you have been, and what you now are; and believe me an honest and industrious Staymaker is a more honourable and more useful Member of Society than such a man as I hold you to be.

Let me ask who has been the Incendiary—who has been the promoter of all the Feuds and Animosities between Individuals in this Colony? You, Sir. You are likewise the man who has had the audacity to accuse me with having acted officially and individually with Injustice, Oppression, and Peculation—nay, even highway Robbery. You who, four years ago, was only a Lieutenant, pennyless but by his pay, and is now reputed worth £8,000. Let this Colony bear witness where lies the strongest presumption, you or me, being the Oppressor, Peculator, or Robber. On this subject, Viper, you bite a file; the day of retribution will come, and believe me it is not far off, when you will be dragged forward by the strong Arm of Justice to public view as a Monster of Society, the Betrayer of private conversation, to answer your own malicious ends, the Assassin of all that constitutes true honour. But why adopt that Epithet when addressing a man to whom it is a perfect Stranger other than by sound, for he never felt it?

I at this period feel myself degraded by devoting a moment in becoming Monitor of such a man. Could you suppose that under any possible point of view your pomposity in promising to support your Charges against me must not recoil more forcibly on yourself, and render you an object of real contempt with every man of real Honour and Veracity? Can you believe that the man who has been guilty of such "Enormities as you are daily practising" can but be detested by all mankind who have a spark of Benevolence and Phylanthropy in their composition? No, you are known too well not to suppose it! You have passed the Rubicon of true Dishonour; you, however, are seared against its sense, and the less pitiable, feeling it not that you are a Leper in reputation, and that you ought to be driven from the Society of all good men least you should be infectious. Shall I go on, or have I said enough to a man who bears "his Sovereign's Commission" and has been called Lyer and Scoundrel, and, if I am not misinformed, received a blow, and still talks of Honour? I assert you have been called these; I apply them again to you, and if your fertile imagination can form any epithets more forcible, take them, for they are your own. The Manners of a Gentleman only causes my subscribing myself,

Your humble Serv't,
RICHARD ATKINS.

I think it proper to acqt. that your late Infamous Transaction respecting me, as well as some other well-authenticated facts, are going home for ye perusal of those whom it may concern; it is not your Signature of a few Letters that will wipe them away.

The second letter was dated 23rd September, 1801 (*see* page 312, volume III).

Note 79, page 286.
Were you ever present . . . . *respecting the stills.*

In a second copy of this examination forwarded to England, this question was not repeated, and the answer was prefaced, "Answer to the first Question put to Mr. Griffin."

Note 80, page 287.
Also page 337.
Any memorial . . . . *from the Judge Advocate.*

The memorial will be found on page 236 *et seq.* In the marginal note attached to the memorial, it was stated, "the purport of it known throughout the Town directly after it was written."

Note 81, page 290.
I did.

According to the statement of Edmund Griffin (*see* page 284), the letter to the members of the criminal court (*see* page 255) was written by Governor Bligh on the advice of George Crossley. In one copy of this examination, this question and answer were omitted.

Note 82, page 302.
A list of the questions.

These questions have been omitted in those cases where they were used in the examination of the respective witnesses, subject to the modifications noted in individual cases.

Note 83, pages 308 and 310.
The Letter.

This letter, dated 14th December, 1807, will be found on page 296.

Note 84, pages 311, 313, and 314.
The Warrant.
The Paper.

The warrant will be found on page 310, and in one copy of these proceedings it was inserted after the words "read accordingly" on page 311 and omitted on page 310. The paper was the memorandum from John Macarthur to Francis Oakes (*see* page 312).

Note 85, page 318.

And if yea.

In the list of questions (*see* note 82), these words were omitted, and " Did or not the Governor direct etc.," formed question numbered 3; the questions, numbered 3 to 15 in this examination, then were numbered 4 to 16 in the list of questions.

Note 86, page 319.

Also pages 322, 336, and 337.

A copy of Macarthur's address.

This was a copy of the paragraph beginning " Mr. McArthur states," which will be found on page 178.

Note 87, page 321.

And particularly in renewing a remembrance of a Person who has been the disturber of the tranquillity of the Colony.

Governor Bligh's despatch to the Duke of Portland was dated 31st October, 1807, and this paragraph formed the third from the end. These words in italics were not included in the copy, which was transmitted by the governor to England.

Note 88, page 323.

And. Thompson.

Andrew Thompson was a native of Scotland, and had been transported to the colony in 1790, when 17 years of age, for setting fire to a stack. On the expiration of his sentence he had settled as a retail storekeeper at the Green Hills. He was a man of wonderful energy, and was one of the pioneers of the Hawkesbury district. In 1799, he was appointed with four others to examine and report on the state of agriculture in the Hawkesbury and adjacent districts. In 1800, he was appointed constable and registrar of agreements at the Hawkesbury. In 1802, he built a floating bridge over the South creek, and was granted the exclusive privilege of levying tolls on persons, stock, and goods crossing the bridge. In 1804, he was the owner of three sloops employed in Bass Strait. In 1806, he built another vessel at the Hawkesbury. In 1807, he was employed by Governor Bligh to manage his farm. Although he had remained loyal to Bligh, he was appointed auctioneer at the Hawkesbury by lieutenant-governor Paterson in 1809. In 1810, he was made chief magistrate at the Hawkesbury by Governor Macquarie. He died at Windsor in his 37th year on the 22nd of October, 1810, and bequeathed one-fourth of his fortune to Macquarie.

Note 89, page 324.

General Order of 1st November, 1806.

Proclamation published on the 3rd of January last.

This order and the proclamation were as follows:—

GOVERNMENT AND GENERAL ORDER.

1st November, 1806.

Whereas the term Currency made use of in this Colony seems not to have carried its proper Signification in the small notes generally circulated, it is hereby declared that its meaning is only applicable to Money and not Barter in goods; so that if any Note is made payable in Copper Coin or the Currency of this Colony, it is to be inferred that Money only is the means by which it is to be liquidated.

And whereas the good faith of Individuals is not to be perverted, it is hereby declared that on or about the first day of January, 1807, all Checks and Promissory Notes issued shall by Public Proclamation be drawn payable in sterling money; and that after the said Proclamation is publicly declared, all outstanding Notes payable in Copper Coin or Colonial Currency shall or may be sued for as if the said term " Copper Coin " or " Colonial Currency " had not been expressed. The Value of Coins already established to be in full force.

PROCLAMATION.

3rd January, 1807.

Whereas by the General Orders dated the 1st of November, 1806, that the term " Currency " was only applicable to Money, and not to Barter in goods, and if a Note was made payable in Copper Coin, as the Currency of this Country, it was to be inferred that Money only was the means by which it is to be liquidated: It is hereby declared, according to the Notice therein given, that from the date hereof all outstanding Notes payable in Copper Coin or Colonial Currency are hereafter to be considered as Sterling Money, and the amount may be sued for as if the said term " Copper Coin " or " Colonial Currency " had not been expressed. And likewise, from the date of this Proclamation, all Checks and Promissory Notes shall be drawn payable in Sterling Money, in consequence of the undefined manner in which Notes have hitherto been given, and the many evils and litigations which have resulted therefrom in the Colony.

By Command of His Excellency,
E. GRIFFIN, Secretary.

Note 90, page 325.

The very flattering Encomium with which so well-informed a Correspondent has been pleased to honor him.

In one copy of these proceedings, these six paragraphs of editorial comments were omitted. It is clear that the editor of the *Gazette* was aware of the identity of " An Oculist." The articles were inspired in consequence of the suit of John Macarthur against Andrew Thompson in the court of appeal before Governor Bligh. Macarthur sued Thompson for recovery on a promissory note expressed in bushels of wheat. During the currency of the bill, an abnormal rise in the value of wheat occurred, and the question arose whether the liability under the note should be assessed according to the price of wheat when the bill was drawn, or when it became due.

Note 91, page 329.

An old man of 60 years of age.

Richard Atkins died on the 21st of November, 1820, aged 75 years. His age was probably 62 years at the date of this trial.

Note 92, page 332.

The paper.

This was a copy of John Macarthur's address to the bench of magistrates (*see* page 178), and in one copy of the proceedings of this trial was filed as exhibit No. 12.

Note 93, page 333.

The Patent.

This was an extract from the letters patent, dated 2nd April, 1787 (*see* volume I, series IV), by which the courts of civil and criminal jurisdiction were established.

Note 94, page 335.
Letter produced and read.

This letter from John Macarthur to Robert Campbell was dated 19th October, 1807 (*see* page 176).

Note 95, page 336.
A Bill of Mr. Bond's between himself and Mr. McA.

In a memorial to Governor Bligh, dated 29th December, 1807 (*see* page 231), John Macarthur detailed the particulars of his dispute with Richard Atkins over a bill drawn in favour of a captain Boyde. This bill was drawn by Atkins on his brother in 1793. In the year 1796, Macarthur and Atkins had a dispute over a bill drawn by the latter in favour of a captain Bond of the East India Service on a Mr. Thornton, an agent in London. It is possible that these two disputes were over the same bill, that Bond and Boyde were identical, and that Thornton was agent for Richard Atkins' brother.

Note 96, page 337.
An order in pencil and it was altered by Mr. Griffin to the shape it was sent in.

This was the circular letter, dated 26th January, 1808, which was sent to each member of the criminal court (*see* page 225).

Note 97, page 338.
Q. 9.

In the list of questions (*see* note 82), questions numbered 9 and 10 in the examination of John Palmer formed one, and questions 11 to 14 were numbered 10 to 13.

Note 98, page 338.
The Paper Writing now produced.
The Paper Writing now produced and shewn.

The first paper mentioned was the letter from John Macarthur to Richard Atkins, dated 14th December, 1807 (*see* page 296), and the second paper was the memorandum from John Macarthur to Francis Oakes, dated 15th December, 1807 (*see* page 312).

Note 99, page 338.
The Paper Writing now produced.

This was a copy of the first warrant for the arrest of John Macarthur (*see* page 310).

Note 100, page 341.
Did not the difference . . . . a deceased brother Officer.

This question referred to the quarrels which arose when lieutenant James Marshall exchanged certain effects belonging to a deceased officer, lieutenant Crawford, for some of his own, at a time, when they were in Marshall's charge. Acting-Governor King wrote a despatch, with full enclosures, on this subject to the Duke of Portland, dated 21st August, 1801 (*see* page 187 *et seq.*, volume III).

Note 101, page 345.
The Paper now produced.

This was the letter from John Macarthur to Richard Atkins, dated 14th December, 1807 (*see* page 296).

Note 102, page 347.

The Letter.

This was the letter from John Macarthur to John Glen, dated 7th December, 1807 (*see* page 295).

Note 103, page 348.

The Note . . . . produced before the Court.

In consequence of w'h I came away with the paper.

John Macarthur's note was dated 15th December, 1807 (*see* page 312). In his evidence at the trial of George Johnston in 1811, Francis Oakes stated that Macarthur "behaved in a very outrageous manner, and made use of a great deal of very improper language."

Note 104, page 350.

The paper produced to the Court.

This was John Macarthur's note, dated 15th December, 1807 (*see* page 312).

Note 105, page 350.

My Nephew.

John Macarthur's nephew was Hannibal Hawkins Macarthur. He was born on the 16th of January, 1788, and had arrived in the colony in the ship *Argo* on the 8th of June, 1805.

Note 106, page 359.

Also pages 361 and 524.

Governor Bligh's Private Concerns at the Hawkesbury.

On the 1st of January, 1807, Governor Bligh purchased, for the sum of £150, two grants belonging to Thomas Tyler, who was then about to return to England. The first of these grants comprised 60 acres, and had been authorised by William Paterson, when administering the government, and had been confirmed by Governor Hunter by a grant, dated 1st May, 1797. The second grant of 110 acres had been issued by Governor King on 12th April, 1803. Shortly after acquiring this land, Bligh purchased, for £100, an adjoining grant of 110 acres, which had been given to James Simpson by Governor King on 31st March, 1802. These grants are numbered 15, 46, and 14 on the parish map of Pitt Town, and are situated due north of Pitt Town on the south bank of the Hawkesbury river. On these grants, Bligh established a dairy, and carried on general farming under the superintendence of Andrew Thompson. The latter managed Captain Putland's farm also, which consisted of a grant of 600 acres made by Governor King to Mrs. Mary Putland, Governor Bligh's daughter. This grant was dated 1st January, 1806 (*see* page x, volume V), and was situated at the modern town of St. Marys.

Note 107, page 371.

Governor King's Boundary.

Adjoining the grant to Mrs. Mary Putland at St. Marys is the grant of 790 acres made by Governor King to his daughter, Mary King. The particulars of this grant and the neighbouring grants to Phillip, Maria, and

Elizabeth King have been detailed in the introduction (*see* page x) to volume V. Andrew Thompson referred to the boundary of this grant as Governor King's boundary.

Note 108, page 371.

Jas. Main.

The reference is to James Meehan, who acted as assistant surveyor during the administration of Governor King.

Note 109, page 374.

We remain, sir, &c.

This address was signed by 833 persons. Among them were: Rd. Atkins, R. Campbell, Thos. Arndell, John Palmer, T. Hobby, John Harris, N. Divine, H. Fulton, A. Thompson, W. Gore, T. Moore, W. Fulton, R. Hassall, R. Fitz, T. M. Pitt, J. Bowman, and George Crossley.

To the papers, which formed this enclosure in the copy preserved in the office of the chief secretary at Sydney, a paper numbered 13 was added. This paper contained a detailed account of labour on the farms of Governor Bligh.

Note 110, page 375.

Officers and Settlers.

The original of this address was presented to the government of New South Wales by some members of the family of major Johnston, and is now preserved in the national art gallery at Sydney. The signatories were:—

Edward Abbott	William Stewart	Peter Hodges
Anthony Fenn Kemp	James Blackman	Absolom West
John Harris	Patrick Moore	William Wall
William Minchin	J. Sutton	Richard Guise
Thomas Jamison	John Reddington	William Thorn
Archibald Bell	Martin Short	Robert Sidaway
Garnham Blaxcell	Joseph Ward	Thomas Stowe
Charles Grimes	Thomas Boulton	Hugh McDonald
John Blaxland	Daniel Cubitt	Edward Riley
John Brabyn	Joseph Underwood	J. Collingwood
William Lawson	Edward Jones	David Bevan
Nicholas Bayly	Lewis Jones	James Larra
William Moore	James Thomson	Edward Wills
Thomas Laycock, Jr.	George Guest	John Griffiths
Thomas Laycock, Sr.	James Parrot	Isaac Nelson
Thomas Moore	William Blake	John Gowen
Ebor Bunker	John Macarthur	James Wilshire
Gregory Blaxland	Edward Macarthur	William Reynolds
Robert Fitz	W. Bennett	James Moran
D'Arcy Wentworth	David Langley	R. Fitzgerald
Hannibal Macarthur	Phillip Tully	Thomas Abbott
John Apsey	George Borch	John Connell
Henry Williams	William Floyd	John Redman
J. W. Lewin	James Bull	James Vanderoom
Simeon Lord	Christopher Friendwriess (?)	William Baker
Isaac Nichols	William Skinner	Richard Tuckwell
Henry Kable	John Driver	Nicholas Divine.
James Badgery	Thomas O'Neil	

The large majority of these signatures were added subsequent to the day on which the address was dated.

Note 111, page 386.

A.

The question preceding this answer is omitted from the transcript of these proceedings.

Note 112, page 394.

Also page 395.

A letter from the Secretary of State's Office.

This letter was signed by Sir George Shee, and is dated 6th October, 1806 (*see* page 25).

Note 113, page 394.

Also pages 395 and 398.

Oliver Russel, now a Convict.

Oliver Russell was convicted of perjury, without trial or indictment, by the criminal court sitting on the 30th of March (*see* page 484). He was sentenced to transportation for seven years. The sentence was annulled by major Johnston's proclamation, dated 3rd April, 1808 (*see* page 277).

Note 114, page 396.

John Holden.

John Holden was a clerk employed by John Macarthur. In a despatch, numbered 4 and dated 14th May, 1809, from Viscount Castlereagh to Governor Macquarie, he was recommended for a pardon.

Note 115, page 396.

General Orders.

Additional papers and correspondence, which arose out of the dispute between John Blaxland and Oliver Russell, were forwarded by major Johnston with his despatch dated 30th April, 1808 (*see* page 457 *et seq.*).

Note 116, page 401.

Proclamation of yesterday.

The proclamation will be found on page 277. Charles Grimes objected evidently to the words "whereas it appears the said Oliver Russell and Robert Daniels were never indicted in due form of Law before the said Court for the said Crime of Perjury, nor allowed the means of Justification to which they were by Law entitled." This statement impugned rightly the informal procedure of the court over which Grimes presided as judge-advocate.

Note 117, page 403.

A Petition from Oliver Russell and Robert Daniels.

This petition or memorial will be found on page 495 *et seq.*

Note 118, page 406.

Document No. 7 in my letter A.

The papers referred to were marked CCC, DDD, and EEE in the enclosure numbered 7 (*see* pages 266 and 267) to major Johnston's despatch, dated 11th April, 1808.

Note 119, page 410.

His Correspondence with me.

This correspondence will be found on pages 419 and 420.

Note 120, page 410.

The imperfect and incorrect manner in which the Documents accompanying my Despatches are Copied.

This statement of major Johnston is fully explanatory of the variations which occur in different copies which are extant of the same papers. It is the probable reason for the difference in the numbering of the enclosures to the despatch, dated 11th April, 1808 (*see* note 70). Two striking examples of " the imperfect and incorrect manner " are discussed in notes 72 and 148.

Note 121, page 416.

Alexander Berry.

The supercargo of the ship *City of Edinburgh* afterwards became the Hon. Alexander Berry, M.L.C. of N.S.W., and owner of the Coolangatta estate in the Illawarra district.

Note 122, page 419.

The enclosed Papers.

Copies of the papers enclosed are not available. It is probable that they were Viscount Castlereagh's despatch to Governor King, dated 13th July, 1805, with two enclosures, the Right Hon. W. Windham's despatch to Governor Bligh, dated 31st July, 1806 (*see* pages 490, 491, and 760, volume V), and the second paragraph of Governor Bligh's despatch, dated 31st October, 1807 (*see* page 182).

Note 123, page 420.

Also pages 424, 430, 432, and 433.

[*1.*]

The first portion of this despatch to the middle of page 434 was repeated by Governor Bligh as the commencement of his despatch, dated 30th June, 1808 (*see* page 520). The latter despatch was paragraphed differently, and the numbers 1 to 54 in brackets indicate the altered paragraphs. The words and sentences enclosed in brackets in the text of the despatch, dated 30th April, were *addenda* incorporated in the despatch dated 30th June. The enclosures will be found attached to the last-mentioned despatch.

Note 124, page 420.

My last Dispatches by the Duke of Portland on the 30th of October.

These despatches to the secretary of state were ten in number, and in the copies available were dated 31st October, 1808 (*see* pages 144, 182, 188, 190, 191, 194, 196, and 197).

Note 125, page 420.

A dutiful Address.

This address was signed by 833 persons (*see* note 109).

Note 126, page 421.

He stands dismissed from the New South Wales Corps for improper Conduct.

Governor Bligh was probably in error in this statement *re* Nicholas Bayly. In 1803, the latter had been concerned in the circulation of certain libellous papers about Governor King. In the same year, on the 10th of February and 8th of March, he was twice tried by court martial for disobedience of orders in beating his convict servants. The court decided at the second trial that the charge was not within its cognizance, and "therefore most honourably acquit him." In the return of the New South Wales Corps, dated 1st March, 1804 (*see* page 579, volume IV), he was entered on the non-active list as "resignation given in, Commg. Officer's leave of absence." In all subsequent returns he occupied a similar status, until the following order appeared in the *Sydney Gazette*, dated 25th December, 1808:—

War Office, 27th February, 1808.
Ensign B. M. Senior to be lieutenant by purchase *vice* Bayly, who retires.

Note 127, page 422.

Bound to India.

In a copy of this despatch sent to England in August, 1808, Governor Bligh added the following marginal note to this statement:—

"Since completing this despatch, one of the missionaries who came from Otaheite has made oath to this circumstance of the convict escaping by the connivance of the master. A copy of his affidavit is enclosed." (*See* the affidavit of James Elder on page 543.)

Note 128, page 424.

A lease.

The lease to John Macarthur was situated to the south-east of St. Phillip's church. The deed of lease was dated 1st January, 1806. This date must be accepted with caution in contradiction of this statement by Governor Bligh. A grant of six hundred acres to Mrs. Mary Putland bears the same date, and this is most probably an antedate for that deed (*see* page x, volume V). If one grant was antedated, it is quite possible that Macarthur's lease was antedated in similar manner.

Note 129, page 426.

Vide full Statement.

Governor Bligh referred to his account of the trial of John Macarthur (*see* page 543 *et seq.*).

Note 130, page 428.

A Memorial.

A copy of the draft of this memorial was transmitted by major Johnston with his despatch, dated 11th April, 1808 (*see* page 236 *et seq.*).

Note 131, page 430.

The enclosed paper from a respectable settler.

The reference is to the affidavit of George Suttor (*see* page 549).

736   *COMMENTARY.*

Note 132, page 432.
Six or seven names.

In a second copy of this despatch, Governor Bligh made the following marginal note:—

"Surgeon John Harris, of the N.S.W. Corps, has since declared to my secretary that not one name was affixed at that time, and also to Mr. Fulton and Mr. Palmer."

Note 133, page 433.
Agreements.

Governor Bligh referred probably to the stipulations proposed in the second paragraph of the address to major Johnston, dated 27th January, 1808 (*see* page 375).

Note 134, pages 434 and 579.
The Box . . . . filled with old paper.

The despatches from Governor King, which were stolen, detailed the reasons for sending John Macarthur under an arrest to England in 1802. The circumstances of the theft have been recorded on page xix and in note 90, volume III.

Note 135, page 437.
A Delegate might be appointed to be sent to England.

In his despatch, dated 30th June, 1808, Governor Bligh enclosed the copy of an agreement (*see* page 550) relating to the expenses of John Macarthur's proposed visit to England. This agreement was not fulfilled owing to dissensions amongst the insurrectionaries. John Macarthur, with major Johnston, sailed in the ship *Admiral Gambier* on the 28th of March, 1809, and travelled in a private capacity.

Note 136, pages 438 and 527.
Annually noted in the Almanacks.

The New South Wales Almanac was published first for the year 1806 (*see* note 233, volume V). No issue for the year 1807 appeared owing to the scarcity of paper. In the issues for the years 1806 and 1808, the name of lieutenant-colonel Paterson appears in the list of officers immediately after that of the governor as holding the office of lieutenant-governor.

Note 137, page 440.
His Servant Marlborough.

Lance-corporal Michael Marlborough made a deposition on the 11th of April, 1808, that he had discovered Governor Bligh under a bed at government house on the evening of the 26th of January (*see* introduction, page xxvi). The facts stated in this affidavit were not confirmed in the evidence given at the court martial on lieutenant-colonel Johnston, 1811. A painting, which is still extant, illustrated this alleged incident, and was exhibited publicly by sergeant-major Whittle in Sydney shortly after the arrest of Bligh. The original deposition is preserved in the national art gallery at Sydney, and is as follows:—

LANCE-CORPORAL MARLBOROUGH came before me this day, and deposeth that he was the Man on duty on the 26th January, after Major Johnston had taken the Command, and was ordered to search for the late Gov. Bligh;

that on himself and a Soldier of the Name of Sutherland examining a Scalene upstairs in the Government House, where a Servant sleeps, he put a Musket under the Bed, and touched Gov. Bligh, which made him make a noise, and, on feeling, caught Gov. Bligh by the Collar, and dragged him out; on his getting up, Gov. Bligh put his hand in his bosom, and Dep't, supposing he might have arms, told him 'if he attempted to resist he would put him to death; and on Gov. Bligh declaring he had no Arms, Dep't told him he would treat him like a Gentleman; and on Gov. Bligh asking Dep't what he was going to do with him, was informed that he would keep him until the Adjutant came, who at the instant came in, when Gov. Bligh said to the Adjutant that if he had done anything wrong he was lead to it. Mr. Minchin, on coming in, assured the Gòvernor his person was perfectly safe, and offered his Arm to take him to the Major, who was downstairs. Dep't further says that he had twice examined the Scalene before; the bedstead had no Curtains, and was extremely low. Gov. Bligh was in his full Uniforms, with his side-Arms and Medal on.

MICH'L MARLBOROUGH.

Sworn before me, 11th of April, 1808,—

E. ABBOTT, J.P.

Note 138, page 440.
A Secret letter from Lieutenant Governor Collins.
This letter was dated 4th April, 1808, and will be found on page 565.

Note 139, page 442.
His letter to Mr. Windham.
This despatch was dated 31st October, 1807 (*see* page 144 *et seq.*), and the passage referred to occurs on page 150.

Note 140, page 455.
The Memorial and Charges.
Mr. McArthur . . . . with Assassination.
. I directed Mr. Grimes.
The memorial will be found on page 376, the details of the alleged plot to assassinate John Macarthur on page 397, and major Johnston's directions to Charles Grimes on page 398.

Note 141, page 456.
My Correspondence with the latter Officer.
I wrote to all the Officers.
The correspondence with surgeon Harris will be found on page 516 *et seq.*, and the letter to the officers, with their reply, on page 518 *et seq.*

Note 142, page 485.
Also page 492.
The Trial of Oliver Russel.
At a bench of magistrates sitting on the 6th of April, 1808, Oliver Russell was committed for trial at the criminal court on a charge of perjury preferred by John Blaxland and Simeon Lord (*see* page 510). The trial was never held, and Oliver Russell was permitted to sail for England on giving his own bond to surrender himself to the secretary of state in answer to the charge (*see* page 516).

Note 143, page 486.

The Protest of John Blaxland.

The copies of the papers attached to this protest are not available. Nine of the papers may be identified. That marked A, No. 1, was probably an extract from the proceedings at the trial of John and Gregory Blaxland and Simeon Lord, relating to the conviction of Oliver Russell (*see* page 484); numbers 3, 4, and 5 were the letters numbered 16, 17, and 18 on page 394, and 6 the letter numbered 19 on page 395; number 8 is numbered 21 on page 395; number 9, "attached to No. 21" on page 396; number 10, number 22 on page 396; and number 11 is number 3 on page 517.

Note 144, page 490.

A Petition of Oliver Russels.

The petition will be found on page 511 *et seq.*, and John Macarthur's reply on page 493.

Note 145, page 494.

Also pages 491 and 511.

Your Honor's Proclamations of the 27th Jany. last, and of the 3rd instant.
These proclamations will be found on pages 240 and 277.

Note 146, page 500.

Question from S. Lord . . . . I believe I did.
Question from Lord . . . . a Villain.

On a comparison of the first two questions and answers with the last question and answer on page 472, and the last question and answer with the second question and answer on page 471, the variations in the evidence as taken by the judge-advocate are apparent.

Note 147, page 502.

The Investigation of his alledged Offence might be postponed.

An application for this purpose from Oliver Russell is not recorded in the proceedings of the criminal court. There is only a brief reference to Russell's desire to abandon the prosecution of John and Gregory Blaxland and Simeon Lord (*see* page 484).

Note 148, page 507.

Bench of Magistrates.

On a comparison of the first and last paragraphs of these proceedings for the 5th of April, 1808, there is a direct contradiction about Oliver Russell's presence in the court. The proceedings, as recorded for this day, are incomplete and illiterate. This is probably one of the enclosures for whose imperfections major Johnston made apologies in his despatch, dated 12th April, 1808 (*see* page 410).

Note 149, page 508.

Bench of Magistrates convened on the 5th day of March last.

The proceedings of this bench will be found on page 385 *et seq.*

Note 150, page 509.

A Letter addressed to me by one of the Parties.

This letter was written by John Blaxland on the 2nd of March, 1808 (*see* page 464).

Note 151, page 519.

As I know some of you are desirous that I should.

George Caley, the botanical collector, in an open letter to major Johnston, dated 7th July, 1808, which he transmitted to Sir Joseph Banks, stated that it was rumoured that John Macarthur was the author of this letter. Caley asserted also that it was recognised generally that Macarthur, not Johnston, held the actual command.

Note 152, page 520.

Governor Bligh to Viscount Castlereagh.

Paragraphs numbered 1 to 54 were a repetition of the first portion of the despatch, dated 30th April, 1808 (*see* page 420 *et seq.*), subject to the modifications mentioned in note 123.

Note 153, page 522.

66.

This is an error in the numbering of the paragraphs which occurs in the original.

Note 154, page 524.

The two Letters from them on the 26th and the Judge Advocate's Memorial to me were missing.

Governor Bligh's account of the proceedings at Macarthur's trial terminates at the conclusion of the sitting on the 25th of January (*see* page 543 *et seq.*). The two letters mentioned will be found on page 224. In the copy from which the proceedings are printed, the two letters appear as one; in another copy, the last paragraph of the letter on page 224 is made into a separate letter, forming the second dated 26th January. The copy of Atkins' memorial (*see* page 236 *et seq.*), transmitted by major Johnston, was a transcript of the rough draft, and as Atkins stated also that he had only a "rough copy," it is not clear what became of the copy presented to the governor.

Note 155, page 525.

Also page 536.

They have executed seven Persons.

On the 30th May, 1808, one man was hanged for the murder of a comrade with whom he escaped from Port Dalrymple. On the 18th June, two men and one woman were hanged at Sydney for burglary, and two days later two men at Parramatta for robbery. The record of a seventh execution has not been discovered.

Note 156, page 529.

The ceremony of marriage.

At the time of the arrest of Governor Bligh, the Reverend Samuel Marsden, chaplain to the colony, was absent in England, and the Reverend Henry Fulton was acting in his place. Fulton remained loyal to Bligh, and was suspended by general orders, dated 30th January, 1808 (*see* page 272). After his suspension, there remained no ordained clergyman to conduct the religious services. The insurrectionary government thereupon established the " New Church," and appointed William Pascoe Crook (*see* note 23, volume IV) as its minister. For reasons unknown, civil marriage was substituted for religious marriage. These actions are indicative of the extremes to which the insurrectionaries were prepared to go.

Note 157, page 531.

The enclosed is a Copy.

The enclosure is numbered 7 (*see* page 550).

Note 158, page 533.

His (Mr. Jamieson's) Letter.

This letter will be found on page 551.

Note 159, page 534.

A Precept from Major Johnston, as here enclosed.

The inclosed Information.

The precept will be found on page 552, and the " information " on page 552 *et seq.*

Note 160, page 535.

Who carried her to sea . . . . and have not since been heard of.

The brig *Harrington* was seized during the evening of Sunday, the 15th of May, 1808. The convicts numbered about fifty, and were under the leadership of a transportee named Robert Stewart, who had been formerly a lieutenant in his Majesty's service. The vessel was boarded whilst the master was on shore, and the mate and twenty-three of the crew were made prisoners. The ship's cables were cut, and passing the fort in the darkness, the convicts cleared the harbour successfully. The mate and crew were then put into the boats and sent back to port, but before their return the loss had been discovered, and a small vessel, the *Halcyon,* with a sergeant and ten privates, sent in pursuit. She returned unsuccessful. When the report of the mate .was received, the ship *Pegasus* was despatched, but returned after an unsuccessful cruize of nine weeks, which cost over £1,000 (*see* page 689).

In March, 1809, H.M.S. *Dedaigneuse* fell in with the *Harrington* near Manilla, in the Philippine islands. After a short engagement, the brig was driven on shore and totally destroyed. Stewart and most of the convicts escaped, and are said to have reached India.

The seizure of the vessel caused a loss of about £4,000 to William Campbell, who was owner, as well as master, of the brig.

Note 161, page 535.

Also page 555.

Tried by a Criminal Court for wilful and corrupt Perjury.

The details of the persecution of William Gore will be found detailed in enclosures numbered 11, 12, and 13 (*see* page 555 *et seq.; see* also note 61).

Note 162, page 537.

An Affidavit.

This was probably a copy of the examination of Robert Fitz, taken on the 27th of January, 1808 (*see* page 352).

Note 163, page 538.
My Dispatch by the Duke of Portland.
The despatch referred to was dated 31st October, 1807 (*see* page 144 *et seq.*).

Note 164, page 543.
The Trial of John Macarthur.

On a comparison of this account of the trial with that (*see* page 221 *et seq.*) transmitted by major Johnston with his despatch, dated 11th April, 1808, it will be noticed that several variations occur. These may be due to "the imperfect and incorrect manner" in which the enclosures to Johnston's despatches were transcribed (*see* note 120) or to other causes. It was customary for the official record of the proceedings at any trial to be kept by the judge-advocate. In this trial no judge-advocate was sworn in, and during most of the proceedings none was present, so technically there was no official record. In Johnston's account, the dispute between Richard Atkins and the members of the court was not recorded. There are marked variations in the first, third, and fifth letters, and minor differences in the second, sixth, and eighth. The omission from Johnston's account of the third paragraph of the fifth letter, as reported by Bligh, must be regarded as prejudicial to the veracity of the insurrectionary record. This paragraph contained most important statements against Richard Atkins, and might have been considered by a critic as showing marked evidence of animus on the part of the members of the court.

Note 165, page 550.
An Agreement.

A memorandum of the proceedings of the meeting, when this agreement was drawn up, has been preserved by the descendants of Governor Bligh. The meeting was held at St. Phillip's church, commencing at 8 p.m., and there were present Garnham Blaxcell, Nicholas Bayly, John Blaxland, D'Arcy Wentworth, William Minchin, "and numerous other gents. of the present establishment."

The proceedings were opened by Garnham Blaxcell, who, supported by Nicholas Bayly, proposed that an address of thanks and a sword "not under the value of one hundred guineas" be presented to major Johnston. This was carried. It was then proposed and carried that addresses of thanks be presented to the New South Wales Corps and to John Macarthur.

It was agreed further that a delegate be sent to England to represent the "grievances the inhabitants of this colony laboured under." John Macarthur was nominated to the position, and a request for his attendance at the meeting was sent to him. After his arrival, he made a speech generally condemning the administration of Governor Bligh, and accepting the appointment of delegate.

At the conclusion of this speech, it was proposed by Blaxcell and carried that a subscription be raised to defray the expenses of Macarthur to England.

Finally John Blaxland proposed that a service of plate be presented to the officers of the New South Wales Corps. After this motion was agreed to, the meeting terminated.

Note 166, page 551.
A very worthless man.

The man appointed by major Johnston was Andrew Hume, who was a notoriously bad character. Under Governor Hunter, he had been storekeeper at Parramatta, and in 1798 on two occasions had been tried by the criminal court on separate charges of malversation of public property and a rape. He was acquitted on both charges, but Hunter dismissed him shortly afterwards for irregularities in his administration. Subsequently he became superintendent of stock, but was dismissed from this office by Governor King in September, 1800, for total neglect of his duties. After his reappointment by major Johnston he was dismissed by lieutenant-colonel Foveaux for dishonesty.

Note 167, page 559.
Captain Kemp's testimony.

This was the evidence given at the examination of captain Kemp on the 1st of March, 1808 (*see* page 235).

Note 168, pages 564 and 565.
To get their Signatures.
I don't know what they are.

These two statements indicate that little importance was attached by the settlers to the act of signing the various addresses to George Johnston, and also that some signatures were obtained through fear.

Note 169, pages 570 and 571.
The Second Paper.
The Sydney Gazette.

The addresses to Governors King and Bligh, with their replies, were published in the issue of the *Sydney Gazette*, dated 17th August, 1806.

Note 170, page 574.
A Proclamation of the 3rd Instant.

This proclamation was forwarded as enclosure numbered 14 (*see* page 563).

Note 171, page 584.
Commission.

All officers on the civil establishment of the colony, of a rank higher than a superintendent, were appointed by commission, when such appointments were made from England. An example of such a commission will be found on page 427, volume V. The Reverend Henry Fulton had arrived in the transport *Minerva* on the 11th of January, 1800, and by orders of Governor King had sailed for Norfolk Island on the 17th of February, 1801, to take up the duties of chaplain, for which he received a salary of £96 *per annum*. As his appointment was made locally, he was liable to be superseded by the arrival from England of a chaplain carrying a full commission.

Note 172, page 584.
He . . . . agreed to transport himself for life to Botany Bay.

It is difficult to understand this statement when the facts of Fulton's status in the colony are considered. On the 8th of November, 1800, Governor King granted him a warrant of conditional emancipation. If Fulton had consented to voluntary transportation, there would have been no assignment of his services, and therefore the conditional emancipation was valueless, as it conferred only freedom from servitude within the colony.

In December, 1805, he was granted an absolute pardon. If he was submitting to voluntary transportation, this amounted to a release from the conditions of his agreement. No such power was delegated to the governor by his commission. It is clear that either Governor King's actions were irregular or the Bishop of Derry's statement was incorrect.

Note 173, page 589.
On the 31st.

This was the 31st of July, 1808.

Note 174, page 590.
An order.

This order was as follows:—

27th August, 1808.

LIEUTENANT-GOVERNOR FOVEAUX has learned, with equal indignation and surprise, that men who have been Prisoners in the Colony have so far forgotten their former condition as to obtrude themselves into the Courts of Justice in the character of Counsellors and Advocates.

Determined to prevent the continuance of a Practice as injurious to decency as it is in fact destructive of Justice, Lieutenant-Governor Foveaux feels it incumbent on him to forbid any person from presuming to interfere with Causes pending before the Courts without an especial License from him for that purpose; and to apprise those who have been Convicts that a disobedience of this injunction will be punished in the most exemplary manner.

All Prisoners, with or without Tickets-of-Leave, who did not appear at the Muster held at Sydney on the 25th Instant, and who are not in the Employment of Government, or indented to Individuals, are directed to report themselves on Saturday next, the 3rd of September, those residing in the Neighbourhood of Sydney, at the Secretary's Office; those of Parramatta, to Captain Kemp; and those of the Hawkesbury to Lieutenant Bell;— when these Gentlemen will require information by whom each man is employed, the Ship in which he came, and the time he has to serve.

Any Prisoner who shall neglect to attend will be ordered into the Gaol-Gang at Sydney.

By Command of His Honor the Lieutenant-Governor.

Note 175, page 593.
Your Proclamation of the 30th.

A copy of this proclamation was transmitted by lieutenant-colonel Foveaux with his despatch, dated 4th September, 1808 (*see* page 631).

Note 176, page 607.
A Copy thereof.

A copy of John Palmer's letter to the secretaries of the treasury will be found on page 613.

Note 177, page 616.
Their Criminal Court.

The members of this court were Anthony Fenn Kemp (judge-advocate), William Kent (acting commander, H.M.S. *Porpoise*), and Edward Abbott, William Moore, Thomas Laycock, William Lawson, and Cadwallader Draffin, officers of the New South Wales Corps.

Note 178, page 623.

The despatches . . . by Major Johnston . . . by the Ships Dart and Brothers.

These despatches were dated 11th April, 12th April, 12th April, 30th April, and 30th April, 1808 (*see* pages 208 *et seq.*, 405 *et seq.*, 407 *et seq.*, 442 *et seq.*, and 453 *et seq.*).

Note 179, pages 625 and 632.

Lord Hobart's Instructions.

An extract of whose letter.

The reference was to the extract of Lord Hobart's letter to lieutenant-colonel Foveaux, which was forwarded as enclosure No. 4 (*see* page 631).

Note 180, page 630.

A piece of Land of equal extent in the vicinity of this town.

The land at Parramatta consisted of 1 acre 3 roods and 12½ perches, and formed part of the Elizabeth Farm estate belonging to John Macarthur. It was situated on the southern bank of the Parramatta river. On the fifth of August, 1808, it was exchanged for a similar area on the west side of the town of Sydney. By this exchange John Macarthur became the first possessor of a land grant within the city of Sydney. The original deed of exchange has been reproduced by photo-lithography in *The Beginnings of Government in Australia.*

Note 181, page 633.

The accompanying correspondence.

Copies of this correspondence were forwarded by Governor Bligh to Viscount Castlereagh with his despatch, dated 31st August, 1808 (*see* page 591 *et seq.*).

Note 182, page 634.

Lord Castlereagh's letter of the 31st of December.

This despatch will be found on page 200 *et seq.*

Note 183, page 642.

The church at the Hawkesbury.

In the report on public buildings at the Hawkesbury, dated 13th August, 1806 (*see* page 97), no church is mentioned, but there is the entry "One New Building, intended School, unfinished." In a similar report, dated 13th August, 1807, it is stated "The Church, School and Granary, Finished" (*see* page 170). It is probable that lieutenant-colonel Foveaux referred to the building which was used as a residence, church, and school by Mr. Harris, the missionary resident in the district (*see* notes 8 and 9, volume V). The church at Ebenezer, Portland, was erected by private subscription, and would not come under the designation of a government building.

Note 184, page 643.

A contract.

The text of this contract will be found on pages 645 and 646.

Note 185, pages 643 and 647.

Wm. Redfern.

William Redfern was born in 1771. He studied for medicine and passed the examination of the Company of Surgeons of London, the predecessor of the Royal College, but did not receive a diploma. He was acting as surgeon's mate at the time of the mutiny at the Nore, and was sentenced to transportation for life for a minor participation in that mutiny. He, with other mutineers, arrived in the colony on the transports *Canada*, *Minorca*, and *Nile*, in December, 1801. He was granted an emancipation in the colony. His appointment by Foveaux was confirmed subsequently by Governor Macquarie and the secretary of state. The examination of William Redfern and that of Edward Luttrell, which was held at the same time, were probably the first medical tests held in the colony. This system was subsequently extended to an examination of all who commenced practice in the colony. Anyone failing to pass the examination was gazetted and ordered to desist from practice.

Prior to the employment of Redfern, John Irving, a transportee in the first fleet, had been appointed by Governor Phillip as assistant to the surgeons, at a salary of £50 *per annum*. He had received the first pardon granted in the colony, dated 16th December, 1791. On the 21st of July, 1801, Daniel McCallum also received a pardon in order that he might practice as a surgeon.

Note 186, page 643.

Also pages 648, 653, 654, and 675.

Enclosure No. 13.

The enclosures to the despatches from lieutenant-colonel Foveaux to Viscount Castlereagh, dated 4th September, 6th September, 6th September, and 8th September, beginning on pages 631, 643, 648, and 653, and those to the despatches from Governor Bligh, dated 31st August, 10th September, and 28th October, beginning on pages 591, 654, and 675, were numbered consecutively in two series.

Note 187, page 653.

Their letter . . . . of the 8th of January last.

The letter from John Barrow to under secretary Cooke will be found on page 205.

Note 188, page 661.

Also page 701.

Lieutenant Colonel Foveaux to ————.

The copy of this letter, preserved in the public records office, London, is not addressed. It was probably the private letter written to under secretary Chapman, which was referred to by Foveaux as dated 6th September in his letter dated 9th November.

Note 189, page 667.

The extraordinary letter.

This letter was as follows :—

REAR-ADMIRAL ISAAC COFFIN TO THE HON. W. W. POLE.

His Majesty's Ship Gladiator, Portsmouth Harbour,

Sir,   13th December, 1807.

The Members of the Court-Martial, assembled this day for the trial of Capt'n Short on charges exhibited against him by Lieut. Tetley, have desired me to state, for the information of the Lords Commissioners of the Admiralty, that he was instigated to bring forward part of the charges by Capt'n Bligh, the Gov'r of N. S. Wales (of which he has been acquitted), whereby Capt'n Short has been deprived of the Command of his Ship; precluded from benefiting by the benign Intentions of Government in locating a tract of Land ordered to be granted to him; obliged, with a Wife, and six Children under twelve years of age, at an inclement season of the year, to return to this Country in a leaky Ship, whose distresses occasioned the loss of his Wife and one Child; from necessity constrained to part with those Implements of Husbandry he carried out with him at a great loss, receiving a Bill to the amount of £740, which has been protested; and finally left in Indigence and Distress.

Under these Circumstances of aggravated suffering, the Members request me to solicit their Lordships' attention to the extreme hardship of his case, which I do in the most earnest manner.

I am, &c.,

Isaac Coffin,

Rear-Admiral.

Note 190, page 668.

No. 228 to No. 245 incl.

Owing to scarcity of paper, the *Sydney Gazette* had been discontinued with the issue numbered 227, and published on the 30th of August, 1807. The publication was re-commenced on the 15th of May, 1808, with the issue numbered 228. This and the succeeding issues consisted of two pages printed on a half sheet of demy. It was published under the supervision of the insurrectionary government, and the customary notice authorising the announcement of general orders was signed by John Macarthur. It was sold on monthly terms at ninepence a copy.

Note 191, page 670.

My letter A.

This was the despatch, dated 4th September, 1808 (*see* page 623 *et seq.*).

Note 192, page 671.

Also page 693.

A substantial brick Barrack, 180 feet in length and two Stories high.

These barracks were erected on the western side of the site now occupied by Wynyard-square. They included a central entrance hall, 12 feet by 22 feet, which contained the staircases. Each floor was similar in arrangement and division into rooms. On each side of the hall there was a large room, 76 feet by 22 feet, and at each end of the building two smaller rooms, each 12 feet by 10½ feet. In front of the barracks, an extensive stone pavement was laid down.

Note 193, page 671.

The proceedings of the Court Martial.

These proceedings were forwarded by lieutenant-colonel Foveaux with a despatch to the judge-advocate general. No copy of them is available (*see* page 701). The charge preferred against James Williamson was one of embezzlement.

Note 194, page 671.

My Despatches by the Rose . . . . in September last.

Governor Bligh's despatches to Viscount Castlereagh by the ship *Rose* were dated 30th June, 31st August, 31st August, 1st September, and 10th September (*see* pages 520 *et seq.*, 588 *et seq.*, 603 *et seq.*, 617 *et seq.*, and 654 *et seq.*).

Note 195, page 672.

Provost-Marshal.

Nicholas Bayly was appointed provost-marshal by an insurrectionary general order, dated 27th January, 1808 (*see* page 271).

Note 196, page 672.

We have heard nothing of her.

The ship *City of Edinburgh* returned to Port Jackson on the 9th of November. She had been given up for lost, as her voyage had occupied twenty-four weeks instead of an anticipated ten. The charter party for this voyage will be found on page 416 *et seq.*

Note 197, page 673.

In continuation of his former Letters.

This was a continuation of the correspondence which will be found on pages 591 to 601 and on pages 654 and 655.

Note 198, page 674.

Copies of two Letters.

The first letter was from Governor Bligh to lieutenant-governor Paterson (*see* page 601), and the second was Paterson's reply (*see* page 679).

Note 199, page 679.

Your Communication of the 8th Inst.

Governor Bligh's letter will be found on page 601 *et seq.*

Note 200, page 686.

The letter . . . . of the 31st August last.

Commissary Palmer's letter will be found on page 603 *et seq.*

Note 201, page 692.

My dispatches to your Lordship by the Rose.

These despatches will be found on pages 623 *et seq.*, 641 *et seq.*, 647 *et seq.*, 653 *et seq.*, and 668.

Note 202, page 694.

Your dispatch of the 16th Ult'o.

This despatch will be found on page 632 *et seq.*

Note 203, page 702.

Account of Land given away.

This account of the lands granted is an incomplete and incorrect record of the actual grants issued by the insurrectionary administrators, and registered prior to the 8th November, 1808. In the land grants preserved in the registrar-general's office at Sydney, no grant to Anthony Fenn Kemp is registered, and the following grants, not mentioned in Governor Bligh's list, are recorded:—23rd July, 270 acres at Parramatta to D'Arcy Wentworth; 9th July, 1,950 acres in St. George and 50 acres at Botany Bay to John Townson; 19th July, 60 acres at Minto to Dorothy Merchant; 19th July, 100 acres at Minto to Aaron Byrne; 1st November, 2,000 acres at Botany Bay to Robert Townson; 1st November, 130 acres at Bankstown to James Meehan. The grant to lieutenant Moore was for 84 acres instead of 83, to ensign Bell 500 acres instead of 600, and to James Wilshire 570 acres instead of 500.

Major Johnston qualified each grant made by him with " the express condition of being subject to the approbation of His Majesty's Ministers and in case of their disapproval is to be considered null and void."

All these grants were confirmed by Governor Macquarie, with the exception of those to George Johnston, junior, and to lieutenants Moore and Minchin.

The grant to William Lawson is of interest, as it contained the reservation of a road one hundred feet wide to the mountains.

The grants to William Faithful, James Wilshire, and Jemima Pitt were given " in consequence of a strong recommendation from the late illustrious and lamented Admiral Lord Viscount Nelson to His Exc'y Gov. King." Mrs. Faithful, Mrs. Wilshire, and Miss Pitt were sisters and nieces of Nelson.

Note 204, page 703.

Despatch per H.M.S. Porpoise.

This despatch was sent on board the *Porpoise* when she sailed for Tasmania under the command of Governor Bligh. It is probable that a duplicate copy was first received in England.

SYNOPSIS.

SYNOPSIS OF DESPATCHES.

From	To	Dated	Despatch endorsed	Transmitted per—	See page	Acknowledged by—	Date of acknowledgment.
		1806.					1807.
King, ...	Windham, Right Hon. W.	18 Aug.		Ship Britannia	19		
..., ...	do	26 Aug.	No. 1	do	19	Castlereagh, Viscount	31 Dec.
Do	do	26 Aug.	No. 2	do	21	do	31 Dec.
Do	..., Secretary	26 Aug.		do	21		
King, ...	Wm., Right Hon. W.	6 Sept.		Ship ... and Mary	23		
Do	Marsden, Secretary	18 Sept.		do	24		
Windham, Right Hon. W.	..., do	do		Ship ...	24	Bligh, Governor	31 Oct.
..., Sir	do			do	25	do	31 Oct.
King, Captain	Commissioners of Navy	1 Nov.	General No. 3	Ship Alexander	25		
..., Governor	Wm., Right Hon. W.	5 Nov.	No. 4 and A	do	26	Castlereagh, Viscount	31 Dec.
Do	do	5 Nov.	No. 5	do	29	do	31 Dec.
Do	do	5 Nov.	No. 6	do	30	do	31 Dec.
Do	do	5 Nov.		do	30	do	31 Dec.
Do	..., Secretary	5 Nov.		do	33		
Do	do	5 Nov.		do	34		
Do	do	8 Nov.		do	36		
King, ..., Right Hon. W.	Bligh, ...	6 Dec.		Transport Duke of Portland.	38		
					39	Bligh, Governor	31 Oct.
Shee, Sir George	do	8 Dec.		H.M.S. Buffalo	39		
Bligh, Governor	Marsden, Secretary	12 Dec.	No. 1	Transport Duke of Portland,	39		
Windham, Right Hon. W.	Bligh, Governor	18 Dec.			55	Bligh, Governor	31 Oct.
Do	do	18 Dec.	No. 2	do	56	do	31 Oct.
Do	do	18 Dec.	No. 3	do	56	do	31 Oct.
Do	do	18 Dec.	No. 4	do	56	do	31 Oct.
Do	do	18 Dec.	No. 5	do	57	do	31 Oct.
Bligh, Governor	Marsden, Secretary	21 Dec.		H.M.S. Buffalo	57		
Do	do	23 Dec.		do	60		
Do	do	27 Dec.	No. 6	do	62		
Windham, Right Hon. W.	Bligh, Governor	30 Dec.	No. 7	Transport Duke of Portland.	70	Bligh, Governor	31 Oct.
Do	do	30 Dec.		do	80	do	31 Oct.
		1807.					
Do	do	— Jan.		do	81	do	31 Oct.

From	To	Dated	Despatch endorsed	Transmitted per—	See page	Acknowledged by—	Date of acknowledgment.
		1807.					1807.
Bligh, Governor	Marsden, Secretary	2 Jan.		H.M.S. Buffalo	84		
Do	do	2 Jan.		do	86		
Do	do	3 Jan.		do	87		
Do	do	7 Jan.		do	89		
Do	do	7 Jan.		do	91		
Do	do	9 Jan.		do	91		
Do	Windham, Right Hon. W.	25 Jan.	No. 1	do	97	Castlereagh, Viscount	31 Dec.
Do	do	1 Feb.	No. 2	do	100	do	31 Dec.
Do	do	1 Feb.	No. 3	do	104	do	31 Dec.
Do	do	1 Feb.	No. 4	do	110	do	31 Dec.
Do	do	1 Feb.	No. 6	do	111	do	31 Dec.
Do	do	1 Feb.	No. 7	do	112	do	31 Dec.
Do	do	1 Feb.	No. 8	do	112	do	31 Dec.
Do	do	1 Feb.	No. 9	do	115	do	31 Dec.
Do	do	4 Feb.	No. 5	do	119	do	31 Dec.
Do	do	7 Feb.	General	do	120	do	31 Dec.
Marsden, Secretary	Bligh, Governor	19 March		Whaler Star	127		
Bligh, Governor	Windham, Right Hon. W.	21 April		Ship Young William	132		
Do	do	6 May		Ship Duchess of York.	133		
Do	do	6 May		do	134		
Do	do	30 Sept.		Whaler Aurora	137		
Do	do	30 Sept.	A	do	142		
Do	do	1 Oct.		do	143		
Do	Pole, Hon. William	30 Oct.		Transport Duke of Portland.	143		1809.
Do	Windham, Right Hon. W.	31 Oct.	General	do	144	Castlereagh, Viscount	15 May.
Do	do	31 Oct.	No. 1	do	182	do	15 May.
Do	do	31 Oct.	No. 2	do	188	do	15 May.
Do	do	31 Oct.	No. 3	do	190	do	15 May.
Do	do	31 Oct.	No. 4	do	191	do	15 May.
Do	do	31 Oct.		do	191	do	15 May.
Do	do	31 Oct.		do	194	do	15 May.
Do	do	31 Oct.		do	196	do	15 May.
Do	Shee, Sir George	31 Oct.	No. 1	do	197		15 May.
Do	do	31 Oct.	No. 2	do	199	do	15 May.
Do					199		

From	To	Dated	Despatch endorsed	Transmitted per—	See page	Acknowledged by—	Date of acknowledgment.
Hawkesbury, Lord	Colonial Governors	4 Nov.		Transport Sinclair	199		1808.
Do	Bligh, Governor	5 Nov.		do	200		
Castlereagh, Viscount	do	30 Dec.	No. 2	do	200		
Do	do	31 Dec.	No. 1	do	200	Foveaux, Lieut. Colonel.	6 Sept.
Cooke, Under Secretary	do	31 Dec. 1808.	Private	do	204	Bligh, Governor	31 Augt.
do	do	11 Jan.		do	205	Foveaux, Lieut. Colonel.	6 Sept. 1809.
Castlereagh, Viscount	do	4 March	No. 3	Ship Star	206	Bligh, Governor	10 June.
Do	do	30 March	No. 4	do	207		
Do	do	30 March	No. 5	do	207		
Do	do	30 March	No. 6	do	208		
Do	do	11 April	A	...Brit	208		
Johnston, Major	Castlereagh, Viscount	12 April		do	405		
Do	do	12 April		...Aer	407		
Do	do	30 April		...this	420	Castlereagh, Viscount	15 May.
Bligh, Governor	Pole, Hon. William	30 April		...Aer	440		
Johnston, Major	Castlereagh, Wnt	30 April		do	442		
Do	do	30 April		do	453		
Cooke, Under Secretary	Bligh, do	5 May		Ship Æolus	520	Paterson, Lieut. Governor.	19 March.
Do	do	7 June		do	520		
Bligh, Governor	Wnt	30 June	Secret.	Ship &c	520	Castlereagh, Viscount	15 May.
Do	do	30 June	No. 7	do	570	do	15 May.
Castlereagh, Viscount	Bligh, Governor	30 June		Transport Duke of Portland.	584		
Do	do	30 June	No. 8	do	585		
Do	do	30 June	No. 9	do	585		
Bligh, Governor	Pole, Hon. William	1 July		Ship Rose	586		
Castlereagh, Viscount	Bligh, Wnt	18 July	No. 10	Transport Duke of Portland.	586		
Johnston, Major	Wnt	31 July		Ship Rose	587	Castlereagh, Viscount	15 May.
Bligh, Governor	do	31 August		do	588	do	15 May.
Do	Pole, Hon. William	31 Augt		do	603		
Do	Wnt	1 Sept.		do	615	Castlereagh, Viscount	15 May.
Do	:			do	617		

From	To	Dated	Despatch endorsed	Transmitted per—	See page	Acknowledged by—	Date of acknowledgment
		1808.					1809.
Foveaux, Lieutenant Colonel.	Castlereagh, Viscount	4 Sept.	A	Ship Rose	623		
Do	do	6 Sept.	B	do	641		
Do	do	6 Sept.	C	do	647		
Do	do	8 Sept.	D	do	653		
Do	do	8 Sept.	E	do	654	Castlereagh, Viscount	15 May.
Bligh, Governor	Pole, Hon. William	10 Sept		do	656		
Foveaux, Lieutenant Colonel.	do	10 Sept.		do	661		
Bligh, Governor	Cooke, Under Secretary	11 Sept.	F	do	667		
Foveaux, Lieutenant Colonel.	Castlereagh, Viscount	13 Sept.		do	668		
Bligh, Governor	Pole, Hon. William	15 Sept.		Transport Experiment	668		
Castlereagh, Viscount	Bligh, Governor	16 Sept.	No. 11	do	668		
Do	Paterson, Lieutenant Governor.	8 Oct.		Transport Sinclair	669		
Foveaux, Lieutenant Colonel.	Cooke, Under Secretary	21 Oct.	Private	Whaler Albion	671		
Bligh, Governor	Castlereagh Viscount	28 Oct.	No. 1	do	681		
Do	do	28 Oct.	No. 2	do	684		
Do	Pole, Hon. William	28 Oct.		do	685		
Do	Castlereagh, Viscount	4 Nov.		do	690		
Do	do	7 Nov.		do	691		
Do	Pole, Hon. William	8 Nov.		do	691		
Do	Cooke, Under Secretary	8 Nov.		do	692		
Foveaux, Lieutenant Colonel.	do	9 Nov.	Private	do	692		
Do	Castlereagh, Viscount	9 Nov.	B	do	699		
Do	do	9 Nov.	Private	do	700		
Do	Chapman, Under Secretary	— Nov.		do	701		
Bligh, Governor	Judge Advocate General	12 Nov.		do	701		
Foveaux, Lieutenant Colonel.	Castlereagh, Viscount	31 Dec.	.	H.M.S. Porpoise.	703		

INDEX.

INDEX.

Abbott, Edward (captain)
appointment of—
  as judge-advocate by Johnston, George,
    271.
  as judge-advocate declined by, 272.
  as magistrate by Johnston, George, 436.
company of, 31.
dismissal of, from magistracy by Bligh,
  Wm., 424.
importation of still for, 160.
judge-advocate of vice-admiralty court, 274,
  534, 552.
land held by, 162.
letter from—
  to Johnston, George, 375, 519.
letter to—
  from Johnston, George, 242, 518.
member of criminal court, 276, 535, 536.
on duty at Parramatta, 32, 131.
opinion of, re arrest of Bligh, Wm., 432.
order issued by, after arrest of Bligh, Wm.,
  549.
orders to, for examination of official papers,
  242, 522.
removal of, from Parramatta to Sydney,
  424.
stock owned by, 164.
witness required by Wm. Bligh in England,
  254.

Abbott, Thomas
signatory to address to Paterson, William,
  574.

Adams, James
warrant of, re crew of *Lady Nelson,* 37.

Addy, William
signatory to address to Bligh, William, 578.

Admiralty
See "Marsden, Wm.," "Pole, Hon. Wm."

Æolus, ship
despatch *per,* 520.

Agriculture
at Castle Hill, 27.
bartering of produce of, for spirits, 124.
blights, prevalence and causes of, 148.
convicts employed at, 179, 180.
encouragement of, in preference to pastoral
  industry, 123.

Agriculture
exotic grasses, cultivation of, 147.
farming carried on by government, 27, 147.
fertilisation of soil necessary, 146.
grain, price of, 121.
impossibility of experimental farming, 146.
improvements in methods adopted in, 146.
Indian corn, cultivation of, 147.
labour required to prepare land for, 145.
maize harvest, prospects of, 128.
potatoes, cultivation of, 26.
results of 1806-7 harvest, 120, 121.
returns, general, of, 161, 162 *et seq.*
seed grain—
  failure of, imported, 20.
  want of, 20, 26.

Aiken, James
master of the *King George,* 193.

Aitken, James
signatory to address to Bligh, William, 572.

Albion, whaler
arrival and particulars of, 113, 192, 618.
cargo of, 113, 194.
departure and particulars of, 114, 193, 619.
despatch *per,* 671, 681, 684, 685, 690, 691,
  692, 699, 700, 701.
fees paid on, 620, 621.

Alexander, ship
arrival and particulars of, 113.
cargo of, 113.
convicts *per,* 20.
departure and particulars of, 114.
despatch *per,* 25, 26, 29, 30, 33, 34, 36, 38.

Allen, James
evidence of, at inquiry re Short, Tetley, and
  Lye, 48.

Allen, Robert
signatory to address to Bligh, William, 542.

Allen, Thomas
removal of, from garden at government
  house, 597.

Allwright, Richard
signatory to address to Bligh, William, 570,
  578.

Hall, George
signatory to address—
 to Bligh, William, 578.
 to Johnston, Geo., 565.
 to Paterson, William, 574.

Hancey, Michael
address of welcome from, to Paterson, Wm.,
 575.

Hancey, William
address of welcome from, to Paterson, Wm.,
 575.
signatory to address to Bligh, William, 570.

Hannah and Sally, ship
arrival and particulars of, 192.
cargo of, 194.
departure and particulars of, 619.

Hansen, Thomas
purchase of land by, 56.
recommendation of, 56.

Hardinge, F. L.
deposition of, to be taken for transmission
 to England, 90.
evidence of, at inquiry *re* Short, Tetley, and
 Lye, 47, 52, 54.

Hardy, Thomas
address of welcome from, to Paterson, Wm.,
 575.

Harrington, brig
departure and particulars of, 193.
detention of, for alleged piracy, 535.
liberation of, 23, 81.
pursuit of, by the *Pegasus,* 689.
seizure of, by convicts, 535.
spirits imported on, 644.

Harris, John (surgeon, N.S.W. Corps)
appointment of, as magistrate, by Johnston, George, 271, 436.
bill drawn in favour of, 137.
commissions received by, 100.
dismissal of, from magistracy, 277, 537.
evidence of, in Macarthur *v.* Campbell, jr.,
 175.
examination of Redfern, William, by, 647.
grain purchased from, 135.
land held by, 162.
lease of land at Sydney to, 155.
letter from—
 to Johnston, George, 375, 517.
letter to—
 from Bayly Nicholas, 516, 517.
 from Johnston, George, 518.
member of bench of magistrates, 385, 506.
on duty at Sydney, 32, 131.

Harris, John (surgeon, N.S.W. Corps)
orders to—
 to carry despatches to England, 456, 516
  et seq., 574.
 from Johnston, George, to proceed to
  England, 220.
questions proposed for the examination of,
 at the trial of Macarthur, John, 302.
report of survey of live stock by, 414.
signatory to address to Bligh, William, 542.
stock owned by, 164.

Hartmann, Thomas
signatory to address to Bligh, William, 572.

Harvey, William
boatswain's mate on H.M.S. *Porpoise,* 48,
 52.
evidence of, at inquiry *re* Short, Tetley, and
 Lye, 48, 52.

Hassall, Rowland
signatory to address to Bligh, William, 542.

Hasselburg, Frederick
appointment of, by Blaxland, John, to command the Brothers, 395.
chief officer of the *Brothers,* 386.
evidence of—
 in prosecution of Russell, O., for perjury,
  506.
 in suit Blaxland *v.* Russell, 386.

Hawkesbury
address of settlers at, to Bligh, William,
 373, 541, 568 *et seq.,* 577, 578.
administration of commissariat at, 356.
church at, 125, 642.
clergyman wanted at, 126.
constable at, 272, 610.
distress caused by floods at, 26, 34.
description of land and soil at, 144, 145.
dues paid on shipping from, 622.
impossibility of protection against floods at,
 641.
magistrate at, 573.
military required at, 130.
public buildings at, report on, 97, 170.
return—
 of convicts employed at, 179, 180, 181.
 of inhabitants at, 105, 106, 107, 139,
  140, 141.
 of live stock at, 415.
 of military at, 106, 130, 140.
 of provisions at, 414.
storekeeper at, 355.
surgeon stationed at, 115.
trade of inhabitants at, 156.

Hawkesbury, Lord
letter from—
 to Governor, 199, 200.

Sydney: William Applegate Gullick, Government Printer.—1916.

Lightning Source UK Ltd.
Milton Keynes UK
UKHW020110231118
332756UK00006B/219/P